THE ENCYCLOPEDIA OF
NORTH AMERICAN INDIAN WARS, 1607–1890

THE ENCYCLOPEDIA OF NORTH AMERICAN INDIAN WARS 1607–1890

A Political, Social, and Military History

VOLUME II: M–Z

Dr. Spencer C. Tucker
Editor

James Arnold and Roberta Wiener
Editors, Documents Volume

Dr. Paul G. Pierpaoli Jr.
Associate Editor

Dr. David Coffey
Dr. Jim Piecuch
Assistant Editors

 ABC-CLIO

Santa Barbara, California Denver, Colorado Oxford, England

Library of Congress Cataloging-in-Publication Data

The encyclopedia of North American Indian wars, 1607-1890 : a political, social, and military history / Spencer C. Tucker, editor ; James Arnold and Roberta Wiener, editors, documents volume ; Paul G. Pierpaoli, Jr., associate editor ; David Coffey, Jim Piecuch, assistant editors.
     p. cm.
  Includes bibliographical references and index.
  ISBN 978-1-85109-697-8 (hard back : alk. paper) -- ISBN 978-1-85109-603-9 (ebook)
  1. Indians of North America—Wars—Encyclopedias.   I. Tucker, Spencer, 1937–   II. Arnold, James R.   III. Wiener, Roberta, 1952–
  E81.E984   2011
  970.004'97003—dc23

2011027913

ISBN: 978-1-85109-697-8
EISBN: 978-1-85109-603-9

15 14 13 12 11   1 2 3 4 5

This book is also available on the World Wide Web as an eBook.
Visit www.abc-clio.com for details.

ABC-CLIO, LLC
130 Cremona Drive, P.O. Box 1911
Santa Barbara, California 93116-1911

This book is printed on acid-free paper ∞
Manufactured in the United States of America

For my girls:
Beverly, Mary Mikel, Paige, and Pam

About the Editors

Spencer C. Tucker, PhD, held the John Biggs Chair of Military History at his alma mater, the Virginia Military Institute in Lexington, for 6 years until his retirement from teaching in 2003. Before that, he was professor of history for 30 years at Texas Christian University, Fort Worth. He has also been a Fulbright Scholar and, as a U.S. Army captain, an intelligence analyst in the Pentagon. Currently the senior fellow of military history at ABC-CLIO, he has written or edited 39 books, including the award-winning *Encyclopedia of the Arab-Israeli Conflict,* the comprehensive *A Global Chronology of Conflict,* and the *Encyclopedia of the Middle East Wars,* all published by ABC-CLIO.

James Arnold is the author of more than 20 military history books and has contributed to numerous others. His published works include *Jeff Davis's Own: Cavalry, Comanches, and the Battle for the Texas Frontier* and *Napoleon Conquers Austria: The 1809 Campaign for Vienna,* which won the International Napoleonic Society's Literary Award in 1995. His two newest titles will be released in 2011: *The Moro War: How America Battles a Muslim Insurgency in the Philippine Jungle, 1902–1913* and *Napoleon's Triumph: The Friedland Campaign, 1807.*

Roberta Wiener is managing editor of the *Journal of Military History.* She coauthored *The American West: Living the Frontier Dream* as well as a number of history books for the school library market and has contributed to several of ABC-CLIO's print and online reference works.

Contents

Volume I: A–L

List of Entries   xi
List of Maps   xxi
List of Tables   xxiii
Preface   xxv
General Maps   xxvii
Overview   xxxvii
Introduction   xlvii
Entries   1

Volume II: M–Z

List of Entries   xi
List of Maps   xxi
List of Tables   xxiii
Entries   463
Appendix: Decorations, Medals, and Military Honors   877
Glossary   883
Chronology   887
Bibliography   895
List of Editors and Contributors   915
Categorical Index   921

Volume III: Documents

List of Documents   vii
Documents   927
Index   1279

List of Entries

Abenakis
Abenaki Wars
Acoma Pueblo, Battle of
Adobe Walls, First Battle of
Adobe Walls, Second Battle of
Agriculture
Albany Conference
Albany Congress
Aleut Rebellion
Algonquins
American Horse
Amherst, Jeffrey
Amherst's Decree
Anglo-Powhatan War, First
Anglo-Powhatan War, Second
Anglo-Powhatan War, Third
Apache Pass, Battle of
Apaches
Apache Wars
Apalachee Revolt
Apalachees
Appalachian Mountains
Appomattocks
Arapahos
Arapahos, Northern
Arapahos, Southern
Arikaras
Arikara Scouts
Arikara War
Artillery
Ash Hollow, Battle of

Athapascans
Atkinson, Henry
Attakullakulla
Augur, Christopher Columbus
Augusta, Congress of

Bacon's Rebellion
Bad Axe, Battle of
Bannock War
Barbed Wire
Barboncito
Bascom Affair
Bear Paw Mountains, Battle of
Bear River, Battle of
Beaver Wars
Beecher Island, Battle of
Belknap, William Worth
Bent, Charles
Bent, William
Benteen, Frederick William
Bent's Fort
Berkeley, William
Bierstadt, Albert
Big Bend, Battle of
Big Foot
Big Hole, Battle of the
Billy Bowlegs
Birch Coulee, Battle of
Birch Creek, Battle of
Black Elk
Blackfoot Confederacy

Blackfoot Sioux
Black Hawk
Black Hawk War
Black Hills, South Dakota
Black Hills Gold Rush
Black Hoof
Black Kettle
Black Point, Attacks on
Black Robes
Black Swamp
Blockhouses
Bloody Brook Massacre
Bloody Knife
Blue Jacket
Blue Licks, Kentucky, Action at
Boomtown
Boone, Daniel
Boonesborough, Kentucky
Bosque Redondo
Bouquet, Henry
Bow and Arrow
Boyer, Mitch
Bozeman, John
Bozeman Trail
Braddock, Edward
Braddock's Campaign
Brant, Joseph
Brims of Coweta
Brodhead Expedition
Brookfield, Siege of
Brown, Thomas
Brulé Sioux
Buffalo
Buffalo Bill's Wild West Show
Buffalo Hump
Buffalo Soldiers
Bureau of Indian Affairs
Burnt Corn Creek, Battle of
Bushy Run, Battle of
Butler, John
Butterfield Overland Mail Route

Caddos
Caesar
Cahokia-Fox Raid
Calhoun, James Silas
Calhoun, John Caldwell
California Gold Rush
Camas Meadows, Battle of
Camels
Cameron, Alexander
Camp Grant Massacre

Canada
Canby, Edward Richard Sprigg
Canby's Campaign
Cannibalism
Canonchet
Canoes
Canyon Creek, Battle of
Canyon de Chelly, Arizona
Captivity Narratives
Captivity of Europeans by Indians
Captivity of Indians by Europeans
Captivity of Indians by Indians
Carbines
Carleton, James Henry
Carleton's Campaign
Carr, Eugene Asa
Carrington, Henry Beebe
Carson, Christopher Houston
Casco, Treaty of
Catawbas
Catlin, George
Cattle Industry
Cavalry, Native American
Cavalry, U.S. Army
Cavalry Regiment, 3rd Colorado
Cavalry Regiment, 4th U.S.
Cavalry Regiment, 5th U.S.
Cavalry Regiment, 6th U.S.
Cavalry Regiment, 7th U.S.
Cavalry Regiment, 8th U.S.
Cavalry Regiment, 9th U.S.
Cavalry Regiment, 10th U.S.
Cayugas
Chacato Troubles
Chaffee, Adna Romanza, Sr.
Champlain, Samuel de
Cherokee Alphabet
Cherokees
Cherokees, Campaigns against
Cherokee War
Cheyenne-Arapaho War
Cheyenne Campaign
Cheyennes
Cheyennes, Northern
Cheyennes, Southern
Chickahominys
Chickamaugas
Chickasaws
Chickasaw Wars
Chillicothe, Ohio, Battles on the Little Miami River
Chivington, John
Choctaw-Chickasaw War

Choctaw Civil War
Choctaws
Church, Benjamin
Cibecue Creek, Incident at
Clark, George Rogers
Clark, William
Clark's Garrison, Battle of
Clark's Ohio Campaign, First
Clark's Ohio Campaign, Second
Clearwater River, Battle of
Clinch, Duncan Lamont
Cochise
Cockacoeske
Cody, William Frederick
Coeur d'Alenes
Coeur d'Alene War
Coffee, John
Colorow
Colt, Samuel
Colt Revolver
Comanche Campaign
Comancheros
Comanches
Connor, Patrick Edward
Connor's Powder River Expedition
Conquistadors
Cooke, Philip St. George
Cooper, James Fenimore
Córdova, Francisco Hernández de
Corn
Corn Liquor
Cornplanter
Cornstalk
Coronado, Francisco Vásquez de
Council on the Auglaize
Counting Coup
Covenant Chain
Crawford, Emmet
Crazy Horse
Creek-Cherokee Wars
Creek-Choctaw Wars
Creeks
Creek War
Croatans
Crockett, David
Croghan, George
Crook, George
Crows
Curly
Curtis, Samuel Ryan
Custer, George Armstrong
Custer, Thomas Ward

Custer's Last Stand in Art

Dade's Massacre
Dakota Sioux
Davis, Jefferson
Dawes Severalty Act
Decanisora
Deerfield, Massachusetts, Attack on
Delawares
Delgadito
Demographics, Historical
Devil's Hole Road, Battle of
Digger Indians
Dime Novels
Dodge, Grenville Mellen
Dodge, Henry
Dog Soldiers
Dover, New Hampshire, Attack on
Dragoon Regiments, 1st and 2nd
Duck River Massacre
Dudley, Joseph
Dull Knife
Dull Knife Fight
Dull Knife Outbreak
Dummer's Treaty
Dummer's War
Duston, Hannah
Dutch-Indian Wars
Dutch-Mohawk Treaty

Easton Conference and Treaty
Econochaca, Battle of
Ecuyer, Simeon
Edged Weapons
Emistisiguo
Emuckfaw Creek, Battle of
Encomienda
Endicott, John
Endicott Expedition
Enitachopco Creek, Battle of
Esopuses
Esopus Wars
Evans, John
Everglades

Fallen Timbers, Battle of
Falls Fight
Falmouth, Battle of
Fetterman, William Judd
Fetterman Massacre
Film and the American Indian Wars
Firearms Trade

Flacco the Elder
Flipper, Henry Ossian
Forsyth, George Alexander
Forsyth, James William
Fort Apache
Fort Armstrong, Treaty of
Fort Bascom
Fort Harmar, Treaty of
Fort Jackson, Treaty of
Fort Laramie
Fort Laramie, Treaty of (1851)
Fort Laramie, Treaty of (1868)
Fort Leavenworth
Fort Mims, Battle of
Fort Phil Kearny
Fort Riley
Fort Robinson
Forts, Camps, Cantonments, and Outposts
Fort Sill
Fort Simcoe
Fort Stanwix, Treaty of
Fort Strother
Fort Sumner
Fort Walla Walla
Fort Washington
Four Lakes, Battle of
Fox Fort, Siege of
Fox Wars
France
Free, Mickey
Frémont, John Charles
French and Indian War
Fur Trade

Gaines, Edmund Pendleton
Gall
Galvanized Yankees and Rebels
Gatewood, Charles Bare
Gatling, Richard
Gatling Gun
Geronimo
Geronimo Campaign
Ghost Dance
Gibbon, John
Girty, Simon
Glaize, The
Gnadenhutten Massacre
Good Friday Massacre
Goshute War
Grant, Ulysses Simpson
Grant's Peace Policy
Grattan Massacre

Great Britain
Great Law of Peace of the Longhouse People
Great Platte River Road
Great Sioux Reservation
Great Sioux War
Great Swamp Fight
Great Swamp Fortress
Greenville, Treaty of
Gregg, John Irvin
Grierson, Benjamin Henry
Grouard, Frank
Gun Merchant of Okchai

Haigler
Hancock, Winfield Scott
Handsome Lake
Harmar, Josiah
Harney, William Selby
Harper's Weekly
Harrison, William Henry
Harrodsburg, Kentucky
Hartford, Treaty of
Hatch, Edward
Havasupais
Hayfield Fight
Hazen, William Babcock
Henderson, Archibald
Hillabee Massacre
Hopewell, Treaty of
Horses
Horseshoe Bend, Battle of
Houston, Samuel
Howard, Oliver Otis
Hualapais
Hudson River School
Hudson's Bay Company
Hunkpapa Sioux

Illinois
Indian Agents
Indian Creek Massacre
Indian Presents
Indian Removal Act
Indian Reorganization Act
Indian Ring Scandal
Indians, Confederate
Indian Territory
Infantry Regiment, 7th U.S.
Infantry Regiment, 24th U.S.
Infantry Regiment, 25th U.S.
Inkpaduta
Iroquois

Iroquois Confederacy
Iroquois Treaties of 1700 and 1701

Jackson, Andrew
Jackson, Helen Hunt
Jamestown
Jefferson, Thomas
Jemison, Mary
Jesup, Thomas Sidney
Johnson, Sir William
Johnson's 1780 Campaign
Joseph, Chief
Julesburg Raids

Kamiakin
Karankawas
Kearny, Stephen Watts
Keepers of the Eastern and Western Doors
Kelly, Luther Sage
Keokuk
Kickapoos
Kieft, Willem
Kieft's War
Killdeer Mountain, Battle of
King George's War
King Philip's War
King William's War
Kintpuash
Kiowas
Kotsoteka Comanches
Kwahadi Comanches

La Barre, Joseph Antoine Le Fèbvre de
Lake Okeechobee, Battle of
Lakota Sioux
Lance
Land Cessions, Northwest Ordinance
Land Rights
Langlade, Charles Michel de
La Salle, René-Robert Cavelier, Sieur de
Lawton, Henry Ware
Legion of the United States
Lewis, Meriwether
Lewis and Clark Expedition
Lipan Apaches
Liquor
Literature and the American Indian Wars
Little Bighorn, Battle of the
Little Crow
Little Turtle
Little Turtle's War
Little Wolf

Logan, Benjamin
Logan, John
Logstown, Treaty of
Lone Wolf
Longhouse
Looking Glass
Lord Dunmore's War
Louisiana Purchase
Lovewell, John
Lovewell's Fight

Mabila, Battle of
Mackenzie, Ranald Slidell
Mackenzie's Mexico Raid
Mahicans
Mangas Coloradas
Manifest Destiny
Manuelito
Marias Massacre
Mariposa War
Mason, John
Massachusetts Bay–Pequot Treaty
Massacre
Massacre Canyon, Battle of
Massasoit
McGillivray, Alexander
McQueen, Peter
Medicine, Military
Medicine, Native American
Medicine Lodge Treaty
Meeker, Nathan Cook
Meeker Massacre
Mendota, Treaty of
Merritt, Wesley
Mesquakies
Metacom
Mexico
Miamis
Miantonomo
Micmac Raids on Nova Scotia
Micmacs
Miles, Nelson Appleton
Military Divisions, Departments, and Districts
Militia
Milk Creek, Battle of
Mingos
Miniconjou Sioux
Minnesota Sioux Uprising
Missionaries
Modocs
Modoc War
Mog

Mohawk-Mahican War
Mohawks
Mohegans
Mojaves
Mojave War
Moniac, David
Moravian Church
Moravian Indian Missions on the Muskingum River
Mormonism
Mortar of the Okchai
Mounted Riflemen, Regiment of
Mourning War
Murray, John, Fourth Earl of Dunmore
Muscle Shoals, Grand Council on
Musgrove, Mary
Muskets
Mystic Fort Fight

Nakoni Comanches
Nakota Sioux
Nansemonds
Narragansetts
Narváez, Pánfilo de
Natchezes
Natchez Revolt
Natchez War
Native Americans
Native Americans, Alliances with Europeans
Native Americans and the American Revolutionary War
Native Americans and the Civil War
Native Americans and the War of 1812
Native American Trade
Native American Warfare
Nativism, Indian
Navajo Removal
Navajos
Navajo War
Neolin
New England Confederation
New Mexico
New Netherland
New Ulm, Battles of
Nez Perces
Nez Perce War
Niagara, Treaty of
Nipmucks
Noble Savage Concept
Norridgewock, Battle of
North, Frank Joshua, and Luther Hedden
Northwest Ordinances of 1785 and 1787
Norton, John

Nottoways
Nutimus

Oatman Family Massacre
Occaneechees
Oconostota
Office of Commissioner of Indian Affairs
Oglala Sioux
Ogoula Tchetoka, Battle of
Ohio Company of Virginia
Ohio Expedition
Ojibwa-Dakota Conflict
Ojibwas
Ojo Caliente Reservation, New Mexico
Ojo Oso, New Mexico
Old Briton
Old Northwest Territory
Old Shawnee Town
Oñate, Juan de
Oneidas
Onondagas
Opechancanough
Oregon Trail
Oriskany, Battle of
Orontony
Osages
Osceola
Otis, Elwell Stephen
Ottawas
Ouray
Overland Trail

Paiutes, Northern
Palo Duro Canyon, Battle of
Palouses
Pamunkeys
Pan-Indianism
Parker, Cynthia Ann
Parker, Ely Samuel
Parkman, Francis, Jr.
Pawnees
Paxton Riots
Payne's Landing, Treaty of
Penateka Comanches
Pennacooks
Pequots
Pequot War
Petite Guerre, La
Petroglyphs
Pettaquamscutt Rock, Treaty of
Pickawillany Massacre

Pima Revolts
Pine Ridge Campaign
Pine Ridge Reservation
Pine Tree Hill, Treaty of
Piqua, Battle of
Piscataway, Siege of
Pistols
Platte Bridge, Battle of
Pocahontas
Point Pleasant, Battle of
Ponce de León, Juan
Pontiac
Pontiac's Rebellion
Pony Express
Popé
Pope, John
Pottawatomis
Powder River Expedition
Powhatan
Powhatan Confederacy
Prairie du Chien, Treaty of
Praying Towns and Praying Indians
Proclamation of 1763
Prophetstown
Pueblo Revolt
Pueblos
Puritans
Pushmataha

Quakers
Quanah Parker
Quapaws
Queen Anne's War

Railroads
Raisin River Massacre
Ranks, U.S. Army
Rappahannocks
Raritans
Red Bird
Red Cloud
Red Cloud's War
Red Jacket
Red River War
Red Shoe
Red Sticks
Remington, Frederic
Reno, Marcus Albert
Reservations
Reynolds, Charles Alexander
Rifles

Rocky Mountains
Rogers, Robert
Rogers's Raid on St. Francis
Rogue River War, First
Rogue River War, Second
Roman Nose
Romanticism
Rosebud, Battle of the
Rowlandson, Mary White
Russell, Charles Marion
Russia

Sacagawea
Sachem
Sagamore
Samoset
San Carlos Reservation
Sand Creek Massacre
Sans Arc Sioux
Santa Fe Trail
Saponis
Sassacus
Sassamon, John
Satanta
Sauks and Foxes
Scalp Bounty
Scalping
Schofield, John McAllister
Schurz, Carl
Scott, Winfield
Scouts, Native American
Seattle
Seminoles
Seminole War, First
Seminole War, Second
Seminole War, Third
Senecas
Senecas, French Attack on
Sequoyah
Shawnee Council
Shawnees
Sheepeater War
Sheridan, Philip Henry
Sherman, William Tecumseh
Shield
Shoshones
Shoshone War
Sibley, Henry Hastings
Sieber, Albert
Sioux
Sitting Bull

Skulking Way of War
Slaughter of the Innocents
Slavery among Native Americans
Slim Buttes, Battle of
Smallpox
Smith, John
Snake War
Sokokis
Solomon's Fork, Battle of
Soto, Hernando de
Spain
Spirit Lake Massacre
Spokanes
Spotted Tail
Springfield, Massachusetts, Burning of
Squanto
Stagecoach
Staked Plains
Standing Bear
Standing Bear v. Crook
Standing Rock Reservation
Standish, Myles
St. Clair, Arthur
St. Clair's Campaign
Steptoe, Edward Jenner
Stevens, Isaac Ingalls
Stillman's Run, Battle of
Stuart, John
Stuyvesant, Petrus
Subsistence Agriculture
Sudbury Fight
Sullivan-Clinton Expedition against the Iroquois
Sully, Alfred
Sully-Sibley Campaigns
Summit Springs, Battle of
Susquehannocks
Susquehannock War
Sutlers
Swansea, Attack on

Tall Bull
Tallushatchee, Battle of
Tanaghrisson
Taos Revolt
Taylor, Zachary
Tecumseh
Teedyuscung
Telegraph
Tenskwatawa
Tequestas
Terry, Alfred Howe
Texas Rangers

Thames, Battle of the
Theyanoguin
Timucuan Revolt
Tippecanoe, Battle of
Tobacco
Tomahawk
Tomochichi
Torture, Ritualized
Trail of Tears
Tres Castillos, Battle of
Trois-Rivières
Trois-Rivières, Treaty of
Tunicas
Turner, Frederick Jackson
Tuscaroras
Tuscarora War

Uncas
Underhill, John
Uprising of 1747
Upton, Emory
Utes
Ute War

Victorio
Virginia-Indian Treaty of 1646
Virginia-Indian Treaty of 1677/1680

Wabash, Battle of the
Wabokieshiek
Waccamaws
Wagon Box Fight
Walking Purchase
Wampanoags
Wampum
Wamsutta
Wappingers
War Belt
War Club
War Department, U.S.
Warren Wagon Train Raid
Washakie
Washington, George
Washita, Battle of the
Watie, Stand
Wayne, Anthony
Wayne's Campaign
Weatherford, William
Wells Fargo
Werowance
Wessagusset Raid
Western Reserve

Westos
Wheaton, Frank
White Bird Canyon, Battle of
Whitestone Hill, Battle of
Whitman Massacre
Willcox, Orlando Bolivar
Williams, Roger
Wilson, Henry
Winnebagos
Winnebago War
Winnemucca
Winnemucca, Sarah
Winthrop, John
Winthrop, John (Fitz-John)
Wolf Mountains, Battle of
Wood, Leonard
Wood Lake, Battle of

Wool, John Ellis
Worth, William Jenkins
Wounded Knee, Battle of
Wovoka
Wright, George
Wyandots
Wyoming, Battle of

Yakima-Rogue War
Yamasees
Yamasee War
Yaquis
Yavapais
Yuma War

Zogbaum, Rufus Fairchild

List of Maps

General Maps

Early Penetration of North America
    by European Nations: xxix
Indian Tribes of North America: xxx
Indian Land Cessions, 1776–1945: xxxi
War on the Northern Plains, 1866–1890: xxxii
War on the Southern Plains, 1866–1890: xxxiii
Warfare beyond the Northern Plains, 1866–1890: xxxiv
Warfare beyond the Southern Plains, 1866–1890: xxxv

Entry Maps

Indian Rebellions against the Spanish
    on the Southern Plains: 5
Campaigns against the Apaches, 1880s: 25
Wagon Roads and Railroads: 88

Creek War, 1813–1814: 213
Southwestern Frontier, 1813–1859: 290
Great Sioux War, 1876: 345
Indian Removal to the West: 382
Indian Territory, 1876: 387
Lord Dunmore's War, 1774: 457
Military Posts in the West, 1874: 496
Modoc War, 1872–1873: 509
Flight of the Nez Perce, June 18–October 5, 1877: 566
Indian Territory, 1854: 613
Proclamation Line of 1763: 645
Red River War, 1874–1875: 672
Seminole Wars, 1816–1858: 720
Indian Rebellions against the Spanish in the Southwest: 749
Northwestern Frontier, 1790–1832: 795
Wounded Knee Campaign, 1890: 860

List of Tables

Types of Fortifications Used during the Early American Indian
    Wars: 76
Buffalo Population Decline: 96
U.S. Government Indian Service Field Units, 1802–1903: 101
Popular Narratives of European Captivity
    by Native Americans: 123
U.S. Army Troops Assigned to Indian Duty, 1862–1865: 139
Population History of Indians in Texas, 1690–1890: 192
American Indian Demographic Change by Region: 235
Massacres during the American Indian Wars: 274
Average Price of a North American Beaver Pelt
    in Britain, 1713–1763: 314
Estimated Population of the Iroquois Confederacy,
    1763: 394
Native American Lands Purchased by the U.S. Government,
    1795–1838: 433
Estimated Casualties at the Battle of the Little Bighorn: 445

Estimated Casualties during the American Indian Wars,
    1775–1890: 473
Native American Conflicts Supported by European Intrigue dur-
    ing the Colonial Period: 511
Firing Mechanisms of Colonial Muskets: 526
Important Native American Affiliations with Europeans
    during the Colonial Era: 538
Prominent Native American Tribes during
    the American Revolution: 539
U.S. Government Indian Service Employees, 1843–1903: 578
Estimated Deaths along the Oregon Trail, 1840–1860: 593
Heads of Indian Affairs, 1824–1905: 610
Total Railroad Mileage in Use by Region, 1830–1890: 659
Estimated Deaths during the Second Seminole War: 719
Probable Smallpox Epidemics, 1520–1797: 740
Important Items in the Columbian Exchange: 797
Important Native American Spiritual Leaders: 862

M

Mabila, Battle of
Event Date: October 18, 1540

Reportedly the most sanguinary engagement ever involving Native Americans, the Battle of Mabila pitted Spanish forces against those of the Choctaws, led by Tascaloosa (Tascalusa). The battle occurred on October 18, 1540, near present-day Selma, Alabama, at the confluence of the Alabama River and the Cahawba River in central Alabama, between a Spanish force of 600 explorers led by Hernando de Soto and several thousand Choctaws.

In March 1539 a Spanish expeditionary force under de Soto sailed from Cuba and landed near present-day Tampa, Florida. The force was an impressive one of some 600 men, divided almost equally between infantry and horsemen. De Soto then set out to explore the American Southeast, leaving a path of destruction as he seized the supplies that he needed to sustain his men from the native villages he encountered.

On October 18, 1540, de Soto arrived at the fortified Choctaw town of Mabila. There he was greeted by Tascaloosa, the leader of Mabila. De Soto promptly seized him and held him hostage to secure what de Soto sought. Tascaloosa finally agreed to cooperate and to lead de Soto and his men into the village, although he insisted on sending ahead messengers to prepare his people.

When de Soto and his men entered the village the Choctaws treated them to a welcoming dance, during which Tascaloosa managed to slip away. This was the signal for the attack, made by warriors armed with bows, spears, and clubs who had been concealed in the settlement's buildings.

The Spaniards managed to cut their way free, but they lost 20 of their number in the immediate fighting. None of the Spanish troops inside the town escaped unscathed, despite armor that proved sufficient to prevent most lethal wounds. During the escape the Spaniards lost virtually all of their baggage and equipment.

After escaping the ambush, the survivors among de Soto's men fought a pitched battle outside Mabila's palisade. In the open, the Spaniards were able to use their horses to advantage and slaughter hundreds of Choctaws. With the Spaniards having regained the advantage, the Choctaws withdrew behind Mabila's wooden walls. De Soto then ordered his men to form four squadrons and assault the palisade surrounding the town from every direction. The Spanish breached the rough-hewn log palisade and then threw torches at the thatched roofs of houses in the town. De Soto kept a mounted patrol on each side of the palisade to kill any Choctaws attempting to escape the inferno.

Although the defenders repulsed the Spanish repeatedly, they suffered heavy casualties in each assault. After a nine-hour battle resistance ended, and every Choctaw defender who had survived the fires was cut down by the Spaniards. The town was burned to the ground in the fighting, destroying all of the captured Spanish baggage.

By the end of the day's fighting, at least 22 Spaniards were dead, including de Soto's own nephew, and an additional 148 were wounded. Some historians estimate Spanish casualties to have been heavier, at 70 dead and hundreds wounded. Most accounts place the Choctaw casualties at between 2,500 and 3,000, although one Spanish witness to the battle claimed that 11,000 Choctaws perished in the fighting and its aftermath. Tascaloosa's remains were never found by the Spanish, but it is likely that he died in the fighting or in the conflagration. In any event, no mention of him is found in any later European account.

Following the battle, de Soto continued his exploration and conquests, despite talk of mutiny among his followers, many of whom wished to abandon the expedition and return to Cuba.

PAUL J. SPRINGER AND SPENCER C. TUCKER

See also

Choctaws; Soto, Hernando de

References

Duncan, David Ewing. *Hernando de Soto: A Savage Quest in the Americas.* Norman: University of Oklahoma Press, 1997.

Hudson, Charles. *Knights of Spain, Warriors of the Sun: Hernando de Soto and the South's Ancient Chiefdoms.* Athens: University of Georgia Press, 1997.

Mackenzie, Ranald Slidell
Birth Date: July 27, 1840
Death Date: January 19, 1889

U.S. Army officer. Born on July 27, 1840, in New York City, the son of U.S. Navy commander Alexander Slidell Mackenzie, Ranald Slidell Mackenzie lacked the flamboyance and celebrity of his peers George Armstrong Custer and Nelson A. Miles but was one of the army's most successful Indian fighters, eventually regarded by General William T. Sherman as the indispensable man in a crisis. After briefly attending Williams College in Massachusetts, Mackenzie went on to attend the U.S. Military Academy at West Point, where he graduated first in his class in 1862. Initially serving as an engineering officer in the Army of the Potomac during the American Civil War (1861–1865), Mackenzie was badly wounded in his first action, the Second Battle of Bull Run (Manassas) on August 29, 1862. He performed engineering duties in the Battle of Fredericksburg (December 13, 1862). Following his participation in the Battle of Chancellorsville (May 1–4, 1863), he was promoted to first lieutenant and brevetted to captain. He was promoted to captain in the regular army after his service at Gettysburg (July 1–3, 1863). In 1864 he saw service in both the Battle of the Wilderness (May 5–7) and the Battle of Spotsylvania Court House (May 7–19).

Promoted to colonel, Mackenzie commanded a regiment in the Shenandoah Valley Campaign, during which he was again wounded, and in the Siege of Petersburg, where he lost two fingers on his right hand, leading the Indians to call him "Bad Hand." At the end of the war Mackenzie was a brigadier general of volunteers, commanding the Cavalry Division in the Army of the James. He led the division at Five Forks and during the Appomattox Campaign (April 3–9, 1865). Mackenzie's abilities and exemplary bravery, reflected in his many wounds (six during the war), led to rapid promotion. He ended the war with brevet promotions through the rank of brigadier general in the regular army and major general of volunteers.

In 1866 on the reorganization of the army, Mackenzie remained in the army but at his permanent rank of captain. In 1867 he accepted command of an African American unit, the 41st Infantry

Regiment, no doubt in part to secure a rare postwar colonelcy. Whatever his motive, he molded the regiment into an efficient outfit. In 1869 he took command of the 24th Infantry Regiment, a consolidation of the 41st and 38th regiments. The following year he took command of the 4th Cavalry, which he transformed into one of the finest regiments on the frontier.

From 1871 to 1874 Mackenzie pursued various Native American tribes in western Texas and led a controversial raid across the Rio Grande some 60 miles into Mexico to attack Lipan and Kickapoo villages. In 1873 he received his seventh wound.

During the Red River War (1874–1875), Mackenzie's surprise attack won the climactic engagement at Palo Duro Canyon on September 28, 1874, capturing some 1,500 Indian horses, most of which he ordered shot to prevent their recapture. Famed Comanche leader Quanah Parker personally surrendered to Mackenzie on June 2, 1875, at Fort Sill, ending the war on the southern Plains.

Following the debacle of the Battle of the Little Bighorn (June 25–26, 1876), Mackenzie and the 4th Cavalry were a key part of the 1876 punitive campaign that ended the Great Sioux War (1876–1877). After forcing Dull Knife's Cheyennes back to the reservation with another devastating surprise attack in November 1876, Mackenzie spent the rest of the decade suppressing banditry in Texas and New Mexico. In 1881 with a bold show of force in Colorado, he singlehandedly prevented a renewed war with the Utes,

U.S. Army colonel Ranald Mackenzie commanded the 4th Cavalry Regiment in the West, molding it into one of the most effective units in the entire army during the Indian Wars of the 1870s and early 1880s. (Library of Congress)

a feat that he regarded as his greatest accomplishment. He then served briefly in Arizona during the early stages of the Geronimo Campaign (1881–1886). Mackenzie's operations on the frontier were distinguished by sound logistics, careful reconnaissance, surprise attacks, concentration of force, and low casualties among his own troops and his enemies alike.

Mackenzie's last campaign was for a brigadier general's star. His many wounds, long frontier service, and high-strung nature were eroding his health, and he sought a less strenuous posting. Sensing that time was running out, supporters convinced President Chester A. Arthur to approve Mackenzie's promotion in October 1882. By that time Mackenzie, serving as commander of the Department of Texas, was already in a noticeable state of decline. Briefly institutionalized after a nervous breakdown in 1883, he spent the rest of his life in various stages of insanity. Recognized as one of the outstanding soldiers in American military history, Mackenzie died at his sister's home in New Brighton, Staten Island, New York, on January 19, 1889.

RAYMOND W. LEONARD

See also

Cavalry Regiment, 4th U.S.; Cheyennes; Dull Knife; Dull Knife Fight; Palo Duro Canyon, Battle of; Powder River Expedition; Quanah Parker; Red River War; Staked Plains; Utes

References

Carter, Robert Goldthwaite. *On the Border with Mackenzie; or, Winning West Texas from the Comanches.* New York: Antiquarian Press, 1961.

Cozzens, Peter, ed. *Eyewitnesses to the Indian Wars, 1865–1890.* 5 vols. Mechanicsburg, PA: Stackpole, 2001–2006.

Dorst, Joseph H. "Ranald Slidell Mackenzie." In *Eyewitness to the Indian Wars, 1865–1890,* Vol. 5, *The Army and the Indian,* edited by Peter Cozzens, 249–261. Mechanicsburg, PA: Stackpole, 2005.

Pierce, Michael D. *The Most Promising Young Officer: A Life of Ranald Slidell Mackenzie.* Norman: University of Oklahoma Press, 1993.

Robinson, Charles M., III. *Bad Hand: A Biography of General Ranald S. Mackenzie.* Austin, TX: State House Press, 1993.

Wallace, Ernest. *Ranald S. Mackenzie on the Texas Frontier.* College Station: Texas A&M University Press, 1993.

Mackenzie's Mexico Raid
Start Date: May 17, 1873
End Date: May 19, 1873

Controversial expedition by Colonel Ranald Slidell Mackenzie and six companies of the 4th U.S. Cavalry Regiment that crossed the Rio Grande to attack Kickapoo and Lipan villages near El Remolino, Coahuila, Mexico, between May 17 and 19, 1873. Tensions had been building along the U.S.-Mexican border since the mid-1860s. While migrating to Mexico in 1865, the Kickapoos had been attacked by a combined force of Texans and Confederate soldiers. Thereafter the Kickapoos and their neighbors, the Lipans, conducted raids into Texas from territory granted to them by the Mexican government. Although these two groups may have been blamed for more than their actual share of frontier strife, it was reckoned that they had caused more than $50 million in property damage and losses to American settlers north of the Rio Grande.

By early 1873, attempts by U.S. secretary of state Hamilton Fish to persuade the Mexican government to allow punitive raids against the Kickapoos had come to naught, so U.S. Army lieutenant general Philip H. Sheridan directed Mackenzie to solve the problem by whatever means necessary. The implication was that the highest authorities, including General William T. Sherman, commanding general of the U.S. Army, and President Ulysses S. Grant, had authorized Mackenzie to invade Mexico and attack the Kickapoo settlements. Although no official order to that effect had been given, the expedition against the Kickapoos and Lipans went forward on Mackenzie's own authority.

On May 17, 1873, Mackenzie's scouts informed him that most of the Kickapoo warriors had departed their three villages near El Remolino to participate in a hunting trip. This was the opportunity that Mackenzie had been waiting for. By nightfall, his cavalry and Black Seminole scouts were crossing the Rio Grande, the first leg of an all-night ride that would get them to El Remolino by dawn. After nearly 16 straight hours in the saddle and 30 hours without sleep, the cavalry came upon the three villages, where they formed up for a full frontal charge. Although a few Native American warriors had stayed to protect the villages, it was a one-sided battle that was over in a matter of minutes.

By Mackenzie's account 19 Native Americans were killed, although the actual number was perhaps significantly greater. Three of the cavalrymen were wounded, 1 mortally. Following the battle, the troops burned the villages and took 40 women and children as hostages.

The most harrowing part of their raid proved to be the journey home. Exhausted and fearful of Mexican retaliation, the men struggled to get back across the Rio Grande, which they finally forded on the morning of May 19. It is estimated that Mackenzie's cavalry traveled 159 miles in 32 hours in the course of invading Mexico, destroying the Kickapoo villages, and returning to the United States.

The public response to Mackenzie's Mexican raid was favorable in the United States, especially in Texas, where cross-border depredations dropped significantly. The Mexican government protested to no avail. Mackenzie was completely sustained by his superiors, just as Sheridan had implied. The Kickapoos were forced to sue for peace, and in an agreement concluded on July 7, 1873, they agreed to return to their former reservation in Indian Territory.

CAMERON B. STRANG

See also

Cavalry Regiment, 4th U.S.; Kickapoos; Lipan Apaches; Mackenzie, Ranald Slidell; Mexico; Seminoles; Sheridan, Philip Henry; Sherman, William Tecumseh

References

Pierce, Michael D. *The Most Promising Young Officer: A Life of Ranald Slidell Mackenzie.* Norman: University of Oklahoma Press, 1993.

Robinson, Charles M., III. *Bad Hand: A Biography of General Ranald S. Mackenzie.* Austin, TX: State House Press, 1993.

Mahicans

Native American group, an eastern branch of the Algonquians, who inhabited the interior northeastern part of North America. The French often called the Mahicans Loups, the French word for "wolves." The name "Mahican" is the Dutch spelling of the tribe's name, while "Mohican," less in favor today, is the English spelling.

The Mahicans' homeland was the upper Hudson River Valley from the Catskill Mountains north to the southern tip of Lake Champlain. From the Schoharie River, their homeland extended east to the Berkshire Mountains of Massachusetts and from northwestern Connecticut to southern Vermont. The Mahicans are not to be confused with the Mohegans of Connecticut.

The five clans of the Mahicans lived in fortified villages, each comprising 20 to 30 longhouses on hills. The Mahicans were agriculturalists who also hunted, fished, and gathered wild foods. In addition, they traded for Great Lakes copper, which they used in jewelry and arrowheads.

Living inland, the Mahicans generally avoided slavery under European ship captains. As such, the Mahicans lacked the hostility toward Europeans that was so evident in coastal tribes. Indeed, the Mahicans were friendly toward and eager to trade with the explorer Henry Hudson in 1609. They also engaged in the fur trade with the Dutch. The Mahicans adapted quickly to Dutch firearms and were excellent marksmen.

The fur trade, however, exposed the Mahicans to European diseases and destabilized their region. The Mahicans fought an intermittent war with the Mohawks, who desired part of the lucrative Mahican wampum production on Long Island Sound as well as a share of the Dutch fur trade. By 1623 the Mahicans were harvesting more furs than nature could replenish, in effect largely exhausting the fur supply. In consequence, when the West India Company acquired the charter for New Netherland in 1624, Dutch policy favored settlement rather than trade.

The Dutch intermarried with the Mahicans but also created difficulties for them. The Dutch demand that the Mahicans arrange trade with the Algonquins and French-allied Montagnais, enemies of the Mohawks, provoked a war with the Mohawks during 1624–1628. The Dutch initially supported the Mahicans, but with the Dutch sustaining casualties, Governor Peter Minuit evacuated Fort Orange (Albany) and began a policy of strict neutrality. The Mahicans lost the war in 1628 and were forced to pay tribute to the Mohawks.

To provide the Mohawks with wampum for the Dutch trade, the Mahicans subdued and absorbed smaller tribes such as the Wappingers. The Mahicans maintained their villages in the vicinity of present-day Albany, New York, although many Mahicans relocated north and east to escape the Mohawks altogether. Disease and war both took their toll.

The Mahicans joined the French anti-Iroquois alliance in 1650 and continued relations with the Dutch and other Europeans and their intermittent war with the Mohawks until the English took New Netherland in 1664. The Mahicans, who had less influence with the English than did the Mohawks and other Iroquois, moved to western Massachusetts and in 1672 fell under the protection of the Iroquois League. The Mahicans played only a limited role in the 18th-century wars between the British and the French, often appearing on the British side as scouts or auxiliaries, and fought on the Patriot side in the American Revolutionary War (1775–1783).

As European settlements encroached, the Mahicans sold their land. By 1775 the last of the Mahican landholdings was at Stockbridge, Massachusetts, where they held only 200 acres. The Mahicans' population plummeted over the course of two centuries. In 1600 the Mahican Confederacy near Albany, New York, may have numbered some 8,000 people. By 1672 the population was only about 1,000, and by 1796 Mahicans numbered just 300 people in Stockbridge, living with the Oneidas and the Brothertons in New York, and 300 people living with the Delawares and the Wyandots in Ohio. Other Mahicans moved to present-day Indiana or beyond the Mississippi River. Today the Mahicans are considered extinct as a separate tribal entity.

James Fenimore Cooper's *The Last of the Mohicans* was loosely based on the Mahicans, although Cooper conflated the Mahican and Mohegan tribes, which were quite different. While the novel took place on territory once inhabited by the Mahicans (Hudson Valley and northern New York), many of the names that Cooper used were actually Mohegan.

JOHN H. BARNHILL

See also

Algonquins; Cooper, James Fenimore; Delawares; Fur Trade; Iroquois; Iroquois Confederacy; Mohawk-Mahican War; Mohawks; Oneidas; Wappingers

References

Brasser, Ted J. *Riding on the Frontier's Crest: Mahican Indian Culture and Culture Change.* Ottawa: National Museums of Canada, 1974.

Dunn, Shirley W. *The Mohican World, 1680–1750.* Fleishmanns, NY: Purple Mountain, 2000.

Frazier, Patrick. *The Mohicans of Stockbridge.* Lincoln: University of Nebraska Press, 1992.

Maize

See Corn

Makataimeshekiakiak

See Black Hawk

Makhpyia-luta

See Red Cloud

Mangas Coloradas
Birth Date: ca. 1790
Death Date: January 18, 1863

Chiricahua Apache leader during the mid-1800s. Born around 1790 in southwestern New Mexico, near present-day Silver City, Mangas Coloradas, from the 1830s until his death in 1863, was the most prominent leader of the Chiricahuas in their struggle for regional dominance with the Mexicans and, beginning in the late 1840s, with the Americans. The Chiricahuas consisted of four major bands: the Chihennes, the Chokonens, the Bedonkohes, and the Nednhis. There was no single tribe in political terms, but all were related, sharing strong linguistic and cultural bonds.

Mangas Coloradas probably was born as a Bedonkohe and married into the Chihenne band. For the first decades of his life he was known as Fuerte and only later received the name Kandazis-tlishishen, or Mangas Coloradas ("Red Sleeves" or "Pink Sleeves"). He came from a prominent family and matured during the period of relative peace between the Spanish and the Indians, when rations and gifts were regularly distributed to the Apaches. Economic and political unrest prompted by the collapse of Spanish power, however, caused this system to crumble.

Struggling Mexican regimes no longer could afford to pay off the Chiricahuas, and escalating warfare became epidemic during the 1830s and continued to devastate both the Chiricahuas and the Mexicans until the 1880s. Because of their policies of extermination and treacherous acts of genocide, the Mexicans of Sonora especially gained Mangas Coloradas's deep hatred.

Character was the single most important factor in Mangas Coloradas's rise to prominence. He excelled as a fierce fighter, a courageous leader, a generous statesman, a wise diplomat, and a loving family man, all traits valued in Chiricahua society. From the 1830s onward his power and prestige among the many Chiricahua bands were exceptional. He not only controlled his own local group, which was a mix of Bedonkohes and Chihennes, but also attracted a wide following of fighting men and many times led a combined force of Chiricahuas from all bands. He gained even more influence by marrying his children wisely. For example, one daughter wed the Chokonen Apache leader Cochise, while others married prominent Navajo, White Mountain Apache, and Mescalero Apache men.

Overall, Mangas was exceptionally well-connected with the many Apache divisions of the Southwest. Mexicans recognized him as the "general" of the Chiricahuas, the most prominent man of that militarily powerful people and whose cooperation and approval were vital for any significant peace initiative to succeed. He was also synonymous with Apache power and cruelty among many Mexicans, and the American invaders knew his reputation when they arrived in the late 1840s.

At first Mangas Coloradas advocated peaceful relations with the Americans, who shared a common enemy with him: the Mexicans. The Americans were rich in trade commodities and thus were useful as partners. However, racial hatred, economic greed, and a lack of mutual respect brought war, and despite peace agreements, several violent incidents caused a deterioration in American–Chiricahua Apache relations throughout the 1850s and early 1860s. During the last years of the prominent chief's life, American miners, ranchers, and farmers began to inundate much of his country.

Mangas Coloradas became engaged in a destructive war with the Americans during the early 1860s and was killed by U.S. volunteers on January 18, 1863, at Fort McLane (southwestern New Mexico) after he had arrived for peace negotiations. Upon his arrival, he was captured and handed over to the American military. While he was a prisoner, soldiers taunted him and burned his feet, and when Mangas Coloradas responded, he was shot and killed. His body was thrown into a ditch after being decapitated for "scientific purposes." Military reports later contained a fabricated story of an escape attempt.

During his lifetime Mangas Coloradas saw Chiricahua power dwindle under the double pressure of Mexican and American colonization. When he was born the Chiricahuas were the dominant group in the region, but his death signaled the beginning of the end for Apache power. In a little more than two decades, all of the surviving Chiricahuas would be exiled to Florida as prisoners of war.

JANNE LAHTI

See also
Apache Wars; Cochise

References
Sweeney, Edwin R. *Mangas Coloradas: Chief of the Chiricahua Apaches.* Norman: University of Oklahoma Press, 1998.
Worcester, Donald E. *The Apaches: Eagles of the Southwest.* Norman: University of Oklahoma Press, 1979.

Manifest Destiny

An ideological mind-set used to rationalize the westward territorial expansion of the United States to the Pacific Ocean during the 1840s and 1850s. Manifest Destiny expressed the belief that the United States had the God-given right and indeed the duty to occupy the remainder of the continent and that such expansion was clearly justified (manifest) and inevitable (destiny). The concept was also later used to legitimize overseas expansion in the 1890s. Although the term was not coined until 1845, the idea of Manifest Destiny had suffused American thinking since the colonial period. Constant westward expansion by English colonists and later by Americans was a recurring feature of American

John Gast's 1873 painting *American Progress* depicts an allegorical female figure of America leading settlers, telegraph lines, and railroads into the untamed West. The concept of Manifest Destiny represented in the painting was the belief that the United States had a moral and divine mandate to control the remainder of the continent to the Pacific. (Library of Congress)

history. To be sure, expansion had momentous effects on Native Americans who had previously inhabited these regions.

The phrase "manifest destiny" was coined in the summer of 1845 by John L. O'Sullivan, a journalist and the editor of the *United States Magazine and Democratic Review*. In an essay supporting the annexation of Texas, he argued for the "fulfillment of our manifest destiny to overspread the continent allotted by Providence for the free development of our yearly multiplying millions." However, Manifest Destiny included more than the will for westward expansion. It was also a belief that the United States was exceptional among all the world's nations—the promised land, the new Israel, and God's own country—and that its people had both a divine mission and the altruistic right to spread the virtue of its democratic institutions and liberties to new realms. Indeed, this thinking can be traced back to the 17th century, when in 1630 the Puritan leader John Winthrop referred to the Massachusetts Bay Colony as a unique "city upon a hill" that would provide an example to the rest of the world.

The theme of American exceptionalism was heightened during the American Revolutionary War (1775–1783), when the colonists fought for the right to implement their own version of freedom. With independence came the promise of expansion, which included cheap and abundant land and economic opportunities west and south of the 13 original colonies. The Louisiana Purchase of 1803 and the acquisition of Florida from Spain in the 1819 Adams-Onis Treaty more than doubled the size of the United States, creating a new frontier that offered relief for a growing population.

The Monroe Doctrine of 1823 also exemplified the ideas and the mood behind Manifest Destiny. When President James Monroe warned Europe that the Americas were no longer "to be considered as subjects for future colonization by any European powers," he paved the way for increasing U.S. hegemony over its neighbors by establishing his nation as the legitimate protector of the Western Hemisphere. Thus, the concept of Manifest Destiny became even more important during the Oregon Boundary Dispute with Great Britain and in U.S. relations with Mexico.

Regarding Oregon, Great Britain and the United States had agreed in the Anglo-American Convention of 1818 to jointly occupy the Oregon Territory. However, in the years following the treaty, thousands of American settlers had migrated to the Northwest, and calls for annexation of the region became very popular in the 1840s. When Great Britain rejected President John Tyler's proposal to divide the area along the 49th parallel, American expansionists responded with demands for a northern border along the 54°40' line (the slogan at the time was "Fifty-Four Forty or Fight").

The question of the annexation of Oregon played an important role in the election of James K. Polk as president in 1844. After the election, however, Polk did not yield to the extremists and settled the boundary dispute with Britain diplomatically, terminating the joint occupation arrangement and establishing the international boundary along the 49th Parallel.

At the same time, expansionist sentiments led to war with Mexico in 1846. Ever since Mexico had opened its province of Coahuila y Texas for colonization in 1823, thousands of settlers from the United States had moved south. The movement was so strong that Mexican authorities soon lost control of the province. During 1835–1836, differences between American settlers and the Mexican government led the newcomers to revolt against Mexico and declare Texas independent. They then sought admittance to the United States. The annexation of Texas was highly controversial among U.S. politicians, however, because it would come in as a slave state. Anxious to keep the delicate balance between slave and free states, the United States rebuffed Texas's request to join the Union. The question of what to do with Texas was an issue in the 1844 presidential campaign because Polk promised annexation should he be elected, which prompted President John Tyler to push an annexation treaty through Congress before Polk took office. Although Polk agreed to settle the boundary dispute over Oregon diplomatically, he refused to compromise with Mexico over the contested Texas-Mexico boundary.

Polk's desire to acquire California as well as the disputed portion of Texas led to war with Mexico in May 1846. In supporting war against Mexico, American expansionists for the first time cited racial reasons for expanding American territory. This reasoning, though, was controversial even among expansionists. Its supporters argued that Manifest Destiny would help improve the Mexicans, while its opponents claimed that Mexicans, as non–Anglo-Saxons, were not qualified to become Americans. When the Mexican-American War (1846–1848) ended with the Treaty of Guadalupe Hidalgo (February 1848), Mexico ceded to the United States present-day Texas with its boundary at the Rio Grande and what would become New Mexico, Arizona, California, and parts of Nevada, Utah, and Colorado. The United States had now accomplished its goal of expanding its territory to the Pacific Ocean.

After decades of internal struggle, civil war, and reconstruction, the belief that Manifest Destiny justified the seizing of Native American and Mexican lands was revived in the 1890s. The ideology behind the term, however, now contained elements of social Darwinism and social determinism. Expansionists believed that it was the white man's burden to lead inferior races in other parts of the world to better lives. This expanded set of beliefs incorporated ideas not only about race and religion but also about culture and economic opportunities.

Expansionists assumed that Americans had the divine right to dominate other lands because they belonged to the most advanced race and had the most developed culture, the best political and economic systems, and the necessary military and technical expertise. By 1898 at the conclusion of the Spanish-American War, the United States had acquired Cuba, Guam, Puerto Rico, and the Philippines. In a separate event, the United States assumed control of the Hawaiian Islands. In Cuba, the United States did not establish de facto political control but certainly maintained strong economic and political ties with the island that endured until the late 1950s. These events made the United States a major world power by 1900.

From the Native American perspective, inexorable westward expansion and ideas of Manifest Destiny proved catastrophic. The United States fought a series of wars with tribes on the Great Plains and in the Far West from the late 1840s to the early 1890s, almost all of which had to do with white encroachment on Native American lands and disputes over land title and ownership. Those tribes that chose not to fight were nevertheless divested of most or all of their lands via treaties. The Indian Wars essentially ended with the Battle of Wounded Knee in December 1890. By then, perhaps as much as 90 percent of all Native American lands had been claimed by white settlers and the U.S. government.

KATJA WUESTENBECKER

See also
Land Cessions, Northwest Ordinance; Louisiana Purchase; Mexico; Wounded Knee, Battle of

References
Haynes, Sam W., and Christopher Morris, eds. *Manifest Destiny and Empire: American Antebellum Expansion.* College Station: Texas A&M University Press, 1997.
Heidler, David S., and Jeanne T. Heidler. *Manifest Destiny.* Westport, CT: Greenwood, 2003.
Stephanson, Anders. *Manifest Destiny: American Expansion and the Empire of Right.* New York: Hill and Wang, 1996.

Manuelito
Birth Date: ca. 1818
Death Date: 1894

Navajo leader. Manuelito, a Spanish name given him by Mexicans, was noted for his resistance to Mexican and American invasions of Navajo territory, or Dinétah. Manuelito was born around 1818 into the Bit'ahni Clan ("Folded Arms People") near Bear Ears in present-day Utah. He trained as a medicine man who followed *hózhó*, the path of harmony and balance to Old Age that the Navajos had been following for many generations. Manuelito's marriage to the daughter of the headman Narbona provided him with the wise leader's insight.

Manuelito was one of the most accomplished of Navajo war leaders. He staunchly resisted Mexican and American encroachments on Navajo territory and was the recognized head chief of the Navajos from 1870 to 1884. (Library of Congress)

Beginning in the late 1500s, Spaniards and then Mexicans had come into the Southwest seeking their fortunes and establishing colonies. The Navajos experienced cultural changes that made them herders and warriors. With the horse, the Navajos ably impeded the foreigners' advances. Manuelito witnessed the shifting relationships of peace and conflict between Navajo and Mexicans. In the 1830s Mexicans rode into Navajo territory determined to break Navajo resistance and to capture women and children for the slave trade. Slavery had been previously known in the Southwest, but the slave trade intensified with Spanish and Mexican invasions. Raiding for Navajo slaves reached a peak during the 1830s. In a battle at Copper Pass in 1835 in the Chuska Mountains, warriors led by Narbona and Manuelito defeated the Mexicans.

By the time the United States laid claim to the Southwest in 1848, Manuelito was a respected war chief, and the cycle of peace and conflict among Navajos, other tribal peoples, and U.S. immigrants began anew. In 1851 the establishment of Fort Defiance on Navajo land preceded a war that would end in the Navajos' defeat. The conflict began over the pasturelands that lay outside the newly established fort. In 1858 Captain (Brevet Major) W. T. H. Brooks asserted control over the pastures for U.S. Army use. In defiance, Manuelito continued to pasture his livestock on the disputed

lands, whereupon Brooks ordered the livestock slaughtered. Soon afterward a Navajo killed Brooks's black slave, and Brooks demanded that the Navajos produce the murderer for American justice. Eventually the Navajos produced a body, most likely that of a Mexican captive. Enraged at what he considered Navajo arrogance, Brooks decided to go on the offensive. In 1860 Manuelito and 1,000 warriors attacked Fort Defiance several times but were unable to take the fort.

The American Civil War (1861–1865) initially turned the U.S. Army's attention away from the Navajos, however, and Fort Defiance was abandoned. During the war, American settlement again threatened the Navajos. Manuelito led the resistance and urged his people to have courage. Finding the Navajos to be obstacles to white expansion, Brigadier General James H. Carleton ordered their removal to a reservation near Fort Sumner, New Mexico, where the Navajos would learn the arts of "civilization."

Carleton enlisted Colonel Christopher "Kit" Carson for the campaign against the Navajo. Carson and his men burned Navajo settlements, destroying cornfields, peach trees, and livestock. By 1863 destitute Navajos began surrendering to the Americans. As prisoners, they endured a 300-mile journey to the internment camp. Some Navajo leaders went with their people, encouraging them to keep heart, even though Navajo bodies littered the trail. The old and sick were abandoned, and pregnant women were shot and killed if they could not keep up. Many Navajos drowned when they tried to cross the Rio Grande. At the Bosque Redondo reservation, which was in reality a prison, the Navajos barely survived.

Manuelito, however, vowed to remain free. U.S. officials, fearing that he would serve as inspiration to others who sought to elude their enemy, hoped to either capture or kill him. In 1865 Navajo leaders, including Herrera, met Manuelito and gave him the army's message to surrender. Manuelito refused.

Finally, in 1866 Manuelito, wounded and ill, surrendered and was interned at Bosque Rodondo. After four years Carleton reluctantly admitted that his plan was not working, and there was talk of returning the Navajos to their former homes. On June 1, 1868, Manuelito and other leaders signed a treaty so that they could return to Dinétah. The treaty stipulated a peaceful relationship between the Navajos and the United States, defined a boundary for a reservation, and required education for Navajo children. Seventeen days later, some 8,000 Navajos began the journey home.

Upon his return to Dinétah, Manuelito remained an influential leader who articulated his concerns for the return of his people's land. He was appointed head of the first Navajo police charged with keeping order on the reservation. In 1874 he traveled with his wife and other Navajo leaders to Washington, D.C., to meet President Ulysses S. Grant. Manuelito died in 1894 in New Mexico from disease and alcoholism.

JENNIFER NEZ DENETDALE

See also
Bosque Redondo; Carleton, James Henry; Carson, Christopher Houston; Navajo Removal; Navajos; Navajo War

References

Iverson, Peter. *Diné: A History of the Navajos.* Albuquerque: University of New Mexico Press, 2002.

Roessel, Ruth. *Navajo Stories of the Long Walk Period.* Tsaile, AZ: Navajo Community College Press, 1973.

Sundberg, Lawrence D. *Dinétah: An Early History of the Navajo People.* Santa Fe, NM: Sunstone, 1995.

Marias Massacre
Event Date: January 23, 1870

Massacre of nearly 200 Blackfoot Piegan Sioux on January 23, 1870, along the Marias River in Montana by a detachment of U.S. cavalry under the command of Major Eugene M. Baker. The Marias Massacre is also often referred to as the Baker Massacre. The bloodshed was the result of ever-increasing tensions between Native Americans and whites in the northern Plains region, largely as a result of the growing influx of white settlers into the area.

The more immediate catalyst for the massacre began in 1867 when a Blackfoot by the name of Owl Child purportedly stole several horses from Malcolm Clark, a white trader in the area. Owl Child claimed that Clark had stolen his horses and that he was simply evening the score. Clark and his son subsequently hunted down Owl Child and severely beat him. In August 1869 Owl Child, bent on revenge, took several Blackfeet with him and murdered Clark; they also seriously wounded Clark's son. The killing outraged white settlers, who demanded retribution. The U.S. Army now insisted that Owl Child be turned over to American authorities, dead or alive, in two weeks' time.

The Blackfeet refused to abide by the ultimatum, and Owl Child went into hiding under the protection of the principal Piegan chief, Mountain Chief. Upon the expiration of the two-week deadline, a detachment from the 2nd Cavalry Regiment, under the command of Major Baker, was ordered to find Mountain Chief's hideout and punish the Native Americans. Baker's order specified that he "strike them hard." The plan had been to attack the village in early morning while most of the Native Americans slept or were huddled inside to keep warm in the frigid January weather.

On January 23 Baker received a report that Mountain Chief's clan was encamped along the Marias River, so he readied his unit for an attack. Mountain Chief, however, had learned of the impending attack and fled. Thus, the encampment that Baker hit that day was not Mountain Chief's but rather that of Chief Heavy Runner, who had generally enjoyed cordial relations with whites. Several scouts had apparently warned Baker that the encampment might not be that of Mountain Chief, but Baker ignored these concerns and struck anyway.

Most of the men in the village were out on a hunt, meaning that the majority of the inhabitants were women, children, and the elderly. What followed was a quick and bloody affair in which at least 173 Blackfeet died, including women and children; another 140 women and children were taken prisoner. U.S. losses included 1 cavalryman who died from a fall from his horse. Chief Heavy Runner was killed in the attack; survivors hid amid ice floes in the frigid waters of the Marias River. Much of the encampment was also torched. Baker came under intense scrutiny for the Marias Massacre, but in the end the army insisted that he had only been following orders, and no official investigation of the incident ever took place.

PAUL G. PIERPAOLI JR.

See also

Blackfoot Sioux

References

Bastien, Betty. *Blackfoot Ways of Knowing: The World View of the Siksi-kaitsitapi.* Calgary, Alberta, Canada: University of Calgary Press, 2004.

Welch, James, with Paul Stekler. *Killing Custer: The Battle of Little Bighorn and the Fate of the Plains Indians.* New York: Norton, 1994.

Mariposa War
Start Date: May 1850
End Date: July 1851

War between Native American tribes of the Yosemite region of central California and white settlers drawn to the area by the California Gold Rush. The first skirmish occurred in May 1850, and the final shot of the war was fired in June 1851. The results of the conflict included the removal of tribes from the central Sierra Nevada mountains and the discovery of unique geological formations and gold deposits in the Yosemite area.

The discovery of gold in California in 1848 attracted a rush of hundreds of thousands of settlers the following year, many of whom headed into the foothills near Yosemite Valley. By the spring of 1850 white settlements, trading posts, and gold claims had been established along the Merced, Fresno, and San Joaquin river systems. Local tribes—particularly the Yosemites, Chowchillas, and Nootchus—resented this encroachment on their lands and in May 1850 decided to take action.

The first attack was launched by the Yosemites in May against a trading post operated by James Savage along the Merced River. A coalition of tribes led by Yosemite chief Tenieya conducted similar attacks and ambushes over the next six months along the many waterways flowing out of the Sierras. Savage attempted to counter Tenieya by creating an opposing alliance of tribes under the leadership of José Juarez, chief of the Tulareno tribe. This failed, however, when Chief Juarez was slighted by Savage and recommended to his fellow chiefs that the whites be driven from the area.

In December 1850 Governor Peter Burnett authorized a U.S. Indian agent, Adam Johnston, to try to settle the dispute between the warring parties. Further Native American attacks convinced Johnston that force would be necessary to pacify the native population, although he cautioned the local militia to keep in mind that it was technically trespassing on Native American lands. James Burney, the sheriff of Mariposa, organized the first militia group, eventually known as the Mariposa Battalion. In early January 1851 Burney led his men to a native encampment near present-day Oakhurst. In the ensuing skirmish, the Native Americans were driven from their camp and suffered about 40 casualties; Burney's unit lost 6 men. Upon returning to Mariposa, Burney requested additional manpower from Governor John McDougal, who had recently succeeded Burnett, and by the end of January Burney had more than 200 militiamen in the Mariposa Battalion.

In February 1851 three Indian commissioners were sent by the federal government to resolve the situation and convince the local tribes to sign treaties and settle on reservations. In addition, Savage replaced Burney as commander of the Mariposa Battalion. From February to June, the battalion conducted operations along the Sierra Nevada, sending three separate expeditions up Mariposa Creek, the Fresno River, and the San Joaquin River. As tribes were subdued and pacified they signed treaties negotiated with the commissioners who had set up camp along Mariposa Creek. The last to come to terms with the U.S. government was the Yosemites, who had holed up in Yosemite Valley and only agreed to surrender when one of Tenieya's sons was killed. In July 1851 the Mariposa Battalion was disbanded, and the Mariposa War officially ended.

On paper the treaties called for reservations totaling more than 8 million acres of good land, but opposition in California's legislature and the U.S. House of Representatives led to major changes in those agreements. The Native Americans thus received very few of the benefits of the negotiated settlements. Similarly, the Mariposa Battalion was never reimbursed for its expenses or losses by the state or federal governments. The Mariposa War forced the relocation of native tribes, which opened the area for future settlement and prospecting by white Americans.

ROBERT W. DUVALL

See also
California Gold Rush

References
Bunnell, Lafayette H. *Discovery of the Yosemite and the Indian War of 1851 Which Led to That Event*. El Portal, CA: Yosemite Association, 1991.
Crampton, C. Gregory, ed. *The Mariposa Indian War, 1850–1851: Diaries of Robert Eccleston; The California Gold Rush, Yosemite, and the High Sierra*. Salt Lake City: University of Utah Press, 1957.

Mason, John
Birth Date: ca. 1600
Death Date: 1672

English-born militia officer best known for leading the assault that destroyed the Pequot settlement on the Mystic River in 1637 in the Mystic Fort Fight. John Mason was probably born in 1600 in England. There are few known details of his life prior to his arrival in North America. Mason served with English forces under Sir Horace Vere in about 1630 in the Netherlands, where he held a lieutenant's commission and befriended Sir Thomas Fairfax.

Mason arrived in Massachusetts Bay Colony in 1632. There he became a militia officer and was commissioned to hunt local pirates and given responsibility for overseeing the construction of fortifications. At one point he became a representative to the Massachusetts General Court. In 1635 Mason helped found what became Windsor, one of the first English settlements on the Connecticut River.

Following the Native American raid on Wethersfield in April 1637, the Connecticut Colony declared war on the Pequots and appointed Captain Mason to lead its forces against them. Mason traveled down the Connecticut River to Fort Saybrook with 90 English militiamen and 60 Mohegans led by Uncas. The Connecticut General Court had instructed Mason to attack the primary Pequot settlement on the Pequot River, but once at Saybrook, Mason decided to sail to Narragansett Bay and march overland to assault the town on the Mystic River.

Obtaining permission from the Narragansetts to travel through their territory, Mason's force attacked Mystic on May 26, 1637, surrounding the village, setting it on fire, and killing or capturing any Pequots who attempted to escape. As many as 700 Pequots—men, women, and children—perished in the attack. Following the successful campaign, Mason led forces to hunt down and capture other bands of Pequots later that summer. After the Treaty of Hartford subjugated the Pequots to the Narragansetts and the Mohegans in 1638, Mason led another expedition later that year against a Pequot group that was trying to live independently.

Shortly after the Mystic Fort Fight, Mason was promoted to major. In 1660 he was also appointed the colony's deputy governor. Mason lived at Fort Saybrook from 1647 to 1659 and later helped found the town of Norwich.

During the Pequot War (1636–1638), Mason established a firm friendship with Uncas. That relationship was a key component of Connecticut's strong support for the Mohegans in later years. From the Pequot War until the end of his life, one of Mason's chief duties was negotiating with local Native American tribes. Mason died in Norwich, Connecticut, sometime in 1672.

MATTHEW S. MUEHLBAUER

See also
Hartford, Treaty of; Mohegans; Mystic Fort Fight; Narragansetts; Pequots; Pequot War; Uncas

References
Mason, John. *A Brief History of the Pequot War*. 1736; reprint, Ann Arbor, MI: University Microfilms, 1966.
Mason, Louis Bond. *The Life and Times of Major John Mason of Connecticut, 1600–1672*. New York: Putnam, 1935.

Massachusetts Bay–Pequot Treaty
Failed peace agreement between the colonists of Massachusetts Bay and the Pequots. In October 1634 the Pequot Nation sent an

envoy to the Massachusetts Bay Colony in hopes of concluding a treaty of friendship and securing protection against their enemies, the Narragansetts. The colonial leaders received the envoy's gifts but refused to negotiate with him because, they held, he was not of sufficient rank. The colonists then told the envoy to summon Pequot sachems (chiefs) for a conference. They also demanded that the Pequots produce the murderers of Virginia merchant ship captain John Stone, who had been killed with his crew in the spring of 1634 while trading along the Connecticut River. Certainly the leaders of Massachusetts Bay used Stone's death as a bargaining advantage. This was ironic, as Massachusetts had earlier charged Stone with adultery, fined him, and threatened him with death should he ever return to that colony.

In November 1634 two Pequot sachems arrived in Massachusetts Bay. Producing a large amount of wampum, they persuaded the English to offer it to the Narragansetts on their behalf. The Pequots also offered Connecticut lands for English settlement, hoping to establish a buffer between themselves and the Narragansetts. The English, fearful of a Narragansett-Dutch alliance against them, hoped to establish peace and accepted.

The English still insisted that the Pequots turn over those natives involved in Stone's murder. The Pequot emissaries explained that Stone had kidnapped two natives to serve as guides and that Stone and his crew had died during an attempt to rescue the two kidnapped natives when gunpowder had accidentally blown up aboard the ship. The Pequots also stated that the Dutch had already killed the grand sachem, Tatobem, leader at the time of Stone's death. The emissaries also claimed that all but two of the Pequots involved had since died of smallpox. On English insistence, the Pequot negotiators agreed to hand over the two who remained and to pay a large indemnity in pelts and wampum. Because of the excessive treaty demands, however, the Pequot council refused to ratify the treaty.

The pretense of Pequot noncompliance with the treaty was the excuse for a Massachusetts Bay expedition against them, led by John Endicott in 1636. This expedition began the Pequot War (1636–1638).

Sarah E. Miller

See also

Endicott, John; Endicott Expedition; Mystic Fort Fight; Pequots; Pequot War

References

Cave, Alfred A. *The Pequot War*. Amherst: University of Massachusetts Press, 1996.

Sylvester, Herbert Milton. *Indian Wars of New England,* Vol. 1. Cleveland, OH: Arthur H. Clark, 1910.

Massacre

Any episode in which wanton, indiscriminate killings are perpetrated. Often the term "massacre" is applied to cases in which large numbers of people are killed, especially women, children,

Estimated Casualties during the American Indian Wars, 1775–1890

	Conflicts with U.S. Government Backing	Conflicts without U.S. Government Backing	Total
Whites	14,000	5,000	19,000
Native Americans	30,000–45,000	8,500	38,500–53,500
Total	44,000–59,000	13,500	57,500–72,500

the elderly, and civilians or noncombatants. The term "massacre" also tends to connote especially savage or brutal modes of murder. In many cases, massacres during the Indian Wars also included mutilation, decapitation, or other forms of disrespect toward the dead. Massacres often occurred as part of a military campaign or battle, but they also took place independent of a war, formal military campaign, or battle. In many cases the perpetrators attacked suddenly to ensure that they would not meet any resistance. Today massacres are considered war crimes or crimes against humanity; they are in violation of international law and the normal rules of warfare to which most nations now subscribe. Massacres in recent times have often been investigated by international tribunals, and their perpetrators have been tried, convicted, and imprisoned. Prior to the early 20th century, however, no such international agreements existed, and massacres thus occurred with great frequency.

Native Americans and Europeans and, later, Americans committed massacres in North America. The earliest ones date to the 17th century. In 1660 approximately 800 Mohawks, Onondagas, and Oneidas massacred a raiding party of about 60 Hurons, Algonquins, and French traders in their camp along the Ottawa River. Those who survived were tortured to death. A combined party of about 48 French troops and their Native American allies launched a surprise raid on Deerfield, Massachusetts, in 1704, killing 48 English colonists; many of the dead were women and children. In 1862 at the beginning of the Minnesota Sioux Uprising, as many as 800 white settlers were systematically murdered by the rampaging Sioux. In 1868 hundreds of Sioux warriors lured Captain William Fetterman and his detachment of 80 soldiers into a trap, killing every man in short order.

Europeans and Americans were just as culpable in the perpetration of massacres. In 1637 colonists in Connecticut and Massachusetts, along with their Native American allies, surrounded and attacked the Pequot village at Mystic Fort, killing at least 500 natives, many of them women and children. In 1863 a unit of California volunteers attacked a Shoshone camp along the Bear River; some 250 Shoshones were killed, and their bodies were mutilated. On November 28, 1864, Colonel John M. Chivington, commanding a detachment of 700 Colorado militiamen, surrounded Cheyenne leader Black Kettle's camp at Sand Creek in Colorado. The next day Chivington attacked, despite the fact that

A telegram from October 7, 1864, from Major General Samuel R. Curtis informing Colonel John Chivington of the presence of a large number of presumed hostile Cheyennes near the Pawnee River. On November 29, Chivington led his 3rd Colorado Volunteers in an attack on Black Kettle's peaceful Cheyenne village. This infamous event is known as the Sand Creek Massacre. (Bettmann/Corbis)

he had known that Black Kettle's band was peaceful. As many as 200 Cheyennes and Arapahos died in the Sand Creek Massacre, many of them women and children. The dead were ritually mutilated, their skulls smashed in and their stomachs slit open. The attack stunned many Americans and led to official investigations. In 1868 Lieutenant Colonel George A. Custer and his 7th Cavalry Regiment attacked Black Kettle's village anew. This time 100 Cheyennes, including Black Kettle, died during what became known as the Battle of the Washita.

As many as 150 Western Apaches—chiefly women and children—died in April 1871 in what came to be known as the Camp Grant Massacre. This time the perpetrators were not soldiers but instead were angry civilian settlers. Perhaps one of the most infamous events occurred at Wounded Knee Creek, South Dakota, where troops of the 7th Cavalry had surrounded Big Foot's Miniconjou Sioux. Although not premeditated and not intended, poor planning and execution on the part of the soldiers led to a tragic and avoidable confrontation on December 29, 1890. A warrior's rifle accidentally discharged, starting a volley of fire that resulted in 150 Native American deaths. Twenty-five U.S. soldiers were also killed. The vast majority of the Native

American deaths at Wounded Knee were innocent women and children.

Clearly both sides in the Indian Wars perpetrated horrific massacres, far too numerous to list or discuss here. But in an era in which there were no national or international norms of warfare and the idea of genocide lay far in the future, massacres were a sad and repetitive part of warfare involving Europeans, Americans, and Native Americans.

Paul G. Pierpaoli Jr.

See also

Bear River, Battle of; Big Foot; Black Kettle; Camp Grant Massacre; Cavalry Regiment, 7th U.S.; Chivington, John; Custer, George Armstrong; Deerfield, Massachusetts, Attack on; Fetterman Massacre; Minnesota Sioux Uprising; Mystic Fort Fight; Sand Creek Massacre; Washita, Battle of the; Wounded Knee, Battle of

References

Dunn, J. P., Jr. *Massacres of the Mountains: A History of the Indian Wars of the Far West.* Mechanicsburg, PA: Stackpole, 2002.

Silver, Peter. *Our Savage Neighbors: How Indian War Transformed Early America.* New York: Norton, 2008.

Utley, Robert M., and Wilcomb E. Washburn. *Indian Wars.* New York: American Heritage Press, 2002.

Massacre Canyon, Battle of
Event Date: August 5, 1873

Military engagement between a group of Pawnee hunters and a large Lakota war party near present-day Trenton, Nebraska, on August 5, 1873. This was the last Native American battle in Nebraska. The Pawnees were a sedentary tribe living in present-day Nebraska and Kansas. They were composed of four autonomous bands that subsisted primarily on corn horticulture supplemented by annual buffalo hunts.

Until the arrival of European-introduced diseases, the Pawnees were one of the great military powers on the central Plains. However, their military hegemony was challenged by the more nomadic Lakota Sioux and Cheyennes, who moved onto the Plains in the late 18th century. The result was increased warfare in which the nomadic tribes frequently raided Pawnee villages and harassed and ambushed Pawnee travelers and hunting parties.

The pressure posed by the Lakotas and Cheyennes ultimately prompted the Pawnees to establish a military alliance with the United States. The military service of Frank North's famous Pawnee Scout Battalion after 1864 further enraged the Pawnees' enemies. Sioux pressure caused some Pawnees to advocate moving to Indian Territory (present-day Oklahoma).

In 1872 while facing starvation largely because of inadequate government rations and annuities, the Pawnees received permission from their government agent to go on a hunting expedition. The hunt was successful, and the next year a group of Pawnees appealed to go on another hunt. As trail agent, 23-year-old John W. Williamson was appointed to accompany the hunters. Williamson was well liked by the Pawnees, but he held little actual influence among them because of his inexperience.

On July 3, 1873, between 350 and 400 Pawnees under Sky Chief (Ti-ra-wa-hut Re-sa-ru), a former Pawnee scout, left the agency for the hunt. After several successful hunts along the Republican River, the Pawnees turned north and began the journey back home. Although a number of white hunters warned that they had seen Sioux warriors lurking in the area, Sky Chief ignored the warnings and decided to push on. His men had found no sign indicating that hostile warriors were nearby, and the Pawnees had no reason to trust the white hunters, who were known for their anti-Indian sentiments. According to one account, the military authorities had also assured the Pawnees that there was no danger in the area. But a large band of Brulé Sioux, supplemented by a group of Oglalas, had been trailing the hunters for several days and were intent on attacking them. Their accompanying agents, Nick Janis and Stephen F. Estes, did little to prevent an attack.

On August 5 the Oglalas moved in, surprising the Pawnee camp. For the first hour the Pawnees, who sought shelter in a deep canyon, were able to hold the Oglalas off. But when the Brulé Sioux arrived, the Pawnees were hopelessly outnumbered. According to

some estimates, there were now more than 2,000 Sioux against some 250 Pawnee warriors. At one point the Pawnees panicked and tried to escape down the canyon. During this desperate retreat, many Pawnees were killed or wounded. According to one account, Sky Chief killed his own infant son rather than have him killed and mutilated by the Sioux. Sky Chief himself died while defending his people. Some Pawnees escaped when the Sioux stopped to kill the wounded and mutilate the dead. The Sioux also took a number of captives.

The Pawnees who had been able to escape later ran into a detachment of the 3rd Cavalry Regiment under Captain Charles Meinhold from Fort McPherson. Meinhold immediately rushed to the scene, but when he arrived there the Sioux had already departed. Meinhold counted 57 dead, but Pawnee agent William Burgess later determined that 20 men, 39 women, and 10 children had died in the massacre. According to some unofficial sources, however, there were more than 100 Pawnee deaths. The prisoners were eventually returned to the Pawnee tribe with the help of Brulé agent Stephen Estes. The number of Sioux dead was never established with certainty but numbered only perhaps 5 or 6.

The fight at Massacre Canyon, as it was soon named, was the last battle between the Sioux and the Pawnees and the last Native American battle in Nebraska. Some scholars also believe that the tragedy was a turning point in Pawnee history. The battle was a major factor in the decision of some Pawnees to leave Nebraska and move to Indian Territory to live with their kinsmen, the Wichitas. Eventually the remainder of the Pawnee tribe followed them there. Later the Pawnees settled on a new reservation in present-day north-central Oklahoma. In 1930 a large granite monument was erected near the site of the Massacre Canyon Battle.

MARK VAN DE LOGT

See also

Brulé Sioux; Lakota Sioux; North, Frank Joshua, and Luther Hedden North; Oglala Sioux; Pawnees

References

Blaine, Garland J., and Martha Royce Blaine. "Pa-re-su A-ri-ra-ke: The Hunters That Were Massacred." *Nebraska History* 58 (Fall 1977): 342–358.

Riley, Paul D. "The Battle of Massacre Canyon." *Nebraska History* 54 (Summer 1973): 221–249.

Williamson, John W. *The Battle of Massacre Canyon: The Unfortunate Ending of the Last Buffalo Hunt of the Pawnees.* Trenton, NE: Republican Leader, 1922.

Massasoit
Birth Date: ca. 1590
Death Date: ca. 1661–1662

Grand sachem of the Wampanoags of New England. The name "Massasoit" is actually a title meaning "grand sachem" or "great leader" bestowed on Ousa Mequin (Yellow Feather), sachem of the Pokanokets and the grand sachem of the Wampanoag Confederacy. Little is known about Massasoit prior to his contact with Plymouth Colony in 1621. He was born about 1590 in Montaup, a Pokanoket village near present-day Bristol, Rhode Island, and rose to leadership over eight large villages.

The first documented contact between Massasoit and the English occurred in 1619. In that year he met with Captain Thomas Dermer following the latter's voyage with Tisquantum (Squanto) to New England. William Bradford, the second governor of Plymouth Colony, described the Pokanoket sachem as "a very lust [sic] man in his best years, an able body, grave of countenance, and spare of speech: In his Attyre, a little or nothing differing from the rest of his followers, only a great Chaine of white bone beades about his neck. . . . His face was painted with a deep red like mulberry and he was oiled both head and face."

Traditionally Massasoit is remembered for his alliance with the Pilgrims and his efforts to aid Plymouth Colony. There is no doubt that he was a calculating and skilled diplomat. He established personal relationships with the principal leaders of Plymouth Colony, including William Bradford and Edward Winslow. Concern over the possibility of conflict with the neighboring Narragansetts led Massasoit to forge an alliance with the colonists at Plymouth in March 1621. The resulting treaty was mutually beneficial, providing security for the colonists and military aid for the Wampanoags in case of hostilities with the Narragansetts. Cemented further by Edward Winslow's resuscitation of the critically ill sachem in 1632, the alliance also served to keep the Wampanoags out of the Pequot War (1636–1638) and enabled Massasoit to resist Puritan efforts to Christianize his people.

Expanding English settlements around Massachusetts Bay brought pressure on Massasoit to cede land to the English. To this he relented, selling land in the 1650s to the colony in exchange for the maintenance of harmony. Until his death in 1661 or 1662, the Wampanoag bands under Massasoit and the colonists of Massachusetts Bay and Plymouth remained at peace. Continued encroachment on Wampanoag lands, however, would lead Massasoit's son, Metacom, known to the English as King Philip, to launch King's Philip's War in 1675.

ALAN C. DOWNS

See also
King Philip's War; Metacom; Narragansetts; Pequot War; Puritans; Squanto; Wampanoags

References
Axtell, James. *Natives and Newcomers: The Cultural Origins of North America.* New York: Oxford University Press, 2001.
Josephy, Alvin M., Jr. *500 Nations: An Illustrated History of North American Indians.* New York: Knopf, 1994.
Philbrick, Nathaniel. *Mayflower: A Story of Courage, Community, and War.* New York: Viking, 2006.

Matoaka
See Pocahontas

McGillivray, Alexander
Birth Date: December 15, 1750
Death Date: February 17, 1793

Creek leader and ally of the British during the American Revolutionary War (1775–1783) who then attempted to unify the Creek Nation to oppose American expansion westward in the 1780s. Alexander McGillivray was born on December 15, 1750, at Little Tallassee on the Coosa River in present-day Alabama. He was the son of Scottish trader Lachlan McGillivray and a Creek woman, Sehoy of the Wind Clan. His mother in turn was the daughter of a French trader, Jean Baptiste Louis Decourtel Marchand, and another Sehoy of the Wind Clan. The Wind Clan was one of the more politically powerful clans among the Creeks. McGillivray's lineage was only one-quarter Creek, but this still gave him advantages within his tribe as a cultural mediator, while his mother's clan gave him a native power base. McGillivray was educated for a time in Charleston, South Carolina, where he learned both Latin and Greek.

Upon the completion of McGillivray's education in the mid-1770s, John Stuart, British superintendent of Indian affairs in the South, secured for him posts as a colonel and an agent of the British Indian Department. Through these positions McGillivray distributed trade goods, which he used to build influence for the British among the Creeks and for himself. Thanks to his mother's clan, his connection to the British through his father, and his education, McGillivray quickly advanced in Creek politics, becoming a leader among the pro-British Upper Creeks.

During the American Revolutionary War, McGillivray persuaded many Creek warriors to fight for the British, believing that they posed less of a threat than did the Patriot side. The war disrupted trade between the Creeks and the colonists, and many Creeks were ruined financially. Alexander McGillivray's father, Lachlan, had his property confiscated and was compelled to return to Scotland. The war also resulted in the deaths of many Creek leaders, particularly those who were pro-British. This facilitated the rise of a new generation of leaders, with McGillivray prominent among them. At a young age he had achieved status as a "beloved man," a title that the Creek gave to prominent councilors, men respected for their acumen and experience. After the war, however, McGillivray became the clear leader of the Upper Creeks.

With the British removal from Florida after 1783, the Lower Creeks chose to make peace with Georgia and to renew economic ties to its white inhabitants. The pro-American Lower Creek Nation made peace with Georgia in the Treaty of Augusta of 1783, which ended hostilities and renewed trade in return for the Creeks' cession of approximately 800 square miles of land. Although this was Lower Creek land, McGillivray nevertheless raised opposition to the treaty, calling for the use of force against settlers.

In 1786 and 1787 McGillivray was involved in the coordination of attacks on the American frontier with the Iroquois, Hurons, and Shawnees, among other tribes. He also ensured a continuous supply of weapons, ammunition, and trade goods with British firms and the new Spanish government in Florida. Through his faction and trade group he directed the Upper Creeks' trade toward Spanish Florida rather than Augusta, Georgia.

In 1790 McGillivray attended a conference in New York that resulted in the Treaty of New York, establishing a brief peace along the southern frontier by setting a firm boundary separating Creek land from Georgia settlements. The Spanish resented the concessions granted by McGillivray to the United States, however. McGillivray next attended a meeting with the Spanish in New Orleans in 1792 to explain his actions. However, he contracted a fever on the return trip from which he never fully recovered. McGillivray died at Pensacola on February 17, 1793. He was an early advocate for greater Indian confederation and Creek resistance to U.S. aggression, ideas that would be influential for future Native Americans, particularly the Creek Red Sticks.

MICHAEL K. BEAUCHAMP

See also

Creeks; Iroquois; Native Americans and the American Revolutionary War; Red Sticks; Shawnees; Wyandots

References

Braund, Kathryn E. Holland. *Deerskins & Duffels: The Creek Indian Trade with Anglo-America, 1685–1815*. Lincoln: University of Nebraska Press, 1993.
Caughey, John Walton. *McGillivray of the Creeks*. Norman: University of Oklahoma Press, 1938.

McQueen, Peter
Birth Date: ca. 1780
Death Date: ca. 1820

Prominent Red Stick Creek chieftain during the Creek War (1813–1814). Peter McQueen was born around 1780 in the Upper Creek town of Tallassee along the Tallapoosa River in present-day Alabama. He was the son of a Scottish trader living among the Creeks and a native woman. Despite his mixed parentage, McQueen identified with his mother's people; he did not even speak English. McQueen soon rose to prominence among the Tallassees (a non-Muskogee–speaking group). As a trader he became wealthy, acquired a large number of African American slaves, and became the Tallassee war leader and trusted lieutenant of the band's chief, Hopoath Mico.

In the autumn of 1811 the Shawnee leader Tecumseh spent several weeks meeting with various Creek groups and urging them to join the Native American confederacy that he was assembling to resist further American expansion. Tecumseh's visit exacerbated an existing dispute among the Creeks between most of the Lower Creeks, who favored an accommodationist policy toward the United States, and a majority of the Upper Creeks, both Muskogee and non-Muskogee speakers, who wished to protect their lands and culture. Inspired by Tecumseh's message, the nativist faction grew more militant. They became known as the Red Sticks, most probably for the red-painted wooden war clubs they carried as a symbol of their movement.

McQueen joined the Red Sticks and along with William Weatherford, Josiah Francis, and a group of Native American prophets, emerged as a leader of the faction. One group of Creeks led by Little Warrior went north with Tecumseh and upon its return in 1813 attacked and killed seven white families in Tennessee.

After these attacks Benjamin Hawkins, the American agent to the Creeks, demanded that the Creeks bring the offenders to justice before U.S. authorities. The Creek chiefs chose to oblige the United States, but so as not to appear as puppets they themselves executed seven of the offenders. In retaliation, the Red Sticks killed nine Creeks who had participated in the execution.

These events initiated the Creek War (1813–1814), which is often considered part of the War of 1812. McQueen and other Red Stick leaders decided that they would first eliminate the accommodationist Creeks and then attack and drive out American settlers.

McQueen and the Red Sticks struck the Lower Creek town of Tuckabatchee in early summer, forced the defenders to retreat after a brief siege, and then burned that town and two neighboring Lower Creek villages. In July, McQueen led a group of 300 Creeks to Pensacola to request arms and ammunition from the Spanish governor to continue the war. The Spanish officials, while privately encouraging the Creeks to resist American expansion, did not want to openly antagonize the U.S. government. They therefore gave McQueen provisions and other supplies but only a limited quantity of gunpowder.

Whites in Alabama learned of the Creek mission to Pensacola, and on July 21, 1813, a militia force under Colonel James Caller attacked McQueen's party at Burnt Corn Creek, less than 100 miles north of Pensacola. The Alabama militia was initially successful, but discipline broke down when the men began to loot the Creek supply train. This allowed McQueen to regroup and counterattack, and the militia then withdrew. This was the first battle of the Creek War, and McQueen's force had won a tactical victory even though it had lost a large quantity of supplies.

McQueen and William Weatherford, known among the Creeks as Red Eagle, then led an attack by more than 700 warriors on Fort Mims, about 40 miles north of Mobile. In a bloody battle, McQueen and Weatherford captured the fort on August 30, killing most of the militia defenders along with American settlers and Lower Creeks who had taken refuge in the post. The Americans accused McQueen, Weatherford, and their followers of slaughtering people after the fort was captured, and the battle came to be known among the whites as the Massacre of Fort Mims. In response, the U.S. government intervened in what previously had been for the most part a Creek civil war.

McQueen actively opposed the American invasion of Creek territory led by Major General Andrew Jackson. On January 22, 1814, McQueen and the Red Sticks attacked Jackson's force at Emuckfaw Creek but were driven off with heavy losses. Continuing his advance, Jackson finally brought the Creek War to an end at the Battle of Horseshoe Bend on March 27, 1814. McQueen along with many other Red Sticks and particularly the leaders escaped to Florida, where they settled among the Seminoles and continued their opposition to the United States and McQueen fought in the First Seminole War (1817–1818). However, after Jackson seized St. Marks, Florida, McQueen again fled. He was not seen again, and reports circulated that he had died in 1820 on an unknown island off the east coast of Florida.

MICHAEL K. BEAUCHAMP AND JIM PIECUCH

See also

Burnt Corn Creek, Battle of; Creeks; Creek War; Emuckfaw Creek, Battle of; Fort Mims, Battle of; Horseshoe Bend, Battle of; Jackson, Andrew; Red Sticks; Tecumseh; Weatherford, William

References

Dowd, Gregory Evans. *A Spirited Resistance: The North American Indian Struggle for Unity, 1745–1815.* Baltimore: Johns Hopkins University Press, 1992.

Hickey, Donald R. *The War of 1812: A Forgotten Conflict.* Urbana: University of Illinois Press, 1989.

Remini, Robert Vincenti. *Andrew Jackson and His Indian Wars.* New York: Penguin, 2001.

Stagg, J. C. A. *Mr. Madison's War: Politics, Diplomacy, and Warfare in the Early American Republic, 1783–1830.* Princeton, NJ: Princeton University Press, 1983.

Wright, J. Leitch, Jr. *Creeks and Seminoles: The Destruction and Regeneration of the Muscogulge People.* Lincoln: University of Nebraska Press, 1986.

Medicine, Military

The evolution of military medicine in the United States between the end of the American Civil War (1861–1865) and the effective end of the Indian Wars with the Battle of Wounded Knee (December 29, 1890) is a story of transition. On an organizational level, the U.S. Army Medical Department went from 204 general hospitals in 1865 to none in 1866. In 1865 there were 12,343 medical officers; at the lowest point in 1866, there were just 213. As striking as those numbers are, the transition in medical care was probably even more significant. Military medicine went from a practice dominated by toxic drugs (compounds containing mercury and arsenic in particular) and amputation to an understanding of the nature and cause of infection and application of that understanding to the practice of surgery and sanitation.

For American military surgeons, the medical care of large numbers of men engaged in organized campaigns changed to looking after small groups engaged in guerrilla warfare. The Medical Department under William Hammond and Jonathan Letterman had made huge improvements by the end of the Civil War. Their organized system of ambulance transport, triage, and stepwise movement of the sick and wounded through field, general, and specialty hospitals had made it possible to manage large numbers of casualties and had measurably improved outcomes. That system, however, was not at all suited to an army of 25,000 scattered among 134 posts, the largest of which had 700 men and more than one-third of the posts had fewer than 60 men. Skills necessary to treat casualties from set-piece battles fought by thousands of men using rifles and artillery were not helpful in treating frostbite, malnutrition, and the occasional arrow wound seen on the western frontier.

After Hammond's removal, the position of surgeon general passed to Joseph K. Barnes, who held the position until 1882. Barnes tried to continue Hammond's reforms, but Barnes's command was so different as to be virtually unrecognizable. Congress set the Medical Department staff at 1 surgeon general; 1 assistant surgeon general (with the rank equivalent to that of colonel); 4 assistant medical purveyors (with rank equivalent to lieutenant colonel), who could also serve as surgeons if needed; 60 surgeons (majors); and 150 assistant surgeons (lieutenants and captains). It quickly became obvious that those numbers were insufficient to staff the widely scattered frontier posts, and in 1866 an additional 264 civilian surgeons were hired under contract, a number that rose to 282 by 1868.

Partially because there was a large pool of military surgeons left from the Civil War and partially because the guaranteed income in the military compared favorably with the generally meager living available to civilian doctors, competition for positions in the medical corps was active, and the caliber of the men coming into the corps was generally quite good. The examination for entry into the medical corps was particularly difficult. The test went on for five hours a day for six days and included Latin, mathematics, English literature, ancient and modern history, chemistry, and physics. The second three days were taken up with oral examinations in medicine and surgery. Of 59 applicants in 1885, only 1 received a commission, and another applicant was hired under contract. Unfortunately, no amount of classical education or dedication could entirely overcome the deficiencies in medical knowledge and the professional isolation that were inevitable concomitants of serving on the frontier.

Prior to 1887, nursing care in army hospitals fell to private soldiers and noncommissioned officers (NCOs) detailed to the Medical Department. The NCOs were assigned as stewards and were generally competent. The privates detailed to patient care were often men whom the line officers did not want and were generally not anxious to do the dirty, heavy work necessitated by bedside care. That situation improved with the formation of a permanent Hospital Corps in 1877, but the use of female nurses would not become general in the army until the Spanish-American War (1898).

The quality of medical services attached to state militia units was not nearly as satisfactory. Most states had no organized medical departments, no hospital corps, and no examinations for their surgeons. Those failures would be manifest and nearly disastrous when the militia was brought to service in the Spanish-American War.

Living conditions for soldiers stationed on the western frontier were generally abysmal. Most forts were either adobe or simple wooden structures with dirt floors and no plumbing or heat. Water was brought in barrels from the nearest stream or well, and there was virtually none available for bathing. During the winter when bathing in streams became impractical, the odor of bunk rooms was usually overwhelming. Privies were so-called earth closets, and the incidence of fecally transmitted disease was a major factor in a sick rate that regularly exceeded 10 percent. Bedding consisted of bags of straw that were inconsistently changed. Vermin were a constant problem until washable sheets, wire spring mattresses, and bed frames became available in the 1880s. Malaria remained a significant problem, and three grains of quinine along with an ounce of whiskey were a standard addition to reveille each morning.

In the 1870s sanitation was the responsibility of camp commanders, who generally had little knowledge of and less interest in the subject. They often had a low opinion of their surgeons and were seldom willing to make changes suggested by them. Diarrheal disease was endemic (as late as 1893 the admission rate for dysentery was over 98 per 1,000), and typhoid outbreaks were not uncommon. By the mid-1880s a new understanding of infectious disease and its transmission pushed responsibility for camp sanitation more into the hands of the medical officers, and regular post sanitary reports were required after 1885. A report that year emphasizing the importance of contaminated water in typhoid transmission resulted in a 50 percent decrease in the incidence of typhoid in the camps.

Inadequate diet was also a pervasive problem on the posts; only 13 cents a day was allowed for a private soldier's rations. Much of the soldiers' diet came from meat they could shoot. The posts were supposed to rely on their own vegetable gardens, but the crops were most often potatoes or beans, and scurvy was common in spite of the fact that effective prevention had been understood for nearly a century. There were 632 cases documented in the army between 1868 and 1874, and complaints of "rheumatism" were very often not joint inflammation but rather pain from hemorrhage into joints or muscles caused by vitamin C deficiency.

The rate of venereal disease in the army hovered around 70 per 1,000, although some posts were much worse. Columbus Barracks in Ohio reported a staggering 334 per 1,000. Admissions for alcoholism were around 30 per 1,000. Through the 1870s, the cumulative sick rate in the army varied between 1,516 and 2,087 per 1,000 men (cumulative sick rate, with many men sick more than once a year) on active duty.

Facilities for providing medical care were little better than the barracks. In 1875 the U.S. Army had 140 post hospitals, but most had fewer than 25 beds, and many had as few as 10 or 12 beds.

None had either operating rooms or laboratories. That year, however, the army did begin construction of permanent hospitals in Washington, D.C., and at West Point, New York. Supplying the posts with medicine and food was a chronic problem. Rivers and railroads went only so far, and most supplies had to be hauled overland, frequently to posts hundreds of miles from the nearest port or railhead.

Much of a unit's time during the Indian Wars was spent on patrol, and medical care had to be at least somewhat mobile. Standard-issue medicines, dressings, and surgical instruments were packed into wooden panniers that weighed 75–100 pounds. Most surgeons added another 50 or so pounds of their own preferred supplies (including chloroform), bringing the total to something that could just be managed by a single mule.

Transport into forts and to men on patrol was not the only problem. It was also difficult to evacuate the sick or wounded. If the men were carried on litters, two mules and four helpers were necessary because the stretcher was slung between the animals, and one man had to direct each mule while another walked on each side to prevent the patient from being rocked out and onto the ground. Travois—litters with one end attached to a mule back and the other end dragging the ground—were more practical where there were no roads but were tortuously uncomfortable.

Because there were no battles comparable to those of the Civil War, the experience gained by military surgeons in that conflict was of little use. The largest number of killed and injured in battle during any year in the 1870s was 267 in 1876, and all but 20 of those occurred in the defeat of Lieutenant Colonel George A. Custer's 7th Cavalry Regiment in the Battle of the Little Bighorn (June 25–26, 1876).

Arrow wounds were a problem unique to the Indian Wars and presented interesting challenges. The arrowheads were usually attached to the shafts with rawhide thongs that softened in the body, making it more likely that the head would stay behind when the arrow was extracted. The retained head was a virtually inevitable source of suppuration. The Native Americans typically aimed at a target's navel so that the arrow would be less likely to be deflected by bone. Penetrating abdominal injuries in the 1870s and 1880s were almost universally fatal either because of hemorrhage from major vessel injury or from peritonitis as a result of bowel perforation. Even arrow wounds were, however, uncommon, and a military surgeon's operative caseload was much more likely to be dominated by amputation from gangrene caused by frostbite.

In 1871 Lord Joseph Lister published his experience using phenol as an antiseptic during surgical procedures. Robert Koch in his 1878 *Study of the Etiology of Wound Infection* described six different microorganisms that could cause specific types of infection. By the 1880s some American military surgeons were operating under clouds of phenol, although many of their more traditional colleagues refused to change. In 1885 the antiseptic method was used in 42 of 170 American military operations; the following year the percentage increased to 60 of 108. Understanding and acceptance of the importance of infection in American military medicine and surgery culminated in the 1893 appointment of bacteriologist George Sternberg as surgeon general. Although sanitation would again be a problem with the widespread mobilization incident to the Spanish-American War, the U.S. Army Medical Department was poised to assume a role at the forefront of research and management of infectious disease.

JACK MCCALLUM

See also
Medicine, Native American

References
Ashburn, P. M. *A History of the Medical Department of the United States Army*. Boston: Houghton Mifflin, 1929.
Gillett, Mary. *The Army Medical Department, 1865–1917*. Washington, DC: Center of Military History, United States Army, 1995.
McCallum, Jack. *Leonard Wood: Rough Rider, Surgeon, Architect of American Imperialism*. New York: New York University Press, 2006.

Medicine, Native American

Native American medicine was (and continues to be) a system of professional practices based on the native concept of health and wellness. Health is seen as a proper balance among the physical, psychological, and spiritual states of the individual as well as personal harmony with the surrounding natural environment. This system predates and is quite similar to the concept of homeostasis that is currently gaining popularity in modern medicine. Native Americans see the natural world as having a significant spiritual nature, and the medicine of Native American culture reflects this concept.

As in Western medicine, Indian medical practice is based on observations of the progression of illness and is strongly rooted in cause and effect. The profession was and still is practiced by specialists who are trained in their medical system of specialized procedures, particular (natural) medicines, and specific rituals. The practitioners fulfill this specialized role in their culture after extensive training and internship with an established healer.

In Native American culture, good health is the result of an individual maintaining a proper balance of his or her own physical, psychological, and spiritual natures. The belief is that a deficiency in any of these aspects can cause illness to the individual. The goal of the medical professional is to restore the person to a proper balance. Therefore, the healer must treat the physical problems as well as perform procedures to address the emotional and spiritual imbalances observed in the patient. It is important to note that the spiritual aspect often involves the group as well as the individual. Thus, medical procedures will often include members of the patient's extended family, acquaintances, and even the entire band or tribe. When balance within the individual is restored, the patient becomes well again.

A Native American healer has knowledge of medical procedures, medicines, and ceremonies. He or she is trained in the use of specific physical procedures to remove objects and toxins from the body, reset bones, relieve stress, and realign muscles and other biological systems. The healer collects, prepares, and administers a large number of naturally occurring plant, fungi, and animal substances (medicines). These medicines are believed to be effective in treating the specific physical symptoms presented by the patient.

Most Native Americans believe that the natural world is directly influenced by spirits of both beneficence and harm; therefore, the effects of these spirits are important in their cultures' practice of medicine. The healers are trained in specific ceremonies that are designed to enhance the effect of beneficial spirits as well as to mitigate the actions of harmful spirits. The healer observes the patient, diagnoses the particular problem, and treats the illness with a particular combination of procedures, medicines, and ceremonies specific to the patient's illness. The healers believe that they are part of a continuum of healing forces in the harmony of nature. Their actions perform a coordinating role in balancing the significant physical, emotional, and spiritual aspects within the patient.

Over the centuries, Native American medicine has been shown to be quite effective in the treatment of numerous illnesses. Western medicine has observed Native American practices over time and has often concluded that many procedures and medicines are useful, and Native American and Western healers continue

Little Big Mouth, a medicine man, seated in front of his lodge near Fort Sill, Indian Territory (Oklahoma). Photograph by William S. Soule, circa 1869–1870. (National Archives)

to exchange knowledge to the benefit of both systems. This was particularly true during the 18th and 19th centuries. Today Native American healers are frequently important partners with Western doctors, particularly in areas with significant Native American populations.

LAWRENCE E. SWESEY

See also
Medicine, Military

References
Bonvillain, Nancy. *Native American Medicine.* Philadelphia: Chelsea House, 1997.

Kavasch, Barrie, and Karen Baar. *American Indian Healing Arts: Herbs, Rituals and Remedies for Every Season of Life.* New York: Bantam Books, 1999.

Medicine Lodge Treaty

Series of three treaties, most commonly referred to in the singular, that were signed in October 1867 between the U.S. government and elements of the Kiowa, Comanche, Kiowa Apache, Cheyenne, and Arapaho tribes at Medicine Lodge Creek, Kansas. The Medicine Lodge Treaty actually comprised three separate accords. The first was signed on October 21 with the Comanches and Kiowas, the second was signed that same day with the Kiowa Apaches, and the third was signed on October 28 with the Cheyennes and Arapahos. The treaty was part of a larger government plan to reduce the size of Native American tribal lands and reservations throughout the West and was also a result of the August 1867 Indian Peace Commission, which had been created by the U.S. Congress in an effort to bring an end to various Native American wars in the region. The commission included leading civilians as well as top officers, among them Lieutenant General William T. Sherman, commander of the Division of the Missouri.

The peace talks, which came in the wake of Major General Winfield Scott Hancock's punitive campaign on the southern Plains, suggested a change in approach by the government from a purely military response to a more humanitarian, if idealistic, solution to the bitter conflict. The treaties established two reservations in western Indian Territory, one for the Kiowas, Comanches, and Kiowa Apaches and the other for the Cheyennes and Arapahos. The treaties also included government promises to provide education and agricultural support in order to foster the Indians' conversion to sedentary farmers. Finally, the government promised army-supervised annual distributions of clothing and other goods. In return the Great Plains tribes yielded all rights to lands outside the reservations other than some hunting privileges. The tribes were no longer to oppose the construction of military posts and railroads on their traditional hunting range. Under the agreement, the Indians were not to threaten settlers or their property.

After initially refusing to sign the accord, chiefs representing the tribes finally agreed when they were threatened with force by the U.S. Army. In spite of the treaty, however, most members of the tribes involved declared that they would not abide by the agreements. Many claimed that their democratic societies required that 75 percent of a tribe had to agree to a treaty for it to be considered legally binding. Even so, young warriors were not bound by agreements made by chiefs, and many leaders simply maintained that they had not agreed to anything. With the majority not recognizing the treaty, it never became operational. Although the government had entered a new phase, which would find fuller expression as President Ulysses S. Grant's Peace Policy, the military found

At Medicine Creek in southwestern Kansas, the U.S. government concluded three separate treaties with the Kiowa, Comanche, Cheyenne, and Arapaho tribes during October 21–28, 1867. The treaties established reservations in western Indian Territory and provided for government assistance, but a majority of Native Americans disapproved of the treaties and within a matter of weeks fighting had resumed. (Library of Congress)

this troubling and gave the change in direction little chance of success. In the end, the Medicine Lodge Treaty failed in almost every regard. Within weeks, both sides returned to fighting.

SETH A. WEITZ AND DAVID COFFEY

See also

Apaches; Arapahos; Cheyennes; Comanches; Kiowas

References

Greene, Jerome A. *Washita: The U.S. Army and the Southern Cheyennes, 1867–1869.* Norman: University of Oklahoma Press, 2004.

Prucha, Francis Paul. *American Indian Treaties: The History of a Political Anomaly.* Berkeley: University of California Press, 1994.

Meeker, Nathan Cook
Birth Date: July 17, 1817
Death Date: September 29, 1879

Journalist, utopian homesteader, and American Indian agent for the White River Ute Agency in Colorado. Nathan Cook Meeker was born in Euclid, Ohio, on July 17, 1817. A devout Christian, he was a strong believer in communal living and cooperative farming. After some years spent as a farmer he began writing articles for local newspapers, and he also taught school. He soon caught the eye of the famed journalist and publisher Horace Greeley and throughout the 1860s was a reporter for Greeley's *New York Tribune,* serving chiefly as an agricultural editor and writer.

Meeker was an adherent of Charles Fourier, a French-born utopian writer who advocated the establishment of communes and cooperative farming arrangements that would make individuals self-sufficient and render them less susceptible to the "evils" of the business world. Fourier's vision was a prototype of socialism, although socialists would later categorize Fourier's prescriptions as "utopian" and not very practical in the real world. Nevertheless, Meeker borrowed freely from Fourier's ideas but wed them with Christianity so that his vision of a utopian society would be centered both on communal economic endeavors and orthodox Christian piety.

Sensing that the unsettled, open lands of the American West would serve as a good incubator for his ideas, Meeker decided to establish a communal agricultural community in Colorado that he named Union Colony, which would later become the town of Greeley. Meeker also hoped to convert the indigenous Native Americans to his way of life. In the spring of 1870 Meeker began his grand agricultural experiment. After convincing some 700 families and individuals to purchase equal shares in the community, Meeker bought 2,000 acres of land, mostly from local Native Americans. Patterning his community after Pueblo towns and the Mormons in Utah, Meeker borrowed heavily to create the Union Colony and keep it running. He borrowed especially large sums from Horace Greeley. In 1870 Meeker also founded the *Greeley Tribune,* a local newspaper that is still published today.

It soon became apparent that the community, for a variety of reasons, could not be entirely self-sufficient, and Meeker fell further into debt. He also became frustrated that his Christian piety had not produced a colony with the highest moral values. By the late 1870s Meeker was forced to augment his income, and in March 1878 he became the Indian agent for the White River Ute Agency in Colorado. While Meeker had previously tried to co-opt the Utes into adopting a communal agricultural lifestyle, his efforts had been largely spurned. The Utes were seminomadic, engaging in seasonal buffalo hunts, and were not interested in becoming completely sedentary farmers. Nor were they much interested in Meeker's brand of Christianity. Nevertheless, Meeker foolishly attempted to use his position to force the Utes into adopting communal agriculture.

From the start Meeker's relations with the Utes were rocky. Worse still, his first substantive decision was to relocate the agency to land better suited for crops, about 15 miles down the White River. That land, however, had been used as pasture for the Utes' horses. Because of their seminomadic lifestyle, horses were a central part of the Ute economy and culture. Meeker nevertheless began to build a commune at the site with white workers, which infuriated the Utes and soon led them to refuse to cooperate and to use as pasture the land set aside for crops.

In 1878, Nathan C. Meeker became the agent at the White River, Colorado, Ute agency and wasted no time attempting to turn the Utes into farmers with little regard for their cultural traditions. Meeker was killed on September 29, 1879, in what became known as the Meeker Massacre. (North Wind Picture Archives)

Meeker, determined to force the Utes to adopt his lifestyle, ordered white workers to plow under the Ute pastureland in September 1879. This provoked a war with the Utes that began on September 29, 1879. That day Ute warriors attacked a column of U.S. troops sent to the area to prevent a conflict. Fighting lasted for the better part of a week. That same day Ute warriors also ambushed Meeker at the White River Agency, killing him and 10 others. His wife and daughter were taken captive but later released. The Meeker Massacre and the Ute War resulted in the forcible removal of the Utes from their ancestral lands to a reservation in Utah by 1881. It is difficult to believe that the tragedy that unfolded beginning in 1879 would have occurred without Meeker's arrogant insistence that the Utes subscribe to his way of living.

PAUL G. PIERPAOLI JR.

See also
Meeker Massacre; Utes; Ute War

References
Overholster, Wayne D., and Lewis B. Patten. *The Meeker Massacre.* New York: Cowles Book Company, 1969.
Werner, Fred H. *Meeker: The Story of the Meeker Massacre and Thornburgh Battle of September 29, 1879.* Greeley, CO: Werner Publications, 1985.

Meeker Massacre
Event Date: September 29, 1879

Killing of white civilians by Ute warriors during the 1879 Ute War. The Meeker Massacre occurred when Ute warriors destroyed the White River Indian Agency in northwestern Colorado and killed Nathan Meeker and 10 other whites on September 29, 1879. The massacre was part of the short-lived conflict known as the Ute War.

A devout utopian, Meeker had become fascinated with creating an ideal agricultural community in the western territories. He attempted this in the spring of 1870 with the founding of Union Colony, Colorado. Later renamed Greeley after Meeker's friend and supporter, Horace Greeley, the settlement failed to meet Meeker's high standards.

By 1877 Meeker's disillusionment with the Greeley agricultural settlement combined with an ever-worsening financial situation forced him to seek employment with the Colorado Indian Agency. On March 18, 1877, he was appointed agent for the White River Ute Agency in Colorado. Meeker's obsession with creating a utopian agricultural society clearly affected his relations with the Ute tribe. Indeed, he believed that the Utes would welcome him and eagerly adopt a sedentary agricultural Christian lifestyle. The Utes, however, engaged in communal buffalo hunts and thus owned a large number of horses.

When Meeker began his new career, he discovered the Utes in bad temperament. Their yearly supply of annuity goods had been withheld, and the Bureau of Indian Affairs had failed to pay for earlier land cessions. Meeker's enthusiasm initially impressed some of the Ute chiefs. This would not last, however, for his first substantive act was to move the agency to land more suitable for farming, 15 miles down the White River. The area chosen had previously served the Utes as pasture for their horses, an integral part of Ute existence.

To help with construction, Meeker also brought in white workers, which irritated the Utes. Many Utes refused to help unless paid. When payments ceased, they returned to their hunting and began using farm fields as horse pastures. Meeker now came to the conclusion that only if Ute culture was destroyed would the Utes be forced to remain at the agency and adopt a sedentary agricultural lifestyle.

Following the relocation of the agency, many of the younger chiefs had become increasingly suspicious of Meeker. In the spring of 1879 an article written by Meeker for the *Greeley Tribune* stated that if the Utes failed to use the land given to them, it would be taken away. The article was later reprinted throughout Colorado under the incendiary title "The Utes Must Go!" Along with blaming numerous wildfires on the Utes, the article greatly increased anti-Indian feelings in the region. The Ute chiefs now believed that Meeker had betrayed them.

As Ute feelings turned against Meeker, he pressed even harder to force their compliance with his policies. In September 1879 he ordered the plowing of a Ute horse pasture. The Utes resisted. Chief Quinkent, whose horses had grazed in the pasture, assaulted Meeker over the provocation. Angered, Meeker threatened to call for troops to evict the Utes from the land.

As the situation deteriorated, the U.S. War Department ordered Major Thomas T. Thornburgh to move with 200 troops to the White River. Upon entering Ute territory along the Milk River on September 29, 1879, Thornburgh's column was attacked by 300 Utes, led by Chief Nicaagat (Jack). Fighting continued on and off for a week.

That same day word of the battle reached the agency, and Chief Quinkent with 25 to 30 Ute warriors proceeded to kill Meeker and all of his white workers (11 people in all). Meeker's wife and daughter and 3 others were taken captive but were all released three weeks later.

Investigations into the massacre failed to establish who had fired the shots that killed Meeker and his employees. Individual guilt mattered little, however, as the incident was used as an excuse to remove the Utes from their land. In August 1881 the U.S. Army herded the Utes onto reservations in Utah.

ROBERT W. MALICK

See also
Meeker, Nathan Cook; Milk Creek, Battle of; Utes; Ute War

References
Brown, Dee. *Bury My Heart at Wounded Knee.* New York: Holt, Rinehart and Winston, 1970.
Overholster, Wayne D., and Lewis B. Patten. *The Meeker Massacre.* New York: Cowles Book Company, 1969.
Werner, Fred H. *Meeker: The Story of the Meeker Massacre and Thornburgh Battle of September 29, 1879.* Greeley, CO: Werner Publications, 1985.

Memeskia

See Old Briton

Mendota, Treaty of

Treaty signed on August 5, 1851, between the U.S. government and the Mdewakanton and Whaphatooka bands of the Dakota (Santee) Sioux. The Treaty of Mendota was signed in Mendota, Minnesota, near Pine Knob on the south bank of the Minnesota River within sight of Fort Snelling. Signing the agreement were U.S. Indian commissioner Luke Lea, Minnesota governor Alexander Ramsey, eight Sioux chiefs, and 57 other Sioux representatives.

The Treaty of Mendota was a follow-up negotiation to the 1837 Treaty of Traverse des Sioux, which had ceded most Sioux lands in Iowa and parts of Minnesota to the United States. In the Treaty of Mendota, the Mdewakantons and Whaphatookas ceded all remaining Native American lands in Minnesota, mainly in the southern portion of the state. In return the two bands received a payment of $1.41 million. The U.S. government also acknowledged a state of peace with the two Sioux bands and reconfirmed existing liquor laws, which tightly regulated the sale of distilled spirits to Native Americans.

After the signing of the Treaty of Mendota, the Mdewakantons and Whaphatookas relocated to the Lower Sioux Agency, located along the Minnesota River near present-day Morton, Minnesota. Along with the earlier Treaty of Traverse des Sioux, the Treaty of Mendota opened all of Minnesota to white settlers.

PAUL G. PIERPAOLI JR.

See also

Dakota Sioux; Sioux

References

Eastman, Mary. *Dahcotah: The Sioux around Fort Snelling.* New York: Echo Library, 2005.

Meyer, Roy W. *History of the Santee Sioux: United States Indian Policy on Trial.* Rev. ed. Lincoln: University of Nebraska Press, 1993.

Merritt, Wesley

Birth Date: June 16, 1836
Death Date: December 10, 1910

U.S. Army officer. Wesley Merritt was born in New York City on June 16, 1836. He attended the U.S. Military Academy, West Point, graduating in the middle of his class in 1860. Commissioned a second lieutenant, Merritt served in Utah with the 2nd Dragoons. The American Civil War (1861–1865) brought Merritt's transfer to the East, where he twice served as aide to generals Philip St. George Cooke, George Stoneman, and Alfred Pleasonton, cavalry commanders in the Army of the Potomac. Merritt turned out to be a superb cavalry officer. As a regular army captain, he distinguished

himself at Chancellorsville (May 1863); at the Battle of Brandy Station (June 1863), the largest cavalry engagement in the history of North America to that time; and in other engagements. On June 29, 1863, he was appointed brigadier general of volunteers. During the Battle of Gettysburg in July, he commanded the elite Reserve Brigade, Cavalry Corps, Army of the Potomac, and saw significant action on the battle's third day.

Commanding his brigade and occasionally a division, Merritt again fought with distinction in the Battle of Todd's Tavern (part of the larger Battle of the Wilderness) on May 7, 1864, and participated in Major General Philip H. Sheridan's raids on Richmond and Trevilian Station, the largest cavalry engagement of the war. Given command of the 1st Cavalry Division of Sheridan's Army of the Shenandoah, Merritt led it with distinction in subsequent battles of the Shenandoah Campaign, including Winchester, Tom's Brook, and Cedar Creek. Promoted to major general of volunteers, during the Appomattox Campaign Merritt commanded Sheridan's Cavalry Corps, fighting conspicuously at Five Forks and in the pursuit of General Robert E. Lee's Confederate army. Merritt then served as one of the three commissioners assigned to accept

Rising to major general during the Civil War, Wesley Merritt remained in the army afterward and helped develop army tactics and equipment during the Indian Wars. As a colonel, he led with distinction the 5th Cavalry Regiment in a number of Indian campaigns. Following service in the Spanish-American War, he retired from the army in 1900 as a major general. (Library of Congress)

the Confederate surrender. For his splendid war service, Merritt won brevets through major general in the regular army.

Following the Civil War, Merritt remained with the regular army as a lieutenant colonel of the 9th Cavalry Regiment, one of two African American cavalry regiments in the army. This began 17 years of service on the frontier and included extensive fighting against the Mescalero Apaches, Kickapoos, Sioux, Cheyennes, and Utes in campaigns from Texas to Montana. His experience earned him a position as cavalry adviser to the Schofield Board in 1869, and in that capacity he helped develop army tactics and equipment for the Indian Wars. In 1876 Merritt received promotion to colonel and took command of the 5th Cavalry Regiment. During the Great Sioux War (1876–1877) he participated in Brigadier General George Crook's Bighorn and Yellowstone expeditions, fighting in the Battle of War Bonnet Creek and the Battle of Slim Buttes. During 1877 Merritt took part in the pursuit of the Nez Perces and in the Bannock War (1877–1878). In 1879 he participated in the Ute War. Under Merritt's command, the 5th Cavalry Regiment was recognized as one of the top cavalry units in the U.S. Army.

In 1882 Merritt became superintendent of West Point, serving in that position until his promotion to brigadier general in 1887. He then assumed command of the Department of the Missouri at Fort Leavenworth, Kansas. From 1895 to 1897 he commanded the Department of the Missouri, the Department of Dakota, and the Department of the East, respectively. In 1893 he wrote a book, *The Armies of Today.* In the book and also in articles, Merritt advocated a large modern regular U.S. Army. He also supported U.S. imperial expansion. He was promoted to major general in 1895.

At the beginning of the Spanish-American War (1898), General Merritt was the second-ranking officer in the army and received command of VIII Corps, dispatched to the Philippines. Merritt arrived there in late July. His command of logistics and his attention to detail contrasted sharply with the disorganized chaos that attended the Cuba campaign. Following negotiations with the Spanish, Merritt staged a small symbolic battle on August 13 to satisfy Spanish honor and then occupied Manila.

At the end of August, Merritt gave up his command to travel to Paris to brief the U.S. peace commissioners there, where he urged that the United States annex the Philippines. In December 1898 Merritt resumed command of the Department of the East. He retired from the army in 1900 and died in Natural Bridge, Virginia, on December 10, 1910.

DAWN OTTEVAERE NICKESON, SPENCER C. TUCKER, AND DAVID COFFEY

See also

Bannock War; Cavalry Regiment, 5th U.S.; Cavalry Regiment, 9th U.S.; Cheyennes; Crook, George; Great Sioux War; Kickapoos; Mackenzie, Ranald Slidell; Miles, Nelson Appleton; Nez Perce War; Sheridan, Philip Henry; Sioux; Slim Buttes, Battle of; Utes; Ute War

References

Alberts, Don E. *General Wesley Merritt: Brandy Station to Manila Bay.* Columbus, OH: General's Books, 2001.

Coffey, David. *Sheridan's Lieutenants: Phil Sheridan, His Generals, and the Final Year of the Civil War.* Lanham, MD: Rowman and Littlefield, 2005.

Feuer, A. B. *America at War: The Philippines, 1898–1913.* Westport, CT: Praeger, 2001.

Starr, Stephen Z. *The Union Cavalry in the Civil War.* 3 vols. Baton Rouge: Louisiana State University Press, 1979–1985.

Mesquakies

An Algonquian-speaking tribe of the Eastern Woodlands cultural group. Culturally and economically, the Mesquakies, also known as the Foxes, followed most of the pursuits of the eastern tribes, which included hunting, fishing, gathering, small-scale agriculture, and trade. In the early 18th century, Mesquakie intractability incurred the wrath of French officials, who waged the Fox Wars (1712–1737) to eliminate the tribe. Seeking refuge from intertribal foes or hoping to retain tribal lands ceded to the United States, some Mesquakies participated in the Black Hawk War (1832).

The Mesquakies inhabited the lower peninsula of Michigan until the Ojibwas drove them from their homelands, probably in the early 17th century. The Mesquakies subsequently took refuge in present-day Wisconsin, where they initially enjoyed stable relations with their Menominee and Ho Chunk neighbors. The tranquility did not endure, however, as Iroquois expansion in the mid-17th century created a refugee crisis in Wisconsin and overburdened the region's ecosystem. Migrating southwest along the Fox-Wisconsin waterway, the Mesquakies encroached on the hunting lands of the Dakota Sioux, in whom the Mesquakies found an enduring enemy. Repelled eastward and denied a meaningful role in the French fur trade, the Mesquakies thus resorted to piracy, demanding tribute from vessels navigating the Fox-Wisconsin waterway.

In 1710 French colonial officials (who referred to the Mesquakies by the name of the Fox Clan, which was responsible for diplomacy and warfare) invited the tribe to relocate to the new trade hub at Detroit. Here those Mesquakies who relocated threatened to take their trade to the British and so annoyed their new Native American neighbors that those tribes asked the French to wage extirpative war against the Mesquakies. In a series of conflicts known collectively as the Fox Wars, the French and their Native American allies pushed the Mesquakies to the brink of extinction. In the 1730s they sought refuge with the Sauks near Green Bay. By the end of the decade, New France authorities and their Native American allies had driven the Sauks and Mesquakies to the shores of the Mississippi, below the mouth of the Wisconsin River. Here the two tribes retained a close relationship and began to restore their populations.

In 1804 Sauk and Mesquakie delegates inadvertently ceded their tribes' lands in Illinois to the United States. Although both tribes subsequently affirmed the cession, certain factions in both tribes rejected its legitimacy. By 1829 the Sauk warrior Black Hawk

Mesquakie (Fox) Indians. Posed (left to right) are Osh U Ton (Winding Stream), Posh O Tu Nic (Bear Scratching Tree), Sho Won (South Wind), Chief On On A Wat (Can't Do It), and Wa Pa Lu Ca (Shining River), circa 1890. (Library of Congress)

emerged as their most prominent leader. Meanwhile, increased competition over hunting lands renewed the Mesquakies' animosity toward the Dakotas and their allies, the Menominees and Ho-Chunks. In May 1830 these tribes attacked a Mesquakie diplomatic party, leading to a Sauk-Mesquakie reprisal the following summer. Most of those responsible for the reprisal sheltered with Black Hawk, who on April 5, 1832, led his band into Illinois and provoked war with the United States.

Although few Mesquakies participated in the Black Hawk War (1832), the U.S. government, which treated the "Sac and Fox" as a single tribe, exacted further land cessions from the tribe as war reparations. Most Mesquakies avoided removal to Kansas in 1845, and a majority of those who went returned to Iowa during the 1850s. In 1856 they obtained legal title to their Iowa lands, and the U.S. government today recognizes them as the Sac and Fox Tribe of the Mississippi in Iowa.

JOHN W. HALL

See also

Black Hawk; Black Hawk War; Dakota Sioux; Fox Wars; Ojibwas; Sauks and Foxes

References

Callender, Charles. "Sauk." In *Handbook of North American Indians,* Vol. 15, *Northeast,* edited by Bruce G. Trigger, 648–655. Washington, DC: Smithsonian Institution Press, 1978.

Edmunds, R. David, and Joseph L. Peyser. *The Fox Wars: The Mesquakie Challenge to New France.* Norman: University of Oklahoma Press, 1993.

Gussow, Zachary. *Sac, Fox, and Iowa Indians.* 3 vols. New York: Garland, 1974.

Hagan, William T. *The Sac and Fox Indians.* Norman: University of Oklahoma Press, 1958.

White, Richard. *The Middle Ground: Indians, Empires, and Republics in the Great Lakes Region, 1650–1815.* New York: Cambridge University Press, 1991.

Metacom
Birth Date: Unknown
Death Date: August 12, 1676

Metacom, also known as Philip, Metacomet, or Pometacom, was the son of Massasoit and sachem (chief) of the Wampanoags (1662–1676). Metacom's precise birth date is unknown, as are the circumstances of his early years. When Massasoit died in 1660, his eldest son, Wamsutta, informed the leaders of Plymouth Colony that he was now sachem. He also asked them to give him and his brother, Metacom, English names. The Plymouth officials drew on classical history and bestowed the name of Alexander Pokanokett on Wamsutta. They dubbed Metacom "Philip."

Wamsutta's cordial relations with the English ended abruptly in 1662 when rumors that he was plotting an attack on Plymouth Colony began to circulate. Wamsutta temporarily mollified the English, but tensions increased when he contracted an illness shortly after he returned from being questioned at Plymouth and died in early 1662. His death raised suspicions among the Wampanoags.

Wamsutta's brother Metacom assumed the role of sachem and on August 6, 1662, agreed on a pact with Plymouth. The Wampanoags accepted that they were the subjects of the English Crown, and Metacom promised not to break any treaty signed by his predecessors. He also agreed that he would not sell land to "strangers," English settlers deemed unacceptable to the colony, nor would he provoke a war with neighboring native tribes. In return the colony promised that all settlers would treat the natives as friends and would advise and aid them, presumably militarily. Metacom thought that the document was binding for seven years, but he could not read, and in actuality the written document that he signed established the terms in perpetuity.

For nearly a decade Metacom maneuvered to maintain his power and ensure his people's welfare as the English population and strength steadily expanded. Wampanoag lands bordered Plymouth Colony, Rhode Island, and the Massachusetts Bay settlement.

Metacom sold tracts of land to various colonists in an attempt to maintain his influence in the politically charged arena, but subsequent conflicts over colonial borders were rarely settled to Metacom's satisfaction. Indeed, colonial courts were biased and unwilling to rule in favor of the Native Americans. The Wampanoags were also angered by colonial efforts to shape native politics, and additional tensions arose as English livestock wandered into Wampanoag fields, destroying crops.

In 1667 the conflict between the Wampanoags and English settlers became more acute when Plymouth, to establish the town of Swansea, violated the agreement with Metacom and authorized the purchase of Wampanoag land that was also claimed by Rhode Island. Believing that his earlier agreement with Plymouth had expired, Metacom had begun selling the same land to Rhode Island colonists.

War parties appeared on the outskirts of Swansea in attempts to intimidate the colonists. Plymouth demanded a meeting with Metacom in 1671 and compelled him to surrender his firearms and sign a treaty that bound him to Plymouth's authority, challenging any previous land sales to other colonies. The colony also insisted on a literal interpretation of the treaty, whereby all Wampanoag guns were to be confiscated. Metacom had assumed that only the guns that he and his men carried to the signing were to be surrendered. He refused the colony's interpretation, and Plymouth then announced that it would confiscate all of the Wampanoags' guns and ordered the Wampanoags' allies to disarm as well. Metacom sought assistance from Massachusetts Bay but found himself confronted by a joint commission from the Bay Colony, Plymouth, and Connecticut, all insisting on strict enforcement of the treaty.

There is evidence that at about this time Metacom sought the backing of other native leaders and peoples, such as the Nipmucks,

Engraving of Metacom, sachem (chief) of the Wampanoags during 1662–1676. Known as Philip to the people of Plymouth, in 1675 he led what became known as King Philip's War against white colonists in southern New England. (Library of Congress)

who felt pressure from the colonists. Metacom also appears to have tried to establish an alliance with the Narragansetts, who were old enemies but also the most powerful tribe in the region. Rumors of his efforts reached colonial authorities, and conflict ignited with the death of John Sassamon, one of Plymouth's native informers, on January 29, 1675. Shortly before his death, Sassamon had warned Plymouth officials of Metacom's plans.

The circumstances of Sassamon's death remain unclear. At first little attention was paid to his demise, which may have been accidental, but Plymouth officials became convinced that the Wampanoags had murdered him. By questionable process, the three Wampanoags accused in Sassamon's death were tried in an English court, found guilty, and hanged. But the jury could not determine if Metacom had known about or ordered the murder.

In June 1675 a band of Pokanokets again appeared at Swansea, rifling through several abandoned homes and slaying livestock. After the death of one of the Pokanokets, retaliation on the part of both natives and colonists led to the Native American siege and destruction of Swansea. A full-scale native uprising ensued, seemingly sparked more by the rage of the Wampanoags than by any plan. Metacom was besieged at his home at Mount Hope (Bristol, Rhode Island) but managed to escape and join with Nipmuck and Podunk allies to attack and burn English settlements west and south of Boston.

King Philip's War had begun. The New England Confederation officially declared war on September 9, 1675. Various Native American groups from the Connecticut River Valley and the Narragansetts joined the uprising after being attacked by English forces, but Metacom was not in formal command. He had left New England in December to seek support from the Mahicans in the upper Hudson River Valley.

As attacks by colonial forces and their native allies became more effective, disease and hunger also took their toll on Metacom's allies. In the spring of 1676 the informal Native American alliance began to disintegrate as many moved north and west to escape the fighting or made peace with the colonies. In June, Mohawks allied with colonial New York attacked Metacom and his forces, killing all but 40 of them and forcing Metacom to return to Massachusetts.

On August 12, 1676, colonial forces surrounded Metacom and his remaining warriors. That day he was shot and killed just outside Mount Hope by a native serving with colonial forces. Metacom's head was cut off, and his body drawn and quartered; the pieces sent to the colonial capitals. For the next 25 years, his head was displayed at the fort at Plymouth as a warning to other natives. Metacom's uprising devastated the native population of southern New England, and his death marked the end of native independence in the region. The Narragansetts, the Wampanoags, the Podunks, the Nipmucks, and several smaller tribes were virtually eliminated, leaving Massachusetts, Connecticut, and Rhode Island fully open to the spread of European colonization.

ANNA KIEFER

See also

King Philip's War; Mahicans; Massasoit; Mohawks; Narragansetts; New England Confederation; Nipmucks; Praying Towns and Praying Indians; Sassamon, John; Wampanoags; Wamsutta

References

Jennings, Francis. *The Invasion of America: Indians, Colonialism, and the Cant of Conquest.* 1976; reprint, Chapel Hill: University of North Carolina Press, 2010.

Lepore, Jill. *The Name of War: King Philip's War and the Origins of American Identity.* New York: Knopf, 1998.

Ranlet, Philip. "Another Look at the Causes of King Philip's War." *New England Quarterly* 61 (March 1988): 79–100.

Mexico

Mexico achieved independence from Spain in 1821, and at that time Mexico also assumed responsibility for a long northern frontier that stretched from the Louisiana line to the Pacific Ocean and northward to the Oregon Territory. When Texas achieved independence in 1836, the Rio Grande became the de facto border between the newly proclaimed Republic of Texas and Mexico, although the Mexicans refused de jure recognition of that line, instead claiming the Nueces River to the north as the official boundary, as it had been for a century. The Mexican-American War (1846–1848) resulted in the cession of most of Mexico's vast northern provinces, including California, Arizona, and New Mexico, to the United States. Although the Rio Grande line was set as the border with Texas, in the other territories there had been no defining river or distinguishing geographical barrier, and this created a problem for both nations.

Long before an international boundary existed, Native Americans from the southern Plains raided deep into central Mexico, carrying off valuable property and captives and terrorizing the population. These raids did not end with the new political realities in 1848, however. In Article XI of the Treaty of Guadalupe Hidalgo, which concluded the Mexican-American War, the United States assumed responsibility for preventing Native American raids launched from American territory south into Mexico, but the Americans could do little to stop such activity. In fact, over the next five years Mexico attributed at least 1,000 deaths to Native American attacks, and hundreds of captives were sold to traders. Mexican complaints and repeated claims for losses yielded little response from U.S. officials. Article XI was finally abrogated as part of the Gadsden Purchase of 1853 in which the United States purchased a narrow sliver of land encompassing what is now southern Arizona and part of southwestern New Mexico.

Meanwhile Mexico, plagued by civil war and political upheaval, found it impossible to protect itself from raiding Indians or to prevent hostile tribes from striking into the United States from Mexican territory. Resentment over the annexation of Texas and the war with the United States made any sort of meaningful cross-border cooperation politically impossible for Mexican leaders. Nor could authorities on either side of the border curtail the continuous irregular warfare, filibustering, and banditry that engulfed the area. The U.S. government established a string of forts along the Rio Grande but government was unprepared to meet the challenges in the border region and never provided for enough troops in the 12 years that followed the Mexican-American War. Thereafter the Confederate government in Texas (1861–1865) did even less.

Comanche and Kiowa raiding parties from the southern Plains as well as Mescalero Apaches from New Mexico found great opportunity in Mexico, ranging deep into the interior to plunder, kill, and kidnap and returning easily to their villages in the canyons of the Texas Panhandle or the mountains of New Mexico, sometimes even to the safety of the reservation. Likewise, the Kickapoos, whose settlement in the northern state of Coahuila the Mexican government had fostered in hopes of creating a barrier against marauding Plains tribes, preyed on the settlements and cattle herds of southern Texas along with Lipan and Mescalero Apaches, only to slip largely untouched back into Mexico. By the

The Treaty of Guadalupe Hidalgo, signed on February 2, 1848, ended the Mexican-American War. The treaty secured for the United States a vast amount of territory, including all or part of the present-day states of California, Nevada, Colorado, Utah, Wyoming, New Mexico, Kansas, and Arizona. (Library of Congress)

early 1870s with the frequency and intensity of raids from Mexico increasing, Texas politicians, merchants, cattlemen, and settlers pushed the Ulysses S. Grant administration to take a more aggressive approach to solving the problems. Efforts to establish a hot-pursuit policy had repeatedly failed, but the army took matters into its own hands.

In 1873 on dubious verbal orders from Major General Philip Sheridan, Colonel Ranald Mackenzie with a large force crossed the Rio Grande south of Fort Clark on May 16 and destroyed a Kickapoo village and two smaller camps near Remolino 40 miles into Coahuila, taking dozens of women and children hostage before returning to U.S. soil. Although Mackenzie narrowly managed to avoid a showdown with Mexican troops, this clear violation of Mexico's sovereignty could have provoked serious consequences, but an ineffectual protest from President Sebastián Lerdo de Tejada was the only response from Mexico. Despite the

illegal nature of Mackenzie's raid and the fact that it fell mostly on women, children, and old men, Kickapoo raiding activity all but ceased, and within a few years most Kickapoos had voluntarily relocated to Indian Territory (Oklahoma).

From 1876 to 1880 the United States repeatedly crossed the Rio Grande to strike tribal villages in Coahuila. Under the aggressive approach of Brigadier General Edward O. C. Ord, commander of the Department of Texas, U.S. soldiers openly defied Mexican authorities but generally avoided contact with the Mexican population as they applied pressure to the remaining Indians in the region. In 1877 newly installed U.S. president Rutherford B. Hayes issued a directive that asserted the U.S. right to hot pursuit, which the Mexicans took as a direct affront. Also in 1877, Division General Porfirio Díaz ousted Sebastián Lerdo de Tejada and assumed control of Mexico. Díaz, who had criticized Lerdo's inaction on the cross-border incursions and vowed to end them, ordered trusted Division General Gerónimo Treviño to reject any incursion with force.

In the meantime, the two governments attempted to negotiate a solution. Díaz wanted recognition, while Hayes wanted a cross-border treaty. The United States recognized Díaz's government in April 1878, and progress on a treaty followed. But to push the issue, in June 1877 Mackenzie led a massive cross-border show of force that included more than 1,000 troops. For his part, Treviño campaigned aggressively against Native Americans on his side of the river, with some positive results. Finally, in 1880 after the Americans dropped their onerous pursuit policy, the Díaz regime opened the door for a cross-border treaty, officially codified in 1882, that played a major role in the final Apache campaigns and remained in effect until 1886.

As events along the Texas-Mexico border heated up, in Arizona and New Mexico they cooled down thanks to some enlightened diplomacy and Lieutenant Colonel (soon Brigadier General) George Crook's innovative campaigning in 1872 and 1873. By the end of the decade, however, the Southwest was again in turmoil, bringing Mexico and the United States together to fight a common enemy. In 1879 Warm Springs Apache leader Victorio conducted a quixotic but bloody campaign on both sides of the border. Victorio, no longer able to use the border to escape pursuit, found his dwindling band harried on all fronts as U.S. troops flowed into Mexico in cooperation with Mexican units. In northern Chihuahua on October 15, 1880, Mexican irregular troops under Colonel Joaquin Terrazas attacked and killed the much-feared chief and most of his followers, women and children included.

Cross-border cooperation played a major but tragic role in the Apache campaigns that followed. White encroachment and deplorable conditions on the reservations led to major breakouts and deadly raids throughout the first half of the 1880s. Apache warrior Geronimo and his followers terrorized both sides of the Arizona border for years. Again U.S. troops followed Native Americans into Mexico, this time largely permitted by the Díaz regime. In 1882 General Crook took command of the Department of Arizona. In 1883 with the new reciprocal crossing treaty now in effect,

General Crook, responding to two violent raids, led a campaign into Sonora's Sierra Madre that netted Geronimo's eventual surrender, although he would not remain quiet for long. In May 1885 a large number of Apaches broke from military control and headed for Mexico, prompting a second campaign deep into the Sierra Madre. On January 11, 1886, as a column led by the gifted Lieutenant Emmet Crawford closed in on Geronimo's band, a party of 150 Mexican irregulars, also pursuing the Apaches, attacked the soldiers, killing Crawford. But the Apaches, with their location now revealed, agreed to meet with Crook. On March 25 and again on March 27, 1886, Crook met with Geronimo and other leaders in Cañon de los Embudos and famously secured Geronimo's pledge to surrender, which was only to be betrayed in short order.

With Geronimo still loose in Mexico, Brigadier General Nelson A. Miles took charge in Arizona. He quickly ordered an extensive campaign that spent weeks in Mexico, with little to show. Miles then reluctantly called upon Lieutenant Charles Gatewood and his Indian scouts, who finally brought the Apaches out of Mexico. Despite the tragedy that befell Crawford, the cooperation of the Mexican government and the vigorous efforts of the Mexican officers in Chihuahua and Sonora played a huge role in finally ending the Indian Wars in the desert Southwest.

DAVID COFFEY

See also

Apaches; Apache Wars; Cochise; Crook, George; Gatewood, Charles Bare; Geronimo; Kickapoos; Mackenzie, Ranald Slidell; Miles, Nelson Appleton; Sheridan, Philip Henry; Victorio

References

Clendenen, Clarence C. *Blood on the Border: The United States Army and the Mexican Irregulars.* Toronto: Macmillan, 1969.

Garner, Paul. *Porfirio Díaz.* New York: Longman, 2001.

Martínez, Oscar J. *Troublesome Border.* Tucson: University of Arizona Press, 1988.

Utley, Robert M. *Frontier Regulars: The United States and the American Indian, 1866–1891.* New York: Macmillan, 1973.

Worcester, Donald E. *The Apaches: Eagles of the Southwest.* Norman: University of Oklahoma Press, 1979.

Miami Campaign

See Little Turtle's War

Miamis

Native American group that chiefly inhabited parts of the present-day U.S. Midwest. The name "Miami" is possibly from the Ojibwa word "Omaumeg" ("People of the Peninsula") or perhaps from their own word for "pigeon." Their original name may have been Twaatwaa, in imitation of the sound that a crane makes. Miami is an Algonquian language. The traditional Miami bands were the Atchatchakangouens, Kilatikas, Mengakonkias, Pepicokias, Weas, and Piankashaws. The Miamis were culturally and linguistically related to the Illinois. From a position possibly south of Lake Michigan, roughly 4,500 Miamis moved into northern Illinois and southern Wisconsin in the mid-17th century.

The six traditional bands had consolidated by the 18th century into four: the Miamis proper, the Pepicokias, the Weas, and the Piankashaws. Of these, the second soon merged with the last two, which by the 19th century acted as separate tribes. Even in the 19th century, each of the three Miami tribes was subdivided into bands.

Each village had a council made up of clan chiefs; the council in turn confirmed a village chief, generally a patrilineally inherited position, who was responsible for civil functions and was in turn supported by the people. There was also a war chief who oversaw military activities. This person generally inherited his position but might obtain it by merit (as was the case with Little Turtle). There were also parallel female peace and war chiefs. The former supervised feasts, and the latter provisioned war parties and could demand an end to various types of hostilities.

The village council also sent delegates to the band council, which in turn sent delegates to the tribal council. All leaders enjoyed respect and a great deal of authority. In fact, early tribal chiefs may have had a semidivine status, reflecting the influence of the Mound Builder culture.

The Miamis recognized roughly five patrilineal clans and possibly a dual division. Names were clan specific, although adults might change names to alter their luck or to avert bad luck. Marriages were either arranged or initiated by couples.

The Miami people built small summer villages in river valleys. Private houses were made of an oval pole framework covered with woven cattail or rush mats. There were also village council houses. Structures in winter hunting camps tended to be covered with elm bark or animal hides. The Miamis developed and grew a particularly fine variety of corn in addition to beans, squash, and (later) melons. Men hunted buffalo on the open prairies, using fire surrounds and the bow and arrow before they acquired horses and firearms. Women also gathered wild roots and other plant food to augment the diet. The Miamis traded agricultural products, pipes, and buffalo products. They acquired shell beads, among other items, through trade.

With the help of the council, war chiefs decided whether to wage war. War rituals, such as the all-night war dance and the homecoming welcome of a successful war party, were clan based, and leaders of war parties were not considered responsible for deaths of members of their own clan. Warriors carried large buffalo-hide shields.

Miami culture evolved at least in part from the prehistoric Ohio Mound Builders. In the mid-17th century, the Miamis effected a temporary retreat west of the Mississippi River in the face of Iroquois war parties during the Beaver Wars (1641–1701). Dakota pressure, including a major military defeat, sent them back east, with French assistance. Peace was established between the Miamis and the Iroquois in 1701.

The Miamis traded with the French from the mid-17th century. Some Miamis guided Jacques Marquette and Louis Jolliet (Joliet) down the Mississippi in the 1670s. The Miami allied with the French during the early colonial wars but in 1747, during King George's War (1744–1748), joined other tribes dissatisfied with French policy and a shortage of trade goods in a revolt against their former ally. At the war's end, under the leadership of Old Briton (Memeskia), the Miamis shifted their allegiance toward the British and permitted the Ohio Company to establish trading posts in their territory. After the French and their Native American allies destroyed the Miami town of Pickawillany in 1752, the Miamis resumed their alliance with the French, which lasted through the French and Indian War (1754–1763). The Miamis participated in Pontiac's Rebellion (1763), after which they ceded most of their Ohio lands to the British and concentrated in Indiana. The Miamis fought with the British against the Americans in the American Revolutionary War (1775–1783).

Little Turtle's War (1785–1795), also known as the Northwest Indian War or the Miami War, was led by the great Miami strategist Michikinikwa, or Little Turtle, and featured a Native American coalition that included the Ojibwas, Ottawas, Delawares, Shawnees, Pottawatomis, and Illinois as well as the Miamis. The war was a defensive one, fought to contain American settlement of the Ohio Valley. The coalition enjoyed significant victories in the early years, thanks mainly to Little Turtle's strategic ability. Although Little Turtle eventually concluded that the war was not winnable and advised a cessation of hostilities, the Native American coalition chose Blue Jacket of the Shawnees to replace him and continued its resistance in 1794 until its defeat in the Battle of Fallen Timbers (August 20, 1794). The ensuing Treaty of Greenville forced the Miamis and other tribes in the Northwest to cede large portions of present-day Ohio and Indiana to the United States.

Afterward the Miamis underwent a dramatic population decline. The United States forcibly removed a group of about 600 Miamis to Kansas in 1846. In 1854 this group joined the remnants of the Illinois tribe and formed the Confederated Peoria Tribe, which was later relocated to Indian Territory (Oklahoma). Other Miamis there joined that confederacy in 1873, which changed its name to the United Peoria and Miami Tribe. The group that remained in Indiana consisted of about 1,500 people whose chiefs had been granted private land.

By the early 20th century, Miami land in both Oklahoma and Indiana had largely been lost through allotment and tax foreclosure. With the loss of their lands, both communities, but especially the one in Indiana, suffered significant population loss as people moved away to try to survive. Forty years after the Indiana Miamis lost federal recognition in 1897, they organized a nonprofit corporation in an effort to maintain their identity.

BARRY M. PRITZKER AND JIM PIECUCH

See also
Algonquins; Fallen Timbers, Battle of; Greenville, Treaty of; Little Turtle; Little Turtle's War; Ohio Company of Virginia; Old Briton; Pickawillany Massacre; Pontiac's Rebellion

References
Anson, Bert. *The Miami Indians.* Norman: University of Oklahoma Press, 1971.
Rafert, Stewart. *The Miami Indians of Indiana: A Persistent People, 1654–1994.* Indianapolis: Indiana Historical Society, 1996.

Miantonomo
Birth Date: Unknown
Death Date: 1643

Key Narragansett leader who played a pivotal role in the early history of New England. Miantonomo (also spelled Miantonomi) presided over the Narragansetts with his uncle Canonicus. Almost nothing is known about the circumstances of Miantonomo's birth and his early years, but he was most likely born in present-day Rhode Island or eastern Connecticut.

The Narragansetts had allied themselves with Rhode Island, a colony that dissented from the Puritan orthodoxy of neighboring Connecticut and Massachusetts Bay. Numerically inferior to the other New England colonies, Rhode Island did not enjoy the support of its sister colonies. However, it did back Massachusetts and Plymouth during the Pequot War (1636–1638) and sought assistance from its Narragansett allies and Miantonomo.

Miantonomo gave advice and military assistance to the English during the conflict. However, he repeatedly admonished them for their mode of warfare, complaining that they killed too many people and did not take enough prisoners. The Narragansetts saw warfare as a way to intimidate and extract tribute from their enemies and as a means to acquire captives. For the Narragansetts, warfare was not principally about killing and destruction.

After the war Miantonomo realized that native peoples had to band together to counter English expansionism. He argued that rather than thinking of themselves as Narragansetts or as Mohegans, the native peoples had to formulate a common identity. Miantonomo employed imagery of a peaceful precontact New England in his efforts to convince the natives to unite. The New England governments became alarmed when they learned about Miantonomo's Pan-Indian activities.

In the 1638 Hartford Treaty, which ended the Pequot War, Miantonomo was granted hunting territory on former Pequot lands. The agreement also stipulated that the Narragansetts and the Mohegans refrain from fighting one another. However, the Mohegans under Uncas routinely attacked Narragansett hunters. In accordance with the treaty, Miantonomo informed Massachusetts Bay Colony of his intent to punish the Mohegans. Wearing armor given to him by a colonist, Miantonomo was weighed down and was easily captured by the Mohegans during a battle in 1642. While a prisoner, Miantonomo discussed with Uncas the possibility of joining forces. But in the end, Uncas turned Miantonomo over to Connecticut authorities.

Connecticut officials were not sure what to do with the sachem. On the one hand they wanted to be rid of Miantonomo, regarding him as a troublemaker. Yet at the same time they did not want his blood on their hands. They handed Miantonomo back to Uncas. In 1643, with colonial representatives in attendance, Uncas's brother slew Miantonomo, the first Native American to propose a Pan-Indian movement.

ROGER M. CARPENTER

See also

Hartford, Treaty of; Mohegans; Narragansetts; Pequots; Pequot War; Uncas

References

Orberg, Michael Leroy. *Uncas: First of the Mohegans.* Ithaca, NY: Cornell University Press, 2003.

Salisbury, Neal. *Manitou and Providence: Indians, Europeans, and the Making of New England, 1500–1643.* New York: Oxford University Press, 1982.

Micmac Raids on Nova Scotia
Start Date: 1744
End Date: 1779

A series of bloody attacks by the Micmac tribe on British outposts in Nova Scotia (Acadia) beginning in 1744 and continuing intermittently until 1779. The Micmacs inhabited the area of present-day Nova Scotia, Prince Edward Island, and parts of New Brunswick. Acadia had been established by the French in 1604. Jesuit priests converted many Micmacs to Catholicism, and French settlers generally lived in harmony with the Native Americans. Intermarriage between the two was common, so much so in fact that by the time trouble began with Great Britain in the late 17th and early 18th centuries, it was difficult to distinguish between those of French descent and those of Micmac ancestry.

The colony, however, had been long neglected by the French, who chose to focus their attention farther west, at Quebec and Montreal. Wedged between New France to the northwest and the English colonies to the southwest, Acadia enjoyed relative peace and prosperity until English colonists began raiding the area in 1690. The Treaty of Utrecht ceded the province to Britain in 1713, which did not sit well with the Micmacs. For the next 30 years the British government entertained different ways to displace the French population and solidify its control of the region. It was finally determined that the best solution would be to inundate the area with British settlers. This was not successful, however, and met with stiff opposition from the Micmacs. When New England fishermen attempted to settle at Canso, a was ensued during 1722–1725.

In King George's War (1744–1748), the Micmacs allied with the French and successfully captured the military outpost at Canso. The Treaty of Aix-la-Chapelle (April 24, 1748) ended the corresponding war in Europe but did not end hostilities in Nova Scotia. A French priest, Father Jean Louis Le Loutre, covertly began encouraging the Micmacs to resist British rule. In the summer of 1749 the British established a large settlement at Halifax, and the Micmacs responded by attacking British stations at Chebucto and Canso. The British retaliated by sending out ranger companies to hunt down the warriors, offering £10 per scalp and £100 for that of Le Loutre. Guerrilla fighting raged throughout the area until a peace treaty was signed in November 1752.

Peace did not last long, however, and the Micmac raids on Nova Scotia commenced once again with the outbreak of the French and Indian War (1754–1763). A favorite target of the Micmacs became British fishing boats. When the British finally expelled the Acadians in 1755, many fled to the woods and joined the Micmacs in guerrilla warfare, restricting the British settlers to their fortified posts. The reward for each Micmac scalp was raised to £30. Although large-scale raids subsided after 1763, violence against British colonists would not officially cease until 1779.

WILLIAM WHYTE

See also

French and Indian War; King George's War; Micmacs; Queen Anne's War

References

Nester, William R. *The Great Frontier War: Britain, France, and the Imperial Struggle for North America, 1607–1755.* Westport, CT: Praeger, 2000.

Plank, Geoffrey. *An Unsettled Conquest: The British Campaign against the People of Acadia.* Philadelphia: University of Pennsylvania Press, 2001.

Micmacs

An Algonquian-speaking Native American tribe that originally inhabited the Gaspé Peninsula, which they called Mi'kma'ki, situated on the eastern tip of the present-day Canadian province of Quebec and immediately to the north of New Brunswick. The Micmacs (Mi'kmaq) at one point commanded a territory that extended to areas of Nova Scotia, Prince Edward Island, the north shore of New Brunswick to the St. John River, parts of Quebec, eastern Maine, part of Newfoundland, and the islands in the Saint Lawrence River. The Micmacs were members of the Wabanaki Confederacy, which was a loose alliance of the Maliseets (Malecites), the Eastern and Western Abenakis, the Penobscots, and the Passamaquoddys. The area inhabited by this confederacy included much of eastern Canada and northern New England.

The Micmacs may have been the original settlers in the area, arriving not long after the end of the last ice age. Since prehistoric times they lived by hunting and gathering in seasonal movements to available food supplies. Later they augmented hunting and

Portrait of a Micmac Native American woman and young man in traditional dress, Nova Scotia, 1865. (National Anthropological Archives, Smithsonian Institution, NAA INV 00290200)

gathering by cultivating seasonal crops, although their northern locale made it difficult to pursue agriculture in a significant way. Micmacs worshiped the so-called Great Spirit and passed down numerous religious legends. Many of these were about a supernatural being named Glooscap, the maker of much of the Micmacs' surrounding landscape.

When the Micmacs first encountered European fishermen (Spanish, Portuguese, and French) in the early 1500s, they did not experience a devastating shock, as did many other tribes. For a long time the Micmacs had held that a spiritual being friendly to the Micmacs had crossed the Atlantic to discover a blue-eyed people. The legend also said that these new people would one day come from the east to disrupt their lives. Some believe that the legend may have sprung from visits by the Vikings around the year 1000. Despite their friendship with the Europeans, the Micmacs were devastated by European diseases, which reduced their numbers from approximately 20,000 before contact to 4,000 or so by 1620.

The Micmacs sought to trade with the Europeans and also tried to employ European technologies, especially in weaponry. When the French explorer Jacques Cartier visited Canada in 1534, he initiated Franco-Micmac trading relations. In 1603 Samuel de Champlain also visited the area, and in 1610 Chief Membertou converted to Roman Catholicism. Eventually, French Jesuit missionaries converted most of the Micmacs to that faith.

In 1710 the British captured Port Royal, the center of French Acadia, in an action during Queen Anne's War (1702–1713). The British renamed the town Annapolis Royal. In 1745 during King George's War (1744–1748), the French, based at Louisbourg, tried to retake Port Royal. With the help of French settlers, Micmacs, and Maliseets, they attacked the British garrison. However, coordination between the French forces, who were led by inexperienced commanders, was poor, and the resultant piecemeal siege proved unsuccessful. Unlike the French and other French-allied tribes, the Micmacs continued to resist the British after King George's War ended; their opposition was sparked by the establishment of a large British settlement at Halifax in 1749. Micmac resistance continued during and after the French and Indian War (1754–1763), although the British expulsion of the French inhabitants from Acadia in 1755 devastated the Micmacs, who by then had developed tight bonds with the French to include significant intermarriage.

In the late 1700s after the French had been expelled from Canada, the Micmacs signed a number of treaties with the British. The Royal Proclamation of 1763 is still the fundamental law between the Micmacs and the Canadian government. During the American Revolutionary War (1775–1783) the Micmacs sided with the Patriots, mainly because the Micmacs mistakenly believed that a British defeat would bring back the French. In 1794 the Micmacs signed the Jay Treaty, allowing them to cross the American-Canadian border freely. Between 1800 and 1900 the Micmac population remained stable at between 3,000 and 4,000 people. That population grew quite dramatically during the 20th century, however. Indeed, the Micmac population increased from about 4,000 in 1900 to more than 15,000 by the turn of the century. Today their population is estimated to be close to 20,000. Most Micmacs live in the Canadian Maritimes, although there has been extensive intermarriage with the French, meaning that a good number of self-identified Micmacs are only part Micmac.

ANDREW J. WASKEY

See also

Abenakis; Champlain, Samuel de; King George's War; Micmac Raids on Nova Scotia; Queen Anne's War

References

Reid, John G. *The "Conquest" of Acadia, 1710: Imperial, Colonial, and Aboriginal Constructions.* Toronto: University of Toronto Press, 2004.

Upton, Leslie Francis Stokes. *Micmacs and Colonists: Indian-White Relations in the Maritimes, 1773–1867.* Vancouver: University of British Columbia Press, 1979.

Middle Plantation, Treaty of

See Virginia-Indian Treaty of 1677/1680

Miles, Nelson Appleton
Birth Date: August 8, 1839
Death Date: May 15, 1925

U.S. Army officer. Nelson Appleton Miles was born on a farm near Westminster, Massachusetts, on August 8, 1839. After attending public school he moved to Boston in 1856, where he worked as a store clerk. Interested in the military, Miles received some instruction from a retired French colonel.

At the outbreak of the American Civil War (1861–1865), Miles recruited some 100 men for a Massachusetts regiment and was commissioned a first lieutenant of volunteers. At first considered too young for battlefield command, Miles initially served in a staff position during the 1862 Peninsula Campaign. He soon demonstrated a natural capacity for battlefield leadership and began a meteoric advance in rank. In 1862 after the Battle of Seven Pines (Fair Oaks), he was promoted to lieutenant colonel in the 61st New York Infantry. He then fought in the Seven Days' Campaign and the Battle of Antietam (Sharpsburg). Promoted to colonel, he was wounded in the Battle of Fredericksburg and again in 1863 in the

Nelson A. Miles was one of the most effective Indian fighters in the frontier army. He was active in campaigns on the Great Plains during the 1870s and 1880s and also conducted a successful campaign against the Apaches, resulting in the final surrender of Geronimo in 1886. Miles went on to command the army during the Spanish-American War. (Library of Congress)

Battle of Chancellorsville. For his actions at Chancellorsville, Miles later (1892) received the Medal of Honor. He commanded a brigade of II Corps in the 1864 Overland Campaign and saw combat in the Battle of the Wilderness and the Battle of Spotsylvania Court House, after which he was promoted to brigadier general of volunteers in May 1864.

Miles commanded a division in the Siege of Petersburg and briefly (at age 26) a corps. He suffered his fourth wound of the war in the Battle of Reams' Station.

Following the war, in October 1865 Miles was advanced to major general of volunteers and assumed command of II Corps. In the reorganization of the army in 1866, he became colonel of the 40th Infantry Regiment, an African American unit. In 1869 he took command of the 5th Infantry Regiment. Miles saw extensive service in the American West and became renowned as one of the army's finest commanders in the ensuing Indian Wars. He was conspicuously active in the Red River War (1874–1875). In 1876 and 1877 he played prominent roles in the Great Sioux War and the Nez Perce War, personally accepting the surrenders of Sioux war chief Crazy Horse and Nez Perce chief Joseph.

Miles was promoted to brigadier general in the regular army in December 1880. From 1880 to 1885 he commanded the Department of the Columbia, and from 1885 to 1886 he had charge of the Department of the Missouri. In 1886 he took command of the Department of Arizona. There he discontinued the wise practice of his predecessor, Brigadier General George Crook, of employing Apaches as scouts, choosing instead to rely mostly on U.S. troops. Following several months of failure, Miles reintroduced Crook's practice and oversaw the final surrender of Geronimo and the Chiricahua Apaches in September 1886. Miles then engaged in a public dispute with Crook over the subsequent exile of the Apaches, including the loyal scouts, to Florida.

In 1888 Miles took command of the Division of the Pacific. Promoted to major general in April 1890, he directed the suppression of the Sioux Ghost Dance uprising in the Dakota Territory but was angered by the bloodshed at Wounded Knee on December 29, 1890. Miles wanted to court-martial Colonel James W. Forsyth, who commanded during that action. Although Miles relieved Forsyth from command, the War Department soon reinstated him.

In 1894 Miles was called upon to employ troops in suppressing the Pullman Strike and then commanded the Department of the East. On October 5, 1895, he succeeded Lieutenant General John M. Schofield as commanding general of the army. Miles opposed the Spanish-American War (1898), believing that diplomacy could resolve the differences between Spain and the United States. When the war began, he favored using regulars in Cuba rather than volunteer forces, which he believed should remain in the United States and maintain its defenses against a possible Spanish attack. He also opposed an invasion of Cuba until the Spanish naval squadron had been destroyed but convinced President William McKinley to shift the main American land assault from Havana to Santiago de Cuba. Once Santiago was secured, Miles received approval to proceed with his own invasion of Puerto Rico, an assignment he had sought early on. He conducted a highly successful campaign in Puerto Rico that was cut short by the armistice of August 12, which denied him the capture of San Juan.

After the war Miles was the central figure in the notorious Embalmed Beef Scandal. He alleged that the Commissary Department had issued spoiled beef to the troops. He was subsequently reprimanded by the Dodge Commission for making charges that were proven to be substantially unfounded.

In June 1900 Miles was promoted to lieutenant general. President Theodore Roosevelt, who called Miles a "brave peacock" for his love of excessive uniform display, also crossed swords with Miles, as did Secretary of War Elihu Root, who found Miles in sharp opposition to his plan to create a General Staff and do away with the position of commanding general of the army, substituting for it the new position of chief of staff.

Miles retired from the army on his 64th birthday in 1903. Combative, vain, and ambitious, Miles was, along with Ranald Mackenzie, one of the finest field commanders during the Indian Wars, amassing a record second to none. Despite Miles's leadership qualities in battle, he was a commanding general who displayed little political sense and did not fit well in the new 20th-century army. In 1917 when the United States entered World War I (1914–1918) Miles offered his service, but it was not accepted. In retirement he wrote articles and several books, including a two-volume memoir. Miles died at Washington, D.C., on May 15, 1925.

JERRY KEENAN AND SPENCER C. TUCKER

See also

Apaches; Crazy Horse; Crook, George; Forsyth, James William; Geronimo; Joseph, Chief; Nez Perce War; Red River War; Wounded Knee, Battle of

References

Cosmas, Graham. *An Army for Empire: The United States Army in the Spanish-American War.* College Station: Texas A&M University Press, 1998.

DeMontravel, Peter R. *A Hero to His Fighting Men: Nelson A. Miles, 1839–1925.* Kent, OH: Kent State University Press, 1998.

Johnson, Virginia. *The Unregimented General: A Biography of Nelson A. Miles.* Boston: Houghton Mifflin, 1962.

Miles, Nelson A. *Personal Recollections and Observations of General Nelson A. Miles.* 2 vols. Lincoln: University of Nebraska Press, 1992.

Wooster, Robert. *Nelson A. Miles and the Twilight of the Frontier Army.* Lincoln: University of Nebraska Press, 1993.

Military Divisions, Departments, and Districts

Beginning in 1813, the United States found it necessary to arrange the growing country into geographically defined military commands, which served as administrative links between forces and installations in a given region and the War Department's national headquarters in Washington, D.C. (or army headquarters when located outside of Washington). Territorial commands held varying designations over the years—divisions, departments, districts (sometimes all three terms were used at once in a tiered arrangement)—that, along with the geographical confines, changed repeatedly. Some arrangements featured divisions with subordinate departments, some featured divisions with independent departments, and one arrangement included divisions with subordinate and independent departments as well as districts. Headquarters could be just as changeable, often owing as much to a commander's preference as to the prominence of a post or a municipality within the jurisdiction.

Often the command structure grew cumbersome, and personal relationships within that structure occasionally proved problematic. Clearly some secretaries of war and commanding generals preferred more direct control over units in the field, while others favored more elaborate chains of command, which accounted for many of the drastic shifts in system structure that occurred in a relatively brief period. Another factor was the philosophical differences over the size and function of the army that always dogged military leaders. But once established, the territorial command structure in whatever guise played an important role in the prosecution of the various Indian Wars.

During the early republic period, the frugal federal government, with little interest in maintaining a large regular military establishment, saw no need for separate territorial jurisdictions until expansion and war demanded such organization. Once the government embraced the idea of territorial commands, however, it adopted an incredibly flexible implementation that allowed for ever-changing definitions, driven largely by philosophical or political shifts among the military and civilian leadership.

In 1813 in the midst of the War of 1812, the government divided the nation into nine military districts; another district was established in July 1814. Following the war, an 1815 reorganization replaced the district model with two divisions—the Division of the North and the Division of the South—each of which was subdivided into military departments with numerical designations. This arrangement lasted until 1821, when the country, now grown well beyond the Mississippi River, was split into two large departments east and west of a line that ran from the Gulf of Mexico to Lake Superior. In 1837 the government returned to a division system, with subordinate departments (the two-department Western Division and the five-department Eastern Division) essentially drawn east and west of the Mississippi River and still reflective of an emphasis on the more established regions of the country. In 1842 the Eastern Division and the Western Division were scrapped in favor of nine independent departments only to be reconstituted in 1844 along with two independent departments, Military Department No. 4 and Military Department No. 9 (the latter was abolished in 1845). In November 1846, reflecting the territorial expansion occasioned by the annexation of Texas, the Mexican-American War (1846–1848), and the settlement of the Oregon boundary dispute, two new departments, Nos. 9 and 10, embracing the Southwest and California, were added. In 1848 with the conclusion of the war

MILITARY POSTS IN THE WEST, 1874

CANADA

Vancouver
Barracks

Blackfeet

Department
of the Columbia

Nez Perce

Department
of Dakota

Klamaths

Bannocks

Department
of the Platte

Lakotas

St. Paul

Modocs   *Paiutes*

Shoshonis

*Northern
Cheyennes*

San
Francisco

Chicago

Omaha

St.
Louis

Department
of California

Utes

Fort
Leavenworth

Department
of the Missouri

Navajos

Kiowas

*Southern
Cheyennes
Arapahos*

Prescott

Comanches

Department
of Arizona

Apaches

Department
of Texas

San
Antonio

New
Orleans

PACIFIC
OCEAN

Gulf of
Mexico

MEXICO

Legend:
- ✪ Division headquarters
- ☆ Department headquarters
- — Department boundary
- ▨ Division of the Pacific
- ▦ Division of the Missouri
- ▩ Division of the Atlantic
- ▧ Indian territory transferred to the Department of the Missouri (1875)

0   200   400 mi
0   200   400 km

100°W   90°W

50°N
40°N
30°N

with Mexico, the Eastern Division and the Western Division were retained with significant changes among the subordinate departments. The Western Division fully incorporated Texas and the New Mexico Territory, with California (No. 10) and the Oregon Territory (No. 11) established as independent departments until the creation of the Pacific Division later in the year. Almost constant realignment followed until this model was abandoned in 1853.

The 1853 reorganization did away with the old divisions and established a system of five departments of geographical rather than numerical designation, which boldly emphasized the new military focus on the West. Four of the five original departments were west of the Mississippi (Department of the West, Department of Texas, Department of New Mexico, and Department of the Pacific); the entire area east of the Mississippi was combined in the Department of the East. This arrangement too saw significant alterations and additions until the outbreak of the American Civil War (1861–1865). The U.S. government retained this basic structure during that war. However, the secession of 11 southern states, military threats from a Confederate invasion of New Mexico, Native American uprisings in Minnesota, Arizona and elsewhere, and ever-changing conditions led to a number of changes and additions, such as the creation of the Department of the Northwest in response to the Minnesota Sioux Uprising in 1862.

With the conclusion of the Civil War in 1865, the United States adopted a territorial command structure that endured, with dozens of alterations, for the duration of the Indian Wars. The 1866 reorganization returned to the division model, with the vast Trans-Mississippi West split into two massive commands, while the East retained the independent department model until 1868, when it too was organized into divisions, the most durable of which was the Division of the Atlantic. Reconstruction politics further complicated matters. Divisions were headed by senior general officers, usually major generals, while brigadiers or senior colonels headed departments. All were prominent Civil War commanders, although some, such as Irwin McDowell and John Pope, owed their postwar appointments more to seniority in the regular army than to their success in the war. In 1867 the former Confederate states were organized into five military districts, all of which were discontinued by the mid-1870s. As the U.S. Army's attention returned to the frontier, the West, with its pioneers, railroads, mining operations, and more than 100,000 Native Americans considered hostile by the federal government, received unprecedented attention.

The Military Division of the Missouri, which included the Department of Arkansas, the Department of Missouri, the Department of the Platte, the Department of Dakota, and, after Reconstruction, the Department of Texas, became the most active theater of war between 1866 and 1890, playing host to major campaigns on the southern Plains, including the Red River War (1874–1875) in Texas, and on the northern Plains, including the Great Sioux War (1876–1877) and the final act of the Indian Wars, the tragedy at Wounded Knee, South Dakota, in December 1890. The division's prominence was also reflected in the fact that its commanding officer for much of the post–Civil War era—William T. Sherman during 1866–1869 and Philip H. Sheridan during 1869–1884—ranked second only to the commanding general and carried the three-star rank. The Military Division of the Pacific—the Department of California, the Department of Columbia, and later the Department of Arizona—saw considerable activity as well, including the Modoc War (1872–1873), the Nez Perce War (1877), and the Apache Wars of the 1880s. Logistical demands, political expediency, and the various contingencies of major campaigns brought continuous change to the configuration of individual departments, as areas shifted from one department to another or departmental boundaries expanded to encompass the scope of a particular campaign.

With the Indian Wars' conclusion in 1890, the War Department once again changed the territorial command structure of the army, abolishing the three existing divisions—the Atlantic, the Missouri, and the Pacific—and adopting a system of eight independent departments.

DAVID COFFEY

See also

Apache Wars; Forts, Camps, Cantonments, and Outposts; Great Sioux War; Minnesota Sioux Uprising; Modoc War; Nez Perce War; Red River War; Sheridan, Philip Henry; Sherman, William Tecumseh; War Department, U.S.

References

Prucha, Francis Paul. *A Guide to the Military Posts of the United States, 1789–1895.* Madison: State Historical Society of Wisconsin, 1964.

United States Army. *American Military History.* Washington, DC: United States Army Center of Military History, 1989.

Utley, Robert M. *Frontier Regulars: The United States and the American Indian, 1866–1891.* New York: Macmillan, 1973.

Utley, Robert M. *Frontiersmen in Blue: The United States and the Indian, 1848–1865.* Lincoln: University of Nebraska Press, 1967.

Militia

Military organization based on a citizen-soldiery organized at the colonial, state, territorial, or local level. Unlike the Spanish who maintained professional soldiers to protect their colonists and maintain control over large indigenous populations, the English colonies were largely devoid of professional armies until the mid-18th century. In part this was because the Native American population in North America was much smaller and was divided into numerous tribes that often warred against one another. Consequently, English colonial defense until the imperial struggles of the 18th century depended on the obligation of able-bodied males to fight in their local militias. Militia officers in the southern colonies were generally appointed by the colonial assembly or governor, while in the New England colonies they were generally elected.

Militia members were expected to provide their own arms, although they could draw ammunition and gunpowder from local arsenals. Periodically the militia mustered for drill, but these

Colonial militiamen fighting the Pequot Indians during the Pequot War of 1636–1638. The war decimated the Pequots and they ceased to exist as an independent people afterward. (Hulton Archive/Getty Images)

occasions grew over time to be generally more social than real military events. Nevertheless, the militia proved to be an effective fighting force against Native Americans in the frontier conditions of North America. It should be emphasized, however, that the militia was often assisted by friendly Native Americans who sought assistance against their traditional enemies. Such was the case in the Pequot War (1636–1638) and King Philip's War (1675–1676) in New England. Without the assistance of Native American allies, the colonial militia would not have been as successful.

During King William's War (1689–1697), Queen Anne's War (1702–1713), King George's War (1744–1748), and the French and Indian War (1754–1763), colonial militia supplemented British regulars in their campaigns against the French and their native allies. British officers generally discounted the effectiveness of militia and were often exasperated by the conditions that the militia demanded in order to fight and their refusal to fight outside their colony's borders. The militia was best suited for the hit-and-run tactics that characterized guerrilla warfare rather than pitched battles. Yet the experience gained in these wars proved beneficial during the American Revolutionary War (1775–1783) by allowing the Continental Army to draw upon volunteers who had prior experience in the colonial and state militias.

After securing independence in 1783, the United States continued to rely on the militia primarily because of fears that a standing

army presented a threat to liberty. This concern was made vocal by Anti-Federalists in the various state conventions that met to ratify the U.S. Constitution in 1787 and 1788. To allay these fears, the Second Amendment guaranteeing the right to bear arms in order to maintain militias was added to the Constitution in 1791. The wording of the amendment continues to raise questions as to whether the right to bear arms was an individual right or a corporate right to guarantee that states would maintain militias. Some clarity can be found in the Militia Act of 1792, which maintained the colonial tradition of a citizen militia by requiring that all able-bodied males between the ages of 18 and 44 enroll in the militia, which would be under state control and would be organized as military units corresponding to the regular army. Although the president could call upon the states to mobilize the militia for national service, the Militia Act of 1792 limited military service to no more than three months and forbade the use of the militia outside the borders of the United States.

With the United States maintaining a small standing army (at least by European standards), reliance upon the militia was vital to securing the ever-expanding frontier against Native Americans. Andrew Jackson's campaign against the Creeks during 1813–1814 was fought almost entirely by volunteer militia forces. In many respects the militia's role in electing officers anticipated Jacksonian Democracy, as many able-bodied males could elect their militia officers but did not meet the property qualifications required for electing public officials. It is not surprising that many elected militia officers, including Jackson, parlayed their election as militia officers into political careers.

The irregular nature of militias often resulted in breakdowns in military discipline. During the Indian Wars of the 19th century, most of the massacres that were committed against Native Americans were carried out by militias. In 1863 California volunteers led by Colonel Patrick Edward Connor attacked Chief Bear Paw's Shoshone village, firing indiscriminately and killing men, women, and children. Once the Shoshones ran out of ammunition, Connor's forces moved into the village, turning the battle into a massacre in which they shot every Native American they could find, raped women, and killed those Native Americans who were wounded. One year later Colonel John M. Chivington led the 3rd Colorado Cavalry Regiment on a raid against Cheyenne chief Black Kettle's peaceful village along Sand Creek approximately 40 miles from Fort Lyon, Colorado. Even though Black Kettle had prominently waved an American flag and a white flag outside his lodge, Chivington's militia ruthlessly and indiscriminately slaughtered more than 300 Cheyennes, mostly women and children, scalping them and mutilating their bodies.

With the end of the Indian Wars the role of the militia became largely obsolete, especially for an emerging urban industrial nation that had become a world power after the 1898 Spanish-American War. In 1903 Congress replaced the Militia Act of 1792 with the Dick Act, which created the National Guard under federal supervision in each state, bringing an end to the general enrollment of able-bodied males in state militias.

JUSTIN D. MURPHY

See also

Black Kettle; Chivington, John; Connor, Patrick Edward; French and Indian War; Jackson, Andrew; King Philip's War; Pequot War; Queen Anne's War; Sand Creek Massacre

References

Cress, Lawrence Delbert. *Citizens in Arms: The Army and the Militia in American Society to the War of 1812.* Chapel Hill: University of North Carolina Press, 1982.

Hoig, Stan. *The Sand Creek Massacre.* Norman: University of Oklahoma Press, 1961.

Madsen, Brigham D. *The Shoshoni Frontier and the Bear River Massacre.* Salt Lake City: University of Utah Press, 1985.

Utley, Robert M. *Frontiersmen in Blue: The United States and the Indian, 1848–1865.* Lincoln: University of Nebraska Press, 1967.

Weigley, Russell F. *History of the United States Army.* New York: Macmillan, 1967.

Milk Creek, Battle of
Event Date: September 29, 1879

Battle fought between 150 cavalrymen under Major Thomas T. Thornburgh and some 300 Ute warriors led by Colorow, Chief Nicaagat (Jack), and Chief Quinkent (Douglas). The battle occurred after Ute warriors had destroyed the White River Indian Agency in northwestern Colorado and killed Nathan Meeker and 10 other whites on September 29, 1879. The massacre and ensuing battle sparked the short-lived conflict known as the Ute War. Milk Creek was located just outside Meeker, Colorado (present-day Greeley).

Indian agent Nathan C. Meeker, head of the White River Ute Agency, had alienated the Utes by pushing them aggressively toward assimilation with white culture, forcing the tribe to relocate to an area better suited for agriculture and attempting to impede the Utes' annual autumn hunt. After a minor altercation between Meeker and Chief Douglas, Meeker requested army assistance to maintain order. Ironically, while the soldiers had been sent to keep the peace, their presence undoubtedly triggered the confrontation.

On September 21 Thornburgh left Fort Fred Steele, near Rawlins, Wyoming, with Troops D and F of the 5th Cavalry, Troop E of the 3rd Cavalry, and Company E of the 4th Infantry, a total of 200 men. His orders were to report to Meeker and assist in maintaining order while the Bureau of Indian Affairs conducted an investigation of the complaints. After leaving the 50 infantrymen and their wagons behind, Thornburgh arrived at Milk Creek on the northern boundary of the White River Agency on September 29. The Utes resented the encroachment of the soldiers on their land and resolved to head off the incursion before the troops could travel the intervening 18 miles to the agency headquarters.

The cavalrymen, however, detected the ambush and were able to fall back behind a corral of their wagons near the creek, where they remained besieged for a week. Thornburgh was killed in the initial attack, and Captain J. Scott Payne assumed command. That same day word of the battle reached the agency, and Chief Douglas along with 25–30 Ute warriors proceeded to kill Meeker and all of his white workers: 11 people in all. Meeker's wife and daughter and three others were taken captive but were all released three weeks later with the help of Chief Ouray of the Uncompaghre Utes.

During the night of September 29–30, four couriers managed to escape the perimeter and ride for help. On October 2 Captain Francis Dodge and 35 buffalo soldiers of Troop D of the 9th Cavalry joined the survivors inside their defensive works but were unable to break the siege. On October 5 Colonel Wesley Merritt arrived with a battalion of the 5th Cavalry from Fort D. A. Russell (the fort's name was changed to F. E. Warren in 1927) in Cheyenne, Wyoming. After moving to Rawlins by rail, Merritt's men rode 170 miles in less than three days to relieve Payne's men. The Utes now escaped to the south. In the battle the army lost 13 killed and 44 wounded, while Ute casualties were estimated at 23 killed. The army awarded a total of 11 Medals of Honor to those who fought in the Battle of Milk Creek.

CHRISTOPHER M. REIN

See also

Buffalo Soldiers; Meeker, Nathan Cook; Meeker Massacre; Merritt, Wesley; Utes; Ute War

References

Decker, Peter R. *"The Utes Must Go": American Expansion and the Removal of a People.* Golden, CO: Fulcrum Publishing, 2004.

Miller, Mark E. *Hollow Victory: The White River Expedition of 1879 and the Battle of Milk Creek.* Niwot: The University Press of Colorado, 1997.

Mingo Chief

See Logan, John

Mingos

Native American group originally inhabiting a broad area of what is now New York state and who then settled in present-day Ohio and western Pennsylvania. The Mingos were often participants in the imperial conflicts of the 18th century, and they unsuccessfully jockeyed for advantage amid competing French, British, and colonial interests in North America. Their name derived from *mingwe,* an Algonquian term meaning "stealthy" or "treacherous," but the Mingos were less a distinct tribe than a multicultural grouping. Included among them were refugees from the Seneca, Wyandot, Shawnee, Conestoga, and Delaware tribes.

By 1740 the Mingos were inhabiting western Pennsylvania, part of the Great Lakes region that the French called the Pays d'en Haut ("Upper Country"). In this borderland between colonial empires, otherwise minor tribes loosely allied themselves with one another for mutual strength. They shared an identity and a sense of mission separate from that of their powerful neighbors in the Iroquois Confederacy.

By 1750 the Mingos, the Delawares, and the Shawnees of the upper Ohio River Valley arranged an alliance known as the Covenant Chain. According to diplomatic agreements, the Mingos were regarded as brothers of the British and nephews of the Iroquois Six Nations because the latter had been granted the role of spokesman for other tribes aligned with the British Crown. But in 1751 the bonds of the Covenant Chain were threatened as the Ohio Company of Virginia established a presence in the region to challenge claims by the French and the Native Americans. A series of events that would spark the French and Indian War (1754–1763) then began.

Virginia lieutenant governor Robert Dinwiddie dispatched Major George Washington into the disputed area in 1753. Dinwiddie assigned Washington the unfamiliar role of emissary to deter the French from expanding their operations. Although the Mingos would generally support the French in the forthcoming conflict, a sachem (chief) known as Tanaghrisson, or Half-King, acted independently to assist Washington. Guided by Mingo warriors, the British surprised the French at Jumonville's Glen in 1754 and, although it is uncertain who initiated combat, defeated them.

The Mingos massacred wounded prisoners, and Washington placed his troops in front of the remaining French soldiers to guarantee their safety. Tanaghrisson, desperate to assert himself as a figure worthy of British support, executed the French commander and died shortly thereafter from what some attributed to French witchcraft. The conclusion of the war forced the Mingos to migrate westward into Ohio.

In 1768 the Mingos rejected the Treaty of Fort Stanwix whereby the Iroquois relinquished much of Ohio to the British. The result was Lord Dunmore's War (1774) in which colonists from Virginia bested the Mingos and the Shawnees. The Mingos also joined the British in battling Patriot forces during the American Revolutionary War (1775–1783). The triumph of the fledgling United States in 1783 forced the Mingos farther into the Ohio Country.

The Mingos participated in Little Turtle's War (1785–1795), and some were present at the disastrous 1794 Battle of Fallen Timbers, in which they and their allies were decisively defeated. Some Mingos migrated farther west, but others stayed in the western part of what would soon become the state of Ohio, where they established fairly successful farms. The 1830 Indian Removal Act, however, effectively forced them to relinquish their Ohio lands, and they moved into eastern Kansas by 1832. In 1869 the surviving Mingos were relocated to Indian Territory (Oklahoma). In 1937 the group officially designated itself the Seneca-Cayuga Tribe of Oklahoma. Today the group, a linear descendant of the Mingos, still lives in Oklahoma. Their number has been estimated at close to 5,000 people.

JEFFREY D. BASS

See also

Covenant Chain; Delawares; Fallen Timbers, Battle of; French and Indian War; Iroquois; Iroquois Confederacy; Little Turtle's War; Lord Dunmore's War; Ohio Company of Virginia; Senecas; Shawnees; Tanaghrisson; Washington, George

References

Anderson, Fred. *Crucible of War: The Seven Years' War and the Fate of the Empire in British North America, 1754–1766.* New York: Vintage Books, 2001.

White, Richard. *The Middle Ground: Indians, Empires, and Republics in the Great Lakes Region, 1650–1815.* New York: Cambridge University Press, 1991.

Miniconjou Sioux

One of the seven major bands of the Lakota Sioux Nation. After their migration from Minnesota, the Miniconjou Sioux were located primarily in western South Dakota, western Nebraska, and Wyoming. By the 1870s, many were also in Montana. The Lakota Nation was split into seven major bands in three groupings. The Miniconjous were part of the central grouping, with the Hunkpapas, Blackfoot Sioux, and Sans Arcs to the north and the Oglalas

Group of Miniconjou Sioux adults and children in a tipi camp on the Pine Ridge Indian Reservation in 1891. (Library of Congress)

and Brulés to the south. The Miniconjous shared the central area of the Lakota range with the Two Kettles band.

Upon moving onto the Great Plains, the Miniconjous and other Lakota groups quickly adopted the Plains way of life. This was characterized by great reliance on the horse (acquired around 1740) to follow the buffalo herds, living in buffalo-hide tepees, and centering their spiritual life on the Sun Dance. Buffalo provided most of their food, clothing, and shelter needs and also figured into their trade relations with other Native Americans as well as with white Americans. In addition to buffalo, smaller game, maple sugar, wild rice, fish, wild potatoes and turnips, and berries supplemented the Miniconjous' diet. Although tribal life was regulated by elders in council governing by consensus, the younger warrior societies were difficult to control. Because exploits in hunting but especially warfare determined a young Lakota warrior's status in the tribe, warfare assumed a central place.

With the advance of white settlement, frequent contact between the Miniconjous and all of the Lakotas with settlers, traders, and soldiers was inevitable, and just as inevitably conflict arose. Beginning in the 1850s, the Miniconjous were often at war

with the U.S. Army. The first major outbreak of violence between the Lakotas and the U.S. government began when a Miniconjou warrior visiting along the Platte River killed a cow, prompting U.S. Army lieutenant John L. Grattan and approximately 30 soldiers to pursue the warrior. The resulting fight resulted in Lieutenant Grattan and his entire command being killed on August 19, 1854. Colonel (Brevet Brigadier General) William S. Harney directed a major punitive expedition to avenge the killings, known as the Grattan Massacre. This conflict waxed and waned until 1859. It did convince some Lakota leaders being held at Fort Leavenworth, Kansas, that peace with the whites, while resulting in changes to the Lakota way of life, was preferable to an unwinnable war.

Most Miniconjous, however, remained resistant to peace with the whites, and many participated in Red Cloud's War (1866–1868) and in the Great Sioux War (1876–1877) during the Battle of the Rosebud (June 17, 1876) and the Battle of the Little Bighorn (June 25–26, 1876). Even after the Miniconjous had been forced onto reservations in the aftermath of the Great Sioux War, they continued to experience the strong arm of the U.S. Army. Indeed, it was a Miniconjou band, led by Big Foot, along with a few Hunkpapa refugees who attempted to flee after the December 15, 1890, death of Sitting Bull. They were surrounded by elements of the 7th U.S. Cavalry, and fighting began on December 29 when the troops attempted to disarm the Lakotas. In the resulting Battle of Wounded Knee (December 29, 1890), approximately 300 of the 350 Miniconjous who had arrived with Big Foot were killed. Today the surviving Miniconjous are concentrated on the Cheyenne River Reservation in north-central South Dakota.

JOHN THOMAS BROOM

See also

Buffalo; Grattan Massacre; Harney, William Selby; Lakota Sioux; Little Bighorn, Battle of the; Red Cloud's War; Rosebud, Battle of the; Sitting Bull; Wounded Knee, Battle of

References

Biolso, Thomas. "The Birth of the Reservation: Making the Modern Individual among the Lakota." *American Ethnologist* 22(1) (February 1995): 28–53.

Gibbon, Guy. *The Sioux: The Dakota and Lakota Nations.* Malden, MA: Blackwell, 2003.

Goldfrank, Esther S. "Historic Change and Social Character: A Study of the Teton Dakota." *American Anthropologist,* n.s., 45(1) (January–March 1943): 67–83.

Hassrick, Royal B. *The Sioux: The Life and Customs of a Warrior Nation.* Norman: University of Oklahoma Press, 1964.

Hyde, George F. *A Sioux Chronicle.* Norman: University of Oklahoma Press, 1956.

Overholt, Thomas W. "The Ghost Dance of 1890 and the Nature of the Prophetic Process." *Ethnohistory* 21(1) (Winter 1974): 37–63.

White, Richard. "The Winning of the West: The Expansion of the Western Sioux in the Eighteenth and Nineteenth Centuries." *Journal of American History* 65(2) (September 1978): 319–343.

Minnesota Sioux Uprising
Start Date: August 17, 1862
End Date: September 23, 1862

Armed clash between the Minnesota Sioux (several of the bands of Dakota people, also known as the Santee Sioux) and U.S. Volunteer forces in August and September 1862. The Minnesota Sioux Uprising began on August 17, 1862, along the Minnesota River in Meeker County in southwestern Minnesota. The uprising ended on September 23, 1862, with the defeat of the Sioux. One of the bloodiest Indian wars in U.S. history, the conflict claimed the lives of 500–800 settlers. Native American casualties are unknown.

Settlers who have fled the Minnesota Sioux Uprising of 1862. (Library of Congress)

In 1851 the United States and the Dakotas signed the Treaty of Traverse des Sioux and the Treaty of Mendota, whereby the Dakota lands became open to white settlers. In return the Native Americans were to receive monetary compensation as well as a stretch of land 20 miles wide and 150 miles long along the upper Minnesota River, where a reservation would be created. However, during the ratification process in the U.S. Senate, Article 3 of each treaty that guaranteed compensation to the Indians for their land was deleted. This along with rampant corruption in the Bureau of Indian Affairs ensured that the Native Americans would never receive the promised compensation.

When Minnesota entered the Union in 1858, its borders shifted from the Missouri River to the Red River. Despite appeals by Sioux chief Little Crow (also known as Taoyateduta) to Washington, the northern half of the reservation was ceded for white settlement. Because of the failed negotiations, Little Crow lost much of his standing with the tribe. The Sioux were ultimately driven out of the state, and those who remained were confined to the remaining small reservation.

White settlement in the region began to have adverse effects on Native American lifestyles. Clearing timber to make room for farmlands interrupted the natural cycle of farming, hunting, and fishing practiced by the Sioux. Also, wildlife populations of bison, elk, whitetail deer, and bear decreased steadily because of excessive hunting by the white settlers. Dwindling lands, lack of game, and crop failures brought starvation, and the Sioux began attacking white settlers in search of food.

On August 4, 1862, representatives of the Minnesota Sioux approached the Upper Sioux Agency to plead for food. After successful negotiations, they returned on August 15 to receive their promised supplies. However, Minnesota state senator and Indian agent Thomas Galbraith refused to distribute the supplies without payment, regardless of the previous agreement. At a subsequent meeting of the Sioux, U.S. government officials, and local traders, the Native Americans pleaded with the lead trader, Andrew Myrick, for his support, to which he essentially replied that they should go away and eat grass.

This offensive and dehumanizing comment enraged the Sioux. With the U.S. Army occupied by the American Civil War (1861–1865), the Dakota chiefs seized the opportunity for an armed uprising. The violence began on August 17, 1862. Four Sioux men, stealing food from a settlement in Meeker County, killed five white settlers. Although Chief Little Crow initially opposed a violent solution to the problem, given the uproar among the Native Americans the other chiefs were able to convince him to lead further attacks. At the council of war, the chiefs decided to attack without warning.

Myrick was one of the first to die in the subsequent attacks. He was found dead with grass stuffed in his mouth, a macabre allusion to his earlier comment. Captain John March then led a force of 44–46 men from Fort Ridgely, but the Sioux attacked them as they were attempting to cross the Minnesota River on the Redwood Ferry on August 18. Either 24 or 25 soldiers died in the ensuing Battle of Redwood Ferry. Sioux casualties are unknown.

Over the next week the Sioux, encouraged by their initial successes, attacked scores of settlements and farms, killing many white settlers in the process. The Sioux also attacked military installations, including Fort Ridgely and Fort Abercrombie. Fort Ridgely, now defended by about 175 men and perhaps 300 settlers who had managed to take refuge there, came under attack by as many as 800 Sioux warriors on August 20. In two days of fighting the defenders managed to drive off the attacking Sioux, thanks in large part to the assistance of three howitzers.

Sioux attacks also targeted the town of New Ulm. Assaults on August 19 and 23 were repulsed, although much of the town was destroyed in the second attack. The inhabitants evacuated the settlement on August 26.

Minnesota governor Alexander Ramsey ordered Colonel Henry Sibley of the militia to lead a force to relieve the settlers. Sibley was soon on the move with 1,500 men. Sibley detached part of his force as a burial detail, and it came under attack at Birch Coulee on September 2, 1862. There 20 soldiers died and 60 more were wounded, but Sibley heard the sounds of battle, and the survivors managed to hold out until the arrival of a relief column the next day.

Sibley then went looking for the hostiles and on September 23, 1862, at the Battle of Wood Lake soundly defeated the Sioux. During the next several days many of the Sioux defected from Little Crow and began releasing captives.

By the end of November, a military tribunal had convicted 303 Native Americans of murder and rape and sentenced them to death. At the trials the Sioux had no representation, and there was no explanation to them of the proceedings. Some trials lasted just five minutes. After a review of the records, President Abraham Lincoln differentiated between the Dakota warriors accused of crimes against the United States and those accused of rape and murder of civilians. Bishop Henry Whipple pleaded with the president for clemency for the Dakotas. Lincoln upheld the convictions of 39 Sioux accused of rape and murder and commuted the death sentences of the others. Those sentenced to death were hanged on December 26, 1862, at Mankato, Minnesota. It was the largest public execution in U.S. history.

In 1863, 1,300 to 1,700 Minnesota Sioux were sent to the Nebraska and Dakota territories. Four years later the surviving imprisoned Sioux were released. Thirty percent of them had died of disease while in prison. The remaining Sioux were sent to Nebraska and Dakota with their families in an attempt to expel the Sioux from Minnesota for good. After that a bounty of $25 was paid for the scalp of any Sioux found within Minnesota borders. The U.S. government also abolished the reservation and voided all previous treaties with the Dakotas. Little Crow and his son, who had returned to Minnesota, were shot and killed by two farmers in the summer of 1863.

ANNA RULSKA

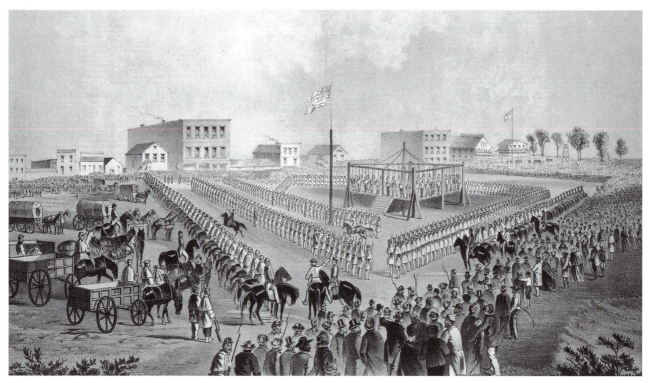

As punishment for their role in the Minnesota Sioux Uprising, 38 Sioux Indians were executed in Mankato in December 1862. It was the largest public execution in U.S. history. (Library of Congress)

See also

Birch Coulee, Battle of; Little Crow; Mendota, Treaty of; New Ulm, Battles of; Sioux; Wood Lake, Battle of

References

Carley, Kenneth. *The Sioux Uprising of 1862*. 2nd ed. St. Paul: Minnesota Historical Society, 1976.

Keenan, Jerry. *The Great Sioux Uprising: Rebellion on the Plains, August–September, 1862*. Cambridge, MA: Da Capo, 2003.

Mishikinakwa

See Little Turtle

Missionaries

The relationship between Christian missionaries and various Native American tribes in the Americas dates back to Spanish efforts to convert Indian tribes in the 16th century. This was later followed by the initial contact with the Puritans of New England and the French Catholic priests in Canada in the early 17th century. On one level, missionaries cultivated relationships with civil governments that provided protection and support for some of their endeavors; on another level, they formed trusting and intimate associations with tribal peoples and sought to protect them from the excesses of paternalism and white aggression.

In the Southeast, the Spanish founded missions beginning in 1565; the last one was created in 1763. Mostly in Florida and coastal Georgia, these missions were created to control the region and safeguard Spanish holdings in the nearby Caribbean. But equally important, the goals of missionaries here were to convert local Indians to Catholicism and try to assimilate them to European/Spanish culture. These first missions were created by the Jesuits, who were not well received by most of the region's Native Americans. A number of missions came under assault, and an especially brutal attack by the Algonquins on a new mission in the Chesapeake Bay area in February 1571 resulted in the wholesale murder of the Jesuit priests there. A year later the Jesuits stopped their activities in the region, having failed because of poor funding, insufficient personnel, a lack of support from the Spanish government, and overzealous efforts to do away with Indian customs and society too quickly.

Beginning in 1573 the Franciscans took over most of the missionary efforts in the Southeast, with considerably more success than their Jesuit predecessors. However, Spanish missionaries faced periodic Indian rebellions until about 1700, at which time most of the region's surviving tribes had been well exposed to Spanish culture and Catholicism. The tribes with whom the Spanish had the most success included the Guales, the Apalaches, and the Timucuas.

The Spaniards began introducing the Catholic faith to the Indians of the Southwest as early as 1598. By the early 1600s, Franciscan priests had established missionary activities at numerous pueblos in New Mexico. In New Spain's vast northern frontier regions, both Franciscans and Jesuits sought to bring the Indians into self-contained communities, where they could be taught European secular customs and practices and could be converted to Catholicism. This system did not always work as planned, however, as some groups, such as the Apaches and Navajos, were nomadic in nature and resisted being confined to a permanent settlement and in close quarters. Most southwestern missionaries sought to introduce Indians to European agricultural practices and skills such as carpentry, weaving, and blacksmithing.

The Spanish missionaries could be heavy-handed, however, and thus Indian rebellions were not uncommon. One of the most successful of these was the 1680 Pueblo Revolt, which witnessed the deaths of more than 400 Spaniards and 21 Franciscan priests. By the early 18th century the Spanish mission system in the Southwest was under siege. Many Spaniards resented the fact that the Indians did not pay taxes and occupied some of the best agricultural lands. And some tribes had steadfastly refused to give up their nomadic ways and Indian customs. As the missionaries in the region struggled with these problems, the mission system in Texas, New Mexico, and Sonora began to disintegrate. By the early 19th century the mission system was all but defunct in these areas. Only in Alta California did the mission system continue to thrive, but such success came at a painful price for that region's Indian tribes. Indeed, by the end of the Spanish colonial era in 1821, nearly 50 percent of California's Indians had died from diseases to which they had no immunity and from forced labor.

Along the East Coast of North America, European missionaries were also at work since the early 1600s. There both Catholic and Protestant missions were set up in an attempt to establish control over the areas in the name of the colonial governments, to acculturate Indians to European culture and agriculture, and, of course, to convert them to Christianity. As early as 1615, the French explorer Samuel de Champlain brought four Franciscan priests with him to New France in an attempt to convert the Wendats to Catholicism. The priests' efforts did not amount to much, however, and the Franciscans soon enlisted the Jesuits in their quest to "civilize" the Indians and make them good Catholics. Until the 1660s, Jesuits played the central role in French missionary efforts. But they soon found their efforts hamstring by Indians who did not wish to give up their seminomadic ways and did not trust Europeans.

In an attempt to increase their success rate, the Jesuits began creating permanent mission settlements for the Hurons in Lower Canada, where Indians were converted, educated in European customs and culture, and kept separate from their unconverted brethren. This arrangement allowed the Jesuits to convert many more Indians but also exposed the converts to deadly disease outbreaks, carried by the priests and other Europeans with whom the Hurons cohabited. For the French, the missions proved to be useful cultural and diplomatic agents and helped in their colonization efforts. In general, the French enjoyed some success in their missionary efforts in part because they tended not to see the Indians in an entirely contemptuous manner. Enlightenment

thinking also helped change the French view of Native Americans from one of untamed savages to noble savages who had inherent worth as beings and who had not been debased by the trappings of civilization.

The English colonial period also witnessed missionary efforts to convert the Indians to Christianity; however, these efforts were far less uniform or successful than those of the Catholic Spanish or Catholic French. Unlike the Spanish and French, the English were chiefly concerned with developing commerce and trade within their colonies; converting Indians to Christianity was of secondary importance. Some English settlers, however, such as the Puritans during the early to mid-1600s, created praying towns, which were akin to French Jesuit missionaries where converted Indians lived separately from their unconverted brethren in self-contained villages. There they were schooled in Christian dogma and taught European customs and culture. None of these towns was very successful, however, and English missionary efforts tended to be more ad hoc affairs undertaken by private missionaries who usually had no connections with or backing from the British Crown.

The English perhaps tried too hard to eradicate all vestiges of Indian culture, and for that reason their missionary efforts were

Feast day at San Estevan del Rey Mission, Acoma Pueblo, New Mexico, circa 1890. (Library of Congress)

largely ineffective. And unlike the French, who usually tried to find accommodation with the Indians, the British often refused to consider any compromises with the Native Americans. Ill feelings and warfare were often the result. When the English colonial period ended after the conclusion of the American Revolutionary War (1775–1783), missionaries continued to minister to Native Americans in North America but without any pretext of advancing a colonial agenda. Many different missionaries, both Catholic and Protestant, continued to operate in North America and Mexico in the late 18th and early 19th centuries.

While there were many points of tension among Christian missionaries, government officials, and native peoples, few were more devastating than those associated with the Indian Wars of 1850–1890. By the middle of the 19th century, all of the major religious denominations—Presbyterian, Quaker, Congregationalist, Methodist, Episcopalian, Baptist, and Roman Catholic—had established missions throughout the nation to instruct and convert Native Americans. Several of the missionaries achieved notoriety—the Episcopalian missionaries Stephen Riggs and Henry Whipple and the veteran Jesuit missionary Jean Pierre DeSmet—through their associations with the Sioux on the northern Great Plains before and after the American Civil War (1861–1865).

During the Indian Wars of the last half of the 19th century, Christian missionaries served in a number of contradictory roles: ministering to warring factions among the tribal nations, serving as informants for the U.S. Army, promoting peace by means of cultural mediation, assuming the task of translation during treaty negotiations, and advocating the rights of Native Americans with government bureaucrats. The unique connection between missionaries and native peoples was complex and was often compromised during periods of hostility and warfare.

In the decade prior to the Civil War, Christian missionaries were posted throughout the nation and worked diligently to observe native customs and beliefs. Many of them, especially Jesuit missionaries, were fully acculturated with the lives of the people and were teaching the tenets of Christianity, preaching the dogma of their particular sect, and translating sacred texts into the native idiom. At the same time, the U.S. government introduced a new Indian policy—concentration—that required the pacification of native cultures and settlement on prescribed reservations. Native American leaders, especially those on the Great Plains, resisted these efforts because they would result in a complete loss of tribal identity. In the 1850s Christian missionaries faced stark alternatives: cooperate with government officials and cajole the tribes into accepting the treaty terms or risk war between the U.S. Army and various Native American groups. In many cases the missionaries sympathized with the Native Americans and believed that the government was perpetrating gross injustices; however, the missionaries frequently served as intermediaries and strongly urged the Native American leaders to negotiate favorable terms with the government.

The influential Father DeSmet was present at Fort Laramie in 1851 when the powerful Plains tribes agreed to terms with the government. He posited that the treaty would be "the commencement of a new era for the Indians—an era of peace." This treaty, however, became the major cause of unrest on the Great Plains until after the Civil War. Intermittent outbreaks of hostilities in the 1850s prompted the government to ruthlessly suppress the Native Americans and paved the way for tribal opportunism during the Civil War.

During the Civil War, many Native American nations recognized that much of the American West was guarded by ill-trained state militias. Militants among them believed that this provided an opportunity for the tribes to reassert their dominance in that region. On August 18, 1862, a band of disgruntled members of the Santee Sioux Nation murdered a small group of white settlers in Minnesota and during the next month were ruthlessly pursued by Union forces. In the aftermath of the Minnesota Sioux Uprising, 303 Sioux were sentenced to death by a military commission; however, Henry B. Whipple, Episcopal bishop of Minnesota, appealed to President Abraham Lincoln on behalf of the accused. Lincoln reduced the sentences of most of the participants and permitted only 39 to be executed. The mass hysteria generated by the Minnesota incident extended to all parts of the frontier. The actions of Whipple illustrated some of the pressures that missionaries faced during the Indian Wars. Whipple believed that his Christian duty was to advocate for the Native Americans.

In the aftermath of the Civil War, the Indian Wars continued in various parts of the Great Plains; however, most tribes gradually accepted the reservation system and peacefully settled on their allotted parcels of land. In order to administer the reservations effectively, the federal government called upon the various Christian denominations to nominate Indian agents and to develop an infrastructure to gradually assimilate the tribes. Between 1870 and 1890, missionaries witnessed and mediated conflicts and cooperated with government programs. The last major battle of the Indian Wars occurred at Wounded Knee, South Dakota, in December 1890 when the wounded and dying natives sought aid and succor from the Christian missionaries at the Holy Rosary Mission.

James F. Carroll and Paul G. Pierpaoli Jr.

See also

Fort Laramie, Treaty of (1851); France; Great Britain; Minnesota Sioux Uprising; Praying Towns and Praying Indians; Pueblo Revolt; Reservations; Sand Creek Massacre; Spain; Wounded Knee, Battle of

References

Niles, Judith. *Native American History.* New York: Ballantine, 1996.

Terrell, John Upton. *The Arrow and the Cross: A History of the American Indian and the Missionaries.* Santa Barbara, CA: Capra, 1979.

Modocs

Native American tribe that resided in northern California and southern Oregon. The Modocs first encountered Europeans—probably Spaniards—either in the late 17th century or the early

18th century. Evidence suggests that the Modocs engaged in trade with Europeans beginning in the 18th century.

The Modocs, like many tribes of the region, relied largely on salmon, which heavily populated the rivers of the Northwest. They led a seminomadic existence, living in easily transported tents or dugouts in the earth. Later in the 18th century the Modocs also engaged in limited small-scale agriculture. When the salmon were not running, the Modocs were on the move in order to hunt and gather other food. Their language was shared mainly by the Klamath Indians, who also inhabited the Pacific Northwest. The Modocs' principal villages were on Lower Klamath Lake, along the Lost River, and on the shores of Tule Lake.

The first significant Modoc contact with English-speaking people occurred in the early to mid-1820s, when the Canadian explorer and trapper Peter Skene Ogden entered into a trade agreement with the tribe. By 1846 American settlers were beginning to intrude on Modoc lands as the South Emigrant Trail emerged from the Oregon Trail. This route avoided the dangers of the Columbia Trail, particularly when President James K. Polk was saber rattling over the joint occupation of the area with Great Britain.

As more settlers journeyed through the area, Modocs conducted raids against them. In 1852 Modoc raiders killed 62 settlers along the Columbia Trail, leaving just 3 survivors. After a survivor of this raid reached Yreka, California, a local leader there, Jim Crosby, organized a punitive expedition against the Modocs. Crosby and his band engaged in one brief skirmish with the tribe before returning to Yreka. A later expedition in 1856, under the command of Yreka settler Ben Wright, resulted in a pitched fight along the Lost River and the death of 80 Modocs.

These engagements further antagonized the Modocs, and they persisted in their raids until 1873. In 1864 the Modocs signed a treaty with the federal government ceding lands along the Lost River and agreeing to inhabit a reservation along with the Klamath tribe in return for a $35,000 payment and an additional $80,000 over a 15-year period. The reservation was not large enough for both tribes, however, and the Modocs requested a separate reservation.

On April 3, 1870, a group of Modocs under Kintpuash, known to Americans as Captain Jack, left the reservation and returned to the lands previously ceded to the United States. The federal government attempted to negotiate with him but failed to persuade the Modocs to return to the reservation. As a result, on November 28, 1872, Major John Green, commanding at Fort Klamath, dispatched Captain James Jackson and 40 soldiers to compel the Modocs to return to the reservation. This ultimately sparked the Modoc War (1872–1873).

Jackson arrived at Captain Jack's camp on November 29 and ordered him to disarm. Captain Jack agreed, but while the Modocs were laying down their weapons a fight broke out between Lieutenant Frazier A. Boutelle and Modoc warrior Scar-Faced Charley. The Modocs then scrambled to recover their weapons. In the ensuing fight, known as the Battle of Lost River, 1 soldier and 2 Modocs died, and Jackson was left in possession of the field. In

their withdrawal to the Lava Beds south of Tule Lake, on the afternoon of November 29 and morning of November 30 a small band of Modocs under Hooker Jim attacked and killed 18 settlers.

Captain Jack then fortified the natural stronghold of the lava beds south of Tule Lake. One Modoc party from this stronghold then raided an ammunition wagon at Land's Ranch on December 21, 1872. On January 16, 1873, troops under Colonel R. F. Bernard attacked the Modocs at Hospital Rock. The next day federal troops attacked the Modoc stronghold in heavy fog. Given the fortified position and the poor weather, the troops were repulsed, suffering 35 casualties, while the Modocs suffered no losses.

The U.S. Department of the Interior then decided to pursue negotiations. After several months of talks with little progress, on April 11, 1873, the Modocs attacked the American negotiators, killing Brigadier General Edward R. S. Canby and the Reverend Eleazar Thomas and wounding Alfred B. Meacham, the Oregon superintendent for Indian affairs. On April 17 federal troops stormed the stronghold, but the Modocs escaped.

On April 26, 1873, a Modoc party under Scar-Faced Charley massacred a U.S. force under Captain Evan Thomas. Following this incident, Colonel Jefferson C. Davis took command of federal forces in the region. On May 10, 1873, at the Battle of Dry Lake, U.S. troops repulsed a Modoc attack, resulting in the deaths of five Modocs including Ellen's Man, a Modoc leader. His death fostered divisions among the Modoc leadership. Shortly thereafter, Modocs under Hooker Jim decided to help federal authorities in the capture of Captain Jack in return for amnesty. On June 4, 1873, Captain Jack was taken. He was put on trial along with five other Modocs for the murder of the peace commissioners. Two of the Modocs received life imprisonment, but Captain Jack and three others were sentenced to death and were hanged on October 3, 1873. The remaining Modocs were subsequently sent to Indian Territory (present-day Oklahoma). In 1909 they were given permission to return to the Klamath Reservation in Oregon.

MICHAEL K. BEAUCHAMP AND PAUL G. PIERPAOLI JR.

See also

Canby, Edward Richard Sprigg; Kintpuash; Modoc War; Oregon Trail

References

Murray, Keith A. *The Modocs and Their War.* 1959; reprint, Norman: University of Oklahoma Press, 2001.

Quinn, Arthur. *Hell with the Fire Out: A History of the Modoc War.* Boston: Faber and Faber, 1997.

Modoc War
Start Date: November 1872
End Date: June 1873

Seven-month-long conflict between the Modoc tribe and U.S. Army forces that exposed the inefficiencies of army tactics against the Native Americans and strained President Ulysses S. Grant's

A reporter takes notes on a battle during the seven-month Modoc War (1872–1873), fought in southern Oregon and northern California. (National Archives)

Native American peace policy. From November 1872 through June 1873, a small faction of Modocs held off a much larger U.S. Army force using the rugged lava beds of northeastern California as a natural redoubt. The Modocs, small in number, were fierce warriors who had wrought havoc against white settlers for decades.

Occupying the border area between Oregon and California, the Modocs were especially adept at using topography to their advantage. Despite their hostility toward whites, they did establish relationships with white miners at Yreka, California. Thus, many of the Modocs were given white nicknames; one in particular was Kintpuash, leader of one of the more militant factions and known to whites as Captain Jack.

Captain Jack refused to honor the Treaty of 1864 in which most of his traditional tribal land had been ceded to white settlers. He and a group of Modocs left the reservation in southwestern Oregon, which they shared with the Klamaths, and moved back to the Lost River basin, where whites demanded their removal. Brigadier General Edward R. S. Canby warned his subordinates that when the time came to attack, they were to use overwhelming force against the formidable warriors. However, Major John Green, commander of the 1st Cavalry Regiment, was pressured by superintendent of Indian affairs Thomas B. Ordeneal to strike quickly, meaning that he was unable to bring preponderant force to bear.

On November 29, 1872, Captain James Jackson, along with 3 officers and 40 enlisted personnel, approached Captain Jack's camp of 17 families along the Lost River and demanded their arms. A melee ensued, and the Modocs fled. Ranchers then attempted to overtake a second encampment of Modocs on the opposite bank but were repulsed. The two Modoc camps then joined forces, killing 14 civilians along the way, and withdrew across Tule Lake. At the southern tip of the lake the Modocs—a mere 60 warriors—occupied a treacherous region of jagged black volcanic rocks and caverns, which the soldiers would dub Captain Jack's Stronghold.

Army reinforcements poured into the area, and on January 16, 1873, two contingents of soldiers approached under cover of darkness in an attempt to surround the lava beds. Two mountain howitzers were positioned for support, but a thick fog rendered them ineffective. Unable to surround the beds entirely, the two

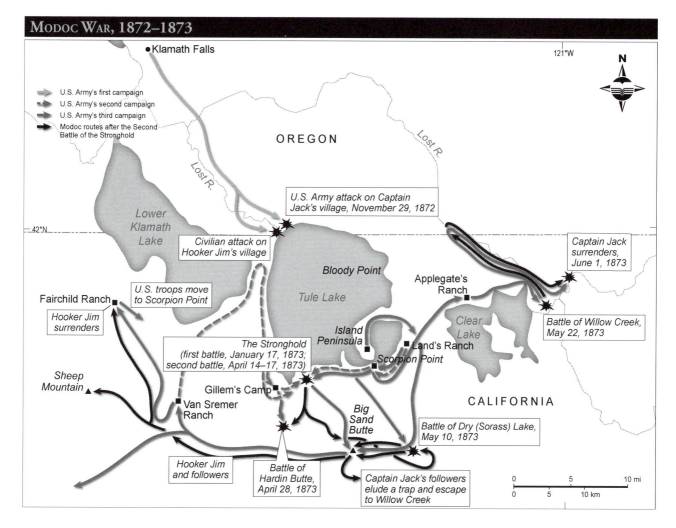

MODOC WAR, 1872–1873

Klamath Falls

121°W

U.S. Army's first campaign
U.S. Army's second campaign
U.S. Army's third campaign
Modoc routes after the Second
Battle of the Stronghold

OREGON

Lost R.

Lost R.

42°N

Lower
Klamath
Lake

U.S. Army attack on Captain
Jack's village, November 29, 1872

Civilian attack on
Hooker Jim's village

Captain Jack
surrenders,
June 1, 1873

Bloody Point

Applegate's
Ranch

Fairchild Ranch

U.S. troops move
to Scorpion Point

Tule Lake

Clear
Lake

Hooker Jim
surrenders

Island
Peninsula

Land's Ranch

Battle of Willow Creek,
May 22, 1873

The Stronghold
(first battle, January 17, 1873;
second battle, April 14–17, 1873)

Scorpion Point

Sheep
Mountain

Gillem's Camp

CALIFORNIA

Van Sremer
Ranch

Big
Sand
Butte

Battle of Dry (Sorass) Lake,
May 10, 1873

Hooker Jim
and followers

Battle of
Hardin Butte,
April 28, 1873

Captain Jack's followers
elude a trap and escape
to Willow Creek

0   5   10 mi
0   5   10 km

companies fell back and tried to join flanks. By early afternoon the fog had lifted, exposing the troops to gunfire from the entrenched Modocs. The snipers pinned down the attackers until they were able to retreat at nightfall. In the exchange of fire the soldiers suffered 9 dead and 28 wounded.

The events unfolding in the Pacific Northwest did not bode well for Grant's conciliatory policy toward Native Americans, so Washington pressed for peace negotiations. When a civilian commission failed to make any headway, Canby was ordered to take direct control of the talks. On April 11 the commission was attacked at the peace table. Canby was shot in the face by Captain Jack, stabbed, and stripped, becoming the sole regular army general officer killed during the Indian Wars. Two civilian commissioners were also attacked, and one of them was slain. This act of treachery brought a call throughout the nation for harsher treatment of the Modocs, and the army renewed its offensive.

Army forces moved against Captain Jack's stronghold again during April 15–17, 1873, employing the same two-pronged attack that had failed earlier in the campaign. A slow methodical battle ensued, with the Modocs firing from protected positions and retreating farther into the lava beds. On April 26 a patrol led

by Captain Evan Thomas was ambushed, suffering 5 officers and 20 enlisted men dead with another 16 wounded. Colonel Jefferson C. Davis took command in early May, but by then the Modocs had fled.

As it turned out, it was not the army that had driven the hostile Modocs out but rather internal dissension. Another Modoc leader, known as Hooker Jim, had decided to retreat. He was later caught and offered to help find Captain Jack.

Captain Jack was finally captured on June 3, 1873. Ultimately six Modocs were tried for the murders of Canby and the other peace commissioner. Four including Captain Jack were hanged, while two had their sentences commuted. The rest of the Modocs were dispersed to reservations throughout Indian Territory (Oklahoma).

The U.S. Army's inability to deal effectively with a small number of Modocs revealed a lack of training, poor tactical planning, and overall ineptitude. On the other hand, the Modocs' cold-blooded murder of a high-ranking army officer and a civilian commissioner helped sway public opinion against Grant's Peace Policy, bringing a much harsher policy toward the Native Americans.

WILLIAM WHYTE

See also
Canby, Edward Richard Sprigg; Grant, Ulysses Simpson; Grant's Peace Policy; Kintpuash; Modocs; Wheaton, Frank

References
Cozzens, Peter, ed. *Eyewitness to the Indian Wars,* Vol. 2, *The Wars for the Pacific Northwest.* Mechanicsburg, PA: Stackpole, 2002.
Murray, Keith A. *The Modocs and Their War.* 1959; reprint, Norman: University of Oklahoma Press, 2001.
Utley, Robert M. *Frontier Regulars: The United States and the American Indian, 1866–1891.* New York: Macmillan, 1973.
Wooster, Robert. *The Military and United States Indian Policy, 1865–1903.* New Haven, CT: Yale University Press, 1988.

Mog
Birth Date: Unknown
Death Date: May 13, 1677

Abenaki headman responsible for a series of Abenaki victories over New England colonists during King Philip's War (1675–1676). Nothing is known about Mog's birth, youth, or early career. Not even his tribal affiliation can be ascertained with certainty. Whether he belonged to the Kennebec or Androscoggin Abenaki communities is unclear. Mog's English contemporaries took him to be a Penobscot Abenaki, which was an error.

By July 1676 Mog had become a sachem, or chief, of his people and made his first appearance in the historical record when he attended a meeting of Abenaki sachems with representatives of Massachusetts. Some Abenaki groups had been caught up in King Philip's War, and as a result the colony had embargoed trade with all Abenakis. The assembled sachems offered peace in return for renewed commerce. However, the Massachusetts representatives rebuffed the offer. Angered by such intransigence, the Abenakis as a whole decided to enter the war.

Presumably Mog led some of the raids that devastated the English settlements in Maine (then part of Massachusetts) in the autumn of 1676. He certainly presided over the greatest Abenaki victory of the campaign when he and his warriors captured the English fort at Black Point on October 12, 1676. Emboldened, he sent word to Boston that he was willing to negotiate for peace. That winter the Massachusetts Council had him brought to Boston by ship for talks. At those talks the council attempted to cajole Mog into signing a treaty conceding Abenaki defeat in the war. It was a concession completely divorced from reality. Nevertheless Mog signed the treaty, presumably out of fear for his life. He then escaped back to Maine, where he repudiated the agreement.

Mog boasted that thanks to his visit, he had found the way to burn Boston. He planned to capture English fishing boats and then use them to mount an amphibious assault on the town. To this end, Abenaki warriors began seizing English vessels. However, they found them too cumbersome to use. Given sufficient time, Mog might have found a way to overcome this, but his time was about to run out.

The English had retaken Black Point over the winter, and on May 13, 1677, Mog led an expedition to recapture it. During the assault he was shot and killed. To honor his father's achievements, Mog's son changed his own name to Mog. He would figure prominently in later Abenaki–New England wars.

ANDREW MILLER

See also
Abenakis; Black Point, Attacks on; King Philip's War

References
Hubbard, William. "A Narrative of the Troubles with the Indians in New-England, from Pascataqua to Pemmaquid" [1677]. In *The History of the Indian Wars in New England,* Vol. 2, edited by Samuel G. Drake, 69–225. 1865; reprint, New York: Burt Franklin, 1971.
Miller, Andrew Malcolm. "Abenakis and Colonists in Northern New England, 1675–1725." Unpublished PhD dissertation, Johns Hopkins University, 2004.

Mohawk-Mahican War
Start Date: 1624
End Date: 1628

Conflict waged by the Mohawks against the Mahicans from 1624 to 1628 to help secure Mohawk access to Dutch traders at Fort Orange (present-day Albany, New York). In many respects, the Mohawk-Mahican War can be considered the prototype for the Beaver Wars (1641–1701). In those conflicts, the Iroquois Confederacy waged war against other native peoples in the Great Lakes and the Ohio Country over access to furs and European trading posts. The Mohawk-Mahican War was the first conflict of the colonial period in which one of the Iroquois Five Nations went to war with the objective of securing trade with a European power.

In 1614 the Dutch established Fort Orange (at first called Fort Nassau) approximately 160 miles north of New Amsterdam, at the confluence of the Mohawk River and the Hudson River. The post gave them access to furs from the north via the Lake Champlain corridor and from the west via the Mohawk River. The fort straddled the territories of two peoples who had maintained an uneasy peace, the Algonquian-speaking Mahicans, whom the Dutch and later the English sometimes called the "River Indians," and the Mohawks, the easternmost nation of the Iroquois Confederacy. Both had long fought the other, seeking captives to replace their dead.

With the establishment of Fort Orange, the Dutch unwittingly introduced a new element to the conflict. Natives quickly realized the advantages of European trade goods. Metal implements were sharper and more durable than stone tools, and woolen cloth was warmer and dried more quickly than leather. Soon the natives became increasingly dependent on European goods. They also realized that it was to their advantage to not only possess metal

Native American Conflicts Supported by European Intrigue during the Colonial Period

Name	Dates	Other Cause(s)
Choctaw-Chickasaw War	1752	Long-standing conflict
Choctaw Civil War	1746–1750	Differences in allegiance
Creek-Cherokee Wars	1716–1754	Land disputes and alliances with other tribes
Creek-Choctaw Wars	1702–1776	Long-standing conflict
Mohawk-Mahican War	1624–1626	Securing of trade with the Dutch

tools and weapons but also deny them to their enemies. This seems to have been the chief motivation behind Mohawk attacks on the Mahicans. If the Mohawks could displace the Mahicans and drive them away from the vicinity of Fort Orange, the Dutch would be forced to trade exclusively with them.

At the start of the conflict most of the Dutch, outnumbered by the natives in the vicinity, dependent on them as trading partners, and not wanting any part of the fighting, departed Fort Orange for New Amsterdam. For the most part the Dutch who remained at Fort Orange wanted the Mahicans to win the war, which began in 1624. But the Dutch stood by as the conflict raged, more concerned about the effects that the war had on trade than anything else.

In 1626 the Dutch entered the fray. Seven Dutchmen from Fort Orange actively sided with the Mahicans, joining them in a war party against the Mohawks. Despite the presence of Dutch soldiers with firearms, the Mohawks, who were armed only with bows and arrows, successfully ambushed them and their Mahican allies. The Mohawks killed four of the Dutchmen. To set an example, the Mohawks allegedly immediately roasted one of the dead men and devoured him in plain sight of the survivors.

Realizing the disastrous effect that this incident could have on trade, the Dutch West India Company moved swiftly to repair relations with the Mohawks. A few days after the incident, Dutch trader Pieter Barentsz visited the Mohawks and apologized for the raid. Peter Minuit, the new director of New Amsterdam, also visited the Mohawks. Within a few days he had appointed a new representative to Fort Orange who was well acquainted with the Mohawk language.

For their part, the Mohawks expressed surprise that the Dutch had meddled in the conflict. They too offered apologies, stating that had the Dutchmen not interfered, there would have been no bloodshed. Following this incident, the Dutch West India Company adopted a policy of strict noninterference with the Five Nations.

The conflict ended sometime in late 1628, with the Mohawks having driven most of the Mahicans east and south. Many of the Mahicans relocated to the Connecticut River Valley. Still others were captured and adopted into Iroquois clans.

The Mohawk-Mahican War is important in that it was the first conflict fought between native peoples primarily over European commerce. Both sides were trying to secure their trade with the Dutch at Fort Orange at the expense of the other. The war also may have served as a template for the Beaver Wars (1641–1701) against the Wyandots (Hurons) and other natives in their quest to gain control of the beaver pelt trade.

ROGER M. CARPENTER

See also

Iroquois; Iroquois Confederacy; Mahicans; Mohawks; Mourning War; Native American Trade; Native American Warfare; New Netherland; Wyandots

References

Dennis, Matthew. *Cultivating a Landscape of Peace: Iroquois-European Encounters in Seventeenth-Century North America.* Ithaca, NY: Cornell University Press, 1993.

Starna, William A., and José António Brandão. "From the Mohawk-Mahican War to the Beaver Wars: Questioning the Pattern." *Ethnohistory* 51(4) (2004): 725–750.

Mohawks

Native American group, part of the Five (later Six) Nations of the Iroquois, or Iroquois Confederacy, whose territory included much of upstate New York. The Mohawks, along with the Senecas, comprised one of the two main fighting wings of the Iroquois Confederacy during the colonial period. They participated in wars against the French and their Huron and Algonquian allies and served as the principal enforcers of British-Iroquois policy following the creation of the Covenant Chain alliance in the late 1600s.

The Mohawks, or Ganienkeh ("People of the Place of the Flint"), occupied the Mohawk River region west of Albany in present-day New York. They guarded the Eastern Door of the Iroquois Confederacy, where they became the first Iroquois to encounter European trade goods, which they acquired during raids against their Algonquian neighbors to the north. Soon the Mohawks discovered Europeans as well.

In July 1609 French-allied Algonquins from the Saint Lawrence River Valley defeated some 200 Mohawks near the southern tip of Lake Champlain. The Algonquins brought along a handful of French soldiers, including Samuel de Champlain, whose firearms helped carry the day. The following year the Algonquins and the French defeated the Mohawks in an even larger battle. Saddled with technological inferiority, the Mohawks, demonstrating the independence of action that characterized membership in the confederation, sought and obtained a trade alliance with the Dutch at Fort Orange (Albany). This agreement brought the firearms that the Mohawks desired.

Armed and aggressive, the Mohawks interjected themselves into the fur trade during the mid-17th century. Handicapped by their limited access to valuable furs and European trade centers, the Mohawks initiated a series of systematic wars, known as the Beaver

Group portrait of St. Regis Mohawk men and women with examples of their baskets, September 1894. (Library of Congress)

Wars (1641–1701), to secure direct access to both fur supplies and European traders. Their main targets were the Mahicans, who also traded with the Dutch at Fort Orange. The Mohawks also targeted the Hurons (Wyandots), who controlled western fur resources and blocked Mohawk access to fur supplies in the Saint Lawrence Valley and the Great Lakes region. In the 1620s the Mohawks drove the Mahicans to the east of Fort Orange. The Mohawks then took control of the fur trade with the Dutch. Conflict between the Mohawks and the Mahicans continued intermittently for the next 50 years, until English authorities brokered a peace deal in 1673. That arrangement formally brought the Mahicans under Iroquois control.

The Hurons fared no better. In the 1640s the Mohawks and the Senecas invaded Huron territory and during the course of the next decade burned Huron towns and villages. The Mohawks also destroyed the Hurons' agricultural fields, systematically exterminated entire groups of Hurons, and forcibly assimilated most of the survivors into Iroquois society. By 1653 the Hurons had been eliminated as an independent political entity.

When the English supplanted the Dutch as the colonial masters of New York, the Mohawks effortlessly shifted their trade interests to the newcomers. The Mohawks became so invested in their new friendship with the English that their leaders refused to ratify a peace agreement between the Iroquois Confederacy and the French. As a result, in 1666 the French twice sent punitive expeditions into Mohawk territory, finally forcing the Mohawks into submission. Yet the evolving Iroquois-English alliance, known as the Covenant Chain, afforded the Mohawks a means to cast off French influence.

As the Iroquois nation closest to Albany, the Mohawks cultivated an especially close relationship with English traders and officials. The Iroquoian wars of the late 17th century gradually merged with the European wars between the French and the British. And the Mohawks, more than any other Iroquoian people, supported the English against the French.

The results, however, did not always favor the Mohawks. During King William's War (1689–1697), the Mohawks suffered heavily at the hands of the French and their native allies. In 1693 in particular, the French destroyed three large Mohawk villages, and French-allied warriors took more than 300 Mohawks into captivity. The rest of the Five Nations suffered similar defeats until at last the Iroquois Confederacy concluded a peace treaty with the French in 1701. In it the confederacy pledged to remain neutral in future disputes between France and England.

Maintaining that neutrality proved difficult for the Mohawks because of their close proximity to the British, whose commerce and culture steadily seeped into Mohawk society. Protestant missionaries were particularly active, winning converts among Mohawk leaders and commoners alike. Not surprisingly, during both Queen Anne's War (1702–1713) and King George's War (1744–1748), Mohawk warriors fought to aid the British cause.

During the French and Indian War (1754–1763), Mohawk military aid to the British intensified even further. This was in no small part due to the influence of Sir William Johnson, the British superintendent of Indian affairs for the northern colonies, who maintained a residence among the Mohawks and twice married Mohawk women. Mohawk war parties helped Johnson achieve victory at the Battle of Lake George (1755) and played an important role in the successful campaign against Fort Niagara in 1759.

A close relationship with the British perhaps afforded the Mohawks greater status than other members of the Iroquois Confederacy during the 18th century but ultimately proved to be their undoing. During the American Revolutionary War (1775–1783), the Mohawks refused to abandon their attachment to the British, a stance that helped to transform the struggle for American independence into an Iroquoian civil war that brought about the end of the confederation.

The Mohawks were bitterly disappointed with the 1783 Treaty of Paris, which virtually ignored Native Americans. Indeed, Mohawk leader Joseph Brant believed that his British allies had betrayed him by giving to the Americans territory that had belonged to the Native Americans. Be that as it may, Brant and his followers continued their allegiance to the British and eventually settled in southern Canada. A number of Mohawks continue to live there today on the Six Nation Reservation in Brantford, Ontario. Several smaller bands of Mohawks settled in northeastern New York, Quebec, and areas of Ontario, where they can still be found today.

DANIEL P. BARR

See also
Algonquins; Beaver Wars; Champlain, Samuel de; Covenant Chain; Dutch-Indian Wars; Dutch-Mohawk Treaty; French and Indian War; Iroquois; Iroquois Confederacy; Johnson, Sir William; King George's War; King William's War; Mahicans; Mohawk-Mahican War; Queen Anne's War; Senecas; Wyandots

References
Brandão, José António. *Your Fyre Shall Burn No More: Iroquois Policy toward New France and Its Native Allies to 1701.* Lincoln: University of Nebraska Press, 1997.
Jennings, Francis. *The Ambiguous Iroquois Empire: The Covenant Chain Confederation of Indian Tribes with English Colonies from Its Beginnings to the Lancaster Treaty of 1744.* New York: Norton, 1984.
Richter, Daniel K. *The Ordeal of the Longhouse: The People of the Iroquois League in the Era of European Colonization.* Chapel Hill: University of North Carolina Press, 1992.
Snow, Dean R. *The Iroquois.* Malden, MA: Blackwell, 1994.

Mohegans

Algonquian-speaking Native American tribe that lived along the Thames River (in colonial times also known as the Pequot River) in Connecticut. Mohegan territory also extended into Massachusetts and Rhode Island. The lifeways of the Mohegans were similar to other Northeast Woodlands natives. The Mohegans roamed the forests, lakes, rivers, bays, and the waters of the Atlantic Ocean to hunt

and fish. They also planted corn and other vegetables in summer locations. The Mohegans fashioned canoes that were either birch bark–covered framed canoes or dugout canoes. The tribe lived in wigwams, which were usually covered with birch bark or hides. They also built more permanent rectangular-shaped housing.

The origins of the Mohegan tribe are somewhat obscure. Formerly scholars thought that the Mohegans were a branch of the Mahicans (Mohicans), another Algonquian-speaking tribe living in the Hudson River Valley in New York. It was also thought that the Pequots of Massachusetts were a subgroup of the Mohegans. Today, scholars believe that the Mohegans were a subgroup of the Pequots who separated from the Pequots about the time that the first English settlers landed at Plymouth in 1620. In 1620 the sachem Sassacus was the chief of the Pequots. Uncas, a subordinate chief, rejected Sassacus's authority and led a splinter group to the Thames River not far from Long Island Sound. The cause of the separation apparently lay in political disagreements among several of their chiefs.

Because the names "Mohegan" and "Mahican" sound very similar, the Mohegans are often confused with the Mahicans. The Mahican were called Loups ("wolves") by the French, possibly

Mohegan chief Etow Oh Koam (King of the River Nation), known as Nocoloas, holds a club and sword. Painting by John Verelst, 1710. (Library and Archives of Canada/1977-35-1)

because the word "Mahican" may have derived from *maingan*, meaning "wolf." However, the name "Mohegan" seems to have come from an Algonquian word meaning "tides." James Fenimore Cooper made the Mahicans famous in his 1826 novel *The Last of the Mohicans*. Adding to the confusion was the fact that Cooper used as a character a "Mohican" who "lived by the sea." Moreover, the names of several other characters seem to have been drawn from the Mohegans. Although they may have been distantly related, the Pequot-Mohegans were a distinctively different group from the Mahicans.

Uncas befriended the English colonists. After the English defeated the Pequots in the Pequot War (1636–1638), the Mohegans became a powerful tribe, laying claim to Pequot lands as well as their own. In addition, they absorbed many of the remaining Pequots.

The Mohegans aided the colonists in King Philip's War (1675–1676). Metacom (King Philip), the chief of the Wampanoags, had allied with the Nipmucks and the Narragansetts. During the autumn of 1675 Metacom's forces had been quite successful in attacks on English settlements and their forces. However, on December 19, 1675, a combined force of colonial troops from Massachusetts Bay, Plymouth, and Connecticut joined forces with 150 Mohegan warriors. They proceeded to attack the main Narragansett village in Rhode Island, which was located in a well-defended swampy area. The swamps were already frozen in bitter winter weather, allowing the militia and Mohegan forces, commanded by Plymouth governor Josiah Winslow, to attack the village. In prolonged fighting, the Narragansett village was destroyed. Probably 1,000 or more of Metacom's allies were killed, including a great many women and children who were burned to death in their fort. Militia losses were fewer than two dozen dead.

The Mohegans were constant allies of the English in the wars against the French. However, eventually their numbers were severely reduced by European diseases, especially repeated epidemics of smallpox. Later, British settlers took much of the Mohegans' lands and sold some Mohegans into slavery in the West Indies. By 1775 a surviving group of the Mohegans had joined with a mixed group of Christianized natives who were living at Brotherton, New York. The group was led by the Reverend Samson Occom, a Mohegan minister. The group was relocated voluntarily by the federal government to the Stockbridge Reservation in Wisconsin in the 1820s. The Mohegan tribe survived, was formally recognized by the federal government in 1994, and has settled land claims with the State of Connecticut.

ANDREW J. WASKEY

See also

Great Swamp Fight; King Philip's War; Metacom; Narragansetts; Nipmucks; Pequots; Pequot War; Sassacus; Uncas; Wampanoags

References

De Forest, John William. *History of the Indians of Connecticut from the Earliest Known Period to 1850.* Hamden, CT: Archon Books, 1964.

Oberg, Michael Leroy. *Uncas: First of the Mohegans.* Ithaca, NY: Cornell University Press, 2003.

Peale, Arthur L. *Uncas and the Mohegan-Pequot.* Boston: Meador, 1939.

Mohicans

See Mahicans

Mojaves

Native American group that traditionally lived in the Mojave Valley and along the northern lower Colorado River. Today the Mojaves (Mohaves) live primarily on the Fort Mojave Reservation (Arizona) and on the Colorado River Indian Reservation (Arizona and California). Their original name was Tzi-na-ma-a. The name "Mojave" is a Hispanicization of the Yuman *aha-makave,* meaning "beside the water." The Mojaves spoke River Yuman, a member of the Hokan-Siouan language family. Roughly 20,000 Mojaves lived along the river in the early 16th century, just prior to European contact. Their number was reduced to 3,000 by 1770.

The Mojaves settled the Mojave Valley around 1150 and farmed soil enriched by sediment deposited during the annual spring floods. They may have encountered nonnatives as early as 1540. Although they served as scouts for Father Francisco Garces's Grand Canyon expedition in 1776, among others, they generally resisted Spanish interference and maintained their independence.

Positions of authority, such as subchiefs or local leaders, derived from dreaming or oratory. Hereditary chiefs in the male line did exist, although what functions they served is unclear. Despite their loose division into bands and local groups, the Mojaves thought of themselves as a true tribe; that is, they possessed a national consciousness and came together for important occasions such as warfare. Men planted the crops, and women harvested them. Leaders addressed the people from rooftops in the morning about proper ways of living. Hunters generally gave away what they killed. Mojaves often traveled widely for trade and recreation.

Bands and families lived in scattered rancherias, or farms. Crops such as corn, beans, and pumpkins (and wheat and melons after the Spanish arrived) constituted 50 percent of the Mojave diet. The Mojaves also caught fish; hunted game such as rabbits and beaver with bows and arrows, traps, or deadfalls; and gathered wild foods. Mesquite beans in particular were a staple, used for food, drink, flour (pith from pods), shoes and clothing (bark), hair dye, instruments (roots), glue (sap), fuel for firing pottery, and funeral pyres.

The Mojaves were fierce fighters. A warrior society (*kwanamis*) led three different fighting groups: archers, clubbers, and stick (or lance) men. They used deer-hide shields, mesquite or willow bows, and arrows in coyote or wildcat fur quivers. War leaders experienced

Four Mojave Native American chiefs with a Yuma Indian, second from left, acting as interpreter, circa 1887. (Library of Congress)

dreams conferring power in battle. Traditional enemies included the Pimas, O'odhams, Pee-Poshes (Maricopas), and Cocopahs. Allies included the Quechans, Chemehuevis, Yavapais, and western Apaches. The Mojaves often took girls or young women as prisoners, giving them to old men as an insult to the enemy.

Contact with nonnatives remained sporadic until the 19th century. At about that time, the Mojaves began raiding American fur trappers. The Mojaves also allowed a band of Paiutes called the Chemehuevis to settle in the southern portion of their territory. The Mexican Cession of 1848 and the discovery of gold in California that same year brought more American trespassers and led to more raids. In 1857 the Mojaves suffered a decisive military loss to their ancient enemies, the Pimas and Pee-Poshes. Two years later the United States built Fort Mojave and Fort Yuma to stem Mojave raiding. By this time, however, the Mojaves, defeated in battle and weakened by disease, settled for peace.

In 1865 the Mojave leader Irrateba convinced a group of his followers to relocate to the Colorado River Valley area. That same year Congress created the Colorado River Reservation for "all the tribes of the Colorado River drainage," primarily the Mojaves and Chemehuevis. Roughly 70 percent of the Mojaves had remained in the Mojave Valley, however, and they received a reservation in 1880. This split occasioned intratribal animosities for decades.

The early 20th century was marked by influenza epidemics and white encroachment. The first assimilationist government boarding school opened at the Colorado River Reservation in 1879. Legal allotments began in 1904. Traditional floodplain agriculture

disappeared in the 1930s, when the great dams reduced the flow of the Colorado River. During World War II (1939–1945), many U.S. citizens of Japanese heritage were interned on the Colorado River Reservation. For this operation the United States summarily appropriated 25,000 acres of Native American land.

Until 1964, the Bureau of Indian Affairs opened the reservation to Hopi and Navajo settlement; tribal rejection of this policy in 1952 was ignored by the bureau. Now members of all four tribes call the reservation home, having evolved into the Colorado River Indian Tribes, a difficult development for the few remaining Mojave elders. In 1963 a federal court case guaranteed the tribes title to federal water rights. They received a deed to the reservation the following year.

Barry M. Pritzker

See also
Apaches; Bureau of Indian Affairs; Navajos; Reservations; Yavapais

References
Sherer, Lorraine M. *Bitterness Road: The Mojave, 1604–1860.* Menlo Park, CA: Ballena, 1994.
Swisher, John. *The Mojave Desert.* Mount Pleasant, SC: Arcadia, 1999.

Mojave War
Event Date: 1859

A brief conflict between the Mojave (Mohave) tribe and the U.S. Army. The Mojaves inhabited lands in the Mojave Valley of the

Colorado River near the convergence of the present states of California, Arizona and Nevada, not far from present-day Las Vegas. Isolated acts of violence had occurred between the tribe and white trappers in the early 19th century, but the amount of contact increased significantly after 1848 because Mojave lands were within the Mexican Cession, territory that came to the United States following its victory in the Mexican-American War (1846–1848). Americans began construction of wagon roads, surveyed railroad routes, and charted the river.

The published five-year ordeal of Olive Oatman also shaded American sentiment toward the tribe during this time. Oatman was captured at age 13 by Native Americans during an attack in which most of her family was killed. She was traded to the Mojaves and eventually released after officers from Fort Yuma learned of her presence. The case hardened the attitude of settlers toward Native Americans, while increased white settlement on Mojave lands sparked clashes.

In 1858 after a band of Mojaves attacked a wagon train bound for California and forced it to turn back, the U.S. government decided to build a fort to secure the Colorado Crossing and protect settlers there. Lieutenant Colonel William Hoffman of the U.S. 6th Infantry Regiment subsequently led a reconnaissance force of dragoons from Fort Tejon, California, in early January 1859. Upon clashing with and killing about a dozen Mojaves in a skirmish by the Colorado River, Hoffman requested a full-scale campaign against the tribe.

In April 1859 the Colorado River Expedition, consisting of six companies and a detachment of artillery, moved from Fort Yuma into the heart of Mojave territory. Hoffman dealt forcefully with the tribe. He threatened to take a chief to Yuma Prison as a hostage and sent emissaries to all of the 22 clans to warn that the army was prepared to use force. The Mojave warriors, who had withdrawn at the approach of the soldiers, elected not to challenge them. On April 23, 1859, Mojave leaders appeared at Hoffman's encampment as ordered and surrendered after hearing an ultimatum from the officer that required them to sign a peace treaty.

Major Lewis Armistead assumed command after Hoffman was ordered to other duties. A fortified stockade in the camp on the eastern bank of the Colorado River evolved into Fort Mojave and served as the focal point of the army's presence in the area. A wagon road from Los Angeles supplied the fort for two years until it was abandoned at the beginning of the American Civil War (1861–1865). Following the end of the war in 1865, the army resumed its control over the post and the surrounding lands. Most Mojaves refused to go to the Colorado River Reservation when it was created in 1865 but did not resist violently. Army leaders opted not to force the members of the tribe onto the reservation and instead allowed them to follow their traditional way of life.

MATTHEW J. KROGMAN

See also
Mojaves; Oatman Family Massacre

References
Baley, Charles Q. *Disaster at the Colorado: Beale's Wagon Road and the First Emigrant Party.* Logan: Utah State University Press, 2002.

Kroeber, A. L., and C. B. Kroeber. *A Mohave War Reminiscence, 1854–1880.* Berkeley: University of California Press, 1973.

Vandervort, Bruce. *Indian Wars of Mexico, Canada and the United States, 1812–1900.* New York: Routledge, 2006.

Mo-ke-ta-va-ta

See Black Kettle

Moniac, David
Birth Date: ca. December 25, 1802
Death Date: November 21, 1836

U.S. Army officer. David Moniac, born near present-day Montgomery, Alabama, on December 25 probably in 1802, was of mixed ancestry but was predominantly Creek. His great-uncle was the noted Creek leader Alexander McGillivray, and his uncle (his mother's brother) was William Weatherford, another well-known Creek leader. During the Creek War of 1813–1814 Sam Moniac, David Moniac's father, served as a scout for U.S. forces.

In 1817 at age 15, Moniac entered the U.S. Military Academy at West Point, making him the first Native American to enter the academy and likely the first nonwhite to matriculate there. Moniac's appointment, which was unheard of at that time, was likely the result of his father's service with the U.S. military. Prior to his enrollment, Moniac studied with a private tutor in Washington, D.C., in order to prepare himself for the entrance exams.

Although Moniac was a model cadet, the novelty of his presence did not go unnoticed. West Point superintendent Sylvanus Thayer referred to him fondly as his "Indian boy." Although Moniac was not an outstanding student, he worked hard and excelled in fencing and other physical activities. After deciding to repeat his first year of studies because of marginal grades, he graduated with the class of 1822 and was commissioned a second lieutenant in the 6th Infantry Regiment. Within months, however, he resigned his commission in December 1822 chiefly because there were few available spots for army officers at that time.

Moniac subsequently returned to his native Alabama, where he became a successful cotton farmer and horse breeder. He also joined the state militia but as an enlisted man instead of an officer. In 1836 shortly after the start of the Second Seminole War, Moniac joined the Mounted Creek Volunteers as a captain and was dispatched to Florida. He was the only Native American officer in the outfit. In October 1836 he led the Mounted Creek Volunteers in an intrepid and successful charge on a Seminole stronghold near Fort Brook (near present-day Tampa), for which he was promoted to major. On November 21, 1836, the Mounted Creeks, along with the members of the Florida Militia and numerous Tennessee Volunteers, entered the foreboding Wahoo Swamp, where a sizable Seminole force had gathered. As Moniac entered the swamp's waters to gauge their depth, he was mortally wounded by a volley of Seminole musket fire.

PAUL G. PIERPAOLI JR.

See also

Creeks; McGillivray, Alexander; Seminole War, Second; Weatherford, William

References

Ambrose, Stephen E. *Duty, Honor, Country: A History of West Point.* Baltimore: Johns Hopkins University Press, 1999.

Griffin, Benjamin. "Lt. David Moniac, Creek Indian: First Minority Graduate of West Point." *Alabama Historical Quarterly* 2 (Summer 1981): 99–110.

Moravian Church

Protestant denomination with spiritual origins in the Unitas Fratrum (Unity of Brethren) that had been part of the Hussite movement in 15th-century Moravia and Bohemia (parts of the present-day Czech Republic). The 18th-century Brethren were important actors in the Pietist trends of their era, and their difficulties reveal the ongoing ambiguity of church and state in Europe in that era as well as the desire for a more personal and ethical religion.

Pietism was a movement that grew in strength in many of the Protestant German states during the last part of the 17th century. In many ways, pietism represented a revolt against authoritarian institutional churches that were affiliated with the states. Pietists did not organize to oppose the governments or even the Lutheran Church, however. They were people seeking individual spiritual awakenings, peace, and happiness rather than any kind of revolutionary social goals. They did not believe that the official churches were truly ethical, but they also did not believe that the official churches could be reformed. They therefore wanted only to proceed privately with their own faith.

These beliefs were nevertheless perceived as threatening to such established sects as the Lutheran and Catholic churches. Particularly in Bohemia and Moravia, areas within the Holy Roman Empire where the Jesuit Order provided the most dynamic Catholic leadership, Pietists became the objects of persecution during the early 18th century. Many Pietists from Bohemia and Moravia left their homes to find a more secure environment in the Protestant states of Germany beginning in the early 1600s.

Very soon after the founding of the Moravian Brethren, their central goal became outreach. By 1727 evangelists were already traveling into other areas of Germany, and by 1732 the first missionaries to the West Indies embarked to work among the enslaved peoples there. Similar missions were funded to work among the native peoples in North America, along with missions to North Africa, Southern Africa, and Greenland. The Moravians most notably founded several missions along the Muskingum River in present-day southeastern Ohio to evangelize and educate Native Americans there, mostly the Delawares.

Although members of the Moravian Church went to Great Britain and a few churches were founded there, the missionaries were more interested in proceeding to North America, as they saw in America the chance to convert Native Americans and the possibility of refuge. The group started in the West Indies, moved briefly to Georgia, and then went to the colony of Pennsylvania, where the large numbers of settlers of Lutheran and Reformed backgrounds appeared as potential members of a united church. This union never came to pass, but the Moravian Church became established in North America.

Although the Moravian Church retained ties to and was controlled in some ways by the European centers, each Moravian community made the decision as to whether to remain open to all or to limit residence to church members. For example, only Brethren were allowed to live in the villages of Bethlehem and Nazareth in Pennsylvania. In both Europe and America, however, Moravian schools continued to educate children from all Protestant denominations. The communities worked hard to sustain the missionary impulse of the church as well. Two Moravian missions in the Muskingum River Valley—Salem and Gnadenhutten—met a tragic end on March 8, 1782, when American militiamen massacred 96 Native Americans (mainly women and children) there. This put an effective end to the cooperation between Native Americans and Moravians in the Ohio Country.

TIM J. WATTS

See also

Delawares; Gnadenhutten Massacre; Moravian Indian Missions on the Muskingum River

References

Hutton, J. E. *A History of the Moravian Church.* Whitefish, MT: Kessinger, 2007.

Langton, Edward. *History of the Moravian Church: The Story of the First International Protestant Church.* London: Allen and Unwin, 1956.

MacMaster, Richard K. *Land, Piety, Peoplehood: The Establishment of Mennonite Communities in America, 1683–1790.* Scottdale, PA: Herald, 1985.

Moravian Indian Missions on the Muskingum River

Missions established in the 1770s by the Moravians to educate Native Americans and convert them to Christianity. Most Moravian Indian Missions were clustered along the Muskingum River in southeastern Ohio. Moravians were a Protestant sect that first arose among the Czechs. Many relocated to the New World to escape religious persecution and to live in communes. A number settled in Pennsylvania and the Ohio Country.

Moravians were pacifists who promoted Native American conversion. As such, they created missions along the Muskingum River over the course of the 1770s, beginning with missions established at Gnadenhutten and Schoenbrunn in 1772 by Moravian missionary David Zeisberger. Johann Schmick was the primary missionary at Gnadenhutten, while Zeisberger oversaw both villages. Mission Indians had frequent contact with their relations in nearby villages, but their way of life demanded that they avoid native religious practices, polygamy, and the consumption of alcohol. The missions attracted a number of Delaware Indians, and the population of the two villages grew to approximately 400. In 1776 Zeisberger founded a third mission at Lichtenau. Like many other missionary efforts, Zeisberger's work split the native society because the converts differed from their tribe in religion as well as in politics and culture.

During the American Revolutionary War (1775–1783) the Moravian Indian missions, despite their putative pacifism, supported the American colonists primarily by giving them information about planned British and British allied tribes' movements. The Delaware tribe as a whole attempted to pursue a neutral policy. The pro-American Coshocton Delawares protected the missions from traditionalist tribes at the start of the war. Even so, in 1777 the Moravians abandoned Schoenbrunn, given the presence of hostile native parties. Because of a growing trend among the Delawares to side with the British and also because of the defection of the previously pro-American Delaware leader Pipe, Zeisberger moved his converts from Lichtenau to new locations called New Schoenbrunn and New Salem. By 1781 the Delawares as a group had moved firmly into the British camp, making the pro-American–leaning Moravian mission Indians' position in the Ohio Country untenable.

In 1781 the Moravian presence was removed from the Ohio Valley, with more than 400 converts forced out of the area. The missionaries were taken to Detroit by a British-allied native force that included the Wyandots and Pomoacans as well as the Delaware leader Pipe. Many of the converts, however, returned to the Ohio Valley. On March 7, 1782, a militia expedition under Colonel David Williamson massacred the natives of Salem and Gnadenhutten, despite their previous aid to the colonists. The incident demonstrated the brutality of warfare along the frontier and its racial dimension. The militiamen were not subject to the discipline of regulars, and Williamson was in no position to enforce it. His force voted on whether to take the natives prisoner or to kill them, and the majority vote ruled. After the massacre, the British allowed the missionaries and their Indian converts to settle in Ontario, recognizing that the Americans had effectively turned against their own allies. The earlier period of cooperation between Moravian Indians and Americans was at an end.

MICHAEL K. BEAUCHAMP

See also

Delawares; Gnadenhutten Massacre; Moravian Church; Native Americans and the American Revolutionary War

References

Dowd, Gregory Evans. *A Spirited Resistance: The North American Indian Struggle for Unity, 1745–1815.* Baltimore: Johns Hopkins University Press, 1992.

Taylor, Alan. *The Divided Ground: Indians, Settlers, and the Northern Borderland of the American Revolution.* New York: Knopf, 2006.

Moraviantown, Battle of

See Thames, Battle of the

Mormonism

Christian denomination founded by Joseph Smith Jr. in 1830 and based on the Latter-day Saint movement of the early 1800s. Two of the more controversial original beliefs of the church were polygamy and the origins of the Native Americans.

Smith was born on December 23, 1805, in Sharon, Vermont. He reported that in 1823 an angel named Moroni had visited him and told him about an ancient book, written on golden plates by ancient prophets. In 1827 Moroni led Smith to the book near his home in Manchester, New York, and Smith published a translation as *The Book of Mormon* in 1830.

The first part tells the story of Lehi, his family, and other Jews whom shortly before the city fell to the Babylonians in 586 BCE God had led from Jerusalem across Arabia and then to the Western Hemisphere. The writings then recount the group's history to about 130 BCE, during which time the community grew and split into two main groups, the Nephites and the Lamanites, who frequently fought each other.

The second part of the book, supposedly written in 385 CE by a Nephite named Mormon, recounts various wars, Mormon's command of Nephite army units, the final destruction of the Nephites, and the idolatrous state of the remaining Lamanite society. Mormon was eventually killed in battle after he handed the records to his son Moroni, the last Nephite prophet. Thus, according to Smith, Native Americans are the descendants of the Lamanites, although there is no archaeological or genetic evidence that validates this claim.

Moroni also wrote a short history of the Jaredites, people whom a man named Jared and his brother led from the Tower of Babel to the Americas. According to this text, the Jaredite civilization existed on the American continent around 2500 BCE and ended before Lehi's arrival in 600 BCE. After completing this alleged history Moroni buried the records, which God promised to reveal in the "latter days."

After publication of *The Book of Mormon,* Smith founded the Church of Jesus Christ of Latter-day Saints (LDS). During the 1830s Smith lived first in Ohio and later in Missouri, where the steadily growing church ran into conflict with local non-Mormons.

Joseph Smith (1805–1844), founder of the Church of Jesus Christ of Latter-Day Saints (the Mormon Church), today one of the fastest-growing Christian denominations. (Library of Congress)

This conflict escalated into the 1838 Mormon War, so Smith and his followers moved to Nauvoo, Illinois. By 1844 Smith's practice of polygamy and his theocratic government of Nauvoo outraged the local populace, and Smith was jailed in Carthage, Illinois, on charges of treason. On June 27, 1844, an armed mob broke into the jail, murdering Smith and his brother Hyrum.

In February 1846 Brigham Young and a large group of Mormons left Illinois on a 1,250-mile trek to the Salt Lake Valley, which was then Mexican territory. They arrived in July 1847 and founded Salt Lake City. In December 1847 the majority of Mormons chose Young as the church president. After the Mexican-American War (1846–1848), Mexico ceded the region to the United States, which established the territory of Utah in 1850. President Millard Fillmore appointed Young as the territory's first governor and superintendent of Indian affairs. Young organized the first legislature at Fillmore, the territory's first capital, and directed the establishment of settlements throughout the northern portion of the Mexican Cession.

On September 7, 1857, at Mountain Meadows in southern Utah, Mormon militiamen, dressed as Native Americans and aided by some Paiutes, attacked a wagon train from Arkansas led by "Colonel" Alexander Fancher that was on its way to California. After a four-day siege, the surviving settlers surrendered. The Mormons then murdered more than 120 men, women, and children and left their bodies to decompose. The militiamen spared only the 17 children under the age of eight, who were given to Mormon families to rear as their own. In 1874 the state government indicted 9 of the militiamen for the massacre, but only 1 was executed.

After receiving reports of widespread obstruction of federal officials in Utah, in 1857 President James Buchanan appointed a non-Mormon, Alfred Cumming, as governor. Young discovered that Cumming was traveling to Utah with 2,500 federal troops to garrison forts in the new territory and mobilized his militia to ambush the federal column. During the so-called Utah War the Mormon forces held out against the army during the winter of 1857–1858. Young also made plans to burn Salt Lake City and move with his followers to Mexico. At the last minute he stepped down as governor, and Buchanan later pardoned Young.

After the American Civil War (1861–1865) the territory's inhabitants applied several times for statehood, but the U.S. Congress steadfastly refused because of the church's practice of polygamy. Mormon leader Wilford Woodruff issued a manifesto in 1890 that officially discontinued the practice, and the U.S. Congress voted statehood for Utah in 1896.

Despite their ideas about Native Americans, the Mormons came to treat them as other Americans did. Shortly after founding the church in 1830, Smith sent four missionaries into the newly created Indian Territory (Oklahoma), but they had little success in converting the Native Americans. After the Mormons arrived in Utah, they initially had amicable relations with the native Utes. However, as more settlers arrived, competition for water and arable land grew, causing friction between the two groups. Also, like other tribes the Utes succumbed to white diseases to which they had no immunity. As the competition for resources grew, church leaders authorized Mormons to attack Native Americans who did not willingly give up their land and water. The Mormon Church rationalized its treatment of Native Americans by stating that the latter's resistance meant rejection of Christ's message and therefore justified retribution. Finally, in 1865 the marginalized Utes, urged by Young, signed a treaty with the U.S. government by which they agreed to move to reservations in northern Utah and Colorado.

ROBERT B. KANE

See also
Paiutes, Northern; Utes

References
Bushman, Richard L., and Jed Woodworth. *Joseph Smith: Rough Stone Rolling.* New York: Knopf, 2005.

Denton, Sally. *American Massacre: The Tragedy of Mountain Meadows, September 1857.* New York: Knopf, 2003.

Farmer, Jared. *On Zion's Mount: Mormons, Indians, and the American Landscape.* Boston: Harvard University Press, 2008.

Vexler, Robert I., ed. *Chronology and Documentary Handbook of the State of Utah.* Dobbs Ferry, NY: Oceana Publications, 1979.

Morning Star

See Dull Knife

Mortar of the Okchai
Birth Date: Unknown
Death Date: November 1774

Influential member of the Upper Creek Nation and a key warrior of the Okchai settlement. Nothing is known of Mortar of the Okchai's birth or early years. Mortar, also called Wolf Warrior in some accounts, became the leader of the Bear Clan of the Okchai faction of the Creek tribe, although he never rose to dominance within the entire Creek Nation.

The settlement of Okchai was located between the Coosa River and the Tallapoosa River, both tributaries of the Alabama River. Mortar feared British incursions onto Creek territory and sought repeatedly to forge alliances with regional tribes to halt the spread of British settlements in Georgia, the Carolinas, and Virginia. However, he was never able to obtain sufficient support to unite even the Creeks, much less the rival Cherokees and Choctaws of the region. He nevertheless maintained close ties with the local Cherokee leadership, and Mortar's sister was married to a Cherokee, providing a close familial connection.

Mortar developed a reputation for farsightedness and diplomacy during the French and Indian War (1754–1763), when he counseled the leadership of the Creek Nation to remain neutral. In particular, a British plan to build fortifications on Creek territory infuriated him. Mortar preferred to side with the French to obtain protection against British expansion, but he realized that the French could never provide sufficient supplies to the Creeks to sustain a war against British colonists. Instead, Mortar maneuvered the French and the British into lowering trading prices for the Creeks by threatening to push the tribe into the war, all the while carefully maintaining neutrality for the duration of the conflict.

In the aftermath of the war, Mortar again sought to forge a regional alliance of 18 tribes to oppose British colonial expansion and possibly overthrow British rule in the Ohio River Valley. The British did successfully entice regional tribes to surrender their French flags, commissions, and medals for British equivalents. But they could never persuade Mortar of their peaceful intentions. In 1766 when several Cherokees were murdered in Augusta County, Virginia, Mortar offered to join a Cherokee war party with 700 warriors in pursuit of revenge, but his offer was refused. Under Mortar's direction, Creeks killed 2 British traders found on Creek land and threatened to kill any other trespassers. This did not, however, provoke a general conflict with the British.

In 1774 during the Creek-Choctaw War, Mortar sought Spanish assistance for the Creeks, asking them to negotiate a peace with the rival Choctaw Nation and then establish a protectorate over the Creeks. While traveling to New Orleans to seek Spanish support in November 1774, Mortar's party was ambushed by Choctaw warriors, and Mortar was mortally wounded in the fighting. His death likely occurred in present-day southern Mississippi or Alabama.

PAUL J. SPRINGER

See also
Cherokees; Choctaws; Creeks

References
Corkran, David H. *The Creek Frontier, 1540–1783*. Norman: University of Oklahoma Press, 1967.
Nester, William R. *"Haughty Conquerers": Amherst and the Great Indian Uprising of 1763*. Westport, CT: Praeger, 2000.
Saunt, Claudio. *A New Order of Things: Property, Power, and the Transformation of the Creek Indians, 1733–1816*. New York: Cambridge University Press, 1999.

Mo-to-vato

See Black Kettle

Mounted Riflemen, Regiment of

U.S. Army mounted regiment. In 1846 the U.S. Congress authorized the organization of a regiment of mounted riflemen. This type of formation was entirely new to the U.S. Army and involved an early and lasting experiment at creating hybrid combat elements. The new Regiment of Mounted Riflemen was not simply a unit of traditional infantry placed on horseback. Soldiers assigned to the regiment were equipped with hunting rifles to provide longer range and more firepower than the smoothbore carbine muskets normally assigned to the cavalry.

Initially the regiment was charged with establishing military stations along the Oregon Trail but was quickly sidetracked by orders sending it south to participate in the invasion of Mexico during the Mexican-American War (1846–1848). En route to Mexico the regiment lost most of its mounts to a storm and subsequently fought as infantry. The hallmark battle of the war for the regiment was Chapultepec. It was there that the men of the Mounted Rifles earned the sobriquet "Brave Rifles" from Major General Winfield Scott.

Once the war in Mexico ended, the regiment returned to its original assignment and under the command of Lieutenant Colonel W. W. Loring set out from Fort Leavenworth for the Oregon Territory. There the regiment patrolled the Pacific Northwest for two years before being ordered to Texas. In Texas the regiment fought against bandits as well as Kiowas, Comanches, and Cheyennes. In 1856 troubles in the New Mexico Territory required additional troops, and the Mounted Rifles moved farther west.

With the beginning of the American Civil War in 1861, the Regiment of Mounted Riflemen was redesignated the 3rd U.S.

Cavalry Regiment. Already located at Fort Bliss (near El Paso), the 3rd Cavalry was prepared to campaign against Confederate forces to prevent them from securing western Texas and the New Mexico Territory. Although the Confederates proved only a limited threat in the region, the many Native American tribes that called the area home remained dangerous. In 1862 elements of the regiment fought several skirmishes at Comanche Canyon in New Mexico Territory. Later that same year the 3rd Cavalry Regiment moved east to campaign in Tennessee, Alabama, Mississippi, and North Carolina.

In 1866 with the end of the American Civil War, the 3rd Cavalry was stationed in New Mexico to face the Apaches. Operating out of Fort Stanton in south-central New Mexico, the regiment campaigned in rugged terrain and fought in more than 20 recorded engagements, mostly against the Apaches. In the process the regiment lost some 45 of its men while killing more than 80 warriors. In one particular fight in the Doña Ana Mountains, a detachment of the 3rd Cavalry chased Apache raiders at a gallop along a six-mile-long mountain pass to recapture 13 stolen cavalry mounts.

In 1870 the regiment was ordered to Arizona for further operations against the Apaches. A year later the regiment was transferred north to the Department of the Platte, which included Wyoming, Montana, the Dakota Territory, and Nebraska. During 1876 the regiment, under Colonel J. J. Reynolds, participated in the Great Sioux War. On June 17, 1876, the regiment fought in the Battle of the Rosebud, the largest battle between the U.S. Army and the Plains tribes in the history of the American West. At Rosebud Creek a force of 1,400 soldiers with their Native American allies faced an attacking force of an estimated 1,500 Lakota Sioux and Cheyennes. Following Lieutenant Colonel George A. Custer's subsequent stunning defeat in the Battle of the Little Bighorn, the 3rd Cavalry participated in the Starvation March and fought well at the Battle of Slim Buttes.

In 1879 elements of the 3rd Cavalry participated in the Ute War (White River Expedition), operating from Fort Fred Steele in Colorado. After setting up a camp near Milk Creek in present-day Arizona, the cavalry, under the command of Major Thomas Thornburgh, was attacked by a band of Ute warriors. Thornburgh was killed early in the battle, but the command held together under tremendous pressure. The men were rescued in a concerted effort by buffalo soldiers of the 9th Cavalry, led by Captain Francis Dodge, and the 5th Cavalry, under the command of Colonel Wesley Merritt.

The regiment continued operations in Arizona and again set off in pursuit of hostile Apaches. In 1883 Brigadier General George Crook launched a raid along the Rio Bavispe, deep inside Apache territory. The command struck a camp near the river and killed 9 warriors. The raid so frightened the Apaches that 123 warriors and 253 women and children surrendered to Crook, among them Geronimo. The Geronimo Campaign essentially signaled the end of the regiment's participation in the Indian Wars.

PATRICK R. JENNINGS

See also

Apache Wars; Buffalo Soldiers; Cheyennes; Comanches; Crook, George; Geronimo; Great Sioux War; Kiowas; Merritt, Wesley; Rosebud, Battle of the; Slim Buttes, Battle of; Ute War

References

Miller, Mark E. *Hollow Victory: The White River Expedition of 1879 and the Battle of Milk Creek.* Niwot: The University Press of Colorado, 1997.

Roberts, David. *Once They Moved like the Wind: Cochise, Geronimo, and the Apache Wars.* New York: Touchstone, 1993.

Utley, Robert M. *Frontier Regulars: The United States and the American Indian, 1866–1891.* New York: Macmillan, 1973.

Webb, George. *Chronological List of Engagements between the Regular Army of the United States and the Various Tribes of the Hostile Indians Which Occurred during the Years 1790 to 1898, Inclusive.* 1939; reprint, New York: AMS Press, 1989.

Mourning War

A social and cultural phenomenon among Native Americans belonging to Iroquois tribes, the purpose of which was to acquire captives as a method of coping with death. The current use of the term "mourning war" stems from historian Daniel K. Richter, who notes that mourning war was the traditional function of warfare for Iroquois warriors prior to contact with Europeans.

The Iroquois believed that an individual's passing robbed his family, clan, and community of spiritual power. To address this problem, communities adopted new persons in requickening ceremonies to take the place and fulfill the social role and duties of the deceased. When the departed was an individual of high status, an adoptee was taken from within the community, but for departees of lower status, adoptees from external sources were often required. Mourning war also provided on outlet for grief.

The Iroquois had several rituals and practices to address bereavement. However, if these failed, the women of the deceased's household could demand that a party of warriors venture out to acquire captives. Most of these people were assimilated into household and family roles previously filled by deceased kin. Some, usually adult men, might be selected for ritual torture and execution in order to assuage the sorrow and pain of grieving family members.

Mourning war fulfilled a number of important social functions in that the adoption of captives maintained population levels, the continuity of village and family life, and the spiritual power of the community. The ritual also provided a means to cope with the emotional trauma of death. Moreover, these functions had two important consequences on Iroquois warfare tactics. First, they stressed the capture of prisoners, not the killing of enemies. Second, they helped minimize Iroquois deaths in battle. As a result, mourning war tactics stressed the use of surprise and ambush (the skulking way of war), foregoing attacks on fortified places, and retreating when an enemy appeared too powerful.

MATTHEW S. MUEHLBAUER

See also

Captivity of Europeans by Indians; Captivity of Indians by Indians; Iroquois; Iroquois Confederacy; Native American Warfare; Skulking Way of War

References

Richter, Daniel K. *The Ordeal of the Longhouse: The People of the Iroquois League in the Era of European Colonization.* Chapel Hill: University of North Carolina Press, 1992.

Richter, Daniel K. "War and Culture: The Iroquois Experience." *William and Mary Quarterly,* 3rd Ser., 40(4) (October 1983): 528–559.

Muddy People

See Spokanes

Murray, John, Fourth Earl of Dunmore

Birth Date: 1730 or 1732
Death Date: February 25, 1809

British colonial administrator, governor of New York (1770–1771), governor of Virginia (1771–1775), and governor of the Bahamas (1787–1796). Born in Scotland in 1730 or 1732, John Murray was a descendant of the Scottish house of Stuart. The eldest son of William Murray, Third Earl of Dunmore, Murray succeeded to the title in 1756. He was a member of the House of Lords from 1761 to 1770, when he was appointed governor of New York.

In 1771 Dunmore was appointed governor of Virginia, Britain's largest and wealthiest North American colony. Very much interested in promoting colonial settlement of the western lands, from 1771 to 1774 Dunmore directed a series of military campaigns against the Native Americans—chiefly the Shawnees—in what became known as Lord Dunmore's War. The fighting ended with the Shawnees ceding to Britain all lands east and south of the Ohio River.

Despite Dunmore's success in fighting those outside of Virginia, he fared much worse with those inside the colony. Although his war with the natives had made him a hero in Virginia, in 1774 his dissolution of Virginia's colonial assembly, the House of Burgesses, for its opposition to British policy led to the creation of a revolutionary convention in Virginia that supplied delegates to the subsequent American Continental Congresses. In 1775 Dunmore's removal of the colony's gunpowder stores from the Williamsburg Magazine led to threats against his life. Dunmore fled Williamsburg, then Virginia's capital, to take refuge aboard a British warship off Norfolk.

While aboard ship on November 7, 1775, Dunmore issued his most memorable declaration, in which he proclaimed martial law and declared as free all indentured servants and slaves owned by persons in rebellion and who were able and willing to bear arms in support of the British cause. This was the first mass emancipation of slaves in British North America. Dunmore's declaration of martial law and offer of emancipation threatened the property rights of all Virginians, moderate and radical alike. It also polarized the colony into two camps: Patriots and Loyalists. Dunmore subsequently organized a number of black Loyalists into the Ethiopian Regiment. His force was defeated in the Battle of Great Bridge near Norfolk on December 9, 1775.

By July 1776, having failed to regain control of Virginia, Lord Dunmore sailed for England. He returned to America in 1781 and again proposed arming the slaves to subdue the American revolutionaries, but the proposal was ignored, and he returned to England. In 1787 he crossed the Atlantic once more to serve as governor of the Bahamas, a position he held until 1796. Retiring to England, Dunmore died there on February 25, 1809.

JOHN F. CHAPPO

John Murray, Fourth Earl of Dunmore, was governor of colonial Virginia from 1771 until he was forced from office in the summer of 1775 by the outbreak of the American Revolution. A firm advocate of colonial settlement of western lands, during 1771–1774, Dunmore directed a series of successful military campaigns against the Native Americans that became known as Lord Dunmore's War. (Library of Congress)

See also

Lord Dunmore's War; Shawnees

References

Galbreath, Charles Burleigh. *The Logan Elm and Dunmore War.* Columbus: Ohio State Archaeological and Historical Society, 1924.

Kellogg, Luise Phelps, and Reuben Gold Thwaites, eds. *Documentary History of Dunmore's War, 1774.* Bowie, MD: Heritage Books, 1989.

Randall, Emilius Oviatt. *The Dunmore War.* Columbus, OH: F. J. Heer, 1902.

Rogers, Alan, and Alan Lawson, eds. *From Revolution to Republic: A Documentary Reader.* Cambridge, MA: Schenkman, 1976.

Muscle Shoals, Grand Council on
Event Date: May 1776

Council between major northern and southern Native American tribes held in May 1776 at Muscle Shoals on the Tennessee River near present-day Florence, Alabama. The principal impetus for the meeting was the commencement of the American Revolutionary War (1775–1783) that had begun a year earlier and that led many Native Americans to take sides in the imperial struggle. With the outbreak of that conflict, the British sought to organize the Trans-Appalachian tribes to fight on their behalf against the American colonists.

Although the British had fought many of these tribes in the past, most recently in the French and Indian War (1754–1763) and Pontiac's Rebellion (1763), Native Americans clearly understood that American settlers from the 13 colonies presented the greatest threat to their independence and survival as a people. Indeed, in 1774 Virginians had launched a campaign against the Shawnees in what became known as Lord Dunmore's War. Consequently Henry Hamilton, the British governor at Fort Detroit, found a receptive audience when he urged Shawnee chief Cornstalk and other tribal leaders from the Delawares (Lenapes), Iroquois, and Ottawas to forge an alliance with southern tribes (the Cherokees, Chickasaws, Creeks, and Choctaws).

In May 1776 Cornstalk and the other northern leaders met with their southern counterparts at Muscle Shoals on the Tennessee River. Although Cornstalk had been an advocate for neutrality after the Shawnees were defeated in the Battle of Point Pleasant in 1774, the bellicosity of other tribes at the council led him to offer his war belt to Cherokee chief Dragging Canoe (although some sources contradict this). Ottawa and Iroquois warriors likewise offered their war belts to Dragging Canoe, and the Delawares offered their war belt to Savanukah, the leader of the Cherokee town of Chota. Before the conference ended, Dragging Canoe led a raid into Kentucky and returned with four white scalps, symbolizing his acceptance of the alliance.

The Grand Council on Muscle Shoals led directly to the Cherokee War of 1776 (sometimes known as the Second Cherokee War) during which Dragging Canoe and his southern allies launched raids all along the southern frontier, stretching from Virginia to Georgia. Unfortunately for the Cherokees, British support was not forthcoming because they had no military presence in the South outside of Florida. Consequently, North Carolina, South Carolina, and Georgia mobilized approximately 4,400 militiamen against the Cherokees in northern Georgia and the western Carolinas, while the Virginia militia attacked Cherokees in Tennessee.

Within a year a Cherokee peace party led by Oconostota and Attakullakulla agreed to peace with Georgia and South Carolina in the Treaty of Dewitt's Corner and with Virginia and North Carolina in the Treaty of Fort Henry. Meanwhile, Cornstalk reverted to a policy of peace upon his return to Ohio. When other members of the tribe appeared determined to go to war, Cornstalk and

his son traveled to Point Pleasant to warn the American garrison, only to be arrested and then killed in retaliation for the murder of white settlers by other members of the tribe. Ironically, American actions helped secure British objectives because the murder of Cornstalk made the Shawnees the most implacable Native American foe the Americans would face for the next 40 years.

JUSTIN D. MURPHY

See also

Attakullakulla; Cherokees; Cherokees, Campaigns against; Chickasaws; Choctaws; Cornstalk; Creeks; Delawares; French and Indian War; Iroquois; Native Americans and the American Revolutionary War; Oconostota; Ottawas; Point Pleasant, Battle of; Pontiac's Rebellion; Shawnees

References

Calloway, Colin G. *The American Revolution in Indian Country: Crisis and Diversity in Native American Communities.* Cambridge: Cambridge University Press, 1995.

Calloway, Colin G. *The Shawnees and the War for America.* New York: Viking, 2007.

Calloway, Colin G. "'We Have Always Been the Frontier': The American Revolution in Shawnee Country." *American Indian Quarterly* 16(1) (1992): 39–52.

Richter, Daniel K., and James H. Merrell, eds. *Beyond the Covenant Chain: The Iroquois and Their Neighbors in Indian North America, 1600–1800.* Syracuse, NY: Syracuse University Press, 1987.

Muscogees
See Creeks

Musgrove, Mary
Birth Date: ca. 1700
Death Date: 1763

Trader, diplomat, interpreter, and cultural liaison of mixed Creek and English descent. Mary Musgrove, also known as Coosaponakeesa, was born around 1700 in Coweta, an influential Lower Creek village in present-day Georgia. She was the daughter of a white English trader and a Creek mother.

Musgrove was brought up with an understanding and respect for both sides of her cultural lineage. She spent her formative years among the Creeks but was also baptized and educated for five years in South Carolina. As such, she became one of the few natives of the period who could read and write. Musgrove returned to Coweta around 1715 and was there when Colonel John Musgrove headed an expedition to the Creeks during the Yamasee War (1715–1717). The two sides confirmed the peace with a pledge of marriage between Mary and John's son and namesake, John Musgrove Jr.

The newlyweds set up a trading post near present-day Savannah and were very successful. Mary Musgrove often facilitated not only economic but also diplomatic and social affairs. When

James Oglethorpe founded Georgia in 1733, he requested Musgrove's help. She encouraged the local natives to provide food and military aid to the fledgling colony, and she herself served as Oglethorpe's official interpreter for almost a decade. During this period, Musgrove did much to foster amicable relations between the British and the Creek Confederacy. Indeed, Oglethorpe himself recognized the colony's indebtedness to her.

The alliance between the British and the Creeks, including Creek military aid against the Spanish in the Anglo-Spanish War (1739–1744), also known as the War of Jenkins' Ear, was largely secured by her and a distant relative, Tomochichi. Musgrove also helped to negotiate the treaties that established Georgia's two main colonial towns: Savannah and Augusta.

After John Musgrove died in 1735, Mary successfully managed the considerable family assets. She married Jacob Matthews a year or so later, and the two set up another trading post called Mount Venture on the Altamaha River, south of Savannah. After Matthews died in 1742, Mary married again in 1744. Her choice of a third husband, Thomas Bosomworth, raised eyebrows. Many considered him an unscrupulous character, and Mary's influence among the British began to decline after their marriage, especially after the couple initiated a series of controversial land claims.

The problem dated back to 1737, when Tomochichi had granted Mary a plot of land near Savannah. In 1747 other Creek chiefs (and possible relatives of Mary) granted her more land, including three of the Georgia Sea Islands. British officials contested the legality of those grants. The debate came to a head in Savannah in 1749, when Mary and many of her Creek relatives arrived in the capital city to press her legal right to the land. The town was a bit intimidated by such a presence, and Mary fell from favor. She was finally able to plead her case before the courts in England in 1754, but a compromise was not reached until 1760. Mary managed to maintain ownership over one of the three islands and acquired a sum of money as reward for her services to the king.

In the wake of the land controversy, Musgrove's involvement in Georgia-Creek relations waned, but the importance of her influence during the early years of the colony cannot be overestimated. She died sometime in 1763 at her home on St. Catherine's Island, off the Georgia coast.

Lisa L. Crutchfield

See also
Creeks; Tomochichi; Yamasee War

References
Gillespie, Michele. "The Sexual Politics of Race and Gender: Mary Musgrove and the Georgia Trustees." In *The Devil's Lane: Sex and Race in the Early South,* edited by Catherine Clinton and Michele Gillespie, 187–201. New York: Oxford University Press, 1997.

Green, Michael D. "Mary Musgrove: Creating a New World." In *Sifters: Native American Women's Lives,* edited by Theda Perdue, 29–47. New York: Oxford University Press, 2001.

Sweet, Julie. *Negotiating for Georgia: British-Creek Relations in the Trustee Era, 1733–1752.* Athens: University of Georgia Press, 2005.

Muskets

The introduction from China of gunpowder into Europe in the 13th century led to a military revolution. Gunpowder consisted of saltpeter (providing oxygen for burning), sulfur (which lowered the temperature at which ignition of the powder occurs), and charcoal (which added bulk to the entire mixture and acted as a burning agent). Gunpowder changed little over the years, and black powder remained the principal propellant for firearms until the end of the 19th century.

Gunpowder when ignited generates great heat, releasing energy in the form of powerfully expanding gases. Properly channeled, these gases could be used to propel a projectile from a barrel at some velocity and distance. Large projectiles could batter down castle walls, and the smallest projectile could penetrate body armor.

Larger cannon led the way, but in the late 14th and early 15th centuries a wide variety of individual hand gonnes appeared. The first primitive types consisted of a tapered wooden pole that was partially hollowed out at its larger end to hold a small, short metal barrel. Metal bands secured the barrel to its gun stock. Behind the barrel a vertical metal spike running through the stock could be hooked over a portable rest in order to absorb recoil.

The earliest firearms were both unwieldy and heavy. Until about 1660, heavy so-called Spanish-style muskets were fired from a simple forked rest. Even the later lighter firearm models were cumbersome and difficult to load.

Although early gunpowder weapons were wildly inaccurate, infantrymen armed with them could employ them to kill or maim knights on horseback. Such weapons in the hands of well-trained individual infantrymen eventually ended the primacy of horse cavalry and knights on the battlefields of Europe.

To fire the gonne, the individual using it would pour a set amount of gunpowder down the muzzle and then ram a round ball (usually of lead) after it in order to seat the ball against the powder charge at the bottom of the barrel (the breach). The ball was wrapped in a cloth wad to ensure a tight fit between ball and barrel and hold the ball in place next to the powder. The individual would ignite the powder charge by means of a slow-burning match applied to the small hole (touch hole) in the top of the breach end of the barrel over the charge.

Until the mid-19th century and the introduction of a new cylindro-conoidal bullet in a rifled barrel, all individual firearms were basically the same: smoothbore muzzle loaders that differed only in the means of their ignition. Improvements in the firing process, however, came steadily after the gun's first appearance. The hand gonne, culverin, or culiver (there are a bewildering number of names for early firearms) gave way to the harquebus or arquebus (a late-16th-century term for any type of long individual firearm) and firelocks.

Shoulder stocks appeared around 1470. By the early 1500s, handheld firearms were on the battlefield to stay, accompanied by the invention of a new wheel-lock mechanism. Pistols made their appearance about 1540, and later that same decade the snap lock appeared. By the first decade of the 17th century and the beginning of European settlement of North America, a true flintlock had emerged. Flintlocks were in widespread use by 1650, and by the end of the century they largely had replaced the matchlock, at least in Europe.

As with most individual firearms through at least the mid-19th century, the matchlock successor to the hand gonne had a long wooden stock. One end of the stock fitted against the individual's shoulder, and the stock itself held the cast-iron barrel and firing mechanism. Unlike the primitive hand gonne, the matchlock had a trigger mechanism. When the trigger was pulled, its mechanism plunged the glowing tip of a slow match into priming powder in a pan, which then ignited the main charge in the barrel. A great many varieties of matchlocks existed, but in most cases the priming pan had to be opened by hand before the trigger was pulled.

Matchlocks did not immediately supplant bows or crossbows. The match proved susceptible to rain and wind and could reveal troop positions at night, inhibiting ambushes and surprise attacks. Matchlocks nonetheless initially had great psychological impact, especially in colonial America against natives. The Native Americans, however, soon overcame their fear of the great smoke, noise, and flame that accompanied the firing of these weapons, and before long they were trading for or capturing matchlocks for themselves.

Among its drawbacks, the matchlock was far slower to load and fire than either the longbow or the crossbow. The matchlock also could not compete with the longbow and the crossbow in terms of accuracy. There was also the concern of an accidental discharge.

The wheel lock improved on the matchlock, but its firing mechanism was very complicated. In the wheel lock, pressing the trigger caused the cover over the pan containing the powder to slide forward. At the same time, iron pyrites known as the spanner, clamped into a cock or dog-head, brushed against a rough-edged wheel as the latter turned, creating sparks that ignited the exposed priming powder. The great expense of the wheel lock meant that it never completely supplanted the matchlock for military use. Wheel locks were not uncommon in America and are known to have been present in the lost colony of Roanoke.

The snap lock was an important step forward from the wheel lock. The snap lock employed flint and steel for the first time. Pulling the trigger opened the pan cover, while at the same time the cock swung forward, scraping the flint against the face of a piece of upright steel, pushing it forward and causing sparks to fall in the exposed pan below.

The flintlock, the last musket of the colonial period, was merely a refinement of the snap lock in which the steel and pan cover were of one piece. Simple and effective, the flintlock replaced both the matchlock and the wheel lock. The flintlock was more reliable and was also far easier to load, safer, and could be carried for a distance. Flintlock firing employed the following procedure: half-cock the weapon (putting it on safety, the origin of the phrase "Don't go off half-cocked"); take out the cartridge and bite off the paper at the

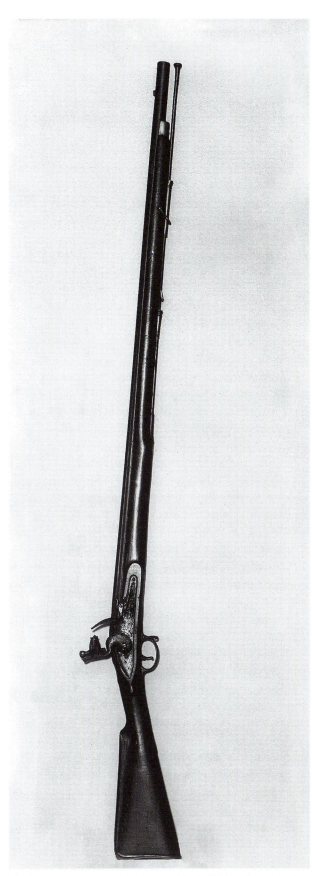

The Brown Bess musket, probably named for its finish or "browning," was the standard infantry firearm of the British Army during most of the 18th century and the first half of the 19th century. (National Archives)

Firing Mechanisms of Colonial Muskets

Type	Mechanism
Matchlock	Tip of slow match plunged into priming powder
Wheel lock	Piece of iron pyrite struck against rotating wheel, creating sparks to ignite powder
Snap lock	Piece of flint struck against steel, creating sparks to ignite powder
Flintlock	Refinement of snap lock, with steel and powder pan cover one piece

top, pouring a small bit of powder into the pan; ram the remaining powder, paper, and ball down the bore; put the musket on full cock; and pull the trigger. Here the lock struck the flint, producing a spark in the powder pan. The cover, or *frissen,* kept the powder dry and prevented it from falling out of the pan and opened when the flint moved forward. (The term "flash in the pan," where there is a sign of something and yet not the desired result, comes from a misfire where there would be a flash only.) The resulting flash raced through the touch hole into the barrel, and the gun fired.

A well-trained soldier could fire three or perhaps four shots a minute from his flintlock. Even so, the flintlock musket was a highly inaccurate and rather unreliable weapon. With the French flintlock musket, 1 misfire might be expected in every 9 shots and 1 hang fire in every 18 shots. The flint had to be changed every 30 shots or so.

The soft lead bullet moving at a relatively low velocity had great knockdown power. As soon as it struck any resistant object, such as human flesh, it began to spread, creating frightful wounds. Because this so often removed chunks of bone, amputations remained a common occurrence.

Despite the advance made with flintlocks, European armies did not immediately forgo the matchlock or the wheel lock. In fact, all three weapons were routinely integrated along with pikes. Well into the 17th century, governments did little to standardize firearm specifications or production. Despite this, the flintlock came to dominate Western armies by the 18th century.

The main drawback to the flintlock was its lack of accuracy. Its great windage (the difference between the diameter of the bore and the diameter of the ball being fired) meant that such weapons were inherently inaccurate. Soldiers could not reliably hit a man-sized target beyond 80 yards. Substantial windage was necessary because of the slightly irregular bullet and the considerable buildup of residue in the barrel from the burning of the black powder. As a result, the bullet actually bounded down the bore (known as balloting) and might take flight from the muzzle of the weapon at an undesired angle.

The inaccuracy in fire meant that most battles between infantry took place at near–dueling pistol range. In firing tactics, commanders sought to mass as many muskets as possible in a short length of firing line, expecting that sheer volume of fire would overcome inaccuracy. The result could be frightful numbers of casualties.

Spain was the first nation to introduce firearms in the Western Hemisphere. Indeed, the word "musket" comes from the Spanish *mosquete.* During his exploration of the Caribbean in the 1490s, Christopher Columbus employed primitive hand cannon.

Under the reign of Holy Roman Emperor Charles V (1519–1556, also king of Spain as Charles I during 1516–1556), the Spanish arms industry greatly expanded. The Spanish are credited with two significant contributions to firearm design. First, the trigger mechanism commonly used on the crossbow was applied to the musket. Second, wooden stocks were designed so that a musket could be fired not braced against the chest as was customary but rather pressed against the shoulder. The latter method allowed better aim and a greater absorption of recoil.

The common Spanish firearm was the *escopeta,* or light musket. Used by both infantry and cavalry, the *escopeta* was also employed by civilians. Unlike mainline army regiments, however, presidios and frontier outposts remained persistently underequipped. Reportedly, in all of New Mexico in 1772 there were only 250 firearms. The variety of calibers and the lack of spare parts also proved a constant problem. As a result, the Spanish tended to retain and repeatedly refurbish older weapons. Cases of 17th-century muskets being used in the 19th century were not uncommon.

The Spanish government did not officially adopt a military musket until the mid-18th century. Heavily influenced by French and German design, its Model 1751 was the first standardized shoulder weapon of the Spanish Army until replaced by the Model 1791.

Like the Spanish, the French did not adopt a standardized infantry musket until the 18th century. Initially, arms used by French troops remained at the discretion of individual commanders as long as the weapons were flintlocks. The French, who officially abandoned the matchlock in 1699, did not adopt a regulation flintlock musket until 1717. Produced in factories at St. Étienne, Maubeuge, Brescia, Tulle, and Charleville (Nozon Manufactory), French muskets were stamped with their place of manufacture. These weapons were routinely all known as Charlevilles. The Model 1717, unlike British and Spanish muskets, underwent numerous changes and modifications during the colonial period. For example, in 1728 metal bands replaced pins to secure the barrel in its wooden stock, making the barrel easier to remove. In 1746 a metal ramrod replaced the older wooden one.

The 1768 model Charleville was lightened and known as the Léger. French armories produced some 150,000 of them. It was a .69-caliber weapon with a barrel length of 44.75 inches and an overall length of 60 inches and weighed 9.47 pounds. The French shipped large numbers of the model to America, and it was the principal musket of the Continental Army in the American Revolutionary War (1775–1783). Later the Charleville formed the basis of the first U.S. military musket, the Model 1795. The French generally produced high-quality muskets, and theirs remained throughout the colonial period second in quality perhaps only to British weapons.

The British, like their Spanish and French counterparts, did not adopt a standardized military musket until the 18th century. Even as late as the 1720s, British regiments purchased their own firearms. Under Queen Anne (r. 1702–1714), however, the British Army officially adopted a standardized shoulder weapon, the so-called Brown Bess. Perhaps the most famous flintlock musket of the colonial period, it may have taken its name from the term "browning," the process whereby the iron barrel was treated. "Bess" may have been a corruption of the German word *büsche,* meaning "gun," or it may have been simply a soldier's nickname. The Brown Bess was introduced into the British Army in 1720 and remained in service until the 1840s. All models were .75 caliber (three-quarters of an inch or 19 millimeters), but barrel length varied. The Long Land musket common to 1760 had a barrel that was 46 inches long, whereas the Short Land model, or Second Model, thereafter had a barrel that was 42 inches long and an overall length of 58.25 inches and weighed 8.8 pounds. The lock for both had a goosenecked cock with a convex surface. The Brown Bess mounted a 17-inch bayonet.

Besides the standard military musket, other types of shoulder weapons found in the colonies included carbines, musketoons, and blunderbusses. Carbines and musketoons were shorter muskets generally intended for so-called light infantry and cavalry and for use aboard ships. No standard archetype of either weapon existed in the colonial period, but most had barrels that measured from 28 to 42 inches in length. Sometimes carbines were rifled. The need for portable shoulder arms in the American woodlands, particularly during the French and Indian War (1754–1763), forced the British military to consider the feasibility of officially adopting such weapons.

The blunderbuss was a large-caliber weapon with a short barrel and a distinctive flaring muzzle. Introduced to England from Holland in the mid-17th century, the blunderbuss was specifically designed to spray a large number of pellets at close range. For this reason, it was the preferred weapon of naval boarding parties and coach guards. At sea, large blunderbusses known as boat guns (often mounted on swivels) could fire up to one pound of shot. Contrary to myth, blunderbusses did not see widespread use in the North American colonies.

One technological innovation that never became widely adopted during the colonial period was the breechloader. Borrowing a concept first used by experiments with early artillery pieces, it was rightly believed that loading a weapon from the breech (rather than the muzzle) would prove more efficient for the soldier. However, despite widespread attempts to develop a viable breechloader, the tolerances necessary were simply not possible with the primitive metallurgical technology of the day. Gases escaping from the breech remained a serious problem for the individual doing the firing. Expense was another factor. As a result, European and American military forces continued to employ the standard muzzle loader well into the 19th century.

A common firearm in the British colonies, the fowler (also referred to as the Kentucky, American, or, most frequently, the Pennsylvania rifle) was a musket with an extra long barrel. Sometimes these barrels were more than seven feet in length. The Pennsylvania Rifle was actually based on a hunting piece introduced by German immigrants. A superb firearm with an effective range of up to 200 yards, the rifle greatly outdistanced the military musket. What made this firearm so lethal was rifling, one of the greatest innovations in the history of weapons technology.

Rifling, or lateral, twisting grooves inside the barrel that imparted a spin to the bullet had been introduced into firearms in Europe by 1550. By spinning a bullet on discharge, rifling allowed bullets to be fired from a weapon with much greater accuracy and distance.

Despite their advantages, most armies did not employ the rifle in any large numbers. The exceptions were specialized units of riflemen formed in the Continental Army during the American Revolutionary War.

Rifled firearms were costly, and they were difficult to load. In order for the rifling to take effect, windage was sharply reduced, and the ball had to be rammed hard down the bore, a time-consuming and more difficult process. Also, because European armies continued to fight in closely compacted ranks at close range throughout the 18th century, accuracy was never a serious concern. Thus, throughout the colonial period, rifles tended to be used primarily by civilians as hunting weapons, whereas smoothbore muskets tended to be used primarily by the military. Muskets gave way to rifles as the weapons of choice of the American military by the mid-1850s and were soon adopted by many Native Americans. This development had been made possible by the introduction of the easily loaded cylindo-conoidal lead bullet, known as the minié ball, and the percussion cap.

Over time the British North American colonies inadvertently acquired a diverse collection of shoulder weapons. Old parts were repeatedly reused and refurbished. More often than not, colonials owned one weapon that served as both a hunting and a militia piece.

Frank Harper and Spencer C. Tucker

See also

Artillery; Edged Weapons; Pistols; Rifles

References

Blair, Claude, ed. *Pollard's History of Firearms.* New York: Macmillan, 1983.

Brinckerhoff, Sidney B., and Pierce A. Chamberlain. *Spanish Military Weapons in Colonial America, 1700–1821.* Harrisburg, PA: Stackpole, 1972.

Brown, M. L. *Firearms in Colonial America: The Impact on History and Technology, 1492–1792.* Washington, DC: Smithsonian Institution Press, 1980.

Lenk, Torsten. *The Flintlock: Its Origin and Development.* New York: Bramhall House, 1965.

Peterson, Harold L. *Arms and Armor in Colonial America, 1526–1783.* Harrisburg, PA: Stackpole, 1956.

Mystic Fort Fight
Event Date: May 26, 1637

Assault on a palisaded Pequot community near the Mystic River in southeastern Connecticut on May 26, 1637. The attack was carried out by a force of English settlers and their Native American allies. The Mystic Fort Fight became the central event of the Pequot War (1636–1638); resulted in the immediate deaths of hundreds of men, women, and children; and led to the longer-term subjugation of the tribe to the Mohegans and the Narragansetts. These two tribes had assisted the English colonists.

Following the outbreak of the conflict with the Endicott Expedition of September 1636, hostilities for the next six months revolved around Pequot harassment of the English at Fort Saybrook at the mouth of the Connecticut River. But in late April 1637 Pequot warriors raided Wethersfield, an English settlement farther up the river, killing six men, three women, and much livestock and capturing two girls. A week later, on May 1, the General Court of the Connecticut Colony declared "offensive war" on the Pequots and duly sent 90 men under Captain John Mason on a retaliatory mission.

Shortly thereafter, Mason's force arrived at Fort Saybrook accompanied by a number of Mohegan warriors under their leader Uncas. There Mason met a smaller group of 20 men under Captain John Underhill, sent out by the colony of Massachusetts.

Mason's original orders specified that he attack the main Native American settlement on the Pequot River (present-day Thames River). However, after considering the difficulties of such an attack and in consultation with other officers and the expedition's cleric, Mason decided to move his force to Narragansett Bay. From there he planned to attack another large fortified Pequot settlement on the Mystic River.

On the evening of May 23, 1637, Mason landed with about 70 men from Connecticut, 19 men from Massachusetts, and some 70 Mohegan warriors. He negotiated with Miantonomo and other Narragansett leaders to pass through their lands and marched his forces westward the following day. The English and the Mohegans then encamped outside and surrounded an Eastern Niantic village, a precaution to ensure that no one alerted the Pequots of their approach and also because of the Niantics' antagonistic attitudes.

On the morning of May 25 several hundred Narragansett warriors joined Mason's expedition. The weather was hot, and the march was a difficult one. Many of the Narragansetts abandoned Mason when his forces reached the Pawtucket River, which was their boundary with Pequot land.

The men rested during the night and then began their attack around daybreak on May 26, 1637. The attackers first surrounded the village and fired a musket volley, surprising the sleeping Pequots inside. Then the men—divided into two forces, one each under Mason and Underhill—simultaneously assaulted the two entrances in the palisade. The Pequots defended themselves with bows and arrows and in hand-to-hand combat. Although the original English intention was to kill the inhabitants, the attackers found the struggle difficult in the tight quarters among the Pequot wigwams, leading their commanders to decide to set fire to the village. The conflagration soon engulfed the settlement, with numerous Pequots dying in the blaze and many warriors fighting to the last. Other Pequots fled the village, but almost all of those attempting to escape were slain by the English or their Native American allies.

Combat did not end with the destruction of the Mystic village, however. Mason's force then had to continue on to the Pequot River to rendezvous with its ships. During the march, warriors from the other main Pequot settlement attacked, although the English managed to keep them at bay. Mason's march was slowed by the exhaustion of his men and the need to transport the wounded. The English reached their ships later that day.

English casualties for the campaign amounted to 2 killed and 20 wounded; casualties among the accompanying Mohegan and Narragansett warriors are unknown. Estimates of Pequots slain at Mystic range from 400 to 700 people. Mason claimed that only 7 were taken captive and that probably a like number escaped. Pequots elsewhere scattered after the assault, with many later being hunted down by the English and their native allies. Although these operations did not result in the wholesale slaughter witnessed at Mystic, hundreds of Pequots were forced into servitude by the English or were incorporated into the Narragansett and Mohegan tribes.

MATTHEW S. MUEHLBAUER

See also
Endicott, John; Endicott Expedition; Mason, John; Miantonomo; Mohegans; Narragansetts; Pequots; Pequot War; Uncas; Underhill, John

References
Cave, Alfred A. *The Pequot War.* Amherst: University of Massachusetts Press, 1996.

Hirsch, Adam J. "The Collision of Military Cultures in Seventeenth-Century New England." *Journal of American History* 74 (March 1988): 1187–1212.

Karr, Ronald Dale. "'Why Should You Be So Furious?': The Violence of the Pequot War." *Journal of American History* 85 (1998): 876–909.

Orr, Charles. *History of the Pequot War: The Contemporary Accounts of Mason, Underhill, Vincent and Gardener.* Cleveland, OH: Helman-Taylor, 1897.

N

Nakoni Comanches

A significant band of Comanches who spoke a language related to the Uto-Aztecan linguistic family. After the Comanches migrated south and east from the Rocky Mountains around 1700, they split from the Shoshones and moved toward Nebraska's North Platte River Valley. As the Comanches moved toward Texas and Oklahoma, they warred with nearly every tribe they came in contact with. They also conducted raids on Spanish settlements.

The Nakonis were known as Nawyehkuh or Nawkohnee ("Those Who Turn Back"). They later changed their name to Dertsahmaw-yekkuh ("Wanderers"). The Nakonis' range was from the Rocky Mountains to Cross Timbers, west of present-day Fort Worth, Texas. Having acquired the horse in the early 1700s, the Comanches became some of the greatest horsemen on the Plains. They moved constantly and covered long distances within just a few days. The Nakonis could also be found in the Colorado plateau or along the banks of the Red River or near Santa Fe in the New Mexico Territory. Like all of the Comanches, the Nakonis' economic system and subsistence patterns were highly dependent upon the buffalo. Indeed, buffalo provided for most of their food, clothing, and shelter needs and also drove their trade with other tribes and white settlers. Horse trading also became a significant component of the Comanche economy.

As with all major Comanche bands, the Nakonis were numerous enough to survive without needing the other bands to replenish their numbers. By 1850 they and their fellow Comanches had all but eliminated or driven out their foes, and few of the neighboring peoples dared to encroach on Comanche lands, which were sizable. The Apaches and Tonkawas lived at the southwestern edge of Comanche territory by the Big Bend Mountains. The Cheyennes and Pawnees were north of the Arkansas River. The Wichitas were the only group that dared to venture close to Comanche lands but were not strong enough to challenge the Comanches. The Kiowas presented the greatest potential challenge, but the Comanches and Kiowas formed a durable if not always friendly alliance that prevented serious conflict between the two formidable tribes.

With their territory enlarged and free from enemies, the Nakonis were able to wander over a vast area without fear of powerful foes. As with other Comanches, they developed their own interests. Although the Nakonis had little contact with other Comanche bands and in spite of their constant wandering, they were able to retain their traditional culture. Like their fellow Comanches, the Nakonis raided Spanish (later Mexican) territory for captives and plunder.

From 1750 to the 1830s, the territory of the Nakonis and their fellow Comanches ranged from the Arkansas River to the Rio Grande in Texas and west almost to the base of the Rockies in New Mexico to the eastern edge of the Plains in Oklahoma and Texas. This was called Comancheria, and its center was the Llano Estacado, or Staked Plains, the flatlands and canyons of the Texas Panhandle. The Nakonis, along with their fellow Comanches, enjoyed considerable freedom and gained respect from tribes outside Comancheria.

Prolific raiders and aggressive warriors, the Comanches terrorized settlements along the Texas frontier. They also drew clear distinctions between Texans and other whites, considering Texans fair game despite treaties with the federal government. In the autumn of 1860 the Nakonis invited trouble for themselves when Peta Nacona and Nakoni warriors raided deep into Parker County, Texas. They found the inhabitants well armed and well organized and were forced to retreat. Peta Nacona and his warriors fled west into the High Plains. Nokoni warriors participated in numerous engagements, including the First Battle of Adobe Walls (November 25, 1864) and the Second Battle of Adobe Walls (June 27, 1874). By 1875 with the success of the U.S. Army's Red River campaign, which rooted the Comanches from their camps on the forbidding Staked Plains, the Nakonis were confined to their reservation in Indian Territory (Oklahoma).

JOHN THOMAS BROOM

See also
Comanches

References
Ferhenbach, T. R. *Comanches: The History of a People.* New York: Anchor Books, 2003.
Hoig, Stan. *Tribal Wars of the Southern Plains.* Norman: University of Oklahoma Press, 1993.
LaVere, David. *Contrary Neighbors: Southern Plains and Removed Indians in Indian Territory.* Norman: University of Oklahoma Press, 2000.
Wallace, Ernest, and E. Adamson Hoebel. *The Comanches: Lords of the South Plains.* 1952; reprint, Norman: University of Oklahoma Press, 1986.

Nakota Sioux

Group of Siouan Native Americans who initially lived in present-day Minnesota and Wisconsin and then migrated west and south onto the Great Plains. The name "Nakota" is from a Siouan dialect spoken by the central group—whose divisions include the Yankton ("end village") and Yanktonai ("little end village") peoples—of the tribe commonly referred to as Sioux. The Yanktonais were divided into upper Yanktonais and lower Yanktonais (Hunkpatinas), from which the Assiniboine/Stoney Native American nation was derived. Nakota is a dialect of Dakota, a Siouan language. "Nakota" means friend or ally, while "Stoney" is the name given to them by white explorers for their use of heated rocks to boil broth.

The Yanktons were organized into eight bands. The upper Yanktonais consisted of six bands, and the Hunkpatinas had seven bands. The governing band council was composed of band chiefs and clan leaders. The Seven Council Fires met approximately annually to socialize and discuss matters of tribal importance. Nakota bands were composed of patrilineal clans.

Small villages were located near lakes and rice swamps when the people lived in the Wisconsin-Minnesota area. While the Nakota Sioux were still in the Great Lakes region, women grew corn, beans, and squash. People also gathered wild rice and ate turtles, fish, and dogs. Large and small game, especially buffalo, which roamed the area in small herds, were also important food sources. With the westward migration, buffalo became increasingly important, although men still hunted deer, elk, and antelope. Women also grew some corn, beans, and squash along river bottomlands and gathered fruits and berries.

As the Missouri River trade developed, the Yanktons controlled the catlinite, or red pipestone, quarry in southwestern Minnesota, supplying its clay to most of the northern Plains groups. During the early 19th century the Yanktonais traded along the Jones River, acting as intermediaries for British goods between the Sisseton and Wahpeton Dakotas and the Tetons farther west.

Dakota-Lakota-Nakota speakers once ranged throughout more than 100 million acres in the upper Mississippi River region, including Minnesota and parts of Wisconsin, Iowa, and the Dakotas, in the 16th to early 17th centuries. At this time the Yanktons and Yanktonais were one tribe, the Assiniboines having separated from them probably by the mid-16th century.

French explorers encountered eastern group tribes around Mille Lacs, Minnesota, in the late 17th century. Shortly afterward the latter probably became directly involved in the fur trade. But conflict with the Crees and Ojibwas, who were well armed with French muskets, in addition to the lure of great buffalo herds to feed their expanding population induced bands to begin moving west onto the Plains.

The Yanktons and Yanktonais separated near Leech Lake in the late 17th century. The Yanktons had moved out of the northern woodlands and onto the southern prairies (near the pipestone quarries of southwestern Minnesota and then west of the Missouri in northwestern Iowa) by the early 18th century. A hundred years later the Yanktons ranged north and northwest into Minnesota and South Dakota.

Portrait of Yanktonai Sioux Yellow Horse. Photograph by Edward S. Curtis, circa 1908. (Library of Congress)

Meanwhile, the Yanktonais left their homes in Mille Lacs by the early 18th century to follow Teton tribes west, making winter villages on the James River (South Dakota) at least as early as 1725. The Yanktonais acquired horses in the mid to late 18th century. By the early 19th century the Yanktonais were hunting buffalo between the Red and Missouri rivers and north to Devils Lake.

A general Yankton decline began during the 1830s. Its causes were smallpox, the growing scarcity of game, and war, particularly with the Pawnees, Otoes, and Omahas. The Yanktons ceded their Iowa lands (2.2 million acres) to the United States in 1830 and 1837 and ceded more than 11 million acres in 1858. They did retain a 430,000-acre reservation near Fort Randall, South Dakota. They also claimed the 650-acre Pipestone Reservation in Minnesota.

By 1860 the Yanktons had ceded all of their remaining lands. Most moved to the Yankton Reservation in South Dakota; others went to the Crow Creek and Lower Brulé reservations in South Dakota and to the Fort Totten (now Devils Lake) Reservation in North Dakota. Yanktons and particularly Yanktonais participated in the Minnesota Sioux Uprising of 1862 and associated conflicts that flared through 1865. The Yanktonais ceded their remaining lands in 1865. They were removed to a number of reservations, including Standing Rock (South Dakota), Devils Lake (North Dakota), Crow Creek (South Dakota), and Fort Peck (Montana). In 1866 they replaced the Santees at Crow Creek when the latter were moved to Nebraska. The Yanktons sold the Pipestone Reservation in 1929 for almost $330,000 plus guarantees of continued access.

BARRY M. PRITZKER

See also

Dakota Sioux; Lakota Sioux; Sioux

References

Carlson, Paul H. *The Plains Indians.* College Station: Texas A&M University Press, 1998.

Gibbon, Guy. *The Sioux: The Dakota and Lakota Nations.* Malden, MA: Blackwell, 2003.

Nansemonds

An Algonquian-speaking Native American tribe inhabiting an area south of the James River in eastern Virginia. The Nansemonds lived in villages along both sides of the Nansemond River near the present-day city of Suffolk. Their chief (*werowance*) lived near Dumpling Island on the Nansemond River in the vicinity of Chuck-atuck. The Nansemonds' way of life was similar to that of other natives of the Eastern Woodlands. They lived a semisedentary existence, moving closer to food supplies based on the season. They also engaged in small-scale agriculture; corn cultivation was an important part of their subsistence. The men engaged in hunting, fishing, and war, while the women tended gardens and performed domestic chores.

At the time of the founding of Jamestown in 1607, the Nansemonds could muster about 300 warriors from a population estimated to have numbered about 1,200. Prior to the arrival of the English, the tribe had been defeated by Chief Powhatan, who compelled the Nansemonds to join the Powhatan Confederacy.

The earliest Nansemond encounters with the English were hostile because of raids carried out by the latter on Nansemond villages. Captain John Smith wrote that two English emissaries had been sent to negotiate the purchase of an island from the Nansemonds in 1608; however, they were tortured and killed. Led by captains John Martin and George Percy, the English in reprisal drove the Nansemonds off the island, burned their dwellings and assembly buildings, stole their corn supplies, and desecrated the resting places of their dead. As English settlers moved into the area of the Nansemond River to farm the rich land there, fierce Nansemond resistance continued. In March 1622 the Nansemonds participated in the native uprising that precipitated the Second Anglo-Powhatan War (1622–1632).

The Nansemonds temporarily mitigated their hostility toward the English in 1638. That year saw the colonist John Bass marrying a Nansemond woman. Converted to Christianity, she was given the baptismal name of Elizabeth. It is believed that everyone in today's Nansemond tribe is descended from that marriage. The unconverted Nansemonds remained hostile toward the English, making war against them again in 1644 during the wider Third Anglo-Powhatan War (1644–1646). After the conflict they fled southwest toward the Nottoway River. There the Virginia colonial government assigned them a reservation in the Hampton Roads area. In the late 1600s the Nansemonds split into two main groups. The Christianized Nansemonds remained along the Nansemond River as English-style farmers. The others stayed on the land reserved for them. After 1744 the reservation was abandoned because the Nansemonds preferred living with the Nottoways on the Nottoway reservation. The old Nansemond reservation was sold in 1792, and the last of these Nansemonds died on the Nottoway reservation in 1806.

The Christianized Nansemonds subsequently moved to an area northeast of the Great Dismal Swamp in far southeastern Virginia. The area had few English settlers and was well suited to their way of life. On May 29, 1677, the Nansemonds along with the Pamunkeys and the Appomattocks signed a peace treaty with the English. By this agreement, known as the Treaty of Middle Plantation and also known as the Virginia-Indian Treaty of 1677/1680, they became tributaries of the English Crown. A small number of Nansemonds still inhabit parts of Tidewater Virginia, mainly the Chesapeake and Suffolk areas; their tribal offices are located in Portsmouth. Until the mid-20th century, the Nansemonds operated their own tribal secondary school, the site of which is now a United Methodist Church still in use as a gathering place for remaining Nansemonds.

ANDREW J. WASKEY

See also

Anglo-Powhatan War, Second; Anglo-Powhatan War, Third; Nottoways; Powhatan; Powhatan Confederacy; Smith, John; Virginia-Indian Treaty of 1677/1680

References

Rountree, Helen C. *Pocahontas's People: The Powhatan Indians of Virginia through Four Centuries.* Norman: University of Oklahoma Press, 1990.

Smith, John. *Travels and Works of Captain John Smith, President of Virginia and Admiral of New England, 1580–1631.* 2 vols. Edited by Edward Arber. Edinburgh, UK: John Grant, 1910.

Nanunteeno

See Canonchet

Narragansetts

Powerful Native American group inhabiting southeastern New England. The Narragansetts lived in present-day Rhode Island, although their authority frequently extended south to Long Island and Block Island. Other area tribes that fell under Narragansett control were the Pawtuxets, the Niantics, the Manisseans, the Cowesets, and the Shawomets. Some Nipmucks and Montauks were also beholden to the Narragansett sachems (chiefs). The Narragansetts came to be known by Europeans through their relationship with Rhode Island founder Roger Williams. Williams was exiled from Massachusetts Bay because of his unconventional ideas, especially in regard to religion. His relationship with the Narragansetts helped him pen *A Key into the Language of America,* written in 1643. It is from this account that much of the knowledge of the Narragansetts is derived.

The Narragansetts spoke an eastern Algonquian language and were governed politically by two sachems, usually an uncle and a nephew. In addition to cultivating maize, squash, beans, and similar crops, the Narragansetts fished and hunted. Because wampum was usually made of shells, the abundance of quahogs (a large clam indigenous to the Northeast) and whelks ensured that the Narragansetts dominated the wampum trade. Indeed, by the mid-1620s the tribe had grown quite wealthy. Wampum was often used as currency for trade, gifts, and even diplomacy, allowing the Narragansetts to develop strong trading ties and tributary relationships with other tribes in New England. When English settlement developed in the 1620s, the Narragansetts were thus quite powerful. Fortunately for them, they had avoided the devastating epidemics of 1616–1619 that had diminished many Native American nations.

During the Pequot War (1636–1638), Williams persuaded the Narragansetts to ally with Massachusetts Bay. The English were intent on a preemptive attack against the Pequots, and Narragansett assistance was critical. Accompanying the English to Mystic Fort in 1637, Narragansett warriors were appalled by the behavior of the English, who burned the entire village. Most Pequot adult males were away from Mystic preparing for war, so primarily women and children remained. As the village burned, fleeing survivors were shot outside the walls. The Mystic Fort Fight killed as many as 700 Pequots and essentially annihilated the tribe. During the fighting, the English had attacked some 20 Narragansetts in the mistaken belief that they were Pequots.

In the 1640s the colonies of Massachusetts, Connecticut, and Plymouth formed the New England Confederation. The loose union was meant to be a military alliance. In 1643 when Narragansett sachem Miantonomo sold a large parcel of land to an enemy of the Puritans, the confederation-allied Mohegans murdered him. Threatened with war, the Narragansetts submitted to the power of the English king but not to the colonists. However, in 1644 a treaty between the two groups placed the Narragansetts in a subordinate position, and they continued to lose ancestral lands to the colonists.

The English continued to covet native lands into the 1670s. Wampanoag leader Metacom, also known as King Philip, organized attacks against the English settlements. In July 1675 the Wampanoags attacked outlying settlements of Plymouth Colony, sparking King Philip's War (1675–1676). Following Metacom's initial success, other tribes joined in the attacks against remote colonial towns. Although the Narragansetts tried to remain neutral while covertly aiding the Wampanoags, the English managed to drag them into the fighting. In retaliation for native attacks, the English organized a force of some 1,000 men who attacked the Narragansetts in late 1675. This offensive culminated in the devastating Great Swamp Fight (December 19, 1675) that devastated the tribe, with more than 600 Narragansetts killed. At least 300 more became prisoners.

The Great Swamp Fight was one of the bloodiest battles of the war and deeply demoralized the tribe, although afterward the Narragansetts openly assisted Metacom. King Philip's War raged on with sporadic attacks until the spring of 1676. Hunger and disease drove many warriors from the field, and Metacom was killed during the summer. Afterward the English sold many of the native captives into slavery and imposed strict regulations on those who remained.

After King Philip's War, the Narragansetts ceased to exist as an independent entity as they joined together with the Niantics, Abenakis, and Mahicans. During the next two centuries the Narragansetts assimilated into American society as the only way to survive. The language and the last full-blooded Narragansetts died in the 1800s. Although the Narragansetts were detribalized in 1880, activists were able to gain recognition of the tribe in 1983.

SARAH E. MILLER

See also

Abenakis; Great Swamp Fight; King Philip's War; Mahicans; Metacom; Miantonomo; Mystic Fort Fight; Nipmucks; Pequots; Pequot War; Wampanoags; Wampum; Williams, Roger

References

Cave, Alfred A. *The Pequot War.* Amherst: University of Massachusetts Press, 1996.

Nash, Gary B. *Red, White and Black: The Peoples of Early North America.* 4th ed. Upper Saddle River, NJ: Prentice Hall, 2000.

Sylvester, Herbert Milton. *Indian Wars of New England,* Vol. 1. Cleveland, OH: Arthur H. Clark, 1910.

Narragansett Treaty of 1675

See Pettaquamscutt Rock, Treaty of

Narváez, Pánfilo de

Birth Date: ca. 1480
Death Date: November 1528

Spanish explorer and conquistador who led an ill-fated expedition to Florida in the early 16th century. Pánfilo de Narváez was born in Tidels or Valladolid, Spain, probably in 1480. As a conquistador, Narváez assisted in the conquest of the island of Cuba in 1511. In 1519 on the orders of the Spanish governor of Cuba, Juan Velasquez, Narváez tried unsuccessfully to seize and imprison Hernán Cortés and claim Mexico for Velasquez. This dispute was adjudicated by the Spanish king Charles V, who took the side of Cortés but granted Narváez land in southeastern North America in 1526.

In 1528 while sailing to the northern Gulf Coast to claim his grant, Narváez accidentally landed on the western coast of Florida after a storm drove his fleet of five ships off the coast of Cuba. Narváez decided to land to replenish his water supply and take advantage of the unintended detour to explore. He set out northward, believing that he was headed toward Bahía Honda (Tampa Bay). Not realizing that he was already north of the location he intended to explore, he marched his 300 men north after he sent his ships ahead to meet them. He never saw the ships again. Narváez's men arrived at the Withlacoochee River, but not finding a bay at its mouth, they headed inland along the river. The party encountered several Timucua villages, and from there they headed north in northwestern Florida.

In territory settled by the Apalachees, Narváez found the natives more numerous and food resources more abundant, but there was no gold. On encountering the first Apalachee village, Narváez ordered an immediate attack. From that point forward, however, the Spanish remained under constant attack by the Apalachees.

Finally low on supplies, the expedition headed west to the coast in the hopes of meeting its ships. When the men reached the Gulf of Mexico the ships were nowhere to be seen, so they built rafts and tried to reach Mexico by sailing along the coastline. During a sudden storm in November 1528, Narváez, who was offshore on a raft, was suddenly swept out to sea and lost. Only a handful of survivors of the expedition finally made it to Mexico after wandering for several years in what is today the southwestern United States

and northern Mexico. One of these men, Álvar Núñez Cabeza de Vaca, published a record of their travails, and this narrative later inspired Hernando de Soto to explore the Southeast and Francisco Coronado to explore the Southwest in attempts to locate the rich lands and cities of gold that Cabeza de Vaca claimed in his narrative to exist. Another survivor of the Narváez debacle, Juan Ortiz, was later found in Florida by the de Soto expedition and proved to be an invaluable guide and translator.

Dixie Ray Haggard

See also

Apalachees; Coronado, Francisco Vásquez de; Soto, Hernando de

References

Cabeza de Vaca, Álvar Núñez. *The Narrative of Cabeza de Vaca.* Edited, translated, and with an introduction by Rolena Adorno and Patrick Charles Pautz. Lincoln: University of Nebraska Press, 2003.

Weber, David J. *The Spanish Frontier in North America.* New Haven, CT: Yale University Press, 1992.

Natchezes

Native American group inhabiting the southwestern part of the present-day state of Mississippi. The center of Natchez culture was present-day Natchez, Mississippi. The Natchez language, related to the Muskogean language family, indicates that the Natchezes were related to other Native American groups in the lower Mississippi River Valley. The word "Natchez" was applied by the Europeans to the people as well as their principal settlement. The Natchez people were successful farmers and grew corn, beans, and squash. They also hunted and fished.

Hernando de Soto was the first European to encounter the tribe, which occurred in 1543. The nation was first designated Natchez in March 1682 when René-Robert Cavelier, Sieur de La Salle, descended the Mississippi River. In the Natchez tribe La Salle found the strongest Native American nation in the area. Of the American Indian groups to survive the wars and disease that came with de Soto's arrival, the Natchezes retained much of their Mississippian mound-building culture, the monarchy, and their so-called Sun Caste.

Natchez society was organized as a chiefdom, which was highly stratified and organized into nobles and commoners. The highest level was known as the Sun Caste. Social standing was determined through the female line. The Natchez chief, known as the Great Sun, inherited his position from his mother's family. Natchez kings were afforded every honor, such as being transported on a litter wherever they went. Indeed, no king's feet were allowed to touch the ground in travel. When a member of the Sun Caste died, many of his family and friends were buried with him in ritual sacrifice.

The Natchez people were mound builders. This had to do with their tribal religion, and they erected sacred buildings on these flat-topped ceremonial mounds. Periodically the dispersed Natchez families gathered at the mounds for social and religious events.

Illustration of Natchez porters transporting a tribal leader; from *Histoire de la Louisiane*, 1758. (Library of Congress)

As with other Native Americans, the Natchezes fell prey to the consequences of contact with the Europeans and their diseases. Indeed, disease accounted for far more casualties than did war. To replace their dwindling numbers, the Natchezes turned to the custom of incorporating smaller groups into their nation.

Following the arrival of La Salle and Christian missionaries in the early 18th century, relations with the French remained relatively cordial. Indeed, a large number of Natchezes had been baptized by the early 1700s. By 1713 the Natchezes were involved in the lucrative task of capturing American Indian slaves for the colonial market. This human trade was a major factor in the eventual extinction of smaller less-powerful tribes.

Relations with the French were not always peaceful, and in 1715 the First Natchez War began. Its basic cause was European encroachment on land that the Natchezes considered their own. Following the murders of 4 Frenchmen, the French governor of Louisiana, Antoine de La Mothe, Sieur de Cadillac, ordered the commander of the Mississippi River, Jean-Baptiste Le Moyne de Bienville, and 34 French troops to deal with some 800 Natchez warriors. Recruiting additional manpower, Bienville moved into Natchez territory and succeeded in taking a number of Natchez nobles hostage and getting the Natchez chiefs to execute the 6 murderers. Bienville then secured the assistance of the Natchezes in the construction in 1716 of Fort Rosalie (present-day Natchez, Mississippi).

French settlers continued to settle on Natchez lands. British agents were also active in trying to stir up the Natchezes against the French. Finally, in November 1729 the commandant at Fort Rosalie provoked the Natchezes into revolt. The Natchezes killed 250 French colonists and took as captives 300 others (women and children) before French reinforcements and superior weaponry turned the tide. The Natchezes finally capitulated in January 1731. Four hundred natives surrendered and were deported to Santo Domingo as slaves.

At war's end in 1733, about 200 Natchezes fled to the Chickasaw Nation in northern Mississippi, where they received refuge. The French subsequently fought two unsuccessful wars with the Chickasaws to have the refugee Natchezes handed over to them.

Eventually the Natchezes who had fled to the Chickasaws or had otherwise scattered split into three groups. One group joined the Upper Creeks in what later became Georgia, the second group joined the Cherokees to the north in what would become Tennessee, and the third group fled to South Carolina. Today the Edisto Nation of South Carolina identifies itself as the Natchez-Kusso Indian Tribe. There is also a small group of Natchez descendants currently living in southeastern Muskogee County, Oklahoma. They are known as the Natchee Creeks and Natchee Cherokees.

THOMAS JOHN BLUMER

See also
Cherokees; Chickasaws; Chickasaw Wars; Creeks; La Salle, René-Robert Cavelier, Sieur de; Natchez Revolt; Natchez War; Soto, Hernando de; Tunicas

References
Barnett, Jim. *The Natchez Indians.* Natchez: Mississippi Department of Archives and History Popular Report, 1998.

Charlevoix, Pierre F. X. de. *Charlevoix's Louisiana: Selections from the History and the Journal.* Edited and translated by Charles E. O'Neill. Baton Rouge: Louisiana State University Press, 1977.

Galloway, Patricia, and Jason Baird Jackson. "Natchez and Neighboring Groups." In *Handbook of North American Indians,* Vol. 14, *Southeast,* edited by W. C. Sturtevant and Raymond D. Fogelson, 598–615. Washington, DC: Smithsonian Institution Press, 2004.

Swanton, John R. *Indian Tribes of the Lower Mississippi Valley and Adjacent Coast of the Gulf of Mexico.* Bureau of American Ethnology, Bulletin No. 43. Washington, DC, 1911.

Natchez Revolt
Event Date: November 28, 1729

Uprising by the Natchez tribe against the French in November 1729. In 1716 the French constructed Fort Rosalie, situated along the eastern bank of the Mississippi River among the Natchez people in Louisiana. This activity was part of an effort to monopolize the fur trade in the Mississippi River Valley.

Natchez relations with the French were tenuous at best, with sporadic episodes of open warfare. In 1728 Sieur de Chepart, a notoriously brash individual, replaced a fairly popular French commander at Fort Rosalie. His relations with the Natchez people were deplorable. Particularly distasteful had been his order for one Natchez village to relocate to make room for a French plantation. Word quickly spread to all Natchez villages of an impending revolt designed to rid the region of the French and prevent further encroachment.

During the autumn of 1729, Natchez villages held celebrations and ceremonies in preparation for the attack. They displayed elaborate decorations and ornaments, and Natchez warriors swore to fight to the death for their people. During these autumn months French settlers began reporting rumors of an impending attack, but Chepart dismissed them.

On November 28, 1729, the Natchez warriors began their planned attack. They moved throughout the French community asking for arms and ammunition for a hunt and promised some of the meat in return, something that did not raise suspicions. With two or three warriors at each French house, the Natchezes simultaneously fell on the French inhabitants at the sound of firing at the commandant's house. Within hours, 145 French men (including Chepart), 36 women, and 56 children had been killed, nearly 10 percent of the white population in Louisiana. Almost 300 black slaves and another 50 white women and children were carried off into captivity.

The Natchez Revolt shocked the colony of Louisiana and halted French settlement around the fort, but the resulting Natchez War (1729–1733) ultimately proved disastrous for the Natchez people. In the long run, the revolt reminded the French how vulnerable they could be to Native American attack, so they redoubled their efforts to build alliances with numerous tribes in the lower Mississippi River Valley. The French also sought to foment suspicion and rivalry among Native American tribes in an effort to prevent them from uniting and launching Pan-Indian offensives.

IAN MICHAEL SPURGEON

See also
France; Natchezes; Natchez War

References
Taylor, Alan. *American Colonies: The Settling of North America.* New York: Viking/Penguin, 2001.

Usner, Daniel H., Jr. *Indians, Settlers, and Slaves in a Frontier Exchange Economy: The Lower Mississippi Valley before 1783.* Chapel Hill: University of North Carolina Press, 1992.

Willis, William S. "Divide and Rule: Red, White, and Black in the Southeast." *Journal of Negro History* 48(3) (July 1963): 157–176.

Natchez War
Start Date: December 1729
End Date: 1733

The last of three conflicts between the French and the Natchez tribe, which lived along the Mississippi River near present-day Natchez, Mississippi. The Natchez War escalated into a regional struggle to include the British as well as a sizable number of southern and northern tribes. Although the Natchezes were devastated and ceased to function as an independent people after the conflict, the war nevertheless accelerated the erosion of French authority and influence in Louisiana as well as in North America as a whole.

The French and the Natchez people had fought previously during 1715–1716 and again in 1722 without reaching any substantial accommodation. Although the French routinely disregarded Natchez culture, other tensions added to this volatile political and military environment. Through their trading partners, the Chickasaws, the British relished antagonizing tribes within the French sphere of influence. The Chickasaws goaded the Natchez people by insinuating that they were merely minions of the French. A flash point occurred in 1729 when the commandant of Fort Rosalie, Sieur de Chepart, demanded that the Natchez people vacate a village containing a sacred burial mound to make room for his plantation.

On November 28, 1729, Natchez warriors rose up in a general revolt that targeted the entire French population within their reach. Roughly 550 French citizens and slaves were killed or captured, with the mutilation and torture of men not uncommon. Some slaves were freed and encouraged to join the fight.

The French assembled an army in Louisiana dominated by 1,500 Choctaw warriors and proceeded into the Natchez heartland. Ensconced within a fort strong enough to resist cannon fire, Natchez warriors taunted their attackers with promises that the Chickasaws and the British would soon come to their rescue. This move only heightened preexisting French suspicions that outside agitation had prompted the Natchez rebellion.

While negotiations were being conducted for the release of women and children, the Natchez defenders quietly left the fort and scattered. One group was captured by Choctaw and Chackchiuma warriors while trying to reach the Chickasaws in early 1730. Some 150 men were executed, whereas women, children, and slaves were freed. The main Natchez body was discovered later in 1730 on an island in the Mississippi. Following a French artillery bombardment, the defenders were largely wiped out. Another sizable contingent was captured by the French and their Caddo allies near Natchitoches, Louisiana. The group was subjected to a wholesale slaughter. Some Natchezes escaped to live among the British, the Creeks, and the Cherokees. But the largest collection of escapees, about 1,000 including 200 warriors, settled among the Chickasaws in 1731.

Believing that the Chickasaw tribe was responsible for the war, the French recruited aggressively among northern tribes for mercenaries to launch a retaliatory strike. The Wyandots (Hurons) and the Illinois responded in the greatest numbers. The French, hoping to deal with the remaining Natchez elements first, did not officially declare war on the Chickasaws. A raid in September 1730 by northern warriors killed or captured some 50 Chickasaw men, but the French feigned ignorance when queried on the motives for the attack. The Chickasaws had some success in using gifts and peace messages to dissuade these distant foes from attacking. Counterattacks by Chickasaws on northern villages enhanced their reputation as the fiercest of tribes east of the Mississippi.

Emboldened by their virtual genocide of the Fox tribe in the Illinois Country in 1730, the French intensified their efforts to eradicate the Natchez people by demanding that the Chickasaws turn over refugees and cease trade with the British. When the Chickasaws refused, French authorities arranged for the Choctaws to burn three Chickasaw prisoners at the stake. By February 1731 there was a clamor among the Choctaws for joining the war, in part because of a rumor that the British had poisoned some cloth acquired through trade. But Red Shoe, an ambitious chief cultivated by the French, objected as part of an effort to play the European powers against one another. The existence of heavily fortified Chickasaw towns further discouraged the Choctaws. But the Chickasaws were plagued by internal divisions of their own concerning the utility of harboring the Natchez refugees. As the pro-Natchez faction gradually prevailed, the Choctaws grew less reluctant to attack their traditional rivals. With Red Shoes settled on a course of war, Choctaws assaulted a Chickasaw hunting party in July 1731 to secure scalps and prisoners.

As the conflict widened, the Choctaws grew adept at using decoys to lure away major Chickasaw forces before raiding their camps. Suffering heavy casualties, the Chickasaws angled for peace with the Choctaws in order to isolate the French. But French officials were adamant that the surrender of the Natchez people must accompany any settlement. By the end of 1732 the French-Choctaw alliance was deteriorating over the French refusal to provide troops for native offensives. On the fringes of New France, Louisiana ranked low among priorities in asserting French authority.

By 1733 the Chickasaws were weakening in their resolve to stand by the Natchezes in the face of this lengthy conflict. A Chickasaw chief known as Courcerai parleyed with the French that spring to secure peace in exchange for handing over all available Natchezes. But the French governor of Louisiana, Jean-Baptiste Le Moyne de Bienville, later incarcerated him in likely retaliation for the capture of two Frenchmen. Courcerai was never heard from again. Meanwhile, the French grew desperate for the Choctaws to demonstrate the sort of initiative lacking among themselves. French officials often assumed cowardice when faced with Choctaw timidity. But Choctaw warriors readied themselves for combat through a series of elaborate rituals deeply rooted in their culture. Expeditions hastily contrived by the French clashed with Choctaw norms and ruined their fighting spirit. In 1733 the Chickasaws concluded a peace with the northern Choctaws that encouraged an abatement of hostilities. When the Chickasaws closed the Mississippi River to French commerce in 1734, the stage was set for another conflict. Only then would the French mount an expedition of their own against the Chickasaws, one that failed in 1736.

JEFFREY D. BASS

See also

Caddos; Chickasaws; Chickasaw Wars; Choctaws; France; Illinois; Natchezes; Natchez Revolt; Red Shoe; Sauks and Foxes; Wyandots

References

Atkinson, James R. *Splendid Land, Splendid People: The Chickasaw Indians to Removal.* Tuscaloosa: University of Alabama Press, 2004.

Axtell, James. *The Indians' New South: Cultural Change in the Colonial Southeast.* Baton Rouge: Louisiana State University Press, 1997.

Native Americans

The term "Native Americans" refers to the first inhabitants or indigenous peoples of the Americas—South, Central, and North—and their descendants. Most scholars, using anthropological, archaeological, and genetic evidence, now agree that the first Native Americans migrated to the Western Hemisphere between 11,000 and 35,000 years ago. This migration took place in four distinct episodes across a land bridge that connected Siberia with Alaska. The last ice age created the land bridge by lowering the sea level.

Although many native groups in North America maintained a nomadic lifestyle, other groups developed sedentary agricultural societies, especially in the Southwest and the Eastern Woodlands. Europeans first encountered American Indians in North America in the late 15th and early 16th centuries. Some native groups were organized into relatively simple bands, and others were organized into complex chiefdoms and confederacies. There were more than 500 different native groups in North America speaking as many as 2,000 different languages and dialects.

European contact and then settlement wrought havoc on American Indian societies. European diseases to which the natives had no natural immunity or resistance killed untold thousands. European settlement and constant land grabs disrupted the societal and political orders of virtually every native nation or tribe. Land disputes with the Europeans also brought destruction to native societies, as many of the disputes resulted in violence and war.

By the end of the colonial period, most Native American populations east of the Mississippi River had been decimated. As white settlement moved farther and farther west in the 19th century, tribes on the Great Plains and in the Southwest and Far West suffered a similar fate. By 1890, Native Americans had lost perhaps 90 percent of their precontact landholdings in North America. Overhunting, which nearly wiped out the buffalo herds on the Plains by the late 1870s, wrought almost unimaginable havoc on societies in which the buffalo was central to their economic, social, and political makeup.

DIXIE RAY HAGGARD

See also

Buffalo; Native American Trade

References

Bonvillain, Nancy. *Native Nations: Cultures and Histories of Native North America.* Upper Saddle River, NJ: Prentice Hall, 2001.

Calloway, Colin G. *First Peoples: A Documentary Survey of American Indian History.* 2nd ed. Boston: Bedford/St. Martin's, 2004.

Dickason, Olive Patricia. *Canada's First Nations: A History of Founding Peoples from Earliest Times.* 3rd ed. Toronto: Oxford University Press, 2002.

Edmunds, R. David, Frederick E. Hoxie, and Neal Salisbury. *The People: A History of Native America.* Boston: Houghton Mifflin, 2005.

Mancall, Peter C., and James H. Merrell, eds. *American Encounters: Natives and Newcomers from European Contact to Indian Removal, 1500–1850.* New York: Routledge, 2000.

Native Americans, Alliances with Europeans

Diplomatic, trade, or military alliances existed between Native Americans and the colonists from the beginning of European settlement. Even after the colonial period ended with the closing of the American Revolutionary War (1775–1783), alliances between Native Americans and Europeans continued well into the 19th century. Native Americans and Europeans created numerous alliances, most of which collapsed soon after agreement. Common in these compacts was the desire on the part of native tribes to secure allies against neighboring tribes and other Europeans and to acquire trade goods, specifically weapons. For the Europeans, the chief motivations were the desire to secure provisions in times of need (especially in the early period of colonization), allies against hostile tribes and competing European powers, and access to native-occupied land.

Colonists of all the major colonial powers present in America sought such alliances from the very beginning of colonization.

Although alliances were dynamic and changed often, tribes in alliance with the Spanish included the Timucuas, the Apalachees, the Guales, and the Pueblos. Among tribes in alliance with the English at various times were the Powhatans, the Narragansetts, the Wampanoags, the Cherokees, the Yamasees, the Chickasaws, and the Iroquois Confederacy.

The French were by far the most successful in securing native alliances. Locked in a struggle for North American mastery with the far more numerous English, the French spent considerable sums on the so-called king's presents to the native peoples in order to secure their loyalty and manpower in time of war. The French were also much more tolerant in their attitudes toward the native peoples and were more likely to marry and live among the natives. Tribes in alliance with the French included the Algonquins, the Illinois, the Hurons (Wyandots), the Ottawas, and the Choctaws.

In the first contacts between the colonists and natives, the alliances were simple and direct, involving only local representatives of both sides and usually an exchange of goods. With continued contact, the demands on both sides became greater, and the alliances involved entire colonies and native nations. The natives were particularly anxious to secure firearms and trade goods, and the colonists took advantage of this to cement alliances against another colonial power or hostile native group and to secure pelts. Alliances between Europeans and natives on occasion involved the exchange of captives.

As with other alliances, these arrangements were rarely static. Intertribal confederations often presented a problem. As tribes shifted locations, new alliances and confederations developed. Sometimes these confederations uniformly bound all villages of the confederation into alliances undertaken with colonists. More often than not, however, elements of these confederations split their allegiances between neighboring European powers. Examples of such instances include the Upper and Lower Creeks, who divided their loyalties between the Spanish and the English. The Chickasaws also experienced divided loyalties between the English and the French. To the north, the French and the English competed for the allegiance of the Huron and Iroquois peoples.

No matter which native tribe or European power was involved in the process, each party sought security for its own people and a means of prosperity through the compacts. The ability of the Europeans to tap into considerable weaponry and other military and population resources often gave them a diplomatic advantage. However, Native American knowledge of the land and its resources and competing European powers allowed larger tribes to exert considerable influence.

After the end of the Revolutionary War, various Native American tribes allied with the British or the Americans during the War of 1812. Tecumseh's Pan-Indian confederacy aligned with the British during that conflict. Most of the Iroquois Confederacy also cast its lot with the British. The Americans made far less use of Native American allies, although some Miamis did support them,

Important Native American Affiliations with Europeans during the Colonial Era

Tribe	Location	Major Alliances/Interactions
Abenakis	Northern New England and Quebec	French
Algonquins	Ottawa River Valley	French
Apalachees	Florida Panhandle	Spanish
Calusas	Southwestern Florida	Spanish
Catawbas	Western Carolinas	British
Cherokees	Southern Appalachian Mountains	British
Chickasaws	Northern Mississippi and Alabama	British
Choctaws	East-central Mississippi and Alabama	French and British
Creeks	Florida, Georgia, and Alabama	Spanish, French, and British
Delawares	Delaware, New Jersey, southeastern New York, and southeastern Pennsylvania	British
Esopuses	Hudson and Delaware River Valleys	Dutch
Hurons	Southern Ontario and southeastern Michigan	French
Illinois	Upper Mississippi River Valley	French
Iroquois Confederacy	New York	British
Kickapoos	Green Bay and Fox River regions	French
Mahicans	Upper Hudson River Valley	Dutch and French
Mingos	New York	British
Mohegans	Connecticut, Massachusetts, and Rhode Island	British
Narragansetts	Southeastern New England	British
Natchezes	Southwestern Mississippi	French
Nipmucks	East-central Massachusetts	British
Nottoways	Southeastern Virginia and northeastern North Carolina	British
Ojibwas	Upper Great Lakes	French
Osages	Upper and lower Mississippi River Valleys	French
Ottawas	Manitoulin Island and northern Lake Huron	French
Pennacooks	New Hampshire	British
Pequots	Southeastern Connecticut	British
Pueblos	Upper Rio Grande Valley	Spanish
Quapaws	Lower Mississippi River Valley	French
Shawnees	South Carolina, Tennessee Cumberland River basin, and southern Illinois	French and British
Tequestas	Miami River and coastal islands of southeastern Florida	Spanish
Tunicas	Louisiana region	French
Wampanoags	Narragansett Bay to Cape Cod	British
Yamasees	Central Georgia and North Carolina	Spanish

as did some Cherokees in the south; however, the alliance with the Cherokees soon broke apart. During the American Civil War (1861–1865), various tribes pledged their loyalty to the Union or the Confederacy, although these loose alliances had almost no impact on the course or outcome of that conflict.

BECCIE SEAMAN AND SPENCER C. TUCKER

See also

Firearms Trade; Native Americans and the War of 1812; Native Americans and the Civil War; Native American Trade; Native American Warfare; Slavery among Native Americans

References

Calloway, Colin G. *First Peoples: A Documentary Survey of American Indian History.* 2nd ed. Boston: Bedford/St. Martin's, 2004.

Edmunds, R. David, Frederick E. Hoxie, and Neal Salisbury. *The People: A History of Native America.* Boston: Houghton Mifflin, 2005.

Jacobs, Wilbur R. *Wilderness Politics and Indian Gifts: The Northern Colonial Frontier, 1748–1763.* Stanford, CA: Stanford University Press, 1950.

Jennings, Francis. *The Invasion of America: Indians, Colonialism, and the Cant of Conquest.* 1976; reprint, Chapel Hill: University of North Carolina Press, 2010.

Usner, Daniel H., Jr. *Indians, Settlers, and Slaves in a Frontier Exchange Economy: The Lower Mississippi Valley before 1783.* Chapel Hill: University of North Carolina Press, 1992.

White, Richard. *The Middle Ground: Indians, Empires, and Republics in the Great Lakes Region, 1650–1815.* New York: Cambridge University Press, 1991.

Native Americans and the American Revolutionary War

For the overwhelming majority of Native Americans, the American Revolutionary War (1775–1783) was a disaster. At least several hundred Native American warriors took part in the conflict on the American side, but they were too few to have any great impact on the conflict. Many thousands fought on the British side but never in large enough numbers to give the British a significantly improved opportunity to achieve victory in any theater of the war. Most tribes remained neutral through much of the conflict, yet nearly all tribes suffered when the independent United States, created by hundreds of thousands of aggressive and often land-hungry settlers from Britain and continental Europe, acquired ultimate sovereignty over the Native Americans' trade and land.

A few key Native American groups were of special importance during the war. These include the tribes of the Iroquois Confederacy and their allies in New York and Pennsylvania, the so-called Five Civilized Tribes in the southern colonies (later states), and the Ohio Valley tribes of the Old Northwest. While some of the distinctions among these three clusters, such as the labels applied to them, are largely the constructions of Europeans, the tribes within each of these groups did have cultural and linguistic similarities as well as common geographic interests that served to delineate their respective memberships. At the same time, they all possessed important commonalities that served to guide European colonial interactions with them. While the ways in which Europeans related to Native Americans covered a wide spectrum, their most important interactions in the American Revolutionary War revolved around Native American military practices and diplomatic rituals.

Most Native American tribes practiced a method of warfare predicated on stealth and concealment. Raids and ambushes punctuated this form of conflict. Most often a small group, or war party, assembled under a leader to execute these activities. Usually the chief action of the group consisted of a brief raid of some sort. The warriors composing the party placed themselves under the direction of the party's leader for the duration of the raid. No set hierarchical command structure existed among most Native American groups, although some leaders, such as Ottawa chief Pontiac and the Mohawk Joseph Brant, did achieve great visibility among several tribes and considerable fame among Europeans.

Once formed, the war party set out for the location of its chosen foe. The preferred time of attack for the war party was at first light, when their enemy would be least prepared. Most engagements were decided in the initial attack. If the warriors were unsuccessful, they usually retired quickly rather than take part in a set battle and risk heavier losses. If the attack was successful, the raiders would immediately take prisoners and seize plunder.

In the 12 years between the end of the French and Indian War (1754–1763) and the outbreak of the American Revolutionary War, diplomatic negotiations with the various Native American groups were carried out almost exclusively by officials of the British government. There were two royal officials who held primary responsibility for this work. These were the Indian superintendents of the Northern Department and the Southern Department who reported directly to the colonial secretary in London. From 1756 to 1774 the British Indian superintendent of the Northern Department was Sir William Johnson; following his death his responsibilities were divided between his relatives John and Guy Johnson. Sir William's death in July 1774 is often cited by historians as one of the reasons for the divisions that wracked the Iroquois Confederacy during the American Revolution. Johnson's responsibilities included all negotiations with the Iroquois Confederacy, the most prominent group in the northern and middle colonies.

Prominent Native American Tribes during the American Revolution

Department	Tribes
Northern	Iroquois Confederacy (Senecas, Mohawks, Oneidas, Onondagas, Cayugas, Tuscaroras)
Southern	Five Civilized Tribes (Cherokees, Chickasaws, Choctaws, Creeks, Seminoles)
Western	Ohio Valley tribes (Shawnees, Delawares, Kickapoos, Miamis, Ottawas, Wyandots)

The Iroquois Confederacy originally included the Onondaga, Oneida, Cayuga, Mohawk, and Seneca tribes. In 1722 the Tuscaroras from the South were admitted, making the confederacy the League of the Six Nations. In addition to the Iroquois, to the west there were the tribes of the Ohio Valley, whose territory stretched from western Pennsylvania through present-day Ohio, Indiana, and Illinois to the Mississippi River. While these people were often considered clients of the Iroquois Confederacy in dealing with Europeans, this relationship proved more nominal than real. Because the Ohio Valley tribes were seen as clients of the Iroquois, they had no separate British superintendent.

The Ohio Valley tribes had been the chief actors in Pontiac's Rebellion (1763). This uprising, which was finally put down by the British, was a primary reason for the Proclamation of 1763. This royal decree curtailed colonial settlement beyond the line marked by the British government and became a source of great tension between settlers on the frontier and the royal government. Indeed, the decree helped set the stage for the American Revolution.

In the Southern Department, the Indian superintendent for most of the prewar period was John Stuart. Following his death in early 1779, he was replaced by several other officials. Stuart was responsible for overseeing diplomacy with the Catawbas, Creeks, Chickasaws, Choctaws, Cherokees, and Seminoles. The most important of these with respect to the Revolutionary War were the Cherokees and the Creeks.

With the beginning of hostilities between Great Britain and the colonists, both sides in the conflict sent diplomatic missions to the various Native American groups. In these early diplomatic efforts Crown officials proved more adept, while the rebel diplomats were initially astounded by the expense attached to the gift-giving aspect of diplomacy, which the British had routinely practiced. The colonies, of course, had to build a diplomatic apparatus from scratch. The Continental Congress set up a plan for the management of Indian affairs that was much the same in its organizational details as that of the British. The plan did, however, include a Middle Department as well as a Southern Department and a Northern Department. The agendas pursued by both sides had much in common.

Early in the Revolutionary War, British policy toward the Native Americans consisted of continuing their friendship while limiting requests for military actions against the rebels. Major

General Guy Carleton, governor-general of Canada, was especially reluctant to call upon the Iroquois for military support and thus unleash an Indian war with all of its attendant depredations on the frontier. The American policy, in turn, consisted of expressing friendship and securing pledges of neutrality from the Native Americans, although some Massachusetts Christian Stockbridge Native Americans were recruited as warriors as early as the siege of Boston. Both British and American emissaries met with considerable failure in their initial efforts.

Among the Iroquois, the first news of conflict between Britain and its American colonies was greeted with confusion and pledges of restraint. While in theory the Iroquois Confederacy was supposed to act as a single unit, in reality the pull of localism, which placed the interests of the various member tribes ahead of the whole, often prevailed. Only the Mohawks would prove a dependable British ally throughout the war. Much of the tribe's reliability came as the result of the efforts of Brant and his sister Mary, who had been the common-law wife of Sir William Johnson for many years.

While the first response of the Iroquois had been to wait and see how developments played out between the British and the colonists, the arrival of Chief Brant on the frontier and Guy Johnson in New York City in July 1776 marked the beginning of a subtle shift in Iroquois policy. The combined efforts of these two men would persuade many of the members of the Iroquois Confederacy to play a much more active role in support of the British. The Continental Congress's lack of experience in the handling of Indian affairs also prompted most tribes to take a more pro-British stance.

In 1777 many warriors from the various tribes of the Iroquois Confederacy began openly aiding the British and their Loyalist auxiliaries, especially in upstate New York and western Pennsylvania. A number of warriors joined the forces of Lieutenant General John Burgoyne in his invasion of New York. A proportionally larger force supplemented the invasion led by Lieutenant Colonel Barry St. Leger (brevetted brigadier general) of the upper Mohawk Valley. These warriors took part in a successful ambush of Colonel Nicholas Herkimer and his militia at Oriskany, New York, in August 1777 but could not capture Fort Stanwix, which the rebel forces eventually relieved.

After Burgoyne's surrender at Saratoga in October 1777, the Iroquois and their Loyalist allies worked to make the western and southern reaches of the Mohawk Valley a no-man's-land. This change in tactics led to the outbreak of brutal raids all along the frontier in 1778. The most destructive of the attacks in that area was known as the Cherry Valley Massacre, although the Wyoming Valley Massacre in northeastern Pennsylvania proved even more devastating to the Americans. But the failure of Burgoyne's invasion also initiated conflict within the Iroquois Confederacy as the various tribes and villages took opposing sides in the conflict. The Onondagas, for example, remained divided among themselves in their loyalties until 1779. And although most Senecas did join the

British, some remained neutral. In contrast, the majority of the Oneidas assisted the Americans.

By this time, however, Major General Frederick Haldimand had replaced Carleton as governor in British Canada. Haldimand was far more willing than Carleton to utilize Native American auxiliaries on the frontier against the Americans. This ensured that raids along the frontier in Pennsylvania and New York would increase in 1778. The severity of these attacks, in turn, gave rise to calls for action by Congress to protect the frontier. In 1779 General George Washington launched two major expeditions against the Iroquois. Colonel Daniel Brodhead commanded the smaller force in western Pennsylvania. A much larger expedition, led by Continental Army major general John Sullivan and New York Militia commander Brigadier General James Clinton, marched through the Iroquois territory in northern Pennsylvania and western New York.

The idea of both campaigns was not so much to kill Iroquois warriors as to devastate their crops, thus simultaneously chastising them and making them a greater supply burden on the British. In this respect the campaigns were a clear success, although they did not end Native American raids on the northern frontier. The importance of these efforts to the Americans, however, is suggested by the fact that the Sullivan expedition was the only major military operation mounted by the Continental Army in 1779.

While there were further attacks by war parties along the northern frontier in both 1780 and 1781, they were greatly reduced in strength, again a signal of the effectiveness of the Brodhead and Sullivan expeditions. Under these reduced conditions, however, frontier warfare continued even after the surrender of Lieutenant General Charles, Lord Cornwallis, at Yorktown, Virginia, in October 1781. But in the later stages of the war the British were increasingly trying to restrain their Native American auxiliaries. The fate of the Iroquois Confederacy was finally decided by treaty with the United States shortly after the peace with Britain. The Six Nations had to cede much of their land to Pennsylvania and New York, and many Iroquois migrated to Canada at the invitation of the British and fared better in the future.

In many ways the same story of division and eventual defeat, with its attendant loss of lands, characterized the experience of Native Americans in the Southern Department. In the South as in the North, the Native Americans' experience in the Revolutionary War was often a struggle for their very survival. Throughout the conflict in the South there appeared the same types of internal divisions among the Native Americans that were seen in New York and Pennsylvania. The only group to remain steadfast in their support of the British was the Chickasaws.

Stuart was the chief motivator of the Native Americans in their support for the British in this region. From the start, however, he had his work cut out for him, as the rebel leaders in his base colony, South Carolina, ran such a successful smear campaign against him among both Native Americans and European settlers that he had to flee to Georgia in 1775. Stuart hoped that Native American warriors would be used in conjunction with British regulars against the rebels. As he was preparing for this, however, the Patriot leaders of South Carolina attempted to send gunpowder to the Cherokees on the frontier as a gift in order to secure good relations. Loyalists in the backcountry seized the powder but promptly expended all of it in their unsuccessful siege of a Patriot force at Ninety Six.

The move to war by Native Americans in the Southern Department came in early 1776 when a delegation of Shawnees, Delawares, and Mohawks from the North came to the Cherokees and urged them to attack the rebel settlers. The Cherokees, over Stuart's objections, agreed to attack the colonists, but their plans were leaked, which cost them the element of surprise. In late June 1776, however, the Cherokees of the Lower Towns, those closest to the colonial frontier, raced through the backcountry of the Carolinas, burning and plundering as they went. These raids were all the more frightful to the colonists for fear that the Creeks might join the Cherokees on the rampage.

In response the newly independent southern states launched a concerted counterattack. South Carolina was the first to respond. On August 2, 1776, Colonel Andrew Williamson of South Carolina began a sweep against the Cherokee Lower Towns. On September 23 he teamed up with Brigadier General Griffith Rutherford and his North Carolina militia. The final prong of the counteroffensive came with the advance of Colonel William Christian of Virginia into Cherokee territory. By the time of Christian's advance, however, the majority of the Cherokees were ready to negotiate. The quick collapse of the Cherokees was disappointing but not necessarily unexpected by the British. Its most serious consequence, however, was to intimidate Britain's other Native American allies in the South, strengthening the peace faction in each tribe and especially making the Creeks more reluctant to aid the British.

Catawba warriors took part in the campaign against the Cherokees and had earlier assisted in the defense of Charleston against a British attack. Stuart had quickly recognized that the Catawbas would assist the rebels, and that nation remained a staunch American ally throughout the war.

The 1776 frontier war broke the power of the Cherokees, and 1777 was a year full of negotiation and little action. Through 1778 most of the attention on the frontier focused on the Creeks, who were threatening settlers in Georgia. But between late 1776 and 1780, relatively little warfare actually took place on the southern frontier. One important reason for Native American inertia in this region was that Loyalists in the southern backcountry had been effectively muzzled by their own defeats in 1775 and 1776.

Beginning in November 1778, the British shifted the focus of their military strategy to the South. The Creeks had more than 300 warriors ready for service with the British in the spring and summer of 1779 but did not support the initial British thrusts into Georgia because they were given no advance notice of British plans. As for the British, their efforts among the Native Americans in the South changed drastically after Stuart's death in March 1779. His former assistants attempted to take his place and carry out his policies, but their efforts were often subverted by Lord George Germain, Britain's secretary of state for the American colonies, who was now taking a more personal interest in military policy. There was also much competition for Stuart's authority at the local level. Thomas Brown, lieutenant colonel of the East Florida Rangers, a Loyalist unit, was also the superintendent of the Atlantic District of the Southern Indian Department. In this role he attempted to stretch his powers to take over all of Stuart's old district. When Creek and Cherokee leaders asked Brown to assist them in driving settlers from their lands in present-day eastern Tennessee and Kentucky, Cornwallis vetoed the operation, dampening the Native Americans' ardor for cooperating with the British.

Faced with American partisan attacks along the Georgia–South Carolina frontier in the summer and autumn of 1780, Cornwallis finally relented and authorized his subordinates to call for Native American assistance. By that time, however, only a small faction of militant Cherokees remained willing to fight; the rest of the tribe had made peace in 1777. The Chickasaws were too few and too distant to do more than harass Americans forces west of the Appalachians. At the same time, the Spanish entry into the war in 1779 drew most of the Creek and Choctaw warriors to the defense of British West Florida. The Creeks and Choctaws helped the British break the first Spanish siege of Pensacola, but the Spanish returned in force. Creeks and Choctaws fought effectively to delay Spanish siege operations, but on May 8, 1781, Brigadier General John Campbell surrendered Pensacola to the Spaniards. This event, along with the British withdrawal from the Georgia and Carolina backcountry that severed direct communication with the Native Americans, signaled the end of the British Southern Indian Department's operations in North America. And the dramatic turn of events in the Southern Department that began with the Battle of Kings Mountain in October 1780, followed by the assumption of the command of the Southern Army by Continental Army major general Nathanael Greene in December and culminating in the surrender of Cornwallis at Yorktown in October 1781, placed much of the South firmly back under Patriot domination.

The last 18 months of the conflict in the Southern Department was a time of retrenchment and decline for both the British and the various Native American tribes, and both awaited the final outcome of peace negotiations before launching any new efforts, diplomatic or military. Yet most of the divisive issues between white settlers and Native Americans that were present at the outbreak of the conflict remained at the war's end.

The only region in which there was something resembling even temporary success for Native Americans during the American Revolutionary War was the West, and that success lasted only as long as the war itself. In the Ohio Valley, with the exception of the expedition of Kentucky Militia lieutenant colonel George Rogers Clark, Native Americans kept white incursions to a minimum. Clark's expedition into the Illinois Country formed the principal defense north of the Ohio for frontiersmen attempting to set up settlements in the area that would become Kentucky.

The fighting in this region, while it did not approach a definitive possession of territory by either side, did set a precedent exploited by American negotiators in the Treaty of Paris. That agreement ceded to the new United States all of the area that encompassed the territory of the Ohio Valley tribes. This region, organized as the Northwest Territory in 1787, quickly became a site of great tension and eventual conflict between the indigenous inhabitants and the United States.

Most historians of the American Revolution now view the frontier conflict with the Native Americans as an expansionist war waged by the colonists and later the independent American settlers in order to gain new territories and view the Proclamation of 1763, with its attendant restraint on colonial encroachment, as one of the key motivators of people along the frontier. The divided loyalties within the various Native American nations, especially the Iroquois Confederacy, are generally seen as a chief cause of their inability to repel American incursions. And the consensus on such Native American support of American independence as did exist is that it led to a gross injustice on the part of the new nation. Tribes that supported the American bid for independence generally received no consideration of their grievances. In fact, they lost territories with as much regularity as those who fought on the British side. The British, for their part, often turned their backs on allies that had contributed valuable service. The major exception was the Iroquois who immigrated to Canada, where the British granted them the Grand River Valley in Ontario.

JAMES R. MCINTYRE

See also

Brant, Joseph; Brodhead Expedition; Brown, Thomas; Cameron, Alexander; Cherokees; Chickasaws; Choctaws; Clark, George Rogers; Creeks; Gnadenhutten Massacre; Iroquois; Iroquois Confederacy; Johnson, Sir William; McGillivray, Alexander; Native American Warfare; Old Northwest Territory; Oriskany, Battle of; Pontiac; Pontiac's Rebellion; Proclamation of 1763; Seminoles; Stuart, John

References

Calloway, Colin G. *The American Revolution in Indian Country: Crisis and Diversity in Native American Communities.* Cambridge: Cambridge University Press, 1995.

Harrison, Lowell Hayes. *George Rogers Clark and the War in the West.* Lexington: University Press of Kentucky, 1976.

Mintz, Max M. *Seeds of Empire: The American Revolutionary Conquest of the Iroquois.* New York: New York University Press, 1999.

Nester, William R. *The Frontier War for American Independence.* Mechanicsburg, PA: Stackpole, 2004.

O'Donnell, James H., III. *Southern Indians in the American Revolution.* Knoxville: University of Tennessee Press, 1973.

Piecuch, Jim. *Three Peoples, One King: Loyalists, Indians, and Slaves in the Revolutionary South, 1775–1782.* Columbia: University of South Carolina Press, 2008.

Richter, Daniel K., and James H. Merrell, eds. *Beyond the Covenant Chain: The Iroquois and Their Neighbors in Indian North America, 1600–1800.* Syracuse, NY: Syracuse University Press, 1987.

Native Americans and the Civil War

On the eve of the American Civil War (1861–1865), the small U.S. Army consisted mainly of garrisons at a few western constabulary outposts used primarily for mapmaking, building roads, and the pacification of Native American tribes. As the war continued, the growing armies of the Union and to a lesser extent those of the Confederacy continued to enforce Indian policies. For example, U.S. forces and volunteers saw action against the Sioux in Minnesota in 1862, the Navajos in Arizona from 1862 to 1864, and the Arapahos and Cheyennes in Colorado in 1864 and 1865 (the Sand Creek Massacre). Native Americans also actively supported both sides in significant numbers. They participated in both conventional battles and guerrilla actions, often in an attempt to further their own tribal goals.

As many as 20,000 Native Americans took an active role in the Civil War. Even when they chose different sides, the reasons for their support were much the same. The poverty of many tribes and their dependence on the U.S. government for protection and survival encouraged their entry into the conflict. Tribes that had been effectively assimilated into the surrounding white populations usually supported the cause espoused by their neighbors. Others were geographically located so as to be vulnerable to one side or the other. This latter was primarily the case for the Creeks, Osages, and Seminoles in Indian Territory (present-day Oklahoma); the Catawbas of South Carolina; and the eastern band of the Cherokees in North Carolina (who became important Confederate allies).

Many Native American groups, such as the Cherokees who followed Stand Watie, one of their leaders and a Confederate Army brigadier general, hoped to settle old grievances by joining the Rebel cause. A number supported the Confederacy simply because they themselves were slaveholders.

Native Americans participated in a number of conventional and unconventional military operations. In the March 7–8, 1862, Battle of Pea Ridge in Arkansas, then-colonel Stand Watie led the Cherokee Mounted Rifles in an assault to capture Union artillery batteries. When members of the 31st U.S. Colored Infantry of the Army of the Potomac fought at the July 30, 1864, Battle of the Crater at Petersburg, Virginia, they were met by Catawba warriors of the 17th South Carolina. Two Seneca brothers served the Union cause faithfully: Isaac Newton Parker was a noncommissioned officer in the 132nd New York State Volunteer Infantry, while his brother, Ely Samuel Parker, was a colonel on Lieutenant General Ulysses S. Grant's staff.

Throughout the war, Confederates formed four infantry regiments from among the Cherokee, Chickasaw, Choctaw, Creek, and Seminole nations. The loyalties of the Cherokee Nation were particularly divided, as many of the original Confederate Cherokees eventually deserted to join the Union cause. Many Native Americans also provided valuable transportation services as river pilots and individuals guarding vital lines of communications and the rail links critical to military operations.

During the Civil War, Seneca Indian Ely S. Parker (third from left) served as a lieutenant colonel and adjutant on the staff of U.S. Army general-in-chief Lieutenant General Ulysses S. Grant. (National Archives)

A particularly sad chapter in U.S.–Native American relations during the war unfolded in the Far Southwest and involved the removal of the Mescalero Apache and Navajo peoples from the District of Arizona. Beginning in October 1862, Colonel Christopher "Kit" Carson was ordered to move against the Mescalero Apaches and Navajos, round them up, and relocate them to the Bosque Redondo reservation in the eastern part of the New Mexico Territory. The forced removal was deemed necessary for white settlement and development in Arizona. Carson was encouraged to embark on a scorched-earth policy in order to move the Native Americans as quickly as possible.

By the winter of 1863 most of the Mescalero Apaches had been subdued and moved to the reservation; most went peacefully. However, the Navajos proved more troublesome, and when a December 1862 delegation of Navajos was rebuffed by American officials, they vowed not to surrender and began a running fight with Carson's forces. Throughout most of 1863 Carson employed brutal tactics to subdue the Navajos, including the destruction of most of their villages and crops.

By late December 1863, Carson's men had cornered the remaining Navajo fighters in Arizona's Canyon de Chelly. On January 6, 1864, with the remaining Navajos trapped in a frigid and snowy canyon, Carson led his men in a brutal assault against them. The Canyon de Chelly Campaign, which ended on January 16, resulted in 23 Navajos killed and 34 captured. An additional 200 capitulated. By March 1, 1864, some 11,500 Navajos had been rounded up and were held at Fort Canby and then were force-marched 400 miles to the reservation. As many as 3,000 Navajos died of starvation, disease, and abuse along the way, and another 2,000 were dead within two years on the tiny reservation.

The legacy of Native American participation in the American Civil War was generally a tragic one. For the Cherokees, Creeks, Chickasaws, Choctaws, and Seminoles—collectively referred to as the Five Civilized Tribes—treaties signed after the war forced huge territorial cessions as a penalty for serving the Confederacy and led to the continued erosion of tribal authority and the physical integrity of their nations. Even though many Cherokees had fought for the Union, the provisions of a July 19, 1866, treaty with the federal government required the tribe to cede parcels of land as railroad rights of way, relinquish a four-mile-wide strip of land that ran the entire length of that nation's border with Kansas, and allow the U.S. government to settle "friendly Indians" west of 96 degrees longitude without the permission of the Cherokee National Council.

Other tribes signed treaties with similar provisions that produced a growing Native American dependence on the federal government. At the conclusion of the war, the U.S. Army could devote even greater efforts to supporting pacification, detribalization, and assimilation policies in regard to all Native Americans. Indeed, the U.S. government pursued these policies generally without regard for the affiliations that Native Americans had expressed during the Civil War.

DEBORAH KIDWELL

See also

Bosque Redondo; Carson, Christopher Houston; Indians, Confederate; Navajo Removal; Parker, Ely Samuel; Sand Creek Massacre; Watie, Stand

References

Abel, Annie Heloise. *The American Indian in the Civil War, 1862–1865.* Lincoln: University of Nebraska Press, 1992.

Colton, Ray C. *The Civil War in the Western Territories.* Norman: University of Oklahoma Press, 1984.

Fischer, Leroy Henry. *The Civil War Era in Indian Territory.* Los Angeles: L. L. Morrison, 1974.

Hauptman, Laurence M. *Between Two Fires: American Indians in the Civil War.* New York City: Free Press, 1995.

Spencer, John D. *The American Civil War in the Indian Territory.* New York: Osprey, 2006.

Native Americans and the War of 1812

Native Americans played a major role in the War of 1812. Before that conflict the tribes of the Northwest Territory had generally allied themselves with the British in Canada chiefly because of the increasing loss of their ancestral lands after the American Revolutionary War (1775–1783) due to constantly encroaching American settlers. To demonstrate the scale, William Henry Harrison, superintendent of the Northwest Indians and governor of the Indiana Territory, secured from Native Americans some 48 million acres in the Old Northwest (the present-day states of Ohio, Indiana, Illinois, Michigan, and Wisconsin) between 1795 and 1809. With the law heavily weighted in favor of white settlers, Native Americans found it all but impossible to secure redress in the courts.

During the first decade of the 1800s, Shawnee leaders Tecumseh and his half brother Tenskwatawa (known as the Prophet) took the lead in opposing further white land acquisitions at Native American expense. Tecumseh believed that the only answer was a confederation of all the tribes, an almost impossible task. Even

had this unity been achieved, Native Americans were now vastly outnumbered by the whites in the Old Northwest. Native Americans could count only some 4,000 warriors in the territory inside the Great Lakes, the Mississippi River, and the Ohio River against at least 100,000 white men of fighting age in the area.

Tecumseh did what he could. Cautioning the Prophet not to initiate hostilities while he was away, Tecumseh traveled south to try to enlist the support of the Creeks. In his absence Harrison precipitated a confrontation by marching some 1,000 regulars and militiamen to Prophetstown (near present-day Lafayette, Indiana). With negotiations to take place the next day, Harrison and his men camped for the night.

In the predawn hours of November 7, 1811, the warriors who were gathered at Prophetstown, whipped into a frenzy by the Prophet's promise that they would be protected against the soldiers' bullets, attacked. Harrison won the Battle of Tippecanoe and went on to burn Prophetstown. Nonetheless, more than anything else this battle led Tecumseh and many of his followers to side with the British in the War of 1812. The battle also convinced the British to aid the Native Americans and convinced American settlers that they would not be safe along the frontier until British influence with the Native Americans could be terminated.

As it turned out, Native American support was critical to the British in the first year of the war. Tecumseh proved a highly effective war leader. Without his assistance, the Americans would have secured much of Upper Canada by the spring of 1813 if not before. The small number of British regulars was hardly sufficient to stem the tide, and the Native Americans helped buttress British strength in isolated garrisons. They proved to be superb guerrilla fighters, adept at stealth, ambush, and irregular warfare. It is true that they often proved mercurial and unreliable, but their indifference to the rules of warfare practiced by regular troops on both sides in the conflict greatly multiplied their impact and was often sufficient to terrify Americans into surrender. Fear of what might be a large Native American force on the British side was a major factor in U.S. brigadier general William Hull's decision to abandon his invasion of Upper Canada in August 1812. British major general Sir Isaac Brock's threat that if American resistance was prolonged he might not be able to control the Native Americans serving with him was a major factor in Hull's decision to surrender Detroit that same month.

On January 22, 1813, at the Raisin River in Michigan Territory, 850 American soldiers, commanded by Brigadier General James Winchester, came under attack by a British force of 1,100 soldiers and Native Americans led by Colonel Henry Procter. Some 300 Americans died in the battle, and after the remainder surrendered, 30 to 60 of them were murdered by drunken warriors. The survivors were marched for 280 miles. Thereafter Americans in the Northwest had a new rallying cry: "Remember the Raisin!" In the spring of 1813 Procter organized an army of 900 regulars plus 1,200 Native Americans, led by Tecumseh, to attack Fort Meigs at the mouth of the Miami River in Ohio. The fort was defended

U.S. Army regulars and militiamen led by William Henry Harrison clash with Native American warriors from Prophetstown in the Battle of Tippecanoe on November 7, 1811. Engraving from a painting by Alonzo Chappel. (Library of Congress)

by 550 Americans under the command of Harrison, who was now a brigadier general. Procter began siege operations on May 1. On May 5 Brigadier General Green Clay arrived with a relief force of 1,200 Kentucky militiamen and drove some British soldiers from their positions. In the Kentuckians' disorganized pursuit almost 600 of them were killed, wounded, or captured, despite Harrison's attempts to rescue them. Once again American prisoners, probably fewer than 40, were massacred by Native Americans. On May 9 the Native Americans deserted with whatever plunder they could find to return home and plant crops. Procter lifted the siege and marched back to Canada.

Late in September 1813 Harrison invaded Canada across the Detroit River with 3,000 men, including 1,200 highly trained Kentucky mounted volunteers under the command of Colonel Richard M. Johnson. On October 5 at the Thames River in southern Ontario, Harrison confronted Procter's army of 800 regulars and 500 warriors under Tecumseh. At Johnson's suggestion, Harrison allowed the mounted volunteers to charge the thin British line. Yelling "Remember the Raisin!" they broke through the British line and captured 600 soldiers as the rest of Procter's men fled. Tecumseh's warriors resisted the Americans longer than their British allies, but when the warriors learned that

Tecumseh had been killed, they also fled. Allegedly the exultant Americans mutilated Tecumseh's body. The battle was a great triumph for the Americans, for it shattered Tecumseh's Indian confederacy.

The British also secured the assistance of many members of the Iroquois Confederacy (Mohawks, Oneidas, Onondagas, Cayugas, Senecas, and Tuscaroras), who lived in both New York state and in Upper and Lower Canada. General Brock approached Teyoninkoharawen early. This Mohawk chief feared that the Americans might take Upper Canada, and he wholeheartedly supported the British. A number of the 1,800 members of the Grand River settlement, just west of the Niagara peninsula, followed Teyoninkoharawen throughout the war. But other members of the Iroquois Confederacy either sided with the Americans or sought refuge in neutrality. Indeed, in June 1812 Little Billy, a New York Iroquois chief, met with his Canadian counterparts, and Iroquois on the two sides of the Niagara River agreed to a truce.

Some Iroquois made a substantial contribution to the British cause. Grand River natives played an important role in the Battle of Queenston Heights, when fear of the Native Americans induced many Americans to surrender. In 1813 Iroquois participated in significant numbers in the battles at York, Fort George, Crysler's Farm, and Châteauguay. Five hundred Iroquois surrounded a larger force of American regulars at Beaver Dams that June, when again fear of massacre brought an American surrender.

Neutrality along the Niagara River changed in July 1813 when the British raided Black Rock, which was close to Seneca land. Young King, a Seneca chief, then went to war against the British. This action led the Iroquois in New York to abandon their position of neutrality in the conflict and to announce that they would defend U.S. soil against any British attack. Indeed, some Senecas volunteered to fight in Canada, and in August near Fort George, New York Iroquois fought Grand River Iroquois. Any pretense of neutrality was lost when Canadian Iroquois burned a Tuscarora village in New York. Senecas in the western part of the state took revenge in early July 1814 when 600 warriors under their chief Sagoyewatha (Red Jacket) invaded Canada with U.S. major general Jacob Brown's forces. In the Battle of Chippewa on July 5, 80 Native Americans perished on both sides, mostly at the hands of other Iroquois. This gave the Native Americans pause and led to a reestablishment of the truce among the Iroquois, which continued for the remainder of the war.

Generally speaking, however, the United States made far less use of Native American auxiliaries in the war than did the British. Partly this was because the Americans were well aware of the deep hostility of the Native Americans toward them, but the Americans also believed at the beginning of the war that they would conquer Canada easily. Erastus Granger, American Indian agent at Niagara, announced to the Iroquois that the U.S. Army was so powerful that it had no use for their services. Nevertheless, in 1812 General Hull employed some Miami warriors in his operations around Fort Dearborn, and as noted, some Iroquois fought alongside American troops on the Niagara front.

In the American South, the Creek (or Muskogee) Confederacy also came to be aligned against the United States. Spanning the territory encompassed by present-day Alabama and part of Georgia, these nations, like their northern brethren, had long-standing grievances against white settlers for encroaching upon their ancestral lands. Tecumseh visited them in 1811 hoping to persuade them to join his confederacy. He received a favorable reception from a faction of Creeks known as the Red Sticks. Early in 1812 a number of whites were killed by disgruntled Creek warriors, and in May 1812 a party of Red Sticks returning from a visit to the Prophet murdered a family of seven white settlers south of Nashville, Tennessee. Tennesseans were outraged with the Creeks and the British, whom they considered complicit. Sentiment for war with Britain ran high along the frontier.

The Creek Confederacy, divided between the nativist Red Stick faction and the White Sticks, who favored accommodation with the Americans, came under assault in 1813 in what came to be known as the Creek War. Major General Andrew Jackson, in command of 2,500 Tennessee militiamen, attacked the Creek towns of Tallushatchee on November 3 and Talladega on November 9. He defeated the Creeks at Emuckfaw Creek on January 22, 1814, and at Enitachopco Creek on January 24. On March 25 he confronted a force of 1,200 Creek warriors at Horseshoe Bend, a peninsula formed by the Tallapoosa River that the Creek had fortified. With an army of 4,000 militia and regulars plus allied Cherokees and White Stick Creeks, he routed the Red Stick Creeks, killing 800 and capturing 350. As a result, both Creek factions were compelled on August 9, 1814, to sign the Treaty of Fort Jackson, which ceded half of Alabama and part of Georgia to the United States.

On December 24, 1814, the War of 1812 officially ended when representatives of the United States and Great Britain signed the Treaty of Ghent. In many ways the treaty was inconclusive, simply returning the belligerents to the status quo ante bellum. For the Native Americans, however, it was a blow from which they would never recover. The negotiators agreed to restore to the Indians all rights and privileges that they had enjoyed in 1811. But the outcome of the war brought a different reality. American forces had weakened the power of the Native Americans by destroying Tecumseh's confederacy in the Northwest and the Creek Confederacy in the South and by eliminating Britain as a supporter of the Native Americans. At Ghent, to protect their former clients, the British had proposed the establishment of permanent Indian reservations and barriers to white settlement. The Americans flatly spurned both proposals.

As British officers finally abandoned forts in the Northwest, some were bitter at the perceived injustice toward the Native Americans, and some angry Indians threatened to attack their erstwhile protectors. But there was no altering the fact that the Native Americans had been humbled on the American frontier and had been left defenseless against America's westward expansion. The War of 1812 had unleashed in the United States a heady sense of national destiny and expansionism that would characterize the country for the remainder of the 19th century. Just or not, the Indians would be swept aside as this destiny was fulfilled. The warriors who fought on the British side and helped save Canada in 1812 and 1813 thus were the war's chief losers.

PAUL DAVID NELSON

See also

Creeks; Creek War; Emuckfaw Creek, Battle of; Enitachopco Creek, Battle of; Harrison, William Henry; Horseshoe Bend, Battle of; Iroquois; Iroquois Confederacy; Jackson, Andrew; Prophetstown; Raisin River Massacre; Red Sticks; Tallushatchee, Battle of; Tecumseh; Tenskwatawa; Thames, Battle of the; Tippecanoe, Battle of

References

Benn, Carl. *The Iroquois in the War of 1812.* Toronto: University of Toronto Press, 1988.

Hickey, Donald R. *The War of 1812: A Forgotten Conflict.* Urbana: University of Illinois Press, 1989.

Horsman, Reginald. *The War of 1812.* New York: Knopf, 1969.

Latimer, Jon. *1812: War with America.* Cambridge: Belknap Press of Harvard University Press, 2007.

Stanley, George F. G. "The Indians in the War of 1812." *Canadian Historical Review* 31 (1950): 145–165.

Native American Trade

Trade between Native Americans and Europeans occurred from the first point of contact in the early 1500s and remained an important mode of exchange into the late 1800s. Europeans and Native Americans regularly exchanged European-made items for furs. Both groups often used trade to create and cement offensive and defensive alliances. In general, the Native American trade network consisted of the exchange of European-produced items such as metal weapons and utensils, cloth and clothing, alcohol, and trinkets for furs that had been trapped and dressed by Native Americans as well as deerskins and foodstuffs and occasionally native slaves. In the Northeast, beaver skins were a major commodity of exchange. In the South, deerskins were exchanged for European goods. In the West and Southwest, a variety of skins, including buffalo, became principal items of exchange.

Although this trade carried distinct economic connotations for American Indians, it also contained spiritual and diplomatic elements that required trading partners to become allies in warfare. The European colonial powers of England, France, the Netherlands, Spain, and Sweden fought for control in North America and continually attempted to co-opt this indigenous process to achieve their imperial agendas in North America. The inclusion of the European powers in these indigenous trade and alliance systems and European attempts to manipulate them often increased the level of hostilities among the native peoples of North America. Additionally, the new weapons introduced by Europeans, such as knives, hatchets, and firearms, made native warfare more dangerous.

The nature of Native American trade varied according to the region. In the northern English colonies, French Canada, the Great Lakes, and the Ohio Valley, the trade centered on the exchange of beaver pelts for European goods. At first the Hurons in Canada and the powerful Iroquois Confederacy (also known as the Five Nations and later the Six Nations) in present-day New York controlled the flow of trade to the interior tribes in the North. By the late 17th century the confederacy had defeated the other tribes of the region in a series of bloody wars known as the Beaver Wars (1641–1701). From that point forward, the confederacy controlled much of the trade until the end of the French and Indian War (1754–1763).

On the European side, the French vied first with the Dutch for the northern Native American trade. That remained the case until the English replaced the Dutch in the second half of the 17th century. Although a majority of the northern native peoples ultimately allied and traded with the French, the English held the upper hand because of their alliance with the Iroquois Confederacy.

In the Southeast, English and French traders competed with each other and the long-established Spanish mission system for Native American trade in the late 17th and early 18th centuries. In this region, American Indians traded war captives (or Native American slaves) and deerskins to the English primarily for guns and ammunition. The French and the Spanish did not participate in the slave trade, but they did accept deerskins for a variety of trade items. The inability of the French to provide sufficient numbers of muskets to their native allies and the reluctance of the

Depiction of Englishmen trading with Native Americans. Engraving by William Faden, 1777. (Library of Congress)

Spanish to provide firearms for their mission natives led to the victimization of these groups by armed slave raiders. Thus, the native slave trade led to a dramatic increase in native warfare in the region.

The increased presence of disease brought by the European settlers to North America combined with the establishment of the native slave trade devastated the Mississippian chiefdoms that had dominated the South prior to the arrival of Europeans. This caused a radical realignment of indigenous peoples in the late 17th century and the 18th century. This realignment created the historic Catawba, Cherokee, Chickasaw, Choctaw, Creek, and Miccosukee Seminole societies.

Throughout North America, the Native American trade eventually forced American Indians into a relationship of dependency on Europeans. This dependency eventually eroded native sovereignty as the colonial period drew to a close. Furthermore, the increased use of alcohol as a trade item by Europeans sped up the process of dependency and the disruption of native societies in the 18th century. Overall, Europeans used native trade to gain control over American Indians. The British, more so than other Europeans, specifically manipulated trade to drive the natives into debt in order to acquire large amounts of land. Later the Americans would do much the same as white expansion continued inexorably westward. Trade in the 19th century would follow similar patterns, both on the Great Plains and in the Southwest and Far West. However, trading patterns were often interrupted by intertribal warfare, warfare with Americans, and overhunting and overtrapping. The beaver was trapped practically to extinction, for example, in the Northeast and in southern Canada by around 1800, and buffalo shared a similar fate in the West by the 1880s. This not only affected trade but also severely disrupted Native American societies. The near disappearance of the buffalo wrought havoc on Plains tribes, as the animals were at the very center of their economic, political, and social activities.

Although largely dependent on the buffalo, the Comanches and other tribes of the southern Plains engaged in a durable and diverse exchange with generations of Hispanic and mixed-blood traders from New Mexico known as Comancheros, who provided manufactured goods, arms, and ammunition in exchange for horses, usually taken from Texas and Mexican ranches; buffalo robes; and captives who were sold into slavery. The Comancheros operated out of isolated trading camps in New Mexico and the canyons of the Llano Estacado (Staked Plains), providing reliable and lucrative commerce until the Red River War (1874–1875) put an end to that relationship in the mid-1870s. Throughout the West, enterprising merchants, many of poor character, traded liberally with the warrior tribes who opposed westward expansion. These traders provided high-quality firearms and ammunition as well as alcohol and trade goods in exchange for a wide range of currency, including stolen property and livestock.

DIXIE RAY HAGGARD

See also

Beaver Wars; Buffalo; Catawbas; Cherokees; Chickasaws; Choctaws; Comanches; Creeks; Firearms Trade; Iroquois; Iroquois Confederacy; Liquor; Wyandots

References

Adair, E. R. "Anglo-French Rivalry in the Fur Trade during the 18th Century." *Culture* 8 (1947): 434–455.

Braund, Kathryn E. Holland. *Deerskins & Duffels: The Creek Indian Trade with Anglo-America, 1685–1815.* Lincoln: University of Nebraska Press, 1993.

Jacobs, Wilbur R. *Wilderness Politics and Indian Gifts: The Northern Colonial Frontier, 1748–1763.* Stanford, CA: Stanford University Press, 1950.

Mancall, Peter C. *Deadly Medicine: Indians and Alcohol in Early America.* Ithaca, NY: Cornell University Press, 1995.

Morris, Michael P. *The Bringing of Wonder: Trade and the Indians of the Southeast, 1700–1783.* Westport, CT: Greenwood, 1999.

Usner, Daniel H., Jr. *Indians, Settlers, and Slaves in a Frontier Exchange Economy: The Lower Mississippi Valley before 1783.* Chapel Hill: University of North Carolina Press, 1992.

White, Richard. *The Middle Ground: Indians, Empires, and Republics in the Great Lakes Region, 1650–1815.* New York: Cambridge University Press, 1991.

Wishart, David J. *An Unspeakable Sadness: The Dispossession of the Nebraska Indians.* Lincoln: University of Nebraska Press, 1994.

Native American Warfare

Combat techniques of Native American warriors evolved with and in response to influences introduced by Europeans, including firearms technology. In fact, native capacities to adopt and employ European weaponry and adjust to European tactics were highly varied and innovative. Moreover, native warfare with Europeans and adoption of the latter's technology occurred on the basis of native perspectives and perceptions that reflected and affected native approaches to conflict.

The most common fighting tactic used by Native Americans was the so-called skulking way of war, which was marked by a reliance on stealth, surprise, taking advantage of terrain, and individual initiative. Contrary to the contemporary European practice of deploying soldiers in close-order formations firing group volleys under strict command, natives moved, aimed, fired, and used cover individually and rarely engaged in sustained fighting when finding themselves at a disadvantage.

Historians disagree over whether the natives' skulking tactics were in widespread use before contact with Europeans or whether they represented an adaptation to the Europeans' introduction of firearms. Some evidence, including early accounts by Samuel de Champlain of New France and Governor Cadwallader Colden of New York, indicate that natives may have fought large-scale battles between massed forces in open terrain until the availability of firearms made such tactics too costly. Other accounts, however, demonstrate that at least some native tribes employed

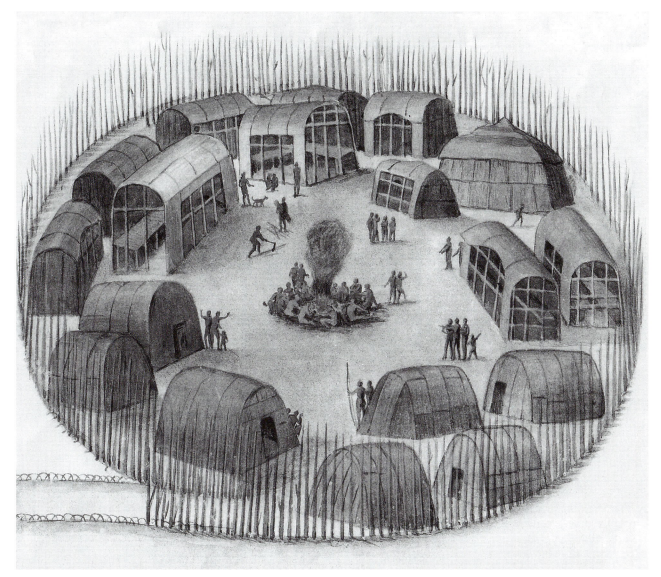

The palisaded Indian village of Pomeioc in present-day North Carolina, painted by John White in 1585. Native Americans employed palisaded settlements as a defense against attack. (National Archives)

skulking methods before European contact because these tactics conformed to the native practice of minimizing casualties in warfare and the desire to obtain captives for adoption into the tribe.

Skulking techniques could not have been used in every form of combat because natives, particularly the Iroquois, sometimes assaulted the palisaded towns of their enemies, which required the attackers to fire on the fortified town with arrows (and later muskets), providing cover while small assaulting parties hacked their way through the wooden palisade. These tactics also required modification, as the defenders adapted by constructing flanking positions to defend their fortifications against such attacks.

Palisades around settlements were used as a means of defense by many native groups, including the Hurons, the Iroquois, and the Susquehannocks. Such fortifications remained in use until the mid-18th century and provided effective protection against native enemies. However, they proved to be of limited use against European attackers and could even make the occupants of fortified towns more vulnerable to colonial attacks, as shown during the Pequot War (1636–1638) and King Philip's War (1675–1676). In both conflicts, English colonists surrounded and set fire to native forts, trapping the natives inside and slaughtering them when they attempted to escape the flames. Natives thus tried to improve their fortifications, observing and adopting European defensive techniques such as adding ditches outside the palisade to obstruct an attacker's approach.

Natives faced with the difficulty of attacking colonial forts, garrison houses, and vessels used a variety of innovations to ease their tasks. In August 1675 during King Philip's War, Nipmucks assaulting Brookfield, Massachusetts, constructed siege engines

Atsina (now known as Gros Ventre) chiefs on horseback. One of the chiefs holds a coup stick. Photograph by Edward S. Curtis, circa 1908. (Library of Congress)

to try to set fire to a fortified garrison house, as did natives who attacked a garrison house in Saco, Maine, a month later. Abenakis in 1724 and Ottawas and Pottawatomis in 1763 used fireships in efforts to destroy British and colonial vessels on rivers. The latter incident took place during the siege of Detroit at the height of Pontiac's Rebellion (1763). The native besiegers also constructed field fortifications to protect their positions around Fort Detroit. In June 1763 Senecas who attacked and captured Fort Presque Isle used approach trenches and tunnels to come safely within attacking distance of their objective.

Skulking tactics, the use and continuing development of fortifications, and the employment of siege engines and fireships demonstrate the wide variety of techniques used in warfare by Native Americans as well as their ability to adapt and innovate to meet new military challenges. Yet although native tactics are well documented, how the Native Americans formulated strategy and what those strategies were remain largely unknown.

The lack of information regarding native strategy is the result of the almost complete absence of native sources that could provide insight into their larger military goals and how native leaders planned to achieve them. Nearly all contemporary accounts of native strategy were recorded by Europeans or colonists, whose efforts to explain the rationale and decisions behind native military operations more accurately reflect the views of the writers rather than those of native leaders. All that can be said with certainty is

that native leaders often worked to form intertribal alliances to counter the numerical superiority of the colonists, that they often sought (as in the Second Anglo-Powhatan War, King Philip's War, and Pontiac's Rebellion) to launch a coordinated series of surprise attacks to catch their enemies off guard and inflict maximum damage at the least possible cost to themselves, and that their ability to conduct sustained operations was impeded by the need to raise crops, hunt, and otherwise provide subsistence for their people, although if a European ally provided food supplies, native forces could remain in the field longer.

The subsistence aspect of native warfare proved to be the natives' greatest vulnerability, and colonists quickly learned that they could force their native enemies to sue for peace by attacking and destroying towns, cornfields, and stored food supplies at less cost in casualties than it would have taken to seek out and engage native warriors in combat.

Another element of native strategy was to lay siege to posts that could not be carried by assault and then focus on interdicting supplies and reinforcements. Pontiac used this method unsuccessfully during the five-month siege of Detroit in 1763, and his allies used the same strategy in an effort to force the surrender of Fort Pitt. In both cases, however, British relief forces were able to fight their way through to the beleaguered garrisons.

Although native strategy and tactics proved insufficient to protect their territory from the European colonists, native fighting methods did prove remarkably successful. King Philip's War checked the expansion of New England for several decades, the Iroquois managed to maintain their hold on their core territory in New York until the American Revolutionary War (1775–1783), and Pontiac's Rebellion caused the British to halt expansion beyond the Appalachian Ridge. The greatest factors that enabled the colonists to overcome native resistance were not the strategic or tactical failures of the natives but rather the epidemic diseases that decimated the native population of North America and internecine warfare among native groups that prevented unified opposition to the European newcomers.

Raiding, especially in the West throughout the 18th and 19th centuries, was an integral part of Native American warfare. In the Southwest, the Apaches and Navajos raided the Pueblos, the Spanish, and later the Americans. Raids involved small bands of warriors on fast horses, and many times horses were the targets of the raids. The Blackfeet may have launched as many as 50 raids per year. Many of the western tribes were expert at launching surprise raids, especially on unsuspecting villages. They frequently carried these out in the predawn hours, or they targeted settlements where they knew most of the men were away on a hunt, thus permitting them to move into the villages with virtually no resistance.

Most tribes did not fight European-style set-piece battles; instead, they relied on guerrilla attacks and ambushes. A few, however, fielded large armies. The Timucuas and Saturiouas of Florida were capable of maintaining a force of as many as 2,000 warriors at one time. In the Southwest, the Pimas, Yumas, Maricopas, and

Mojaves sometimes fought set-piece battles during which warriors lined up in rows and attacked the opposing force with clubs and poles.

Warfare on the open Plains followed similar patterns. Military campaigns or raids involved small groups of warriors, oftentimes acting independently. However, there are notable examples of Plains tribes combining forces to field large armies of hundreds of warriors. Although the Battle of the Little Bighorn (June 25–26, 1876) was something of an anomaly, it did reveal the potential for large-unit action by allied Indian forces. Horses made raiding and ambushing far more practical and lethal, and the adoption of firearms by Native Americans saw a further reduction in the size of raiding and war parties. Before firearms, many Native Americans, especially on the Plains and in the Southwest, employed body armor made of animal hides. Many tribes on the northern and central Plains also employed a type of psychological warfare using a coup stick. That is, instead of killing an opponent, a warrior would touch him with a coup stick. This was meant to suggest that the warrior holding the coup stick could have easily hurt or killed his opponent had he desired to do so.

As with the Native Americans in the East, the Native Americans of the Plains and the West were intrepid and highly effective fighters. They fought valiantly to hold on to their lands and resist white encroachment. That they lost most of their territory to Americans does not mean that they were not good military strategists or tacticians. Indeed, many historians argue that Native Americans were better horsemen than U.S. cavalrymen. What made the difference, then, were diseases, which wrought havoc on Native American peoples, and the superior firepower of the U.S. Army.

MATTHEW S. MUEHLBAUER AND JIM PIECUCH

See also

Anglo-Powhatan War, Second; Bow and Arrow; Brookfield, Siege of; French and Indian War; Horses; King Philip's War; Mourning War; Muskets; Pequot War; Pontiac's Rebellion; Rifles; Skulking Way of War; Tomahawk

References

Calloway, Colin G. *The Western Abenakis of Vermont, 1600–1800: War, Migration, and the Survival of an Indian People.* Norman: University of Oklahoma Press, 1990.

Hirsch, Adam J. "The Collision of Military Cultures in Seventeenth-Century New England." *Journal of American History* 74 (March 1988): 1187–1212.

Jennings, Francis. *The Invasion of America: Indians, Colonialism, and the Cant of Conquest.* 1976; reprint, Chapel Hill: University of North Carolina Press, 2010.

Lee, Wayne E. "Fortify, Fight, or Flee: Tuscarora and Cherokee Defensive Warfare and Military Culture Adaptation." *Journal of Military History* 68 (July 2004): 713–770.

Malone, Patrick M. *The Skulking Way of War: Technology and Tactics among the New England Indians.* Lanham, MD: Madison Books, 2000.

Richter, Daniel K. *The Ordeal of the Longhouse: The People of the Iroquois League in the Era of European Colonization.* Chapel Hill: University of North Carolina Press, 1992.

Starkey, Armstrong. *European and Native American Warfare, 1675–1815.* Norman: University of Oklahoma Press, 1998.

Nativism, Indian

Philosophy and phenomenon of spiritual revitalization among Native American communities coping with the loss of power to European colonial regimes and later the United States. Often combining traditional beliefs with selected elements of the colonial culture, nativist movements of the late 18th century and the 19th century contributed to the development of a Pan-Indian identity and sometimes inspired militant resistance.

European colonization of North America wrought tremendous changes among the continent's indigenous populations. While geographic isolation or colonial competition helped preserve the autonomy of many Native American groups, all eventually had to contend with a balance of power that tipped in favor of the Europeans and their descendants. The erosion of autonomy created political, social, economic, and spiritual crises occasioned by a lost way of life and deteriorating self-confidence. Once-vibrant communities descended into internal dissension, fear of malevolent spiritual forces, and alcohol abuse. Confronted with alien customs that appeared at once superior and at the root of their suffering, Native American communities often divided over the proper response. Some Native American leaders sought to regain power by making the best possible accommodation with whites; scholars have variously termed such individuals "progressives," "cosmopolitans," or "accommodationists." Others looked to spiritual sources for salvation. Because they drew on traditional beliefs and sometimes rejected white culture, scholars have called these Native Americans "conservatives," "primordialists," or "nativists."

Nativists often blamed Native American suffering on their departure from traditional ways and spirituality. Conceiving all Native Americans to be inherently alike but unlike whites, some nativists believed that it was unnatural to emulate another race. While many white colonists held that the Native Americans could only be redeemed through assimilation, most nativists believed the opposite: their woeful condition was a consequence of their having tried to live like Europeans. Yet the distinction between nativists and accommodationists is easily overdrawn. While nativists rejected certain European practices (most commonly the consumption of alcohol), they routinely incorporated elements of European culture and Christian beliefs into a new worldview. Preaching to the Iroquois at the dawn of the 19th century, the Seneca prophet Handsome Lake used nativist ideology to encourage acculturation with whites.

Handsome Lake was but one of a host of prophets who professed access to sources of spiritual power and pathways to salvation. In the early 1760s the Delaware prophet Neolin rose to prominence by promising spiritual power to Native Americans still coming to terms with France's calamitous defeat in the French and Indian War (1754–1763). Advocating renewed faith in native rituals, temperance, and the gradual abandonment of European manufactures, Neolin evoked a Pan-Indian consciousness among the tribes of the Ohio Country and beyond. When in 1763 the British made it clear that they would treat the Native Americans as conquered subjects rather than sovereign nations, Neolin's

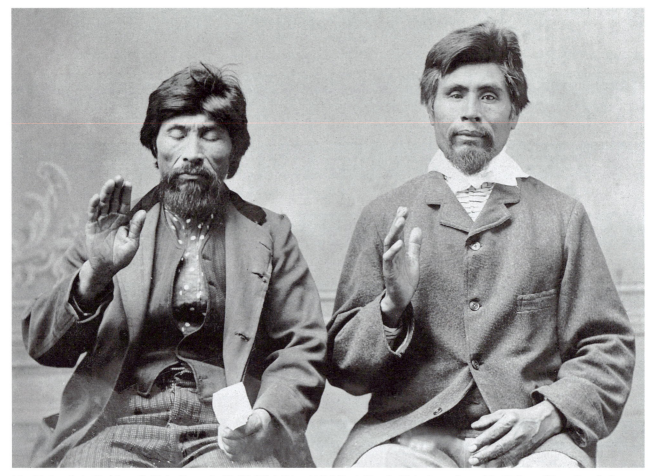

Messiah Squ-Sacht-Un (also called John Slocum) with Chief High Priest Ai-Yal (Louis Yowaluch), both members of the Shakers of Puget Sound, circa 1892. (National Anthropological Archives, Smithsonian Institution, NAA INV 06487500)

teachings provided the ideological foundation for a multitribal response. Pontiac's Rebellion (1763) failed to evict the British but compelled the reformation of British Indian policy and solidified a Pan-Indian ideology of resistance east of the Mississippi River.

This ideology persevered in various forms through the 1830s but reached its high-water mark in the early 19th century under the stewardship of the Shawnee prophet Tenskwatawa and his charismatic brother Tecumseh. Like many other nativist prophets, Tenskwatawa lived a debauched life before a vision in 1805 showed him the path to salvation. Tenskwatawa encouraged followers to avoid Americans and reject their ways while resurrecting traditional Native American practices. Meanwhile, Tecumseh traveled among the eastern tribes assembling a broad confederacy to stem American expansion. Dealt a significant setback at the Battle of Tippecanoe (November 7, 1811), Tenskwatawa and Tecumseh's movement disintegrated with the defeat of their British allies and Tecumseh's death in the War of 1812.

Nativist movements surfaced among the more diffuse tribes of the Trans-Mississippi West as the tide of American expansion swept over them. Messianic visions gave rise in the 1850s to the Dreamer religion in the Columbia River Valley and in the 1880s to the Indian Shakers around Puget Sound. Perhaps the most

significant nativist movement of the late 19th century was the Ghost Dance religion of the Paiute shaman Wovoka. Although Wovoka's message was essentially peaceful, it expressed antiwhite sentiments that resonated with some militant Sioux. Hoping to preempt a violent uprising, federal troops instead invited a tragedy on December 29, 1890, when they attempted to disarm a recalcitrant band of Miniconjou Sioux. The ensuing Battle of Wounded Knee became a touchstone for adherents to a nativist ideology and Pan-Indian identity that persists to this day.

JOHN W. HALL

See also

French and Indian War; Ghost Dance; Glaize, The; Miniconjou Sioux; Native Americans and the War of 1812; Neolin; Pontiac; Pontiac's Rebellion; Senecas; Tecumseh; Tenskwatawa; Tippecanoe, Battle of; Wabokieshiek; Wounded Knee, Battle of; Wovoka

References

Dowd, Gregory Evans. *A Spirited Resistance: The North American Indian Struggle for Unity, 1745–1815.* Baltimore: Johns Hopkins University Press, 1992.

Ostler, Jeffrey. *The Plains Sioux and U.S. Colonialism from Lewis and Clark to Wounded Knee.* Cambridge: Cambridge University Press, 2004.

Wallace, Anthony F. C. *The Death and Rebirth of the Seneca.* New York: Knopf, 1970.

Navajo Removal
Event Date: 1864

Forced relocation of the Navajos by U.S. volunteer forces in 1864. As with the Cherokees' Trail of Tears 26 years earlier, the removal of the Navajos (Dinés) from their traditional homeland in 1864 marked a pivotal event in Navajo history and culture. At the outset of war with Mexico in 1846, U.S. troops under the command of Colonel Stephen Watts Kearny occupied Santa Fe, New Mexico, on their way to California. In October of that year Kearny sent Colonel Alexander William Doniphan into present-day northeastern Arizona to inform the Navajos that they now fell under the authority of the U.S. government. There Doniphan concluded the first of seven peace treaties negotiated between the Navajos and the United States during 1846–1868.

For many Navajos, however, Doniphan's treaty had no validity. In an effort to bring broader compliance to U.S. demands, the army launched military expeditions into Navajo country, specifically targeting the stronghold of Canyon de Chelly. In September 1847 a battalion under the command of Major Robert Walker invaded the upper reaches of the canyon but encountered few people with whom to treat. Two years later Colonel John Macrae Washington made a similar foray, this time with some success. Washington's expedition resulted in a treaty signed on September 9, 1849, and ratified by the U.S. Senate a year later that gave the U.S. government the power to establish military posts, agencies, and trading posts in

Navajo country. However, the unfortunate death of seven Navajo men, including a respected elder, at the hands of Washington's men led to continued resistance to the designs of the United States.

Between 1850 and 1860 animosity between the Navajos and the United States intensified. The U.S. Senate, unwilling to pay Native Americans or to set aside land for their use, was loath to ratify further treaties with the Navajos. In 1860 an attack by 1,000 Navajo warriors against U.S. troops at Fort Defiance in the southern part of Navajo country nearly met with success. Accordingly, the commander of the Department of New Mexico, Colonel Edward R. S. Canby, became increasingly convinced that the best way to handle the problem was simply to move the Navajos out of their homeland and onto a reservation. Canby's threatened removal policy resulted in an 1861 treaty signed by 49 Navajo leaders who had led the attack on Fort Defiance the previous year. The treaty, like many of its predecessors, never passed the Senate.

As the American Civil War (1861–1865) engulfed the country, Canby's focus necessarily shifted away from Native American problems and toward the Confederate presence in New Mexico. Following his victory over Confederate forces at Glorieta Pass (March 26–28, 1862), Canby was promoted to brigadier general and transferred to Washington, D.C. Command of the Department of New Mexico now fell to Brigadier General James Henry Carleton. With the Confederate threat to New Mexico eased, Carleton returned to the execution of the removal policy articulated by his predecessor. Carleton sought to remove the Navajos (as well as the

A number of Navajos being held at Fort Sumner, New Mexico, in 1866, following their removal from their ancestral lands by soldiers under Colonel Christopher ("Kit") Carson two years earlier. (Courtesy Palace of the Governors Photo Archives (NMHM/DCA), 038194)

Mescalero Apaches) from Navajo country and isolate the Native Americans at Bosque Redondo along the Pecos River in eastern New Mexico Territory.

Realizing that the Navajos would not leave on their own accord, Carleton sent soldiers under the command of Colonel Christopher "Kit" Carson into Navajo country to force its inhabitants to depart. Carson recognized that control of Canyon de Chelly was the key to the operation. A brief but devastating campaign in the snow-blanketed canyon in January 1864 proved successful, as thousands of Navajos were forced out of their homes, rounded up, and sent first to Fort Wingate near present-day Gallup, New Mexico, and then on the infamous Long Walk to Fort Sumner at the Bosque Redondo. The trip took 20 days, during which a great many Navajos died. Many more died at Bosque Redondo, a place singularly ill-suited for habitation. To make matters worse, the Mescalero Apaches, with whom the Navajos had been forced to share the reservation, had been their traditional adversaries. After several years of virtual incarceration, the Navajos signed a treaty with the U.S. government on June 1, 1868, allowing them to return to a portion of Navajo country: 3.328 million acres, including most of Canyon de Chelly.

ALAN C. DOWNS

See also

Bosque Redondo; Canby, Edward Richard Sprigg; Canby's Campaign; Canyon de Chelly, Arizona; Carleton, James Henry; Carleton's Campaign; Carson, Christopher Houston; Navajos

References

Dunlay, Thomas W. *Kit Carson and the Indians.* Lincoln: University of Nebraska Press, 2000.

Iverson, Peter. *Diné: A History of the Navajos.* Albuquerque: University of New Mexico Press, 2002.

Navajos

Native American tribe of the American Southwest. The Navajos, or Dinés (meaning "the People"), are the largest reservation tribe in the United States with a population of more than 200,000 people. The Navajo Nation comprises 25,000 square miles in New Mexico, Arizona, and southern Utah in an area known as Dinétah. Navajo lineage can be traced to the Athabascan tribes of northwestern Canada and Alaska that migrated southward and arrived in the American Southwest by the early 1500s. Their language, Navajo, is derived from their Athabascan heritage. Navajo culture is matrilineal, based on clan kinship, and their religion is polytheistic. The center of Navajo life is the home (*hogan*).

Early Navajo subsistence, predicated upon trade, demanded the creation of trading agreements with neighboring tribes. Navajo and Pueblo trade existed for generations, as did commerce with the Utes, Hopis, and Comanches. Tribal interaction was mostly positive, but issues such as land control, horse stealing, and human slave trafficking led to bloodshed. Intertribal conflict and the Navajos' desire to expand their territory led to them being considered warlike, a reputation they carried into the 20th century.

During the Spanish occupation of the Southwest, the Navajos remained nomadic traders and expansionists. These ideals eventually brought the Navajos and Pueblos into conflict. Navajo and Spanish trade was extensive, as were land disputes and horse theft. Fighting between the two nations was sporadic throughout the Spanish colonial period. The Navajos refused to relinquish sovereignty over their ancestral land to Spain; however, contact with Spanish settlers brought the introduction of domestic livestock, especially sheep. Sheepherding soon became an integral part of Navajo life, as did seasonal farming. Early Navajo units were wanderers and without a singular identity. Thus, herding tied them to the land and acted as a strong tribal unifier. The protection of their land would eventually bring them into direct conflict with a westward-bound United States.

During the Mexican-American War (1846–1848), the United States sought control of the Southwest. Newly commissioned governor of the New Mexico Territory Brigadier General Stephen Watts Kearny quickly declared the Navajos enemies. Occupation of Dinétah by an outside power was unacceptable to the Navajos and resulted in a series of raids by both sides. One such raid occurred on August 31, 1849, and resulted in the killing of the elderly Navajo leader Narbona. Narbona was replaced by his son-in-law Manuelito, who witnessed the killing and was particularly outraged. The following September the U.S. Congress ratified the Navajo Treaty of 1849, which allowed the United States to establish posts and agencies and set restrictions on Navajo boundaries.

Many of the Navajos, including Manuelito, who was not a party to its signing, despised the treaty. In 1851 the United States constructed and began operations at Fort Defiance, situated on ancestral Navajo land. On April 30, 1860, Manuelito and Barboncito led an unsuccessful attack on the fort in an attempt to take the stronghold and reclaim lost territory, but the attack only resulted in the strengthening of anti-Navajo sentiment.

With the outbreak of the American Civil War (1861–1865), the control of the territory soon fell to Brigadier General James H. Carleton. He decided on a plan of removal for the Navajos to end conflict and thus encourage white settlement in the western interior. The plan involved forcibly removing the Navajos from Dinétah to an area on the Pecos River in eastern New Mexico known as Bosque Redondo. Colonel Christopher "Kit" Carson, a Mexican-American War veteran and frontiersman, was appointed to oversee the removal. He decided that a mixed force of U.S. volunteers working with neighboring tribes could force the Navajos into exile.

Beginning in 1863, attacks on Diné settlements were overwhelmingly destructive and brutal and culminated in a showdown in the Navajo stronghold of Canyon de Chelly in January 1864. Those Navajos not killed faced starvation and exposure during a freezing winter. With few options left, some 9,000 Dinés began

Navajo family group in Canyon de Chelly, New Mexico Territory. The woman is weaving at a loom; the man holds a bow and arrow. Photograph by Timothy H. O'Sullivan, 1873. (National Archives)

their southeastern migration, known as the Long Walk, to Fort Sumner in the Bosque Redondo. Hundreds died en route.

Known to the Navajo as Hweeldi, Fort Sumner was inadequately provisioned to provide for the 7,300 Navajos who had survived the harrowing journey. Timber for building *hogans* was scarce, food supplies were limited, and the water was polluted. Diseases and attacks by other Native American groups resulted in the deaths of one-third of the Dinés.

After four years of incarceration, peace negotiations began between American representatives and Navajo leaders, including Manuelito and Barboncito. On June 1, 1868, the Treaty of Bosque Redondo ended the Navajos' exile. The return of the Navajos to Dinétah was contingent upon their acceptance of a land reduction equal to less then 10 percent of their original territory, or 3.5 million acres. By 1886 more land was returned to the Navajos. Today the Diné Bikéyah, or Navajo Country, is a semiautonomous homeland covering some 26,000 square miles (17 million acres) and occupying all of northeastern Arizona, the southeastern portion of Utah, and northwestern New Mexico. These territorial holdings represent the largest land area assigned primarily to a Native American jurisdiction within the United States. The 2000 census reported 298,215 Navajo people in the United States, of which 173,987 were within the Navajo Nation boundaries.

JASON LUTZ AND JIM PIECUCH

See also

Barboncito; Bosque Redondo; Carleton, James Henry; Carleton's Campaign; Carson, Christopher Houston; Fort Sumner; Kearny, Stephen Watts; Manuelito; Navajo Removal; Navajo War; Pueblos

References

Iverson, Peter. *Diné: A History of the Navajos.* Albuquerque: University of New Mexico Press, 2002.

Sandweiss, Martha A., ed. *Denizens of the Desert: A Tale in Word and Picture of Life among the Navaho Indians, the Letters of Elizabeth W. Forster.* Albuquerque: University of New Mexico Press, 1988.

Navajo War
Start Date: 1846
End Date: 1864

A series of mid-19th-century battles and skirmishes occurring approximately between 1846 and 1864 that pitted Americans against the Navajo tribe in the American Southwest. The 12,000 Navajos lived on the Colorado Plateau west of the Rio Grande in what is today northern Arizona and New Mexico.

The U.S. government assumed de facto control of the region encompassing the Navajo lands in 1846 during the Mexican-American War (1846–1848), and U.S. Army brigadier general Stephen Watts Kearny promised settlers and immigrants protection from the local tribes. In the years that followed, the army built a string of forts in the region and occasionally launched expeditions against the Native Americans. In one such endeavor, under Military Governor and Brevet Lieutenant Colonel John M. Washington, a strong army detachment marched into Navajo lands, skirmished with warriors, and killed a chief. The result was a peace treaty in which the Navajos promised to allow forts to be constructed on their lands in return for annual payments. As with most of the treaties concluded within the larger conflict, this one had little effect, and the Navajos and white settlers continued to raid each other.

In 1851 Colonel Edwin Sumner established Fort Defiance in the middle of Navajo territory, which placed settlers in close proximity to the Navajos and thus increased both tensions and the number of violent interactions. Tension had reached a boiling point in 1860, when 1,000 Navajo warriors attacked Fort Defiance. Some 400 members of the New Mexico Militia then raided Navajo lands, and the army launched seven separate expeditions during the last three months of 1860. At the beginning of the American Civil War (1861–1865), the U.S. Army abandoned its forts in the region, but conflict between the tribe and American settlers continued as private citizens and the militia frequently raided the Navajos.

In a major change in policy, Brigadier General Edward R. S. Canby determined in 1863 that the Navajos would have to be removed to more remote areas in order to ensure the protection of settlers. After Canby was promoted and reassigned, Brigadier

General James Henry Carleton, a veteran of the recent campaign against the Apaches, replaced him. Carleton also wanted to clear Navajo lands for various reasons, including to serve his own ambition and to make mining easier should gold be discovered in the territory. He decided that Bosque Redondo on the Pecos River in eastern New Mexico would be an appropriate place to relocate the Navajos because they would be far from settled areas and could be monitored from nearby Fort Sumner.

Even moderate Navajos rejected the idea of moving to barren lands nearly 300 miles distant. Carleton gave them an ultimatum in June 1863 to leave their lands or be treated as hostile. Colonel Christopher "Kit" Carson, who had served as a scout for Carleton in previous campaigns, was ready by the deadline with a command of more than 1,000 soldiers. Instead of trying to battle the Navajos, however, the Americans decided to target their food supplies and slowly erode the morale of the people. Carson's troops, with the help of Native American guides, ranged through Navajo lands for six months destroying crops, confiscating livestock, and burning homes while fighting relatively few skirmishes. The campaign drastically reduced the tribe's ability to survive and sapped the resolve of many of its members.

The climactic event was the assault in January 1864 on the traditional Navajo stronghold of Canyon de Chelly, a labyrinthine canyon with steep walls more than 100 feet high. Carson methodically blocked all of the exits before sending a detachment straight into the canyon. Rather than fight, the Navajos sought to escape only to find themselves trapped between groups of soldiers. For many Navajos, the capitulation at the canyon signaled the certainty of the tribe's defeat, and two-thirds of them surrendered by the end of the winter. Twenty-three Navajos lost their lives at Canyon de Chelly, while 34 others were captured. The army then marched various groups of Navajos to Bosque Redondo in the infamous Long Walk, which was marked by horrific suffering. As many as several thousand Navajos died along the way.

In 1866 the last of the Navajos submitted and joined their brethren at Bosque Redondo. Two years later the U.S. government investigated numerous testimonials about the poor quality of life at the site, decided that the land could not be farmed, and relocated the tribe to a new reservation that included some of its traditional ancestral lands.

Matthew J. Krogman

See also

Bosque Redondo; Canby, Edward Richard Sprigg; Canyon de Chelly, Arizona; Carleton, James Henry; Carson, Christopher Houston; Kearny, Stephen Watts; Navajo Removal

References

Sides, Hampton. *Blood and Thunder: An Epic of the American West.* New York: Doubleday, 2006.

Stewart, Richard W., ed. *American Military History,* Vol. 1, *The United States Army and the Forging of a Nation, 1775–1917.* Washington, DC: Center of Military History, 2005.

Tebbel, John. *The Compact History of the Indian Wars.* New York: Hawthorne, 1966.

Wooster, Robert. *The Military and United States Indian Policy, 1865–1903.* New Haven, CT: Yale University Press, 1988.

Neolin
Birth Date: Unknown
Death Date: Unknown

Native American prophet. Neolin (meaning "four") was also known as the Delaware Prophet and the Enlightened One. Although the specifics of Neolin's birth and death are unknown, he first attracted the attention of colonists as a young man preaching his beliefs on the Old Northwest frontier in 1762.

Neolin proclaimed his new nativist religion from his home in a Delaware village on the Cuyahoga River in present-day northeastern Ohio. His new religion exhibited Christian overtones, undoubtedly influenced by contact with Protestant Christian missionaries who lived and preached among the Delawares. Neolin's descriptions of the universe featured a graphic Christian hell, complete with horned devils and pitchforks, and purgatory. But his central teaching held that contact with whites, principally the British, was the cause of the Native Americans' declining fortunes. The only way for Native Americans to achieve salvation was by breaking off relations with Europeans and returning to the ways of their forefathers.

Neolin was especially vehement about prohibitions against alcohol, polygamy, and witchcraft, and he advocated a return to precontact native rituals and beliefs. He prepared religious charts—his so-called Indian Bible—for his followers on deerskins. The charts outlined separate paths for Native Americans and white men to enter heaven.

According to tradition, Neolin received his first vision and instructions in 1760 from the Delaware Great Being, Keesh-she'-lamil'-lang-up, after earlier smallpox epidemics in 1756 and 1758. Neolin informed his listeners that after sitting at the feet of the Great Being, he had been told to return to Earth with the message that the Master of Life was angry with his Native American children because they had adopted white ways. Hence, he had punished them by removing fur-bearing and other animals deep into the forests. Once natives had severed ties with whites, the animals would be restored to them. Neolin preached a nativist return to precontact traditions and a rejection of social, moral, religious, and commercial dependence on Europeans.

Significantly, Neolin allegedly reported that the Master of Life had told him that not all Europeans had to be banished from native communities. The French reportedly would be spared because they did not covet native lands and always gave gifts to their Native American friends. The land-hungry British, meanwhile, would have to go to the place set aside for them by the Master of Life. Some evidence indicates that the Ottawa leader Pontiac altered Neolin's teachings to favor the French while organizing native tribes to drive the British from native lands. Pontiac hoped that native success would induce the French to return. Other research, however, suggests that Pontiac accurately related Neolin's ideas to tribal audiences. Certainly Neolin's message reached outside of the Delaware refugee communities of the Ohio Valley and influenced the western nations of the Ottawas, the Pottawatomis, the Ojibwas, and the Wyandots in the 1760s. Pontiac capitalized on Neolin's ideas to assemble his alliance and launch his uprising in 1763 upon the end of the French and Indian War (1754–1763).

Uncertainty shrouds Neolin's activities during the years after 1764. There is some indication that, having predicted British defeat, the suppression of Pontiac's Rebellion undermined his influence. There is also evidence that in his last years the prophet took a renewed interest in conventional Christianity.

R. J. Gilmore and Bruce Vandervort

See also

Delawares; France; French and Indian War; Great Britain; Ojibwas; Old Northwest Territory; Ottawas; Pontiac; Pontiac's Rebellion; Pottawatomis

References

Dixon, David. *Never Come to Peace Again: Pontiac's Uprising and the Fate of the British Empire in North America.* Norman: University of Oklahoma Press, 2005.

Dowd, Gregory Evans. *A Spirited Resistance: The North American Indian Struggle for Unity, 1745–1815.* Baltimore: Johns Hopkins University Press, 1992.

Dowd, Gregory Evans. "Thinking and Believing: Nativism and Unity in the Ages of Pontiac and Tecumseh." *American Indian Quarterly* 16 (1992): 309–335.

Hunter, Charles E. "The Delaware Nativist Revival of the Mid-Eighteenth Century." *Ethnohistory* 18 (1971): 39–49.

Wallace, Anthony F. C. "New Religions among the Delaware Indians." *Southwest Journal of Anthropology* 12 (1956): 1–21.

New England Confederation

Union of four New England colonies first chartered on September 7, 1643, that lasted, despite several periods of stagnation, until 1691. The New England Confederation, or the United Colonies of New England, was a union of the colonies of Connecticut (Hartford), Massachusetts Bay (Boston), Plymouth, and New Haven. This marked the first attempt at a European-style federation in North America.

Colonial officials founded the confederation chiefly to provide protection from the threat presented by Native Americans and other European colonizing powers. The confederation was also intended to mediate boundary disputes involving the confederated colonies. Maine (nominally under Massachusetts's control), New Hampshire, and Rhode Island did not take part in the union.

Massachusetts hoped to annex both Maine and New Hampshire, which were barred from membership because the confederation's charter guaranteed colonial borders. As such, Massachusetts would not be able to take control over Maine and New Hampshire. The confederation refused to allow Rhode Island to join because of its religious tolerance, which was at great odds with Puritan thinking. Leaders of the other colonies hoped to be able to annex Rhode Island.

The articles of confederation contained provisos for joint military actions, defensive steps, and the raising and financing of troops in proportion to the colonies' ability to pay and the number of available men. Each colony selected two commissioners to coordinate the actions of the confederation. These commissioners held both regular and extraordinary meetings. However, the internal affairs of the member colonies were beyond the purview of the alliance.

The New England Confederation had no means to compel members to act. Commissioners simply had the power to ask for cooperation among members. The confederation's primary role was to deal with local Native Americans. This included mediating disputes between tribes or keeping peace between colonists and the natives.

The confederation was born out of several concerns, chief among them the Pequot War (1636–1638). In that conflict, New England colonists and their Native American allies vanquished the hated Pequots. Following the war, colonists and natives streamed into the vacated Pequot lands. In order to ensure an orderly settlement of Pequot territory, the interested parties entered into the 1638 Treaty of Hartford. Additionally, unrest caused by the English Civil War (1642–1649) had created concerns.

Religion was a strong motivation behind the New England Confederation. The four colonies that made up the union were all stoutly Puritan. The Puritans saw themselves as God's agents in the New World, in direct competition with the "forces of darkness" for control of New England. Accordingly, the colonists saw the need to band together for protection from the heathen natives, the Catholic French, the overly secular Dutch, and the heterodoxy of Rhode Island.

From 1643 to 1652 the confederation indeed preserved peace in the area. In 1653, however, tensions between the Dutch and the New England colonies reached a climax during the First Anglo-Dutch War (1652–1654). When Massachusetts Bay refused to join the other colonies in a proposed offensive against the Dutch, the confederation all but collapsed. The union, though still in existence after the Anglo-Dutch crisis, ceased to be a legitimate political entity for a number of years. Nevertheless, the threat from Native Americans continued unabated.

The confederation was revived in 1672 and now included the colonies of Plymouth, Massachusetts Bay, and Connecticut. New Haven Colony had been annexed by the larger Connecticut Colony in 1655. This new New England Confederation's primary goal was to provide protection from restive Native Americans. Tensions between Native Americans and the colonists erupted into the bloody King Philip's War (1675–1676), a conflict that forever destroyed Native American power in New England.

The New England Confederation witnessed a brief resurgence between 1689 and 1691. The union helped deal with an Abenaki uprising in northern New England and assisted in negotiations for a friendship treaty with the Mohawks. The confederation dissolved for good in 1691, when Massachusetts lost its charter and became a Crown colony.

RICK DYSON

See also

Abenakis; Hartford, Treaty of; King Philip's War; Mohawks; Pequots; Pequot War; Puritans

References

Lister, Frederick. *The Early Security Confederations: From the Ancient Greeks to the United Colonies of New England.* Westport, CT: Greenwood, 1999.

Pulsifer, David, ed. *Acts of the Commissioners of the United Colonies,* Vols. 9 and 10, *Records of the Colony of New Plymouth.* Boston: William White, Printer to the Commonwealth, 1859.

Vaughan, Alden T. *New England Frontier: Puritans and Indians, 1620–1675.* 3rd ed. Norman: University of Oklahoma Press, 1995.

Ward, Harry M. *The United Colonies of New England, 1643–90.* New York: Vantage, 1961.

New France

See France

New Mexico

Frontier region controlled by New Spain and then Mexico and since 1846 by the United States. In the early 16th century, survivors from the 1528 Pánfilo de Narváez expedition to Florida, having been shipwrecked on the coast of present-day Texas, journeyed across northern Mexico in hopes of making their way home. Following his eventual rescue, Alvar Núñez Cabeza de Vaca, the leader of the group, reported rumors of cities to the north that contained an abundance of wealth.

These stories appeared to validate Aztec mythology, so the viceroy of New Spain authorized exploratory expeditions into the northern frontier of Mexico in search of cities of gold and silver. Francisco Vásquez de Coronado, governor of the province of New Galicia in northern Mexico, led the largest of these expeditions from 1540 to 1542. Coronado, with approximately 300 Spanish cavalry and infantry and more than 1,000 Tlaxcalan natives, journeyed up the Rio Grande Valley into the land of the Pueblos only to find none of the anticipated opulent cities. Instead the Spanish conquistadors discovered desert towns of stone and mud-plastered dwellings containing not riches but stores of maize and beans.

Coronado's accounts of his unprofitable expedition dissuaded further official forays into the northern Mexican frontier for some 50 years. There were, however, occasional unsanctioned ventures northward during this period by Franciscan priests and civilian opportunists. One such expedition was led by Gaspar Castaño de Sosa, who in January 1590 led 170 settlers up the Rio Grande to the Pecos River in hopes of finding productive silver mines. Pursued by the viceregal agent, Captain Juan Morlete, Sosa was arrested and sent back to Mexico in chains.

In 1595, however, the Spanish court commissioned Juan de Oñate, the son of a wealthy silver mine owner, to lead an expedition up the Rio Grande to spread the Catholic faith, pacify the natives, and establish a permanent colony in the northern provinces of New Spain. In 1598 Oñate and 500 men, women, and children entered New Mexico near present-day El Paso, Texas, and claimed possession of the land and its people. Oñate arrived at the confluence of the Chama River and the Rio Grande in July and established his headquarters at Ohke Pueblo, which he renamed San Juan, the capital of the new colony.

From San Juan, Oñate personally conducted a reconnaissance of the province. Native hospitality turned to resistance at Acoma Pueblo in January 1599, leaving 11 Spanish soldiers dead. In retaliation, Oñate sent a punitive expedition against the town, killing 800 men, women, and children and taking another 580 captive. In 1601 Oñate moved the capital across the Rio Grande to Yunque Ouinge Pueblo and renamed it San Gabriel. Nine years later the capital moved again, this time to its permanent location at Santa Fe.

Throughout much of the 17th century, New Mexico existed mainly as an outpost on the fringes of the Spanish Empire. There was no Spanish military garrison in the colony, and the settlers were expected to serve as soldiers if necessary. With only one urban center (Santa Fe) in the province, most of New Mexico's 3,000 colonists lived in scattered settlements near the Pueblos along the Rio Grande and profited from the exploitation of native labor. The realization that there were few riches to be found among the Pueblos persuaded many colonists to return to Mexico and offered little incentive for new colonists to venture northward. Life challenged those who remained, and support from Mexico was rarely forthcoming. Warding off Apache, Ute, and Navajo raiders proved especially problematic. Church and civil authorities seldom got along, and corruption and abuse of power were commonplace.

The repressive policies of the Spaniards toward the Native Americans, particularly in the realm of religion, reached a boiling point in 1680. Popé, a spiritual leader from San Juan Pueblo, preached the maintenance of traditional religious practices and railed against all things Spanish and Christian. As Popé's message spread throughout the Pueblos, Governor Juan Francisco Treviño ordered the arrest of native spiritual leaders in the province. Because of the loss of their religious leaders, the Rio Grande Pueblos threatened to rebel against the Spanish and prompted a worried Treviño to free his captives. On his release, Popé devised plans for a widespread revolt. He unified the majority of Pueblos in a coordinated uprising against their oppressors in early August 1680.

The success of the Pueblo Revolt kept the upper reaches of the Rio Grande free from Spanish control for 12 years. When the Spanish returned to New Mexico in 1692 under Diego de Vargas, the Pueblos responded with minimal resistance. Spanish officials quickly repressed any opposition that they encountered.

Effective Spanish control of the province resumed in 1696 but with a decidedly different approach toward the Pueblos. Natives were allowed to retain their religious icons and ceremonies. Labor and food requisitions were moderated. Spanish officials went so far as to arm the Pueblos to help them ward off raiding tribes. Throughout the remainder of the colonial period, the Pueblos were spared the repressive policies of the pre-1680 era, as Spain grew more concerned about encroachments along the fringes of its provinces than it was about the conversion of natives to Catholicism.

As French traders along the Gulf of Mexico and the upper reaches of the Mississippi River Valley began seeking trading partners among the inhabitants of New Mexico and as Comanche raiding parties began threatening New Mexican settlements, the viceroy of New Spain responded by increasing the Spanish military presence in the province. The construction of presidios at El Paso del Norte in 1681 and at Santa Fe in 1693 were followed by punitive campaigns against nomadic natives and unwanted Frenchmen.

After the War of the Quadruple Alliance (1718–1720)—in which Britain, France, Holland, and Austria fought against Spain—erupted in Europe, New Mexican governor Antonio Valverde y Cosío dispatched his lieutenant governor, Lieutenant General Pedro de Villasur, to seize French fur traders who had entered New Mexico illegally and to gather information about French activities along the northern frontier.

Villasur and his force of 45 soldiers, 60 Pueblo Indian allies, some Apache scouts, and Father Juan Minguez marched to the confluence of the Platte and Loup rivers in present-day Nebraska before Pawnee and Oto warriors (possibly aided by a few French fur traders) attacked them at dawn on August 14, 1720. The general, 31 soldiers, 11 Pueblo Indians, and the priest were killed. The defeat, which the survivors blamed on the French fur traders, demoralized Spanish forces in New Mexico and spawned fears of a French invasion.

The conclusion of the French and Indian War (1754–1763) and the terms of the 1763 Treaty of Paris removed the French threat from New Spain's frontier, only to replace it with worries about roving natives and, until 1783, the British Empire. In 1779 the governor of New Mexico, Juan Bautista de Anza, led 800 soldiers on a punitive expedition against the western Comanches who had been systematically raiding New Mexican settlements for years. Anza decisively defeated the Comanches north of present-day Pueblo, Colorado, and established long-term peaceful relations with their leaders.

With the exception of a brief foray in 1807 by a party of U.S. explorers under Lieutenant Zebulon Pike (who was detained by Spanish officials in Santa Fe), American interest in New Mexico did not really materialize until the 1820s with the establishment of the Santa Fe Trail. For the remainder of the colonial period until Mexican independence in 1821, New Mexico existed as part of the Comandancia General de las Provincias Internas (General Command of Inland Provinces), a semiautonomous administrative entity designed by the Spanish court to boost morale among the presidios, coordinate military campaigns across the northern frontier, promote immigration, and foster economic development in the region.

Between 1821 and 1848, at which time the Mexicans had ceded New Mexico to the United States, the Mexican government fought a number of battles with the region's Native Americans. There were perhaps 30,000 Mexicans living in New Mexico by the eve of the Mexican-American War (1846–1848), but the area remained sparsely populated and, like other northern border areas, received relatively little attention from settlers and the central government in Mexico City. In 1846 following the outbreak of hostilities between the United States and Mexico, Colonel (soon to be brigadier general) Stephen Watts Kearny arrived in New Mexico to assert U.S. authority over the region.

After the 1848 Mexican land cession to the United States, some Americans had hoped to bring New Mexico into the Union as a state. However, this raised concerns about the spread of slavery, so statehood was long postponed. Further complicating matters were Texas land claims on eastern portions of New Mexico, which were finally settled by the Compromise of 1850. That same year the New Mexico Territory was created and encompassed virtually all of the present-day states of New Mexico and Arizona. In 1912 just one month apart, both were admitted to the Union.

Throughout the 1850s, Navajo and Apache raids on American and Mexican settlers in the territory posed a continuing problem for the United States. Beginning in 1853 when Christopher "Kit" Carson became the U.S. Indian agent for New Mexico, he oversaw a number of fairly successful expeditions designed to break the back of tribal resistance. Upon the beginning of the American Civil War in 1861, Confederate forces briefly occupied northern New Mexico before their defeat at the Battle of Glorieta Pass in March 1862. In the meantime, Carson mounted several campaigns against the Comanches, Apaches, and Navajos in New Mexico and western Texas, resulting in the forced relocation of the Navajos and Mescalero Apaches to the barren Bosque Redondo Reservation in eastern New Mexico. In 1863 Arizona became part of a separate territory, so the New Mexico Territory generally encompassed all of present-day New Mexico. Occasional Apache raiding continued after the war ended in 1865, highlighted by Victorio's vigorous raiding in the late 1870s and Geronimo's numerous outbreaks, and did not cease until Geronimo's capture in 1886. In 1874 a column of troops under Major William R. Price, based in New Mexico, participated in the Red River War that brought the final subjugation of the Comanches.

Alan C. Downs

See also

Acoma Pueblo, Battle of; Apaches; Carson, Christopher Houston;
  Comanches; Coronado, Francisco Vásquez de; Geronimo; Mexico;

Missionaries; Narváez, Pánfilo de; Navajos; Navajo War; Oñate, Juan de; Popé; Pueblo Revolt; Pueblos; Santa Fe Trail; Spain; Utes

References

Chávez, Thomas E. *An Illustrated History of New Mexico.* Albuquerque: University of New Mexico Press, 1992.

Kessell, John L. *Spain in the Southwest: A Narrative History of Colonial New Mexico, Arizona, Texas, and California.* Norman: University of Oklahoma Press, 2002.

Simmons, Marc. *New Mexico: An Interpretive History.* Albuquerque: University of New Mexico Press, 1988.

New Netherland

Dutch colony in North America. The Dutch commenced their colonial experiment in North America in 1609 upon Henry Hudson's discovery of the river that bears his name. New Netherland refers to Dutch colonial holdings in North America that were seized by the English in 1664 upon the capture of New Amsterdam. Relations between Dutch settlers and Native Americans unfolded amid a setting influenced by favorable ecological conditions and based on economics, mutual dependency, and political parity.

In this milieu the Hudson River tribes, predominantly the Mohawks and Mahicans, provided the Dutch with the motive and means to establish permanent settlements in New Netherland: Fort Orange (Albany, New York), Rensselaerswyck (near present-day Albany), and New Amsterdam (New York City). They did so by creating a profitable fur trade that became dependant on Native American military prowess, provisions, diplomacy, and economic cooperation. At the same time, Dutch goods—specifically firearms—afforded the Mohawks a tactical advantage over their Native American neighbors that enabled them and their fellow tribes in the Iroquois Confederacy to become the dominant Native American group in an area stretching from the Atlantic seaboard to the Mississippi River and from Lake Erie south to present-day Virginia. This power balance remained relatively intact until the American Revolutionary War (1775–1783).

In 1568 after years of economic and religious persecution at the hands of King Philip II of Spain, the Protestant inhabitants of the Dutch lowlands revolted and battled their would-be masters across the globe to achieve their independence. Like many international conflicts of the 16th and 17th centuries, the war between the Dutch and the Spanish proved to be a protracted affair, lasting 80 years and occurring in two distinct phases. In this epic contest, colonization and economic expansion proved to be a double-pronged tactic employed by the Dutch to disrupt the flow of goods and wealth coming out of Spain's colonies, the very things that fueled the Spaniards' ability to wage war on the Netherlands. Employing these strategies throughout the entirety of the conflict, the Dutch won for themselves an independent state by 1609 and temporarily halted hostilities between the warring nations by negotiating and signing the Twelve Years' Truce. However, in their bid for independence

the Dutch alienated themselves from the rich colonial markets of the Spanish Empire. Realizing that peace was just a momentary pause in their bid for complete autonomy, the Dutch government, the States General, actively sought new markets to fuel its nation's economy in case of a renewal of hostilities with Spain.

Dutch–Native American relations in New Netherland essentially unfolded in three distinct phases: the exploration phase (1609–1614), the trading phase (1614–1623), and the settlement phase (1624–1664). The exploration phase began when the Englishman Henry Hudson sailed for the Dutch East India Company in his ship the *Half Moon* to the Arctic Ocean in search of a sea route to China. Hoping to find and open new economic markets for Holland in China, Hudson instead stumbled upon the woodlands of present-day New York, which abounded with fur-bearing animals, wild fruits and vegetables, fish, fowl, and thousands of Native Americans, who were adept at harvesting these various commodities and were willing to interact with the Dutch. Although trading with Native Americans had not been the purpose of his journey, Hudson successfully met and exchanged both goods and information with the various native peoples along the Hudson River, laying the groundwork for Dutch exploration and initial settlement of New Netherland.

Although the *Half Moon* was perhaps the first ship on record to navigate up the Hudson River, the region's Native Americans already knew of Europeans and their trade goods. Indeed, since 1608 Native Americans had acquired European-made items from neighboring tribes who had access to the French trade in Quebec. Seldom aware of the intended purpose of many of the European goods they obtained, the Native Americans used the items within the context of their own culture, employing axes and hoes as necklaces, copper pots for arrowheads and earrings, and stockings as tobacco pouches. In some cases the Native Americans used European goods to replace more traditional items, such as their practice of using duffels (cloth) in place of furs to make leggings, loincloths, and capes. Like many of the more prized traditional commodities such as wampum, the Hudson River tribes held European goods in high regard, assigning to them a social significance that allowed individuals the opportunity to rise in rank and prestige by acquiring and redistributing such valuable items to their neighbors through the use of their gift economies. As such, the Hudson River tribes and their neighbors actively sought European goods more for the social benefit they provided than for their actual utility.

As Holland's traders became more involved and interested in the region, the Dutch and the Hudson River tribes developed a general understanding of one another and created a middle ground upon which to interact. In their process of mutual discovery, the Dutch and the Native Americans saw each other from the perspectives of their own cultures, inhibiting each group's ability to understand fully the intricacies of their counterparts' society.

Three critical outcomes resulted from Dutch–Native American interaction during the exploration phase. First, the Dutch and the Native Americans created a trade jargon and sign language

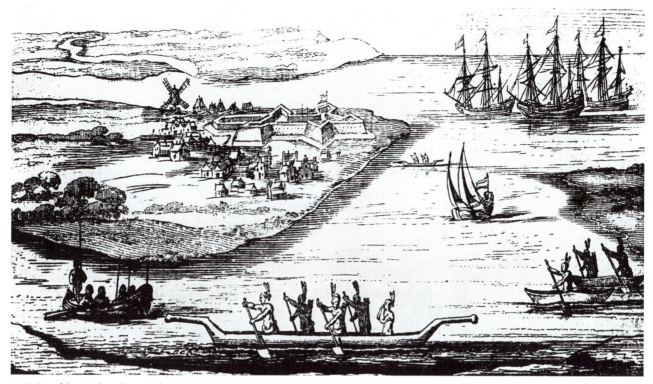

Depiction of the Dutch settlement of New Amsterdam. Engraving published by Joost Hartgers, Amsterdam, 1651. (Corbis)

that transcended the linguistic barriers that existed between the two peoples, facilitating the flow of information and goods. Second, the Native Americans included the Dutch in their preexisting indigenous trade network, causing a shift in the political and economic dynamics of the northeastern frontier from Quebec in Canada to the Atlantic shores of New England by giving the Iroquois Confederacy direct access to European goods that Huron middlemen had heretofore monopolized from Quebec beginning in 1608. And third, the profits generated by the fur trade coupled with the information that traders learned and disseminated about New Netherland's rich and prosperous landscape motivated the Dutch to attempt permanent settlement in the region.

The trading phase of the Dutch development of New Netherland began with the creation of the New Netherland Company in 1614. Granted a government charter, the New Netherland Company planned to exploit the Hudson River fur trade by establishing a year-round post where Native Americans could bring furs on a regular basis. The company planned to locate a post near present-day Albany, New York, where the Hudson River intersected with the Mohawk River. There the Native Americans could trade easily and more amicably, and from there large oceangoing ships could maneuver with little difficulty. For this purpose the company chose for its location a defensible and strategic spot south of the Mohawk River junction, where its personnel built Fort Nassau on Castle Island (present-day Van Rensselaer or Westerlo Island).

From the moment the Dutch arrived, the Hudson River tribes welcomed the company's merchants and assisted them with the establishment of Fort Nassau in three key ways. They approved of the company's occupation of Castle Island, kept the post provisioned with critical foodstuffs, and entered into a trade agreement with the Dutch that broadened the scope of the company's fur market to include the Saint Lawrence River, the Mohawk Valley, and the Delaware River. More importantly, the trade agreement introduced the Dutch to the importance of the New England and Long Island wampum trade and broadened their fur markets. The Hudson River tribes actively supported the Dutch because doing so enabled them to further counter Huron and Algonquian monopolization of the fur trade.

By procuring European trade goods, both the Mohawks and the Mahicans strengthened themselves against each other as well as against their northern neighbors. However, the constant strain of competition among the rival Native American groups eventually led to hostilities. The Mohawk victory in this contest established the Iroquois Confederacy as the dominant power in the region and led to a virtual Mohawk monopoly over the Dutch trade. All of these developments changed forever the political dynamics of the Hudson Valley and spurred Holland's government and merchants to push for permanent colonization in New Netherland.

The settlement phase of Dutch–Native American interaction in New Netherland occurred during 1624–1664. Concerned that their truce with Spain was about to end, the States General organized a state-sponsored armed mercantile organization, the Dutch West India Company, to resist rival European powers from interloping on Holland's colonial possessions. To accomplish this, the States General granted the company a 24-year monopoly over trade in the Western Hemisphere, provided troops and ships to protect any and all territory claimed, and gave 1 million guilders (nearly half a million dollars) to fund its efforts. In turn the States General expected the company to establish forts, settlements, and trade routes and to negotiate treaties and alliances with the rival European groups and native inhabitants.

Challenged with the task of developing markets on three continents, the company elected to focus on African gold, Brazilian sugar, and Caribbean salt while adopting a policy of agricultural colonization in New Netherland. By 1624 the company found its ideal colonists and enlisted 30 Walloon families (French Protestants from southern Holland) along with a multiethnic group of traders and clerks to build and populate four posts in New Netherland, two of which were Fort Orange and New Amsterdam.

As they did during the exploration and trading phases, the Hudson River tribes, primarily the Mohawks, used the Dutch and their trade goods as a means to gain an advantage over their Native American neighbors. In so doing the Mohawks provided a shield of protection around the Dutch West India Company's settlements at Fort Orange and Rensselaerswyck that helped protect the Dutch from their European rivals and hostile tribes. Additionally, the Mohawks increased the profitability of the wampum and fur trades by provisioning the Dutch with much-needed foodstuffs. Because of this support, the Hudson River tribes induced direct conflict with the Atlantic seaboard tribes and their English allies as well as the Hurons and their French allies. Not surprisingly, this led to frequent hostilities including Kieft's War (1639–1645), the Peach War (1655), the First Esopus War (1659–1660), and the Second Esopus War (1663–1664). This pattern of interaction and hostilities continued until the Second Anglo-Dutch War (1664–1667), which ended Dutch involvement in North America.

JOSEPH P. ALESSI

See also
Algonquins; Dutch-Indian Wars; Dutch-Mohawk Treaty; Esopus Wars; France; Fur Trade; Great Britain; Iroquois Confederacy; Kieft's War; Mahicans; Mohawks; Native American Trade; Wampum; Wyandots

References
Donck, Adriaen Van der. *A Description of New Netherland.* Translated by Diederick William Goedhuys. Faerie Glen, South Africa: D. W. Goedhuys, 1992.
Jameson, J. Franklin, ed. *Narratives of New Netherland, 1609–1664.* New York: Scribner, 1909.
Rink, Oliver A. *Holland on the Hudson: An Economic and Social History of Dutch New York.* Ithaca, NY: Cornell University Press, 1986.

New Ulm, Battles of
Event Dates: August 19 and 23, 1862

Battles fought at New Ulm, Minnesota, precipitated by Native American attacks on that town as part of the Minnesota Sioux Uprising. The attacks occurred on August 19 and August 23, 1862. New Ulm, located in south-central Minnesota, was the largest white settlement near the Dakota Sioux Reservation and was home primarily to German immigrant farmers and their families. However, the population of the town, which was normally about 900, had mushroomed to nearly twice that number, as many farmers living on the outskirts of the settlement had moved there to seek temporary safety after the outbreak of hostilities with the Sioux. The town was weakly defended by a small inexperienced and poorly armed militia. Making matters even worse, most of the town's dwellings and buildings were scattered about on two promontories on a bluff, which made them difficult to defend and easy prey for surprise assault.

The first attack on New Ulm occurred on August 19, 1862, when some 100 Dakota Sioux warriors began firing on the town from a wooded area above the settlement. They were well concealed in a thick stand of trees. The town's militia fired back but with only marginal success. Fire was exchanged for several hours until a sudden storm forced the Sioux to call off the assault. Six townspeople were killed, and another five were wounded. Native American casualties are not known.

Colonel Charles E. Flandreau, who had charge of the local militia, was determined to bolster his town's defenses in case of further attack. During the course of the next few days he tried to improve the militia's effectiveness and gathered all of the town's residents in a small defensible area enclosed by barricades.

The Sioux attacked New Ulm again on August 23 with approximately 650 warriors under chiefs Wabasha, Big Eagle, and Mankato. The newly enlarged militia had about 225 men under arms. The warriors stormed the town, shouting war cries as they closed in and forcing the militiamen to retreat. The defenders soon regrouped, however, and engaged in fierce combat with the Sioux, who had in the meantime set several homes ablaze. Amid a pall of smoke about 50 warriors approached the barricaded area but were driven back by an unexpected charge by the militia. After several hours of combat, some of it hand to hand, the warriors retreated. By early evening the fighting had ended. Flandreau reported 34 of the defenders killed on August 23; Native American losses are not known. The next day Flandreau prepared to vacate the town and ordered all remaining buildings destroyed. Fires raged all night, and by morning the settlement was little more than a smoldering heap of debris. In all at least 190 buildings had gone up in smoke.

On August 26 more than 2,000 people and refugees from New Ulm loaded into 153 wagons, most with nothing more than the clothes on their back. Escorted by 150 federal troops, they traveled about 30 miles to the east seeking safety in Mankato, Minnesota. The wagon train arrived safely there late that evening.

PAUL G. PIERPAOLI JR.

See also
Dakota Sioux; Little Crow; Minnesota Sioux Uprising

References
Carley, Kenneth. *The Sioux Uprising of 1862.* 2nd ed. St. Paul: Minnesota Historical Society, 1976.
Lass, William E. *Minnesota: A History.* 2nd ed. New York: Norton, 1998.

Depiction of fighting at New Ulm, Minnesota. The largest Anglo-American settlement near the Sioux Reservation, New Ulm was attacked twice during the 1862 Minnesota Sioux Uprising. (Library of Congress)

Nez Perces

Native American people whose traditional lands ranged from the Pacific Northwest to the Great Plains until the close of the 19th century. This territory included much of present-day Washington, Oregon, and Idaho. The Nez Perce people aided the Lewis and Clark expedition in 1805, and after a series of failed treaties with the federal government, some bands fought the U.S. Army during the Nez Perce War (1877).

The name "Nez Perce" means "pierced nose," a misnomer attributed to a French interpreter with Lewis and Clark. The tribe refers to itself as Ni Míi Puu ("Real people") and never practiced nose piercing as a regular part of the culture, although native groups farther south did. The Nez Perces traditionally relied on salmon and camas (a versatile edible root) for their food staples. But the introduction of horses in the early 18th century greatly expanded their ability to hunt, and they soon ranged onto the Great Plains for buffalo. Therefore, the Nez Perces can be said to have been seminomadic, following herds for hunting but also engaging in some agriculture. They also engaged in trade with whites and other friendly native tribes. Territorial expansion led to frequent conflict with other Plains peoples, however, particularly the Blackfeet and the Shoshones, and the Nez Perces developed leadership structures and tactics that made them successful warriors.

The Nez Perces traveled in autonomous bands that occasionally joined together for hunting or war. These large groups would temporarily form a supreme council that included leaders from each band, who would then select a war chief to direct military operations and a camp chief to oversee travel and maintain harmony. Diplomatic skills, negotiation, and oral argument were as important to this structure as was military prowess.

Through the late 19th century, the horse also played a significant role in the Nez Perces' military and economic success. Using selective breeding, they created the foundation for the Appaloosa horse, developing a line of animals remarkable for their temperament, soundness, and color. The Nez Perces amassed large herds, becoming both wealthy and highly mobile. They also refined techniques and procedures for hunting and fighting on horseback, making them formidable raiders.

The Nez Perces first encountered white Americans in September 1805, when they extended traditional hospitality to the Lewis and Clark expedition. They fed the starving strangers, furnishing them with supplies and information on both their westward and homeward journeys.

The 1815 Treaty of Ghent that ended the War of 1812 opened the unorganized Oregon Territory to both white American and British settlement. Thus, Nez Perce lands were at the center of an imperial dispute that lasted until 1846, when the Oregon Treaty ceded the territory to the United States and established the 49th Parallel as the border with Canada. These events ultimately led to the Nez Perce War and the subsequent Nez Perce diaspora.

The Nez Perces were divided into two chief factions. The more sedentary Christianized bands farmed and raised cattle, advocating interracial tolerance, while many traditionalist bands adhered to the Dreamer religion and rejected white culture altogether. During the treaty period, from 1855 to 1877, these factions became more polarized. Hallalhotsoot, or Lawyer, aided missionaries and advocated cooperation with whites, while Old Joseph of the Wallowas spoke adamantly of retaining rights to all the land.

Expansion and white settlement led the United States to negotiate the Nez Perce Treaty of Camp Stevens, signed on June 11, 1855. This treaty reduced Nez Perce lands to less than one-third what they had been but allowed the natives to retain a reservation of about 5 million acres on their homeland. Congress failed to ratify the treaty for four years, and the Nez Perces received none of the promised goods or services even though settlers began claiming the ceded lands. Gold was discovered in Nez Perce territory in 1860, so hundreds of miners flooded the reservation in violation of the 1855 treaty.

The 1863 Lapwai Treaty and the Third Nez Perce Treaty of 1868 contributed to further discontent on both sides. Most non-Christian bands rejected these negotiations, while Lawyer and his people agreed to live on a drastically reduced reservation. Consequently, the 784,996-acre reservation preserved the Christian Nez Perces' property while ceding lands occupied by the more traditional Nez Perces. The nontreaty Nez Perces refused to recognize the boundaries and continued horse herding and hunting throughout the region.

Old Joseph died in 1871, and his son, Young Joseph, became camp chief of the Wallowa band. Friction between settlers and the Nez Perces prompted Brigadier General Oliver Otis Howard to meet with the chiefs in July 1876. Chief Joseph and his brother Ollokot represented the nontreaty Nez Perces, testifying about crimes committed against their people by white settlers. A series of meetings failed to resolve the situation, and in January 1877 Howard sent an ultimatum to Joseph demanding that his band move to the reservation in Idaho by April 1. Joseph refused, and Howard promptly sent two companies of the 1st Cavalry from Fort Walla Walla to the mouth of the Wallowa Valley. Joseph sought peace and counseled his people against violence. Joseph and Howard again met, negotiating at Fort Lapwai in early May. Howard issued a new ultimatum, and under threat of military action Joseph finally agreed to move his people to the reservation.

On June 14, 1877, three Nez Perce warriors killed four white men, sparking the Nez Perce War. A small war party continued the attacks on white settlements during June 14–15, while others fled. Joseph decided that he would not take the Wallowas to the reservation and embarked on a running tactical retreat of more than 1,500 miles that impressed many U.S. Army officers. U.S.

forces ultimately chased Joseph to the Bear Paw Mountains in northern Montana, less than 40 miles from sanctuary in Canada. With most of his men killed or wounded and hopelessly outnumbered, he was forced to surrender to Colonel Nelson Miles on October 5, 1877.

Some Nez Perces were able to flee to Canada, but most of the nontreaty natives were transported to Indian Territory. Many eventually made their way back to Oregon, but they were never allowed to return to their traditional homelands. Today the Nez Perces live on the Colville Reservation (Washington) and the Nez Perce Reservation (Idaho).

DAWN OTTEVAERE NICKESON

See also
Big Hole, Battle of the; Canyon Creek, Battle of; Howard, Oliver Otis; Joseph, Chief; Miles, Nelson Appleton; Nez Perce War

References
Greene, Jerome A. *Nez Perce Summer, 1877: The U. S. Army and the Nee-Me-Poo Crisis.* Helena: Montana Historical Society Press, 2000.
Josephy, Alvin M. *The Nez Perce Indians and the Opening of the Northwest.* New Haven, CT: Yale University Press, 1965.
Moulton, Candy. *Chief Joseph: Guardian of the People.* New York: Tom Doherty, 2005.

Nez Perce War
Event Date: 1877

Military conflict between the Nez Perces and the U.S. Army. In 1855 most Nez Perce bands signed a treaty with the United States accepting a reservation in present-day Idaho. Some bands, however, refused to sign and did not agree to a second treaty in 1863 that greatly reduced the size of the Nez Perce Reservation. For more than a decade no action was taken against the Nez Perces who had not signed the treaties, but under mounting pressure from white settlers in northeastern Oregon and southeastern Washington in 1877, the government sent Brigadier General Oliver O. Howard to remove those recalcitrant bands to the reservation. Howard met several times with Nez Perce leaders Joseph and Ollokot of the Wallowa band, White Bird of the Salmon River band, and Looking Glass of the Asotins before issuing them an ultimatum on May 14, 1877, to move to the reservation within 30 days or face military action.

The Nez Perce leaders reluctantly began moving their people, but during the journey some young Nez Perce warriors killed several white settlers. Howard then sent troops in pursuit, and Joseph moved to White Bird Canyon. Still hoping to preserve peace, Joseph sent a truce party to meet with U.S. soldiers on June 17, but the troops opened fire, sparking a battle in which they were badly defeated by the Nez Perces.

Joseph tried to escape, while Howard called out troops across the Northwest to pursue and capture the Nez Perces. Some of these

Soldiers under Colonel Nelson Miles charge the Nez Perce camp during the Battle of Bear Paw Mountains, September 30–October 5, 1877, the culminating battle of the Nez Perce War. Illustration by G. M. Holland, from *Frank Leslie's Illustrated Newspaper*, November 3, 1877. (Library of Congress)

soldiers attacked Looking Glass's village on July 1, and he and his people joined the other fleeing Nez Perces, bringing their numbers to about 700, including 200 fighting men.

Sporadic fighting ensued as the fleeing Nez Perces encountered army detachments. Howard's troops defeated the Nez Perces in a battle at the Clearwater River during July 11–12, although the surviving Nez Perces managed to escape.

On the night of July 15 Looking Glass proposed crossing the Bitterroot Mountains into Montana, where the Nez Perces could take refuge with their Crow allies or, if that failed, escape north to Canada. They set out the next day and reached the Big Hole River on August 7, where they stopped to rest. The halt allowed Colonel John Gibbon's column to catch up and attack them on August 9. Recovering from the surprise assault, the disciplined Nez Perce warriors drove back the soldiers and held them off while the noncombatant Nez Perces escaped. Nevertheless, 90 Nez Perces had been killed in the melee.

The Nez Perces eluded several army units as they moved across Montana. Having encountered Crow scouts assisting the soldiers, the Nez Perces realized that they would get no assistance from their ally and directed their march toward Canada, where Sitting Bull established his followers after the Great Sioux War (1876–1877).

Howard now ordered Colonel Nelson Miles at Fort Keough, Montana, to block their escape. While the Nez Perces were taking advantage of another rest break suggested by Looking Glass, on September 30 Miles caught them in the Bear Paw Mountains less than 40 miles from sanctuary in Canada. In the five-day siege that followed, during which Howard arrived with his command, about 300 Nez Perces escaped to Canada, but Joseph, with most of his fighting men killed or wounded, surrendered the remainder of his force to Colonel Miles on October 5. Looking Glass was killed in a final exchange. During the course of this remarkable campaign, the Nez Perces covered some 1,500 miles and defeated or eluded several quality army units in the process. Despite Miles's promise to Joseph that the Nez Perces would be sent to the Idaho reservation, the government exiled them to the Indian Territory (present-day Oklahoma), where many died.

Jim Piecuch

See also
Big Hole, Battle of the; Clearwater River, Battle of; Gibbon, John; Howard, Oliver Otis; Indian Territory; Joseph, Chief; Looking Glass; Miles, Nelson Appleton; Nez Perces; White Bird Canyon, Battle of

References
Brown, Dee. *Bury My Heart at Wounded Knee.* New York: Holt, Rinehart and Winston, 1970.
Josephy, Alvin M. *The Nez Perce Indians and the Opening of the Northwest.* New Haven, CT: Yale University Press, 1965.
Nerburn, Kent. *Chief Joseph and the Flight of the Nez Perce: The Untold Story of an American Tragedy.* New York: HarperCollins, 2005.
Utley, Robert M. *The Indian Frontier of the American West, 1846–1890.* Albuquerque: University of New Mexico Press, 1984.

FLIGHT OF THE NEZ PERCE, JUNE 18–OCTOBER 5, 1877

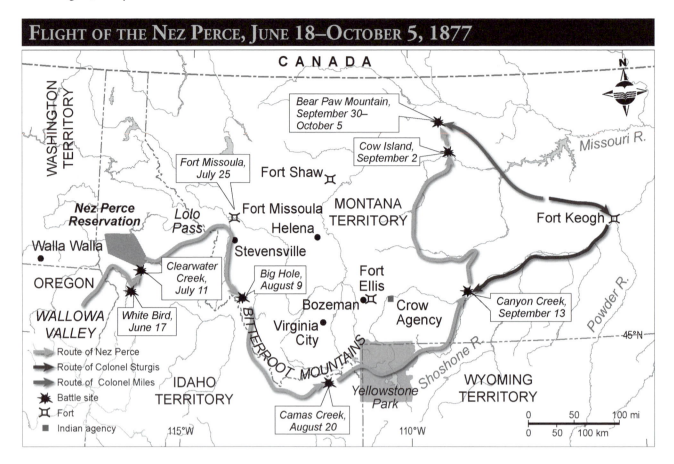

Niagara, Treaty of

Agreement between some 44 Native American nations and the British signed at Fort Niagara (New York) in August 1764. The British undertook the negotiations in an attempt to end hostilities with Native Americans that had begun with Pontiac's Rebellion (1763). The treaty also affirmed the Proclamation of 1763 and recognized the nation-to-nation relationship between the American Indians and the British. In a significant way, the negotiations attempted to deal with the postwar order after the long and destructive French and Indian War (1754–1763).

In late 1763 Sir William Johnson, Britain's superintendent of Indian affairs for the northern colonies, called for a peace conference to take place in the summer of 1764. He sent messengers carrying strings of wampum and copies of the Proclamation of 1763 to the natives. The message reached as far away as Nova Scotia in the east, Hudson Bay in the north, the Gulf of Mexico in the south, and the Mississippi River in the west. As a result, approximately 2,000 indigenous people representing roughly 44 nations attended the peace conference. Chief Pontiac, one of the key leaders of the anti-British faction, was not present. He would sign a separate peace in 1765.

The Niagara Congress convened and met in July 1764. During the negotiations Johnson attempted to use a divide-and-conquer technique to ensure a swift agreement. The chiefs, though they met with Johnson independently, kept each other abreast of their discussions. The final agreement was reached in August. A hybrid of two worlds, the accord was symbolized in wampum, with the two-row wampum belt used to symbolize native understanding of the agreement. The treaty was also written out for British officials.

The terms of the treaty included an exchange of prisoners, reestablishment of British gift giving, promises to prosecute whites who committed crimes against natives, compensation for white traders' losses, a schedule of value for trade goods, and promises of open and free trade. The treaty also stipulated that there must be protection against mutual enemies, no settler encroachments on native territory, free passage across the frontier for natives and traders alike, and a native promise to cease contact with Britain's enemies.

Details of the Niagara Treaty continued to influence negotiations involving Native Americans, Canadian, and the British into the 19th century. For example, in 1836 when negotiating a treaty on Manitoulin Island, Chief Assickinack reminded the lieutenant governor of Upper Canada, Sir Francis Bond Head, of the terms of the Niagara Treaty. In Canada the 1764 Treaty of Niagara and the Proclamation of 1763 represented a charter for the Native Americans' relationship with the Crown.

KARL S. HELE

See also

French and Indian War; Great Britain; Johnson, Sir William; Pontiac; Pontiac's Rebellion; Proclamation of 1763; Wampum

References

Borrows, John. "Wampum at Niagara: The Royal Proclamation, Canadian Legal History, and Self-Government." In *Aboriginal Treaty Rights in Canada: Essays on Law, Equity, and Respect for Difference*, edited by Michael Asch, 155–172. Vancouver: University of British Columbia Press, 1997.

Dickason, Olive Patricia. *Canada's First Nations: A History of Founding Peoples from Earliest Times*. 3rd ed. Toronto: Oxford University Press, 2002.

Nicholas

See Orontony

Ni Míí Puus

See Nez Perces

9th U.S. Cavalry Regiment

See Cavalry Regiment, 9th U.S.

Nipmucks

Native American people belonging to the Algonquian linguistic group who lived primarily in east-central Massachusetts. Several small bands of Nipmucks lived in northeastern Connecticut and northern Rhode Island as well. The name "Nipmuck" means "Fresh Water People" and refers to their living inland, away from the coast. The Nipmucks were relatively small in number, perhaps 5,000 people in 1620. They were very loosely organized and militarily weak. As such, they frequently saw their territory dominated by neighboring tribes, particularly the Wampanoags, Pequots, Narragansetts, Massachusetts, and Pennacooks. The Iroquois Confederacy and the Mohegans also viewed the Nipmucks as their enemy.

As with other New England Algonquian speakers, the Nipmucks lived in local bands of a few hundred people. Each band settled in a village for part of the year and traveled over its territory to hunt and gather food the rest of the year. A head sachem (chief) and a council of lesser sachems led each band, making decisions such as whether to go to war. Limited warfare among rival bands occurred frequently. But slaughter with the goal of total annihilation did not take place until English colonists introduced their own brand of take-no-prisoners warfare.

Most of the Nipmuck bands had bowed to the authority of the Massachusetts Bay Colony by the mid-1600s. With their population depleted by European diseases and intertribal warfare, a number of the remaining Nipmucks turned to Christianity. Under the influence of such Puritan preachers as John Eliot, they viewed their plight as a sign of the English god's supremacy over their own. During the early 1670s, the Christianized Nipmucks began living in the so-called praying towns of Massachusetts.

English offenses against the Nipmucks soon outweighed Christian influences, however. Matoonas, once a loyal Nipmuck convert, became a leading adversary when the English executed his son on a false charge. On August 1, 1675, a Nipmuck force led by former converts Matoonas and Muttawump ambushed a group of English troops that had come to open peace negotiations. When the surviving English took refuge in Brookfield, some 200 Nipmucks laid siege to the town until English reinforcements arrived three days later. By the autumn of 1675 most of the recently converted Nipmucks deserted the praying towns to join Metacom and the Wampanoags in prosecuting King Philip's War (1675–1676) against the English. Only a few Nipmucks remained loyal to the Puritans and relocated to another tribe's praying town. During the war, bands of Nipmucks joined other combatant bands in raiding Massachusetts frontier towns, including Deerfield, Hadley, Northampton, and Springfield. At peak strength, Muttawump commanded a mixed force of some 700 warriors from Nipmuck and allied bands.

Probably fewer than 1,000 Nipmucks survived the war. The English sold some survivors into slavery in the West Indies and consigned others to reservations or praying villages. A few escaped to take refuge with other native bands and joined in attacks on English frontier towns during later uprisings.

The presence of Nipmuck refugees among the Pennacooks of New Hampshire brought about another episode of betrayal and revenge in New England–native relations. In 1676 New Hampshire Militia commander Richard Waldron invited a party of Pennacooks and Nipmucks to visit him and then seized the Nipmucks and shipped them off for punishment, execution, or slavery. His betrayal enraged and humiliated the Pennacooks. They waited 13 years for the opportunity to take revenge, when they tortured Waldron to death.

After King Philip's War, an undetermined number of Nipmucks sought refuge with the Abenakis and Mahicans. Today about 500 Nipmucks live on two small reservations, one in Webster, Massachusetts, and the other in Grafton, Massachusetts. They have long enjoyed official recognition by the Commonwealth of Massachusetts, but the federal government continues to claim that they do not meet all of the requirements to be recognized as a nation.

ROBERTA WIENER

See also

Abenakis; Brookfield, Siege of; King Philip's War; Mahicans; Metacom; Pennacooks; Praying Towns and Praying Indians

References

Bourne, Russell. *The Red King's Rebellion: Racial Politics in New England, 1675–1678*. Oxford: Oxford University Press, 1990.

Daniell, Jere R. *Colonial New Hampshire: A History*. Millwood, NY: KTO, 1981.

Taylor, Alan. *American Colonies: The Settling of North America.* New York: Viking/Penguin, 2001.

Vaughan, Alden T. *New England Frontier: Puritans and Indians, 1620–1675.* 3rd ed. Norman: University of Oklahoma Press, 1995.

Ni-U-Ko'n-Skas

See Osages

Noble Savage Concept

A glorification of indigenous peoples as living in peace and harmony with nature, untouched by the negative aspects of Western civilization. During the 18th century, Europeans deliberately applied this stereotype to native peoples in North America. Writers, scholars, and artists alike have used similar constructs to critique Western society, idealizing characteristics such as the love of equality, of nature, and of liberty as uniquely Indian.

European observers in the 15th and 16th centuries expressed considerable fascination about indigenous peoples in the Americas. The cultures that Europeans encountered did not reflect European social mores and were perceptually the "other." Despite the romantic imagery surrounding peoples of the New World, however, colonizers increasingly feared native populations as threats. Thus, European governments and settlers emphasized religious

Drawing of a Native American in an idyllic tropical scene, 1771. (Library of Congress)

conversion to Christianity as well as domination, and sometimes eradication, of native populations.

The origins of the noble savage myth are contested. The French explorer Marc Lescarbot (ca. 1570–1629) included philosophical comparisons of French and Canadian Indian societies in his 1609 history of the French colony of Acadia. The actual phrase "noble savage" first appeared in English playwright John Dryden's *The Conquest of Granada* (1670). Although Louis Armand, Baron de Lahontan (1666–1715), proposed a similar idea in 1703, the myth of the noble savage is most frequently attributed to the French philosopher Jean-Jacques Rousseau (1712–1778). Rousseau's 1755 essay *Discourse on Inequality* idealized "the natural man" as possessing traits of liberty and independence not found in "civilized" society.

The polarizing viewpoints of "noble" and "savage" overshadowed authentic depictions of American Indian peoples and their diverse cultures in the 18th and 19th centuries. European land acquisition and governance were legitimized throughout New World colonization by assuming that American Indians lacked cohesive cultures, civilized societies, or legal title to the lands they inhabited. At the same time, Indian culture and identity were used to symbolize both America and its political causes. Indeed, nonnative colonists before the American Revolutionary War (1775–1783) appropriated Indian dress and identity to show opposition to British authority, as demonstrated by the Boston Tea Party of December 16, 1773. American Indian images were similarly used in Europe to symbolize America and all Americans, whether native or not. By the mid to late 18th century, Europeans of all sorts were utterly fascinated by American Indian images, perhaps because they represented such a stark material and philosophical difference from European society.

The rise of industrialization in the 19th century and urban life further spurred the romanticized image of the noble savage. By the turn of the 20th century, Old World immigrants were encouraged to assimilate by exposure to American patriotic and cultural imagery. This included plays, poems such as Henry Wadsworth Longfellow's *The Song of Hiawatha* (1855), and other cultural cues that reinforced the myth to new audiences. More recently, the myth of the noble savage has become less popular. Today it is contested as a stereotype of Native American peoples.

LISA HEUVEL

See also

Native Americans; Native Americans and the American Revolutionary War

References

Clifton, James A., ed. *The Invented Indian: Cultural Fictions & Governmental Policies.* 2nd ed. New Brunswick, NJ, and London: Transaction Publishers, 2003.

Deloria, Philip J. *Playing Indian.* New Haven, CT: Yale University Press, 1998.

Dickason, Olive Patricia. *The Myth of the Savage and the Beginnings of French Colonialism in the Americas.* Edmonton: University of Alberta Press, 1984.

Ellingson, Terry Jay. *The Myth of the Noble Savage.* Berkeley: University of California Press, 2001.

Strickland, Rennard. *Tonto's Revenge.* Albuquerque: University of New Mexico Press, 1997.

Trachenberg, Alan. *Shades of Hiawatha: Staging Indians, Making Americans, 1880–1930.* New York: Hill and Wang, 2004.

Norridgewock, Battle of
Event Date: August 12, 1724

New England militia raid against the Eastern Abenakis' main village at Norridgewock, Maine (then part of Massachusetts), on August 12, 1724, during Dummer's War (1722–1727). The objective of the raid was to capture or kill Father Sébastien Râle, a French Jesuit missionary believed by New Englanders to have fomented the conflict. After years of increasing tensions, Governor Samuel Shute of Massachusetts declared war on the Abenakis in July 1722, beginning Dummer's War. New Englanders blamed Abenaki resistance on French machinations rather than on their own land hunger and duplicitous trade and diplomacy.

To English thinking, the French mission at Norridgewock, some 75 miles up the Kennebec River, was the heart of the rebellion. The New England colonists portrayed Râle as a religious fanatic who had encouraged the Abenakis to purge English Protestant heretics from North America. The reality was far more complex. For more than two decades, the Jesuits had lived among the Abenakis and championed their interests, often forcefully, against English demands.

After two years of a frustrating guerrilla war, the New Englanders targeted Norridgewock. They did so to arrest Râle but in reality to break the rebellion. On August 8, 1724, Captain Johnson Harmon and a force of some 200 militiamen and a few native scouts left Fort Richmond, a small post 25 miles up the Kennebec. The group traveled by whaleboat upstream to a point just south of Norridgewock. Leaving 40 men to guard the boats, Harmon's force marched overland.

The attackers were undetected and reached the village's outskirts by midday on August 12. Harmon took half the force to scour surrounding cornfields, leaving the actual attack on the village to his second-in-command, Captain Jeremiah Moulton.

Moulton's men approached Norridgewock from the west and soon cordoned off the northern and southern approaches. This left the only avenue of escape eastward by means of the Kennebec River. Achieving near-total surprise, the attackers fired into the village while Abenaki warriors scrambled from their dwellings, trying to purchase time for their families to escape. The New Englanders, however, quickly overran the village and pursued their escaping foes, shooting many as they sought to cross the river.

In the fighting roughly 30 Abenakis were killed, among them many prominent warriors. Some historians have suggested that the death toll may have been higher, however. Moulton's force lost 1 New Englander and 1 native scout. As many as 150 Abenakis escaped to other French missions. Râle was among the dead. English and Abenaki accounts offer several versions of his death. The English portrayed the Jesuit as either actively leading the Abenakis or firing on the militia from a dwelling. Abenaki accounts, relayed by French missionaries, depicted the unarmed missionary confronting his attackers and dying at the foot of a cross. Allegedly his body lay amid several of his converts, who died shielding him with their own bodies.

With dusk approaching, the English spent the night in Abenaki dwellings. After pillaging and burning the town the following morning, Harmon's force returned to English territory. Harmon arrived in Boston to a hero's welcome, complete with a number of Abenaki scalps and that of Râle in order to collect a £100 reward.

The attack on Norridgewock eliminated a major obstacle to further English expansion in the Kennebec River Valley. Râle had openly challenged New England's aggressive policies, and his death and the destruction of the Eastern Abenaki village at Norridgewock weakened that nation, although the war continued for three more years.

Stanley J. Adamiak

See also
Abenakis; Dummer's War

References
Ekstorm, Fannie H. "The Attack on Norridgewock, 1724." *New England Quarterly* 7 (1934): 541–578.

Morrison, Kenneth M. *The Embattled Northeast: The Elusive Ideal of Alliance in Abenaki-Euramerican Relations.* Berkeley: University of California Press, 1984.

Morrison, Kenneth M. "Sebastien Rasle and Norridgewock, 1724: The Ekstrom Conspiracy Thesis Reconsidered." *Maine Historical Society Quarterly* 14(2) (1974): 75–98.

North, Frank Joshua and Luther Hedden
Birth Dates: March 10, 1840 (Frank); March 6, 1846 (Luther)
Death Dates: March 14, 1885 (Frank); April 18, 1935 (Luther)

U.S. Army officers who led the famous Pawnee Scout Battalion. Frank Joshua North was born on March 10, 1840, in Tompkins County, New York. Luther Hedden North, the third son of the family, was born on March 6, 1846, in Richland County, Ohio. In 1856 the North family settled in Columbus, Nebraska, near the Pawnee Indian Reservation, where Frank North was appointed clerk and interpreter in 1861.

At the request of Major General Samuel R. Curtis, Frank North helped to organize the Pawnee Scout Battalion in August 1864, which was charged with assisting the army in controlling hostile

Map from 1788 showing the organization into townships of the Old Northwest Territory as provided by the Northwest Ordinance of 1785. (Library of Congress Geography and Map Division)

Native Americans and thus freeing regular troops for service in the East during the American Civil War (1861–1865). Despite suffering from asthma and lacking military experience, North was commissioned a lieutenant of volunteers. Although the scouts did not engage hostile tribes that year, Curtis deemed the experiment a success and ordered North to reenlist the battalion for the following year.

In 1865 North, now at the rank of major, and the scouts joined the Powder River campaign of Brigadier General Patrick E. Connor and scored some military successes against the Cheyennes and Arapahos. In 1866 Frank North's brother, Luther, joined the battalion as a lieutenant. Although Luther had served in the Civil War, he had no experience in Native American warfare. In fact, few of the all-white officer corps of the battalion had any prior military experience. Consequently, in battle the Pawnees usually acted independently, employing their own tactics and extemporaneous command structure.

Between 1866 and 1868 the North brothers commanded the scouts, mainly protecting railroad construction crews of the Union Pacific Railroad. In 1869 they led the scouts during the Republican River Expedition under Major Eugene A. Carr. The campaign climaxed with the Battle of Summit Springs in which the power of the Cheyenne Dog Soldiers was broken. When the Pawnee Battalion was inactive, the North brothers continued to serve as scouts, guides, and interpreters.

In 1870 Frank North accompanied Professor Othniel C. Marsh on a fossil-hunting expedition. Luther North accompanied ethnologist George Bird Grinnell on Lieutenant Colonel George Armstrong Custer's Black Hills Expedition in 1874. The last time the North brothers were ordered into action with the Pawnee Battalion was for the Powder River Expedition of 1876, during which they helped defeat the Northern Cheyennes under Dull Knife and Little Wolf.

After the Pawnee Battalion was permanently disbanded in 1877, Frank went into business with William ("Buffalo Bill") Cody and established the Cody-North Ranch on the North Platte River in Nebraska. In 1882 Frank sold his interest in the ranch and was elected to the Nebraska legislature on the Democratic Party ticket. In 1884 he joined Buffalo Bill's Wild West Show. The following year Frank fell ill while traveling to Omaha on business for the show. He died at Columbus, Nebraska, of "congestion of the lungs" on March 14, 1885.

Luther North spent the remainder of his life in a variety of pursuits in Omaha and Columbus, where he wrote extensively on the brothers' experiences with the Pawnee scouts. He died at Columbus on April 18, 1935.

MARK VAN DE LOGT

See also

Arapahos; Buffalo Bill's Wild West Show; Carr, Eugene Asa; Cheyennes; Cheyennes, Northern; Cody, William Frederick; Connor, Patrick Edward; Curtis, Samuel Ryan; Custer, George Armstrong; Dog Soldiers; Dull Knife; Little Wolf; Pawnees; Powder River Expedition; Scouts, Native American; Summit Springs, Battle of

References

Bruce, Robert. *The Fighting Norths and Pawnee Scouts: Narratives and Reminiscences of Military Service on the Old Frontier.* New York: n.p., 1932.

Danker, Donald F. "The North Brothers and the Pawnee Scouts." *Nebraska History* 42 (1961): 161–178. Reprinted in *The Nebraska Indian Wars Reader, 1865–1877,* edited by R. Eli Paul, 73–87. Lincoln: University of Nebraska Press, 1998.

Danker, Donald F., ed. *Man of the Plains: Recollections of Luther North, 1856–1882.* Lincoln: University of Nebraska Press, 1961.

Grinnell, George Bird. *Two Great Scouts and Their Pawnee Battalion: The Experiences of Frank J. North and Luther H. North, Pioneers in the Great West, 1856–1882, and Their Defence of the Building of the Union Pacific Railroad.* Cleveland, OH: Arthur H. Clarke, 1928.

Northern Arapahos

See Arapahos, Northern

Northern Cheyennes

See Cheyennes, Northern

Northern Paiutes

See Paiutes, Northern

Northwest Indian War

See Little Turtle's War

Northwest Ordinances of 1785 and 1787

Congressional ordinances designed to organize and govern the Old Northwest Territory, essentially lands located west of the Appalachians, east of the Mississippi River, and north of the Ohio River. The Northwest Ordinance of 1785 was created on May 20, 1785, by the Confederation Congress in New York City. The ordinance was written by a committee chaired by Thomas Jefferson and was part of an attempt by the federal government to organize and distribute the land ceded to the United States by Great Britain in the Treaty of Paris (1783). Today the area encompasses the states of Ohio, Michigan, Indiana, Illinois, and Wisconsin and part of Minnesota.

Part of the reasoning that led to the 1785 ordinance lay in the fact that the Articles of Confederation (1781), the first document uniting the states, had no provision for taxation; the primary way of raising money was to request funds from the states. This proved to be an unsatisfactory approach, and some states, such as New Jersey, soon protested and refused to make their contributions. Congress suggested that a more acceptable way of raising money was through the sale of land in the Old Northwest Territory to private entities.

Almost immediately the question arose as to who actually owned the territory. Several of the existing eastern states claimed colonial rights to portions of the territory. These states included New York, Virginia, Massachusetts, and Connecticut. Their claims were often referred to as the Western Reserve. The problem of ownership was solved when New York and Massachusetts ceded their claims entirely and when Virginia and Connecticut ceded their claims in lieu of land reserved for them to sell.

The first legal step toward the creation of the territory came in 1784 with passage of the Ordinance of 1784. This ordinance simply designated that the territory would eventually become 10 states, but there were no provisions for how to accomplish this.

The following year the Confederation Congress met and created the Northwest Ordinance of 1785. The ordinance designated a means for dividing up the territory and set aside reserves for education and for grants to qualifying former members of the Continental Army. In addition, the ordinance created a township system in which each town was 36 square miles in area. Surveyors were assigned the task of drawing up boundaries, and the land was to be sold at $1 per acre in 640-acre sections.

In 1787 another piece of legislation, the Ordinance of 1787, set rules for governance and statehood, allowing for the creation of up to five territories. When the population of a territory reached 60,000, the territory could apply for statehood.

To the dismay of settlers, the Treaty of Paris had not relinquished claims by Native Americans to the territory. The federal government, through treaties, began a system of purchasing the lands in the Old Northwest Territory from the tribes that lived there. These purchases became a source of friction involving the settlers, Native Americans, and the British in Canada. Land disputes sparked not only Little Turtle's War (1785–1795), also known as the Northwest Indian War, but also served as one of the catalysts for the War of 1812 between Britain and the United States.

WILLIAM TOTH

See also

Greenville, Treaty of; Land Cessions, Northwest Ordinance; Little Turtle's War; Native Americans and the War of 1812; Old Northwest Territory; Western Reserve

References

Barr, Daniel P., ed. *The Boundaries between Us: Natives and Newcomers along the Frontiers of the Old Northwest Territory, 1750–1850.* Kent, OH: Kent State University Press, 2006.

Sword, Wiley. *President Washington's Indian War: The Struggle for the Old Northwest, 1790–1795.* Norman: University of Oklahoma Press, 1985.

Norton, John

Birth Date: ca. 1770
Death Date: ca. 1831

Mohawk leader who sided with the British during the War of 1812. Little is known about John Norton's early years or the precise circumstances of his birth. It is believed that he was born circa 1770, probably in Scotland, the son of a Scottish mother and a Cherokee father, who had been captured by British soldiers as a youth and then transported to Great Britain. By the mid-1780s Norton had joined the British Army as a private and was soon dispatched to Canada.

After being stationed at Fort Niagara in 1787, Norton deserted. A year later he was formally discharged from service. Soon thereafter he began teaching school among the Mohawks in Upper Canada. From 1791 to 1795 he worked as a fur trader in the vicinity of Detroit.

Returning to Upper Canada, Norton became an interpreter for the British Indian Department. Soon Mohawk leader Joseph Brant, who had strong ties to the British, adopted Norton as a nephew and made him his chief interpreter and diplomat. Norton's principal role was to act as an emissary and diplomat to the British in Canada, especially when Brant began to press questionable Canadian land claims with the British government in the early 1800s. As Brant grew older and his grasp on power waned, Norton's influence among the Mohawks and the larger Iroquois Confederacy increased, particularly among those natives allied with the British.

Between 1804 and 1806 Norton was in England, where he met with numerous British leaders in an attempt to convince London to honor old land deeds, some predating the American Revolutionary War (1775–1783). Although he was unsuccessful in this endeavor, he made many important contacts while there, which ultimately served him in good stead. During 1809–1810 Norton toured the western frontier of the United States and made contact with Cherokee relatives. It is probable that he also met with Shawnee leader Tecumseh at this time. Norton certainly supported Tecumseh's attempt to form a Pan-Indian alliance to deter further American encroachment on Indian lands.

When the War of 1812 commenced, Norton supported the British cause and mobilized and trained a group of prowar Mohawks (and other Iroquois warriors) to engage in the fighting. Norton personally led troops at the October 13, 1812, Battle of Queenston Heights, and he is credited with helping secure a British victory there. Norton was also at the Battle of Fort George (May 25–27, 1813) and may have been present for the Battle of Stoney Creek (June 6, 1813). The following year Norton led some 200 warriors in the Battle of Chippewa (July 5, 1814) during which his men took heavy casualties, and he led an Indian contingent at the Battle of Lundy's Lane (July 25, 1814). Norton was also on hand for the Battle of Fort Erie (August 4–21, 1814).

After the war Norton remained an influential Mohawk leader in Canada, and the British government granted him a generous pension for his service during the war. He traveled to England at least several times after 1815 and became a large landowner along the Grand River in Upper Canada. Norton died around 1831 in Upper Canada.

PAUL G. PIERPAOLI JR.

See also

Brant, Joseph; Creeks; Iroquois Confederacy; Mohawks; Native Americans and the War of 1812; Tecumseh

References

Benn, Carl. *The Iroquois in the War of 1812.* Toronto: University of Toronto Press, 1988.

Fenton, W. N. "Cherokee and Iroquois Connections Revisited." *Journal of Cherokee Studies* 3 (1978): 239–249.

Nottoways

Native American tribe that lived along the Nottoway River in present-day southeastern Virginia and northeastern North Carolina. When the English founded Jamestown in 1607, the Nottoway population was estimated at some 1,500 people. They were of Iroquoian background, which sometimes led to tensions between them and their Algonquian neighbors. The name "Nottoway" is an Algonquian term meaning "snake" or "adder." The name stuck when Europeans began using it.

Initially the 40-mile distance between Nottoway villages and Jamestown limited their interaction with white colonists. The relative proximity of the Nottoways to the coasts of Virginia and North Carolina, however, placed them directly in the path of future English colonial expansion. During his infamous rebellion in 1676, for example, Nathaniel Bacon attacked the Nottoways and surrounding tribes, leading the natives to sign a 1677 treaty promising friendship to Virginia.

The outbreak of the Tuscarora War (1711–1713) in North Carolina divided the Nottoways. Governor Alexander Spotswood of Virginia marched a militia force to the main Nottoway town to prevent its inhabitants from joining the uprising. This action had some success, and in 1712 the Nottoways pledged peace in return for the right to trade for muskets and ammunition. Not all of the Nottoways apparently agreed, however, as some joined their Iroquoian neighbors, the Tuscaroras. When the Tuscaroras were defeated in the Tuscarora War, they and some of the Nottoways fled to New York, where they became the sixth nation in the Iroquois Confederacy. Those Nottoways who remained behind in Virginia thereafter enjoyed relatively good relations with their white neighbors. These Nottoways supported the British colonists in the French and Indian War (1754–1763) and then the American side during the American Revolutionary War (1775–1783).

A possible exception to this friendly pattern was an outbreak of violence along the South Carolina frontier during the late 1740s and early 1750s. Two white Charles Town (present-day Charleston) traders, George Haig and Thomas Brown, were killed by a mixed group of "Notowega" natives. Contemporaries identified some of them as Conestogas or Senecas. But the clear Iroquoian identification of the group has led to speculation that at least some of them were Nottoways. After several years of clashes with South Carolina settlers, these Nottoways retreated to Cherokee territory and disappeared.

After the Tuscarora War, the Nottoways in Virginia declined in numbers. In 1728 William Byrd estimated their population at just 300. A 1764 report described the Nottoways and their lesser neighbors as collectively having 60 warriors. The pattern continued so that by the end of the American Revolutionary War, Thomas Jefferson exaggeratedly reported that not a single male Nottoway still lived. A census in 1825 counted only 47 Virginia Nottoways. Although the name "Nottoway" is still used by some northern Iroquois tribes, descendants of the Virginia band today call themselves the Cheroenhakas. They live primarily in Southampton County, Virginia.

ANDREW C. LANNEN

See also

Algonquins; Bacon's Rebellion; French and Indian War; Iroquois Confederacy; Tuscaroras; Tuscarora War

References

Briggs, Martha Wren, and April Cary Pittman. "The Metes and Bounds of a Circle and a Square: The Nottoway Indians in Virginia." *Virginia Cavalcade* 46 (Winter 1997): 132–143.

Swanton, John R. *The Indians of the Southeastern United States.* Washington, DC: Smithsonian Institution Press, 1946.

Nova Scotia, Micmac Raids on

See Micmac Raids on Nova Scotia

Numas

See Paiutes, Northern

Nutimus

Birth Date: ca. 1680
Death Date: 1763

Delaware (Lenni Lenape) sachem (chief) who became the principal spokesperson for the tribe, particularly in regard to relations with British settlers. Nutimus (meaning "one who spears fishes") was born around 1680, most likely in present-day New Jersey in the region of the upper Delaware River Valley. His tribe occupied territory in present-day Northampton County in eastern Pennsylvania near the Lehigh River and the Delaware River. Thanks to the beneficence of its founder, William Penn, the colony dealt fairly with Native Americans. But rising debt among Penn's heirs to the proprietorship, sons John and Thomas, set the stage for a betrayal.

In 1735 Thomas Penn produced a dubious treaty purportedly negotiated in 1686 that ceded to the proprietors as much native-held territory as could be traversed in a day and a half of walking. Nutimus objected and threatened to press his case through the Iroquois Confederacy. The Penns, however, forestalled the move through separate negotiations with the Onondagas, who were members of the confederacy. Iroquois leaders ignored the fraud because they saw an opportunity to establish themselves as the sole agents for the British in handling questions of land rights.

In 1737 Nutimus officially acquiesced and subjected his people to the so-called Walking Purchase. He cried foul as the whites hired as walkers took few breaks and ran for portions of their trek. The Penns ultimately claimed 1.2 million acres based on a 65-mile journey. By 1740 Nutimus had resumed efforts to enlist the support of other tribes in redressing his grievance. But in 1742 the Onondaga chief Canasatego, with prompting from Governor George Thomas of Pennsylvania, admonished Nutimus. Referring to the Delawares as "women," Canasatego evicted them from their land without allowing them any right to sell it.

The Delawares relocated to Pennsylvania's Wyoming Valley along the northern branch of the Susquehanna River. Their ongoing lobbying for the abrogation of the bogus treaty lasted 19 years but came to naught. One of Nutimus's followers and a subsequent chief, Teedyuscung, secured a royal investigation into the matter. Quakers disenchanted with the Penn family had by then taken up the cause of the Delaware tribe. Teedyuscung withdrew his claim before a hearing could be held, however. Nutimus lived out his remaining years in relative solitude, although he did engage in diplomacy with superintendent of Indian affairs Sir William Johnson in 1756 to earn his tribe recognition as an independent nation.

Nutimus died in 1763 during Pontiac's Rebellion. Although neither he nor his village was involved in the hostilities, the settlement was nonetheless raided and destroyed by colonial forces. It is believed that Nutimus died during the attack.

JEFFREY D. BASS

See also

Delawares; Iroquois Confederacy; Johnson, Sir William; Onondagas; Pontiac's Rebellion; Quakers; Teedyuscung; Walking Purchase

References

Harper, Steven. *Promised Land: Penn's Holy Experiment, the Walking Purchase, and the Dispossession of Delawares, 1600–1763.* Bethlehem, PA: Lehigh University Press, 2006.

Jennings, Francis. *The Ambiguous Iroquois Empire: The Covenant Chain Confederation of Indian Tribes with English Colonies from Its Beginnings to the Lancaster Treaty of 1744.* New York: Norton, 1984.

O

Oatman Family Massacre
Event Date: February 18, 1851

Massacre of the Royce Oatman family in western Arizona probably by the Western Yavapai or Tolkepaya peoples. Only three siblings of the nine family members survived the attack, and two of the three—Olive and Mary Ann Oatman—were taken captive by the Native Americans. The attack occurred on February 18, 1851, on a ridge overlooking the Gila River about 85 miles east of Fort Yuma, which is located at the confluence of the Gila and Colorado rivers. At the time Mary Ann Oatman, the mother of the family and wife to Royce, was pregnant with her eighth child, bringing the effective death toll to seven.

In May 1850 the Oatmans, a Mormon family that included father Royce, mother Mary Ann, and seven children ages 1 to 16, joined a wagon train bound for California with other Mormons. The band was led by James C. Brewster, who had openly disagreed with Mormon leaders and sought to find a gathering place for like-minded Mormons in the West. The allure of unsettled land and a more salubrious climate also attracted the Oatmans to make the trek.

Eventually the Mormon wagon train gathered in Independence, Missouri, where its members laid in supplies, planned the remainder of the journey, and waited for all of the travelers, including Brewster and his family, to arrive. It is believed that there were about 17 families who made the journey, totaling perhaps 85 to 95 people. On August 9, 1850, the wagon train finally got under way west of Independence. The decision had already been made to follow the Santa Fe Trail toward the southwest.

Along the arduous journey dissension arose among some families, and a few turned back. Upon reaching Santa Fe, New Mexico, the train split, with Brewster and some of his followers choosing to take a more northerly route to California. Royce Oatman and several other families decided to press on toward the southwest via Santa Cruz and Tucson. Oatman was determined to reach the mouth of the Colorado River, where he believed that the climate and soil would support agriculture. The other families traveling with the Oatmans ultimately decided not to press on, having heard rumors of hostile Native Americans in western Arizona. By early February 1851 the Oatmans were traveling alone, making them a prime target for the area's hostile tribes.

On February 18, 1851, as they encamped along a high ridge overlooking the Gila River less than 100 miles from their intended destination near Fort Yuma, the Oatmans encountered a band of Native Americans. Royce Oatman invited them to sit with the family and provided them with tobacco and pipes, which the Native Americans had requested. What happened next is subject to speculation, but in short order the family was nearly wiped out. Only three survived the ensuing attack: Lorenzo, age 14; Olive, age 13; and Mary Ann, age 8. Lorenzo, who had been badly wounded, managed to escape and sought help and refuge in a nearby settlement. Olive and Mary Ann, however, were taken captive and led into the nearby mountains. Lorenzo claimed that the family had been clubbed after Royce Oatman refused to give the Native Americans food that he considered crucial to the family's survival.

Ultimately the two sisters were taken to a Native American village perhaps 100 miles from the site of the massacre. The girls were put to work but were frequently beaten, probably because of miscommunication. Sometime in 1852 a band of Mojaves acquired the two girls for food, blankets, and horses. The girls were then taken to a Mojave village on the Colorado River probably in or near present-day Needles, California. The girls were treated far better by the Mojaves, and the band's chief took a special interest in their welfare. Within a year, however, a severe drought brought starvation to the Mojaves, and Mary Ann died, presumably of disease or starvation.

Sometime later the commander at nearby Fort Yuma learned of Olive's whereabouts and sent a party to the Mojave settlement to seek her release. After some wrangling the Mojaves agreed to release Olive in exchange for horses and other goods. She arrived at Fort Yuma in 1856 to a tumultuous welcome and was soon reunited with her only surviving sibling, Lorenzo. Her story was an instant sensation in the press.

In 1857 a best-selling book on the massacre and captivity titled *Captivity of the Oatman Girls* was published by Royal B. Stratton. The following year Olive and Lorenzo went back East, and she went on a speaking tour, becoming a sought-after celebrity. Olive eventually married and settled in Texas, where she lived until her death in 1903. The Oatman Massacre and the captivity of the Oatman sisters remained a high-profile story for much of the 1850s, capturing the public's imagination and shaping easterners' perceptions of the far West and its Native American population.

PAUL G. PIERPAOLI JR.

See also
Santa Fe Trail; Yavapais

References
Braatz, Timothy. *Surviving Conquest: A History of the Yavapai Peoples.* Lincoln: University of Nebraska Press, 2003.

McGinty, Brian. *The Oatman Massacre: A Tale of Desert Captivity and Survival.* Norman: University of Oklahoma Press, 2006.

O'Bail, John

See Cornplanter

Obwandiying

See Pontiac

Occaneechees

A Siouan-speaking Native group indigenous to the Virginia Piedmont. For a brief time the Occaneechee dominated the southern Indian trade in Virginia, acting as native middlemen, but they eventually fell victim to both Native American and Virginia colonial attacks in the late 17th century and faded into oblivion during the 18th century. As with most eastern tribes, the Occaneechees engaged in small-scale agriculture supplemented by hunting and gathering in addition to trade. During the second half of the 16th century, the Occaneechees occupied the Roanoke River Valley and its tributaries in southern Virginia and North Carolina.

The Occaneechees are first mentioned in the historical record in 1650 by an English explorer named Edward Bland. The exploration team of Thomas Batts and Robert Fallam may also have encountered the Occaneechees in 1671. In 1673 while on their way to the Appalachian Mountains, James Needham and Gabriel Arthur encountered the Occaneechees. The next year Needham was slain by an Occaneechee guide.

During this period, the Occaneechees' main town occupied a strong defensible position on an island in the Roanoke River. This island was situated on the primary trading path connecting southern tribes with the colony of Virginia. By 1676 the Occaneechees dominated trade between native peoples and the colonists in Virginia.

The Occaneechees' situation changed dramatically with the eruption of Bacon's Rebellion in Virginia in 1676 and nearly simultaneous attacks by other tribes. In early 1676 the Susquehannocks sought refuge with the Occaneechees because of their hostilities with the colonists of Virginia and Maryland. The Susquehannocks had fled to the Occaneechees because the Occaneechees had been their primary supplier of guns and ammunition. Nevertheless, the Susquehannocks turned on their hosts in an effort to seize their island stronghold and gain control of the Indian trade for themselves. The Occaneechees ultimately defeated the Susquehannocks, but disruptions caused by the Susquehannock attacks eventually compelled the Occaneechees to abandon part of their Virginia homeland.

Responding to Susquehannock attacks on Virginia's northwestern frontier in 1676, Nathaniel Bacon became the leader of a small ad hoc army of disgruntled landless colonists. Bacon's purported goal was to attack hostile Native Americans to the north, but instead he attacked allied groups, including the Occaneechees in southern Virginia, and then turned his force against the colonial government. In the summer of 1678 the Iroquois from the north attacked the Occaneechees and the other Siouan groups in Virginia. Coming on the heels of the devastation caused by Bacon's Rebellion, these attacks forced the Occaneechees and the other Siouan groups to abandon Virginia and move south into North Carolina.

Following their withdrawal from Virginia, the Occaneechees became more closely associated with their Siouan neighbors, the Tutelos and Saponis. At the turn of the 18th century, the Saponis and Tutelos settled near present-day Salisbury, North Carolina, at the same time that the Occaneechees established themselves near Hillsborough, North Carolina. Eventually all three groups moved back into Virginia. By 1728 the Occaneechees had merged with the Saponis and lost their separate identity.

DIXIE RAY HAGGARD

See also
Bacon's Rebellion; Iroquois; Saponis; Susquehannocks

References
Briceland, Alan Vance. *Westward from Virginia: The Exploration of the Virginia-Carolina Frontier, 1650–1710.* Charlottesville: University Press of Virginia, 1987.

Davis, R. P. Stephen, Jr. "The Cultural Landscape of the North Carolina Piedmont at Contact." In *The Transformation of the Southeastern Indians, 1540–1760*, edited by Robbie Ethridge and Charles Hudson, 135–154. Jackson: University Press of Mississippi, 2002.

Washburn, Wilcomb E. *The Governor and the Rebel: A History of Bacon's Rebellion in Virginia*. Chapel Hill: University of North Carolina Press, 1957.

Oconostota
Birth Date: ca. 1712
Death Date: 1783

Primary war leader of the Cherokees in the third quarter of the 18th century and later a revered statesman during some of the most violent and turbulent events in Cherokee history. Born about 1712, by 1753 Oconostota had become the great warrior for the Overhill town of Chota, which had gained preeminence over all the Cherokee towns. This in effect made Oconostota the great warrior for all the Cherokees.

During the years leading up to the French and Indian War (1754–1763), Oconostota favored an alliance with the French over the existing Cherokee alliance with the British. Another great Cherokee chief, Attakullakulla, a staunch leader of the more popular pro-British faction, opposed Oconostota on these matters.

Despite his desire to ally with the French, Oconostota led numerous war parties against French-allied natives during the 1750s as the Cherokees' alliance with the British strengthened. In 1753 he led some 400 warriors against the Choctaws to assist the Chickasaws at the behest of Governor James Glen of South Carolina. Oconostota and his Cherokees administered a decisive defeat against the Creeks in the Battle of Taliwa, forcing the Creeks to leave northern Georgia. Then in 1755 Oconostota led numerous war parties against the French-allied natives in Illinois. Finally, in 1757 he led raids against French trading boats and canoes on the Mississippi River and the Ohio River.

Unfortunately for the Cherokees and the colony of South Carolina, relations between the Cherokees and the British soured in 1759 when unscrupulous Virginia rangers attacked a Cherokee war party returning home after fighting for the British in the Ohio Valley. This incident led to an outbreak of hostilities along the Carolina frontier known as the Cherokee War (1759–1761). Oconostota led a Cherokee peace delegation to Charles Town (present-day Charleston, South Carolina) to resolve the situation, but Governor William Henry Lyttelton took the Cherokee delegates hostage and then accompanied them and South Carolina forces to Fort Prince George among the Cherokee Lower Towns. There Lyttelton demanded that in exchange for the release of the chiefs, the Cherokees surrender those responsible for the killing of two dozen settlers. Lyttelton had hoped to use his military force to chastise the Cherokees, but an outbreak of smallpox dispersed his men.

Oconostota, chief of the Cherokees. His capture of Fort Loudoun in present-day Tennessee in 1760 was the worst defeat of a British force at the hands of Native Americans until Pontiac's Rebellion in 1763. Eighteenth-century engraving attributed to James McArdell, after a painting by Francis Parson. (National Archives of Canada/e002139936)

Eventually Attakullakulla secured the release of some of the chiefs, including Oconostota. The latter immediately led a Cherokee attack on Fort Prince George, which brought the immediate execution of the remaining Native American hostages. The attack also invited a South Carolina punitive expedition. The British troops and militia destroyed many of the Cherokee Lower Towns. On June 1, 1760, Oconostota and the Cherokees repulsed British lieutenant colonel Archibald Montgomery at Etchoe, about six miles south of present-day Franklin, North Carolina, whereupon Montgomery retired to Charles Town.

Oconostota then led a Cherokee siege of Fort Loudoun in present-day Tennessee. The garrison surrendered in August, marking the worst defeat of a British force at the hands of Native Americans until Pontiac's Rebellion (1763).

In 1761 Oconostota traveled to New Orleans to seek French assistance, but he was unable to secure any meaningful aid. In the spring of 1761 Colonel James Grant led some 2,400 South Carolinians and British troops against the Cherokees and was ultimately victorious. Grant and his men then attacked the Cherokee Middle Towns, destroying some 15 towns and a great many crops. The Cherokee War was concluded that same year.

Although the war had been a serious setback for the Cherokees, Oconostota remained an important leader. Indeed, from 1764 he was effectively leader of all the Cherokees. In 1768 he led delegations to meet with both the Iroquois and representatives of Virginia to draw a new boundary line between Cherokee lands and that colony. The Virginians almost immediately broke the agreement.

Preferring peace to war, in 1775 Oconostota signed an agreement with North Carolina lawyer Richard Henderson that ceded more than 20 million acres of Cherokee land in Tennessee and Kentucky. In 1776 some Cherokees attacked colonial settlements along the frontier from Virginia to Georgia, leading to savage settler reprisals against Cherokee towns. The Cherokees agreed to peace in the spring of 1777, with Oconostota playing a key role in the talks.

Some Cherokees fought on the British side in the American Revolutionary War (1775–1783), but Oconostota opposed this. He remained the revered leader of the Cherokees until his death in the spring of 1783.

DIXIE RAY HAGGARD

See also

Attakullakulla; Cherokees; Cherokee War; Chickasaws; Choctaw-Chickasaw War; Choctaws; Creek-Cherokee Wars; French and Indian War

References

Fabel, Robin F. A. *Colonial Challenges: Britons, Native Americans, and Caribs, 1759–1775.* Gainesville: University Press of Florida, 2000.

Hatley, Tom. *The Dividing Paths: Cherokees and South Carolinians through the Revolutionary Era.* New York: Oxford University Press, 1995.

Kelly, James C. "Oconostota." *Journal of Cherokee Studies* 3 (Fall 1979): 221–238.

Oliphant, John. *Peace and War on the Anglo-Cherokee Frontier 1753–63.* Baton Rouge: Louisiana State University Press, 2001.

Office of Commissioner of Indian Affairs

Administrative office created by Secretary of War John C. Calhoun in 1824 to oversee the newly created Bureau of Indian Affairs (BIA). Later, in his professional papers and public remarks, Calhoun often referred to an operating BIA, despite the fact that such a bureau had not yet been approved by Congress. When in 1832 Congress finally did officially recognize the existence of the BIA, its mandate was to finalize treaties with Native American nations. As more settlers appeared in the western United States, treaties took on an ever-increasing importance. Although the BIA was not given cabinet status, Congress did approve the creation of the Office of the Commissioner of Indian Affairs (OCIA) as the administrative head of the BIA. In 1849 both the OCIA and the BIA were shifted from the Department of War to the Department of the Interior.

Throughout the 19th century treaty talks continued, but in the meantime the OCIA took on the additional task of turning Native Americans into "civilized" Americans. Such a change could occur, claimed the BIA, through the imposition of a reservation system for dwelling and a network of specific laws designed to encourage "civilized" behavior and society. Communal landholdings and

tribal councils became illegal, and treaties came to include provisions for forced relocation, although this was often not disclosed to Native American signatories.

By the end of the American Civil War (1861–1865), schooling was imagined to be yet another tool to aid in the civilizing process. Because of what were claimed to be budgetary restraints, however, commissioners announced that religious institutions were to be placed in charge of reservation schools. Furthermore, passage of the Dawes Severalty Act in 1887 forbade any indigenous community from holding titles to land. The OCIA claimed in 1901 that these policies were carried out so as to transform Native Americans into "self-supporting, self-respecting and useful citizens of the United States."

The OCIA's enforcement of BIA policies continued into the 20th century. Eventually it became apparent, however, that the type of transformation sought by the federal government was not likely to occur. In fact, it became necessary to attempt, through additional government assistance, to repair damage caused by earlier policies that had adversely affected conditions on the reservations. In 1938 a team of social scientists led by Lewis M. Meriam prepared the Meriam Report, officially titled "The Problem of Indian Administration," that detailed for nonnatives the appalling mortality rates and poor labor conditions being experienced by native communities. Native American political movements and public sympathy in the 1950s and 1960s among nonnatives came to reinforce this point and encourage dialogue.

In recent decades, several laws and acts have sought to alleviate these problems. The Indian Self-Determination and Educational Assistance Act of 1975 aimed at improving state schooling and housing projects. The Indian Child Welfare Act of 1978 permits

U.S. Government Indian Service Employees, 1843–1903

Year	Washington Office	Inspectors and Super-intendents	Agency Services	Miscellaneous	Total Employees
1843	16	11[1]	232	16	275
1853	19	19[2]	176	17	231
1863	34	37[3]	371	42	484
1873	44	22	1037[4]	—	1,103
1883	77	11	1592	96[5]	1,776
1893	93	11	1795	1430	3,329
1903	141	11	1813	2465[6]	4,430

[1] Excludes two territorial governors serving as ex officio superintendents.
[2] Excludes four territorial governors serving as ex officio superintendents; includes eight agents, four subagents, and one special agent attached to superintendents.
[3] Excludes five territorial governors serving as ex officio superintendents; includes two superintending agents in California and five interpreters, four physicians, and two special agents attached to the Southern Superintendency.
[4] Incomplete; 15 agencies out of a total of 78 did not report.
[5] Includes employees of two off-reservation boarding schools, Carlisle (Pennsylvania) and Forest Grove (Oregon).
[6] Includes 4 members and 160 employees of the Commission to the Five Civilized Tribes.

important evaluations of Native American children's custody arrangements. Most significantly, the Tribal Self-Governance Demonstration Project Act of 1991 allows Native American communities significant control over any property or assets held in a community's trust.

SIGNA DAUM SHANKS

See also
Bureau of Indian Affairs; Dawes Severalty Act

References
Jackson, Curtis. *A History of the Bureau of Indian Affairs and Its Activities among Indians.* San Jose, CA: R & E Publishing, 1977.
Taylor, Theodore W. *The Bureau of Indian Affairs.* Boulder, CO: Westview, 1984.

Oglala Sioux

One of seven subdivisions of the Teton Lakota Sioux living in the southwestern Dakota Territory by the second half of the 19th century. The Oglala Sioux were commonly included with other Lakota bands in the generalized designation "Sioux," a derogatory term derived from a fragment of *nadouessioux,* the French derivation of an Ojibwa word meaning "little snake." (The term is also interpreted as "enemy.") Traditionally hunters and gatherers, the Oglalas' lifestyle on the northern Plains was largely dependent on buffalo, from which they derived food, clothing, and shelter. Skilled horsemen armed with lances, bows, or rifles, Oglala mounted warriors constituted some of the finest light cavalry in the world.

As Manifest Destiny and perceived economic opportunity led white settlers across the northern Plains, the Oglalas witnessed disruption to the migratory patterns of the buffalo. The Bozeman Trail, with its three military garrisons, proved particularly intolerable because of its northwesterly route across traditional hunting grounds to the Montana goldfields. From 1866 to 1868 Oglala warriors led by Red Cloud along with other Lakota bands and their Northern Cheyenne and Arapaho allies effectively placed the army's forts along the trail under siege. With the Treaty of Fort Laramie in 1868, the U.S. government in effect admitted defeat and agreed to close the Bozeman Trail and abandon its military outposts. The treaty also created the Great Sioux Reservation—setting aside land that included their sacred Black Hills—for the Oglalas and the six other Teton Lakota bands.

The discovery of gold in the Black Hills in 1874 soon led to encroachment onto the reservation by nonnatives. Red Cloud, representing the Oglalas, along with Sicangu chief Spotted Tail and other Lakota tribal leaders, met with President Ulysses S. Grant in Washington, D.C., during the summer of 1875 in an unsuccessful effort to persuade the U.S. government to honor its treaty and remove the trespassers. A subsequent government directive ignoring the treaty's provision for Lakota hunting rights beyond the western boundaries of the Great Sioux Reservation and requiring all tribes to be on the reservation by January 31, 1876, served

Oglala chiefs American Horse (left) and Red Cloud (right) shake hands in front of a tipi—probably on or near Pine Ridge Reservation, 1891. (Library of Congress)

only to heighten tensions and instigate the so-called Great Sioux War (Black Hills War).

Led by Oglala war chief Crazy Horse and Hunkpapa chief and holy man Sitting Bull, the Great Sioux War embroiled the Oglalas and their allies in warfare with the United States from 1876 to 1877. Oglala warriors were instrumental in winning military victories over U.S. Army contingents in the Battle of the Rosebud (June 17, 1876) and the Battle of the Little Bighorn (June 25–26, 1876). The victories were short-lived, however, and by 1877 the Oglalas and their allies, having suffered a series of military setbacks—including the surrender and assassination of Crazy Horse—were back on the reservation.

During the last decades of the 19th century, the Oglalas and their Lakota brethren witnessed the systematic dissection of the Great Sioux Reservation. With their lands shrinking, their traditional culture under attack, and their dependency on scarce government handouts ever increasing, Oglala leaders embraced the Ghost Dance, a revitalization movement spawned by the prophecy of a Paiute man named Wovoka. Hoping to assuage white fears of renewed Native American militancy, the government sent troops to the Pine Ridge Reservation to suppress the Ghost Dancers. The resulting tragedy at Wounded Knee Creek on December 29, 1890, ended—at least for 80 years—large-scale Native American resistance to U.S. government Indian policy on land occupied by the Oglalas. Today a number of Oglala Sioux continue to live on what became the Pine Ridge Reservation in the southwestern corner of South Dakota.

ALAN C. DOWNS

See also

Crazy Horse; Fort Laramie, Treaty of (1868); Ghost Dance; Great Sioux War; Little Bighorn, Battle of the; Manifest Destiny; Pine Ridge Reservation; Red Cloud; Red Cloud's War; Rosebud, Battle of the; Sioux; Sitting Bull; Spotted Tail; Wounded Knee, Battle of; Wovoka

References

Larson, Robert W. *Red Cloud: Warrior-Statesman of the Lakota Sioux.* Norman: University of Oklahoma Press, 1997.

Utley, Robert M. *Frontier Regulars: The United States and the American Indian, 1866–1891.* New York: Macmillan, 1973.

Ogoula Tchetoka, Battle of
Event Date: March 25, 1736

French attack on the Chickasaw village of Ogoula Tchetoka on the lower Mississippi River (near present-day Memphis, Tennessee). As allies of the British, the Chickasaws were important in helping Britain gain supremacy over France in the southern part of North America. The Chickasaw Nation's location on the Mississippi River and the stranglehold that it imposed on French commerce and communication cut New France virtually in two, separating Louisiana from the rest of the colony. The Chickasaws had supported the Natchez people when they revolted against the French in 1729, adding insult to France's grievances against the tribe and leading to the French decision to destroy the Chickasaws in the same manner as they had destroyed the Fox and Natchez tribes.

In the spring of 1736 two French forces set out against the Chickasaws. The northern column, under the command of the Illinois Territory's governor, Pierre d'Artaguette, included 30 French regulars, 100 militiamen, and almost 300 Illinois, Weas, Miamis, and Piankashaws led by the Illinois chief Chicagou and François de la Valterie, Sieur de Vincennes. The southern force included some 600 French troops and 1,000 Choctaw warriors commanded by Jean-Baptiste Le Moyne de Bienville. The original plan was for both armies to meet at the main Chickasaw town of Ackia (Tupelo, Mississippi) at the end of March.

Bienville's force, which followed the Tombigbee River north from Mobile, was delayed for several weeks by heavy rains, but Bienville had no means of informing d'Artaguette of his position. The northern force arrived at the Chickasaw Bluffs (Memphis) in early March as planned and built a small fort as a supply base. After three weeks, however, d'Artaguette was running short of food and decided to attack on his own. The Chickasaws were well aware of the presence of the French and were waiting in their fortified towns. Realizing that his force was not strong enough to defeat the Chickasaws in their main town of Ackia, d'Artaguette chose to attack Ogoula Tchetoka on March 25.

The Chickasaw village was heavily fortified, and the French and their allies were pinned down by cross fire. Worse yet, 400 Chickasaw warriors arrived from a nearby town and hit the French flank. Most of France's native allies fled the battlefield, joined by some of the French regulars. Seventeen Frenchmen were captured, including d'Artaguette and Vincennes. When the Chickasaws realized that a second force was approaching from the south, they no longer hoped to ransom their captives and burned d'Artaguette and the others alive.

Learning of d'Artaguette's death when he approached Chickasaw territory, Bienville was determined to avenge him by attacking Ackia, which hosted Natchez refugees. The Chickasaws, however, had used the interval to fortify the town with the help of British traders. Nevertheless, as the French forces outnumbered the Chickasaw and Natchez defenders three to one, the Chickasaws sent a delegation of intermediaries to arrange for a truce, but the Choctaws killed them after their arrival.

The French then attacked Ackia and employed grenades against the village's fortified houses while protecting themselves against musket balls with heavy woolen bags, but the defenders caught them with cross fire between houses. Several French officers were killed, which added to the confusion among the soldiers. The French finally retreated, and Bienville led his diminished force back to Mobile. The Battle of Ogoula Tchetoka was the worst defeat that the French had suffered to that point in their clashes with Native Americans.

KATJA WUESTENBECKER

See also

Chickasaws; Choctaws; France; Natchezes; Natchez Revolt

References

Foreman, Grant. *The Five Civilized Tribes: Cherokee, Chickasaw, Choctaw, Creek, Seminole.* Norman: University of Oklahoma Press, 1934.

Woods, Patricia Dillon. *French-Indian Relations on the Southern Frontier, 1699–1762.* Ann Arbor: University of Michigan Research Press, 1980.

Ohio Company of Virginia

A land speculation company formed in July 1749 and officially dissolved in May 1771. The official name of the enterprise was the Ohio Company of Virginia. Stockholders in the Ohio Company included members of some of the most prominent families in the colony, such as Augustine Washington, Thomas Lee, John Mercer, and Robert Dinwiddie. The company's most effective advocate was John Hanbury, a wealthy Quaker merchant in London. Hanbury had presented the Ohio Company's petition for the land grant to the king's Privy Council. After hearing the company's petition for land in 1749, King George II sent instructions to Lieutenant Governor William Gooch of Virginia directing him to grant 200,000 acres to the company in the Ohio River Valley, which was within Virginia's extensive western land claims.

The company did not fulfill the obligations outlined in its charter, namely to settle 100 families on its land grant, but managed to capitalize on an expanding Native American trade network. By the end of 1749 company traders and agents had constructed a storage house on a western branch of the Potomac River. Within the next two years the company began planning a road northwest toward the Monongahela River. The company also sought to purchase more land in western Maryland, while company representative Christopher Gist began surveying Ohio Company land for larger-scale settlement.

The Ohio Company's attempts to advance its claims raised fears among natives in the region. In 1752 officials representing Virginia and the Ohio Company negotiated the Treaty of Logstown with the Iroquois, Shawnee, Delaware, and Wyandot nations. This treaty required the natives to recognize Virginia's claims along the eastern Ohio River and required the Ohio Company to build a fort near present-day Pittsburgh, Pennsylvania, to protect the allied natives and white settlers. This provision brought the company and the colony of Virginia into direct confrontation with the French, who also claimed the area.

After the French in 1753 rejected Virginia lieutenant governor Robert Dinwiddie's demand that they leave the region, Dinwiddie dispatched a force under George Washington to assert Virginia's and the company's claim. Shortly after Washington built a fort in 1754 it was surrounded by an armed French and native force, which secured Washington's surrender after a brief battle. This action set in motion the events that precipitated the French and Indian War (1754–1763).

Following the French and Indian War, the Ohio Company met more obstacles to settlement, the most important being the royal Proclamation of 1763, which forbade white settlement west of the Appalachians. The company finally merged with another land company before the official expiration of its charter in 1771.

CRESTON LONG

See also

French and Indian War; Logstown, Treaty of; Washington, George

References

Anderson, Fred. *Crucible of War: The Seven Years' War and the Fate of the Empire in British North America, 1754–1766.* New York: Vintage Books, 2001.

Hofstra, Warren R. *The Planting of New Virginia: Settlement and Landscape in the Shenandoah Valley.* Baltimore: Johns Hopkins University Press, 2004.

Jennings, Francis. *Empire of Fortune: Crowns, Colonies, and Tribes in the Seven Years War in America.* New York: Norton, 1988.

Ohio Expedition
Event Date: 1764

Campaign orchestrated in the autumn of 1764 by British colonel Henry Bouquet, designed to compel Native American insurgents to sue for peace. The 1764 Ohio expedition was carried over from the French and Indian War (1754–1763) and Pontiac's Rebellion (1763). In concert with a northern force led by Colonel John Bradstreet, Bouquet set out to attack Delaware, Mingo, and Shawnee villages that had taken part in the insurrection.

Bradstreet's contingent did not complete all of its assigned duties, however. This left Bouquet's force to face the region's Indian war parties alone. Delays in raising colonial forces and adequate supplies to equip 1,200 troops under Bouquet's command slowed offensive preparations, and the final preparations were not completed until the late summer.

Colonial legislators were reluctant to provide manpower for this combined effort. The Pennsylvania Assembly agreed to provide 1,000 men, but many of them deserted before reaching the operational theater. Consequently, regulars drawn from the 42nd (Royal Highland) Regiment of Foot and the 60th (Royal American) Regiment of Foot did not take the field with provincial counterparts from Pennsylvania and Virginia until October 1. On that date the expedition began its slow advance from Fort Pitt toward the upper Muskingum River Valley.

Bouquet's command of irregular warfare was demonstrated during the 130-mile march through the wilderness to a fortified encampment constructed deep in the heart of native territory. His late start was not a detriment, because offensive operations were most effective after autumn frost had denuded vegetation that provided natural cover for ambushes. The soldiers moved at a guarded pace along three parallel paths cut by pioneers, much as during Forbes's march on Fort Duquesne in 1758. Bouquet had been de facto field commander of that campaign and had learned the basics of North American frontier warfare.

Bouquet's tactical thinking had evolved in the intervening six years, however. His infantrymen now adopted a novel configuration based on the hollow square used to defend against cavalry attack. In this instance, when fired on they were to deploy into a defensive shell instead of an extended line. Regulars formed the front and right of the square, Pennsylvanians composed the left and rear of the square, and 50 light horse and Virginia volunteers provided the rear guard. The center was reserved for the baggage train that moved down the middle lane ahead of troops, who would close the square behind the 300 or so drovers and camp followers. Such innovations protected both the troops and the vulnerable pack horses from surprise.

The approach of Bouquet's force alarmed natives, who realized their untenable position and hurried to the negotiating table. Delaware messengers were the first to come, since their confederates near Detroit had already reconciled with the British months earlier. Mingo and Shawnee representatives appeared shortly thereafter. The Royal American commander displayed his diplomatic skills by receiving native emissaries gallantly but without affection to emphasize the solemnity of the occasion.

The ensuing conference held at Tuscarawas met on October 17, 1764, in a special arbor built some distance away from the lines.

Illustration from a general map of the country on the Ohio and Muskingham showing the situation of the Indian towns with respect to the Army under the command of Colonel Bouquet March of His Majesty's troops from Fort Pitt to the forts of Muskingham in 1764. Illustration from *An Historical Account of the Expedition against the Ohio Indians, in the Year 1764 [] By Tho. Hutchins*, published in 1765. (Library of Congress)

There an honor guard of light horse, regulars, and provincials were posted to impress arriving dignitaries with the strength of the forces marshaled against them.

Bouquet censured native chiefs for breaking the peace, killing innocent civilians, and besieging Fort Pitt. Old native refrains that warriors had been compelled to participate in the insurrection or that parties still raiding backcountry settlements were beyond the control of community headmen fell on deaf ears. Bouquet assured his listeners that a new armistice would not be signed until every previous treaty obligation was honored by their communities. In particular, he stipulated that all British captives, including slaves and deserters, must be returned to the colonies. Natives were required to provide provisions and transportation for this exodus. Bouquet also insisted that all war parties were to be recalled and that appropriate tribal deputies were to be sent to Sir William Johnson, superintendent of Indian affairs for the northern colonies, to make peace. A grace period of 12 days allowed prisoners to be collected from distant villages at the Muskingum Forks, where the army marched to receive them.

Bouquet then advanced another 30 miles into the very heart of Shawnee territory and built an entrenched camp. Meanwhile, he awaited delivery of the prisoners. Native raiders had captured approximately 2,000 colonists through 1764, with many still awaiting redemption by the autumn of that year. Shawnee communities held the largest number of British colonists taken during the French and Indian War and Pontiac's Rebellion. They had also exhibited remarkable unwillingness to release them, despite repeated promises to do so. The intimidating presence of Bouquet's troops overcame their recalcitrance and also prompted the release of many captives and the surrender of 6 hostages as surety for the delivery of the balance soon after. Initially taken into army custody were 207 captives, who were housed in special accommodations constructed within British lines.

Lists recording the names of captives as well as their ages, dates and places of capture, and physical descriptions were compiled before they were discharged into the care of custodians, who accompanied them eastward to Pittsburgh. From there the captives were returned to their counties of origin. Nine more Shawnee prisoners were released to authorities within weeks of the first group's arrival at Fort Pitt on November 28, 1764.

Pennsylvania legislators, in a rare moment of equanimity, offered public thanks to Bouquet for restoring tranquility to their western frontiers, a peace that would last until the outbreak of Lord Dunmore's War (1774). Their address recognized the Royal American officer's expertise in partisan warfare, citing his actions at Bushy Run and the Muskingum Valley expedition as concrete evidence of military prowess.

Alexander V. Campbell

See also

Bouquet, Henry; Delawares; French and Indian War; Lord Dunmore's War; Mingos; Pontiac's Rebellion; Shawnees

References

Dowd, Gregory Evans. *War under Heaven: Pontiac, the Indian Nations, and the British Empire*. Baltimore: Johns Hopkins University Press, 2002.

McConnell, Michael N. *A Country Between: The Upper Ohio and Its Peoples, 1724–1774*. Lincoln: University of Nebraska Press, 1992.

Ojibwa-Dakota Conflict
Start Date: Unknown
End Date: 1850s

Intertribal Indian conflict. It is not possible to ascertain with certainty when the Ojibwa (also called Anishinabe or Chippewa) and Dakota (Sioux) peoples began to war against each another. The origins of the conflict, according to Ojibwa accounts recorded by William Warren, date back to pre–European contact times. Forced westward because of their conflicts with the Iroquois, the Ojibwas moved into the territory west of the Great Lakes. Many of the native peoples in the region, including the Dakotas, regarded the Ojibwas as intruders. The origins of the Dakota-Ojibwa wars are also usually attributed to treachery on the part of one side or the other. The fighting lasted from precontact times into the mid-19th century.

The Ojibwa-Dakota conflict, however, would take on a very different aspect with the arrival of Europeans. By the end of the 17th century, native peoples of the Great Lakes and beyond had discovered the advantages of European tools and weapons, and they realized that possessing them gave them an advantage over their enemies. Even before they encountered Europeans, the Dakotas recognized the value of metal trade goods.

The arrival of French traders in the 17th century introduced a new and deadlier aspect to the Ojibwa-Dakota conflicts. Having easier access to French traders because of their location, the Ojibwas obtained firearms earlier than the Dakotas. Thus, they were able to gain and for the most part keep the advantage in the conflict. Concerned with the ruinous effects of warfare on the fur trade, French traders—and their later British and American counterparts—did their best to arrange truces between the two sides. Traders realized that they were in a delicate situation. Commerce with one side in the conflict could bring an attack by the other.

By the mid-18th century, the main battleground between the two sides was the area of present-day Minnesota. Not only were furs and fur trapping territories at stake, but also at stake were the abundant waterways of the region with large quantities of wild rice, which was the staple food of both peoples. Another primary objective of both the Ojibwas and the Dakotas, in addition to the traditional goals of honor and captives, was to keep the other side from trading with the French and acquiring European weaponry.

By the beginning of the 19th century the Ojibwas had succeeded in pushing the Dakotas and their allies, the Cheyennes, out of most of the Minnesota Territory. The conflict between the two continued into the 1850s, and some Dakotas remained in Minnesota until the 1860s, when they departed to join their brethren on the Great Plains, becoming part of the Plains horse culture.

ROGER M. CARPENTER

See also

Beaver Wars; Cheyennes; Dakota Sioux; Ojibwas; Sioux

References

Anderson, Gary C. "Early Dakota Migration and Intertribal War: A Revision." *Western Historical Quarterly* 11 (1980): 17–36.

Hickerson, Harold. *The Chippewa and Their Neighbors: A Study in Ethnohistory*. New York: Holt, Rinehart and Winston, 1970.

Warren, William W. *History of the Ojibway People*. St. Paul: Minnesota Historical Society Press, 1984.

Ojibwas

Native American nation of the upper Great Lakes region. At the time of first European contact, the Ojibwas (who called themselves Anishinabe, meaning "original people," and were also known as Ojibwes or Chippewas) constituted the largest Native American group in the upper Great Lakes area. Their population was estimated at some 35,000 people. Located in present-day Michigan, Wisconsin, Minnesota, Ontario, and Manitoba, the Ojibwas lived in widely separated bands linked by clan and kinship. They had no centralized leadership structure. They were allied with the Ottawas and Pottawatomis through the Three Fires Confederacy, and the three nations may in fact have constituted a single tribe at one time.

The Ojibwas spoke an Algonquian language that comprised five regional dialects. Some bands that subsisted by hunting, fishing, and gathering moved seasonally, while others that raised maize and wild rice lived in sedentary towns. All bands also engaged in trade with other Ojibwas and neighboring native nations. The Dakotas (Sioux) were traditional enemies of the Ojibwas, and the two nations engaged in sporadic warfare. The most intensive conflict began around 1650. In addition to traditional native motives of honor, captives, and access to regions that produced wild rice, the war was also caused by the Ojibwa desire to block Dakota access to the fur trade and the supply of European goods that the trade provided. By 1800 the Ojibwas had managed to push most of their rivals onto the Great Plains.

In the early 1600s the Ojibwas encountered French fur traders and Jesuit missionaries probing westward across the Great Lakes. The Ojibwas established trade ties with the French, which made the tribe the target of Iroquois attacks during the Beaver Wars (1641–1701), when the Iroquois sought access to furs and control of the trade. Equipped with firearms by the French, the Ojibwas defeated the Iroquois in a series of battles in present-day Ontario and northern Michigan. Casualties sustained in the fighting caused the Ojibwa population to suffer a considerable decline, but their numbers recovered quickly afterward. They became concentrated in the vicinity of Detroit and other French trading posts at the start

Saulteaux (Ojibwa) family of the Upper Assiniboine River area, Manitoba, Canada, in 1887. The Saulteaux are a branch of the Ojibwa Nation in Canada. The name is derived from the French phrase meaning "people of the rapids," referring to the location of Sault Ste. Marie. (Library and Archives Canada)

of the 18th century. Band leaders' control of trade strengthened their authority, and leadership positions became hereditary.

The Ojibwas did not participate in the early Anglo-French wars in North America but allied with the French during the French and Indian War (1754–1763). Ojibwa warriors participated in the defeat of the Braddock expedition in 1755 and in the 1756 and 1757 French operations at Fort Oswego, Fort Edward, and Fort William Henry. However, the refusal of the Marquis de Montcalm to reward the Ojibwas and other native allies with captured goods and captives to adopt after the surrender of Fort William Henry led the Ojibwas and other natives to return home in frustration.

The end of the French and Indian War in 1763 saw France expelled from the North American mainland and its previous possessions ceded to Great Britain. Distrusting the British and angered by Major General Jeffrey Amherst's parsimony in the distribution of gifts that most natives had come to depend on, such as gunpowder and lead, the Ojibwas were receptive to calls from the Ottawa war leader Pontiac to join in a war against the British. The fact that Pontiac's mother was an Ojibwa and that the two nations were allies convinced the Ojibwas to join in Pontiac's Rebellion in

1763. Ojibwa warriors participated in a number of battles during the war. The most important for the Ojibwas occurred on June 2, 1763, at the British Fort Michilimackinac on Mackinac Island in the Straits of Mackinac, which separate Lake Michigan and Lake Huron. The fort's garrison was unaware of the uprising and did not know about Pontiac's attacks on other British forts. The Ojibwas arrived at the fort and began playing a game of lacrosse outside its walls. The garrison looked on, with the gates to the post left open. During the game the ball was lofted over the wall into the fort, and the players pursued it through the gates while their women handed them weapons that they had concealed underneath blankets. Seizing the fort, the Ojibwas killed 15 of its 35-man garrison and took the remainder prisoner. By the end of 1763, however, Pontiac's Rebellion had ended.

After Pontiac's Rebellion most Ojibwas remained peaceful and engaged in trade with the British and, after 1776, the United States. A few Ojibwa assisted the British in operations against Spanish St. Louis (in present-day Missouri) during the American Revolutionary War (1775–1783), and others later joined the Shawnees and Miamis in their war against Americans in the Ohio Country during the 1790s. Some Ojibwas showed interest in the Pan-Indian movement organized by the Shawnee leader Tecumseh and the prophet Tenskwatawa in the early 19th century. But the Ojibwas blamed Tenskwatawa's witchcraft for an epidemic that struck some of their eastern towns and responded with a raid on his settlement at Prophetstown in present-day Indiana. They took no further part in the movement, and later most avoided participation in the War of 1812.

During subsequent decades as the natural resources on which their traditional lifestyle depended became exhausted, the Ojibwas ceded or sold much of their territory in Canada to the British government and most of their lands in Michigan, Wisconsin, and Minnesota to the United States. The Ojibwas resettled on reservations, retaining their rights to hunt, fish, and harvest wild rice. A few Ojibwas were removed to Kansas. Most of the Ojibwas on the reservations turned to farming and raising livestock for sustenance. Thereafter the Ojibwas remained at peace with their white neighbors except for one instance in October 1898 when a handful of warriors on the Leech Lake Reservation in Minnesota, angered by recent land transfers, declared war on the United States. They fortified themselves on Big Bear Island and repulsed an attempt by U.S. troops to dislodge them. The situation was quickly resolved when Ojibwa leaders arranged a truce.

ROGER M. CARPENTER AND JIM PIECUCH

See also

Beaver Wars; Braddock's Campaign; French and Indian War; Iroquois; Johnson, Sir William; Neolin; Ojibwa-Dakota Conflict; Ottawas; Pontiac's Rebellion; Pottawatomis; Tecumseh; Tenskwatawa

References

Eid, Leroy V. "The Ojibwa-Iroquois War: The War the Five Nations Did Not Win." *Ethnohistory* 26(4) (Autumn 1979): 297–324.

Hickerson, Harold. *The Chippewa and Their Neighbors: A Study in Ethnohistory.* New York: Holt, Rinehart and Winston, 1970.

Warren, William W. *History of the Ojibway People.* St. Paul: Minnesota Historical Society Press, 1984.

Ojo Caliente Reservation, New Mexico

Located northwest of present-day Truth or Consequences in southwestern New Mexico, Ojo Caliente is the site of a series of hot springs at the base of the San Mateo Mountains, which Native Americans of the region held as sacred. For generations the waters and their environs were favored by the eastern branch of the Chiricahua Apaches, commonly referred to as the Warm Springs or Mimbres Apaches. Foremost among the leaders of this branch were Mangas Coloradas and Victorio. In the years immediately following the American Civil War (1861–1865), the U.S. government

Apache Indians bathe at Ojo Caliente in New Mexico. The Ojo Caliente Reservation was occupied by the Warm Springs Apaches, led by Chief Victorio. (Library of Congress)

sought to concentrate the diverse bands of southern Apaches onto five reservations in Arizona Territory and New Mexico Territory. In 1871 Ojo Caliente became the designated reservation for the Warm Springs Apaches.

Owing to its long-established importance as a sanctuary for the Chiricahuas, Ojo Caliente quickly became a refuge for disgruntled Apaches including Victorio and Geronimo, who detested U.S. concentration policies and encroaching white miners. Tensions between Native Americans and nearby settlers led to the establishment of a U.S. Army outpost on the Alamosa River near the springs. In 1875 the U.S. Indian Bureau decided to close four of its reservations, including Ojo Caliente, and concentrate all southern Apache bands onto the desolate San Carlos Reservation in western Arizona.

Opposition to their removal led to a series of confrontations between the Warm Springs Apaches, led by Victorio, and the U.S. Army. One of the most costly occurred on September 4, 1879, near Ojo Caliente. Five buffalo soldiers of the 9th U.S. Cavalry were killed and 3 were wounded in the encounter before Victorio and his approximately 300 followers fled south with 46 captured horses.

ALAN C. DOWNS

See also
Cavalry Regiment, 9th U.S.; Geronimo; Mangas Coloradas; San Carlos Reservation; Victorio

References
Cozzens, Peter, ed. *Eyewitnesses to the Indian Wars, 1865–1890.* 5 vols. Mechanicsburg, PA: Stackpole, 2001–2006.
Thrapp, Dan L. *Victorio and the Mimbres Apaches.* Norman: University of Oklahoma Press, 1974.

Ojo Oso, New Mexico

Site in northwestern New Mexico just outside present-day Gallup in McKinley County and the location for treaty negotiations in November 1846 between U.S. Army colonel Alexander W. Doniphan and the Navajos. After securing Santa Fe, New Mexico, in August 1846, Brigadier General Stephen W. Kearny, commanding the Army of the West, became concerned over reports that the Navajos and Apaches were raiding and committing acts of violence against non–Native American New Mexicans, many of them Mexicans by birth. Charged with protecting New Mexicans now that the United States had claimed the region as its own, Kearny decided to hold a summit with Navajo and Apache leaders in order to negotiate a security agreement with them. Only a few leaders appeared in Santa Fe, however. Nevertheless, Kearny explained to them that New Mexico was no longer Mexican territory, that the United States now controlled it, and that U.S. officials would not permit continued attacks against New Mexicans. The Navajos continued their depredations, however, and armed units that Kearny sent to protect New Mexicans were doing little good.

In September 1846 when Kearny departed for California, he left Colonel Doniphan in charge of U.S. forces at Santa Fe. Doniphan was determined to end the violence being perpetrated by the Navajos and decided to go to them to seek an accommodation. On October 26 he set out for the northwestern mountains with a force of some 300 men, frequently traveling through heavy mountain snows. After visiting some Native American villages and talking with village leaders, he managed to gather about 500 Navajos who agreed to meet with him at Ojo Oso (Bear Spring). Those leaders who were reluctant to attend were escorted at gunpoint to the council.

Doniphan explained that the Navajos would face war and extinction if they did not cease their depredations. He also told them that the New Mexicans were now American citizens who were protected under the laws of the United States. The Navajos countered that they harbored no ill will against the Americans but despised the Mexicans because of the violence they had perpetrated against the Navajos.

On November 22, 1846, after several days of talks, Doniphan along with Lieutenants Congreve Jackson and William Gilpin signed an agreement with senior Navajo leaders. That agreement bound the Navajos to cease their attacks. In return the U.S. government agreed to protect the Navajos from attacks by Mexicans and New Mexicans. Signing for the Navajos were Sarcilla Largo, Caballada de Mucho, Sandoval, Kiatanito, Alexandro, Narbona, Sagunda, Tapio, Pedro José Manuelito, and Savoietta Garcia, among others. As acts of good faith, Doniphan presented the Navajos with numerous gifts, including cattle and sheep. The Navajos gave the Americans blankets.

Doniphan left Ojo Oso a day or two later. On his way back to Santa Fe he went to the Zuni Pueblo, where he hoped to bring an end to the Zunis' war with the Navajos. After three days of mediating talks between the two warring parties, he managed to get leaders to agree to a treaty on November 26, 1846. In the end, however, Doniphan's efforts came to naught, as the Zunis and Navajos continued to fight, and the Navajos kept up their raids against New Mexicans.

PAUL G. PIERPAOLI JR.

See also
Apaches; Kearny, Stephen Watts; Navajos; New Mexico

References
Hughes, John Taylor. *Doniphan's Expedition: Containing an Account of the Conquest of New Mexico.* New York: Arno, 1973.
Iverson, Peter. *Diné: A History of the Navajos.* Albuquerque: University of New Mexico Press, 2002.

Old Briton
Birth Date: Unknown
Death Date: June 21, 1752

A Miami sachem (chief) who forged ties first with the French and then with the British in the vicinity of western Ohio. Nothing is known of the date and circumstances of birth for Old Briton (Memeskia) or of his early years. Initially Memeskia backed the

French during the early stages of King George's War (1744–1748). By 1747, however, a shortage of trade goods and dwindling French gifts had badly strained relations between the Miamis and the French. This led Memeskia and the Miamis to join an unsuccessful rebellion, led by the Wyandot sachem Orontony, against the French.

Following the war, Memeskia formed an alliance with the British and allowed Ohio Company traders to move into the new village of Pickawillany in western Ohio. To underscore his transfer of loyalty, Memeskia was thereafter known by the nickname of "Old Briton" instead of the French moniker "La Demoiselle."

Pickawillany flourished as a major economic center, channeling to the British the trade of numerous native nations from as far away as Illinois. The French had claimed possession of Pickawillany and its surrounding countryside, but they felt powerless to counter the British presence because of their increasingly weak hold on the entire Great Lakes region. French officials tried without success to pressure Old Briton into expelling the British.

In early 1752 the French finally organized a military expedition of 250 Ottawa and Ojibwa warriors under the command of Charles Langlade, a leader of mixed French and Native American heritage. On June 21, 1752, the numerically superior French-led force overwhelmed and destroyed Pickawillany. In the process, Old Briton was taken captive. To foster a proper fear of French power, Langlade executed Old Briton. He then handed over the body to be cooked and eaten by the Ottawas.

The Miamis returned to their alliance with the French in 1753, a temporary accommodation that lasted only until the British permanently drove the French out of the region during the French and Indian War (1754–1763).

ANDREW C. LANNEN

See also
King George's War; Orontony; Pickawillany Massacre

References
Hurt, R. Douglas. *The Ohio Frontier: Crucible of the Old Northwest, 1720–1830*. Bloomington: Indiana University Press, 1996.
Trent, William. *Journal of Captain William Trent from Logstown to Pickawillany, A.D. 1752*. New York: Arno, 1971.

Old Man's Creek, Battle of

See Stillman's Run, Battle of

Old Northwest Territory

The Old Northwest Territory encompassed the present-day states of Ohio, Indiana, Illinois, Michigan, and Wisconsin. The Congress of the Confederation officially organized the territory in the Northwest Ordinance of July 13, 1787. The territory was to be governed initially by a governor, a secretary, and three judges appointed by Congress. The ordinance also provided that three to five states could be formed from the territory. Because it had a large Native American population and settlers anxious to secure their lands, the territory saw notable armed conflict between 1763 and 1832.

In 1763 at the conclusion of the French and Indian War (1754–1763), Ottawa chief Pontiac led a revolt against the British in the Old Northwest Territory. Pontiac had been inspired by the teachings of Neolin (the Delaware Prophet), who rejected accommodation with whites. Pontiac was angered by the expulsion of the French from North America in 1763 and was equally insulted by the suspension of traditional diplomatic gifts by the new British regime. Pontiac's Rebellion resulted in the capture of every British fort in the region with the exceptions of Pitt, Niagara, and Detroit. Pontiac's warriors were forced to suspend their military efforts to hunt for food in the autumn of 1763, however, and the rebellion soon disintegrated.

After the American Revolutionary War (1775–1783), the tribes of the Old Northwest formed a loose confederacy to oppose American expansion onto their lands. Led by Miami chief Little Turtle and the Shawnee war chief Blue Jacket, the Native Americans fought repeatedly against U.S. troops. Indeed, they defeated American forces led by Brigadier General Josiah Harmer in Ohio in October 1790 and by Major General Arthur St. Clair in November 1791. Major General "Mad" Anthony Wayne finally defeated the Native Americans in the Battle of Fallen Timbers on August 20, 1794. A year later Little Turtle and other Native American leaders signed the Treaty of Greenville, which had been negotiated chiefly by General Wayne. The treaty ceded much of present-day Ohio and Indiana to the United States.

The visions of Tenskwatawa (the Shawnee Prophet) during 1804 and 1805 launched yet another wave of Native American resistance in the Old Northwest Territory. Tenskwatawa saw the Americans as "the offspring of an evil serpent." Tenskwatawa's brother Tecumseh, himself a powerful warrior, wanted to unite all Native American peoples in an alliance to oppose American expansion. He thus traveled throughout the Old Northwest and the Old Southwest gathering support and began caching military stores at his brother's village of Prophetstown on the Wabash River in Indiana.

In November 1811, taking advantage of Tecumseh's absence, Indiana Territory governor William Henry Harrison led a force of regular troops and militia to Prophetstown with the intention of destroying it. Young warriors talked Tenskwatawa into attacking Harrison's men, but the Americans scattered the Native Americans at the Battle of Tippecanoe, burning Prophetstown and all of its provisions. With his supplies now destroyed, Tecumseh turned to the British in Canada for assistance just as the War of 1812 began. The British appointed Tecumseh a brigadier general in the British Army, but he perished at the Battle of the Thames near Chatham, Ontario, on October 5, 1813. His death essentially ended another phase of Native American resistance in the Old Northwest.

The last major conflict in the region was the Black Hawk War of 1832. Chief Black Hawk was a Sauk leader who was angered by a series of land cessions to the United States. In late 1828 he led his band of warriors on a winter hunt west of the Mississippi River. In the spring of 1829 he and his forces returned to their homes at Saukenk, located on the Illinois side of the Mississippi. They were more than surprised to find white settlers living there. When Black Hawk was told that the land had been sold, he protested, and the Sauks and settlers spent an uneasy summer together.

Black Hawk left on another winter hunt in late 1831, and when he returned the next spring settlers panicked. A conflict began involving the U.S. Army, Illinois volunteers, and the outnumbered Sauks. Black Hawk was ultimately captured, and most of the Sauks were sent to Indian Territory (present-day Oklahoma), ending the last Native American war in the Old Northwest.

ROGER M. CARPENTER

See also

Black Hawk; Black Hawk War; Blue Jacket; Fallen Timbers, Battle of; Greenville, Treaty of; Harmar, Josiah; Harrison, William Henry; Little Turtle; Native Americans and the War of 1812; Neolin; Pontiac; Pontiac's Rebellion; Sauks and Foxes; Shawnees; St. Clair, Arthur; Tecumseh; Tenskwatawa; Thames, Battle of the; Wayne, Anthony

References

Dowd, Gregory Evans. *War under Heaven: Pontiac, the Indian Nations, and the British Empire.* Baltimore: Johns Hopkins University Press, 2002.

Downes, Randolph C. *Council Fires on the Upper Ohio: A Narrative of Indian Affairs in the Upper Ohio Valley until 1795.* Pittsburgh: University of Pittsburgh Press, 1940.

Edmunds, R. David. *The Shawnee Prophet.* Lincoln: University of Nebraska Press, 1983.

Edmunds, R. David. *Tecumseh and the Quest for Indian Leadership.* Boston: Little, Brown, 1984.

Nichols, Roger L. *Black Hawk and the Warrior's Path.* Arlington Heights, IL: Harlan Davidson, 1992.

Trask, Kerry A. *Black Hawk: The Battle for the Heart of America.* New York: Holt, 2006.

Old Shawnee Town

A Shawnee settlement located on the Ohio River at the mouth of the Scioto River in present-day Scioto County near Portsmouth, Ohio. Old Shawnee Town's nucleus was the council house, described by Christopher Gist in 1751 as a bark-covered structure about 90 feet in length. This structure would have been used for council meetings, rituals, secular celebrations, the seclusion of warriors after a raid, or occasionally as a fort. Gist stated that the town had 140 bark lodges and 300 men, suggesting a total population of about 1,200, which was unusually large for a Shawnee settlement.

The village was established sometime before 1739 and was destroyed by a flood in 1753. One of two Shawnee chief towns, or capitals, the village was also known as Lower Shawnee Town or Lowertown. The French called it Sonnioto or Sonnontio. In addition, any Shawnee chief town could be called Chillicothe. Some of these same names were used at different times for other villages or for the same villages moved to new locations.

An example of what the French called an Indian Republic, Old Shawnee Town was an ethnically mixed community of refugee peoples (Mingos, Delawares, and some Miamis in addition to Shawnees) not controlled by a European alliance system though nominally linked to the Iroquois-English Covenant Chain. Having been expelled from the Ohio Country by the Iroquois in the mid-17th century, the Shawnees began returning in the 1730s. In this they were encouraged by the French, who hoped to incorporate them into the French alliance system. Although the Shawnees came to the area in part to use the French as an alternative source of trade goods, British traders followed them there as well. The town was also visited regularly by Susquehannock and Potomac traders. Moreover, Shawnee efforts to establish peace among the natives without French mediation vexed the French greatly.

Captain Pierre-Joseph Céloron de Blainville was met with suspicion and hostility at the town when he came to assert France's claim to the Ohio Country in 1749. He ordered the British traders out, stating that they had no right to be in the territory. At Old Shawnee Town, Céloron received word that the Detroit-based natives would not be reinforcing his expedition as promised. He then decided to withdraw without pillaging the British traders' goods, as he had been instructed to do.

In August 1752, following the destruction of Pickawillany by French-allied natives, the Miamis, Mingos, Delawares, and Shawnees of the Ohio Valley met at Old Shawnee Town and called on the British and the Iroquois for support under the Covenant Chain. No aid was forthcoming. Believing themselves abandoned, the Shawnees shifted their allegiance to the French until the fall of Fort Duquesne in 1758.

SCOTT C. MONJE

See also

Covenant Chain; Delawares; Iroquois; Iroquois Confederacy; Miamis; Mingos; Shawnees

References

Gipson, Lawrence Henry. *The British Empire before the American Revolution,* Vol. 4, *Zones of International Friction: North America South of the Great Lakes, 1748–1754.* New York: Knopf, 1939.

White, Richard. *The Middle Ground: Indians, Empires, and Republics in the Great Lakes Region, 1650–1815.* New York: Cambridge University Press, 1991.

Old Winnemucca

See Winnemucca

Oñate, Juan de

Birth Date: ca. 1552
Death Date: 1626

Spanish explorer and the first governor of the province of New Mexico. Juan de Oñate was born around 1552 in Nueva Galicia

Inscription by Mexican governor of New Mexico Don Juan de Oñate, carved over an ancestral Puebloan petroglyph at El Morro. It reads: "Passed by here, the Adelantado Don Juan de Oñate, from the discovery of the Sea of the South, the 16th day of April, 1605." (National Park Service)

(New Galicia), located in western Mexico. As a young man he participated in the campaigns against the Chichimec natives along the northern frontier and helped administer the family silver mines in Zacatecas, the largest silver mining site in northern Mexico. Oñate married Isabel de Tolosa Cortés Moctezuma, the great-granddaughter of the Aztec ruler Moctezuma II (Montezuma) and granddaughter of Hernán Cortés. The combined wealth of these two families made Oñate one of the richest men in Mexico.

In 1595 Oñate received an appointment from the Spanish court to lead an expedition up the Rio Grande to spread the Catholic faith, pacify the natives, and establish a permanent colony in the northern reaches of New Spain. After a series of delays, Oñate and 500 men, women, and children entered New Mexico in early 1598 near present-day El Paso, Texas. The explorer immediately claimed possession of the land and its people.

By late May 1598 the expedition reached the upper Rio Grande and encountered the first of many pueblos that Oñate formally claimed for Spain. In July, Oñate arrived at the confluence of the Chama River and the Rio Grande and established his headquarters at Ohke Pueblo, which he renamed San Juan, the capital of the new colony. In doing so, he effectively extended the Camino Real another 600 miles.

From San Juan, Oñate inaugurated his missionary program by dispersing friars to the Pueblos while he personally conducted a reconnaissance of the province. Native hospitality turned to open resistance in January 1599 when natives at Acoma Pueblo attacked Spanish soldiers who had entered the pueblo in search of food. Eleven Spanish soldiers died. In retaliation, Oñate sent a punitive expedition against the town that killed 800 men, women, and children and took another 580 captive. Adolescents were sentenced to 20 years of servitude, and adult men were subjected to public mutilation to be conducted in the plazas of pueblos along the Rio Grande as a lesson to those who might question Spanish authority.

In 1601 Oñate moved the capital across the Rio Grande to Yunque Ouinge Pueblo and renamed it San Gabriel. Despairing over the apparent lack of riches in the colony, he set out in June of that year in hopes of finding wealth in Quivira, a location (most likely Wichita villages) in present-day Kansas visited by Francisco Vásquez de Coronado in 1541. The journey proved fruitless, and Oñate returned to his colony only to lead a final and equally unrewarding expedition in 1604 westward to the Colorado River and the Gulf of California. During his absence, growing discontent in the colony led many Spaniards to return to Mexico.

With Spanish interests in New Mexico on the verge of failure, government officials recalled Oñate to Mexico City in 1606 to face charges related to the poor condition of the colony and the governor's conduct toward the Acoma natives. Oñate resigned his office in 1607 but remained in New Mexico long enough to see the establishment of a new provincial capital at Santa Fe. In Mexico City, the Spanish court found the former governor guilty of misconduct toward the inhabitants (Spanish and native) of his colony and permanently banished him from New Mexico. Despite a successful appeal that cleared him of all charges, Oñate departed Mexico for Spain, where he became a mining inspector. He died there sometime in 1626.

ALAN C. DOWNS

See also

Acoma Pueblo, Battle of; New Mexico; Pueblos

References

Knaut, Andrew L. *The Pueblo Revolt of 1680: Conquest and Resistance in Seventeenth-Century New Mexico.* Norman: University of Oklahoma Press, 1995.

Simmons, Marc. *The Last Conquistador: Juan de Oñate and the Settling of the Far Southwest.* Norman: University of Oklahoma Press, 1991.

Oneidas

One of the five original tribal nations of the Iroquois Confederacy. The Iroquois called themselves Haudenosaunee, or "People of the Longhouse." The name "Oneida" was derived from the Iroquois word *onayotekaona,* which referred to a great boulder that was located in their territory. The Oneidas joined with the Senecas, the Cayugas, the Onondagas, and the Mohawks to form the Iroquois Confederacy. Around 1570 the prophet Deganawidah and his disciple Hiawatha founded the confederation with the goal of ending constant intertribal warfare.

The Oneidas' territory was in what is now central New York state. They lived near Lake Oneida southward to the Susquehanna River. To their immediate east were the Mohawks, and to their immediate west were the Onondagas. Although they were part of the Iroquois Confederacy, the Oneidas were distinct from their fellow allied natives. They were also the least numerous of the Iroquois, numbering just 1,500 at first European contact.

The Oneidas shared the general culture and history of all the northeastern indigenous peoples and the Iroquois in particular. The Oneisas built palisades to surround their villages and lived as families in longhouses in arrangements according to matrilineal descent. The women raised corn, tobacco, beans, and squash, and the men hunted and fished. Women were socially honored and held in generally high regard. The Oneidas believed that the world had been created when a woman fell from the sky world. The water creatures were concerned for her, so they built the land to be a platform for the woman, who was mother earth. This myth and many others were part of the rich spiritual lore of the Oneida people.

In the mid-1600s the Oneidas made a temporary peace with the French while they played the Mohawks and the Onondagas against each other to preserve their independence. King William's War (1689–1697) wrought great destruction on the Oneidas, and in 1696 French forces raided a key Oneida village and destroyed its structures and surrounding fields. This led to the division of the Oneidas into the Upper Oneidas and the Canawarogheres. Finally in 1701, the Iroquois Confederacy—including the Oneidas—made peace with the French and their native allies. In 1722 the Tuscaroras, an Iroquoian-speaking tribe from North Carolina, moved to New York. They sought protection from the Iroquois and were given a place next to the Oneidas to live. The Tuscaroras soon became the sixth nation of the confederation. For some time thereafter, the Oneidas sent war parties into North Carolina to punish the Tuscaroras' enemies.

The Iroquois Confederacy held an annual Great Council in Onondaga territory. Nine sachems, or chiefs, would attend as representatives of the Oneidas. The Oneidas were organized into three clans: Bear, Turtle, and Wolf. Each clan was represented by three sachems nominated by the women of their respective clans. These sachems after 1722 also served as representatives for the Tuscaroras.

In general, the Oneidas tried to remain neutral in the various colonial conflicts. Nevertheless, their locale helped them to develop strong economic ties to the English, particularly in the Hudson River Valley. They courted natives in the Great Lakes but frequently warred with southern native groups. In this way the Oneidas—and all of the Iroquois Confederacy—could achieve maximum economic and military benefits from their allies.

During the American Revolutionary War (1775–1783), the Oneidas broke with the other Iroquois and supported the Americans against the British. The Oneidas had tried to remain neutral so that they could avoid attacking the Loyalists, who were their neighbors. Eventually the Reverend Samuel Kirkland, a Presbyterian minister, brought most of the Oneidas over to the Patriot cause. Some Oneidas served as scouts for the colonists, and others served in other ways. During the desperate winter at Valley Forge, a party of Oneidas led by Chief Skenadoah brought 600 bushels of corn to General George Washington's starving army.

Oneidas participated in several major battles of the Revolutionary War. On August 6, 1777, they fought in the Battle of Oriskany. After the Revolutionary War some Oneidas returned to their homes in central New York, but the new state government had seized most of their land. At this time they took in some of the remnants of the Mohegans. Other Oneidas moved to a reservation on the Thames River in Ontario, Canada. In the early 1800s most of the New York Oneidas relocated to Green Bay, Wisconsin. Today, Oneidas continue to live in New York, Wisconsin, and Ontario.

ANDREW J. WASKEY

See also

Iroquois; Iroquois Confederacy; King William's War; Native Americans and the American Revolutionary War

References

McLester, L. Gordon, et al. *The Oneida.* Austin, TX: Raintree Steck-Vaughn, 2001.

Oxley, Shelley. *The History of the Oneida Indians.* Madison: Wisconsin Department of Public Instruction, 1981.

Richards, Cara Elizabeth. *The Oneida People.* Phoenix: Indian Tribal Series, 1974.

Onondagas

Founding nation of the Iroquois Confederacy. The Onondagas ("People of the Hills") controlled the heart of Iroquois territory in much of present-day upstate New York. They were hunters as well as agriculturalists, and their hunting territory ranged from present-day Onondaga County as far north as Lake Ontario and as far south as the Chenango Forks.

As the most centrally located of the original Iroquois Five Nations (the others were the Senecas, the Oneidas, the Cayugas, and the Mohawks), the Onondagas hosted the confederation's yearly councils beneath the Tree of the Great Peace. They also provided the chief who presided over these gatherings. This pivotal position rendered Onondaga political sentiments crucial to how the confederation aligned itself with respect to European powers.

The Onondagas acted as mediators of sorts in deliberations at the annual councils. If the elder house or brotherhood of the Senecas and the Mohawks could not agree with its junior counterparts among the Cayugas, the Oneidas, and later the Tuscaroras, then the Onondagas supplied the deciding vote. But they had no veto power in the event that the other Iroquois nations presented a united front. The Onondagas also served as archivists for the confederation by maintaining its wampum belts and consequently boasted the most chieftainships within the league. Their council house was one of the largest and most elaborate Native American structures of its time.

According to an Iroquois legend known as the Deganawidah (Peacemaker) Epic, the peoples of the Five Nations warred frequently on one another until Hiawatha and Deganawidah promoted reconciliation. But an Onondaga chief and sorcerer, Tadadaho, rejected this message of peace and, in his resultant madness, grew misshapen with a bed of snakes for hair. Hiawatha and Deganawidah subsequently cured Tadadaho with wampum beads, which symbolically spurred the creation of the Great League of Peace and Power. This alliance, which dated at least as

An 1850s illustration, possibly taken from a Native American drawing, by U.S. Army captain Seth Eastman. It depicts the Onondaga legend of a snake-covered Tadadaho smoking a pipe, approached by the peacemakers Hiawatha and Dekanawidah. (Getty Images)

far back as the 16th century, emphasized internal stability and asserted authority over weaker native nations.

The Onondagas participated in the Beaver Wars (1641–1701). During this period they warred with western nations such as the Hurons and the Eries over hunting rights and access to trade with Europeans and other native groups.

Periodically relocating for better access to natural resources, the Onondagas generally confined themselves to inhabiting two large fortified villages at a time. They employed fire to clear land for agriculture and forest underbrush for hunting. As with the rest of the league, they relied on adopting members of defeated nations to replenish their numbers. Some captives suffered ritualistic torture and execution as a means of grieving for lost loved ones. The Hurons (allied with the French) and the Susquehannocks comprised the principal indigenous enemies of the Onondagas.

During the 17th and 18th centuries, Protestants and Catholics proselytized among the Onondagas with limited success. The Jesuits established missions that proved short-lived because of dramatic shifts in support for the French.

The Onondagas became factionalized through scheming among Anglophiles, Francophiles, and neutralists. This constant intrigue influenced the diplomacy of the confederacy and threatened to draw it into larger conflicts. Although neutral at first, by 1759 most Iroquois supported the British during the French and Indian War (1754–1763). The demise of New France in 1763 left the Six Nations (with the addition of the Tuscaroras in 1722) without its former position as the arbiter of the balance of power in North America.

In the Proclamation of 1763, King George III established a limit for westward migration by American colonists. Settlers largely ignored the rule that prohibited expansion beyond the Appalachian Mountains, and Onondaga landholdings came under increased pressure. The Treaty of Fort Stanwix (1768) reconfirmed the Great Covenant Chain through which the Iroquois dissuaded subsidiary tribes from attacking colonists. In 1776 with the American Revolutionary War (1775–1783) under way, both sides courted the league for an alliance. The Great Council opted to let each of the Six Nations decide for itself. The Senecas, the Mohawks, and the Cayugas joined the British, and the Oneidas and the Tuscaroras assisted the United States. Accounts vary as to where a majority of the Onondagas stood on this question, but U.S. authorities regarded them as hostile.

Pro-British Iroquois conducted raids alongside Loyalist Rangers in New York and in Pennsylvania. An American offensive in 1779 destroyed the Onondaga villages. The British loss of the 13 colonies spelled disaster for the Iroquois Confederacy, as Britain ceded the Iroquois homeland to the United States in the Treaty of Paris (1783). The Onondagas then split between those who remained in New York and those who followed the Mohawk chief Joseph Brant to Canada. A small reservation was later set aside in New York state for those Onondagas who chose to remain there, where their descendants continue to live. In more recent years the tribes of the old Iroquois Confederacy reunited, and the Onondagas' New York reservation serves as the capital of the Iroquois Confederacy. The chief of the reunited tribes is chosen only from the Onondagas.

JEFFREY D. BASS

See also

Beaver Wars; Brant, Joseph; Covenant Chain; French and Indian War; Iroquois; Iroquois Confederacy; Native Americans and the American Revolutionary War; Proclamation of 1763; Wampum

References

Anderson, Fred. *Crucible of War: The Seven Years' War and the Fate of the Empire in British North America, 1754–1766.* New York: Vintage Books, 2001.

Aquila, Richard. *The Iroquois Restoration: Iroquois Diplomacy on the Colonial Frontier, 1701–1754.* Detroit: Wayne State University Press, 1983.

Richter, Daniel K. *The Ordeal of the Longhouse: The People of the Iroquois League in the Era of European Colonization.* Chapel Hill: University of North Carolina Press, 1992.

O-non-dowa-gahs

See Senecas

Opechancanough
Birth Date: 1575
Death Date: 1646

Pamunkey chief and paramount leader of the Powhatan Confederacy (1622–1646) in Virginia's Chesapeake region. Opechancanough was sometimes referred to as the "King of the Pamunkeys," a name given to him by Jamestown leader Captain John Smith. Opechancanough was born sometime in 1575, probably in the eastern part of present-day Virginia. Nothing is known of his early life, but Opechancanough's half brother was the powerful Chief Powhatan, leader of a confederacy of local natives. In 1617 Powhatan migrated north toward the Potomac River, leaving his half brother in charge of the Chesapeake region. When Powhatan died in 1618, Opechancanough succeeded him as the *werowance* ("chieftain") of the confederacy.

Unlike Powhatan, Opechancanough took a dim view of the English settlers. He saw them as interlopers who had to be driven away or destroyed. In March 1622 he staged a daring attack against English settlements around Jamestown. Only weeks before, Opechancanough had given English leaders the impression that he advocated peace and tranquility. The settlers thus had little reason to prepare to defend themselves against a potential attack. In any event, Opechancanough's offensive killed 347 colonists, or some 25 percent of the English population.

The stunned but furious survivors sought a hasty retribution. Although Opechancanough escaped capture, a large number of his

Captain John Smith captures Pamunkey leader Opechancanough. Reproduction of engraving from the *Originals in the True Travels of Captaine John Smith, 1629.* (Library of Congress)

subjects fell to blistering attacks and starvation at the hands of the English. Within a year Opechancanough sued for peace. In 1644 a frail and failing Opechancanough authorized yet another broad offensive against the English settlements, allegedly to avenge the murder of a Pamunkey leader. His decision launched the Third Anglo-Powhatan War (1644–1646) in which roughly 500 of Virginia's 8,000 white inhabitants died. The natives, however, again suffered disproportionately.

In 1645 Virginians managed to track down Opechancanough and took him captive. He died in 1646 in Jamestown, murdered by a militiaman.

JAIME RAMÓN OLIVARES

See also
Anglo-Powhatan War, Second; Anglo-Powhatan War, Third; Jamestown; Pamunkeys; Powhatan; Powhatan Confederacy; Virginia-Indian Treaty of 1646

References
Axtell, James. *The Rise and Fall of the Powhatan Empire: Indians in Seventeenth-Century Virginia.* Williamsburg, VA: Colonial Williamsburg Foundation, 1995.
McCary, Ben C. *Indians in Seventeenth-Century Virginia.* Charlottesville: University Press of Virginia, 1957.
Shea, William L. *The Virginia Militia in the Seventeenth Century.* Baton Rouge: Louisiana State University Press, 1983.

Oregon Trail

The primary route for travelers heading west to California and the Oregon Territory between 1840 and 1860. Beginning in Independence, Missouri, the 2,000-mile-long Oregon Trail extended through the Great Plains and the Rocky Mountains. Settlers joined wagon trains in Independence and then trekked for five or six months before reaching their destination.

The movement of settlers to Oregon as well as California and Texas was part of a sizable movement of Americans to the far western regions of North America between 1840 and 1860. An estimated 300,000 Americans traveled west seeking new opportunities during those decades, most of them coming from the Old Northwest. The majority of these travelers were white, although some blacks did migrate to the West. In general these people traveled in family groups, with the exception of the single men attracted by the California Gold Rush.

Most of these new settlers were fairly prosperous; some were even wealthy. Poorer travelers tended to join wagon trains as laborers in order to afford the trek west. Groups heading toward the western regions where lumber and mining provided the majority of jobs tended to be made up of men, while farmlands attracted families.

The majority of these migrants headed west along the great overland trails, gathering at departure points in Iowa or Missouri, such as Independence, where they joined a wagon train. Hired guides led the way as these settlers traveled in covered wagons with their livestock following along. The primary route was the Oregon Trail, which began in Independence, crossed the Great Plains, and worked its way through the South Pass of the Rocky Mountains. From there settlers could move north into Oregon or take the California Trail to the California coast. Other branches led to mining sites in Montana and Nevada or to the Mormon settlements in Utah.

The westward journey was difficult, lasting five or six months usually from May to November. The Rocky Mountains had to be crossed before winter set in, as the passes were blocked by snow in the cold months. The slow rate of movement, often no more than 15 miles a day, made reaching the Rockies in time difficult. Most of the travelers walked the entire way to ease the burden on the oxen or mules that were pulling the wagons. Women especially worked

Estimated Deaths along the Oregon Trail, 1840–1860

Cause	Deaths
Disease	6,000–12,500
Indian attacks	500–1,000
Hypothermia	300–500
Scurvy	300–500
Crushed by wagon	200–500
Drowning	200–500
Firearms-related	200–500
Miscellaneous	200–500
Total	7,900–16,500

Emigrants Crossing the Plains, an 1869 painting by F. O. C. Darley depicting settlers in covered wagons pulled by oxen. (Library of Congress)

hard preparing meals and washing clothes after a long day's journey. Disease, cholera in particular, was one of the many hazards confronting these pioneers as they made their way west.

The danger from hostile Native Americans remained, for the trail crossed lands held primarily by the Cheyenne and Pawnee tribes. Native American attacks along the Oregon Trail between 1840 and 1860 killed as many as 400 settlers. However, many Native Americans were helpful to the pioneers, offering their services as guides or trading with them. It was not uncommon for wagon trains to obtain fresh food, clothing, and horses by bartering with the Native Americans they encountered.

The journey west was often a communal experience. Many wagon trains were made up of friends or families who had joined together to seek out new opportunities in the Oregon Territory. Because there was little or no contact with outsiders other than Native Americans during the arduous journey, the travelers soon learned the value of cooperation if they were to reach their destination successfully.

A. GREGORY MOORE

See also

Cheyennes; Overland Trail; Pawnees; Rocky Mountains

References

Dary, David. *The Oregon Trail: An American Saga.* New York: Knopf, 2004.

McLynn, Frank. *Wagons West: The Epic Story of America's Overland Trails.* London: Jonathan Cape, 2002.

Unruh, John David. *The Plains Across: The Overland Emigrants and the Trans-Mississippi West, 1840–1860.* Urbana: University of Illinois Press, 1993.

Oriskany, Battle of
Event Date: August 6, 1777

Battle of the American Revolutionary War (1775–1783) involving members of the Iroquois Confederacy under Chief Joseph Brant. Even before Lieutenant General John Burgoyne's army had departed Canada for New York in the summer of 1777, word had reached the Continental Congress that a second British force might attempt to attack Albany via the Mohawk Valley. Continental Army major general Philip Schuyler, commander of the Northern Department, alerted the local authorities and ordered them to assist. At the beginning of July, New York Militia brigadier general Nicholas Herkimer met with Mohawk leader Joseph Brant, who was allied with the British, in an effort to keep him neutral. This failed. Two weeks later Herkimer tried to mobilize a force of militia to assist in the defense of Fort Stanwix but had to abandon the project when only 200 men turned out.

On July 30 a friendly Oneida warrior warned Herkimer that a British force under Brevet Brigadier General Barry St. Leger was about to cross Lake Oneida. Herkimer promptly ordered all males between 16 and 60 years of age to gather at Fort Dayton. Five days later he had 800 men, organized into four regiments. Herkimer departed Fort Dayton with this force on August 4, covering 12 miles before halting for the night at Stirling Creek. The following day the column crossed the Mohawk River and was just 8 miles from Fort Stanwix by nightfall.

Meanwhile, on the evening of August 5 St. Leger had been informed that the Patriot relief force was within striking distance of the fort. If the two Patriot forces could link up, this might be fatal to St. Leger's own force, of which a majority were Native Americans. St. Leger promptly dispatched Brant and Sir John Johnson with 150 Loyalists and 400 Iroquois to ambush Herkimer's column before it could reach Fort Stanwix.

Herkimer was aware that imprudent action could bring defeat and leave both the fort and the communities of the Mohawk Valley defenseless. Nevertheless, his four colonels demanded an immediate advance, and at least two of them reportedly accused him of cowardice and even treason. Against his better judgment and perhaps feeling more confident after the arrival of 60 Oneida warriors and 50 rangers who could act as scouts and flank guards, Herkimer gave in and, possibly to allay suspicions as to his bravery or loyalty, rode at the head of the column. At some point that morning he also sent messengers ahead to the fort to inform Gansevoort of his approach and to ask him to carry out a sortie against the British lines. The signal that the message had been received was to be three cannon shots.

By 9:00 a.m. Herkimer's column had reached a point where the military road was intersected by two steep-sided ravines; both were heavily shaded by tall trees growing within a few feet of the track. As Herkimer's leading regiment emerged from the second ravine, the men heard three whistle blasts.

Johnson had planned the ambush and had chosen the site well. His own unit, the King's Royal Regiment of New York, blocked the road and lined the sides of the second ravine. The rest of the trail was flanked by Iroquois under Brant and Loyalist rangers under John Butler. The plan was to allow the leading militia to enter the smaller ravine, by which time the wagons and rear guard would be inside the larger ravine. The trap would then be sprung.

Around 10:00 a.m. Johnson's men fired the first volley, wounding Herkimer and throwing the head of the column into confusion. Unfortunately, the Iroquois attacked the rear guard too soon and ended up having to chase the militiamen eastward, back toward Fort Dayton. While this destroyed one militia regiment as a fighting unit, it also left a gap in the Iroquois line through which the other units could fight their way off the road and onto higher ground. As the militia rallied in circular formation, Herkimer was propped against his saddle under a beech tree. There he dispensed orders but was unable to move because of a shattered leg.

About an hour after the fighting began, the area was hit by a thunderstorm. The lull gave Herkimer time to reorganize his defenses. He had noticed that once a man fired, one or more warriors would be on him with their knives and tomahawks before he could reload. Herkimer ordered his men to operate in pairs, with at least one having a loaded weapon at any moment to prevent these deadly enemy rushes. The plan worked, and as native casualties began to mount, the Iroquois became restless.

Around noon the Loyalists attempted to break the deadlock by subterfuge. Major Stephen Watts had his men turn their coats (which were green with gray-white facings and lining) inside out and approached the enemy as if they were a relief party coming from Fort Stanwix. The ruse might have worked, but Captain Jacob Gardenier of the militia recognized a neighbor. In the ensuing fighting Gardenier, who killed three of the Loyalists himself with his spontoon, was himself bayoneted and badly wounded, but the rest of the force was now fully alerted.

Fierce hand-to-hand fighting followed, and as both sides withdrew to recover, three cannon shots were heard. Herkimer and his men knew instantly what they meant; their enemies found out soon enough as messengers arrived to tell Brant that their camp was being sacked. Already demoralized by heavy losses, the remaining warriors now departed. Unable to fight on unaided, Johnson and Butler also withdrew.

Herkimer's messengers had arrived at the fort around 10:00 a.m., almost at the same time as the ambush was sprung. By the time a sortie had been planned, the garrison was forced to wait for the storm to pass. As the weather cleared, 250 men led by Marinus Willett, second-in-command at the fort, attacked the Loyalist and Iroquois camps and removed 21 wagonloads of supplies without losing a single man. Coming on top of their own casualties at Oriskany, this loss infuriated the Native Americans, who promptly sacked the camps of their allies in frustration.

As his enemy withdrew, Herkimer ordered his surviving troops to fall back to Fort Dayton. Little more than one-fourth of the 600 men from his three leading regiments were unhurt. Herkimer died 10 days later from complications following the amputation of his leg. St. Leger claimed to have taken 200 prisoners; this seems unlikely. However, 2 captured officers were sent into the fort the next day to inform Gansevoort of the disaster and encourage him to surrender. Combined Loyalist and Iroquois losses were probably around 150. While the siege went on officially until August 21, St. Leger's chances of capturing the fort had effectively been ended 15 days earlier at Oriskany.

Brendan D. Morrissey

See also

Brant, Joseph; Iroquois Confederacy; Native Americans and the American Revolutionary War

References

Foote, Alan. *Liberty March: The Battle of Oriskany.* Utica, NY: North Country Books, 1998.

Wood, W. J. *Battles of the Revolutionary War, 1775–1781.* Chapel Hill, NC: Algonquin, 1990.

Orontony

Birth Date: Unknown
Death Date: 1750

Wyandot (Huron) leader in the Ohio River Valley noted for his consistent hostility toward the French. Nothing is known about the circumstances of Orontony's birth or his early years. In 1738 Orontony (sometimes referred to as Orontondi, Rondoenie, Wanduny, or Nicholas) helped the British-allied Cherokees ambush a Detroit war party. This action earned him the enmity of French-allied natives, including some other Wyandots. Soon afterward he and his followers left the Detroit region and founded a new settlement near Sandusky Bay. The site was within easy reach of British merchants and their lower-priced trade goods.

When King George's War (1744–1748) began, most Wyandots rallied to support the French. Orontony's group, however, instead strengthened its relationship with the British. Orontony entered into an alliance treaty with them in 1745 and allowed Pennsylvania traders to build a strong blockhouse near his village. A wartime British blockade of Canada soon cut the flow of both gifts and French trade goods. This development greatly disrupted French relations with natives in the Great Lakes region. Emboldened by this apparent weakness, in 1747 Orontony quietly recruited the Miamis and several other regional nations into a general armed uprising against the French. The plot was revealed prematurely in June 1747, however, when an overeager group of Wyandots killed five French traders and tipped off the commandant of Detroit to the danger.

With the 1747 conspiracy uncovered, several of the native nations involved denied any knowledge of Orontony's plans. Instead, they pledged their loyalty and friendship to the French. Violent clashes between Orontony's remaining allies and the French flared briefly in the summer of 1747 and then abruptly died out. Later that year Orontony visited Detroit in a bid for peace, but he returned to Sandusky without any firm guarantees from the French commander. In 1748 the French renewed their demand that Orontony break off all relations with the British. Meanwhile, the pro-French Ottawas began preparing a large expedition to send against him should he refuse.

Faced with these threats, Orontony burned the Sandusky village and moved his followers south and west to the White River in what is today Indiana. Yet Orontony's impact on the Ohio region lingered on after his departure. Indeed, a 1749 French expedition from Canada found the Ohio natives resistant to any French presence. Orontony died in present-day Indiana in 1750.

ANDREW C. LANNEN

See also

King George's War; Ottawas; Wyandots

References

Lajeunesse, Ernest J., ed. *The Windsor Border Region, Canada's Southernmost Frontier: A Collection of Documents.* Toronto: Champlain Society, 1960.

Sioui, Georges E. *Huron Wendat: The Heritage of the Circle.* Lansing: Michigan State University Press, 2000.

Osages

Native American group located in the upper Mississippi River Valley and the lower Missouri River Valley. In colonial times, the Osages were seminomadic and eventually controlled present-day Missouri, southern Illinois, northern Arkansas, northeastern Oklahoma, and southeastern Kansas. Originally they were probably part of a single tribe that split and developed into the Osages, the Kasaws, the Omahas, the Poncas, and the Quapaws. In colonial times the Osages probably numbered around 10,000 people, but as time progressed their numbers dwindled significantly. Linguistically, the Osages were part of the Siouan-speaking nations.

The Osages called themselves the Ni-U-Ko'n-Ska, or "People of the Middle Waters." The word "Osage" came from the name of one of their clans, the Wazhazhes. During French explorations of the Illinois River Valley and the Mississippi River Valley in the late 17th century, French explorers gallicized the name as Ouazhagi. The English later anglicized the name to Osage.

The Osages lived in semipermanent villages in wooded river valleys most of the year. They cultivated corn, beans, squash, and other vegetables. During buffalo hunting season they made use of temporary shelters. The buffalo not only provided an important food source but also served as a key source of clothing and trade.

The Osages were organized into two groups (moieties). The Tsizhu moiety had 9 clans that were associated with the sky and peace. The 15 clans of the Honga moiety were linked with earth and war. The clans each occupied a separate section of their villages and operated as separate military units.

Osage political and religious organizations were closely interconnected and were integrated on both the village and tribal levels. At the tribal level were two hereditary chiefs, one from each moiety. The Osage Nation was divided into five permanently named bands of villages, each with its own set of chiefs, and a council of Nonhonzhinga ("Little Old Men"). The council was primarily a religious body, but it could also deal with civil affairs on occasion.

Europeans first mentioned the Osages in 1683 when Father Jacques Marquette, a Jesuit missionary, encountered them while exploring the Mississippi River Valley. During the 1700s the French and the Osages shared a robust trade in furs, guns, horses, and European goods. This trade gave the Osages great influence with many natives of the region and also enabled them to act as mediators between the woodlands natives to the east and the natives of the Great Plains to the west.

The profitable trading enabled the French to establish a strong military alliance with the Osages. During the French and Indian War (1754–1763), the Osages actively aided the French. Indeed, Osage warriors fought with the French when the British, under Major General Edward Braddock, approached Fort Duquesne on

July 9, 1755. After the French defeat in 1763, the Osages developed contacts with the Spanish, who had gained control of the Louisiana Territory. Eventually, however, the Osages engaged in hostile actions against the Spanish.

Numerous Osage warriors later allied themselves with U.S. military forces, acting as scouts and soldiers. In the years immediately after the American Civil War (1861–1865) when Major General William T. Sherman was in command of the Military Division of the Missouri, which encompassed all territories west of the Mississippi River, Osage scouts frequently led U.S. Army forces in campaigns against hostile Plains tribes. In 1868 Osage scouts guided the 7th Cavalry Regiment under Lieutenant Colonel George A. Custer to Black Kettle's Cheyenne village, sparking the Battle of the Washita (November 27, 1868).

Between 1808 and 1865 the Osages ceded most of their lands to the U.S. government in a series of treaties. By 1870 they had located to a reservation in Indian Territory (Oklahoma). The 1896 discovery of large oil deposits there made many Osages wealthy.

ANDREW J. WASKEY

See also

Black Kettle; Braddock's Campaign; French and Indian War; Quapaws; Sherman, William Tecumseh; Washita, Battle of the

References

Baird, W. David. *The Osage People.* Phoenix: Indian Tribal Series, 1972.
Chapman, Carl H. *The Origin of the Osage Indian Tribe.* New York: Garland, 1974.
Mathews, John J. *Osages: Children of the Middle Waters.* Norman: University of Oklahoma Press, 1961.

Osceola
Birth Date: ca. 1804
Death Date: January 31, 1838

Native leader in the Second Seminole War (1835–1842). Born near the Tallapoosa River in present-day Alabama circa 1804, Osceola was the son of a mixed-blood Creek mother. His father was probably the Scottish trader William Powell. Osceola in his youth was called Billy Powell, although he later asserted that he had been born before his mother's relationship with Powell and that his father was Creek. Following the Creek War (1813–1814), Osceola and his mother moved to Spanish Florida and settled in a Seminole town at Peas Creek. There Osceola's hunting and leadership skills gained him prominence.

When Major General Andrew Jackson invaded Florida in 1818, Osceola and his mother were captured but soon released. They eventually moved to a Seminole reservation in central Florida, where Osceola worked for the U.S. government in the 1820s policing the Seminole boundaries against intruders.

In 1834 the Seminoles became divided over acquiescence to the Treaty of Payne's Landing in which many members of the

A Seminole leader born around 1804, Osceola achieved his status not as a hereditary chief but through his clearly demonstrated leadership skills during the Second Seminole War of 1835–1842. (Library of Congress)

tribe accepted removal to the west. Osceola's denunciation of the treaty earned him a leadership position among the Seminoles who opposed removal. Wiley Thompson, U.S. agent to the Seminoles, tried to convince Osceola to sign the treaty on April 22, 1835, but Osceola refused. Some accounts say that Osceola thrust a knife into the document in an act of defiance. Fearing Osceola's influence, Thompson had him arrested. After five days' imprisonment, Osceola consented to sign the treaty and was released. However, he immediately fled to the swamps and began preparing for war.

Osceola and his followers began their campaign by killing Charley Emathla, a chief who had favored removal, and attacking his supporters. On December 28, 1835, Osceola attacked Fort King, killing Thompson and an army officer. The same day the Seminoles ambushed an army baggage train and killed all but 3 of 110 soldiers. At the Withlacoochee River on December 31, Osceola turned on a force of 600 regulars and militia sent to attack him. Catching them as they crossed the river, he mauled 250 men on one side while the remainder watched. Osceola was, however, wounded in the battle.

Osceola's offensive ignited the Second Seminole War. U.S. officials and Florida governor Richard K. Call recognized Osceola's importance as the leader of Seminole resistance and targeted him for death or capture. Eventually 8,000 troops were in the field pursuing Osceola, but for two years the Seminole leader evaded them while launching hit-and-run raids against vulnerable detachments and posts. In one such operation in June 1837, Osceola freed several hundred Seminoles held in a detention compound.

Throughout the campaign, army officers had made overtures to the Seminoles, urging them to meet and negotiate peace. Osceola accepted Brigadier General Joseph M. Hernandez's offer of a parley on October 22, 1837. On the orders of his superior, Major General Thomas S. Jesup, Hernandez violated the truce and arrested Osceola and 80–100 of his followers.

Osceola was imprisoned in St. Augustine until December 31, 1837, when he was transferred to Fort Moultrie in Charleston, South Carolina. He became ill but refused treatment because he distrusted the fort's doctor, Frederick Weedon, who was the brother-in-law of Wiley Thompson. Osceola died in Charleston on January 31, 1838.

JIM PIECUCH

See also
Dade's Massacre; Payne's Landing, Treaty of; Seminoles; Seminole War, Second

References
Bland, Celia. *Osceola: Seminole Rebel.* New York: Chelsea House, 1994.
Oppenheim, Joanne. *Osceola: Seminole Warrior.* Mahwah, NJ: Troll Associates, 1979.

Otis, Elwell Stephen
Birth Date: March 25, 1838
Death Date: October 21, 1909

U.S. Army officer. Born in Frederick, Maryland, on March 25, 1838, Elwell Stephen Otis graduated from the University of Rochester in 1858 and from Harvard Law School in 1861. During the American Civil War (1861–1865) he was commissioned a captain of volunteers in the 140th New York Infantry Regiment on September 13, 1862. He was advanced to lieutenant colonel in December 1863 and later to colonel. Seriously wounded in battle, Otis was mustered out of the army on January 14, 1865. In recognition of his distinguished wartime service, he received a brevet promotion to brigadier general of volunteers on March 13, 1865.

Otis found military life to his liking and secured a regular army commission upon his recovery after the war. In March 1869 he was appointed a lieutenant colonel and was assigned to the 22nd Infantry Regiment. After the Battle of the Little Bighorn (June 25–26, 1876) he campaigned extensively in the Dakotas and Montana and was influential in the eventual submission of Sitting Bull. In August 1876 Otis successfully reinforced Brigadier General George Crook's force at Glendive, Montana. In 1878 Otis published *The Indian Question*, a book based on his many encounters and experiences with Native Americans. Otis was perceived as firm but fair with the Native Americans, although he refused to be intimidated by hostile tribes. Promoted to colonel and assigned to the

U.S. Army colonel Elwell Stephen Otis saw considerable service in the American West during the late Indian Wars and established the school for army officers at Fort Leavenworth, Kansas, in 1880. Otis distinguished himself in the Spanish-American War and retired from the army as a major general. (*Photographic History of the Spanish-American War*, 1898)

20th Infantry Regiment in February 1880, Otis saw considerable service in the American West during the latter years of the Indian Wars. At Fort Leavenworth, Kansas, in 1880, Otis established a school for army officers. He remained at Fort Leavenworth as commandant until 1885. He was advanced to brigadier general in November 1893.

With the outbreak of war with Spain in 1898, Otis was appointed major general of volunteers on May 4, 1898, and was sent to the Philippines as second-in-command to Major General Wesley Merritt. In August 1898 he succeeded Merritt as commander of VIII Corps and military governor of the Philippines, when Merritt was relieved of the command at his own request.

A 36-year army veteran when he arrived in the Philippines, Otis had the misfortune to direct affairs in the Philippines during the initial stages of U.S. involvement in the Filipino insurrection. In this capacity he had to make critical decisions when there were no clear guidelines regarding U.S. policy except for President William McKinley's desire to see the Philippines pacified in a kind and compassionate manner. Benevolent assimilation, as it came to be known, was not, however, an easy policy to implement. Furthermore, Otis generally disliked Filipinos. He considered Emilio Aguinaldo's insurgents "a band of looters" and promptly ordered them from Manila. Otis also issued the proclamation of January 4, 1899, in his capacity as military governor of the Philippines that announced U.S. sovereignty over the islands.

Otis rarely left his office and constantly sent off overly optimistic reports that led the McKinley administration to underestimate the troop strength required to win the war. Otis's refusal to acknowledge the limitations of his military resources exacerbated a difficult situation. He also had to deal with the problem posed by volunteer troops who wanted to go home once the war with Spain had ended.

Otis was succeeded as military governor of the Philippines in May 1900 by Brigadier General Arthur MacArthur. Otis was promoted to major general on June 16, 1900. On his return to the United States, in October 1900 he took command of the Department of the Lakes, headquartered in Chicago. He reached mandatory retirement age on March 25, 1902. Otis retired to Rochester, New York, and died there on October 21, 1909.

JERRY KEENAN AND SPENCER C. TUCKER

See also
Crook, George; Great Sioux War; Little Bighorn, Battle of the; Sioux; Sitting Bull

References
Gates, John Morgan. *Schoolbooks and Krags: The United States Army in the Philippines, 1898–1902.* Westport, CT: Greenwood, 1973.

Linn, Brian McAllister. *The Philippine War, 1899–1902.* Lawrence: University Press of Kansas, 2000.

Otis, Elwell S. *The Indian Question.* 1878; reprint, Whitefish, MT: Kessinger, 2007.

Ottawas

Native American people who inhabited Manitoulin Island along the northern reaches of Lake Huron. The Ottawas belonged to the Algonquian linguistic and cultural group, being closely related to the Ojibwas, the Pottawatomis, and the Algonquins. The Ottawas entered the written record when Samuel de Champlain encountered people he referred to as the *Cheveux relevés* ("raised hairs") in 1615.

French observers were impressed by the Ottawas' martial skills, and Champlain himself claimed that they were formidable warriors. Similar to other Great Lakes groups, the Ottawas practiced scalping, torture, adoption of prisoners, and symbolic eating of human flesh. They preferred to engage in guerrilla-style warfare. The Ottawas supported themselves by agriculture, trading, hunting, fishing, and gathering. Indeed, the French soon discovered that the Ottawas were perceptive and highly effective traders.

The Ottawas traditionally occupied the north shore of Georgian Bay (Lake Huron), Manitoulin Island, and the Bruce Peninsula in Ontario. They fled to the western shores of Lake Superior after 1649 to avoid attacks by the Iroquois. By 1670 the Ottawas began to return east after clashing with Dakota and Winnebago groups in present-day Wisconsin.

By 1701 the Ottawas had settled throughout the Great Lakes–Ohio Valley region, and by the 1770s they had begun to venture into Manitoba. The name "Ottawa" means "trader," which reflects the role that the Ottawas played in the Great Lakes region. The term, however, also applied to anyone engaged in trade. This led 17th-century French observers to give the name to all non-Huron traders from the upper Great Lakes. This broad use has hindered identification of the Ottawas prior to the 18th century. By the early 1700s the French recognized several subdivisions among the Ottawas, who usually acted independently of other related native nations.

The Ottawas warred with the Iroquois, the Foxes, and the Mascoutens and belonged to the Three Fires Confederacy, a sociopolitical and military alliance with the Ojibwas and the Pottawatomis. As allies of the Wyandots (Hurons), the Ottawas became allied to the French and thus became involved in the Beaver Wars (1641–1701). In 1670 the French thwarted Ottawa attempts to conclude a peace treaty with the Iroquois. In 1701 under the auspices of the French, several branches and chiefs of the Ottawa Nation signed the Treaty of Montreal.

A number of Ottawas settled in the Detroit region after 1701. On the instigation of Lamothe Cadillac, clashes that involved the Ottawas, the Foxes, the Miamis, and the French soon erupted, which led to Ottawa involvement in the Fox Wars of 1710–1738. The Ottawas in the Detroit region also grew to distrust their Wyandot allies, accusing them of conspiring with the Iroquois and other enemies.

The Ottawas participated in the colonial wars as allies of France, especially during the French and Indian War (1754–1763). In 1763 Ottawa leader Pontiac united several native nations in the Great Lakes–Ohio Valley region and attempted to drive the British from that area. After the Niagara Peace Treaty of 1764, the Ottawas became allies of the British. Despite the broad alliance patterns, internal divisions among the Ottawas often permitted groups and individuals to hold neutral, anti-French, or anti-British sentiments.

Due to the Treaty of Fort McIntosh (1785) and the Treaty of Fort Harmar (1789), the Ottawas were compelled to move westward, away from their ancestral homeland. Eventually most surviving Ottawas wound up in Indian Territory (Oklahoma). Today a number of them still reside in Oklahoma and Kansas, but some have returned to the Great Lakes region, where they purchased land in Ontario and Michigan.

KARL S. HELE

See also
Algonquins; Beaver Wars; Champlain, Samuel de; Fort Harmar, Treaty of; Fox Wars; French and Indian War; Iroquois Confederacy; Ojibwas; Pontiac; Pontiac's Rebellion; Pottawatomis; Wyandots

References

Cash, Joseph H., and Gerald W. Wolf. *The Ottawa People.* Phoenix: Indian Tribal Series, 1976.

Landau, Elaine. *The Ottawa.* Danbury, CT: Franklin Watts, 1996.

Ouray
Birth Date: ca. 1833
Death Date: August 24, 1880

Principal chief of the Utes. Born most likely in Taos (New Mexico) around 1833 to an Uncompahgre Ute father and a Jicarilla Apache mother, Ouray spent his youth with his mother in Taos, where he learned to speak both Spanish and English before joining the Uncompahgres in southwestern Colorado at age 18. Upon his father's death in 1860, Ouray succeeded him as the chief of the Uncompahgres and developed a close relationship with Ute Indian agent Christopher "Kit" Carson. After traveling with other Ute leaders to Washington, D.C., in 1862, Ouray returned as a committed peace advocate, convinced that resistance to whites was futile. In October 1863 he and other Ute leaders met with Colorado territorial governor John Evans at Conejos and signed a treaty in which the Utes agreed to withdraw from the rich farmlands of the San Luis Valley. Unfortunately for the Utes, the agreement at Conejos proved to be a mere prelude to further land cessions.

With increasing numbers of prospectors moving into the mountains of Colorado, in 1868 the federal government insisted that the seven Ute bands appoint a principal chief who could negotiate a new treaty in order to prevent hostilities. Chosen by tribal leaders to be their spokesman, Ouray traveled with a delegation of Utes to Washington, where they agreed that the Utes would surrender their lands in central Colorado and move west to a new reservation encompassing approximately one-third of present-day Colorado. The Yamo and Grand River bands settled in the northern section of the reservation, where the federal government established the White River Agency near present-day Meeker, while the Tabeguache, Uncompahgre, Moache, Capote, and Wiminuche bands settled in the southern section of the reservation, where the federal government established the Los Pinos Agency along Cochetopa Creek. Ouray himself took up residence near the Los Pinos Agency, where the government provided him with a house and an annual salary of $1,000. Within five years, however, white miners had moved into the San Juan Mountains, forcing Ouray to agree to a further cession of 4 million acres in the Brunot Treaty of 1873.

Although Ouray maintained peaceful relations at the Los Pinos Agency, he was unable to prevent conflicts from arising at the White River Agency, where chiefs Jack and Douglas resented the efforts of Nathan C. Meeker, who had been appointed Indian agent in the spring of 1878, to force the Utes to become farmers. As tensions escalated at White River in the late summer of 1879, Meeker appealed to federal authorities to send troops to protect whites at the agency, leading to the Ute War of 1879. On September 29 Chief Jack and 100 Ute warriors ambushed a force of 153 cavalry led by Major Thomas T. Thornburch at Milk Creek, approximately 15 miles from the White River Agency, killing Thornburch and 11 troops.

Later in the afternoon Chief Jack and his warriors attacked the agency, killing Meeker and 10 other whites and abducting Meeker's wife, daughter, and 3 others (a mother and her 2 children). Within two weeks the U.S. Army had mobilized some 1,500 soldiers under Colonel Wesley Merritt. U.S. Army commander General William Tecumseh Sherman and Lieutenant General Philip Sheridan were determined to punish the Utes. Fearing that a punitive expedition against the Utes at the White River Agency would lead to a general Ute uprising, Secretary of the Interior Carl Schurz intervened to halt the offensive by appealing to Ouray to mediate. Ouray ordered Chief Jack to stop fighting and successfully secured the release of the 5 white captives.

Although Ouray had prevented an outbreak of war, Coloradoans demanded that the Utes be removed from the state altogether. In the spring of 1880 Ouray, who was suffering from Bright's disease, traveled to Washington, where he was forced to sign a new

Ouray, the principal chief of the Utes, served as a spokesman for the seven Ute bands and as a peacemaker during the Ute War of 1879. (Library of Congress)

treaty under which the White River Utes were to be removed to the Uintah Reservation in Utah, the Uncompahgre Utes were to be removed to a smaller reservation either along the junction of the Gunnison and Colorado rivers or on land close to the Uintah Reservation in Utah, and the remaining southern Utes were to be confined to a smaller reservation on the La Plata River along the Colorado–New Mexico border. Upon returning to Colorado, Ouray worked diligently to secure acceptance of the treaty before his death on August 24, 1880.

JUSTIN D. MURPHY

See also
Carson, Christopher Houston; Meeker, Nathan Cook; Meeker Massacre; Milk Creek, Battle of; Utes; Ute War

References
Simmons, Virginia McConnell. *The Ute Indians of Utah, Colorado, and New Mexico.* Niwot: University Press of Colorado, 2000.
Smith, P. David. *Ouray: Chief of the Utes.* Ridgway, CO: Wayfinder, 1986.
Utley, Robert M. *Frontier Regulars: The United States and the American Indian, 1866–1891.* New York: Macmillan, 1973.

Outposts

See Forts, Camps, Cantonments, and Outposts

Overland Trail

Important land route used roughly between 1840 and 1869 by an estimated 250,000–500,000 settlers moving west and also utilized by freight and stagecoach companies as well as the U.S. military. The Overland Trail was an alternative route on the Oregon Trail that traversed a tortuous course beginning in western Nebraska and eastern Colorado and ending in western Wyoming. The trail swung south from the North Platte River route; followed the South Platte River to the southwest; turned northwest along the Cache la Poudre River at Latham, Colorado, for approximately 35 miles; turned north at LaPorte and then west across the Laramie Plains to Bridger Pass; and finally rejoined the main trail system at Fort Bridger, Wyoming. A loop on the trail also followed the South Platte to Denver from Latham and then returned north to rejoin the route at LaPorte.

Most of the Overland Trail was also known as the Cherokee Trail because of its use by Cherokees during the 1849 migration to California in the midst of the California Gold Rush. The trail had the benefit of being shorter than the northern route and was considered safer at a time in which more Indian attacks on the traditional California Trail and Oregon Trail were occurring, particularly in the 1860s. The Overland Trail gained its name when Ben Holladay began using the route in 1862 for his Overland Stage Line, providing U.S. mail, express freight, and passenger service to California. Holladay developed this route system when the American Civil War (1861–1865) caused the U.S. Postal Service to shift its overland contract to the north in 1861. Butterfield Overland Mail had operated the southern route to California through El Paso, Texas, and Tucson, Arizona, since 1858.

In 1861 the Central Overland California and Pikes Peak Express (COCPPE) had initially gained the government mail contract, carrying the California mail on the Oregon Trail while also providing mail service to Denver and Salt Lake City. However, the COCPPE faced significant financial challenges, and the mail contract was taken over by Holladay in 1862. He established the Overland Stage Line and shifted the operations to the old Cherokee Trail, which quickly was renamed in popular usage to reflect the stage line's use of the route. Migrant and freight traffic also shifted to this southern route from the main Oregon Trail, with an estimated 20,000 persons a year moving west on the Overland Trail between 1862 and 1868.

Although the Indian threat was lower on the Overland Trail, sporadic attacks on stations, stagecoaches, and wagon trains continued to occur until after the Civil War, when the U.S. Army was able to devote more forces to security operations in the West. The use of the Overland Trail steadily declined as the Union Pacific Railroad moved farther west to provide faster and more secure service.

The term "Overland Trail" has also been used to generically describe the broader network of trails supporting westward migration across the continent in the 19th century. Additionally, other individual trails, such as the southern mail route used by Butterfield Overland Mail, have at times been referred to as the "Overland Trail."

JEROME V. MARTIN

See also
Butterfield Overland Mail Route; California Gold Rush; Cherokees; Oregon Trail; Pony Express

References
Lass, William E. *From the Missouri to the Great Salt Lake: An Account of Overland Freighting.* Lincoln: Nebraska State Historical Society, 1972.
Moody, Ralph. *Stagecoach West.* Lincoln: University of Nebraska Press, 1998.
Utley, Robert M. *Frontiersmen in Blue: The United States and the Indian, 1848–1865.* Lincoln: University of Nebraska Press, 1967.

P

Pais

See Havasupais; Hualapais

Paiutes, Northern

Native American group that includes a number of seminomadic, culturally distinct, and politically autonomous Great Basin bands. The name "Paiute" is a modern construction; aboriginally, these groups were tied together only by the awareness of a common language. The term "Paiute" may have meant "True Ute" or "Water Ute" and was applied only to the Southern Paiutes until the 1850s. Their self-designation is Numa, or "People." Nonnatives have sometimes called these people Digger Indians, Snakes (Northern Paiutes in Oregon), and Paviotsos. The Bannocks were originally a Northern Paiute group from eastern Oregon.

Traditionally, the groups now known as Northern Paiutes ranged throughout present-day southeastern Oregon, extreme northeastern California, extreme southwestern Idaho, and northwestern Nevada. Bannock territory included southeastern Idaho and western Wyoming (the Snake River region). The highly diverse environment included lakes, mountains, high plains, rivers, freshwater marshes, and high desert. Elements of California culture entered the region through groups living on or near the Sierra Nevada. Presently the Northern Paiutes live on a number of their own reservations, on other nearby reservations, and among the area's general population. The Paiute population in the early 19th century was roughly 7,500, excluding about 2,000 Bannocks.

The nuclear family, usually led by senior members, was the main political and economic unit. Where various families came together, the local camp was led by a headman who advised, gave speeches on right behavior, and facilitated consensus decisions. The position of the headman was often inherited in the male line. Camp composition changed regularly. Other elders were selected to take charge of various activities, such as hunts and irrigation projects.

Diet varied according to specific location. Plants supplied most food needs and included roots, bulbs, seeds, nuts, rice grass (ground into meal), cattails, berries, and greens. Pine nuts and acorns were especially important. Animal foods included fowl (and eggs), squirrel, duck, and other small game as well as mountain sheep, deer, buffalo, and elk. Paiutes hunted rabbits in communal drives. Small mammals were either pit roasted or boiled or were dried for storage. Lizards, grubs, and insects also provided food. Trout and other fish were crucial in some areas and less important in others. The Paiutes usually dried and stored fish for winter consumption. Some groups cultivated wild seed-bearing plants. The Bannocks also fished for salmon in the Snake River and hunted buffalo in the autumn.

People later called the Bannocks, or Snakes, acquired horses as early as the mid-18th century. They soon joined the Northern Shoshones in southern Idaho in developing fully mounted bands and other aspects of Plains culture, including buffalo hunting, extensive warfare, and raiding for horses. Early Northern Paiute contacts with American fur traders were generally friendly.

Most Northern Paiutes remained on foot until the late 1840s and 1850s. Around this time, heavy traffic on the Oregon Trail and the California Trail and the gold rush of 1849 brought many nonnatives through the Northern Paiute territory. The nonnatives cut down piñon trees for fuel and housing, and their animals destroyed seed-bearing plants and fouled water supplies. Mining resulted in extensive and rapid resource degradation. New diseases also took a heavy toll during this period. The Paiutes responded by moving away from the invaders or attacking wagons for food and materials. White traders encouraged theft by trading supplies for stolen items and animals. Some Paiutes began to live at the fringes of and work at white ranches and settlements.

Gold and silver strikes in the late 1850s fueled a cycle of conflict and violence. Local conflicts during this period included the brief Pyramid Lake War in 1860, the Owens Valley conflicts during 1862–1863, and the Coeur d'Alene War (1858–1859), which grew out of the Yakima-Rogue War over white treaty violations. In the Snake War (1866–1867), chiefs Paulina and Weawea led their warriors to early successes, but eventually the former was killed and the latter surrendered. Survivors settled on the Malheur Reservation (Oregon) in 1871.

Winnemucca, who represented several hundred Northern Paiutes in the 1860s and 1870s, participated in the Pyramid Lake War and, with his daughter Sarah, went on to serve as a negotiator and peacemaker. In 1873 he refused to take his band to the Malheur Reservation, holding out for a separate reservation. The Bannocks too rebelled in a short-lived war over forced confinement on the Fort Hall Reservation in Idaho and white treaty violations.

Beginning in 1859, the United States set aside land for Northern Paiute reservations. Eventually a number of small reservations were created, but ultimately much of the designated land was lost to nonnative settlers. Most Northern Paiutes, however, drifted between reservations, combining traditional subsistence activities with a growing dependence on local settler economies. Conflict on several reservations remained ongoing for decades over issues such as water rights, white land usurpation, and fisheries destruction. Refugees from the Bannock War were forced to move to the Yakima Reservation; from there many ultimately moved to the Warm Springs Reservation.

The U.S. government also established day and boarding schools from the late 1870s into the 1930s, including Sarah Winnemucca's school at Lovelock, Nevada. Sarah Winnemucca, who published *Life among the Paiutes* in 1884, also worked tirelessly although ultimately unsuccessfully, for a permanent Paiute reservation. New economic activities included cattle ranching at Fort McDermitt, haying, and various businesses.

In 1889 the Northern Paiute Wovoka, known to the whites as Jack Wilson, established a new Ghost Dance religion. It was based on the belief that the world would be reborn with all Native Americans, alive and dead, living in a precontact paradise. For this to happen, Native American peoples had to reject all nonnative ways, especially alcohol; live together in peace; and pray and dance. The Ghost Dance movement of 1889 followed a similar movement established at Walker River in 1869.

By about 1900 the Northern Paiutes had lost more than 95 percent of their original territory. Most groups accepted the Indian Reorganization Act and adopted tribal councils during the 1930s. Shamanism has gradually declined over the years. The Native American Church has had adherents among the Northern Paiutes since the 1930s, and the Sweat Lodge movement became active during the 1960s.

BARRY M. PRITZKER

See also

Coeur d'Alene War; Ghost Dance; Snake War; Winnemucca; Winnemucca, Sarah; Wovoka; Yakima-Rogue War

References

Heizer, Robert F. *The Destruction of the California Indian.* Lincoln, NE: Bison Books, 1993.

Hurtado, Albert L. *Indian Survival on the California Frontier.* New Haven, CT: Yale University Press, 1988.

Palo Duro Canyon, Battle of
Event Date: September 28, 1874

Decisive engagement of the Red River War (1874–1875) that led to the final subjugation of the Comanches and Kiowas. The Battle of Palo Duro Canyon occurred in the Texas Panhandle. In the summer of 1874 Lieutenant General Philip H. Sheridan, commander of the massive Military Division of the Missouri, responding to escalating violence on the southern Plains, most notably a fierce battle between buffalo hunters and a large force of Native American warriors at Adobe Walls on June 27, and increased unrest on the reservations of Indian Territory (Oklahoma), which also served as safe havens for marauding Cheyenne, Comanche, and Kiowa bands, ordered a five-pronged campaign to converge on previously impregnable Native American sanctuaries on the Llano Estacado (Staked Plains) in the Texas Panhandle.

One of the largest of the five columns, led by Colonel Ranald S. Mackenzie, pressed northwest from Fort Concho, Texas, with eight companies of the 4th Cavalry, arguably the most potent frontier regiment, and five companies of infantry. After establishing a forward supply base and leaving three companies of infantry to protect it, Mackenzie pushed onward in a cold, heavy rain. By late September his force approached Palo Duro Canyon, near the site of an inconsequential engagement on August 30 between Colonel Nelson Miles's command pushing south from Kansas and a formidable array of Cheyenne, Comanche, and Kiowa warriors. Supply problems had curtailed Miles's effort, however, leaving the field to Mackenzie. On September 26 a Comanche party failed to stampede the well-picketed army horses and was easily driven off by the soldiers. Meanwhile, scouts reported the location of a large encampment, miles in length, containing hundreds of lodges within the canyon.

In the predawn darkness of September 28, 1874, Mackenzie's cavalry descended into the canyon single file on a precarious trail that was completely exposed. At daybreak as each company reached the bottom, the troops charged through the villages, scrambling surprised Cheyennes, Comanches, and Kiowas who attempted in vain to defend their homes. Typical of a Mackenzie fight, casualties were amazingly low, with only three Indians killed and one soldier badly wounded. However, so complete was the surprise that the Indians could only escape with what they could carry, leaving behind almost all food, shelter, and other supplies, which they had painstaking stockpiled for winter. Almost all of the supplies went up in smoke when Mackenzie ordered the villages torched.

More significant and even more devastating for the warriors was the loss of some 1,500 ponies, captured by the quick-thinking and hard-riding troops of Captain Eugene Beaumont's company. A final heartbreaking blow came when Mackenzie deprived the Native Americans of any hope of recapturing the herd. As a long-time practitioner of total war, Mackenzie understood the value of the ponies. After culling out some 350 horses for his men and his scouts, he ordered the remainder—more than 1,000—shot.

The Battle of Palo Duro Canyon cemented Mackenzie's reputation as one of America's most successful Indian fighters. The battle also revealed the vulnerability of the Indian refuge on the Staked Plains and signaled the end to a cherished way of life for the tribes of the southern Plains. Although campaigning continued into 1875, the Indians' ability to sustain themselves in the field had been destroyed. Within a year the last of the holdouts trickled into the reservation at Fort Sill in Indian Territory.

DAVID COFFEY

See also
Adobe Walls, Second Battle of; Cheyennes; Comanches; Kiowas; Mackenzie, Ranald Slidell; Miles, Nelson Appleton; Quanah Parker; Red River War; Sheridan, Philip Henry; Staked Plains

References
Haley, James L. *The Buffalo War: The History of the Red River Indian Uprising of 1874.* Norman: University of Oklahoma Press, 1985.
Pierce, Michael D. *The Most Promising Young Officer: A Life of Ranald Slidell Mackenzie.* Norman: University of Oklahoma Press, 1993.
Utley, Robert M. *Frontier Regulars: The United States and the American Indian, 1866–1891.* New York: Macmillan, 1973.

Palouses

Native American group that inhabited the Columbia Plateau in eastern Washington, north-central Idaho, and eastern Oregon. The Palouses (often referred to as the Paluses) lived in three principal groups—upper, middle, and lower bands—along the Columbia, Snake, and Palouse rivers. Initially nomadic, following food sources according to the season, the Palouses later became somewhat more sedentary and took up seasonal agricultural pursuits. They frequently congregated with neighboring Native American peoples for activities that included hunting, gathering, trading, and religious observances.

In October 1805 Meriwether Lewis and William Clark during their expedition encountered a number of Palouses, probably in present-day eastern Washington or northern Idaho. Lewis and Clark noted in their journal that much of the tribe was away on a hunting expedition. Nevertheless, the explorers presented Chief Kepowhan with a silver peace medal. While some whites confused the Palouses with the Nez Perces because they were culturally related, they were distinctly separate ethnic groups.

The Palouses were considered outstanding horsemen, and at their peak in the early 1800s they possessed 1,000 or more horses. It is believed that the term "Appaloosa," a particular breed of horse known for its distinguishing physical characteristic of a leopard-spotted coat pattern and speed and stamina, is derived from the word "Palouse." In an 1855 treaty between the Yakimas and the U.S. government, the Palouse tribe was recognized as one of the original 14 bands of the Yakima Nation.

In 1858 the Palouses became involved in the on-again, off-again Yakima-Rogue War along with the Yakima, Spokane, and Coeur d'Alene tribes. The Palouses were soundly defeated, and this conflict marked the beginning of a steady and rapid decline in Palouse fortunes. Indeed, in an attempt to curtail the war-making ability of the Palouses, the U.S. Army systematically killed or corralled hundreds of the tribe's horses.

The Palouse tribe is also represented by descendants who compose 1 of 12 aboriginal tribes enrolled in the Confederate Tribes of the Colville Reservation, mostly composed of the Salishan people and their descendants. The Colville Reservation is located in the eastern part of Washington state in Okanogan and Ferry counties. The 2000 census showed a total population of 7,587. It is believed that there are approximately 8,700 total descendants in the United States today.

PAUL G. PIERPAOLI JR.

See also
Coeur d'Alenes; Lewis and Clark Expedition; Nez Perces; Spokanes; Yakima-Rogue War

References
Glassley, Ray Hoard. *Indian Wars of the Pacific Northwest.* Portland, OR: Binfords and Mort, 1972.
Miller, Christopher. *Prophetic Worlds: Indians and Whites on the Columbia Plateau.* Seattle: University of Washington Press, 2003.
Trafzer, Clifford E., and Richard D. Scheuerman. *Renegade Tribe: The Palouse Indians and the Invasion of the Inland Pacific Northwest.* Pullman: Washington State University Press, 1986.

Pamunkeys

An Algonquian-speaking Native American group that belonged to the Powhatan Confederacy and lived along the Pamunkey River in Tidewater Virginia. The Pamunkey River is formed by the confluence of the North Anna River and the South Anna River. The Pamunkey River then joins the Mattaponi River to form the York River near present-day West Point, Virginia. The Pamunkeys were among the 31 nations that formed the Powhatan Confederacy and one of the tribes that Chief Powhatan (Wahunsonacock) had inherited from his parents late in the 16th century. Powhatan's three

Engraving depicting the capture in 1607 of Captain John Smith by the Pamunkey Indians of the Powhatan Confederacy in Virginia. (John Smith, *The True Travels, Adventures, and Observations of Captaine John Smith,* 1630)

brothers—Opichapam, Opechancanough, and Kekataugh—were chiefs (*werowances*) in the Pamunkey territory.

The Pamunkeys' way of life was similar to that of other natives living in the Eastern Woodlands. Men engaged in hunting and fishing, while women practiced limited agriculture and also made clay pots, jars, and pipes.

In the winter of 1608–1609 the English captain John Smith, accompanied by 38 men, visited the Pamunkeys, who were then living along the York River. After a tense verbal exchange with the Powhatans who were present, Smith threatened to kill a Pamunkey. Smith then intimidated a group of warriors, forcing them to load the English ship with grain. Two days later, Smith's party arrived at Opechancanough's town. After a bit of trading in exchange for corn, Smith found himself surrounded by hostile warriors. In the tension of the moment, he allegedly challenged Opechancanough to individual combat.

In 1622 the natives of the Powhatan Confederacy attacked the settlers in the colony of Virginia, sparking the Second Anglo-Powhatan War (1622–1632). The Pamunkey took part in the uprising. Opechancanough, the brother of the late Chief Powhatan, had assumed leadership of the Powhatan Confederacy and planned and led the native attack. His actions placed the Pamunkeys in a difficult situation. In July 1624 the Pamunkeys were forced to defend their enormous cornfields from the English. Following a

two-day pitched battle, the English were able to destroy virtually all of the corn. This event was quite damaging to the Pamunkeys, who lost much of their reputation as keen warriors.

The fighting between the Pamunkeys and the English continued until 1632, when the settlers made peace with both the Chickahominys and the Pamunkeys. Nevertheless, the peace treaty forbade English trade or other contact with the natives. The Second Anglo-Powhatan War wrought dramatic and negative consequences on all of the Powhatan tribes. Their populations were greatly reduced, and many of the old ways of life were lost.

In 1644 Opechancanough led the Powhatan Confederacy into another conflict against the English, the Third Anglo-Powhatan War (1644–1646). Once more the Pamunkeys joined the fray. The fighting took a particularly devastating toll on the Pamunkeys, for much of the turmoil unfolded on their ancestral lands near the headwaters of the York River. Opechancanough's death brought an effective end to the conflict and to the Powhatan Confederacy.

In 1646 Opechancanough's successor, Necotowance, believed also to have been a Pamunkey, signed a treaty with the English. He agreed to relinquish land to the settlers, while his people would become tributaries to the English Crown presumably for reasons of defense and protection.

With the collapse of the Powhatan Confederacy, individual chiefs moved to gain power. In the case of the Pamunkeys, the *weronsqua* (female leader) Cockacoeske sought the leadership of the nation from her inherited relationship with the late Opechancanough. However, the colonial government misunderstood that she was in effect the new tribal leader and regarded her husband Totopotamoi as the new chief of the Pamunkeys.

In 1656 the English sought the help of the Pamunkeys and the Chickahominys in fighting other Native Americans. The Pamunkeys paid dearly for the action because the English commander acted incompetently, resulting in an unnecessary defeat in which Totopotamoi was killed.

In 1676 Virginia was wracked by Bacon's Rebellion. In such tense times, colonial militias often attacked friendly natives as well as those who were hostile. To the natives' way of thinking, such bloodshed required retribution in blood. During Bacon's Rebellion, the Pamunkeys found themselves caught in the middle. Governor Sir William Berkeley rightly interpreted the 1646 Virginia-Indian Treaty as offering the natives protection against all rebels. Thus, he was obliged to protect them from Nathaniel Bacon and his rebels. Bacon's followers, however, saw Berkeley as trying to monopolize trade with the natives, and the rebels soon launched attacks against the Pamunkeys.

The Pamunkeys were so frightened by Bacon's followers that they fled their villages and hid in the surrounding swamps. In the autumn of 1676 Bacon's followers located the Pamunkeys in their swamp hideouts. When Bacon's forces attacked, the Pamunkeys did not resist, yet many were shot. Pamunkey prisoners were paraded to Jamestown to demonstrate Bacon's skill as an "Indian fighter." Bacon died a few weeks later, but hostile attitudes among the rebel colonists almost resulted in the captured Pamunkeys being sold into slavery.

After Berkeley's return to Jamestown in 1677, a new treaty was signed between several native nations (including the Pamunkeys) and the colony of Virginia. The Virginia-Indian Treaty of 1677/1680 created a new reservation for each nation. Cockacoeske was also recognized as the *weronsqua* of the Pamunkeys. By the late 1700s the Pamunkeys had declined to a small number of people. Today the Pamunkeys and the Mattaponis are the only two tribes of the Powhatan Confederacy to own state-reserved lands in Virginia.

ANDREW J. WASKEY

See also

Anglo-Powhatan War, Second; Anglo-Powhatan War, Third; Bacon's Rebellion; Cockacoeske; Opechancanough; Powhatan Confederacy; Smith, John; Virginia-Indian Treaty of 1646; Virginia-Indian Treaty of 1677/1680

References

Feest, Christian F. *The Powhatan Tribes.* New York: Chelsea House, 1990.

Rountree, Helen C. *The Powhatan Indians of Virginia: Their Traditional Culture.* Norman: University of Oklahoma Press, 1989.

Pan-Indianism

A conglomeration of intertribal Native American people who organize in an effort to accomplish a set of specific goals. Pan-Indianism has historically been a reaction to the arrival of Europeans and westward expansion. Pan-Indian movements have always had proponents and critics from all segments of society. Simultaneously, Pan-Indianism is evidence of the diversity of Native American culture and proof that European cultural imperialism has successfully erased many tribes from existence.

The earliest examples of Pan-Indianism are typically linked to Native American revolts. Native Americans pooled their intertribal resources to resist colonization, as exemplified by the several revolts between 1675 and 1700, including King Philip's War (1675–1676) and the Pueblo Revolt (1680). Pan-Indian resistance continued in the United States with leaders such as Pontiac, Neolin the Prophet, and Tecumseh, who created Pan-Indian alliances across tribal lines. Their collective goal involved preserving Native American autonomy and control of land by preventing European settlers from spreading westward.

The late 1800s saw the emergence of at least three Pan-Indian movements. First came the movement to make present-day Oklahoma an intertribal Native American state to be governed by a Pan-Indian set of laws and cultural practices based on the traditions of several tribes. Second was the Ghost Dance movement that spread across the Great Plains, promising to return the land to its condition prior to European arrival. U.S. agents interpreted Ghost Dance activities as a revolt and targeted Sitting Bull, who was murdered in custody, as an instigator. The Ghost Dance movement ended with the tragic Battle of Wounded Knee (December 29, 1890). Many former Ghost Dancers became active in the so-called Peyote Cult, forming the third Pan-Indian movement. Peyote use is most commonly linked to the Native American Church, which merges intertribal groups with Christian and Native American spiritual practices.

As European colonial activity evolved, so did the Native Americans' reaction evolve, promoting considerable Pan-Indian activity. Perhaps a product of European efforts to assimilate Native Americans via boarding schools, many graduates went on to form Pan-Indian organizations based on the notion of a shared national Indian identity. The process of assimilation allowed for the emergence of middle-class educated Native Americans who attempted to utilize U.S. laws to make improvements in the lives of reservation and urban Native Americans. These organizations tended to take practical approaches to promoting the needs of impoverished Native Americans by advancing integration into mainstream U.S. political and economic institutions.

An early example of a Pan-Indian integration organization was the Society of American Indians (SAI), formed in 1911 to monitor U.S. policy and its effect on Native American communities. Although the SAI was concerned with improving the education and integration of Native Americans, the group could not agree on how best to accomplish these goals. Its drive for U.S. citizenship for all Native Americans was realized in 1924, the same year that the SAI disbanded.

Another successful Pan-Indian organization is the National Congress of American Indians (NCAI). The NCAI initially focused on Native American education and legislation, much like the SAI, but expanded its efforts to job training and legal aid for Native American people. Today the NCAI serves as a beacon for federal policy and legislation impacting tribal government and individual Native Americans. Since its inception, the NCAI has expanded its focus to include environmental resource management, elder and youth health care, and the promotion of religious freedom for Native Americans.

Amid the tide of ethnic movements during the 1950s and 1960s for increased integration and self-determination, a Pan-Indian civil rights movement emerged. These civil rights organizations followed a pattern similar to other ethnic groups. As the 1960s progressed, newer civil rights organizations emerged with more extreme ideologies and actions than the previous organizations.

In 1961 the National Indian Youth Council (NIYC) emerged as a predominantly college student–based organization that worked to promote political visibility for Native American youths. The NIYC resorted to civil disobedience as a way of focusing attention on the issues it deemed important. In 1968 the most famous Pan-Indian organization, the American Indian Movement (AIM), began patrolling the streets of Minneapolis and St. Paul, Minnesota, to monitor police abuses in Native American communities. AIM would emerge on the national scene because of its tactics and its involvement with many acts of disobedience against U.S. authority.

AIM is credited with bringing many issues to national visibility but, in the process, lost some members to prison and death. AIM worked with many other Pan-Indian organizations to reclaim Alcatraz Island, the former site of a prison in San Francisco Bay, on November 9, 1969. The resulting media attention was utilized to bring forward a long-existing Pan-Indian consciousness that rejected many of the principles of U.S. legitimacy. For the first time in U.S. history, notions of Manifest Destiny, U.S. nationalism, and American Indians as conquered people were being challenged in front of a national mainstream audience.

Members of AIM took controversial stands on issues in Indian country as well. By challenging the authority of tribal reservation governments, AIM risked alienating traditional Native Americans and the most powerful of Native Americans relative to all reservation residents. One of the most famous examples of such a challenge came from the Pine Ridge Reservation in the mid-1970s, when Guardians of the Oglala Nation (GOONs), a private police force hired by the Lakota Sioux tribal government, were accused of overstepping their authority and killing reservation residents unjustifiably. AIM members began to monitor GOONs' activity. After several altercations between AIM and GOONs, the Federal Bureau of Investigation (FBI) was brought in to control the situation. Although no one agrees on the details, the outcome was the arrest and conviction of AIM member Leonard Peltier for the murder of two FBI agents. Peltier remains incarcerated to this day for what many believe is a crime he did not commit.

As access to economic, educational, and political institutions increased, Pan-Indianism took a less militant approach. Today, many Pan-Indian organizations represent groups of professional Native Americans in the private sector, in the U.S. government, and on university campuses throughout the nation.

Also expanding in universities is the Pan-Indian discipline of American Indian (or Native American) studies. Emerging in the late 1970s, bachelor's, master's, and doctoral programs have proliferated. Several philosophies of education, community building, and integration with mainstream U.S. institutions have developed. The diversity of approaches to Native American issues has led to criticism that the discipline lacks focus as a whole. One example of this inconsistency may be the very name for the discipline. Academic programs founded in the 1980s use the name American Indian studies, newer programs use the name Native American studies, Canadian programs call themselves First Nations' studies, and programs being formed today are tentatively called applied indigenous studies programs. Despite the label changes, all these programs share a common concern for the future of Native American people in terms of economic development, access to education, cultural sensitivity in research, and cultural revitalization.

Today, academics who study and teach political philosophy are emerging and promoting theories of Pan-Indianism as an explanation of world power structures. On the basis of the premise that the world is composed of developed and developing nations, indigenous studies scholars argue that developing nations can never truly become developed nations. Rather, developed nations are developed only because of their relationship with first nations' resources. Members of the first nations' culture generally saw themselves as part of their environment, whereas developed nations saw themselves as masters of their environment. Colonialism allowed developing nations from Europe to become developed at the expense of first nations' resources. Only those capable of functioning in their environment in nonexploitative ways will emerge from the inevitable resource depletion. Academics in indigenous studies believe that only a Pan-Indian movement will be capable of leading the world once developed nations consume resources beyond the point of sustainability.

Often taken as a double-edged sword, Pan-Indianism is interpreted in terms of positive and negative impacts. The danger of Pan-Indianism is that it threatens the purity of tribal cultures that have survived into the modern era. Pan-Indianism contains no language and adheres to a so-called powwow culture potentially in conflict with individual tribal cultures. On the other hand, without a Pan-Indian movement, many Native Americans throughout the world who have lost their former tribal affiliations would be left without a connection to Native American identity.

MICHAEL LERMA

See also

Ghost Dance; King Philip's War; Neolin; Pontiac; Pontiac's Rebellion; Pueblo Revolt; Sitting Bull; Tecumseh; Wounded Knee, Battle of

References

Deloria, Vine. *Tribes, Treaties, and Constitutional Tribulations.* Austin: University of Texas Press, 1999.

Grande, Sandy. *Red Pedagogy: Native American Social and Political Thought.* Lanham, MD: Rowman and Littlefield, 2004.

Smith, Linda Tuhiwai. *Decolonizing Methodologies: Research and Indigenous Peoples.* London: Zed Books, 1999.

Parker, Cynthia Ann
Birth Date: ca. 1825
Death Date: ca. 1870–1871

American woman abducted by Comanches in 1836. Born to Lucy Duty and Silas M. Parker in Crawford County, Illinois, probably in 1825, Cynthia Ann Parker moved to central Texas with her family when she was nine. The Parkers and other families of the community prepared themselves against possible Native American attacks by constructing Fort Parker in present-day Limestone County, east of Waco.

On May 19, 1836, Comanche, Kiowa, and Kichai warriors attacked Fort Parker. Several settlers were killed, and five were captured alive, including Parker and her brother John. Over the years the captives, except for Parker and her brother, were sold to other tribes and eventually returned to their families. Parker gradually acculturated with the Comanches; married Peta Nocona;

had three children, Quanah, Pecos, and Topsannah Parker; and remained with the Comanches for 25 years.

Sometime in the 1840s Cynthia's brother John sought her out to bring her home, but she explained that she was committed to her husband and children. After that John remained with the Comanches for several years. The tribe left him when he contracted smallpox. He recovered, lived in Mexico for some time, and returned to the United States to fight on the Southern side in Texas during the American Civil War (1861–1865).

The Comanches valued Parker and refused a ransom for her return, which had been offered by Colonel Leonard G. Williams in April 1846. Then in December 1860 Parker's family's camp was attacked by Texas Rangers under Captain Lawrence Sullivan "Sul" Ross. Peta escaped with their sons, but Parker and daughter Topsannah were captured, taken to Camp Cooper, and later identified by her uncle, Colonel Isaac Parker. Parker accompanied him through Birdville and Fort Worth, Texas, and was finally reunited with her birth family. The Texas legislature granted her $500 over five years and land on which to settle. The legislature also placed her under the guardianship of brothers Isaac and Benjamin Parker.

Parker's repeated attempts to return to her Comanche family were foiled. Her birth family kept close watch on her and took turns hosting her in their homes. She was never reunited with her Comanche family and learned that her son Pecos had died of smallpox in 1863. Several months later Topsannah died of influenza. Beset with grief, Parker refused food and starved herself to death in 1870 or 1871.

Parker's son Quanah grew in reputation as an excellent hunter, fighter, and leader of the Comanches. He founded the Native American Church, integrating Christianity with the peyote religion. Eventually he made peace with whites and prospered as a cattle rancher. After learning of his mother's death, he had her body and that of Topsannah disinterred from Anderson County, Texas, and moved to Fort Sill, Oklahoma, where he was buried at their sides when he died.

REBECCA TOLLEY-STOKES

See also
Comanches; Kiowas; Quanah Parker

References
"Cynthia Ann Parker." In *American National Biography,* Vol. 17, edited by John A. Garraty, 15–16. New York: Oxford University Press, 1999.
Exley, Jo Ella Powell. *Frontier Blood: The Saga of the Parker Family.* College Station: Texas A&M University Press, 2001.

Parker, Ely Samuel
Birth Date: 1828
Death Date: August 30, 1895

Seneca leader, U.S. Army officer, and commissioner of Indian affairs. Ely Samuel Parker, whose Seneca name was Do-ne-ho-ga-wa (Keeper of the Western Door), was born sometime in 1828 on the Tonawanda Reservation near Indian Falls, New York. At about age 10 after being ridiculed for his poor English by soldiers at an army post where he worked as a stable boy, he enrolled in a Baptist mission school on the reservation. He later attended Cayuga Academy.

After completing his studies in 1845, Parker traveled to Washington, D.C., with a delegation of Seneca leaders to defend their land claims. Upon his return he studied law, but despite having taken an English name, he was denied admission to the New York Bar because the state prohibited nonwhites from practicing law. Parker then studied civil engineering at Rensselaer Polytechnic Institute, graduated in 1851, and worked as an engineer on the Erie Canal.

In 1855 the U.S. government hired Parker to be chief engineer of the Chesapeake and Albemarle Canal in Virginia. Two years later he was appointed to supervise a project in Galena, Illinois, where he befriended a tanner named Ulysses S. Grant.

At the start of the American Civil War (1861–1865), Parker volunteered to raise an Iroquois regiment for New York, but the governor refused to allow Native Americans to serve. Parker next

Ely Parker, a Seneca Indian from New York, was named commissioner of Indian Affairs by President Ulysses S. Grant in 1871 as part of his "peace policy" that transferred responsibility for the management of Native American matters from the U.S. Army to the Department of the Interior. (Arthur C. Parker, *The Life of General Ely S. Parker,* Buffalo Historical Society, 1919)

Heads of Indian Affairs, 1824–1905

Name	Title	Dates in Office
Thomas L. McKenney	Head of Office of Indian Affairs[1]	1824–1829
Samuel S. Hamilton	Head of Office of Indian Affairs	1830–1831
Elbert Herring	Head of Office of Indian Affairs	1831–1832
	Commissioner of Indian Affairs[2]	1832–1836
Carey A. Harris	Commissioner of Indian Affairs	1836–1838
Thomas H. Crawford	Commissioner of Indian Affairs	1838–1845
William Medill	Commissioner of Indian Affairs	1845–1849
Orlando Brown	Commissioner of Indian Affairs[3]	1849–1850
Luke Lea	Commissioner of Indian Affairs	1850–1853
George W. Manypenny	Commissioner of Indian Affairs	1853–1857
James W. Denver	Commissioner of Indian Affairs	1857–1859
Charles E. Mix	Commissioner of Indian Affairs (interim)	1858
Alfred B. Greenwood	Commissioner of Indian Affairs	1859–1861
William P. Dole	Commissioner of Indian Affairs	1861–1865
Dennis N. Cooley	Commissioner of Indian Affairs	1865–1866
Lewis Vital Bogy	Commissioner of Indian Affairs	1866–1867
Nathaniel G. Taylor	Commissioner of Indian Affairs	1867–1869
Ely S. Parker (Seneca)	Commissioner of Indian Affairs	1869–1871
Francis A. Walker	Commissioner of Indian Affairs	1871–1872
Edward P. Smith	Commissioner of Indian Affairs	1873–1875
John Q. Smith	Commissioner of Indian Affairs	1875–1877
Ezra A. Hayt	Commissioner of Indian Affairs	1877–1880
Rowland E. Trowbridge	Commissioner of Indian Affairs	1880–1881
Hiram Price	Commissioner of Indian Affairs	1881–1885
John D. C. Atkins	Commissioner of Indian Affairs	1885–1888
John H. Oberly	Commissioner of Indian Affairs	1888–1889
Thomas J. Morgan	Commissioner of Indian Affairs	1889–1893
Daniel M. Browning	Commissioner of Indian Affairs	1893–1897
William A. Jones	Commissioner of Indian Affairs	1897–1905

[1] From 1789 to 1832, the secretary of war was officially in charge of Indian affairs, but in 1824 an Office of Indian Affairs was created within the War Department, and a head of Indian affairs was appointed to oversee it.

[2] In 1832 the secretary of war created the position of commissioner of Indian affairs within the War Department to manage Indian affairs.

[3] In 1849 the Bureau of Indian Affairs and its head, the commissioner of Indian affairs, moved from the War Department to the Department of the Interior.

offered his services to the federal government and was again rejected for the same reason. However, in May 1863 his friend Grant, now a Union general, arranged for him to be commissioned a captain of volunteers. Parker served with Grant for the remainder of the war, eventually joining the general's staff as his military secretary and attaining the rank of lieutenant colonel. Parker also won brevets through brigadier general. Joining the regular army, he continued to serve as Grant's aide after the war and was promoted to colonel. When Grant became president in 1869, he appointed Parker commissioner of Indian affairs.

The Bureau of Indian Affairs had a reputation for corruption, and Parker set out to reform the agency. He appointed tribal agents on the recommendation of religious groups rather than on the basis of political connections and created a citizens' Board of Indian Commissioners to oversee the bureau's activities. Eager to maintain peace in the West, he invited Red Cloud and other Plains Indian leaders to Washington in 1870 for talks. Parker's intervention helped resolve disputes over treaty terms.

Parker's efforts to protect the Plains tribes and to reform the Bureau of Indian Affairs aroused the anger of the Indian Ring, a politically connected group that had profited from the agency's corruption and sought further gain from the opening of western lands to mining and settlement. Their friends in Congress delayed providing funds in 1870 to support the tribes on western reservations. To prevent starvation, Parker bypassed the bidding process to purchase and transport supplies.

Seizing upon this violation of government rules, Parker's enemies accused him of corruption. The House Appropriations Committee launched an inquiry that exonerated Parker of all charges; however, the ordeal and continual attacks from the press caused him to resign in August 1871.

Parker moved to New York City, where he became a successful businessman. He died on August 30, 1895, in Fairfield, Connecticut.

JIM PIECUCH

See also

Bureau of Indian Affairs; Grant, Ulysses Simpson; Indian Ring Scandal; Red Cloud; Senecas

References

Armstrong, William H. *Warrior in Two Camps: Ely S. Parker, Union General and Seneca Chief.* Syracuse, NY: Syracuse University Press, 1978.

Brown, Dee. *Bury My Heart at Wounded Knee.* New York: Holt, Rinehart and Winston, 1970.

Conn, Steven. *History's Shadow: Native Americans and Historical Consciousness in the Nineteenth Century.* Chicago: University of Chicago Press, 2004.

Parkman, Francis, Jr.
Birth Date: September 16, 1823
Death Date: November 8, 1893

Noted U.S. historian whose writings on the West and Native Americans are regarded as among the best narrative and romantic treatments of the 19th century. Francis Parkman Jr. was born in Boston, Massachusetts, on September 16, 1823. He came from a well-to-do family that traced its heritage in New England back many generations. Parkman's share of his family's fortune enabled him, in spite of years of poor health, to carry on his historical writings.

In 1840 Parkman entered Harvard College. Much influenced by his extensive outside reading, he later claimed that he chose his life work while a second-year student when he fell in love with writing, the rapidly vanishing wilderness, and the history of the French and Indian War (1754–1763). Parkman earned his degree in 1844. He then entered law school with no intention of practicing but instead merely for mental training. Meanwhile, he published his first five stories based on his rambles and traveling adventures during 1845 in the *Knickerbocker, or New-York Monthly Magazine.*

Trying to prove himself hardy, Parkman left St. Louis, Missouri, on April 28, 1846, for the great adventure of his life, a journey along the Oregon Trail. He linked up with a band of Sioux and lived with them for some weeks, observing their habits, customs, and ways of thought. He also studied the white hunters, trappers, and travelers in the region.

Parkman returned to Boston in October 1846 much weakened but with some knowledge and experience of the frontier. Beginning in February 1847 he published a narrative of his trip as a series in *The Knickerbocker* that was published in 1849 as a book titled *The California and Oregon Trail,* one of his most popular and enduring writings.

In 1848 Parkman began to write his *History of the Conspiracy of Pontiac,* the first of his long series on the struggle of the French and the British for the possession of the continent. He expected that his history of the French and Indian War would take about 20 years to complete. His health soon took another turn for the worse, however.

Writing very little for a time, Parkman eventually was able to work more. Helped by his mostly female friends, he continued conducting research from books and manuscripts sent to him from libraries in Europe and throughout America. Amazingly, he completed *The History of the Conspiracy of Pontiac* in less than two and a half years and published it in two volumes in 1851.

Suffering a nervous disorder in 1853, Parkman laid aside historical work and published an unsuccessful novel in 1856. He then turned to the study of horticulture and successfully raised new varieties of lilies and roses. He was so good at it that he was elected president of the Massachusetts Horticultural Society and was appointed a professor of horticulture at Harvard in 1871.

In 1858 following the deaths of his only son and his wife within a year of each other, Parkman suffered a breakdown and traveled to Europe. In 1865 he published *Pioneers of France in the New World,* the first volume in his massive study titled *France and England in North America. Pioneers* cemented his reputation and popularity as a historian. The rest of the series appeared regularly for the next 27 years. During the same period and despite continued ill health, he frequently contributed to the *Atlantic Monthly* and the *North American Review.*

In combination with his gifts of literary power and narrative skill, Parkman's reputation must also stand within the context of his 19th-century beliefs in progress and political elitism and his racist views about Native Americans as well as his unsympathetic contempt for Catholic, clerical-ridden, and fanatical regimes but not Catholicism itself. Parkman was, however, critical of British and French immoral treatment of Native Americans. He was scrupulous with sources, but his knowledge of the Iroquois, for example, was spotty at best. Nonetheless, he was an excellent storyteller who interwove tales of significant heroes. Those heroes were often idealized images of what he believed that he himself should be. His histories of the primeval wilderness and "savage peoples" contending with civilization must be read with critical care, but his prose can still be read with pleasure. Parkman died on November 8, 1893, in Jamaica Plain, Massachusetts.

Paul G. Pierpaoli Jr.

See also
French and Indian War; Iroquois; Oregon Trail; Pontiac's Rebellion; Sioux

References
Jacobs, Wilbur R. *Francis Parkman: Historian as Hero.* Austin: University of Texas Press, 1991.
Kraus, Michael, and Davis D. Joyce. *The Writing of American History.* Norman: University of Oklahoma Press, 1985.

Paviotsos
See Paiutes, Northern

Pawnees
Plains Indian tribe composed of the Skiri, Chawi, Pitahawirata, and Kitkahahki bands. Before removal to Indian Territory (Oklahoma) in the 1870s, the Pawnees lived in semipermanent earth lodge villages along the Platte and Republican rivers in present-day Nebraska and Kansas. Corn-based agriculture supplemented by annual buffalo hunts was their basic means of subsistence. The

Pawnee lodges at Loup, Nebraska, circa 1873. The Pawnees were a major military force on the Great Plains. The Pawnees never went to war against the United States and were among the first western Indians to serve as U.S. Army scouts. (National Archives)

Pawnees cultivated an elaborate ritual and ceremonial religious complex based on the careful study of stars, planets, and other celestial phenomena.

Until European-introduced diseases caused massive population losses among the Pawnees in the late 1700s and early 1800s, they were one of the great military powers on the Plains. They fought numerous wars with neighboring tribes, such as the Kansas (Kaws), Osages, Omahas, Poncas, Iowas, Missourias, Kiowas, Comanches, and Apaches. During the first half of the 19th century, the Pawnees came under increasing pressure from the Sioux, Cheyennes, and Arapahos. Warfare with these three nomadic tribes was particularly disruptive and explains the decision of many Pawnees to serve as scouts for the U.S. Army in the 1860s and 1870s. Notably, the Pawnees never went to war with the United States and signed treaties of peace and friendship with the U.S. government in 1825, 1833, 1848, and 1857.

When war erupted between the United States and the Sioux and Cheyennes in the 1850s and 1860s, the U S. Army began to consider the use of Native American auxiliary forces. In 1857 Colonel Edwin V. Sumner of the First Cavalry recruited five Pawnee warriors to serve as scouts in a campaign against the Cheyennes. Nevertheless, the army remained reluctant to employ the Pawnees as scouts. It was not until 1864 that the army fully recognized the potential of a military alliance with the Pawnees. That year a unit of Pawnee scouts under the command of white officers was formed. This unit, sometimes referred to as the Pawnee Battalion, was organized periodically between 1864 and 1877, during which time it rendered valuable services to the U.S. Army and contributed significantly to the military pacification of the Plains.

Although nominally under command of a white officer, the Pawnee scouts often acted independently, employing their own tactics. Attempts to drill them like regular army soldiers were terminated when the Pawnees resisted, and this reduced their effectiveness in the field. Consequently, military service reinforced the Pawnees' traditional martial practices rather than preparing them for "civilized" life, as General William T. Sherman and other high-ranking generals suggested.

The Pawnee scouts participated in several major campaigns, such as the Powder River Expedition of 1865. During these campaigns they guided the troops, scouted the area, protected the flanks of army columns, carried mail and dispatches, and spearheaded attacks against enemy villages. In addition to several well-known battles, such as the Battle of Summit Springs (1869) and the Dull Knife Fight (1876), the scouts fought several other successful but less publicized engagements, including one at Plum Creek, Nebraska, in 1867 when they were employed to protect railroad surveying and working crews of the Union Pacific Railroad company against hostile Native Americans.

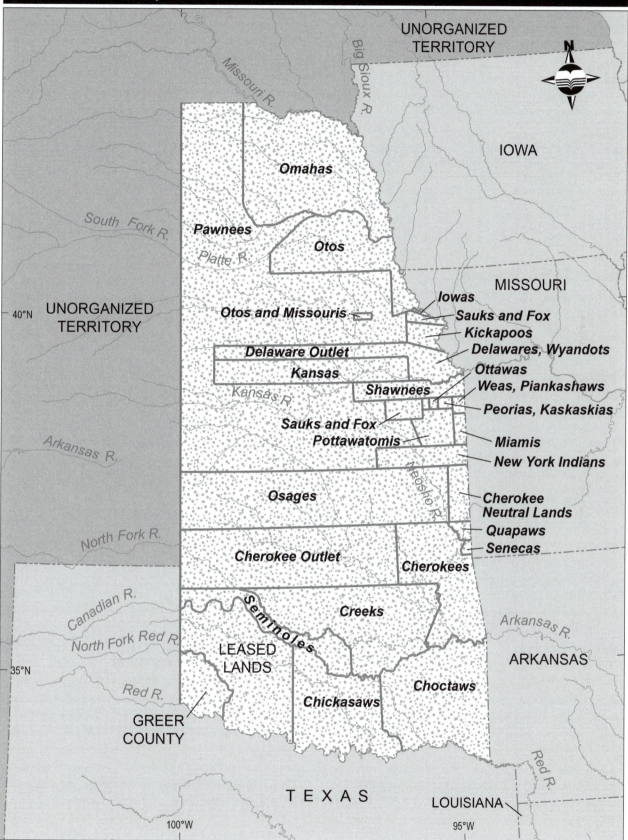

INDIAN TERRITORY, 1854

UNORGANIZED
TERRITORY

N

IOWA

Omahas

Pawnees

Otos

MISSOURI

40°N UNORGANIZED
TERRITORY

Iowas

Otos and Missouris

Sauks and Fox

Kickapoos

Delawares, Wyandots

Delaware Outlet

Ottawas

Kansas

Weas, Piankashaws

Shawnees

Peorias, Kaskaskias

Sauks and Fox

Pottawatomis

Miamis

New York Indians

Osages

Cherokee
Neutral Lands

Quapaws

Cherokee Outlet

Senecas

Cherokees

Creeks

Seminoles

LEASED
LANDS

ARKANSAS

Chickasaws

Choctaws

GREER
COUNTY

T E X A S

LOUISIANA

100°W

35°N

95°W

South Fork R.

Missouri R.

Big Sioux R.

Platte R.

Kansas R.

Arkansas R.

Neosho R.

North Fork R.

Canadian R.

North Fork Red R.

Red R.

Arkansas R.

Red R.

After the Great Sioux War of 1876–1877, the Pawnee Battalion was permanently disbanded. The Pawnee people today take special pride in the contributions of the scouts, whose service is honored each year at the annual Pawnee Homecoming Powwow.

MARK VAN DE LOGT

See also
Cavalry, Native American; Dull Knife Fight; Great Sioux War; Scouts, Native American; Summit Springs, Battle of

References
Dunlay, Thomas W. *Wolves for the Blue Soldiers: Indian Scouts and Auxiliaries with the United States Army, 1860–90.* Lincoln: University of Nebraska Press, 1982.
Hyde, George E. *The Pawnee Indians.* Norman: University of Oklahoma Press, 1974.

Pawnee Scouts Massacre
See Massacre Canyon, Battle of

Paxton Riots
Start Date: December 14, 1763
End Date: January 1764

Uprising in which residents of western Pennsylvania, believing that the Quaker establishment in Philadelphia had failed to adequately defend the frontier from Native American attacks, massacred members of the peaceful Conestoga tribe in Lancaster County before marching on Philadelphia. The violence began on December 14, 1763, and was largely extinguished by late January 1764. More a massacre than a riot, it exemplified both the racial conflict along the colonial frontier as well as internal divisions between colonial elites and western settlers. Moreover, the Paxton Riots point to many colonists' disgust with King George III's Royal Proclamation of 1763, which forbade white settlement beyond the Appalachians and effectively created Native American territories to the west and north.

During the French and Indian War (1754–1763), thousands of residents along the colonial frontier were killed in a wave of war and bloodshed that reached a crescendo during Pontiac's Rebellion (1763). Many of the Scotch Irish settlers on the Pennsylvania frontier blamed the Quaker government in Philadelphia for not supplying adequate funds and troops to defend the frontier. The so-called backcountry of western Pennsylvania was also underrepresented in the colonial assembly, holding only 10 seats compared with 26 for Philadelphia alone.

On December 14, 1763, a group of frontier ruffians from the village of Paxton took out their frustrations on a small community of Christian Conestogas about eight miles west of Lancaster,

Pennsylvania. Six inhabitants were killed and scalped, including a child. Fourteen other Conestogas were placed in a workhouse adjacent to the Lancaster jail, ostensibly for their own protection. But on the evening of December 27 a mob surged past token security provided by the authorities and slaughtered the 14 Conestogas in protective custody. Although rewards were offered for the perpetrators of the murders, no arrests were made as the frontier community closed ranks behind the so-called Paxton Boys.

In January 1764 with their support growing in western Pennsylvania, the Paxton Boys, constituting a force estimated at 500 to 1,500 men, marched on Philadelphia, where 140 Moravian Native Americans had sought refuge. In response to the march, an army of approximately 500 citizen volunteers and 200 royal troops were mustered in Philadelphia to defend the city and the Moravian natives. However, the Paxton Boys' march halted in February at Germantown, outside of Philadelphia, where Benjamin Franklin helped broker a deal that avoided more potential violence. The rebels thereby agreed to disband in exchange for amnesty and an opportunity to present their grievances to colonial authorities.

While the agreement was honored, there was little change in colonial policy, and frontier grievances against colonial elites as well as Native American populations were major issues in the American Revolutionary War (1775–1783). Violent outbreaks such as the Paxton Riots against Native Americans help explain why many Native Americans looked upon the British more favorably than the colonists during the American Revolution.

RON BRILEY

See also
French and Indian War; Pontiac's Rebellion; Proclamation of 1763

References
Jacobs, Wilbur, ed. *The Paxton Riots and the Frontier Theory.* Chicago: Rand McNally, 1967.
Taylor, Alan. *American Colonies: The Settling of North America.* New York: Viking/Penguin, 2001.
Vaughan, Alden T. *Roots of American Racism: Essays on the Colonial Experience.* New York: Oxford University Press, 1995.

Payne's Landing, Treaty of

Treaty signed between the Seminoles and the U.S. government on May 9, 1832, at Payne's Landing on the Oklawaha River in Florida. In 1819 the United States acquired Florida from Spain and in 1823 signed the Treaty of Moultrie Creek with the Seminoles. In signing this treaty, the Seminoles agreed to move onto land set aside for them in central Florida. In return the United States was to offer the Seminoles protection, pay them compensation for agricultural losses, and pay a yearly stipend of $5,000 for 20 years.

Seven years later the Seminoles were asked to move again after President Andrew Jackson signed the Indian Removal Act of 1830. That legislation called for all Native American tribes in the

Southeast to be relocated west of the Mississippi River. Each tribe was to sign an individual treaty with the government expressing its willingness to relinquish all claims to land that it currently inhabited.

Two years after the Indian Removal Act, James Gadsden, who had been charged with working with the Seminoles after the Treaty of Moultrie Creek, was now asked to negotiate a new treaty that would move the tribe out of Florida for good. The U.S. government wanted the Seminoles to move onto land given to the Creeks in what became Indian Territory (present-day Oklahoma).

According to the Treaty of Payne's Landing, the Seminoles were expected to move to their new land within three years. The treaty also granted them the right to send representatives to the new land to see if it was suitable. Gadsden also informed the Seminoles that they would be required to return all runaway slaves whom they had been long protecting.

The Seminoles resented the demands made by the government in the treaty but tentatively agreed to the terms in 1833 after several chiefs had visited the Creek lands. After they returned to Florida, however, some of the chiefs claimed that they had not signed the treaty, while others claimed that they had signed it under duress. In spite of the fact that the Seminoles now refused to leave Florida, Congress ratified the treaty in 1834. The Seminoles were supposed to vacate their land by 1835.

When the government dispatched Indian agent Wiley Thompson to Florida to discuss the removal plans with the Seminoles in the late autumn of 1834, they refused to recognize the treaty and refused to move. In response, Thompson asked the government to send more troops to persuade the Seminoles to abide by the treaty. President Jackson meanwhile bluntly informed the Seminole chiefs that if they refused to relocate, U.S. troops would forcibly remove them from the land.

Tensions mounted between the U.S. government and the Seminoles, and in late December 1835 the Seminoles attacked a column of more than 100 U.S. soldiers moving through central Florida. This marked the official beginning of the Second Seminole War (1835–1842). During and after the war, hundreds of Seminoles moved to the Creek Reservation in Indian Territory, but several hundred remained in Florida and moved into the Everglades in southern Florida. To this day the Seminoles claim to be the only unconquered Native American tribe in the United States.

SETH A. WEITZ

See also

Creeks; Indian Removal Act; Indian Territory; Jackson, Andrew; Seminoles; Seminole War, Second

References

Gannon, Michael. *Florida: A Short History*. Gainesville: University Press of Florida, 1993.

Knetsch, Joe. *Florida's Seminole Wars, 1817–1858*. Charleston, SC: Arcadia Publishing, 2003.

Missall, John, and Mary Lou Missall. *The Seminole Wars: America's Longest Indian Conflict*. Gainesville: University Press of Florida, 2004.

Pedadumies

See Pottawatomis

Penateka Comanches

A major band of the Comanches. The Penatekas spoke a language related to the Uto-Aztecan linguistic family. They along with their Comanche cousins migrated south and east from the Rocky Mountains. Around 1700 the Comanches split from the Shoshones and moved toward the North Platte River in Nebraska. The Comanches fought with nearly every tribe they encountered as they moved toward present-day Texas and Oklahoma. They also raided Spanish and later Mexican settlements in search of booty and captives. By the 1750s the Comanches had fully adopted the Plains culture and had assembled large herds of horses. Seminomadic, their lifestyle and movement patterns followed the great buffalo herds and other game.

The Penatekas were known as Pehnahterkuh ("Honey Eaters") and also as Pehnahner ("Wasps") or Hohees ("Timber People"). The Spanish and Americans knew them as southern Comanches. Their range was within the Edwards Plateau of Texas, where they found honey for eating and trees for other uses. They relied chiefly on the buffalo, which they used for food, clothing, shelter, tools, and household supplies.

The Penatekas, like the other larger Comanche bands, were sufficiently populous to survive without needing the other bands to replenish their numbers. They frequently fought their ancient foes the Apaches, especially the Lipan Apaches, as well as the Tonkawas. By 1750 the Penatekas and their fellow Comanches were so strong that few of the surrounding peoples dared to enter Comanche land. The Apaches and Tonkawas remained at the southwestern trans-Pecos region. The Cheyennes and Pawnees stayed north of the Arkansas River. The Utes rarely ventured eastward past the Rocky Mountains. The Wichitas were the sole tribe that dared to venture from the east, but they were not sufficiently strong to challenge the Comanches.

With their expanded territory largely free from enemies, the Penatekas lived apart from other tribes, developed their own interests, and had little contact with other Comanche bands. They did, however, share the Comanche hatred of the Apaches and retained the Comanche culture, with slight differences in ceremonies, dances, and accents.

Despite the large size of the Comancheria (as the Comanche homeland was called), the increasing encroachment of white settlers and a long drought began to reduce the ability of the Penatekas to feed themselves. By the 1850s impoverished Penatekas frequented Fredericksburg, Texas, to barter meager goods for food and merchandise. To the east the Penatekas faced a threatening encroachment of white settlers who had pushed into a wide zone between the San Antonio and Trinity rivers.

The Penatekas responded to the encroachments by raiding through Texas and deep into Mexico. To counter this, the U.S. Army placed seven frontier garrisons nearly 100 miles deeper into the Comancheria. These were situated at key watering places where infantry could intercept raiding parties heading to Texas and Mexico. By the autumn of 1853 the Texas frontier had engulfed the Comancheria all the way to Comanche Peak, and Penateka raiding in Texas dwindled to sporadic actions along the Rio Grande.

Gradually three Penateka factions appeared and settled in different areas: one along the middle of the Colorado River; another north of the Brazos River, where they blended with Tenewa Comanches; and the third on 23,000 acres of land set aside for them on the Clear Fork of the Brazos. Within a year, hunger drove the other Penatekas in as well. More than 500 Comanches were collecting annuities on the Clear Fork Reservation. However, problems between the Comanches and both Texans and other Native Americans in the area resulted in the Clear Creek Reservation being closed and the band being moved to Indian Territory (Oklahoma) in 1859.

JOHN THOMAS BROOM

See also

Buffalo; Comanches

References

Ferhenbach, T. R. *Comanches: The History of a People.* New York: Anchor Books, 2003.

Hoig, Stan. *Tribal Wars of the Southern Plains.* Norman: University of Oklahoma Press, 1993.

LaVere, David. *Contrary Neighbors: Southern Plains and Removed Indians in Indian Territory.* Norman: University of Oklahoma Press, 2000.

Powers, William K. *Indians of the Southern Plains.* New York: Capricorn Books, 1972.

Wallace, Ernest, and E. Adamson Hoebel. *The Comanches: Lords of the South Plains.* 1952; reprint, Norman: University of Oklahoma Press, 1986.

A woodcut of a Pennacook chief known as Passaconaway the Bashaba, circa late 1600s. (North Wind Picture Archives)

Pennacooks

Native American group that lived within present-day New Hampshire along the Merrimack River watershed and around Lake Winnipesaukee. The Pennacooks were prominent participants in New England's early imperial wars. A numerous people before European contact, the Pennacooks were ravaged by the New England pandemics of 1619 and 1633. As a result, they welcomed the English colonists of New Hampshire and Massachusetts Bay as friends and allies. In their weakened state, the Pennacooks hoped that the newcomers might help in the struggle against rival tribal groups, particularly the Mohawks.

Enmity between the Pennacooks and the Mohawks predated European movement into New England. However, that intrusion had given the Mohawks new interest in captives and furs and new weapons in firearms to satisfy that interest. The two sides fought an ongoing war with each other between the 1650s and the 1670s in which the Pennacooks generally fared poorly.

When King Philip's War (1675–1676) began, the Pennacooks attempted to remain neutral. This neutrality was sorely tested, for at the war's beginning Massachusetts sent soldiers to burn the Pennacooks' principal town (present-day Concord, New Hampshire) for fear that they were hostile. Worse was to come. After the war's conclusion, many natives who had fought for Metacom took refuge among the Pennacooks. The colonial government of Massachusetts, concerned by this, asked its northern agent, Major Richard Waldron, to settle the situation. Waldron, under pretext of friendship, invited Pennacook leaders and their guests to his home and then arrested those suspected of participating in the war and sent them to Boston. There they were executed or sold into slavery.

During their wars with the Mohawks, the Pennacooks had frequently relied on the French for aid. But by the 1680s Pennacook amity with the French and dissatisfaction with the English were so strong that when King William's War (1689–1697) began, the Pennacooks abandoned their neutrality and attacked Waldron's estate. Having cast their lot with the French, they maintained the alliance throughout that war. That bond continued throughout Queen Anne's War (1702–1713).

The pressure of Mohawk and English hostility in the period 1660–1713 encouraged many Pennacooks to withdraw permanently from their traditional lands. A number moved to Canada. Others opted for Abenaki or Sokoki lands that were more remote from English settlements. By 1713 the Pennacook population of New Hampshire was insufficient to prevent English occupation and settlement of the Pennacook homeland.

Although some Pennacook warriors continued to participate in wars against the English, the age of wholesale Pennacook resistance to New England was over. The Pennacooks essentially ceased to exist as a separate tribe by the late 1700s. Today, some Abenakis in northern New England and southern Canada trace their lineage back to the Pennacooks.

ANDREW MILLER

See also

Abenakis; France; King Philip's War; King William's War; Mohawks; Queen Anne's War; Sokokis

References

Belknap, Jeremy. *The History of New Hampshire.* 3 vols. New York: Arno, 1972.

Calloway, Colin G. *The Western Abenakis of Vermont, 1600–1800: War, Migration, and the Survival of an Indian People.* Norman: University of Oklahoma Press, 1990.

Stewart-Smith, David. "The Pennacook Indians and the New England Frontier, Circa 1604–1733." PhD dissertation, Union Institute, 1998.

Pequots

Algonquian-speaking tribe that inhabited southeastern Connecticut, centered around present-day New London, between the Pawcatuck River and Niantic Bay. At the height of Pequot dominance, the tribe's territory encompassed nearly 2,000 square miles.

The Pequots dominated the area for many years before the arrival of the Europeans and for a short time after. Many tribes in the Connecticut River Valley paid tribute to the Pequots, and their military dominance is best illustrated by their Algonquian name, which translates as "destroyer." Only five years after their first sustained contact with whites, the Pequots were nearly exterminated by disease and the Pequot War (1636–1638) at the hands of the English and their Native American allies.

Pequot livelihood centered on agriculture, foraging, trade, hunting, and fishing. The Pequots lived in small dispersed familial villages of 10 to 20 dwellings each. These villages were not stationary but instead were relocated throughout the year, allowing the Pequots to follow seasonal changes that affected the availability of game, fish, and crop cultivation. In the summer months the tribe lived near the coast and planted, hunted, and fished. In the winter the tribe moved inland, taking with them as much food as possible gathered in the summer. For subsistence in the winter, the tribe depended on hunting and stores from its summer and autumn plantings.

A sachem (sagamore or chief) headed the tribe. The position was patrilineal in that the office was held by men who were related. However, female sachems were not unknown. A council of elders composed of prominent warriors and other notables within the tribe advised the sachem. The sachem ruled through persuasion and the granting and receiving of gifts.

The arrival of Europeans in the region and their eventual penetration into the Connecticut Valley presented the Pequots with new rivals to their dominance in the region. Unfortunately for the Pequots, the high tide of European confrontation occurred at a most inopportune time. The Pequots, like most Native American tribes, were devastated by disease. Two outbreaks of European-imported diseases in 1616–1619 and 1633 occurred just as the Pequots were confronting the brunt of European incursions onto their lands.

The Puritans chose to regard the Pequots as little more than bloodthirsty savages. This view helped precipitate the tragic Pequot War in 1636. The English allied with the Pequots' enemies, the Narragansett and Mohegans, to destroy the Pequots and nearly succeeded in their aim.

According to some estimates, the Pequot population numbered 13,000 people just before European contact. By 1636 the population had fallen to 3,000. With the conclusion of the Pequot War, fewer than 1,500 Pequots remained. The great majority of these were sold into slavery or took refuge with neighboring tribes. The Pequots all but disappeared, as the English refused to allow them to use their tribal name. Today the tribe survives on small reservations in eastern Connecticut.

RICK DYSON

See also

Algonquins; Hartford, Treaty of; Mohegans; Narragansetts; Pequot War

References

Apess, William. *On Our Own Ground: The Complete Writings of William Apess, a Pequot.* Amherst: University of Massachusetts Press, 1992.

Axtell, James. *The Invasion Within: The Contest of Cultures in Colonial North America.* New York: Oxford University Press, 1985.

Hauptman, Laurence M., and James D Wherry, eds. *The Pequots in Southern New England: The Rise and Fall of an American Indian Nation.* Norman: University of Oklahoma Press, 1990.

Vaughan, Alden T. *New England Frontier: Puritans and Indians, 1620–1675.* 3rd ed. Norman: University of Oklahoma Press, 1995.

Pequot War

Start Date: July 1636
End Date: September 21, 1638

Conflict between the Pequot people of the lower Connecticut River Valley and the English colonies of Massachusetts Bay and Connecticut, resulting in the near-destruction of the Pequots. The Pequot War grew out of a series of confrontations and growing tensions between the Pequots and English settlers in Connecticut and Massachusetts Bay in the early 1630s. The Pequots and English settlers seemed to be expanding their influence at the same time. The Pequots were growing as a regional trading power just as English settlers extended trading posts and settlements into the Connecticut River Valley. While the Pequots were interested in trading with the English, a few violent incidents quickly changed the tone of interaction.

In the spring of 1634 a Virginia merchant, John Stone, was exploring the Connecticut River area for trading prospects on a return voyage from Massachusetts. Stone apparently provoked the Pequots, and they or a subordinate tribe killed Stone and his crew. Because the Pequots were then embroiled in conflict with the Narragansetts in Rhode Island and eastern Connecticut and the Dutch in New Netherland, they quickly made a treaty with the English. Pequot sachems (chiefs) claimed that Stone had provoked the incident by kidnapping two of the Pequots to serve as guides up the Connecticut River and that during a Pequot rescue attempt some powder on board the ship had ignited, destroying the ship. The sachems also claimed that most of the murderers had since died of smallpox, but they agreed to hand over the two who remained. They also agreed to pay a large indemnity of wampum and pelts. Negotiations slowly ground to a halt as Pequot sachems failed to ratify the treaty, thus confirming Puritan notions that the natives were not to be trusted. Only a portion of the tribute was ever paid, but Massachusetts did not pursue the issue.

The negative attitude of Puritan settlers in Massachusetts Bay toward the Pequots was fueled by charges brought by Uncas, sachem of the rival Mohegans, that the murderers of Stone and his crew continued to live among the Pequots. Uncas also reported that the Pequots were planning a preemptive war against the English.

In this increasingly charged atmosphere another English trader was murdered. In July 1636 a ship captained by John Gallop discovered Captain John Oldham's pinnace adrift off Block Island. Seeing only natives on deck, Gallop assumed that they had taken the vessel. Gallop and his crew attacked the pinnace and retook it at a cost of 10 to 11 Native American dead and discovered Oldham's body. Because of the proximity of the vessel to Block Island, the government of Massachusetts held the natives there as well as the Narragansetts responsible because the Massachusetts leaders believed that the Block Islanders paid tribute to the Narragansetts. The Narragansett sachem, Canonicus, agreed to return both property and captives taken from Oldham's vessel, but to deflect

English anger, he claimed that Oldham's murderers had fled to the Pequots. Subsequently signing a peace treaty with Massachusetts, Canonicus agreed to help avenge the murders.

The Narragansetts' claims, Uncas's efforts to discredit his rivals, Puritan preconceptions about Native Americans, and the murders of Stone and Oldham all combined to produce a violent response. In August 1636 Massachusetts dispatched a force of some 90 volunteers, led by captains John Endicott and John Underhill, to punish the Block Islanders. Endicott and Underhill had orders to seize the island, kill the men, and take the women and children prisoner. As the colonial force moved ashore, it was immediately assaulted by warriors who had concealed themselves in the brush. Scattering the natives with a volley, the Massachusetts volunteers searched the island but failed to come to grips with the warriors, who had taken refuge in a swamp.

Following two days of pillaging and burning the villages they encountered, the English expedition set off for Pequot territory. There Endicott demanded the extradition of Oldham's murderers, payment of 1,000 fathoms of wampum, and hostages. Meanwhile, the Pequots quietly evacuated their women and children. Misunderstanding or refusing the English demands, the Pequots then refused to do battle. Again unable to bring the natives to decisive battle, the English turned on the Pequots' village, burning wigwams and corn. Having suffered no casualties itself, the expedition then returned to Massachusetts Bay.

The Pequots responded to this Massachusetts attack by raiding settler communities in the Connecticut River Valley. Fort Saybrook, at the mouth of the Connecticut River, came under intermittent siege for the better part of a year. Soon after the Endicott expedition, soldiers gathering corn outside of the fort in preparation for possible Pequot attacks were set upon, and the Pequots captured and subsequently tortured to death two men.

On February 22, 1637, Fort Saybrook itself came under attack. Lieutenant Lion Gardiner and nine men were clearing a wooded area to provide better fields of fire when several hundred Pequots attacked, killing three of the soldiers. The Pequots also struck undefended settlements along the river. Most notable was the attack on Wethersfield, Connecticut, on April 23, 1637, in which nine English inhabitants died. The Pequots also captured two young women.

Fearing the English response, the Pequots attempted to enlist the support of neighboring native nations. The Mohegans under Uncas, enjoying their influence with the English, spurned overtures of alliance, while the timely intervention of Roger Williams, the banished Puritan minister, prevented the more powerful Narragansetts from siding with the Pequots.

The Pequots had been right to fear retribution. Both Massachusetts Bay and Connecticut approved raising troops for expeditions against the Pequots. Assuming command of the Connecticut forces, Captain John Mason led a force of 80 soldiers and 80 Mohegans under Uncas. The expedition stopped at Fort Saybrook before moving on to Pequot territory, where Gardiner

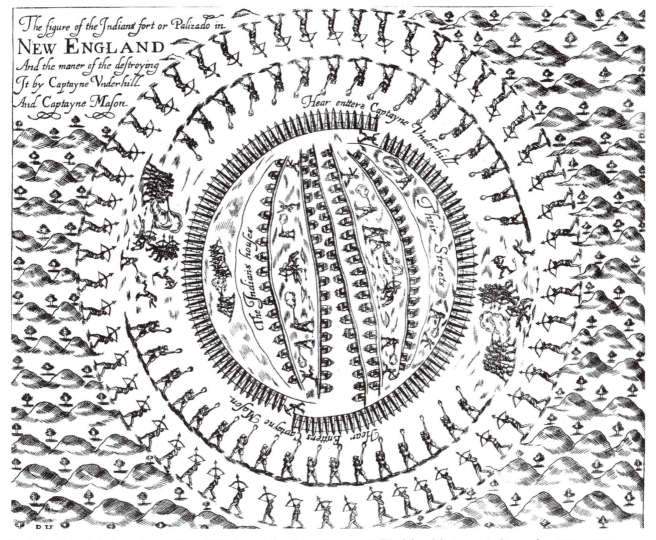

Depiction of a battle during the Pequot War in 1637. The English and their Narragansett allies defeated the Pequots in this war, from 1636 to 1638. Illustration from *Newes from America*, 1638. (Library of Congress)

questioned Uncas's loyalty. To prove their allegiance, the Mohegans killed four Pequots seen lurking in the fort's vicinity and captured another.

At this point Captain John Underhill and 20 Massachusetts militiamen joined Mason, replacing a number of wounded Connecticut soldiers. Mason then discussed with his officers the expedition's goals. The Connecticut General Court had ordered him to attack the Pequots at the mouth of the Pequot River (today the Thames River). Mason was certain that the Pequots, who were far more numerous than his own force, would be watching the river and would repel any frontal assault. He thus proposed sailing farther east and marching overland through Narragansett territory, flanking the Pequots. Several of Mason's officers opposed the plan, but after the expedition's chaplain averred that God was in agreement with it, the expedition proceeded.

Sailing past Pequot Harbor, Mason and his force arrived in Narragansett Bay. There Mason convinced the Narragansett sachems Miantonomo and Canonicus to support his efforts. They supplied both guides and warriors, most of whom deserted before the battle, however.

On May 25, 1637, Mason's force approached the smaller of two Pequot forts on the Mystic River. At daybreak on May 26 Mason moved in, positioning his men in a circle around Mystic village, with his Mohegan and Narragansett allies in a second outer ring. Detected by dogs, the Englishmen acted quickly, firing through the palisade and storming the village's two entrances. As the Pequots responded, Mason feared being overwhelmed and ordered a retreat. His men blocked the two gates and, with the aid of gunpowder, torched the wigwams. The two rings of soldiers and warriors prevented most Pequots from escaping. Of an estimated population of 400 to 700 Pequots, only 7 were captured alive, and a reported 7 escaped.

Despite this overwhelming victory, Mason was deep in hostile territory, and 20 of his own men were wounded. He was also perilously close to a larger Pequot village. Indeed, some 500 Pequots converged on Mason's men as they marched to a rendezvous with their boats, seven miles distant. Although the warriors harried the

English for most of this distance, frequent volleys of musket fire prevented them from overrunning the small English force.

The so-called Mystic Fort Fight largely broke Pequot resistance. Massachusetts forces led by Captain Israel Stoughton, assisted by Narragansetts, pursued the surviving Pequots during the summer of 1637. These forces ultimately captured more than 100 Pequot women and children and executed more than 20 warriors. The fighting effectively ended in July, when a large number of Pequots were surrounded in a swamp near present-day New Haven.

The Treaty of Hartford, signed on September 21, 1638, officially ended the Pequot War. With it the Pequots ceased to exist as an independent people. The Mohegans, the Narragansetts, and the Eastern Niantics absorbed the surviving Pequots in return for paying an annual tribute to the English. The destruction of the Pequots shifted the balance of power from New England's natives to the English. The war also demonstrated to the English that European methods of warfare could be successful in America, particularly encirclement and the use of Native American allies.

DAVID M. CORLETT

See also

Endicott Expedition; Hartford, Treaty of; Mason, John; Miantonomo; Mohegans; Mystic Fort Fight; Narragansetts; Pequots; Uncas; Underhill, John; Wampum

References

Cave, Alfred A. *The Pequot War.* Amherst: University of Massachusetts Press, 1996.

Chet, Guy. *Conquering the American Wilderness: The Triumph of European Warfare in the Colonial Northeast.* Amherst: University of Massachusetts Press, 2003.

Leach, Douglas Edward. *Arms for Empire: A Military History of the British Colonies in North America, 1607–1763.* New York: Macmillan, 1973.

Vaughan, Alden T. *New England Frontier: Puritans and Indians, 1620–1675.* 3rd ed. Norman: University of Oklahoma Press, 1995.

Peskeompskut Massacre

See Falls Fight

Petite Guerre, La

A French term from the 18th century literally meaning "little war," referring to the small units and tactics used. Broadly speaking, *la petite guerre* refers to partisan or irregular warfare. Indeed, *la petite guerre* is essentially the same as guerrilla warfare, which comes from Spain during the Peninsular War against Napoleon (1808–1814) and is the diminutive of *guerra* ("war"). *La petite guerre* may well have originated in the small-scale raids against isolated troops, food supplies, crops, and civilians that characterized this mode of warfare. Native Americans frequently employed tactics of *la petite guerre.*

In Europe, nations typically fought wars against each other using professional armies. The devastation wrought by the Thirty Years' War (1618–1648) across large swaths of continental Europe convinced many leaders that destructiveness should be limited; warfare would thus follow strict codes of conduct and pursue clear and limited objectives. War would be conducted by armies against armies, with clear rules dictating legitimate targets and actions. For most Europeans, *la petite guerre* was a distasteful ancillary to more organized campaigning. Often, skirmishers and scouts along the fringes of armies on the move would pursue the objectives of *la petite guerre,* from harassing enemy supply trains to disrupting communications. These operations ultimately served as a support for the main operations of the army. By the mid-18th century, most European nations had developed military doctrines that included the limited use of *la petite guerre.* In other words, while Europeans held an ideal of organized, orderly war, they also developed the doctrine of *la petite guerre* to respond to the messy day-to-day realities of conflict.

The strategic and tactical situation in North America also encouraged the practice of *la petite guerre,* although both the French and British employed regular troops in their respective colonies. The vast spaces of North America, the raiding tactics of the Native Americans, and the lack of large field armies often prevented the employment of regular army units. Indeed, historian John Grenier has argued that *la petite guerre* found its fullest application in North America and that the Americans developed it to its most extreme form: wanton and indiscriminate attacks upon Native Americans that failed to acknowledge the difference between combatant and civilian. In the end, Americans found *la petite guerre* the most effective method to employ against Native Americans. The Americans drew upon already established doctrine and the European practice of small war; they did not simply adopt the war fighting practices of the Native Americans.

In colonial North America, two types of units exemplified the demands of the small war. In New France, the colonial troops of the Department of the Marine were organized to operate independently and to adjust their tactics accordingly. These troops participated alongside Native American allies in the raid against Deerfield, Massachusetts, in 1704. The British replied with ranger units, the most famed of which was the command of Major Robert Rogers during the French and Indian War (1754–1763).

PETER C. LUEBKE

See also

Deerfield, Massachusetts, Attack on; France; French and Indian War; Native American Warfare; Rogers, Robert

References

Grenier, John. *The First Way of War: American War Making on the Frontier.* Cambridge: Cambridge University Press, 2005.

Haefeli, Evan, and Kevin Sweeney. *Captors and Captives: The 1704 French and Indian Raid on Deerfield.* Amherst: University of Massachusetts Press, 2003.

Petroglyphs

Engravings made by cutting into the surface of rock using bone, antler, or hard stone chips. Petroglyphs depict spirits, victories, and an association between martial might and supernatural forces. Although such images can be found across the globe, the most notable sites are found in Europe, in Australia, and throughout the Americas. Petroglyphs throughout North America were crafted by Native Americans primarily during the last 5,000 years but may date from as early as the end of the Ice Age (ca. 10,000 BCE) to the early 1900s.

Rock art was characteristic of the native cultures found in every corner of North America. Usually these sites are located on vertical rock faces near water. These areas were and in some traditions still are considered sacred spaces that facilitate communication with the spirit world or actualization of spiritual power. A variety of methods were used to create petroglyphs including incising, pecking, and abrading. To create incised petroglyphs, Native American shamans or warriors used the bone, antler, or stone tools to cut deep grooves into the rock. Pecked or chiseled petroglyphs were made by striking an area repeatedly with a harder tool to produce a shallow indentation that could then be enlarged into a form. The least common method of creation was abrasion, in which a rough cliff wall would be smoothed and flattened by the rubbing of a harder rock to create forms and designs.

Petroglyphs depict anthropomorphic and zoomorphic figures as well as a diverse spectrum in between representing creatures and structures found in either natural or supernatural landscapes. Rock art images also occur in nonrepresentational forms such as abstract, geometric, or amorphous shapes including spirals, mazes, geometric designs, and vertical marks. Individual representational traditions varied by region and era from highly naturalistic to extremely abstract.

Rock images appear in both iconic and narrative modes. Iconic images are static, detailed depictions that represent mythological beings and sacred forces. Narrative images are active and integrative scenes that depict mythological and historical events. While some of these carvings are strictly associated with supernatural powers and mythological tales, many have more mundane associations as well. Petroglyphs celebrating a warrior's exploits appear in a vast corpus of rock art across North America, particularly in the northwestern Plains. Rock art war records were often inscribed at sacred locations, which reinforced the relationship of war honors to spiritual powers. These public records of an individual's or group's deeds of honor served to commemorate exemplary

Fremont Indian petroglyph in Nine Mile Canyon (near Price, Utah) featuring hunters with bows and arrows, a horned shamanic figure, and a shield figure among bighorn sheep. Interpretations of the panel have been centered around bringing good luck to the hunt or describing a particularly plentiful hunt. (iStockPhoto.com)

members of society, encourage children to emulate these heroes' virtues, and reaffirm the notion of community.

During the Indian Wars, the heightened significance of war honors and counting coup was reflected in the shift in the narrative mode of rock art away from visions and symbols of power to recording biographical and historical events. This shift to narrations of victories and tallies of war trophies indicates a changing status system and the belief in a close correlation between success in war and the presence of supernatural powers.

MICHAEL P. GUENO

See also
Counting Coup; Native American Warfare

References

Moore, Sabra. *Petroglyphs: Ancient Language, Sacred Art.* Santa Fe, NM: Clear Light Publishers, 1998.
Whitley, David S., ed. *Handbook of Rock Art Research.* Walnut Creek, CA: Alta Mira, 2001.

Pettaquamscutt Rock, Treaty of

Treaty signed by the Narragansetts and Massachusetts Bay colonists on July 15, 1675. The Treaty of Pettaquamscutt Rock is also known as the Narragansett Treaty of 1675. Although the treaty was designed to guarantee the neutrality of the Narragansetts during King Philip's War (1675–1676), it quickly unraveled.

The Narragansetts, who were for the most part situated in southern Rhode Island, were the most powerful Native American nation in New England. In July 1675 a body of heavily armed English colonists coerced them to sign the Treaty of Pettaquamscutt Rock. The English feared that the Narragansetts might join their neighbors in raids on English settlements. In order for them to prove their loyalty, the English demanded that the Narragansetts surrender any Wampanoag warriors captured on Narragansett land. Furthermore, the English demanded four hostages from the natives as a sign of good faith.

Differing concepts of the terms led to confusion, however. The Narragansetts assumed that the hostages would be released in exchange for Wampanoag captives. Such was not the case. Colonists and the Narragansetts also interpreted the term "neutrality" in different ways. Thus, when the Narragansetts did not closely confine Wampanoags and immediately transfer them to English control, the colonists decided that the Narragansetts were in violation of the treaty. They then proceeded to launch a punitive expedition against a major Narragansett settlement. In the ensuing Great Swamp Fight (December 19, 1675), 600 or more Narragansett villagers were killed, and 300 others were taken prisoner. This unprovoked attack drove the Narragansetts into an alliance with Metacom's Wampanoags and was a major blow to the survival of the Narragansetts.

PAUL J. SPRINGER

See also
Great Swamp Fight; King Philip's War; Narragansetts; Wampanoags

References

Bourne, Russell. *The Red King's Rebellion: Racial Politics in New England, 1675–1678.* Oxford: Oxford University Press, 1990.
Drake, James D. *King Philip's War: Civil War in New England, 1675–1676.* Amherst: University of Massachusetts Press, 1999.
Leach, Douglas Edward. *Flintlock and Tomahawk: New England in King Philip's War.* East Orleans, MA: Parnassus Imprints, 1992.

Philip

See Metacom

Pickawillany Massacre
Event Date: June 21, 1752

Devastating French attack on a fortified British fur-trading post and Miami village on June 21, 1752. Some consider the assault to have been the first battle of the French and Indian War (1754–1763). The westernmost British commercial post in the early 1750s, Pickawillany was located on the Great Miami River in present-day western Ohio.

Piankeshaw Miami chief Memeskia (Old Briton) first settled his people at Pickawillany in 1748. The tribe had cooled in its loyalty to the French during the 1740s. The site eventually attracted some 50 British commercial agents including Pennsylvanian George Croghan, whose commercial ventures were so successful that the French put a price on his head. British traders engaged in a brisk business with the natives, primarily in beaver, deer, bear, fox, and raccoon pelts in return for manufactured products. By 1751 Pickawillany, then home to as many as 400 native families, threatened the French fur trade as well as their western military posts.

In 1749 French captain Celeron de Blainville had warned the native peoples at Pickawillany of the dangers of an alliance with the British traders. The residents failed to pay heed. The French threats did, however, lead Pickawillany's traders and natives to fortify the post with a log stockade by 1750.

Several years of confrontation in the region led to the French decision to send an expedition to destroy the settlement at Pickawillany in June 1752. French ensign Charles Michel Mouet de Langlade led a few dozen French militiamen from Detroit, along with some 200 allied Ottawa, Pottawatomi, and Ojibwa warriors under Chief Pontiac, in an expedition against Pickawillany. Langlade and Pontiac attacked the village early on the morning of June 21, when most of its defenders were away hunting. The attackers burned the village to the ground.

The French and their allied native forces then plundered and destroyed the site. Memeskia, 13 of his followers, and 1 British trader were killed. Allegedly Memeskia was ritually eaten after his death by his native enemies. Several British traders were taken captive and sent to Detroit.

The British could no longer claim the trans-Appalachian West by right of occupation. Their influence now waned among most Ohio native tribes, many of which chose to side with the French in the approaching French and Indian War. The fort at Pickawillany was never reoccupied.

JOHN R. MAASS

See also

Croghan, George; French and Indian War; Miamis; Native American Trade; Old Briton; Pontiac

References

Anderson, Fred. *Crucible of War: The Seven Years' War and the Fate of the Empire in British North America, 1754–1766.* New York: Vintage Books, 2001.

Baker-Crothers, Hayes. *Virginia and the French and Indian War.* Chicago: University of Chicago Press, 1928.

Hurt, R. Douglas. *The Ohio Frontier: Crucible of the Old Northwest, 1720–1830.* Bloomington: Indiana University Press, 1996.

Pima Revolts
Event Dates: 1695 and 1751

Violent uprisings by the Pimas in northern Sonora (Mexico and part of present-day Arizona) against Spanish rule. The growing volatility of Spanish relations with Indians on the northern frontier of New Spain resulted in revolts by the Upper Pima people in northern Sonora (Pimería Alta) in 1695 and 1751. Throughout the 17th century, Spanish missions and members of the Franciscan and Jesuit orders served as the principal vehicles for the extension of Spanish influence in the northern reaches of New Spain. Accordingly, in 1687 a Jesuit missionary, Father Eusebio Francisco Kino, arrived in Pimería Alta and established a mission at Dolores. However, the cultural diversity of the Upper Pimas complicated his efforts to broaden the mission system in northern Sonora.

The natives living in eastern Pimería Alta inhabited easily accessible small villages, or *rancherías,* and practiced subsistence agriculture. Their western kinsmen, however, led a more nomadic lifestyle. The attitude of most Spanish settlers in central Sonora, who resented the mission program's control of prospective land and labor, was also troubling for the priest. Nevertheless, Kino traveled extensively throughout Pimería Alta baptizing hundreds of natives, winning over converts to the mission program, and encountering little native opposition. By 1693 four missionaries were working in northern Sonora, and the mission system appeared to be functioning well.

Kino's system was shattered in 1695 when Pimas at the Tubutama mission fomented a revolt against the Spanish. Growing animosity stemming from injustices suffered at the hands of Spaniards and their Opata cohorts persuaded a faction of Pimas at Tubutama to kill their Opata overseer and 2 other Christian natives. The action sparked an uprising by other mission Pimas, resulting in the death of a young priest at Caborca. Spanish reprisals were swift and deadly. Kino's efforts to work out a peaceful resolution to the problem led to the slaughter of 50 Pimas by Spanish soldiers at El Tupo. Pima leaders had agreed to assemble there under the promise of immunity in order to turn in the guilty parties. However, much to Kino's horror, Spanish soldiers reneged on the deal and went on a rampage. These senseless deaths further inflamed Pimería Alta and led to the destruction of the missions at Tubutama, Caborca, San Ignacio, and Imuris.

Failing to find sizable bodies of Pimas to engage in battle, Spanish forces moved about the countryside killing indiscriminately and destroying Pima crops. Peace and stability returned to the region after Father Kino once again convinced Pima leaders to hand over those natives responsible for the murders of the Opata overseer at Tubutama and the priest at Caborca. Following Kino's successful negotiations, the Spanish military turned its attention to Apache raiders and ended the campaign against the Pimas. Peace now returned to Pimería Alta. Nevertheless, the revolts severely shook Kino's missionary program.

When Kino died in 1711, missionary activities in northern Sonora began to decline. Disenchanted Spaniards called for the removal of the Jesuits and the breakup of the mission system. Native lands appeared to be the most fruitful for farming and ranching but remained unavailable for Spanish settlement. Despite the colonizers' dissatisfaction with the mission system, revitalization of the Jesuit missions began in 1732. By 1750 nine missionaries were working among the Upper Pimas.

In 1751 a second Pima revolt led to a short-lived but more widespread uprising that succeeded in once again weakening the Jesuit presence in northern Sonora. Luís Oacpicagigua, an overly ambitious Pima from Saric, devised a plan to remove the Spanish from Pimería Alta. Beginning with the murders of 15 Spaniards he had invited to his home, Oacpicagigua and his followers killed more than 100 Spanish settlers, including the missionaries at Caborca and Sonoita. Although the revolt spread eastward and found collaborators across northern Sonora, it never garnered much support among the general Pima population. The movement began to wane with the arrival of Spanish forces under Captain Diego Ortiz Parillas, who proceeded to kill 40 Pimas in retribution. Oacpicagigua's revolt soon lost momentum and collapsed as its leader agreed to negotiations. He and other rebels were subsequently imprisoned.

Although neither Pima revolt enjoyed overwhelming collaboration among the Pimas of northern Sonora, they each effectively undermined the Jesuit presence in the region. The revolt of 1751 in particular left the mission system quite weak. Following Spain's expulsion of the Jesuits from all its territories in 1767, Franciscans attempted to continue missionary work among the Upper Pimas but with little success. The principal vehicles for the Spanish conquest of Pimería Alta withered during the remainder of the colonial era.

ALAN C. DOWNS

See also
Mexico

References
Shaw, Anna M. *A Pima Past*. Tucson: University of Arizona Press, 1994.
Spicer, Edward H. *Cycles of Conquest: The Impact of Spain, Mexico, and the United States on the Indians of the Southwest, 1533–1960*. Tucson: University of Arizona Press, 1962.

Pine Ridge Campaign
Start Date: 1890
End Date: 1891

Last major campaign of the Indian Wars, which ended with the Battle of Wounded Knee on December 29, 1890, and the surrender of the last hostile Sioux the following month. Despite having been deprived of their traditional lifestyles and forced onto reservations, many Native Americans remained defiant and resisted the U.S. government's attempts to assimilate them into white civilization. In this atmosphere of despair, many sought solace and hope in religious movements that promised deliverance from the reservations and a return to the lifestyles that they had enjoyed before the arrival of whites.

The late 19th century saw a number of such movements, which were similar to Tenskwatawa's religious revival in the Old Northwest at the beginning of the 19th century. The most important of these was the Ghost Dance message preached by Wovoka, a Paiute shaman in Nevada who attracted attention from many western tribes. Influenced by Christian teachings, Wovoka emphasized a strict moral code and promised a future world in which Native Americans would be reunited with the dead and would live a life free from sickness, death, and whites. By dancing the Ghost Dance, believers would be able to glimpse this future world.

Although Wovoka's message was peaceful and specifically warned against fighting, when the Ghost Dance was introduced to the Sioux by Short Bull and Kicking Bear, it morphed into a message of defiance and resistance that sought to hasten the arrival of the new millennium by eliminating whites. Short Bull and Kicking Bear preached that dancing the Ghost Dance and wearing ghost shirts would protect the Sioux against the white man's bullets.

By November 1890 the spread of the Ghost Dance among the Oglalas on the Pine Ridge Reservation and the Brulés on the Rosebud Reservation, where the Sioux defied agents' efforts to stop the dance, so alarmed Pine Ridge Indian agent Daniel F. Royer and nearby white settlers that they called for military intervention. On November 13 President Benjamin Harrison ordered the War Department to restore order on the reservations. By November 20,

600 soldiers from the 2nd and 8th Infantry regiments and the 9th Cavalry Regiment had occupied the Pine Ridge and Rosebud agencies, and Brigadier General John R. Brooke, commander of the Department of the Platte, moved his headquarters to Pine Ridge. The arrival of troops split the Sioux asunder, as friendly Sioux who feared war flocked to the agency headquarters while hostile Sioux moved to remote corners of the reservations, where they continued to dance. By early December the Brulé and Oglala hostiles had joined together in a village of 600 lodges on a high plateau between the Cheyenne and White rivers in the northwest corner of the Pine Ridge Reservation.

Meanwhile, Division of the Missouri commander Major General Nelson A. Miles moved to suppress the Ghost Dance movement at other Sioux reservations before it became as powerful as it had become on the Pine Ridge and Rosebud reservations. Toward that end, he ordered the arrest of Sitting Bull at the Standing Rock Reservation and Big Foot at the Cheyenne River Reservation. When Native American police arrested Sitting Bull on December 15, his Ghost Dance followers attempted to rescue him, resulting in a firefight that left six policemen and five Ghost Dancers, along with Sitting Bull, dead.

News of Sitting Bull's death produced great outrage among the Ghost Dancers, leading 38 Hunkpapa dancers to seek refuge with Chief Big Foot's Miniconjous. Ironically, Big Foot had by this time begun to lose faith in the Ghost Dance movement. More important, Oglala chiefs had invited him to the Pine Ridge Reservation to make peace among the different factions. On the night of December 23 Big Foot's village—a total of 350 people including the Hunkpapas who had fled after Sitting Bull's death—headed south toward the Pine Ridge Reservation.

Unaware of Big Foot's intentions and fearful that a concentration of Ghost Dancers on the Pine Ridge Reservation would spark a war, Miles, who had taken personal command of the campaign after relocating to Rapid City, ordered units of the 6th and 9th Cavalry regiments to prevent Big Foot from reaching the Ghost Dance village on the Pine Ridge Reservation, while Major Samuel M. Whitside led four troops of the 7th Cavalry Regiment to scout eastward from the Pine Ridge Agency. On December 28, 1890, Whitside confronted Big Foot's party and convinced Big Foot, who was now ill with pneumonia, to accept a military escort to the Pine Ridge Agency. During the night of December 28 as Big Foot's people camped with the soldiers along Wounded Knee Creek approximately 20 miles from the agency, Colonel James W. Forsyth arrived with the remainder of the 7th Cavalry and Light Battery E of the First Artillery. Ordered to arrest Big Foot, disarm his people, and march them to the railroad so they could be moved to Omaha, Forsyth recognized that force might be necessary to ensure compliance.

Consequently, when the Sioux awoke on the morning of December 29, they found themselves surrounded by 500 soldiers who were supported by four Hotchkiss cannon located on a nearby hilltop and pointed directly at the village. After assembling

Artist Frederic Remington's interpretation of the Oglala Sioux Ghost Dance at Pine Ridge Indian Reservation, South Dakota. Illustration in *Harper's Weekly* magazine December 6, 1890. (Library of Congress)

the 120 Sioux men and ordering the 230 women and children to begin packing for the march, Forsyth ordered the warriors to turn over their repeating rifles. When the warriors refused, Forsyth's soldiers began searching through the lodges and underneath the blankets of the men and women.

As the search continued, Yellow Bird, a medicine man, began performing the Ghost Dance and calling on the warriors to resist. It was at this point that a scuffle between a warrior and a soldier resulted in a rifle discharging. Soldiers and warriors instinctively opened fire on each other at close range. The artillery then opened fire with the Hotchkiss guns, sending exploding shells into the middle of the camp, hitting both soldiers and Native Americans, and a ravine where the Sioux had fled to find shelter. By the time the smoke cleared, 150 Sioux, including Big Foot, lay dead, and another 50 were wounded. At least 62 of the Sioux dead were women and children. Army casualties totaled 25 dead and 39 wounded, many from friendly fire. More significant, news of the tragedy at Wounded Knee galvanized the Ghost Dance movement on the Pine Ridge Agency, where Brooke was beginning to enjoy success in negotiating an end to the crisis. Indeed, Kicking Bear and Short Bull were in the process of leading the members of the Ghost Dance village back to the Pine Ridge Agency. Now they halted approximately 15 miles from the agency in a massive village along White Clay Creek. Other Sioux quickly joined them.

In the aftermath of the Battle of Wounded Knee, Miles moved to the Pine Ridge Agency and concentrated his forces against the Ghost Dance village on White Clay Creek. Although the village contained perhaps 1,000 warriors and 3,000 women and children, the Ghost Dancers had no real chance at resistance, as Miles surrounded the village with approximately 2,500 troops with another 2,000 in reserve. Seeking to avoid another Wounded Knee, Miles relied upon gentle pressure and negotiations to finally convince the Ghost Dancers to submit on January 15, 1891. With their surrender the Pine Ridge Campaign came to an end, but controversy over the campaign persisted. The large number of women and children killed at Wounded Knee led many eastern newspapers to condemn the action as a massacre, although it should be noted that this was no deliberate action, as had been the case at Sand Creek in 1864. Nevertheless, Miles relieved Forsyth of his command and ordered a military inquiry, which eventually cleared Forsyth and resulted in him being restored to command. In reality, the chief cause of the tragedy was the order to disarm Big Foot's people. Had they been allowed to continue on the march to the agency under military escort, the confrontation of December 29 would have been avoided. In any event, the Pine Ridge Campaign crushed the Ghost Dance movement and ended Indian resistance once and for all.

JUSTIN D. MURPHY

See also
Big Foot; Brulé Sioux; Forsyth, James William; Ghost Dance; Hunkpapa
    Sioux; Miles, Nelson Appleton; Oglala Sioux; Paiutes, Northern; Pine
    Ridge Reservation; Sand Creek Massacre; Sioux; Sitting Bull; Stand-
    ing Rock Reservation; Wounded Knee, Battle of; Wovoka

References
Brown, Dee. *Bury My Heart at Wounded Knee.* New York: Holt, Rinehart
    and Winston, 1970.
Coleman, William S. E. *Voices of Wounded Knee.* Lincoln: University of
    Nebraska Press, 2000.
Utley, Robert M. *Frontier Regulars: The United States and the American
    Indian, 1866–1891.* New York: Macmillan, 1973.
Utley, Robert M. *The Last Days of the Sioux Nation.* 2nd ed. New Haven,
    CT: Yale University Press, 2004.

Pine Ridge Reservation

Major Sioux reservation. Located on the Nebraska border in southwestern South Dakota just east of the Black Hills, the Pine Ridge Reservation is currently the eighth-largest Indian reservation in the United States and home to the Oglala Sioux. The reservation covers 3,468.86 square miles, more than the area of the states of Delaware and Rhode Island combined. Originally part of the Great Sioux Reservation established by the Fort Laramie Treaty of 1868, Pine Ridge emerged first as an agency in 1878 and then as a separate reservation 11 years later when the U.S. government dismembered the Great Sioux Reservation in favor of five smaller entities.

Undoubtedly, many Oglala inhabitants of the expanse that would become the Pine Ridge Reservation participated with chiefs Red Cloud and Crazy Horse during their operations against the U.S. Army in the 1860s and 1870s, including the Great Sioux War of 1876–1877. Pine Ridge is best known as the location of the Battle of Wounded Knee, which occurred on December 29, 1890.

The passage of the 1887 Dawes Severalty Act not only paved the way for the division of the Great Sioux Reservation, but its emphasis on farming and individual land ownership also undermined Oglala cultural principles and practices at Pine Ridge. The prevalence of hunger stemming from poor agricultural productivity and inadequate government rations combined with the ever-increasing presence of white bureaucrats, missionaries, and homesteaders in and around the reservation served only to heighten Oglala anxieties about the future and yearnings for the past.

Within a year of the creation of the Pine Ridge Reservation, its residents were in a crisis and ripe for the cultural revitalization proffered by the Ghost Dance movement. When the U.S. government attempted to suppress the apparent growing popularity of the Ghost Dance, the reservation's expanse and geology fostered the movement's longevity. Ghost Dance camps appeared in remote areas away from the agency and in the seemingly inhospitable gullies and ravines found in the arid Badlands. It was in these Ghost Dance camps on Pine Ridge that the Miniconjou chief Big Foot hoped to find protection for his followers when he was apprehended by troops from the 7th Cavalry. The resulting catastrophe at Wounded Knee Creek signaled the end of the brief but tragic role that Pine Ridge Reservation played in America's Indian conflicts.

The federal government built schools like the Pine Ridge Indian Boarding School, seen here, to "civilize" Native American children and to assimilate them to white American ways. The Civilization Fund Act of 1819 provided money for the establishment of these schools. (Library of Congress)

Conditions at Pine Ridge have remained difficult, and it is the poorest reservation (according to income) of all the existing U.S. reservations. The U.S. Army—in the guise of the National Guard—returned again to the reservation in 1973 to participate in the 71-day siege of Wounded Knee. A recent census placed the Pine Ridge Reservation population at 27,787 people.

ALAN C. DOWNS

See also

Big Foot; Dawes Severalty Act; Fort Laramie, Treaty of (1868); Ghost Dance; Great Sioux Reservation; Great Sioux War; Oglala Sioux; Red Cloud; Red Cloud's War; Sioux; Wounded Knee, Battle of

References

Starita, Joe. *The Dull Knifes of Pine Ridge: A Lakota Odyssey.* Lincoln, NE: Bison Books, 2002.

Utley, Robert M. *The Last Days of the Sioux Nation.* 2nd ed. New Haven, CT: Yale University Press, 2004.

Pine Tree Hill, Treaty of

Land cession agreement negotiated between the Catawba Nation and British settlers in North and South Carolina in July 1760. Before European migration to North America, the Catawbas laid claim to roughly 55,000 square miles of territory. Their land claims stretched from south-central Virginia in the north through central North Carolina east of the Appalachian Mountains and much of South Carolina to the Savannah River. These claims remained relatively secure until the founding of Charles Town (present-day Charleston) in 1670 on the southern coast of South Carolina. From that point on the Catawbas were under constant pressure from English settlers. The situation grew worse with the settling of North Carolina from the early to mid-18th century.

By 1760 the leaders of both North and South Carolina were eager to negotiate a land cession from the Catawbas. Unfortunately, the text of the important treaty, signed sometime in July 1760 by the Catawbas and representatives of the two Carolinas, has been lost. Extensive research on both sides of the Atlantic by historians as well as Catawba tribal attorneys has failed to discover it. Some facts are known about the accord, however. In 1760 the Catawbas, led by King Haigler, agreed to the cession. In it the Catawba people agreed to cede most of their land claims in both Carolinas, reserving only a tract of some 2 million acres. In return for signing the treaty, King Haigler received a gold gorget, and his queen was presented with a silver plate.

Samuel Wyly began to survey these lands immediately after the treaty was signed, but he did not complete the work. Soon North Carolina leaders began to complain that the Catawbas had retained too much land. Complicating matters, King Haigler was killed, allegedly by Shawnee warriors. In 1763 when Catawba representatives traveled to Augusta, Georgia, to attend a conference, they found themselves unable to resist further settler encroachment and felt compelled to agree to the Treaty of Augusta. After

1763 the Catawbas were limited to a reservation of 15 square miles located along the North Carolina–South Carolina border, adjacent to the Catawba River.

THOMAS JOHN BLUMER

See also

Augusta, Congress of; Catawbas; Haigler

References

Brown, Douglas S. *The Catawba Indians: The People of the River.* Columbia: University of South Carolina Press, 1966.

Merrell, James H. *The Indians' New World: Catawbas and Their Neighbors from European Contact through the Era of Removal.* Chapel Hill: University of North Carolina Press, 1989.

Piqua, Battle of
Event Date: August 8, 1782

Military engagement between members of the Kentucky County (Virginia) Militia and the Shawnees on August 8, 1782. The Battle of Piqua was fought at Piqua, near present-day Springfield in southwestern Ohio. The engagement was part of a larger western campaign during the American Revolutionary War (1775–1783) that saw sporadic fighting west of the Appalachian Mountains in what would become the Old Northwest Territory. Much of the fighting involved Native Americans, many of whom were allied with the British.

In early August 1782 Brigadier General George Rogers Clark with some 1,050 militiamen, including Daniel Boone, launched a raid across the Ohio River from a location near present-day Cincinnati against five Shawnee villages in present-day northern Kentucky; all were destroyed. Clark also ordered a British trading post burned in what would become Shelby County, Ohio. After the raids the Shawnees retreated to gather their forces for a retaliatory blow. Meanwhile, Clark divided his force into three bodies. One moved toward the Mad River and took up positions along its bank to prevent the Shawnees from escaping east. Another forded the river, with artillery in tow, to take up a position in the center, while a third would engage the Shawnee left flank, which would come under heavy fire.

On August 8 the Shawnees struck Clark's force about seven miles from present-day Springfield, Ohio. The battle lasted only a few hours but proved costly for both sides. It was nevertheless considered a Patriot victory, as the Shawnees were prevented from moving farther north, and for a time their raids became less frequent. Shawnee losses are unknown, but Clark's men suffered 20 killed and 40 wounded. Another 9 militiamen died during the preceding raid on the Shawnee villages.

Although the campaign against the Shawnees and the Battle of Piqua clearly discouraged Native American raids in Kentucky and the Ohio Country in general, in the long term they heightened the animosity between Native Americans and white settlers in the

Shawnee elders bear gifts to seated U.S. Army colonel George Rogers Clark following his victory in the Battle of Piqua (Pickawe) in Ohio in 1782. A 1923 photograph of the mural by Arthur Thomas. (Library of Congress)

Old Northwest Territory. Also of note, the Battle of Piqua was the only battle of the Revolutionary War fought within the confines of present-day Ohio.

PAUL G. PIERPAOLI JR.

See also
Boone, Daniel; Clark, George Rogers; Native Americans and the American Revolutionary War; Shawnees

References
Harrison, Lowell Hayes. *George Rogers Clark and the War in the West.* Lexington: University Press of Kentucky, 1976.

Hurt, R. Douglas. *The Ohio Frontier: Crucible of the Old Northwest, 1720–1830.* Bloomington: Indiana University Press, 1996.

Juday, Richard Roland. *The Battle of Piqua: Revolutionary Encounter in Ohio.* Dayton, OH: Grove-Merrit Publications, 1976.

Piscataway, Siege of
Start Date: September 1675
End Date: October 1675

Military engagement during the Susquehannock War that ultimately contributed to Bacon's Rebellion. The establishment of European colonies in the 17th century had exacerbated traditional rivalries between Native American tribes, resulting in the Beaver Wars (1641–1701) in which the Iroquois Confederacy sought to establish control over the lucrative fur trade. Armed by the Dutch, the Iroquois first fought French-allied tribes to their north in the Saint Lawrence River Valley and to their west in the Great Lakes region before attacking the Susquehannocks to their south in the region of the Delaware Bay and the upper Chesapeake Bay. By 1652 the hard-pressed Susquehannocks, who had originally resisted the English in Maryland and Virginia, allied with the two colonies in order to obtain the arms needed to defend themselves against the Iroquois. Consequently, the Susquehannocks provided a military buffer that protected English colonists in Virginia and Maryland.

Although the English conquest of New Netherland in 1664 during the Second Anglo-Dutch War (1665–1667) eased tensions considerably, in August 1673 the Dutch temporarily regained control of New York during the Third Anglo-Dutch War (1672–1674), part of the greater Dutch War (1672–1678), also known as the Franco-Dutch War, in Europe. Fearing that the return of the Dutch would lead to renewed conflict with the Iroquois, Maryland governor Charles Calvert invited the Susquehannocks—some sources indicate that he gave them an ultimatum—to move from Delaware Bay and settle at Piscataway Fort, an abandoned site located on the falls of the Potomac River, in order to minimize the potential for conflict between the Iroquois and Susquehannocks. More important, the removal of the Susquehannocks would advance Calvert's efforts to negotiate a permanent peace with the Iroquois. In February 1674, however, the Dutch returned New Netherland to the English in the Treaty of Westminster in exchange for England abandoning its alliance with France.

Although the conditions that had contributed to Calvert's invitation (ultimatum) were made moot by the end of the Third Anglo-Dutch War, in February 1675 the Susquehannocks abandoned Delaware Bay and arrived in Maryland, where they settled at Piscataway Fort. Shortly thereafter in July 1675, members of the Doeg tribe from Maryland seized hogs belonging to Virginia planter Thomas Mayhew, who they claimed owed them for previous trade items. When Mayhew's servants pursued and attacked the Doegs, the Doegs retaliated by killing Mayhew's overseer. This led to a series of Doeg raids to which Virginian frontiersmen responded with counterraids in which they indiscriminately attacked any Native Americans they encountered, including the newly arrived and ostensibly allied Susquehannocks.

Angered by the unprovoked attacks against them, the Susquehannocks launched attacks against colonial farms in the Piedmont region of Virginia and Maryland. In retaliation, 750 Virginia militia under Colonel John Washington (the great-grandfather of George Washington) and 250 Maryland militia under Captain John Truman placed Piscataway Fort under siege in September 1675. When

Truman, possibly with Washington's concurrence, ordered the murder of 5 Susquehannock chiefs who had come to a parley under a flag of truce, the Susquehannocks held out for six weeks before escaping during the night in mid-October and then launched a series of raids that claimed the lives of some 50 colonists.

In response to the Susquehannock raids that followed the siege of Piscataway Fort, Virginia governor William Berkeley blamed Truman for provoking the Susquehannocks and demanded that he be punished in hopes of bringing the raids to an end. Although the Maryland Assembly tried and convicted Truman, the only punishment inflicted was a required security bond. More important, frontier outrage at Berkeley's reluctance to wage a vigorous war, which stood in sharp contrast to the bruising campaign that New England colonies were waging against Metacom in King Philip's War (1675–1676), served as a catalyst for Bacon's Rebellion in 1676. Although Bacon's Rebellion collapsed after Nathaniel Bacon's untimely death from disease in October 1676, Bacon and his followers inflicted much damage on the Susquehannocks as well as other tribes in Virginia. By the early 1680s the Susquehannocks had fled Virginia and Maryland, with part of the tribe merging with the Senecas in New York and the remainder settling in Pennsylvania, where they became known as the Conestogas.

JUSTIN D. MURPHY

See also

Bacon's Rebellion; Beaver Wars; Susquehannocks; Susquehannock War

References

Hatfield, April Lee. *Atlantic Virginia: Intercolonial Relations in the Seventeenth Century.* Philadelphia: University of Pennsylvania Press, 2004.

Jennings, Francis. "Glory, Death, and Transfiguration: The Susquehannock Indians in the Seventeenth Century." *Proceedings of the American Philosophical Society* 112 (February 1968): 15–53.

Pistols

Pistols are small handheld firearms used primarily for short-range targets. They have long been a favored weapon for cavalry and other mounted troops. The effective range of bullets from pistols was generally shorter than that for rifles or carbines; however, pistols were more portable. The pistol had the shortest barrel of a personal firearm, no shoulder stock, and could be fired effectively with one hand. Pistols could be single-shot weapons; however, by the 1840s they were generally multishot weapons.

Pistols have been utilized throughout the entire period of firearm use. In the early 18th century, pistols, like most muskets and rifles, were generally single-shot muzzle-loaded weapons fired using a flintlock system of ignition. The development of the percussion firing system ushered in one of the most significant eras of pistol advancements. This system allowed the powder and bullet to be loaded directly into the chamber and a separate igniter to be placed in a convenient location. This greatly improved the

flexibility and reliability of the pistol. The next and arguably the greatest advancement in pistol technology was the development of the revolving chamber firing system. In this type of system, several chambers, usually a half dozen, were arranged around an axis. The charges were loaded into the chambers and the (movable) chamber system closed to align one chamber with the barrel. After each round was fired, the mechanism turned to bring the next chamber in line with the barrel, ready to be fired.

In early models, the rotation was accomplished by pulling the hammer to the rear with the thumb, cocking the weapon. A later system allowed this to be done as part of the firing sequence. This allowed the user to fire five, six, or even more shots in very short order. The two systems, percussion firing and revolving multichambered cylinder, could be easily incorporated into a single weapon. The multiple chamber cylinder was usually pivoted out of the frame to ease loading. The firing caps were individually placed on the cylinder to the rear of each chamber on most models.

Samuel Colt is often credited with inventing the revolver, even though the concept was centuries old. He did, however, patent his revolver in 1835 and led the continuing development of revolvers for the next several decades. Colt's 1851 Navy and 1861 Army revolvers are excellent examples of pistols from this era.

The next significant advancement in pistol technology followed the development of self-contained metal cartridges. These cartridges had the powder, bullet, and igniter all contained in a single rigid metal container. The use of these cartridges greatly increased the reliability and speed of reloading the pistol. There were several manufacturers of the revolver in the United States and Europe; however, Colt continued to be the primary company in both development and manufacture of pistols in the late 19th century.

Colt's Army Model 1873 (Peacemaker) was perhaps the most famous pistol of all time. Adopted by the U.S. Army as the standard side arm, it saw significant use in the final stages of the Indian Wars. This was a solid-frame revolver whose cylinder was loaded from a gate in the rear. There were a number of variants in revolver design; the two most significant were the rigid frame and the hinged frame. The cylinder in a solid frame revolver could pivot out of line, with frame, to load the cartridges, or alternatively, a loading gate was provided to the rear. In hinged-frame models, the frame itself pivoted on a pin to expose the chambers for loading. There were few other modifications of pistol design during this period; however, multiple-barrel models were not uncommon. In this type of pistol, the barrels themselves were mounted on a cylinder and revolved into firing position.

The pistol was the most flexible and useful of the personal firearms in use during the various Indian Wars. This was particularly true of the revolver with self-contained metal cartridges. Pistols were usually issued to officers in the military as well as mounted troops, as the weapons were small and portable as well as easy to reload. The pistol was easy to conceal and therefore had been a traditional personal weapon for nonmilitary persons from the beginning. Pistols also enjoyed popularity as dueling weapons during the latter part of the 18th century and the early 19th century. The revolver remains the symbolic weapon of the West of the mid to late 19th century. Accordingly, Colt's Peacemaker is often referred to as "the gun that won the West."

LAWRENCE E. SWESEY

See also

Carbines; Colt, Samuel; Colt Revolver; Muskets; Rifles

References

Bilby, Joseph G. *A Revolution in Arms: A History of the First Repeating Rifles.* Yardley, PA: Westholme Publishing, 2006.

Bilby, Joseph G. *Small Arms at Gettysburg: Infantry and Cavalry Weapons in America's Greatest Battle.* Yardley, PA: Westholme, 2008.

Myatt, Frank. *Firearms: An Illustrated History of the Development of the World's Military Firearms during the 19th Century.* New York: Crescent Books, 1979.

Pizi

See Gall

Platte Bridge, Battle of
Start Date: July 25, 1865
End Date: July 26, 1865

An ambush devised by an alliance of the Cheyenne, Sioux, and Arapaho tribes against the 11th Ohio Cavalry Regiment stationed at Platte Bridge Station near present-day Casper, Wyoming, some 130 miles west of Fort Laramie. The tribes had formed the alliance in response to the Sand Creek Massacre of November 29, 1864, when Colorado militia under the command of Colonel John Chivington killed more than 200 Cheyennes and Arapahos along the banks of Sand Creek in Colorado.

In 1853 a fur trader named John Richard established a toll bridge over the North Platte River. This crossing became a pivotal point along the Oregon Trail, where immigrants began the passage over the Rocky Mountains. The strategic location of the crossing was not overlooked by the military commanders at Fort Laramie, who established the post of Platte Bridge in December 1857 to protect the supply line to Utah during the Mormon War.

The Battle of Platte Bridge at Platte Bridge Station (later Fort Caspar) during July 25–26, 1865, near present-day Casper, Wyoming. Watercolor by William Henry Jackson. (Denver Public Library, Western History Collection, William Henry Jackson, hand-colored by Clarence S. Jackson, WHJ-10621)

The station was no stranger to conflict. On July 25, 1863, a company of soldiers led by First Lieutenant Henry C. Bretney broke up a gathering of Native Americans, destroying their shelters and seizing 30 horses. Two years later the Native Americans were poised to strike back. The first move by the natives was to cut the telegraph lines below the bridge. This prompted the dispatch of a repair party that was ambushed, suffering one killed.

On July 25, 1865, a large number of Native Americans gathered conspicuously across from the bridge. A patrol dispatched to disperse the hostiles was recalled just before the warriors could cut off its retreat. The next day, Second Lieutenant Caspar Collins moved out with 20 troops to meet an incoming supply train, and he and his men were quickly surrounded. Collins ordered a series of charges in an attempt to break out. Although most of the cavalrymen made it back to the station, Collins and 4 soldiers were killed.

Meanwhile, the supply train, about five miles away, came under attack. The escort, led by Sergeant Amos Custard, circled the wagons, trying in vain to repel the onslaught. Troops from Platte Bridge Station attempted a rescue but could not penetrate the Native American defenses in front of the bridge. Custard and the supply train were soon overrun. The warriors then retreated north to the Powder River. The battle resulted in the deaths of 27 U.S. soldiers. Native American casualties were 60 dead and some 130 wounded.

The Battle of Platte Bridge, although considered a minor skirmish, demonstrated the animosity of the Plains tribes toward white encroachment and their refusal to honor the 1851 Fort Laramie Treaty in the wake of the Sand Creek Massacre.

WILLIAM WHYTE

See also

Arapahos; Cheyennes; Chivington, John; Fort Laramie; Fort Laramie, Treaty of (1851); Sand Creek Massacre; Sioux

References

McChristian, Douglas C. *Fort Laramie: Military Bastion of the High Plains.* Norman: University of Oklahoma Press, 2008.

McDermott, John D. *Frontier Crossroads: The History of Fort Caspar and the Upper Platte Crossing.* Casper, WY: City of Casper, 1997.

Vaughn, J. W. *The Battle of Platte Bridge.* Norman: University of Oklahoma Press, 1963.

Pocahontas
Birth Date: 1595 or 1596
Death Date: March 20, 1617

Daughter of the powerful Chief Powhatan and influential intermediary in the first years of the Virginia settlement. Born in 1595 or 1596 in present-day Virginia, Pocahontas has assumed many identities and spawned many controversies both in life and on death. The name "Pocahontas" is a nickname meaning "mischievous" or "playful one." Her public name was Amonute, and

Pocahontas (1596–1617), depicted here during her voyage to England, supposedly saved English captain John Smith from death by pleading with her father, Powhatan, on Smith's behalf. (Library of Congress)

her personal name was Matoaka. She was one of approximately 30 children of Powhatan, the paramount chief of the Algonquian-speaking peoples known as the Powhatans, who dominated the Tidewater region of Virginia.

In 1607 Pocahontas encountered Captain John Smith, the military head of the fledgling Jamestown settlement. Still only a girl, she allegedly saved Smith's life, which was about to be extinguished on her father's orders. The exact details of the occurrence are subject to much debate and interpretation, but conventional wisdom claims that she threw herself on top of Smith to protect him from the blow of a war club. From then on Pocahontas became well known to the English colonists.

Probably in 1610 or 1612 Pocahontas married a Powhatan named Kocoum. In 1613 Pocahontas was captured by Samuel Argall, who hoped to exchange her for English prisoners being held by the Powhatans. While in captivity Pocahontas learned English and was exposed to Christianity, and before her ordeal was over the following year she had converted and was baptized as "Rebecca." She also met John Rolfe while in captivity, and the two were married in 1614. The marriage temporarily suspended most of the hostilities between the natives and the English.

In 1616 Pocahontas accompanied her husband on a journey to England. Pocahontas was something of a phenomenon in London, and as such she and her husband were lavished with attention and hospitality. It is believed, although it cannot be positively substantiated, that Pocahontas had an audience with King James I, whom she found so humble that she did not believe she had met the king until after the visit.

In 1617 Rolfe, who was anxious to return to his plantation along the James River, decided to set sail for Virginia. But before the ship cleared the River Thames, Pocahontas became desperately ill. Taken ashore near Gravesend, she died there on March 20, 1617.

Records referring to Pocahontas are sparse and contradictory, which has led to many debates surrounding her life. The debates largely revolve around her rescue of Smith in 1607 as well as her role as European Americans' symbol of a "good Indian" because of her Christian conversion and subsequent marriage to Rolfe as well as her previous compassionate rescue and alleged love affair with Smith. The rescue and the meaning behind it are controversial because Smith failed to mention it until after Pocahontas had become very popular in England. Finally, the alleged love interest between Pocahontas and Smith seems to have been entirely constructed from a reencounter in 1616, when both met again in England. During this meeting Pocahontas reminded Smith of his obligations to her and the Powhatan people.

KARL S. HELE

See also
Jamestown; Powhatan; Powhatan Confederacy; Smith, John

References
Abrams, Ann Uhry. *The Pilgrims and Pocahontas: Rival Myths of American Origin.* Boulder, CO: Westview, 1999.

Allen, Paula Gunn. *Pocahontas: Medicine Woman, Spy, Entrepreneur, Diplomat.* San Francisco: Harper San Francisco, 2003.

Gleach, Frederic W. *Powhatan's World and Colonial Virginia.* Lincoln: University of Nebraska Press, 1997.

Rountree, Helen C. *Pocahontas, Powhatan, Opechancanough: Three Indian Lives Changed by Jamestown.* Charlottesville: University of Virginia Press, 2005.

Point Pleasant, Battle of
Event Date: October 10, 1774

The only major battle of Lord Dunmore's War of 1774. This war between the British colonists and Native Americans began in April 1774 when numbers of frontiersmen attacked native settlements in the Ohio River Valley. Subsequent retaliatory raids by the natives prompted Virginia governor John Murray, Fourth Earl of Dunmore, to send 2,000 men into the area. The desire of many in Virginia and Pennsylvania to expand colonial settlement beyond the boundary delineated by the Proclamation of 1763 had much to do with the war.

Two major militia columns—one headed by Dunmore and the other by Colonel Andrew Lewis—moved into Indian country. On July 12, 1774, Dunmore ordered Lewis to proceed from Camp Union (present-day Lewisburg, West Virginia) to the mouth of the Kanawha River, where Dunmore's army was to link up with Lewis from Fort Pitt. Lewis arrived at the rendezvous point with 1,100 men on October 6, 1774, and camped at Point Pleasant, a triangle of land at the confluence of the Kanawha and Ohio rivers and site of the present-day city of Point Pleasant, West Virginia. Dunmore changed his plans, however, ordering Lewis to join him in attacks on the Shawnee settlements along the Scioto River. Before Lewis could depart Point Pleasant, he came under a fierce Indian attack.

Shawnee scouts had located Lewis's force on October 6, and the warriors sought an immediate attack. Chief Cornstalk, an advocate of peace negotiations, insisted on a council to discuss the issue. When the council voted in favor of an attack, at dawn on October 10 Cornstalk led a force variously estimated at 300–1,000 Shawnee, Mingo, Delaware, Wyandot, and Ottawa warriors against the unsuspecting militiamen.

The battle was hard fought and lasted all day. Lewis sent some of his men around to outflank the attackers, who were finally driven off at nightfall. In the Battle of Point Pleasant (also known as the Battle of Kanawha), the militiamen sustained some 75 killed and 150 wounded, while the Shawnees and their allies are reported to have lost only 33 dead. Nonetheless, the battle is counted as a militia victory because the militiamen held the field and because Cornstalk now entered into negotiations with Lord Dunmore, securing peace on October 19, 1774, with the Shawnees surrendering all claims to lands south and east of the Ohio River. Eventually the other tribes also agreed, bringing the war to an end.

SPENCER C. TUCKER

See also
Cornstalk; Lord Dunmore's War; Murray, John, Fourth Earl of Dunmore; Proclamation of 1763; Shawnees

References
Brand, Irene. "Dunmore's War." *West Virginia History* 40 (Fall 1978): 28–46.

Dowd, Gregory Evans. *A Spirited Resistance: The North American Indian Struggle for Unity, 1745–1815.* Baltimore: Johns Hopkins University Press, 1992.

Downes, Randolph C. *Council Fires on the Upper Ohio: A Narrative of Indian Affairs in the Upper Ohio Valley until 1795.* Pittsburgh: University of Pittsburgh Press, 1940.

Holton, Woody. "The Ohio Indians and the Coming of the American Revolution in Virginia." *Journal of Southern History* 60 (August 1994): 453–478.

Sosin, Jack M. "The British Indian Department and Dunmore's War." *Virginia Magazine of History and Biography* 74 (1966): 34–50.

Thomas, William H. B., and Howard McKnight Wilson. "The Battle of Point Pleasant." *Virginia Calvacade* 24 (Winter 1975): 100–107.

Po-i-to
See Winnemucca

Pometacom

See Metacom

Ponce de León, Juan
Birth Date: 1460
Death Date: July 1521

Spanish soldier and explorer. Juan Ponce de León was born sometime in 1460 in San Sérvas de Campos, Spain, into a noble family of modest means. As a young man he became a soldier, and in the early 1490s he fought against the Moors in the southern part of Spain. In 1493 he set sail for the New World on Christopher Columbus's second voyage to the Americas. Ponce de León did not return to Spain with Columbus but instead stayed in the Caribbean and in 1502 settled on the island of Hispaniola. Ponce de León became the governor of Higuey Province on Hispaniola in 1504.

In 1508 Ponce de León, while purportedly searching for gold, began the conquest of the island now called Puerto Rico. He went on to serve as its governor beginning in 1509, in the process amassing a fortune from gold and land speculation. His brutal treatment of the natives in Puerto Rico resulted in his ouster in 1511. The Spanish Crown granted him the right to find, explore, and conquer the island of Bimini (in the Bahamas) in 1512.

On his voyage to locate Bimini and perhaps the fabled Fountain of Youth, Ponce de León happened upon Florida. He first sighted the Florida peninsula on March 27, 1513, naming it Pascua de Florida (Feast of Flowers) because of its discovery on Palm Sunday. By making several trips to Florida, Ponce de León eventually charted most of peninsular Florida by 1521. He also discovered the Gulf Stream, a warm current of water that passes through part of the Caribbean and parallels the southeastern coast of North America. Meanwhile, in 1514 he had returned to Spain for a brief visit during which the king appointed him a captain general.

Still believing that Florida was an island, Ponce de León left for Florida from Puerto Rico on February 20, 1521, determined to reach Bimini. His expedition of some 200 men instead landed on the western coast of Florida. Ponce de León hoped to establish a Spanish colony there, but the fledgling settlement soon fell under attack by hostile natives, and the Spaniards abandoned the site in short order. Wounded during one of the skirmishes, Ponce de León died soon after arriving in Havana, Cuba, in July 1521.

DIXIE RAY HAGGARD AND PAUL G. PIERPAOLI JR.

See also
Spain

References
Fuson, Robert H. *Juan Ponce de Leon and the Spanish Discovery of Puerto Rico and Florida.* Blacksburg, VA: McDonald and Woodward, 2000.
Stefoff, Rebecca. *Accidental Explorers: Surprises and Side Trips in the History of Discovery.* New York: Oxford University Press, 1992.

Pontiac
Birth Date: ca. 1720
Death Date: April 20, 1769

Ottawa leader who gave his name to Pontiac's Rebellion (also known as Pontiac's Conspiracy and Pontiac's War) in 1763. Little is known about the early life of Pontiac (also known as Obwandiyng). Most historians place his birth at around 1720, although dates range widely from 1703 to 1725. Many sources believe that his father was an Ottawa and his mother an Ojibwa. Pontiac's birthplace also is unknown but most likely was near present-day Detroit, Michigan, or Defiance, Ohio.

As a young man, Pontiac probably participated in the fighting between the French and the British. In 1745 he fought for the French in King George's War (1744–1748) and in 1755 probably participated, as an Ottawa war chief, in the ambush of British forces under Major General Edward Braddock advancing against Fort Duquesne during the French and Indian War (1754–1763). Colonial ranger officer Robert Rogers claimed to have met with Pontiac in 1760, although most historians now believe this to be apocryphal. In any case, Rogers's subsequent publication *Pontieach; or the Savages of America* (1765) began the process of mythologizing the native leader.

Pontiac rose to prominence following the British defeat of the French in North America during the French and Indian War. Major General Jeffrey Amherst, British commander in chief in North America, failed to understand the need to alleviate native fears and cultivate their friendship. Despite advice from British Indian agents George Croghan and Sir William Johnson, Amherst raised prices on Native American trade goods and curtailed the French practice of gift giving. Both actions angered the Native Americans.

At the same time, the Delaware prophet Neolin influenced many of the Northwest natives, including Pontiac. Neolin's call for nativist religion required a return to the old ways, including abandonment of many European conveniences and the ousting of Europeans from native territory.

In April 1763 Pontiac convened a meeting of the tribes of the Northwest near Detroit on the Ecorse River. He passionately restated Neolin's message to the assembled natives but insisted that the French were allies and should be left alone. Only the British were to be attacked.

The subsequent Pontiac's Rebellion was a series of coordinated attacks against British forts in the Great Lakes–Ohio Valley region. The centerpiece of native strategy was an attack in May 1763 led by Pontiac against Fort Detroit that, however, miscarried. Pontiac then initiated a siege of that post, the longest such sustained military operation in North American native history, that eventually failed. He then withdrew to the Illinois Country. It is by no means clear how much he was able to influence native operations. Probably he was more an inspiration for the uprising than its actual field commander.

Although the native attacks overwhelmed a number of garrisons, the British rushed reinforcements to the region. One by one

Ottawa chief Pontiac, shown here passing a pipe to British major Robert Rogers in 1760 during the French and Indian War. In 1763, Pontiac led a coalition of tribes in a revolt against British rule. (Library of Congress)

the tribes reached accommodation with the British. Pontiac himself made peace in August 1765.

In July 1766 Pontiac and other chiefs met with Johnson, the British superintendent of Indian affairs in the North, at Fort Ontario to negotiate a formal peace treaty. The British identified Pontiac as a chief, but the Ottawa likely did not have such a position at the time. Nonetheless, the British negotiated with him as if he held such authority as leader of a broad native coalition. Native American protocol, however, called for war chiefs to step down in favor of civil chiefs when negotiations took place. Despite custom, Pontiac sought to speak for all the natives of the Northwest, both assembled and absent. This action alienated him from many natives, including a number of Ottawas.

Pontiac's arrogance in treating with the British may have led to his death. Forced to quit his Ottawa village on the Maumee River in 1768, he returned to the Illinois Country and on April 20, 1769, in the village of Cahokia, across the Mississippi River from present-day St. Louis, Missouri, was stabbed in the back by a Peoria Native American. Pontiac was left to die in the open.

SARAH E. MILLER

See also

Braddock's Campaign; French and Indian War; Neolin; Ottawas; Pontiac's Rebellion

References

Cave, Alfred A. *The French and Indian War.* Westport, CT: Greenwood, 2004.

Dowd, Gregory Evans. *War under Heaven: Pontiac, the Indian Nations, and the British Empire.* Baltimore: Johns Hopkins University Press, 2002.

Nester, William R. *"Haughty Conquerers": Amherst and the Great Indian Uprising of 1763.* Westport, CT: Praeger, 2000.

Peckham, Howard H. *Pontiac and the Indian Uprising.* Princeton, NJ: Princeton University Press, 1947.

Pontiac's Rebellion
Event Date: 1763

Conflict between Native Americans and British troops and colonists that followed the French and Indian War (1754–1763). Pontiac's Rebellion, also known as Pontiac's War or Pontiac's

Uprising, was named for its principal leader, the Ottawa Indian Pontiac.

The conflict sprang from the defeat of the French. Most Native Americans had allied themselves with the French against the British in the contest between the two great colonial powers. Indeed, the alliance between the French and most natives had been both long-standing and warm as well as beneficial to both sides. Many Frenchmen lived among the natives and married native women. French policies toward the natives were also far more benign than were those of the British.

The reason for the benevolent attitude of the government of New France toward the natives is obvious. Vastly outnumbered by the British, the French desperately needed Native American support in times of war. That the arrangement worked may be seen in the fact that most Native Americans repeatedly fought on the French side in the wars against the British. It was therefore most disquieting to Native Americans of the Great Lakes and Ohio Valley region to have their long-standing friends depart and be replaced by their enemies. As early as 1761, the Senecas of New York had circulated a wampum belt among the natives of the region calling for the formation of a confederation to continue the armed struggle against the British. Although this Seneca appeal elicited little response, it nonetheless was indicative of the widespread native discontent.

Native American policy fell to Major General Jeffrey Amherst, the British commander in chief in North America. Amherst thought little of the natives and did not understand the need for policies that would allay their fears and win their friendship. Although George Croghan and Sir William Johnson, two men with wide knowledge of native affairs, sought to dissuade him, Amherst proceeded to raise the price of trade goods and end the long-standing French practice toward the natives of gift giving as part of diplomatic negotiations. These decisions outraged and deeply offended many native people and increased the natives' desire to resist the British. By the spring of 1763, natives from western New York to the Illinois River were prepared to go to war.

Two Native Americans had a decided influence on subsequent events. The first was the Delaware mystic Neolin, known as the Delaware Prophet. In part influenced by Christianity, Neolin preached a nativist religion that called on his people to reform their habits but also to break off relations with the Europeans and return to the ways of their forefathers. Neolin had an immense influence on the people of the Great Lakes.

The second individual was Pontiac. He too was deeply upset over the British victory and now decided that the time had come to oust the British from the region. Pontiac issued a call for a meeting, and in April 1763 the Great Lakes nations sent representatives to a place near Detroit on the Ecorse River.

For about a month the natives discussed the course of action to be followed. Pontiac added his impassioned oratory to the Prophet's teachings and assured the representatives that the time for action was at hand. For practical reasons, Pontiac assured his

listeners that the Delaware Prophet's teachings regarding Europeans did not include the French, who were to be left alone. It was the British and the few natives allied with them who were to be attacked and annihilated. After the native representatives had reached agreement to go to war, they returned to their villages to build support for the effort. Each native group was assigned certain military objectives to attain.

The British military presence in the Great Lakes area was concentrated at Fort Detroit and at Fort Pitt in the Ohio Valley. Another dozen smaller British posts were scattered throughout the region. Pontiac himself took responsibility for the reduction of Detroit, while in semicoordinated assaults warriors of various nations were to attack British forts all along the frontier.

On May 7 Pontiac and a large party of warriors entered Fort Detroit. He had arranged with the commander of the post, Major Henry Gladwin, to hold a ceremonial dance there, with the plan that once the dance had begun, the natives, who would carry concealed weapons, would fall upon the unsuspecting British. Either because he had been forewarned or because he was naturally skeptical, Gladwin forestalled the plan. His men were fully armed and prepared, leading Pontiac to call off the attack.

After he and his men had departed the fort, Pontiac found himself the object of heavy criticism from a number of his warriors and therefore allowed his followers to open hostilities by mounting attacks on those settlers who remained outside the fort. On May 10 Pontiac called for a parley with Gladwin, who refused. Captain Donald Campbell then offered to meet with Pontiac. Gladwin sought to dissuade him but allowed Campbell to depart. When the British captain reached the designated meeting place outside the fort, the natives immediately took him hostage. Pontiac then demanded that Gladwin surrender the fort. Gladwin refused, whereupon Pontiac initiated what would become the longest North American native siege of a fortified position.

While the siege of Detroit went forward without result, the natives were enjoying great success in their operations elsewhere. On May 16 warriors secured entrance to Fort Sandusky by pretending to call a council. They then killed or captured all the men at the fort, both soldiers and traders, and secured the trade goods there. At Fort Miami (near present-day Fort Wayne, Indiana) on May 27, the native mistress of fort commander Robert Holmes asked his assistance in bleeding her sick sister. As Holmes exited the fort, he was killed. A second soldier responded to the gunfire and was captured. The remaining nine men of the garrison then surrendered to an overwhelming number of warriors.

To the north, on June 2 at Fort Michilimackinac, the largest of the forts taken by the natives, Ojibwas and Sauks staged a game of *bag'gat'iway,* similar to lacrosse, outside the fort. Native women and other spectators watched with guns and other weapons hidden under blankets. After several hours of play, the ball was launched into the fort. Securing weapons from the spectators, the players then entered the fort, supposedly to retrieve the ball, and seized the post in the last of the surprise attacks on British garrisons.

In a two-week span, eight forts had fallen to the natives. The British forts lost also included St. Joseph (Niles, Michigan), Ouiatenon (Lafayette, Indiana), Venango (Franklin, Pennsylvania), Le Boeuf (Waterford, Pennsylvania), and Presque Isle (Erie, Pennsylvania), all of which had been held by fewer than 30 men each. The British abandoned Fort Burd and Fort Edward Augustus. Fort Pitt, Fort Ligonier, and Fort Bedford were all attacked but held out, as did Fort Detroit.

On May 28 a British force of 96 men in 10 bateaux under Lieutenant Abraham Cuyler put in to Point Pelee on the western end of Lake Erie on their way from Niagara to Detroit with supplies. Not long after making camp, they came under surprise native attack. Cuyler and only a handful of his men managed to escape in 2 bateaux.

Attacks after mid-June 1763 confronted a now-alert British military. Various Native Americans, including but not limited to the Senecas, Mingos, Shawnees, Delawares, and Wyandots, assaulted the string of forts leading to Detroit and the roads that supplied it.

The key was Detroit, and victory there eluded the natives. At Detroit, Pontiac led a coalition of Ojibwas, Pottawatomis, Wyandots, and Ottawas in a loose siege. Although the natives could block access to the fort by land, they could not do so on the water. Two ships, the schooner *Huron* and the sloop *Michigan,* were able to reach Detroit and resupply it. Pontiac ordered fire rafts floated down the Detroit River into the anchored ships, but the latter were moved in time to avoid destruction. A native attempt to board the ships and take them by storm was discovered and beaten back. In November, a frustrated Pontiac ended the siege and withdrew his forces to the Maumee River.

The British were not idle, and soon reinforcements were on their way to the northwest. Able British colonel Henry Bouquet led 400 men from Fort Niagara to relieve Fort Pitt, which had been under considerable pressure since the beginning of the fighting. Its commander, Simeon Ecuyer, refused to yield to Delaware demands for surrender and reportedly sent smallpox-infected clothing among the natives that led to an epidemic.

About 30 miles from Fort Pitt, Bouquet's relief column came under heavy attack by a large force of Delawares, Wyandots, Mingos, and Shawnees. In the Battle of Bushy Run (August 5–6, 1763), Bouquet's men drove off the attackers and marched on to Fort Pitt, relieving it.

The Battle of Bushy Run proved to be the turning point in the struggle. Although sporadic warfare continued for another two years, isolated native groups began to conclude peace with the British. Pontiac himself eventually recognized the hopelessness of his position and made peace in August 1765. His dream of a final victory over the English would not be realized.

SARAH E. MILLER AND SPENCER C. TUCKER

See also

Amherst, Jeffrey; Bouquet, Henry; Bushy Run, Battle of; Delawares; Ecuyer, Simeon; French and Indian War; Johnson, Sir William; Neolin; Ottawas; Pontiac

References

Dowd, Gregory Evans. *War under Heaven: Pontiac, the Indian Nations, and the British Empire.* Baltimore: Johns Hopkins University Press, 2002.

Nester, William R. *"Haughty Conquerers": Amherst and the Great Indian Uprising of 1763.* Westport, CT: Praeger, 2000.

White, Richard. *The Middle Ground: Indians, Empires, and Republics in the Great Lakes Region, 1650–1815.* New York: Cambridge University Press, 1991.

Pontowattimies

See Pottawatomis

Pony Express

Mail service of express riders that regularly crossed the North American continent between St. Joseph, Missouri, and Sacramento, California, from April 1860 to October 1861. The average transit time was 10 days. In early 1860 William H. Russell and Alexander Majors of the freighting firm Russell, Majors, and Waddell conceived the idea of a mail service employing riders and horses to deliver mail faster and more reliably across the continent than via stagecoaches, hoping thereby to win the government mail contract. They acquired between 420 and 500 horses and established about 190 relay stations for the mail service. Each station was about 10 miles apart—roughly the maximum distance that a horse could travel at full gallop—along the approximately 2,000-mile route between Missouri and California. The owners charged $5.00 for each half-ounce letter and $3.50 for every 10-word telegram, which was quite expensive for the day.

The riders were paid $25 per week (the comparable wage for unskilled labor was about $1 per day for 12 hours of work). The rider, who could not weigh more than 125 pounds, rode at a full gallop for about 10 miles to the next station, where he changed to a fresh horse. A fresh rider replaced the incoming rider about every 75–100 miles. They rode day and night in all seasons and types of weather across the prairies, plains, mountains, and deserts of the western United States. In case of emergencies, a given rider rode two stages back to back (150–200 miles) for approximately 20 hours on a galloping horse.

Each rider carried a specially made pouch, which could carry 20 pounds of mail in four padlocked compartments, and a personal pouch of 20 pounds. Originally the rider's pouch included a water sack, a Bible, a horn for alerting the relay station master to prepare the next horse, a revolver, and a choice of a rifle or another revolver, but the owners removed everything except one revolver and the water sack to reduce weight. As a result, the rider had to depend on speed to outrun outlaws and hostile Native Americans. The employers stressed the importance of the pouch, often saying that it should get through even if the horse and rider did not.

Frank E. Webner, a Pony Express rider, circa 1861. In 1860, the Central Overland California and Pikes Peak Express Company created the Pony Express to carry mail from St. Joseph, Missouri, to Sacramento, California, in 10 days. (National Archives)

Pony Express riders rode westward and eastward from the route's two endpoints. The route roughly followed the Oregon Trail and the California Trail to Fort Bridger, Wyoming, and then the Mormon Trail to Salt Lake City, Utah. From there the Pony Express route roughly followed the Central Overland Route to Carson City, Nevada, and then passed over the Sierra Nevada Mountains to Sacramento, California. At any given time there were up to 80 riders in the saddle. During the 16 months of operation of the Pony Express, its riders traveled about 650,000 miles, with the loss of only one mail pouch.

On the first day of operations, April 3, 1860, the founders had scheduled riders to leave San Francisco and St. Joseph simultaneously. However, the messenger bringing the pouch from New York and Washington missed a connection in Detroit and arrived in Hannibal, Missouri, two hours late. The first pouch contained 49 letters, 5 private telegrams, and some papers for San Francisco and intermediate points. The westbound rider left St. Joseph around 7:15 p.m. and reached his destination, San Francisco, on April 14, at 1:00 a.m., a little more than 10 days later. The *Weekly West* of April 4, 1860, reported that the first rider was Johnson William Richardson. James Randall is credited as the first rider from the Alta Telegraph Company in San Francisco. William (Sam) Hamilton was the first rider to begin the journey from Sacramento.

The Pony Express proved that a central and northern mail route was viable. In the turbulent months of late 1860, a Pony Express rider carried the news to California of Abraham Lincoln's election as president of the United States in November 1860 and the secession of South Carolina from the Union in December. Unfortunately, Russell, Majors, and Waddell did not get the contract to deliver mail. Instead in March 1861 the contract went to Jeremy Dehut, who had taken over the southern congressionally favored Butterfield Overland Mail Stage Line. Ben Holladay, owner of the Central Overland Stage Line, then purchased the Pony Express stations for his stagecoaches, but the start of the American Civil War in April 1861 caused the stage line to go out of business.

From March to October 1861 the Pony Express only ran mail between Salt Lake City and Sacramento. The Pony Express grossed $90,000 but had losses of $200,000, forcing it to end operations on October 26, 1861, two days after the Transcontinental Telegraph reached Salt Lake City, Utah, and connected Omaha, Nebraska, and Sacramento, California. Soon other telegraph lines connected points along the line and other cities on the East Coast and the West Coast. The telegraph could send short messages much faster and cheaper than the Pony Express.

The Pony Express nevertheless demonstrated that a unified transcontinental system could be built and operated continuously year-round. Also, the Pony Express may have contributed, at least indirectly, to keeping California in the Union. In 1866 Holladay sold the Pony Express assets along with the remnants of his stage line to Wells Fargo for $1.5 million. Wells Fargo and subsequent owners continued to use the Pony Express logo.

ROBERT B. KANE

See also
Butterfield Overland Mail Route; Oregon Trail; Wells Fargo

References
Billington, Ray Allen. *The Far Western Frontier, 1830–1860.* New York: Harper and Brothers, 1956.
Corbett, Christopher. *Orphans Preferred: The Twisted Truth and Lasting Legacy of the Pony Express.* New York: Broadway Books, 2003.
Gardiner, Dorothy. *West of the River.* New York: Thomas Y. Crowell, 1941.
Moody, Ralph. *The Old Trails West.* New York: Thomas Y. Crowell, 1963.
Moody, Ralph. *Riders of the Pony Express.* 1958; reprint, Lincoln, NE: Bison Books, 2004.

Popé
Birth Date: Unknown
Death Date: 1688

Spiritual leader from San Juan Pueblo near present-day Santa Fe, New Mexico, and leader of one of the most effective Native American revolts in North American history. There are no detailed written or oral accounts about the birth or early life of Popé (also known as El Popé). He first appears in the historical record in the early 17th century, when Spanish colonists strove to gain control over the northern provinces of New Spain.

The repressive policies of the Spaniards toward the Pueblo peoples drove Popé onto the path of rebellion. Worst of all for Popé was the effort by Franciscan friars to eradicate Pueblo religious icons and ceremonies. In reaction to these moves, Popé began preaching the maintenance of traditional religious practices and railed against all things Spanish and Christian.

As Popé's message spread throughout the Pueblo settlements, in 1675 Governor Juan Francisco Treviño ordered the arrest of native spiritual leaders and medicine men in the province of New Mexico. Popé and 46 other medicine men were taken by force to the capital in Santa Fe and charged with witchcraft. Four of the prisoners were condemned to death, although 1 committed suicide before the sentence could be carried out. The remainder were whipped and imprisoned.

Owing to the loss of their spiritual leaders, the Rio Grande Pueblos threatened to revolt against the Spanish. This prompted a worried Treviño to release his captives. Later in 1675 Popé returned to San Juan Pueblo and then fled to Taos Pueblo after he had been implicated in the stoning death of his son-in-law and the governor of the pueblo, whom Popé suspected of spying for the Spanish. At Taos, Popé devised plans for a widespread revolt.

Popé successfully overcame obstacles created by distance and language barriers to unify at least 24 pueblos in a coordinated revolt against the Spanish in early August 1680. Using cords of maguey fibers, Popé devised a method for synchronizing the attack with knots symbolizing the number of days remaining before the commencement of the uprising. Runners carried the cords to the leaders of each pueblo, who then untied one knot per day until there were none remaining, the sign to strike.

The Pueblo Revolt began on August 10, 1680. Approximately 8,000 of Popé's followers killed nearly 400 Spanish colonists and 21 of the 33 Franciscan friars in the region. Those Spaniards who were not killed or wounded initially sought safety at the Governor's Palace in Santa Fe (and at the few pueblos that had not participated in the uprising) before fleeing southward toward El Paso del Norte and Mexico.

Following his successful revolt, Popé ordered the destruction of the remaining vestiges of Spanish culture, including objects associated with Christianity. He likewise banned the use of the Spanish language and surnames and annulled marriages consecrated by the Catholic Church. In their place, Popé insisted on a return to traditional cultural practices.

Exulting in his victory, Popé chose to remain in Santa Fe and reside in the former governor's palace. He soon became overbearing, demanding tribute payments from all the pueblos and punishing those that refused to comply. As Popé's authoritarianism increased, his support eroded, and the alliance collapsed as villages returned to their familiar practice of autonomy. When Popé died sometime in 1688, probably in Santa Fe, the stage was set for the Spanish to reconquer New Mexico.

ALAN C. DOWNS

See also

New Mexico; Pueblo Revolt; Pueblos

References

Josephy, Alvin M., Jr. *The Patriot Chiefs: A Chronicle of American Indian Resistance.* New York: Penguin, 1989.

Knaut, Andrew L. *The Pueblo Revolt of 1680: Conquest and Resistance in Seventeenth-Century New Mexico.* Norman: University of Oklahoma Press, 1995.

Pope, John
Birth Date: March 16, 1822
Death Date: September 23, 1892

U.S. Army officer. John Pope was born in Louisville, Kentucky, on March 16, 1822, but grew up in Kaskaskia, Illinois. He graduated from the U.S. Military Academy, West Point, in 1842 and then served as a topographical engineer. During the Mexican-American War (1846–1848) he distinguished himself in the Battle of Monterrey and the Battle of Buena Vista.

After the war Pope carried out surveys in Minnesota and the American Southwest. In 1856 he was promoted to captain. By the late 1850s Pope was known as an expert horseman and an intrepid soldier. He was also known for his impetuosity and caustic personality.

When the American Civil War (1861–1865) began, Pope was commissioned a brigadier general of volunteers for the Union Army in June 1861. He held various district and field commands until February 1862, when he was assigned to command the Army of the Mississippi as a major general of volunteers.

Pope's army captured two key Confederate positions on the Mississippi River: New Madrid, Missouri, in mid-March 1862 and, with the assistance of the navy, Island No. 10 and its 5,000 defenders in early April. These successes earned him promotion to brigadier general in the regular army and a summons to Washington, D.C., to command the new Army of Virginia.

Pope led his troops during the Second Battle of Bull Run (August 29–30, 1862) but was convincingly defeated there by General Robert E. Lee's Confederates. Pope was removed from command the following month and was assigned to head the Department of the Northwest, where the army had just defeated an uprising by the Santee Sioux in Minnesota. A military tribunal had sentenced 303 Santees to death for their participation in the fighting. Responsibility for reviewing the sentences and carrying out the executions now fell to Pope. Although he favored executing the condemned Santees, he referred the matter to President Abraham Lincoln, who reduced the number of death sentences to 39.

In 1863 and 1864 Pope supervised operations against other Sioux groups in the Dakotas. Impressed by Pope's leadership, Lieutenant General Ulysses Grant created the Division of Missouri in 1864 that extended his command westward to the Rocky Mountains. Pope considered all of the Plains tribes hostile, rejected the advice of civilian Indian agents to negotiate, and prepared to impose peace by force. Cheyenne, Arapaho, and Sioux attacks in retaliation for the Sand Creek Massacre (November 29, 1864) convinced him that his view was correct.

Pope thus organized the army's largest campaign to that date against the Plains tribes. He assigned several thousand troops to guard forts, roads, and settlements while an additional 6,000 troops undertook offensive operations. In the spring of 1865 Brigadier General Patrick Connor marched into the Powder River area with three columns of soldiers, Brigadier General Alfred Sully headed an expedition on the upper Missouri River, and Brevet Brigadier General James H. Ford moved against the Kiowas and Comanches south of the Arkansas River.

All three offensives failed. The large units moved slowly, enabling the Native Americans to easily evade them. Supplying the units also became a problem, and as provisions ran short, many soldiers simply deserted.

Pope's inability to defeat the Plains tribes and public horror at the Sand Creek Massacre gave rise to demands that the government make peace with the Plains tribes. Pope continued to favor military action and argued that civilian interference with the army was a major obstacle to defeating the hostile tribes. He therefore urged that the Bureau of Indian Affairs be placed under the control of the War Department. Although his views won widespread support among western settlers and with some politicians, Congress rejected the idea, opting instead to pursue a peace policy. Having alienated many influential officials, Pope was transferred to the South to supervise Reconstruction efforts.

In 1870 Pope returned to the Department of Missouri, one of three districts into which the large and unwieldy Division of Missouri had been divided. From his headquarters at Fort Leavenworth, Kansas, he closely supervised operations during the Red River War (1874–1875) against the southern Plains tribes, forcing the Comanches, Kiowas, and Southern Cheyennes to submit to government control. He also developed a more humanitarian attitude toward the Native Americans, advocating a policy of religious conversion and cultural assimilation, although he continued to favor giving the army full authority over Indian affairs.

Pope dispatched troops in the summer of 1879 to quell unrest on the Ute reservation in Colorado. The soldiers' arrival only worsened the crisis, and fighting broke out in late September. However, Pope rushed more army units to the scene, and their appearance quickly ended the conflict. Because his department included New Mexico, Pope was later involved in directing operations against the Apaches from 1881 to 1883, when he took command of the Division of the Pacific with the rank of major general (from 1882).

In 1886 Pope retired from the army. He died in Sandusky, Ohio, on September 23, 1892.

JIM PIECUCH

See also
Connor, Patrick Edward; Minnesota Sioux Uprising; Red River War; Sand Creek Massacre; Sully, Alfred; Ute War

References
Cozzens, Peter. *General John Pope: A Life for the Nation.* Champaign: University of Illinois Press, 2000.
Utley, Robert M. *Frontier Regulars: The United States and the American Indian, 1866–1891.* New York: Macmillan, 1973.

Pottawatomis

Native people of the northern Great Lakes region (present-day Michigan and Wisconsin). The Pottawatomis (also Potewatmis, Pedadumies, Pontowattimies, Potawatomis) belong to the Algonquian linguistic and cultural group, being closely related to the Ojibwas, Ottawas, and Algonquins. The name "Pottawatomi" is linguistically unanalyzable and roughly corresponds to the self-designation of *potewatmi.* Traditional interpretations of the name suggest that the name "Pottawatomi" means the "leading tribe," "chosen people," "people of the fire," or "fire keepers."

The Pottawatomis entered the written record around 1634 when the French explorer Jean Nicolet visited Green Bay (northern Wisconsin). Other French explorers and Catholic missionary priests noted that the Pottawatomis had a very strong sense of identity. Like other Great Lakes groups, the Pottawatomis practiced a complicated system of alliances and undertook warfare that involved guerrilla-style campaigns. They regularly engaged in trade throughout the Great Lakes region with other tribes and later with Europeans. The Pottawatomis practiced agriculture and also exploited seasonal variations in game, fishing, and plant life.

Oral tradition indicates that the Pottawatomis, along with the Ojibwas and Ottawas, migrated from the East to present-day Sault Ste. Marie as a single large group. There they split into three separate nations, with the Pottawatomis becoming the "keepers of the fire." This early unity can be seen by the Pottawatomis' key place within the Three Fires Confederacy, which was a political, military, and religious alliance in which they participated along with the Ojibwas and Ottawas.

In the early 1600s the Pottawatomis lived chiefly along the southeastern shores of Lake Michigan. Here they may have experienced raids from various Iroquoian groups such as the Five Nations (Iroquois Confederacy) and the Hurons. By the late 1660s the Pottawatomis began to relocate to the western shores of Lake Michigan along the Green Bay Peninsula. After the Great Peace of 1701, the Pottawatomis began once again to return to their eastern homelands. Eventually they occupied the lands east of the Mississippi River, west of the Detroit River, north of the Illinois River, and south of the Grand River.

As early as the 1640s the Jesuits had reported on raids conducted against the "Fire Nation" by the Hurons and the Ottawas, the Pottawatomis' erstwhile allies. Rivalry with the Ottawas over control of the fur trade at Green Bay required Médard Chouart des Groseilliers to mediate a peace in 1655. During the Beaver Wars (1641–1701), the Pottawatomis mustered warriors to counter

Group portrait of Pottawatomi men, women, and children in western dress, circa 1906. Photograph attributed to T. R. Hamilton. (Library of Congress)

invasions of their territory as well as to attack Iroquois settlements. They also fought alongside their Ojibwa allies against the Dakotas in the 1600s and 1700s. The Pottawatomis participated in the Fox Wars (1712–1737) and by the mid-1700s were raiding Chickasaw villages and British colonial settlements.

Following the defeat of France in the French and Indian War (1754–1763), the Pottawatomis sided with Great Britain in the American Revolutionary War (1775–1783) and the War of 1812. At the conclusion of both wars, many Pottawatomis, while acknowledging the dominance of the United States, nevertheless clung to their British ties. Groups of Pottawatomis regularly visited British military and Indian Department officials to receive presents in recognition of past military service and their alliance with Britain.

By 1867 the Pottawatomis had signed more than 50 treaties with the United States, beginning with the 1789 Treaty of Fort Harmar. The most significant treaties for the Pottawatomis were undertaken in the 1800s. The increasing influx of white settlers into southern Michigan and Wisconsin as well as northern Indiana and Illinois led to a series of removal treaties. This resulted in the establishment in 1867 of the Citizen's Band in Indian Territory (Oklahoma), with hundreds of Pottawatomis seeking refuge in Canada. Once in Canada, many of the Pottawatomis were classified as "wandering" Indians and through various policy measures

were forced either to merge with local Ojibwa or Ottawa bands or return to the United States.

Today there are three federally recognized bands of Pottawatomis in the United States, located in Oklahoma, Wisconsin, and Michigan. There are other groups that claim ancestry with the Pottawatomis in the United States, but they do not have federal recognition. In Canada there are many people who are descended from the refugee Pottawatomis, but there are no Canadian-recognized Pottawatomi bands.

KARL S. HELE

See also
Algonquins; Beaver Wars; Chickasaws; Fort Harmar, Treaty of; Fox Wars; French and Indian War; Iroquois Confederacy; Native Americans and the American Revolutionary War; Native Americans and the War of 1812; Ojibwas; Ottawas; Wyandots

References
Clifton, James A. *A Place of Refuge for All Time: Migration of the American Potawatomi into Upper Canada, 1830 to 1850.* Ottawa: National Museums of Canada, 1975.

Clifton, James A. "Potawatomi." In *People of the Three Fires: The Ottawa, Potawatomi, and Ojibway of Michigan,* edited by James A. Clifton, George L. Cornell, and James M. McClurken, 39–74. Grand Rapids: Michigan Indian Press, 1986.

Clifton, James A. *The Prairie People: Continuity and Change in Potawatomi Indian Culture, 1665–1965.* Lawrence: Regents Press of Kansas, 1977.

Edmunds, R. David. *The Potawatomis: Keepers of the Fire.* Norman: University of Oklahoma Press, 1978.

Powder River Expedition
Start Date: November 1876
End Date: December 1876

A U.S. military campaign that took place in the autumn of 1876 during the Great Sioux War (1876–1877) and essentially ended any further resistance from the Northern Cheyennes, who were allied with the Sioux. The successful Powder River Expedition was overshadowed by defeats earlier in the year, including Brigadier General George Crook's defeat at the Battle of the Rosebud (June 17, 1876) and Lieutenant Colonel George A. Custer's debacle at the Battle of the Little Bighorn (June 25–26, 1876).

The Great Sioux War had been a direct consequence of the discovery of gold in the Black Hills of South Dakota in July 1874, which attracted a large influx of white prospectors. The Black Hills was sacred Sioux territory and contained some of their best hunting grounds, so the Sioux were outraged at the escalating white encroachment. When the U.S. government decided not to stop whites from entering the region in violation of the 1868 Fort Laramie Treaty, the Sioux went to war and gathered many northern Plains tribes as allies. After a series of army blunders throughout the spring and summer of 1876, U.S. forces regrouped, were reinforced, and again took the offensive.

At Fort Fetterman in the Wyoming Territory, General Crook assembled a formidable force consisting of 11 cavalry troops, 15 infantry companies, 400 Native American scouts, and more than 300 civilians to man the supply train. His objective was to destroy the Lakota-Cheyenne coalition by capturing Crazy Horse, the audacious Lakota chief. Crook's force departed on November 14, 1876, and marched north up the Bozeman Trail toward Rosebud, Montana, the scene of Crook's defeat that prior June. A blizzard stalled the column for four days when word came that a large Cheyenne village of Chief Dull Knife (Morning Star) was nearby.

Crook ordered Colonel Ranald S. Mackenzie to take 10 troops of cavalry and the Indian scouts to seek out and destroy the village. The Cheyennes were encamped in a canyon along the Powder River. Mackenzie attacked at dawn on November 25, driving the sleepy Cheyennes from their lodges into the high bluffs above the village. There they made their stand, and a bloody close-quarter battle ensued. The village was seized later that day and burned. Among the items looted by the soldiers were items belonging to Custer's 7th Cavalry Regiment. The army suffered 1 officer and 5 enlisted men killed, with 24 wounded. The Cheyennes lost 40 dead, but the loss of their housing, horses, and supplies that late in the year proved devastating. Many Cheyennes froze during a three-week trek to unite with Crazy Horse on the upper Tongue River.

The harsh winter weather forced Crook to call off his expedition in December and return to the fort. The campaign was successful in that Mackenzie's destruction of Dull Knife's village rendered any future Cheyenne resistance futile. Crook's campaign coincided with similar efforts by other army elements in the region that largely subdued the Sioux by early 1877, making the Great Sioux War a significant success for the army.

WILLIAM WHYTE

See also
Black Hills, South Dakota; Black Hills Gold Rush; Bozeman Trail; Cavalry Regiment, 7th U.S.; Cheyennes; Crazy Horse; Crook, George; Custer, George Armstrong; Dull Knife; Great Sioux War; Little Bighorn, Battle of the; Mackenzie, Ranald Slidell; Rosebud, Battle of the; Sioux

References
Greene, Jerome A. *Morning Star Dawn: The Powder River Expedition and the Northern Cheyennes, 1876.* Norman: University of Oklahoma Press, 2003.
Utley, Robert M. *Frontier Regulars: The United States and the American Indian, 1866–1891.* New York: Macmillan, 1973.

Powhatan
Birth Date: ca. 1547
Death Date: 1618

Paramount chief over a loose confederacy of Algonquian-speaking nations on the coastal plain of Virginia when the English established Jamestown in 1607. Powhatan (his throne name) inherited leadership of at least 5 native nations, whose territory adjoined the fall lines of three rivers: the James, the Pamunkey, and the Mattaponi. The rest he brought under his control through a combination of force, persuasion, and intimidation in the decades preceding English settlement. By 1618 Powhatan presided over roughly 30 Native American groups.

Powhatan's powers as paramount chief were limited. He usually ruled by prestige rather than force, with his ceremonial powers outweighing his real political or legal authority. He did not control much of the day-to-day lives of his people, and ordinary natives had considerable personal freedom.

Powhatan's success in building his paramount chiefdom was based in part on his personal qualities. The English described the chief as tall, kingly, and charismatic. However, these qualities do not explain why he created the Powhatan Confederacy. He might have wanted to rebuild a population ravaged by disease or monopolize the European seaborne trade for copper, firearms, and other high-status goods. He may also have been reacting to other unknown internal native issues.

Powhatan initially welcomed the English outpost at Jamestown, for a permanent English presence meant easy access to trade goods. The English might also have become useful allies in his wars with the Siouan-speaking Monacans to the west. His goal was to maintain an English presence while not allowing

Powhatan (Wahunsonacock) was the principal chief of the so-called Powhatan Confederacy in Virginia when the English colonists established Jamestown in 1607. (Library of Congress)

the English to become too powerful or to make contact with his enemies.

Powhatan's relations with the English quickly soured. The newcomers' insistence on exploring beyond Powhatan's territory and expanding onto Powhatan lands greatly agitated the Powhatans. The situation was made worse when English colonists stole supplies of corn from the Powhatan settlements near Jamestown.

These tensions ultimately resulted in the First Anglo-Powhatan War (1610–1614), which ended when the English captured Powhatan's favorite daughter, Pocahontas. Following this event, Powhatan's power waned. The conflict seemed to have had a profound effect on Powhatan. He lost any will to fight white encroachments and instead chose to live a life of quiet solitude. Although he remained paramount chief until his death sometime in 1618, his younger brother and successor Opechancanough and others with great antipathy toward the English dominated Powhatan foreign policy in the 1610s.

JENNIFER BRIDGES OAST

See also

Anglo-Powhatan War, First; Jamestown; Opechancanough; Pocahontas; Powhatan Confederacy

References

Axtell, James. *After Columbus: Essays in the Ethnohistory of Colonial North America.* New York: Oxford University Press, 1988.
Rountree, Helen C., ed. *Powhatan Foreign Relations, 1500–1722.* Charlottesville: University Press of Virginia, 1993.
Rountree, Helen C., and E. Randolph Turner III. *Before and After Jamestown: Virginia's Powhatans and Their Predecessors.* Gainesville: University Press of Florida, 2002.

Powhatan Confederacy

Confederation of Native American nations in eastern Virginia. Powhatan, a powerful chief, created the Powhatan Confederacy in the late 16th century as a loose collection of approximately 30 Algonquian-speaking tribes along the Virginia coastal plain. Tsenacomoco, as the Powhatans referred to this area, contained about 13,000 native inhabitants when the English arrived in 1607. Powhatan inherited control over several nations, including the Powhatans, Arrohatecks, Appomattocks, Pamunkeys, Youghtanunds, and Mattaponis. He may also have inherited control of the Werowocomocos, Chiskiacks, and Orapaks, according to contemporary English sources. Powhatan brought the other neighboring tribes into his chiefdom through a combination of warfare, intimidation, and personal persuasion.

Sometimes referred to as a miniempire, the Powhatan Confederacy might best be viewed as a paramount chiefdom in which Powhatan received tribute and homage from local chieftains of individual tribes. Powhatan usually ruled through prestige rather than by force, as his ceremonial powers outweighed his real legal and political authority. He in fact had little control over the day-to-day lives of his people.

Following Powhatan's death in 1618, the paramount chieftaincy fell to his younger brothers, Opitchapam (Otiotan) and Opechancanough. It was Opechancanough who held the real power in the Powhatan Confederacy from the last years of Powhatan's reign until his own death in 1646. Opechancanough organized two massive assaults against the English, in 1622 and 1644. His capture by the English in 1646 ended Powhatan resistance. After 1646 the Powhatans were subject people of the English. In 1649 the paramount chiefdom was dismantled, and after that time local chiefs negotiated with the English independently.

JENNIFER BRIDGES OAST

See also

Anglo-Powhatan War, First; Anglo-Powhatan War, Second; Anglo-Powhatan War, Third; Opechancanough; Powhatan; Virginia-Indian Treaty of 1646; Virginia-Indian Treaty of 1677/1680

References

Axtell, James. *After Columbus: Essays in the Ethnohistory of Colonial North America.* New York: Oxford University Press, 1988.
Rountree, Helen C., ed. *Powhatan Foreign Relations, 1500–1722.* Charlottesville: University Press of Virginia, 1993.

Rountree, Helen C., and E. Randolph Turner III. *Before and After Jamestown: Virginia's Powhatans and Their Predecessors.* Gainesville: University Press of Florida, 2002.

Prairie du Chien, Treaty of

Treaty signed on August 19, 1825, between agents of the U.S. government and Native American tribes of the upper Midwest and eastern Great Plains. The agreement was negotiated and affirmed at Prairie Du Chien, Michigan Territory (Wisconsin), at the confluence of the Wisconsin and Mississippi rivers. The site had long been a neutral meeting place for Native American tribes and also served as a hub of the French fur trade.

Nearly 1,000 Native Americans reportedly attended the meeting, which was designed principally to stop fighting among the regional tribes. Representing the United States were William Clark, Lewis Cass, Thomas Forsyth, and several other negotiators. The treaty included the Dakota Sioux, Ojibwa, Sauk, Fox, Menominie, Iowa, and Winnebago tribes and select bands of Ottawas and Pottawatomis.

The catalyst for the treaty, which came at the request of the federal government, was increasing violence and intertribal warfare in the region. This had been the result of greater encroachment by whites onto Native American lands, the relocation of eastern tribes to the upper Midwest and Great Plains, shifting and shaky relations among the U.S. government and Native American tribes, and ever-greater competition for shrinking resources in the area.

Article Ten of the treaty asserted that the United States had control over all the territory in question. Other clauses stipulated that while current boundaries between tribes would remain in place, further negotiations would be needed to finalize certain boundaries. The Treaty of Fond du Lac (1826) and the Treaty of Butte des Morts (1827) served as follow-ups to the Prairie du Chien agreement.

While it is important to note that the Treaty of Prairie du Chien did not result in any Native American land cessions per se, some historians have argued that the agreement in fact established a foundation upon which future land cessions would be based. Indeed, large land purchases by individual white Americans and the U.S. government soon occurred in the region. Native American landholdings were sharply reduced after 1825. The Dakotas claimed landholdings that encompassed parts of five states in 1825. By 1851, however, their holdings had been reduced to a narrow strip of land in Minnesota that was just 5 miles wide and 70 miles long. Two subsequent treaties, also signed at Prairie du Chien in 1829 and 1830, witnessed land concessions from the Ojibwas and several other tribes, including the Dakotas. In the end it is hard to believe that intertribal peace was the only motivating factor behind the Treaty of Prairie du Chien.

PAUL G. PIERPAOLI JR.

Native Americans assembled at the U.S. Army encampment at Prairie du Chien in Michigan Territory (Wisconsin) for the presentation of the treaty signed on August 19, 1825. Painting by James O. Lewis, 1835. (Library of Congress)

See also
Clark, William; Dakota Sioux; Ojibwas; Ottawas; Pottawatomis; Sauks and Foxes; Sioux

References
Danziger, Edmund J., Jr. *The Chippewas of Lake Superior.* Norman: University of Oklahoma Press, 1979.
Prucha, Francis Paul. *American Indian Treaties: The History of a Political Anomaly.* Berkeley: University of California Press, 1994.

Praying Towns and Praying Indians

Algonquian-speaking natives who lived in New England and converted to Protestant Christianity became known as praying Indians, and many of them lived in segregated communities known as praying towns. Unlike the French or the Spanish, for whom Christianization of the natives was conceived of as a sacred duty, English Christianization efforts had as much to do with strategic and economic concerns as religious imperatives.

Systematic efforts to Christianize the natives did not take place until after 1644 in New England. In other areas of English North America, efforts to Christianize the natives did not occur until the end of the 17th century. But all English missionaries shared the desire to "reduce" the Native Americans to civilization, meaning the destruction of their native identities and reconstruction along English lines. Simultaneously, English missionaries attempted to teach European political philosophy as a means of imposing order in an uncertain colonial environment. This served the dual purpose of rendering the natives harmless dependents and preventing English settlers from adopting native "lawlessness."

To accomplish these ends, the English adopted the French practice of segregating native converts in the praying towns. There they were immersed in the English manner of living as they were instructed in Christianity. Devised by the Puritan missionaries John Eliot (1604–1690) and Daniel Gookin (ca. 1612–1687), the praying towns were never very successful, however. Natick, Massachusetts, established in 1650, had a population of only 145 at its height in 1674. Unlike neighboring white towns and villages, the praying towns were governed according to far stricter legal and social codes. This rendered them essentially theocracies.

Sachems (chiefs) were the preferred leaders for the praying towns because natives were accustomed to paying tribute to them. The loss of tribute from those who refused to convert was most prohibitive, and praying Indians were barred from paying tribute to "pagan" sachems. The English offered bribes to sachems, which in native eyes were simply the requisite gifts exchanged before and after all negotiations. This critical misunderstanding constituted yet another disincentive for natives to convert and for sachems to live in the praying towns.

The settlements also served as staging areas for the application of pressure on nearby Native American villages to conform to English standards of diplomacy at the very least. In the ideal, it was hoped that the natives would convert to English civilization by means of emulation. Oftentimes lands successfully cleared and cultivated by praying Indians were appropriated by neighboring whites, using both legal and illegal means. Such scheming added to the natives' frustration and reinforced the unattractiveness of conversion.

Gookin complained on the eve of King Philip's War (1675–1676) that "many" of the praying Indians had "not yet come so far as to be able or willing to profess their faith in Christ and yield obedience and subjection to him in his church." Indeed, he estimated that only 1,100 praying Indians inhabited the 14 praying towns of Massachusetts. Only 45 of the natives had been baptized, and fewer than 74 were in communion.

It had been hoped that praying towns would act as buffers between Puritan towns and hostile natives. The English hoped too that praying Indians would inform them of impending native attacks. More often than not, however, the praying Indians served neither mission particularly well. The outbreak of King Philip's War in 1675 dealt a virtual death blow to the praying towns and their residents, who were widely distrusted by the colonists.

JOHN HOWARD SMITH

See also
Algonquins; Captivity of Indians by Europeans; King Philip's War; Missionaries

References
Axtell, James. *The Invasion Within: The Contest of Cultures in Colonial North America.* New York: Oxford University Press, 1985.
Eliot, John. *John Eliot's Indian Dialogues: A Study in Cultural Interaction.* Edited by Henry W. Bowden and James P. Ronda. Westport, CT: Greenwood, 1980.
Jennings, Francis. *The Invasion of America: Indians, Colonialism, and the Cant of Conquest.* 1976; reprint, Chapel Hill: University of North Carolina Press, 2010.

Presents, Indian

See Indian Presents

Proclamation of 1763

Royal dictate that forbade white settlement west of the Appalachian Mountains. A direct consequence of the British victory in the French and Indian War (1754–1763), the Proclamation of 1763 closed western lands to colonial expansion. The population of British North America had been ecstatic with the outcome of the war, which removed the French threat and, they believed, would open the western lands to settlement. They were thus profoundly disappointed with the royal proclamation. King George III and his council, however, saw the proclamation as a means to calm Native American anxieties and to secure the frontier and

PROCLAMATION LINE OF 1763

90°W   80°W   70°W   60°W   50°W

Hudson Bay

RUPERT'S LAND HUDSON'S BAY COMPANY

LABRADOR

NEWFOUNDLAND

Gulf of Saint Lawrence

Saint Pierre **(FRANCE)**

Miquelon **(FRANCE)**

NOVA SCOTIA

QUEBEC

MAINE (MASSACHUSETTS)

L. Superior

L. Ontario

L. Michigan   *L. Huron*

NEW YORK

L. Erie

NEW HAMPSHIRE

MASSACHUSETTS

RHODE ISLAND

CONNECTICUT

PENNSYLVANIA

NEW JERSEY

INDIAN COUNTRY

DELAWARE

MARYLAND

VIRGINIA

LOUISIANA

NORTH CAROLINA

SOUTH CAROLINA

GEORGIA

ATLANTIC

OCEAN

WEST FLORIDA

EAST FLORIDA

Gulf of Mexico

50°N

40°N

30°N

20°N

British territory
Indian Country (British territory)
Spanish territory
French territory
Proclamation Line of 1763

0   150   300 mi
0   150   300 km

protect the colonists from Native American attacks. The British settlers perceived the proclamation as a direct infringement of their land rights.

The Treaty of Paris, signed by Britain, France, and Spain in February 1763, recognized New France (Canada) and all North American lands east of the Mississippi River as British territory. Colonial administrators, assured of Great Britain's dominant position in North America, responded by implementing postwar policies designed to reduce the expense of imperial administration.

Native American uprisings attributed to Neolin, a Delaware prophet, and Pontiac, an Ottawa war chief, necessitated immediate action on the part of London. The king's ministers responded quickly to the reports of frontier hostilities. Their plan provided for the orderly settlement of all lands recently acquired from France and Spain. The Proclamation of 1763, issued in the name of King George III on October 7, 1763, defined the boundaries and intentions for civil government in four new colonies: Quebec, East Florida, West Florida, and Grenada. In addition, the measure prohibited British governors and military commanders from issuing warrants for survey or patents for lands beyond the crest of the Appalachians, where they were now forbidden. British colonists living in the so-called Indian country were ordered to leave at once.

The Proclamation of 1763 reflected the Crown's awareness that frontier hostilities between Native Americans and colonists would continue indefinitely unless the colonists were confined to the Atlantic seaboard. The pacification program, however, was offset by throngs of colonists who defied the demarcation line. To complicate matters, royal officials in the colonies often connived with land speculators in schemes involving tribal lands. Illegal land grants, surveys, and private purchases of lands from the Creeks and Cherokees, tribes that did not recognize the right of the British government to demarcate boundaries, also occurred.

British Indian agents, particularly Sir William Johnson of the Northern Department, sought to ease tensions through diplomacy. Johnson and the Iroquois fixed the northern boundary line by the Treaty of Fort Stanwix in 1768. Additional treaties and land purchases occurred. In particular, the Treaty of Hard Labor, negotiated by John Stuart with the Cherokees in October 1768, extended the reach of the king's boundary line farther north, south, and west.

The Proclamation of 1763 promised Native Americans a barrier to British expansion that was never fulfilled. Not surprisingly, the intrusion of westward-moving settlers beyond the Appalachians and the Alleghenies sparked frequent retaliatory raids. By 1768 frontier hostilities became commonplace. Angry Shawnees, Wyandots, Delawares, and Mingos fought to retain their ancestral lands, particularly after the settlement of eastern Kentucky. Those tensions later culminated in Lord Dunmore's War of 1774. The repeated violations of the proclamation's prohibition against western settlement also persuaded several western tribes to cast their lot with the British during the American Revolutionary War

(1775–1783). At the same time, this intrusion by London in North American affairs upset the colonists, who dreamed of westward expansion, and was thus an underlying cause of the American Revolution.

Jon L. Brudvig

See also
French and Indian War; Johnson, Sir William; Lord Dunmore's War; Neolin; Pontiac; Pontiac's Rebellion

References
Bailyn, Bernard. *The Peopling of British North America: An Introduction.* New York: Vintage Books, 1988.

Countryman, Edward. *The American Revolution.* New York: Hill and Wang, 1985.

Jennings, Francis. *Empire of Fortune: Crowns, Colonies, and Tribes in the Seven Years War in America.* New York: Norton, 1988.

Prucha, Francis Paul. *American Indian Policy in the Formative Years: Indian Trade and Intercourse Acts, 1790–1834.* Cambridge: Harvard University Press, 1962.

Sosin, Jack M. *Whitehall and the Wilderness: The Middle West in British Colonial Policy, 1760–1775.* Lincoln: University of Nebraska Press, 1961.

Prophetstown

Native American town at the juncture of the Tippecanoe and Wabash rivers, near present-day Lafayette, Indiana, and also near the site of the Battle of Tippecanoe (November 7, 1811). Popular American perceptions of British complicity in this conflict helped encourage a U.S. declaration of war against Great Britain in 1812.

Following their humiliating capitulation at the 1795 Treaty of Greenville, demoralized Ohio Country Native Americans faced difficult choices, all of which led to further disruptions of tribal authority and traditional life ways. Over the next two decades, some would opt to assimilate into the advancing white society, optimistically struggling to achieve some measure of cultural compromise by acknowledging U.S. suzerainty and its related—if undependable—dole. Among this group, some accommodating Native Americans made a modest living authorizing questionable land sales to Americans.

Yet most Ohio Native Americans continued to embrace their traditional cultural patterns, choosing to migrate west into increasingly dense multitribal communities. Once resettled in northwestern Ohio Country, they encountered fierce competition for the use of communally held agricultural and hunting lands. Among these groups, a small and bitter minority repudiated past land transfers and treaties made by self-professed chiefs and for decades would resist white settlement and authority. These holdouts, often called renegades by American settlers, saw themselves as freedom fighters defending Native American cultural rights and property.

While an evangelical Christian Second Great Awakening ignited in the American backcountry, a quasi-religious separatist movement blazed in the Indian territories as well. Thus, religiously derived American doctrines of Manifest Destiny and Native American cultural superiority collided in western Ohio.

Many proponents of a forceful defense of traditional Amerindian homelands embraced a radical doctrine espoused by a prophet from the Turtle Clan of the Shawnees. Tenskwatawa prophesied that whites could be forcefully ejected from the Ohio Country by a Pan-Indian alliance. But first, he cautioned, the Native Americans must learn to coordinate their efforts, abstain from alcohol, purge witchcraft, and return to traditional Native American cultural practices. Then, a surprise attack against all western American settlements would be planned and led by Tenskwatawa's older brother, Tecumseh. Until that time, conspirators would feign peaceful intentions while the brothers recruited, trained, and indoctrinated warriors from dozens of Native American tribes. In 1808 Tenskwatawa moved his followers to a new village, called Prophetstown, on the then most recent border between Native American and white lands.

Before 20th-century dams were built, the Wabash River (Wah-Bah Shik-Ki, or "Pure White River") drained the hills of western Ohio and then meandered through the fertile lowland prairies of northern and western Indiana, flowing south into the Ohio River and washing finally into the Mississippi. To the Native American leaders, Shawnee culture seemed to be following the same westward course. Tenskwatawa laid out Prophetstown in symmetrical rows of cabins and bark huts in a site just downstream from the conjunction of the Tippecanoe and Wabash rivers. A frontier hotel of sorts welcomed converts, and a large council house could accommodate 200 participants. With its proximity to river transportation, its nearby fertile bottomland for farming, and its symbolic position on the contested boundary with the United States, the site proved to be an attractive vortex for a radical new religion.

As Tenskwatawa directed the construction of Prophetstown, his older brother attended to intertribal politics. Tecumseh toured southern Canada, met with western tribes, and visited Native Americans living near the Gulf of Mexico. Wherever he spoke, Tecumseh decried "white land hunger" and the dangers of accommodation, warnings that resonated with the recent experience of most Native Americans.

Neither the rapid growth of Prophetstown nor the expanding influence of the Shawnee brothers escaped the notice of the governor of the Indiana Territory, William Henry Harrison. He had grown alarmed by intelligence reports of British involvement in the conspiracy and from hearing secondhand accounts of the brothers' threats of imminent attack. Thus, Harrison led an expedition of nearly 1,000 U.S. Army troops, Indiana militia, and Kentucky volunteers toward Prophetstown in September 1811, when he knew Tecumseh was away recruiting. At the time Harrison was acting on his own authority and as such held no commission or military rank. He had, however, attained the rank of captain in the U.S. Army before he resigned in 1798 to become secretary for the Northwest Territory.

As Harrison and his force approached Prophetstown on the evening of November 6, 1811, a delegation of villagers met him to request a parley on behalf of the Prophet. The Native Americans denied hostile intent and insisted that Tenskwatawa hoped to prevent bloodshed. Agreeing to this request for discussions the next day, Harrison huddled his forces into a makeshift encampment a mile west of Prophetstown. That night, outnumbered more than two to one, short of ammunition, with the war leader absent, and with families still in the village, Tenskwatawa prepared for his predawn preemptive attack.

Surprised shortly before 5:00 a.m. on November 7, Harrison's forces fought from a surrounded position, regaining the initiative after dawn. American losses (68 killed and 120 wounded) outnumbered the best available estimates of Native American casualties. But in their retreat, the Native Americans abandoned Prophetstown, which Harrison's men sacked and burned the next day. Although the town was rebuilt following Harrison's departure, Tenskwatawa's personal credibility and religious mystique never recovered. Tecumseh's long-planned Pan-Indian alliance would never materialize, although he returned to battle against the United States in the War of 1812. Harrison's victory, however inconclusive, would fuel his successful run for president of the United States in 1840. In addition, the events at Prophetstown helped feed American's perceptions that the British were encouraging the Native Americans to resist the Americans. This would become an important factor in the American decision to declare war on Britain in 1812.

JOE PETRULIONIS

See also
Greenville, Treaty of; Harrison, William Henry; Nativism, Indian; Shawnees; Tecumseh; Tenskwatawa; Tippecanoe, Battle of

References
Edmunds, R. David. *The Shawnee Prophet*. Lincoln: University of Nebraska Press, 1983.
McConnell, Michael N. *A Country Between: The Upper Ohio and Its Peoples, 1724–1774*. Lincoln: University of Nebraska Press, 1992.
Sugden, John. *Tecumseh: A Life*. New York: Holt, 1997.
White, Richard. *The Middle Ground: Indians, Empires, and Republics in the Great Lakes Region, 1650–1815*. New York: Cambridge University Press, 1991.

Pueblo Revolt
Start Date: August 10, 1680
End Date: August 21, 1680

Revolt of the Pueblo Native Americans against the Spaniards in New Mexico. The Spanish conquest of New Mexico began with Francisco Vásquez de Coronado's 1540–1542 quest for the mythical Seven Golden Cities of Cíbola. Intermittent Spanish forays into New Mexico occurred thereafter, although permanent European settlements were not begun until Don Juan de Oñate y Salazar formally established New Mexico in 1598. Franciscan missionaries, eager to convert the sedentary horticulturalists they called *Indios de los pueblos* (village Indians), soon took up residence in the scattered pueblos.

Relations between the Spanish and the Pueblos took a turn for the worse in 1675 when Governor Juan Francisco Treviño imprisoned 47 Native Americans whom he termed "sorcerers." These men were shamans who were perpetuating their sacred ceremonies. Three of the detainees were executed. Another committed suicide before angry Pueblo warriors forced the zealous governor to release the remaining prisoners.

Nearly a century of colonial encroachments, smallpox outbreaks, prolonged drought, forced conversions, demands for tribute, and the suppression of traditional practices led most Pueblos to long for an end to Spanish oppression. Popé, a Tewa shaman from San Juan Pueblo, made this wish reality after experiencing a powerful vision that had followed his 1675 detention.

The Pueblos' plot to drive out the Spanish unfolded on August 9, 1680, when runners carried knotted cords and instructions to two dozen villages as far south as Isleta in New Mexico, a distance of some 400 miles. Tribal leaders receiving the knotted yucca cords were instructed to untie one knot each day until none remained. After the last knot was untied, the warriors would attack the Spanish.

Governor Don Antonio de Otermín downplayed the seriousness of the planned uprising on learning about it from native informants. The rebellion, Otermín had learned, was to begin during the night of the new moon. In addition, the attacks would coincide with the arrival of the triennial Spanish supply caravan dispatched from Mexico City. The governor then ordered the torture of Nicolás Catua and Pedro Omtua, captured runners from Tesuque, for further details. Confident that the uprising would not commence until August 13, 1680, Otermín adopted a strategy of watchful waiting.

Pueblo raiders, however, attacked unsuspecting Spanish outposts on August 10, 1680, after learning that the Spaniards had captured the two runners. The stunned Otermín responded by dispatching soldiers to subdue the warriors. In addition, he ordered all Spanish colonists to gather within the safe confines of Santa Fe's defenses.

Spanish settlements in northern New Mexico as far west as the Hopi mesas in present-day Arizona felt the fury of war. The uprising claimed the lives of 19 Franciscan friars and 2 assistants. In all, some 380 Spaniards, including women and children, perished. Alonso García, New Mexico's lieutenant governor residing in Ro Abajo, learned about the devastation on August 11. On the receipt of false reports that all Spanish settlements had been destroyed in the attack and that no colonists had survived, García organized a withdrawal of all remaining Spaniards in the region to El Paso del Norte (present-day Juárez) instead of marching north to the settlers' relief.

Governor Otermín, waiting at Santa Fe for reinforcements that never arrived, prepared for a long siege. Nearly 500 Pueblo warriors attacked the capital of New Mexico on August 15, 1680. Within two days more than 2,500 Pueblos had joined the fight. Otermín, severely wounded in a desperate counterattack designed to drive off the attackers, abandoned Santa Fe on August 21 after the attackers cut off the city's water supply. The Spaniards then withdrew down the Rio Grande Valley.

After the Spanish had departed, Popé and other leaders of the rebellion launched a purification campaign, destroying Catholic churches, statues, and relics. All Pueblos who had received the sacraments were ordered to cleanse themselves by scrubbing their bodies with yucca fibers while bathing in the Rio Grande. Pueblo traditionalists constructed kivas (partially subterranean ceremonial chambers) to replace those that the Spanish colonizers had earlier destroyed.

Otermín attempted to reclaim New Mexico for Spain in November 1681, but Pueblo warriors repelled his invading forces. Spain's interest in New Mexico waned until French explorers visited the lower Mississippi River Delta. Eager to secure the Southwest lest it fall to France, Spanish officials dispatched soldiers there in 1688 and 1689. Although unsuccessful, these expeditions revealed fissures in Pueblo civilization. Officials also learned that Ute, Apache, and Navajo raids, combined with drought and famine, had created severe hardship for the Pueblos. On August 10, 1692, 12 years to the day of the Pueblo Revolt, Governor Diego José de Vargas vowed that he would retake New Mexico.

By September 13, 1692, a force of 40 Spanish soldiers, 50 Mexican natives, and 2 missionaries reached Santa Fe. Vargas, anxious to assure the defenders that he meant them no harm, pardoned Tewa leaders for their past transgressions. Amazingly, the governor eventually entered the city without having to fire a shot. Maintaining constant vigilance, Vargas also visited the outlying pueblos to assure villagers of his desire for peace.

Despite the governor's efforts, violence returned to the region in 1693 when hostile Pueblos recaptured Santa Fe. A furious Vargas retook the city on December 29, 1693, after cutting off the defenders' water supply. The governor's reconquest of New Mexico ended in December 1696, when Vargas secured a lasting peace.

Although the Spanish colonizers and missionaries returned, they had learned an important lesson. After 1696 the villages were allowed to govern themselves, and the missionaries tolerated residents' traditional practices. The Pueblo Revolt of 1680 had thus succeeded in ensuring the perpetuation of cherished tribal languages, dances, and ceremonies for centuries to come.

JON L. BRUDVIG

See also

Apaches; Navajos; New Mexico; Oñate, Juan de; Popé; Pueblos; Utes

References

Bowden, Henry Warner. "Spanish Missions, Cultural Conflict, and the Pueblo Revolt of 1680." *Church History* 44 (June 1975): 217–228.

Knaut, Andrew L. *The Pueblo Revolt of 1680: Conquest and Resistance in Seventeenth-Century New Mexico.* Norman: University of Oklahoma Press, 1995.

Roberts, David. *The Pueblo Revolt: The Secret Rebellion That Drove the Spanish out of the Southwest.* New York: Simon and Schuster, 2004.

Pueblos

Native American groups that lived along the upper reaches of the Rio Grande Valley in the American Southwest (principally in present-day New Mexico and parts of Arizona). The Pueblos had prospered for thousands of years prior to European contact. Population estimates vary, but their numbers probably reached as high as 60,000, divided into 80 towns, by the end of the 16th century. With sufficient water to sustain agriculture, the Pueblos cultivated maize, beans, and squash and used artificial means to irrigate their crops. They dwelled in terraced apartment-like buildings built of adobe and stone, which were usually two to three stories high. Towns were often situated on elevated terrain (cliffs and mesas), offering security for the community. The people were called Pueblos because they resided in permanent settlements, or *pueblos* in Spanish.

Pueblo government was theocratic, and ceremonial life dominated community affairs. Each pueblo was politically autonomous, with leadership originating from the community's priesthood. This along with the presence of multiple languages and dialects (Keresan or the Tanoan tongues: Tano, Tewa, Tiwa, or Towa) made collaboration between pueblos very rare.

In the early 16th century the viceroy of New Spain authorized expeditions north of Mexico in hopes of discovering riches rumored to be found among the adobe towns scattered across the landscape. Francisco Vásquez de Coronado, governor of the province of New Galicia in northern Mexico, led the largest of these expeditions from 1540 to 1542. With approximately 300 Spanish cavalry and infantry and more than 1,000 Tlaxcalan warriors, Coronado journeyed up the Rio Grande into the land of the Pueblos. He found none of the anticipated opulent cities. Instead, the Spanish conquistadors discovered desert towns of stone and mud-plastered dwellings whose stores of maize and beans offered inviting targets for raids and consumption.

Despite the efforts of the Pueblos to welcome the strangers, conflict was commonplace. Resistance to Spanish incursions proved futile at Zuni Pueblo, where Spanish horses, lances, and guns overwhelmed attempts by the Zunis to protect their foodstuffs. At the Tiwa Pueblos, the approaching winter led Coronado to commandeer buildings, clothing, and food supplies for the benefit of his soldiers. Tiwa resistance to these demands instigated three months of merciless Spanish reprisals. When Coronado's expedition returned to Mexico in 1542 after venturing all the way to present-day Kansas, it left behind a wide swath of devastation among the Pueblos it had encountered.

San Buenaventura's Day Corn Dance at Cochiti Pueblo, circa 1888. (Library of Congress)

Coronado's accounts of his profitless expedition dissuaded further forays into Pueblo country for more than half a century. In 1595 Don Juan de Oñate, the son of a wealthy silver mine owner, was charged by the Spanish court with leading an expedition up the Rio Grande to spread the Catholic faith, pacify the natives, and establish a permanent colony in the northern provinces of New Spain. In 1598 Oñate and 500 men, women, and children entered New Mexico near present-day El Paso, Texas, and claimed dominion over the land and its people. By late May 1598, Oñate reached the upper Rio Grande and encountered the first of many pueblos he would formally claim for Spain. Despite the expedition's habit of requisitioning food from the Pueblos it encountered, the indigenous population generally welcomed the newcomers, choosing to suppress the memory of Coronado and any desire for retribution.

In July 1598 Oñate arrived at the confluence of the Chama River and the Rio Grande and established his headquarters at Ohke Pueblo, which he renamed San Juan, the capital of the new colony. From San Juan, Oñate inaugurated his missionary program by dispersing friars to the pueblos while he personally conducted a reconnaissance of the province. Native hospitality turned to resistance at Acoma Pueblo in January 1599, leaving 11 Spanish soldiers dead. In retaliation Oñate sent a punitive expedition against the town that killed 800 men, women, and children and took another 580 captive. Adolescents were sentenced to 20 years of servitude, while adult men were subjected to public mutilation to be conducted in the plazas of pueblos along the Rio Grande. In 1601 Oñate moved the capital across the Rio Grande to Yunque Ouinge Pueblo and renamed it San Gabriel. Nine years later the capital was moved again, this time to its permanent location in Santa Fe.

By 1610 the realization that there were few riches to be found among the pueblos led many colonists to return to Mexico. There was little incentive for new colonists to venture northward. Those who remained in New Mexico lived in scattered settlements along the Rio Grande and profited from the exploitation of native labor.

For the Pueblo people, the 70 years following the establishment of the Spanish capital at Santa Fe proved intolerable. Spanish labor demands on native people were burdensome. Native children were placed into permanent servitude, Franciscan friars strove to abolish Pueblo religious icons and ceremonies, epidemic diseases became rampant, and to make matters worse, Apache, Ute, and Navajo raiding parties preyed on Pueblo livestock. Sporadic revolts against the Spanish materialized on occasion in isolated pueblos but were easily put down, mostly because of the lack of cooperation between the native towns.

All of this dramatically changed in 1680 when Popé, a spiritual leader from San Juan Pueblo, led one of the most effective native revolts in American history. Popé successfully overcame obstacles created by distance and language barriers to unify at least 24 pueblos in a coordinated revolt against the Spanish in early August 1680. His 8,000 followers killed more than 400 Spanish colonists and 21 of the 33 Franciscan friars. Those Spaniards who were not killed or wounded fled back to Mexico, and the victors destroyed the vestiges of Spanish rule.

The success of the Pueblo Revolt kept the upper reaches of the Rio Grande free from Spanish control for 12 years. The Pueblos' alliance was short-lived, however, as native towns soon returned to their familiar practice of autonomy. When the Spanish under Diego de Vargas returned to New Mexico in 1692, the Pueblos responded with minimal resistance. What opposition the Spanish did encounter was quickly suppressed. Effective Spanish control of the province resumed in 1694 but with a decidedly different approach toward the Pueblos.

Natives were now allowed to retain their religious icons and ceremonies. Labor and food requisitions were moderated. Spanish officials went so far as to arm the Pueblos to help them ward off raiding tribes. Throughout the remainder of the colonial period, the land of the Pueblos was spared the repressive policies of the pre-1680 colonists and quickly evolved into a military buffer zone protecting Mexico's northern provinces from native and European incursions. Ironically, what emerged in effect was a Pueblo-Spanish alliance that helped to preserve Pueblo culture for generations to come. In 1820 Pueblo lands came under Mexican control, and in 1848 after the Mexican land cession to the United States, they came under American control. There were few instances of violence between the Pueblos and Americans. Today Pueblo natives continue to thrive in various pueblos, mainly in New Mexico.

ALAN C. DOWNS

See also

New Mexico; Oñate, Juan de; Popé; Pueblo Revolt

References

Josephy, Alvin M., Jr. *The Patriot Chiefs: A Chronicle of American Indian Resistance.* New York: Penguin, 1989.

Knaut, Andrew L. *The Pueblo Revolt of 1680: Conquest and Resistance in Seventeenth-Century New Mexico.* Norman: University of Oklahoma Press, 1995.

Puritans

Term, originally an epithet, referring to individuals who sought to rid the Church of England of any vestiges of Catholic ritual and hierarchy. The term "Puritans" refers variously to wings of radical 16th- and 17th-century English Protestants who adhered to the rigid doctrines of John Calvin. Indeed, the Puritans sought to purify the Anglican Church of all things Catholic. A few branches of Puritanism did emerge with slightly differing ideas about church governance, but all agreed on the diluting of ecclesiastical authority, ranging from radical independence to Presbyterianism. They were also broadly divided between a mainstream that never disavowed its connection to the Church of England and a Separatist fringe eventually led by Robert Browne (1550–1633).

The Separatists became known by their contemporaries as Brownists. Many of them fled England for the Netherlands and other parts of Europe during the reign of Queen Mary (r. 1553–1558), a Catholic. Some found their way to Geneva, Switzerland, where they sought to refine their Calvinist theology under the tutelage of Calvin.

On Queen Mary's death and the accession to the throne of Elizabeth I in 1558, all but the most radical Puritans returned to England in order to participate in the process of Reformation begun by Henry VIII. Nevertheless, Elizabeth made it clear that she was not favorably disposed to their religious opinions. A steadily mounting atmosphere of official persecution ensued and accelerated during the reigns of James I (r. 1603–1625) and Charles I (r. 1625–1649).

The Separatists in Holland, concerned that their children were gradually losing their English identity, became determined to reestablish themselves in the New World. Thus, they formed the Plymouth Company, under the leadership of William Bradford, that was granted a charter in 1619. Sailing to America aboard the *Mayflower,* the Pilgrims, as they called themselves, landed at Cape Cod in present-day Massachusetts in 1620. There they established Plymouth Plantation.

Encouraged by this example and frustrated by their straitening circumstances, English Puritans began considering the prospect of founding an American colony of their own. Their effort was spearheaded by John Winthrop, who founded the Massachusetts Bay Company and secured a royal charter for a colony in New England in 1629. Carried to the New World in the *Arabella,* Winthrop's settlers sailed to the Massachusetts Bay area in 1630 and founded the colony of that name, which Winthrop hoped would be a "city on a hill," a religious utopia for the rest of the world—primarily England—to emulate.

To that end, the initial form of government in the Puritan colonies of New England was dependent on its congregational church organization. That governance established strict standards for achieving church membership and the sociopolitical perquisites conferred by it. Most important in that regard was the right to vote and hold elective office in the towns and the assembly. Although clergy were barred from elective office, thus avoiding the creation of a theocracy, the Puritan colonies were not democratic. Magistrates, for example, did not believe that they represented voters or the general population. Bradford and Winthrop both envisioned a holy commonwealth, but that never precluded robust commercial activity. This along with the New Englanders' shared sense of religious purpose and demographic balance created healthy and economically successful communities in relatively short order.

These success stories resulted in the Great Migration of Puritans and other Britons to New England throughout the 1630s. Growing through natural population increases and steady immigration, towns and villages sprung up quickly. Encroaching white settlements pushed inexorably westward into lands claimed by the Massachusett, Pawtuxet, Pequot, Narragansett, and Wampanoag peoples. In short order, the American Indians of the region had been devastated by disease and wars among themselves and with the English over land and trade.

The Pequot War (1636–1638) brought the Pequots to the edge of extinction, and King Philip's War (1675–1676) swept away what little southern Algonquian resistance still remained. By the 1680s New England's frontiers stretched into French-allied Abenaki lands in New Hampshire and Maine. And territory claimed by the Dutch-allied Mohawks and Mahicans in western Massachusetts and Connecticut inevitably enmeshed the Puritan colonies in international imperial rivalries. These tensions sparked a series of colonial wars between 1652 and 1763.

Although New England Puritanism moved away from the radical Calvinism and idealism of the founding generation, it never relinquished its eschatological sense of purpose as the New Canaan in the 18th century. The revivalism of the Great Awakening (ca. 1730–1750) served to reinforce this mentality. Such was especially the case with the interpretive influence of the New Light theologian Jonathan Edwards (1703–1758) of Massachusetts, among others. The French and Indian War (1754–1763) against Catholic France and pagan natives took on a critically apocalyptic significance in New England, as the clergy exhorted their male parishioners to enlist in provincial regiments. Indeed, they were exhorted to combat the "Enemies to God, to Religion, Liberty, and the pure Worship of the Gospel," in the words of Sylvanus Conant (1750–1843). The victorious conclusion of the war in 1763 inspired Puritan thinker Jonathan Mayhew (1720–1766) to envision "mighty cities rising on every hill," thus evoking the language and ideals of Winthrop.

JOHN HOWARD SMITH

See also
Abenakis; King Philip's War; Narragansetts; Pequots; Pequot War; Praying Towns and Praying Indians; Wampanoags; Winthrop, John

References
Jennings, Francis. *The Invasion of America: Indians, Colonialism, and the Cant of Conquest.* 1976; reprint, Chapel Hill: University of North Carolina Press, 2010.
Miller, Perry. *The New England Mind: From Colony to Province.* Cambridge: Harvard University Press, 1953.
Miller, Perry. *The New England Mind: The Seventeenth Century.* 2nd ed. Cambridge: Harvard University Press, 1953.

Pushmataha
Birth Date: ca. 1764
Death Date: December 24, 1824

Choctaw chief and diplomat. Known as the "Indian General," Pushmataha was the greatest Choctaw leader of his day. Little is known about Pushmataha's early life beyond the fact he was born probably in 1764 near present-day Macon, Mississippi. As an adult, Pushmataha often stated that he had no mother, father, brother, or sister but had instead emerged fully grown with a rifle in his hand out of a pine tree that had shattered in a thunderstorm.

As a young man, Pushmataha won fame as a skillful warrior in raids against the Osages and Caddos in present-day Arkansas and

Oklahoma. These conflicts had been caused by fierce competition over hunting grounds that were needed to sustain the fur trade. The Choctaws fought doggedly to maintain their way of life and to protect the holiest site of their nation, a 50-foot-high mound called Nanih Waya located in present-day Winston County, Mississippi. The Choctaws believed that their ancestors had either emerged from this mound or had settled around it after they had migrated from the west.

After Pushmataha was elected a district chief in 1800, he became involved in treaty negotiations with the U.S. government. He was certain that he could maintain peaceful relations with the United States and protect Choctaw territory in the Old Southwest (Mississippi and Alabama). Pushmataha negotiated the Treaty of Fort Confederation in 1802 that redefined the eastern border of the Choctaw Nation and the Treaty of Mount Dexter in 1805 that surrendered 4 million acres of land to the United States in exchange for the government paying off tribal debts to traders. Pushmataha and the other district chiefs also received many gifts from the U.S. government.

Such cozy relations with the United States soon brought Pushmataha into open conflict with Shawnee chief Tecumseh, who was seeking to organize a Pan-Indian confederation in an attempt to stop the sale of land to the Americans. Tecumseh considered chiefs such as Pushmataha enemies of their people. In the autumn of 1811 Tecumseh made a tour through the South to win supporters for his confederation. He visited the Chickasaws and Cherokees, who were not interested in joining him, and the Creeks, who became some of his most loyal followers.

Pushmataha allowed the gifted orator to speak to the Choctaws but countered his arguments at every turn. Tecumseh urged the Choctaws to join his confederation and admitted that he was planning to launch a war against the Americans to stop their relentless conquest of Native American lands. Equally as eloquent as the Shawnee chief, Pushmataha argued that the Choctaws had never fought the Americans and that to do so now would be dishonorable. He condemned Tecumseh as a "tyrant" who expected the Choctaws to follow his commands without question. Pushmataha warned his tribe that joining a war against the more powerful U.S. government would be disastrous. Pushmataha then had Tecumseh escorted from Choctaw territory and threatened to murder any warrior who followed him.

During the War of 1812, Pushmataha joined the Americans against the British and their Native American allies. He raised a company of 500 Choctaw warriors and fought alongside Major General Andrew Jackson in his campaign against the Creeks, which culminated in the Battle of Horseshoe Bend on March 27, 1814. Pushmataha also may have been among the handful of Choctaws who fought with Jackson at the Battle of New Orleans in January 1815.

After the war ended, Pushmataha was elected the primary chief of the Choctaws. He advocated adopting educational and farming techniques from the Americans but resisted every attempt to convert his people to Christianity. He also came to regret his unquestioning devotion to the United States. Instead of rewarding the Choctaws for their loyalty, the U.S. government demanded treaties that would open more tribal land to settlement. In the Treaty of Fort Stephens in 1816, the Choctaws surrendered more than 3 million acres, which was not a great loss because the land had been overhunted. But the Treaty of Doak's Stand, negotiated in 1820, had a more devastating impact because it exchanged the traditional Choctaw homeland in Alabama for territory in Arkansas and Oklahoma. Concerns over the treaty brought Pushmataha to Washington, D.C., where he died of pneumonia on December 24, 1824, and was buried with great ceremony in the Congressional Cemetery.

MARY STOCKWELL

See also
Choctaws; Horseshoe Bend, Battle of; Jackson, Andrew; Native Americans and the War of 1812; Shawnees; Tecumseh

References
Carson, James Taylor. *Searching for the Bright Path: The Mississippi Choctaws from Prehistory to Removal.* Lincoln: University of Nebraska Press, 1999.
Debo, Angie. *The Rise and Fall of the Choctaw Republic.* Norman: University of Oklahoma Press, 1989.
Galloway, Patricia. *Choctaw Genesis, 1500–1700.* Lincoln: University of Nebraska Press, 1995.

Pyramid Lake, First Battle of

See Big Bend, Battle of

Q

Quaker Peace Policy

See Grant's Peace Policy

Quakers

Protestant religious group, also known as the Society of Friends, founded in England in the mid-17th century. Standing out from British society, the Quakers attracted much persecution and migrated in large numbers to North America, particularly Rhode Island and Pennsylvania.

The Quakers were founded by George Fox in the 1650s. Although raised an Anglican, Fox began to preach in 1647 after a spiritual vision inspired him to minister to others. He called for a profound spiritual renewal within England, supported the prohibition of alcohol, and preached against holidays, sports, and all other activities that diverted attention from the spirit. Fox supported peace, and when he was imprisoned for his beliefs, he converted his jailer. Fox's inclination toward humility eventually morphed into Quaker pacifism.

The group to whom Fox ministered professed the belief that Jesus Christ provided individuals with an inner light so that believers could experience personal illumination from God in their daily lives. Followers of Fox became known as Quakers because they reportedly shook when filled with the Holy Spirit. As part of what was considered a radical religious fringe, the Quakers were subjected to considerable persecution in both England and the New World. They especially stood apart due to their distinctive code of dress and manners and their refusal to observe status distinctions, swear oaths, or pay tithes to the established church. The Quakers were helped somewhat by the Toleration Act of 1689, which modified laws against religious dissenters.

The Quakers had no clergy, so church services consisted of long periods of sitting together in silence, waiting for the Holy Spirit to move someone to speak. Initially men and women met together for religious services, and women were often moved to speak. By the 18th century the Friends held segregated meetings, and from 1737 on Quakers followed a yearly Book of Discipline designed to provide church cohesion and instruct followers in proper behavior.

Rhode Island was an early refuge for Quakers in North America and sheltered William Penn during the 1660s. When Penn inherited the large tract of land that became Pennsylvania, he established a Quaker haven with abundant space in which to practice their religious beliefs and from which to gain a comfortable living. Penn attempted to foster positive relations with local Indians by dealing fairly in treaty negotiations and land acquisitions, but his example failed to spread much beyond his immediate influence. Although the Quakers were never an established church or officially linked to the colony's government, the importance of individual Quakers among the early proprietors gave them considerable power in the colonial assembly long after they ceased to be a majority of the population.

Quakers used their political clout to pursue the abolition of African slavery and to minister to Native American groups in the region and pursue peaceful relations with them. Slave importation to Pennsylvania was outlawed in 1711. In England, Quakers were prominent in antislavery and prison reform campaigns. John Woolman, an influential leader during the first half of the 18th century, preached that war and slavery were inherently evil and that the materialism of non-Quakers showed spiritual degradation. In 1755 during the French and Indian War (1754–1763), 21 Quakers opposed the payment of taxes because their tax revenue went to finance the war. This caused something of a schism among Quakers, drawing a sharp distinction between those who denounced all violence and those who did not. As the American Revolutionary War (1775–1783) approached, Quakers again refused to pay taxes or to support the war effort in any way. By the 1770s, however, the Quakers lost political clout in Pennsylvania, as many chose to withdraw entirely from politics.

During the 19th century Quakers abandoned the strict code of dress that they had previously followed, which helped them assimilate into the larger society. Quakers figured prominently in the so-called Peace Policy (sometimes called the Quaker Peace Policy) instituted by Ulysses S. Grant upon assuming the presidency in 1869. Pressed by reformers and driven by his own sincere desire to promote the protection and "civilization" of what he termed the "original occupants of this land," Grant broke from the policy of using patronage appointees as Indian agents in favor of selfless religious servants appointed by the major Christian denominations in America, with each participating denomination given responsibility for a particular Indian group or agency. While the policy never fully developed, the Society of Friends assumed their roles with earnest determination. To the Quakers fell arguably the most difficult assignment: jurisdiction over the southern Plains and some of the most formidable warriors in North America, the Comanches, Kiowas, Cheyennes, and Arapahos. Although laudably well intentioned, the attempt to transform the nomadic Plains tribes into self-sustaining farmers, Christians, and educated citizens largely failed.

The Quakers' antiwar views and commitment to pacifism further set them apart in the 20th century, when they were again seen by some as radicals.

JOHN HOWARD SMITH

See also

Grant's Peace Policy; Missionaries

References

Brock, Peter. *Pacifism in the United States: From the Colonial Era to the First World War*. Princeton, NJ: Princeton University Press, 1968.

Marietta, Jack D. *The Reformation of American Quakerism, 1748–1783*. Philadelphia: University of Pennsylvania Press, 1984.

McFeely, William S. *Grant: A Biography*. New York: Norton, 1981.

Quanah Parker
Birth Date: ca. 1845
Death Date: February 23, 1911

Comanche chief known for his tenaciousness and skills as a guerrilla leader in an effort to keep the Quahada (Antelope) band of Comanche free on the Llano Estacado (Staked Plains) of western Texas and also known for his mother Cynthia Ann Parker. Natives

Quanah Parker (ca. 1845–1911) was a Comanche war chief, highly acclaimed for his skills in guerrilla warfare. He fought at the Second Battle of Adobe Walls in 1874. (National Archives)

had seized Cynthia Ann in 1836 when she was nine years old during a raid on Parker's Fort in Central Texas. Adopted into a family of the Noconi (Wanderer) band of Comanches, she received the name Naudah. Quanah, born in western Texas as early as 1845, was the eldest child of her marriage to Peta Nocona.

Historians dispute whether Quanah was a chief before the Quahadas surrendered in 1875. Quanah spoke openly in the councils of the Quahadas, a mark of high standing and respect. He was also among those who denounced the Medicine Lodge Treaty Council of 1867, which the Quahadas refused to attend. He was designated in 1871 to lead his village away from advancing U.S. troops and provided leadership in the attack against buffalo hunters during the Second Battle of Adobe Walls in the Texas Panhandle on June 28, 1874. Quanah was a respected leader during the Red River War (1874–1875).

No record indicates when Quanah learned that his mother had been adopted. His father may have told him only after Naudah was captured in 1860 during a raid led by Texas Rangers under Captain Lawrence S. "Sul" Ross against Comanches camped on Pease River. Quanah did not see his mother again, as she was returned to her Texas relatives. She never renounced her Comanche ways. Quanah was known as Quanah Parker to Colonel (later Brigadier General) Ranald S. Mackenzie, who pursued the Quahada from 1871 to 1875. Mackenzie's troops weakened but never captured the band.

In 1875 following the disastrous Red River War, the Quahadas agreed to go to Fort Sill (Oklahoma) and settle on the reservation. Mackenzie's emissary, Dr. Jacob J. Sturm, reported that Quanah had spoken positively of relocating to the area. Quanah was also among a small group sent ahead to Fort Sill as messengers to inform Mackenzie of the success of Sturm's mission.

Mackenzie very much respected the Quahadas. He knew their skill and determination as warriors, and he also knew that they had never lived a lifestyle such as that which would be required on a reservation. Quanah's band was allowed to keep many of its horses, and no one was imprisoned in the Fort Sill guardhouse or the uncompleted icehouse stockade.

By late 1875, Quanah had been appointed by reservation agent James M. Haworth as one of 30 band leaders for distributing beef and other supplies owed to the Comanches. Quanah sometimes undertook assignments from Mackenzie to locate runaways, returning them to the reservation while insisting that they not be imprisoned. In 1878 when the U.S. government insisted on a single chief for all the Comanches, Mackenzie named Quanah as the designated leader. This came with the agreement of many, though not all, Comanches, and the support of Indian agent P. B. Hunt. From 1886 to 1901 Quanah also served as one of three judges on the Court of Indian Offenses.

As chief, Quanah encouraged his people to develop cattle herds to replace the bison, which were then all but extinct. He also took the lead in leasing unused reservation land to American cattle owners to generate income from the large herds of Texas cattle already being grazed on the reservation. From 1892 to 1901 Quanah worked diligently to delay the allotment of Native American lands, which would open reservation space for settlement by American farmers.

A leading practitioner of traditional peyote rituals, Quanah defended the ancient ceremonies against agents and missionaries who sought to stamp them out. He also advised the Comanches to stay away from the Ghost Dance religion in the 1890s. Quanah became friends with missionaries such as the Reverend A. E. Butterfield (whose father Quanah had captured in 1865) but never formally became a Christian.

Quanah's polygamous family, a traditional prerogative of leading Comanches, was controversial. He had at least three wives when he arrived in Fort Sill in 1875. Later he had as many as seven wives. Quanah died on February 23, 1911, at Cache, Oklahoma.

CHARLES ROSENBERG

See also

Adobe Walls, Second Battle of; Buffalo; Comanches; Fort Sill; Ghost Dance; Mackenzie, Ranald Slidell; Medicine Lodge Treaty; Red River War

References

Baker, T. Lindsay, and Billy R. Harrison. *Adobe Walls: The History and Archeology of the 1874 Trading Post.* College Station: Texas A&M University Press, 1986.

Hagan, William T. *Quanah Parker, Comanche Chief.* Norman: University of Oklahoma Press, 1993.

Neeley, Bill. *The Last Comanche Chief: The Life and Times of Quanah Parker.* New York: Wiley, 1995.

Quapaws

Native Americans whose territory covered the lower Mississippi River Valley near its confluence with the Arkansas River in present-day Arkansas. Quapaw territory abutted that of the Osages in northwestern Arkansas. Their Algonquian-speaking neighbors referred to the Quapaws as the Akanseas, leading the French to call them Akensas or Akansas. It is believed that the Quapaws had once lived east of the Allegheny Mountains but, pressed by other native groups, moved first west and then down the Ohio River.

The Quapaws' first contact with Europeans occurred in 1541 when Spaniard Hernando de Soto came upon their palisaded and moated principal town, which reportedly contained several thousand people. The Quapaws' next contact with Europeans was in 1673 when Frenchmen Louis Jolliet (Joliet) and Jacques Marquette visited Quapaw settlements near the juncture of the Mississippi and Arkansas rivers. When French explorer René-Robert Cavelier, Sieur de La Salle, passed by in 1682, the Quapaws had five villages situated along both waterways. La Salle negotiated a treaty of peace with the Quapaws and claimed the territory for France. Subsequently, other Frenchmen tried to convert the Quapaws to Christianity.

For the most part, Quapaw-French relations were cordial. Indeed, because of the strategic location of Quapaw territory, the French went to considerable lengths to ensure the Quapaws' allegiance. The French realized early on that a key to controlling the Mississippi Valley was peaceful relations with its native peoples.

The Chickasaws were perennial rivals of the Quapaws. When they fought the Chickasaws, the Quapaws actively advanced French interests. Indeed, keeping the British-allied Chickasaws on the defensive helped alter the Franco-British balance in the region. During the Natchez War (1729–1733) in which the French practically destroyed the Chickasaw tribe, the Quapaws fully backed the French.

In 1739–1740 the French set out to annihilate the Chickasaws and lay exclusive claim to their territory. Toward that end the French amassed an army of about 3,600 men, including hundreds of eager Quapaw warriors. Several months into the campaign, however, the Quapaws left the expedition, which had failed to make contact with the Chickasaws. During the French and Indian War (1754–1763) the Quapaws remained steadfast French allies, although their small numbers meant that they had little impact on the outcome.

The Quapaws numbered between 5,000 and 10,000 people at first European contact, but a virulent outbreak of smallpox in 1698 killed a large majority of them. Subsequent wars, relocations, epidemics, and general decline reduced Quapaw numbers to 3,200 in 1687, 1,600 in 1750, and only 700 in 1763. Indeed, by 1763 the Quapaws had dwindled to the point that they inhabited only three tiny settlements along the Arkansas River. By 1910 the Quapaw population was estimated at just 307, including those with mixed ancestry. Nevertheless, their sliver of territory proved rich in zinc and lead deposits. By the 1920s the few surviving Quapaws enjoyed substantial royalties from the lease of mining rights.

JOHN H. BARNHILL AND PAUL G. PIERPAOLI JR.

See also

Chickasaws; Chickasaw Wars; France; French and Indian War; La Salle, René-Robert Cavelier, Sieur de; Natchez War; Osages; Soto, Hernando de

References

Arnold, Morris S. *The Rumble of a Distant Drum.* Fayetteville: University of Arkansas Press, 2000.

Baird, W. David. *The Quapaw Indians: A History of the Downstream People.* Norman: University of Oklahoma Press, 1980.

Thompson, Vern E. *Brief History of the Quapaw Tribe of Indians.* Pittsburg, KS: Mostly Books, 1994.

Queen Anne's War
Start Date: May 1702
End Date: April 1713

A series of engagements fought in North America and tied to the greater European conflict known as the War of Spanish Succession (1702–1713). Charles II (1661–1700), the Habsburg king of Spain, was childless. On the urging of King Louis XIV, French diplomats worked successfully to secure the inheritance for Louis's grandson, Philippe, Duc d'Anjou. On his death in November 1700, Charles left his considerable European and overseas possessions to Philippe on the condition that they not be divided. European leaders had long dreaded the Spanish succession and held discussions over possible partition plans (along the lines of the eventual settlement in 1713). A diplomatic solution would have averted a long and costly war, but Louis rejected any such arrangement.

The union of France with Spain and its possessions would be a formidable power bloc. To prevent this, the threatened powers assembled a coalition, and fighting in Europe began in March 1701. The war has sometimes been called the first world war, for the fighting took place around the globe in Europe, India, and North America. England became a leading player in the coalition to stymie French ambitions, allying itself with Austria,

the Netherlands, Prussia, and most of the other German states against France, Spain, and Bavaria. In May 1702 England formally declared war, and John Churchill, Earl of Marlborough, arrived in Holland as captain general of English and Dutch forces.

In North America, the war became the second of four conflicts fought for control of the continent. The English colonists there called it Queen Anne's War for the English ruler Queen Anne (r. 1702–1714). They saw the war as an opportunity to break the ring of French and Spanish settlements extending in a great arc from Canada (New France) to the Gulf of Mexico.

The first fighting in the New World occurred in 1702, when the English moved against French and Spanish holdings in the Caribbean. English forces moved from their possessions in the Leeward Islands to occupy the French portion of the island of Saint Kitts. This early success led to the unsuccessful siege of French Guadeloupe in the spring of 1703.

British North American colonists saw the war as an opportunity to raid and plunder French and Spanish colonial holdings. South Carolina raised a force of militia and native warriors. Under the command of Governor James Moore Jr., this force moved southward against Spanish Florida in October 1702. Moore destroyed several outposts along the St. Johns River and then moved on St. Augustine. The Spanish abandoned the town and withdrew to the Castillo de San Marcos. Moore's forces burned the town and returned to their ships on the approach of Spanish warships. Moore later mounted another expedition to strike at the Spanish outposts in western Florida. He used the promise of plunder to enlist native allies to participate in attacks against Spanish missions. This expedition proved a success, capturing all but 1 of the 14 missions and taking nearly 1,000 mission natives as slaves. The Carolinians were unable to push through the Choctaws, however, to get at the French settlements on the Gulf of Mexico.

In June 1703 the French colonial government enlisted the help of the Abenaki Native Americans for a series of raids along the northern frontier of New England. The purpose of the attacks was to prevent the expansion of the British colonists into the interior near New France. With French assistance and leadership, nearly 500 warriors swept into the English settlements in Maine (then part of Massachusetts). Towns such as Wells and Saco were destroyed, and a number of their inhabitants were either killed or carried off into captivity.

During these attacks, the New England colonies were left to their own devices to protect their settlements. Britain was heavily committed to fighting on the European continent, and the New York colony had made a separate peace with the natives and was not subject to native raids. The New England colonies therefore continued to suffer severe losses amid increasing rumors regarding New Yorkers' trade with the natives.

During the night of February 29, 1704, a force numbering 48 Frenchmen and Canadians and 200–250 native allies attacked Deerfield, Massachusetts. They achieved complete surprise. The raid resulted in the deaths of 50 English colonists and the capture of 112 more. Twenty-one of the captives died during the 300-mile trek back to Montreal. Eventually the survivors were ransomed and returned to Deerfield.

In response to the numerous French and native raids on New England, Massachusetts raised troops to carry the war to the French in the spring of 1704. In June of that year, Colonel Benjamin Church led a force of 500 New Englanders north to destroy Abenaki supplies and to take control of the Acadian fisheries. Church destroyed Abenaki villages at Minas and Beaubassin in July and then besieged the French Acadian fortress of Port Royal. Unable to take it, the troops then voted to return home. In Newfoundland, a force of French and Native Americans mounted a raid from Placentia against an English settlement at Bonavista during August 18–29, 1704.

In 1705 there was a lull in the fighting in North America, and the French governor proposed a prisoner exchange with the New England colonies. Both sides had taken large numbers of captives over the previous two years in raids along the frontier, but the negotiations yielded only a small number of exchanges. The governments of New France and Massachusetts actually considered a separate peace, but the negotiations failed.

In 1706 a commissioner from Massachusetts, Samuel Vetch, sailed for Britain to obtain military assistance from the Board of Trade to settle the conflict. That same year, the French and Spanish combined their forces to strike at the British in the American South and in the Caribbean. A combined force of Spanish troops and French privateers sailed from Havana, Cuba, and St. Augustine, Florida, to raid Charles Town (present-day Charleston), South Carolina. The South Carolinians were able to defeat the poorly led landing force and then raised a naval force to defeat the French ships.

South Carolina then attempted to enlist native allies to attack Spanish holdings around Pensacola and Mobile. Although an attack was mounted on Pensacola in 1707, it was not successful.

New Englanders again attempted to attack the seat of the French colonial government in Acadia by attacking Port Royal in the spring and summer of 1707. Colonel John March led a force of roughly 1,500 men funded by the government of Massachusetts. The force landed and drove the French back into their defensive works. A lack of discipline and poor colonial leadership, however, enabled the French to reinforce the garrison. By August the attempt to take Port Royal had failed, and the troops returned to Massachusetts.

In the summer of 1708 the French took the initiative by launching another series of raids along the New England frontier. A large force of 400 French Canadians and their native allies set out, but a significant number of Native Americans left the expedition. On August 29, 1708, the now-reduced force attempted to strike at Haverhill, Massachusetts. The raiders faced a spirited defense and were forced to withdraw on the arrival of Massachusetts reinforcements. The French did succeed in capturing St. John's on January 2, 1709, bringing all the eastern shore of Newfoundland under their control.

Throughout 1706–1709, colonial representatives worked to obtain military assistance from the Board of Trade in Britain. In 1709 Queen Anne granted approval for a military force to be sent to New England that would move in concert with a colonial military force commanded by Colonel Francis Nicholson. Provincial troops gathered in Albany, New York, in preparation for an advance on Montreal to support the planned British advance on Quebec and Port Royal. In October, however, word was received that European demands had led the British to cancel their participation and send the forces to Portugal instead, whereupon the entire operation was called off. The colonial representatives then dispatched another team of delegates to plead their case before the Board of Trade.

Representatives of Massachusetts, New Hampshire, Connecticut, and Rhode Island petitioned Queen Anne for a new British military operation against the French in 1710. The representatives also voted to assemble their own expedition to take Port Royal as soon as possible. Toward that end, in September 1710 a colonial force of 3,500 men under the command of Nicholson sailed from Boston for Port Royal. This time the British supplied a naval contingent of 36 vessels, including a bomb ketch. Captain George Martin had command. The British also contributed a regiment of Royal Marines. The siege of Port Royal opened on September 24, 1710, and the badly outnumbered French surrendered the citadel on October 1. The British renamed the town Annapolis Royal.

In 1711 the British government approved plans to send a military force to New England for an invasion of New France. The colonial representatives agreed to raise provincial troops to assist in this invasion. The British force of more than 60 ships and 5,000 men arrived in June 1711, but a fractured British command structure prevented any rapid movement northward. By August 1711, the force sailed for the Saint Lawrence River. At the mouth of the Saint Lawrence, an incompetent pilot led some of the British ships onto the rocks, with the loss of 8 transports. More than 700 soldiers and 200 sailors died. British admiral Sir Hovenden Walker abandoned the operation and returned with his remaining ships to England. With the loss of British military assistance, the colonial forces again disbanded.

A new Tory government in London opened negotiations for peace with the French in December 1711, and in April 1713 the warring parties agreed to peace in the Treaty of Utrecht. Philippe, Duc d'Anjou, became King Philip V of Spain, with the proviso that the French Crown and the Spanish Crown could never be united in one person. Spain was also forced to cede territory in Europe to the Austrian Habsburgs. In the New World the English received recognition of their claim to Hudson Bay and control of both Acadia and Newfoundland. The French retained both Cape Breton Island and the islands of the Saint Lawrence. The French then moved to build an even stronger fortification than Port Royal. Located on Cape Breton Island, it was later known as Louisbourg.

Although many New England colonists were unhappy with the settlement, it considerably advanced British fishing, fur-trading, and commercial interests in North America and opened up new lands for British settlement. The failure to define the frontiers precisely, however, led to renewed conflict. In 1744 the English and French colonists in North America again went to war.

WILLIAM H. BROWN AND SPENCER C. TUCKER

See also

Church, Benjamin; Deerfield, Massachusetts, Attack on; France; Great Britain; Spain

References

Eccles, William J. *France in America*. New York: Harper and Row, 1972.

Haefeli, Evan, and Kevin Sweeney. *Captors and Captives: The 1704 French and Indian Raid on Deerfield*. Amherst: University of Massachusetts Press, 2003.

Miquelon, Dale. *New France, 1701–1744: A Supplement to Europe*. Toronto: McClelland and Stewart, 1987.

Peckham, Howard Henry. *The Colonial Wars, 1689–1762*. Chicago: University of Chicago Press, 1964.

Taylor, Alan. *American Colonies: The Settling of North America*. New York: Viking/Penguin, 2001.

R

Railroads

The spread of railroads into the American West, especially after 1865, accelerated the movement of white settlers into areas previously controlled by Native Americans. At the same time, the promise of free or inexpensive land for farming and the succession of discoveries of gold and silver were great enticements to new immigrants. The expansion of the railroads, which had a tremendous impact on the buffalo range, led to the transformation of tribal hunting territories into farming and ranching areas as well as towns and commercial centers.

Since the founding of the nation, westward expansion was marked by conflict between native tribes and settlers. Railroads initially played only a minor role in westward expansion as the new transport system was first concentrated in the East along the Atlantic seaboard. By the 1850s there were slightly more than 9,000 miles of railways in the United States, but the overwhelming majority of these tracks connected cities in the East and were designed to move goods and people to and from the major seaports along the Atlantic coast and major rivers and canals.

From the 1840s through the close of the 19th century, the United States experienced a period of rapid territorial expansion. The first significant movement of settlers into the West began with the widespread use of wagon trains, headed for the Oregon Territory, in 1841. However, large-scale migration and settlement were haphazard and perilous because of the vast distances involved, the lack of efficient means of communication, and the difficulty in obtaining supplies during the westward journey.

The invention of the telegraph in 1844 and improvements in railroad technology dramatically increased the safety and efficiency of transcontinental migration. In addition, the discovery of gold in California in 1848 created an unprecedented demand for travel to the West. During a three-year period, some 250,000 Americans made the journey to California. Also in 1848, Mexico

Total Railroad Mileage in Use by Region, 1830–1890

States/Territories	1830	1840	1850	1860	1870	1880	1890
Maine, New Hampshire, Vermont, Massachusetts, Rhode Island, Connecticut	30	513	2,596	3,644	4,327	5,888	6,718
New York, Pennsylvania, Ohio, Michigan, Indiana, Maryland, Delaware, New Jersey, Washington, D.C.	0	1,484	3,740	11,927	18,292	28,155	40,826
Virginia, West Virginia, Kentucky, Tennessee, Mississippi, Alabama, Georgia, Florida, North Carolina, South Carolina	10	737	2,082	7,908	10,610	14,458	27,833
Illinois, Iowa, Wisconsin, Missouri, Minnesota	0	0	46	4,951	11,031	22,213	35,580
Louisiana, Arkansas, Oklahoma	0	21	107	250	331	1,621	5,154
North Dakota, South Dakota, New Mexico, Wyoming, Montana, Idaho, Utah, Arizona, Washington, Nebraska, Kansas, Texas, Colorado, California, Nevada, Oregon	0	0	0	239	4,578	15,466	47,451
Total	40	2,755	8,571	28,919	49,169	87,801	163,562

In 1862, the U.S. Congress chartered the Central Pacific Railroad to build east from Sacramento and the Union Pacific Railroad to build west from Omaha. Here, workers join the tracks at Promontory Point in Utah on May 10, 1869, creating the first transcontinental railroad. (National Archives)

lost claim its to its northern provinces, including Arizona, California, Texas, New Mexico, and the southern portions of Colorado, Nevada, and Utah as a result of the Mexican-American War (1846–1848).

The U.S. acquisition of these new territories and the resultant American presence on both the Atlantic and Pacific coasts reinforced the need for a transcontinental railroad to connect both ends of the continent. Even in the midst of the American Civil War (1861–1865), Congress recognized the need for a transcontinental railroad, and in 1863 the legislature passed the Pacific Railroad Act, which stipulated that a transcontinental railroad would be built. Meanwhile, the Homestead Act of 1862 opened up vast new territories to settlement. With these two important steps, an era of conflict over the unsettled American central plains began.

In 1862 the first transcontinental telegraph began operation. However, the Civil War diverted resources toward the war effort, including the need to build and often rebuild railroad tracks to move goods and supplies to support the various military campaigns. The end of the Civil War marked the onset of a period of

rapid expansion of rail lines, including resumption of the quest for a transcontinental line. From 1860 through 1890, rail expansion west of the Mississippi increased from 2,175 miles to more than 72,389 miles. By 1890, the United States had more than 163,597 miles of railroad.

The period 1860–1890 saw dramatic improvements in railroad technology. For instance, in 1868 Eli Janney invented a semiautomatic device known as a knuckle coupler for quickly connecting and disconnecting cars. This increased the ability of rail companies to load and move cars. In 1869 the first transcontinental railway was completed, meeting at Promontory Summit, Utah. This dramatically sped the transport of goods and services across the continent. In 1872 the automatic air brake was invented; this is the same system used to this day. In 1880 the first practical refrigerated cars came into use. Second and third transcontinental railways were completed in 1883.

U.S. expansion began to narrow the corridor granted to Native Americans in past agreements with the U.S. government. With the railroad came vast numbers of people and settlements in the lands populated by the nomadic Plains tribes. The permanent bisection of the land by the railroad coupled with the need for wood, food, and grazing and farming lands proved to be a serious danger for the buffalo and the Plains tribes. Buffalo, the main source of food for several of the Great Plains tribes, were nearly hunted to extinction to supply meat for workers engaged in the construction of the rail lines and to fill the eastern appetites for exotic buffalo robes. Railroads also brought sportsmen who left the prairie littered with rotting buffalo carcasses.

At rail intersections and other commercial hubs, new towns emerged that further eroded the territory of the tribes. Railroads also proved a far more efficient means to move settlers and expand farm and ranchlands at the expense of the native peoples. The inability of native peoples to adapt to the rapidly changing environment resulted in constant conflict.

With expanding encroachment upon traditional Native American lands, skirmishes between the tribes and settlers supported by federal troops occurred with increasing frequency.

The tribes viewed the railroads with increasing hostility. Each train brought more white settlers onto Native American lands and took out valuable resources. Native Americans began to harass work crews, rustle livestock, and attempt to sabotage rail travel. In response, the powerful railroad companies exerted increasing pressure on Congress to suppress the tribes and constrain them through the reservation system. With the Wounded Knee tragedy in 1890 and the end of substantial Native American resistance, the railroad had left its indelible mark on the land and on Native Americans.

TOM LANSFORD

See also

Buffalo; California Gold Rush; Manifest Destiny; Sand Creek Massacre; Wounded Knee, Battle of

References

Martin, Albro. *Railroads Triumphant: The Growth, Rejection and Rebirth of a Vital American Force.* New York: Oxford University Press, 1992.

Stover, John F. *American Railroads.* 2nd ed. Chicago: University of Chicago Press, 1997.

Raisin River Massacre
Start Date: January 22, 1813
End Date: January 23, 1813

Bloody clash between U.S. troops and British forces and their Native American allies that occurred at Frenchtown (present-day Monroe) in the Michigan Territory on January 22–23, 1813. The Raisin River Massacre was a significant event in the Northwest during the War of 1812 and was a sharp defeat for the Americans.

Following the surrender of Detroit on August 16, 1812, President James Madison appointed Major General William Henry Harrison commander in chief of the Northwestern Army. Harrison had under his command a mix of regulars and militia, both untrained, with whom he hoped to recapture Detroit. He ordered an autumn campaign, beginning in September, to restore the American position. While detachments reinforced American forts on the Mississippi River, Harrison divided his main force into three columns. Brigadier General James Winchester led the column through Indiana Territory. Harrison hoped to unite his columns on the Maumee River and then move against Detroit.

The campaign proceeded slowly. Native Americans in the region (mainly the Shawnees) had allied themselves with the British, but the Americans were unable to bring the Native Americans to battle. Instead, the Shawnees destroyed their villages and the food supplies that the Americans needed. This put Harrison's troops in a precarious situation because American logistics were in a shambles, made worse by corrupt contractors and a wet autumn. By December, Harrison suspended the operation. He ordered Winchester to remain on the Maumee, at Fort Defiance.

Winchester's column, however, was short of supplies, and the men were anxious to fight. They were mostly volunteers from Kentucky whose enlistments would expire in February. Winchester feared that inactivity would cause many to leave when their time was up.

Winchester lent a sympathetic ear to the citizens of Frenchtown. The settlers there had been raided by British and Native American parties and promised Winchester food and fighting. Thus, he sent Lieutenant Colonel William Lewis ahead with 660 Kentuckians. After a hard-fought skirmish, Lewis dispersed a small party of British near Frenchtown. Winchester's men then occupied the village and enjoyed the fruits of their victory. Winchester's tired column, with many men sick or overindulged with food and drink, failed to organize a proper defense. Winchester joined them the next day with another 300 men. When Harrison heard of Winchester's advance, he recognized the danger and ordered his forces forward immediately.

Colonel Henry Procter, the British commander in Detroit, was keenly aware of the danger posed by Winchester's presence and quickly gathered a force of about 600 regulars, militia, and sailors, including those driven out of Frenchtown. Another 600–800 Native Americans joined him. These were mostly Wyandots and Pottawatomis under the Wyandot chief Roundhead (the Shawnee chief Tecumseh was away). Procter also managed to collect six pieces of artillery. The mixed British–Native American force was encamped near Frenchtown by January 21. The Americans failed to reconnoiter the area, however, and had no idea of their danger.

At dawn of January 22 the British attacked, concentrating on the American right. The surprised Americans nevertheless managed to form ranks and put up a fight. For a half hour they held their own. At that point ammunition began to run low, and although a large supply was with Winchester, his headquarters was nearly a mile behind the lines. When the right wing collapsed, Winchester was captured. Many of the Americans who fled were killed by pursuing warriors. The American center and left continued to hold out for several more hours. Finally Winchester convinced his remaining commanders to surrender on the promise that they would not be killed. Out of 934 Americans, only 33 escaped to reach Harrison.

Procter captured more than 500 Americans. Approximately 350 died in the fighting. His own losses amounted to 24 killed and 161 wounded among the British. Although Procter had won the victory, his scouts reported that Harrison's column was only 15 miles away. Fearing a counterattack, Procter ordered his men to withdraw to Malden. Sufficient sleds were available to carry the British wounded, and those Americans who could walk were rounded up to be marched to Malden also. Some were prisoners of the Native Americans, who were reluctant to give them up. The British traded whiskey for the prisoners, and the spirits were quickly consumed.

About 80 Americans were too wounded to walk, so they were left in Frenchtown. A British officer and several interpreters were left with them to protect them from the 50 or so warriors who remained as guards. Winchester protested the delay in moving his men, although Procter promised to send sleds back as soon as possible. During the night several drunken warriors killed some of the prisoners. By early morning, about 100 other Native Americans had returned to Frenchtown. They wanted revenge for their losses in the battle of January 22. Many of the wounded were now put into houses that were set on fire, and they either burned to death or were killed trying to escape. At least 30 American wounded died before help arrived.

The defeat at the Raisin River was one of the worst suffered by the Americans in the Northwest. When he heard of the battle and that Procter had withdrawn, Harrison called off his own advance and returned to the Maumee. He gave up his idea of marching on Detroit and decided to wait until the U.S. Navy had secured control of Lake Erie.

The massacre of wounded American soldiers on the Raisin River caused outrage among many Americans, especially among Kentuckians. They blamed Procter for allowing the Native Americans to massacre defenseless men and also blamed regular army leadership for the way the battle had been bungled. While many men flocked to the militia, they avoided enlisting in the regulars. Thousands of militiamen turned out for Harrison's successful 1813 campaign. Their battle cry was "Remember the Raisin," and they were especially reluctant to take prisoners.

TIM J. WATTS

See also

Harrison, William Henry; Native Americans and the War of 1812; Pottawatomis; Shawnees; Wyandots

References

Clift, G. Glenn. *Remember the Raisin! Kentucky and Kentuckians in the Battles and Massacre at Frenchtown, Michigan Territory in the War of 1812.* Frankfort: Kentucky Historical Society, 1961.
Quimby, Robert S. *The U.S. Army in the War of 1812: An Operational and Command Study.* East Lansing: Michigan State University Press, 1997.

Ranks, U.S. Army

All armies during the period of the Indian Wars had two primary classes of soldiers: officers and enlisted men. This distinction reflected the social class distinctions of American society as a whole. An officer was by definition a gentleman; a common soldier was not. Nonetheless, the officer ranks of American military organizations during the Indian Wars period were far more accessible to men of capability from a wider range of socioeconomic classes than in almost any other army in the world.

Officers, who traditionally have comprised 10–15 percent of the American military, are further divided into three basic groups. Company-grade officers (second lieutenants, first lieutenants, and captains) are responsible for the leadership of platoons and companies. Field grade officers (majors, lieutenant colonels, and colonels) lead battalions and regiments. General officers command the higher echelons and also coordinate the overall direction of the army and its military operations. It is the generals who answer directly to the political leadership.

Enlisted soldiers are divided into two basic categories, enlisted men and noncommissioned officers (NCOs). The NCOs, which include corporals and sergeants, have always been the backbone of the American military. They are the ones responsible for training individual soldiers and for training and leading squads and gun crews. NCOs hold key leadership positions in platoons and companies. At the higher levels they assist staff officers in the planning and execution of operations. As in all other armies, the larger majority of the American enlisted ranks denoted the distinctions within the NCO corps.

Throughout virtually all of the colonial period the various American militia organizations were patterned on the British model. Organized initially as self-defense forces against England's European rivals and the native inhabitants, the American colonial units gained extensive practical experience in operations against the French and their Native American allies during the four collective conflicts between 1689 and 1763 popularly known as the French and Indian Wars. America's first army, the Continental Army, was established on April 19, 1775, and adopted the organization and rank structures of its British opponents. Many of the battles of the American Revolutionary War (1775–1783) included operations against Britain's Native American allies.

The officer rank structure of the Continental Army was almost the same as the U.S. Army has today. Brigadier general (one star) and major general (two stars) were the only two general officer ranks. The commander in chief, George Washington, was simply referred to as "general." When he was recalled to active duty in 1798 to assume command of the U.S. Army during the period of increasing tensions with France, President John Adams made Washington the first officer to hold the rank of lieutenant general (three stars). After Washington died in 1799, the rank was abolished until Winfield Scott received a brevet promotion to lieutenant general in 1855. During America's bicentennial in 1976, the U.S. Congress posthumously promoted Washington to general of

U.S. Army major general with staff and line officers in full dress, circa 1885. (Getty Images)

the armies, with an effective date of rank of July 4, 1776, thereby ensuring that Washington would always be America's senior-ranking military officer.

Promoted to lieutenant general in March 1864 during the American Civil War (1861–1865), Ulysses S. Grant was the first officer to hold that substantive rank since Washington. On July 25, 1866, Grant became America's first general (four stars). Following the Civil War, William T. Sherman succeeded Grant as commanding general of the U.S. Army in March 1869 and was promoted to full general that same month. Philip Sheridan, who became commanding general of the U.S. Army in November 1883, remained a lieutenant general but wore the special insignia of his office, which consisted of two stars flanking an eagle as depicted on America's Great Seal. Sheridan was promoted to full general just weeks before his death in 1888. When Sheridan died in office in June 1888, major general reverted to the highest rank in the U.S. Army throughout the remainder of the 19th century. The senior ranking major general (as determined by date of rank) was assigned as the commanding general of the U.S. Army. That position was transformed into the chief of staff of the U.S. Army in 1903.

Field-grade officer ranks remained consistent from the Continental Army through the 19th century and indeed to the present. Typically, a regiment was commanded by a colonel, assisted by one or two lieutenant colonels and one or two majors. A regimental staff in the Continental Army also had a number of specialist officers designated by titles such as adjutant, quartermaster, paymaster, and surgeon. By the late 19th century most of the officers serving in those positions held the rank of captain.

The positions of company-grade officers in the Continental Army varied by type of unit. Companies were commanded by captains. Infantry company commanders generally were assisted by a first lieutenant, a second lieutenant, and an ensign, the lowest officer rank whose primary responsibility was to carry the unit's flag. In cavalry units the officer holding that duty bore the rank of coronet. Artillery companies also had four distinct officer ranks, but none that equated to ensign or coronet. Below captain but above first lieutenant was the rank of captain lieutenant, which was only used for a few years. By the end of the Revolutionary War, the junior-most officer in an artillery company held the rank of lieutenant fireworker, which equated to ensign in the infantry and coronet in the cavalry. The U.S. Army abolished the ranks of ensign and coronet in 1800, leaving captain, first lieutenant, and second lieutenant as the standard structure for company-grade ranks, still in use today.

When Washington assumed command of the Continental Army on July 3, 1775, the identification of officers was one of the immediate problems he faced. In one of his first orders, Washington called for "some badge of distinction" between officer ranks in the form of different-colored cockades in their hats. Field officers were to be identified by red or pink cockades, captains by yellow or buff, and lieutenants by green. For general officers and their aides-de-camp, Washington ordered the aides to wear a green sash diagonally across their shoulders between their uniform coats and waistcoats. Brigadier generals wore a purple sash, major generals wore a pink sash, and as commander in chief, Washington himself wore a light blue sash.

The 1780 regulations stipulated that major generals wear two stars on the epaulettes of their uniform coats, while brigadier generals wore one star. Initially there was no specific insignia of rank for the field-grade and company-grade officers, but their respective ranks were distinguished by the size and the length of the fringe of their epaulettes. In 1832 the eagle insignia was authorized for colonels. Infantry officers wore silver epaulettes with gold insignia; all other officers wore gold epaulettes with silver insignia.

In 1836 shoulder straps were adopted for field uniforms, while epaulettes remained for dress uniforms. Lieutenant colonels were authorized to wear the oak leaf insignia, and captains and first lieutenants wore two bars and one bar, respectively. Majors and second lieutenants still had no specific insignia. In 1851 silver was adopted as the insignia color for colonels and lieutenant colonels of all branches, and gold was adopted for the bars of captains and first lieutenants.

Shoulder knots replaced epaulettes on the dress uniform in 1872; shoulder straps remained on the field uniform. Majors that year were authorized a gold leaf to distinguish them from second lieutenants, and the bars of captains and first lieutenants were changed to silver. Although second lieutenants wore shoulder straps with no insignia, the shoulder straps identified them as officers and thus second lieutenants by default.

The khaki and olive drab field uniforms introduced at the beginning of the 20th century had neither shoulder knots nor shoulder straps but rather pin-on rank insignia. As the uniforms became simpler and more utilitarian, it became increasingly difficult to distinguish a second lieutenant from a private, and in 1917 the single gold bar was adopted as the rank insignia for a second lieutenant. Thus, the curious situation in which a given insignia design in silver outranks the same design in gold was not the result of a conscious decision at any given point but instead was the result of an evolutionary period of some 100 years.

A brevet promotion was an advancement in an officer's rank without an accompanying advancement in pay or assigned position. Adopted from British practice by the Second Continental Congress, the brevet promotion was the primary means through which the large numbers of foreign volunteer officers were brought into the Continental Army. At the end of the Revolutionary War, the Congress on September 30, 1783, conferred a general brevet, advancing by one rank all officers below the rank of major general. Eighteen days later Congress voted to disband the Continental Army, with the exception of a single company to guard the military stores at West Point.

After the adoption of the U.S. Constitution in 1787, the brevet system was retained as the U.S. military slowly built back up. On April 6, 1818, Congress passed an act requiring that all brevet promotions be confirmed by the Senate. During the 19th century, brevet promotions were conferred on officers for valor in the presence of the enemy or for distinguished service. Prior to the Civil War, brevet promotions were also conferred upon officers for 10 years of faithful service at the same rank if no regular vacancies were available in the next higher rank. Until the Medal of Honor was established in 1861, the brevet promotion was the sole means of formally recognizing an officer's heroic conduct in combat. Fifty-five U.S. Army officers received brevet promotions for distinguished conduct during the Second Seminole War (1835–1842).

Militia and volunteer rank further complicated the army officer rank structure throughout the 19th century. From the War of 1812 through the Spanish-American War (1898), the U.S. Army depended heavily on state militia and volunteer units in times of crisis. Separate from the standing state militia units that could be called into federal service, the volunteer units were federal formations hastily raised for the duration of the war at hand and then just as quickly disbanded. Typically, the volunteer units were led by regular army officers detailed to command the volunteers at much higher ranks than they held in the regular army. The situation was complicated even further with the authorization of brevet volunteer rank in March 1863. By 1865, then, an officer could hold any or all of five different ranks, all of which were duly recorded in his permanent record: regular army rank, regular army brevet rank, volunteer rank, volunteer brevet rank, and militia rank of some state.

George Armstrong Custer is a case in point. An 1861 graduate of the U.S. Military Academy at West Point, Custer was promoted to captain in the regular army in May 1864. He also received five regular army brevet promotions, the last being to brevet major general in March 1865. Meanwhile, he was made a brigadier general

of volunteers in June 1863, a brevet major general of volunteers in October 1864, and a major general of volunteers in April 1865. In February 1866 Custer was mustered out of volunteer service, and that July he was promoted in the regular army to lieutenant colonel, the highest substantive rank he ever held. His brother Thomas W. Custer held ranks under all five systems during his military career, starting in 1864 as a militia second lieutenant in the 6th Michigan Cavalry. Although he had held brevet rank as a lieutenant colonel in the Civil War, he was a regular army captain at the time of his death at the Battle of the Little Bighorn (June 25–26, 1876).

During the Civil War large numbers of brevet promotions were awarded, and the system was rife with abuse. On March 13, 1865, the army gave brevet promotions to a huge number of officers for "faithful and meritorious service," including many staff officers who had spent the entire war sitting behind desks at the War Department. Those brevets fostered a great deal of anger and resentment among the officers who had received their brevets for heroic conduct in the face of the enemy. Two other large groups of Civil War brevet promotions were conferred on March 2 and November 6, 1867. The three waves of end-of-war brevets covered almost every officer who had served the Union.

Congress reacted on March 1, 1869, by passing an act requiring that all future brevet promotions be awarded only for "distinguished conduct and public service in the presence of the enemy." Congress further tightened the brevet promotion system by passing a law on July 15, 1870, stipulating that "Hereafter no officer shall be entitled to wear while on duty any uniform other than that of his actual rank, on account of having been brevetted; nor shall he be addressed in orders or official communications by any title other than that of his actual rank."

The restrictive language of the March 1869 congressional act effectively held up all brevet promotions for the next 25 years. Although officers were nominated for brevet promotions after March 1869 and those nominations were processed and submitted to the Congress, the Senate refused to confirm the nominations on the basis that military actions against Native Americans did not qualify under the "in the presence of the enemy" language of the act. On February 27, 1890, Congress finally passed a law titled "An Act to Authorize the President to Confer Brevet Ranks, &c., for Gallant Services in Indian Wars." Even so, it took more than four years before President Grover Cleveland sent to the Congress the consolidated list of the brevet nominations since 1869. The list of 158 officers was submitted on April 20, 1894, but the brevets were confirmed and entered in the officers' records with an effective date of February 27, 1890.

By the end of the Indian Wars, brevet promotions were almost extinct. A few were conferred during the early years of the 20th century, but the system essentially died out from disuse. The introduction of the Medal of Honor during the Civil War marked the beginning of the end of the brevet system, and the introduction in the early 20th century of the subordinate-level awards for valor completely eliminated the justification for brevet promotions.

U.S. Army enlisted men, circa 1885. (Getty Images)

The militia units of the colonial period all included NCOs based on the British model. As early as 1609, the militia of Jamestown, Virginia, was organized into squads led by NCOs. The small squads were particularly effective in operations against Native American hit-and-run tactics in heavily wooded areas. By the start of the Revolutionary War in 1775, NCOs were sergeants, corporals, or specialists whose rank titles also identified their functions. In 1775 a Massachusetts artillery company, for example, consisted of 3 sergeants, 3 corporals, 6 bombardiers, 6 gunners, and 32 privates, which in artillery units of the time were called matrosses. A Continental infantry company of 1776 had 4 sergeants, 4 corporals, 1 drummer, 1 fifer, and 76 privates.

Field musicians such as drummers, fifers, and buglers were key NCOs. Through the very end of the 19th century their most important function was the transmission of orders on the field of battle. Along with the field musicians, other NCO specialist and non-NCO specialist ranks remained in wide use into the early years of the 20th century.

When General Washington issued his first uniform order in 1775, he also stipulated that sergeants be identified by an epaulette or stripe of red cloth on the right shoulder, with the corporals wearing one of green. While officers wore more ornate epaulettes of gold or silver color, the simpler NCO epaulettes were of a worsted wool or sometimes silk material. In 1779 Washington authorized sergeants to wear two silk epaulettes and corporals to wear one worsted epaulette on the right shoulder. The color of the epaulette designated the branch of the NCO's unit: white for infantry, yellow for artillery, and blue for cavalry.

As the Revolutionary War progressed, the ranks of sergeants expanded to differentiate their levels of responsibility. The staff of a Continental Army infantry regiment in 1776 included a sergeant major, a quartermaster sergeant, a drum major, and a fife major. The drum and fife majors were the senior NCOs responsible for training the drummers and fifers of the subordinate companies. The sergeant major was the senior-ranking NCO of the regiment. By 1781 the Continental Army infantry regiment had first sergeants as the senior NCOs within companies.

The system of colored epaulettes to distinguish sergeants and corporals remained in use throughout the War of 1812. The new uniform regulations of 1821 introduced for the first time chevrons as the distinctive insignias of rank for NCOs. Sergeants wore a single large point-up chevron between the elbow and the shoulder. Corporals wore the single chevron below the elbow, just above the wrist. The insignia for sergeant major was introduced in 1825 and consisted of a horizontal bar connecting the two extreme points of the chevron, resulting in a large triangle.

The uniform regulations of 1847 identified five specific NCO ranks. All of the insignia consisted of chevrons worn between the shoulder and the elbow, and all were worn points up except for soldiers in mounted units, who wore theirs points down. At the company level corporals wore two chevrons, sergeants wore three chevrons, and first sergeants wore three chevrons above a diamond. At the regimental staff level the quartermaster sergeant wore three chevrons tied together with three horizontal bars. The sergeant major wore three chevrons tied together with three arcs. In the 20th century, the arcs that distinguished the various higher NCO ranks came to be called "rockers."

The uniform regulations of 1851 established the pattern that remained in effect until 1902. Points-down chevrons became the standard for all branches. The rank of ordnance sergeant, consisting of three chevrons and a star, was added to the regimental staff. The specialist rank of hospital steward consisted of a single green diagonal half-chevron 1.75 inches wide and embroidered with a gold caduceus. At the company level the new specialist rank of pioneer consisted of a pair of crossed axes but no chevrons or stripes. Regimental NCOs wore insignia made from silk, whereas company NCOs wore worsted insignia.

The insignias were very large by modern standards. The chevrons were 10 inches across at their widest point, and the sergeant major chevron was 8 inches from top to bottom. The chevrons on the field uniform were made from a single piece of felt, with the individual stripes delineated by chain stitching, usually black. The basic color of the chevron matched the color of the uniform trouser stripe and indicated the NCO's branch of service: yellow for cavalry, red for artillery, and light blue for infantry. Artillery soldiers to this day are called "redlegs."

The uniform regulations issued between 1872 and 1899 introduced a wide range of NCO and non-NCO specialist ranks. The 1872 regulations authorized at the regimental level a principal musician, wearing three chevrons and a bugle, and at the company

A group of U.S. Army officers, photographed in March 1882. (Getty Images)

or battalion level a quartermaster sergeant, wearing three chevrons and a single horizontal bar. The 1882 regulations authorized a chief trumpeter, wearing the three chevrons and bugle of the principal musician, plus a single arc; a commissary sergeant, wearing three chevrons and a crescent moon; and a saddler sergeant, wearing three chevrons and a saddler's round knife.

The 1884 regulations changed the color of the chevrons for infantry NCOs from light blue to white. The 1884 regulations also eliminated the diagonal half-chevron for a hospital steward and replaced it with three green chevrons surmounted by a red cross with a single green arc. The new rank of acting hospital steward wore the same insignia with only the three chevrons and no arc. Two other newly introduced NCO ranks included post quartermaster sergeant, wearing three buff chevrons surmounted by a crossed key and feather pen, and regimental and battalion color sergeant, both of whom wore three chevrons surmounted with a circle 1.25 inches in diameter. The insignia for the new specialist rank of farrier was a horseshoe in the branch color of the unit. Like the pioneer insignia, it was sewn onto the uniform sleeve as a rectangular patch or worn as an armband.

A War Department circular in August 1890 established uniforms for Native American scouts, who wore white chevrons with red stitching. A general order in May 1891 authorized the rank of lance corporal "to test the capacity of privates for the duties of noncommissioned officers." Lance corporals wore a single chevron. Also authorized in 1891 was the rank of sergeant first class

of the signal corps, the first NCO rank to carry the designation of sergeant first class. The rank insignia consisted of three black chevrons and a single arc delineated by white stitching, with the full-color signal corps branch insignia of crossed signal flags and a flaming torch in the center.

The 1899 uniform regulations introduced even more new ranks, both NCO and specialist. Among the most significant, the new rank of battalion or squadron sergeant major was designated by three chevrons and two arcs. The rank of chief musician was indicated by three chevrons, a bugle, and two arcs. Signal Corps sergeants, corporals, and lance corporals were also authorized to wear above their chevrons the crossed flags and torch insignia that signal corps sergeants first class had been authorized in 1891. The specialist insignia of privates first class that continued to be worn on armbands included saddlers (round knife), farriers (horseshoe), cooks (cook's hat), mechanics (crossed hammers), and gunners (cannon projectile). All were in the branch color of the soldier's assigned unit except for the gunner's insignia, which was always red because gunners were only assigned to artillery units.

Aside from adding a few more specialist NCO ranks, the 1902 uniform regulations did little to alter the enlisted rank structure. What did change completely was the look of enlisted rank insignia. The basic arrangement of chevrons, arcs, bars, specialist marks, and branch colors remained the same, but they were all converted to a points-up configuration and reduced in size to the standard 3-inch width still worn on U.S. Army uniforms today. A single chevron was still a lance corporal. By World War I (1914–1918), virtually every branch had a unique specialist insignia (now worn on the sleeve on 2.5-inch disks) to designate their privates first class. All of the specialist insignia were eliminated in 1920 along with the rank of lance corporal, and the single chevron became the rank insignia of private first class.

David T. Zabecki

See also

Custer, George Armstrong; Custer, Thomas Ward; Grant, Ulysses Simpson; Sheridan, Philip Henry; Sherman, William Tecumseh; Washington, George

References

Bell, William Gardner. *Commanding Generals and Chiefs of Staff: 1775–1995*. Washington, DC: Center of Military History, 1997.

Emerson, William K. *Chevrons: Illustrated History and Catalog of U.S. Army Insignia*. Washington, DC: Smithsonian Institution Press, 1983.

Heitman, Francis B. *Historical Register and Dictionary of the United States Army*. Washington, DC: U.S. Government Printing Office, 1903.

Hogan, David W., Arnold G. Fisch, and Robert K. Wright. *The Story of the Noncommissioned Officer Corps: The Backbone of the Army*. Washington, DC: Center of Military History, 2003.

Lelle, John E. *The Brevet Medal*. Springfield, VA: Quest Publishing, 1988.

Ogden, H. A., and Henry Loomis Nelson. *Uniforms of the United States Army: First Series*. New York: Thomas Yoseloff, 1959.

Ogden, H. A., and Marvin H. Pakula. *Uniforms of the United States Army: Second Series*. New York: Thomas Yoseloff, 1960.

Wright, Robert K., Jr. *The Continental Army*. Washington, DC: Center of Military History, 1983.

Rappahannocks

A small Algonquian-speaking Native American group that lived on the Rappahannock Peninsula in the Tidewater area of eastern Virginia. The principal Rappahannock village was at Cat Creek Point on the north side of the Rappahannock River. The Rappahannocks had a lifestyle similar to that of other Eastern Woodlands and Northeast Woodlands American Indians. They lived in small villages built in clearings that contained about 200 people. The men engaged in hunting and fishing, and the women grew corn (maize) and other vegetables. Crops were gathered and stored in hand-woven baskets. The men used flint knapping to create arrowheads for hunting and for war.

In the late spring and summer of 1608 Captain John Smith sailed west from the new English colony at Jamestown to explore, going up the great rivers that empty into Chesapeake Bay. One of these tributaries was the Rappahannock River. Smith explored the Rappahannock roughly 130 miles from Chesapeake Bay to the fall line. On his journey he was entertained by a group of friendly natives called the Moraughtacunds. They advised him not to go to the Toppahanocks (Rappahannocks), who were deemed a dangerous people. Furthermore, they claimed that the Rappahannocks would kill the Moraughtacunds if they discovered that they had helped Smith.

Smith ignored the Moraughtacunds' warnings and sailed to a place where some Rappahannocks were located. The encounter soon turned violent. Smith recorded that one of the Rappahannocks was killed, and one colonist was shot with an arrow.

The Rappahannocks were at the time a member of the Powhatan Confederacy, organized by Chief Powhatan. He had inherited dominion over 6 native tribes: the Arrohattocs, the Appomattocks, the Mattaponis, the Pamunkeys, the Powhatans, and the Youghtanunds. Powhatan had then by various means added some 25 more tribes to the confederation. Each of the approximately 30 tribes forming the Powhatan Confederacy was ruled by a *werowance,* or chief. They in turn were subject to Powhatan.

The Rappahannocks participated in the native attacks on the colony of Virginia in 1622 and again in 1644. In addition, there was specific trouble between the colonists and the Rappahannocks in 1655. By then, English settlers had begun to encroach on Rappahannock lands.

In 1656 the Virginia House of Burgesses ordered a march against the Rappahannocks, and 170 men took part in the raid. The attacks caused serious damage to Rappahannock villages.

That same year the English signed a treaty with the Rappahannocks that delineated territories. The treaty was almost immediately ignored, however, by settlers moving west. By the late 1660s the Rappahannocks had been forced to give up their lands guaranteed by the treaty and began to move toward the falls of the Mattaponi River.

In the 1670s and 1680s war between the Rappahannocks and white settlers resulted in many deaths and a forced migration of the Rappahannocks farther west. The Virginia-Indian Treaty of 1677/1680 made the Rappahannocks tributaries to the English Crown and subservient to the Pamunkeys. That arrangement lasted for less than a year, however. By the 1680s the Rappahannocks had retreated to a reserve along Portobago Bay. By the beginning of the 18th century the Rappahannocks had dwindled to perhaps fewer than 50 families, nearly all of whom were living in Virginia's Essex County.

Today, 200 to 300 descendants of the Rappahonnocks and related tribes live in Essex, Caroline, and King and Queen counties in eastern Virginia. They incorporated as a tribe in 1921, and in 1983 they were officially recognized by the Commonwealth of Virginia.

ANDREW J. WASKEY

See also

Anglo-Powhatan War, Second; Anglo-Powhatan War, Third; Pamunkeys; Powhatan; Powhatan Confederacy; Virginia-Indian Treaty of 1677/1680

References

Bastow, Thelma Wilkerson de Shields. *What Happened to the Rappahannocks? The Story of This Once Mighty Tribe of the Great Nation of Powhatan from the Time of the Coming of Those First Englishmen to Jamestown until the Present.* Indian Neck, VA: Board of Trustees for the Preservation of the Rappahannock Indian History, 1975.

Speck, Frank G. *The Rappahannock Indians of Virginia.* New York: Museum of the American Indian Heye Foundation, 1925.

Raritans

A segment of the Delaware (Lenni Lenape) tribe. The Raritans occupied the lower Raritan River Valley in present-day New Jersey until the 1640s, when a series of conflicts with the Dutch drove them away from the coast and into the interior of New Jersey. Relations between the Dutch colony of New Netherland and the Raritans turned violent during the 1640s because of unfortunate decisions by Governor Willem Kieft and demands placed on the Raritans by the growing settler population. As with most Native Americans of the Northeast, the Raritans' main economic activities were derived from small-scale agriculture, hunting and gathering, and trade with other Native American groups and Europeans.

Initially, all of the native groups in the vicinity of New Amsterdam (later New York City) prospered from their relations with the Dutch. However, as the city's population grew, Dutch demands for native labor, land, and food escalated at the same time that the Dutch developed a contemptuous attitude toward the local natives, including the Raritans. Relations between the Dutch and the natives became further strained as the Dutch stopped trading for firearms with the Delawares and other local groups but continued to trade guns to the Iroquois, enemies of the Delawares and other Algonquian-speaking tribes in the area. Additionally, Dutch hogs and cattle herds began destroying native agricultural fields. Finally, Kieft demanded that all Delawares and other Algonquians pay an annual tribute in maize or wampum. By 1641 the strife between the Dutch and local natives reached a boiling point.

The key event that opened hostilities between the Raritans and the Dutch occurred in 1641, when some pigs belonging to Dutch settlers were stolen from Staten Island. Governor Kieft assumed, without investigation, that the culprits were the Raritans and sent a detachment of 50 men to exact retribution. They killed several Raritans and burned their crops. In retaliation for the attack, the Raritans attacked a Dutch-owned plantation on Staten Island. They killed four workers and burned the home and the tobacco house. This was just the first in a series of events that eventually escalated into a full-blown conflagration that engulfed the lower Hudson River Valley and northeastern New Jersey. In another incident, Kieft sent a detachment of soldiers to Manhattan Island to massacre a group of 80 natives seeking sanctuary among the Dutch from attacks by other natives farther north. This group consisted primarily of women and children. Some 1,000 natives lost their lives in what became known as Kieft's War (1639–1645) before peace was finally restored in 1645.

The Delawares and other Algonquians fought the Dutch in three other wars in 1655, during 1659–1660, and during 1663–1664. All of these conflicts with native people in the area hurt the Dutch because they diminished immigration of new colonists to New Netherland. The first of these wars helped to eventually drive the Raritans out of their homeland near the New Jersey shore along the Raritan River. Afterward the Raritans lost their individual identity among the larger Delaware population.

DIXIE RAY HAGGARD

See also
Delawares; Iroquois; Kieft, Willem; Kieft's War

References
Kraft, Herbert C. *The Lenape: Archaeology, History, and Ethnography.* Newark: New Jersey Historical Society, 1986.
Weslager, C. A. *The Delaware Indians: A History.* New Brunswick, NJ: Rutgers University Press, 1972.

Red Bird
Birth Date: ca. 1788
Death Date: February 16, 1828

Winnebago (Ho-Chunk) warrior who in June 1827 led retaliatory attacks against white settlers and boatmen in western Wisconsin. The resulting Winnebago War, also known as Red Bird's Uprising, failed to end American transgressions and instead aroused calls for the removal of all Native Americans from the Old Northwest Territory. Red Bird (Waunigsootshkau) was born probably in 1788 in west-central Wisconsin. Little is known of his early years.

In 1822 the U.S. government began issuing leases to mine lead in northwestern Illinois and southwestern Wisconsin. Droves of miners soon flooded the region and abused the Native American population, which included the Winnebagos, who had not ceded these lands for white exploitation. Already strained, the Winnebagos' patience broke in early 1827 with the false rumor that the United States had turned two Winnebago prisoners over to Ojibwa executioners.

Winnebago chiefs selected Red Bird, a warrior known and liked by whites around Prairie du Chien, to seek retribution. On June 26, 1827, Red Bird and two accomplices visited the home of Registre Gagnier, who treated his guests hospitably. The Winnebagos nevertheless attacked the unsuspecting family, killing Gagnier and another man and scalping an infant (who survived). On June 30 Red Bird gathered a larger party of warriors and attacked the keelboat *O. H. Perry* as it descended the Mississippi River. Regular army forces under Brigadier General Henry Atkinson and Illinois militiamen now deployed to the heart of Winnebago country, and a chastened Red Bird surrendered at the Wisconsin-Fox River portage on September 3. On February 16, 1828, he died in American captivity at Fort Crawford (Prairie du Chien). Red Bird's action prompted a brief conflict, known as the Winnebago War, that was quickly won by U.S. forces.

Instead of teaching the Americans a lesson, the Winnebagos learned how tenuous their hold on their ancestral lands had become. In consequence, they lent the Sauk warrior Black Hawk only tepid support when he waged his own war against the Americans in 1832.

JOHN W. HALL

See also
Atkinson, Henry; Black Hawk; Black Hawk War; Ojibwas; Old Northwest Territory; Sauks and Foxes; Wabokieshiek; Winnebagos; Winnebago War

References
McKenney, Thomas L. *Memoirs, Official and Personal.* Lincoln: University of Nebraska Press, 1973.
Zanger, Martin. "Red Bird." In *American Indian Leaders: Studies in Diversity,* edited by R. David Edmunds, 64–87. Lincoln: University of Nebraska Press, 1980.

Red Cap
See Inkpaduta

Red Cloud
Birth Date: ca. 1821–1822
Death Date: December 10, 1909

Oglala Sioux war leader. Red Cloud (Makhpyia-luta) was born in 1821 or 1822 possibly near the forks of the Platte River in present-day Nebraska. In conflicts against the Pawnees, Crows, and other rival tribes, he demonstrated great courage and earned the position of war leader for the Teton Lakota Sioux, which included Red Cloud's Oglala band. The discovery of gold in Montana drew numerous white immigrants to the Bozeman Trail that passed through the Powder River region of Wyoming and Montana, territory claimed by the Sioux, Arapahos, and Northern Cheyennes.

Oglala Sioux war chief Red Cloud was one of the greatest of Native American military leaders against white American encroachments on Indian lands. (Library of Congress)

The influx began in 1864, and by early 1865 the Sioux, at Red Cloud's urging, had begun to attack these interlopers.

American peace commissioner E. B. Taylor invited the Sioux to Fort Laramie in Wyoming Territory for talks. Red Cloud along with Man-Afraid-of-His-Horses and other leaders arrived in June 1866. During the negotiations, Colonel Henry Carrington arrived with troops to build forts along the Bozeman Trail. Red Cloud denounced this as treachery, promised to fight anyone who intruded onto Sioux lands, and promptly left the conference.

Throughout the summer and autumn of 1866, Sioux, Cheyenne, and Arapaho warriors under Red Cloud and other leaders attacked travelers and the soldiers building three forts along the trail. The raids culminated in the Fetterman Massacre of December 21, 1866. Lured from Fort Phil Kearny by a Sioux decoy party, Captain William Fetterman and his 79 men were ambushed and annihilated.

Native raids continued during 1867, including an unsuccessful assault against woodcutters from Fort Phil Kearny that Red Cloud led in person. Meanwhile, after much debate the U.S. government agreed to a conciliatory approach to the Native Americans of the Powder River region.

Red Cloud, on the advice of Man-Afraid-of-His-Horses, rejected an invitation to a peace conference in November 1867. When Red Cloud received a second invitation the following spring, he agreed to attend on the condition that the soldiers first evacuate the forts on the Bozeman Trail. American officials complied, and the forts were evacuated in July and August 1868. Red Cloud and his followers then burned the abandoned forts.

In November, Red Cloud arrived at Fort Laramie for negotiations. The resulting treaty ended the war, recognized Sioux claims to a vast tract of land in Montana and Wyoming, and set aside most of present-day western South Dakota as the Great Sioux Reservation.

Red Cloud apparently chose to ignore the terms of the treaty by remaining near Fort Laramie, regardless of government efforts to have him move to the reservation. In 1870 he visited Washington, D.C., and met with President Ulysses Grant. In 1873 the government created the Red Cloud Agency in northwestern Nebraska for Red Cloud and his followers, but in 1878 the agency was relocated within the confines of the old Great Sioux Reservation in the Dakota Territory and redesignated the Pine Ridge Agency. There Red Cloud feuded with the Indian agent, Dr. Valentine T. McGillycuddy, who wanted the Sioux to abandon hunting and take up farming.

Despite his conflict with McGillycuddy, repeated violations of the Fort Laramie Treaty by the U.S. government, and pressure from Sioux militants to join them in armed resistance, Red Cloud played no role in the Great Sioux War (1876–1877) or the Ghost Dance movement that ended with the tragedy at Wounded Knee. For the remainder of his life Red Cloud honored his commitment to remain at peace. He died on December 10, 1909, at Pine Ridge.

JIM PIECUCH

See also

Bozeman Trail; Fetterman Massacre; Fort Laramie, Treaty of (1851); Fort Laramie, Treaty of (1868); Oglala Sioux; Pine Ridge Reservation; Red Cloud's War; Sioux

References

Brown, Dee. *Bury My Heart at Wounded Knee.* New York: Holt, Rinehart and Winston, 1970.

Olson, James C. *Red Cloud and the Sioux Problem.* Lincoln: University of Nebraska Press, 1965.

Utley, Robert M. *The Indian Frontier of the American West, 1846–1890.* Albuquerque: University of New Mexico Press, 1984.

Red Cloud's War
Start Date: 1866
End Date: 1868

Conflict between Native Americans and the U.S. government over control of the Powder River Country, through which passed the Bozeman Trail leading to the Montana goldfields. Fought from

1866 to 1868, and also known as the Powder River War, the conflict is named after Red Cloud, an Oglala Sioux war leader, who led the most successful war Native Americans had ever waged against the U.S. Army. Red Cloud's determined resistance led to the abandonment of the Bozeman Trail and three U.S. Army forts in the summer of 1868.

The discovery of gold in 1862 and 1863 in Idaho and Montana opened a new front in the ongoing conflict between white settlers and the Plains Indian tribes. Although the American Civil War (1861–1865) was still in progress, thousands of adventurers and fortune seekers nevertheless flocked to the area, and pressure mounted to establish more direct lines of access to the Virginia City goldfields. To respond to these challenges, army officials finally adopted the route pioneered by John Bozeman that extended from Fort Laramie on the North Platte River and the Oregon Trail northwestward along the eastern base and around the northern shoulder of the Bighorn Mountains and on to Virginia City. Although the Bozeman Trail was nearly 400 miles shorter than other routes to the region, it also cut through hunting grounds reserved for the Sioux, Northern Cheyennes, and Arapahos by the Harney-Sanborn Treaties of 1865.

In 1866 U.S. government representatives, under considerable public pressure and also lured by the gold in the region that might relieve the financial stress of the Civil War, engaged the tribes in new negotiations in an effort to gain passage through their lands. Although a few chiefs signed new treaties at Fort Laramie, others led by Red Cloud quit the discussions when Colonel Henry B. Carrington marched in with a battalion from the 18th Infantry on his way to establish posts along the Bozeman Trail. This occurred well before agreements with all the tribes had been reached.

On June 17, 1866, Carrington's battalion of about 700 men, plus several cavalry units and hundreds of mule teams hauling large quantities of equipment and supplies, departed Fort Laramie and headed toward the Bighorn Mountains. At Fort Reno, located on the Powder River many miles from the nearest telegraph station, Carrington relieved two companies of the 5th U.S. Volunteers, comprised of former Confederate prisoners who had aligned with the Union and agreed to frontier service in exchange for their freedom. Farther to the northwest some 225 miles from Fort Laramie, Carrington constructed his headquarters on the Piney tributary of the Powder River, which he named Fort Phil Kearny. Five companies stayed at Fort Phil Kearny, while the remaining two marched another 90 miles to establish Fort C. F. Smith on a bluff some 500 yards from the Bighorn River.

Fort Phil Kearny almost immediately came under Native American attack and, during its brief existence, remained in an almost continual state of siege. On December 21, 1866, Red Cloud's warriors attacked a wagon train six miles from the fort. Captain William Fetterman, who had boasted that he could ride through the whole Sioux Nation with just 80 men, asked to lead a relief column. Native decoys lured Fetterman from the fort, and, against Carrington's orders, Fetterman crossed the ridge toward hundreds of waiting warriors. In a carefully executed ambush, the Sioux annihilated Fetterman's entire force, including 2 civilians who had accompanied the soldiers to test their new Henry repeating rifles.

The army was more successful in two other notable actions on the Bozeman Trail. In August 1867 Cheyenne and Sioux warriors launched separate but seemingly coordinated attacks known as the Hayfield Fight (August 1, 1867) and the Wagon Box Fight (August 2, 1867). In the Hayfield Fight, 19 soldiers and 6 civilians from Fort C. F. Smith under Lieutenant Sigismund Sternberg, equipped with converted breech-loading Springfields and several repeating rifles, held off a superior force with the loss of 3 killed and 3 wounded. In the Wagon Box Fight near Fort Phil Kearny, Captain James Powell and 31 men positioned themselves behind wagons that had their running gear removed. There they managed to hold at bay a force of several hundred warriors for four hours with only 3 killed and 2 wounded.

Despite these small victories, the days of the Bozeman Trail were numbered. After eight months of negotiations, the majority of the tribal leaders finally agreed to the terms of a new treaty, but it was not until November 6, 1868, that Red Cloud signed the document at Fort Laramie that officially ended Red Cloud's War. The 1868 treaty met almost all of the Sioux demands, including the abandonment of Fort Reno, Fort Phil Kearny, and Fort C. F. Smith and the closing of the Bozeman Trail. The treaty also recognized Native American dominion over the Powder River Country and vast hunting grounds in Wyoming and Montana and set aside most of the Dakota Territory west of the Missouri River as the Great Sioux Reservation. For the first time in its history, the U.S. government had negotiated a peace that had conceded everything demanded by the opposing party and that had extracted nothing in return.

BRETT F. WOODS

See also

Arapahos; Black Hills Gold Rush; Bozeman Trail; Cheyennes, Northern; Fetterman Massacre; Fort Laramie, Treaty of (1851); Fort Laramie, Treaty of (1868); Fort Phil Kearny; Hayfield Fight; Oglala Sioux; Powder River Expedition; Red Cloud; Wagon Box Fight

References

Bell, William G. "Winning the West: The Army in the Indian Wars, 1865–1890." In *American Military History,* edited by Maurice Matloff, 300–318. Washington, DC: Office of the Chief of Military History, 1973.

Cohen, Felix S. *Handbook of Federal Indian Law.* Washington, DC: U.S. Department of the Interior, Office of the Solicitor, 1945.

Mattes, Merrill J. *Fort Laramie Park History, 1834–1977.* Washington, DC: U.S. Department of the Interior, 1980.

Schuetz, Janice E. *Episodes in the Rhetoric of Government-Indian Relations.* Westport, CT: Greenwood, 2002.

Red Eagle

See Weatherford, William

Red Jacket
Birth Date: 1758
Death Date: January 20, 1830

Seneca leader. Red Jacket was born sometime in 1758 in Canoga, New York. As a youth, Red Jacket's budding oratorical skills earned him the name Sagoyewatha ("He Who Keeps Them Awake"). The Senecas fought on the British side during the American Revolutionary War (1775–1783), but Red Jacket earned no distinction as a warrior in that conflict. In recognition for his service as a messenger, however, British officers presented him with a red coat that he wore proudly, earning him the name Red Jacket by which he was known among whites.

During the War of 1812, Red Jacket initially negotiated a defensive alliance with the Americans. The Senecas would defend their lands in New York but would not cross into Canada. However, this stance changed in the face of repeated British raids onto Seneca lands along the Niagara River. Thus, in 1814 Red Jacket and approximately 500 Seneca warriors joined the American invasion of Upper Canada. Attached to forces under New York Militia major general Peter Porter, Red Jacket and the Senecas fought with distinction in the Battle of Chippewa (July 5, 1814). The Senecas earned the Americans' respect and goodwill that Red Jacket would later use in his campaign to defend native lands and traditions.

Over the years, Red Jacket met with presidents George Washington, John Quincy Adams, and Andrew Jackson to plead the case of the Iroquois Confederacy and negotiated to preserve Seneca lands and sovereignty over internal tribal affairs. Translations of

his speeches routinely appeared in newspapers and other publications of the time, and Red Jacket became a celebrity. As a result of his efforts, the Seneca tribe retains reservations on its traditional lands in New York to this day. Red Jacket died at Buffalo Creek, New York, on January 20, 1830.

RICHARD V. BARBUTO

See also
Iroquois Confederacy; Native Americans and the War of 1812; Senecas

References
Densmore, Christopher. *Red Jacket: Iroquois Diplomat and Orator.* Syracuse, NY: Syracuse University Press, 1999.
Stone, William L. *Life and Times of Red-Jacket.* New York: Wiley and Putnam, 1841.

Red River War
Start Date: June 27, 1874
End Date: June 2, 1875

Major conflict on the southern Plains. The Red River War began on June 27, 1874, and officially ended on June 2, 1875. The Medicine Lodge Treaty of 1867 created two new reservations in Indian Territory (Oklahoma), one for the Comanches and Kiowas and another for the southern Cheyennes and Arapahos. The treaty ensured that the American government would provide the tribes with food, clothing, and other goods in return for which the tribal leaders agreed to prevent warriors from launching raids on settlers. The tribes were also given permission to hunt buffalo on any lands south of the Arkansas River.

However, the activities of commercial buffalo hunters were not curbed, and by 1874 the number of buffalo had plummeted. Also, many of the U.S. officials providing the tribes with the goods specified in the treaty were either inefficient or corrupt, the quality of the items delivered to the tribes was poor, and the quantity was insufficient. Thus, many warriors chose to leave the reservations for the freedom of the Texas plains. Rising tensions as whites pastured cattle on the reservations in violation of the treaty and stole the Native Americans' horses also compelled Native Americans to leave. All of these factors led to a major Native American uprising.

By 1874 Isa-tai, a Comanche shaman, rose to prominence on the Comanche reservation. He claimed to have talked with the Great Spirit, who had granted him supernatural powers. Isa-tai, having convinced many Comanches of his spiritual power, began to urge war on the white settlers. He had a personal reason for doing so, as his uncle had been killed in battle with U.S. forces. Isa-tai convinced many tribal leaders that conflict with the Americans was inevitable and that it would be better if the Comanches struck first.

Isa-tai brought the Comanches together for a sun dance in May 1874. Small numbers of Kiowas and Southern Cheyennes also joined the gathering. Initially tribal leaders wanted to attack the Tonkawas, who provided scouts for the U.S. Army. However,

Portrait of Seneca chief Red Jacket, by 19th-century American painter Charles Bird King, from *The Indian Tribes of North America.* (McKenney, Thomas L. and James Hall. *The Indian Tribes of North America,* 1836–1844)

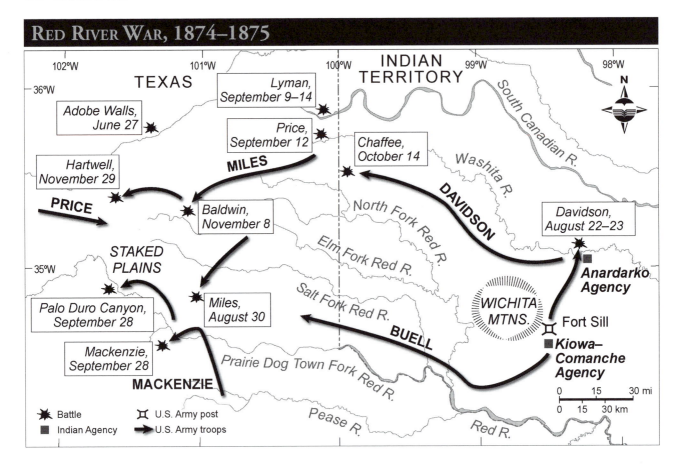

RED RIVER WAR, 1874–1875

they later decided that the attack should be focused on the buffalo hunters at a trading post known as Adobe Walls, located in the Texas Panhandle.

On June 27, 1874, a war party numbering several hundred Cheyenne and Comanche warriors attacked Adobe Walls. Among the leaders was the Comanche Quanah Parker, son of an influential Comanche chief and his captured settler wife. Isa-tai did not join in the attack but watched from a nearby hill. Despite the odds, the Native Americans were held at bay by long-range rifle fire and were unable to close in on a small group of buildings defended by 28 men and 1 woman. Fifteen warriors died in the failed attack.

Isa-tai claimed that the failure was because of a warrior violating a sacred taboo. Several Cheyenne warriors refused to accept this explanation, however, and publicly beat Isa-tai, who was now disgraced. Most of the Kiowas had not joined in the attack, but on July 12 a small party of 50 warriors under Lone Wolf attacked a force of Texas Rangers near Jacksboro, killing 2.

U.S. Army general William T. Sherman ordered the commander of the Military Division of the Missouri, Lieutenant General Philip Sheridan, to end the uprising. Both Sherman and Sheridan were advocates of total war, and neither was well disposed toward the Native Americans. Sheridan's plan was the largest attempted by the army against the Native Americans of the American West.

Sheridan's plan called for five independent army columns to converge on the Native Americans of the Texas Panhandle and exact such retribution that there would not be another uprising. The five columns consisted of those under Colonel Nelson A. Miles from Fort Dodge, Kansas; Colonel Ranald S. Mackenzie from Fort Concho, Texas; Major William R. Price from Fort Bascom, New Mexico; Lieutenant Colonel John W. Davidson from Fort Sill in Indian Territory (Oklahoma); and Lieutenant Colonel George P. Buell from Fort Griffin in Texas. Altogether the force numbered more than 2,000 soldiers and Native American scouts.

Beginning in August 1874, the army units moved onto the reservations to separate the hostile from the peaceful Native Americans. Most of the Arapahos were judged to be friendly, while the majority of the Cheyennes were considered hostile. At Fort Sill a confrontation occurred between Davidson's cavalrymen and Comanches supported by Kiowas under Lone Wolf. Altogether the army estimated that there were some 5,000 hostile Native Americans, including 1,200 warriors.

The first column in action was that of Colonel Miles. He departed Fort Dodge on August 11, 1874, with eight companies of cavalry and four of infantry, all supported by Gatling guns and artillery. During August 27–31 Miles fought a series of running battles near Palo Duro Canyon with Cheyenne warriors, who were then joined by Kiowas. Although the soldiers drove off the Native Americans in these engagements, Miles was short of supplies and was forced to halt and await them. On September 7 his column joined Price's cavalry squadron. Two days later Miles's supply train under the command of Captain Wyllys Lyman came under attack and was besieged for three days until the Native Americans broke off their effort.

Miles sent out scouting parties to learn what had happened to his supply train. One of these groups, composed of six men, was attacked on September 12 and sought refuge in a buffalo wallow. One man was killed, and the remainder were wounded. On the same day Price reached the beleaguered wagon train.

By now a third column was in the field. Colonel Mackenzie's eight cavalry troops and five infantry companies advanced from Fort Concho. Mackenzie fought a skirmish in Tule Canyon on September 26, frustrating a Comanche attack. Two days later, on September 28, his men located a large group of Native Americans in the upper Palo Duro Canyon. After a harrowing descent into the canyon, Mackenzie's 4th Cavalry attacked at dawn, forcing dozens of Native Americans to surrender. The troops then destroyed the camp, lodges, supplies, and food stores for the coming winter. They also captured some 1,500 ponies, 1,000 of which Mackenzie ordered slaughtered. The Battle of Palo Duro Canyon and the loss of the horses had a major impact on the fighting capacity of the Comanches, and by October many began to move back toward the reservations. The weather had now turned cold and treacherous, but the soldiers nonetheless continued to tighten their grip. On November 8, 1874, Lieutenant Frank Baldwin from Miles's command destroyed a large Cheyenne camp. The other columns were then reinforced with the additional two columns under Davidson and Buell.

Throughout the winter and spring of 1875, the number of Native American surrenders increased. In late February 1875 Lone Wolf came in with some 500 Kiowas. On March 6 some 800 Cheyennes under Gray Beard surrendered. On June 2 Quanah Parker and some 400 Comanches surrendered at Fort Sill.

The Red River War that ended the Native American threat on the southern Plains was certainly among the most successful U.S. campaigns against Native Americans in the history of North America and confirmed the total war approach and the effectiveness of winter campaigning.

RALPH MARTIN BAKER AND SPENCER C. TUCKER

See also

Adobe Walls, Second Battle of; Arapahos; Cheyennes; Comanches; Kiowas; Mackenzie, Ranald Slidell; Medicine Lodge Treaty; Miles, Nelson Appleton; Quanah Parker; Sherman, William Tecumseh

References

Hayley, James L. *The Buffalo War: The History of the Red River Indian Uprising of 1874.* Sacramento, CA: State House Press, 1998.

Jauken, Arlene F. *The Moccasin Speaks: Living as Captives of the Dog Soldier Warriors, Red River War, 1874–1875.* Lincoln, NE: Dageforde Publishing, 1998.

Leckie, William, ed. *Indian Wars of the Red River Valley.* Newcastle, CA: Sierra Oaks Publishing, 1987.

Marshall, J. T., and Lonnie J. White, eds. *Miles Expedition of 1874–1875: An Eyewitness Account of the Red River War.* Austin, TX: Encino, 1981.

Red Shoe

Birth Date: ca. 1705
Death Date: June 23, 1747

Choctaw war chief also known as Soulier Rouge, Soulouche Oumastabé, and Shulush Homa. The term "Red Shoe" was a title given to all Choctaw war chiefs, but the name has been linked historically to this particular leader. Red Shoe was born around 1705 in the village of Couechitto in present-day Mississippi. While still a warrior, he was named speaker for the Choctaws' civil chief, Mingo Tchito, an office that required Red Shoe to explicate the chief's positions. Such a role ultimately testified to Red Shoe's persuasiveness; persuasiveness and generosity were key qualities expected of a Choctaw leader. Through his success in the Chickasaw Wars (1736–1740), Red Shoe rose to war chief, the highest position to which someone of his status could normally aspire. Although war chief was normally a temporary position, he appears to have retained it on a permanent basis.

Mingo Tchito, the head chief of Couechitto, had been recognized by the French (if not by all Choctaws) as the leader of the Choctaw Nation. The French cemented their alliance, as was the custom, with a stream of trade goods as gifts, which Mingo Tchito and other civil chiefs redistributed to bolster their positions as tribal leaders. Mingo Tchito occasionally played the colonists against each other and sent Red Shoe to contact British traders whenever corruption, mismanagement, or accidents made French gifts scarce. In 1729 Red Shoe advocated a permanent alliance with the more reliable though distant British. Mingo Tchito, who was content to use the British to keep the French pliable, ignored the advice.

Also in 1729, the French called on the Choctaws to help suppress the Natchez tribe, which had revolted with British and Chickasaw support. Red Shoe managed to recover women, children, and African slaves whom the Natchezes had seized and handed the captives over to the French in exchange for a substantial quantity of trade goods. This act provided him for the first time with the wherewithal to establish his own generosity and build a faction within the tribe.

In 1732 after Mingo Tchito resisted French entreaties to attack the Chickasaws, Red Shoe led 30 young warriors against a Chickasaw hunting party. Essentially Red Shoe had plunged his people into war on his own initiative. In doing so, he earned the gratitude of the French and became the only war chief to receive gifts regularly. He also disrupted the traditional Choctaw social and political hierarchy and alienated Mingo Tchito and the other civil chiefs, who refused to accept him as an equal.

During the 1730s and 1740s, Red Shoe was preoccupied with warfare and the search for European trade goods. The French would reward him for attacking the Chickasaws, and the British would reward him for making peace with the Chickasaws. These gifts made it possible to hold his faction together despite the resentment of the traditional chiefs and the distrust of virtually all sides. Red Shoe also manipulated a growing gulf between the common warriors and the civil chiefs, whom he accused of not redistributing goods sufficiently.

In 1743 Pierre de Rigaud de Vaudreuil, the new governor of Louisiana, restructured the gift-giving system, eliminating Red Shoe. Red Shoe then sought to forge an alliance with the Chickasaws, the Creeks, and the British. Meanwhile, the French tried to form an alliance with the Chickasaws, the Creeks, and the Choctaw civil chiefs. The outbreak of King George's War (1744–1748), however, disrupted the flow of French goods. Support among the Choctaws shifted back toward Red Shoe as the supply of French gifts and trade dried up. But Red Shoe's killing of three Frenchmen initiated a crisis in French-Choctaw relations and among the tribal factions. In response, Vaudreuil put a price on Red Shoe's head, and on June 23, 1747, just as Red Shoe had achieved an alliance with South Carolina, he was assassinated. The tribal code of revenge, triggered by the assassination, added to the already growing divisions within Choctaw society and sparked the Choctaw Civil War (1746–1750).

SCOTT C. MONJE

See also

Chickasaws; Choctaw-Chickasaw War; Choctaw Civil War; Choctaws; Creeks; Natchez War

References

Galloway, Patricia. "Choctaw Factionalism and Civil War, 1746–1750." In *The Choctaw before Removal*, edited by Carolyn Keller Reeves, 120–156. Jackson: University Press of Mississippi, 1985.

White, Richard. "Red Shoes: Warrior and Diplomat." In *Struggle and Survival in Colonial America,* edited by David G. Sweet and Gary B. Nash, 49–68. Berkeley: University of California Press, 1981.

Red Sticks

A militant faction of the Creek Nation that resided in present-day Alabama and chose armed resistance to the United States during the War of 1812 rather than assimilation, unlike many of their fellow tribesmen. The Creeks spoke Muskogean and were a loosely organized confederation of some 60 townships. The name "Red Stick" arose from the Creek practice of taking away sticks from a bundle of red sticks to count the number of days until an important occasion or event. Red Stick Creeks advocated resistance to the whites and maintenance of the traditions of hunting and the use of communal lands.

During the American Revolutionary War (1775–1783), the Creeks allied with the British and afterward remained on good terms with them, largely through the efforts of British traders. In addition, the Creeks were in contact with the Spanish in Florida. The British and the Spanish saw the Creeks as a useful proxy to limit American expansion, and the Creeks in turn found the Europeans helpful in securing trade goods and arms. In the aftermath

of the Revolution, half-Scottish Creek chief Alexander McGillivray unsuccessfully attempted to forge an intertribal alliance in the South to curb American expansion.

A number of younger Creeks, unhappy with the official Creek policy toward the United States that allowed large land sales and also upset about the general cultural trend toward greater assimilation, began to support a more militant stance toward white Americans. These Red Sticks numbered perhaps 4,000 warriors. In the midst of this growing unrest, Shawnee leader Tecumseh arrived among the Creeks and spoke at a council meeting on September 30, 1811.

Tecumseh argued for Pan-Indian resistance to encroachments on native land. However, at a Creek council Chief Big Warrior opposed his proposal. Tecumseh, angered by this resistance, predicted a climactic event. The occurrence of an earthquake a few months later enhanced his reputation. Nevertheless, the Creek leadership still refused to aid him. Tecumseh's efforts were not entirely without result, for a group of young Creeks under Little Warrior journeyed with him to the North and fought with the British against the Americans, participating in the River Raisin Massacre of January 1813. When these Creeks, now known as Red Sticks, returned in 1813 from Detroit, they began to attack white settlements.

After these attacks Benjamin Hawkins, the U.S. government agent to the Creeks, demanded that the Creeks bring the offenders to justice before U.S. authorities. Creek chiefs chose to oblige the United States but to comply without seeming to appear as puppets. They executed Little Warrior and six of his compatriots. This event initiated a Creek civil war in which U.S. forces ultimately became involved. This conflict from 1813 to 1814 is usually called the Creek War and formed part of the War of 1812.

The Red Sticks, who were centered in upper Creek villages, soon began to attack the lower Creek villages, taking care to destroy implements of white civilization except those useful for warfare. The Creeks had large numbers of mixed-blood tribe members, and ironically among the Red Stick leaders who opposed assimilation, there were many of mixed ancestry, such as Red Stick prophet Josiah Francis and war leaders Peter McQueen and William Weatherford, also known as Red Eagle.

Not surprisingly, the Spanish and the British were supportive of the Red Stick efforts. Fighting began on July 21, 1813, with a Creek victory in the Battle of Burnt Corn Creek and largely concluded in the decisive Battle of Horseshoe Bend on March 27, 1814, in which the Creeks were defeated, with some 800 Creeks killed out of 1,000 who fought that day.

The Creek War and the War of 1812 devastated the Creek Nation. On August 9, 1814, Major General Andrew Jackson imposed on the Creeks the Treaty of Fort Jackson in which the entire Creek Nation, including Creeks who had fought alongside Jackson, was treated harshly. Under the treaty terms the Creeks ceded to the United States some 23 million acres of land. Most

Creeks ended their warfare on the signing of the treaty, although some continued to fight when British forces arrived on the Gulf Coast bound for New Orleans. Another Red Stick, Osceola, was active in the Second Seminole War (1835–1842) against the United States.

MICHAEL K. BEAUCHAMP AND SPENCER C. TUCKER

See also
Creeks; Creek War; Fort Jackson, Treaty of; Jackson, Andrew; McQueen, Peter; Native Americans and the War of 1812; Tecumseh; Weatherford, William

References
Dowd, Gregory Evans. *A Spirited Resistance: The North American Indian Struggle for Unity, 1745–1815.* Baltimore: Johns Hopkins University Press, 1992.
Hickey, Donald R. *The War of 1812: A Forgotten Conflict.* Urbana: University of Illinois Press, 1989.
Wright, J. Leitch, Jr. *Creeks and Seminoles: The Destruction and Regeneration of the Muscogulge People.* Lincoln: University of Nebraska Press, 1986.

Red Stick War
See Creek War

Remington, Frederic
Birth Date: October 4, 1861
Death Date: December 26, 1909

Painter, illustrator, and sculptor whose images of the West shaped American perceptions of the vanishing frontier. Frederic Remington was born in Canton, New York, on October 4, 1861. His father served as a lieutenant colonel in the American Civil War (1861–1865), a fact that influenced Remington's art themes of war and conflict on horseback. In 1878 Remington enrolled at Yale University, studying at the school of art and architecture. His new passion became football, and he was a starter on the varsity team. His first published illustration was a cartoon in the *Yale Courant* of an injured football player. Despite his mother's objections, Remington left Yale after only two years upon the death of his father in 1880.

Remington worked as a clerk in the office of the governor of New York and in other state offices in 1880 but was dissatisfied with the regimen. Frustrated, he decided to experience the American West. His travels to Montana and Wyoming resulted in his first illustration of the frontier, an image of a Wyoming cowboy published by *Harper's Weekly* in February 1882.

Remington bought land in Kansas in 1883 after receiving a modest inheritance from his father the year before. His attempt at sheep farming was not successful, however, and he sold the ranch, returning to friends and family in New York a year later.

Married in 1884, Remington and his new wife moved to Kansas City, Missouri. He used the remainder of his inheritance to invest in a saloon there. The venture was successful, but Remington eventually lost his share due to unscrupulous partners. His wife Eva returned to New York within the year, as Remington could not find steady work. He spent the next year traveling through the American Southwest, working as a cowboy and scout and sketching Native Americans. He returned to New York in 1885, and he and Eva moved to Brooklyn, where Remington began to sell his illustrations of the West to major magazines. His big break came in 1886 when his illustration *The Apache War: Indian Scouts on Geronimo's Trail* became the cover of *Harper's Weekly.*

To develop his artistic talents further, Remington enrolled in classes at the Art Student League, where he worked with watercolors. His exhibition in the National Academy of Design and American Water-Color Society brought him to the attention of Theodore Roosevelt, who asked Remington to illustrate an article that Roosevelt was writing about ranching and hunting in the West. From this initial contact, the two men began a long friendship.

Frederic Remington (1861–1909) was a painter, illustrator, and sculptor best known for his images of the Old West. (Library of Congress)

Remington spent each summer in the West and Canada under publisher sponsorship, sketching and photographing scenes for later illustrations as well as collecting Native American and frontier artifacts. In 1888 and 1890 he documented the wars against the Apaches and Plains Indians.

The demand for magazine illustrations was constant because the number of magazine publications had grown from about 700 in 1865 to some 3,000 in 1885. Remington published more than 2,700 illustrations in 41 journals. He also illustrated more than 140 books, including Henry Wadsworth Longfellow's *The Song of Hiawatha,* Francis Parkman's *The Oregon Trail,* and Elizabeth B. Custer's *Tenting in the Plains.*

In the late 1880s Remington began to develop an oil-painting career, filling more than 700 canvases with scenes of soldiers, horses, Native Americans, and cowboys. When the Spanish-American War began in 1898, *Harper's Weekly* and William Randolph Hearst's *New York Journal* sent Remington to Cuba to cover the conflict, assignments that he quickly found frustrating. Nevertheless, his painting *Charge of the Rough Riders at San Juan Hill* depicting his friend Colonel Theodore Roosevelt became extraordinarily well known and helped to foster the image of Roosevelt as war hero, a crucial element in his future political career.

Remington's first sculpture in 1895 was *The Bronco Buster,* which the Rough Riders later gave to Roosevelt when they returned from Cuba. Remington produced 25 bronze sculptures, all but 1 emphasizing a Western theme. He was a highly prolific and successful artist, and his illustrations have been praised for the authenticity of Native American garb, soldiers' uniforms, and accurate horse anatomy in all poses. His later paintings were more romantic and captured the disappearing spirit of the Western frontier. Remington said he knew that "the wild riders and the vacant land were about to vanish forever.... Without knowing exactly how to do it, I began to record some facts around me and the more I looked the more the panorama unfolded." Indeed, he captured his era and the feelings toward it with considerable sentiment.

Remington's life and career were cut short when he died from complications from an appendectomy at his home in New Rochelle, New York, on December 26, 1909. He was only 48 years old.

JOSÉ VALENTE

See also

Apache Wars; Geronimo; *Harper's Weekly;* Literature and the American Indian Wars

References

Baigell, Matthew. *The Western Art of Frederic Remington.* New York: Ballantine, 1976.

Buckland, Roscoe L. *Frederic Remington, the Writer.* New York: Twayne, 2000.

Nemerov, Alexander. *Frederic Remington and Turn-of-the-Century America.* New Haven, CT: Yale University Press, 1995.

Samuels, Peggy, and Harold Samuels. *Frederic Remington: A Biography.* Garden City, NY: Doubleday, 1982.

Reno, Marcus Albert
Birth Date: November 15, 1834
Death Date: March 30, 1889

U.S. Army officer famous for what many consider to be his questionable judgment during the disastrous Battle of the Little Bighorn (June 25–26, 1876). Marcus Albert Reno was born on November 15, 1834, in Carrollton, Illinois. In 1851 he entered the U.S. Military Academy at West Point, where he was an average student who often chafed under the strict discipline of the academy. Graduating in 1857, Reno was commissioned a second lieutenant in the 1st Dragoons Regiment and was assigned to garrison duty in the Pacific Northwest.

During the American Civil War (1861–1865), Reno was promoted to first lieutenant in April 1861 and to captain in the 1st Cavalry Regiment soon thereafter. He was wounded at the Battle of Kelly's Ford on March 17, 1863, and was subsequently brevetted through colonel in the regular army. Reno continued to see considerable action and after a brief stint as colonel of the 12th Pennsylvania Cavalry Regiment was brevetted brigadier general of volunteers in March 1865.

Reno remained in the army after the Civil War, and in 1868 he was appointed a major in the 7th Cavalry Regiment, commanded by Lieutenant Colonel George Armstrong Custer. Although not personally close to Custer, Reno was second-in-command at Fort Abraham Lincoln and helped prepare the 7th Cavalry for its spring 1876 campaign against the Cheyennes and Sioux, part of the Great Sioux War (Black Hills War) of 1876–1877.

The overall campaign was under the command of Brigadier General Alfred H. Terry. Reno was assigned six companies of the regiment and on June 10, 1876, made a reconnaissance of the Powder and Tongue rivers, discovering a large Native American encampment that had moved upstream along Rosebud Creek. Terry's strategy was to employ a hammer-and-anvil operation in which Custer's 7th Cavalry would drive the Native Americans into the anvil of Colonel John Gibbon's infantry. Custer, however, moved before Gibbon was ready and on June 25 located Sitting Bull's encampment along the Little Bighorn River. Thus began the ill-fated Battle of the Little Bighorn. Custer then split his command, with Reno's battalion sent to attack the encampment, while Custer moved his forces farther downstream.

When Reno's advance met with greater resistance than anticipated, he withdrew to the bluffs along the Little Bighorn, where he was joined by Captain Frederick Benteen's battalion and the regiment's supply train. During this retreat more than a third of Reno's force was lost. By most accounts, Reno was stunned by the day's events and largely ineffectual. The besieged men were unable to break free and aid Custer and his men, who were soon wiped out. Finally, on the evening of June 26 the Native Americans ended their attacks on Reno's position with the arrival of reinforcements under Terry. Reno returned to Fort Abraham Lincoln in command of what remained of the 7th Cavalry, but detractors blamed him for not having gone to Custer's aid.

In 1877 Reno was assigned to Fort Abercrombie along the Red River in Dakota Territory, where he was court-martialed for alleged improper advances toward the wife of a fellow officer. Reno was suspended from rank and pay for two years. Continually plagued with allegations of cowardice at Little Bighorn, he demanded a military court of inquiry, which resulted in his being cleared of any wrongdoing. However, the decision of the military court, convened in Chicago in 1879, found that while there was no basis for the charges against Reno, his actions at Little Bighorn had not been particularly well executed. Reno was reinstated to active duty later that year, but he was quickly in trouble again with allegations of improper conduct toward fellow officers. He was dismissed from the army on April 1, 1880. Reno struggled economically as a pension clerk during the 1880s and died on March 30, 1889, in Washington, D.C. In 1967 a military board of review reversed Reno's 1877 court-martial, and the status of his discharge was changed to honorable.

RON BRILEY

See also

Custer, George Armstrong; Gibbon, John; Great Sioux War; Little Bighorn, Battle of the; Sitting Bull; Terry, Alfred Howe

References

Connell, Evan S. *Son of the Morning Star: Custer and the Little Bighorn.* New York: North Point Press, 1984.

Nichols, Ronald H. *In Custer's Shadow: Major Marcus Reno.* Norman: University of Oklahoma Press, 2000.

Terrell, John Upton, and George Walton. *Faint the Trumpet Sounds: The Life and Trial of Major Reno.* New York: D. McKay, 1966.

Reservations

Today approximately 22 percent of Native Americans in the United States live on reservations, land set aside for their tribes by treaties with the federal government. These preserved pieces of territory vary in size from a few hundred acres to the more than 17 million–acre Navajo Reservation, which is the nation's largest. These reservations are all that remain of the immense landholdings of the numerous Native American nations that once dominated the North American continent.

The first attempt to set aside land for Native Americans can be traced to colonial Massachusetts. John Eliot, a minister who hoped to convert the local Massachusett tribe to Christianity, proposed that the tribe live near the English. In 1641 he thus established Natick, a settlement for Christian Native Americans within the town of Dedham. During the next 25 years, 14 towns for so-called praying Indians were founded throughout the Massachusetts Bay Colony.

New York, Virginia, and North Carolina also established a few reserves for various tribes during the colonial period. Still, these arrangements were rare, and the idea that there was a boundary between American settlements and Native American territory remained the dominant attitude in colonial times. For the colonists, this line was a fluid one that moved steadily westward as they pushed up river valleys and into the mountains in search of more land for farming.

After the American Revolutionary War (1775–1783), the boundary between the Native Americans and the United States moved west from the Appalachian Mountains to the Mississippi River. President George Washington was determined to open the land west of the Appalachians for settlement. He thus implemented a policy by which the United States recognized the Native Americans as owners of the land and convinced them to sell it in exchange for annuities and other incentives. The idea of setting aside reserves for the tribes on land they had surrendered to the Americans first took shape under the presidency of Thomas Jefferson, who believed that the Native Americans must abandon hunting and settle down as sedentary farmers. This belief necessitated granting tracts of land to the tribes on already-surrendered territory.

Following the War of 1812, many tribes living on reserves east of the Mississippi River made a successful transition to farming. Others, however, fell prey to whiskey and the violence prevalent on the frontier. President James Monroe recommended the removal of the eastern tribes across the Mississippi as a solution. While some tribes took Monroe up on his offer, the majority preferred to remain on their reserves. They did not leave until forced west following the passage of the 1830 Indian Removal Act under President Andrew Jackson. By the mid-1840s, approximately 100,000 Native Americans from a dozen eastern tribes were living in the Indian Territory, which included the present-day states of Nebraska, Kansas, and Oklahoma. Northern tribes lived on a patchwork of small reserves in Nebraska and Kansas, while the Five Civilized Tribes lived on larger reserves in Oklahoma. The frequent forced relocation of tribes to the west resulted in much suffering and many deaths among Native Americans. One of the most tragic, the removal of the Cherokees, is known as the Trail of Tears.

Once on the reservation, most Native Americans found life difficult at best and miserable at worst. Many times they were forced to share land with traditional adversaries and fell prey to unscrupulous Indian agents. The land that the Native Americans were given was also frequently inhospitable to agricultural pursuits.

Despite their many hardships, the tribes living in Indian Territory were able to maintain their cultural identity to a remarkable degree. However, new problems soon developed. Kansas and Nebraska were subsequently opened for settlement in the mid-1850s, and tribes living there were forced south onto smaller reserves in Oklahoma. The Five Civilized Tribes in Oklahoma lost half of their remaining land as punishment for their support of the Confederacy in the American Civil War (1861–1865).

Tribes living on the Great Plains and farther west were able to survive behind a boundary line between themselves and the

Bird's-eye view of a large Lakota camp of tipis, horses, and wagons on the Pine Ridge Indian Reservation in 1891. Originally part of the Great Sioux Reservation established by the Fort Laramie Treaty of 1868, Pine Ridge became one of seven separate reservations in 1889. (Library of Congress)

Americans, at least for a time. That line was breached, however, in several places as settlers headed to Texas, Oregon, and California beginning in the 1830s. The U.S. government dealt with conflicts in the West with the 1851 Fort Laramie Treaty, which was signed by the United States and eight major nations on the Great Plains. The treaty allowed the government to concentrate the Sioux in the Dakotas, the Cheyennes in the foothills of the Rockies, and the Comanches near Texas. Subsequent treaties created reservations in the Southwest for Navajos, Apaches, and other tribes, many of which proved to be short-lived or, like the Bosque Redondo in New Mexico, to be abject failures with tragic human consequences.

It was not until the Treaty of Medicine Lodge in 1867 that the far western tribes were subjected to the reservation system. By this time, many of them were at war with the United States in a desperate attempt to preserve their way of life and their ancestral lands. The treaty signed at Medicine Lodge permitted the U.S. government to force many of these tribes onto reservations in the Indian Territory or onto arid western lands that no settlers wanted and that did not support agriculture. The Fort Laramie Treaty of 1868, while an Indian victory by closing the Bozeman Trail and three federal forts, also established the framework for a reservation system that would eventually house the great Sioux and Cheyenne bands of the northern Plains. Within a dozen years, 30 western tribes had been rounded up and sent to Oklahoma.

By the 1880s, Native Americans were living on 441 reservations in 21 states. Life on these reservations was difficult for many

reasons. Promised supplies and annuity payments often arrived late and in insufficient quantity, and some of the funds and supplies that did arrive were often stolen by the agents who ran the reservations and who were often corrupt. Native American religious practices were banned, and children were sent to boarding schools to be Americanized. Adults often fell into drunkenness, despair, and destitution. The situation grew worse in 1887 when Congress passed the Dawes Severalty Act, which granted individual members of the tribes up to 160 acres of land each. Reformers had hoped that private ownership of land would end the acute poverty on the reservations. Ultimately the Dawes Act robbed the Native Americans of millions of acres of territory. Even more land was lost in 1889 when the government opened the Indian Territory to white settlement.

During the twentieth century, Native Americans in successive generations left the reservations in large numbers, mainly to find work. Still, their ties to their people remained strong, and they were determined to see their reservations survive into the future. Support for improving reservation life came during the administration of Franklin D. Roosevelt with the passage of the Indian Reorganization Act. This law made it possible for tribes to reestablish their tribal government, practice their own culture, and educate their children at home. Since the 1930s, most Democratic administrations have supported efforts to improve the quality of life on reservations. However, several Republican presidents, most notably Dwight Eisenhower, advocated closing reservations and helping Native Americans assimilate fully into American culture. With the passage of the Indian Gaming Regulatory Act in 1988, which has transformed numerous reservations into money-making enterprises, the debate continues.

MARY STOCKWELL

See also

Dawes Severalty Act; Fort Laramie, Treaty of (1851); Indian Reorganization Act; Indian Territory; Medicine Lodge Treaty; Trail of Tears

References

Confederation of American Indians. *Indian Reservations: A State and Federal Handbook.* Honolulu: University Press of the Pacific, 2000.

Frantz, Klaus. *Indian Reservations of the United States.* Chicago: University of Chicago Press, 1999.

Strickland, Rennard. *The Indians of Oklahoma.* Norman: University of Oklahoma Press, 1981.

Revolutionary War

See Native Americans and the American Revolutionary War

Reynolds, Charles Alexander
Birth Date: March 20, 1842
Death Date: June 25, 1876

Civilian scout for the U.S. Army. Born in Warren County, Illinois, on March 20, 1842, Charles Alexander "Lonesome Charley" Reynolds attended Abingdon College and then relocated to Kansas. In 1860 he set out for Pikes Peak in search of gold, but Cheyenne warriors attacked his wagon train. Escaping, Reynolds briefly trapped furs in Colorado. At the beginning of the American Civil War (1861–1865), Reynolds enlisted in the 10th Kansas Volunteers and saw action in Missouri and Arkansas. Receiving an honorable discharge after three years of service, he drifted during the next several years.

In 1865 Reynolds set up a trading operation in southwestern Kansas, but Native Americans killed his partner and looted his goods. After working as a guide along the Santa Fe Trail, Reynolds went to Colorado and Nebraska, where he hunted buffalo in 1866. Again troubles with Native Americans interfered. In 1869 he began work in the Dakotas as a guide and hunter.

By 1872 Reynolds was well known on the Upper Missouri, and Lieutenant General Philip H. Sheridan recruited him to escort Russian grand duke Alexis on the latter's buffalo hunt in Nebraska. It was in this capacity that Reynolds met Lieutenant Colonel George Armstrong Custer. The following year Reynolds scouted for Custer during the Northern Pacific Railroad's Yellowstone survey expedition. In 1874 while again scouting for Custer, Reynolds carried news of the expedition's discovery of gold in the Black Hills to Fort Laramie, inciting a gold rush. That winter he helped Custer's men capture the Sioux warrior Rain in the Face, who allegedly killed several civilians during the Yellowstone expedition.

When guiding Custer's 7th U.S. Cavalry during the Great Sioux War (1876–1877), Reynolds was the most trusted hunter and scout in the Dakota Territory, yet his contemporaries remarked that he was not a rough man like many of his counterparts. Educated, quiet, and modest, Reynolds lived by himself without even a dog, earning him the sobriquet "Lonesome Charley." Native scouts called him "Lucky Man," perhaps referring to his superb marksmanship. On June 24, 1876, the day before the Battle of the Little Bighorn, Reynolds, seemingly anticipating his own fate, distributed his belongings to his comrades. Although his ability to fire a gun was hampered by a seriously infected right thumb, he nevertheless rode with the 7th Cavalry toward the large Sioux encampment on the Little Bighorn River. Exactly how he died on June 25, 1876, like much else of what happened on that day, is lost to history, but he perished with Major Marcus A. Reno's command. The most widely accepted explanation is that Reynolds was shot through the heart while helping Dr. Henry Porter assist a wounded cavalryman.

ADAM R. HODGE

See also

Custer, George Armstrong; Great Sioux War; Little Bighorn, Battle of the; Reno, Marcus Albert; Sheridan, Philip Henry

References

Connell, Evan S. *Son of the Morning Star: Custer and the Little Bighorn.* New York: North Point Press, 1984.

Scott, Douglas D., et al. *They Died with Custer: Soldiers' Bones from the Battle of the Little Bighorn.* Norman: University of Oklahoma Press, 1998.

Utley, Robert M. *Cavalier in Buckskin: George Armstrong Custer and the Western Military Frontier.* Rev. ed. Norman: University of Oklahoma Press, 2001.

Rickahocans

See Westos

Rifles

The rifle is an individual firearm. The first rifles were muzzle loaders identical to smoothbore muskets in firing mechanism, means of loading, and general outward appearance. The difference was that the rifle had a spiral twist of lands and grooves on the internal surface of the barrel. Known as rifling, these imparted spin to the round ball and gave it far greater accuracy at much greater distances. Ironically, rifling seems to have been introduced not as a means to improve accuracy but rather to collect fouling, which occurred with the black powder charge, and thus to ease the loading of the bullet, which had to be pushed down the bore with a ramrod. Rifling, however, proved to be one of the most important inventions in the history of weaponry.

While the range at which an individual with a smoothbore musket would be expected to hit a man-sized target might be only

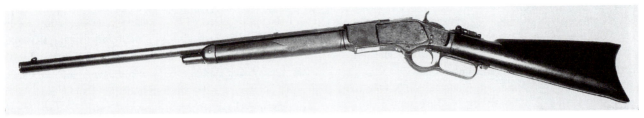

A Winchester 1873 rifle, owned by D. W. Peckham. The lever-action Winchester was touted as "the gun that won the West." (AP/Wide World Photos)

50 to 100 yards, the rifle had an effective range of up to 200 or even 300 yards. Such advantage, however, was offset for a military weapon by its much slower rate of fire because of the reduced windage (the difference between the diameters of the ball and of the bore) in order that the soft lead ball would take to the rifling. The difficulty of loading meant that the rifle could be fired only about once a minute, as opposed to three to four shots per minute for the smoothbore musket by a well-trained soldier. Hence, rifles were not suited for the tactics of the day that stressed massed close-in fire. Units of riflemen could prove important, however, in picket duty, sniping, and long-range fire in a general engagement.

Rifles were employed in virtually every conflict between American settlers and Native Americans from the early 17th century through the late 19th century. By the mid-1850s the introduction of the easily loaded cylindo-conoidal lead bullet, known as the minié ball, made the rifled musket the shoulder arm of choice for the American military. Rifles were readily available for private purchase, however, and often the models issued to U.S. troops were obsolete when compared to their free-market counterparts. As a result, soldiers occasionally found themselves confronted by Native American warriors armed with superior weapons.

In the earliest conflicts with Native Americans in colonial Virginia, the American colonists had few rifles. Rifled muskets, however, became prized on the frontier for hunting because of their superior range. Although rifles were certainly used in New England in the Pequot War (1636–1638) and King Philip's War (1675–1676), they did not become a truly important element of the North American battlefield until the 18th century. In this period, American militiamen and scouts often reported for duty with their own weapons. Their commanders found that militiamen could serve as extremely effective skirmishers when armed with their flintlock rifles, even if the colonial units did not have the training and discipline to prove effective in the linear battlefield tactics of the day. Riflemen continued to be a key component of American military successes throughout the American Revolutionary War (1775–1783), notably in the Battle of Saratoga and the Battle of King's Mountain; the War of 1812 (1812–1815), including the Battle of New Orleans; and the Mexican-American War (1846–1848).

U.S. armed forces in the Old Northwest were armed with smoothbore muskets rather than rifles, but because militias often constituted a major element in fighting Native Americans, rifles remained a key component of frontier fighting throughout the period. Shortly after the end of the American Revolutionary War, some Native Americans took up arms against American settlers who were moving onto Native American land in the Old Northwest. Many of these Native American raiders were armed and supplied by British merchants operating in the Great Lakes region, and some of their weapons were flintlock rifles. This was the so-called golden age of the legendary Kentucky rifle. It was characterized by a long barrel and a caliber of .40 to .45. The rifles also often had elaborate metallic inlays.

In 1794 following two abortive expeditions against hostile Native Americans in the Old Northwest, Congress authorized the formation of the Legion of the United States. President George Washington selected Major General Anthony Wayne to command the legion. Each of its four sublegions contained, among other units, a battalion of riflemen. These men proved themselves in the Battle of Fallen Timbers (August 20, 1794) that broke the power of Native Americans in the Old Northwest.

Among the most significant technological advances of the early 19th century was the introduction of the percussion cap. Capable of use in all weather conditions, it also greatly improved reliability and ease of firing. The percussion-cap rifled musket was the standard infantry weapon of the American Civil War (1861–1865) for both the North and the South. Breech-loading weapons had begun to appear, however. These were a great advantage in that they allowed the weapon to be reloaded while the user was in a prone position or on horseback. The problem here lay in inadequate sealing that allowed the emission of gasses from the breech, which endangered the individual firing the weapon. Improved metallurgical techniques and better machining solved this. Percussion caps were also soon incorporated into the base of metal cartridge cases, which greatly increased the speed of loading and the efficiency of rifles.

In the years after the Civil War, the final pacification of the Trans-Mississippi West occurred. U.S. cavalry units were the most visible American military presence on the western frontier. Most units after 1865 were armed with carbines, rifles with a shorter barrel that facilitated their employment from horseback. Although the technology for repeating rifles was in common use after 1865, most cavalry regiments were issued single-shot carbines by the government as a cost-saving measure. Members of the Bureau of Ordnance argued that repeaters encouraged wasteful shooting and were thought to be less effective than relying upon the aimed fire of a trained marksman. Native American warriors, who purchased their weapons on the open market, did not suffer from such a short-sighted policy and thus often secured the most effective rifles available.

One prominent example of the rejection of effective rifles by the army can be seen in the case of the Henry repeater rifle, Model 1860. The Henry repeater rifle was the forerunner of the Winchester rifles. Manufactured by the New Haven Arms Company, the Henry fired the .44 rimfire cartridge with a copper case. The breech was opened by means of a breech block, operated by means of a lever under the stock. The Henry had a 16-shot magazine. The powder charge of 25 grains of black powder propelled a 216-grain bullet. Although the Henry was never officially adopted for service by the army, many Union soldiers purchased Henry rifles with their own funds. A well-trained soldier could fire the Henry at up to 28 rounds per minute, as opposed to 4 rounds per minute for the standard-issue rifled musket. Ironically, concerns over excessive ammunition expenditure helped to prevent official military adoption. Henry rifles were frequently used by scouts, skirmishers, flank guards, and raiding parties rather than in regular infantry formations.

The Henry rifle evolved into the famous Winchester Model 1866 lever-action rifle. That same year, the New Haven Arms Company became the Winchester Repeating Arms Company. The Spencer Model 1860 also incorporated breech-loading technology, allowing seven rounds to be loaded into a magazine tube. The Model 1860 was easily loaded and could be quickly fired, with the user toggling a lever to eject a spent cartridge and replace it with a fresh round. Once again, the rifle was rejected by the military as too wasteful of ammunition, although some cavalry units in the years following the Civil War carried Spencers.

In 1871 the Springfield Armory began producing rifles on a Remington pattern, paying a royalty to the Remington Arms Company for each gun produced at the federal arsenal. Eventually 10,000 Model 1871 rifles and carbines were issued to the U.S. Army frontier regulars. The gun fired a .50-caliber metallic cartridge that loaded at the breech. The Model 1871 was simple and quick to use and included a simple leaf sight that could be adjusted for targets at a range of up to 1,000 yards. However, because it was a single-shot weapon, the Model 1871 limited the firepower of individual soldiers.

The Model 1873 Trapdoor Springfield was the U.S. Army's first standard-issue breech-loading rifle, although some earlier Model

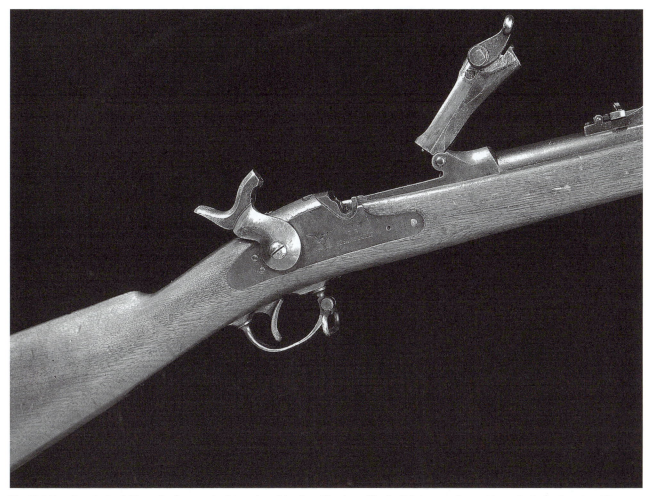

The 1873 Trapdoor Springfield was the first standard-issue breechloading rifle adopted by the U.S. Army and saw wide service in the American West. (Picture Desk)

1866 Trapdoors were issued to troops along the Bozeman Trail in 1867. The Model 1873 saw extensive army use during the Great Sioux War (1876–1877) and in many other conflicts with Native Americans.

The Model 1873 was named for its hinged breechblock that opened like a trapdoor and was produced in two versions: an infantry rifle with a 32⁵/₈-inch barrel and a cavalry carbine with a 22-inch barrel. The Model 1873 fired a .45-70-405 cartridge (a .45-caliber 405-grain lead bullet propelled by 70 grains of black powder). The carbine utilized a .45-55-405 cartridge, that is, a powder charge of only 55 grains of powder for reduced recoil for cavalrymen.

As with the Henry, the rifle originally utilized a copper cartridge case, but the soft copper expanded with heat and sometimes could not be extracted, rendering the rifle useless except as a club. Complaints that this had contributed to the army's defeat at the Battle of the Little Bighorn (June 25–26, 1876) led to the substitution of a brass cartridge case.

Perhaps the most popular and well-known rifle on the western frontier was the Winchester Model 1873. This weapon was very similar to the Henry Model 1860 but had a much-improved loading system. Users needed only to work a lever to reload the weapon, allowing very rapid fire of its .44-40 caliber cartridges. The Winchester is often referred to as the "gun that won the West," but it was never formally adopted for military use. Military testers argued that it was less accurate over great distances than the Springfield Model 1873 single-shot breechloader.

The decision to emphasize marksmanship over volume of fire was most starkly and famously illustrated by the experiences of Lieutenant Colonel George A. Custer and his 7th Cavalry Regiment at the Battle of the Little Bighorn on June 25, 1876. Custer's detachment of more than 200 soldiers encountered a much larger force of Lakota Sioux and Northern Cheyennes near Little Bighorn Creek. In the fight, Custer's troops were armed with Model 1873 Springfield carbines, while many of the Native Americans carried Spencer and Winchester repeater rifles. Predictably, the numerically superior warriors annihilated Custer's troops in a brief but intense firefight, amply demonstrating the importance of rapid-fire shoulder arms in modern combat.

PAUL J. SPRINGER AND SPENCER C. TUCKER

See also

Carbines; Fallen Timbers, Battle of; Little Bighorn, Battle of the; Muskets; Pistols; Rifles

References

Behn, Jack. '.45–70' Rifles. Harrisburg, PA: Stackpole, 1956.

Butler, David F. United States Firearms: The First Century. New York: Winchester, 1971.

Chapel, Charles Edward. Guns of the Old West. New York: Coward-McCann, 1961.

Gluckman, Arcadi. Identifying Old U.S. Muskets, Rifles & Carbines. Harrisburg, PA: Stackpole, 1965.

Shields, Joseph W., Jr. From Flintlock to M1. New York: Coward-McCann, 1954.

Sword, Wiley. President Washington's Indian War: The Struggle for the Old Northwest, 1790–1795. Norman: University of Oklahoma Press, 1985.

Rocky Mountains

Major mountain range traversing the North American continent in a generally northwest to southeast direction. The Rocky Mountains, often referred to as the Rockies, encompass much of western Canada (British Columbia and Alberta). In the United States the Rockies cover parts of Idaho, Montana, Wyoming, Utah, Colorado, New Mexico, and Texas. The entire mountain chain stretches nearly 3,000 miles; its tallest peak is 14,440 feet above sea level (Mount Elbert in central Colorado). The Rocky Mountains have numerous subranges, including the Wasatch (Utah) and Bitterroots (Idaho-Montana borderland). The Continental Divide, the point at which waters run either into the Atlantic or the Pacific, can also be found in the Rocky Mountains.

Portions of the mountain range were formed as many as 100 million years ago. Since then the mountains have undergone many changes and shifts due to volcanic and seismic activity, water action, and glaciation during the Ice Age. Parts of the Rocky Mountains, especially in the northern regions, have active glaciers. Because of their elevation and sheer size, the Rockies posed a formidable barrier for those individuals seeking to traverse the North American continent.

The Rocky Mountains have offered abundant natural resources, which eventually attracted European and American interest. Indeed, the range is rich in mineral deposits, including copper, lead, molybdenum, tungsten, zinc, silver, and gold. Parts of the Rockies, especially the Wyoming Basin, are also home to oil, natural gas, shale, and coal deposits. Minerals first attracted white settlers and prospectors to the region in the early 19th century, and to this day there are significant and lucrative mining operations in progress. The Rockies have also been home to sizable logging operations and livestock grazing and agricultural concerns in the lower altitudes and valleys.

Much of the Rocky Mountain chain has a highland climate (sometimes referred to as an Alpine climate). Climate and precipitation vary greatly according to elevation. The highest peaks have snow cover year-round; lower elevations experience major winter snow accumulations that recede or melt by late spring. July is the warmest month, while January is the coldest. Summers in most of the Rockies are dry and sunny because the high western summits block ocean-borne moisture from moving east.

The Rocky Mountains were home to many Native American tribes, including the Apaches, Arapahos, Bannocks, Blackfeet, Cheyennes, Crows, Flatheads, Shoshones, Sioux, Utes, and Sekanis and many other smaller groups. These people usually migrated during the winter to the plains and valleys where they hunted buffalo, a key staple of Native American life in this region. The buffalo provided food, clothing, and shelter needs as well as tools and other implements. In the summer when the lowlands were hot these tribes would move to the higher elevations, where they had ample supplies of pure mountain water and where they fished and gathered berries. In Colorado, researchers have found evidence of Native American habitation dating back some 5,500 years.

Rocky Mountain National Park, Colorado. (Reciprocityimages/Dreamstime.com)

In 1540 Spanish explorer Francisco Vásquez de Coronado was the first European to arrive in the Rocky Mountain region. The introduction of horses, metal tools, and firearms gradually transformed Native American life in the Rockies. So too did the introduction of European diseases, to which the Native Americans had no natural immunity. Disease devastated many Native American groups, who by the early 1800s had been forced to leave much of their ancestral territory because of intertribal warfare, tensions with Europeans, and encroachment of white settlers.

In 1739 French fur traders moving west encountered the Rocky Mountains, and they were the first to officially document their findings. The Native Americans they encountered had named the range "Rocky Mountains," and the name stuck. Few Europeans attempted to cross the Rocky Mountains directly, but that changed with the 1803–1805 Lewis and Clark expedition, which was an overland expedition from St. Louis, Missouri, to the West Coast and back. Meriwether Lewis and William Clark painstakingly recorded the flora, fauna, and geography of parts of the Rocky Mountains, which encouraged others to cross the mountains thereafter.

Thanks to abundant waterways and wildlife, Europeans and Americans soon discovered that the Rockies offered a potential windfall for fur traders. Beginning in the early years of the 19th century, European fur traders began moving into the region in significant numbers. They included William Henry Ashley, John Colter, Thomas Fitzpatrick, Jim Bridger, and Jedediah Smith. Indeed,

as early as 1793 fur-trading posts had sprung up in present-day British Columbia. The North West Company and Hudson's Bay Company were two large fur-trading concerns that conducted extensive business in the Rocky Mountain region.

The Rocky Mountain fur-trading system was fundamentally different than that of other systems farther east. In the Rockies few permanent trading posts were created. Beginning in 1825, William Ashley established the rendezvous system whereby once a year he sent a supply train to a different spot in the Rockies. There Native Americans, American trappers, and Mexicans congregated to trade their wares. The rendezvous system became a key part of the Rocky Mountain fur-trading business. Many trappers, who led solitary lives, eagerly anticipated the rendezvous, where they could interact with others, play cards and games, drink, tell stories, and dance. By the 1840s, however, the Rocky Mountain trapping system had eroded substantially, mainly because fur-bearing animal populations had been significantly diminished by overzealous trappers. This gave way to the rise of the buffalo-hide trade in which the Native Americans initially played a central role. However, overhunting by whites drastically reduced the buffalo herds, and the buffalo was nearly extinct by the late 19th century.

Today the Rocky Mountains remain an icon of American vastness and strength as well as unspoiled natural beauty. Even in the 21st century, much of the Rocky Mountain chain is desolate and hard to reach. The population density is, on average, just 10 people per square mile, and there are few cities with populations that exceed 50,000 people. Salt Lake City and Denver remain the two largest cities within the Rockies region.

PAUL G. PIERPAOLI JR.

See also

Apaches; Arapahos; Blackfoot Sioux; Buffalo; Cheyennes; Crows; Fur Trade; Hudson's Bay Company; Lewis and Clark Expedition; Shoshones; Sioux; Utes

References

Cole, Virginia C., and Maurine Carley. *The Shoshinis: Sentinels of the Rockies.* Norman: University of Oklahoma Press, 1964.

Thybony, Scott. *The Rockies: Pillars of a Continent.* New York: National Geographic Society, 1996.

Wisehart, David. *The Fur Trade of the American West, 1807–1840.* Lincoln: University of Nebraska Press, 1979.

Rogers, Robert

Birth Date: November 7, 1731
Death Date: May 17, 1795

British colonial militia officer, best known for his service in the French and Indian War (1754–1763) and his leadership of Rogers' Rangers. Born in Methuen, Massachusetts, on November 7, 1731, Robert Rogers was raised in New Hampshire, where he received only a rudimentary education but developed keen skills as a woodsman and hunter. Rogers served briefly as a scout for the New Hampshire Militia during King George's War (1744–1748) but did not achieve true military distinction until the French and Indian War.

Following service early in the war with militia forces supporting British regulars in the expedition against Crown Point, New York, and battles around Lake George in 1755, Rogers received a promotion to captain. In 1756 he received orders to raise a company of rangers. Most of the men in the unit were handpicked by Rogers himself and were equipped from his own means. In 1758 Rogers was promoted to major and expanded his rangers to include nine companies numbering roughly 200 men.

Rogers' Rangers, as his outfit became known, specialized in scouting and reconnaissance missions. Working in small groups, the rangers often operated behind enemy lines gathering intelligence or engaging in raids and ambushes. All of Rogers's men were accomplished woodsmen, adept at moving swiftly through rough terrain and living resourcefully off the land. They even wore green jackets as an attempt at camouflage. The rangers demonstrated their unique mobility during the Battle on Snowshoes (1758), when they launched raids against enemy encampments in the dead of winter using snowshoes.

After taking part in Major General Jeffrey Amherst's capture of Fort Ticonderoga and Crown Point in July 1759, Rogers achieved his greatest military success to date by executing a daring surprise attack on an Abenaki village near St. Francis, Canada, in October 1759 as retribution for the Abenakis' repeated raids, which had

Major Robert Rogers achieved renown during the French and Indian War (1754–1763) when he organized Rogers' Rangers, a unit adept at irregular woodland warfare and regarded as the forerunner of today's U.S. Army Rangers. (Library of Congress)

killed as many as 600 British colonists. Rogers' Rangers also supported Major General James Wolfe's campaign against Quebec as well as Amherst's capture of Montreal in 1760.

After the British took Montreal, Amherst reassigned Rogers to the Great Lakes region to seize the remaining French fortifications there. Rogers' Rangers continued their success with several key victories, including the capture of Fort Detroit in November 1760, a feat that made Rogers an even greater hero in the colonies. His rangers returned to the Detroit territory again three years later to assist the British Army in suppressing Pontiac's Rebellion (1763).

In 1765 Rogers traveled to England to compile his war memoirs and publish accounts of his heroics against the French and their native allies. He boldly asked King George III for money to fund an expedition to explore the Mississippi River to the Pacific Ocean. The king refused this audacious request but did reward Rogers with command of Fort Michilimackinac in present-day Michigan. As commandant of the fort, Rogers followed a path of corruption and insubordination mostly in trying to pursue his obsession of creating an expedition to find the elusive Northwest Passage. He was arrested and tried for treason by the royal government. Acquitted in 1768, Rogers returned to England in hopes of securing another command but succeeded only in landing in debtors' prison.

At the outbreak of the American Revolutionary War (1775–1783) Rogers offered his services to the Patriot cause, but the Continental Congress did not trust his allegiance and rejected the offer. An embittered Rogers then joined the British side, receiving a commission as a lieutenant colonel in command of Loyalist rangers. Although he fought in several campaigns during 1776–1777, he failed to earn any notable distinction. Captured in 1781, he was released the next year on parole and returned to England, where he lived in poverty and obscurity until his death in London on May 17, 1795.

BRADFORD A. WINEMAN

See also

Abenakis; French and Indian War; Rogers's Raid on St. Francis

References

Cuneo, John R. *Robert Rogers of the Rangers.* New York: Oxford University Press, 1959.

Smith, Bradford. *Rogers' Rangers and the French and Indian War.* New York: Random House, 1956.

Rogers's Raid on St. Francis
Start Date: September 13, 1759
End Date: October 6, 1759

Attack by Rogers' Rangers on the Canadian town of St. Francis during the French and Indian War (1754–1763). From their town of St. Francis, the French-allied Abenakis raided British settlements to the south.

The Abenaki mission town of St. Francis was located close to the mouth of the river of the same name between Montreal and Trois Rivières. Known as Odanak to the natives, the town contained more than 60 dwellings, a Jesuit chapel, and a council house. The Abenakis used St. Francis as a base from which they launched raids against the northern British colonies. According to some reports, as many as 600 English scalps taken by the raiding parties were displayed in the town. The strong native position at St. Francis also blocked communication between British forces moving to attack Quebec and other British and colonial forces in New York and New England.

To remove this obstacle to wresting Canada from the French and their native allies, British commander in North America Major General Jeffrey Amherst ordered Major Robert Rogers, an expert at irregular warfare, to attack St. Francis. The operation was fraught with considerable risk, as it required Rogers's force to penetrate deep into French-controlled territory, country that was unfamiliar to the attackers.

Rogers set out from the British post at Crown Point on September 13, 1759, with a force of about 200 men, most of them rangers, with a few British regulars and more than 20 Stockbridge Native Americans. The party traveled in whaleboats across Lake Champlain to Missisquoi Bay in present-day Vermont, where they disembarked and moved overland to St. Francis. During the march Rogers lost about one-fourth of his men to accident and disease. Also, shortly after the raiders landed, the French discovered and destroyed their whaleboats, depriving Rogers's men of the means to return to their base by water and leaving them completely cut off in hostile territory.

Undeterred by the loss of the boats, Rogers convened a council of war, which decided to proceed with the attack on St. Francis. Rogers then planned to withdraw overland to Fort Number Four on the Connecticut River.

Rogers and his remaining 142 men reached their objective on the night of October 5 after a dangerous crossing of the St. Francis River. The French and their native allies were aware of the rangers' presence in the area and had parties out searching for them but expected Rogers to attack elsewhere. Learning from some prisoners that none of the French and native parties were near St. Francis, Rogers decided that it was safe to conceal his force and attack early the next morning.

Some accounts suggest that the Abenakis received a warning on the night of October 5 that an attack on St. Francis was imminent and that many of the town's inhabitants chose to leave. Nonetheless, there were approximately 500 people in the town the next morning. Exhausted after a night spent celebrating a harvest festival (or wedding, according to some accounts), the Abenakis apparently took no precautions to guard against an attack.

Rogers carefully positioned his men and then launched his assault before dawn on October 6. Some rangers forced their way into houses and killed the occupants with tomahawks; others set fire to dwellings and shot down the inhabitants as they attempted to flee. Another body of rangers posted along the St. Francis River fired on any natives seen escaping the growing conflagration. The assault was over quickly, as the surprised Abenakis were unable to offer effective resistance.

When the fighting ended, the rangers gathered as much corn as they could carry to sustain them on their return journey. They also plundered the Jesuit chapel of its gold and silver religious artifacts. They then withdrew to escape certain pursuit. The rangers took with them a half dozen captured Abenaki women and children as well as some captives who had been held at the town. Among the latter were three members of Rogers's own unit who had been taken prisoner earlier in the war.

Rogers later claimed to have killed 200 natives in the battle, thus breaking the Abenakis' ability to conduct offensive operations. French officials visiting St. Francis shortly after the attack, however, reported having seen only 30 dead, two-thirds of whom were women and children. The actual native death toll is probably somewhere between these two extremes. The rangers suffered no casualties themselves in the engagement.

The attackers then withdrew up the St. Francis River to the site of present-day Sherbrooke and then moved on to the southeast. Near Lake Memphremagog their provisions ran out, so Rogers ordered his men to disperse into smaller parties, thus making it easier both to find game and to elude their pursuers. Slowed by hunger, exhaustion, and exposure to the cold, some groups were caught and killed by the pursuing French and natives. Fewer than 100 members of the expedition eventually made their way to safety. The remainder were killed by the French and Abenakis or succumbed to starvation and exposure.

Despite the large number of casualties suffered, Rogers's raid proved a strategic success. The loss of life among the Abenakis and the destruction of their base, along with the British capture of Quebec the month before, effectively ended the Native American threat to the British settlements on the northern frontier.

JIM PIECUCH

See also

Abenakis; French and Indian War; Rogers, Robert

References

Cuneo, John R. *Robert Rogers of the Rangers.* New York: Oxford University Press, 1959.

Rogers, Robert. *The Journals of Major Robert Rogers.* New York: Corinth Books, 1961.

Rogue River War, First
Event Date: 1853

The first of two wars fought between the Rogue River tribe of Native Americans and volunteer forces and the U.S. Army. The fighting in the First Rogue River War occurred in southwestern Oregon during 1853. An influx of settlers and especially gold miners into the territory, prompted by the California Gold Rush, as well as the language barrier and clash of cultures all led to violence. Ironically, the Rogue River tribe was apparently blamed for a raid most likely committed by Shasta Native Americans from northern California, which led to action by the army and settler volunteers.

In response to the raid, a small detachment of 10 members of the U.S. Army's 4th Infantry Regiment under the command of Captain Bradford Alden set out from Fort James, just across the border in Scotts Valley, California, in pursuit of the Rogue River tribe. At Yreka the regiment was joined by one volunteer company, and at Jackson three other companies joined. The territorial delegate Joseph Lane also joined and insisted that he take command, with Alden relegated to second-in-command.

The volunteers and regulars pursued the Native Americans into the rugged Cascade Mountains and in a single engagement on August 24, 1853, fought some 200 warriors. As a consequence of this one battle, the Rogue River Native Americans sued for peace.

Following a truce, the two sides signed the Table Rock Treaty of September 10, ratified on April 12, 1854. The treaty was negotiated by Joel Palmer, superintendent of Indian affairs, and Samuel H. Culver, Indian agent, with Jo-aps-er-ka-har (Horse Rider), principal chief of the Rogue River tribe, along with several subordinate chiefs. The Native Americans agreed to cede their lands in the Bear Creek Valley and settle temporarily on a 100-square-mile reservation (the Table Rock Indian Reservation) until a permanent reservation could be found. The government promised to pay the tribe $60,000 for the loss of its lands, $15,000 of which was to be used to recompense settlers for property destroyed in the fighting. Quiet prevailed along the Rogue River for the next two years until the resumption of fighting in 1855.

SPENCER C. TUCKER

See also

Rogue River War, Second

References

Beckham, Stephen Dow. *Requiem for a People: The Rogue Indians and the Frontiersmen.* Norman: University of Oklahoma Press, 1971.

Douthit, Nathan. *Uncertain Encounters: Indians and Whites at Peace and War in Southern Oregon, 1820s to 1860s.* Corvallis: Oregon State University Press, 2002.

Schwartz, E. A. The *Rogue River Indian War and Its Aftermath, 1850–1980.* Norman: University of Oklahoma Press, 1997.

Utley, Robert M. *Frontiersmen in Blue: The United States and the Indian, 1848–1865.* Lincoln: University of Nebraska Press, 1967.

Rogue River War, Second
Start Date: 1855
End Date: 1856

War fought in southwestern Oregon between the Rogue River tribe of Native Americans and both civilian volunteers and U.S. Army regulars. Most of the fighting occurred in the Rogue River Valley. Shorter in duration than the wider conflict with which it became entangled—the Yakima-Rogue War in the Washington Territory—the Rogue River War stemmed from frustrations and bitterness over the September 1853 treaty that had relocated Native Americans to the Table Rock Reservation north of the Rogue River. A lack of water, a hard winter, and disease led some of the natives to leave the Table Rock Reservation and return to their former village on Little Battle Creek on the upper Rogue River.

At the same time, increasing numbers of settlers prospecting for gold heightened tensions. In the summer of 1855, settlers had accused Native Americans living on the reservation of conducting attacks on miners and settlements, including a massacre of 20 whites on the Klamath River in July 1855. The Native Americans charged in turn that settlers were raiding their camps and complained that the reservation afforded them little protection.

Fearing a major Native American uprising, U.S. Army captain Andrew J. Smith of the 1st Dragoons Regiment at Fort Lane and George Ambrose, the local Indian agent, refused to hand over the Native Americans accused of these acts to the Siskiyou County volunteer force. A similar situation occurred in August, when Smith rejected an ultimatum by Yreka volunteers to deliver to them Native Americans suspected of killing whites. This further exacerbated tensions and led militia to mobilize.

The Rogue River War began on October 8, 1855, when James Lupton and his volunteer company carried out a raid near Fort Lane on the Native Americans at Little Bear Creek, who had remained defiant when ordered to return to the reservation. The attack killed 23 Native Americans, including women and children. This event prompted reservation warriors to join with nonreservation bands to combat the volunteer militia. Within days Native American warriors had killed some 20 white men, women, and children living farther downriver and then moved west to strike homesteads and mining camps. Believing that he and his people were largely unprotected by the U.S. Army in the face of enraged volunteers, Chief Old John (Tecumtum) left Table Rock to lead the rebellion against the white settlers and miners.

Captain Smith and Joel Palmer, Oregon's superintendent of Indian affairs, attempted to quell the violence in the wake of the October massacre, believing the conflict to be a war of extermination waged by white volunteers on mostly peaceful Native Americans. This did not stop George Curry, Oregon territorial governor, from raising eight companies of mounted volunteers to conduct major engagements against the Native Americans. In the Battle of Hungry Hill (October 31–November 1, 1855), 300 warriors won a major victory when they held back a force of nearly 500 volunteers and regulars by establishing a strong defensive position on a steeply forested hill. A few weeks later some 200 warriors successfully defended an encampment against 386 volunteers and 50 regulars at Battle Bar, below Grave Creek.

Fighting subsided in December, perhaps because of Brevet Major General John E. Wool's public condemnation of unruly whites, although volunteer companies operating outside of the army's command renewed their search for Native Americans along the upper Rogue River in January 1856. Fierce fighting broke out on the lower Rogue River on February 22, 1856, even as Superintendent Palmer began a forced removal of nearly 400 Native Americans from the Table Rock Reservation to the Grand Ronde Reservation on the Yamhill River in the upper Willamette Valley.

During the course of the next several weeks, warriors guided by Enos Thomas, a mixed-blood Native American, attacked volunteers and settlements along the river to the coast, killing 31 settlers including Indian agent and volunteer leader Benjamin Wright. They burned some 60 cabins over a two-day span. At Gold Beach at the mouth of the Rogue River, some 130 whites fled to a fortification on the north bank, where they lost 6 men to Native American assaults in the next month until army regulars arrived on March 20.

Through the spring, General Wool directed 270 regulars in a three-pronged attack on the hostile warriors, while Governor Curry raised a force of 865 Oregon mounted volunteers to pursue the Native Americans downriver. By late May, with little food or supplies available after a harsh winter, most Native Americans had agreed to stop fighting and move to reservations. Nevertheless, Chief Old John remained a formidable opponent. His band of 150 warriors struck Captain Smith's 80 regulars at Big Meadows

(Bend) on May 27, 1856, killing 11 and wounding 20. The attack could well have ended in disaster for the Americans but for a warning by Chief George (Cholcultah) to Smith and the arrival of Captain C. C. Augur's relief force the next day.

Coastal Native Americans and both upper and lower Rogue River tribes surrendered in greater numbers over the following weeks as volunteers and regulars continued to press them. On June 20, 1856, the war essentially ended with the surrender of Old John, who was incarcerated at Fort Alcatraz in San Francisco Bay. Enos Thomas also eventually surrendered and was hanged in 1857. Other warriors were sent to an area near Fort Hoskins. The remaining members of the Rogue River tribe were relocated to the Grande Ronde and Siletz reservations.

Casualties among the Native Americans and the soldiers and volunteers in the war are estimated at 225 Native Americans and 50 whites (33 volunteers and 17 regulars) killed and 61 whites (39 volunteers and 22 regulars) wounded. The number of Native American wounded is unknown. Having lost a third of its male population because of the conflict, the Rogue River tribe ceased to be a military threat, and southern Oregon remained permanently open to white settlement.

MICHAEL F. DOVE

See also
Rogue River War, First; Wool, John Ellis; Yakima-Rogue War

References
Beckham, Stephen Dow. *Requiem for a People: The Rogue Indians and the Frontiersmen.* Norman: University of Oklahoma Press, 1971.

Douthit, Nathan. *Uncertain Encounters: Indians and Whites at Peace and War in Southern Oregon, 1820s to 1860s.* Corvallis: Oregon State University Press, 2002.

Schwartz, E. A. The *Rogue River Indian War and Its Aftermath, 1850–1980.* Norman: University of Oklahoma Press, 1997.

Roman Nose
Birth Date: ca. 1830
Death Date: September 17, 1868

Southern Cheyenne war leader. Also known as Wakini (Hook Nose), Roman Nose was born around 1830. Little is known of his early life, but by the 1860s he had emerged as a leader of the Cheyennes' Crooked Lance Society and had closely aligned the group with another Cheyenne society, the Dog Soldiers. In the summer of 1864 he led many Cheyennes to the Powder River area to hunt and thus escaped the Sand Creek Massacre in November.

Roman Nose learned of the events at Sand Creek in January 1865. He and his warriors, yearning for vengeance, joined Red Cloud's Sioux, who had decided to drive out white intruders on the Bozeman Trail. On July 26 while the Sioux attacked a cavalry detachment on the North Platte River, Roman Nose led his followers in an attack on a nearby army wagon train. Wearing a special headdress of eagle feathers made for him by a shaman and believing that this medicine bonnet rendered him immune to bullets and arrows, Roman Nose drew the soldiers' fire, and the Cheyenne followed him in a charge that overran the circled wagons and annihilated the soldiers.

On September 1 Roman Nose led a force of Cheyenne, Sioux, and Arapaho warriors in an attack on a detachment of soldiers along the Powder River. Protected by his medicine bonnet, he rode several times along the full length of the soldiers' line to expend their ammunition before the Native Americans attacked. His horse was killed, but Roman Nose remained unscathed. The soldiers, however, withstood the Native Americans' assault.

By 1866 Roman Nose and his followers had returned to their home territory. At a council at Fort Ellsworth, Kansas, Roman Nose protested against the Union Pacific Railroad's encroachment into Cheyenne hunting grounds. When railroad construction continued and growing numbers of settlers began moving westward along the Smoky Hill Road, the more militant among the Cheyennes resolved to attack the stagecoach stations. In the autumn Roman Nose visited Fort Wallace to announce that he would commence attacks in 15 days if travel on the road was not halted. However, a harsh winter limited Cheyenne operations to a few raids.

In April 1867 Major General Winfield Scott Hancock arrived at Fort Larned with 1,400 men, intending to force the Cheyennes to allow settlers unimpeded passage on the roads and railways. Hancock presented his demands at a council with Cheyenne chiefs and also insisted on meeting Roman Nose, who had not attended the meeting because he was not a chief. Hancock then marched his force toward the Cheyenne camp at Pawnee Fork. The Cheyennes believed that Hancock intended to attack their camp. While they gathered their possessions and fled, Roman Nose, at the head of 300 warriors, met Hancock on April 14. Roman Nose wanted to kill Hancock but was restrained by one of the Cheyenne leader's lieutenants. After Hancock insisted that Roman Nose instruct the fleeing Cheyennes to return to their camp, the meeting broke up. Hancock's troops then destroyed the abandoned village.

Once the Cheyenne women and children were safe, Roman Nose and his followers unleashed the offensive they had planned earlier, attacking wagon trains, railroad work crews, and settlers in western Kansas. Roman Nose refused to attend the Medicine Lodge Council in October 1867 at which Kiowa, Comanche, Arapaho, and some Cheyenne leaders signed a treaty that restricted the tribes to a joint reservation and accepted construction of the railroad.

Roman Nose and his 300 warriors, assisted by some Sioux and a few Arapahos, continued their raids into the autumn of 1868. On September 16 a Sioux party discovered a company of 53 army scouts under Major George Forsyth. The Sioux sent a message to Roman Nose urging an immediate attack. When the message arrived, Roman Nose was in his lodge undergoing a purification ritual; several days earlier he had inadvertently eaten food prepared with metal utensils, which supposedly rendered his medicine bonnet ineffective. The Native Americans attacked the scouts'

camp the next morning in what became known as the Battle of Beecher's Island. Roman Nose joined them in the afternoon without properly completing the ritual. While leading an unsuccessful charge on the scouts' position, he was mortally wounded and died later that night.

Robert W. Malick and Jim Piecuch

See also
Beecher Island, Battle of; Cheyennes; Forsyth, George Alexander; Hancock, Winfield Scott; Medicine Lodge Treaty

References
Brown, Dee. *Bury My Heart at Wounded Knee.* New York: Holt, Rinehart and Winston, 1970.
Grinnell, George Bird. *The Fighting Cheyenne.* 1915; reprint, Norman: University of Oklahoma Press, 1989.
Nye, Wilber S. *Plains Indian Raiders: The Final Phase of Warfare from the Arkansas to the Red River.* Norman: University of Oklahoma Press, 1968.

Romanticism

Literary, artistic, and intellectual movement that began in Europe at the end of the 18th century. By the early 19th century, Romanticism had spread to the United States. In general, Romanticism sought to cast away rigid classical thinking and assert the validity of subjective experiences, which included individual emotions. Romanticism was strongly rooted in the subjective experiences of

Famed western artist George Catlin's rendering of representatives of three different Native American tribes—the Osages, the Iroquois, and the Pawnees—circa 1850. (Getty Images)

nature and those who communed with it. Thus, Native Americans were frequent subjects of American artists and writers during the Romantic era.

The American Indian Wars of 1866–1890 were fought largely over ownership of the land in the West. Although there were originally more than 500 Native American nations and societies, a great number were entirely wiped out in the brutal wars that claimed thousands of lives and devastated native cultures. Facts were usually ignored in the portrayal of these wars, with art, literature, and later the movies romanticizing the role of the Native American. An aura and fascination developed around these people and their daily lives, giving rise to a plethora of idealized and romantic representations. Hence, they became homogenized and stereotyped to the extent of becoming "the Indian," devoid of individuality, unique language, and culture.

Native Americans were portrayed either as the noble savage (good, peaceful, helpful) or the ignoble savage (bad, hostile, and barbaric), labels that inferred that the individual was a primitive being at the beginning of civilization. The settlers, although fascinated by the Native Americans, saw it as their right to dominate and conquer them. Artists and writers perpetuated these images

to validate and justify the various wars, the taking of Native American lands, and the slaughter of entire nations to make way for white settlement. The many different Native American languages were frequently reduced to simple guttural utterances (e.g., "ugh" and "how") to suit the image conveyed, and, of course, such images had very little to do with the realities of Native American life, as they were not generally based on actual contact with them.

The romanticizing of the Indian Wars reinforced the popular belief that the white society was superior. The settlers believed then that the Native Americans would see the fruitlessness of the wars and in turn embrace white society, along with its religion and politics.

Native Americans were usually portrayed as the aggressor, while settlers were portrayed as the victim. Paintings, illustrations, and traveling shows depicted Native Americans in full battle regalia riding their horses and attacking wagon trains or stage coaches. Buffalo Bill's Wild West Show was a testament to this romantic portrayal of the Indian Wars, reinforcing this view.

Authors such as James Fenimore Cooper helped to perpetuate the romantic images, writing about the strong, the brave, and the wise and the last of a powerful Indian nation. Making use of

Sioux chiefs. Photo taken by Edward S. Curtis, circa 1905. (Library of Congress)

poetic terms, authors intimated that Native Americans were from another time, either living in harmony and peace or, on the other hand, being the violent abductor of innocent women and children, therefore justifying the massacres that occurred.

Edward S. Curtis and George Catlin, both visual artists, sympathized with and romanticized the Native Americans, believing that they were a vanishing people. The artists would sometimes stage the representations to characterize the Native Americans' heroism and nobility, most evident in the poses of the chiefs, always standing with their arms crossed and in full battle regalia.

Almost all romantic representations of the Native Americans during the time of the Indian Wars were a form of propaganda aimed at appeasing the guilt of the white settlers for pushing the tribes from their native lands in the name of progress.

SHELLEY G. ALLSOP

See also

Buffalo Bill's Wild West Show; Catlin, George; Cooper, James Fenimore; Custer's Last Stand in Art; Literature and the American Indian Wars; Remington, Frederic

References

Berkhofer, Robert. *The White Man's Indian: Images of the American Indian from Columbus to the Present.* New York: Vintage, 1978.
Donovan, James. *A Terrible Glory: Custer and the Little Bighorn.* New York: Little, Brown, 2007.
Goldensohn, Lorrie, ed. *American War Poetry: An Anthology.* New York: Columbia University Press, 2006.

Rondoenie

See Orontony

Rosebud, Battle of the
Event Date: June 17, 1876

Military engagement between the Lakota Sioux and Northern Cheyennes and U.S. Army forces. The Battle of the Rosebud, also known as the Battle of the Rosebud Creek, occurred on June 17, 1876. Army forces led by Brigadier General George Crook confronted the allied Native Americans along the Rosebud Creek in present-day Big Horn County, Montana. The clash was part of the Great Sioux War (Black Hills War) of 1876–1877.

In the spring of 1876, the U.S. Army launched a campaign against hostile tribes by sending three columns from western posts to converge on Indian encampments in southeastern Montana Territory. Crook's force was one of the three. From Fort Fetterman, Wyoming, Crook marched north along the south fork of the Rosebud Creek to converge with the other two columns in an attempt to locate and defeat the Native Americans, who had left the reservations in large numbers in response to white encroachment into the Black Hills and other violations of the Fort Laramie Treaty of 1868.

During a halt in Crook's march, a force of Lakotas and Cheyennes found and attacked the resting army column. Crook's Crow and Shoshone scouts engaged the attacking warriors first and fought an effective delaying action, which gave Crook enough time to organize and deploy his troops. Situated on low ground, Crook deployed troops of the 3rd Cavalry to seize the high bluffs to the south while he marched the remainder of his command against the warriors to the north. Hampered by Native American fire on his flank, Crook ordered seven troops of the 3rd Cavalry to charge in an attempt to disrupt his enemy and hasten his own advance. The Lakotas then withdrew from their position and reestablished themselves along the crest of the next ridgeline. While Crook's troops converged and established their command post, his second-in-command, Lieutenant Colonel William Royall, assembled several unengaged troops and led them against the warriors who had emerged to the west and had begun harassing the rear of Crook's column. After pushing the Native Americans back nearly a mile, Royall, in fear of being cut off, finally halted his advance near the head of Kollmar Creek.

Although his initial actions seized key terrain, Crook's efforts did little to weaken or slow the Native American attack. Realizing the vulnerability of the U.S. position, the Lakotas and Cheyennes shifted their efforts to the west against Royall's detachment, virtually ignoring the troops to the south. For an hour the Native Americans and U.S. forces engaged in a series of cat-and-mouse charges, countercharges, and retreats. Neither side, however, gained the upper hand.

In an effort to strike a decisive blow against the warriors, Crook attempted to consolidate his forces while simultaneously deploying his cavalry to find and pressure the Lakota and Cheyenne camps that he suspected to be in the area but to no avail. For six hours the engagement continued until the Native Americans finally withdrew. While Crook claimed a victory because he was left in command of the field, the Lakota Sioux and Northern Cheyennes effectively stopped the American advance. Crook reported losses of 10 killed and 21 wounded, although most historians put the losses much higher, perhaps three times as many. The Native Americans suffered about 100 killed or wounded.

The Native Americans could claim a strategic victory because Crook was forced to break off his advance and, significantly, was unable to send news of his setback to the other two columns. Crook next marched his command south to Big Goose Creek, Wyoming, and established a base camp there, waiting seven weeks for reinforcements rather than continuing north and converging with the other two columns, one of which included Lieutenant Colonel George Armstrong Custer's ill-fated 7th Cavalry Regiment, which was all but wiped out on June 25 at the Battle of the Little Bighorn (June 25–26, 1876).

JOSEPH P. ALESSI

See also

Cheyennes, Northern; Crook, George; Great Sioux War; Lakota Sioux; Little Bighorn, Battle of the; Scouts, Native American

Warriors advance in the Battle of the Rosebud in Montana on June 17, 1876. Although the army claimed it a victory, the protracted Native American stand here forced soldiers under Brigadier General George Crook to fall back and regroup, preventing their union with the other two army columns. Engraving from *Frank Leslie's Illustrated Newspaper*, August 12, 1876. (Library of Congress)

References
Bourke, John G. *On the Border with Crook.* Lincoln: University of Nebraska Press, 1971.
Brown, Dee. *Bury My Heart at Wounded Knee.* New York: Holt, Rinehart and Winston, 1970.
Finerty, John F. *Warpath and Bivouac: The Big Horn and Yellowstone Expedition.* Chicago: R. R. Donnelley, 1955.
Mangum, Neil A. *Battle of the Rosebud: Prelude to the Little Big Horn.* El Segundo, CA: Upton, 1987.

Rowlandson, Mary White
Birth Date: ca. 1637
Death Date: ca. 1710–1711

Englishwoman captured by Native Americans in 1676 and author of a narrative of her time in captivity. Mary White was born in England around 1637. Her parents left for North America in 1639, taking their daughter with them. The family settled in Lancaster, Massachusetts, where White married Joseph Rowlandson in 1656. He became a Puritan minister in Lancaster in 1660.

In February 1676 during King Philip's War (1675–1676), a band of Narragansett and Nipmuck warriors attacked Lancaster and in the process burned most of the settlement. The warriors took a number of captives, Mary Rowlandson among them. After her capture, she was transported with other English captives along a meandering trek through western Massachusetts before returning to an area near Lancaster, where her husband paid her ransom. Her captivity lasted three months. In all Rowlandson endured 20 "removes" (relocations), during which she suffered from exposure to the elements, hunger, and the psychological shock of captivity and fear of death.

On her release the noted Puritan minister Increase Mather encouraged Rowlandson to publish an account of her captivity. He counseled this to help quell rumors that she had been sexually abused by her captors and to provide a timely moral lesson for a spiritually backsliding society. Lascivious rumors and innuendo about the sexual assault of female captives prompted Rowlandson to set down the facts of the matter to deflect such gossip. She also hoped to dispel the falsehoods that might have compromised her prominent position as the wife of a clergyman.

In her captivity narrative titled *The Sovereignty and Goodness of God,* which was published in 1682, Rowlandson gave a vivid and candid account of her ordeal, carefully noting that no warrior had made any sexual advances toward her or any of the other female hostages. She heaped scorn on the Christian praying Indians, however, whom she regarded as spies and traitors. She interpreted her experience as a divine chastisement for her pride and spiritual laxity, and Mather intended that New Englanders would interpret King Philip's War as a collective punishment.

A classic in the popular genre of the captivity narrative, the book went through several editions throughout the rest of the 17th century and the 18th century, confirming Anglo-American society's negative assumptions about Native Americans. Meanwhile, Rowlandson moved to Wethersfield, Connecticut, where her husband had a congregation. Rowlandson died in either 1710 or 1711.

JOHN HOWARD SMITH

See also

Captivity Narratives; Captivity of Europeans by Indians; King Philip's War; Praying Towns and Praying Indians

References

Leach, Douglas Edward. "The 'Whens' of Mary Rowlandson's Captivity." *New England Quarterly* 34(3) (September 1961): 352–363.

Rowlandson, Mary. *The Sovereignty and Goodness of God.* Edited by Neal Salisbury. Boston: Bedford Books, 1997.

Russell, Charles Marion

Birth Date: March 19, 1864
Death Date: October 24, 1926

Artist, author, and humorist who created more than 2,000 paintings depicting the life of cowboys and Native Americans on the western landscape. Charles Marion Russell, also known as C. M. Russell, was born in St. Louis, Missouri, on March 19, 1864.

In 1880 at the age of 16, having learned to ride horses at a farm in Illinois, Russell left school and became a cowboy in Montana. It was the bitterly cold winter of 1886–1887 that ultimately changed his life forever. While working as a wrangler at the O-H Ranch in central Montana he was approached by the ranch foreman, who had with him a letter from the owner inquiring about the condition of the surviving cattle. Russell's response was to take a small piece of cardboard on which he drew an impressive watercolor sketch depicting a thin starving cow surrounded by hungry wolves. Russell sent the report along with the sketch, which he titled *Waiting for Chinook.*

The ranch owner shared the picture with friends and business acquaintances and then had it prominently displayed in a shop window in downtown Helena, Montana. New settlers to the territory who were experiencing rough financial times also related to the sketch. Russell's depiction became so popular that postcards bearing the painting were dispatched throughout the United States and Europe. As the depiction grew in stature, Russell later drew a more detailed version, which became known as *The Last of the Five Thousand* and would remain one of his most celebrated works.

In 1888 as his stature as an artist grew, Russell spent the summer with a Native American tribe known as the Bloods. They were part of the Northern Blackfoot Nation. He quickly immersed himself in their culture, learning their language, customs, and legends. Gaining their trust and respect, he grew his hair long and wore their clothes. As the frontier gradually closed and Native Americans were forced to assimilate or live on reservations, Russell remained steadfast in his sympathy to their plight.

In 1890 Russell's *Studies in Western Life,* a portfolio of 21 color pictures, was unveiled. A number of the pictures highlighted his admiration for those who lived in nature. Other notable portraits include *Blackfeet Indian with Capote* (1896), *Indian Women Moving Camp* (1897), *Peace* (1899), and *Indian on Horse Shooting a Buffalo* (1906).

In 1897, a year after he married, Russell moved to Great Falls, Montana, where he spent the majority of his life from that time forward. His wife, Nancy Russell, is credited with making him an internationally known artist. She set up many art shows for Russell in the United States and in London. The same year he moved to Great Falls, he also turned to publishing short stories, capturing and recording the pioneering spirit of the West. He thus entertained friends and audiences with amusing stories about his experiences and counted among his associates and collectors of his works Douglas Fairbanks and Will Rogers.

One of Russell's best-known publications, which was richly illustrated, is *Back-Trailing on the Old Frontiers* (1922). A year after his death, a collection of his short stories, patterned after the dime novel, was published as *Trails Plowed Under.* Russell died on October 24, 1926, in Great Falls. Local schools and businesses closed that day to watch the funeral procession. A museum named in his honor in Great Falls houses more than 2,000 artworks, personal memorabilia, and artifacts. His popular mural *Lewis and Clark Meeting the Flathead Indians* hangs in the state capitol building in Helena, Montana.

CHARLES FRANCIS HOWLETT

See also

Blackfoot Sioux

References

Adams, Ramon, and Homer E. Britzman. *Charles M. Russell, the Cowboy Artist: A Biography.* Pasadena, CA: Trail's End Publishing, 1948.

Gales, Robert L. *Charles Marion Russell.* Boise, ID: Boise State University Press, 1979.

Hassrick, Peter H. *Charles M. Russell: The Life and Legend of America's Cowboy Artist.* New York: Harry N. Abrams, 1989.

Russia

The history of Native interactions with Russians in Alaska and the far Northwest (present-day far northwestern Canada) is really a history of two institutions that often operated at cross-purposes: the Russian Orthodox Church and the Russian American Company. The church, like so many other religious groups in colonial North America, charged itself with saving the souls of the Native Americans. The company's self-defined purpose was making a profit from the colony's extensive fur resources. The political interaction involving the Russian American Company, the Russian Orthodox Church, and the Russian government in St. Petersburg would profoundly affect changes both in the short-lived nature of the company's mission and the permanent structure of the church.

In the 17th century Russia began expanding eastward toward Siberia and China, and the Orthodox faith accompanied Russian colonization efforts from the beginning. Although small transitory Russian settlements had been built by profit-seeking *promyshlenniki* ("fur hunters") throughout the mid-18th century, the first verifiable permanent settlement in Alaska was established on Kodiak Island in 1784 by Grigorii I. Shelikov, later to head the Russian American Company. Shelikov was among the first to anticipate the possible profits and benefits of Alaskan colonization. Fifteen years later, the Russian American Company was granted a monopoly on the exploitation of the natural resources and governmental control of Alaska, and the city of Novo-Arkhangel'sk (later named Sitka) was established as the capital of Russian America.

Orthodox missionaries played a major role in the settlement process in Siberia and the Far East during this early period of Russian expansion eastward. Native people were baptized by the thousands and given Russian names. Many of these newly Russified Native Americans were rewarded for their conversion by being released from paying taxes to the Cossack rulers and by promises of employment by the hunters and traders. This conversion of native people, marriages between Russians and natives, the baptizing of children, and promises of religiously determined economic gain laid a foundation for the religious conversion policies that would be used later in North America.

Between the first Russian American settlement at Three Saints Harbor, near Kodiak, in 1784 and the establishment of the first mission, the explorers themselves were primarily responsible for these rudimentary rituals. The Orthodox mission in Russian America was first authorized by Catherine II in 1793 and then established at Kodiak, the first capital of the colony, on September 24, 1794, by a group of monks sent from the Valaam monastery in St. Petersburg. One of these monks, Archimandrite Ioasaph, was elected the first bishop of the new colony.

Ioasaph complained to Shelikov about conditions in Russian America in a letter he wrote in May 1795. The company's general manager, Alexander Baranov, was unwilling to assist the priests and even showed outright hostility toward the initial efforts to found a mission church in Kodiak. Ioasaph complained of Baranov's exploits with women, of his encouraging the hostility of the *promyshlenniki*

Illustration of St. Paul Harbor, Kodiak Island, Alaska, from Russian explorer Urey Lisiansky's journal of 1814. (Urey Lisiansky, *Voyage Round the World in the Years 1803, 4, 5, & 6,* 1814)

against the priests, and of insufficient resources and food. The company was proving a hindrance to the monks rather than a help. After being consecrated as bishop in April 1798, Ioasaph died in a shipwreck on the way back to America with all but three of the other monks. For the next two decades only those three surviving monks remained in Russian America, and a state of constant enmity existed between them and Baranov. Religious rituals and missionary activities were almost nonexistent because of the lack of trained clergy in the colony. Finally, in 1816 a small church was erected in the new city of Novo-Arkhangel'sk, and Aleksei Sokolov came to serve as its first priest, performing baptisms and other church rituals for people who came from all over Russian America.

Among the first group of monks sent to America from the Valaam monastery in St. Petersburg in 1794 was a monk named Herman who was to become the Native Americans' most adamant defender against the Russian American Company. When Herman arrived in Alaska, relations between the Russians and the Native Americans were very poor, and during 1819–1823 there were only two other monks besides Herman left in Russian America. This period between the first settlements and the reorganization of the Russian American Company in 1821 was a time of great persecution by the profit-seeking *promyshlenniki,* both of the Orthodox Church and the Native American populations in Russian America. After the death of Ioasaph, Herman, as the superior among the three remaining monks in the colony, reported on these incidents in letters back to Russia.

Because the *promyshlenniki* were not adept at the hunting of sea otter furs and the Aleut and Kodiak populations were, the Russians soon found that they would need to either buy or coerce the assistance of the Native Americans to exploit this resource. In some cases the pelts were a form of tribute paid by the Aleuts to the Russians, with hostages being held by the Russians to ensure payment. Later a quasi-feudal system developed in which the Aleuts were required to work for the Russian American Company and received the goods that they needed for survival in return for sea otter pelts. This system was a reaction to the system in place in Russia. Aleut men were separated from their families for long periods of time and were forced to hunt in distant regions. As time passed, many of the Native Americans began to rebel against this system. In the 1760s, armed Aleuts killed the crews of three (or four, according to some reports) Russian ships.

Incidents such as these made it clear to Shelikov that greater support of the church by the company would be necessary to control the Native American population, but as of 1820 only one priest and one monk remained in Russian America. However, after the reorganization of the Russian American Company in early 1821, the relationship between the Orthodox Church and the company became one of codependence. When the Russian American Company's charter was renewed by the czar, Nicholas I stipulated that the company was to provide adequate financial resources from its own profits for the needs of the Orthodox Church and its Russian, Creole, and Native American parishioners. A string of mediocre leaders filled the position of bishop of Alaska from that point until 1840, when Ivan Veniaminov (later named Saint Innocent), who had been working as a diocesan priest on Unalaska Island and at Novo-Arkhangel'sk since 1822, became bishop. Under his guidance, the Russian Orthodox Church gained a truly permanent foothold on the North American continent.

Veniaminov reported that between 1799 and 1828, the Native American population had decreased rapidly. This was due in large part to fatalities that occurred during the long hunting expeditions on which the Russian American Company sent parties of Native Americans. Also, the absence of the Aleut men on these parties caused starvation among the remaining Native American people in their villages. Veniaminov also noted that the state of the education of the Native Americans was extremely poor and that Herman was the only monk teaching in a school for Native Americans. Because he was held in high esteem, Herman's letters back to church and government officials in Russia were effective in that they were one of the causes of the reorganization of the Russian American Company, which eventually led to a stronger ecclesiastical presence in America. Only because of a new company charter from the czar was there renewed interest in both education and ecclesiastical leadership. Although the Russian American Company paid the priests' salaries, not many newly ordained clergy were interested in making the hazardous journey into an unknown area where some had already been martyred. To the extent that the ecclesiastical situation had deteriorated, so had the education of Native Americans, Creoles, and Russians in America.

Veniaminov designed and built the Church of the Holy Ascension along with his own home and a school in 1826. He and his wife taught in the school, which had about 100 pupils of both genders, instructing them in scholastic subjects and trades. This education, like all assistance to Native Americans in Alaska, did not come without a price, however. All men educated in company schools were obligated to serve the Russian American Company for 10 to 15 years.

Veniaminov then undertook the task of learning the local language and put it into writing. Although Russian was the primary language taught in the school, after he had gained enough proficiency, he taught a course in the Native American language, called Aleutian-Fox. He then translated into Aleutian-Fox the Orthodox Catechism, the entire Gospel of Matthew, the book of Acts, and part of the Gospel of Luke along with a sermon he had authored.

Veniaminov took many trips to the surrounding islands of Akun and Unga, where sizable Native American populations lived. While on these islands he performed and explained the rites of the church including the sacraments of baptism and confession for the Native Americans. He also blessed all of the marriages, allowing them to be recognized in the sight of the Orthodox Church. Interestingly, in a demonstration of the overlapping of civil and ecclesiastical authority, Veniaminov also had to administer the oath of allegiance to the czar to all Russians, Creoles, and Native Americans to whom he ministered. Veniaminov even encouraged

Ivan Veniaminov (1797–1879), later Saint Innocent, served as bishop of Russian Alaska. Mount Veniaminov is named in his honor. (Alaska State Library, Portrait Photograph Collection, P01-1983)

the older Native Americans to continue to tell their myths and legends, and he himself was not an apologist for earlier Russian atrocities committed against the Aleut population. Veniaminov's journals, letters, and edicts verify a view of him as a missionary who did not use forced conversion as a tactic but who instead attempted to integrate Russian and Native American beliefs.

After the death of his wife, Veniaminov was transferred to Novo-Arkhangel'sk, the new episcopal seat of Russian America, becoming bishop of Alaska in 1840. The Russian American Company was seeking a renewal of its charter at the time, and because the Russian government was very concerned with the welfare of the church in America, the construction of a new cathedral was a high priority to the company. Veniaminov's growing influence can be seen in the new company charter in that Russians working in America were forbidden to use force against the Native Americans, except in keeping peace, and could not establish any posts without the consent of the local Native American population. Governmental and church authority overlapped in this period to prevent abuse of the Native Americans. This was not always out of sympathy. The fact that the company was prospering created less pressure to exploit the Native American population for monetary gain. Veniaminov also became an ambassador to the other colonial powers in the region and entertained foreign visitors such as Hudson's Bay Company chief George Simpson.

From Novo-Arkhangel'sk, Veniaminov directed the expansion of Orthodox mission work in the vast Alaskan interior, whereas earlier missions had been established only near the coastline. With the establishment of many missions, he helped to create communities of Native American Orthodox believers that still exist today. The long-term success of these missions was based on Veniaminov's emphasis on the enculturation of the liturgy and theology of the Orthodox Church. Just as he had learned the Aleut language, Veniaminov strove to learn the Tlingit language upon his arrival in Novo-Arkhangel'sk. Other priests were not as willing or able to learn the Native American languages as was Veniaminov, so a seminary was established in 1845 to train Native American clergy, whom Veniaminov thought were necessary to the long-term success of the church in America. Most Russians were in America only temporarily, whereas the Native American clergy were permanent residents and had a stake in the future of the region. The seminary trained priests, deacons, and lay readers. Some of these people went on to train further at seminaries in Russia before returning to Alaska. This indigenization of the Orthodox clergy would prove essential to the survival of the faith (and, with it, Russian influence) in Alaska after the sale of the region to the United States in 1867.

Veniaminov's methods may explain the continued strength of the Russian Orthodox Church among Native Americans in Alaska, even more than 140 years after the end of Russian rule in the region. During the initial period after the sale of Alaska to the United States, most Russians returned home, and the Aleuts primarily continued the operation of schools, churches, and trading posts. After 1920, nearly all clergy were Native Americans. Veniaminov's vision of an indigenized church is what would allow it to survive both in the changing political climates and in the lives of Native American converts.

In 1806 a Russian envoy traveled to northern California, where the Russians hoped to expand their interests. At the time, this area was under Spanish control. Eventually the Russian American Company established an outpost near Monterey Bay. The Russians generally cultivated cordial relations with the Native Americans of the region and even negotiated a treaty in 1817 that gave them certain land grants. By 1840, however, the Russians had pulled out of the area because the expansion south had not proven to be financially viable.

STEVEN L. DANVER

See also
Aleut Rebellion; Fur Trade; Hudson's Bay Company

References
Chevigny, Hector. *Russian America: The Great Alaskan Venture, 1741–1867.* New York: Viking, 1965.

Oleksa, Michael, J., ed. *Alaskan Missionary Spirituality.* New York: Paulist Press, 1987.

Starr, S. Frederick, ed. *Russia's American Colony.* Durham, NC: Duke University Press, 1987.

Veniaminov, Ioann. *Journals of the Priest Ioann Veniaminov in Alaska, 1823 to 1836.* Fairbanks: University of Alaska Press, 1993.

S

Sacagawea
Birth Date: ca. 1787
Death Date: December 20, 1812

Native American woman who accompanied the Lewis and Clark expedition during its journey to the Pacific Ocean between 1804 and 1806. Although her name has been traditionally spelled as "Sacajawea" and sometimes "Sakakawea," "Sacagawea" is probably the most accurate spelling. Meriwether Lewis noted in his journal that her name was "Sah ca gah we ah" and meant "bird woman" in the Hidatsa language. Sacagawea was born around 1787 into the Lemhi band of the Shoshones, whose home was in the Lemhi Valley of present-day Idaho. Around 1800 Hidatsas captured her in a raid on the Lemhi band's camp near the Three Forks of the Missouri River in present-day Montana. Toussaint Charbonneau, a French Canadian fur trader, purchased Sacagawea from the Hidatsas sometime between 1800 and 1804.

In 1804 Charbonneau and Sacagawea were living with a band of Hidatsas on the Missouri River in present-day North Dakota. In November 1804 Charbonneau met Meriwether Lewis and William Clark at their Corps of Discovery's winter camp, Fort Mandan, and signed on with the expedition as an interpreter. Sacagawea gave birth to a son, Jean Baptiste (whom Clark called "Pompey"), on February 5, 1805. In April 1805 when the party proceeded westward with Charbonneau, Sacagawea accompanied them.

Sacagawea has been mythologized as Lewis and Clark's guide to the Pacific. She was not. In fact, most of the territory through which the expedition passed was as new and unfamiliar to Sacagawea as it was to the explorers. Despite her much-heralded role in helping the party obtain horses from the Lemhi Shoshones,

Sacagawea, a Shoshone Native American woman who accompanied the Lewis and Clark Expedition as an interpreter and guide. From a drawing by E. S. Paxson, circa 1810. (Getty Images)

Lewis and Clark's success was due more to promises of trade and firearms than to Sacagawea's kinship with the band.

Nevertheless, Sacagawea did make contributions to the success of the Corps of Discovery. In August 1805 she recognized landmarks that helped the party locate the Lemhi Shoshones and their horses. In 1806 she helped Clark locate Bozeman Pass. Although not the party's principal interpreter, she did help translate when the party encountered the Shoshones and other tribes that had Shoshone prisoners, such as the Flatheads, the Nez Perces, and the Walulas. Sacagawea's foremost contribution to the party was her mere presence, which helped convince tribes along the way that the party came in peace. Clark wrote of Sacagawea's role in this regard that "The Wife of Shabono our interpreter We find reconsiles all the Indians, as to our friendly intentions. A woman with a party of men is a token of peace."

Sacagawea remained with Charbonneau at the Mandan villages when Lewis and Clark returned to St. Louis in 1806. In 1809 Clark persuaded them to come to St. Louis, where he educated Jean Baptiste while Charbonneau and Sacagawea joined a fur-trading expedition back up the Missouri River. Although there is considerable debate about the date and place of her death, Sacagawea probably died on December 20, 1812, at the Fort Manuel (Fort Manuel Lisa, Fort Lisa) trading post in the Dakota Territory.

PAUL G. PIERPAOLI JR.

See also
Clark, William; Lewis, Meriwether; Lewis and Clark Expedition; Shoshones

References
Howard, Harold P. *Sacajawea.* Norman: University of Oklahoma Press, 2001.
Ronda, James P. *Lewis and Clark among the Indians.* 2nd ed. Lincoln: University of Nebraska Press, 2002.

Sachem

Term for the leaders of certain northeastern Native American groups. The term "sachem" can be traced back to four Northeastern bands that all used the word for a similar purpose. In Narragansett, the term is *sachem;* in Delaware, it is *sakimam;* in Micmac, it is *sakumow;* and in Penobscot, it is *sagamo* (which became *sagamore*). The term "sachem" has come to mean any leader who is working for the best interest of his tribe and has developed into such words as "sachemship," "sachemdom," and "sachemic."

Whereas the position of chief was based on skill, sachem was an inherited civil position. Sachems fulfilled many roles within their tribes, but their main duties concerned land distribution, meting out justice, collecting tribute, and receiving guests. They also sometimes supervised the direction of war and rituals. Most sachems were men, but women could also be sachems.

The position of sachem was extremely prestigious. Although the position was inherited, it carried with it great responsibility and obligation. These leaders were expected to act in the common interest at all times. They needed their people's support in order to do their job effectively and had to demonstrate skill and competence. Although sachems theoretically had ultimate authority, they had no way of enforcing it and thus had to rely on persuasion and consensus for their power.

The leaders of the powerful Iroquois Confederacy came to be known as sachems, and today the leaders and prominent members of many aboriginal tribes are known by this traditional title.

TAKAIA LARSEN

See also
Delawares; Iroquois Confederacy; Micmacs; Narragansetts

References
Morgan, Lewis H. *League of the Ho-de-no-sau-nee or Iroquois.* New York: Dodd, Mead, 1901.
Underhill, Ruth Murray. *Red Man's America: A History of Indians in the United States.* Chicago: University of Chicago Press, 1953.
Wilson, James. *The Earth Shall Weep: A History of Native America.* New York: Atlantic Monthly Press, 1998.

Sagamore

From the Algonquian language, synonymous with the term "sachem" and used to describe the rank of tribal leader or chief. The distinction between the terms has been used to differentiate the Algonquian-speaking tribes of the Atlantic coast of North America, with the northernmost tribes preferring the term "sagamore," while tribes of the lower region preferred the term "sachem." This geographic theory is problematic, however, as the Delawares of the Mid-Atlantic region use *sakimam,* while the Micmacs of Nova Scotia prefer *sakumow.* The term "sagamore" is an anglicized version of these terms and derives from English contact with the Penobscots of Maine, who used *sagamow.* The Algonquian language permeated the northeastern Atlantic coast of North America, with at least 13 separate dialects.

The prestigious role of sagamore was gained through heredity; however, power was not absolute. To remain in this position, the sagamore had to promote the communal welfare rather than individual goals. The sagamore's responsibilities included, but were not limited to, the roles of diplomat, hunter, conveyor of punishment, allocator of land allocation, and warrior. The sagamore would remain in power until death unless removed for poor behavior. Algonquian societies were democratically inclined, so the sagamore rarely acted without consultation with tribal elders. The concept of tribe, or clan, was of kinship; therefore, sagamores ruled over their extended family rather than an unknown constituency. This served as a significant check on the power of the sagamore.

Familial bonds created a singular interest within the group, and therefore a centralized system of government was not required, nor was obedience to the sagamore. The sagamore gained authority through the voluntary submission of the tribe, resulting from the persuasive skills of sagamores and their commitment to the community's interests. The role of leader in these tribes was not limited to men; several women served as sagamores and sachems along the Atlantic coast.

The role of sagamore during wartime varied among the tribes of the Northeast. Some tribes preferred to divide power between a civil leader and a war chief, while others entrusted their sagamores with both roles. In either case, the men serving under a sagamore did so voluntarily. The military accomplishments and strategic abilities of the sagamore were the avenues of persuasion used to raise war parties and to secure fidelity within fighting bands. These war parties could engage in fighting, raiding, or scouting against either other tribes or European settlers.

During the early colonial era, even the fiercest of the Algonquian-speaking tribes, such as the Pequots, Narragansetts, Wampanoags, Massachusetts, and Penacooks, fell prey to the neighboring Iroquois, who imposed a system of tributary payment upon them. These periods of subjugation led to the deposing of sagamores by many Algonquian nations. During the French and Indian War (1754–1763), many tribes of the Algonquian-language group fought under their sagamores alongside their British or French allies.

JASON LUTZ AND JIM PIECUCH

See also

Algonquins; Iroquois; Iroquois Confederacy; Sachem

References

Haviland, William A., and Marjory W. Power. *The Original Vermonters: Native Inhabitants, Past and Present.* Hanover, NH: University Press of New England, 1981.

Russell, Howard. *Indian New England before the Mayflower.* Hanover, NH: University Press of New England, 1980.

Sagoyewatha

See Red Jacket

Salt Creek Prairie Massacre

See Warren Wagon Train Raid

Samoset
Birth Date: Unknown
Death Date: Unknown

An Abenaki from the southern coast of Maine who is believed to have been the first Native American with whom the Plymouth colonists interacted. Samoset's birth and death dates are unknown. On March 16, 1621, Samoset, who had recently traveled south from his home in present-day Maine to the land of the Wampanoags, entered the Pilgrim settlement at Plymouth and stunned the newcomers by welcoming them in broken English. Samoset had learned the language from European fishermen who had fished the waters around Monhegan Island off the coast of Maine.

Edward Winslow, the future governor of the colony, described Samoset as "starke naked, only a leather about his waist, with a fringe about a span long, or a little more; he had a bow & 2 arrowes, the one headed, and the other unheaded; he was a tall straight man, the haire of his head blacke, long behind, only short before, none on his face at all." Far from taciturn, Samoset spent much of the day of their first encounter conversing with the colonists. He informed them of the shipborne plague that was introduced to the area by English slave traders in 1616 that had wiped out the original inhabitants of the village of Patuxet, the land that the colonists were currently inhabiting.

Documentation exists for three trips by Samoset to Plymouth. On his third visit, which occurred on March 22, 1621, he was accompanied by Tisquantum (Squanto), the last surviving member of the village of Patuxet. Kidnapped in 1614 by an English sea captain and subsequently sold into slavery, Squanto was absent when the deadly diseases swept through Patuxet. Having escaped the bonds of slavery in Spain, he fled to England, where he learned English and was befriended by John Slaney, a wealthy English merchant who facilitated Squanto's return to his homeland.

Whereas Samoset's command of the English language was limited—often tainted by the use of fishermen's jargon—that of Squanto was not. Samoset's introduction of Squanto to the Plymouth colonists gave both the Wampanoags and the colonists a capable translator who would aid in establishing harmonious relations between the two peoples in the coming years.

ALAN C. DOWNS

See also

Abenakis; Squanto; Wampanoags

References

Axtell, James. *Natives and Newcomers: The Cultural Origins of North America.* New York: Oxford University Press, 2001.

Philbrick, Nathaniel. *Mayflower: A Story of Courage, Community, and War.* New York: Viking, 2006.

San Carlos Reservation

Reservation established in 1871 to house a number of Apache bands relocated from various parts of New Mexico and Arizona. In June 1897 an act of Congress divided the reservation into the San Carlos Reservation in the south and the White Mountain (Fort Apache) Reservation in the north. The two reservations are in eastern Arizona approximately 100 miles east of Phoenix. The San Carlos portion comprises 2,910 square miles with a current population of 10,709 people, and the White Mountain portion comprises 2,626 square miles with 12,429 residents. The

An irrigation ditch under construction at San Carlos Indian Agency in Arizona in 1886. Established in 1871, the San Carlos Reservation was at the center of the Apache Wars and the various uprisings led by Geronimo and Victorio in the 1870s and 1880s. (National Archives)

combined reservation has been home to Aravaipa, Chiricahua, Coyotero, Mimbres, Mogollon, Pinal, and Tsiltaden Apaches. The land includes deserts, alpine meadows, and 750,000 acres of Ponderosa, pinion, juniper, and oak forest.

On April 17, 1871, Colonel (Brevet Major General) George Stoneman issued a general order that directed all Apaches in Arizona to be removed to the reservation, which had been reserved for them because of its remote location. Once there, the Native Americans were forbidden to leave the reservation without permission "for any reason whatever." The directive was confirmed by executive order from Washington, D.C., on December 14, 1872.

The reservation experienced difficulty from the outset. The various Apache bands had been uprooted from ancestral lands and crammed together with bands that in many cases had been their traditional enemies. About 80 percent of the roughly 5,000 Native Americans brought to the reservation lived within 10 miles of the San Carlos Agency because they were reliant on government rations, which were only issued once a week and had to be picked up at the agency headquarters. Unfortunately, the agency was in one of the least hospitable parts of the reservation, a gravelly plain between the San Carlos and Gila rivers that was plagued with hordes of gnats, flies, and mosquitoes and where the temperature often hovered near 110 degrees in the summer.

The traditionally nomadic Apaches were expected to become farmers but had no training or inclination for that job, besides which the land around the agency was entirely unsuited for agriculture. This left the idle men to occupy themselves with gambling, abusing their wives, and drinking tizwin, a harsh liquor made from maize (corn).

Their situation was made a great deal worse by the endemic corruption of the agents assigned to supervise the reservation. Rations intended for the tribes were routinely sold for profit to nearby settlements and mining camps, and the Apaches were pushed to the edge of starvation. One of the worst agents, J. C. Tiffany, was indicted for corruption by a local grand jury. John Philip Clum, who assumed control of the agency in August 1874, was an exception to the generally abysmal performance of Indian agents. He was a brash, arrogant 23-year-old who shared a mutual antipathy with the local military commanders but was scrupulously honest and made a concerted effort to allow the Apaches a degree of self-government and to supply them with useful employment. His efforts were complicated when the government forced an additional group of tribes uprooted from New Mexico and Arizona onto the reservation.

San Carlos is perhaps best known for its role in the last Native American uprising in the southwestern United States. Following another attempt to concentrate the Apaches, in April 1877 a group of Apaches including Victorio, Loco, and Geronimo were brought to San Carlos from the Warm Springs Reservation in chains. Victorio and his followers soon left in a quixotic effort to reestablish themselves in New Mexico. Geronimo was unable to adapt to farming and rebelled against restrictions on his drinking and wife beating and left the reservation in September 1881. He was brought back to the reservation by Brigadier General George Crook after a year of raiding in Mexico and Arizona but escaped a second time in May 1885. He was the subject of a prolonged chase through the Sierra Madres in northern Mexico until his final surrender in September 1886, after which he and his followers were removed to Florida before eventually settling at Fort Sill in the Indian Territory (Oklahoma).

JACK McCALLUM

See also

Apaches; Apache Wars; Corn Liquor; Crook, George; Geronimo; Reservations; Victorio

References

Betznez, Jason. *I Fought with Geronimo*. New York: Bonanza Books, 1959.
Davis, Britton. *The Truth about Geronimo*. Chicago: Lakeside, 1951.
Thrapp, Dan L. *The Conquest of Apacheria*. Norman: University of Oklahoma Press, 1967.

Sand Creek Massacre
Event Date: November 29, 1864

Infamous attack by Colorado militia on a peaceful Cheyenne village. Located in southeastern Colorado some 50 miles from present-day Lamar, Sand Creek was the site of a deliberate and unprovoked 1864 attack on a peaceful Southern Cheyenne village by Colorado volunteers. In a little more than an hour 148 Native Americans lay dead, many of their bodies mutilated for souvenirs.

Included in the land guaranteed to the Cheyennes and the Arapahos in Article V of the Fort Laramie Treaty of 1851 was eastern Colorado, from its border with Kansas and Nebraska westward to the Rocky Mountains and south to the Arkansas River. The discovery of gold at the confluence of the South Platte River and Cherry Creek, however, drew a multitude of prospective miners into Cheyenne territory during the latter half of the 1850s. New trails traversed Cheyenne hunting grounds, opening the way for immigrants who constructed settlements on land promised to the Native Americans. Soon buffalo and other wildlife grew scarce. Tensions mounted as hunger and disease spread through Native American bands.

The U.S. government sought to relieve the friction by further reducing Native American lands. Believing that obstinacy and delay would result in a less favorable settlement, Cheyenne leaders Black Kettle and White Antelope, along with an Arapaho

delegation led by Little Raven and Left Hand, met with government agents on February 8, 1861, and placed their "X" on the Treaty of Fort Wise. The document ceded to the United States the vast territory granted to the Native Americans in the 1851 Fort Laramie agreement in exchange for annuity payments and a small reservation of 600 square miles in southeastern Colorado between the Big Sandy and Arkansas rivers.

The reservation was unable to sustain the Native Americans who were compelled to live there. Unsuitable for agriculture, the desolate, gameless terrain proved to be a breeding ground only for epidemic diseases. With the nearest buffalo herd more than 200 miles away, young Cheyenne men left the reservation in search of food. Raids on livestock and passing wagon trains became more and more frequent. Between 1861 and 1864, sporadic violence spread across eastern Colorado and the plains of Kansas and Nebraska as men from Cheyenne and Arapaho bands clashed with soldiers and volunteer militia units. Fear and panic swept among white homesteaders, who were fully aware of the incidents associated with the Dakota Sioux uprising of 1862.

In June 1864 John Evans, who had become the second governor of Colorado Territory two years earlier, issued a proclamation inviting all "friendly Indians" to certain designated forts, where they would be fed and allowed to camp under the protection of the military. Those Native Americans who chose not to comply with this directive would be considered hostile and subject to punitive raids. With most of the territory's regular troops away fighting the Confederates in the American Civil War (1861–1865), Evans called for civilians to join the new 3rd Colorado Cavalry for 100 days to carry out his plan, stressing that "Any man who kills a hostile Indian is a patriot . . . and no one has been or will be restrained from this."

The commander of the Colorado volunteers was Colonel John M. Chivington, a 43-year-old Methodist minister turned soldier and politician. In 1862 Chivington replaced his clerical attire with a major's uniform in the 1st Colorado Volunteer Regiment and won acclaim for his role in defeating Confederate troops at the battle of Glorieta Pass in eastern New Mexico (March 26–28, 1862). Now he was to lead an expedition against the Native Americans.

Black Kettle and six other chiefs decided to accept the governor's invitation and traveled with Major Edward Wynkoop, the commander of Fort Lyon, to Denver to meet with Evans and Chivington. Meeting at Camp Weld on September 28, 1864, the Native Americans were told to submit to military authority as represented by the garrison at Fort Lyon. Black Kettle believed that he had secured peace and safety for his band and others. Unbeknownst to the Native Americans, Chivington received an order that same day from Major General Samuel R. Curtis, commanding officer of the Department of Kansas, instructing him not to make peace. To this Chivington readily assented, with the blessing of Governor Evans.

On November 4, 1864, Major Wynkoop was relieved of command of Fort Lyon. His replacement, Major Scott Anthony, proceeded to disperse the Native Americans, sending them away from the fort toward Sand Creek. Chivington meanwhile moved his column of nearly 600 men down the Arkansas River toward Fort Lyon, arriving at the post on November 28. The enlistment of his 100-day volunteers was about to expire, and the men were already disappointed at not having experienced a battle. Also, Chivington had been ridiculed in the press for his inactivity. Accompanied by 125 men under Major Anthony and four mountain howitzers, the volunteers started for Black Kettle's camp at 8:00 p.m. Having covered the 40 miles to the village that night, Chivington's men were in position to attack as dawn broke on November 29.

Black Kettle's camp along Sand Creek was composed of approximately 450 Southern Cheyennes and 40 Arapahos split into separate groups of lodges, each headed by a chief. While a few women were up starting fires for cooking, most of the village was still asleep when the volunteers struck. Major Anthony drove away the herd of Native American ponies and then approached the village from the west. Three companies of the 1st Colorado crossed the mostly dry creek bed and attacked from the east and north, while the 3rd Colorado Cavalry under Colonel George L. Shoup charged straight into the center of the encampment. Cheyenne oral history is replete with accounts of confusion and chaos as the Colorado volunteers swept through the village, firing indiscriminately into the lodges. The mountain howitzers positioned on the south bank of the creek began to rain grapeshot down on the fleeing Native Americans. Black Kettle tied an American flag that he had received in Denver, along with a white flag of truce, to one of his lodge poles in an unsuccessful effort to halt the slaughter. Black Kettle and Left Hand were left with no choice but to try to escape. White Antelope chose to remain and was shot in front of his lodge.

The bloodletting continued as Chivington's men chased the remaining Cheyennes and Arapahos for miles up Sand Creek, overtaking and killing as many men, women, and children as they could find. Some of the refugees, including Black Kettle, managed to escape by digging into the sandy soil or hiding under the embankments of the creek. Returning to the village, the Colorado volunteers proceeded to kill all the remaining wounded and mutilate the bodies. Chivington did nothing to halt the carnage. On December 1 the remains of the village and its inhabitants were set on fire, and the Colorado volunteers left the area bound for Denver. Chivington's casualties at Sand Creek were 9 killed and 38 wounded. The Cheyenne and Arapaho dead numbered 148, only 60 of them men.

At first Chivington and his volunteers were wildly praised and rewarded for their actions. Soon, however, rumors and testimonials about what really happened at Sand Creek convinced the U.S. Congress to order a formal investigation of the affair. Although never formally punished for his actions, Chivington nevertheless resigned from military service and withdrew from political life. Black Kettle, having miraculously escaped the carnage, returned to his efforts to bring peace on the plains. On October 14, 1865, Cheyenne and Arapaho representatives agreed to a treaty that called for giving up the Sand Creek Reservation in Colorado in exchange for a reservation in southwestern Kansas and Indian Territory.

ALAN C. DOWNS

See also

Arapahos; Black Kettle; Cheyennes; Chivington, John; Dog Soldiers; Evans, John

References

Hoig, Stan. *The Sand Creek Massacre.* Norman: University of Oklahoma Press, 1961.

Hughes, J. Donald. *American Indians in Colorado.* Boulder, CO: Pruett Publishing, 1977.

Josephy, Alvin M., Jr. *The Civil War in the American West.* New York: Knopf, 1991.

Utley, Robert M. *Frontiersmen in Blue: The United States and the Indian, 1848–1865.* Lincoln: University of Nebraska Press, 1967.

Sans Arc Sioux

One of the seven major bands of the Lakota Sioux Nation also known as the Itazipcos, a Siouan word that refers to their habit of not marking their arrows so that all could share in the spoils of a hunt. The Sans Arc name is derived from the French name for this band, meaning "without bows." The Sans Arc Sioux were originally known to the French in Minnesota. Later in the late 1700s the Sans Arc Sioux migrated west to the Great Plains with the other Lakota bands.

The Sans Arcs were part of the northern cluster of Lakota bands, which included the Hunkpapas and the Blackfoot Sioux. After crossing the Missouri River in the late 1700s, the Sans Arcs tended to range across the western Dakotas, eastern Montana, and northwestern Wyoming. Prior to their westward migration, the Sans Arcs followed a traditional woodlands lifestyle in Minnesota, where they were semisedentary. They subsisted chiefly on grains, local small-game hunting, and fishing and participated in occasional buffalo hunts on the prairies and plains. By the early 1800s, however, the Sans Arcs exhibited the complete Plains cultural complex, including the extensive use of horses, a nomadic existence, buffalo-hide tepees, great reliance on the buffalo, and the Sun Dance.

By the late 1830s and early 1840s, the Sans Arcs, along with their Lakota cousins, were beginning to feel the pressure of increasing American encroachment on their new hunting ranges. The Sans Arcs participated in the Sioux uprising of the 1850s, which began along the Platte River basin and resulted in Brevet Brigadier General William S. Harney's and Colonel Edwin Sumner's expeditions of 1855 and 1857, respectively.

The Sans Arcs also went to war in the 1860s especially during Red Cloud's War (1866–1868), fought because of white movement through the Powder River Country. They were resistant to reservation life and were considered to be part of the so-called wild Sioux in the 1870s. Many of the Sans Arcs were present at the major engagements of the Great Sioux War (1876–1877), fighting Brigadier General George Crook at the Battle of the Rosebud (June 17, 1876) and Lieutenant Colonel George A. Custer at the Battle of the Little Bighorn (June 25–26, 1876). A number of Sans Arcs fled to Canada with Sitting Bull and his Hunkpapa band but returned in 1880. The Sans Arcs were subsequently sent to the Cheyenne River Reservation and became participants in the Ghost Dance movement of the late 1880s. Most continue to reside on the Cheyenne River Reservation.

JOHN THOMAS BROOM

See also

Buffalo; Blackfoot Sioux; Crook, George; Custer, George Armstrong; Harney, William Selby; Hunkpapa Sioux; Lakota Sioux; Little Bighorn, Battle of the; Red Cloud's War; Rosebud, Battle of the; Sitting Bull

References

Gibbon, Guy. *The Sioux: The Dakota and Lakota Nations.* Malden, MA: Blackwell, 2003.

Goldfrank, Esther S. "Historic Change and Social Character: A Study of the Teton Dakota." *American Anthropologist,* n.s., 45(1) (January–March 1943): 67–83.

Hassrick, Royal B. *The Sioux: The Life and Customs of a Warrior Nation.* Norman: University of Oklahoma Press, 1964.

Hyde, George F. *A Sioux Chronicle.* Norman: University of Oklahoma Press, 1956.

White, Richard. "The Winning of the West: The Expansion of the Western Sioux in the Eighteenth and Nineteenth Centuries." *Journal of American History* 65(2) (September 1978): 319–343.

Santa Fe Trail

Transportation route linking the lower middle West and the Southwest. First scouted and used in 1821, the Santa Fe Trail began in the west-central Missouri town of Franklin, on the north bank of the Missouri River, but later shifted westward to Independence, Missouri. The trail then wound its way west and south to Santa Fe, New Mexico. From there travelers could link up with the El Camino Real, which proceeded due south into Mexico. Stretching some 900 miles, the Sante Fe Trail traversed plains, deserts, and mountains. The trail also cut through the lands of several Native American tribes.

Pushing westward, the trail struck the Arkansas River near present-day Great Bend, Kansas, and followed the stream to the southwest. Near present-day Dodge City the trail split on several spurs that took travelers to the more direct but more hazardous route, known as the Cimarron Cutoff. This trail, which featured long dry sections, cut across the Cimarron grasslands, the Oklahoma Panhandle, and the plains of eastern New Mexico before crossing the Rocky Mountains at Glorieta Pass and passing on to Santa Fe. In addition to the dangerous lack of water, the route also passed through Kiowa and Comanche lands.

The so-called Mountain Route continued along the Arkansas River to Bent's Old Fort in southeastern Colorado before turning southward through Raton Pass and then merging with the Cimarron route south of where the army established Fort Union in 1851. This route was well watered for most of the journey and passed

Settlers cross a dry tributary of the Gila River on the Santa Fe Trail, circa 1846. (Library of Congress)

through lands frequented by Cheyenne and Arapaho bands. In addition to Fort Union, the United States would establish numerous posts to protect traffic along the Santa Fe Trail.

The Santa Fe Trail was an economic lifeline that connected the United States and Mexico. Santa Fe was the capital and commercial center of Spain's (and later Mexico's) northernmost province and was connected to the rest of the nation via the Santa Fe–Chihuahua Trail. Goods transported to Santa Fe made their way farther south to Mexico's interior and the Pacific coast via the Santa Fe–Chihuahua Trail. The main purpose of the Santa Fe Trail was commercial, although the majority of overland trails of the period served the primary function of providing a route west for settlers.

In 1821 William Bucknell, a Missouri trader, was the first U.S. merchant to use the trail. He realized the economic potential that would flow from Mexico having won its independence from Spain. After selling his goods in Santa Fe for a tidy profit, Bucknell returned to Missouri and reported his success, opening up a lucrative trading route. He returned the next year with three wagons of goods, blazing the trail to Santa Fe that others soon followed.

The overland trip was arduous, taking travelers across arid plains, harsh desert, and rugged mountains. Conestoga wagons pulled by mules or oxen were loaded with trade goods in Independence, Missouri. These wagons then formed into larger wagon trains for protection. Rarely did single wagons travel alone. Before the wagon train set out, its members selected a leader who designated other assignments, such as night guards. The 900-mile trip to Santa Fe took two to three months to complete.

Trade between Missouri and Santa Fe exploded during the Mexican period of the existence of the Santa Fe Trail (that is, prior to 1848). The trade was so lucrative that Missouri senator Thomas Hart Benton was able to persuade the U.S. Congress to authorize a survey to map out the route and allocate funding to negotiate rights of way with Native American tribes through their lands and, for a while, to provide military escorts. The latter ended in 1830, however.

The trail found military uses as well. Colonel Stephen Watts Kearny's column used the route for its march westward to capture Santa Fe during the Mexican-American War (1846–1848). Following the war, trade along the trail grew rapidly. Trade was spurred by several factors: the ending of Mexican tariffs, the construction of army forts to protect wagon trains from raiders, and the creation of stagecoach and mail services. Trade along the Santa Fe Trail in 1855 amounted to more than $5 million dollars. The construction of the Atchison, Topeka, and Santa Fe Railroad, which pushed through Raton Pass and into New Mexico in 1878, essentially closed the Santa Fe Trail.

RICK DYSON AND DAVID COFFEY

See also
Bent's Fort; Forts, Camps, Cantonments, and Outposts; Kearny, Stephen Watts; New Mexico; Overland Trail

References
Boyle, Susan C. *Los Capitalistas: Hispano Merchants and the Santa Fe Trade.* Albuquerque: University of New Mexico Press, 1997.
Dary, David. *The Santa Fe Trail: Its History, Legends, and Lore.* New York: Knopf, 2000.
Gregg, Josiah. *Commerce of the Prairies.* Norman: University of Oklahoma Press, 1954.
Hyslop, Stephen G. *Bound for Santa Fe: The Road to New Mexico and the American Conquest, 1806–1848.* Norman: University of Oklahoma Press, 2002.

Saponis

Native American people of the Mid-Atlantic region. The word "Saponi" is evidently a corruption of the word "Monasiccapano" or "Monasukapanough," signifying "shallow water." The Saponis belonged to the Siouan linguistic family, their closest relations being the Tutelos. At the time of European colonization, the Saponis and Tutelos probably numbered only about 2,700 people.

The Saponis lived in central and southwestern Virginia. A Saponi village site has been identified near present-day Charlottesville. Their principal settlement, bearing the tribe's name, may have been near present-day Lynchburg. The Saponis seem to have been constantly on the move in order to escape their enemies. By the 1670s the Saponis and the Tutelos had moved to avoid attack by the Iroquois and then lived on islands in the Roanoke River in present-day Mecklenburg County. By the beginning of the 18th century they had moved again to lands along the Yadkin River near present-day Salisbury, North Carolina. Prior to the Tuscarora War (1711–1713), the Saponis had established themselves near present-day Windsor, North Carolina.

Although the Saponis sought incorporation with other native groups, including the Tutelos, Occaneechis, and Stakanoxes, they still feared attack from larger tribes and thus sought the status of tributary Indians, living under the protection of colonial settlements. Governor Alexander Spotswood of Virginia listed them as such in 1712.

Spotswood planned to settle the Saponis and other small native groups on the Virginia frontier, where they might help protect colonial settlements. By 1715 the Saponis had moved to Fort Christanna and there were incorporated with the Oconeechis, Stakunoxes, and Totteros. These splinter groups were joined by the Enos and Saraws, who also sought protection. While at Fort Christanna, all of the natives who settled there, no matter their tribal affiliation, were called Saponis, and in 1716 a visitor identified 200 "Saponis" at Fort Christanna.

In the Treaty of Albany of 1722 the Iroquois agreed to halt their incursions into Virginia, whereupon some Saponis moved north into Pennsylvania and south into North Carolina. The latter group incorporated with the Catawbas. At that point the Saponis disappeared as a distinct tribal entity, although there is a small community known as the Hallowa-Saponis in North Carolina, and others live among the Iroquois.

THOMAS JOHN BLUMER AND SPENCER C. TUCKER

See also
Catawbas

References
Brown, Douglas S. *The Catawba Indians: The People of the River.* Columbia: University of South Carolina Press, 1966.
Merrell, James H. *The Indians' New World: Catawbas and Their Neighbors from European Contact through the Era of Removal.* Chapel Hill: University of North Carolina Press, 1989.

Sassacus
Birth Date: ca. 1560
Death Date: ca. July 1637

Pequot leader and key figure in the Pequot War (1636–1638). Sassacus (meaning "the wild one"), the son of Pequot sachem Tatobem (Wopigwooit), was born about 1560 near present-day Groton, Connecticut, and lived in the palisaded town of Weinshaunks on the Thames River, where Groton is now located.

Sassacus fought in many campaigns against neighboring tribes, during which the Pequots expanded their dominion from Rhode Island west to the Hudson River Valley and subordinated the Montauks on Long Island. He earned a reputation as a great warrior and was said to have killed a large number of enemies in battle. His fellow Pequots bestowed on him great honors for his fighting abilities, believing that he possessed supernatural powers. The Pequots' Narragansett enemies considered Sassacus to be virtually divine and very much feared him.

In 1632 on his father's death at the hands of the Dutch, Sassacus assumed leadership of the 26 towns of the Pequot Nation. When New England officials wrongly accused the Pequots of murdering several traders in 1636, Sassacus refused to submit to the colonists' demands. The New Englanders responded by invading Pequot territory in company with their Narragansett and Mohegan allies. Sassacus led the Pequot resistance in what became known as the Pequot War and was in command of a war party searching for colonial forces when New England troops destroyed the Pequots' Mystic Fort in May 1637, killing hundreds of natives.

Although the carnage convinced many Pequots to surrender, Sassacus continued to resist and traveled to Mohawk territory with several warriors in an effort to win that tribe's assistance. Instead of assisting the Pequots, however, the Mohawks killed Sassacus, probably in July 1637, and delivered his scalp to the governor of Massachusetts. Sassacus's death ended the possibility of any further Pequot resistance and ensured the colonists' complete victory in the Pequot War.

JIM PIECUCH

See also
Mohawks; Mohegans; Mystic Fort Fight; Narragansetts; Pequots; Pequot War

References
Cave, Alfred A. *The Pequot War.* Amherst: University of Massachusetts Press, 1996.
Hauptman, Laurence M., and James D. Wherry, eds. *The Pequots in Southern New England: The Rise and Fall of an American Indian Nation.* Norman: University of Oklahoma Press, 1990.

Sassamon, John
Birth Date: ca. 1620
Death Date: January 1675

Influential Wampanoag leader and interpreter whose death in January 1675 helped precipitate King Philip's War (1675–1676). Little is known of Sassamon's life. John Sassamon (Wussausmon) was likely born in the early 1620s to a Wampanoag father who, along with his wife, died in the smallpox epidemic of 1633. They likely left their son to be raised by English colonists. A protégé of the Roxbury minister John Eliot, Sassamon converted to Christianity, studied at Harvard College, and preached among the so-called praying Indians of Natick.

Sassamon's unusual background, especially his literacy and multilingualism, gave him opportunities in both the Native American and English communities. Evidence suggests that he served as an interpreter or a scribe for the great Pokanoket and Wampanoag sachem Massasoit and later for his two successor sons, Wamsutta (Alexander) and Metacom (Philip). Moreover, Sassamon's ties to the ruling elite were reinforced by his marriage to Metacom's daughter, Assowetough. Provincial authorities, especially in Plymouth Colony, also drew upon the talent, language skills, and position of Sassamon. Indeed, they repeatedly employed him as a translator, a messenger, an arbiter, and a proselytizer. As such, he helped keep open lines of communications between the two peoples. However, despite or because of having a foothold in each world, he was not completely trusted in either.

By 1671 relations between Sassamon and Metacom became strained, as did those between Plymouth officials and the Wampanoag sachem. Plymouth sought to force Metacom to accept the colony's sovereignty over his people, a demand that the leader resented and rejected. He was further incensed to learn that Sassamon, who was involved in the negotiations, had reported to Plymouth authorities Metacom's attempt to ally with the Narragansett tribe in Rhode Island against the colonists. Although conflict was avoided, tensions resurfaced three years later when Metacom sold tribal lands without Plymouth's approval, a requirement that the colony had insisted upon. This time he prepared for war. Twice in 1674 Sassamon warned the colonists of Metacom's belligerence. The second time, late in the year, Sassamon went to the

Marshfield home of Plymouth governor Josiah Winslow, warned him of an impending attack, and confessed his fear that Metacom would kill him for this perceived treachery. Winslow chose to ignore the warning, and in January or early February 1675 Sassamon was found dead.

Little is known about Sassamon's death or the subsequent trial. Several Wampanoags discovered his body beneath the ice on a pond near his home and buried it. Upon hearing the news, Winslow ordered the body exhumed, which resulted in murder charges. Three Native Americans were arrested, tried, and declared guilty by a jury of 12 Englishmen, supported by 6 Christian Indians. The defendants declared their innocence, but the jury decided otherwise largely on the testimony of a Native American who claimed to have witnessed the murder from a nearby hill. On June 8, 1675, the three men were hanged, but a rope snapped, and 1 of the men was not killed. Given the opportunity to exchange a confession for a reprieve, the last defendant claimed that the other 2 men, upon Metacom's order, had committed the crime. Despite the deal, the man was again hanged, this time to death. The tensions produced by Sassamon's death and the trial contributed to the conflict that broke out late in June 1675.

MARK THOMPSON

See also

King Philip's War; Massasoit; Metacom; Praying Towns and Praying Indians; Wampanoags; Wamsutta

References

Kawashima, Yasuhide. *Igniting King Philip's War: The John Sassamon Murder Trial.* Lawrence: University Press of Kansas, 2001.

Schutz, Eric B., and Michael J. Tougias. *King Philip's War: The History and Legacy of America's Forgotten Conflict.* Woodstock, VT: Countryman, 1999.

Satanta
Birth Date: ca. 1820
Death Date: September 11, 1878

Prominent Kiowa warrior. Born in present-day northern New Mexico or Oklahoma around 1820 into the Onde (prominent warriors) caste, which comprised about 10 percent of the Kiowa tribe, Satanta emerged as a leading warrior and spokesman for his people while in his early 20s. Accustomed to leading raids into Texas, New Mexico, and Mexico to capture horses and obtain captives to augment their numbers, the Kiowas began to face pressure to stop their raids after Texas entered the United States in 1845. But despite increased warnings from U.S. Indian agents and military officers, Satanta and other Kiowa leaders considered these threats to be mere bluffs. The outbreak of the American Civil War (1861–1865) served to reinforce this attitude because at that time the whites were virtually powerless to prevent the Kiowas from raiding.

Kiowa war chief Satanta, circa 1869–1874. Also known as White Bear, Satanta emerged as a leading warrior and spokesperson for his people while still in his twenties. (National Archives)

The one government effort to suppress the Kiowas and their Comanche allies came in November 1864, when Brigadier General James Carleton, commanding in the Department of New Mexico, dispatched a volunteer force of 350 men under Colonel Christopher "Kit" Carson to attack the Kiowas and Comanches along the South Canadian River in the Texas Panhandle. The ease with which the Kiowas and Comanches defeated Carson's volunteers at Adobe Walls further convinced Satanta that the Kiowas could remain masters of the southern Plains.

Despite their victory, not all Kiowas shared Satanta's bellicose outlook toward the whites. Kicking Bird and Stumbling Bear in particular believed that tribal survival required peace with the whites. In 1865 they and other Kiowa leaders signed a peace treaty in which the Kiowas agreed to remain between the Red and Arkansas rivers and surrender claims to land in Colorado, Kansas, and New Mexico. Satanta, Lone Wolf, and Satank, however, ignored the treaty and continued to raid into Texas.

In April 1867 Satanta was the leading voice against concessions at a meeting between Kiowa leaders and Major General Winfield Scott Hancock at Fort Dodge, Kansas. In October 1867 Satanta was among the many leaders of southern Plains tribes who attended the peace commission at Medicine Lodge Creek in Kansas. Once again he eloquently rejected demands that the Kiowas confine themselves to a reservation in Indian Territory (Oklahoma) and adopt white culture. In an effort to conciliate Satanta, the U.S. government recognized the right of the Kiowas to leave the reservation to hunt buffalo on the southern Plains.

Although Satanta joined the Kiowas on the reservation, the failure of the government to provide sufficient rations and the decline of the buffalo herds led him to return to the time-honored pattern of raiding, first against the nearby Caddos and Wichitas and then into Texas. Following Lieutenant Colonel George Armstrong Custer's attack on Cheyenne chief Black Kettle's village along the Washita River on November 27, 1868, Satanta and Lone Wolf went under a flag of truce to meet with Major General Philip Sheridan, who promptly had them arrested and taken to Fort Cobb, where they were held for three months. Angered at their captivity, Satanta and other Kiowa leaders launched raids into Texas during the next three years.

On May 18, 1871, Satanta took a leading role in an attack on a civilian wagon train owned by Henry Warren as it crossed the Salt Creek Prairie near Fort Richardson in northern Texas. The raiders tortured and killed a number of teamsters and drove off some 40 mules. Satanta and other leaders then returned to the Fort Sill Reservation, where they boasted of their participation in the raid. U.S. Army commander General William Tecumseh Sherman, who had narrowly missed the attack that struck the wagon train and who too had moved on to Fort Sill, had Satanta, Satank, and Big Tree arrested and sent them to Jacksboro, Texas, to be tried. Satank, an aged warrior chief, was killed when he tried to escape, but Satanta and Big Tree were convicted and sentenced to death; however, Governor Edmund J. Davis succumbed to federal pressure and commuted the sentences to life imprisonment at the state penitentiary in Huntsville.

In an effort to conciliate the Kiowas, federal authorities pressured Davis to parole Satanta and Big Tree to Fort Sill in 1873 on the promise that they refrain from further raids. Although Satanta remained at peace, he was nevertheless held responsible for the Kiowas who attacked buffalo hunters in the Second Battle of Adobe Walls (June 27, 1874) and carried out raids in Texas in 1874. Even though Indian agents at the Kiowa Reservation confirmed that Satanta had not participated in either the battle or the raids, Sheridan ordered that Satanta be arrested and returned to Huntsville. After four years' captivity and realizing that he would never be freed, Satanta took his own life by leaping from the second floor of the prison on September 11, 1878.

JUSTIN D. MURPHY

See also
Adobe Walls, Second Battle of; Fort Sill; Kiowas; Medicine Lodge Treaty; Warren Wagon Train Raid; Washita, Battle of the

References
Mayhall, Mildred P. *The Kiowas.* Civilization of the American Indian Series. 1971; reprint, Norman: University of Oklahoma Press, 1984.
Worcester, Donald. "Satanta." In *Studies in Diversity: American Indian Leaders,* edited by R. David Edmunds, 107–130. Lincoln: University of Nebraska Press, 1980.

Sauks and Foxes

Two closely allied Native American groups in the western Great Lakes region that banded together in response to attacks by other native groups from the eastern Great Lakes and French attempts to exterminate the Foxes (Mesquakies). The Sauks and Foxes were two distinct but related tribes that spoke two different dialects of the same Algonquian language. Both peoples originated in the western Great Lakes area. The Sauks and Foxes were related to the Mascoutens and Kickapoos, with whom they periodically maintained military alliances.

At the time that the French first made contact with them, the Sauks occupied upper present-day Wisconsin. The Foxes lived in central Wisconsin. There is some evidence that both groups may have lived in Michigan prior to 1600 and were driven out of that area by Iroquois or Huron raids.

In the early 1600s the Sauks and Foxes secured Wisconsin for themselves by defeating the Winnebagos in a brief conflict. By the end of the 17th century the Sauks had hesitantly accepted Jesuit missionaries among them. However, the Foxes refused to allow the outsiders into their midst. In the early 18th century the Foxes fought two wars with the French, one during 1712–1716 and another during 1728–1737. During both conflicts the French attempted to exterminate the Foxes. Finally in 1734 the Foxes took refuge with the Sauks, and both groups moved to Iowa in 1735 to put distance between themselves and the French. In 1766 both groups moved back to Wisconsin, only to return to Iowa by the end of the century.

In the 19th century the U.S. government removed both groups to Indian Territory (Kansas and Oklahoma). This occurred after the 1832 Black Hawk War in which a number of Sauks fought the U.S. Army in Illinois. Today the Sauks and Foxes can be found in Missouri, Kansas, Iowa, and Illinois; however, most live in Oklahoma.

DIXIE RAY HAGGARD

See also
Beaver Wars; Black Hawk War; Fox Wars; Kickapoos; Wyandots

References
Callender, Charles. "Fox." In *Handbook of North American Indians,* Vol. 15, *Northeast,* edited by Bruce G. Trigger, 636–647. Washington, DC: Smithsonian Institution Press, 1978.
Edmunds, R. David, and Joseph L. Peyser. *The Fox Wars: The Mesquakie Challenge to New France.* Norman: University of Oklahoma Press, 1993.
Gussow, Zachary. *Sac, Fox, and Iowa Indians.* 3 vols. New York: Garland, 1974.
White, Richard. *The Middle Ground: Indians, Empires, and Republics in the Great Lakes Region, 1650–1815.* New York: Cambridge University Press, 1991.

Sauk and Fox Indians by Karl Bodmer, a 19th-century Swiss painter. (Library of Congress)

Scalp Bounty

Remuneration paid by governments for enemy scalps. During the 17th century, colonial governments adopted the practice of rewarding with bounties individuals who returned from combat with the scalps of their opponents. As early as 1616, Spanish authorities had relied on head bounties to suppress an indigenous insurrection in Durango. In 1637 the English colony of Connecticut was the first to adopt a similar policy, promising goods to allied Mohegans who would bring back Pequot heads or scalps (the records are ambiguous). The Dutch in New Amsterdam followed suit four years later, offering bounties for the heads of Raritans.

It was not until 1675, however, that the first unequivocal references to scalp bounties appeared. During King Philip's War (1675–1676), New England authorities offered such rewards to both Narragansett warriors and white settlers. By 1692 New France also began to pay its native allies for enemy scalps. It was around this period, within the context of King William's War (1689–1697), that bounty policies that had originally rewarded only the scalping of hostile natives were extended to include the scalping of enemy colonists.

Both the French and the British infamously continued to offer scalp bounties intermittently until the end of their struggle in North America. However, there existed rather important differences in their respective policies. Bounties in the Anglo-American colonies were primarily aimed at soldiers and colonists, providing them with an incentive to risk their lives in the pursuit of hostile natives. Each British colonial government promulgated and abrogated its own scalp acts. The amounts promised fluctuated widely according to available financial resources, the degree of perceived threat, the age and gender of the victim, and the status of the scalp taker.

French colonial authorities, however, made no distinction as to age and gender. They also extended their offer of scalp bounties only to native allies as a means of subsidizing war parties. Furthermore, the value of the trade goods offered by the French remained surprisingly stable throughout the period (around 30 livres per scalp). French bounties dipped only in the few years that preceded the capitulation of New France.

The strongest opposition to such bounties generally came from one's colonial adversary. Indeed, French and British governors mutually accused the other of having been the first to promote by this dubious means the savage murder of seemingly innocent white Christians. Because the survival of colonists and of empires was believed to be at stake, however, moral misgivings were few. It is quite telling, for example, that several Puritan ministers joined scalping parties or that some French missionaries are known to have served as intermediaries in the payment of bounties.

That the newcomers manipulated an indigenous practice leaves no doubt. Yet it remains unclear what repercussions bounties may have had on the customs and values of native warriors. Although Anglo-American colonists transformed scalping into a profit-making exercise, it can be argued that native warriors in fact understood bounties within a relatively traditional context of reciprocal gift exchanges.

The practice of paying bounties for scalps did not end with the colonial era. Governors of several Mexican states, including Chihuahua and Sonora, for example, offered lofty sums for Apache and Comanche scalps. Numerous state, territorial, and municipal governments and civilian organizations in the United States offered bounties at various times. And small bands of American bounty hunters found lucrative employment in the scalp trade, usually dealing with Mexican officials who often were not particular about the source of a scalp. This led to the frequent murder of friendly natives, including women and children.

JEAN-FRANÇOIS LOZIER

See also
King Philip's War; King William's War; Native American Warfare; Scalping

References
Axtell, James, and William C. Sturtevant. *The European and the Indian: Essays in the Ethnohistory of Colonial North America.* New York: Oxford University Press, 1981.
Axtell, James, and William C. Sturtevant. "The Unkindest Cut, or Who Invented Scalping?" *William and Mary Quarterly* 37(3) (1980): 451–472.
Lozier, Jean-François. "Lever des chevelures en Nouvelle-France: La politique française du paiement des scalps." *Revue d'Histoire de l'Amérique Française* 56(4) (2003): 513–542.

Scalping

The practice of removing the skin—or scalp—from an enemy's skull with the hair still attached. In the early modern imagination, no act of violence typified the brutal nature of North American warfare more aptly than scalping. Although generally performed on the bodies of those who had been killed, the operation in itself was not fatal. Occasionally a lucky victim left for dead and scalped on the battlefield survived to tell of his or her experience. If the bone tissue regenerated properly, which was not always the case, a scalping victim could live a long and productive life.

Although there have been allegations that scalping originated with European newcomers, archaeological evidence has firmly established that the custom was widely practiced among the indigenous peoples of the Americas during the pre-Columbian period. The earliest reference to scalping in the historical record can be found in the writings of the French explorer Jacques Cartier. During his 1535 voyage to the Saint Lawrence River Valley,

the Iroquoian inhabitants of Stadacona proudly displayed "the skins of five men's heads, stretched on hoops, like parchment." They were prizes that had been taken from their Micmac enemies. Spanish explorers encountered similar practices around the same period in what is today the southeastern United States. The renewed French, English, and Dutch explorations of the early 17th century produced additional reports of scalping among most, if not all, of the native peoples of the Eastern Woodlands.

It is clear that the act of scalping had profound meaning in Native American thought. A substitute for decapitation, it secured not only a physical victory but also a spiritual one over an opponent. Although the highly ritualized integration of the scalp within local belief systems varied from one native group to the next, the basic elements seem universal. A warrior cried out immediately after removing a scalp, and likewise he sang a special song when he returned to his village. The flayed skins were then stretched on hoops and dried. They were often carefully painted and decorated, later to be used in dances and ceremonies. They could also be worn about the body and displayed in lodges and on palisades.

The head, and by extension its skin, was widely believed in indigenous cultures to be a repository of vital energy. Accordingly, the scalp was much more than a mere war trophy; it was the embodiment of the victim. Scalping thus served as an acceptable substitute for a living captive and could be a replacement for a dead relative.

Contemporary observers conditioned by European notions of war as well as later historians persisted in viewing the custom of scalping as a testament to the cruel and barbaric nature of American Indians. Yet beginning in the late 17th century, many colonists took up the practice themselves, and colonial governments frequently subsidized the practice by offering scalp bounties, as did several Mexican states during the 19th century. Several state and local governments of the United States as well as civilian organizations offered scalp bounties at times. Not surprisingly, the complex indigenous cultural meanings were lost on the newcomers. From their perspective, a scalp offered little more than evidence that an enemy had been killed. By the close of the 18th century, scalping became a widespread practice among both warriors and white Europeans. Scalping remained a part of warfare throughout the Indian Wars but was effectively ended when those conflicts came to a conclusion in 1890.

JEAN-FRANÇOIS LOZIER

See also
Native American Warfare; Scalp Bounty

References
Abler, Thomas S. "Scalping, Torture, Cannibalism and Rape: An Ethnohistorical Analysis of Conflicting Cultural Values in War." *Anthropologica* 34(1) (1992): 3–20.
Axtell, James, and William C. Sturtevant. *The European and the Indian: Essays in the Ethnohistory of Colonial North America.* New York: Oxford University Press, 1981.
Axtell, James, and William C. Sturtevant. "The Unkindest Cut, or Who Invented Scalping?" *William and Mary Quarterly* 37(3) (1980): 451–472.

Scarlet Point

See Inkpaduta

Schofield, John McAllister
Birth Date: September 29, 1831
Death Date: March 4, 1906

U.S. Army officer. John McAllister Schofield was born in Gerry, New York, on September 29, 1831, the son of a Baptist minister. Raised in Illinois, Schofield graduated from the U.S. Military Academy, West Point, in 1853. Commissioned a second lieutenant, he served for two years in the 1st U.S. Artillery and then returned to West Point as an instructor of physics. He was promoted to first lieutenant in 1855 but, disillusioned by the lack of promotion, secured a leave of absence in 1860 and took a position teaching physics at Washington University in St. Louis.

In April 1861 at the beginning of the American Civil War (1861–1865), Schofield was commissioned a major in the 1st Missouri Volunteers. He favorably impressed Brigadier General Nathaniel Lyon, the local Union commander, who appointed Schofield as his chief of staff. In this capacity Schofield accompanied Lyon in a

Major General John M. Schofield was commanding general of the army during 1888–1895. In contrast with his predecessors, Schofield recommended that Native Americans be admitted to the army as regular soldiers. (Hayward Cirker, ed., *Dictionary of American Portraits,* 1967)

series of small Union victories over Confederate forces but advised against engaging numerically superior Confederate forces at Wilson's Creek on August 10, 1861. Lyon attacked anyway and was killed. Schofield particularly distinguished himself in the battle and in 1892 was formally awarded the Medal of Honor for his role in it.

On November 21, 1861, Schofield was advanced to brigadier general of volunteers. In October 1862 he took command of the Army of the Frontier and the District of Southwest Missouri. Enjoying some success driving Confederate guerrillas from Missouri and Kansas, he also sought a more important command. On May 12, 1863, he was named major general of volunteers and given command of the Department and Army of the Ohio. He then participated in Major General William T. Sherman's Atlanta Campaign, during which Schofield did battle with Confederate forces under General John B. Hood. Hood invaded Tennessee and attempted to cut off Schofield's smaller force from Nashville. Schofield eluded Hood and entrenched at Franklin. In the Battle of Franklin on November 30, 1864, Schofield's men destroyed the attacking Confederates. For this victory Schofield was advanced from captain to brigadier general in the regular army to date from the battle. Moving his forces by sea to Fort Fisher, North Carolina, Schofield occupied Wilmington on February 22, 1865.

Following the war, President Andrew Johnson appointed Schofield a confidential agent of the State Department and sent him to France, charged with negotiating with Emperor Napoleon III the withdrawal of French forces from Mexico. This mission was accomplished successfully, and Schofield next commanded the Department of the Potomac from August 1866 to June 1868. President Johnson then appointed him secretary of war. In March 1869 Schofield was promoted to major general of regulars and took charge of the Department of the Missouri until May 1870. He then commanded the Division of the Pacific and in 1873, under secret orders from Secretary of War William Belknap, traveled to Hawaii to evaluate the strategic usefulness of those islands to the United States. Upon Schofield's recommendation, the government purchased Pearl Harbor as a naval facility. In September 1876 Schofield returned to West Point as a commandant, remaining there until January 1881 when he succeeded to command of the Division of the Gulf. In 1878 he also headed a board that reconsidered the court-martial of Major General Fitz John Porter and absolved him of misconduct at the Second Battle of Bull Run in 1862.

After successive tours with the Division of the Pacific and the Division of the Missouri, in August 1888 Schofield succeeded Lieutenant General Philip H. Sheridan as commanding general of the army. During his seven-year tenure, Schofield pressed for improvements in the lives of common soldiers through better rations, higher pay, and improved standards of living. He also sought to foster professionalism among the officer corps by a system of examinations for promotion, the creation of post libraries, and strong support for service schools.

In sharp contrast with his predecessors Sherman and Sheridan, Schofield disagreed with the prevailing national policy toward Native Americans. Indeed, he urged that they be allowed to join the military as regular soldiers. He believed that in this capacity Native Americans and their dependents could be cared for while at the same time performing useful national service. Owing to the racism prevalent at the time, however, this policy was never adopted.

Schofield proved to be an able administrator. He clarified the military chain of command by ending a long feud with the secretary of war, subordinating the post of commanding general to the secretary's office, and agreeing to function as his senior military adviser. Schofield's final act was to advocate the adoption of a general staff on the German model to better formulate grand strategic planning. This scheme was not adopted. Schofield was promoted to lieutenant general on February 5, 1895, and retired from the army soon thereafter.

In 1902 Schofield appeared before a congressional committee to support the creation of a general staff concept, contrary to the opinions of commanding general Lieutenant General Nelson A. Miles. Schofield also argued strongly in favor of U.S. intervention in Cuba in order to end the suffering of the Cuban people. During the Spanish-American War (1898), President William McKinley, who distrusted both Miles and Secretary of War Russell Alger, often sought the counsel of the retired Schofield regarding military issues. Schofield also played a major role in McKinley's decision to call for an increase in the size of the regular army. Schofield died in St. Augustine, Florida, on March 4, 1906. He is generally regarded as one of the finest peacetime commanding generals of the army.

JOHN C. FREDRIKSEN AND SPENCER C. TUCKER

See also

Miles, Nelson Appleton; Sheridan, Philip Henry; Sherman, William Tecumseh

References

Connelly, Donald B. *John M. Schofield and the Politics of Generalship.* Chapel Hill: University of North Carolina Press, 2006.
McDonough, James L. *John M. Schofield: Union General in the Civil War and Reconstruction.* Tallahassee: University of Florida Press, 1972.
Schofield, John M. *Forty-Six Years in the Army.* 1897; reprint, Norman: University of Oklahoma Press, 1999.

Schurz, Carl
Birth Date: March 2, 1829
Death Date: May 14, 1906

U.S. Army officer, U.S. Senator (1869–1875), and secretary of the interior (1877–1881). Carl Schurz was born on March 2, 1829, in Liblar near Cologne (Köln), Germany. He attended the University of Bonn but did not complete his degree. In 1852 he immigrated to the United States as a political refugee from the failed German revolutions of 1848. Schurz established himself in business in Philadelphia and then moved to Wisconsin, where he studied law and was admitted to the bar. He almost immediately took an active

role in American politics. A supporter of the newly established Republican Party, Schurz headed the Wisconsin delegation to the Republican National Convention and was appointed to the foreign department of the Republican National Committee. He rallied German American support for Abraham Lincoln's presidential nomination and candidacy in 1860. Following Lincoln's election, Schurz received appointment as minister to Spain. What he had really wanted, however, was a commission in the U.S. Army.

Before departing for Spain in 1861, Schurz helped raise German cavalry regiments, and he returned from Spain in January 1862 to accept a commission as a brigadier general of volunteers in April 1862. Schurz served effectively in command of a division in the Second Battle of Bull Run (August 28–30, 1862) and received promotion to major general on March 17, 1863. He was nevertheless criticized for his performance in the Battle of Chancellorsville (May 1–4, 1863) and the Battle of Gettysburg (July 1–3, 1863). This criticism continued during the Chattanooga Campaign, when he arrived late for the night attack on Wauhatchie on October 28–29, 1863. A court of inquiry later cleared him of incompetence, but Schurz never again held a field command.

Schurz stayed in the western theater until the late spring of 1864, at which point he took a leave of absence to help coordinate Lincoln's 1864 reelection bid. Following the Confederate surrender at Appomattox Court House in April 1865, Schurz resigned his commission. After the war he worked as a journalist and represented Missouri as a Republican in the U.S. Senate from 1869 to 1875.

Schurz then served as secretary of the interior from 1877 to 1881 in the Rutherford B. Hayes administration. In this role Schurz helped professionalize the civil service and was an early conservationist. He also successfully fended off efforts to move the Bureau of Indian Affairs to the War Department and attempted to rid the bureau of rampant corruption, which met with far less success. Initially he generally continued his predecessors' policies of relocating Native Americans to reservations, but he later changed that position and sought policies that were more compassionate toward Native Americans. In 1879 he was influential in reaching a peaceful settlement of the Ute War. After he left office, he expressed his support for the Dawes Severalty Act and backed assimilationist efforts designed to educate Native Americans and break up tribal affiliations. Following his lengthy government service, he again pursued a career as a journalist, winning broad public approval for his principles. Schurz died in New York City on May 14, 1906.

THERESA L. STOREY

See also

Bureau of Indian Affairs; Dawes Severalty Act; Ute War

References

Schurz, Carl. *The Autobiography of Carl Schurz: An Abridgement in One Volume by Wayne Andrews.* New York: Scribner, 1961.
Trefousse, Hans L. *Carl Schurz: A Biography.* Knoxville: University of Tennessee Press, 1982.

Scott, Winfield
Birth Date: June 13, 1786
Death Date: May 28, 1866

U.S. Army general. Born at Laurel Branch near Petersburg, Virginia, on June 13, 1786, Winfield Scott briefly attended the College of William and Mary in 1805 and then studied law. In the aftermath of the 1807 *Chesapeake-Leopard* Affair, Scott enlisted in a Virginia cavalry troop. He then secured a direct commission as a captain of artillery in 1808 and was assigned to New Orleans. Following a direct letter to President Thomas Jefferson in which Scott sharply criticized the demonstrated incompetence of his commanding officer, Brigadier General James Wilkinson, Scott was suspended without pay for a year during 1809–1810. He then returned to New Orleans in 1811 and was promoted to lieutenant colonel in July 1812.

Assigned to the Niagara frontier at the beginning of the War of 1812, Scott saw combat at the Battle of Queenston Heights on October 13 and was taken prisoner. Exchanged, he was promoted to colonel in March 1813. Known as a demanding trainer who nonetheless was greatly concerned for the welfare of his men, Scott led the successful attack on and capture of Fort George, Ontario, on May 27, during which he was wounded. Promoted to brigadier general in March 1814, Scott led a brigade in Major General Jacob Brown's invasion of Canada, greatly distinguishing himself in the Battle of Chippewa on July 5 and the Battle of Lundy's Lane on July 25; he was wounded twice in the latter battle. His performance in these contests made him a national hero and won him the thanks of Congress, a gold medal, and a brevet promotion to major general.

Following the war Scott wrote the drill manual *Infantry Tactics* that became the standard on the subject in the U.S. Army for a generation. Appointed to command the Northern Department in 1815, he twice traveled to Europe to study its military establishments. In 1829 he assumed command of the Eastern Division. Scott's astute diplomacy helped smooth relations with South Carolina in the Nullification Crisis of 1832 and with Britain over the U.S.-Canadian border in 1838 and 1839. He was also heavily involved in Native American affairs, negotiating the Treaty of Fort Armstrong with the Sauks and Foxes in September 1832, commanding U.S. forces in 1836 during the Second Seminole War (1835–1842), and overseeing the Cherokee removal to Indian Territory (Oklahoma) in 1838. The latter led to numerous deaths by starvation, exposure, and exhaustion on the aptly named Trail of Tears.

Appointed commanding general of the U.S. Army with the permanent rank of major general in July 1841, Scott worked to professionalize the officer corps. During the Mexican-American War (1846–1848) he planned and then carried out the march to Mexico City that began with an amphibious landing at Veracruz on March 9, 1847. Outnumbered, moving through hostile territory, often short of supplies, and plagued by political generals, Scott conducted a brilliant campaign. He won a series of victories at Cerro Gordo, Puebla, Contreras, Churubusco, Molino del Rey, and Chapultepec and then occupied Mexico City. He ignored President James K. Polk's orders to recommence fighting and helped to secure a treaty with Mexico at Guadalupe Hidalgo on February 2, 1848.

Scott's performance in the war brought the thanks of Congress and the enmity of President Polk. Scott returned to the United States in April 1848 to find that Polk had set out to ruin him. Viewing Scott as a political rival, Polk ordered an inquiry into Scott's relationship with his subordinate commanders in the war, especially Major General Gideon Pillow, a political appointee. Although Scott was exonerated, the inquiry tarnished his reputation. Running as the Whig candidate in the 1852 presidential election, he carried only four states.

Brevetted lieutenant general in 1855, Scott was sent west by President Franklin Pierce to end tensions with the British over the Puget Sound area, specifically a dispute over San Juan Island. Scott urged preparations for war in 1860. Too old for the job himself, he tried without success to persuade Colonel Robert E. Lee to accept the field command of the army. One of the few in Washington to understand that the war would be long and difficult, Scott developed the strategic plan to impose a naval blockade of the Confederate coasts while training a large army and then operate with the navy to bisect the South along its great rivers. Critics dubbed the strategy the "Anaconda Plan" for the giant snake that squeezes its victims to death, but it ultimately brought victory for the Union.

After 54 years in military service and the longest tenure as a general officer in U.S. history, Scott retired from the army in November 1861. He moved to West Point, New York, where he wrote his memoirs. Scott died on May 28, 1866, in West Point. Known as "Old Fuss and Feathers," he loved display. A brilliant trainer, careful planner, consummate strategist, and highly effective field commander, Scott ranks as one of the most important military leaders in U.S. military history.

SPENCER C. TUCKER

See also
Black Hawk War; Cherokees; Fort Armstrong, Treaty of; Sauks and Foxes; Seminole War, Second; Trail of Tears

References
Eisenhower, John S. D. *Agent of Destiny: The Life and Times of General Winfield Scott.* New York: Free Press, 1997.
Johnson, Timothy D. *Winfield Scott: The Quest for Military Glory.* Lawrence: University Press of Kansas, 1998.
Scott, Winfield. *Memoirs.* 2 vols. New York: Sheldon, 1864.

Scouts, Native American
Native American allies or auxiliaries who lent services to Europeans or American military organizations. These groups frequently depended on Native Americans because of their familiarity with relevant terrain and the indigenous populations or simply because they were an additional source of military manpower.

Apache scouts drill with rifles at Fort Wingate, New Mexico, in a photograph from the 1880s. Native Americans often rendered invaluable service to the U.S. Army in the West. (National Archives)

The use of native scouts dates to the initial stages of European contact with the indigenous populations of the Americas. Meso-americans helped the Spaniards topple the Aztecs, for example, while the Dutch, French, and English all relied on Native American allies to maintain their tenuous footholds in North America and to challenge the hegemony of their European rivals. These allies provided not only scouts but also sizable contingents of warriors who often operated in concert with, but usually independently of, European forces.

As sovereign powers, Native Americans entered into alliances with European nations to obtain military advantage over their Native American enemies, to gain access to European manufac-tured goods, and to seek revenge on a European enemy by ally-ing with their enemy's enemy. Individual warriors meanwhile relished the opportunity to distinguish themselves in battle and reap the spoils of war. Given the diffuse nature of political authority among most Native American societies, Europeans allied with groups as small as individual villages or as large as multitribal confederacies. Competition between colonial powers often worked to the advantage of many Native Americans, who offered their military service and trade to competing suitors and thus played them against one another. The demise of New France in consequence of the French and Indian War (1754–1763) and Great Britain's successive losses in the American Revolutionary War (1775–1783) and the War of 1812, however, gradually elimi-nated this advantage. From 1815 onward, few Native American

groups retained the power to treat with the United States as sov-ereign entities.

Some eastern tribes, devastated by disease and subsumed by the advance of the English colonial frontier, had been reduced to subject status as early as the 17th century. As a means of sus-taining their people in the face of wrenching change, they offered military service to the Europeans not as allies but instead as aux-iliaries. This form of cooperation between Americans and Native Americans predominated in the Trans-Mississippi West of the mid and late 19th century and is most commonly associated with the term "Indian scout."

Native American motivations for allying with Europeans and Americans are relatively easy to discern, but understanding their auxiliary service is more complicated. Often regarded as merce-naries or race traitors by other natives, Native American auxil-iaries have endured the scorn of some scholars and even their own descendants. Almost invariably, however, auxiliary service permitted Native Americans to provide for their communities in accordance with their cultural and societal values. Intending to "civilize" the Native Americans, U.S. officials forbade intertribal warfare and encouraged Native American men to abandon hunt-ing in favor of intensive sedentary agriculture. As most Native American societies regarded farming as women's work and held accomplished warriors in the highest esteem, federal officials were, in effect, requiring Native American men to surrender their manhood. Auxiliary service thus provided some men with an attractive opportunity to distinguish themselves, provide for their families, and perhaps exact revenge from Native American antagonists. Although some Americans valued Native American auxiliaries for the presumed psychological benefit of pitting Native American against Native American, auxiliaries consistently performed their duties in accordance with their interests and sympathies.

For their part, Europeans and Americans were often ambivalent about the employment of Native American allies and auxiliaries. Military necessity demanded the practice initially, but English colonists in particular feared that it advertised weakness to potential enemies. These colonists and their American descendants relied on Native American allies only as an expedient of last resort and regularly punished their allies as harshly as their enemies. These concerns diminished by the mid-19th century, however, with the erosion of Native American sovereignty east of the Mississippi River.

In the sparsely populated West, army commanders found ready Native American auxiliaries among sedentary tribes that had been victimized by their horse-mounted aggressive neighbors. Deprived of manpower, local commanders increasingly turned to auxiliaries during the American Civil War (1861–1865), for example. Congress regularized the practice on August 1, 1866, when it authorized a force of 1,000 Native American auxiliaries, who were to receive the same pay as regular U.S. Army cavalrymen.

Some officers opposed the enlistment of Native American auxiliaries because it offended their sense of military professionalism or seemed to retard the process of "civilization." Others simply doubted Native American loyalty. With the exception of a single mutiny among Apache scouts at Cibecue Creek in 1881, however, Native American troops proved not only loyal but also invaluable to U.S. Army operations in the West.

The more prominent and numerous Native American scouts hailed from among the Pawnees, Apaches, Navajos, Crows, Seminoles, and Arikaras. The most forceful advocate for the use of Indian scouts was Brigadier General George Crook, who employed them widely in his many campaigns, most notably against Geronimo's Apaches. Apache scouts accompanying Lieutenant Charles Gatewood located Geronimo and helped to secure his surrender.

Black Seminole (Seminole Negro) scouts played a conspicuous role in campaigns along the Texas-Mexico border, including Colonel Ranald S. Mackenzie's cross-border incursions. A number of Indian scouts rode to their deaths with Lieutenant Colonel George A. Custer's 7th Cavalry during the Battle of the Little Bighorn (June 25–26, 1876). In fact, Indian scouts contributed meaningfully to most of the major campaigns of the post–Civil War era.

Private civilian companies such as railroads also employed Native American scouts. Native American scouts were also frequently employed by surveyors, explorers, and pioneers. The Shoshone Sacagawea is perhaps the most famous example; she accompanied the Lewis and Clark expedition of 1803–1806.

Undeniably, scouts' and auxiliaries' service facilitated American conquest of the West, yielding a historical legacy as ambiguous as it was important.

JOHN W. HALL

See also

Apaches; Arikaras; Cibecue Creek, Incident at; Crook, George; Crows; Curly; French and Indian War; Gatewood, Charles Bare; Grouard, Frank; Langlade, Charles Michel de; Lewis and Clark Expedition; Native Americans and the American Revolutionary War; Native Americans and the War of 1812; Navajos; North, Frank Joshua, and Luther Hedden North; Pawnees; Sacagawea; Seminoles; Sieber, Albert

References

Dunlay, Thomas W. *Wolves for the Blue Soldiers: Indian Scouts and Auxiliaries with the United States Army, 1860–90.* Lincoln: University of Nebraska Press, 1982.

Hall, John W. *Uncommon Defense: Indian Allies in the Black Hawk War.* Cambridge: Harvard University Press, 2009.

Starkey, Armstrong. *European and Native American Warfare, 1675–1815.* Norman: University of Oklahoma Press, 1998.

Seattle
Birth Date: ca. 1786
Death Date: June 7, 1866

Chief of the Suquamish and Duwamish tribes in the Puget Sound region of present-day Washington state. Seattle was born around 1786 (some sources say 1788) in the Puget Sound area. Perhaps because Seattle's mother may have been a slave, he opposed the poor treatment of slaves when he became a tribal leader. Seattle gained leadership in his tribe when he led tidewater tribes in small intertribal wars against the Green and White River tribes. He then became primary chief of the Suquamish and Duwamish nations, which he united.

The Pacific Northwest's fertile lands attracted many white settlers throughout the early 1800s. When Seattle was in his forties he became a Catholic, taking the name Noah when he was baptized. He became friends with the white leaders of the area and was acquainted with Isaac I. Stevens, the territorial governor and superintendent of Indian affairs in the Washington area. As tribal chief, Seattle advised his people to offer the settlers open trade and friendship. When gold was discovered in California in 1848, Washington and Oregon became the second most-popular destinations for settlers looking for land and resources, bringing white settlers by the thousands.

The white settlers honored Seattle's friendship by naming their Puget Sound settlement Seattle in 1852. With the increasing white population, the U.S. government pressured the natives to sell their land. Seattle met with Stevens in December 1854 to negotiate reservation land and government annuities in exchange for the sale of tribal land. He specifically asked that a medical doctor be assigned to the tribes.

During this meeting with U.S. government officials, Seattle made a famous speech. His words were recorded by Dr. Henry A. Smith, a poet. In 1960 the poet William Arrowsmith updated the speech into modern English: "The Great Chief in Washington sends word that [he] wishes to buy our land. The Great Chief also sends us words of friendship and goodwill. This is kind of him, since we know he has little need of our friendship in return. But we will consider your offer. For we know that if we do not sell, the white man may come with guns and take our land. How can you buy or sell the sky, the warmth of the land? The idea is strange to us."

Seattle returned with other tribal leaders in January 1855 as the first signer of the Port Elliot Treaty between the U.S. government and the Puget Sound tribes. At the time Seattle was about 67 years old. He and his tribe subsequently moved to the Madison Reservation on the east shore of Bainbridge Island across from the present-day city of Seattle.

Within months, white settlers had broken the terms of the treaty. Puget Sound warriors joined with Yakima allies from the Cascade Mountains to try to prevent settlers from occupying tribal land. For the next three years a series of uprisings occurred, eventually resulting in the U.S. government's execution of Nisqually chief Leschi. Seattle condemned the government's failure to ratify the Port Elliot Treaty for four years as well as failing to deliver services to native people as outlined in the treaty. While still maintaining his friendship with whites, Seattle defended Native American warriors who fought white settlers in the 1856–1857 uprising. By 1858 the white settlers had completely suppressed the Native Americans. Seattle died on the reservation on June 7, 1866.

JOSÉ VALENTE

See also

Stevens, Isaac Ingalls; Yakima-Rogue War

References

Gifford, Eli, and R. Michael Cook, eds. *"How Can One Sell the Air?" Chief Seattle's Vision.* Summertown, TN: Book Publishing Company, 1992.

Nerburn, Kent. *The Wisdom of the Great Chiefs: The Classic Speeches of Chief Red Jacket, Chief Joseph, and Chief Seattle.* San Rafael, CA: New World Library, 1994.

2nd Dragoon Regiment

See Dragoon Regiments, 1st and 2nd

Seminoles

Native American group whose traditional territory was located chiefly in Florida. The name "Seminole" means "pioneer" or "runaway" and is possibly derived from the Spanish *cimarrón* ("wild"). The Seminoles, known as such by 1775, formed in the 18th century from members of other Native American peoples, mainly Creeks but also Oconees, Yamasees, and others. The Creeks, Choctaws, Chickasaws, Cherokees, and Seminoles were known by non-Native Americans in the 19th century as the Five Civilized Tribes.

The Seminoles spoke two mutually unintelligible Muskogean languages: Hitchiti, spoken by the Oconees and today mostly by the Miccosukees (Mikasukis), and Muskogee.

Before the First Seminole War (1817–1818), Seminole towns had chiefs and councils of elders. After the Third Seminole War (1855–1858) there were three bands (two Miccosukee bands and one Creek band), based on language. Each band had its own chief and council of elders. Matrilineal clans helped provide cultural continuity among widely scattered bands after the wars. There was also a dual division among the people. Particularly after 1817, the Seminoles lived in small extended families.

Owing to a fairly mobile and decentralized existence, the early towns were much less organized than were those of the Creeks. Seminole women grew corn, beans, squash, and tobacco. They made hominy and flour from corn and and the coontie plant. They also grew such nonnative crops as sweet potatoes, bananas, peanuts, lemons, melons, and oranges. They gathered wild rice; cabbage palmetto; various roots and wild foods, such as persimmon, plum, honey, and sugarcane; and nuts, such as hickory and acorns. Men hunted alligators, bears, opossums, rabbits, squirrels, wild fowl, manatees, and turkeys. The Seminoles ate fish, turtles, and shellfish in abundance.

Traditional trade items included alligator hides, otter pelts, bird plumes, and foods. Bird plumes and alligator hides in particular were very much in demand in the late 19th century. The Seminoles were also known for their fine patchwork clothing and their baskets. Their geometric designs were often in the pattern of a snake. Ribbon appliqué, previously consisting mainly of bands of triangles along borders, became much more elaborate during the late 19th century.

The Apalachees and Timucuas had been the original inhabitants of northern Florida. By about 1700, however, most had been killed by disease and raids by more northerly tribes. Non-Muskogee Oconee people from southern Georgia, who moved south during the early 18th century, formed the kernel of the Seminole people. They were joined by Yamasee refugees from the Yamasee War (1715–1717) as well as by some Apalachicolas, Calusas, Hitchitis, and Chiahas and escaped slaves. The Chiahas were known as Miccosukees by the late 18th century. Several small Muskogean groups joined the nascent Seminole Nation in the late 18th century.

Seminoles considered themselves Creeks; the Seminoles supported the Creeks in war and often attended their councils. By the outbreak of the American Revolutionary War (1775–1783), the Seminoles' ties to the Creeks were diminishing. Under the leadership of Cowkeeper (Ahaya of Cuscowilla), the Seminoles allied with the British but saw little action, given their homeland's distance from the main theaters of combat. When Spain resumed control of the Florida peninsula in 1785, the Seminoles generally enjoyed good relations with the Spanish.

The Seminoles experienced considerable population growth after the Creek War (1813–1814), mainly from Muskogean immigrants from Upper Creek towns. From this time on the dominant language among the Seminoles was Muskogee, or Creek. However, Seminole settlements, mainly between the Apalachicola and Suwannee rivers, were too scattered to permit the reestablishment of Creek towns and clan structures.

Prior to the American Civil War (1861–1865) some Seminoles owned slaves, but the slaves' obligations were minimal, and the Seminoles welcomed escaped slaves into their communities. Until 1821, U.S. slaves might flee across an international boundary to Florida. Even after that year the region remained a haven for escaped slaves because of the presence of free African American and mixed African American and Seminole communities.

The Seminoles first organized to fight the United States in 1817–1818 (they did not engage in intertribal warfare). The conflict was begun by state militias chasing runaway slaves and resulted in the Spanish cession of Florida. In the Treaty of Moultrie Creek (1823), the Seminole traded their north Florida land for a reservation in central Florida. The 1832 Treaty of Payne's Landing, which was signed by unrepresentative chiefs and was not supported by most Seminoles, called for the tribe to relocate west to Indian Territory (Oklahoma). By 1838, up to 1,500 Seminoles had been rounded up and penned in concentration camps. These people were forcibly marched west, during which time as many as 1,000 died from disease, starvation, fatigue, heartbreak, or attacks from whites. Although under pressure to do so, the Seminoles consistently refused to give up the considerable number of African Americans among them. In 1856 the Seminoles in Indian Territory, who wished to remain free of Creek domination, were given a strip of land of about 2 million acres west of the Creeks.

Resistance to relocation and to white slave-capturing raids led to the Second Seminole War (1835–1842). Under Osceola, Jumper, and other leaders, the Seminoles waged a guerrilla war against the United States, retreating deep into the southern swamps. Although Osceola was captured at a peace conference and soon died in captivity and although at war's end most Seminoles (about 4,500 people) were forced to move to Indian Territory, the Seminoles were not militarily defeated. The war ended because the United States decided not to spend more than the $30 million it had already spent or to lose more than the 1,500 soldiers who had already been killed.

The Third Seminole War took place during 1855–1858. From their redoubt in the Everglades, the Seminoles attacked nonnative surveyors and settlers. The army, through its own attacks and by bringing in some Oklahoma Seminoles, succeeded in persuading another 100 or so Seminoles to relocate, but about 300 remained, undefeated, in Florida. There was never a formal peace treaty.

In the 1870s as the first nonnatives began moving south of Lake Okeechobee, there was another call for Seminole removal, but the government decided against an attempt. In the late 19th century a great demand for Seminole trade items led to close relationships being formed between Florida Native Americans and nonnative traders.

The Western Seminoles settled in present-day Seminole County, Oklahoma, in 1866. By the 1890s they had formed 14 bands, including 2 composed of freedmen, or black Seminoles. Each band was self-governing and had representation on the tribal council. Most of the Western Seminole Reservation, almost 350,000 acres, was allotted in the early 20th century. Through fraud and other questionable and illegal means, nonnatives by 1920 had acquired about 80 percent of the land originally deeded to the Seminoles. Tribal governments were unilaterally dissolved when Oklahoma became a state in 1907.

Most Seminoles still in Florida relocated to reservations during the 1930s and 1940s. There they quickly acculturated, adopting cattle herding, wage labor, schools, and Christianity. With the help of Florida's congressional delegation, the tribe avoided termination in the 1950s. At that time the tribe adopted an Indian Reorganization Act–style corporate charter. Formal federal recognition came in 1957. By the 1950s, a group of more traditional Miccosukee-speaking Seminoles, mostly living deep in the Everglades, moved to separate themselves from the Seminoles, whom they regarded as having largely renounced their native traditions. The Miccosukees won recognition as a separate nation in 1962.

BARRY M. PRITZKER

See also
Osceola; Seminole War, First; Seminole War, Second; Seminole War, Third; Slavery among Native Americans

References
Debo, Angie. *A History of the Indians of the United States*. Norman: University of Oklahoma Press, 1970.

Iverson, Peter. *"We Are Still Here": American Indians in the Twentieth Century*. Arlington Heights, IL: Davidson, 1998.

Power, Susan C. *Early Art of the Southeastern Indians: Feathered Serpents and Winged Beings*. Athens: University of Georgia Press, 2004.

Rawls, James. *Chief Red Fox Is Dead: A History of Native Americans in the Twentieth Century*. Fort Worth, TX: Harcourt Brace, 1996.

Seminole War, First
Start Date: 1816
End Date: 1818

First of three conflicts between Seminoles and the United States. The Seminoles inhabited southern Georgia and much of Spanish Florida and had once been part of the Creek Confederacy. In the early 19th century the Seminoles came into conflict with Americans encroaching onto their lands and retaliated with occasional raids on frontier settlements. The Seminoles' practice of harboring fugitive slaves also increased friction with the American settlers.

These tensions led to hostilities during the War of 1812. In March 1812 a group of Georgians invaded northern Florida, hoping to convince the inhabitants there to declare independence from Spain. The invaders were later joined by regular U.S. Army troops and militiamen from Georgia. Concerned that the Americans would seize their land, the Seminoles joined forces with blacks who feared being returned to slavery. On July 25, 1812, they attacked pro-American planters along the St. Johns River. On September 12 another force of African Americans and Seminoles ambushed a supply train escorted by U.S. marines and Georgia militia at Twelve Mile Swamp. The ambush sparked an extended period of fighting that culminated in an American expedition that destroyed several Seminole towns. American troops withdrew from Florida in May 1813.

The Seminoles continued to launch occasional raids into southern Georgia and Alabama while also continuing to provide refuge to fugitive slaves. Some of the latter fortified a former British post on the Apalachicola River. To eliminate this magnet for runaway slaves, Brigadier General Edmund P. Gaines dispatched an expedition that destroyed the so-called Negro Fort on July 27, 1816. Angered at this attack on their allies, the Seminoles retaliated with new raids into the United States.

In 1817 Gaines responded by insisting that Neamathla, chief of Fowltown on the Flint River in Georgia, turn over to the American government Seminoles who had killed whites. Neamathla rejected the demand, and Gaines ordered Major David Twiggs and 250 men to arrest Neamathla. Most of the Seminoles fled, and Twiggs burned Fowltown on November 12.

The attack on Fowltown marked the beginning of the First Seminole War. Neamathla's people meanwhile took refuge with their fellow Seminoles in Florida. From there the Seminoles and their African American allies launched a series of raids into the United States. On November 30 they attacked a boat on the Apalachicola River, killing 36 soldiers and 10 women and children.

President James Monroe then ordered Major General Andrew Jackson to defeat the Seminoles. Jackson assembled more than 3,000 troops and about 1,500 Creeks and invaded Florida in March 1818. He established a post at the site of the demolished Negro Fort before moving against Spanish Fort San Marcos, which surrendered on April 7. Jackson then set out eastward through Seminole territory, overcoming sporadic opposition from parties of Seminoles and blacks. The American force occupied the town inhabited by Peter McQueen and his Red Stick Creek followers on April 12.

Jackson pushed toward the predominantly black settlement headed by Nero, where on April 16 some of the inhabitants fought a rearguard action that allowed most of the people to escape. Nero's defense also enabled the Seminoles in nearby Billy Bowlegs's town to flee before Jackson arrived that evening. Jackson burned the abandoned towns.

After unsuccessfully scouring the surrounding region for the fugitives, Jackson marched on Pensacola and forced the Spanish garrison to surrender on May 24. Jackson also ordered the execution of four prisoners who had been captured by his supporting naval force. Hillis Hadjo, a Seminole leader also known as Francis or the Prophet, and Himollemico, an elderly Red Stick Creek chief, were tried by court-martial on charges that they had instigated the war. They were found guilty and sentenced to death. The court found Scottish trader Alexander Arbuthnot guilty of inciting the Native Americans to war against the United States and hanged him. The fourth captive, Robert Armbrister, a former British marine, was sentenced to a year's imprisonment for arming, training, and leading Seminoles and blacks against American forces. Jackson overruled the court, however, and ordered Armbrister shot.

Having put an end to Seminole and black resistance, Jackson began his withdrawal from Florida on May 30, 1818. However, his invasion and the executions outraged Spain and Great Britain. Monroe distanced himself from Jackson's actions by noting that the general had not been ordered to attack the Spanish, although the government's instructions to Jackson had been deliberately vague. American officials blamed Spain for the incidents, accusing the Spanish of failing to control the Seminoles and blacks in Florida.

Jackson's invasion convinced the Spanish government that it could no longer hold on to Florida, and in 1819, under the terms of the Adams-Onis Treaty, Spain sold Florida to the United States.

JIM PIECUCH

See also

Billy Bowlegs; Creeks; Gaines, Edmund Pendleton; Jackson, Andrew; McQueen, Peter; Native Americans and the War of 1812; Seminoles; Seminole War, Second; Seminole War, Third

References

Heidler, David S., and Jeanne T. Heidler. *Old Hickory's War: Andrew Jackson and the Quest for Empire.* Mechanicsburg, PA: Stackpole, 1996.

Missall, John, and Mary Lou Missall. *The Seminole Wars: America's Longest Indian Conflict.* Gainesville: University Press of Florida, 2004.

Peters, Virginia Bergman. *The Florida Wars.* Hamden, CT: Archon Books, 1979.

Seminole War, Second
Start Date: 1835
End Date: 1842

The second and most costly of the three major conflicts between the United States and the Seminoles. The Second Seminole War (1835–1842) resulted from President Andrew Jackson's policy of forced Native American relocation and the Indian Removal Act of 1830. To provide more land for white settlement, the U.S.

The Second Seminole War (1835–1842) was the largest and most expensive of U.S. wars against Native Americans as the American forces endeavored to track down Florida's indigenous Seminoles and remove them to the West. (Library of Congress)

government offered southern Native Americans land in present-day Oklahoma in exchange for the surrender of their territory east of the Mississippi River. Many Seminoles in Florida, either willingly or under pressure, signed treaties accepting removal. Others refused to leave their lands, however. While Seminole leader Osceola organized opposition to removal, the U.S. Army in November 1835 hastened to move the Seminoles gathered at Fort Brooke on Tampa Bay to the west because officers feared that poor conditions at the post would drive many to join Osceola.

Before the army could remove all of the Seminoles, Osceola confronted Charley Emathla, a leader of the faction favoring removal, and killed him on November 26, 1835. Osceola then attacked a detachment of Florida militia on December 18, and other Seminole parties launched raids in the area south of St. Augustine.

On December 28, 108 regular army troops commanded by Major Francis Dade were ambushed while marching to Fort King. The Seminole attackers virtually annihilated Dade's force. Brigadier General Duncan Clinch, commander of U.S. troops in Florida, retaliated by trying to strike a Seminole stronghold on the Withlacoochee River. Clinch's force suffered heavy casualties in inconclusive fighting on December 31.

President Jackson appointed Brigadier General Winfield Scott to replace Clinch in January 1836, but Scott did not arrive at his new post until March. Meanwhile, Brigadier General Edmund P. Gaines, who commanded the army's Western Division, learned of the trouble in Florida and sailed from New Orleans with regular troops and volunteers. He landed in Tampa and on February 13 advanced into the Florida interior with 1,100 men. Gaines reached the Withlacoochee River but was prevented from crossing by heavy fire from Osceola's Seminoles. The troops constructed makeshift fortifications and, although surrounded, withstood Seminole attacks until forces under Clinch forced Osceola to withdraw on March 5.

Shortly afterward, Scott mounted his own offensive at the head of 2,000 regular troops. He reached the Withlacoochee in late March, came under constant harassment from small parties of Seminoles, became bogged down in the swamps, and withdrew. A supporting column of 1,200 Louisiana and Alabama volunteers withstood two Seminole attacks, but its commander decided to turn back. Jackson then replaced Scott with Brigadier General Thomas Jesup.

Low-level fighting continued throughout the summer. In the autumn, expeditions marched into the Florida interior. The troops

Estimated Deaths during the Second Seminole War

Category	Deaths
Seminoles	700
U.S. Army	1,466
U.S. Navy	69
White noncombatants	400
Total	2,635

and militia destroyed some of the Seminoles' crops but accomplished little else.

Jesup dispatched new expeditions in the spring of 1837 and succeeded in preventing the Seminoles from planting crops. Osceola, suffering from an unknown illness, was unable to lead the Seminole opposition. Jesup also used flags of truce to lure Seminole parties into the open and then take them prisoner. The ruse succeeded twice, and on October 27 he attempted it a third time, this time capturing Osceola.

Despite these successes, U.S. battlefield victories remained elusive. A detachment of 1,000 troops under Colonel Zachary Taylor attacked 400 Seminoles near Lake Okeechobee on December 25, 1837, and drove off the Native Americans; however, Taylor's loss of 150 troops was six times the loss that the Seminoles suffered.

In 1838 Jesup tried a new strategy, offering the African Americans fighting alongside the Seminoles freedom in exchange for military service against the warring tribe. This appeal compelled some 400 blacks to switch sides. Jesup resigned shortly afterward, having been harshly criticized for using a flag of truce to capture Osceola. Taylor assumed command in May 1838, and with the war seemingly over, the government ordered him to end the campaign even though Seminole raids continued. Taylor soon asked to be relieved, and in April 1839 Major General Alexander Macomb replaced him. By that time the war had settled into a pattern of army forays into the interior that suffered from Seminole harassment as well as Seminole retaliatory raids that likewise achieved little.

The government continued to change the army's commanders, sending Brevet Brigadier General Walker Armistead to succeed Macomb and then Colonel William Worth as Armistead's replacement. Worth's aggressive forays drove the Seminoles into the Everglades, where he continued to assail them with help from the navy. With the cost of the war approaching $20 million, in 1842 American officials decided to make concessions to achieve peace. An August 1842 agreement granted the 600 Seminole survivors (those captured had already been sent west) a reservation in southern Florida and officially ended hostilities, although sporadic fighting continued into 1843.

JIM PIECUCH

See also

Clinch, Duncan Lamont; Dade's Massacre; Gaines, Edmund Pendleton; Indian Removal Act; Jackson, Andrew; Osceola; Scott, Winfield; Seminoles; Seminole War, First; Seminole War, Third; Taylor, Zachary; Worth, William Jenkins

References

Debo, Angie. *A History of the Indians of the United States.* Norman: University of Oklahoma Press, 1970.

Mahon, John K. *History of the Second Seminole War, 1835–1842.* Rev. ed. Gainesville: University Press of Florida, 1991.

Peters, Virginia Bergman. *The Florida Wars.* Hamden, CT: Archon Books, 1979.

Seminole War, Third
Start Date: 1855
End Date: 1858

Third in a series of wars that pitted U.S. forces and Florida militia against the Seminole tribe in Florida. The war lasted from 1855 to 1858, and by its end there were perhaps as few as 100 Seminoles left in the entire Florida peninsula.

Having been defeated by American forces in the Second Seminole War (1835–1842), the majority of the Seminole people had been relocated to Indian Territory (Oklahoma). Those who remained in Florida, an estimated 300 to 400 men, women, and children, were left in the remote southern portions of the peninsula. Scattered into various Seminole subtribes, leadership fell primarily to Alachua leader Billy Bowlegs.

The Seminoles sought to maintain peace by keeping to their reservation and avoiding contact with white settlers. This changed, however, on July 12, 1849, when 5 rogue Seminoles attacked a white-owned farm east of Fort Pierce. Later, on July 17, 1849, the same group launched an assault on a trading post at Charlotte Harbor. Fearing a general Seminole uprising, settlers began to seek refuge within military fortifications, while local militias were called to arms. Some 1,400 federal troops were also dispatched to Florida.

Fearing the repercussions of the rogue incidents, Billy Bowlegs quickly ordered the capture of the outlaws. Three were eventually captured and turned over to the U.S. military, while another of the outlaws was killed. Bowlegs's quick action calmed the immediate situation, but the continual fear of an uprising and the government's desire to settle southern Florida undermined his efforts. In 1850 Congress passed the Swamp and Overflowed Land Act. Under this legislation, all federal lands at least half covered with water and that might be drained were turned over to the states. In Florida this amounted to about 20 million acres. Developers and land speculators soon rushed to southern Florida, while various plans for draining the Everglades were proposed to the state legislature. All that stood in the way, it appeared, were the few remaining Seminoles.

Efforts to persuade the Seminoles to relocate west of the Mississippi now increased, while several old forts were reactivated in an attempt to intimidate the tribe. At the same time, Seminole chiefs who had moved west were brought back in an effort to convince Bowlegs and his followers to make the journey west

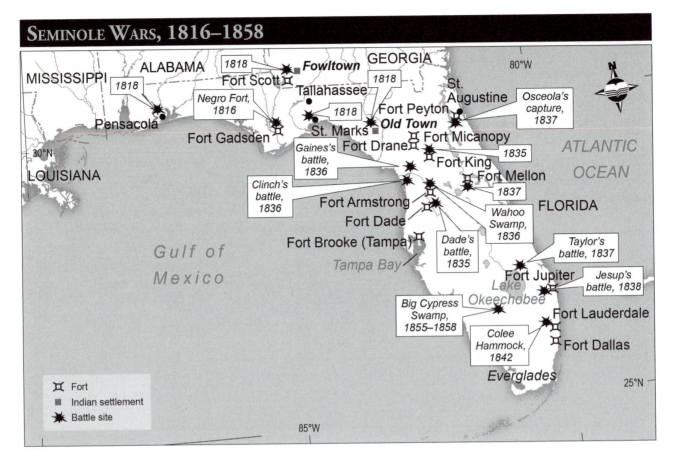

SEMINOLE WARS, 1816–1858

and leave Florida. When this failed, Bowlegs and other Seminole leaders were invited to tour Washington, D.C.; Baltimore; and New York City. Treated as celebrities, the Seminoles even met President Millard Fillmore. The purpose of the trip was to impress upon Bowlegs and his followers the power of the United States. The government offered thousands of dollars to every Seminole who peacefully relocated west, but Bowlegs and the majority of the Seminoles still refused to go.

The federal government then proceeded to construct more forts, including one on the edge of the Big Cypress Swamp. Soldiers and survey parties continued to move throughout southern Florida marking the location of Seminole villages and trails. On December 20, 1855, a survey detachment of 11 men was ambushed by 40 Seminole warriors. Four of the party died, while another 4 were wounded. The Third Seminole War had begun.

Fighting primarily a guerrilla war, the Seminoles appeared to strike at will along the frontier. On January 7, 1856, a war band attacked a flour mill near Fort Dallas. In February, two oystermen were killed on their boats in Charlotte Harbor. No one in southern Florida appeared safe. By late March, the Sarasota home of state senate president H. V. Snell was attacked by a dozen Seminoles. In the meantime, state militia and volunteers offered feeble resistance, and there was little desire to invade the Everglades, a massive swampy junglelike wetland that occupied much of southern Florida. Many people preferred to remain near their homes and

crops. As fear of Seminole raids grew, however, many settlers fled southern Florida. Pressure began to mount on the government for its handling of the war.

The Battle of Tillis Farm on June 14, 1856, marked the turning point in the conflict. It was initially a successful Seminole raid against a white homestead, but the natives were forced to retreat when militia was dispatched from nearby Fort Meade. Reinforced, they discovered a Seminole camp and killed the war chief Oscen Tustenuggee and several of his warriors. The death of their chief and the realization that they did not possess the manpower to carry the battle to the whites resulted in the Seminoles' withdrawal into their territory. They then conducted only minor raids.

With the Seminoles on the defensive, the federal government prepared to go on the offensive. Regular army and militia forces had begun to gather near Fort Meade and Fort Dallas. Command of the force was given to Brevet Brigadier General William S. Harney, a veteran of the Second Seminole War (1835–1842). Harney realized that the only way to defeat the Seminoles was to invade and drive them from their territory. When negotiations failed, Harney began his offensive in January 1857. Outnumbered and with families to protect, the Seminoles were forced from one hiding place to another as Harney's forces moved deeper into Seminole territory. Those Seminoles and their families who were captured were taken to Egmont Key off Tampa Bay, there to await removal west.

In April 1857 Harney was transferred to Utah, and command of southern Florida fell to Colonel Gustavus Loomis. Loomis continued the offensive into Seminole territory and developed the use of alligator boats. Flat-bottomed and more than 30 feet long, they could operate efficiently in shallow water and could transport up to 16 soldiers each. In them, companies of soldiers traveled throughout the Everglades and the Kissimmee River harassing Seminole camps.

As the war progressed, efforts continued to convince Bowlegs and the Seminoles to surrender and voluntarily move west. Western Seminoles were again brought in. It was also decided that the Seminoles would be allowed their own territory in Oklahoma, separate from the hated Creeks. The government also agreed to establish a $500,000 trust for Seminoles whenever Bowlegs and his followers relocated. Exhausted, Bowlegs finally accepted the arrangement on March 27, 1858. On May 4, 38 men and 85 women and children, including Billy Bowlegs, boarded a ship for the West. About 100 Seminoles refused to go and were allowed to remain. On May 8, 1858, Loomis announced an end to all hostilities. The Third Seminole War marked the end of effective native resistance in Florida.

ROBERT W. MALICK

See also

Billy Bowlegs; Harney, William Selby; Seminole War, Second

References

Covington, James W. *The Billy Bowlegs War, 1855–1858: The Final Stand of the Seminoles against the Whites.* Chuluota, FL: Mickler House, 1982.

Covington, James W. *The Seminoles of Florida.* Gainesville: University Press of Florida, 1993.

McReynolds, Edwin C. *The Seminoles.* Norman: University of Oklahoma Press, 1967.

Missall, John, and Mary Lou Missall. *The Seminole Wars: America's Longest Indian Conflict.* Gainesville: University Press of Florida, 2004.

Senecas

One of the five original Iroquois nations comprising the Iroquois Confederacy. The Senecas were among the most aggressive members of the confederation during the colonial period. They actively participated in wars against the French and their Algonquian allies in Canada, especially during the Beaver Wars (1641–1701).

The Iroquois styled themselves the "People of the Longhouse," and the Senecas were the "Keepers of the Western Door" of the confederation. The Senecas occupied the region from the Genesee River to Canandaigua Lake in western New York. Known in their own language as O-non-dowa-gah ("Great Hill People"), they were the largest in population of all Iroquois nations and remained so throughout the colonial period. Senecas made up perhaps half of the total Iroquois population and in the colonial period could place in the field upward of 1,000 warriors.

In the 1620s trade with the Dutch allowed the Mohawks, the easternmost Iroquois nation, to obtain guns and metal weapons.

They disseminated these through the confederation to the Senecas, who then carried them into war against their enemies to the north and west.

Beginning in the 1640s, the Iroquois attacked their Huron (Wyandot) neighbors to the north and other nations to the west in what became known as the Beaver Wars. Although the warfare had an economic component to it, it was also driven by the Iroquois' need to reconstitute their population. Indeed, their population had been greatly reduced by epidemic disease over the previous two decades. To that end, the Iroquois conflict with the Hurons served also as a so-called mourning war, whereby enemy captives would be assimilated into Iroquois culture to replace the dead.

Whatever the cause of the Iroquois conflict with the Hurons, it was the Senecas who did the majority of the fighting. During the summer of 1648 Seneca war parties ravaged Huron towns, including the large fortified village of Taenaostaiae. Some 700 Hurons were killed or captured, and 1,000 others were forced to flee. Soon afterward the Mohawks joined the Senecas, and together they killed or captured thousands of Hurons, driving survivors north and west of Lake Ontario before the Hurons finally stopped the Iroquois assault. Victorious but badly battered, the Senecas and the Mohawks decided to withdraw, leaving the Huron survivors to seek refuge among other tribes or flee farther west. Although the Hurons were not completely exterminated by the Iroquois, the political and economic entity that had been the Huron Nation ceased to exist.

The Senecas turned their attention to neighboring tribes on their western border. Beginning in 1651, the Senecas attacked a Native American group known as the Neutrals, who occupied the Ontario peninsula. After some initial setbacks the Senecas soon overcame the Neutrals, scattering or absorbing their entire population by 1653. An Iroquoian-speaking people known as the Eries were the next to face Seneca hostility. The Eries occupied desirable hunting grounds south of Lake Erie. In 1655 the Senecas, along with the Onondagas, attacked the Eries, dispersing and defeating them by 1657.

Following these victories, the Senecas along with the Onondagas, the Oneidas, and the Cayugas reached a peace settlement with the French. These four western Iroquois nations, jealous of the Mohawk monopoly over trade with the Dutch at Albany, sought to replace the Hurons as the principal French trading partner. With their northern border secured, the Senecas then joined their Mohawk cousins in a war against the Susquehannocks, another Iroquoian-speaking people living in Pennsylvania and Maryland. But the Susquehannocks put up a fierce fight, and when Mohawk raids along the Saint Lawrence River fractured the peace agreement with the French, the Senecas pulled their warriors back to their homelands along the Genesee River. The Senecas sought to maintain their alliance with the French, but peace proved fleeting.

Anxious to bring ever-greater quantities of furs to their new English partners at Albany, the Iroquois struck westward and attacked the tribes of the Ohio Valley and the Ottawas north of the Great Lakes. The Ottawas were the main fur suppliers for the French, and retaliation from New France fell hard and swiftly on the Senecas. In 1687 some 2,000 French Canadians and allied natives invaded Seneca homelands, destroying villages, cornfields, and storehouses. Additional punitive raids followed. Finally, the Senecas, exhausted by two decades of war, joined the Onondagas in making peace with the French in 1701.

Over the next 50 years the Senecas remained neutral, although they increasingly gravitated toward the French in part because of their dependence on French trade goods from Fort Niagara. During King George's War (1744–1748) and the French and Indian War (1754–1763), Seneca warriors, especially western Senecas in the upper Ohio Valley, often supported the French. Moreover, the Seneca attachment to the French did not immediately dissolve after the French withdrew from North America in 1763. Many Senecas joined Pontiac's Rebellion that same year, during which they assisted in the capture of British forts in northwestern Pennsylvania. But the failure of the uprising and the removal of the French forced the Senecas to seek accommodation with the British. Their alliance was strained at best, although the Senecas remained true to their new ally, eventually siding with the British during the American Revolutionary War (1775–1783).

In the course of the Revolutionary War, two powerful chiefs achieved prominence: Cornplanter and Red Jacket, both of whom played important roles in the late 18th and early 19th centuries. Handsome Lake, Cornplanter's half brother, had meanwhile founded the Longhouse religion, which was widespread among the Iroquois by 1799. Some Iroquois continue to practice it today. Gradually the Senecas' land was appropriated by white settlers, although the tribe did retain some lands in New York state. In 1869 Ely Parker, a Seneca, became the first Native American commissioner of the Bureau of Indian Affairs. In recent times, the Senecas have maintained four reservations in New York: Allegany, Tonawanda, Oil Springs, and Cattarangus. Smaller numbers of other Senecas reside in Ontario on the Six Nations Reserve or in Oklahoma alongside the Cayugas.

DANIEL P. BARR

See also
Algonquins; Beaver Wars; Cayugas; Cornplanter; French and Indian War; Iroquois Confederacy; Iroquois Treaties of 1700 and 1701; King George's War; Mohawks; Mourning War; Oneidas; Onondagas; Ottawas; Parker, Ely Samuel; Pontiac's Rebellion; Red Jacket; Senecas, French Attack on; Susquehannocks; Wyandots

References
Barr, Daniel P. *Unconquered: The Iroquois League at War in Colonial America.* Westport, CT: Praeger, 2006.
Brandão, José António. *Your Fyre Shall Burn No More: Iroquois Policy toward New France and Its Native Allies to 1701.* Lincoln: University of Nebraska Press, 1997.
Jennings, Francis. *The Ambiguous Iroquois Empire: The Covenant Chain Confederation of Indian Tribes with English Colonies from Its Beginnings to the Lancaster Treaty of 1744.* New York: Norton, 1984.
Richter, Daniel K. *The Ordeal of the Longhouse: The People of the Iroquois League in the Era of European Colonization.* Chapel Hill: University of North Carolina Press, 1992.

Senecas, French Attack on
Event Date: 1687

French invasion of Iroquois territory in 1687 during the Beaver Wars (1641–1701). The French alliance with the Hurons in the early 17th century brought Quebec colonists into conflict with the Five Nations of the Iroquois, who were the Hurons' traditional enemies. When the Iroquois tried to expand their control of the fur trade in the Illinois region, challenging the French position there, Governor Joseph-Antoine Le Febvre de La Barre pronounced the existing French-Iroquois peace treaty dissolved and marched against the Five Nations in 1684. However, by the time La Barre's force of 1,200 French soldiers and native allies reached the eastern end of Lake Ontario, supply shortages and disease had rendered them ineffective. Surrounded by the Onondagas, La Barre was forced to sign a rather humiliating treaty recognizing Iroquois rights to the Illinois trade and abandoning French support for their native allies in the area.

On learning of the treaty, King Louis XIV was incensed. He quickly dismissed La Barre and replaced him with Jacques-René de Brisay, Marquis de Denonville, a capable and well-tested soldier. Louis provided Denonville with 1,600 French troops and ordered the new governor to settle the Iroquois problem by any means necessary. Realizing that the English in New York were encouraging the Iroquois attacks and would urge the Five Nations not to negotiate, Denonville decided that force was required to end the Iroquois threat.

Denonville marched into Iroquois country in late June 1687. A few Onondagas and Oneidas came to the French camp in an effort to negotiate, but Denonville captured them. He then marched into Seneca territory with a combined force of 2,000 French troops and native warriors. Most of the Senecas, including all the women and children, fled, but several hundred men stayed behind to defend their land. After a brief skirmish in which the Senecas suffered at least 20 dead and the French suffered about half that many dead, the Senecas offered no further resistance. Denonville then proceeded to burn two large Seneca towns and two smaller villages and destroy all the stored provisions and crops that his soldiers could find, amounting to an estimated 1.2 million bushels. He correctly predicted that this loss of foodstuffs would cause the Senecas great distress. The French and their allies also desecrated and looted Seneca burial grounds.

When the Iroquois learned of the impending invasion, they dispatched emissaries to Albany to seek English assistance but received only a small amount of ammunition and some critical comments about their lack of courage. English officials subsequently provided the Iroquois with additional arms and ammunition. The Iroquois launched retaliatory raids into New France during the next several months until both sides agreed to open peace negotiations in the summer of 1688. The negotiations failed, however, and sporadic French-Iroquois warfare continued until the outbreak of King William's War (1689–1697) further intensified the strife.

JIM PIECUCH

See also

Beaver Wars; France; Iroquois; Senecas

References

Richter, Daniel K., and James H. Merrell, eds. *Beyond the Covenant Chain: The Iroquois and Their Neighbors in Indian North America, 1600–1800.* Syracuse, NY: Syracuse University Press, 1987.

Richter, Daniel K. *The Ordeal of the Longhouse: The People of the Iroquois League in the Era of European Colonization.* Chapel Hill: University of North Carolina Press, 1992.

Sequoyah
Birth Date: ca. 1770
Death Date: ca. 1843

Native American leader. Born to a white father, the trader Nathaniel Gist, and a Cherokee mother, Sequoyah was best known for having invented the Cherokee syllabary. Sequoyah was born probably in 1770 in the Cherokee village of Taskigi near present-day Knoxville, Tennessee. He was raised as a Cherokee, however, and spoke only limited English. In his early years he was a hunter and trapper, and during the Creek War (1813–1814) he served under Major General Andrew Jackson. A hunting accident sometime thereafter left Sequoyah permanently disabled; he then became a silversmith.

Unable to move around as he once did, Sequoyah decided to focus his attention on the development of a Cherokee alphabet, which he hoped would eliminate illiteracy among his people and help preserve the Cherokees' culture and language. He began his endeavor in 1809 but soon came to realize that the Cherokee language did not lend itself to a coherent alphabet. Thus, he decided that a phonetic syllabary (a system of symbols that represent spoken syllables) would be the best way in which to codify the Cherokee language. After much work over a period of nearly 12 years he perfected his system, which contains 86 symbols, or characters.

Some Cherokees were skeptical, if not suspect, of Sequoyah's work, but in 1821 he demonstrated the syllabary to the Cherokee Council, which advocated its use. Before long the system was in wide use, and literacy rates among the Cherokees rose substantially. Just seven years later the Cherokee Constitution was written in Cherokee using Sequoyah's system.

The invention and dissemination of the syllabary served to empower the Cherokees during a time in which the Cherokee

Portrait of Sequoyah, inventor of the Cherokee alphabet, by 19th-century American painter Charles Bird King, from *The Indian Tribes of North America.* (Thomas L. McKenney and James Hall, *The Indian Tribes of North America*, 1836–1844)

Nation was coming under increasing pressure from the U.S. government. Indeed, the syllabary helped the tribe maintain unity of purpose and retain its cultural identity at a time in which other Native American groups had been torn apart by U.S. government relocation efforts.

In 1838 Sequoyah and many other Cherokees were forcibly removed from their ancestral lands for resettlement in Indian Territory (Oklahoma). This movement came to be called the Trail of Tears because of the high incidence of deaths due to exposure, starvation, and disease. Around 1840 Sequoyah became leader of the western Cherokees and helped promulgate the Cherokee Act of Union, which united the western and eastern Cherokees. In 1842 he set out on an expedition, probably to Mexico, in search of a lost band of Cherokees who had likely left Cherokee territory in the late 18th century. Sequoyah did not return, and his remains have never been located. It is believed that he died in Mexico, perhaps in 1843. Sequoyah nevertheless is revered by the Cherokees, who still use his syllabary in parts of North Carolina and Oklahoma. He was the only person to invent a written language entirely by himself.

PAUL G. PIERPAOLI JR.

See also

Cherokee Alphabet; Cherokees; Creek War; Indian Removal Act; Jackson, Andrew; Trail of Tears

References

Bender, Margaret. *Signs of Cherokee Culture: Sequoyah's Syllabary in Eastern Cherokee Life.* Chapel Hill: University of North Carolina Press, 2002.

Mooney, James. *Myths of the Cherokee.* New York: Dover, 1996.

7th U.S. Cavalry Regiment

See Cavalry Regiment, 7th U.S.

7th U.S. Infantry Regiment

See Infantry Regiment, 7th U.S.

Shawnee Council

Political organization of the Shawnee Nation. Prior to the arrival of Europeans, the Shawnees were arranged into five major divisions based on the role each played within tribal society. Each division lived in separate villages. The Chalagawthas and Thawegilas provided political leaders (peace chiefs), the Piquas served as religious leaders, the Kispokathas supplied war chiefs, and the Maykujays, noted for their knowledge of herbs, provided medical care. Leaders from each division, generally drawn from the most important clans, not only furnished leadership over their respective towns but also represented their division and towns at general tribal councils. While these distinct divisions persisted well into the 18th century, the expansion of the colonial frontier disrupted traditional tribal organization and resulted in villages comprising most (and often all) of the tribal divisions. Although the amalgamation of the tribal divisions often resulted in intratribal rivalries and dissension, the principle of government by council helped prevent the outbreak of tribal civil war.

Peace chiefs (generally from the Chalagawtha or Thawegila divisions) were usually middle-aged or older men who were respected for their wisdom and experience. They represented the tribe in its dealings with outside groups and mediated disputes within the tribe, yet their authority was actually rather limited because decisions were made after consulting the leaders of the various clans within the village council or the leaders of the various towns in the tribal council. More important, the role of war chiefs became increasingly prominent within the tribe because the Shawnees were almost constantly at war with the United States after the American Revolutionary War (1775–1783).

As a consequence, important warriors such as Tecumseh gained greater influence within tribal councils and often replaced the peace chief as the primary spokesmen of the tribe with outside groups. Likewise, the religious fervor fomented by Tenskwatawa (the Shawnee Prophet), Tecumseh's brother, enabled Tenskwatawa to exert tremendous influence over the tribe. Yet even Tenskwatawa's power was limited by the extent to which the council would support him. Following his defeat at the Battle of Tippecanoe in 1811, Tenskwatawa's influence within the council was effectively ended, as even Tecumseh denounced him for the debacle.

Although dissension between peace chiefs and war chiefs within other tribes, such as the Creeks, enabled the United States to play the game of divide and conquer, the Shawnee Council provided a stable vehicle for maintaining tribal unity. Consequently, the Shawnees presented by far the greatest obstacle to American expansion between the American Revolution War and the War of 1812.

Justin D. Murphy

See also

Creeks; Little Turtle's War; Native Americans and the American Revolutionary War; Shawnees; Tecumseh; Tenskwatawa; Tippecanoe, Battle of

References

Calloway, Colin G. *The Shawnees and the War for America.* New York: Viking, 2007.

Edmunds, R. David. *Tecumseh and the Quest for Indian Leadership.* Boston: Little, Brown, 1984.

Warren, Stephen. *The Shawnees and Their Neighbors, 1795–1870.* Urbana: University of Illinois Press, 2009.

Shawnee Prophet

See Tenskwatawa

Shawnees

An Algonquian-speaking people whose name, *chawunagi,* means "southerners" in Algonquian. The name came from the fact that the Shawnees lived south of other Algonquians. While the Shawnees are generally classified as natives of the Northeast Woodlands, their migrations taught them to adopt the lifeways of other Native Americans, especially those of the Southeast.

Although nomadic, the Shawnees in the warm months inhabited villages, around which they grew crops. Winter brought more scattered habitation patterns as small groups went out to hunt. The Shawnees moved many times throughout their history. Their original homeland was in present-day southern Ohio, West Virginia, and western Pennsylvania. In the mid-1600s, however, the Iroquois drove them out of these areas. The Shawnees were scattered to South Carolina, Tennessee's Cumberland River basin, and southern Illinois. By the 1730s, most had returned to their original lands. In the following decades, they fought hard against encroaching white settlements in Ohio and Pennsylvania.

As the several Shawnee bands moved, they also changed their alliances between the French and the English. Many of the Shawnees sided with the French in the period from 1689 until the end of the French and Indian War (1754–1763). However, some did ally themselves with the British because they believed that British trade goods were better than those of the French. As a result, the British were able to establish an important trading post at Pickawillany in Shawnee territory in Ohio. Most of the Shawnees, however, fought the British along with other natives, including the Ottawas, in Pontiac's Rebellion (1763). And in 1774 the Shawnees fought against Virginians in Lord Dunmore's War.

Illustration of a Shawnee Indian from Georges-Henri-Victor Collot's *Voyage dans l'Amérique Septentrionale*, published in 1826. (Library of Congress Geography and Map Division)

tried to unite the natives of the Mississippi Valley against the Americans, but Tenskwatawa's defeat at the Battle of Tippecanoe (November 7, 1811) combined with the death of Tecumseh in Canada at the Battle of the Thames (October 5, 1813) during the War of 1812 effectively ended Shawnee resistance.

Tecumseh's alliance splintered after his death, and soon the Shawnees began to divide into factions, largely a result of nearly constant warfare that badly weakened the Shawnee Nation. In the years after the War of 1812, some Shawnees moved to Missouri; others migrated as far west as Texas. By the early 1830s, most Shawnees had settled in northeastern Kansas. In 1870 they were forced to move to Indian Territory (Oklahoma), where they resided near the Cherokees. One Shawnee band, however, remained in the Ohio area and still has small landholdings there.

ANDREW J. WASKEY

See also

Boone, Daniel; Cornstalk; French and Indian War; Lord Dunmore's War; Mingos; Native Americans and the War of 1812; Old Briton; Pickawillany Massacre; Pontiac's Rebellion; Proclamation of 1763; Tecumseh; Tenskwatawa; Tippecanoe, Battle of

References

Clark, Jerry E. *The Shawnee.* Lexington: University Press of Kentucky, 2007.
Noe, Randolph. *The Shawnee Indians: An Annotated Bibliography.* Lanham, MD: Scarecrow, 2001.

Sheepeater War
Event Date: 1879

Six-month military campaign in the second half of 1879 to subdue remaining rebellious tribes in the Pacific Northwest. At the conclusion of the 1878 Bannock War, a small band of Native Americans, primarily from the Bannock, Weiser, and Shoshone tribes and known as the Sheepeaters, retreated to the mountains of central Idaho to continue their resistance against white settlers by raiding livestock and stealing horses. When five Chinese miners were found murdered in Oro Grande and two ranchers were also murdered on the South Fork of the Salmon River in May, authorities blamed the crime on renegade Sheepeaters. However, there was no proof that they had been responsible for the attacks.

Brigadier General Oliver O. Howard, commander of the Department of the Columbia, ordered a detachment of federal troops to apprehend the guilty for prosecution. The campaign, which began at the end of May 1879, employed three separate forces that converged on the Sheepeaters' stronghold in the Weiser Valley from separate directions: Bannock War veteran Captain Reuben Bernard led 56 men of the 1st Cavalry Regiment north from Boise Barracks, Lieutenant Henry Catley led 48 mounted soldiers from the 2nd Infantry Regiment south from Camp Howard, and 28 scouts and sharpshooters under Lieutenant Edward S. Farrow marched eastward from the Umatilla Reservation in Oregon.

King George III's Proclamation of 1763 had all but promised Native Americans the lands west of the Appalachian Mountains. However, the governor of Virginia, John Murray, Earl of Dunmore, began parceling out western lands to veterans of the French and Indian War. Thus, Shawnee chief Cornstalk led Shawnee warriors in an armed attempt to drive the settlers out of trans-Appalachian lands, sparking Lord Dunmore's War. After a series of bloody raids and counterraids, on October 6, 1774, Colonel Andrew Lewis, commanding 1,100 militiamen, defeated chiefs Cornstalk and Logan (of the Mingos) in a fierce battle at Point Pleasant in present-day West Virginia. Cornstalk subsequently signed a peace treaty that punished the Shawnees with forfeiture of some of their lands.

During the American Revolutionary War (1775–1783), the Shawnees sided with the British. In 1778 the Shawnees even managed to capture the famed frontiersman Daniel Boone. He was held prisoner at Chillicothe, Ohio, but subsequently escaped. From 1783 to 1790 a Shawnee-led coalition killed perhaps as many as 1,000 white settlers in the Old Northwest Territory. By 1794 the Shawnees and other natives in the Northwest Territory had fought several pitched engagements with forces dispatched by the U.S. government. The most famous of the Shawnees were Tecumseh and his brother Tenskwatawa (also known as the Prophet). They

In spite of the departure at the beginning of the summer, bad weather and the rugged terrain encumbered the movement of each column. Eight-foot snowdrifts sequestered Catley's troops in the town of Warren for nearly three weeks in early July. Bernard lost several pack mules in the mountains, forcing his troops to subsist on reduced rations. After resting at Rains Ranch on July 11, Catley continued southward, camping at Big Creek on the night of July 28. He ignored scouts' reports of warriors in the area, however, and moved his troops the next morning into the valley of the creek bed. There a band of Native Americans ambushed his column from the surrounding high ground, severely wounding two of his men. Catley retreated, rendezvoused with his pack train that night, and used the baggage to construct a hasty defense at Vinegar Hill. The next morning the Native Americans attacked again with long-range rifle fire. Failing to dislodge the soldiers, they set fire to the surrounding woods and would have succeeded in flushing out the troops had Catley's first sergeant preemptively not burned the underbrush around their position to prevent them from being driven out by the conflagration. The besieged troops escaped during the night, leaving behind much of their equipment or losing it in the darkness of the hasty departure.

When Bernard learned of Catley's disaster, he reported it to his superiors and coordinated with both Catley and Farrow to consolidate their columns. The three separate forces united at Elk Creek on August 11 and, with reinforcements under Captain Albert G. Forse from Camp Howard, proceeded back toward Big Creek to find Catley's attackers. The rugged terrain continued to wear on the soldiers' mounts, forcing them to shoot nearly 20 worn-out horses and mules along the way. On August 1 Farrow's scouts made contact with a small party of warriors and chased them for several miles. After Catley's command withdrew to a neighboring settlement for supplies the following day, Native Americans attacked Bernard's pack train, killing one soldier, Harry Eagan, the army's only fatality of the campaign.

Bernard, Farrow, and Forse continued to follow the trail of the Sheepeaters for the next several weeks without any contact. With exhausted horses, being short on rations, and the onset of winter weather, Bernard and Forse disengaged and returned to their home posts in early September. Farrow remained behind in one last effort to subdue the renegade bands. After following the trails of abandoned Sheepeater camps for several days, Farrow's scouts captured several dozen Sheepeater women and children. On September 25 one of Farrow's lieutenants and a scout encountered Tamanmo (known as War Jack), the leader of the insurgents, who confessed that he was tired of the fight and offered to surrender his people. It took several weeks to escort the various warriors and families out of the remote mountains, but by October the Native Americans had been moved to the Columbia River. Farrow then sent them to Vancouver for internment. They were transferred to Fort Hall the following spring.

The few remaining Sheepeater warriors never admitted to the murders of which they were accused but were kept in prison under presumed guilt. Lieutenant Catley was tried at a court-martial for his debacle at Big Creek and was dismissed from the service; he won reinstatement from President Rutherford B. Hayes. The Sheepeater War of 1879 ended Native American resistance in the Pacific Northwest, as it forcefully eliminated the last hostile bands and compelled all other remaining tribes onto reservations.

BRADFORD A. WINEMAN

See also

Bannock War; Howard, Oliver Otis; Shoshones

References

Brown, W. C. *The Sheepeater Campaign, Idaho-1879*. Boise, ID: Syms-York, 1926.

Glassley, Ray Hoard. *Pacific Northwest Indian War*. Portland, OR: Binfords and Mort, 1953.

Sheridan, Philip Henry
Birth Date: March 6, 1831
Death Date: August 5, 1888

U.S. Army general. Born in Albany, New York, to Irish immigrant parents on March 6, 1831, Philip Henry Sheridan grew up in Somerset, Ohio. Too young to serve in the Mexican-American War (1846–1848), he attended the U.S. Military Academy at West Point. Suspended for one year for disciplinary reasons, he graduated in 1853 and was commissioned a second lieutenant in the infantry. Sheridan then served with the 1st Infantry Regiment in Texas and with the 4th Infantry Regiment in Oregon, being promoted to first lieutenant in March 1861 on the eve of the American Civil War (1861–1865).

Assigned to the western theater, Sheridan was promoted to captain in May 1861 and served in the 13th Infantry Regiment in southwestern Missouri and then as quartermaster for the Department of the Missouri under Major General Henry W. Halleck during the latter's Corinth Campaign during May–June 1862. Sheridan intensely disliked staff duty and secured a transfer to the volunteer establishment as colonel of the 2nd Michigan Cavalry in May. His subsequent victory at Booneville, Mississippi, earned him promotion to brigadier general of volunteers that September.

Sheridan commanded an infantry division and distinguished himself in Kentucky in the Battle of Perryville and especially at Stones River, where he perhaps saved from defeat Major General William S. Rosecrans's Army of the Cumberland. For this action Sheridan was promoted to major general of volunteers in March 1863. In the Battle of Chickamauga that September, Sheridan gained laurels for his division's tenacious fighting. His men played a key role in the Union victory in the Battle of Chattanooga that November.

When Ulysses S. Grant was promoted to lieutenant general and became the army's general in chief, he selected Sheridan to command the Army of the Potomac's three-division cavalry corps. During the spring and summer of 1864 Sheridan's men won a number of victories against the Confederate cavalry. His forces took part in Grant's Overland Campaign and disrupted Confederate lines of communication. Sheridan was victorious in the Battle of Yellow Tavern (May 1864) in Virginia, although his forces suffered defeat at Trevilian Station the next month.

Grant gave Sheridan command of the Army of the Shenandoah in August 1864 and instructed him to drive the Confederates south and destroy any supplies that might be of use to the Confederate Army. Sheridan defeated Confederate forces under Lieutenant General Jubal Early in the Shenandoah Valley in the Third Battle of Winchester and at Fisher's Hill that September. This accomplishment led to Sheridan's advancement to brigadier general in the regular army. Although caught off guard by Early's attack at Cedar Creek in October, Sheridan helped to rally his army to victory. Sheridan then laid waste to the Shenandoah Valley, depriving the Confederates of much-needed supplies. The extent of this destruction is seen in his boast that "A crow couldn't fly from Winchester to Staunton without taking its rations along."

Promoted to major general in the regular army in November 1864, Sheridan raided from Winchester to Petersburg, where he joined Grant. Sheridan played a major role in the final defeat of General Robert E. Lee's Army of Northern Virginia in April 1865, besting the Confederates at Five Forks and Sayler's Creek before trapping Lee's army near Appomattox Court House.

Sheridan was then ordered to Texas with a large force to encourage the French to quit Mexico. He remained in Texas as commander of the Military Division of the Gulf from May 1865 to March 1867, when he was named to command the Fifth Military District of Louisiana and Texas, but his harsh policies brought his removal that September.

Sheridan took over the Department of the Missouri in September 1867 and as such was responsible for the federal effort against hostile western Native Americans. In his new position he aggressively prosecuted a winter campaign in the Washita Valley in Indian Territory (Oklahoma) and on the southern Plains during 1868–1869, attacking the Cheyennes, Kiowas, and Comanches and destroying their livestock and supplies. Units from his department also fought in Colorado in the Battle of Beecher's Island (September 17, 1868) and the Battle of the Washita River (November 27, 1868).

When Grant became president and William T. Sherman moved up to command the army as a full general, Sheridan was promoted to lieutenant general in March 1869 and assumed command of the Military Division of the Missouri. Sheridan then traveled to Europe, where he was an official observer attached to the Prussian Army during the Franco-Prussian War (1870–1871).

Returning to the United States, Sheridan planned the campaign of three converging columns against the Sioux that resulted in the Battle of the Little Bighorn (June 25–26, 1876) and directed the punitive effort that followed. He also directed the final operations that prevented Chief Joseph and most of his Nez Perces from reaching Canada in 1877. Under Sheridan's direction, the army fought the Ute War of 1879. Sheridan succeeded Sherman as

commanding general of the U.S. Army in 1884 and was promoted to general in June 1888. As commanding general Sheridan oversaw the final operations of the army against the Apaches under Geronimo. Sheridan was also a prime mover behind the creation of Yellowstone National Park. He died at Nonquitt, Massachusetts, on August 5, 1888. Known as "Little Phil," Sheridan was blunt and outspoken. He was also industrious, offensive-minded, and aggressive and was a superb tactical commander.

SPENCER C. TUCKER

See also
Beecher Island, Battle of; Geronimo; Joseph, Chief; Little Bighorn, Battle of the; Washita, Battle of the

References
Hutton, Paul Andrew. *Phil Sheridan and His Army.* Lincoln: University of Nebraska Press, 1985.
Morris, Roy, Jr. *Sheridan: The Life and Wars of General Phil Sheridan.* New York: Crown, 1992.
O'Connor, Richard. *Sheridan the Inevitable.* Indianapolis: Bobbs-Merrill, 1953.

Sherman, William Tecumseh
Birth Date: February 8, 1820
Death Date: February 14, 1891

U.S. Army general. Born in Lancaster, Ohio, on February 8, 1820, William Tecumseh Sherman graduated fifth in his class of 42 students from the U.S. Military Academy, West Point, in 1840 and was commissioned a second lieutenant of artillery. He fought in the Second Seminole War (1835–1842) in Florida and was promoted to first lieutenant in November 1841. During the Mexican-American War (1846–1848), Sherman was a staff officer under Colonel Stephen Watts Kearny in California, winning a brevet promotion to captain. Sherman made permanent captain two years later in June 1850.

Resigning his commission in 1853, Sherman became the agent for a St. Louis–based banking firm, but the parent bank failed in 1857. He briefly practiced law in Kansas and was then superintendent of Alexandria Military Academy (later Louisiana State University) from 1859 to 1861. Sherman had great affection for the South, but when Louisiana seceded from the Union he resigned his position in January 1861 and moved to St. Louis.

Sherman reentered the U.S. Army as colonel of the 13th Infantry Regiment in May 1861 and commanded a brigade in the First Battle of Bull Run (Manassas) in July 1861. Commissioned a brigadier general of volunteers that August, he was ordered to the western theater to help hold Kentucky for the Union. There his eccentric behavior prompted questions about his sanity. Temporarily relieved of his duties, he returned to duty as commander of the Cairo Military District.

Assuming command of a division in Major General Ulysses S. Grant's Army of the Tennessee, Sherman distinguished himself

A major general during the Civil War, William T. Sherman is remembered for declaring "War is Hell." Sherman did not hate the Indians, but during his tenure as commanding general of the army from 1866 to 1883, he adopted the same tough tactics he had employed during the Civil War to bring the Indian Wars to a close. (National Archives)

in the Battle of Shiloh in April 1862 during which he was slightly wounded. Promoted to major general of volunteers in May, he developed a close friendship with Grant and by that summer was Grant's principal subordinate. Sherman participated in the Corinth Campaign and the effort to take Vicksburg, during which he was rebuffed in the Battle of Chickasaw Bayou in December 1862. He then led XV Corps and took part in the capture of Arkansas Post in January 1863. Sherman aided Grant in the capture of Vicksburg in July, for which Sherman was promoted to regular army brigadier general that same month.

When Grant took charge in the western theater, he assigned Sherman command of the Army of the Tennessee in October 1863. Sherman then led the Union left wing in the Battle of Chattanooga in November. When Grant became Union Army general in chief, Sherman took command of the Military Division of the Mississippi in March 1864, for all practical purposes overall command of the western theater. Sherman then launched a campaign against General Joseph E. Johnston's Confederate Army of Tennessee in May 1864, driving toward Atlanta and capturing the city in September. For this accomplishment Sherman received the thanks of Congress and promotion to regular army major general.

Destroying such military stocks as would not be of use to him and detaching part of his force to deal with Confederate general John B. Hood in Tennessee, Sherman began his March to the Sea in November 1864. He practiced total war, believing that destroying property would likely bring the war to a speedier end than would the taking of lives. Sherman encouraged his armies to forage liberally off the land, cutting a wide swath of destruction through Georgia. Reaching the coast, his forces occupied Savannah in December.

Turning northward, Sherman began a drive through the Carolinas in early February 1865, taking Columbia, South Carolina, in midmonth. The city was burned, but retreating Confederate troops rather than Sherman were probably to blame. Sherman then accepted the surrender of the Confederate army under General Johnston near Durham Station, North Carolina, in April.

Following the war, in June 1865 Sherman took command of the Division of the Missouri. When Grant was promoted to general in July 1866, Sherman was advanced to lieutenant general, and when Grant became president in March 1869, Sherman moved up to become commanding general of the army as a full general. During his years in command the army successfully ended the wars with Native Americans in the West. Here a chief concern was protection of the railroads across the West. Sherman did not hate Native Americans, but he was adamant in his belief that the West had to be made safe for settlers. In the Indian Wars, Sherman practiced against the Native Americans the same sort of war as he had during 1864–1865, seeking to destroy food stocks and other resources in order to bring the fighting to a speedier conclusion. At the same time, however, he insisted that the Indians be treated fairly, and he strongly opposed speculators and corrupt Indian agents who profited at Native American expense. Sherman was involved in the Medicine Lodge Treaty of 1867 and was an active participant in the negotiations for the Fort Laramie Treaty in 1868. On June 19, 1879, he delivered his famous "War Is Hell" speech at West Point.

As commanding general, Sherman took a deep interest in professionalism and in military education, establishing the School of Application for Infantry and Cavalry (today the Command and General Staff College) at Fort Leavenworth, Kansas, in 1881. He also encouraged the publication of military journals. Sherman stepped down as commanding general on November 1, 1883. He retired from the army on February 8, 1884, and lived in New York City. His two volumes of memoirs, *The Memoirs of General William T. Sherman,* are, like the man who wrote them, plainspoken and direct. Refusing to run for president on the Republican ticket, Sherman died in New York City on February 14, 1891. An intelligent and aggressive commander who is often credited with originating modern total war, he was also an able administrator and a notable military reformer.

SPENCER C. TUCKER

See also
Fort Laramie, Treaty of (1868); Grant, Ulysses Simpson; Medicine Lodge Treaty; Railroads; Sheridan, Philip Henry

References

Kenneth, Lee. *Sherman: A Soldier's Life.* New York: HarperCollins, 2001.

Marszalek, John F. *Sherman: A Soldier's Passion for Order.* New York: Free Press, 1993.

Sherman, William T. *Memoirs of General William T. Sherman.* 2 vols. 1886; reprint, Bloomington: Indiana University Press, 1957.

Shield

Personal defensive armament carried by Europeans and some Native American groups. Shields came in various shapes and sizes and were fashioned from a variety of materials, depending on the group that created them.

Shields of European manufacture were most commonly made of steel-reinforced wood. They were carried by the earliest Europeans to come to America before firearms had completely supplanted edged weapons. Shields made and carried by Europeans came in a variety of styles and shapes. The Scots carried small round shields known as targets that were roughly a foot in diameter. Larger shields were rectangular or triangular in shape and were several feet in height and more than a foot in width.

Native American shields, on the other hand, were made of animal hides, shrunken to increase their density. This process also increased the shield's deflective capability. They were most often round and roughly a foot in diameter, although design and size varied widely.

JAMES R. MCINTYRE

See also

Bow and Arrow; Edged Weapons; Lance; War Club

References

Ashdown, Charles H. *British and Foreign Arms and Armor.* London: T. C. and E. C. Jack, 1909.

Yenne, Bill, ed. *The Lost Field Notes of Franklin R. Johnston's Life among the American Indians.* Cobb, CA: First Glance Books, 1997.

Shoshones

Native American group of the Great Plains, Great Basin, and West divided into three groups: the Eastern, Northern, and Western Shoshones. The Eastern Shoshones, sometimes referred to as the Wind River Shoshones, lived in present-day western Wyoming since at least the 16th century. Thereafter they moved into the northern Great Plains, and by the late 18th century they inhabited areas of Wyoming, northern Colorado, and Montana. The Comanches separated from the Shoshones around 1700, moving toward Texas.

Buffalo hunting and fur trading provided the bulk of the Eastern Shoshones' food, clothing, shelter, and economic activity. Buffalo hunts were augmented by small-scale seasonal agriculture and the use of wild plants and trees. Because of the centrality of the buffalo hunt, the Eastern Shoshones were seminomadic. As with many Native American tribes, the Eastern Shoshones were decimated mainly by European-introduced diseases; by 1840 the tribe had dwindled to as few as 3,000 people.

The Eastern Shoshones divided themselves into three to five bands during the winter months, setting up camp principally in the Wind River Valley. Each band had its own chief, military society, and warriors. Warfare with enemy tribes was highly destructive to the Shoshones and from the early to mid-18th century onward proceeded nearly uninterrupted. In the 19th century the Eastern Shoshones frequently allied themselves with white Americans and, as a result, underwent a renaissance, enhancing themselves both demographically and materially.

From 1810 to about 1840 the Eastern Shoshones were major players in the buffalo hide trade. When settlers began arriving on their lands in the 1850s, they tried their best to coexist under the leadership of their chief, Washakie. The Eastern Shoshones often allied with the U.S. Army to fight the Lakota Sioux. The Eastern Shoshones became disenchanted, however, when in 1878 the U.S. government forced the Arapahos, one of their perennial enemies, to join them on their reservation. Destruction of the buffalo herds essentially ended the traditional Shoshone cultural and economic ways by the 1880s. Until well into the 20th century, the surviving Eastern Shoshones lived a hard-scrabble existence as their numbers continued to decline.

The Northern Shoshones demonstrated more of a cultural delineation than an ethnic or even geographic orientation. They shared some cultural traits with the Bannock, Ute, and Paiute tribes as well as the Eastern Shoshones. As such, the Northern Shoshone culture blended features of tribes found in the Great Plains, the Northwest Plateau, and the Great Basin. By the early 19th century the Northern Shoshones inhabited eastern Idaho, western Wyoming, and northeastern Utah. They numbered some 30,000 people prior to European contact, but by the mid-1800s they numbered just 3,000 or so. Seminomadic, the Northern Shoshones divided themselves into impermanent bands that often lacked long-term leadership; indeed, some bands had no discernible leadership at all. Like the Eastern Shoshones, the Northern Shoshones were largely reliant on buffalo for their economic activity and daily subsistence. They augmented this by hunting elk, deer, and mountain sheep and employing local flora that they used for food and medicinal purposes. Salmon also formed a key part of their diet.

After they integrated horses into their culture in the late 17th century, the Northern Shoshones, along with the Bannocks, adopted some of the Great Plains cultural traits, including warrior societies and tepees. By the mid-19th century the Northern Shoshones had come in conflict with the Blackfeet and were prevented from moving farther west. As whites moved into Northern Shoshone lands, competition for resources was keen, and by the 1860s most of the beaver and buffalo had been hunted to near extinction, forcing radical lifestyle and cultural changes. This led to raids against American settlements and wagon trains. After increased

Shoshone Native Americans at Fort Washakie, Wyoming, in 1892. This is the last photograph of Chief Washakie, who is on the extreme left, standing and pointing. (National Archives)

conflict with whites, the Northern Shoshones were placed on reservations by the mid to late 1870s. Perhaps the most famous Northern Shoshone was Sacagawea, who served as a guide during the 1804–1806 Lewis and Clark expedition.

The Western Shoshones' territory ranged from south-central Idaho, northwestern Utah, and central Nevada south and west to California's Death Valley. From as many as 10,000 people before European contact, the Western Shoshones dwindled to perhaps only 2,000 by 1820. The group lived in loosely organized bands, the membership of which was quite fluid. Chiefs had few powers other than directing hunting and gathering and allocating resources. Because of the harsh climate and terrain that predominated within their territory, buffalo were not prevalent. Thus, the seminomadic Western Shoshones relied primarily on native plants and small game for sustenance.

The influx of Mormons into the Great Salt Lake region beginning in the 1840s placed much pressure on the Western Shoshones. The discovery of the Comstock Lode in Nevada in 1857 attracted a flood of new white settlers, which further disrupted the Shoshones' way of life. Falling victim to disease and near starvation, the Western Shoshone sometimes resorted to raids on white settlements. After 1860 when the Pony Express routinely traversed their lands, the Western Shoshones began staging raids, which almost always brought retaliation by local or U.S. military forces. During the 1870s some Western Shoshones joined the Bannocks

and Northern Paiutes in their struggle against white encroachment. Many refused to be relocated to reservations, and they tried their best to retain as much of their original culture as they could.

PAUL G. PIERPAOLI JR.

See also

Arapahos; Buffalo; Comanches; Paiutes, Northern; Pony Express; Sacagawea; Utes; Washakie

References

Bial, Raymond. *The Shoshone*. Tarrytown, NY: Benchmark Books, 2001.
Dramer, Kim. *Shoshone*. New York: Chelsea House, 1996.

Shoshone War
Event Date: 1863

Key conflict fought for control of the Great Basin of the West (centered on the present-day state of Utah) involving the Shoshone (Shoshoni) tribe and federal volunteer troops from January to October 1863. The culmination of a quarter century of raids and skirmishes, the Shoshone War compelled the U.S. government to recognize those Native Americans occupying the territory through which the western trails passed and to make a concerted attempt at peace through treaties combined with the threat of overwhelming military force.

The primary cause of the Shoshone War was the steady encroachment of white settlers onto the traditional homelands of three distinct Shoshone populations: the Eastern Shoshones, the Northern Shoshones, and the Western Shoshones. Major developments that had placed increased pressure on Shoshone lands and resources included the influx of Mormon settlers beginning in 1847; the California Gold Rush (1848–1849); the mail route running through Deep Creek, completed in 1854; the creation of the Overland Stage Route in 1858; the 1859 Comstock Lode Silver Rush; the Oregon Gold Rush of 1860; the establishment of the Pony Express (1860); and the Grasshopper Creek Gold Rush of 1862. The establishment of farms, ranches, and mail stations near the best springs and the most productive lands provoked frustrated and starving Shoshone bands to raid for horses and food supplies.

The late summer of 1862 found the Shoshones particularly desperate and aggressive when Colonel Patrick Edward Connor and his California Volunteers (the 3rd California Infantry) arrived in the Great Basin to protect the overland route between Carson City and Fort Bridger. Worried about California's vulnerability to Confederate forces during the American Civil War (1861–1865), the U.S. government ordered Connor to secure lines of communication and sources of gold and silver vital to the Union war effort. Numerous attacks by separate Native American bands along the trails, including the Western Shoshones' killing of 12 whites at Gravelly Ford in September 1862, spurred Connor to dispatch Major Edward McGarry and two companies to the Humboldt River to kill all Shoshones they encountered. This order resulted in 25 Native American deaths. Connor continued to batter the Shoshones, while Utah superintendent of Indian affairs James Doty postponed assistance and treaties until May 1863 when he could also negotiate with the Bannocks and Utes. The delay proved disastrous, as hunger led Native American bands to increase the frequency and ferocity of their attacks.

Chief Bear Hunter of the Northern Shoshones concentrated his attacks on the mail and stage lines, and he and his followers became the primary target of Connor's military campaign. In November 1862 Connor sent McGarry to rescue a boy taken by the Shoshones some two years earlier. McGarry proceeded to attack Bear Hunter's camp, chasing him and others into a canyon where three more Indians died. Bear Hunter surrendered and was held hostage until the boy was returned. In retaliation, the Shoshones killed two miners within a half mile of their winter camp at Bear River.

When raids on white settlements continued, Connor sent McGarry to retrieve the stolen stock. At Bear River Crossing on December 6, McGarry executed four Shoshones for their failure to cooperate. A flurry of Shoshone attacks ensued through January 1863, prompting Utah Territory Supreme Court chief justice John F. Kinney to issue arrest warrants for chiefs Bear Hunter, Sagwitch, and Sanpitch.

Connor decided that a massive assault on the Shoshones' winter camp was the most effective approach. Sending Captain Samuel Hoyt with 69 infantrymen, 13 wagons, and 2 howitzers toward Cache Valley on January 22, 1863, Connor waited two days before he and McGarry led 220 cavalrymen to a rendezvous point in hopes of misleading Shoshone scouts as to his intentions. At Bear River on January 29, 1863, Connor's four-hour attack killed at least 224 Shoshones and wounded 70 men, women, and children while capturing 170 horses and destroying all winter provisions and supplies. The California Volunteers lost 17 men.

This attack is often referred to as a massacre by historians. The number of Shoshone killed was likely closer to 300. Bear Hunter died. Sanpitch and Sagwitch escaped, as did Chief Pocatello of the Fort Hall Shoshones days before the attack.

Although the battle was an important victory for the government, removing one of its most troublesome opponents and convincing the Shoshones of the military's superior firepower, the engagement would stand as perhaps the single greatest loss of Native American lives in western battles with whites and precipitated major unrest among bands.

Eluding U.S. troops for months, the hostile Shoshones could manage little more than small raids. Attacks were met with military counterattacks, none larger than Captain Samuel Smith's killing of 53 Goshutes in early May 1863. Connor strengthened the area around Fort Ruby to the west and Fort Bridger to the east while establishing Camp Connor near Soda Springs to the north. By the summer Doty negotiated five treaties with the Shoshones: the Treaty of Fort Bridger with the Eastern Shoshones (July 2), the Treaty of Box-Elder with the Northwestern Shoshones (July 30), the Treaty of Ruby Valley with the Western Shoshones (October 1), the Treaty of Tooele Valley with the Goshutes (October 12), and the Treaty of Soda Springs with the Fort Hall Bannock-Shoshones (October 14). All of the treaties contained nearly identical terms, promising 20 years of annuity payments in exchange for guarantees of safe passage and settlement. Thus, by October 1863 the Shoshone War had been brought to a close. The conflict and the agreements concluding it demilitarized the Shoshones and demonstrated the fundamental role of U.S. troops in safeguarding the western trails.

Michael F. Dove

See also

Bear River, Battle of; Connor, Patrick Edward; Goshute War; Shoshones

References

Christensen, Scott R. *Sagwitch: Shoshone Chieftain, Mormon Elder, 1822–1887*. Logan: Utah State University Press, 1999.

Madsen, Brigham D. *Glory Hunter: A Biography of Patrick Edward Connor*. Salt Lake City: University of Utah Press, 1990.

Madsen, Brigham D. *The Shoshoni Frontier and the Bear River Massacre*. Salt Lake City: University of Utah Press, 1985.

Shulush Homa

See Red Shoe

Sibley, Henry Hastings
Birth Date: February 20, 1811
Death Date: February 18, 1891

Businessman, politician, Minnesota Militia officer, and U.S. Army officer. Henry Hastings Sibley was born on February 20, 1811, in Detroit, Michigan. He had little formal education but became a shrewd and effective businessman. As a young man he moved to the Minnesota frontier, where he worked for the American Fur Company as a clerk and fur trapper.

Sibley proved adept at turning a profit in the fur business, and in 1835 he constructed the first private residence in all of Minnesota. In 1849 he was elected to the U.S. House of Representatives as a territorial delegate and worked hard to establish the Minnesota Territory. He served until 1853. After Minnesota was admitted to the Union, Sibley served as the state's first governor (1858–1860).

In August 1862 the Santee Sioux, led by Little Crow, staged an armed rebellion throughout the Minnesota River Valley. The Sioux were reacting to increased white encroachment onto their lands and had been emboldened to fight back after most Union troops serving in the region had been sent to the East to fight in the American Civil War (1861–1865), which was then under way. The violence began on August 17, 1862, when Native Americans attacked a white settlement in Meeker County during which 5 settlers were killed. Similar attacks occurred in rapid succession, stunning white Minnesotans. Sibley offered his services to the state's governor, who appointed him colonel in the state militia with the task of putting down the Minnesota Sioux Uprising. Sibley assembled some 1,500 militiamen and went in search of the Santee Sioux warriors.

Sibley fought several engagements, finally subduing the Native Americans at the Battle of Wood Lake on September 23, 1862. This effectively ended the uprising, which had nonetheless claimed between 500 and 800 lives among whites. On September 29 Sibley was given a commission as a brigadier general of volunteers in the U.S. Army largely because of his efforts during the uprising. Sibley never actually held a command after that time, and the U.S. Senate failed to confirm his commission, which expired on March 4, 1863. Nevertheless, within days Sibley was reappointed, and the Senate confirmed this on March 20. Meanwhile, Little Crow and a number of his followers had managed to escape into the Dakotas.

After establishing a headquarters at St. Paul and augmenting his force with Brigadier General Alfred Sully's cavalrymen, Sibley launched an offensive into the Dakotas to ensure that the Sioux would not mount further attacks. The resulting Sully-Sibley Campaign ended with the July 28, 1863, Battle of Stony Lake. During the campaign Sibley's forces suffered only some dozen casualties; the Sioux lost at least 150 men. After that Sibley was charged with providing security along the western frontier. In November 1865 Sibley was brevetted major general for his "efficient and meritorious" service. He mustered out of the service in April 1866.

After the war Sibley continued his business and public service career with considerable success. He was president of a gas company, an insurance company, and a bank. He also served in the Minnesota legislature and was a member of the Board of Regents for the University of Minnesota. Sibley died in St. Paul, Minnesota, on February 18, 1891.

Paul G. Pierpaoli Jr.

See also
Little Crow; Minnesota Sioux Uprising; Sully, Alfred; Sully-Sibley Campaigns

References
Gilman, Rhoda R. *Henry Hastings Sibley: Divided Heart.* St. Paul: Minnesota Historical Society Press, 2004.
Pedersen, Kern. *Makers of Minnesota: An Illustrated History of the Builders of Our State.* St. Paul: Minnesota Centennial Commission, 1949.

Sieber, Albert
Birth Date: February 27, 1843
Death Date: February 19, 1907

Soldier, prospector, and U.S. Army scout. Albert Sieber was born on February 27, 1843, in Mingolsheim, Baden, Germany, the 13th of 14 children. He was only two years old when his father died, and in 1848 Sieber's mother immigrated to the United States with her surviving 8 children (6 others had already died). The family settled first in Pennsylvania and then in Minnesota.

Sieber received little formal education and took on a variety of menial jobs before enlisting in the 1st Minnesota Volunteer Infantry Regiment in March 1862. He saw action in a number of campaigns during the American Civil War (1861–1865), mainly in the East, and mustered out in late 1865.

Briefly returning to Minnesota after the Civil War, Sieber soon headed west, where he was a prospector in Nevada and California. Between 1868 and 1871 he managed a ranch in the Arizona Territory. In 1871 he was chosen by Brigadier General George Crook to be his chief scout. As such Sieber participated in most of Apache expeditions from 1871 to 1873. After most of the campaigning had ended, he remained in the Arizona and New Mexico territories and helped round up Yavapais and Apaches for placement on the San Carlos Reservation in Arizona.

In 1883 Sieber accompanied Crook's force into Mexico's Sierra Nevada mountains in a campaign to pursue and capture Geronimo, a Chiricahua Apache leader who had been waging a guerrilla war against both Americans and Mexicans. Geronimo finally surrendered in 1886. The following year Sieber was shot and wounded during an attempted rebellion at the San Carlos Reservation. He stayed at San Carlos for a number of years and became an advocate for the Native Americans there, who he believed were being ill-treated by the U.S. government.

Disenchanted with government policies, Sieber left the employ of the government in 1891 and once again turned to prospecting. On February 19, 1907, he was killed in a construction accident on the Apache Trail in present-day Gila County, Arizona. Sieber had been supervising an Apache work crew building a road designed to supply the planned Roosevelt Dam on the Salt River.

PAUL G. PIERPAOLI JR.

See also

Apaches; Apache Wars; Crawford, Emmet; Crook, George; Gatewood, Charles Bare; Geronimo; San Carlos Reservation; Scouts, Native American; Yavapais

References

Bourke, John G. *On the Border with Crook.* Lincoln: University of Nebraska Press, 1971.

Cruse, Thomas. *Apache Days and After.* Norman: University of Oklahoma Press, 1987.

Robinson, Charles M., III. *General Crook and the Western Frontier.* Norman: University of Oklahoma Press, 2001.

Sioux

A northern Plains nation made up of three major tribes: the Eastern Sioux or Dakotas, the Middle Sioux or Yanktonai-Yanktons, and the Western Sioux or Lakotas. The Sioux speak mutually intelligible dialects of the same Siouan language. The groups were closely aligned at the time French explorer Pierre Radisson found them located in western Wisconsin and northeastern Minnesota. They lived in a woodlands pattern, subsisting on a mixture of farming, gathering, and hunting. Their principal crops were maize, beans, and squash in the southern region and wild rice in the northern region. They also frequently ventured out onto the prairies in search of bison.

Under pressure from the better-armed Ojibwas, the Sioux moved west and south. By 1804 the Sioux were situated on the prairies between the Mississippi and Missouri rivers and moving westward. The Dakotas were in southern Minnesota, while the Yanktonai-Yanktons were in what would become the eastern Dakotas. The Lakotas migrated onto the Great Plains and were west of the Missouri River when they encountered the Lewis and Clark expedition (1804–1806). The Lakotas drove the Kiowas from the Black Hills and were pushing against the Crows in the Powder River Country of Wyoming and Montana. The Dakotas and the Yanktonai-Yanktons were now sedentary, relying on farming and hunting for subsistence. The Lakotas, however, adopted the nomadic Great Plains culture of horses, bison, and tepees. The Lakotas become the prototypical Indians of the Plains, although they adopted the horse later than their neighbors.

The U.S. government tried to maintain peace between the Dakotas and Ojibwas with some success. The Dakotas lived in peace with the whites of Minnesota, northern Iowa, and the eastern Dakotas until the 1862 Sioux uprising in Minnesota. During the uprising, which lasted six weeks, the Dakotas raided the Minnesota River Valley, killing 500 whites while losing many of their own people to volunteer troops and civilians. The uprising ended with the dispersion of the Dakotas as far as Canada and out to their Yankton and Yanktonai cousins. Some 400 were sentenced to be hanged, but President Abraham Lincoln pardoned all but 38, who were known to have committed murder and rape during the unrest. Those individuals were hanged in Mankato, Minnesota, in early 1863. By 1870 fewer than 100 Sioux remained in Minnesota, although many subsequently moved back onto reservations established in the state. The Yankton-Yanktonais attempted to resist settler pressure in central South Dakota but succumbed to the inevitable, signing a treaty in 1858 that restricted them to small reservations there.

Moving west, the Lakotas made many tribal enemies. By holding their territory against all comers, they made more. As the Lakotas moved onto the Plains, war became an integral part of their culture. Manhood and social respect for men were determined by their abilities and bravery in warfare; in this way young men acquired respect and also obtained wealth in horses. Women and children captives were integrated into the tribe, building its population further.

The Lakotas were often at war with their neighbors. To the west, the Crows were their most constant opponents. The Lakotas finally pushed the Crows out of the Powder River region of Wyoming and Montana. To the north the Lakotas warred with the Blackfeet and the Assiniboines. To their east the Lakotas raided the Mandan, Arikara, and Hidatsa tribes. To the south the Lakotas fought with the Pawnees of Nebraska and Kansas. The Lakotas were also capable of making allies among their neighbors, however. Although the Lakotas had pushed the Cheyennes from the Black Hills region, as the two moved farther west, they came to be close allies, often traveling together along with the Arapahos. By 1800 the three peoples had an alliance, and Lakota war parties often included Cheyenne and Arapaho warriors.

The Lakotas had little contact with whites until the 1850s as more settlers traversed the southern edges of Lakota territory. The first significant conflict, known as the Grattan Massacre of 1854, resulted from the overconfidence of U.S. Army lieutenant John Grattan. Ordered to arrest a Lakota warrior accused of killing cattle near Fort Laramie in Wyoming, Grattan's escort of 30 men attacked the suspected Lakota village and was quickly wiped out. The U.S. government responded by sending a 600-man expedition under Brevet Brigadier General William Harney. Harney's force advanced into Nebraska and attacked a village, killing and capturing many Lakotas. Sporadic conflict continued throughout the late 1850s as more settlers moved west and plans unfolded to begin building railroads through the Plains.

The Lakotas were not easily subdued. Between the mid-1850s and 1877, they actively resisted white encroachment. Under Chief Red Cloud, they were successful in driving whites out of the Powder River Country and from the Bozeman Trail after Red Cloud's War

A group of Sioux posed in front of a tipi, 1908. (Library of Congress)

(1866–1868), which witnessed the siege of Fort Phil Kearny and the Fetterman Massacre. The great Sioux war chief Crazy Horse rose to prominence during this war, but it was only later in the 1870s that he became an iconic figure both to the Lakotas and the whites.

By 1870 the Lakotas and their allies numbered more than 20,000 people, about a quarter of whom were warriors. War parties could number 500–1,000 warriors, numbers unheard of in earlier times. The climax of warfare came with the government decision to push the Native Americans onto reservations. By restricting the Plains Indians to reservations, millions of acres opened for white settlement, the huge bison herds disappeared, and railroad construction expanded.

In 1874 Lieutenant Colonel George Custer led an expedition into the Black Hills. This exploratory endeavor discovered gold, which brought more pressure on the Lakotas and led to the final campaigns of the Plains Indian wars, including the Great Sioux War (1876–1877). In the process, Custer and more than 260 of his men of the 7th Cavalry were killed in the Battle of the Little Bighorn (June 25–26, 1876) by the Lakota alliance led by Sitting Bull, Crazy Horse, Spotted Tail, and the Cheyenne and Arapaho warriors, led by Dull Knife and Black Bear. This was the largest defeat and loss of life by the U.S. Army in the Plains wars.

A concerted effort by the U.S. Army under colonels Ranald Mackenzie, Wesley Merritt, and Nelson A. Miles resulted in the pursuit and capture of many of the Lakotas, with Crazy Horse surrendering in May 1877; he was later killed in a scuffle with an arresting soldier. Sitting Bull fled to Canada with many of his people, remaining there until 1881, when he returned and surrendered himself and his people to the army.

The Lakotas were placed on reservations in the western Dakotas, where they remained. In 1890 the Ghost Dance movement, promising the return of the buffalo and, in the Lakota version, the disappearance of the whites, swept across the northern Plains. The Standing Rock Reservation agent, James McLaughlin, ordered the arrest of Sitting Bull, who was killed by a native policeman in the scuffle. Chief Big Foot and his band then fled from the Cheyenne River Agency, pursued by soldiers of the 7th Cavalry. The troops soon caught up with Big Foot's followers. Something triggered an outbreak of gunfire. When the smoke had cleared on Wounded Knee Creek, as many as 200 Lakotas lay dead, including women and children. The December 29, 1890, Battle of Wounded Knee (Wounded Knee Massacre) is regarded as the final event of the Indian Wars on the Great Plains.

STEFAN M. BROOKS

See also

Arapahos; Cheyennes; Crazy Horse; Fetterman Massacre; Fort Phil Kearny; Grattan Massacre; Great Sioux War; Little Bighorn, Battle of the; Mackenzie, Ranald Slidell; Merritt, Wesley; Miles, Nelson Appleton; Nakota Sioux; Pine Ridge Reservation; Red Cloud; Red Cloud's War; Sitting Bull; Standing Rock Reservation; Wounded Knee, Battle of

References

Carlson, Paul H. *The Plains Indians.* College Station: Texas A&M University Press, 1998.

Gibbon, Guy. *The Sioux: The Dakota and Lakota Nations.* Malden, MA: Blackwell, 2003.

Goodrich, Thomas. *Scalp Dance: Indian Warfare on the High Plains, 1865–1879.* Mechanicsburg, PA: Stackpole, 1997.

Hassrick, Royal B. *The Sioux: The Life and Customs of a Warrior Nation.* Norman: University of Oklahoma Press, 1964.

Hedren, Paul L., ed. *The Great Sioux War, 1876–77.* Helena: Montana Historical Society Press, 1991.

Olson, James C. *Red Cloud and the Sioux Problem.* Lincoln: University of Nebraska Press, 1965.

Sandoz, Mari. *Crazy Horse: The Strange Man of the Oglalas.* 3rd ed. Lincoln: University of Nebraska Press, 2008.

Utley, Robert M. *The Lance and the Shield: The Life and Times of Sitting Bull.* New York: Ballantine, 1993.

Sioux War

See Great Sioux War

Si Tanka

See Big Foot

Sitting Bull
Birth Date: ca. 1831
Death Date: December 15, 1890

Hunkpapa Lakota chief and holy man under whom the Lakota tribes in the mid-1870s united in their struggle against encroaching white settlement on the northern Plains. Sitting Bull (Tatanka-Iyotanka) was born around 1831 at a place the Lakota called Many Caches on the Grand River in present-day South Dakota. He received the name Tatanka-Iyotanka, which describes a buffalo bull sitting on its hind legs. At 14 years old he experienced his first battle in a raid against the Crow Nation. He first encountered American soldiers in June 1863 during a campaign in retaliation for the Minnesota Sioux Uprising in which the Lakotas had not participated. The next year Sitting Bull fought the U.S. volunteers at the Battle of Killdeer Mountain, and in 1865 he led a siege against Fort Rice in present-day North Dakota. Widely respected for his bravery and insight, he became head chief of the Lakota Nation around 1868.

In 1874 Lieutenant Colonel George Armstrong Custer led an army expedition that confirmed the presence of gold in the Black Hills of the Dakota Territory, an area sacred to many native tribes and placed off-limits to whites by the 1868 Fort Laramie Treaty. Despite this ban, white prospectors began to move into the Black Hills and provoked the Lakotas into defending their land. The U.S. government tried to purchase the Black Hills, but the tribes refused to sell. The government then set aside the Fort Laramie Treaty, and the commissioner of Indian affairs decreed that all Lakotas must return to their reservation by January 31, 1876, or be considered hostile. Sitting Bull and his people refused to return to the reservation.

In March 1876 brigadier generals George Crook and Alfred Terry and Colonel John Gibbon led separate army columns into the Yellowstone Valley. At his camp on Rosebud Creek in Montana Territory, Sitting Bull led the Lakota, Cheyenne, and Arapaho nations in the sun dance ritual, offering prayers to Wakan Tanka, their Great Spirit. During this ceremony Sitting Bull had a vision in which he saw soldiers falling into the Lakota camp like grasshoppers falling from the sky.

Inspired by Sitting Bull's vision, the Oglala Lakota war chief Crazy Horse, with 500 warriors, surprised Crook's troops on June

Hunkpapa Sioux Sitting Bull is one of the most celebrated Indian leaders in American history. He participated in many famous battles, most notably the Battle of the Little Bighorn in 1876, then joined Buffalo Bill's Wild West Show in 1885. (Library of Congress)

17, forcing them to retreat at the Battle of the Rosebud. The Lakotas now moved their camp to the valley of the Little Bighorn River, where 3,000 more Native Americans who had left the reservations joined them. On June 25 in the Battle of the Little Bighorn, the badly outnumbered troops of the 7th Cavalry, commanded by Custer, attacked the camp but were overwhelmed by the unexpectedly large Indian force. Custer and a large portion of the regiment were annihilated.

After this disaster the army sent thousands of troops into the Yellowstone Valley and the Black Hills and over the next year relentlessly pursued the Lakotas. Because the Lakotas had split up after the Battle of the Little Bighorn, the army was able to defeat them piecemeal. However, the defiant Sitting Bull led his band into Canada in May 1877. There he refused a pardon offered by General Terry, who had traveled to Canada for that purpose, in exchange for settling on a reservation.

After three years Sitting Bull, unable to feed his people, returned to the United States and surrendered to the commanding officer of Fort Buford in Montana on July 19, 1881. The army sent him to the Standing Rock Reservation and soon afterward farther down the Missouri River to Fort Randall because of fears that he might inspire a new uprising. Sitting Bull and his followers remained there as prisoners of war for almost two years.

On May 10, 1883, Sitting Bull rejoined his tribe at Standing Rock. James McLaughlin, the Indian agent in charge of the reservation, was determined not to give Sitting Bull any special privileges and even forced him to work in the fields. However, Sitting Bull still knew his own authority and spoke forcefully, although futilely, to a delegation of U.S. senators who presented him with a plan to open a part of the reservation to white settlers.

In 1885 Sitting Bull joined Buffalo Bill Cody's Wild West Show and earned $50 a week for riding once around the arena in addition to any fees that he obtained for his autograph and picture. During that time Sitting Bull shook hands with President Grover Cleveland, a sign to Sitting Bull that he was still regarded as a great chief. Unable to tolerate white society, he left the show after only four months. He returned to Standing Rock and lived in a cabin on the Grand River near where he had been born. He maintained his traditional ways despite the rules of the reservation, living with his two wives and rejecting Christianity. Sitting Bull did send his children to a nearby Christian school so they could learn to read and write.

Soon after his return, Sitting Bull had another vision in which a meadowlark sat beside him on a hill and said to him that a Lakota would kill him. In the autumn of 1890 a Miniconjou Lakota named Kicking Bear told Sitting Bull about the Ghost Dance, a ceremony that promised to rid the land of white people and restore the Native Americans' way of life. Because many Lakotas at the Pine Ridge and Rosebud reservations had already adopted the ceremony, U.S. Indian agents had called for troops to control the growing movement. Some authorities at Standing Rock, fearing that Sitting Bull would join the Ghost Dancers, sent 43 Lakota policemen to

apprehend him. Before dawn on December 15, 1890, the policemen forced their way into Sitting Bull's cabin and dragged him outside. During an ensuing gunfight between Sitting Bull's supporters and the Lakota policemen, one of the policemen shot Sitting Bull in the head. Sitting Bull was buried at Fort Yates in North Dakota, but in 1953 his remains were moved to Mobridge, South Dakota, where a granite shaft marks his grave.

ROBERT B. KANE

See also

Black Hills, South Dakota; Black Hills Gold Rush; Buffalo Bill's Wild West Show; Cavalry Regiment, 7th U.S.; Cheyennes; Crazy Horse; Crook, George; Custer, George Armstrong; Fort Laramie, Treaty of (1851); Fort Laramie, Treaty of (1868); Gall; Ghost Dance; Great Sioux War; Hunkpapa Sioux; Lakota Sioux; Little Bighorn, Battle of the; Pine Ridge Reservation; Rosebud, Battle of the; Terry, Alfred Howe

References

Larson, Robert W. *Gall: Lakota War Chief.* Norman: University of Oklahoma Press, 2007.
Michno, Gregory F. *Lakota Moon: The Indian Narrative of Custer's Defeat.* Missoula, MO: Mountain Press Publishing, 1997.
McMurtry, Larry. *Oh What a Slaughter: Massacres of the American West, 1846–1890.* New York: Simon and Schuster, 2005.
Utley, Robert M. *The Indian Frontier of the American West, 1846–1890.* Albuquerque: University of New Mexico Press, 1984.

Sitting Bull's War

See Great Sioux War

6th U.S. Cavalry Regiment

See Cavalry Regiment, 6th U.S.

Skitswishes

See Coeur d'Alenes

Skulking Way of War

A form of warfare in which attackers used stealth to surprise their enemies that was employed largely by Native Americans and later adopted by Europeans in North America. Ambushes were typical of the skulking way of war, as were raids on small isolated garrisons or settlements. Skulking tactics relied on detailed knowledge of local terrain and the cover of darkness to conceal movements and acquire positions from which to waylay foes. Attackers also exercised individual initiative, advancing or retreating in open order. Many times, individual combatants aimed and fired at specific targets on their own volition. Combatants usually did not press attacks against enemies who were well prepared to receive an assault, avoided pitched battles, and retreated if they were themselves ambushed.

Native Americans pursued skulking warfare throughout the era of the Indian Wars. Although other forms of combat occurred in particular cases, skulking tactics prevailed among American Indian warriors throughout the period. Over time, Native American combatants also replaced indigenous arms (bow and arrows, edged weapons, etc.) with firearms of European and later American manufacture as their primary weapon.

In contrast to the skulking way of war, conventional European warfare of the colonial period emphasized the role of prescribed orderly battle. Infantry moved in unison in compact close-order formations, handling and discharging weapons together in volleys fired under the direction of officers. Europeans and their colonial descendants varied in their abilities to adapt to or cope with skulking warfare. Militiamen from New France were largely successful in employing these tactics. In fact, they often joined with their American Indian allies in raiding the English colonial frontier during wars between the two countries.

English forces often had more difficulty coping with skulking foes, particularly in conflicts such as King Philip's War (1675–1676), in which effective military responses emphasized direct assaults on American Indian communities or employed native allies against aboriginal foes. However, by the mid-18th century, some British colonial units such as Rogers' Rangers were primarily employing skulking tactics. Skulking tactics saw widespread use among both Native American and U.S. forces in most of the Indian Wars that transpired from the 1790s to the 1890s.

Matthew S. Muehlbauer

See also

King Philip's War; Native American Warfare; Rogers, Robert

References

Hirsch, Adam J. "The Collision of Military Cultures in Seventeenth-Century New England." *Journal of American History* 74 (March 1988): 1187–1212.

Malone, Patrick M. *The Skulking Way of War: Technology and Tactics among the New England Indians.* Lanham, MD: Madison Books, 2000.

Otterbein, Keith F. "Why the Iroquois Won: An Analysis of Iroquois Military Tactics." *Ethnohistory* 11 (1964): 56–63.

Starkey, Armstrong. *European and Native American Warfare, 1675–1815.* Norman: University of Oklahoma Press, 1998.

Slaughter of the Innocents
Start Date: February 25, 1643
End Date: February 26, 1643

Attack by Dutch troops outside New Amsterdam (present-day New York City) during February 25–26, 1643, in which two camps of Wappinger natives were overrun without warning, resulting in the deaths of more than 100 men, women, and children. The attack occurred during Kieft's War (1639–1645).

New Netherland's fifth governor, Willem Kieft, arrived in the New World in 1638. His tenure was marked by a succession of crises and controversies. Conflict between various Native American peoples and the Dutch had become routine. Aggressive territorial expansion also contributed to the tensions. When Kieft arrived, he was not pleased with the condition of New Amsterdam, the main settlement in the colony. Defenses, especially the main fort, were in poor condition. To correct these problems, he made numerous reforms in government and military administration.

Among Kieft's changes was a heavy tax on the local natives, who were part of the Algonquian group, in return for protection against hostile natives such as the Mohawks. The Mohawks were important trading partners with the Dutch, and Kieft used them to terrorize other native peoples who refused to pay the tax. In 1641 several tribes refused to pay the tax and then attacked an outlying Dutch settlement. This led to a four-year struggle between the Dutch and various Native American groups.

In the spring of 1642 the governor sent an expeditionary force to subdue the Raritans, one of the offending tribes. A treaty with them, however, prevented further bloodshed. Yet Kieft was determined to collect the tax from other Native Americans. In early 1643 he put pressure on the Wappingers, who lived above Manhattan Island along the lower Hudson River. Kieft ordered a large party of Mohawks to collect the tribute that had not been paid. Numbering about 500 people, the Wappingers fled ahead of the invaders. Most took refuge with the Hackensacks at Pavonia (present-day Jersey City, New Jersey). Others fled to Corlaer's Hook in northern Manhattan.

Kieft badly mismanaged the situation. The fleeing Native Americans arrived seeking Dutch protection and had no intention of waging battle. Kieft did not see it that way, however. In late February without any warning or provocation, the governor dispatched a Mohawk party to Pavonia to initiate an attack. Eighty Dutch soldiers followed closely behind. At the same time, a smaller number of Dutch troops killed the native refugees at Corlaer's Hook.

During the night of February 25–26, 1643, some 100 Native American men, women, and children were brutally murdered in what was later known as the Slaughter of the Innocents. The Dutch soldiers returned to New Amsterdam the following day carrying with them the severed heads of nearly 80 natives. Some of the Dutch then used the heads like footballs. Kieft also ordered the public torture of some 30 native captives.

Kieft took immense delight at the success of the raid, but this Dutch atrocity served to further incense the local natives. A number of them subsequently united in waging war against the Dutch, burning farms and killing settlers. Throughout the remainder of the year, the Dutch suffered numerous losses fighting the natives. In February 1644 Dutch forces managed to kill more than 500 natives in the region of Westchester. Finally, in 1645 after four years of steady conflict, Kieft negotiated a treaty ending a war that had claimed more than 1,000 lives on both sides.

CHARLES FRANCIS HOWLETT

See also

Algonquins; Dutch-Indian Wars; Kieft, Willem; Kieft's War; Mohawks

References

Ellis, David M., et al. *A History of New York State*. 2nd ed. Ithaca, NY: Cornell University Press, 1967.

Jennings, Francis. *The Invasion of America: Indians, Colonialism, and the Cant of Conquest*. 1976; reprint, Chapel Hill: University of North Carolina Press, 2010.

Shorto, Russell. *The Island at the Center of the World: The Epic Story of Dutch Manhattan and the Forgotten Colony That Shaped America*. New York: Doubleday, 2004.

Slavery among Native Americans

Traditions of slavery arising from Native American cultures and from European settlement in America overlapped in the wars fought between native inhabitants of America and the fledgling United States. American Indians took both European and African captives as slaves, welcomed runaway European-descended servants and African slaves into their tribes, and at various times and places bought African slaves from European and American settlers.

The United States did not in general practice enslavement of Native Americans, but this was fairly widespread in colonial times from Massachusetts to South Carolina. Hundreds of natives were sold to planters in the West Indies after King Philip's War (1675–1676). The enslaved portion of the American population after the American Revolutionary War (1775–1783) included many with mixed African and Indian as well as European blood.

The Westo tribe, which settled along the Savannah River, sold captives from neighboring tribes to the Virginia colony in the 17th century. Although also selling deer skins, the Westos found that they could get a higher return for slaves from tobacco farmers facing a limited supply of labor. The Yamasees captured members of other tribes to sell as slaves to the South Carolina colony based in Charles Town (Charleston) for 40 years. When the Yamasees turned on the British colony in 1715 and lost, they in turn were sold by the thousands to the West Indies.

The force that defeated the Yamasees included 600 European settlers, 400 African slaves, and 100 free Native Americans. People designated with the status of servant were almost universally included in colonial militia in the 1600s, when the main duty of the militia was guarding against attacks by neighboring Native American nations. The word "slave" was not yet in common use; the term "servant" included indentured servants and servants "for life."

A Massachusetts ordinance of 1652 specified that "Negroes, Indians and Scotchmen" were required to train in the militia. A 1656 ordinance exempted "Negroes and Indians," but a 1660 ordinance reduced the exemption to "one servant of every magistrate

and teaching elder." In 1693 "Indians and Negroes" were exempted from military training, but all persons exempt from training were to be provided with arms and ammunition.

Connecticut and New Jersey militia laws from 1672 and 1682 required all males ages 16 to 60 to bear arms and made several occupational exemptions but none for race or servitude. A New Jersey law for training and mustering of the militia adopted in 1668 has a footnote specifying that blacks or persons of color were not exempt. By the early 1700s Connecticut exempted "Indians and Negroes" from military service, while New Jersey provided that no man under 21 years of age and no slave or indentured servant could be enlisted without the written permission of a parent, guardian, master, or mistress. Rhode Island in 1665 and again in 1667 provided allowances for poor people to maintain arms for militia duty and specified that parents and masters use the allowance to maintain their sons and servants in arms.

By the 1700s many colonies either routinely excluded slaves from the militia, excluded all "Negroes and Indians," or provided that free blacks and Indians report without arms to perform labor duties or serve as drummers in the militia. However, South Carolina continued well into the 1700s to provide fines for any slave owner who avoided the enlistment of his slaves in the militia.

Many Native Americans nations practiced some form of slavery before the arrival of Europeans. Taking captives as slaves was part of the culture of the Mississippian communities and remained in succeeding cultures of the Southeast. The peoples known as the Five Civilized Tribes (the Cherokees, Choctaws, Creeks, Chickasaws, and Seminoles) and, to a lesser extent, the Shawnees and the Delawares came to adopt slavery on a large scale in the manner of their European and American neighbors. The northwestern Pacific coast was also notable for a ranked society whereby acquisition of property, including slaves, increased a man's status. Nomadic tribes such as the Comanches put captives who were not killed outright to work as slaves, eventually adopting into a family those who proved themselves.

The Comanches, Hopis, Navajos, and other peoples of the Southwest were subjected to slave raiding by Mexican landowners. The Comanches and Apaches in particular launched counterraids on northern Mexican villages. Large numbers of captives from raids into Mexico became Comanches; smaller numbers of white and African captives were treated in the same manner. Although there are some reports that the Comanches believed that black men had no souls, this is contradicted by the fact that some warriors had black scalps on their shields. Captive women often became second wives and were given the more menial household work.

Words that could be translated into English as "slavery," "slave," "adoption," and "prisoner" were used interchangeably in many American Indian languages. For example, the Cherokee word *ah-hutsi* means "captive" in all of these senses. Mohawk chief Joseph Brant, who fought as a British ally in the American Revolutionary War, had estates at Burlington Bay and Grand River where, by contemporary accounts, "runaway Negroes remained working and living with Indians." Reports conflict as to whether these may have been free people or may have been Brant's slaves. Lieutenant Alexander Fraser wrote that the Illinois tribe had "a great many Negroes who are obliged to labor very hard." These would most likely have been acquired from the French or the Spanish who dominated the Mississippi River Valley until the early 19th century.

Many members of the Creek tribe owned African slaves. During the American Revolutionary War and the War of 1812, British officers rewarded their Creek allies with slaves, while the Creeks also captured slaves during raids on American plantations. The Creeks known as Red Sticks, who responded to Tecumseh and Tenskwatawa's call for a unified war against expansion by the United States, were forced from Alabama into Spanish-ruled Florida during 1813–1814. After losing the Battle of Horseshoe Bend (March 27, 1814) to an army led by Andrew Jackson, they allied with bands of runaway African slaves. Among the Creeks, black people who were free had high status, and there was no aversion to intermarriage, although courts of the United States often refused to recognize such marriages.

Removal of the five southern tribes during the Andrew Jackson administration to land in what is now Oklahoma also removed the slaves belonging to tribal members. By the time that removal began in 1835, 209 Cherokees owned 1,600 slaves. Adoption of a plantation economy worked by slaves had required and made possible the replacement of communal land cultivation with individual ownership in the shrinking land area not taken up with European settlement. In fact, the designation "Five Civilized Tribes" may have derived not only from their adoption of a written language and formal government, as was the case with the Cherokees, but from the tribes' adoption of a slave-based economy. There was even a revolt by Cherokee-owned slaves in 1842 that was joined by slaves of Creek and Choctaw masters.

The Seminoles did not depend on slavery to the same extent and welcomed runaway slaves more consistently than did most tribes. The very name of the Seminole tribe derives from the Creek word *simanoli,* meaning "wild" or "runaway," and is closely related to the Spanish word *cimarron,* which is in turn the root of the word "maroon," used in Caribbean lands for communities of runaway slaves. The Seminole tribe emerged from the remnants of several tribes native to Florida, some Lower Creeks, and descendants of runaway slaves who left South Carolina and Georgia as early as 1687. The tribe became firmly established in Florida after 1750.

At the beginning of the American Civil War (1861–1865), the Confederacy signed treaties with the Creeks, Choctaws, Chickasaws, Seminoles, Cherokees, Osages, Senecas, Shawnees, Quapaws, Wichitas, and Comanches (or whatever portion of tribal leadership was favorable to the South) that offered statehood to several tribes at whatever time they chose to accept it. A history of slave ownership combined with attractive possibilities in the doctrine of states' rights motivated many from the Indian Territory to enlist in the Confederate Army. The result was to split most tribes between mixed-blood slaveholders and full-blood nonslaveholders together with African-descended free tribal members and slaves.

CHARLES ROSENBERG

See also

Brant, Joseph; Cherokee War; French and Indian War; Indian Removal Act; King Philip's War; Pequot War; Red Sticks; Seminole War, First; Seminole War, Second; Yamasee War

References

Berlin, Ira. *Many Thousands Gone: The First Two Centuries of Slavery in North America.* Cambridge: Belknap Press of Harvard University Press, 1998.

Gallay, Alan. *The Indian Slave Trade: The Rise of the English Empire in the American South, 1670–1717.* New Haven, CT: Yale University Press, 2002.

Slim Buttes, Battle of
Start Date: September 9, 1876
End Date: September 10, 1876

Battle fought between the U.S. Army and members of the Miniconjou and Oglala Sioux in the Great Sioux War of 1876–1877. The engagement took place at the Great Sioux Reservation in present-day South Dakota. Following Colonel Joseph Reynolds's defeat in the Battle of the Powder River (March 17, 1876), the disappointing action in the Battle of the Rosebud (June 17, 1876), and the disaster at the Battle of the Little Bighorn (June 25, 1876), Brigadier General George Crook, in command of elements of the 2nd and 3rd Cavalry regiments as well as a detachment from the 4th Infantry Regiment, linked up with the 5th Cavalry Regiment under Colonel Wesley Merritt in early August and continued to pursue the Lakotas and Northern Cheyennes.

In a manner more suited to the guerrilla fighter in Crook, he ordered his column stripped down to bare essentials so that no supply wagons or excess remounts would slow his movements. Supplies were carried by mules, and the men were expected to take excellent care of their mounts. This force marched down Rosebud Creek and along the Tongue and Powder rivers. The column eventually shifted across rough country to the Little Missouri River and then swung south toward the Black Hills, a march of nearly 1,800 miles across some of the most demanding terrain in North America. All along the route the column found evidence that the Native Americans were near starvation and abandoning valuable supplies as they moved, but contact eluded Crook's weary force as the terrain and summer weather punished both pursued and pursuers. So depleted was Crook's column that his pursuit earned the nickname "Horsemeat March," as men were forced to kill their mounts for food.

Finally on September 9 after four and a half months in the field, Captain Anson Mills and 130 troops of the 3rd Cavalry caught up

A horsedrawn stretcher transports a soldier wounded in the Black Hills of South Dakota during the Battle of Slim Buttes, part of the Great Sioux War, during September 9–10, 1876. (National Archives)

with Chief American Horse and his camp of 37 Lakota lodges near present-day Reva, South Dakota. Mills's cavalrymen then drove the stunned Lakotas toward the bluffs of Gap Creek. The Lakotas put up a stubborn defense until Crook arrived later in the afternoon with the balance of his command. Crook continued to pressure American Horse and his force until Crook was attacked by warriors from a nearby camp, led by Crazy Horse. By nightfall the battle was stalemated.

On the morning of September 10 Crook, despite his overwhelming numbers, resumed his plodding advance against the Sioux while guarding against further attacks from Crazy Horse. Once the soldiers cleared the bluffs, Crook had 23 Lakota prisoners and 15 wounded soldiers to care for. As night fell he destroyed the village, buried his dead, and prepared to resume his march.

Throughout the next day Crook pushed his exhausted force toward Deadwood, all the while fighting an effective rear-guard action. By September 12 Crook's column was resupplied but effectively broken. That the men were able to engage the small Lakota force at Slim Buttes was a notable feat. In the battle Crook lost 2 soldiers and 1 civilian guide killed in action, while 15 soldiers were wounded. Crook reported 14 Lakotas killed and Chief American Horse mortally wounded. All 23 Lakota warriors captured in the battle were returned to the Rosebud Agency.

PATRICK R. JENNINGS

See also

American Horse; Crazy Horse; Crook, George; Great Sioux War; Lakota Sioux; Little Bighorn, Battle of the; Merritt, Wesley; Miniconjou Sioux; Oglala Sioux; Powder River Expedition; Rosebud, Battle of the

References

Gray, John S. *Centennial Campaign: The Sioux War of 1876.* Norman: University of Oklahoma Press, 1988.

Rickey, Don, Jr. *Forty Miles a Day on Beans and Hay.* Norman: University of Oklahoma Press, 1963.

Stewart, Edgar I. *Custer's Luck.* Norman: University of Oklahoma Press, 1989.

Smallpox

A systemic viral disease that occurs in two forms: variola major, which carries 25 percent mortality, and variola minor, with a 1 percent mortality rate. The disease is caused by an orthopoxvirus. This DNA-based organism is the largest virus that infects animals. The virus initially multiplies in the bloodstream before infecting internal organs, especially the lungs, liver, and spleen. About 12 days after exposure there is a secondary viremia, at which time

Probable Smallpox Epidemics, 1520–1797

Year	Location
1520–1524	Total geographic area unknown; possibly from Chile across present United States
1592–1593	Central Mexico to Sinaloa; southern New England; eastern Great Lakes
1602	Sinaloa and northward
1639	French and British northeastern North America
1646–1648	New Spain north to Nuevo Leon; western Sierra Madres to Florida
1649–1650	Northeastern United States; Florida
1655	Florida
1662–1663	Mid-Atlantic; northeastern United States; Canada
1665–1667	Florida to Virginia
1669–1670	United States and Canada
1674–1675	Texas; northeastern New Spain
1677–1679	French and British northeastern North America
1687–1691	French and British northeastern North America; Texas
1696–1699	Southeastern North America and the Gulf Coast
1701–1703	Northeastern North America to Illinois
1706	Texas; northeastern New Spain
1715–1721	Northeast to Texas
1729–1733	New England; California; Southeastern North America
1738–1739	Southeast to Hudson Bay; Texas
1746	New York; New England; New Spain
1750–1752	Texas north to Great Lakes
1755–1760	From Canada, New England, and Great Lakes south to Virginia, the Carolinas, and Texas
1762–1766	From central Mexico through Texas and the Southeast north to the Great Lakes and the Northwest coast
1779–1783	From central Mexico across all of North America
1785–1787	Alaskan coast across northern Canada
1789	New Mexico
1793–1797	New Spain

Woodcut of Native Americans suffering from an epidemic in colonial Massachusetts. Large numbers of Indians died from European diseases to which they had no immunity. (North Wind Picture Archives)

the organism infects the skin and causes a rash that develops into vesicles after 2 to 3 days. Fluid from either infected lungs or from weeping vesicles carries viral particles and can spread the infection, although human-to-human transmission is usually by inhalation of infected airborne fluids. The disease is relatively contagious, with one drop of pulmonary secretion typically carrying 1,000 or more viral particles that can cause infection, although a carrier is typically infectious for only 3 to 4 days.

There is no treatment for an established infection; however, smallpox was the first disease successfully prevented by creating immunity in potential hosts. For centuries the Chinese and later the Turks intentionally exposed susceptible people to infectious material from patients suffering from mild forms of smallpox. This variolation, or "buying the pox," carried a mortality of some 1–10 percent but conferred permanent immunity. In 1796 English physician Edward Jenner proved that exposure to cowpox (Vaccinia) was almost universally safe and, in 99 percent of cases, conferred lasting immunity to the genetically related smallpox virus.

Smallpox has played intentional and unintentional military roles over the centuries. A probable smallpox epidemic in Rome in 165 CE cost the city one-third of its population. Crusaders brought the disease to Western Europe on their return from the Levant. A combination of smallpox, influenza, and measles reduced the Native American population of the central Mexican plateau by 90 percent in less than five generations and made the military and cultural conquest of the Aztec and Inca empires by the Spanish possible. In North America in 1763 the British commander in chief, Major General Jeffrey Amherst, attempted to use smallpox as a weapon by ordering that infected blankets be distributed to Native Americans during Pontiac's Rebellion. Smallpox devastated many Native American tribes that had not previously been exposed to it.

In 1958 smallpox was still killing 2 million people a year, and the Soviet Union asked the World Health Organization (WHO) to sponsor a worldwide program to eradicate the disease. The program was begun in 1967, and the last naturally occurring case of smallpox was documented in Somalia in 1977, making smallpox the first disease intentionally eradicated. Samples of the virus have been maintained at the Centers for Disease Control and Prevention (CDC) in Atlanta and at the Russian State Research Center of Virology and Biotechnology (Vector) in Siberia, presumably for scientific research. The risk that smallpox will reappear as a bioweapon has resulted in vaccination programs for the military and for health care providers and in discussions of widespread civilian vaccination.

JACK McCALLUM

See also
Medicine, Military; Medicine, Native American

References
Levine, Arnold. *Viruses.* New York: Scientific American Library, 1992.
McNeill, William. *Plagues and Peoples.* New York: Doubleday, 1977.

Smith, John
Birth Date: January 1580
Death Date: June 21, 1631

English explorer, soldier, author, and leader of the English settlement at Jamestown, Virginia. Born in Willoughby, Lincolnshire, England, in January 1580, John Smith attended school but left home at age 16 on the death of his father and traveled to the Netherlands. There Smith joined Dutch forces fighting against the Spaniards. He served for a brief time and then returned to England. Smith improved his martial skills by studying books on military history and strategy and by learning horsemanship.

In 1600 Smith left England to join the Austrian forces under Archduke Ferdinand fighting the Turks. Smith attained the rank of captain in the Austrian Army and won accolades for killing three Turkish opponents in tournament combat. Later he was wounded in battle in Transylvania, left for dead, and captured by the Turks, who enslaved him. Smith killed his master, escaped from the Ottoman Empire, and eventually made his way back to England in 1603.

Smith sailed to America in 1606 with the English expedition to Chesapeake Bay, under the auspices of the joint stock venture known as the Virginia Company of London. In May 1607 he helped to found Jamestown, the first permanent English settlement in North America. The company appointed him as resident councilor; however, other leaders in the fledgling colony of Virginia feared Smith's domineering personality and prevented him from exercising much authority. When the colonists ran into difficulty, however, they turned to him for leadership. The colonists elected him president in September 1608, a post he held until August 1609.

Recognizing the colony's weakness and the threat posed by the Powhatan Confederacy, Smith placed the colony on a military footing. He organized the settlers into companies, drilled them weekly, and assigned them various duties such as raising crops and strengthening Jamestown's defenses. One of his favorite mantras was "He who does not work will not eat." To protect the colony and enable the settlers to procure needed supplies from the natives, Smith adopted a confrontational policy toward the Powhatans. Smith's stance was designed to keep the Powhatans in awe of the English without, however, provoking a full-scale war.

In December 1607 Powhatan warriors captured Smith in an ambush. Chief Powhatan, the leader of the confederacy,

The English soldier and adventurer Captain John Smith (1580–1631) not only helped to found the Virginia Colony in 1607 but, through his bold and vigorous leadership, played a crucial role in its survival. (Library of Congress)

sentenced him to death. In what was probably a ritual intended to impress Smith and win better treatment from him, Powhatan's daughter, Pocahontas, intervened to prevent Smith's execution and win his release.

Smith was not intimidated, however, and continued his tough policies. He used threats to obtain food from the Powhatans. When he met resistance, he confiscated corn, burned houses, killed natives, and took others hostage to ensure that his demands were met. On one such expedition in January 1609, a battle nearly erupted when Smith believed Opechancanough's Pamunkey warriors were poised to attack. Smith seized Opechancanough and threatened him with a pistol, thereby averting a crisis. Relations between the English and the natives improved after this confrontation. When Smith learned that settlers at outlying posts frequently were abusing the natives, he ordered the colonists to behave in a more conciliatory manner so as not to provoke a war. His orders were ignored.

In September 1609 Smith was badly injured in a gunpowder explosion and subsequently returned to England. Although he did not return to Virginia, he received much credit for his work in establishing the colony. He would later journey to New England as an explorer for the Plymouth Company. In England, Smith wrote and published extensively about his experiences in North America. Perhaps the most famous of his works was *The General*

Historie of Virginia, New-England, and the Summer Isles (1624). Smith remained an ardent promoter of colonization until his death in London on June 21, 1631.

JIM PIECUCH

See also

Anglo-Powhatan War, First; Jamestown; Opechancanough; Pamunkeys; Pocahontas; Powhatan; Powhatan Confederacy

References

Lemay, J. A. Leo. *The American Dream of Captain John Smith.* Charlottesville: University Press of Virginia, 1991.

Vaughan, Alden T. *American Genesis: Captain John Smith and the Founding of Virginia.* Boston: Little, Brown, 1975.

Snakes

See Paiutes, Northern

Snake War

Start Date: 1864
End Date: 1868

A series of small conflicts between Native American tribes and white settlers that occurred in areas of California, Nevada, Oregon, Utah, and Idaho from 1864 to 1868. This war waged by the Northern Paiute and Shoshone tribes, called "Snakes" by early French explorers, against Americans was precipitated by the continuous expansion of white settlement into these regions. Although not widely discussed in history books, the Snake War was among the deadliest Indian wars in American history.

When the Mexican-American War ended in 1848, the U.S. government and Native Americans west of the Mississippi River witnessed a new outburst of westward migration. This was largely due to the discovery of gold in California in 1848. A series of incidents throughout the 1850s eventually led to the Snake War, which officially began in 1864. In October 1851 Shoshone warriors killed 8 men at Fort Hall, Idaho. In September 1852 Ben Wright and a group of miners responded to a Native American attack by invading the Modoc village near Black Buff, Oregon, killing some 40 people. The Shoshones attacked several wagon trains along the Snake River in August 1854, resulting in the deaths of some 20 whites. Throughout this period each side carried out small attacks, resulting in numerous deaths.

During the American Civil War (1861–1865), new gold mines were opened near Boise, Idaho, in 1862 and in the Owyhee Canyon lands in 1863. These led to an influx of white settlers. In 1864 open warfare erupted between the white settlers and volunteer militias on one side and various Native American bands in southwestern Idaho, northern California, northern Nevada, Utah, and eastern Oregon on the other side. Among tribal leaders waging war against the whites and the U.S. military were Chief Egan of the Paiutes in Owyhee Canyon and Nevada; Howluck, one of the principal chiefs of the Shoshones in Oregon; and Wewawewa, the principal leader of the Shoshones in southern Idaho.

The war was not characterized by one major battle or even several small battles. Rather, it was a series of skirmishes during a four-year period. Most of the encounters were directly attributable to the actions of volunteer militia led by inexperienced and overly enthusiastic junior officers seeking to make higher rank as well as to the actions of groups of armed citizens. The majority of the troops deployed during the initial stages of the Snake War were from volunteer regiments from California and the surrounding states.

The Snake War was not widely covered in the press at that time because the Paiutes and Shoshones were not considered formidable warriors, as were the Apaches and Cheyennes. The many smaller skirmishes, best characterized as guerrilla warfare, also did not produce any notable leaders. The only American military commander of note associated with the Snake War was Lieutenant Colonel George Crook of the 23rd Infantry, who played a significant role in the Civil War and was later in command during the Apache Wars. The conclusion of the Civil War allowed for a return of regular army troops to the West.

In 1866 after a plea by the governor of Idaho to halt the Native American attacks, Crook was dispatched to Fort Boise. He arrived on December 11 and began a relentless campaign to defeat the warring tribes. His strategy was to give the Native Americans no time to rest, regroup, or accumulate supplies. His most successful tactic was to embark on winter expeditions, a practice used in later conflicts with the Plains tribes, and establish temporary posts at strategic locations within hostile territory.

In May 1868 the Indian Peace Commission sent Brigadier General C. C. Augur to Fort Bridger, Wyoming, to negotiate with the warring tribes. As peace talks commenced, Crook continued pursuing the fighting factions. That same month, Chief Egan and his Paiutes consisting of 10 lodges were captured. In June, Howluck and 60 of his people were taken by surprise in eastern Oregon. These actions forced Shoshone leader Wewawewa to sue for peace. He surrendered to Crook at Fort Harney, Idaho, and by June 1868 the Snake War was over. This conflict was one of the deadliest of the Indian Wars in terms of casualties. The total number of whites and Native Americans killed, wounded, or captured totaled some 1,750 people.

CHARLES FRANCIS HOWLETT

See also

Augur, Christopher Columbus; California Gold Rush; Crook, George; Paiutes, Northern; Shoshones

References

Corless, Hank. *The Weiser Indians: Shoshoni Peacemakers.* Caldwell, ID: Caxton, 1996.

Hook, Jason, and Martin Pegler. *To Live and Die in the West: The American Indian Wars.* Chicago: Fitzroy Dearborn, 2001.

Michino, Gregory. *The Deadliest Indian War in the West: The Snake Conflict, 1864–1868*. Caldwell, ID: Caxton, 2007.

Wooster, Robert. *The Military and United States Indian Policy, 1865–1903*. New Haven, CT: Yale University Press, 1988.

Society of Friends
See Quakers

Sokokis

Native American people belonging to the larger Abenaki Nation. The Sokokis' western Abenaki territory covered an area in the northern Connecticut River Valley roughly between present-day Northfield, Massachusetts, and Bellows Falls, Vermont. Before European contact and a series of epidemics in the 16th century, there were 20,000 eastern, 10,000 western, and 10,000 Canadian Maritime Abenakis. In the decade prior to English settlement of Plymouth Colony in 1620, three epidemics killed 75 percent of the eastern Abenakis. The Sokokis, who were more isolated, lost about half of their original population of 10,000 people. They regained some of this by absorbing southern New England Algonquians, but by the time of the American Revolutionary War (1775–1783) the Abenakis numbered little more than 1,000 people.

Like other Abenakis, the Sokokis grew corn, beans, and squash. They also hunted, fished, and gathered. Where the soil was poor, they used fish to enrich it. They lived in oval longhouses or wigwams, depending on the season. Until 1670 all Abenakis organized at the tribal level. After that time they established the Abenaki Confederacy in response to ongoing war with the English and the Iroquois.

The Abenaki-French fur trade began in 1604 but faded because of perennial French-English disputes. The Abenakis first encountered the English at the Kennebec River in Maine in 1607, at which time they counted the Pemaquids as their allies. Other Sokoki allies included the Mahicans and the neighboring Pennacooks, who were the first to deal with the English extensively.

When the Mohawks attacked the Sokokis in 1629, the French and English ignored Sokoki-Pennacook pleas for help. Another outbreak of smallpox hit New England during 1633–1634, further reducing Sokoki numbers. By 1637 the Sokokis possessed firearms and demonstrated a willingness to trade. However, most traders did not wish to encounter the Mohawks, who were still on Sokoki territory.

Eventually the Sokokis found themselves tied to the French. The French had better resources, and the English, for their part, did not trust New France's native allies. In 1642 the Sokokis allied with the Mohawks and Mahicans against the Montagnais in an effort to monopolize trade with the French.

In 1650 the Sokokis and the French formed an abortive alliance against the English-allied Mohawks. The Sokokis also had sought alliance with other New England natives. The Mohawks fought additional wars with the Sokokis until 1658, by which time the English had taken Port Royal in Acadia and isolated the Sokokis from the French. By 1670 because of the ongoing conflicts involving the French, the Sokokis, the English, and the Mohawks, most Sokokis were refugees under French protection living along the Saint Lawrence River. The Abenakis migrated to and from Canada in the 18th century before finally settling on a reserve in northern Maine at century's end. The Sokokis fought on the French side against the British during the imperial wars of the 18th century, participating in the 1704 attack on Deerfield, Massachusetts.

Today there are about 1,200 self-recognized Sokokis, many of whom live in Vermont. The tribe was briefly recognized by Vermont in 1976, but after protests from white hunters and fishermen, recognition was rescinded the following year. The tribe continues to lobby for official recognition by the federal government. The Sokokis are one of only three Abenaki groups still residing in the United States.

JOHN H. BARNHILL

See also
Abenakis; Deerfield, Massachusetts, Attack on; Iroquois; Longhouse; Mahicans; Mohawks; Pennacooks

References
Calloway, Colin G. *The Abenaki*. New York: Chelsea House, 1989.

Calloway, Colin G. *The Western Abenakis of Vermont, 1600–1800: War, Migration, and the Survival of an Indian People*. Norman: University of Oklahoma Press, 1990.

Day, Gordon M. "The Identity of the Sokokis." *Ethnohistory* 12 (1965): 237–247.

Thomas, Peter A. "In the Maelstrom of Change: The Indian Trade and Cultural Process in the Middle Connecticut River Valley, 1635–1665." Unpublished PhD dissertation, University of Massachusetts, 1979.

Solomon's Fork, Battle of
Event Date: July 29, 1857

Engagement between Cheyenne warriors and the U.S. 1st Cavalry Regiment (augmented) in north-central Kansas on July 29, 1857. Throughout 1857 the Cheyennes had sought to exert their claim over the vast central Plains, attacking wagon trains, immigrant camps, and white hunting parties. In response to these raids, Brevet Lieutenant General Winfield Scott ordered Colonel Edwin V. Sumner to hunt down and punish the Cheyennes. Sumner organized his force around the majority of his 1st Cavalry, adding a detachment of the 6th Infantry Regiment, a small contingent of artillery, and a handful of Pawnee scouts. The force departed Fort Leavenworth on May 20, 1857.

Sumner's plan was to cut loose from his pack train as soon as possible and move southeast toward the Republican River. In order to move at a pace equal to that of the Cheyennes, Sumner's command stripped down to little more than clothes, saddle blankets, weapons, and ammunition. A mule train carried rations sufficient for 20 days and ammunition. The column followed the South Platte River for three days before venturing out onto the open plains in pursuit of the Cheyennes. The terrain over which the command traveled was so expansive that Sumner had his screening units and scouts out as far as 12 miles from the main body.

After three weeks of fruitless searching, the force discovered a fresh trail near a tributary of the Republican River. Following the trail, Sumner reached the South Fork of the Solomon River, where his scouts at last encountered the Cheyenne rear guard.

Anxious to strike the Cheyennes before they dispersed into smaller bands, Sumner ordered his cavalry to give chase. Passing over broken terrain and through creek beds, on July 29 the command soon dropped into a wide valley and saw some 300 Cheyenne warriors assembled for battle. The Cheyennes had recently performed ceremonies at a sacred lake that was supposed to make them immune to army bullets.

Sumner quickly realized that he had been drawn into terrain of the Cheyennes' choosing and ordered his men into line for attack. While the Cheyennes rode about, Sumner calmly ordered his troops forward first at a walk and then at a trot. Despite his substantial advantage in firepower, Sumner shocked his troops by ordering a saber charge. The sudden onslaught of flashing steel, massed horse cavalry, and screaming soldiers unnerved the Cheyennes, and many broke and fled. The 1st Cavalry pursued at full gallop, cutting down nine warriors and wounding a host of others before the buglers sounded recall. In the action Sumner lost two troops killed and eight wounded. With his force reorganized, he waited a day and then moved toward the Cheyenne village, where he destroyed lodges, food, and the animals that were left behind. Despite the stunning success of the charge, many officers in Sumner's command complained about his decision to use sabers instead of carbines and pistols. Although he continued to patrol the Plains until September 2, Sumner never again encountered a concentration of Cheyenne warriors.

PATRICK R. JENNINGS

See also

Cheyenne Campaign; Cheyennes; Dragoon Regiments, 1st and 2nd; Scott, Winfield

References

Ball, Durwood. *Army Regulars on the Western Frontier, 1848–1861.* Norman: University of Oklahoma Press, 2001.

Grinnell, George Bird. *The Fighting Cheyenne.* 1915; reprint, Norman: University of Oklahoma Press, 1989.

Soto, Hernando de
Birth Date: ca. 1496
Death Date: May 21, 1542

Spanish explorer and conquistador credited with having discovered the Mississippi River. Hernando de Soto was born about 1496 in Jerez de los Caballeros, Badajoz, Spain, and led a Spanish military expedition during 1539–1542 into what is now the southeastern United States. His expedition firmly established Spain's early claim to the region and devastated many of the Native American populations that inhabited it. De Soto had earlier been one of Francisco Pizarro's lieutenants during Pizarro's conquest of the Inca Empire. After de Soto had been appointed governor of Cuba in 1535, he undertook the conquest of Florida at his own expense in hopes of surpassing the success of Pizarro's exploits and gaining additional wealth and fame.

On May 30, 1539, de Soto's force of 1,000 men with a few hundred horses and a herd of swine landed at Tampa Bay, Florida. The Spanish then headed north into the interior Southeast. Over the next three years de Soto's men were almost constantly fighting because of their brutal treatment of the natives they encountered. Usually de Soto followed the tactics of seizing the leader whenever he met a new group of natives. Holding their leader hostage, de Soto would then force the natives to provide him with bearers to carry the expedition's supplies. He also took whatever food he needed. Often the Spaniards left a region physically devastated. They ravaged women, consumed scarce food supplies, tainted water with human and animal wastes, and killed many native

Spanish conquistador and explorer Hernando de Soto (ca. 1496–1542) is credited as being the first European to discover the Mississippi River. (Library of Congress)

warriors. De Soto's brutality provoked one of the largest battles between Europeans and natives in North America when the Choctaws attacked the Spaniards at Mabila on October 18, 1540.

In 1541 de Soto's expedition traveled through the present-day states of Alabama, Arkansas, Florida, Georgia, the Carolinas, Mississippi, Tennessee, and parts of Texas. During his trek westward and then back east, de Soto is believed to have "discovered" the Mississippi River. De Soto was stricken with a fever and died on May 21, 1542, somewhere along the Mississippi River in present-day Louisiana. By this time, after almost three years of near-constant hostilities, his force was only a shattered remnant of its former self. De Soto's successor, Luis de Moscoso de Alvarado, disposed of his chief's body in the Mississippi River so that local natives would not find it and learn that the Spanish had lost their leader. The expedition then floated down the Mississippi on makeshift rafts while under constant native attack. The survivors finally made it to Mexico.

DIXIE RAY HAGGARD

See also
Captivity of Indians by Europeans; Mabila, Battle of

References
Akridge, Scott. "The De Soto Expedition through North Mississippi in 1540–41." *Mississippi Archaeology* 22 (1987): 61–73.
Akridge, Scott. "De Soto's Route in North Central Arkansas." *Field Notes: Newsletter of the Arkansas Archaeological Society* 211 (1986): 3–7.
Clayton, Lawrence A., Vernon James Knight Jr., and Edward C. Moore, eds. *The De Soto Chronicles: The Expedition of Hernando de Soto to North America in 1539–1543.* 2 vols. Tuscaloosa: University of Alabama Press, 1993.
Hudson, Charles. *Knights of Spain, Warriors of the Sun: Hernando de Soto and the South's Ancient Chiefdoms.* Athens: University of Georgia Press, 1997.

Soulier Rouge/Soulouche Oumastabé

See Red Shoe

Southern Arapahos

See Arapahos, Southern

Southern Cheyennes

See Cheyennes, Southern

Spain

For three centuries after the voyages of the Genoese voyager Christopher Columbus at the end of the 15th century, Spain possessed the world's most extensive overseas empire. For much of this period Spain also maintained a powerful navy, and its army was among the best trained and most feared of those of European states. Spain's early success in empire building, however, brought confrontation with other states that also sought to carve out overseas empires in the Americas and Asia. Initially Spain's chief rival was Portugal, but other antagonists—the English, the Dutch, and the French—soon appeared.

By 1500 Spain was well positioned to lead European expansion in the New World. Geographically Spain was closer to the New World than any other colonial power except Portugal. Spain also had a long commercial and seafaring tradition based on extensive trading with Africa, the islands of the Mediterranean, and other European states. In addition, Spain had resolved its internal divisions and emerged as a unified state ready to assume foreign challenges.

In 1492 Spanish troops under King Ferdinand of Aragon and his wife Queen Isabella of Castile conquered the Kingdom of Granada, ending centuries of Moorish (Muslim) power on the Iberian Peninsula. That same Columbus secured funding from Ferdinand and Isabella for a voyage westward to reach Asia. The voyages of exploration were fueled by the desire of Spanish leaders to secure a direct trade with China and other Asian markets without having to go through Muslim middlemen. Because an earlier treaty with Portugal prohibited Spanish competition on the southerly route to Asia around Africa, Spanish leaders sought a western route.

Prior to its unification, Spain had been a handful of small states. Thus, there was little sense of a Spanish identity. That identity came through the Catholic Church. To be Spanish was to be Catholic. Missionary zeal and the desire to see Catholicism triumph everywhere were both motives and ready justifications for Spain's expansionary impulses.

In 1492 Columbus "discovered" America and initiated Spanish colonization of the Americas. Spain first secured the Caribbean islands. Spaniards settled Hispaniola in the early 1500s. From there, Juan Ponce de León acquired Puerto Rico, and Diego Velásquez took Cuba. Major Spanish settlements on these islands followed. Spanish rule was hardly benign, for the settlers enslaved the native populations, which in any case quickly succumbed to European diseases against which they had no immunity.

In 1512 Vasco Núñez de Balboa established the first Spanish settlement on the mainland, located at Darién in Panama. Numerous small expeditions of Spanish explorers soon fanned out throughout the New World, in the process opening up vast new territories to exploitation and colonization. These warrior-explorers were known as conquistadors. More concerned with the quest for riches than with colonization or religious conversion, their appetites were fueled by the discovery of rich deposits of gold and silver.

Although the native populations vastly outnumbered the conquistadors, success was made possible by European firearms and horses, both of which the natives had never before seen. The Spaniards were also fortunate in encountering the Aztec and Inca

Explorer Christopher Columbus, shown here bidding farewell to Queen Isabella and King Ferdinand in this 17th-century illustration from *Nova Typis Transacta Navigatio*. (Library of Congress)

empires when they were already in decline. Internal dissension and alliances with tribes that had been enslaved by the Aztecs and Incas also aided the Spanish, as did European diseases such as smallpox from which the natives had no immunity.

Perhaps the most successful of the conquistadors was Hernán Cortés. From 1519 to 1521, allying himself with American Indians opposed to the Aztecs, he led a relatively small force in the defeat of the once-powerful Aztec Empire, bringing what became modern Mexico under Spanish control. To the south, Francisco Pizarro destroyed the Inca Empire in what became Peru. Rumors of fabled cities of gold (Quivira and Cibola in North America and El Dorado in South America) led to a series of other expeditions. Although unsuccessful in finding riches, they did bring Spain considerable additional territorial claims.

The gold and silver of America became the chief source of Spanish wealth and power. Soon the Spaniards were shipping vast amounts of these precious metals across the Atlantic (one source estimates this trade from 1500 to 1650 at 181 tons of gold and 16,000 tons of silver). Overreliance on this mineral wealth,

the failure to build an infrastructure in Spain itself, overly ambitious government spending on maintaining Spain's international position, and a vast Catholic military crusade all contributed in the long run to the ruin of Spain. Local industry declined as Spain used its wealth to buy finished goods from abroad. Manual work was held to be a sign of inferior social status, and catastrophic inflation set in.

Increasingly the Spanish economy became dependent on the regular arrival of the treasure ships. At the same time, however, that economic lifeline came under attack from state-sponsored piracy encouraged by the Dutch, French, and, above all, English governments.

The Spanish monarchy ignored the signs that pointed to the need for reform, and in the short run all seemed well. Indeed, the 16th and 17th centuries came to be known in Spanish history as the Siglo de Oro (Golden Age). Spain's vast empire included much of the Americas and extended to the Philippines in Asia.

At the same time that Spanish explorers were creating a vast overseas empire, Spain itself had embarked on a great military effort in Europe. The motivations were to defend Europe against the threat posed by the Ottoman Turks but also to maintain and expand Spanish influence throughout the continent and above all to crush the Protestantism espoused by Martin Luther in the German states. King Charles I (r. 1516–1556; Holy Roman Emperor Charles V, r. 1519–1556) was as near a universal monarch as Europe had seen in a long time or would see again until Napoleon. In 1525 in a decisive encounter, Charles's armies defeated French forces in Italy at Pavia, even taking as prisoner French king Francis I. King Charles also waged extensive warfare with the Protestant German princes but was unable to crush them and indeed was obliged to conclude peace with them in 1555 at Augsburg.

Disheartened by his inability to achieve decisive success, Charles abdicated his many crowns and retired to a monastery in 1556. His and Spain's vast crusade reached its peak under Charles's son and successor, King Philip II (r. 1556–1598). With religious zeal and grim persistence, Philip poured all his nation's resources into the vast religious enterprise of advancing the Catholic faith. At first he enjoyed success, defeating the Turks at sea in the Battle of Lepanto in the eastern Mediterranean in 1571, but he experienced a major failure in his efforts to subdue England.

War with England had come about in consequence of a revolt in the Netherlands against Spanish rule. Queen Elizabeth I of England (r. 1558–1603) provided assistance to the Protestant Dutch—at first covertly and then openly in the form of an expeditionary force—while at the same time English freebooters such as Sir Francis Drake attacked Spanish treasure ships on the high seas. Determined to crush England, in 1588 Philip sent his powerful Armada to the English Channel, only to meet humiliating defeat in the form of English warships and a great storm (the so-called Protestant Wind).

This rebuff at the hands of the English did not at the time seem to seriously weaken Spanish power, but in retrospect it was a major turning point that marked the beginning of the rise of England as a major international force. Spanish troops also invaded France in an unsuccessful effort to prevent Henry of Navarre from becoming king. The Netherlands, meanwhile, had become a bloody quagmire. All of this drove the Spanish government to declare bankruptcy in 1596. Finally, in 1609 Spain signed the Twelve Years' Truce with the United Provinces, bringing to a temporary end the fighting in the Netherlands.

The conclusion of the truce provided an opportunity for the Spanish government to get the nation's economic house in order and scale back commitments to meet revenues. Spain needed peace to be able to reform, but this was not to be. In 1618 fighting again broke out in Europe, producing the conflagration known as the Thirty Years' War (1618–1648). In 1621 warfare also resumed in the Netherlands.

For a time it appeared as if the Catholic powers might prevail. Finally, for reasons of sheer realpolitik, France entered the fighting openly on the side of the Protestants and against Spain. The French shattered the seemingly invincible Spanish infantry in the Battle of Rocroi in 1643, ending the long period of Spanish military

greatness. On the seas, the Spanish Navy was unable to adequately resupply the nation's troops in the Netherlands, and Spain was forced to make peace with the Netherlands and recognize its independence. War with France continued even after the Peace of Westphalia in 1648 that ended the Thirty Years' War. Not until the Peace of the Pyrenees in 1659 was peace with France achieved but with the Spanish ceding territory to France.

To add to Spain's woes, Portugal, which had fallen under Spanish control, rebelled in 1640. Spanish efforts to subdue Portugal failed, and Spain finally recognized its independence in 1688. Lost along with Portugal was Brazil.

In 1700 King Charles II, the unfortunate product of Habsburg inbreeding, died childless and unlamented. During the last year of Charles's sad life, King Louis XIV of France won the commitment that the entire Spanish inheritance would pass to the French king's grandson. Even the ambitious Louis must have hesitated at the prospect, for this decision touched off the War of the Spanish Succession (1702–1713). Known in English America as Queen Anne's War, it has also been called the first world war, for fighting occurred all over the globe as France and Spain stood against much of the rest of Europe.

The war ended in the Peace of Utrecht of 1713. The Bourbon Philip V was confirmed as king of Spain with its American possessions, but Spain was forced to cede considerable possessions in Europe. Britain retained both the island of Minorca and Gibraltar. Spain was also forced to cede to Austria its possession of the Spanish Netherlands.

Although the Bourbon monarchy did bring reform to Spain in the form of centralization, the introduction of mercantilist principles, and the creation of departments of the army and navy, these came too late to completely reverse the decline brought on by generations of neglect. Throughout much of the 18th century Spain remained closely tied to France—the so-called Family Compact—following that nation into war against Britain in the French and Indian War (1754–1763) and the American Revolutionary War (1775–1783).

As noted, the Spanish overseas empire directly impacted developments in Spain itself. Columbus had sailed under the aegis of Castile, and the new lands passed under its control. At first on the mainland, Spain had allowed those conquering the land to control it under royal patent, but within a few years the Crown moved to consolidate its authority over the newly acquired lands and remove the conquistadors from ruling positions. By the 1570s all the machinery of government in the colonies was firmly in place. As early as 1503 and the beginning of trade with the West Indies, the government created the Casa di Contractación at Castile. By the 1530s a new body, the Conseillo de Indias (Council of the Indies), had full executive, judicial, and ecclesiastical authority in the Indies and over the Casa di Contractación. Other institutions came into being to control the movement of the Spanish Army and Spain's fleets.

In 1542 the Crown created two viceroyalties. That of Peru with its capital at Lima had authority over all of Spanish South America, except Venezuela, extending north to include Panama.

INDIAN REBELLIONS AGAINST THE SPANISH IN THE SOUTHWEST

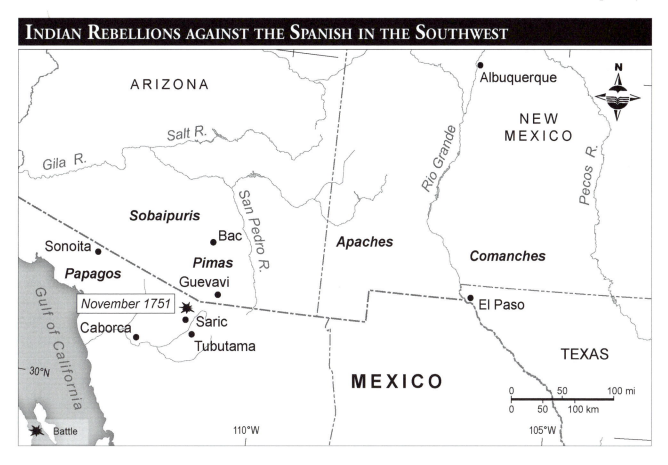

The viceroyalty of New Spain, with its capital at Mexico City, had authority over all Spanish territory north of Panama as well as the West Indies, Venezuela, and the Philippine Islands. The two vice-royalties, as the direct representatives of the Spanish sovereign, had wide-ranging civil and military powers as well as some ecclesiastical powers.

Beneath the viceroyalties, the empire was further divided into *audiencias* ("law courts"), a combination of a legislature, cabinet, and court that drafted laws, advised the viceroy, and conducted major judicial proceedings. The king appointed the members of the *audiencias*. The governing structure in the colonies was intended solely to safeguard the power and wishes of the government in Spain, which approved all major decisions.

The Catholic Church enjoyed considerable influence in the colonies. The conversion of natives was always held to be a prime motive for Spain's conquests, and priests accompanied the con-quistadors and explorers in their travels. Missions soon sprang up throughout the viceroyalties of New Spain and Peru.

The Crown rigidly controlled emigration, only allowing Catholics in good standing to settle in the New World. The vast majority of settlers came from the territories of Castile. A number of nobles immigrated to the New World, including many younger sons seeking adventure and wealth denied them by inheritance laws in Spain.

During the initial conquests the Spanish had enslaved the natives, but the New Laws of 1542–1543 prohibited this, making the natives wards of the Crown. The beneficent attitude of the Crown was, however, to a considerable measure negated by the actions of individual administrators, although many Spaniards attempted to act as advocates for the native peoples. Spanish treatment of the native populations, which had come under considerable condemnation, was in fact outdone by the English treatment of African slaves in the Caribbean. The Spanish much resented the English perpetuation of the so-called Black Legend. The English held that their own rule was more benign than that of Spain and used it to justify their own acquisition of Spanish territory.

The Spanish Crown also introduced African slavery, although chiefly in the West Indies and in northern South America. With its large tracts of land suitable for settlement and cultivation, Mexico was the primary place of settlement. The number of immigrants grew rapidly, and by 1574 the Spanish population was estimated at 160,000 people. Intermarriage between Spaniards and the native population produced a caste known as mestizos. Upper-class Spaniards possessed virtually all of the colonial wealth.

Spanish colonial expansion to the north in the present-day United States came both in the West from New Spain and along the Gulf Coast and in Florida and the Carolinas. In the West and operating from New Spain, legends of the fabled Seven Cities of Cibola prompted expeditions northward. In 1539 Franciscan Fray Marcos de Niza reached Zuni Pueblo. The next year Francisco Vásquez de Coronado led another northern expedition, while

Hernando de Alarcón proceeded by sea along the Pacific coast. Coronado reached Zuni Pueblo, and his lieutenants traveled as far as the Grand Canyon of the Colorado River. Coronado then explored present-day northern Texas, Oklahoma, and eastern Kansas before returning south in 1542.

From 1598 to 1608 Spain established its control over New Mexico. Explorers also traveled into Kansas and up the Pacific coast of present-day California. In 1535 Cortés attempted to establish a colony in Baja, California, and by the mid-1540s the Spanish had explored as far up the Pacific coast as Oregon.

In 1680 a revolt of the Pueblos drove the Spanish from New Mexico, although they reestablished their control there in 1696. Meanwhile, the Spanish extended their exploratory efforts into Florida and the Great Plains of present-day New Mexico, Arizona, Texas, and California. From 1720 to 1722, contesting the area with the French, Spain established its control over present-day Texas, and from 1769 to 1786 small Spanish forces took upper California, including San Diego (1769), Monterey (1770), Los Angeles (1781), and San Francisco (1776). The Spanish established a series of presidios (fortified outposts) and missions run by the Franciscan order.

To the east, in 1521 Juan Ponce de León attempted without success to colonize Florida. During 1526–1528 Lucas Vásquez de Ayllón established a colony in the Carolinas, but it was abandoned when he died. That same year, 1528, Pánfilo de Narváez arrived in Florida with colonists from Spain. Trying to reach the area of the Pánuco River, the members of the expedition were shipwrecked, with most dying of hunger or disease or at the hands of the natives.

In 1539 Hernando de Soto arrived in Florida from Spain at the head of a sizable force of 600 men and then proceeded to explore much of what is today the southeastern United States. In 1541 the members of his expedition were the first Europeans to see the Mississippi River. De Soto then traveled as far west as present-day Arkansas and Oklahoma before descending the Arkansas River to the Mississippi. De Soto died in 1542 during the subsequent passage down the Mississippi, although members of his expedition did reach the Pánuco area the next year.

The Spanish sent out a large expedition under Tristán de Luna in 1559 to colonize the Carolinas. Luna established a post at Pensacola and then moved inland, although these colonists were later removed to Pensacola. Efforts to establish a settlement in the Carolinas met with failure, and the garrison at Pensacola was also withdrawn. In 1561 King Philip II, faced with numerous previous failures, issued an order forbidding further colonization of Florida. The need for a naval base to protect the Bahama Channel used by the Spanish treasure fleets sailing to Spain and French efforts beginning in 1564 to establish a Huguenot colony in South Carolina from which they might attack the Spanish ships prompted Philip to reverse his earlier order. In 1565 Pedro Menéndez de Avilés founded St. Augustine in Florida, hailed today as the oldest city in the United States. Menéndez de Avilés then proceeded to capture the French settlement at Fort Caroline on the St. Johns River, killing its garrison and ending French colonization efforts in

Hernando de Soto's capture of the fortified Native American town of Alibamo on the Yazoo River, Mississippi, 1541. Illustration from *Herrera, Historia General*, Madrid, 1615. (Library of Congress)

the region. During the next decade, Menéndez de Avilés expanded the Spanish settlements in Florida. Although Menéndez de Avilés was successful in securing Florida for Spain, his efforts to the north, which reached as far as present-day Virginia, failed.

Spain's success in colonization in the New World and the flow of gold and silver to the mother country early excited the colonial ambitions of other powers. These and the decline of Spain would bring a steady erosion of Spanish overseas holdings.

Spanish settlements and Spain's trade and treasure fleets early came under attacks mounted by the French, the English, and the Dutch. French corsairs attacked Spanish ships off the Iberian coasts and in the Caribbean, where they also razed Spanish coastal towns. In the mid-16th century the English Crown encouraged freebooters such as Sir Francis Drake and Sir John Hawkins to attack the Spanish treasure fleets and raid Spanish settlements. When England and Spain formally went to war in 1557 this activity intensified, creating considerable economic loss for Spain.

Spain neglected the Lesser Antilles, and in the 17th century the French, the English, and the Dutch moved into that area. The Dutch and the French also contested with the Spanish for control of Brazil, and in 1628 a Dutch fleet captured a large plate fleet sailing from New Spain. England continued to inflict heavy financial losses on Spain during this period, and in 1668 the Englishman Sir Henry Morgan captured and looted Portobello in Panama.

In 1655 the English took Jamaica from Spain and retained it. In the Treaty of Ryswick of 1697 that ended the War of the League of Augsburg (King William's War in America), Spain ceded Western Hispaniola (Haiti), where French irregular forces had landed during the war, to France.

The 18th-century wars involving Spain in Europe had immense repercussions in the Americas. British control of the seas made it next to impossible for Spain to protect its colonies or to preserve its monopoly in trade. English, Dutch, and French illicit trade with the Spanish colonies increased. During the War of the Spanish Succession (1702–1713), known as Queen Anne's War in America, considerable fighting occurred between the allied Spanish and French and the English in both Florida and the West Indies. Among concessions won by the English in the Treaty of Utrecht of 1713 ending the war was the *asiento* ("agreement"), a 30-year monopoly on slave trading in Spanish America, as well as the right to send one trading ship a year to trade with the Atlantic ports of the Spanish colonies. This proved a license both for expanded English trade and illicit smuggling.

When Philip V sought to overturn provisions of the peace settlement, in 1718 Britain, France, the Netherlands, and Austria concluded the Quadruple Alliance and went to war against Spain. During 1718–1720 fighting took place in both Europe and the Americas, and Spain abandoned its claims in Italy. In fighting with France in Florida and Texas, however, Spain secured its hold over Texas.

Reforms under the Bourbon monarchy led to successful defense by Spain of its overseas possessions in the Anglo-Spanish War (1739–1744), also known as the War of Jenkins' Ear, that merged into the War of the Austrian Succession (1740–1748). In the New World, considerable fighting occurred along the Georgia-Florida border and in Florida, where Spain retained its hold. The Spanish also turned back a powerful British naval expeditionary assault on Cartagena (Colombia). The resultant Treaty of Aix-la-Chapelle produced no important colonial transfers.

This was not the case during the French and Indian War. Spain entered that war in 1761 as an ally of France. The following year, British expeditionary forces captured both Havana and Manila. By the Treaty of Paris ending the war in 1763, Spain ceded all of Florida to Britain in return for the restoration of Havana and Manila. To compensate for the loss of Florida, France transferred to Spain control of Louisiana, although this met some opposition from French colonists there.

Convinced that Britain was determined to take all of Spain's New World colonies and that a showdown with Britain was inevitable, Spanish king Charles III (r. 1759–1788) oversaw a series of military, fiscal, and administrative reforms in both Spain and the colonies to prepare for the inevitable. In 1779 Spain entered the American Revolutionary War on the side of France (but not the Patriots) in America. Spanish forces captured Mobile, Pensacola, and the Bahamas and blocked British efforts to secure the Mississippi. Under the terms of the peace in 1783, Spain relinquished the Bahamas but regained Florida.

During the Napoleonic Wars, Spain lost Trinidad to Britain and in 1800 was forced to return Louisiana to France. Despite its pledge to Spain not to cede that territory to any other power than Spain, France then sold Louisiana to the United States. Considerable pressure from the United States then led Spain to sell Florida to the United States in 1819.

The loss of Spain's northern territories in the New World was perhaps inevitable. The scattered settlements, missions, and forts in the territory that Spain claimed north of Mexico were never adequately supported, in large measure because the Crown was already overextended in Central and South America. In addition, Spain's concomitant decline in power in relation to other European states conspired against a major effort in North America.

The Spanish Latin American colonies, largely cut off from the mother country during the Napoleonic Wars, broke away from Spain in a series of wars of liberation in the 1820s. The final blow to Spanish imperial power came at the hands of the United States in the Spanish-American War of 1898.

RICK DYSON AND SPENCER C. TUCKER

See also

Acoma Pueblo, Battle of; Apalachee Revolt; Apalachees; Córdova, Francisco Hernández de; Coronado, Francisco Vásquez de; French and Indian War; Karankawas; Kickapoos; Louisiana Purchase; Mabila, Battle of; Missionaries; New Mexico; Oñate, Juan de; Ponce de León, Juan; Pueblos; Queen Anne's War; Soto, Hernando de; Timucuan Revolt; Yamasees

References

Bakewell, Peter. *A History of Latin America.* 2nd ed. Malden, MA: Blackwell, 2004.

Elliott, J. H. *Imperial Spain, 1469–1716.* New York: St. Martin's, 1963.

Kamen, Harry. *Spain, 1469–1714: A Society of Conflict.* London: Longman, 1991.

Kessell, John L. *Spain in the Southwest: A Narrative History of Colonial New Mexico, Arizona, Texas, and California.* Norman: University of Oklahoma Press, 2002.

Taylor, Alan. *American Colonies: The Settling of North America.* New York: Viking/Penguin, 2001.

Thomas, Hugh. *Rivers of Gold: The Rise of the Spanish Empire, from Columbus to Magellan.* New York: Random House, 2003.

Wright, James Leitch. *Anglo-Spanish Rivalry in North America.* Athens: University of Georgia Press, 1971.

Spirit Lake Massacre
Start Date: March 8, 1857
End Date: March 9, 1857

Santee Sioux massacre of white settlers in northern Iowa that took place during March 8–9, 1857. In the years leading up to the Spirit Lake Massacre, several factors combined to increase unrest among the Wahpekute band of the Santee Sioux (Dakota). In 1851 the Sisseton and Wahpeton bands of the Santee Sioux had signed the Treaty of Traverse de Sioux, which ceded all Sioux lands in northwestern Iowa to the U.S. government. The Wahpekutes, however, who had not been a party to the treaty, refused to abide by its terms. As white settlers began moving into traditional Sioux hunting grounds, conflict became virtually inevitable. In January 1854 the whiskey trader Henry Lott and his stepson killed Sisseton chief Sintomniduta, the chief's wife, and their five children. Wahpekute chief Inkpaduta demanded justice from U.S. military officials at Fort Dodge, but Lott fled before he could be apprehended, although he was indicted in absentia.

When a Wahpekute hunter was beaten by a white settler for shooting the settler's dog in the winter of 1856, Wahpekute warriors retaliated by stealing cattle from white settlements to feed their starving families. Militia captain Seth Smith led 20 armed settlers to Inkpaduta's camp and confiscated all the firearms in his village. Outraged by these insults and the threats to his band's survival, Inkpaduta launched raids across northern Iowa in February 1857.

On March 7, 1857, the Wahpekutes arrived at Okoboji and Spirit lakes in present-day Dickinson County, which lies along Iowa's northern border with Minnesota. The Wahpekutes had long considered the lakes sacred and had forbidden tribal members from fishing or even using a canoe in the waters. Outraged to find that white families, numbering approximately 40 men, women, and children, had established settlements along the shores of the lakes during the previous summer, the Wahpekutes attacked with a vengeance. During March 8–9, 4 families were wiped out entirely; in all 32 men, women, and children were killed. Four women—Elizabeth Thatcher, Lydia Noble, Abigail Gardner, and Margaret Marble—were taken captive. Only 2 men from the settlement survived the massacre because they had been away at the time.

Following the massacre, Inkpaduta led his band and the 4 captives along the Big Sioux River into Minnesota, where Thatcher was killed when she had difficulty crossing the river. Although Lieutenant Alexander Murray and 24 soldiers from Fort Ridgely attempted to pursue the Wahpekutes, heavy snows caused them to lose the trail, and 2 soldiers froze to death. The soldiers returned empty-handed. Meanwhile, the Wahpekutes headed west to South Dakota. After their arrival in May, Inkpaduta's son clubbed Noble to death. Marble was sold to local Sioux, who then took her to white officials in St. Paul, Minnesota, while Gardner was sold to 3 Sioux sent to ransom her.

Although the Spirit Lake Massacre was the last event of its kind in Iowa, it served as a precursor to the 1862 Santee Sioux Uprising in Minnesota that resulted in the deaths of between 500 and 800 white settlers. Inkpaduta was in Minnesota at the time of the uprising, but it is unclear if he played a role in the violence.

JUSTIN D. MURPHY

See also

Inkpaduta; Dakota Sioux; Minnesota Sioux Uprising; Sioux

References

Bakeman, Mary Hawker. *Legends, Letters, and Lies: Readings about Inkpaduta and the Spirit Lake Massacre.* Roseville, MN: Park Genealogical Books, 2001.

Teakle, Thomas. *The Spirit Lake Massacre.* Iowa City: State Historical Society of Iowa, 1918.

Spokane Plain, Battle of

See Four Lakes, Battle of

Spokanes

A Plateau tribe having three geographic divisions—upper, lower, and middle—who lived along the Spokane River in eastern Washington state and northern Idaho. The Spokanes (Spokans) have also been known as Muddy People as well as Sun People, probably after a faulty translation of their name. Their self-designation was Spoqe'ind, meaning "round head." Today they live on reservations in Washington and Idaho as well as in regional cities and towns. Spokane is a dialect of the interior division of the Salishan language family.

The Spokanes probably originated in British Columbia along with other Salish groups. Each division of the Spokanes was composed of a number of bands, which were in turn composed of groups of related families. Bands were led by a chief and a subchief, who were selected on the basis of leadership qualities. Several bands might winter together in a village and at that time select an ad hoc village chief. Decisions were made by consensus. In the historic period, as authority became more centralized, there was also a tribal chief.

The Spokanes were seminomadic for nine months a year; during the other three months they lived in permanent winter villages. The men's realm consisted of tool making, warring, hunting, fishing, and later caring for horses, as they were expert horsemen.

The Spokanes built typical Plateau-style semiexcavated, cone-shaped wood-frame houses covered with woven matting and/or grass. Longer lodge-style structures of similar construction were used for communal activities. Temporary brush shelters served as summertime houses. Later, skin tepees replaced the original structures.

Fish, especially salmon, was the staple of the Spokane diet. Trout and whitefish were also important. These were mostly smoked, dried, and stored for the winter. Men hunted local big game and, later, buffalo on the Plains. Important plant foods included camas, bitterroot and other roots, bulbs, seeds, and berries.

Women made coiled baskets of birch bark and/or cedar root; they also wove wallets and bags of strips of hide and sewed tule mats and other items. These goods were sometimes traded with other Native American peoples and with whites.

After they acquired horses from the Kalispel people around the mid-18th century, the Spokanes began hunting buffalo on the Great Plains. This was especially true of the upper division. By the time they encountered the Lewis and Clark expedition in 1805, their population had already declined significantly as a result of smallpox epidemics.

Following the Lewis and Clark visit, the North West, Hudson's Bay, and American Fur companies quickly established themselves in the area. Missionaries arrived in the 1830s and found the Spokanes to be reluctant converts, and the influence of Christianity acted to create factionalism within the tribe. Interracial relations declined sharply in the late 1840s with the November 29, 1847, Whitman Massacre and the closing of the Protestant mission. Severe smallpox epidemics in 1846 and again in 1852 and 1853 helped spur the rise of the Prophet Dance and the Dreamer Cult.

After white miners had effectively dispossessed the Spokanes from their territory, they joined with the Coeur d'Alenes, Yakimas, Palouses, and Paiutes in the short-lived 1858 Coeur d'Alene War (part of the Yakima-Rogue War). The Spokanes then remained on their land when they could or settled on various reservations. Despite pleas from Chief Joseph, they remained neutral in the 1877 Nez Perce War. In that year the lower division agreed to move to the Spokane Reservation (officially declared a reservation in 1881 and encompassing 154,898 acres). Ten years later the other two divisions as well as some remaining lower Spokanes agreed to move to either the Flathead, Colville, or Coeur d'Alene reservations. The local fort, Fort Spokane, became a Native American boarding school from 1898 to 1906. There were also conflicts over land with nonnatives in and around the city of Spokane at this time.

In the early 20th century, much tribal land was lost to the allotment process as well as to "surplus" land sales to non–Native Americans. Dams built in 1908 (Little Falls) and 1935 (Grand Coulee) ruined the local fishery. Uranium mining began in the 1950s. The Spokane tribe successfully fought off termination proceedings begun in 1955. In 1966 the tribe received a land claims settlement of $6.7 million.

BARRY M. PRITZKER

See also
Coeur d'Alenes; Coeur d'Alene War; Fur Trade; Hudson's Bay Company; Joseph, Chief; Lewis and Clark Expedition; Nez Perce War; Palouses; Whitman Massacre

References
Carpenter, Cecelia S. *They Walked Before: The Indians of Washington State.* Tacoma, WA: Tahoma Publications, 1989.
Ruby, Robert H., and John A. Brown. *The Spokane Indians: Children of the Sun.* Norman: University of Oklahoma Press, 1982.

Spoqe'inds
See Spokanes

Spotted Elk
See Big Foot

Spotted Tail
Birth Date: 1823
Death Date: August 5, 1881

Upper Brulé Lakota Sioux leader. Spotted Tail (Sinte Gleska) was born in 1823 in the Ring band (*tiyospe*), a community of bilaterally related extended families on the White River in south-central South Dakota. Spotted Tail learned to hunt bison, conduct raiding expeditions against the Pawnees, protect his community's southern lands that lay beyond the Platte River in western Nebraska, and take the proper path toward leadership under the guidance of Little Thunder, leader of the Ring band. By midcentury, Spotted Tail became a Shirt Wearer (Wicasa), the official band executive for the council (Wiscas Itacans) responsible for locating good hunting and campgrounds, deciding family disputes, and negotiating with nontribal officials.

Traders were part of Spotted Tail's early life, but increased white migration to Oregon in 1843, to Utah in 1847, and to California in 1849 brought overland travelers through the Brulés' Platte River territories, and soon the American military followed to protect the travelers. These events forever changed Spotted Tail's life.

In 1854 a Mormon abandoned a lame cow, and a Miniconjou Lakota killed the animal. This so-called Mormon cow affair convinced the brash Lieutenant John Lawrence Grattan to lead a detachment and demand that Little Thunder's Brulé band pay

Spotted Tail, a Brulé Sioux chief, circa 1870. Although he took part in the Grattan Massacre of 1854, he refused to join the Sioux War of 1876–1877. (Library of Congress)

compensation and release the guilty Lakota to military control. After fruitless negotiation, Grattan's men fired their artillery, and the Lakotas retaliated, annihilating the entire unit. After learning of Grattan's fate, Secretary of War Jefferson Davis ordered Brevet Brigadier General William S. Harney to prepare a punitive campaign against the tribe. Sometime later at Ash Hollow in western Nebraska, Harney's expedition attacked Little Thunder's band, killing 86 people and taking prisoners. Harney then demanded the surrender and imprisonment of the leading men. Spotted Tail, among others, surrendered at Fort Laramie in the autumn of 1855. He was incarcerated at Fort Leavenworth and later Fort Kearny before returning to his people the following autumn. Upon his return, he decided to stand with Little Thunder and avoid war with the whites but to continue to fight the Lakotas' traditional Pawnee foes.

In 1866 Spotted Tail succeeded Little Thunder as headman of the Ring band and joined with Swift Bear of the Corn band for protection. Together they stood for peace, signing the Fort Laramie Treaty of 1868 and moving to the Whetstone Agency on the Missouri River. There Spotted Tail killed Big Mouth during a leadership dispute in 1869. The agency was moved to northwestern Nebraska shortly afterward. The discovery of gold in the Black Hills, within the boundaries of the Great Sioux Reservation, sparked an invasion of miners that led to the Great Sioux War of 1876–1877.

While Crazy Horse, Sitting Bull, and their followers fought, Spotted Tail's agency was known as a peace camp. As Colonel Nelson Miles pursued the warring chiefs, Brigadier General George Crook sought Spotted Tail's help and in the autumn of 1876 unilaterally and illegally declared that the United States "recognized Spotted Tail as chief of all the Sioux." Spotted Tail, with U.S. backing, maintained his status by signing the Black Hills Treaty in 1876 that enabled the United States to take control of that region.

In early 1877 at Crook's urging, Spotted Tail went north on a peace mission seeking Crazy Horse's surrender. The two men met, and Crazy Horse accepted the terms that Spotted Tail presented. The war essentially ended when Crazy Horse surrendered in late spring and Sitting Bull and his people fled to Canada in an effort to retain their independence.

After briefly moving their people to the old Ponca Agency on the Missouri River, Spotted Tail and other upper Brulé leaders moved in the summer of 1878 to the Rosebud Agency in south-central South Dakota. At Rosebud, old tribal conflicts grew into new battles. Spotted Tail tried to follow Lakota tradition but lacked credibility because he owed his position to U.S. intervention. As he attempted to maintain control over all the Brulé bands, Spotted Tail encountered increasing tension between himself and Two Strike, White Thunder, Crow Dog, and Hollow Horn Bear. Rosebud leaders sent some children to the Carlisle boarding school in 1879, and Spotted Tail removed the children without Brulé authority, violating tribal political protocol. These ill feelings erupted following a meeting on August 5, 1881, when Crow Dog shot Spotted Tail, killing him instantly.

RICHMOND L. CLOW

See also

Ash Hollow, Battle of; Brulé Sioux; Crazy Horse; Crook, George; Fort Laramie, Treaty of (1868); Grattan Massacre; Great Sioux War; Sitting Bull

References

Clow, Richmond L. "The Anatomy of a Lakota Shooting: Crow Dog and Spotted Tail." *South Dakota History* 28(4) (1998): 209–227.
Hyde, George E. *Spotted Tail's Folk: A History of the Brulé Sioux.* The Civilization of the American Indian Series 57. Norman: University of Oklahoma Press, 1961.
Worcester, Donald F. "Spotted Tail: Warrior, Diplomat." *American West* 1(4) (1964): 38–46, 87.

Springfield, Massachusetts, Burning of
Event Date: October 5, 1675

Attack on Springfield, Massachusetts, by Agawam and allied Nipmuck warriors on October 5, 1675, during King Philip's War (1675–1676). Springfield was the preeminent English settlement along the Connecticut River.

In the summer and autumn of 1675, King Philip's War spread from a localized conflict between Wampanoags, whose chief was Metacom (also known as King Philip), and Plymouth Colony to include other New England colonies and American Indian peoples. In the Connecticut River Valley, local natives had already attacked Squakeag, Deerfield, and nearby Brookfield. The Springfield area had suffered some minor raids, but townspeople continued to believe that the neighboring Agawams were still loyal to the English or at least were neutral.

In late September and early October, the commissioners of the United Colonies of New England ordered the gathering of troops at the town of Hadley, Massachusetts. There they readied themselves for an expedition against enemy Native Americans north of Springfield. In response, Springfield community leader and military commander Major John Pynchon marched most of that town's troops north. With the town virtually undefended, a messenger arrived on October 4 with intelligence that Springfield's Agawam neighbors were plotting with Metacom to attack the town.

The next morning, October 5, Lieutenant Thomas Cooper and Constable Thomas Miller rode out of Springfield intending to talk with the local natives and dispel rumors of attack. Warriors ambushed the two men. Miller fell dead, but the mortally wounded Cooper managed to ride back to town and warn the inhabitants. Springfield's residents were thus able to withdraw safely to fortified garrison houses. They could do nothing, however, to prevent warriors from burning the settlement's undefended houses, barns, and outbuildings.

On learning of the native attack, two English forces under Pynchon and Major Robert Treat immediately marched south to relieve Springfield. Treat arrived first and attempted to cross the Connecticut River to assist the town's defenders, but his forces were driven back. The attacking natives, who had been reinforced by Nipmuck warriors, then withdrew with the arrival in midafternoon of Pynchon's forces from Hadley.

The English suffered only minor casualties in the attack, with three dead and three or four wounded, but the town was virtually destroyed. More than 30 houses, countless outbuildings, corn and hay stores, and indispensable mills all burned to the ground. Nearly a third of the town's families were left homeless and destitute. Despite the tremendous destruction, English settlers and soldiers remained in Springfield, maintaining an English presence in the upper Connecticut Valley. Not surprisingly, the "treachery" of supposedly friendly natives led to greater suspicion of all neutral or English-allied natives, resulting in the internment of Massachusetts's Christian natives on Deer Island in Boston Harbor. Furthermore, the events at Springfield reignited the debate over colonial military policy. Clearly, the concentration of troops for offensive actions against hostile natives had left Springfield and other towns virtually undefended. As a result, the colonies began employing a combination of garrison forces to protect exposed settlements and raiding forces to combat native enemies on their own ground.

DAVID M. CORLETT

See also

King Philip's War; Metacom; Nipmucks; Wampanoags

References

Drake, James D. *King Philip's War: Civil War in New England, 1675–1676.* Amherst: University of Massachusetts Press, 1999.

Drake, James D. *The Northern Colonial Frontier, 1607–1763.* Albuquerque: University of New Mexico Press, 1974.

Leach, Douglas Edward. *Flintlock and Tomahawk: New England in King Philip's War.* East Orleans, MA: Parnassus Imprints, 1992.

Squanto
Birth Date: Unknown
Death Date: 1622

Patuxet native perhaps best known for his services as an interpreter for the Pilgrims. Squanto also showed the Pilgrims how to survive in New England. No information is known about Squanto's birth or early years. In 1614 Thomas Hunter seized a number of native captives including Squanto, who was then taken to Spain to be sold as a slave.

A carved bust of Patuxet Native American Squanto. Believed to have been taken from America in 1614, Squanto returned to become the principal interpreter for the New England colonists. (AP/Wide World Photos)

Little is known about Squanto's time in Spain. However, by 1617 he was living in the London home of the Newfoundland Company's treasurer, John Slany. Hoping to use Squanto as an interpreter and intermediary, the English took him to Newfoundland in 1618. Squanto returned to Patuxet while serving as a guide for Thomas Dermer's 1619 expeditions to Cape Cod and Martha's Vineyard. On his return to Patuxet he discovered that the village had been wiped out by smallpox.

The Wampanoags subsequently took Squanto captive, and he remained with them until March 1621. Working with an Abenaki named Samoset, Squanto helped the Wampanoags establish relations with the new English settlement at Plymouth. Squanto soon began spending more time with the English, serving as an interpreter between the Plymouth leadership and the Wampanoag sachem Massasoit.

The Wampanoags then permitted Squanto to live with the English. There he acted as an interpreter and a mediator for the English. He also obtained a quantity of maize and trained the English settlers in the planting and harvesting of the crop. His instruction in the cultivation of corn may indeed have helped the Pilgrims survive the first few harsh winters of New England.

Squanto also attempted to rebuild the Patuxet tribe, scouring the region for survivors of the smallpox epidemic. This angered the Pokanokets, who saw this as a challenge. Thus, Plymouth Colony vowed to protect Squanto. Despite his difficulties with the Pokanokets, Squanto did exercise a degree of influence among native peoples. Toward the end of his life, which was spent among the Pilgrims, he lost some of that prestige when he was accused of playing the Wampanoags and Pilgrims against each other. Squanto died sometime in 1622 in the vicinity of Plymouth Colony.

ROGER M. CARPENTER

See also
Abenakis; Massasoit; Puritans; Samoset; Wampanoags

References
Salisbury, Neal. *Manitou and Providence: Indians, Europeans, and the Making of New England, 1500–1643*. New York: Oxford University Press, 1982.
Salisbury, Neal. "Squanto: Last of the Patuxet." In *The Human Tradition in Colonial America*, edited by Ian K. Steele and Nancy L. Rhoden, 21–36. Wilmington, DE: Scholarly Resources, 1999.

Stagecoach

A horse-drawn four-wheeled covered or enclosed coach designed to transport passengers or cargo over medium to long distances. Stagecoaches reached their peak of popularity in the 1840s and early 1850s but were soon superseded by railroads. There were a great variety of stagecoaches, but they can be divided into four main types: the Concord coach, a large carriage named after the U.S. manufacturer; the mail (or post) coach, designed to carry mail; the mud coach, smaller and lighter than the Concord; and the road coach, which was between a mud coach and a Concord coach in size.

Stagecoaches used in the American West invaded the traditional trade and travel routes employed by Native Americans, which strained relations between them and the white settlers. Regular mail service and passenger routes provided means of communication and travel that encouraged miners, settlers, and traders to move into a given area, but this led to population increases that created more friction between whites and Native Americans.

Stagecoaches were typically slow, traveling at 5 to 12 miles per hour, and regularly scheduled coach stops were made to change horses and drivers at designated stations along the route. Poor roads, especially in the hinterland, frequently impeded stagecoach travel.

Prior to the organization of the express companies, communication with the West Coast was usually by steamship twice a month to San Francisco. On March 3, 1857, however, Congress authorized the U.S. postmaster to take bids for mail delivery between the Missouri River and San Francisco. Eight stage and express companies were outbid six months later by John Butterfield Sr. of Butterfield Overland Mail, who won the yearly contract for $600,000 to provide mail every 25 days or less between the two destinations. The federal agency required inclusion in the 2,600-mile so-called Ox Bow Route of Fort Smith, Arkansas; El Paso, Texas; and Fort Yuma, California.

The route took the stagecoaches directly through the territory of numerous Native American nations. Newspapers reported frequent attacks on stages. Sometimes these were by white robbers in the guise of Native Americans in that particular area.

Overland Mail began delivering mail twice a week beginning on September 15, 1858, with service between San Francisco and Missouri. The Butterfield Line was named to honor the company's president. Each stagecoach began the route in Missouri and then dipped south through El Paso and then west to Los Angeles before shifting north to San Francisco, through California's Central Valley.

The American Civil War (1861–1865) required a change in stagecoach routes northward, traveling across the centermost part of the Great Plains, a route that the Pony Express riders took from 1860 to 1861. The Pioneer Stage Line first operated coaches from San Francisco to Virginia City, Nevada, where the Overland Mail Company picked up mail and passengers and transported them to Salt Lake City, Utah. Ben ("the Stagecoach King") Holladay's Pioneer Stage Line then completed the route through Denver into Missouri. Butterfield forced Holladay to sell out to him, after which Holladay organized his men, dressed as Native Americans, to burn Butterfield's stages and rob riders, forcing Butterfield into financial distress. Holladay took back his line and sold out at a huge profit to Wells, Fargo & Company, a major stagecoach enterprise.

Wells Fargo (as the company is commonly known), under the leadership of Henry Wells and William Fargo, took over all the routes along this path (including Holladay's). These were then combined into the largest stagecoach company in history by 1866. New stops were added in the mining towns of Colorado, Utah, Montana, and Idaho. The stage empire came to an end with the completion of the transcontinental railroad in 1869, but rural stage lines continued to operate into the early part of the 20th century. While the railroads dealt a crippling blow to stagecoaches, so too did the stagecoach bring paralyzing changes to Native American culture.

PAMELA LEE GRAY

See also

Butterfield Overland Mail Route; Overland Trail; Pony Express; Railroads; Wells Fargo

References

Fradkin, Philip L. *Stagecoach: Wells Fargo and the American West.* New York: Simon and Schuster, 2002.

Moody, Ralph. *Stagecoach West.* Lincoln: University of Nebraska Press, 1998.

Staked Plains

A high dry plateau in eastern New Mexico and western Texas rising to a height of 3,000 feet in the south, where it joins with the Edwards Plateau and gradually ascends toward the north and west to about 5,000 feet. The Staked Plains are also known as Llano Estacado (Spanish for "Palisaded Plains").

The origin of the name "Llano Estacado" goes back to Spanish explorer Francisco Coronado, who observed the area in 1541. The surface of the plateau itself is nearly flat, and the very gradual rise is scarcely noticeable. The plateau is bounded by sharply rising escarpments, which is what led Coronado to describe it as a palisaded plain. It is an area measuring about 250 miles north to south and 150 miles east to west. The Staked Plains are windswept and arid, with very little natural vegetation except scrub, sage, and seasonal grasses.

The Staked Plains formed the heart of Comancheria, the Comanche homeland. For decades the area was thought to be impenetrable to whites. However, Comancheros, Hispanic traders from New Mexico, routinely trekked onto the forbidding plains to trade with the Comanches and their Kiowa allies. In the mid-19th century the Comanches and Kiowas used the Staked Plains as a natural sanctuary to elude the U.S. Army and as a base from which to raid Texas settlements. The dry climate made conditions very difficult for the grain-fed and well-watered cavalry horses, although Native American ponies, which had originated from escaped Spanish horses in the 16th and 17th centuries, were able to survive in the inhospitable environment. The canyons on the plateau, leading down into the surrounding plains area, served as winter campsites for the Comanches. Although the area was

The Llano Estacado (Staked Plains) figured prominently in the Indian conflicts of the Southwest against the Comanches, Kiowas, and Cheyennes. The First Battle of Adobe Walls in 1864 and the Red River War in 1874–1875, which included the Second Battle of Adobe Walls and the Battle of Palo Duro Canyon, were fought on the Llano Estacado. (Tom Bean/Corbis)

forbidding, army explorations conducted by Captain Randolph Marcy in the 1850s and later expeditions by various army units began to unravel the mystery of the Staked Plains and eventually dispelled the notion of the region's impregnability. Comanche and Kiowa hideouts on the Staked Plains became the target of a massive five-pronged military effort in 1874, the Red River War. The last significant battle of the southern Plains was fought in Palo Duro Canyon on September 28, 1874, with Colonel Ranald S. Mackenzie and the 4th U.S. Cavalry attacking a large Comanche village, occupied principally by the Kwahadi (Quahadi) Band led by Chief Quanah Parker. After the destruction of the village and the pony herd there, the Kwahadis eventually surrendered, to be relocated to the Comanche reservation in Indian Territory (Oklahoma).

In the late 1800s and early 1900s settlers attempted to raise cattle on the Staked Plains, but the cattle quickly destroyed the natural grasses. Today, irrigation produces significant quantities of cotton. The cities of Lubbock and Amarillo, Texas, are located on the Staked Plains and draw water from underground aquifers.

JOHN THOMAS BROOM AND DAVID COFFEY

See also

Comanche Campaign; Comanches; Kwahadi Comanches; Mackenzie, Ranald Slidell; Palo Duro Canyon, Battle of; Quanah Parker; Red River War

References

Ferhenbach, T. R. *Comanches: The History of a People.* New York: Anchor Books, 2003.

Hoig, Stan. *Tribal Wars of the Southern Plains.* Norman: University of Oklahoma Press, 1993.

Matthews, W. A., III. *The Geologic Story of Palo Duro Canyon.* Guidebook 8, Bureau of Economic Geology. Austin: University of Texas, 1969.

Wallace, Ernest, and E. Adamson Hoebel. *The Comanches: Lords of the South Plains.* 1952; reprint, Norman: University of Oklahoma Press, 1986.

Whitlock, V. H. *Cowboy Life on the Llano Estacado.* Norman: University of Oklahoma Press, 1970.

Standing Bear
Birth Date: 1829
Death Date: September 1908

Ponca leader and plaintiff in an important U.S. District Court case in 1879 establishing Native American rights (*Standing Bear v. Crook*). Standing Bear was born in 1829 near the Niobrara River in what is now northeastern Nebraska. The Poncas initially enjoyed good relations with the United States, and Standing Bear and other leaders favored peace. In 1858 they ceded part of their territory to the federal government in a treaty that guaranteed the Poncas' right to their remaining land along the Niobrara and protection from their enemies.

The 1868 Fort Laramie Treaty, to which the Poncas were not a party, inadvertently placed their land within the boundaries of the Great Sioux Reservation. Standing Bear and other Ponca leaders repeatedly protested this violation of the 1858 treaty, particularly because the Sioux and the Poncas were traditional enemies. However, the government limited its response to the appropriation of funds to reimburse the Poncas for their loss of life and property at the hands of Sioux raiders.

Despite the Poncas' difficult situation, Standing Bear continued to advocate peace. In 1876 following the Battle of the Little Bighorn (June 25–26, 1876), Congress decided to move many of the northern tribes, including the Poncas, to Indian Territory (present-day Oklahoma). The legislation stipulated that the Poncas had to agree to be relocated.

In January 1877 federal Indian agent Edward C. Kemble arrived at the Ponca Reservation and told the Poncas that they had to move. When tribal leaders questioned the order, Kemble allowed 10 of them, including Standing Bear, to accompany him to Indian Territory and examine the land.

Upon their arrival, Standing Bear and his fellow chiefs expressed dismay at the barren environment. Kemble offered to take them to see other areas, but the Poncas, who had twice been stricken with illness, declined. Angered by their refusal, Kemble abandoned them in Indian Territory and refused their request for funds that would have allowed them to return home by train.

Ponca chief Standing Bear filed a lawsuit (*Standing Bear v. Crook*) that in 1879 resulted in the U.S. government's recognition of constitutional rights for Native Americans. (Library of Congress)

Instead, Standing Bear and the other leaders were forced to make the 500-mile journey on foot in winter. They reached the Niobrara River after a 40-day trek.

Kemble reported the Poncas' reaction to his superiors, and General William T. Sherman decided to use federal troops to force the Poncas to relocate. Kemble returned to the reservation in April and used the threat of military action to convince some of the Poncas to accept removal. Standing Bear protested vigorously and was arrested. He was released, but troops forced the Poncas to leave their homes on May 21, 1877. They arrived in Indian Territory on July 9. About one-third died from hardship, disease, and starvation on the journey and shortly after reaching their new reservation.

In late December 1878 Standing Bear's eldest son died after obtaining his father's pledge to bury him on the old tribal lands. Standing Bear thus set out for Nebraska with about 30 followers in January 1879.

Whites saw the party and, thinking that the Native Americans were hostile, reported them to federal authorities, who ordered Brigadier General George Crook to arrest them. The troops found Standing Bear and his party on the Omaha Reservation in March and confined them at Fort Omaha. Crook, however, sympathized with Standing Bear and brought his story to the attention of reporter Thomas H. Tibbles. His articles inspired much public sympathy for Standing Bear and his people. Two attorneys volunteered to assist the Poncas and served Crook with a writ of habeas corpus demanding that he show cause for the detention of Standing Bear.

The U.S. district attorney asserted that Native Americans were not considered persons under the U.S. Constitution and therefore had no legal rights. Federal judge Elmer Dundy convened a trial on April 30 and after two days of testimony issued his ruling on May 12. Dundy declared that Standing Bear was in fact a person under U.S. law and was entitled to his rights, including the ability to go where he pleased. Dundy stated that the government had lacked the authority to remove the Poncas without their consent and ordered Standing Bear and his followers released.

Standing Bear and the Poncas continued their journey, and in 1880 the government granted them a small reservation on the Niobrara River. The following year Congress compensated them for the losses they had suffered during removal. Upon learning of Dundy's decision, the Poncas in Indian Territory prepared to return home. Agent William H. Whiteman, however, with assistance from the army, prevented them from leaving.

From 1879 to 1883, Standing Bear made several tours of the eastern United States to advocate for Native American rights. He then returned to the Ponca Reservation in Nebraska, where he died in September 1908.

JIM PIECUCH

See also
Crook, George; Fort Laramie, Treaty of (1851); Fort Laramie, Treaty of (1868); *Standing Bear v. Crook*

References
Brown, Dee. *Bury My Heart at Wounded Knee.* New York: Holt, Rinehart and Winston, 1970.
Tibbles, Thomas H. *The Ponca Chiefs: An Account of the Trial of Standing Bear.* Edited by Kay Graber. Lincoln: University of Nebraska Press, 1972.

Standing Bear v. Crook

Landmark U.S. court case establishing constitutional rights for Native Americans. The events that led to the case of *Standing Bear v. Crook* began in 1877, when the U.S. Army forcibly removed the Poncas from their land in northeastern Nebraska to Indian Territory (present-day Oklahoma). Standing Bear was a Ponca leader and the chief plaintiff in the U.S. District Court case. Standing Bear's eldest son died in late December 1878 and on his deathbed obtained his father's promise to bury him in the Poncas' homeland.

In accordance with his son's wishes, Standing Bear set out for Nebraska from Indian Territory with about 30 followers in January 1879. White settlers saw the party, believed them to be hostile, and promptly notified federal authorities, who ordered Brigadier General George Crook to take them into custody. Crook's soldiers found Standing Bear on the Omaha Reservation in March, arrested him and the other Poncas with him, and confined them at Fort Omaha.

Crook felt pity for Standing Bear, however, and informed Omaha journalist Thomas H. Tibbles of the Poncas' plight. Tibbles publicized the affair, and the news spread widely, winning Standing Bear considerable public support. After reading and hearing about the situation, John L. Webster, an Omaha attorney, volunteered to represent Standing Bear and was soon joined by Andrew Poppleton, the chief attorney for the Union Pacific Railroad.

Webster and Poppleton served Crook with a writ of habeas corpus demanding to know the grounds on which Standing Bear was being held. When Crook appeared before federal judge Elmer Dundy to show his orders, U.S. district attorney G. M. Lambertson argued that Standing Bear could not demand the writ because Native Americans were not citizens of the United States, nor were they "persons within the meaning of the law." Therefore, no Native American could initiate legal action against the federal government.

Dundy allowed each side to present arguments at a trial that began on April 30, 1879. Webster and Poppleton insisted that Native Americans were indeed persons entitled to legal rights. Lambertson countered that Native Americans were completely subject to federal authority but with no rights to challenge that authority. Dundy overruled Lambertson's objections and permitted Standing Bear to testify. The Ponca leader eloquently asserted his humanity and made a moving plea for his legal rights. After two days of testimony, the trial adjourned.

On May 12, 1879, Dundy issued his ruling. In a carefully reasoned decision, Dundy declared that Native Americans were in fact persons under U.S. law and that Standing Bear's habeas corpus action was valid. He ruled that the Poncas and all Native Americans had the same right as whites to travel so long as they obeyed the law, and therefore the prisoners at Fort Omaha were illegally held. Dundy added that the U.S. government had no legal authority to remove the Poncas to Indian Territory without their consent and ordered the immediate release of Standing Bear and his followers. Spectators in the courtroom responded to the decision with a standing ovation.

Standing Bear and the Poncas were freed and returned to their homeland. In 1880 Congress granted them a small reservation on the Niobrara River and a year later compensated them for the losses they had suffered during removal. The U.S. Army, however, refused to allow the remaining Poncas in Indian Territory to return home, limiting the effects of Dundy's decision.

JIM PIECUCH

See also

Crook, George; Fort Laramie, Treaty of (1851); Fort Laramie, Treaty of (1868); Standing Bear

References

Brown, Dee. *Bury My Heart at Wounded Knee.* New York: Holt, Rinehart and Winston, 1970.

Tibbles, Thomas H. *The Ponca Chiefs: An Account of the Trial of Standing Bear.* Edited by Kay Graber. Lincoln: University of Nebraska Press, 1972.

Standing Rock Reservation

Reservation straddling the border of present-day North and South Dakota created for the Sioux in 1889. The reservation currently encompasses 3,572 square miles. Standing Rock Reservation was originally part of the Great Sioux Reservation established by the Fort Laramie Treaty in 1868 following Red Cloud's War (1866–1868). Under the terms of the treaty, the U.S. government established several agencies in Sioux territory. The Standing Rock Agency was established in 1874 to supervise relations with the Upper and Lower Yanktonai, Cut Head, Blackfoot, Hunkpapa, Lakota, and Dakota Sioux bands and was located on the western bank of the Missouri River near Fort Yates in the Dakota Territory.

Within a decade after the signing of the Fort Laramie Treaty, tensions between the Sioux and encroaching whites led to renewed conflict. The discovery of gold in the Black Hills in 1874 brought an influx of prospectors into Sioux lands. When Native American leaders protested this violation of the treaty, government officials attempted to purchase the Black Hills, but the Sioux refused. Angered by the Native Americans' stubbornness, in December 1875 the Bureau of Indian Affairs ordered all of the Native Americans to report to their agencies or face military action. However, a lack of provisions at the agencies made it impossible for most of the Native Americans who did go to the agencies to remain there.

The army began a campaign against the Native Americans in the spring of 1876 that featured the Battle of the Little Bighorn

Census-taking at Standing Rock Agency, South Dakota, circa 1880–1900. (Library of Congress)

(June 25–26, 1876) and culminated in a punitive response from the army that compelled most Sioux and Cheyennes to return to their reservations. Shortly afterward the government put the Sioux reservation under military control. In August 1877 Congress, claiming that the Sioux had violated the 1868 treaty, unilaterally appropriated 7.7 million acres in the Black Hills, along with other tracts of the Great Sioux Reservation.

As more settlers moved westward, the U.S. government became eager to take more Sioux land. In 1882 a commission headed by Newton Edmunds bullied, cajoled, and deceived the Sioux into ceding an additional 14,000 square miles, or nearly half of their remaining territory. However, questions about the validity of the agreement were raised in Washington, and the following year a second commission led by Senator Henry Dawes traveled to the Dakota Territory to investigate the matter. At Standing Rock the commissioners conferred with Sitting Bull who, like other Sioux leaders, denounced the treaty. The agreement was subsequently withdrawn.

This Native American victory was short-lived. In 1889 yet another government commission arrived, and this time, by threatening to take the land if the Sioux did not sell it, succeeded in purchasing the desired territory. Standing Rock Reservation was carved from the remaining Sioux holdings. Its boundaries were the Cannonball River on the north, Cedar Creek on the northwest, and Lake Oache on the Missouri River to the east.

Frustrated by his people's decision to sell their land, Sitting Bull, like many Native Americans across the West, developed an interest in the Ghost Dance movement, a Native American spiritual revival that promised the return of the dead and renewal of the earth through performance of ritual dances. Upon further inquiry, Sitting Bull became skeptical of Ghost Dance teachings, but he allowed his followers at Standing Rock to practice the rituals. Agent James McLaughlin, a longtime enemy of Sitting Bull, accused the Sioux leader of promoting the movement and ordered his arrest. On December 15, 1890, Native American police attempted to carry out McLaughlin's instructions, sparking a confrontation in which Sitting Bull and several others were killed. The incident ended Sioux resistance at Standing Rock.

In 1910 the U.S. government took additional land at Standing Rock, reducing the reservation to its present size. The inhabitants engaged primarily in farming and raising cattle. The reservation's population in 2000 was 8,259 according to the U.S. census.

PAMELA LEE GRAY AND JIM PIECUCH

See also

Fort Laramie, Treaty of (1868); Ghost Dance; Lakota Sioux; Sioux; Sitting Bull

References

Brown, Dee. *Bury My Heart at Wounded Knee*. New York: Holt, Rinehart and Winston, 1970.

Utley, Robert M. *The Indian Frontier of the American West, 1846–1890*. Albuquerque: University of New Mexico Press, 1984.

Utley, Robert M. *The Lance and the Shield: The Life and Times of Sitting Bull*. New York: Ballantine, 1993.

Standish, Myles
Birth Date: ca. 1584
Death Date: October 3, 1656

First military adviser and captain general of Plymouth Colony; from 1644 to 1649 he served the colony in a number of capacities, including treasurer. Myles Standish was born about 1584 most likely in Chorley, Lancashire, England, and was commissioned as a lieutenant in the army in 1602. He eventually caught the attention of the Reverend John Robinson, spiritual leader of the refugee Pilgrims in Leiden, Holland, where Standish was serving during the Twelve Years' Truce in the Dutch revolt against Spain.

Opting to leave the Netherlands and migrate to the New World, the Pilgrims recruited Standish to manage the defense of the colony. Outfitted with his armor, helmet, rapier, dagger, and a musket, Standish—now a captain—was militarily the most well equipped of all the colonists when they set sail in August 1620. The diminutive Standish, with his deep red hair and prickly temperament, proved a formidable adversary to the New World natives, whom he regarded with much distrust.

On November 11, 1620, Standish and 40 other male passengers aboard the *Mayflower* anchored off present-day Provincetown, Massachusetts, and signed the Mayflower Compact, creating a civil government for Plymouth Colony. Standish immediately oversaw a reconnaissance of Cape Cod and ultimately approved of the site selected for settlement. During the first difficult winter in Plymouth, Standish was among only 7 colonists untouched by illness. Among the stricken was his first wife, Rose, who died in January 1621.

With growing anxiety over the ever-diminishing number of colonists and anticipating trouble from the natives from whom the colonists had previously commandeered corn, in February 1621 Standish removed four cannon from the *Mayflower* and positioned them on high ground near the settlement. Tensions subsided the following month, however, when Massasoit (Ousa Mequin), the grand sachem of the nearby Wampanoag Confederacy, forged an alliance with the colonists.

Meanwhile, Standish was elected captain general of the settlement. The alliance was mutually beneficial, providing security for Plymouth and military aid for the Wampanoags in case of hostilities with their traditional adversaries, the Narragansetts. Standish did not hesitate to use aggression when faced with a perceived native threat. In 1623 he led a band of eight Plymouth men on a raid against the Massachusetts tribe after rumors surfaced of an imminent attack against Wessagusset, a small rival English fur-trading colony to the north (present-day Weymouth, Massachusetts). Standish saw the reportedly hostile natives as a threat to all colonists. Pretending to have come for the purpose of trade, Standish drew the suspected natives close to his party and then killed eight of them including the sachem Wituwamet, whose head was later placed on display in Plymouth. In retaliation, Massachusetts warriors killed three Englishmen from Wessagusset.

Fearing further reprisals, the remainder of the Wessagusset colonists abandoned their outpost and sailed back to England, leaving Plymouth, for the time being, with a monopoly on the fur trade.

Standish's heavy-handed preemptive strike did little for relations between the English and the natives and did not escape criticism. On learning of the incident, Reverend Robinson wrote Plymouth governor William Bradford from Holland about his concern that Standish had become "a terrour to poor barbarous people." Thomas Morton, a non-Pilgrim fur trader who was later arrested by Standish for "interracial cavorting" with the natives and who referred to his jailor as "Captain Shrimp," reported that Standish's ruthlessness led natives to regard all the English as "Wotowequenage" or "Cutthroats."

Standish held a number of military and civil positions while at Plymouth. In 1635 he participated in an abortive attempt to reclaim a Plymouth trading post in Maine recently seized by the French. As a colonial agent and representative, Standish made several trips back to England to secure trade goods and negotiate debt repayments with the colony's merchant sponsors. From 1644 to 1649 he served as the treasurer of the colony. Standish died on October 3, 1656, in nearby Duxbury, a town that he helped establish in the 1630s.

ALAN C. DOWNS

See also

Massasoit; Narragansetts; Wampanoags; Wessagusset Raid

References

Cave, Alfred A. *The Pequot War.* Amherst: University of Massachusetts Press, 1996.

Jennings, Francis. *The Invasion of America: Indians, Colonialism, and the Cant of Conquest.* 1976; reprint, Chapel Hill: University of North Carolina Press, 2010.

Philbrick, Nathaniel. *Mayflower: A Story of Courage, Community, and War.* New York: Viking, 2006.

St. Clair, Arthur
Birth Date: March 23, 1734
Death Date: August 31, 1818

Politician and Continental Army officer. Arthur St. Clair was born at Thurso in Caithness, Scotland, on March 23, 1734. In May 1757 he purchased an ensign's commission in the 60th Foot, Royal American Regiment, to serve in the French and Indian War (1754–1763). He then went to Boston, married, and resigned his commission in 1762. St. Clair left Boston in 1764 when the Penn family asked him to look after its interests on the Pennsylvania frontier. He settled at Fort Ligonier and then held a succession of local offices.

In May 1775 St. Clair became involved with the American Revolutionary War (1775–1783) when he attended a protest meeting against actions by the Crown. In December 1775 St. Clair secured a commission as a colonel in the Continental Army and assumed command of the 2nd Pennsylvania Regiment. By March

12, 1776, he had completed his recruiting and left Philadelphia en route to Quebec to help withdraw American forces from Canada. Arriving in May, St. Clair was able to cover the Americans' retreat from Quebec. The Americans finally aborted the Canadian campaign, eventually withdrawing to Fort Ticonderoga, where St. Clair remained for most of the summer.

On August 9, 1776, St. Clair was appointed brigadier general. Three months later he joined Continental Army commander General George Washington on the Delaware River. In late December with the enlistments of most of his men about to expire, Washington risked everything on a daring attack against the British outpost of Trenton. On the night of December 25–26, 1776, Washington's troops crossed the Delaware River into New Jersey. St. Clair led a column under Major General John Sullivan in the ensuing Patriot success at Trenton. St. Clair also played an important role in the Patriot victory at Princeton on January 3, 1777. After the battle on the march to Morristown, St. Clair commanded the rear guard, destroying bridges along the road.

St. Clair was rewarded for his performance with promotion to major general on February 19, 1777. In the summer of 1777 he took command of Fort Ticonderoga. He arrived with 2,200 men to strengthen the garrison but neglected to fortify Mount Defiance that overlooked the fort. The British invasion force under Lieutenant General John Burgoyne arrived at Ticonderoga on June 20, and by July 5 Burgoyne had placed guns on Mount Defiance. St. Clair knew that his position was hopeless, so he and his men escaped the fort on the night of July 6. His force eventually joined Major General Horatio Gates to fight in the Battles of Saratoga (September 19 and October 7, 1777), but St. Clair did not join them. Removed from command, St. Clair found himself accused of both cowardice and incompetence in the loss of Ticonderoga. He demanded and received a court-martial.

While awaiting his court-martial proceedings, St. Clair joined Washington at the Battle of Brandywine in Pennsylvania in September. St. Clair was not present at the Battle of Germantown in October because he was visiting family. He remained with the army during the winter of privation at Valley Forge (1777–1778) and fought in the Battle of Monmouth the next June. He was restored to command after his court-martial exonerated him in August 1778. St. Clair spent most of 1779 campaigning with Sullivan against the Iroquois in western New York.

St. Clair helped to end the mutiny of several Pennsylvania regiments during the winter of 1780–1781, and when Washington finally moved south in the summer of 1781 during the Yorktown Campaign, the commander in chief ordered St. Clair to stay in Philadelphia and raise more men. St. Clair did not join the army at Yorktown until October 15, by which time the siege and campaign were nearly over. After the British surrender, Washington sent St. Clair to the Carolinas to join Major General Nathanael Greene. St. Clair did not reach Greene's army, near the South Carolina coast, until December 27. St. Clair remained with the Continental Army until November 5, 1783.

Following the war, St. Clair quickly assumed a role in the central government, winning election to Congress in 1785. He was elevated to the presidency of Congress on February 2, 1787, and was appointed the first governor of the Northwest Territory in 1788.

In 1791 St. Clair led a campaign against Native Americans in the Old Northwest Territory during Little Turtle's War (1785–1795). Ill much of the time, he neglected to train his men and on November 4, 1791, was soundly defeated in a battle with Native Americans known as St. Clair's Defeat, the Columbia Massacre, or the Battle of the Wabash; it was the greatest defeat of the U.S. Army by Native Americans in history. Following the debacle, St. Clair resigned his army command at the request of President George Washington. Ultimately cleared by court-martial, St. Clair continued to serve as governor of the Northwest Territory until 1802, when he retired. He died on August 31, 1818, in Greensburg, Pennsylvania.

RYAN STAUDE

See also

Little Turtle's War; Old Northwest Territory; St. Clair's Campaign; Wabash, Battle of the

References

Middlekauf, Robert. *The Glorious Cause: The American Revolution, 1763–1789.* Oxford: Oxford University Press, 2005.

St. Clair, Arthur. *The St. Clair Papers: The Life and Public Services of Arthur St. Clair.* 2 vols. Edited by William Henry Smith. Cincinnati: Robert Clarke, 1882.

St. Clair's Campaign
Start Date: September 6, 1791
End Date: November 4, 1791

U.S. Army campaign during the wars for the Northwest Territory marked by the worst defeat ever inflicted upon the U.S. Army by Native American forces in the Battle of the Wabash (November 4, 1791). When Brigadier General Josiah Harmar's attack on Miami villages in the Northwest Territory failed in October 1790, President George Washington blamed undisciplined militia as the cause of the failure rather than the skill of Native American warriors commanded by Miami chief Little Turtle. In March 1791 Secretary of War Henry Knox secured the appointment of Arthur St. Clair, governor of the Northwest Territory, as a major general and ranking officer in the U.S. Army to command a new expedition into Native American country. St. Clair hoped to raise a force of about 3,000 men and to establish a fort near the Miami villages to secure the territory for white settlers and deter further Native American attacks.

During the late summer of 1791, St. Clair tried to organize his force but faced numerous delays because of inadequate logistics, including poor-quality gunpowder and a limited number of horses. Recruiting for the army was slow, many men suffered from smallpox, and others were lost to accidents and attempted desertion. St. Clair himself was ill much of the time and did little to train his men. Beyond that, he had never served on the frontier and knew little of American Indian warfare. To make the situation worse, he failed to listen to advice proffered by knowledgeable subordinates. Eventually his force consisted of the 1st and 2nd regular army regiments, two Kentucky Militia regiments, a battery of 6 cannon, and about 400 noncombatant civilian camp followers, including women and children. On September 6, 1791, some three months behind schedule, St. Clair's army departed its base at Fort Washington (Cincinnati, Ohio) for the movement into the Northwest Territory.

The lack of roads required the army to carve one out of the wilderness and establish a series of fortifications to guard their line of communication and supply back to Fort Washington. Inclement late autumn weather that saw much rain and cold hampered operations, and in two months the expedition had advanced just a little more than 100 miles. By the beginning of November, St. Clair's force had been reduced by illness and desertion to only 1,400 effectives.

On November 3, 1791, St. Clair's army encamped in a clearing near a tributary of the Wabash River (near the border of present-day Ohio and Indiana). The clearing was too small for the whole army, so the militia was forced to encamp a few hundred yards on the other side of the river. Believing that he was still 15–20 miles from the main Indian villages, St. Clair posted sentries but made no attempt to fortify the camp or send out patrols to ensure that hostile warriors were not nearby. In fact, the Americans were less than a mile from about 1,200 Miami, Wyandot, Ottawa, and Delaware warriors led by Little Turtle and Blue Jacket.

At dawn on November 4, Little Turtle and his warriors attacked the Americans just as they were arousing in camp. The Indians hit the militia first, forcing them to flee into the main camp and spreading panic among the rest of the army. The Americans heard a noise that sounded like the howling of wolves as the warriors surrounded them and destroyed all form of military organization. After several hours of fighting, the American perimeter had been constricted to a point where men huddled together in a bewildered crowd. By 9:30 a.m. the Battle of the Wabash (also known as St. Clair's Defeat) was over. St. Clair's command had been decimated. He had lost 632 killed and 264 wounded, a 64 percent casualty rate and three times what Lieutenant Colonel George Custer would lose at the Battle of the Little Bighorn (June 25–26, 1876). More significantly, Little Turtle had effectively destroyed almost the entire existing U.S. Army.

Two years later Major General Anthony Wayne would avenge St. Clair's defeat by organizing and training a new army, the Legion of the United States, which decisively defeated the Native Americans at the Battle of Fallen Timbers (August 20, 1794).

STEVEN J. RAUCH

See also

Blue Jacket; Fallen Timbers, Battle of; Harmar, Josiah; Legion of the United States; Little Turtle; Little Turtle's War; St. Clair, Arthur; Wabash, Battle of the; Wayne, Anthony; Wayne's Campaign

References

Guthman, William H. *March to Massacre: A History of the First Seven Years of the United States Army 1784–1791.* New York: McGraw-Hill, 1970.

Lytle, Richard. *The Soldiers of America's First Army, 1791.* Lanham, MD: Scarecrow, 2004.

Sword, Wiley. *President Washington's Indian War: The Struggle for the Old Northwest, 1790–1795.* Norman: University of Oklahoma Press, 1985.

St. Clair's Defeat

See Wabash, Battle of the

Steptoe, Edward Jenner

Birth Date: 1816

Death Date: April 17, 1865

U.S. Army officer. Edward Steptoe was born near Lynchburg, Virginia, in 1816. He attended the U.S. Military Academy, West Point, and graduated in 1837. Commissioned a second lieutenant of artillery, Steptoe subsequently held a number of assignments and saw action during the Second Seminole War (1835–1842), earning promotion to first lieutenant in 1838. Promoted to captain in 1847 during the Mexican-American War (1846–1848), Steptoe saw combat in numerous battles and operations, including at Cerro Gordo and Chapultepec, for which he was brevetted twice for meritorious service to major and to lieutenant colonel.

Posted to Utah during 1854–1855, Steptoe attempted to soothe relations among Mormons, non-Mormon settlers, and Native Americans. Promoted to major in 1855, he was then sent farther west, where he commanded a relief force organized by Colonel George Wright during the Yakima-Rogue War (1855–1858). Steptoe then became commander of Fort Walla Walla in present-day Washington state.

In the spring of 1858 Steptoe became involved in an engagement that would spark the 1858 Coeur d'Alene War, part of the Yakima-Rogue War. On May 6, 1858, a small white settlement at Colville requested military assistance from Steptoe's garrison. The settlers feared that they would soon come under attack by the Palouse, Spokane, Coeur d'Alene, and Nez Perce tribes, as several white miners had already been killed. Steptoe decided to grant the request and personally led a column of 164 troops from Fort Walla Walla and across the Snake River. The local Native American tribes mistook his action, believing that Steptoe was on an offensive mission. On May 16 a much larger force of Native Americans (as many as 1,000) approached and surrounded Steptoe's force. This precipitated the Battle of Pine Creek on May 17.

Vastly outnumbered and with inferior weapons, Steptoe managed to engineer a retreat early the next day but not before he suffered 8 dead and 11 wounded. Native American losses included 9 dead. Because U.S. troops withdrew so quickly, they were forced to leave behind their artillery and camp supplies, which were seized by the Native Americans.

Shortly after the encounter at Pine Creek, Steptoe's health began to deteriorate. He went back East but was compelled to resign his commission in 1861 after reaching the rank of lieutenant colonel. That same year Steptoe suffered a serious stroke that left him nearly paralyzed. He died on April 17, 1865, in Lynchburg, Virginia.

PAUL G. PIERPAOLI JR.

See also

Coeur d'Alenes; Coeur d'Alene War; Fort Walla Walla; Nez Perces; Palouses; Spokanes; Wright, George; Yakima-Rogue War

References

Gibson, Elizabeth. *Walla Walla.* Mount Pleasant, SC: Arcadia, 2004.

Utley, Robert M. *Frontiersmen in Blue: The United States and the Indian, 1848–1865.* Lincoln: University of Nebraska Press, 1967.

Stevens, Isaac Ingalls

Birth Date: March 25, 1818

Death Date: September 1, 1862

U.S. Army officer, territorial governor (1853–1857), and U.S. congressman (1857–1861). Isaac Ingalls Stevens was born in Andover, Massachusetts, on March 25, 1818. Frail and plagued by ill health as a child, he stood barely five feet tall as an adult. Nevertheless, his keen intellect and driving ambition served him well. After attending Phillips Academy for a brief time, he enrolled at the U.S. Military Academy, West Point, and graduated first in his class in 1839. He was commissioned a second lieutenant of engineers and served along the East Coast constructing defensive fortifications, earning quick promotion to first lieutenant in 1840. Stevens saw action during the Mexican-American War (1846–1848) in the Battle of Cerro Gordo, the Battle of Churubusco, and the Battle of Contreras. He was brevetted to captain and then to major and was seriously wounded during the drive on Mexico City in September 1847.

During a long convalescence Stevens wrote *Campaigns of the Rio Grande and of Mexico,* which was published in 1851. In the autumn of 1849 he began serving as the chief assistant to Alexander Bache, head of the U.S. Coast Survey in the War Department. In 1852 Stevens staunchly supported Franklin Pierce's Democratic Party presidential bid. Stevens delivered a number of electrifying speeches on behalf of Pierce and also penned numerous editorials backing his candidacy. As a result, after Pierce became president in 1853 he promptly rewarded Stevens with the governorship of

Isaac I. Stevens, governor of the Washington Territory during 1853–1857, negotiated a number of treaties with tribes in the Northwest. Several of these treaties figured in the later Indian Wars, especially those with the Nez Perces and Yakimas. (Library of Congress)

the Washington Territory. Stevens resigned his army commission in March 1853 to take up his new position. Along the way he oversaw a major surveying effort employing 125 men to plot the course of a proposed transcontinental railway that would link the Pacific Northwest with the Mississippi River.

Stevens's tenure as governor was steeped in controversy. Although he worked indefatigably and in accordance with policies set in Washington, his handling of Native Americans especially left much to be desired. Indeed, both whites and Native Americans accused him of extreme hubris and having dictatorial proclivities. In an attempt to reserve land for white settlement and to make room for the proposed railway, Stevens entered into a frenzy of negotiations with the various Native American tribes in the area. He sought the purchase of millions of acres of land and also sought to limit tribes to prescribed reservations. When tribes balked he frequently dispatched troops, which only further raised tensions between whites and Native Americans. His heavy-handedness helped provoke war with the Yakima, Palouse, Spokane, and Coeur d'Alene tribes in eastern Washington and western Idaho.

The fighting began in earnest in July 1855 and ended temporarily in November.

In 1856 Stevens declared martial law for two months in response to rising tensions between whites and Native Americans. This move was most controversial, including among many white settlers. In July 1858 war began anew between U.S. forces and the Yakimas and their allies. The renewed conflict came to a head on September 1, 1858, at the Battle of Four Lakes, which saw the Native Americans crushed. Stevens ordered the execution of several tribal leaders who had participated in the military struggle. As a result of these heavy-handed tactics, there were numerous calls for Stevens's recall. Some local officials who criticized Stevens were arrested, which did nothing to ameliorate his gubernatorial reputation. In 1856 Stevens successfully ran for a seat in the U.S. House of Representatives. He took office in March 1857 and was reelected in 1858 and 1860.

When the American Civil War (1861–1865) began in April 1861, Stevens promptly sought an army commission. His strong ties to the Democratic Party and pro-Southern politicians, however, prevented him from immediately rejoining the armed forces. Finally in July 1861 he was commissioned colonel of the 79th New York Infantry Regiment, a unit that had been plagued by poor leadership and mutiny. Within weeks Stevens had whipped the regiment into shape, taking it south to Virginia and then South Carolina. In September 1861 he was promoted to brigadier general of volunteers. He commanded the army post in Beaufort, South Carolina, and in June 1862 led an infantry division in the failed assault on Secessionville, south of Charleston.

After that Stevens was ordered, along with IX Corps, to join the Army of Virginia. He saw early action at the Second Battle of Bull Run (August 26–September 1, 1862) and brought up the rear of Major General John Pope's army during the withdrawal to Washington, D.C. Stevens's force was assaulted by Confederate troops under Major General Thomas J. Jackson near Chantilly, Virginia, on September 1. During the melee Stevens was struck in the head by a rifle ball and was killed instantly. He was posthumously promoted to major general of volunteers.

PAUL G. PIERPAOLI JR.

See also

Coeur d'Alenes; Coeur d'Alene War; Four Lakes, Battle of; Palouses; Spokanes; Yakima-Rogue War

References

Doty, James, ed. *Journal of Operations of Governor Isaac Ingalls Stevens of Washington Territory in 1855*. Fairfield, WA: Ye Galleon, 1978.

Miller, Christopher. *Prophetic Worlds: Indian and Whites on the Columbia Plateau*. Seattle: University of Washington Press, 2003.

Richards, Kent D. *Isaac I. Stevens: Young Man in a Hurry*. Provo, UT: Brigham Young University Press, 1979.

St. Francis, Canada, Rogers's Raid on

See Rogers's Raid on St. Francis

Stillman's Run, Battle of
Event Date: May 14, 1832

First military engagement of the Black Hawk War (1832). The Battle of Stillman's Run, also known as the Battle of Old Man's Creek or the Battle of Sycamore Creek, occurred in northern Illinois on May 14, 1832. Illinois militia under Major Isaiah Stillman encountered members of the Sauk and Fox tribes under the leadership of Black Hawk at a small stream near the present-day town of Stillman Valley. The ensuing skirmish was a confused affair, after which the pejorative moniker "Stillman's Run" was attached to it because of the militia's hasty withdraw from the field of battle.

Stillman had about 275 men under his command as he moved north from Dixon, Illinois, in search of Black Hawk and his British Band (so-named because they had supported the British during the War of 1812). The so-called Sucker Militia (a name of which Illinoisans at the time were proud, having derived from a species of fish found in Illinois waterways) moved only as fast as its supply train, especially the whiskey wagons. By happenstance, on the evening of May 14 Stillman's men encamped along Old Man's Creek where it emptied into the Rock River, a mere seven miles from Black Hawk's camp. What then transpired has been the subject of study and speculation ever since.

Some sources put Black Hawk's numbers at only 40 warriors, while others insist that there were more than 500 Sauk, Fox, Kickapoo, and Pottawatomi warriors present. Some historians assert that Black Hawk sent emissaries to negotiate surrender, while others insist that a small group of warriors lured some of the militia into chasing them into a trap. Regardless of the actual numbers and who attacked whom, the result was that the militia, well lubricated with intoxicating spirits, broke in the face of an attack and then scampered 25 miles back to Dixon, insisting that all of the Native Americans in Illinois were hot on their tails.

The battle cost the lives of 12 Illinois militiamen and perhaps as many as 5 of Black Hawk's men. While Black Hawk may have rejoiced in the ease of the victory, the dead militiamen would soon incite more white men to take up the pursuit of the native warriors.

Much of the confusion as to the actual events of that May evening in 1832 stems from the fact that those of the militia who were willing to talk or write about the debacle in later years were inclined to recount different versions with each telling.

EDWARD F. FINCH

See also
Black Hawk; Black Hawk War; Kickapoos; Pottawatomis; Sauks and Foxes

References
Black Hawk. *Black Hawk: An Autobiography.* Edited by Donald Jackson. 1833; reprint, Urbana: University of Illinois Press, 1964.
Jung, Patrick J. *The Black Hawk War of 1832.* Norman: University of Oklahoma Press, 2007.
Stevens, Eugene C. *Last Stand at Old Man's Creek.* Baltimore: Publish America, 2009.

Stuart, John
Birth Date: September 25, 1718
Death Date: March 21, 1779

British merchant, frontier diplomat, and superintendent of Indian affairs (1762–1779) in the southern colonies. Born in Inverness, Scotland, on September 25, 1718, John Stuart was educated in local schools and in London before traveling to Spain in 1736. There he worked as a clerk.

Returning to London, Stuart joined Commodore George Anson's 1740 expedition to the Pacific during the Anglo-Spanish War (1739–1744). Stuart's performance in this difficult operation earned him both high praise from Anson and substantial prize money. These funds enabled Stuart to begin a career as a merchant.

Stuart lived in Portsmouth and London before migrating in 1748 to Charles Town (present-day Charleston), South Carolina, where he established himself in business. In 1749 he traveled to England and married, and in 1751 he returned to South Carolina. He held various political offices there, including a seat in the provincial assembly. His business ventures failed, however, in 1752.

Shortly after the outbreak of the French and Indian War (1754–1763), Stuart secured a commission as a captain in the provincial militia and led his company to the frontier. His mission was to protect the pro-British Cherokees from Native Americans allied with the French. During his sojourn in the backcountry, he developed an admiration for the Cherokees and became close friends with one of their principal chiefs, Attakullakulla. Stuart was reassigned to oversee the construction of defenses at Port Royal (Beaufort) the following year. In 1759 he received orders to return to Fort Loudoun on the frontier when hostilities began between the Cherokees and South Carolina. In August 1760 the Cherokees forced the surrender of Fort Loudoun following a five-month siege.

Although the garrison was permitted to march to another post with their arms, the Cherokees attacked the column on August 10, 1760. Stuart was among those captured in the ensuing battle, but Attakullakulla ransomed him shortly afterward. Attakullakulla personally guaranteed his safe return to Charles Town. Stuart then helped negotiate the 1761 treaty ending the Cherokee War (1759–1761), and his intervention mitigated some of the colonists' harsher demands.

With the French and Indian War ending, the British government created two departments to manage native affairs. London named Edmond Atkin as superintendent of the Southern Department, which encompassed all natives living south of the Ohio River. On Atkin's death in 1761, Stuart became superintendent in early 1762.

Dedicating himself to the welfare of the American Indians, Stuart recognized that the colonists' unfair trading practices and land hunger were the chief sources of conflict between natives and settlers. He therefore worked to regulate traders and vigorously opposed the efforts of southern governors and colonists to force the natives to cede land. These policies won Stuart the respect of the American Indians but made him extremely unpopular with the colonists.

When the American Revolutionary War (1775–1783) erupted, Stuart worked to keep the southern natives neutral until the British government was capable of supporting them with regular troops. The Patriots, however, accused Stuart of planning to order the natives to attack the frontier. Mobs subsequently forced him to flee first from Charles Town and then from Savannah. He eventually established his headquarters at Pensacola, capital of the province of West Florida. Stuart indeed did not incite the 1776 Cherokee attacks on the southern frontier, but the colonists nonetheless held him responsible.

Stuart worked hard to keep the natives well disposed toward the British. With the defeat of the Cherokees in mind, he remained reluctant to encourage them to attack the colonists. This along with the natives' own ambivalence limited their contributions to the British. Stuart soon came under criticism from his superiors, who complained that the heavy expenses incurred to maintain native allegiance had yielded no substantial results. By 1778, illness had reduced Stuart's ability to perform his duties. He died at Pensacola on March 21, 1779.

JIM PIECUCH

See also

Attakullakulla; Cherokees; Cherokee War; French and Indian War; Native Americans and the American Revolutionary War

References

Alden, John Richard. *John Stuart and the Southern Colonial Frontier.* Ann Arbor: University of Michigan Press, 1944.

Snapp, J. Russell. *John Stuart and the Struggle for Empire on the Southern Frontier.* Baton Rouge: Louisiana State University Press, 1996.

Stuyvesant, Petrus
Birth Date: ca. 1610
Death Date: February 1672

Dutch soldier, colonial official, and the last director general of the Dutch colony of New Netherland (present-day New York). Petrus Stuyvesant was born in Scherpenzeel, near Wolvega, Netherlands, about 1610. His father was a pastor in the Dutch Reformed Church. Little is known about Petrus Stuyvesant's youth except that he entered military service at an early age and attended Franeker University during 1629–1630. By 1632 he was serving in the Dutch West India Company, which sent him to Brazil in 1635.

In 1643 Stuyvesant was appointed governor of Curaçao and other Dutch possessions in the West Indies. While participating in a campaign against the Portuguese in the West Indies in 1644, he was wounded in his right leg, which later was amputated and replaced by a silver-ornamented wooden leg. This elaborately decorated leg became popularly known as his "silver leg."

On July 28, 1646, the States General of the Netherlands commissioned Stuyvesant director general of New Netherland and other Dutch possessions in the New World. That same year Stuyvesant sailed to Curaçao. He then went on to New Amsterdam (present-day New York City), landing there on May 11, 1647. Although he was an effective administrator who made determined efforts to provide New Netherland with an honest and efficient administration, Stuyvesant's religious intolerance and arbitrary methods made him an extremely unpopular governor.

Under Stuyvesant, a marked change in the appearance of New Amsterdam soon occurred as a result of numerous public works projects. Stuyvesant also made extensive changes in the city government. He created the Board of Nine Men on September 25, 1647, to assist him in governing the settlement. Stuyvesant soon proved to be so autocratic, however, that the citizens of New Amsterdam, aided by directors of the West India Company, forced him to grant independent municipal control of the city on February 2, 1653.

Stuyvesant was also not very successful in settling a long-standing dispute between Connecticut and New Netherland. By way of the humiliating Treaty of Hartford in 1650, Stuyvesant virtually relinquished Dutch control of the Connecticut River Valley. Pressures exerted by English colonists also resulted in Stuyvesant granting several Long Island towns the right to elect their own officials.

As a devout member of the Dutch Reformed Church, Stuyvesant was autocratic in his religious policies. He regarded all nonconformists as likely to foment rebellion and therefore dealt harshly with them, particularly Lutherans and Quakers.

With the West India Company on the verge of bankruptcy, Stuyvesant resorted to a policy of taxation to provide for badly needed improvements during his years as director general. Furthermore, he strove to eliminate smuggling to prevent loss of revenue. He also sought to improve relations with Native Americans by attempting to eliminate unscrupulous business practices long used by the merchants of New Amsterdam and Fort Orange (present-day Albany). Nonetheless, Stuyvesant was adamantly opposed to any governmental reforms that might lessen his own authority over New Netherland. Throughout his directorship he rejected all demands for the creation of a popularly elected legislative assembly.

From 1653 to 1664 Stuyvesant's primary concern was to prevent the decline of Dutch influence on Long Island. Despite his arduous efforts, Stuyvesant met with only mixed success. His most notable achievement in this period occurred in 1655 and involved a long-standing dispute over Swedish colonization of the Delaware Valley. To deal with this problem, he invaded New Sweden and forced its surrender. He was also able to keep the Native Americans restrained.

Despite his successes with the Swedes and the natives, Stuyvesant's dealings with aggressive colonists were far less successful. Increasing difficulties with the English over boundaries and trade eventually climaxed with the appearance of an English fleet in the harbor of New Amsterdam in 1664. Its commander, Colonel Richard Nicolls, demanded that the city capitulate to the Duke of York, who laid claim to all the land between the Connecticut River and the Delaware Valley. Stuyvesant, whose plans for the defense of the city were opposed by the local burghers, was compelled to surrender New Netherland to the English without resistance on September 8, 1664.

In October 1665 Stuyvesant arrived in the Netherlands to defend himself against charges of misconduct. Returning to America, he retired to New York in 1667 and lived on his farm, or *bouwerij*, from which New York City's Bowery takes its name. He died in February 1672 and was buried beneath the chapel on his farm, which is now the site of St. Mark's Episcopal Church.

BRUCE VANDERVORT

See also
Dutch-Indian Wars

References

Abbott, John S. C. *Peter Stuyvesant, the Last Dutch Governor of New Amsterdam.* 1873; reprint, Glacier, MT: Kessinger, 2004.

Gehring, Charles T. *Correspondence, 1654–1658.* Syracuse, NY: Syracuse University Press, 2003.

Innes, J. H. *New Amsterdam and Its People: Studies, Social and Topographical, of the Town under Dutch and Early English Rule.* Princeton, NJ: Princeton University Press, 1902.

Kessler, Henry H., and Eugene Rachlis. *Peter Stuyvesant and His New York: A Biography of a Man and a City.* New York: Random House, 1959.

Subsistence Agriculture

Small-scale agricultural production that is based on the needs of individual families or local communities rather than larger market prices or other outside variables. Most Native Americans practiced subsistence agriculture, planting only what they believed would be needed for the yearly agricultural cycle. Subsistence agriculture is still practiced in many parts of the world today, most notably in Africa, Asia, and Latin America. Subsistence agriculture largely disappeared in Europe by the turn of the 20th century and was not practiced among whites in the United States in large measure after the late 1930s. Today large agricultural concerns, which gave rise to agribusiness, dominate American agriculture. Farms are often very large and are owned by large business conglomerates or multiparty cooperatives rather than by individuals or families. Today most agricultural yields are designed exclusively to be sold on national and international markets based on market prices, supply, and demand.

The Native Americans were excellent farmers who were among the first to cultivate staple crops, particularly corn, beans, and squash. They learned how to plant crops that would thrive in their locales and carefully planned their crops based on the needs of their communities. Native Americans would sometimes plant crops for individual family consumption, but they mainly planted crops that would serve the entire village or community. Agriculture was dominated by women, whose job it was to tend to the crops except in the case of tobacco, which was often overseen by men. Realizing that corn quickly depleted the soil, Native Americans learned to rotate crops and intersperse corn with beans, which added nitrogen to the soil through their roots. Native Americans in arid regions, such as the Pueblos, devised clever ways in which to take advantage of sparse rainfall by way of irrigation systems. Tribes in areas where rainfall was more abundant also employed effective agricultural methods to keep weeds to a minimum and to conserve soil moisture in times of drought. Native Americans also bred many different varieties of plants, especially corn, to make them more suitable for cultivation in their specific climate and soil.

Native Americans usually did not engage in agricultural pursuits designed to produce a large surplus, and they did not usually use agricultural products for trade or barter. They planted only what the community needed but often with an eye toward production that would ensure some surplus to tide the village over during the winter months. Because many products could not be stored long term, however, corn became a principal product earmarked for surplus production because of its longevity well after it had been harvested.

A 17th-century Indian village in the Chesapeake Bay region as depicted in an illustration by explorer and artist John White (engraved by Theodor de Bry). (Library of Congress)

In the New England and Mid-Atlantic regions, the Iroquois Confederacy began practicing large-scale agriculture sometime around 1000 CE. In this case they purposefully cultivated corn to produce a sizable surplus. This ran counter to subsistence agriculture techniques but was used by the confederation as a means by which to wield political power. This enabled the Iroquois to form alliances and contend with outside groups that might have challenged their supremacy in the region. Corn was thus used as a system of intertribal trade and barter that helped maintain the cohesiveness of the confederacy. In addition to corn, the Iroquois also raised beans and squash, often referred to as the "three sisters." In the 19th century when many Native American tribes were driven off their lands and onto reservations (or given individual tracts of land) by the U.S. government, they practiced subsistence agriculture.

PAUL G. PIERPAOLI JR.

See also

Agriculture; Corn; Iroquois Confederacy; Pueblos

References

Ballantine, Betty, and Ian Ballantine. *The Native Americans: An Illustrated History*. Atlanta: Turner Publishing, 1994.

Cronon, William. *Changes in the Land: Indians, Colonists, and the Ecology of New England*. New York: Hill and Wang, 1983.

Hughes, J. Donald. *American Indian Ecology*. El Paso: Texas Western Press, 1993.

Sando, Joe S. *The Pueblo Indians*. San Francisco: Indian Historian Press, 1976.

Sudbury Fight
Event Date: April 21, 1676

Native American attack on Sudbury, Massachusetts. By mid-April 1676, almost a year into King Philip's War (1675–1676), the Massachusetts Bay General Court decided that it could not afford to abandon the western frontier in the face of Native American attacks. The colony's leader decided to make a stand at Sudbury, the westernmost town still boasting a civilian population and located only 17 miles from Boston.

On the evening of April 20, 1676, between 500 and 1,000 Wampanoag, Nipmuck, and Narragansett warriors, possibly led by Metacom (King Philip) himself, invested Sudbury. The next morning they attacked. The inhabitants had taken safety in garrison houses, and the natives, unable to penetrate these strong defenses, instead burned several uninhabited homes and barns. Assistance for the beleaguered settlers soon arrived from nearby Watertown. The men of the two towns were then able to drive the attackers back to the western side of the Sudbury River.

As that fighting took place, captains Samuel Wadsworth and Samuel Brocklebank arrived from Marlborough with their two companies of militia, some 50–60 men in all. Arriving on the outskirts of Sudbury, the relief force spotted a party of retreating natives and quickly pursued them. Suddenly the militiamen found themselves confronting several hundred warriors. The militia had fallen into a trap. The men fought their way to nearby Green Hill, where they waged a pitched battle with the natives throughout the afternoon. Local militia forces from Sudbury tried to break through to the two surrounded companies but failed.

As the afternoon wore on, the natives set fire to the brush on the hillside, blinding and choking the colonial defenders. In a moment of panic, some of the militiamen bolted and ran down the hill in an effort to escape. This action caused others, who could barely see, to believe that a retreat was under way, and they followed. As the colonial defenses splintered, the natives, sensing a rout, fell on the militiamen and hacked them to pieces. Wadsworth and Brocklebank both were killed, as were some 30–40 of their men.

Following this slaughter, the native force withdrew from the town. The next day a force of men from Sudbury, accompanied by a contingent of Christian native allies, crossed the river to bury the dead. To their surprise, they discovered 13 militia survivors in a nearby mill.

The fighting at Sudbury was a demoralizing defeat for the colonial forces. However, the native alliance that had made possible the attack was starting to splinter, as Mary Rowlandson noted in her diary on the return of the native victors from Sudbury.

KYLE F. ZELNER

See also

King Philip's War; Metacom; Narragansetts; Nipmucks; Rowlandson, Mary White; Skulking Way of War; Wampanoags

References

Bodge, George Madison. *Soldiers in King Philip's War*. 3rd ed. Baltimore: Genealogical Publishing, 1967.

Leach, Douglas Edward. *Flintlock and Tomahawk: New England in King Philip's War*. East Orleans, MA: Parnassus Imprints, 1992.

Schultz, Eric B., and Michael J. Tougias. *King Philip's War: The History and Legacy of America's Forgotten Conflict*. Woodstock, VT: Countryman, 1999.

Sullivan-Clinton Expedition against the Iroquois
Event Date: 1779

Savage military campaign during the American Revolutionary War (1775–1783) aimed at breaking the power of the Iroquois Confederacy and seizing control of the Ohio Country. Sometimes touted as the largest military operation against Native Americans, the Sullivan-Clinton Expedition was conducted chiefly by Continental Army officers Major General John Sullivan and Brigadier General James Clinton in 1779. The operation brought near catastrophe for the Native Americans and unfolded mainly in upstate New York, western Pennsylvania, and Ohio. After the 1779 scorched-earth attacks by Sullivan, Clinton, and colonels Goose Van Schaick and Daniel Brodhead, the Patriots were known to eastern Native Americans as the "Town Destroyers."

Militiamen burn an Indian village. The Sullivan-Clinton Expedition of 1779 against the Iroquois amounted to genocide. In addition to the outright deaths of Native Americans, it destroyed some 60 of their towns and their means of subsistence. (North Wind Picture Archives)

Typically, American histories reduce the coordinated assaults by these military forces down to the Sullivan Expedition, ignoring the full intent and extent of the orders of Continental Army commander in chief General George Washington. Washington ordered his lead general, Sullivan, to utterly destroy the Iroquois not because of their alliance with the British but very specifically because Washington considered them the enemy. He consequently ordered that their settlements be annihilated.

Washington thus ordered total war, for the people included were women, children, and the elderly. The American battle cry of danger to settlers on the frontier served as a pretext and a rationale for committing genocide, the preferred method for clearing the land of its original people in favor of white settlers. Furthermore, Washington had what today would be viewed as a serious conflict of interest in ordering the attacks, for the ultimate prize was Ohio, and the Washington family owned a significant stake in the Ohio Company, which speculated heavily in real estate that was then in the fiercely protected possession of Native American nations. He had personally surveyed Ohio Company land for speculation before the French and Indian War (1754–1763).

Moreover, the Continental Congress paid its army recruits in land warrants, issued on property to be seized in Ohio. The only way to pay its debts was to break the Iroquois Confederacy and

appropriate Ohio, a move that would personally enrich Washington. Should the new United States fail to take Ohio, to pay its debts, and to establish its financial and political credit, European nations could possibly reclaim the states as their colonies. These complex interactions explain the absolute and driving need of Washington to break the Iroquois and seize Ohio.

Washington's plan called for a two-pronged attack by the forces under Sullivan at Easton, New Jersey, and under Clinton at Canajoharie, New York, converging in upstate and western New York. Van Schaick was specifically to target the Onondagas, the perceived seat of Iroquoian government. In the meantime, Brodhead was to drive north from Fort Pitt to meet up with the combined forces of Sullivan, Clinton, and Van Schaick in western New York, thus cutting the New York Iroquois off from aid from Pennsylvania and Ohio natives. If possible, after devastating the Iroquois the armies were to march on Niagara, the British headquarters, but that was always more of a desire than an actual war goal.

In fact, because of Sullivan's dawdling, Van Schaick's attack occurred in April 1779, well before the main force left. Also ready in April, Brodhead was told to stand down, but he went ahead with his original orders, setting up forts along the Allegheny Mountains in the spring and summer and setting off on August 6, 1779, to meet Sullivan's force. Finally, on August 9, 1779, Sullivan and

Clinton simultaneously lumbered out of their separate headquarters, meeting up at Tioga. Whereas Van Schaick marched with the main body, Brodhead never quite met up with it, only reaching Olean Point, 40 miles distant from the main force.

It is important to understand that the Iroquois did not want the war, avoided participating in it as long as they could, and, once coerced into it, chose removing women, children, and elders from harm's way over standing to fight the Continental Army. At the outset of British and American hostilities in 1775, Iroquois speakers explicitly told both sides that they were neutral. This did not stop the Americans from attacking any and all tribes, including those allied with them, nor did it stop the British from deliberately engineering an attack by the Americans on the neutral Senecas at the Battle of Oriskany (August 6, 1777) to drag the Iroquois into the war on the Crown's side. The resultant disagreement among Iroquois nations as to their loyalty simply meant that the issue was tabled, with each of the constituent nations free to form its own policy. The Iroquois Confederacy itself was not dissolved, as many historians still erroneously assert.

To ensure the defeat of the Iroquois, Congress authorized Washington to raise an army of 5,163 troops, to be shared among Van Schaick (558 men), Clinton (1,500), and Sullivan (2,500), with Brodhead to join the fray, bringing his 605 men from Fort Pitt. By contrast, the Iroquois at their peak in 1777 had but 1,000 warriors. By 1779 those numbers had dwindled. By the time of the one set-piece engagement of the Sullivan-Clinton Expedition, fought at Newtown (Elmira, New York) on August 29, 1779, the confederated forces under Joseph Brant (Thayendenegea), the Mohawk war chief, and Colonel John Butler, the Loyalist ranger commander, had been seriously thinned.

According to Butler, the combined strength of the British and Native American forces amounted to fewer than 600 men the day of the Newtown battle. In his formal report Sullivan greatly exaggerated this number to 1,500, but even his own commanders falsified that count at the time, and historians since then have pegged the Native American numbers at those reported by Brant and Butler. Meanwhile, whereas Sullivan's men had been feasting their way across Iroquois land on native crops before destroying what they did not consume, the British and their Native American allies were starving. The Battle of Newtown was therefore a complete rout of the Iroquois, but the Native Americans' goal had never been to defeat Sullivan's army. The Iroquois were simply buying time to evacuate their people.

The American attacks of 1779 had the intended genocidal effect, destroying a total of at least 60 towns. Van Schaick razed 3 towns, Brodhead razed 16 towns, and Sullivan and Clinton razed 41 towns. The destruction was complete, with all housing within the sweep of the combined forces completely burned, all crops looted or burned, all household and farm implements destroyed or looted, and all of the once-magnificent peach and apple orchards of the Iroquois Confederacy cut down. The American soldiers also took numerous scalps for the lucrative bounties that the states and Congress offered on Native American dead. American soldiers also skinned Native Americans, making shoes and other items from their tanned hides.

Because previous American attacks in 1778 had already induced famine in Iroquoia, there was no buffer for the effects of the Sullivan-Clinton Expedition. In addition, the winter of 1779–1780 was the severest on record, with New York Harbor freezing solid and snows drifting several feet high from New York through Ohio. Thousands died as an immediate result of the starvation caused by the attacks. Many more died as refugees: 5,036 at Niagara and another 5,000 at British Detroit. The Americans lost no time in seizing the land that had recently hosted Iroquoian farms.

Barbara Alice Mann

See also

Brant, Joseph; Brodhead Expedition; Iroquois Confederacy; Native Americans and the American Revolutionary War; Washington, George

References

Cook, Frederick. *Journals of the Military Expedition of Major General John Sullivan against the Six Nations of Indians in 1779.* 1887; reprint, Freeport, NY: Books for Libraries Press, 1972.

Graymont, Barbara. *The Iroquois in the American Revolution.* Syracuse, NY: Syracuse University Press, 1972.

Mann, Barbara Alice. *George Washington's War on Native America, 1779–1782.* Westport, CT: Praeger, 2005.

Sully, Alfred
Birth Date: May 22, 1821
Death Date: April 27, 1879

U.S. Army officer. Alfred Sully was born on May 22, 1821, in Philadelphia, Pennsylvania. The son of celebrated painter Thomas Sully, Alfred Sully was also an accomplished artist who produced a series of drawings and watercolors depicting scenes encountered throughout his career as an army officer.

In 1841 Sully graduated from the U.S. Military Academy at West Point, was commissioned a second lieutenant, and was assigned to the 2nd Infantry Regiment. Later that year he began his long career as an Indian fighter by pursuing Native American warriors led by Osceola during the Second Seminole War (1835–1842). Sully saw combat again during the Mexican-American War (1846–1848), and on March 11, 1847, he was promoted to first lieutenant during the Siege of Veracruz. When the Rogue River War began in southern Oregon in 1853, Sully, now a captain, was dispatched there. Two years later the army transferred him to Fort Pierre in the Nebraska Territory to pursue hostile Lakota Sioux.

Sully was in the Great Plains campaigning against the Cheyennes when the American Civil War (1861–1865) began. He entered the volunteer army as colonel of the 1st Minnesota Volunteer Infantry Regiment on March 4, 1862, and shortly thereafter was promoted to major in the regulars. On June 1, 1862, he was

Brigadier General Alfred Sully, who in September 1863 ended the Minnesota Sioux Uprising. (Denver Public Library, Western History Collection, D.F. Barry, B-592)

wounded at the Battle of Seven Pines in Virginia. Nevertheless, he led his regiment throughout the Peninsula Campaign (March–August 1862) and the Seven Days Battles (June 25–July 1, 1862). On September 26, 1862, after the Battle of Antietam (September 17, 1862), Sully was promoted to brigadier general. He fought in the Battle of Fredericksburg (December 13, 1862) and was again wounded.

Realizing that Sully's experience would be valuable in suppressing the Minnesota Sioux Uprising, the army appointed him to command the Military District of Dakota on June 1, 1863. Three weeks later Sully marched 1,200 soldiers north from Sioux City, Iowa, to Whitestone Hill, North Dakota, where on September 3, 1863, his men encountered a large Sioux encampment and battled nearly 1,000 Native warriors under Inkpaduta. Sully's troops won a decisive victory and inflicted further damage by destroying most of the Sioux's winter food stocks.

On December 4 Sully took command of the Military District of Iowa. Pursuing the hostile Sioux, he led an expedition up the Missouri River in June 1864. On July 28 at Killdeer Mountain

northwest of Bismarck (present-day North Dakota), Sully's command battled nearly 2,000 Sioux, eventually routing them with an artillery bombardment. Sully lost only 5 men while killing some 150 Sioux. Following his victory, he ordered his men to destroy all of the supplies abandoned by the Sioux.

Following the Civil War, Sully was brevetted major general of volunteers and brigadier general in the regular army before mustering out of the volunteers. He rejoined the regular establishment as lieutenant colonel of the 3rd Infantry Regiment. In 1868 Sully pursued Kiowa, Comanche, Southern Cheyenne, and Southern Arapaho warriors in the southern Plains. At the Battle of Sand Hills (September 11–15, 1868) in Oklahoma, Sully commanded the 7th Cavalry Regiment and a detachment of the 3rd Infantry Regiment against the Cheyennes and Kiowas. In 1873 he became colonel of the 21st Infantry and thereafter held several administrative assignments. Sully died on April 27, 1879, after a long illness while serving as commander of Fort Vancouver, Washington Territory.

Angela D. Tooley and Jim Piecuch

See also

Inkpaduta; Great Sioux War; Killdeer Mountain, Battle of; Minnesota Sioux Uprising; Seminole War, Second; Sully-Sibley Campaigns; Whitestone Hill, Battle of

References

Clodfelter, Michael. *The Dakota War: The United States Army versus the Sioux, 1862–1865.* Jefferson, NC: McFarland, 1998.
O'Neal, Bill. *Fighting Men of the Indian Wars.* Stillwater, OK: Barbed Wire, 1991.

Sully-Sibley Campaigns
Start Date: 1863
End Date: 1865

Military campaigns conducted during 1863–1865 by brigadier generals Alfred Sully and Henry Hastings Sibley against the Dakota Sioux in the northern Great Plains. In 1862 as the American Civil War (1861–1865) raged in the East, the Dakota Sioux began attacking white settlements in Minnesota, sparking the so-called Minnesota Sioux Uprising. In 1863 Major General John Pope directed General Sibley to march from Camp Pope near Fort Ridgely, Minnesota, to drive the Native Americans west toward the Missouri River.

Sibley departed Camp Pope on June 16 and established his field base at Camp Atcheson, North Dakota. His campaign was initially successful and witnessed the defeat of the Dakotas at Big Mound (Kidder County) on July 24, at Dead Buffalo Lake on July 26, and at Stony Lake on July 28. Retreating Dakota warriors, however, held back Sibley's army until their families crossed the Missouri River to the western side. Sibley then set up camp at the mouth of Apple Creek near present-day Bismarck, North Dakota.

Between August 1 and August 23 he marched to Fort Abercrombie by way of Camp Atcheson.

Meanwhile, General Sully had marched up the Missouri to intercept the Dakotas before they could cross to the river's west side. Sully established his headquarters at Sioux City, Iowa, and set up a base camp at Fort Pierre, South Dakota. On August 13 he marched northward and then on September 3 defeated the Dakotas near White Stone Hill, North Dakota. He then returned to his headquarters at Sioux City for the winter.

In the summer of 1864 Sully, accompanied by two steamboats with supplies, led his force up the Missouri River from Sioux City to meet Sibley near the new army post at Fort Rice, North Dakota. The fort's garrison consisted of six companies of the 1st U.S. Volunteers, mostly so-called Galvanized Yankees, Confederate prisoners of war who had sworn allegiance to the United States and had then been sent to the West, where they would not fight against their former comrades. Sully left part of his force to construct the fort and marched the rest northwest to the Dakota camp located in the Killdeer Mountains. Once there he defeated the Dakotas on July 28 and scattered the survivors.

In the summer of 1865 Sully returned to Fort Rice and marched north of Devils Lake. On August 2, 1865, he marched to the Mouse (Souris) River and then southwest to Fort Berthold. His force returned to Fort Rice on September 8 and went into winter quarters at Sioux Falls, South Dakota. The Sully-Sibley Campaigns of 1863–1865 essentially ended the Minnesota Sioux Uprising and helped secure the area from Native American threats, allowing for the westward advancement of the frontier.

ROBERT B. KANE

See also

Dakota Sioux; Galvanized Yankees and Rebels; Minnesota Sioux Uprising; Sibley, Henry Hastings; Sully, Alfred

References

Clodfelter, Michael. *The Dakota War: The United States Army versus the Sioux, 1862–1865*. Jefferson, NC: McFarland, 1998.

Jones, Robert Huhn. *The Civil War in the Northwest: Nebraska, Wisconsin, Iowa, Minnesota, and the Dakotas*. Norman: University of Oklahoma Press, 1960.

Utley, Robert M. *The Indian Frontier of the American West, 1846–1890*. Albuquerque: University of New Mexico Press, 1984.

Summit Springs, Battle of
Event Date: July 11, 1869

Battle between the 5th U.S. Cavalry Regiment, commanded by Major Eugene A. Carr, and the Southern Cheyenne Dog Soldiers, led by Chief Tall Bull. The Battle of Summit Springs occurred in Logan County, situated in northeastern Colorado, on July 11, 1869. The U.S. victory effectively ended the military resistance of the Dog Soldiers between the Arkansas and Platte rivers.

Major Carr's mission was to stop Cheyenne raiding into western Kansas and move the Native Americans to a reservation in Indian Territory (Oklahoma). On July 9, 1869, some 500 men, including 244 members of the 5th Cavalry and a battalion of Pawnee Indian scouts, departed Fort McPherson. The most famous individual in the force was the scout William F. Cody, already known as "Buffalo Bill."

Unaware that they were being closely pursued, some 200 Cheyennes camped while waiting for the South Platte River to subside before crossing. Believing that they were in no danger, the Cheyennes allowed their horses to graze at a distance. At 3:00 p.m. on July 11, troops of the 5th Cavalry and the Pawnee scouts located the Cheyennes. As cavalry bugles sounded, the troops formed two parallel columns and charged from about one mile distant. The Pawnee scouts reached the Cheyenne village first, while the cavalrymen encircled the camp to prevent the Dog Soldiers from reaching their horses. Terrified, the Indian women and children fled from the village to a ravine that led to the South Platte River. Chief Tall Bull and about 20 Dog Soldiers fought to cover their escape. After directing his family to safety, Tall Bull moved to the mouth of the gully, killed his horse to provide cover, and then fought to the death. Other warriors scattered to shallow depressions, where they fought with bows and arrows until they too were killed.

In its resounding victory, the 5th Cavalry sustained only 1 man wounded. Carr reported that 52 Cheyennes had been killed and 17 women and children taken prisoner. The soldiers also recovered 2 captured white women. A total of 84 lodges complete with military supplies, food, clothing, and camp equipment were also taken and burned. Some 274 Cheyenne horses and 144 mules were herded away as well. The loss of their supplies and horses rendered the remaining Cheyennes virtually powerless.

The battle ended Cheyenne Dog Soldier occupation of western Kansas and eastern Colorado. Although some of the survivors under White Horse joined the Northern Cheyennes, most of them simply moved south under Bull Bear and surrendered at Camp Supply.

DONALD L. WALKER JR.

See also

Carr, Eugene Asa; Cavalry Regiment, 5th U.S.; Cheyennes, Southern; Cody, William Frederick; Dog Soldiers; Tall Bull

References

Broome, Jeff. *Dog Soldier Justice: The Ordeal of Susanna Alderdice in the Kansas Indian War*. Lincoln, KS: Lincoln County Historical Society, 2003.

Utley, Robert M. *Frontier Regulars: The United States and the American Indian, 1866–1891*. New York: Macmillan, 1973.

West, Elliott. *The Contested Plains: Indians, Goldseekers, and the Rush to Colorado*. Lawrence: University Press of Kansas, 1998.

Sun People
See Spokanes

Susquehannocks

Native American group concentrated in the Susquehanna River Valley. Among the most powerful tribes of the Mid-Atlantic region at the time of the European arrival in North America, the Susquehannocks were exterminated in 1763.

The Susquehannocks, who spoke a dialect of the Iroquois language, lived in about two dozen fortified villages along the Susquehanna River and its tributaries in Maryland, central Pennsylvania, and southern New York. Their villages, the largest of which was located near present-day Lancaster, Pennsylvania, were vast stockades that surrounded longhouses. The longhouses were framed with logs and had a rectangular shape and vaulted roofs. They were 50 to 100 feet long and 18 to 25 feet wide, were covered with bark, and had vent holes in the roof to allow smoke from fires to escape. Families slept together on raised platforms on either side of the structure and used animal furs for covers. Because the Susquehannocks were matrilineal, the oldest female was the head of the longhouse.

The Susquehannocks arrived from the north and occupied the Susquehanna Valley from at least 1150. Their earliest known village dates back to 1550. At the height of their power during the early 17th century, they numbered some 7,000 people.

The Susquehannocks were farmers, fishermen, and hunters. They planted corn, beans, and squash in the spring and then went south to the Chesapeake Bay area to fish. They returned in the fall to harvest and hunt. Their first recorded European contact was with Captain John Smith in 1608 near Chesapeake Bay.

"Susquehannock" was a descriptive term used by Smith's Algonquian-speaking guide to describe the tall Susquehannocks he met. "Susquehannock" is an Algonquian word meaning "people of the muddy river," a reference to the Susquehanna River.

The Susquehannocks frequently fought with their neighbors, such as the Delawares (Lenni Lenapes) to the east and the Powhatan Confederacy to the south. Although linguistically and culturally related to the Iroquois, the Susquehannocks were allies of the Hurons and bitter enemies of the Iroquois. During the first half of the 17th century the Susquehannocks were the only natives in the region to become major trading partners with the French, the English, the Dutch, and the Swedes. As such, the Susquehannocks made huge profits from the fur trade.

In their search for greater supplies of furs, the Susquehannocks became involved in increased intertribal rivalry between 1630 and 1700. As the Susquehannocks expanded their search for furs westward they were drawn into the Beaver Wars (1641–1701), a period of intense native rivalry in the Great Lakes and Ohio River Valley region. Although the Beaver Wars were primarily a competition between the Hurons and the Iroquois, the Susquehannocks contributed to the escalation of the conflict.

Because of their multiple alliances with European colonial powers, the Susquehannocks had more European weapons than any other natives in the region. They even possessed a cannon,

A Susquehannock warrior; detail from *Map of Virginia as described by John Smith*, engraved by William Hole and published in 1612. (Library of Congress)

a weapon not held by any other natives at the time. The Susquehannocks were placed in jeopardy when the Iroquois Confederacy overwhelmed the Hurons during 1648–1649. The Iroquois had also been strengthened when they absorbed many of the defeated Hurons into their ranks. In 1651 the Mohawks attacked the Susquehannocks and fought a war with them that lasted until 1656. During the course of that conflict, the Susquehannocks were pushed farther south along the banks of the Susquehanna River.

In return for assistance from the English in Maryland, the Susquehannocks ceded much of their Maryland territory to the English in 1652. In 1654 a smallpox epidemic hit the Susquehannocks, which further weakened their ability to resist the Mohawks. The Susquehannocks also lost their major arms supplier when the Dutch seized the Swedish colony in Delaware in 1655.

Although the Susquehannocks eventually made peace with the Mohawks in 1656, the Iroquois attacked the Susquehannocks in 1658. Another smallpox epidemic struck the Susquehannocks in 1661, further inhibiting their ability to withstand the Iroquois attack. In 1663 Maryland settlers, fearful of the Iroquois, provided the Susquehannocks with weapons. In 1664, however, the English took New Netherland (New York) from the Dutch and formed an alliance with the Iroquois. Weakened by war and disease, the Susquehannocks were defeated by the Iroquois in 1675 and were also driven out of Pennsylvania.

The governor of Maryland then offered the Susquehannocks refuge on the upper bank of the Potomac River, much to the chagrin of the English colonists living there. The English colonists subsequently attacked the Susquehannocks, sparking the Susquehannock War (1675–1676). The Susquehannocks responded with retaliatory raids on colonial settlements but in 1676 were forced to flee north. Ultimately the Susquehannocks either surrendered to the Iroquois or were dispersed among other regional tribes.

The Iroquois resettled what was left of the Susquehannocks among the Mohawks and the Oneidas in New York. The Susquehannocks thus became part of the so-called Covenant Chain. In 1706 the Iroquois allowed 300 Susquehannocks to return to the Susquehanna Valley and establish the village of Conestoga. Quaker missionaries converted many of the Susquehannocks there to Christianity. In protest, the traditional Susquehannocks left to join the Mingos in Ohio. By 1763 there were only 20 Susquehannocks remaining in Conestoga. Although these 20 natives were living peacefully and causing no harm, the Paxton Boys, enraged by Pontiac's Rebellion (1763), which did not involve the Susquehannocks, decided that all natives in the region were a threat and should be exterminated. Local officials arrested 14 members of the Conestoga community and placed them in a jail in Lancaster for their own protection. Meanwhile, the Paxton Boys killed the 6 Susquehannock Christians remaining in Conestoga. The Paxton Boys then proceeded to the Lancaster jail, where they murdered the remaining Susquehannocks. By the end of 1763 the Susquehannocks ceased to exist as a separate tribe; thereafter individual families joined other neighboring tribes. A few Susquehannock descendants currently live in Oklahoma among the Cayugas and Senecas.

MICHAEL R. HALL

See also

Algonquins; Beaver Wars; Covenant Chain; Delawares; Iroquois; Iroquois Confederacy; Longhouse; Mingos; Mohawks; Oneidas; Paxton Riots; Powhatan Confederacy; Smallpox; Smith, John; Susquehannock War; Wyandots

References

Chadwick, Joseph L. *Susquehannock: The Rogue Iroquois Nation and Its Descendants.* Mechanicsburg, PA: Stackpole, 2001.
Eshleman, H. Frank. *Annals of the Susquehannocks and Other Indian Tribes of Pennsylvania, 1500–1763.* Philadelphia: Pennsylvania Historical Society, 2000.
Uhler, S. *Pennsylvania Indian Relations to 1754.* New York: AMS, 1983.
Wallace, Paul A. W. *Indians in Pennsylvania.* Harrisburg: Pennsylvania Historical and Museum Commission, 2000.

Susquehannock War
Start Date: 1675
End Date: 1676

Frontier war between backcountry settlers in Virginia and Maryland and Susquehannock Native Americans in the upper Potomac River region. In 1676 Virginia frontiersmen under the leadership of Nathaniel Bacon rebelled against their provincial government and burned Jamestown. The primary cause of their dissatisfaction was the colonial government's reluctance to prosecute a war between the backcountry inhabitants and the Susquehannocks, an Iroquoian people situated just north of the Potomac River.

The Susquehannock War began in 1675 when a dispute over stolen hogs escalated into a full-scale war. Virginia frontiersmen killed a group of Doeg natives who were trying to confiscate a farmer's hogs as payment for goods they had sold him. The killings set off a series of raids and counterraids. These quickly expanded to involve both Maryland residents and the Susquehannocks.

The Susquehannocks were relative newcomers to the upper Potomac River area. They had only recently accepted an invitation from Maryland to settle closer to their principal trading partners. Early in the conflict, Susquehannock leaders sought to negotiate a peaceful resolution. Nearly 1,000 Virginians and Marylanders led by John Washington, however, surrounded a principal Susquehannock town and murdered several Susquehannock headmen.

Outnumbered by the Virginians, the enraged Susquehannocks nonetheless wrought devastation across the Potomac frontier region, raiding and pillaging the settlers' isolated farms. Hard-pressed by the natives, the frontier populace sought aid from the Virginia government. Colonial officials, fearful of potential disruptions in the profitable Native American trade, responded only with a bland and ineffective defensive strategy. Incensed, frontier settlers rallied around the leadership of Bacon, a young but out-of-favor Virginia aristocrat. Under Bacon's leadership, settlers began indiscriminately killing Native Americans, not only the hostile Susquehannocks but also friendly Algonquian-speaking groups such as the Pamunkeys and the Appomattocks.

Bacon's attacks greatly troubled Virginia lawmakers, who sought to avoid a general war with the natives. Thus, in early 1676 Governor William Berkeley of Virginia declared Bacon an outlaw. That move touched off the brief but violent frontier uprising known as Bacon's Rebellion (June 1676–January 1677).

Disaffected and disenfranchised frontier residents quickly rallied to Bacon's aid. In September 1676 his makeshift army chased Berkeley from Jamestown and then burned the town. However, Bacon died of dysentery only a month later, and the rebellion quickly collapsed.

The Susquehannock War ended in 1676 as well. Reluctantly the Susquehannocks migrated back into Pennsylvania, where they soon dispersed. Some joined the Delawares (Lenni Lenapes) in southeastern Pennsylvania, whereas others were forcefully assimilated into the Iroquois Confederacy and still others returned to their old home in the Susquehanna River Valley, where they became known as the Conestogas. After the war the Susquehannocks in essence ceased to exist, reduced instead to a small constituency in other tribes or reconfigured as only a shadow of their former selves.

DANIEL P. BARR

See also

Appomattocks; Bacon's Rebellion; Berkeley, William; Iroquois Confederacy; Pamunkeys; Susquehannocks

References

Jennings, Francis. *The Ambiguous Iroquois Empire: The Covenant Chain Confederation of Indian Tribes with English Colonies from Its Beginnings to the Lancaster Treaty of 1744.* New York: Norton, 1984.

Richter, Daniel K. *Facing East from Indian Country: A Native History of Early America.* Cambridge: Harvard University Press, 2001.

Richter, Daniel K. *The Ordeal of the Longhouse: The People of the Iroquois League in the Era of European Colonization.* Chapel Hill: University of North Carolina Press, 1992.

Taylor, Alan. *American Colonies: The Settling of North America.* New York: Viking/Penguin, 2001.

Sutlers

Individuals who traveled with troops in the field and sold provisions and other goods to soldiers. Sutlers were vitally important to the morale of the troops, as the sutlers sold quality-of-life items that were otherwise difficult for soldiers to acquire. Irregular pay meant that many soldiers were often unable to buy simple necessities from local merchants, who refused to extend credit to transient soldiers. Sutlers usually accepted credit, and typically they sold such items as tobacco, soap, paper, needles, thread, sugar, and tea.

Liquor was by far the most lucrative item sold by sutlers, however. Despite problems of drunkenness, it was impossible to outlaw alcohol among the troops. Moderate alcohol consumption was generally regarded as a cheap means of pacifying the troops. Sutlers were happy to meet the demand.

Most sutlers were men, but it was not unheard of for women during the colonial period to work as sutlers. Although they were important for troop morale, unscrupulous sutlers could also cause dissension, and some sold goods that had been looted from civilians. Such plundering tended to increase when there were too many sutlers within a regiment.

In an attempt to maintain order, sutlers were usually required to register with the commanding officer of a unit. Efforts were made to ensure that they were of good reputation, and commanders impressed on them the need to charge fair prices for their goods if they were to retain the privilege of remaining with the unit. Sutlers were used during the American Revolutionary War (1775–1783), the War of 1812 (1812–1814), the Mexican-American War (1846–1848), and the American Civil War (1861–1865).

They also operated during many of the postcolonial Indian Wars. In the latter periods, sutlers frequently provided gambling and prostitution services, much to the chagrin of military commanders. Sutlers diminished in importance after the 1890s.

DOROTHY A. MAYS

See also

Native Americans and the American Revolutionary War; Native Americans and the Civil War; Native Americans and the War of 1812

References

Mayer, Holly A. *Belonging to the Army: Camp Followers and Community during the American Revolution.* Columbia: University of South Carolina Press, 1999.

Tapson, Alfred J. "The Sutler and the Soldier." *Military Affairs* 21 (Winter 1957): 175–181.

A sutler's price list from 1863. Sutlers were businessmen who located near military establishments and offered to soldiers commodities not provided by the military, such as alcohol, candy, and cigars. (National Archives)

Swansea, Attack on
Start Date: June 20, 1675
End Date: June 25, 1675

The opening attack of King Philip's War (1675–1676), carried out intermittently during June 20–25, 1675, by the Wampanoags. The attack on Swansea convinced the New England colonies that the Wampanoags were hostile, igniting war between the two groups.

Swansea, a Plymouth Colony village, was located on the border between English and Wampanoag lands. On June 20, 1675, Wampanoag warriors began to loot and burn outlying Swansea farms. The farmers fled north to Swansea proper and alerted their neighbors, who sent for aid and then retreated to their garrison houses. Colonial militiamen from nearby Bridgewater and Taunton arrived on June 21. In the meantime, the Wampanoags had left the area.

Evidence of what happened next is scant and contradictory. Apparently on June 23, Wampanoag looters returned to Swansea. In the process a Plymouth youth shot and killed one warrior. The following day Wampanoag parties ambushed several groups of colonists that had left their garrison houses. Nine English settlers were killed, and two were mortally wounded. These deaths persuaded the governments of Plymouth and Massachusetts Bay that the Wampanoags intended a full-scale war, and colonial militias mustered accordingly.

Metacom (King Philip), the Wampanoag sachem, had been preparing for war against New England for some time. However, it seems unlikely that he would have chosen to begin the war in such fashion. Probably disaffected Wampanoags attacked Swansea on their own initiative, sparking the conflict before Metacom had intended.

ANDREW MILLER

See also
King Philip's War; Metacom; Wampanoags

References
Hubbard, William. "A Narrative of the Troubles with the Indians in New-England, from Pascataqua to Pemmaquid" [1677]. In *The History of the Indian Wars in New England,* Vol. 2, edited by Samuel G. Drake, 69–225. 1865; reprint, New York: Burt Franklin, 1971.
Leach, Douglas Edward. *Flintlock and Tomahawk: New England in King Philip's War.* East Orleans, MA: Parnassus Imprints, 1992.

Sycamore Creek, Battle of
See Stillman's Run, Battle of

T

Tachnedorus

See Logan, John

Tahkahokuty Mountain, Battle of

See Killdeer Mountain, Battle of

Tallapoosa Indians

See Creeks

Tall Bull

Birth Date: ca. 1830
Death Date: July 11, 1869

Cheyenne warrior and leader of the Cheyenne Dog Soldiers. Tall Bull (Hotoa-qa-ihoois) was born sometime around 1830. Little is known of his early years, and his place of birth is uncertain. An accomplished warrior, Tall Bull became well known for his leadership of the Dog Soldiers, an elite society of warriors renowned for their intrepid fighting skills. During the American Civil War (1861–1865), numerous Colorado volunteer militia groups waged sporadic warfare against Cheyenne villages, most of which were peaceful. This unwarranted violence led Tall Bull to wage his own war against the white population.

Between 1865 and 1867 Tall Bull led numerous raids on white settlers and U.S. Army units. He refused to submit to peace negotiations in early 1867, but in October 1867 he agreed to sign the Medicine Lodge Treaty. Despite such attempts to secure a truce, violence on the southern Plains continued. In 1868 Tall Bull's Dog Soldiers took part in a failed attack on 50 frontiersmen and scouts employed by the army at Beecher's Island.

As bloodshed increased in the region in the late 1860s, Tall Bull launched a series of fairly effective guerrilla-style raids against U.S. forces. Indeed, his success now attracted allies, including some Sioux and Arapaho bands. Tall Bull's campaign was effectively terminated on July 11, 1869, when an army contingent led by Major Eugene A. Carr attacked his encampment, resulting in the Battle of Summit Springs. Tall Bull died in the battle.

PAUL G. PIERPAOLI JR.

See also

Arapahos; Beecher Island, Battle of; Carr, Eugene Asa; Cheyennes; Dog Soldiers; Medicine Lodge Treaty; Sioux; Summit Springs, Battle of

References

Afton, Jean, David Fritjof Halaas, and Andrew E. Masich. *Cheyenne Dog Soldiers: A Ledgerbook History of Coups and Combat.* Niwot: University Press of Colorado, 1997.

Goodrich, Thomas. *Scalp Dance: Indian Warfare on the High Plains, 1865–1879.* Mechanicsburg, PA: Stackpole, 1997.

Tallushatchee, Battle of

Event Date: November 3, 1813

Engagement fought between Tennessee militiamen and Red Stick Creeks on November 3, 1813. Tallushatchee, an Upper Creek village, was located in present-day Calhoun County, Alabama, in the northeastern part of the state. Major General Andrew Jackson assembled an army of 2,500 Tennessee militiamen for an expedition against the Creeks. His primary goal was to destroy the Red Stick faction.

The Red Sticks constituted a minority of the Creek Nation. Inspired by several religious prophets, they aggressively promoted traditional views of Creek society. The Red Sticks vehemently opposed the U.S. government and American settlers.

After a band of Red Sticks had massacred settlers, militia, and even some of their Creek rivals at Fort Mims, Alabama, on August 30, 1813, Jackson marched his army southward into the Mississippi Territory. His army attempted to construct Fort Strother along the Coosa River, where the troops suffered from supply shortages. As he tarried, Jackson received a report from Path Killer, a Cherokee chief, informing him of a large party of Red Sticks gathering only 15 miles away at the Creek village of Tallushatchee. Jackson then ordered his trusted subordinate, Brigadier General John R. Coffee, to organize a concentrated strike on the village. Jackson's goals were to destroy the village and occupy the Creek lands before the onset of winter.

On November 3 Coffee led about 1,000 mounted militiamen and Indian allies to Tallushatchee. Seemingly pleased that the villagers refused to flee, he divided his force into two columns. The militiamen quickly encircled the village. Two companies then advanced into Tallushatchee to draw out the poorly armed Red Stick warriors, who tried to protect their families. The trap worked, and the warriors broke from cover in a desperate charge. Coffee closed the circle on them and ordered his own advance, which forced the warriors to retreat back into the village's buildings.

Hand-to-hand combat ensued. All of the Creek men in the village died in the course of the assault. Numerous women and children were also killed, and 84 others were taken prisoner. Before the fighting ended that day, Coffee's men had killed at least 180 Red Sticks while losing just 5 killed and 41 wounded.

The Battle of Tallushatchee was the first major military operation in Jackson's campaign against the Creek Nation. The battle clearly demonstrated that if his better-armed men could reach the Creek villages, they would be successful. By the end of 1813, Jackson's men would kill more than 1,000 Creeks.

BRAD D. LOOKINGBILL

See also

Coffee, John; Creeks; Creek War; Crockett, David; Fort Mims, Battle of; Fort Strother; Jackson, Andrew; Red Sticks

References

Grenier, John. *The First Way of War: American War Making on the Frontier.* Cambridge: Cambridge University Press, 2005.

Martin, Joel W. *Sacred Revolt: The Muskogees' Struggle for a New World.* Boston: Beacon, 1991.

Owsley, Frank L., Jr. *Struggle for the Gulf Borderlands. The Creek War and the Battle of New Orleans, 1812–1815.* Gainesville: University Presses of Florida, 1981.

Tanaghrisson
Birth Date: Unknown
Death Date: Late 1754

Catawba-born Seneca leader and diplomat in the Ohio Country. The Iroquois captured Tanaghrisson during his youth and raised him as a Seneca. As with most Iroquois men who aspired to positions of leadership, Tanaghrisson had a career as a warrior, but he did not attract the attention of the British and the French until he became a diplomat.

In the wake of the Walking Purchase of 1737, the Iroquois, acting on the behalf of Pennsylvania, ordered the Delawares (Lenni Lenapes) to the westernmost reaches of the colony. At the same time, the Iroquois also assigned supervisors who would keep an eye on the Delaware, Shawnee, and Mingo peoples in the Ohio Country and report on their activities. The British and French referred to these administrative diplomats as "half-kings." When a half-king died, the Iroquois resuscitated the title and bestowed it on the man they selected as the new supervisor. Sometime in the late 1740s, the confederation council at Onondaga assigned Tanaghrisson to oversee the Mingo village of Logstown in what is now western Pennsylvania.

The British quickly recognized Tanaghrisson as being authorized to speak for the British-allied tribes in the Ohio Country. As such Conrad Weiser, Pennsylvania's representative to the Iroquois, negotiated with Tanaghrisson, as did British trader George Croghan. Virginia agents also treated with Tanaghrisson in 1752.

Tanaghrisson most probably would have remained relatively unknown to most historians. However, in the last year of his life he participated in an action that ignited a global conflict. A British partisan, Tanaghrisson was concerned with the dispute between the French and the British over control of the Ohio Country and resented what he regarded as French intrusions. As a half-king, Tanaghrisson's authority rested in part on the acquiescence of the Delaware and Shawnee peoples he purported to lead. Their cooperation resulted from what he could provide them in the way of British trade goods, which were often of much better quality than comparable French wares.

Based on a 1744 treaty with the Iroquois, Virginia also laid claim to the Ohio Country. Troubled by French activity in the area of the Monongahela and Allegheny rivers, in 1754 Lieutenant Governor Robert Dinwiddie of Virginia dispatched a mission led by Lieutenant Colonel George Washington to force the French from the contested territory.

However, Washington and his men could not locate the French. At that point they met Tanaghrisson and some of his Mingo warriors, who led them to the French encampment. Tanaghrisson and Washington's men encircled the French position and opened fire. The French soon surrendered, ending what came to be known as the Battle of Jumonville's Glen. Washington learned from the French officer in charge of the detachment that his was a diplomatic mission, sent to tell the British that this was the territory of the French king. To the surprise of Washington and the other Virginians, Tanaghrisson and his warriors began killing the wounded Frenchmen, including the officer in charge. Afterward Tanaghrisson and his men accompanied Washington to the newly constructed Fort Necessity. Tanaghrisson realized that the position was not defensible, and he and his warriors departed before the French attacked the post. Tanaghrisson fell ill and died in late 1754.

ROGER M. CARPENTER

See also

Catawbas; Croghan, George; Delawares; French and Indian War; Iroquois; Mingos; Senecas; Shawnees; Walking Purchase; Washington, George

References

Anderson, Fred. *Crucible of War: The Seven Years' War and the Fate of the Empire in British North America, 1754–1766*. New York: Vintage Books, 2001.

Jennings, Francis, et al., eds. *The History and Culture of Iroquois Diplomacy: An Interdisciplinary Guide to the Treaties of the Six Nations and Their League*. Syracuse, NY: Syracuse University Press, 1985.

Taos Revolt

Start Date: January 19, 1847
End Date: February 3, 1847

Uprising of Mexicans and Taos Indians in Don Fernando de Taos, New Mexico, in January–February 1847 during the Mexican-American War (1846–1848). In August 1846 U.S. Army forces under Colonel Stephen Watts Kearny from Fort Leavenworth, Kansas, had easily captured Santa Fe, where Mexican governor Manuel Armijo surrendered without firing a shot. President James K. Polk then advanced Kearny to brigadier general and ordered him to California. Before departing, Kearny detached troops under Colonel Sterling Price to garrison New Mexico and named Charles Bent New Mexico's first territorial governor. Following Kearny's departure, opposition forces in Santa Fe began plotting an uprising. The uprising was planned for Christmas 1846, but when the plot was discovered by American authorities, the uprising was put off until January 1847.

On the morning of January 19, 1847, in Don Fernando de Taos, Mexican national Pablo Montoya and Taos Indian Tomás Romero (Tomasito) led attacks on Americans throughout the town. Tomasito led a force of Native Americans to Governor Bent's residence. There they shot Bent with arrows, killing and scalping him within sight of his wife and children. At least three other government officials were killed and scalped: Stephen Lee (county sheriff), Cornelio Vigil (prefect and probate judge), and J. W. Leal (circuit attorney).

Later that same day some 500 Mexicans and Native Americans attacked Simeon Turley's mill in Arroyo Hondo, a few miles outside of Taos. One of Turley's employees escaped to ride to Santa Fe and inform the U.S. forces there. Of 8 to 10 men left defending the mill, only 2 managed to escape. Simultaneously, other Mexican insurgents killed 7 American traders in the village of Mora.

U.S. captain Jesse I. Morin and a small army force defeated the insurgents in fighting at Mora on January 24, 1847. At the same time Price, with 300 U.S. troops and 65 volunteers, departed Santa Fe for Taos. Some of the volunteers were New Mexicans organized by Ceran St. Vrain, Bent's business associate. On the way to Taos, Price defeated a force of some 1,500 Mexicans and Native Americans at Santa Cruz de la Cañada and Empudo Pass. The rebels then retreated to Don Fernando de Taos and sought refuge in the church there.

The siege of the church at Don Fernando de Taos was the final action of the Taos Revolt. On February 3 the American soldiers shelled the church, but the artillery fire had little effect against its thick adobe walls. By the next day, however, Price's men had entirely surrounded the town and attacked. Pursued by U.S. troops, a number of the rebels fled into the surrounding mountains. Two days later the remaining insurgents surrendered. Approximately 150 rebels were killed and 400 captured, while Price lost 7 soldiers killed and 45 wounded.

Price imposed martial law in Taos and then set up a court to try the imprisoned rebels. Finding an adequate jury pool presented problems, for the American community was very small and was, in any case, prejudiced against the rebels. Ultimately 15 men were found guilty of murder and treason and were sentenced to death. Six of them were hanged in Taos Plaza on April 9, and on April 25 another 5 were executed. Altogether, some 28 people were executed for having taken part in the revolt. Romero was murdered in his cell before trial, while Montoya was among those tried, sentenced to death, and hanged.

A year later U.S. secretary of war George W. Crawford reviewed the court proceedings and found that one of the insurgents sentenced to death—Pablo Salazar—might have been wrongfully convicted. The U.S. Supreme Court supported Crawford's finding, but all other convictions were upheld. There was no further opposition to U.S. rule in New Mexico.

ANNA RULSKA

See also

Kearny, Stephen Watts; New Mexico

References

Coldsmith, Don. *Trail from Taos*. New York: Bantam, 1990.

Crutchfield, James Andrew. *Tragedy at Taos: The Revolt of 1847*. Plano: Republic of Texas Press, 1995.

McNierney, Michael. *Taos 1847: The Revolt in Contemporary Accounts*. Boulder, CO: Johnson Publishing, 1980.

Taoyateduta

See Little Crow

Tatanka-Iyotanka

See Sitting Bull

Taylor, Zachary
Birth Date: November 24, 1784
Death Date: July 9, 1850

U.S. Army officer and president of the United States (1849–1850). Born near Barboursville in Orange County, Virginia, on November 24, 1784, Zachary Taylor moved with his family to Kentucky and grew up on a plantation near Louisville, receiving only a rudimentary education. In May 1808 he secured a commission as a first lieutenant in the 7th Infantry Regiment.

Taylor's first duty assignment was New Orleans. He then commanded Fort Pickering near present-day Memphis, Tennessee. In November 1810 Taylor was promoted to captain and commanded Fort Knox in Vincennes, Indiana. Shortly before the beginning of the War of 1812, he assumed command of Fort

Major General Zachary Taylor, who went on to become president of the United States, achieved renown commanding U.S. forces in northern Mexico during the Mexican-American War (1846–1848) but also had extensive experience fighting Native Americans, including during the War of 1812, the 1832 Black Hawk War, and the Second Seminole War (1835–1842). (Library of Congress)

Harrison (present-day Terre Haute) along the Wabash River in the Indiana Territory. During the war in September 1812, Taylor and 50 men held off an attack on the fort by some 500 native warriors. For this rare American victory in the region, Taylor was brevetted major. In the summer of 1814 he led an expedition against Native Americans in the upper Mississippi region, but a British and Native American force at Rock River forced him to turn back that September.

After the war Taylor reverted to his permanent rank of captain and soon resigned his commission. He returned to the army in 1816 when President James Madison ordered his rank of major restored. Taylor then directed the construction of Fort Howard along the Fox River in Green Bay, Wisconsin, an important center of the fur trade and Wisconsin's first white settlement.

Promoted to lieutenant colonel in 1819, Taylor relocated to Louisiana, where he served in recruitment and helped build a military road and fortifications. Reassigned to posts in present-day Minnesota and Wisconsin in the late 1820s, Taylor received promotion to full colonel in April 1832. Later that year he led troops in the Black Hawk War (1832), participating in the Battle of Bad Axe (August 1–2, 1832).

Taylor's experience fighting Native Americans proved helpful for his next combat assignment during the Second Seminole War (1835–1842), when he oversaw construction of a series of strongholds to support the army's advance into Native American territory. On Christmas Day 1837 Taylor won the biggest engagement of the war in the Battle of Lake Okeechobee and was rewarded with a brevet to brigadier general. In May 1838 he assumed command of the Department of Florida and spent the next two years continuing the campaign against the Seminoles. His boldness in battle and indifference to etiquette and military dress (including his wearing of a wide-brimmed straw hat) earned him the affectionate nickname from his men of "Old Rough and Ready." In 1841 Taylor assumed command of Fort Gibson in Indian Territory, where he attempted to keep the peace among Native Americans.

In July 1845 following its annexation, President James K. Polk ordered Taylor to Texas in command of the Army of Observation of some 3,500 men. In March 1846 Polk, seeking a confrontation with Mexico, ordered Taylor to cross the Nueces River, long the southern boundary of Texas, and take up position along the Rio Grande to its south, which Polk and Texans claimed as the southern border of Texas. On April 25, 1846, a Mexican cavalry unit attacked part of Taylor's force on the Rio Grande, inflicting several American casualties. Polk used this incident as the excuse for war.

Taylor's Army of Occupation won the Battle of Palo Alto on May 8, the first major engagement of the Mexican-American War (1846–1848). He was again victorious the next day at Resaca de la Palma, forcing the Mexican Army to withdraw across the Rio Grande. Congress declared war on Mexico on May 11.

Brevetted major general for these two victories and named commander of the Army of the Rio Grande in July, Taylor crossed the Rio Grande to occupy Matamoros. His army remained there until late summer while struggling with logistical problems. In September 1846 Taylor advanced toward the heavily fortified city of Monterrey. Following the Battle of Monterrey (September 19–21, 1846) with his own forces taking casualties and short of supplies, Taylor agreed to an armistice that allowed the Mexican garrison to depart, enraging Polk. The American public saw only another victory, however. Polk worried that Taylor might seek to convert his growing popularity into political capital and thus endeavored to keep the general from further combat by siphoning off much of his northern Mexico force for Major General Winfield Scott's Mexico City Campaign.

Learning of the American plans, Mexican president and general Antonio López de Santa Anna saw an opportunity to march against Taylor's weakened force and then deal with Scott's invaders. Outnumbered 20,000 to his 5,000 men, Taylor won the Battle of Buena Vista (February 22–23, 1847). Believing the war to be virtually over, Taylor departed Mexico in November 1847, having now developed a considerable dislike for both Polk and Scott.

Whig Party leaders convinced Taylor to run for the presidency in 1848. He won the election that November with Millard Fillmore as his running mate. Taylor's tenure as chief executive was consumed by the matter of slavery. He often acted independent of party interests and was fully prepared to veto the Compromise of 1850. President for only 16 months, Taylor died of acute gastroenteritis at the White House on July 9, 1850. His death removed the obstacle to passage of the Compromise of 1850.

JEFFREY W. DENNIS AND SPENCER C. TUCKER

See also

Bad Axe, Battle of; Black Hawk War; Lake Okeechobee, Battle of; Seminole War, First; Seminole War, Second

References

Bauer, K. Jack. *Zachary Taylor: Soldier, Planter, Statesman of the Old Southwest.* Baton Rouge: Louisiana State University Press, 1985.

Dyer, Brainerd. *Zachary Taylor.* New York: Barnes and Noble, 1967.

Hamilton, Holman. *Zachary Taylor: Soldier of the Republic.* 1941; reprint, Hamden, CT: Archon Books, 1966.

Singletary, Otis A. *The Mexican War.* Chicago: University of Chicago Press, 1960.

Tecumseh
Birth Date: ca. March 1768
Death Date: October 5, 1813

Shawnee chief and organizer of a Pan-Indian resistance movement. Little is known with certainty about Tecumseh's early life. He was born around March 1768 in a Shawnee village along the Scioto River in Ohio near present-day Piqua. His father was a war chief of the Kispoko band. At the time of Tecumseh's birth, the Shawnees were trying to resist white settlers flooding into the Ohio Country. The result was Lord Dunmore's War (1774). When the American Revolutionary War (1775–1783) broke out, the Shawnees sided with the British in an attempt to retain their land. In 1777 Tecumseh's people were forced to flee westward to a village on the Mad River and then moved farther west in 1780. These experiences instilled in Tecumseh a hatred for whites in general and for Americans in particular.

Beginning at age 16, Tecumseh participated in war parties that raided white settlements, but the advance by white settlers continued. In 1786 Kentucky militia burned Tecumseh's village, forcing his people to flee to a new location on the Maumee River. Under the leadership of his older brother Cheeseekau, Tecumseh earned a reputation as a brave and skillful warrior. Cheeseekau was killed in 1792 in an attack on Nashville, and Tecumseh succeeded him as war chief of the Kispoko band.

Tecumseh supported a loose confederacy of tribes organized by Blue Jacket and Little Turtle in 1790. When American armies under brigadier generals Josiah Harmar and then Arthur St. Clair marched against the tribes in Ohio, Tecumseh was among those who ambushed and defeated them. On August 20, 1794, Tecumseh participated in the Battle of Fallen Timbers in which Major General Anthony "Mad Anthony" Wayne decisively defeated Blue Jacket and broke the Pan-Indian confederacy.

Tecumseh refused to attend the signing of the Treaty of Greenville in 1795 in which Native Americans ceded most of Ohio to the United States. Instead, he led his followers into Indiana Territory, where he could get away from white influence. In 1797 the band settled near present-day Anderson, Indiana. Meanwhile, Native American settlements continued to decline because of alcoholism and renewed attempts by whites to take their lands. During this time Tecumseh joined his brother, the prophet Tenskwatawa, in calling for a return to traditional values and a rejection of all white influences. In 1805 Tecumseh moved his band back to Ohio, settling at Greenville. Soon Tecumseh and Tenskwatawa began to exert growing influence among other tribes. Delegations visited Tecumseh and listened to ideas of an Indian confederacy to prevent white encroachment.

While Tecumseh's message found favor among the younger warriors, older leaders opposed him. Whites were also uncomfortable with Tecumseh's presence so close to the border. Although he was careful to give no pretext for attacks by whites, Tecumseh realized that he was in danger in Ohio. The most damaging and dangerous charges against Tecumseh were that he was plotting with the British in Canada and receiving arms from them. To avoid possible conflict before he was ready, Tecumseh moved his band back to Indiana in the spring of 1808. They settled along the Wabash River, just below the mouth of the Tippecanoe River. Tecumseh now became more outspoken in his criticism of American expansionism.

In 1809 in the Treaty of Fort Wayne, Indiana territorial governor William Henry Harrison secured the cession of 3 million acres from tribes in Indiana. The outraged Tecumseh demanded that these land cessions halt, believing that the land belonged to all tribes and that none could be sold or given away without the consent of all. At a meeting with Harrison, the two nearly came to blows. Realizing that only strength could stop American settlements, Tecumseh began traveling widely to recruit followers for his confederacy. Although many favored his message, only the nativist Red Stick faction of the Creeks was willing to commit to joining his confederacy. While Tecumseh was away in 1811, Harrison brought an American army to attack Tecumseh's village on the Wabash. Tenskwatawa launched an unsuccessful surprise attack on Harrison but was decisively defeated at the Battle of Tippecanoe (November 7, 1811). This defeat diminished Tecumseh's power and following among the Indians.

Tecumseh was now forced to turn to the British for aid. When word reached Tecumseh in July 1812 that war had been declared, he gathered a band of followers and led them into Canada, joining British major general Isaac Brock in defending Fort Malden against an invasion by Brigadier General William Hull from Detroit. There is a tradition that Tecumseh was commissioned a brigadier general in the British Army, the only Indian to be so recognized. While Hull proved to be an indecisive leader, Tecumseh led his band into Michigan and destroyed a supply column in an ambush on August 5. He continued to harass American forces around Detroit, helping to convince Hull to retreat from Canada and later to surrender Detroit.

The victory over Hull caused large numbers of warriors to join Tecumseh. Brock now led a combined British and Native American army against Ohio. They fought a series of battles against American columns under Harrison, who sought to recapture Detroit. Tecumseh was in Indiana in January 1813 when an American force was destroyed on the Raisin River and the wounded were massacred. Tecumseh returned in time to join Brigadier General Henry Procter in the siege of Fort Meigs from April 28 to May 9. Tecumseh's warriors destroyed an American relief column on May 5 before the allies gave up the siege. A second attempt to capture Fort Meigs in July also failed, and many of the warriors began to lose confidence in the British.

When Procter, now a major general, retreated to Canada after the American victory in the Battle of Lake Erie, Tecumseh was outraged. He did not understand how the naval defeat would prevent the British from resupplying the army and the thousands of Native American families massed around Fort Malden. Nevertheless, Tecumseh and a small group of warriors joined the British in their retreat eastward from Fort Malden. To pacify Tecumseh, Procter agreed to make a stand on the Thames River on October 5, 1813. Tecumseh was killed in the battle. After Tecumseh's death and the British defeat, the Native Americans lost heart and dispersed.

TIM J. WATTS

See also
Blue Jacket; Fallen Timbers, Battle of; Greenville, Treaty of; Harrison, William Henry; Little Turtle; Native Americans and the War of 1812; Old Northwest Territory; Tenskwatawa; Thames, Battle of the; Tippecanoe, Battle of; Wabash, Battle of the

References
Dowd, Gregory Evans. *A Spirited Resistance: The North American Indian Struggle for Unity, 1745–1815.* Baltimore: Johns Hopkins University Press, 1992.
Edmunds, R. David. *Tecumseh and the Quest for Indian Leadership.* Boston: Little, Brown, 1984.
Sugden, John. *Tecumseh: A Life.* New York: Holt, 1997.

Teedyuscung
Birth Date: ca. 1700
Death Date: April 19, 1763

Delaware (Lenni Lenape) sachem (chief) who rose to prominence rather suddenly in the mid-1750s at the onset of the French and Indian War (1754–1763). Teedyuscung was born sometime around 1700 probably near Trenton, New Jersey. Before the 1750s he made a marginal living making brooms and baskets for British settlers in New Jersey. Teedyuscung became a Moravian Christian convert in 1755, taking the name Gideon. Disliking the life of a convert, he soon left the Moravians. Teedyuscung then settled with other Delaware people along the Susquehanna River.

In December 1755 during the French and Indian War, Teedyuscung led a successful war party against the British, striking across the upper Delaware River. The British soon retaliated, driving most Delawares deeper into the French camp. Teedyuscung then reversed course and opened peace negotiations with Pennsylvania on behalf of the Susquehanna Delawares. Assuming a leadership role despite his lack of any hereditary claim to do so, Teedyuscung used the negotiations as a platform on which to challenge the terms of the 1737 Walking Purchase, a controversial Delaware land cession to Pennsylvania.

Teedyuscung also used his newfound influence to challenge the Iroquois' domination of the Delawares. Bombastic and with a profound liking for liquor, Teedyuscung boasted that he represented 18 Native American nations, and he insisted that he be provided a clerk to record conference minutes.

Pennsylvania authorities doubted Teedyuscung's claims. Be that as it may, he knew that he had the backing of politically powerful Philadelphia Quakers. The Quakers hoped that Teedyuscung's allegations about the Walking Purchase would embarrass the colony's proprietors, the non-Quaker heirs of William Penn.

The matter soon came to the attention of the Privy Council, which then ordered Sir William Johnson, the British superintendent of Indian affairs for the northern colonies, to investigate. Johnson, who had close ties to the Iroquois, depicted Teedyuscung as a drunkard and blamed the Quakers for the controversy, accusing them of having inflamed the Delawares. Iroquois representatives also attempted to discredit Teedyuscung, arguing that he did not have any real authority. Teedyuscung then backed away from his accusations, stating that the Quakers had misled him. Pennsylvania's governor subsequently presented him with gifts to distribute to his followers, which many viewed as a reward for withdrawing his claims regarding the Walking Purchase.

By about 1760, Teedyuscung had asked Pennsylvania to deed land to the Delawares in Pennsylvania's Wyoming Valley. The colony did send laborers to build cabins for the Delawares. However, this was really an attempt to thwart Susquehanna Company claims to the area. Teedyuscung perished in the Wyoming Valley on April 19, 1763, when his cabin burned. Many historians suspect that arson was the cause of the fire, with the Iroquois and the Susquehanna Company being the most likely suspects.

ROGER M. CARPENTER

See also

Delawares; French and Indian War; Iroquois; Iroquois Confederacy; Johnson, Sir William

References

Wallace, Anthony F. C. *King of the Delawares: Teedyuscung, 1700–1763.* Philadelphia: University of Pennsylvania Press, 1949.

Weslager, C. A. *The Delaware Indians: A History.* New Brunswick, NJ: Rutgers University Press, 1972.

Teganissorens

See Decanisora

Tekestas

See Tequestas

Telegraph

Device used to communicate over long distances using an electrified wire. The telegraph comprised several approaches to communicating over wire. One such device used a dial to register the polarity, as invented by Charles Wheatstone and William Fothergill Cooke in June 1837 and widely used in continental Europe. Another involved keying pulses in combination of long and short durations, also patented in October 1837 and most commonly known as Morse code, after its primary inventor Samuel F. B. Morse (1791–1872). However, Morse's copatentees Alfred Vail and Leonard Gale made the invention marketable. Telegraphy in the United States was dominated by the use of Morse code and sets of instruments.

Unlike in Europe, the telegraph was immediately exploited for commercial, government, and military purposes in the United States. The telegraph proved invaluable to military commanders during the Indian Wars beginning in the early 1850s and was employed extensively during the American Civil War (1861–1865). The Spanish-American War of 1898 was the last major conflict in which the telegraph played a central role. After the turn of the century, telephones and teletypes predominated.

The first experimental telegraph line was commissioned by Congress in 1842 with a grant of $30,000 to Morse and Vail. The line ran between Baltimore and Washington, D.C., sending its first message on May 24, 1844, and later delivering news from the Democratic National Convention and gaining widespread popular and congressional support. With private financing Morse built additional lines between other major cities in the Northeast as did other entrepreneurs, ushering in a period of intense litigation. The telegraph market was nevertheless very competitive despite the high entry costs, expanding from six large providers in the eastern United States in 1855 to some 217 in 1886 and covering the entire country, including many rural areas.

By 1870 Western Union held a virtual monopoly in telegraphy. Western Union began as the New York and Mississippi Telegraph Company and expanded rapidly by acquisition and by partnership with the railroads. The union between telegraph and railroad began in 1852 and benefited the former by providing clear tracts of land on which to run wire and benefited the latter by improving safety through increased operational efficiency of signaling and better communications. Many telegraph wires were strung immediately adjacent to railroad tracks.

Slightly less than a decade later Congress again took an active role in promoting the telegraph when, in 1860 with the Pacific Telegraph Act, it commissioned Hiram Sibley of Western Union to build a telegraph line connecting the East Coast and the West Coast for an annual subsidy of $40,000 if the line was completed by July 31, 1862. Edward Creighton surveyed the route used by the Pony Express, which ran from Omaha, Nebraska, to Sacramento, California. He concluded that this was the best route for the line and gained the approval of Native Americans to traverse their land while exacting a pledge that they would not disturb the wires. Construction of the line began on May 27, 1861, and was completed ahead of schedule on October 24, 1861. This considerable feat was accomplished by employing separate labor gangs from the Overland Telegraph Company and the Pacific Telegraph Company to complete their own segments of the line. The Pony Express was financially induced to keep running, and progress was monitored via telegraph as the line was erected. The outbreak of the Civil War in 1861, however, forced the eastern terminus of the line to move from St. Louis north to Chicago.

The transcontinental railroad followed nearly the same course as the transcontinental telegraph line, and once the former was completed, the latter was moved to run parallel to the tracks. The proximity of rail and telegraph enabled more efficient repairs of wires, while rail stations doubled as telegraph offices. Multiple lines were eventually strung, and the reliability of the lines increased.

As the telegraph extended westward, the military was linked to and linked by its wires. Soldiers not only protected gangs as they erected the transcontinental line but also engaged in manual labor to establish their own lines. Following the Civil War, another effort was begun in the District of Texas at the behest of its commander to link forts from the Red River to the Rio Grande, resulting in more than 1,200 miles of wire being erected. As a military telegraph network, it was operated by soldiers at the various stations, of which Fort Concho was the hub, although civilians often made use of the military lines for personal and business purposes. Other military networks were established in the Midwest and the Northwest.

The telegraph linked military outposts to the rest of the country, thereby providing forts and nearby homesteads with access to news and weather reports. Army unit commanders during campaigns against Native American tribes telegraphed their headquarters to report on operations, enemy strength, and the logistical situation as well as to request reinforcements. News also flowed from the battlefield, such as at Slim Buttes on September 8 and 9, 1876, during the Great Sioux War (Black Hills War) of 1876–1877 in which scouts with unofficial reports of the battle raced the official messenger to the nearest telegraph station to be the first to release the story. The telegraph could also be a liability and required frequent maintenance and policing. Lines were often targeted by Indians throughout the period, and soldiers either did the repairs themselves or accompanied repair crews. Nevertheless, the telegraph was a force multiplier that provided better means of coordinating smaller units in a struggle against highly mobile Native American bands in skirmishes, battles, and campaigns.

MARCEL A. DEROSIER

See also

Black Hills, South Dakota; Pony Express; Railroads; Slim Buttes, Battle of

References

Beauchamp, Ken. *History of Telegraphy*. London: Institute of Electrical Engineers, 2001.

Coe, Lewis. *The Telegraph: A History of Morse Invention and Its Predecessors in the United States*. Jefferson, NC: McFarland, 1993.

Lubrano, Annteresa. *The Telegraph: How Technology Caused Social Change*. New York: Garland, 1997.

Tenskwatawa
Birth Date: ca. 1775
Death Date: November 1836

Shawnee religious prophet and political leader in the early 19th-century Great Lakes–Ohio Valley region. Tenskwatawa was born around 1775 at Old Piqua, Ohio; he was also known as the Shawnee Prophet or simply the Prophet. He was born as one of triplets into a family of at least six older brothers and sisters. Just prior to Tenskwatawa's birth, his Shawnee war chief father, Puckeshinwa, died in the 1774 Battle of Point Pleasant, Ohio. Their Creek mother, Methoataske, left the Ohio Valley in 1779 and entrusted her children—Tenskwatawa, Tecumseh (who would be one of the most famous Native American orators and military leaders of all time), and another child—to an older sister, Tecumapease.

Tenskwatawa's childhood name was Lalawethika. In 1804 he assumed the role of community shaman when the renowned

shaman Penagashea died. Lalawethika had been studying with him since 1795. After a series of visions in 1805, Lalawethika changed his name to Tenskwatawa, meaning "The Open Door." In the visions Tenskwatawa met the Master of Life, who showed him heaven and hell and gave him instructions on how to avoid the latter while gaining admission to the former. Tenskwatawa preached that Native Americans must give up alcohol, reject Christianity, destroy their medicine bags, and respect all life. If the Master of Life's teachings were followed, Tenskwatawa claimed, the dead would be brought back to life, and animal populations would be restored. Adherents were given prayer sticks inscribed with prayers for the Master of Life. Tenskwatawa also claimed that Americans were products of the evil Great Serpent who, assisted by witches, spread death and destruction.

Tenskwatawa nonetheless proposed that trade continue with the Americans but only on terms set by the Native Americans until trade was no longer needed. Finally, the nativist vision of Tenskwatawa and Tecumseh included a call for Pan-Indian unity to resist encroachments on ancestral lands by whites. Of the brothers, Tenskwatawa's approach was more spiritual, while Tecumseh's was more pragmatic, but both were very persuasive.

Immediately following his vision and explanations, Tenskwatawa and Tecumseh established a village near Greenville, Ohio, and called for all Native American peoples to settle there. This settlement was a direct challenge to the 1795 Treaty of Greenville. Tenskwatawa participated in witchcraft trials among the Delawares and Wyandots in 1806. Those accused of witchcraft were individuals who appeared to be acculturated to the white immigrants' ways. As Tenskwatawa's prestige and popularity grew, the settlement of Greenville proved to be inadequate, resulting in the establishment of Prophetstown in 1808 at the mouth of the Tippecanoe River.

Here the brothers' influence was interpreted as a threat by Indiana governor William Henry Harrison. In 1811 when Tecumseh was in the South building his Pan-Indian coalition, Harrison moved into the area with a force of 970 men with the goal of destroying Prophetstown. Tenskwatawa promised to meet with Harrison and suggested that he camp for the night at a location some two miles distant from Prophetstown. Tecumseh had warned his brother not to give battle, but that night Tenskwatawa incited some 500–700 of his followers to strike first, promising them that the white men's bullets could not harm them, as their powder had already turned to sand and their bullets to soft mud.

Early on the morning of November 7, the Native Americans struck. During the battle Tenskwatawa stood on a high rock and chanted war songs to encourage his followers. Informed early that some of his warriors had been slain, he insisted that his followers fight on, promising an easy victory. Although Harrison lost up to a quarter of his force in casualties, the Battle of Tippecanoe ended in a Native American defeat, and the next day Harrison went on to destroy Prophetstown.

A Shawnee mystic and brother of Tecumseh, Tenskwatawa was known as the Shawnee Prophet. His precipitous actions led to the Native American defeat in the Battle of Tippecanoe on November 7, 1811, and the subsequent destruction of Prophetstown. (Thomas L. McKenney and James Hall, *The Indian Tribes of North America*, 1836–1844)

Tenskwatawa's followers almost killed him in their fury over the outcome of the Battle of Tippecanoe. It was clearly the nadir of his influence among the Great Lakes nations. The battle was nonetheless of great importance. It drove many Native Americans of the region to side with the British in the War of 1812. The British also decided to assist the Native Americans there against the United States.

The Native Americans rebuilt Prophetstown shortly after Harrison left the area, and Tenskwatawa participated in the major events of the War of 1812, although he did not take part in any of the actual fighting. In the Battle of the Thames on October 5, 1813, Tenskwatawa fled with the British, leaving Tecumseh and dozens of other warriors to die protecting their retreat. The American victory in this battle effectively ended British and Native American power in the Old Northwest.

Denied admission to the United States in 1815, Tenskwatawa and a few Shawnee followers remained in Upper Canada until 1824. In 1826, two years after his return, Tenskwatawa and the Shawnees were removed from the Ohio Valley. They traveled to Kaskaskia and western Missouri, eventually reaching the Shawnee Reservation in Kansas in 1828. Tenskwatawa sat for an iconic portrait by American artist George Catlin in 1832 and died in November 1836 in present-day Kansas City, Kansas.

KARL S. HELE

See also

Catlin, George; Greenville, Treaty of; Harrison, William Henry; Native Americans and the War of 1812; Nativism, Indian; Point Pleasant, Battle of; Prophetstown; Shawnees; Tecumseh; Thames, Battle of the; Tippecanoe, Battle of

References

Dowd, Gregory Evans. *A Spirited Resistance: The North American Indian Struggle for Unity, 1745–1815.* Baltimore: Johns Hopkins University Press, 1992.

Dowd, Gregory Evans. "Thinking and Believing: Nativism and Unity in the Ages of Pontiac and Tecumseh." *American Indian Quarterly* 16 (1992): 309–335.

Edmunds, R. David. *Tecumseh and the Quest for Indian Leadership.* Boston: Little, Brown, 1984.

Gilbert, Bil. *God Gave Us This Country: Tekamthi and the First American Civil War.* New York: Atheneum, 1989.

10th U.S. Cavalry Regiment

See Cavalry Regiment, 10th U.S.

Tequestas

An Arawak-speaking group of Native Americans who lived along the Miami River and on the coastal islands of southeastern Florida. Estimates of the Tequesta (Tekesta) population at the time of European contact vary from 1,000 to 5,000. In large part, this wide variance is because the Spanish did not clearly distinguish between them and their more powerful neighbors, the Calusas. Europeans usually interacted only with the villages along the Atlantic shore, but it is believed that Tequesta villages may once have stretched far inland, into the Everglades.

The Tequestas showed a high degree of technical sophistication, as demonstrated by the 1998 archaeological discovery of the so-called Miami Circle, a stone arrangement 38 feet across. Postholes around the perimeter have led to speculation that the Miami Circle may have been an imposing ceremonial structure.

Early relations between the Spanish and the Tequestas varied widely between open hostility and peace. Juan Ponce de León encountered the Tequestas in 1513 and believed that he established peaceful contact. In 1521, however, Ponce de León was fatally wounded in a clash with a Calusa force that may also have included Tequesta warriors.

In 1565 Governor Pedro Menéndez de Avilés attempted to repair the relationship with the Tequestas by leaving Francisco de Villareal and a company of soldiers to construct a mission in a Tequesta village. Villareal erected crosses and built meeting huts for converting the natives.

The Tequestas and the Spanish were soon again at odds. For unknown reasons, the Spanish garrison killed an important tribe member in 1568. In response the Tequestas tore down the crosses, burned the meeting huts, and harassed Spanish soldiers. Whenever the Spanish attempted to leave the village to forage or retrieve water, the Tequestas ambushed them. Finally, Villareal and the Spanish company decided to abandon the settlement for the safety of Santa Lucia. An attempt in 1569 to build a missionary station also ran afoul of intercultural tensions. The Spanish withdrew entirely the following year.

Once a real power in the region, the Tequestas were already in decline when the Europeans arrived, mainly because of competition with large, aggressive rival tribes. The Tequestas continued to dwindle in numbers and importance over the course of the 17th century. European diseases weakened them further, as did ongoing warfare with the Calusas. The Tequestas also drew the ire of the Spanish from time to time for taking in runaway African slaves.

The Tequestas' decline accelerated further in the 18th century. In 1704 an English raid destroyed Tequesta settlements near the mouth of the New River. When Spain formally ceded Florida to the British in 1763, the Tequesta population stood at only a few hundred people. The majority of these soon successfully petitioned the Spanish to resettle them in Cuba. The remnants left behind in Florida assimilated into surrounding tribes.

ANDREW C. LANNEN

See also
Ponce de León, Juan

References
McGoun, William E. *Ancient Miamians: The Tequesta of South Florida.* Gainesville: University Press of Florida, 2002.

Swanton, John R. *The Indians of the Southeastern United States.* Washington, DC: Smithsonian Institution Press, 1946.

Terry, Alfred Howe
Birth Date: November 10, 1827
Death Date: December 16, 1890

U.S. Army officer. Alfred Howe Terry was born into a wealthy New England family on November 10, 1827, in Hartford, Connecticut. After briefly attending Yale University Law School from 1848 to 1849, he served as a law clerk for the New Haven County Superior Court from 1854 until the outbreak of the American Civil War (1861–1865).

After the Civil War began, Terry raised a volunteer regiment in Connecticut and was commissioned its colonel. The regiment saw action in the First Battle of Bull Run (Manassas) in Virginia (July 21, 1861). Terry subsequently recruited and led another Connecticut volunteer regiment, helping to secure Port Royal, South Carolina, on November 7, 1861. On April 11, 1862, Terry's regiment helped to capture Fort Pulaski, at the mouth of the strategic Savannah River. On April 26 Terry was promoted to brigadier general of volunteers. He then commanded a division of X Corps and took part in operations against Charleston, including the capture of Fort Wagner in September 1863. In 1864, X Corps was assigned to Major General Benjamin Butler's Army of the James in Virginia, and Terry saw extensive action in the Bermuda Hundred Campaign. On the death of Major General David

B. Birney in October, Terry briefly commanded X Corps before it was disbanded.

Terry's greatest recognition during the Civil War came when he received command of a provisional corps, later designated X Corps, for an attack on Fort Fisher. He and Rear Admiral David D. Porter worked well together, and Fort Fisher fell to Union forces on January 13, 1865. Terry's success won him an official thanks from the U.S. Congress, a brigadier general's commission in the regular army, and a major general's commission in the volunteer army. His promotion to brigadier general in the regular army was a rare accomplishment for someone who had not graduated from the U.S. Military Academy. Terry finished the war in the Carolinas, where he was part of Major General John M. Schofield's Army of the Ohio, which was operating under Major General William T. Sherman.

After the Civil War, Terry commanded the Department of Dakota from 1866 to 1868 and again from 1873 to 1886. He was a key architect of the 1867 Medicine Lodge Treaty that temporarily ended the fighting with the southern Plains Kiowa, Apache, Cheyenne, and Arapaho tribes. Terry also participated in the 1868 Treaty of Fort Laramie negotiations, which helped to end the fighting in the northern Plains known as Red Cloud's War (1866–1868).

In 1873 Terry returned to command the Department of Dakota and participated in the Great Sioux War (Black Hills War) of

Brigadier General Alfred H. Terry commanded the Department of Dakota during 1866–1868 and during 1873–1886. He played a leading role in the Great Sioux War of 1876–1877. (Library of Congress)

1876–1877. He commanded one of the three converging columns designed to locate and destroy the hostile Native Americans. This led to the disastrous Battle of the Little Bighorn (June 25–26, 1876) in which the 7th Cavalry Regiment, commanded by Lieutenant Colonel George A. Custer, spearheading Terry's column, attacked without waiting for the supporting columns and suffered a devastating defeat, including the annihilation of Custer and the men with him. Afterward Terry refused to say anything that might tarnish Custer's reputation.

In October 1877 Terry went to Canada to negotiate the surrender of the Sioux leader Sitting Bull. These talks were not successful, but in 1881 Terry was the man to whom Sitting Bull surrendered. Still commander of the Department of Dakota during the Nez Perce War of 1877, Terry sent troops to help intercept Chief Joseph and his people. In 1878 Terry joined Major General John Schofield and Colonel George W. Getty on the so-called Schofield Commission, a board charged with reexamining the Civil War court-martial of Major General Fitz John Porter.

In 1886 Terry was promoted to major general, one of only three men to hold that rank in the army at the time. He was also the first Civil War volunteer officer to attain that rank in the regular army. Terry received command of the Division of the Missouri, with headquarters in Chicago. He retired from the army in 1888 and died on December 16, 1890, in New Haven, Connecticut.

ALAN K. LAMM

See also

Apaches; Arapahos; Cheyennes; Custer, George Armstrong; Fort Laramie, Treaty of (1851); Fort Laramie, Treaty of (1868); Gibbon, John; Great Sioux War; Joseph, Chief; Kiowas; Little Bighorn, Battle of the; Medicine Lodge Treaty; Nez Perce War; Red Cloud's War; Schofield, John McAllister; Sioux; Sitting Bull

References

Bailey, John W. *Pacifying the Plains: General Alfred Terry and the Decline of the Sioux, 1866–1890.* Westport, CT: Greenwood, 1979.

Hutton, Paul Andrew. *Phil Sheridan and His Army.* Lincoln: University of Nebraska Press, 1985.

Utley, Robert M. *Cavalier in Buckskin: George Armstrong Custer and the Western Military Frontier.* Rev. ed. Norman: University of Oklahoma Press, 2001.

Warner, Ezra J. *Generals in Blue: Lives of the Union Commanders.* 1964; reprint, Baton Rouge: Louisiana State University Press, 2006.

Teton Sioux

See Lakota Sioux

Texas Rangers

Texas law enforcement organization that frequently operated as a paramilitary force. In 1823 Stephen F. Austin organized small armed groups to range over the Texas countryside to protect settlers from Native American raids and bandits. The Texas Rangers were formally established on October 17, 1835, by the Provisional Government of Texas, and the force, which grew to 300 men, played an important role in the Texas Revolution of 1835–1836. During the late 1830s and early 1840s, Texas president Mirabeau B. Lamar employed the rangers against the Cherokees and Comanches along the frontier of the new Republic of Texas. During the Mexican-American War (1846–1848) rangers joined federal forces in the invasion of Mexico, where they earned a reputation for bravery as well as cruelty toward the Mexican people.

Following Texas's annexation by the United States, the protection of the Texas frontier became the responsibility of the U.S. Army, and the rangers were used sparingly. In 1857, however, Texas governor Hardin Richard Runnels commissioned John S. "Rip" Ford, a ranger veteran of the Mexican-American War, to form a company of 100 rangers. Ford's command subsequently battled the Comanches in the Canadian River Valley, and on December 27, 1859, the rangers engaged the irregular forces of Mexican bandit hero Juan Cortina at the Battle of Rio Grande City.

After Texas joined the Confederacy on March 5, 1861, during the American Civil War (1861–1865), the rangers were disbanded. Many former rangers volunteered for Confederate service, however. The 2nd Texas Cavalry, commanded by Ford, was stationed along the Rio Grande and battled Native Americans and Juan Cortina while protecting trade between the Confederacy and Mexico. During the Civil War years, Texans endured numerous Native American raids along the western and southern frontiers. The 8th Texas Cavalry contained many former rangers and was popularly known as Terry's Texas Rangers after its first commander, Benjamin Franklin Terry. Extolled for its fearlessness and tenacity, the 8th Texas Cavalry had a combat record among Texas units second only to General John B. Hood's Texas Brigade.

The Texas Rangers were officially reconstituted in 1874. The law enforcement organization subsequently gained legendary fame for subduing such outlaws as Sam Bass and John Wesley Harding. On the other hand, the rangers drew considerable criticism for their racist attitudes during the Mexican Revolution (1900–1917). In 1935 the rangers were professionalized and placed under the control of the Texas Department of Public Safety.

RON BRILEY

See also

Cherokees; Comanches; Mexico; Native Americans and the Civil War

References

Davis, John L. *The Texas Rangers: Their First 150 Years.* San Antonio: Institute of Texas Cultures, 1975.

Smith, David Paul. *Frontier Defense in the Civil War: Texas' Rangers and Rebels.* College Station: Texas A&M University Press, 1992.

Utley, Robert. *Lone Star Justice: The First Century of the Texas Rangers.* New York: Oxford University Press, 2000.

Thames, Battle of the
Event Date: October 5, 1813

Climactic battle of the War of 1812 in the Northwest. Also known as the Battle of Moraviantown, the Battle of the Thames signified the end of British and Native American influence on the Great Lakes frontier. The engagement occurred near present-day Chatham, Ontario, Canada, along the Thames River. Throughout 1813, the British and their Native American allies, commanded by Major General Henry Procter and Tecumseh, had frustrated efforts by Major General William Henry Harrison to regain U.S. control over the region. When U.S. Navy master commandant Oliver Hazard Perry defeated the British in the Battle of Lake Erie on September 10, 1813, the Americans regained control of Lake Erie. This naval victory enabled Harrison to undertake an offensive to recapture Detroit, farther west, and to invade Canada.

With his logistical support now all but cut off, Procter hoped to withdraw from Detroit by moving through Upper Canada along the Thames River. Tecumseh strongly opposed Procter's decision, viewing it as evidence of abandonment by the British, who had promised the Native Americans their own lands. Eventually the allies reached a compromise to retreat but to make a stand somewhere along the route. The British march from Sandwich began on September 24 with about 880 troops and perhaps 500 Native American warriors and their families. The withdrawal was not well organized and proceeded slowly, encumbered with considerable personal baggage.

Soon the men were on half rations. Morale was low, and the officers were reportedly dissatisfied with Procter's leadership, although Lieutenant Colonel Augustus Warburton, second-in-command, resisted calls that he intervene to remove Procter.

On September 27 Harrison's army landed in Canada. He had almost 5,000 U.S. regulars and Kentucky militia. Harrison left Sandwich on October 2, the speed of his advance greatly enhanced by mounted Kentucky riflemen led by Colonel Richard M. Johnson. On October 4 the American column reached the third and unfordable branch of the Thames. Tecumseh and his warriors had dismantled the bridge there and were then on the opposite side. Harrison ordered up two 6-pounders and used these to drive away the Native Americans, then ordered his men to repair the bridge. In just two hours Harrison was again on the move. Johnson's Kentuckians caught up with Procter a few miles from Moraviantown along the Thames River, the British having already set fire to the craft they were using to transport some of their baggage and supplies on the river.

By the morning of October 5, it was clear to Procter that he would have to stand and fight. He deployed his regulars in a wedge-shaped clearing in a beech forest. The left flank rested on the river beside which ran the road to Moraviantown some three and a half miles to the east. The line ran about 250 yards to the north, ending at a small swamp. It then extended from the small swamp another 250 yards, where it ended at a large swamp. The left portion of the British line was held by 540 men of the 41st Regiment of Foot and

Death of Tecumseh at the Battle of the Thames during the War of 1812. (Library of Congress)

290 men of the Royal Newfoundland Regiment. Procter positioned a 6-pounder artillery piece in the road to provide some support. The portion to the right of the small swamp was held by Tecumseh's 500 Native Americans. The British had not erected any sort of earthworks or abatis by felling trees.

The Americans arrived before the British position at about 8:00 a.m. The American force numbered 140 regulars, 1,000 Kentuckians in Johnson's regiment, and about 2,300 Kentucky volunteers. There were also perhaps 160 allied Native Americans. As Harrison was making his dispositions prior to an attack, Johnson learned that the British left was only thinly held by men standing about three feet apart. The situation seemed tailor-made for Johnson's mounted men, and he asked permission from Harrison to make an immediate charge. Harrison agreed. With many of the attackers screaming "Remember the Raisin!" (a reference to the Raisin River Massacre), the Kentuckians in only a few minutes drove through the British line—the British artillery piece having failed to fire—and then dismounted and used their rifles to attack the British from the rear. Under attack from both front and rear, the British line quickly crumbled, and most of the British troops surrendered.

The Native Americans, protected somewhat by the swamp, held their ground and halted Johnson's horsemen with musket fire, killing or wounding 15 of them. Johnson himself was wounded several times. Tecumseh, who had a premonition of his own death, was slain. His body was never recovered (the Native Americans said it had been lifted up to heaven), but Johnson claimed to have killed him and was generally so credited. With the sizable American force converging on their position, most of the Native Americans fled.

The Battle of the Thames lasted less than an hour, with the British suffering 12 killed, 22 wounded, and some 600 captured. Thirty-three Native Americans were also slain. American casualties were 7 killed and 22 wounded. Procter, who escaped, was widely blamed for the defeat. He blamed his men, saying that they had not carried out his orders. Procter demanded a court of inquiry, and when this was not held, he wrote directly to the British commander, Frederick, Duke of York. This led to a court-martial and a finding that Procter was guilty of failing to properly prepare for the retreat and of exercising poor tactical judgment. The court recommended that he be reprimanded and suspended from duty for six months. In the end he was only reprimanded, in July 1815.

Although a relatively minor action, the Battle of the Thames proved decisive and provided a rare victory for the United States. Even though the Americans had enjoyed the advantage of greatly superior numbers, they had defeated British regulars. The victory was received with great enthusiasm in Kentucky and helped renew public support for the war. Certainly the battle destroyed the British position west of the head of Lake Erie and broke forever Native American power in the Old Northwest. This opened that territory for white settlement west to the Mississippi River. After their victory, the American troops burned Moraviantown, a peaceful Native American settlement. Then, lacking naval support that was needed elsewhere, they departed Canada for Detroit.

STEVEN J. RAUCH AND SPENCER C. TUCKER

See also

Harrison, William Henry; Native Americans and the War of 1812; Raisin River Massacre; Tecumseh

References

Antal, Sandy. *A Wampum Denied: Procter's War of 1812.* Ottawa: Carleton University Press, 1997.

Sugden, John. *Tecumseh's Last Stand.* Norman: University of Oklahoma Press, 1985.

Thayendanega

See Brant, Joseph

Theyanoguin
Birth Date: ca. 1680
Death Date: September 8, 1755

Mohawk sachem (chief), warrior, orator, and diplomat as well as a notable ally of British settlers and interests in western New York and beyond. Theyanoguin (Deyohninhohakarawenh) was born in western Massachusetts about 1680 to a Mohegan father and a Mohawk mother. Both tribes being long-standing allies of Dutch colonists in New York and English settlers in New England, Theyanoguin was raised in the tradition of friendship with those two colonial powers, including conversion to Anglicanism and adoption of an English name, Hendrick, around 1690. During the next 60 years this Mohawk sachem played a major role in military operations against New France, epitomizing his Iroquois name, which translates as "the western door is open."

Despite his allegiance to the English, Theyanoguin's first loyalty was always to his own people. In 1698 he joined another Christian Mohawk in accusing English and Dutch speculators of fraudulent land claims and in getting those claims overturned by the governor of New York, Richard Coote, Earl of Bellomont. Three years later Theyanoguin worked with other Iroquois chiefs to conclude a pact of neutrality with New France.

For the most part, however, Chief Theyanoguin was a friend to the English colonists in peace and war alike. In 1709 he participated in an abortive attack on New France, and he visited England the following year. There Theyanoguin obtained permission from Queen Anne to serve as a lay preacher for the Church of England. On returning from London, Theyanoguin settled and grew apples along the Mohawk River, near the mouth of East Canada Creek, and spent much of the succeeding 30 years preaching and consolidating his power.

Mohawk chief Theyanoguin (Hendrick), a close ally of the British, was killed in the Battle of Lake George on September 8, 1755, during the French and Indian War. (Library of Congress)

Theyanoguin joining Colonel William Johnson in an expedition against Crown Point.

During the Battle of Lake George on September 8, 1755, Theyanoguin's Mohawk warriors were among the first to be attacked on the so-called Bloody Morning Scout. Theyanoguin himself became separated from the main body in the disorderly retreat and was subsequently killed and scalped by some of his own distant brethren, the Caughnawagas, Iroquois allies of the French. Theyanoguin was not forgotten, however; his fellow Mohawks continued to serve the British with distinction throughout the French and Indian War and helped open the door to westward Anglo-American expansion.

MATT SCHUMANN

See also

Beaver Wars; French and Indian War; Iroquois; Iroquois Confederacy; Iroquois Treaties of 1700 and 1701; Johnson, Sir William; King George's War; King William's War; Mohawks; Mohegans; Queen Anne's War

References

Anderson, Fred. *Crucible of War: The Seven Years' War and the Fate of the Empire in British North America, 1754–1766.* New York: Vintage Books, 2001.

Fenton, William N. *The Great Law and the Longhouse: A Political History of the Iroquois Confederacy.* Norman: University of Oklahoma Press, 1998.

Flexner, James Thomas. *Mohawk Baronet: A Biography of Sir William Johnson.* Syracuse, NY: Syracuse University Press, 1989.

Steele, Ian K. *Betrayals: Fort William Henry & the "Massacre."* Oxford: Oxford University Press, 1990.

It was after a second visit to London in 1740 that Theyanoguin truly distinguished himself as a friend of Great Britain. During King George's War (1744–1748), he led a negotiating party to Montreal to plead for peace. There he accepted French gifts and then attacked a French outpost at Île Lamothe in present-day Vermont. His warriors also aided Colonel William Johnson's attack on Montreal in 1746, and they harassed French forts and military expeditions in the region around Lake Champlain.

Following King George's War, Theyanoguin looked westward and attempted to enlist British support against French expansion into the Ohio Valley. For several years his calls went unheeded, and he drifted somewhat from his traditional allies. The rift came to a head at the Albany Congress in June 1754, when Theyanoguin, now chief sachem of the Mohawks, chastised the colonial delegates: "Look at the French. . . . They are fortifying everywhere; but, we are ashamed to say it, you are . . . bare and open, without any fortifications. It is but one step from Canada hither, and the French may easily come and turn you out of doors." Shortly thereafter, the British colonists received substantial assistance from the mother country to challenge the French, including 1,000 men of the 44th and 48th regiments under Major General Edward Braddock, the new commander in chief in North America. Braddock decided to launch four simultaneous attacks in 1755, with

3rd Colorado Cavalry Regiment

See Cavalry Regiment, 3rd Colorado

3rd U.S. Cavalry

See Mounted Riflemen, Regiment of

Thocmentony

See Winnemucca, Sarah

Timucuan Revolt
Event Date: 1656

Violent uprising of the Timucuas, a loose confederation of Native Americans inhabiting northern Florida and southern Georgia, against the Spanish in 1656. After first contact with the Spanish in the 16th century, the Timucuas permitted the establishment of Franciscan missions throughout their territory. The Spanish paid Timucuas affiliated with the missions to clear roads, supply crops, and build new missions. The missions came at a terrible cost in terms of the spread of deadly disease, however. The Timucuas may have lost half their population to epidemics between 1612 and 1616.

By the mid-17th century, tensions between the Spanish and the Timucuas were mounting. Food shortages, disease, and the demoralizing effect of Spanish authority had eroded the authority of the Timucua chiefs. The Spanish governor, Diego de Rebolledo, also regularly requisitioned Timucua men for service at the Castillo de San Marcos in St. Augustine. Many Timucuas resented such servitude and disliked Spanish intrusions into their affairs.

In early 1656 Rebolledo, fearing an attack by the English, summoned an additional 500 men, including the chiefs, from Timucua and Apalachee provinces. The men were instructed to carry their own food and supplies with them. Timucuan society was highly stratified, and the suggestion that chiefs should carry their own food was an affront to their status as leaders.

Timucua chief Lúcas Menéndez refused to send his warriors and encouraged other chiefs to rebel against the Spanish. Careful not to disavow loyalty to the Spanish king or the Franciscan friars, the Timucuas limited their assaults to Spanish soldiers. The Timucuas attacked only sporadically, but the violence led to seven Spanish deaths in three separate skirmishes. Thereafter the Timucuas abandoned the missions and left the fields unplanted.

In the meantime, the ringleaders of the revolt constructed a small palisaded fort and attempted to spread the rebellion to neighboring Apalachee tribes. Their efforts failed, for most Apalachees anticipated Spanish retaliation.

Because Rebolledo refused to be diverted from his defensive preparations against an English assault, the insurrectionist Timucuas had time to fortify their palisade. The fort proved to be a doubled-edged sword, however. Although offering a degree of protection for the rebels, it also concentrated them in a single location, ultimately making it easier for the Spanish to suppress the rebellion.

After several months of tension, rank-and-file Timucuas began losing faith in their leaders. Rather than spreading the rebellion to neighboring tribes, the rebellion appeared to have driven the Apalachees into an even tighter alliance with the Spanish, leaving the Timucuas dangerously isolated.

Four months passed before Rebolledo turned his attention to the rebellious Timucuas. He then sent 60 Spanish soldiers to suppress the revolt and persuade the Timucuas to return to the missions. The Spanish offered negotiations rather than warfare, which the Timucua leaders reluctantly accepted. Most of the rebels were allowed to disperse. But the Spanish placed the chiefs and principal warriors on trial. Ultimately the Spanish executed 11 Timucuas and sentenced another 10 to hard labor at St. Augustine. The bodies of the executed chiefs were publicly displayed near their villages.

The revolt accelerated the destruction of Timucuan culture. The demoralizing defeat, ongoing epidemics, and periodic slaving raids from the Caribbean whittled away the vitality and population of the villages. When Spain ceded Florida to England in 1763, it is believed that there were only 89 surviving Timucuas.

DOROTHY A. MAYS

See also
Apalachees

References
Hann, John H. *A History of the Timucua Indians and Missions.* Gainesville: University Press of Florida, 1996.
Milanich, Jerald T. *The Timucua.* Oxford, UK: Blackwell, 1996.

Tippecanoe, Battle of
Event Date: November 7, 1811

Battle between American forces and Native American warriors that occurred on the banks of the Wabash River near Prophetstown (near present-day Lafayette, Indiana) on November 7, 1811. The Battle of Tippecanoe served to blunt Shawnee leader Tecumseh's growing native confederation. Tecumseh opposed any concessions to the white settlers who were expanding westward into Indian lands but realized that in order to mount an effective resistance, he had to form an alliance extending beyond the Shawnees. He thus worked to create a Native American coalition of many tribes that would be dedicated to the goal of protecting their lands against white expansion.

Tecumseh and his half brother Tenskwatawa, known as the Prophet, had founded Prophetstown in May 1808 as the capital of their growing native confederacy. The town was not only the center for diplomatic activities among the tribes but was also a training ground for warriors. At its peak, more than 1,000 people resided there.

In November 1811 Tecumseh was absent from Prophetstown, recruiting other Native American groups in the southern states for his confederation, and Tenskwatawa was in charge in Tecumseh's absence. At the same time, governor of the Indiana Territory William Henry Harrison was determined to destroy Prophetstown. Harrison had aggressively pursued land cession treaties with the Native Americans. These treaties often included the payment of small sums of money for vast tracts of land. Oftentimes, officials played one tribe or individual against another to help secure the cessions or plied native leaders with alcohol to get them to sign away their lands. Tecumseh's growing Native American confederation was a threat to this process. To western whites, Prophetstown had become a symbol of British influence, although the native raids on American frontier settlements almost certainly did not originate with them. Governors Ninian Edwards of the Illinois Territory and Benjamin Howard of the newly formed Missouri Territory both approved Harrison's proposed plan for a march up

The Battle of Tippecanoe, November 7, 1811. Fought near present-day Lafayette, Indiana, it was trumpeted as a victory over the Indians, but army and militia casualties had been heavy and the battle led many Native Americans to side with the British in the War of 1812. Illustration by Kurz & Allison, circa 1889. (Library of Congress)

the Wabash River to the limits of the purchase of 1809. Harrison so informed Secretary of War William Eustis, who responded that he favored approaching the Prophet, asking him to disperse his followers, and, should he refuse, attacking him. Eustis also authorized Harrison to establish a new frontier post, but in no circumstances was he to antagonize the British.

The most important element of Harrison's expeditionary force, Colonel John Boyd's 4th U.S. Infantry Regiment, arrived at Vincennes, Indiana, from Philadelphia on September 19, 1807, having covered the 1,300 miles on foot and in boats. Six days later on September 25, Harrison gave the order to move out. A total of 970 men responded: 350 members of the 4th Regiment, 400 Indiana Militia infantry, 84 mounted Indiana riflemen, 123 Kentucky dragoons, and 13 scouts and guides. The march order, adopted from Major General Anthony Wayne's practice in the Fallen Timbers Campaign of 1794, consisted of a company of riflemen leading, followed 100 yards behind by a mounted troop and 50 yards behind it the infantry in column. Another mounted troop took up the rear 100 yards behind the infantry. Detached troops protected the flanks of the column 100 yards to either side. Each night the men prepared a fortified camp to protect against possible native attack.

As a consequence of these precautions, it took Harrison more than two weeks to cover the 65 miles from Vincennes to the bend in the Wabash River at present-day Terre Haute. There the men completed Fort Harrison on October 27 before moving to the mouth of the Vermillion River. Harrison now ordered the construction of a blockhouse, later called Fort Boyd, at the site.

Harrison had warned that whether he advanced farther would depend on Native American conduct, so when some natives stole horses from the camp and someone fired into the camp, wounding a man on October 10, Harrison took these incidences as justification to cross the Vermillion into Native American territory. More shots were fired into Harrison's advancing forces but without casualties. Harrison was now determined to destroy Prophetstown, and his officers urged that he attack without delay. However, on November 6 a native delegation requested talks, and Harrison, against the advice of his subordinate commanders, accepted, with the parley scheduled for the next day.

The native delegation then suggested the campsite for Harrison's force. Harrison's enemies later claimed that the natives had selected an ideal ambush position, but in fact it was the best site in the area for defensive purposes. Located some two miles west

NORTHWESTERN FRONTIER, 1790–1832

90°W

85°W

80°W

N

45°N

Lake Superior

St. Croix R.

Wisconsin R.

Mississippi R.

Lake Michigan

Lake Huron

Georgian Bay

Lake Ontario

Fort Howard

Bad Axe, August 1832

Wisconsin Heights, July 1832

Milwaukee

Fort Koshkonong

Prairie du Chien

Thames R.

Thames, October 1813

Fort Malden

Raisin R.   Detroit

Moravian Town

Lake Erie

Allegheny R.

Winnebago Uprising, 1827

Galena

Rock R.

Stillman's Run, May 1832

Fort Dearborn (Chicago)

Tippecanoe R.

Fallen Timbers, August 1794

Fort Miami

Fort Meigs

Cleveland

Fort Armstrong

Prophet's Village

Fort Wayne

Fort Defiance

Legionville

Fort Pitt

Saukenuk (Rock Island)

St. Clair's battle, November 1791

Harmar's battle, September 1790

Peoria

40°N

Keokuk

Fort Edwards

Illinois R.

Tippecanoe, November 1811

Prophetstown

Fort Recovery

Fort Greenville

Fort Jefferson

Muskingum R.

Monongahela R.

Fort St. Clair

Fort Harmar

Kickapoo Resistance, 1819–1824

Kaskaskia R.

Wabash R.

Fort Harrison

Miami R.

Fort Hamilton

Ohio R.

Scioto R.

Vincennes

Fort Washington (Cincinnati)

St. Louis

Mississippi R.

Ohio R.

35°N

Battle site

Fort

0   50   100 mi

0   50   100 km

of Prophetstown on an oak-covered knoll, it was a wedge-shaped area covering about 10 acres, bordered by wet prairie land and by Burnet's Creek on its west side. On its east the knoll rose about 10 feet above the prairie and on its west about 20 feet before the creek.

Harrison ordered the men to bed down for the night fully clothed, with their weapons loaded and bayonets fixed. It was a cold night, and Harrison did not restrict fires to help the men stay warm. In case of native attack, Harrison instructed that the men rise, advance a pace or two, and form a line of battle and return fire. Harrison was confident that he could hold during a night attack and then take the offensive when it was light. The horses were kept within the camp, and to warn of any attack, Harrison ordered the posting of a sizable night guard of 108 men. He did not, however, order the construction of breastworks, nor was he concerned about the possibility of fires illuminating the American positions.

Although Tecumseh had warned his brother against fighting until the confederation was stronger and fully unified, the Prophet ignored the advice. On the night of November 6 the natives discussed their options. Later Shabonee, a Pottawatomi chief, testified that two Englishmen were present during the deliberations and had urged an attack. A captured African American wagon driver informed the Prophet that Harrison had no artillery with him and that he planned to attack Prophetstown after his discussions with the natives the next day.

That night some 550 to 700 natives, largely Kickapoos, Pottawatomies, and Winnebagos but also including Ojibwas, Wyandots, Mucos, Ottawas, Piankashaws, and Shawnees, worked themselves into a frenzy. Using fiery speeches, Tenskwatawa urged action. He claimed that the white man's bullets could not harm them, that the whites' powder had already turned to sand and their bullets to soft mud.

The warriors left Prophetstown during the night, and by 4:00 a.m. on November 7 they had surrounded Harrison's camp. One of the American sentinels, Stephen Mars, heard movement in the darkness and fired a shot or two before fleeing for the safety of the camp. He was killed before he could reach it, but his shot alerted Harrison's men. The Indians then let out war whoops and opened fire. The battle opened first on the northwest side of the camp. Unfortunately for Harrison's men, when they rose many were silhouetted against their campfires, making them easy targets. Harrison himself mounted and rode to the sound of the firing. His own white horse had broken its tether during the night, and he rode a dark one. This probably saved his life, for the natives were looking for him on a white horse. (Harrison's aide Colonel Abraham Owen, who found and rode Harrison's white horse, was shot and killed.) Firing then broke out on the east side of the camp, and the battle became general. During the battle, the Prophet stationed himself on a high rock to the east and chanted war songs to encourage his followers. Informed early that some of his warriors had been slain, the Prophet insisted that his followers fight on, promising an easy victory.

After two hours of fighting and when it was sufficiently light, Harrison sent out mounted men to attack the natives on their flanks. Soon the natives were in retreat. In the battle, Harrison lost 68 men killed and 126 wounded, a significant casualty rate of up to a quarter of his force. The number of Native American dead is not known for certain. Thirty-seven bodies were found at the battle site, but this did not account for those who were carried off or died later from their wounds. Native American losses are estimated at no fewer than 50 killed and 70 or more wounded.

Worried by a false report that Tecumseh was nearby with a larger native force, Harrison ordered his men to fortify their position. A reconnaissance the next day revealed, however, that Prophetstown had been abandoned, and Harrison then advanced on it. Among supplies abandoned there by the natives in their hasty withdrawal was some new British equipment. Again wary about the possibility of Tecumseh being nearby, Harrison ordered the men to take what supplies they could and destroy the rest. Prophetstown, its supplies, and its food stocks were soon ablaze. In order to move swiftly and provide for his wounded in carts, Harrison also ordered much of the expedition's private property, including his own, destroyed. His force then set out for Vincennes, 150 miles distant. The return march was an agony for the wounded who, tossed about in the carts, died at the rate of two or three per day.

The native warriors came close to killing the Prophet for his false predictions. Certainly the Battle of Tippecanoe also badly damaged Tecumseh's vision of building a confederation to stave off white settlement. Tecumseh returned to Prophetstown several weeks later to find only ruins. He was never able to recover the momentum behind his confederation movement after the battle, although Prophetstown was rebuilt.

In the end, the battle only hardened positions on both sides. Frontiersmen were convinced that the British had been behind native aggression, while the battle drove many natives to side with the British during the War of 1812. The British were also convinced of the need to aid the natives. In effect, Tippecanoe served to cement the British–Native American alliance. For all these reasons, many have called it the opening battle of the War of 1812. For Harrison, the Battle of Tippecanoe had mixed results. Although he described the battle as "a complete and decisive victory," his political enemies charged that he had been guilty of poor leadership and undue aggressiveness. Among his attackers was Colonel Boyd, angered at least in part by Harrison staying his harsh disciplinary measures during the march to Prophetstown. Boyd claimed that Harrison had given the militia too much credit for the victory. Harrison's friends, however, claimed that he had saved the Old Northwest from the natives. Certainly the battle helped establish his national reputation and clearly assisted him in securing the presidency in the election of 1840, during which the slogan "Tippecanoe and Tyler Too" was used.

Daniel W. Kuthy and Spencer C. Tucker

See also
Fallen Timbers, Battle of; Harrison, William Henry; Prophetstown;
    Shawnees; Tecumseh; Tenskwatawa

References

Cave, Alfred. "The Shawnee Prophet, Tecumseh, and Tippecanoe." *Journal of the Early Republic* 22(4) (Winter 2002): 637–673.

Edmunds, R. David. *The Shawnee Prophet.* Lincoln: University of Nebraska Press, 1983.

Edmunds, R. David. *Tecumseh and the Quest for Indian Leadership.* Boston: Little, Brown, 1984.

Mahon, John K. *The War of 1812.* Gainesville: University of Florida Press, 1972.

Todd, Charles Stewart, and Benjamin Drake. *Sketches of the Civil and Military Services of William Henry Harrison.* New York: Arno, 1975.

Tobacco

Agricultural commodity that was first cultivated for use by Native Americans. It was used principally for smoking, chewing, snuffing, and dipping. Many Native Americans revered tobacco as a sacred and powerful substance that was used in ceremonies, including peace treaties and prayers. Nicotiana tabacum, N. rustica, and other species of tobacco were used as narcostimulants, psychotropic substances that aided shamans' abilities to serve as a medium between the ordinary world of humans and the supernatural world of spirits. These strains were domesticated by native peoples of North America between 160 and 720 CE.

The earliest use of tobacco in the New World was likely the result of the same shamanistic predisposition to seek psychotropic or mind-altering effects that led to the development and use of other hallucinogenic plants. Tobacco was employed in numerous ceremonies, rituals, and everyday occurrences. In ceremonies throughout North America, there were many ritual movements that involved lighting pipes, smoking, and sharing them with others. Tobacco was also offered as an invocation to the spirits of the objects and forces of the natural world. Therefore, it was also cast into fires, water, and rock crevices to appease supernatural forces. In this way, the tobacco could be sent to the supernatural beings in the terrestrial or underwater realms as well as to those in the celestial realm, who generally received such gifts in the traditional form of smoke. It was because it was both an effective means to consume tobacco and to simultaneously appease the spirits of the supernatural realm that combustion and inhalation became the more popular form of tobacco offering.

The proliferation of tobacco, with its sacred and shamanistic associations, contributed to a rise in democratized shamanism in which all members of a society had the potential to dream, acquire spiritual power, and perform supernatural feats for themselves and their community. However, shamans continued to use tobacco, and the leaf was still esteemed as being sacred and supernaturally potent. According to Native American tradition, tobacco fire in a pipe bowl was related to the sun and its supernatural powers. Smoking the pipe of peace together invoked some of this power and acknowledged the importance of the pipe in forming alliances. Many Native American tribes, including the Chitimachas of

Important Items in the Columbian Exchange

New World to Old World	Old World to New World
Avocados	Apples
Beans	Bananas
Chewing gum	Barley
Chocolate	Carrots
Corn	Cattle
Guinea pigs	Chickens
Llamas	Coffee
Peanuts	Horses
Peppers	Influenza
Potatoes	Oats
Squash	Measles
Sweet potatoes	Melons
Syphilis	Pigs
Tapioca	Plums
Tobacco	Smallpox
Tomatoes	Sugarcane
Turkeys	Wheat

Louisiana, the Five Civilized Tribes, and Plains tribes, used a peace pipe with European delegates to begin a peace ceremony. To call the gods to witness a treaty, a tribe's members blew smoke to the sky and the earth and to the four points of the compass.

However, tobacco did not always lead to peace in America. Cultivated by Europeans in Virginia in 1612, tobacco rapidly depleted nutrients in the soil, driving the colonists to demand ever-increasing amounts of land from the Native Americans. Needing to meet the growing European demand for tobacco and unwilling to marshal the effort necessary to prepare new areas for agriculture, Captain John Smith and others intimidated, threatened, and sometimes killed Native Americans for their farmland. The resulting resentment led to a series of violent outbreaks and small wars that are seldom documented. Tobacco consumption continued to increase in popularity in Europe, leading more colonists to cultivate it. In the tidal and Piedmont regions of Maryland, Virginia, and North Carolina, tobacco became big business, and numerous large plantations—worked by slave labor—were established during the 17th and 18th centuries.

Michael P. Gueno

See also

Anglo-Powhatan War, Second; Ghost Dance; Smith, John

References

Utley, Robert M., and Wilcomb E. Washburn. *Indian Wars.* New York: American Heritage Press, 2002.

Winter, Joseph C., ed. *Tobacco Use by Native North Americans.* Norman: University of Oklahoma Press, 2000.

Tomahawk

Derived from the Algonquian word *tamahak* or *tamahakan*, which designates a type of cutting tool, the tomahawk was primarily a melee and missile weapon used by Native Americans. Tomahawks generally resembled lightweight hatchets. Although they varied in size, most tomahawks measured less than 18 inches long and were light enough to be used singlehandedly. Initially natives sharpened bone, stone, or wooden blades and fastened them to short wooden handles. However, European colonists introduced superior iron and brass blades and themselves began using the weapons for military, trading, and other practical purposes. Well-crafted tomahawks remained prized trade items well into the 19th century. Even in the 21st century, armies continue to employ tomahawks as both tools and weapons.

Although the tomahawk traditionally served as a hand or short-ranged missile weapon, it had other purposes. American Indians and Europeans both used tomahawks as tools in everyday work. They were often used to chop smaller pieces of wood, to drive stakes into the ground, or to dress game after a hunt. Native Americans in particular employed tomahawks as ceremonial objects and symbols of leadership. Some Native American groups, such as the Lakota Sioux, equipped tomahawks with pipe bowls and hollow stems to create smoking pipes. Others elaborately decorated ceremonial tomahawks for burial and to signify peace with an enemy. Although certainly not used solely by Native Americans, the tomahawk has become a popular—and stereotypical—symbol of native culture alongside the tepee and the feathered headdress.

Jason Mann Frawley

See also

Edged Weapons; Lakota Sioux; Native American Warfare

References

McLemore, Dwight C. *The Fighting Tomahawk*. Boulder, CO: Paladin, 2004.

Peterson, Harold L. *American Indian Tomahawks*. New York: Museum of the American Indian, 1965.

Starkey, Armstrong. *European and Native American Warfare, 1675–1815*. Norman: University of Oklahoma Press, 1998.

Tomochichi
Birth Date: ca. 1650
Death Date: October 5, 1739

Yamacraw (Creek) chief who allied with the British and served as an emissary to Governor James Oglethorpe of Georgia. Little is known about the majority of the life of Tomochichi (Tomochachi). He was born about 1650 and apparently spent most of his years among the Creeks in the vicinity of southern South Carolina and Georgia as a warrior and leader. Tomochichi participated in the Creek negotiations with South Carolina in 1721. Around 1728 he broke from the Creek Confederacy to form his own band and relocated with them farther east.

Accompanied by about 200 followers of both Creek and Yamasee descent, Tomochichi settled along the Savannah River

Tomochichi (ca. 1650–1739), chief of the Yamacraw Indians, with his son Tooanahowie, who holds an eagle in his arms. Tomochichi allied with the British. Painting by Verelst, circa 1700. (Getty Images)

near the present-day site of Savannah, Georgia. Once there, he negotiated with the officials of South Carolina to secure ownership of the territory and cement peaceful relations. As leader of this small band called the Yamacraws, Tomochichi remained in contact with nearby traders and maintained cordial relations with the British. When Oglethorpe founded Georgia in 1733, he immediately sought out Tomochichi to secure his support and friendship for the new settlement.

In the earliest years of the nascent colony, Tomochichi proved a staunch ally and provided invaluable assistance to Oglethorpe. The Yamacraws welcomed the British to the immediate area and signed a treaty of friendship with them on May 18, 1733. The Yamacraws also served as hunters, fishers, and guides for the colonists.

Tomochichi himself intervened for peace and justice whenever problems arose. Peace with the larger Creek Nation was accomplished primarily through Tomochichi's negotiations on Oglethorpe's behalf. As his ally and personal friend, Tomochichi traveled with Oglethorpe first to Charles Town (Charleston) in March 1733 and later to England as an emissary to meet with King George II in the summer of 1734.

The visit to England reinforced the alliance between the English and the Yamacraws, and Tomochichi became convinced that his people should learn as much as they could of the white English culture. In 1735 Tomochichi teamed with John Wesley, among others, to establish a school for the Yamacraws where they could learn the English language and religion. When political problems between the British and the Spanish developed in 1735, the Yamacraws allied themselves with the British.

Four years later Tomochichi was again an important force in strengthening the British alliance with all the Creek tribes. Their loyalty to the British was reconfirmed with the Treaty of Coweta on August 21, 1739, which was the last great diplomatic achievement of Tomochichi. Before his death on October 5, 1739, near Savannah, Georgia, Tomochichi requested that he be buried within the town of Savannah near his British friends, and the citizens happily complied.

LISA L. CRUTCHFIELD

See also
Creeks; Yamasees

References

Jones, Charles Colcock, Jr. *Historical Sketch of Tomochichi: Mico of the Yamacraws.* Savannah, GA: Oglethorpe, 1998.

Todd, Helen. *Tomochichi: Indian Friend of the Georgia Colony.* Marietta, GA: Cherokee Publishing, 1977.

Torture, Ritualized

The Native American peoples living in the Americas and throughout the Caribbean tended to rely on a variety of forms of ritualized torture as they waged warfare against their neighbors and Europeans. Types of torture ranged from dismemberment to burning at the stake and from physical beatings to human sacrifice and even at times cannibalism. Such practices led European explorers and colonists to conclude that the American Indians with whom they were making contact were uncivilized. What Europeans failed to understand was that the ritualized torture practiced by the Native Americans held deep-rooted cultural meanings that aided those societies in maintaining a delicate social balance.

While not all American Indians practiced ritualized torture, the groups that did embrace such acts did so to instill social order. Eastern Woodlands Indians, for example, tended to go to war for social reasons. So-called mourning wars allowed kinship groups within larger tribes to replace lost family members or to find opportunities for revenge. The object of a mourning war was to capture individuals who could then replace lost members or serve as the focus for the release of violent emotions and for the taking of revenge for previous losses. Those not accepted for adoption into the tribe became the focus of torture and execution. In this manner, the entire tribe was able to participate in its warriors' victory and experience a catharsis as the members of the tribe released pent-up aggression through torturing the victim.

Those who were actually adopted could expect to live a long life if they truly attempted to become active members of the tribe.

In this manner, American Indian warfare and ritualized torture promoted group cohesion and allowed younger warriors to learn how to die bravely if they ever found themselves captured and the focus of another tribe's catharsis. American Indians expected victims not only to refrain from showing any pain as they endured an agonizing death but also to literally sing their identity without pausing or wavering. If the victim did not cry out in pain or stop singing his identity song that recounted his exploits in previous battles, then the victim retained his identity, his honor, and if the victim impressed his torturers, he might retain his life.

Traditionally, Native Americans perceived the taking of prisoners to be a great honor for the warrior. The catharsis that prisoners allowed tribes to experience was an essential component of Iroquois, Wyandot (Huron), and other Eastern Woodland American Indian societies, as aggression could escape the tribe's members as a captured warrior felt their rage unleashed on his body. Among the Wyandots, for example, individuals could express rage, grief, and anger only in this manner.

The Shawnees engaged in a torture ritual known as the gauntlet in which the prisoner or victim was forced to run between two rows of men, women, and children armed with clubs. The victim was beaten as he proceeded to run the gauntlet. If he stumbled, fell, or hesitated, he had to begin the process anew. The ritual ended when the prisoner died or when he made his way successfully to the end of the line. In a sense, torture, execution, and sometimes even cannibalism allowed tribal members to purge themselves of emotions that might otherwise materialize in ways considered dangerous and unacceptable to their tribe. What was savage and barbarous to Europeans was simply social control to the Native Americans.

Europeans also occasionally engaged in torture of Native Americans, although not usually in ritual fashion. During the Tuscarora War (1711–1713), for example, a British settler tortured and killed a chief of the Coree tribe. In general, however, Europeans and later Americans preferred outright killing to torture.

B. SCOTT CRAWFORD

See also
Cannibalism; Iroquois; Mourning War; Native American Warfare; Shawnees; Tuscarora War; Wyandots

References

Anderson, Karen. *Chain Her by One Foot: The Subjugation of Native Women in Seventeenth-Century New France.* New York: Routledge, 1991.

Axtell, James, and William C. Sturtevant. *The European and the Indian: Essays in the Ethnohistory of Colonial North America.* New York: Oxford University Press, 1981.

Merritt, Jane T. *At the Crossroads: Indians and Empires on a Mid-Atlantic Frontier, 1700–1763.* Chapel Hill: University of North Carolina Press, 2003.

Richter, Daniel K. "War and Culture: The Iroquois Experience." *William and Mary Quarterly,* 3rd Ser., 40(4) (October 1983): 528–559.

White, Richard. *The Middle Ground: Indians, Empires, and Republics in the Great Lakes Region, 1650–1815.* New York: Cambridge University Press, 1991.

Trail of Tears
Event Date: 1838

Name given to the forced movement of the Cherokee tribe from their homelands in the Southeast by the U.S. Army. This movement, which consisted of a series of brutal forced marches, began on May 26, 1838, and was part of the U.S. government's Indian Removal Policy. Some 17,000 Cherokees were gathered together, mostly in Georgia and Tennessee, and were then forced to travel nearly 1,200 miles to Indian Territory (Arkansas and Oklahoma). In the Cherokee language, the removal was referred to as "the trail where we cried," a name that has described the grim event ever since.

Tensions between the Cherokee Nation and white settlers had reached new heights in 1829, when gold was discovered in Dahlonega in northwestern Georgia. The Cherokees considered this area their tribal land and insisted on exercising sole sovereignty over it. In 1830 the State of Georgia sought legal clarification of the land dispute in a case that ultimately went to the U.S. Supreme Court, which refused to hear the case because the Court did not consider the Cherokee Nation a sovereign state. However, in another U.S. Supreme Court case in 1832, the Court ruled that state governments could not invoke sovereignty over the Cherokees, arguing that this was the prerogative of the federal government. After his landslide 1832 reelection to the presidency, Andrew Jackson was more determined than ever to pursue with vigor the removal of the Cherokees and other eastern tribes, which had been made easier by the 1830 Indian Removal Act.

Soon thereafter a splinter faction of the Cherokees, called the Ridge Party or the Treaty Party, was formed, led by Cherokees Major Ridge, Elias Boudinot, and Stand Watie. They began negotiations with the Jackson administration to secure equitable treatment, believing that removal was inevitable. However, Ridge and others acted without the support of the elected Cherokee Council, headed by Chief John Ross, who was firmly opposed to any kind of removal and thus unwilling to negotiate such terms. This created a split among the Cherokees, with the Ridge contingent forming its own ruling council and becoming known as the Western Cherokees. Those loyal to Chief Ross were then known as the Eastern Cherokees.

In 1835 President Jackson appointed Reverend John Schermerhorn as a treaty commissioner to enter into detailed negotiation with the Cherokees. That same year the U.S. government proposed to pay $4.5 million to the Cherokees as compensation for their land. In return, they were to vacate the area voluntarily. Schermerhorn then organized a meeting with a small number of Cherokee Council members who were prepared to accept removal. Not more

Depiction of the Trail of Tears by western artist Robert Lindneux. This painting was created in 1942 and is part of the collection of the Woolarac Museum in Bartlesville, Oklahoma. (Native Stock Pictures)

than 500 Cherokees (out of many thousands) parleyed with the commissioner, but nevertheless, 20 Cherokees—including Major Ridge—signed the Treaty of New Echota on December 30, 1835. It was signed later by Ridge's son John and Stand Watie. No members of the main Cherokee Council signed the document, however.

This treaty ceded all Cherokee lands east of the Mississippi River. Naturally, Chief Ross rejected the treaty out of hand. The U.S. Senate nevertheless ratified it—just barely—on May 23, 1836, and set the date of May 23, 1838, as the deadline for the removal of the Cherokees. Although Chief Ross presented a 15,000-signature petition to Congress in support of the Cherokees and against the treaty, this appeal fell on deaf ears. Meanwhile, Cherokees who had supported the removal policy began to migrate from Georgia to Oklahoma and Arkansas. It is estimated that by the end of 1836, at least 6,000 Cherokees had voluntarily left their ancestral lands. However, some 17,000 remained.

In May 1838 with the removal deadline looming, President Martin Van Buren appointed Brigadier General Winfield Scott to oversee the forcible removal of the recalcitrant Cherokees. By May 17 Scott had reached New Echota, Georgia, the heart of Cherokee country, with 7,000 troops. They began to round up the Cherokees in Georgia beginning on May 26. Operations in Tennessee, North Carolina, and Alabama began on June 5. Systematically the Cherokees were forced from their homes at gunpoint and marched to a series of camps. They were allowed to take no belongings with them, and they offered little resistance.

Thirty-one forts—basically makeshift detention camps—had been built to aid in the removal. Thirteen of them were in Georgia. The Cherokees were then moved from these temporary encampments to 11 fortified camps, of which all but 1 was in Tennessee. By late July 1838, some 17,000 Cherokees and an additional 2,000 black slaves owned by wealthy Native Americans were in the camps.

Conditions in the camps were appalling, and diseases including dysentery were rife. As a result, there was a high mortality rate in the camps. The Cherokees were then gradually removed to three transfer points: Ross's Landing (Chattanooga, Tennessee), Gunter's Landing (Guntersville, Alabama), and the Cherokee Agency (Calhoun, Tennessee).

Three groups of Cherokees, totaling 2,800 people, were moved from Ross's Landing by steamboat along the Tennessee, Ohio, Mississippi, and Arkansas rivers to Sallisaw Creek in Indian Territory by June 19. However, the majority of the Cherokees were moved in groups of between 700 and 1,500 people, along with guides appointed by Chief Ross, on overland routes. Chief Ross had received the contract to oversee the relocation under Cherokee supervision despite resistance from within his own nation and members of Congress who resented the extra cost. In the end, the army was to be used only to oversee the removal and to prevent outbreaks of violence. There was one exception to this mass removal, which was the small group of Cherokees who had signed the Treaty of New Echota. They were escorted by Lieutenant Edward Deas of the army, mainly for their own protection.

The movement of detachments began on August 28, 1838. It was customary for the detachments to be accompanied by a physician and a clergyman. For most Cherokees, the journey was about 1,200 miles. Although there were three distinct overland routes, the majority took the northern route through central Tennessee, southwestern Kentucky, and southern Illinois. These groups crossed the Mississippi at Cape Girardeau, Missouri, and trekked across Missouri to northern Arkansas. They then entered present-day Oklahoma near Westville, having met troops from Fort Gibson.

The conditions on the march varied. The first groups to undertake the journey experienced high temperatures, and many suffered from heat exhaustion. In the winter, many Cherokees suffered from frostbite and hypothermia while waiting to cross frozen rivers. Most Cherokees marched on foot, but some were loaded into overcrowded wagons. Many died on the way. The official government total was 424, but the most widely cited number is 4,000, half of them in the camps and half on the march. A recent scholarly study, however, has come up with a much higher figure of 8,000 dead.

Many of the Cherokees settled around Tahlequah, Oklahoma, which became the center for the tribal government. Local districts were established that in turn elected officials to serve on the new National Council. Bilingual schools were created, and missionaries from the American Board of Commissioners for Foreign Missions built churches on the reservations. There was great resentment on the part of many Cherokees against Ridge, Boudinot, Watie, and the signatories of the Treaty of Echota Treaty. Ridge and his son John were killed on June 22, 1839, in separate incidents, and Boudinot was also murdered. The Trail of Tears is generally considered to be one of the most deplorable eras in American history.

Ralph Martin Baker and Paul G. Pierpaoli Jr.

See also

Cherokees; Indian Removal Act; Jackson, Andrew; Scott, Winfield

References

Carter, Samuel, III. *Cherokee Sunset: A Nation Betrayed: A Narrative of Travail and Triumph, Persecution and Exile.* Garden City, NY: Doubleday, 1976.

Ehle, John. *Trail of Tears: The Rise and Fall of the Cherokee Nation.* New York: Doubleday, 1988.

Foreman, Grant. *Indian Removal: The Emigration of the Five Civilized Tribes of Indians.* Norman: University of Oklahoma Press, 1989.

Remini, Robert Vincenti. *Andrew Jackson and His Indian Wars.* New York: Penguin, 2001.

Tres Castillos, Battle of
Start Date: October 15, 1880
End Date: October 16, 1880

Military engagement between Mimbres Apache leader Victorio and his followers and Mexican forces in the northern state of Chihuahua, south of the Rio Grande and the New Mexican border. The

Battle of Tres Castillos ("Three Castles") occurred during October 15–16, 1880, and marked the end of the so-called Victorio War.

During the late 1870s, Victorio and his band had been relocated several times to various reservations in the Southwest. Between 1877 and 1880 Victorio and his followers had been consigned to live first on the San Carlos Reservation (Arizona), a desolate place that the Apaches disliked, and then on the Ojo Caliente Reservation, which the federal government had declared closed. Victorio then led his people to the Mescalero Apaches' reservation, where they hoped to take up residence, but that arrangement proved unworkable. In September 1879 Victorio and some 60 warriors attacked a unit of buffalo soldiers near Ojo Caliente, which began a yearlong battle between Victorio and U.S. and Mexican forces.

For a time Victorio was successful in evading both American and Mexican forces. In April 1880 he launched a raid against a white settlement in Alma, New Mexico, during which numerous settlers were killed. U.S. forces then redoubled their efforts to seek out Victorio and capture him, dead or alive. Once again Victorio proved elusive, and by early autumn he had been forced to cross into Mexico to keep ahead of pursuing U.S. troops.

By mid-October, Victorio and as many as 150 warriors were camped in northern Chihuahua amid three small rocky peaks that the Mexicans called Tres Castillos. At daybreak on October 15 Mexican militia troops caught Victorio and his men by surprise and immediately launched a full-scale assault on the encampment. The Mexicans were aided by Tarahumara warriors, who had allied with the Mexicans to capture Victorio. Leading the force was Colonel Joaquín Terrazas, who had ordered his men to scatter Victorio's horses just prior to the attack to hinder their escape.

Victorio's force ascended one of the three peaks and engaged in a firefight with the Mexicans and their allies for the entire day and well into the night. Victorio attempted an escape, but his force had been virtually surrounded. He then ordered his men to erect makeshift stone fortifications and vowed to fight to his death. At dawn on October 16 the Mexicans and their allies rushed the stone walls and engaged Victorio's men directly; much of the fighting was hand to hand. Victorio's band was defeated, suffering 78 dead and 68 taken prisoner. Victorio was among the dead. The Battle of Tres Castillos marked one of the last large military engagements of the Apache Wars (1861–1886).

PAUL G. PIERPAOLI JR.

See also
Apaches; Apache Wars; Buffalo Soldiers; Ojo Caliente Reservation, New Mexico; San Carlos Reservation; Victorio

References
Kaywaykla, James, and Eva Ball, eds. *In the Days of Victorio: Recollections of a Warm Springs Apache.* Tucson: University of Arizona Press, 1972.
Thrapp, Dan L. *Victorio and the Mimbres Apaches.* Norman: University of Oklahoma Press, 1974.

Trois-Rivières

French fort and trading site. Trois-Rivières ("Three Rivers") is located on the western shore of the St. Maurice River at its confluence with the Saint Lawrence River, about halfway between Quebec and Montreal. Samuel de Champlain founded the settlement there in 1634. Trois-Rivières was the second French settlement in Canada and one of the oldest European settlements in North America.

Named after the three-armed delta formed by the islands at the St. Maurice River's mouth, Trois-Rivières was chosen for its strategic location as a military and fur-trading site. It was built on the site of an Algonquin stockade that had been abandoned some 30 years earlier because of Iroquois incursions. Once Trois-Rivières was established, a number of Algonquins returned to live near or within the village, and many more natives visited the site to trade with the French.

From 1636 Trois-Rivières was under almost constant Iroquois attack, creating serious problems for the French, who were unable to venture far from the fort. In July 1645 the French concluded a treaty there with the Mohawks, but efforts to secure peace with the other four Iroquois nations were not successful. Peace with the Mohawks did not last long, and they resumed their attacks in 1647. By 1649 the Iroquois had nearly halted the French fur trade and threatened French control of the Saint Lawrence Valley.

Despite such setbacks, Trois-Rivières grew into a prosperous fur-trading hub and a place for converting the natives to Catholicism. Boasting a deep-water port, Trois-Rivières provided access for large merchant ships and warships. Many Jesuit missionaries and Ursuline nuns chose to locate there, building, among other institutions, the St. Joseph Seminary in 1663 and the Ursuline Convent in 1697. During the wars between the French and the English in North America, Trois-Rivières served on several occasions as an assembly point for French and native warriors raiding southward.

The French never heavily populated Trois-Rivières, however, and there were only 800 people in residence there at the time of the British conquest of New France in the French and Indian War (1754–1763). Thereafter Trois-Rivières remained an important strategic and economic location. On June 8, 1776, during the American Revolutionary War (1775–1783), British forces turned back a Patriot attack at Trois-Rivières.

JONATHAN A. CLAPPERTON

See also
Algonquins; Beaver Wars; Champlain, Samuel de; France; French and Indian War; Fur Trade; Iroquois; Mohawks; Trois-Rivières, Treaty of

References
Anderson, Fred. *Crucible of War: The Seven Years' War and the Fate of the Empire in British North America, 1754–1766.* New York: Vintage Books, 2001.
Leach, Douglas Edward. *Arms for Empire: A Military History of the British Colonies in North America, 1607–1763.* New York: Macmillan, 1973.

Trois-Rivières, Treaty of

Temporary peace agreement between the Mohawk Nation and New France reached in July 1645 at Trois-Rivières in New France (Canada). The Treaty of Trois-Rivières was the last serious attempt by one of the Iroquois Five Nations to secure peace with the French and the Wyandots (Hurons) in the earliest stages of the Beaver Wars (1641–1701).

Almost from the founding of the Iroquois Confederacy, the Iroquois sought to convince the Hurons, who were linguistically and culturally related to them, to join the Longhouse. The 1645 effort at Trois-Rivières, however, was not an attempt by the Iroquois as a whole to secure peace. Instead, it was undertaken solely by the easternmost of the Five Nations, the Mohawks, for their own benefit.

By the 1630s, the Iroquois had found that overtrapping had virtually wiped out the beaver in their own territory. Dependent on European trade goods, the Iroquois had to find another source of furs to maintain their relationship with their Dutch trading partners at Fort Orange (present-day Albany, New York). Huronia, which lay between Lake Huron's Georgian Bay and Lake Simcoe, had relatively few fur-bearing animals. Nevertheless, the Hurons took advantage of their geographical position, trading maize to other native peoples farther north and west in exchange for furs. The Hurons then transported the furs to the French in Quebec and traded them for manufactured items such as pots, hatchets, knives, and cloth. In 1642, however, the French established the post of Montreal, which by virtue of its location interfered with Mohawk trade and the Mohawks' raids on Huron fur-trading parties on the Saint Lawrence River.

The principal Mohawk diplomat, Kiotseaeton, went to Trois-Rivières with two goals in mind. The first was to secure a trade agreement with the French that would allow the Mohawks to trap on lands north of the Saint Lawrence. The second was to secure access to Huron trade routes. Written into the treaty was a secret clause in which the French agreed not to extend protection to Algonquins, who had not converted to Christianity. Supposedly this clause was inserted in an attempt to secure Mohawk and Huron goodwill.

The Treaty of Trois-Rivières is interesting from an ethnohistorical standpoint in that French Jesuits who witnessed the meeting were able to record the proceedings in detail. Kiotseaeton began by standing in the bow of a shallop (open boat), draped in wampum, and greeting the French, the Hurons, and the Algonquins with words of peace. Using belts and strings of wampum as mnemonic devices, Kiotseaeton acted out the history of Huron-Iroquois relations and his voyage to Trois-Rivières. He also brought two French prisoners, whom he then ceremoniously handed over to Governor Charles Huault Montmagny of New France.

The Treaty of Trois-Rivières remained in effect for only a little more than one year. Although the French encouraged the Mohawks to convince other Iroquois Confederacy members to seek peace with New France, their efforts came to naught. The Senecas and the Onondagas, for instance, persisted with their raids against French interests. In the autumn of 1646 Mohawk warriors killed the French Jesuit missionary Isaac Jogues, and by 1649 the Beaver Wars were in full swing. The treaty had done nothing to stem long-term tensions.

ROGER M. CARPENTER

See also
Algonquins; Beaver Wars; Iroquois; Iroquois Confederacy; Mohawks; Trois-Rivières; Wyandots

References
Dennis, Matthew. *Cultivating a Landscape of Peace: Iroquois-European Encounters in Seventeenth-Century North America.* Ithaca, NY: Cornell University Press, 1993.

Jennings, Francis, et al., eds. *The History and Culture of Iroquois Diplomacy: An Interdisciplinary Guide to the Treaties of the Six Nations and Their League.* Syracuse, NY: Syracuse University Press, 1985.

Tunicas

Native American people inhabiting the Louisiana region along the Mississippi River. The first historical reference to the Tunica tribe may have been in the chronicles of Hernando de Soto. Here they were identified as the "Tanico" people. On European contact, the Tunicas were reportedly living along the Yazoo River in present-day northwestern Mississippi. There they produced and traded salt. The French found them in the same general area in the late 17th century, and the Tunicas and the French soon became firm allies.

The Tunicas were noteworthy for their support of the French against the Natchez tribe. This hostility apparently stemmed from a long-standing feud of unknown origin. During the Natchez War (1729–1733), Natchez warriors, knowing that the Tunicas were allied with the French, attacked them in April 1731 and killed the principal Tunica chief. The Tunicas reported many other casualties as well. In 1736 the Tunicas turned against the Chickasaws during the Chickasaw Wars (1736–1740) because the Chickasaw were allied with the British. The French long considered the Tunicas vital to the defense of the lower Mississippi Valley.

The Tunicas also served important commercial roles. Indeed, they became key middlemen between European traders and other Native American tribes, handling both European- and native-made goods. The Tunicas were also pivotal in the trading of horses from eastern Texas to Louisiana.

The Tunicas remained staunch allies of the French until 1763, when the French were forced from the region. From that time the dwindling number of Tunicas assimilated with other tribes. By 1783 the Tunica population was down to only 80 people. The U.S. government finally recognized the Tunica-Biloxi tribe in 1989. Currently the Tunicas inhabit a 415-acre reserve in Avoyelles Parish, Louisiana. The 2000 census of the reservation listed a Tunica population of 89 people.

THOMAS JOHN BLUMER

See also

Chickasaws; Chickasaw Wars; France; Natchezes; Natchez War; Native American Trade; Soto, Hernando de

References

Brian, Jeffrey P. *The Tunica Treasure.* Salem, MA: Peabody Museum of Archaeology and Ethnology and Harvard University Press, 1979.

Brian, Jeffrey P., George Roth, and Willem J. De Reuse. "Tunica, Biloxi, and Ofo." In *Handbook of North American Indians,* Vol. 14, *Southeast,* edited by Raymond D. Fogelson, 856–897. Washington, DC: Smithsonian Institution Press, 2004.

Swanton, John. *The Indian Tribes of North America.* Washington, DC: Smithsonian Institution Press, 1952.

Turner, Frederick Jackson
Birth Date: November 14, 1861
Death Date: March 14, 1932

Eminent U.S. historian and writer whose provocative essay "The Significance of the Frontier in American History" (1893) opened up a new period in the interpretation of American history and, some argue, helped justify U.S. overseas expansionism in the 1890s. Frederick Jackson Turner was born on November 14, 1861, in Portage, Wisconsin. Educated in local schools, he earned both his bachelor's degree (1884) and master's degree (1888) at the University of Wisconsin in Madison. He received his PhD in 1890 from Johns Hopkins University, where he studied under Herbert Baxter Adams. Adams was one of a group of American historians who applied social Darwinism to the study of history. Turner retained the evolutionary thrust of Adams's thinking while significantly modifying it.

In 1893 as a young professor at the University of Wisconsin, Turner presented his famous paper "The Significance of the Frontier in American History" at a meeting of the American Historical Association in Chicago. In Turner's view, American democracy had begun in American rather than German forests, as his mentor Adams had postulated. American history, Turner maintained, was to a great extent the history of the conquest of the West, the relentless move westward that had begun when the first English colonists arrived in the New World at the beginning of the 17th century. The availability of free land had drawn settlers farther and farther westward, and as each successive wave of immigrants struggled with the primitive conditions of the frontier, they were transformed by the experience. Thus if America's national character was to be identified, it was to be found in the individual and shared experiences of the western pioneers. This meant, Turner claimed, that Americans were continually moving away from their European roots and instead moving toward a unique and independent American mind-set. To ignore this powerful movement would be to ignore the very basis of American history.

Turner believed that the frontier had molded the American character. From it stemmed the Americans' toughness, resourcefulness, resiliency, and individualism as well as American democracy itself. He also believed that the frontier had served as a kind of safety valve for Americans, allowing upward mobility and the promise of new opportunities. "So long as free land exists," he wrote, "the opportunity for a competency exists, and economic power secures political power." Turner did not, however, analyze how this westward-looking pioneering spirit affected Native Americans, whose populations were decimated during America's love affair with Manifest Destiny.

Yet Turner cited a recent bulletin from the superintendent of the census showing that as of 1893 the western frontier was officially gone. Turner therefore fretted about what the future held in store for Americans without a western frontier, but he hoped that because of their frontier heritage and ingenuity Americans would avoid many of the social ills that had beset Europeans.

More recent historians have pointed to Turner's so-called frontier thesis to argue that while he had announced the end of the frontier, many Americans were looking toward new frontiers to conquer. These included industrialism and economic expansion, inventions and technology, and overseas territorial expansion. While it is not possible to conclude that Turner's thesis prodded

U.S. historian Frederick Jackson Turner's provocative 1893 essay, "The Significance of the Frontier in American History," opened a new period in interpretation of American history and some say helped justify subsequent U.S. imperialism. (Library of Congress)

America into the imperial expansionism of the 1890s, his thesis certainly provides an instructive way of looking at U.S. expansionism, which Turner might have argued had been part of America's character from the very beginning.

Turner's essay catapulted him to instant celebrity. By focusing on an area that until then had been neglected, he brought about a major shift in the interpretation of American history. While previous American historians had concentrated on the nation's European origins, Turner was the first to look for what was unique about the American experience. He was also among the first to apply interdisciplinary techniques and scientific techniques to the study of history in the seminars he taught at the University of Wisconsin.

Turner's dedication to teaching combined with the painstaking process by which he gathered and verified facts meant that his writing output was relatively slight. Turner remained at the University of Wisconsin until 1910, when he became a professor at Harvard University. From 1909 to 1910 he served as president of the American Historical Association, and from 1910 to 1915 he was on the board of the *American Historical Review*. Upon his retirement from Harvard in 1924, he worked as a research associate at the Huntington Library in Pasadena, California. There he devoted himself to an analysis of such problems as population explosions, the depletion of natural resources, and the prospect of another world war more terrible than the first. Turner died in San Marino, California, on March 14, 1932.

PAUL G. PIERPAOLI JR.

See also
Manifest Destiny

References

Bogue, Allan G. *Frederick Jackson Turner: Strange Roads Going Down.* Norman: University of Oklahoma Press, 1998.

Turner, Jackson, and John Mack Faragher. *Rereading Frederick Jackson Turner: "The Significance of the Frontier in American History" and Other Essays.* New York: Henry Holt, 1995.

Tuscaroras

Iroquoian-speaking Native Americans whose territory included most of eastern North Carolina during the colonial period. The Tuscaroras were a loose confederacy of three tribes with an estimated population of around 25,000 people prior to European contact. The Tuscarora Nation was the most powerful in a vast region of the Southeast running from Virginia in the north to South Carolina in the south. The Tuscaroras later became the sixth nation to join the Iroquois Confederacy in 1722.

Drawing depicting four Tuscarora Native American men. Note the plumed hats, long coats, leggings, and sashes. (National Anthropological Archives, Smithsonian Institution, NAA INV 797200)

The Tuscaroras were farmers, hunters, gatherers, and saltwater fishers along the lower Neuse, Tar, Pamlico, and Roanoke rivers. Many Tuscarora towns were comprised of oblong and oval houses, each serving several families. The longhouse was more typical in the Tuscarora-Iroquoian tradition. Structural frames of pine, cedar, and hickory were secured with bark and moss to form the shell of the longhouses. Cedar and cypress bark covered quadrangular arched roofs, which had smoke holes in the centers. Animal skins covered mats of reed sprawled over bed benches skirting the inner structure. Windowless granary structures and houses encircled the villages' council meeting area. Many times situated on slopes along waterways, some strategic villages were heavily fortified and palisaded.

Weapons and dress were tied to regional tribes and climate, but Tuscarora adornment was elaborate. Tattooing displayed tribal symbols, usually on the right shoulder. Regalia included pendants of bone and teeth, wampum ear pendants, necklaces, and beads of bone, copper, and colored stones. Chieftain adornments included pearls.

By 1650 the Tuscaroras were fully involved in the fur trade and the slave trade with Europeans. The Tuscaroras' primary town of Kentenuaka came to be regarded as a center for Native American commerce by 1670. Described in 1701 as the largest tribe in the region, their population was greatly diminished by 1707. Both disease and slave traders exacerbated the population decline.

The Tuscaroras' relationship with the English deteriorated in the early 18th century. In 1710 Baron Christoph von Graffenried founded the German and Swiss colony of New Bern, North Carolina. Not content to stay there, he continued surveying along the Trent and Neuse rivers, the heart of Tuscarora country. Graffenried's bold encroachments, combined with abuses on the part of colonial traders in South Carolina, North Carolina, and Virginia, forced the Tuscaroras to war in 1711.

In what became known as the Tuscarora War (1711–1713), the Tuscaroras raided white settlements, killing some 200 Europeans. The war had two phases. The first was a conflict between the Tuscaroras and English settlers, and the second witnessed the Tuscaroras fighting Europeans and rival tribes, including their northern Tuscarora kin as well as the Creeks and the Yamasees.

The war ended in March 1713 with a Tuscarora capitulation. After that, in 1715 a number of Tuscaroras were forced onto a small North Carolina reservation. Some 2,000 others fled northward to live among tribes of the Iroquois Confederacy. The Tuscaroras were officially recognized as the confederation's sixth nation in 1722. The Tuscaroras tried to remain neutral during the course of the American Revolutionary War (1775–1783), but most ended up siding with the Patriots.

Alongside the Oneidas, many Tuscaroras warriors fought the British at the Battle of Oriskany (August 6, 1777). The Tuscaroras then helped to defeat the British campaign down the Hudson River from Canada. After the war, New York confiscated land that the Tuscaroras shared with the Oneidas and forcibly removed the Tuscaroras to the Seneca Reservation near present-day Lewiston, New York. There the Tuscaroras eventually purchased land in 1796 and in 1804 where their descendants live today. The Tuscaroras who sided with the British eventually moved to the Six Nations Reserve in Ontario, Canada.

RAESCHELLE POTTER-DEIMEL

See also
Iroquois Confederacy; Native Americans and the American Revolutionary War; Oriskany, Battle of; Tuscarora War

References
Gallay, Alan. *The Indian Slave Trade: The Rise of the English Empire in the American South, 1670–1717*. New Haven, CT: Yale University Press, 2002.

Swanton, John R. *The Indians of the Southeastern United States*. Washington, DC: Smithsonian Institution Press, 1946.

Wright, J. Leitch, Jr. *The Only Land They Knew: The Tragic Story of the American Indians in the Old South*. New York: Free Press, 1981.

Tuscarora War
Start Date: September 22, 1711
End Date: April 14, 1713

Major war between Native Americans and colonists in North Carolina. The Tuscarora War began on September 22, 1711, when Tuscarora and allied Algonquian militants attacked colonial settlements on the Neuse and Pamlico rivers. The uprising, proprietary North Carolina's largest and costliest Native American war, was the result of the colonists' fraudulent trading practices, land seizures, and forced enslavement of Native Americans. When peace returned in 1713, political, religious, and economic reforms fueled North Carolina's growth. The defeat of the Tuscaroras also removed the last obstacle blocking European expansion in the colony.

The Iroquoian-speaking Tuscaroras, the largest tribe in North Carolina's central coastal plain, occupied several towns along the Pamlico, Neuse, and Trent rivers. Resentment toward Europeans began when Baron Christoph von Graffenried occupied a vacated Tuscarora town. Other colonists followed suit, establishing communities on or abutting tribal lands. Although colonial expansion increased trade between Native Americans and Europeans, mistreatment, cultural prejudice, and fraud engendered hard feelings. The prohibition of hunting in newly settled areas also enraged the Tuscaroras.

The enslavement of children, however, produced the greatest outcry. Although the colony's lord proprietors forbade the practice, Native American slavery flourished throughout the Carolinas. The Tuscaroras discovered, however, that their children, entrusted to neighboring colonists for apprenticeships, were in fact often enslaved.

By 1710 the Tuscaroras sought to escape the abuses and encroachments by moving north. Pennsylvania's leaders, however,

Storming of the great Tuscarora fortress of Nehucke in 1713 by a combined force of Cherokee and English forces. Painting by Ron Embleton. (Bridgeman Art Library)

rejected the tribal diplomats' petition to relocate there. Hancock, chief of the southern Tuscaroras, responded with force.

On September 22, 1711, some 250 Bear River, Pamlico, Neusiok, Coree, Machapunga, and Tuscarora warriors visited the homes of unsuspecting white settlers. Once welcomed into the colonists' abodes, the warriors brandished weapons and killed the inhabitants. Nearly 130 men, women, and children perished during the attacks. Many others, including Baron von Graffenried, were captured. News of the onslaught shocked colonial leaders. Political instability, civil unrest, disease, and drought initially prevented Governor Edward Hyde from organizing a military response or providing relief to those in need.

Thomas Pollock, president of the provincial council, immediately marched militia to the war zone. Problems resulted, however, when soldiers from Bath Town refused to cross the Pamlico River to join troops from New Bern. As a result, New Bern's forces were stranded without reinforcements in hostile territory.

Governor Hyde meanwhile appealed to neighboring colonies for assistance. Lieutenant Governor Alexander Spotswood of Virginia responded by securing the neutrality of several tribes with promises of trade, bounties for enemies, recognition of tribal boundaries, and protection. He also dispatched Peter Poythres, a veteran scout and interpreter, to neutral Tuscarora settlements. Poythres's diplomacy produced treaties with the eight upper towns, thereby halving the Tuscaroras' fighting power and diminishing the hostiles' chance of victory. Spotswood also secured the safe release of Baron von Graffenried and other prisoners while ratifying treaties with the Nottoways, the Saponis, and the Meherrins, thereby further isolating the militant Tuscaroras.

In 1712 Spotswood sent blankets and clothing to help ease the plight of war refugees. He also readied Virginia's militia, bolstered by 100 Native American allies, to march against the hostiles. Plans for the expedition fell through, however, when North Carolina's leaders failed to provide provisions for Spotswood's force.

South Carolina officials responded to Hyde's pleas by recruiting Catawba and Yamasee warriors to march against their traditional enemies. Many volunteers saw the campaign as an opportunity to secure Native American slaves, a line of reasoning encouraged by Governor Hyde.

Colonel John Barnwell, a South Carolina trader and experienced soldier, commanded an army of 495 Native Americans and 30 colonists. On reaching New Bern in February 1712, Barnwell's force encountered fierce resistance. A short time later the colonel learned that two-thirds of his force had deserted, taking a large supply of slaves and goods with them. Sixty-seven locals bolstered what remained of Barnwell's force in a campaign against Fort Hancock, a fortified Tuscarora town along the Neuse River. Although Barnwell's first assault was unsuccessful, his use of cannon ultimately produced a negotiated settlement.

The truce did not last long. Shortly after negotiating the agreement, Barnwell enslaved those who had accepted his terms. Not surprisingly, the colonel's treachery sparked a series of Tuscarora raids during the summer of 1712, a situation exacerbated by food shortages, Quaker politicians' refusal to support the war, and Governor Hyde's death in September 1712.

Once again South Carolinians responded with military force. In March 1713 Colonel James Moore Jr. led 50 colonists and 1,000 Native American allies against Nehucke, a Tuscarora town protected by palisades, blockhouses, and escape tunnels. Moore achieved victory only after setting fire to the town's palisades. He subsequently estimated that 558 Native Americans had perished in the fight. Nearly 400 others were taken prisoner. Following the victory, all but 180 of Moore's soldiers deserted him, taking their slaves and plunder with them back to South Carolina.

Moore's campaign signaled the end of the Tuscarora War. By 1713 both the Native Americans and North Carolina officials lacked the resources needed to prolong the conflict. News of Nehucke's destruction also prompted residents of other lower Tuscarora settlements to escape a similar fate by fleeing west to the headwaters of the Roanoke River.

On April 14, 1713, Thomas Pollock concluded peace with the remaining Tuscaroras. Tom Blunt, declared "king" of all Tuscaroras, accepted a reservation established for the tribe between the Neuse and the Pamlico. Although the treaty did not end hostilities, it marked the end of Tuscarora dominance.

Peaceful Tuscaroras, now the targets of frequent enemy raids, depended on their colonial neighbors for supplies and protection. North Carolina officials approved relocation to a new reservation along the Roanoke River following Catawba attacks during the 1720s. Later removals to New York to join the Iroquois Confederacy, which had adopted the Tuscaroras around 1722, finally brought the promise of revitalization to a defeated people.

JON L. BRUDVIG

See also

Captivity of Indians by Europeans; Iroquois Confederacy; Tuscaroras; Yamasees

References

Parramore, Thomas C. "The Tuscarora Ascendancy." *North Carolina Historical Review* 59 (October 1982): 307–326.

Richter, Daniel K., and James H. Merrell, eds. *Beyond the Covenant Chain: The Iroquois and Their Neighbors in Indian North America, 1600–1800.* Syracuse, NY: Syracuse University Press, 1987.

Robinson, W. Stitt. *The Southern Colonial Frontier, 1607–1763.* Albuquerque: University of New Mexico Press, 1979.

24th U.S. Infantry Regiment

See Infantry Regiment, 24th U.S.

25th U.S. Infantry Regiment

See Infantry Regiment, 25th U.S.

Tzi-na-ma-a

See Mojaves

U

Uncas

Birth Date: ca. 1588
Death Date: 1683

Leader of the Mohegans. Most Americans remember Uncas as the fictional character in James Fenimore Cooper's *The Last of the Mohicans.* The historical Uncas, however, was a Mohegan, not a Mahican, nor was he the last of his tribe. Uncas closely allied himself with the New England colonies and presided over the rise of the Mohegans. Born around 1588, Uncas gave military assistance to the colonies at Plymouth, Connecticut, and Massachusetts Bay during the Pequot War (1636–1638) and King Philip's War (1675–1676). These alliances, along with his part in the slaying of the Narragansett sachem (chief) Miantonomo, have caused some historians to cast Uncas as a traitor to native peoples. However, his actions strengthened the Mohegans and helped them retain a measure of independence in colonial New England.

A small tributary group dominated by the more powerful Pequots, the Mohegans occupied the lands between the Connecticut River and the Thames River. When the Pequot War erupted in 1636, Uncas participated in planning and leading the attack on the Pequots' Mystic River fort. As a reward for his services he was given a large share of Pequot prisoners, most of whom were incorporated into the Mohegan tribe.

Uncas proved useful to the colonists yet again when Miantonomo, an English ally during the Pequot War, began to speak out against them. At the same time, Uncas's Mohegans began attacking Narragansett hunters. Following a treaty that he had signed with Massachusetts, Miantonomo sought and was granted permission to attack the Mohegans. The Mohegans captured Miantonomo, and Uncas turned him over to the colony of Connecticut.

Not wanting Miantonomo's blood on their own hands, Connecticut authorities gave Miantonomo back to Uncas, who had him executed.

During King Philip's War, Uncas allied the Mohegans to Massachusetts and assisted the colonists in crushing the resistance. After the war he reaffirmed his alliance with the colony. Uncas died in 1683.

ROGER M. CARPENTER

See also

Cooper, James Fenimore; King Philip's War; Mohegans; Mystic Fort Fight; Narragansetts; Pequots; Pequot War

References

Jennings, Francis. *The Invasion of America: Indians, Colonialism, and the Cant of Conquest.* 1976; reprint, Chapel Hill: University of North Carolina Press, 2010.

Orberg, Michael Leroy. *Uncas: First of the Mohegans.* Ithaca, NY: Cornell University Press, 2003.

Underhill, John

Birth Date: 1597
Death Date: July 21, 1672

English-born mercenary, privateer, and militia officer. John Underhill was born sometime in 1597 at Bagington, Warwickshire, England. He gained his first military experience in the Netherlands, where he also married a Dutch woman. Underhill arrived in Massachusetts in 1630 to train the colonial militia. He also served as a Boston town official.

Underhill served as a captain in command of a Massachusetts Militia contingent during the Pequot War (1636–1638). In May

1637 Underhill's force participated in the massacre of the inhabitants of a Pequot village on the Mystic River in Connecticut. The village contained between 400 and 700 people, mostly women, children, and elderly men. The New Englanders set the village afire and killed everyone trying to escape the flames. Underhill later wrote an account of the Pequot War titled *News from America.*

A 1639 accusation of heresy led to Underhill's banishment from the Massachusetts Bay Colony. He subsequently moved to New Hampshire, then to Connecticut, and finally in 1643 to New Netherland. There he lived among other English settlers on Long Island. Governor Willem Kieft hired Underhill to command militia during the early phase of the Dutch-Indian Wars (1641–1664). Underhill's unit participated in another massacre of a native village in February 1644. This time his men burned and shot a reported 500–700 inhabitants of an Algonquian village near present-day Westchester, New York. Toward the end of the war, however, Kieft abruptly dismissed Underhill.

Continuing to live in New Netherland, Underhill served as the sheriff of Flushing, Long Island, and defended English interests there. Following the outbreak of the First Anglo-Dutch War (1652–1654), Connecticut officials wrote to him in 1653 and asked him to investigate a possible Dutch conspiracy to arm natives against the English. Dutch officials then arrested Underhill when he publicly accused them of inciting the natives against the English. On his release, Underhill openly worked against Dutch rule on Long Island, calling on English residents there to overthrow the Dutch. When the English failed to heed his calls, he fled to Rhode Island. There he accepted a privateer's commission to raid Dutch shipping and was called on to organize an English force to attack New Netherland.

When the English seized New Netherland in 1664, Underhill returned to Long Island. There he held a number of official posts. Underhill died on July 21, 1672, in an area then known as Killingworth on Long Island.

Roberta Wiener

See also
Kieft, Willem; Kieft's War; Mystic Fort Fight; Pequot War

References
Cave, Alfred A. *The Pequot War.* Amherst: University of Massachusetts Press, 1996.
Rink, Oliver A. *Holland on the Hudson: An Economic and Social History of Dutch New York.* Ithaca, NY: Cornell University Press, 1986.
Underhill, John. "News from America." *Massachusetts Historical Society,* 3rd ser., 6 (1837): 1–28.
Van der Zee, Henri, and Barbara Van der Zee. *A Sweet and Alien Land: The Story of Dutch New York.* New York: Viking, 1978.

United Colonies of New England
See New England Confederation

United Kingdom
See Great Britain

Uprising of 1747
Start Date: Spring 1747
End Date: September 1747

Revolt of Ohio Country Native Americans against the French during King George's War (1744–1748). The Uprising of 1747 reflected the volatile interplay of tribal rivalries and imperial ambitions on the North American continent. By the early 1740s, the area south of Lake Erie had become an arena for commercial competition between New France and rapidly encroaching English traders from Pennsylvania. In this borderland between colonial empires, gaining the allegiance of a recently relocated tribe of Wyandots (Hurons) was a key factor in regional politics.

Wyandot chief Orontony had requested resettlement deep within French territory to protect the Wyandots from predations by the French-allied Ottawas, located near Detroit. His collaboration with the Cherokees in an earlier assault on an Ottawa war party had ruined his standing within the Great Lakes region, however. Rejected by French colonial officials whom he likened to slave owners hostile toward his confederation, he moved his people instead to the periphery of French power. The Wyandots finally settled at Sandusky Bay. Ambitious and prone to conspiracy, Orontony immediately cultivated relations with the English by traveling to Albany and obtaining trading privileges.

This new partnership brought Orontony into contact with the most successful and charismatic merchant in the region, George Croghan. It also earned Orontony the enmity of the French. An Irish immigrant well versed in native languages and customs, Croghan was developing a vast economic network. By 1746 he had secured permission to build a blockhouse at the Wyandot village of Sandusky, located between Detroit and the Cuyahoga River in what was the first British military post in the Ohio Country. Already apprehensive over losing influence with the powerful Iroquois Confederacy as a bulwark against the British, French authorities placed a bounty on Croghan's head. Quick to joke about his newfound notoriety, Croghan remained undeterred. Meanwhile, Orontony agitated among the Miami (Twightwee), Ottawa, and Shawnee tribes to stage assaults on overextended French positions with an emphasis on taking Detroit. His plan was to establish himself as a figure worthy of leading a new nation, independent of French authority.

The onset of King George's War in 1744 created an opportunity for Orontony to strike at the French and gain leverage by requesting British support. The threat of a British invasion of Quebec received the highest priority in French military preparations, which left the Ohio Country sparsely defended. In the spring of 1747 five French traders who were unaware of Orontony's machinations were murdered while visiting Sandusky. Then a French fort on the Maumee River was partially burned, and the Miamis razed a trading post within their territory.

The Uprising of 1747 had begun. Orontony arrived at Detroit purportedly to seek peace, but a party of natives killed several Frenchmen nearby. Natives, including some Ottawas, planned a massive attack against the settlement, but the work of an informant scuttled the operation.

Although not always acting in coordination with one another, numerous native villages rose against the French as the entire frontier became destabilized. Croghan's precise role in encouraging Orontony remains unclear, but the trader likely promised British assistance to him and provided gunpowder to the native rebels. Sensitive of his own credibility, Croghan convinced the governor of Pennsylvania to provide logistical support lest the rebelling tribes reassess their loyalties. The French proved quick to identify British intrigue as the primary cause of the uprising, but the true explanation was more complex. Indeed, the ongoing success of the British Royal Navy in denying supplies to Canada had impeded the ability of the French to trade with the natives. The desire for trade goods caused many tribes to turn against the French and ally with the British.

In September 1747 the deployment of French reinforcements compelled Orontony to destroy Sandusky and retreat eastward into the Ohio River Valley and then Pennsylvania, where he died in 1750. The Wyandots ceased hostilities, but the Miamis continued to resist the French until 1752. Only the employment of French troops and native allies from distant locations brought the insurgency to a close. Although ultimately successful in quelling the revolt, the French suffered heavy losses at their commercial outposts and were fortunate to retain Detroit.

Slowly during the early 1750s the French improved their standing with the tribes of the Great Lakes. The Uprising of 1747 was in part an attempt by natives to renegotiate their position within a rapidly deteriorating French alliance system. One measure of mounting desperation among the French was the abrogation of the policy of pardoning warriors who had fought against them. Clearly France's native allies were growing more cognizant of the shifting balance of power in favor of the British.

Jeffrey D. Bass

See also
Croghan, George; France; King George's War; Native American Trade; Orontony; Ottawas

References
Axtell, James. *The Invasion Within: The Contest of Cultures in Colonial North America.* New York: Oxford University Press, 1985.

White, Richard. *The Middle Ground: Indians, Empires, and Republics in the Great Lakes Region, 1650–1815.* New York: Cambridge University Press, 1991.

Upton, Emory
Birth Date: August 27, 1839
Death Date: March 15, 1881

U.S. Army officer and military theorist. Emory Upton was born on August 27, 1839, to a farming family in Batavia, New York. After a year at Oberlin College (Ohio), he entered the U.S. Military Academy, West Point, in 1856, graduating near the top of his class in May 1861. A week later, Upton was promoted to first lieutenant of artillery.

During the American Civil War (1861–1865), Upton fired the opening gun of the First Battle of Manassas (Bull Run) (July 21, 1861) and was wounded there. The following year he fought in the Peninsula Campaign (March–August 1862) and at the Battle of Antietam (September 17, 1862). To avoid an assignment teaching at West Point, Upton transferred to the infantry as a colonel of the 121st New York Volunteer Regiment. The regiment saw little action despite its presence at the Battle of Fredericksburg (December 13, 1862), the Battle of Chancellorsville (May 1–4, 1863), and the Battle of Gettysburg (July 1–3, 1863).

Just before the Battle of Gettysburg, Upton received command of a brigade in VI Corps, which he led with great effectiveness at Rappahannock Station (November 7, 1863). He especially distinguished himself during Lieutenant General Ulysses S. Grant's

Emory Upton (1839–1881), U.S. Army officer, military theorist, and reformer. (Library of Congress)

Overland Campaign of 1864 that brought the Union Army to the gates of Richmond.

Upton's experiences on the battlefield led him to advocate an important change in infantry tactics, chiefly advancing the men in columns close to the enemy line, when they would deploy in line and charge. Applying this method, Upton led 12 regiments in breaking through Confederate defenses during the Battle of Spotsylvania Courthouse (May 7–19, 1864). The attack ultimately failed for lack of support, but Upton had demonstrated its potential for breaking through a strongly defended position.

Still only 24 years old, Upton was rewarded with promotion to brigadier general, to date from May 12, 1864. Given command of an infantry division a few months later in Major General Philip H. Sheridan's Shenandoah Valley Campaign, Upton was wounded at Opequon (Winchester) and brevetted major general. He was then transferred to Nashville, where he led a cavalry division in a campaign against Selma, Alabama, and Columbus, Georgia.

Following the war, Upton reverted to his permanent rank of captain, but in July 1866 he was appointed lieutenant colonel of the 25th Infantry Regiment. He soon became one of the army's leading intellectuals and reformers. During 1866–1867 he was assigned to West Point as an instructor. There he also produced *A New System of Infantry Tactics* (1867), which was adopted by the army the same year. This system became the basis for the army's tactics in the Spanish-American War (1898) and into the two 20th-century world wars.

From 1870 to 1875, Upton was commandant of cadets and instructor in tactics at West Point. With the United States then involved in fighting the Native Americans in the West, Commanding General of the Army William T. Sherman sent Upton on a yearlong world tour to Asia and Europe to study the fighting there, especially the British India campaigns. Upton returned as an admirer of the German model of a strong standing army with a large officer cadre and skeleton formations. In time of need, such an army could be rapidly expanded. This system would do away with volunteer units entirely, for all volunteers would serve in the regular army under its officers. Upton also applauded the German general staff system and its frequent rotation of officers between staff and line assignments. He advocated conscription but dared approach this only indirectly. Upton chiefly wanted the United States to abandon its dual system of federal and state control in favor of assigning all military duties to the regular army. He also argued against civilian control of the military.

Upton presented these views in his report, published as *The Armies of Asia and Europe* (1878), and in an influential manuscript, *The Military Policy of the United States*. The latter, the first professional military history of the United States, was published posthumously in 1904. Congress and the country largely ignored his recommendations.

In 1880 Colonel Upton took command of the 4th Artillery Regiment at the Presidio, San Francisco, where on March 15, 1881, plagued by agonizing headaches perhaps caused by depression heightened by the death of his wife, he took his own life.

NEIL HEYMAN AND SPENCER C. TUCKER

See also

Sheridan, Philip Henry; Sherman, William Tecumseh

References

Ambrose, Stephen E. *Upton and the Army*. Baton Rouge: Louisiana State University Press, 1964.

Michie, Peter S. *The Life and Letters of Emory Upton, Colonel of the Fourth Regiment of Artillery, and Brevet Major-General, U.S. Army*. New York: D. Appleton, 1885.

Reardon, Carol. *Soldiers and Scholars: The U.S. Army and the Uses of Military History, 1865–1920*. Lawrence: University Press of Kansas, 1990.

Upton, Emory. *The Military Policy of the United States*. Washington, DC: U.S. Government Printing Office, 1904.

Weigley, Russell F. *Towards an American Army: Military Thought from Washington to Marshall*. New York: Columbia University Press, 1962.

Utes

Native American people who initially occupied western Colorado and eastern Utah. The Utes were divided into 11 bands, with the eastern bands living in Colorado and the western bands residing primarily in Utah. The eastern bands were the Capotes, Muaches, Uncompahgres, Parusanuchs, Weeminuches, and Yampas. The western bands were the Moanunts, Pahvant Sanpits, Timpanogots, and Uintahs.

The Ute economic system centered on hunting, gathering, and raiding. The Utes traditionally raided the Apaches, Hopis, Navajos, Pueblos, and Shoshones, and once the Spanish arrived in New Mexico, the Utes began raiding them as well. However, hostilities with these groups were sporadic.

The Eastern Utes encountered Europeans sooner than their western counterparts and, as a result, acquired horses sooner. By the early 17th century the Eastern Utes began participating in the horse culture that had developed on the Great Plains. Therefore, they began to spend more time on the Plains hunting buffalo. The Western Utes did not gain access to horses until the turn of the 18th century. In the 17th and early 18th centuries, the Utes used their horses to expand their raiding to Paiute communities in western Utah and Nevada in order to enslave women and children and sell them to the Spanish in New Mexico.

As the Utes began to spend more time on the Plains and in the eastern valleys of the Rocky Mountains, they began to encounter hostile groups of people. These included the Arapahos, Cheyennes, Comanches, and Lakota Sioux. The Comanches had previously been Ute allies living in the Colorado and Nevada areas before they acquired horses and moved to the Plains. Because of the tense relations with these groups, the Utes began to participate in a larger network of captive exchanges that extended from the upper Mississippi River Valley westward to Arizona and Nevada.

When Americans first began moving into the Southwest, the Utes maintained good relations with them but over time ceded

A Ute warrior and his bride on horseback in northwestern Utah. Photograph by John K. Hillers, 1874. (National Archives)

land to the U.S. government. In treaties signed in 1855, 1863, 1868, and 1873, the Utes saw their landholdings reduced to fewer than 12 million acres. Utes living on the White River Agency briefly rebelled in 1879 against federal control. This incident, known as the Ute War, occurred after the local agent, Nathan C. Meeker, tried to force the Utes to plow up their pastureland to plant crops. The failure of this uprising forced the Utes to give up most of their land in Colorado and move to the southwestern part of the state or to a new reservation in Utah in 1882.

In 1887 the U.S. Congress passed the Dawes Severalty Act to end communal control of native land by the tribe and divide it among individual members. Excess land was to be given to whites for settlement. The implementation of the Dawes Act diminished the Utes' landholdings to just 40,600 acres. Fortunately for the Utes, the passage of the Indian Reorganization Act in 1933 aided their reacquisition of some former tribal land, and by the end of the 1960s the Utes controlled 304,700 acres of land.

DIXIE RAY HAGGARD

See also

Apaches; Arapahos; Cheyennes; Comanches; Dawes Severalty Act; Indian Reorganization Act; Lakota Sioux; Meeker Massacre; Navajos; Paiutes, Northern; Pueblos; Shoshones; Ute War

References

Decker, Peter R. *"The Utes Must Go!" American Expansion and the Removal of a People.* Golden, CO: Fulcrum, 2004.

Miller, Mark E. *Hollow Victory: The White River Expedition of 1879 and the Battle of Milk Creek.* Niwot: The University Press of Colorado, 1997.

Simmons, Virginia McConnell. *The Ute Indians of Utah, Colorado, and New Mexico.* Niwot: University Press of Colorado, 2000.

Ute War
Start Date: September 1879
End Date: October 1879

Little more than a minor skirmish, the Ute War of late September and early October 1879 reflected the frustrations of the Ute tribe with attempts by the U.S. government to transform the Utes into yeoman farmers. The war also set the stage for the final removal of a majority of the tribe from the state of Colorado.

Originally the Utes were divided into 11 independent bands. After contact with Europeans, decimation by European-introduced diseases, and U.S. government efforts to put the Utes on reservations, the Ute population and the number of different bands diminished significantly. The eastern Ute bands had encountered the Spanish as early as 1600. After acquiring horses, the Utes raided the Spanish and other natives in the Southwest and on the southern Great Plains. Until 1850, most Utes had little contact with Americans. By the 1870s, however, the remaining Ute bands lived on reservation land located along the Colorado, San Juan, and White rivers in western Colorado and eastern Utah. The U.S. government administered these reservations, and until 1879 the Utes had a long history of peaceful relations with settlers.

Because of silver strikes on Ute reservations during the early and mid-1870s, Coloradans began to demand that the Utes be removed to Indian Territory in Oklahoma. The federal government exacerbated the situation by appointing Nathan C. Meeker as the Indian agent to the White River Agency in the spring of 1878. Uniquely unqualified as an agent and with no experience dealing with Native Americans, Meeker attempted to force the Utes to plow their meadows used for pasturage to grow crops. This threatened the Utes' large pony herds, on which they depended heavily for their survival. Meeker's insistence upon initiating this policy and his assertion that the Utes had too many horses, some of which should be killed, compelled a Ute chief to throw Meeker out the front door of the agency. In response, U.S. Army troops were dispatched to the area from Fort Fred Steele, Wyoming.

Major Thomas T. Thornburgh led this force south from Wyoming to the White River Agency. His command consisted of 175–200 men, most of whom were from the 5th Cavalry, but some soldiers from the 4th Infantry were also present primarily to protect the supply train. Upon his arrival, Thornburgh agreed to a council with the Utes to resolve the conflict but then decided to advance with his cavalry to Milk Creek. On September 29, 100 Ute warriors confronted Thornburgh's command there. Although it appeared at first that conflict might be avoided, a single gunshot from an undetermined rifle sparked the Battle of Milk Creek (September 29–October 5, 1879).

After the initial exchange, the soldiers fell back to their wagon train. During the retreat, Thornburgh was killed by a shot to the head. The Utes kept the soldiers pinned down for six days, but a detachment of buffalo soldiers from the 9th Cavalry reinforced the besieged soldiers on October 2. Eventually Colonel Wesley Merritt arrived with a larger number of reinforcements, which forced the Utes to leave the battlefield on October 5.

During the Battle of Milk Creek, Ute warriors also attacked and burned the White River Agency, killing most of the men there, including Meeker. The Utes took the women and children captive. Eventually Charles Adams, a former agent to the Utes, and Ouray, the chief of the Uncompahgre band, negotiated an end to hostilities. As part of the terms, the Utes gave up their captives. Although the government planned to prosecute 12 Ute warriors for the massacre of Meeker and his subordinates, none ever stood trial. However, the Ute War led even more Coloradans to take part of the land held in reserve for the Utes. Eventually the tribe lost most of its land in Colorado and was forced to settle on small reservations in southwestern Colorado and eastern Utah.

DIXIE RAY HAGGARD

See also

Cavalry Regiment, 4th U.S.; Cavalry Regiment, 5th U.S.; Cavalry Regiment, 9th U.S.; Meeker, Nathan Cook; Meeker Massacre; Merritt, Wesley; Milk Creek, Battle of; Ouray; Utes

References

Dawson, Thomas Fulton. *The Ute War.* New York: Garland, 1976.

Decker, Peter R. *"The Utes Must Go!" American Expansion and the Removal of a People.* Golden, CO: Fulcrum, 2004.

Miller, Mark E. *Hollow Victory: The White River Expedition of 1879 and the Battle of Milk Creek.* Niwot: The University Press of Colorado, 1997.

Simmons, Virginia McConnell. *The Ute Indians of Utah, Colorado, and New Mexico.* Niwot: University Press of Colorado, 2000.

V

Victorio

Birth Date: ca. 1825
Death Date: October 15, 1880

Mimbres (Mimbreño) Apache chief, one of the greatest guerilla fighters and military strategists of the 19th-century Indian Wars. Victorio was born about 1825 in southwestern New Mexico. Legends about his origins persist, most holding that he was a captured Mexican boy raised among the Apaches, but proof is lacking. Biduyé, as he was called by tribal members, was renamed by his enemies when he became a respected war leader, even though he tried very hard to find a course other than war. The Mimbres Apaches initially lived near what is today known as Monticello, New Mexico. Their most notable early leader was Mangas Coloradas. At about age 16 Victorio, as an apprentice, rode along on the first of four raids during which the older warriors acted as his teachers and tested his skills in the many aspects of warfare. By 1850 U.S. military leaders had begun to take note of Victorio's military prowess. In 1855 Victorio conducted a successful raid, taking his followers into the Mexican states of Sonora and Chihuahua to bring back large numbers of captives and livestock. In July 1862 he took part in the noteworthy Battle of Apache Pass near Tucson, Arizona, and continued to participate in numerous skirmishes and raids against white settlers and the U.S. military.

In 1863 after the death of Mangas Coloradas, Victorio assumed leadership of the Mimbres Apaches. In 1869 he settled near Fort Craig, New Mexico. There he and his followers awaited completion of a reservation near Ojo Caliente, New Mexico. Apparently Victorio and his band remained quiescent until after April 20, 1877, when the U.S. government ordered them removed to the San Carlos Reservation. In September 1879 he and 60 warriors raided a U.S. cavalry unit camped near a small settlement in southwestern New Mexico. The Apaches killed 5 soldiers and 3 civilians and then made off with 68 horses and mules. The attack signaled the start of what is sometimes known as the Victorio War.

By January 1880 Victorio had led his people in battles across three states. He fought Anglo and Mexican settlers, Mexican regulars, Texas Rangers, and the black troops of the 9th U.S. Cavalry Regiment in New Mexico, Texas, and Mexico, winning almost every engagement. On April 6, 1880, 71 members of the 9th Cavalry, led by Captain Henry Carroll, cautiously approached Victorio's camp in the Hembrillo Basin, a natural stronghold, in south-central New Mexico. They were immediately surrounded by a larger force of about 150 Apaches under Victorio. The Apache force fired volley after volley from behind stacked breastworks erected on the surrounding ridge tops. However, a relief column sent by 9th Cavalry commander Colonel Edward Hatch drove off Victorio's warriors from their positions. Undeterred, Victorio raided extensively throughout May and June before slipping into Mexico, in the process wearing out the buffalo soldiers of the 9th Cavalry.

In July, anticipating Victorio's return through western Texas, Colonel Benjamin Grierson of the 10th Cavalry Regiment posted his command at the few essential water holes that the Apaches would need and waited. Grierson himself, with 2 officers and 21 black troops, held a position in Quitman Canyon when Victorio and some 150 warriors attacked on July 30. The soldiers held out until relieved, while Victorio's band, denied water, fell back into Mexico. On August 2 Victorio tried to drive again only to be turned back by Grierson's troops at Rattlesnake Springs four days later.

Driven back into Mexico, Victorio became the target of both U.S. and Mexican efforts. Although a large U.S. force entered Mexico for the proposed campaign, the Americans were soon ordered out, leaving Victorio to the Mexicans. Victorio eventually took his people to a site on the plains, three rocky peaks called Tres Castillos, where they were attacked by a group of Mexican irregulars and Tarahumara auxiliaries. Fighting continued for hours until dawn on October 15, 1880, when Victorio was killed, possibly by his own hand but most likely by a bullet fired by an Indian auxiliary. Sixty warriors and 18 women and children also lay dead. Sixty-eight other women and children were taken captive, along with 180 animals. After the prisoners were gathered, the adolescent boys were taken to a nearby arroyo and shot, while the remaining women and children were enslaved.

H. HENRIETTA STOCKEL

See also

Apache Pass, Battle of; Cavalry Regiment, 9th U.S.; Mangas Coloradas

References

Laumbach, Karl W. *Hembrillo: An Apache Battlefield of the Victorio War.* White Sands, NM: White Sands Missile Range, 2000.

Thrapp, Dan L. *Victorio and the Mimbres Apaches.* Norman: University of Oklahoma Press, 1974.

Utley, Robert M. *Frontier Regulars: The United States and the American Indian, 1866–1891.* New York: Macmillan, 1973.

Virginia-Indian Treaty of 1646

Treaty between Virginia and the remnants of the Powhatan Confederacy that concluded the Third Anglo-Powhatan War (1644–1646). Faced with the rapid expansion of the Virginia colony, Powhatan leader Opechancanough launched a full-scale attack on the settlers in March 1644 in a desperate bid to preserve native sovereignty. Despite his initial successes that claimed the lives of as many as 500 Virginians, the colonists quickly regrouped and counterattacked, devastating Powhatan towns and crops. Opechancanough, taken prisoner, was ultimately murdered by one of his guards in the late summer of 1646.

Following Opechancanough's death, his successor, Necotowance, began peace negotiations with Virginia governor William Berkeley. The war had reduced the once-extensive Powhatan lands to a small core of communities. In a treaty signed on October 5, 1646, Necotowance agreed that the Powhatans would be confined to small territories (in effect, the first native reservations in America) north of the York River. He further conceded that the natives' remaining land was held by them as if granted by the English Crown. Future Powhatan leaders would be confirmed by the Virginia government, to which the Powhatans acknowledged their dependency and pledged loyalty. Other provisions of the treaty required the natives to return runaway servants to Virginia officials and pay an annual tribute of 20 beaver skins to the colonial government.

In return for these concessions, Virginia authorities promised the Powhatans legal and military protections and strict policing of the new Anglo–Native American boundaries. Native messengers

wishing to enter colonial territory were required to wear special striped shirts for identification. Unauthorized contact between settlers and natives was punishable by the death penalty for all offenders, with an exception made for young native servants. To prevent traders from cheating the natives—an issue that Virginia officials believed had helped provoke the war—trade was restricted to designated frontier forts.

Over time, however, the impracticality of these draconian measures became clear, and penalties were reduced. Eventually the colonial government relaxed its control over trade and ignored settlers' encroachment on native lands. After 1649, Virginia ended its policy of dealing with the Powhatan Confederacy and began renegotiating treaties with the separate constituent tribes. Virginia's native policy continued to undergo piecemeal alteration until it was recodified by the Virginia-Indian Treaty of 1677/1680.

STEPHEN D. FEELEY AND JIM PIECUCH

See also

Anglo-Powhatan War, Third; Berkeley, William; Opechancanough; Powhatan Confederacy

References

Rountree, Helen C., ed. *Powhatan Foreign Relations, 1500–1722.* Charlottesville: University Press of Virginia, 1993.

Vaughan, Alden T., ed. *Early American Indian Documents: Treaties and Laws, 1607–1789,* Vol. 2, *Virginia Treaties, 1607–1722.* Frederick, MD: University Publications of America, 1983.

Virginia-Indian Treaty of 1677/1680

Following Bacon's Rebellion in 1676–1677, representatives of King Charles II negotiated the Virginia-Indian Treaty of 1677/1680, also known as the Treaty of Middle Plantation, with several Virginia native tribes to rectify the wrongs done to the natives during Bacon's campaigns. Bacon's Rebellion began with skirmishes between a few natives and colonists on the Virginia frontier but quickly expanded into an attack on innocent Indians who had no part in the original dispute. Following the conflict, commissioners sent by the Crown to investigate the rebellion exonerated the native tribes who had been unfairly attacked and concluded the Virginia-Indian Treaty of 1677/1680 to strengthen the tribes' rights as loyal subjects of the king.

A first version of the treaty was signed on May 29, 1677, at Middle Plantation (rechristened Williamsburg in 1699) by Queen Cockacoeske of the Pamunkeys and her son, a Nansemond chief. As word spread of the treaty's fairness, representatives of several other tribes, including the Meherrins, the Monacans, the Saponis, the Pattanouchus, and the Portabaccos, signed the agreement between April and June 1680.

This liberal treaty granted tributary natives the same civil rights enjoyed by the English. For example, individual natives could settle disputes in county courts, where they would be treated as any subject of the Crown would be. The treaty also established protections for natives employed by English colonists so that they would not become de facto slaves.

Additionally, the treaty sought to resolve problems surrounding land use. Tribes would have perpetual ownership of land in a three-mile radius from their towns for foraging and hunting. Tributary natives could also hunt on unfenced English lands and forage almost anywhere for items not valued by the colonists, such as the edible tuckahoe found in the marshes.

In return the tribes that signed the treaty accepted their status as subjects of the king and agreed to pay an annual tribute to the Virginia governor. They also had the responsibility of reporting the presence of foreign natives and, when necessary, to take up arms against them alongside the English.

The treaty represented the objectives of the royal government rather than those of the colonists in Virginia. Although London officials ordered strict observance of the treaty, the governor quietly allowed the rights of the natives under the treaty to erode in the quarter century following its enactment. Various laws brought native land into English hands and curtailed natives' civil rights. Most significant was a 1705 law directed against all nonwhites that took away the natives' rights to vote, bear arms, testify in court, or hold civil, military, or religious office. Thus, the Virginia-Indian Treaty of 1677/1680 ultimately did little to protect the natives from colonists increasingly anxious over issues of race and power.

JENNIFER BRIDGES OAST

See also

Bacon's Rebellion; Cockacoeske; Nansemonds; Powhatan Confederacy

References

Rountree, Helen C., ed. *Powhatan Foreign Relations, 1500–1722.* Charlottesville: University Press of Virginia, 1993.

Rountree, Helen C., and E. Randolph Turner III. *Before and After Jamestown: Virginia's Powhatans and Their Predecessors.* Gainesville: University Press of Florida, 2002.

Virginia-Indian Wars

See Anglo-Powhatan War, First; Anglo-Powhatan War, Second; Anglo-Powhatan War, Third

W

Wabash, Battle of the
Event Date: November 4, 1791

Military engagement between American forces under the command of Major General Arthur St. Clair and Miami, Shawnee, and Delaware warriors along the Wabash River near what is now Fort Wayne, Indiana. The Treaty of Paris of 1783 that ended the American Revolutionary War (1775–1783) gave the new United States sovereignty over former British lands east of the Mississippi River. Native Americans living in the Old Northwest were not a party to this treaty, however, and increasing incursions by white settlers onto their lands led to widespread Native American anger especially among the Miamis and Shawnees, who refused to recognize American claims to the territory northwest of the Ohio River. British authorities in Canada meanwhile encouraged the Native Americans' resistance.

Increasing numbers of casualties among the settlers and their retaliatory raids on the Native Americans led to growing sentiment for action among members of the government in Philadelphia, and President George Washington and Secretary of War Henry Knox authorized the use of force to bring the area firmly under U.S. control. In 1790 Brigadier General Josiah Harmar was ordered into the territory in the first major military expedition by the standing army of the United States, augmented by militia units from Kentucky and Pennsylvania. In all Harmar had 320 regulars of the 1st Infantry Regiment (virtually the entire army) and 1,133 militia. Harmar proved unusually inept, dividing his force and then dividing it again, allowing the Native Americans to defeat it in detail. One-fourth of his troops became casualties. Worse lay ahead.

President Washington now called on St. Clair, a former Revolutionary War general, to lead a new expedition. On September 17, 1791, Secretary of War Knox ordered St. Clair, with a commission as a major general, to force the Native Americans into submission and to establish a strong permanent military post at Kekionga, the principal Miami village near present-day Fort Wayne, Indiana, to offset British influence over that tribe. To assist St. Clair in this endeavor, Congress authorized establishment of the 2nd Infantry Regiment.

Unfortunately, St. Clair was ill much of the time and did little to prepare his men. Washington had insisted that the campaign occur in the summer months, but delays occasioned by supply problems intruded, and it was not until the autumn of 1791 that St. Clair departed Fort Washington (present-day Cincinnati, Ohio). He commanded 2,000 men: the entire regular army of some 600 men, 800 six-month conscripts, and 600 militia drawn principally from Kentucky.

Desertions soon reduced St. Clair's force to about 1,500 men and some 200 women and children camp followers. As his force moved northward, it engaged in occasional skirmishes with the Native Americans who were shadowing its every move. St. Clair, suffering from "rheumatic asthma" and gout, had difficulty controlling the men, and disciplinary problems were rife. In an effort to establish order he had three men brought up before a court-martial, two of them for desertion and the third for shooting another soldier. All three were executed before the drawn-up army.

Food was now in short supply, and the weather turned cold, with drenching rains followed by sleet and snow. Morale was at a nadir. Even though he then had food sufficient for only several days, St. Clair resolved to press on to his objective. Leaving behind 120 mostly sick men and 2 of his 10 artillery pieces to secure Fort Jefferson, St. Clair departed that place on October 21. By the beginning of November, desertion and illness had reduced St. Clair's force to about 1,000 men.

On November 3 St. Clair set up camp on roughly seven acres of high ground near the headwaters of the Wabash River at what is today the location of Fort Recovery, Ohio. He did not order the construction of any defensive works on the elevated meadow where his troops encamped. On that day St. Clair then had 52 officers and 868 enlisted men ready for duty.

That night a Native American force of some 700 warriors led by Little Turtle of the Miamis and Blue Jacket of the Shawnees, joined by 480 warriors led by Buckongahelas of the Delawares (Lenni Lenapes), moved into attack positions. At first light on November 4 as the soldiers were preparing breakfast, the Native Americans charged from the woods in a surprise attack. The troops attempted a number of bayonet charges. The Native Americans simply gave way and then encircled the advancing soldiers and destroyed them. St. Clair's artillery never got into the fray. As it wheeled into position, Native American marksmen shot down the gun crews. Exasperated, St. Clair tried to rally his men, riding among them and berating them as "cowards." During the fighting, he had three horses shot from beneath him.

After three hours of fighting, half of St. Clair's force was dead or dying. The American commander then met with his remaining officers, and they decided on a last bayonet charge and escape. The wounded were simply abandoned where they lay. The warriors later threw many of them onto the American campfires to burn to death.

Almost 90 percent of the officers were casualties, and close to 97 percent of the soldiers were killed, wounded, or captured, with 69 percent of these dead. Nearly all the camp followers, a number of whom had seized weapons and fought with the soldiers, were slain. The total number of killed in St. Clair's force, including camp followers, was 832. The Native American casualty total was estimated at about 61, with at least 21 killed.

The Battle of the Wabash, also known as the Battle of the Wabash River and St. Clair's Defeat, was arguably a great Native American victory over a U.S. military force and was also one of the greatest defeats ever for the U.S. Army, with the highest percentage casualty rate of any battle in its history. The next day the survivors reached the nearest U.S. military outpost at Fort Hamilton and then proceeded on to Fort Washington.

President Washington, who had warned St. Clair not to be taken by surprise, was furious. Washington made no attempt to conceal the extent of the disaster from the American people, and he immediately communicated the dire news to Congress. St. Clair traveled to Philadelphia to report in person, placing blame on the War Department and quartermaster services. He asked for a court-martial, planning to resign after he was exonerated, but Washington forced him to resign first.

The U.S. House of Representatives then proceeded to launch its own inquiry into the matter with its first-ever investigation of the executive branch and demanded that the War Department release to it certain documents. President Washington and his advisers refused to do so, thereby invoking the first instance of executive privilege in American history. The House committee did not attempt to fix blame, although it largely came down in favor of St. Clair, finding that the War Department had indeed failed to support him adequately. St. Clair was ultimately cleared by a court-martial.

The battle led directly to the raising of the 5,000-man Legion of the United States, commanded by Major General Anthony Wayne. This well-trained and well-prepared force achieved quite different results in 1794 in the next foray into Indian territory.

CHARLES FRANCIS HOWLETT AND SPENCER C. TUCKER

See also

Blue Jacket; Delawares; Harmar, Josiah; Little Turtle; Little Turtle's War; Miamis; Shawnees; St. Clair, Arthur; Washington, George

References

Dowd, Gregory Evans. *A Spirited Resistance: The North American Indian Struggle for Unity, 1745–1815.* Baltimore: Johns Hopkins University Press, 1992.

Guthman, William H. *March to Massacre: A History of the First Seven Years of the United States Army 1784–1791.* New York: McGraw-Hill, 1970.

Palmer, Dave R. *1794: America, Its Army, and the Birth of the Nation.* Novato, CA: Presidio, 1994.

Sugden, John. *Blue Jacket: Warrior of the Shawnees.* Lincoln: University of Nebraska Press, 2000.

Sword, Wiley. *President Washington's Indian War: The Struggle for the Old Northwest, 1790–1795.* Norman: University of Oklahoma Press, 1985.

Van Trees, Robert V. *Banks of the Wabash.* Fairborn, OH: Van Trees Associates, 1996.

Wabokieshiek
Birth Date: ca. 1794
Death Date: 1841

Winnebago (Ho-Chunk) prophet who unintentionally helped incite the Black Hawk War (1832) by encouraging the Sauk war leader Black Hawk to reoccupy ceded lands in Illinois. A half-Sauk and half-Winnebago shaman, Wabokieshiek (White Cloud) was born around 1794; little is known of his early life. He ultimately preached a message of native perseverance in the face of white encroachment in the Old Northwest in the 1820s and 1830s. Wabokieshiek attracted a following of approximately 200 disaffected Native Americans from various tribes to his village, Prophetstown, on the Rock River in Illinois.

While Wabokieshiek's specific teachings remain obscure, he does not appear to have endorsed violent resistance. Indeed, he dissuaded his followers from joining other Winnebago bands in the Winnebago War of 1827. Regardless, white residents in Illinois (perhaps recalling the militant messages of earlier Native American prophets) feared Wabokieshiek and his followers.

In the winter of 1828–1829, Wabokieshiek became a counselor to Black Hawk, leader of Sauk and Mesquakie bands that rejected

Oil portrait of Winnebago leader Wabokieshiek (White Cloud), also known as the Prophet, by Robert Sully, 1833. Wabokieshiek unintentionally helped bring about the Black Hawk War of 1832. (Wisconsin Historical Society/79800)

the legitimacy of an 1804 treaty in which those tribes had ceded their lands east of the Mississippi River. Although U.S. officials forbade it, Black Hawk and his followers reoccupied their summer village on the Rock River in the spring of 1831. Joining him, Wabokieshiek assured Black Hawk that the U.S. Army would not harm Black Hawk's followers so long as they remained at peace. Black Hawk did not doubt Wabokieshiek's dream-inspired advice but feared the Illinois militiamen who appeared eager for a fight and beyond federal control. In June 1831 Black Hawk returned to Iowa.

That winter, however, Wabokieshiek invited Black Hawk and his followers to plant corn at Prophetstown in the coming spring. Wabokieshiek still insisted that the Americans would not harm peaceful tribes. Meanwhile, another of Black Hawk's advisers, Neapope, assured Black Hawk that British forces in Canada and a Pan-Indian confederation would support Black Hawk in the event of war. Both assurances proved hollow, but they induced Black Hawk and about 1,000 followers to cross the Mississippi into Illinois on April 5, 1832.

Regarding this movement as an invasion, U.S. officials demanded that Wabokieshiek explain why he had invited Black Hawk to Prophetstown. Wabokieshiek disingenuously explained that he saw no harm in inviting kinsmen to farm at his unceded village. Although unapologetic, Wabokieshiek assured the officials that his intentions were peaceful, and he subsequently sheltered a U.S. Indian agent from militants in Prophetstown. Here Black Hawk learned that few Native Americans and no British were disposed to

aid him. He resolved to make peace with the U.S. government, but Illinois militiamen attacked before he had the chance.

Wabokieshiek remained Black Hawk's closest adviser during the ensuing war. Both Black Hawk and Wabokieshiek survived the decisive Battle of Bad Axe (August 2, 1832) but surrendered to a Winnebago hunting party and were remanded to American custody on August 27. Imprisoned for less than a year, Wabokieshiek and Black Hawk met with President Andrew Jackson and toured eastern cities in 1833. Wabokieshiek remained a counselor to Black Hawk during treaty proceedings in 1836 but retired to obscurity shortly thereafter. Wabokieshiek died sometime in 1841.

JOHN W. HALL

See also

Bad Axe, Battle of; Black Hawk; Black Hawk War; Mesquakies; Nativism, Indian; Red Bird; Sauks and Foxes; Winnebagos; Winnebago War

References

Black Hawk. *Black Hawk: An Autobiography.* Edited by Donald Jackson. Urbana: University of Illinois Press, 1964.

Jung, Patrick J. *The Black Hawk War of 1832.* Norman: University of Oklahoma Press, 2007.

Waccamaws

Native Americans who were Catawban speakers of the Pee Dee branch. In the 15th and 16th centuries the Waccamaws lived in what is now southeastern North Carolina south of the Cape Fear River. They originally lived in six villages. In the 1520s the Spaniard Francisco de Chicora was the first European explorer to identify the Waccamaws.

The Waccamaws were skilled in the domestication of animals, including deer. They also kept poultry and raised crops such as corn, beans, squash, melons, pumpkins, and tobacco. European diseases, however, wiped out much of the population.

By 1715 the Waccamaws were living about 100 miles northeast of Charles Town (present-day Charleston), South Carolina. At that time they numbered some 610 people in four villages. For a short time the Waccamaws fought on the side of the Yamasees in the Yamasee War (1715–1717), but they soon made peace with the British.

In 1715 British traders helped the Waccamaws build a trading post. The tribe fought the Waccamaw War of 1720 against the settlers, in the process losing some 60 of its men, women, and children. Others were deported and sold into slavery. In 1755 Cherokee and Natchez war parties killed additional Waccamaws.

In the mid-1700s the Waccamaws established a settlement near Doug Bluff, South Carolina. It is believed that they continued to exist as a separate tribe until well into the 1770s. Some Waccamaws incorporated with the Catawbas, and descendants of others remained in southeastern North Carolina. Others live in Conway, South Carolina, where they are recognized as a native nation by the state government.

THOMAS JOHN BLUMER

See also

Catawbas; Cherokees; Natchezes; Yamasees; Yamasee War

References

Lerch, Patricia B. "Indians of the Carolinas Since 1900." In *Handbook of North American Indians,* Vol. 14, *Southeast,* edited by Raymond D. Fogelson, 328–336. Washington, DC: Smithsonian Institution Press, 2004.

Lerch, Patricia B. *Waccamaw Legacy: Contemporary Indians Fight for Survival.* Tuscaloosa: University of Alabama Press, 2004.

Swanton, John. *The Indian Tribes of North America.* Washington, DC: Smithsonian Institution Press, 1952.

Wagon Box Fight
Event Date: August 2, 1867

An engagement between Native Americans and U.S. soldiers that occurred some 20 miles south of present-day Sheridan, Wyoming, during Red Cloud's War (1866–1868). On August 1, 1867, Captain James Powell with 31 men from Company C of the 27th Infantry Regiment took up protection of a 50–60-man party cutting wood for the construction of Fort Phil Kearny along the Bozeman Trail in Wyoming Territory. It was common practice to form the hauling wagons into a corral to prevent the Native Americans from running off draft animals.

Early on August 2, some 1,500 Sioux warriors led by Red Cloud attacked the camp. Some of the woodcutters and soldiers found safety in the woods, while 26 soldiers and 6 civilians took refuge in the makeshift corral formed of 14 wagons with their wheel assemblies detached; the wagons were arranged in an oval-shaped defensive perimeter some 25 by 60 feet in size. The defenders cut portholes in the wagon boxes through which to fire at the attackers. In the ensuing 5-hour fight, Powell lost 3 men killed and 2 wounded, but he reported Native American losses as 60 killed and 120 wounded; other estimates for Native American losses are much higher. The battle ended with the arrival of a relief force from Fort Phil Kearny.

That the fight turned out as it did was undoubtedly because of the recent issuance of the Springfield Model 1866 Trapdoor .50-caliber breech-loading rifle, supplied to the military in the West as a result of the earlier Fetterman Massacre. In his attack plan Red Cloud had counted on the long reloading time necessary for muzzle-loading weapons, but with the breechloaders the soldiers were able to deliver a considerably greater volume of fire.

SPENCER C. TUCKER

The Wagon Box Fight of August 2, 1867, between a detachment of the 27th Infantry Regiment and Sioux warriors led by Red Cloud. Painting by William Henry Jackson. (Denver Public Library, Western History Collection, Edward William Milligan, X-33606)

See also

Bozeman Trail; Fetterman Massacre; Fort Phil Kearny; Red Cloud; Red Cloud's War

Reference

Keenan, Jerry. *The Wagon Box Fight.* Boulder, CO: Lightning Tree, 1992.

Wahunsonacock

See Powhatan

Wakini

See Roman Nose

Walapais

See Hualapais

Walkara/Walker

See Colorow

Walking Purchase

Land agreement between the Delawares (Lenni Lenapes) and colonial Pennsylvania. From the time of first European settlement of Pennsylvania in the 1680s, the Delawares enjoyed generally good relations with the colony. However, as the colony expanded, the English began to encroach on more of the natives' land. In 1735 James Logan, the colony's chief justice and acting head of native affairs, presented Delaware chiefs with a purported copy of a 1686 deed that granted Pennsylvania most of the Lehigh Valley. The deed also seemed to grant the colony as much land west of present-day Wrightstown as a man could walk in a day and a half. The Delaware chiefs protested that they knew of no such document. Furthermore, they quickly pointed out that the colony's founder, William Penn, had guaranteed them their lands.

In 1737 Logan, despite Delaware protests, persuaded the Delawares to have the boundaries paced off in accordance with the 1686 deed. To ensure that they would acquire as much land as possible, Pennsylvania officials arranged for trees and brush to be cut, clearing a path through the woods. They also designated three men who had trained specifically for the walk to carry out the task. They would be followed by mounted men carrying food and provisions for them. The walkers ended up running most of the course, traversing an area of approximately 60 miles.

The Delawares immediately complained that the walk was not conducted in accordance with the deed. Indeed, they pointed out that the wording on the document said "walk," while the men who had paced off the land had run almost the entire way. As a consequence, the Delawares subsequently refused to vacate their lands. Unwilling to use force against the Delawares, Pennsylvania officials approached the Iroquois Confederacy for assistance in removing the Delawares. The Iroquois agreed to act as the final arbiter of native land disputes in Pennsylvania.

Now outnumbered and potentially outgunned, the Delawares had little choice but to capitulate. In August 1737 Delaware leaders met with Logan and signed the so-called Walking Purchase. During a 1742 conference in Philadelphia, the Onondaga leader Canestego ordered the Delawares to leave for Shamokin or Wyoming, Pennsylvania, and to vacate eastern Pennsylvania. Although most Delawares did go to the specified areas of Pennsylvania, many of them went farther west and settled in the Ohio Country.

ROGER M. CARPENTER

See also

Delawares; Iroquois Confederacy; Logan, John; Onondagas

References

Jennings, Francis. *The Ambiguous Iroquois Empire: The Covenant Chain Confederation of Indian Tribes with English Colonies from Its Beginnings to the Lancaster Treaty of 1744.* New York: Norton, 1984.

Wallace, Anthony F. C. *King of the Delawares: Teedyuscung, 1700–1763.* Philadelphia: University of Pennsylvania Press, 1949.

Weslager, C. A. *The Delaware Indians: A History.* New Brunswick, NJ: Rutgers University Press, 1972.

Wampanoags

Native American group that once inhabited a region ranging from the eastern shore of Narragansett Bay to the tip of Cape Cod, including the islands of Martha's Vineyard and Nantucket. The Wampanoags, or "People of the Morning Light," were farmers, fishermen, hunters, and gatherers. At the time of European contact, there were approximately 12,000 Wampanoags divided among 40 villages. The term "Pokanoket," the name of one of the principal Wampanoag villages and home to Ousa Mequin (Massasoit), the grand sachem (chief) who treated with the Pilgrims, was often mistakenly used in the early 17th century to identify the Wampanoags.

Epidemic diseases introduced by European fishermen and slave traders in the late 16th and early 17th centuries devastated the indigenous population of New England. The coastal Wampanoags were especially affected. By the time of the establishment of the English colony at Plymouth in 1620, there were perhaps no more than 2,000 Wampanoags left on the mainland. Some villages, such as Patuxet (site of Plymouth Colony), were entirely wiped out. Island Wampanoag populations fared slightly better owing to their relative isolation.

Portrait of Tewileema, the last female descendant of King Philip, in native dress, 1885. (National Anthropological Archives, Smithsonian Institution, NAA INV 00799600)

colonists who interpreted his land deals as a threat, Wamsutta was taken to the Plymouth court in 1662 and forced to defend his actions. Before he could do so, the grand sachem fell ill and died. His untimely death—there is some circumstantial evidence that he was poisoned by the English—shifted power to Wamsutta's younger brother Metacom, known to the English as King Philip.

During the course of the next decade, Metacom grew increasingly distrustful of the colonists. English encroachments onto Wampanoag land, interference in native political affairs, and establishment of Christian missions and praying towns of converted natives ultimately drove the Wampanoag grand sachem to the breaking point. The resulting conflict, known as King Philip's War (1675–1676), proved devastating to the Wampanoags as well as to the indigenous population of southern New England. One-fourth of the estimated 3,000 natives killed in the war were Wampanoags, and many of the Wampanoags who were captured or who surrendered were subsequently sold into slavery. The survivors (possibly as few as 400 people) were relocated, along with remnants of other native communities, onto Cape Cod or into praying towns. Their descendants can be found today around Gay Head on Martha's Vineyard and at Mashpee on the mainland.

ALAN C. DOWNS

See also

King Philip's War; Massasoit; Metacom; Micmacs; Narragansetts; Pequots; Pequot War; Praying Towns and Praying Indians; Wamsutta

References

Philbrick, Nathaniel. *Mayflower: A Story of Courage, Community, and War*. New York: Viking, 2006.
Steele, Ian K. *Warpaths: Invasions of North America*. New York: Oxford University Press, 1994.

In addition to the devastation wrought by disease, the Wampanoag Confederacy was weakened in the early 17th century by raids from Micmac war parties to the north and encroaching Pequots to the south. The formidable Narragansetts, essentially untouched by the epidemics because of their isolation on the islands of Narragansett Bay, grew in power and prestige during this period, ultimately forcing the Wampanoags to pay them tribute.

Seeing his power diminish, Massasoit skillfully concluded a treaty of alliance with the colonists at Plymouth in 1621. The treaty provided security for the vulnerable Englishmen in exchange for aid to the Wampanoag Confederacy in case of hostilities with their rivals. The alliance also served to keep the Wampanoags out of the Pequot War (1636–1638) and enabled Massasoit to resist Puritan efforts to Christianize his people.

The death of Massasoit in 1661 or 1662 ushered in a dramatic change in the relationship between the Wampanoags and the English colonists. Massasoit's eldest son, Wamsutta, succeeded his father as grand sachem and began selling land to colonies other than Plymouth. Seized at gunpoint by Plymouth

Wampum

Native American form of currency and exchange also used as a sign of friendship and alliance and sometimes worn as jewelry or adornment. The word "wampum" comes from the Narragansett word for "white shell beads." Wampum beads were in two colors: white (*wòmpi*) beads (*wompam*) from the heavy whelk clamshell (*meteaûhock*) and purple-black (*súki*) beads (*suckáuhock*) obtained from the growth rings of the quahog shell (*suckauanaûsuck*). The purple beads were the more valuable.

Native Americans have treasured shell beads for thousands of years; indeed, the oldest beads found in archaeological digs are quite large. Working with stone drills meant that bead manufacture was both tedious and difficult, so the beads were highly valued. Before Native American contact with Europeans, wampum often was made of wood. The resulting wooden beads were then painted white and black.

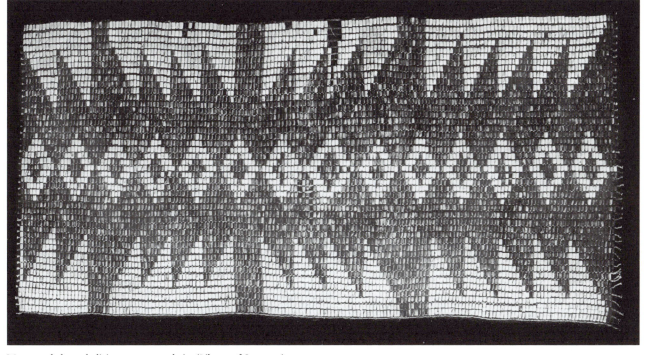

Wampum belt symbolizing a covenant chain. (Library of Congress)

With the introduction of metal awls obtained from white traders, particularly from the Dutch, the manufacture of wampum enjoyed a golden age. Small holes could be drilled in the shell, and coastal natives soon set up primitive factories. In the process they often created large shell middens (refuse heaps) of cast-off shell fragments. Because European coins of silver and other metals were scarce in the colonies, wampum soon became crucial as a medium of exchange. For instance, six feet of strung wampum beads was worth 10 shillings. Six feet of purple wampum was worth 12 shillings. Belts of wampum were worth far more than that on the open market.

Wampum was used as currency, jewelry, and ornamentation and for bonds between nations. Wampum, when exchanged, sealed a pledge. Wampum belts, such as the famous Hiawatha Belt, were used to seal the agreement that created the union of the five original Iroquois nations. A belt found in the Vatican Library represented a concordat between the Roman Catholic Church and the Micmacs of French-held Nova Scotia. This wampum belt, presented in 1610, is thought to be the oldest in existence.

THOMAS JOHN BLUMER

See also

Iroquois; Iroquois Confederacy; Micmacs; Narragansetts; Native American Trade

References

Massey, J. Earl. "Early Money Substitutes." In *Studies on Money in Early America,* edited by Eric Newman and Richard Doty, 15–24. New York: American Numismatic Society, 1976.

Taxay, Don. *Money of the American Indians and Other Primitive Currencies of the Americas.* New York: Nummas, 1970.

Wamsutta
Birth Date: Unknown
Death Date: 1662

Leader of the Wampanoags in the early 1660s. Wamsutta (known to the English as Alexander) was the son of Massasoit, the Wampanoag grand sachem (chief) who signed a peace agreement with Plymouth Colony in 1621. Massasoit kept the peace with Plymouth and occasionally sold land to the English. Wamsutta became the leader of the Wampanoags on the death of his father sometime in the period 1660–1662.

Shortly after Wamsutta came to power, Plymouth officials became concerned when he sold land to the colony at Rhode Island. Plymouth officials informed Wamsutta that he could only sell land to Plymouth Colony. Apparently this had little effect on Wamsutta, as he continued to sell land to the Rhode Island settlers.

Frustrated with what they regarded as Wamsutta's intransigence, Plymouth resorted to sterner measures in 1662, sending an armed party under Major Josiah Winslow to seize the sachem. Winslow captured Wamsutta while he was hunting and took him and his son under guard back to Plymouth. There the Plymouth authorities questioned Wamsutta at length and, according to some reports, attempted to get him to abrogate an earlier agreement that gave the Wampanoags full control over their lands. The authorities finally released Wamsutta but held his son hostage to ensure the Wampanoag leader's good behavior.

There are conflicting versions as to what happened next. Some sources claim that Wamsutta became ill while in English custody; others say that he became sick on the way home. The English claimed that his illness was brought on by hot weather, but the Wampanoags believed that the colonists poisoned him. In any case, Wamsutta died shortly thereafter.

On Wamsutta's death, his brother Metacom (known to the English as King Philip) became the sachem of the Wampanoags. If anything, Metacom was a more implacable foe of the English than his brother, launching the conflict that came to be known as King Philip's War (1675–1676).

ROGER M. CARPENTER

See also
King Philip's War; Massasoit; Metacom; Wampanoags

References
Leach, Douglas Edward. *Flintlock and Tomahawk: New England in King Philip's War.* East Orleans, MA: Parnassus Imprints, 1992.
Lepore, Jill. *The Name of War: King Philip's War and the Origins of American Identity.* New York: Knopf, 1998.

Wanduny

See Orontony

Wappingers

Conglomeration of American Indian nations in the Hudson River Valley. At the time of European contact, seven Algonquian-speaking bands, including the Wappingers proper, constituted the Wappinger Confederacy. The Wappingers were situated on the eastern side of the Hudson River Valley; the word "Wappinger" has been translated as "easterner." The French referred to them as *loups* ("wolves").

The Wappingers were an agricultural people who raised corn, beans, squash, and tobacco. They also fished and during the winter months relied on hunting. The Wappingers lived in a mix of wigwams and wooden longhouse dwellings but in the winter moved into larger fortified dwellings. Estimates vary widely as to the confederacy's population in 1600, from as many as 20,000 people to a more reasonable figure of 3,000. This great variance was due in part to the difficulty of knowing which people considered themselves Wappingers.

During the 17th century the Wappingers engaged in more than two decades of intermittent warfare with the Dutch, who settled the region. Beginning in the 1620s, Dutch settlers increasingly moved into the Hudson River Valley. The pace of European settlement picked up further in the early 1640s, putting pressure on Dutch governor-general Willem Kieft to remove or exterminate the Wappingers to open land for expansion.

Kieft therefore orchestrated a conflict—known as Kieft's War (1639–1645)—by ordering the February 1643 massacre of Wappinger men, women, and children. This sad incident came to be known as the Slaughter of the Innocents. Enraged, the Wappingers

and allied Mahicans declared war and drove the Dutch back into last-ditch fortified positions. Finally, with help from English mercenaries led by Captain John Underhill from New England, Kieft turned the tide of the war. He also brutally punished his opponents, slaughtering more than 1,600 Wappingers before concluding a peace treaty with the survivors in 1645.

Wappinger anger against the Dutch continued to simmer, and the killing of a Delaware woman in 1655 triggered the Peach War (1655). That conflict saw the Wappingers ally with the Delawares and later the Esopuses. The Dutch-Indian Wars dragged on until 1664, when Governor Petrus Stuyvesant used hostages as leverage to force the natives to surrender. When the English attacked and conquered New Netherland the same year, the Wappingers lent their support to the invaders. The Wappingers continued to support the English in future wars.

The long period of warfare proved utterly destructive to the Wappingers. The nation began a steady decline in influence, and its population plummeted. By the 1730s only a few hundred Wappingers remained in the Hudson River Valley. Some joined nearby tribes, and some settled in other areas of New York.

The last great sachem of the Wappingers was Daniel Nimham, whose people had relocated near Stockbridge, Massachusetts, in the mid-1700s. For decades he lobbied colonial and British courts to return native lands taken from his people. During the French and Indian War (1754–1763) he fought on the British side, perhaps with the hope of improving his legal claims. The effort proved fruitless. British courts denied Wappinger petitions at every turn. When the colonists went to war against Great Britain, it was thus understandable that Nimham chose to support the Patriots against the British Crown. The American Revolutionary War (1775–1783) claimed the lives of nearly half of the remaining Wappinger men. In the 19th century many of the surviving Wappingers were relocated to a reservation in Wisconsin.

ANDREW C. LANNEN

See also
Delawares; Dutch-Indian Wars; Esopuses; Esopus Wars; French and Indian War; Kieft, Willem; Kieft's War; Mahicans; Slaughter of the Innocents; Stuyvesant, Petrus

References
Kammen, Michael. *Colonial New York: A History.* New York: Scribner, 1975.
Trelease, Allen W. *Indian Affairs in Colonial New York: The Seventeenth Century.* Ithaca, NY: Cornell University Press, 1960.

War Belt

A form of wampum used in various diplomatic capacities, primarily among the Native American nations of the Northeast and the northern Plains. The colors and designs on the belts transmitted various messages. War belts thus served an important function in Native American diplomatic proceedings.

War belts were made up of dark red or purple beads. The darker-colored beads were considered more valuable in trade as well. The specific design signified the precise meaning of the belt. The belts could transmit various messages, including declarations of war, the summoning of natives to make war, or appeals for assistance in a conflict. The belts did not, however, automatically constitute an order to go to war.

JAMES R. MCINTYRE

See also
Native American Warfare; Wampum

References
Axtell, James, and William C. Sturtevant. *The European and the Indian: Essays in the Ethnohistory of Colonial North America.* New York: Oxford University Press, 1981.

Leach, Douglas Edward. *Arms for Empire: A Military History of the British Colonies in North America, 1607–1763.* New York: Macmillan, 1973.

War Club

A blunt-force weapon used by Native American warriors for close-in fighting. Usually made of maple or ironwood, the war club possessed a long shaft and a heavy ball end. The ball end could be fabricated out of wood or stone. Clubs were often decorated, sometimes with a record of the accomplishments of the warrior who carried it.

The war club and the bow and arrow were the principal weapons of the various Native Americans from New England to the Great Lakes before Europeans introduced the musket. Raiding parties throughout these regions employed the war club in their ceremonies and in combat. During the 18th century, the tomahawk gradually replaced the war club among these natives.

JAMES R. MCINTYRE

See also
Bow and Arrow; Native American Warfare; Tomahawk

References
John, Michael G. *American Woodland Indians.* Oxford, UK: Osprey, 1990.

Schultz, Eric B., and Michael J. Tougias. *King Philip's War: The History and Legacy of America's Forgotten Conflict.* Woodstock, VT: Countryman, 1999.

War Department, U.S.

Executive department responsible for U.S. defense and military operations against Native Americans during the Indian Wars. Perhaps nothing better symbolizes the relationship between the United States and Native American tribes than the decision of

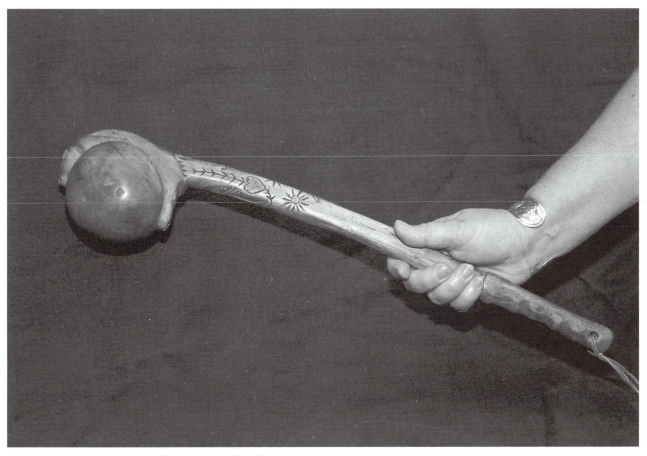

Shawnee hardwood war club with ball head and painted handle. (Native Stock Pictures)

the first Congress in 1789 to place relations with Native American tribes under the jurisdiction of the Department of War rather than the Department of State. This clearly revealed that the United States regarded Native American tribes to be in a subordinate position and potentially hostile; thus, the United States reserved the right to impose terms by military force if necessary. With the exception of campaigns by Josiah Harmar, Arthur St. Clair, and Anthony Wayne in the Old Northwest during the early 1790s, however, the War Department generally succeeded in avoiding armed conflict with Native Americans during the first two decades of its existence. During that time, Indian commissioners such as William Henry Harrison negotiated treaties that secured title to Native American lands, thereby avoiding conflict.

At the same time, the War Department controlled trade with Native Americans through the so-called factory system, whereby the department licensed merchants to trade with specific tribes. In part this was designed to prevent the sale of alcohol to Native Americans for fear that its use would lead to violence. In addition, the fortifications that the War Department established along the western frontier were designed not only to protect white settlers from Native American attack but also to prevent whites from encroaching upon Native American lands.

In the aftermath of the War of 1812, the War Department found itself in a much stronger position when dealing with Native American tribes east of the Mississippi because British influence had effectively been ended in the Old Northwest. Moreover, the Spanish sold Florida to the United States in 1819, meaning that Spain no longer exercised meaningful influence in North America. Major General Andrew Jackson, commander of the Department of the South, negotiated a series of treaties with the Cherokees, Creeks, Choctaws, and Chickasaws during and immediately after the War of 1812 that forced the tribes to cede millions of acres of land to the United States, a prelude to the removal policy that Jackson would impose as president in the 1830s and that the War Department would be charged with carrying out. It should be noted, however, that during this same period the War Department was also responsible for the federal government's efforts to assimilate Native Americans to white culture.

Between 1819 and 1842 a total of $214,500 was disbursed by the War Department through the so-called Civilization Fund to missionary societies for the purpose of educating Native American children. The program was so successful that in 1861 on the eve of the American Civil War (1861–1865), the literacy rate among the Cherokees and Choctaws was higher than that of whites living in Texas and Arkansas.

Although management of Indian affairs was officially transferred to the Interior Department when it was established in 1849, the War Department continued to play a leading role in the relationship between the United States and Native American tribes until the end of the Indian Wars in 1890. Whereas the Interior Department was responsible for operating the reservations established for tribes, the War Department was responsible for forcing tribes to move to the reservations and to remain on them. Consequently, it is not surprising that conflicts often arose between Indian agents appointed by the Interior Department and army officers stationed at posts within or near the agencies or reservations. In some cases military officers made an Indian agent's task difficult by mistakenly attacking peaceful Native Americans. A good example of this is Lieutenant Colonel David T. Chandler's attack on Delgadito's peaceful Mimbres Apache band in 1856, which infuriated Indian agent Michael Steck. In many cases, however, the War Department asserted that the incompetence and corruption of civilian Indian agents was the chief cause of unrest among tribes and that this warranted returning Indian affairs to the War Department's jurisdiction.

In many respects President Ulysses S. Grant's peace policy, which sought to rely on Quakers and other religious groups as Indian agents, was intended to combat corruption and thereby ensure that tribes remained at peace on their reservations. In the end, however, it was the military power exercised by the War Department that broke the resistance of the Plains tribes and the Apaches and established peace on white terms.

JUSTIN D. MURPHY

See also

Bureau of Indian Affairs; Grant's Peace Policy; Indian Agents; Indian Removal Act; St. Clair's Campaign; Wayne's Campaign

References

Bolt, Christine. *American Indian Policy and American Reform.* London: Unwin Hyman, 1987.

Tyler, S. Lyman. *A History of Indian Policy.* Washington, DC: U.S. Department of the Interior, 1973.

Utley, Robert M. *Frontier Regulars: The United States and the American Indian, 1866–1891.* New York: Macmillan, 1973.

Utley, Robert M. *Frontiersmen in Blue: The United States and the Indian, 1848–1865.* Lincoln: University of Nebraska Press, 1967.

War of 1812

See Native Americans and the War of 1812

Warren Wagon Train Raid
Event Date: May 18, 1871

Kiowa and Comanche assault against a wagon train near present-day Graham, Texas, on May 18, 1871. In the late 1860s, Texas was rife with tensions between Native Americans and whites. The frontier was unsafe, and raids were frequent. Furthermore, the 1867 Medicine Lodge Treaty, signed in Kansas by the Comanches, Kiowas, and U.S. officials, had not been honored by either the Native Americans or the federal government. The repeated encroachment onto reservation lands by outlaws and the extensive slaughter of the buffalo herds provoked numerous Native American raids on white settlements.

In the spring of 1871, U.S. Army commanding general General William Tecumseh Sherman conducted a tour of all Texas forts to investigate complaints of raids on the frontiers. Sherman was traveling with Inspector General Randolph Marcy and a small escort of the African American 10th Cavalry Regiment (buffalo soldiers).

Perhaps as a show of force, on May 18, 1871, more than 100 Kiowas, Comanches, and other Native Americans traveled from the Fort Sill Reservation and positioned themselves in an open area known as Salt Creek Prairie. Kiowa chiefs Satanta, Satank (Tsatangya), Big Tree, Big Bow, and Eagle Heart led the raiding party and watched silently as Sherman and his well-armed detachment passed, unaware that the nondescript military ambulance carried America's ranking soldier. Soon afterward a wagon train belonging to a freight company owned by Henry Warren heading to Fort Griffin appeared. The raiding party then attacked it suddenly and in full force. The warriors thoroughly plundered the wagons and killed and mutilated 7 teamsters. Three Kiowas were also killed during the raid. Five members of the wagon team managed to escape. After the attack, the raiding party retreated to the Fort Sill Reservation with 40 mules and other booty taken from the wagon train.

Sherman was at Fort Richardson when a wounded teamster reported the attack. The general then ordered Colonel Ranald S. Mackenzie of the 4th Calvary Regiment to search for the raiding party. Sherman also repealed his earlier order prohibiting soldiers from pursuing Native Americans living on reservations. He personally traveled to Fort Sill and found Big Tree, Satank, and Satanta boasting about their actions. Sherman and post commander Colonel Benjamin Grierson of the 10th Cavalry then confronted the leaders. Although they denied their involvement in the raid, they were arrested and taken into custody.

Mackenzie and his command subsequently led the captives in a taxing journey to Jacksboro, Texas, where they were to be tried. Old Satank, a revered member of an elite Kiowa warrior society, was able to loosen his restraints and, while attempting to escape, stabbed a guard before he was shot to death. Satanta and Big Tree were found guilty and sentenced to death, although their sentences were later commuted to life imprisonment. Ultimately the Warren Wagon Train Raid helped to doom President Ulysses S. Grant's peace policy toward the Native Americans. Sherman unleashed the army in Texas and elsewhere. Within four years with the conclusion of the Red River War (1874–1875), the Indian threat to Texas settlements was largely ended.

LORIN M. LOWRIE, PAUL G. PIERPAOLI JR., AND DAVID COFFEY

See also
Comanches; Grierson, Benjamin Henry; Kiowas; MacKenzie, Ranald Slidell; Medicine Lodge Treaty; Sherman, William Tecumseh

References
Capps, Benjamin. *The Warren Wagontrain Raid: The First Complete Account of an Historic Indian Attack and Its Aftermath.* Dallas, TX: Southern Methodist University Press, 1989.
McConnell, Joseph Carroll. *The West Texas Frontier; Or, A Descriptive History of Early Times in Western Texas.* Jacksboro, TX: Gazette Print, 1933.
Meadows, William C. *Kiowa, Apache, and Comanche Military Societies: Enduring Veterans, 1800 to the Present.* Austin: University of Texas Press, 1999.

Washakie
Birth Date: ca. 1798–1804
Death Date: February 20, 1900

Shoshone leader who allied with Plenty Coups' Crow tribe to assist the U.S. Army in its campaign against the Cheyennes, Sioux, and others who were defined by the United States as "hostile" during the final phases of the Plains Wars beginning in the 1870s. Various accounts place Washakie's birth at between 1798 and 1804, likely in the Bitterroot Valley of Montana. His father, Pasego, was of mixed blood; his mother was Shoshone. Pasego died when Washakie was a child. As a young man, Washakie developed his skills as a warrior by riding for several years with a band of Bannocks. Washakie was renowned for his buffalo-hunting skills and was for a time a key figure in the regional fur trade.

By the late 1840s, large numbers of gold seekers on their way to California were passing through the Shoshone homeland in present-day Wyoming, but few settled in the area. Soon thereafter a large party of Mormons under Brigham Young settled on the southern edge of the Shoshone homeland at the Great Salt Lake.

Shoshone chief Washakie (ca. 1798–1900) allied his people with the U.S. Army against the Cheyennes and Sioux in the last of the wars on the Great Plains of the 1870s. (National Archives)

Washakie became a friend of Young's and helped his fledgling settlement; Washakie converted to Mormonism in 1880. In 1851 Washakie rejected the terms of a proposed treaty that would have diminished Shoshone lands and allied for a time with the Mormons before the federal government asserted authority over them as part of Utah's bid for statehood. In 1869 Washakie negotiated the Treaty of Fort Bridger, which set aside 3 million acres for the Shoshones in their traditional homeland.

By the mid-1870s the Plains Wars (including the Great Sioux War) were drawing to a close. At the time, Washakie had allied with the Crows and the U.S. Army at the Little Bighorn in Montana. Plenty Coups, Washakie's Crow ally, worried that Brigadier General George Crook was not prepared for Crazy Horse's Lakota Sioux when they met in battle, along with Washakie's Shoshone, at the Battle of the Rosebud (June 17, 1876). Plenty Coups was correct. Crazy Horse staggered Crook and his Native American allies in a fight that presaged Custer's disastrous defeat at the Little Bighorn nine days later.

Despite his general support for the white settlers, Washakie and his people experienced their share of troubles with broken treaties. In 1870 land that had been set aside for the Shoshones and Bannocks by a treaty signed in 1864 was demanded for white settlement. Many young Shoshone warriors called for war, but Washakie forbade it. He allied with the whites out of necessity, not choice, and chafed at being confined on a reservation.

During Washakie's later years, his eldest son (also named Washakie) was killed in a drunken brawl with a white man. The elder Washakie was grieved by the fact that his son had passed onto the Spirit World in disgrace but did not seek retribution. Washakie also opposed the Ghost Dance, but he urged his people to continue the Sun Dance, which they had borrowed from the Sioux.

Washakie was such a source of support for the U.S. Army that in 1878 it named a frontier fort after him in the Wind River Valley. In 1897 he became an Episcopalian. Washakie died on February 20, 1900, on the Wind River Reservation in west-central Wyoming. He was buried with military honors accorded an army captain in the post cemetery at Fort Washakie, the first-known Native American to be so honored. Two statues of Washakie memorialize him in the Salt Lake City area. The most notable is located downtown and is part of the Brigham Young Monumental Group, which includes statues of other individuals (all American nonnatives) who gave great aid to initial Mormon settlement in the Salt Lake Valley.

BRUCE E. JOHANSEN

See also

Crows; Ghost Dance; Great Sioux War; Little Bighorn, Battle of the; Rosebud, Battle of the; Shoshones; Sioux

References

Armstrong, Virginia Irving. *I Have Spoken: American History through the Voices of the Indians.* Chicago: Swallow, 1971.
Hebard, Grace Raymond. *Washakie: Chief of the Shoshones.* Lincoln: University of Nebraska Press, 1995.

Washington, George
Birth Date: February 22, 1732
Death Date: December 14, 1799

Commander in chief of the Continental Army during the American Revolutionary War (1775–1783) and first president of the United States (1789–1797). Born in Westmoreland County, Virginia, on February 22, 1732, George Washington was one of seven children of Augustine Washington, a wealthy farmer. Washington had little formal education. His mother blocked his plans to join the Royal Navy, and he became a surveyor in Culpepper County in 1749, spending several years surveying Virginia's western lands. With his brother Lawrence's assistance, Washington received an appointment as a major in the Virginia Militia in 1752. Following Lawrence's death in July 1752 and that of Lawrence's daughter in September, Washington inherited the family estate of Mount Vernon.

Washington became involved in the struggle between the British and French for supremacy in North America when he volunteered to investigate reports of French incursions into the Ohio River Valley from October 1753 to January 1754. When Virginia lieutenant governor Robert Dinwiddie ordered formation of a regiment to oppose the French in the west in the spring of 1754, Washington received a commission as lieutenant colonel of militia and was appointed second-in-command. On the death of the colonel in May, Washington assumed command and led 160 men across the Alleghenies. His preemptive attack on the French at Great Meadows on May 28 in effect began the French and Indian War (1754–1763). The French then sought out Washington's force and obliged it to surrender at hastily constructed Fort Necessity on July 4.

Allowed to return home with his men, Washington learned that the Virginia Militia would be broken into independent companies. Facing the prospect of reduction in rank to captain, he resigned his commission in October 1754. In the spring of 1755 Washington volunteered to accompany British major general Edward Braddock as aide-de-camp without rank on the latter's ill-fated expedition against French Fort Duquesne, located at present-day Pittsburgh, Pennsylvania. The British met disaster in the Battle of Monongahela on July 9. In the battle Washington exhibited both leadership and personal courage and helped bring the remnants of Braddock's force to safety.

Refusing to blame Braddock and winning wide public approval for his own role in the fiasco, Washington in August 1755 accepted command of the Virginia regiment as a full colonel, training the men and supervising the construction and manning of a number of western frontier forts, which then turned back a number of Indian raids in 1756 and 1757. Washington established an excellent reputation, leading by example and manifesting concern for the welfare of his men.

Washington failed in his attempts to secure incorporation of the Virginia regiment into the British Army, but he commanded a brigade of some 700 provincial troops as part of Brigadier General John Forbes's successful expedition against Fort Duquesne (July–November 1758), gaining valuable command experience in the process.

Resigning his military post in December 1758, Washington married the wealthy widow Martha Custis and was elected to the Virginia House of Burgesses. He also represented Virginia at the First and Second Continental Congresses in Philadelphia in 1774 and 1775. With the beginning of the American Revolutionary War in April 1775, Washington lobbied for military command. Because he was native-born, had some military experience, and was from the wealthiest colony (Virginia), on June 15 Congress named Washington the commander in chief of the newly created Army of the United Colonies, also known as the Continental Army. His formidable leadership skills, recognition of the primacy of civil authority in Congress, reputation for honesty, humility, and ability to pick able subordinates all proved to be valuable assets. Merely keeping the Continental Army together was a considerable achievement, but Washington worked hard to train the army. Within three years he had developed a small well-disciplined force capable of meeting the British on equal terms in selective battles.

Although Washington was successful in causing the British to evacuate Boston on March 17, 1776, the resulting New York campaign was a near disaster, fueled in part by his mistakes. Forced to withdraw across New Jersey, Washington escaped across the Delaware River into Pennsylvania. He then risked everything by recrossing the Delaware to launch a daring raid on the British outpost at Trenton, New Jersey, and was successful on December 26. He then went on to defeat the British at Princeton on January 3, 1777. These two victories restored confidence both in the patriot cause and in Washington as a military leader.

Although he actively sought the advice of his subordinates and usually heeded it, Washington was an aggressive commander when opportunities arose. Defeated before Philadelphia at Brandywine Creek on September 11, 1777, he mounted a surprise attack on the British camp outside of Philadelphia at Germantown on October 4. The attack failed but only because of inept subordinates and an overly complex plan. At the same time Washington, recognizing an important opportunity, sent units north to assist in the capture of an entire invading British army under Major General John Burgoyne at Saratoga, New York, on October 17. Washington held his army together, despite the suffering of the encampment at Valley Forge during the bitter winter of 1777–1778, and then on June 28, 1778, attacked the British on their withdrawal from Philadelphia at Monmouth Court House, New Jersey, where his inept subordinate Major General Charles Lee threw away a splendid chance for victory.

Informed of the American victory at Saratoga, the French signed a formal treaty of alliance in February 1778 and were at war with Britain that June. Washington was able to take advantage of the arrival in North American waters of a powerful French fleet under Admiral François Joseph Paul, Comte de Grasse. Marching south from New York with French land forces under Lieutenant General Jean Baptiste Donatien de Vimeur, Comte de Rochambeau, Washington laid siege to the British army under the command of Lieutenant General Charles, Earl Cornwallis, at Yorktown and after a month-long siege (September 26–October 19, 1781) forced it to surrender. This defeat brought the downfall of the ministry in London and a new policy on the part of the British government, leading to the end of the war and the Treaty of Paris of September 3, 1783. Washington quelled a would-be mutiny among his officers over pay at Newburgh, New York, during February–March 1783 and then resigned his commission in December to return to his beloved Mount Vernon.

Washington was selected as president of the convention that produced the U.S. Constitution in 1787. He then became the first president of the United States in April 1789. His leadership was invaluable in establishing the new institutions of government and making them work effectively. Granted the rank of lieutenant general by Congress, Washington took field command of militia forces during the Whiskey Rebellion of 1794. His leadership and calls for restraint proved invaluable in ending the crisis.

During Little Turtle's War (Northwest Indian War) of 1785–1795, Washington acted decisively to secure the Old Northwest Territory, authorizing a force of 300 regulars and 1,000 militiamen to be dispatched to the region in the autumn of 1790. After the expedition's failure Washington, in conjunction with Congress, expanded the army in the spring of 1791 and then that summer sent to the region a larger force under the command of Major General Arthur St. Clair. On November 4, 1791, St Clair's force was defeated at the Battle of the Wabash. The next year Washington authorized Colonel John Hardin to engage in peace talks with the Shawnees. However, Hardin's death at the hands of Shawnee warriors served only to raise tensions in the region.

Determined to defeat the Native Americans, Washington tapped Major General Anthony "Mad Anthony" Wayne to head the new 5,000-man Legion of the United States. Wayne thoroughly trained the legion and then systematically moved against the Native Americans. He dealt a decisive blow to the hostile tribes at the Battle of Fallen Timbers on August 20, 1794. The defeat effectively ended Little Turtle's War and buoyed Washington tremendously. In 1795 he instructed delegates to negotiate the Treaty of Greenville, which saw all of the disputed Indian lands in the Old Northwest ceded to the United States.

Refusing to stand for a third term, Washington retired to Mount Vernon in 1797 and died there on December 14, 1799.

SPENCER C. TUCKER

See also

Braddock's Campaign; Fallen Timbers, Battle of; French and Indian War; Greenville, Treaty of; Little Turtle's War; Old Northwest Territory; Shawnees; St. Clair, Arthur; Wabash, Battle of the; Wayne, Anthony

References

Ellis, Joseph J. *His Excellency: George Washington.* New York: Knopf, 2004.

Flexner, James T. *George Washington in the American Revolution, 1775–1783.* Boston: Little, Brown, 1968.

Lengal, Edward G. *General George Washington: A Military Life.* New York: Random House, 2005.

Washita, Battle of the
Event Date: November 27, 1868

U.S. Army attack on a Southern Cheyenne village in western Indian Territory (Oklahoma) two miles from present-day Cheyenne. A tranquil bend in the Washita River was the site of a surprise winter attack on November 27, 1868, by the U.S. 7th Cavalry Regiment under the command of Lieutenant Colonel George Armstrong Custer on Chief Black Kettle's peaceful band of Southern Cheyennes. Black Kettle, a survivor of the Sand Creek Massacre four years earlier, died along with his wife and 101 other men, women, and children.

Custer's attack was the result of the U.S. Army's evolving strategy for imposing the government's reservation policy on noncompliant Indians of the Great Plains. In October 1867 peace commissioners from the U.S. government met with representatives of the Arapahos, Comanches, Kiowas, Kiowa Apaches, and Southern Cheyennes in a grove of trees along Medicine Lodge Creek, 60 miles south of Fort Larned, Kansas. There the principal leaders of the southern Plains tribes signed treaties promising to move onto two reservations in western Indian Territory and to take no action to impede the construction of nearby railroads, wagon roads, and government facilities. In exchange for their compliance, signatory tribes were promised agricultural implements, clothing, education for their children, annuity payments, and the prohibition of white settlement on reservation land.

Of the five nations represented at the Medicine Lodge Council, the Southern Cheyennes were the least united in support of the treaty. Black Kettle was reluctant to sign the document until the militant Cheyenne Dog Soldiers agreed to its terms. Unable to convince war chief Roman Nose and his band of the merits of peace under the terms of the treaty, Black Kettle nevertheless affixed his mark to the paper. Despite the lack of a unified following, the Cheyenne chief settled peaceably into reservation life below the Arkansas River.

Throughout the winter of 1867–1868, food stores from the autumn buffalo hunts sustained the reservation Cheyennes. As spring approached and supplies dwindled, the promised government support materialized in insufficient quantities. Most disconcerting for the Cheyennes was the absence of the promised guns and ammunition needed for hunting. Notwithstanding the best efforts of Agent Edward W. Wynkoop to reassure the disaffected, some young Cheyenne men, angered by the duplicity of the white peace commissioners, ventured northward away from the reservation to join Roman Nose and the leaders of other resistant factions.

In response to the growing defiance of the government's reservation policy among Native American peoples on the southern Plains, Major General Philip Sheridan, commander of the Department of the Missouri, with the support of Lieutenant General William Tecumseh Sherman, commander of the Military Division of the Missouri, orchestrated a strategy to force submission. Sheridan envisioned a winter operation utilizing converging columns of cavalry and infantry to round up warriors whose limited supplies and grass-fed ponies would make them virtually immobile and susceptible to capture. Accordingly, on November 18, 1868, Major Andrew W. Evans left Fort Bascom, New Mexico, with 563 men and marched eastward down the South Canadian River. Two weeks later Major Eugene Carr and 650 men left Fort Lyon, Colorado, and moved southward (guided by Buffalo Bill Cody) toward Antelope Hills in Indian Territory. The third and largest column, comprising the 800 troops of the 7th U.S. Cavalry under the command of Custer, departed Camp Supply, a depot on the North Canadian River 100 miles south of Fort Dodge, Kansas, on November 23 and headed south toward the Washita River. Sheridan instructed Custer to follow a fresh trail in the snow, suspecting its creators to be a Cheyenne raiding party returning from Kansas.

That same autumn as Sheridan put the finishing touches on his planned winter campaign, Black Kettle and his followers set up an encampment on a bend in the Washita River 40 miles east of the Antelope Hills. Consisting of 51 lodges, the village was populated by Cheyenne women, children, and elders as well as recently returned young warriors who were now more willing to accept the peaceful ways of Black Kettle after Roman Nose's death on September 17 at the Battle of Beecher's Island. Downriver, Arapaho, Kiowa, and additional Cheyenne camps dotted the landscape. Learning that U.S. troops were on the move, Black Kettle and other Cheyenne and Arapaho leaders traveled 100 miles down the Washita River Valley to Fort Cobb to meet with the garrison's commander, Brigadier General William B. Hazen, to seek protection for their people. To their dismay, the heretofore convivial Hazen maintained that he lacked the authority to allow the Cheyenne and Arapaho bands to move closer to the fort and instructed Black Kettle to return to his camp.

On November 26 Custer's undetected column drew near the bend in the Washita River occupied by the Cheyenne chief and his band. The trail that Custer's column followed led directly to the encampment. Without bothering to adequately determine the size and strength of his foe, Custer ordered an attack for the following day. Just before daybreak on November 27, troops from the 7th Cavalry, with the regimental band playing "Garryowen," charged into Black Kettle's sleeping village from four directions. The shaken and surprised Cheyennes could do nothing except run for safety. A few warriors vainly fought back. Black Kettle and his wife

Lieutenant Colonel George Armstrong Custer leads an attack by the 7th Cavalry against a Cheyenne encampment along the Washita River on November 27, 1868, known as the Battle of the Washita. Reproduction of an 1878 painting by James E. Taylor. (Library of Congress)

attempted to escape across a ford in the river, only to be gunned down in the mud. Within 10 minutes, the 7th Cavalry troops controlled the village.

Estimates vary, but it is probable that 103 Cheyenne men, women, and children died in the attack, while 53 women and children were taken captive. For his part, Custer lost 2 officers and 19 enlisted men, most of whom were under the command of Major Joel H. Elliott. Attempting to corral a group of Indians fleeing downriver, Elliot and his men were themselves surrounded and killed by members of the nearby Arapaho and Cheyenne camps who were coming to Black Kettle's aid.

As more and more mounted warriors arrived at the scene, Custer's troops set up a defensive perimeter and then systematically set fire to the lodges, destroying the Cheyennes' winter supply of food and clothing. The cavalry likewise slaughtered more than 800 Cheyenne ponies and mules. To remove his command from an increasingly foreboding environment, Custer abandoned efforts to locate Major Elliott, feigned an attack in the late afternoon against

Indian encampments farther downriver, and then escaped back across the river after dark. The 7th Cavalry returned triumphantly to Camp Supply on December 2, much to the satisfaction of General Sheridan.

More of a massacre than a battle, Washita proved to be a debilitating blow to the Southern Cheyennes. With their winter supplies destroyed along with their herd of mules and ponies, the majority of the Cheyenne bands found themselves with little choice but to submit to reservation life. Perhaps of equal consequence, the Battle of the Washita demonstrated to the noncompliant tribes of the Plains that winter no longer provided the element of security that it once had.

ALAN C. DOWNS

See also

Beecher Island, Battle of; Black Kettle; Carr, Eugene Asa; Cheyennes, Southern; Cody, William Frederick; Custer, George Armstrong; Dog Soldiers; Medicine Lodge Treaty; Roman Nose; Sand Creek Massacre; Sheridan, Philip Henry; Sherman, William Tecumseh

References

Greene, Jerome A. *Washita: The U.S. Army and the Southern Cheyennes, 1867–1869*. Norman: University of Oklahoma Press, 2004.

Utley, Robert M. *Frontier Regulars: The United States and the American Indian, 1866–1891*. New York: Macmillan, 1973.

Watchful Fox

See Keokuk

Watie, Stand

Birth Date: 1806
Death Date: September 9, 1871

Cherokee leader and the only Native American to hold the rank of brigadier general in the Confederate Army. Stand Watie (also known as Isaac S. Watie) was born near present-day Rome, Georgia, in 1806 and was named Degataga (meaning to stay or stand firm). He was educated at a Moravian mission school in Springplace, Georgia, and subsequently served as a clerk for the Cherokee Supreme Court. He was also Speaker of the Cherokee National Council.

In the early and mid-1830s when the Cherokee Nation split over the decision to accede to forcible removal to present-day Oklahoma by the U.S. government, Watie sided with the faction that opted to move west and vacate the Cherokees' ancestral lands in Georgia. Watie was one of the signatories to the 1835 Treaty of New Echota, which provided federal compensation for Cherokee lands in the East and established land for their relocation in the Indian Territory. Watie and others who supported the removal believed that it was the only way to keep the Cherokee Nation from being irreparably harmed by white encroachment. Many vehemently rejected Watie's reasoning and asserted that personal greed fueled his decision.

Once he had resettled in the Indian Territory, Watie became a successful planter and the de facto leader of the Cherokee faction in Oklahoma. When the American Civil War (1861–1865) began the Cherokee Nation declared its neutrality, but by late August 1861 Watie decided to ally his Cherokee faction with the Confederacy. He proceeded to assemble a volunteer regiment, the Cherokee Mounted Rifles, and was named colonel of the unit.

Operating mostly in the Indian Territory, Watie proved to be an intrepid cavalry raider who enjoyed great success in numerous hit-and-run guerrilla-style raids against Union troops and their Native American allies. Watie's force played a significant role in the Battle of Pea Ridge, Arkansas (March 7–8, 1862), capturing Union artillery and covering the ultimate Confederate retreat. Indeed, Watie virtually ensured that the war in the region would be waged using unconventional warfare, and in May 1864 he was promoted to brigadier general for his efforts.

In June 1864 Watie led a successful raid on the Union steamer *J. R. Williams* that was plying the Arkansas River. The taking of

Cherokee leader Stand Watie was, during the American Civil War, the only Native American to serve as a Confederate brigadier general. (National Archives)

that vessel resulted in the capture of valuable Union supplies estimated to be worth some $120,000. On September 19, 1864, Watie's force seized a major Union wagon supply train at the Second Battle of Cabin Creek; the loot from that raid is believed to have been worth more than $1 million.

Watie's daring and successful raids bolstered Confederate morale in the West and won him many accolades from his superiors. He was the last Confederate general to surrender to the Union, laying down his arms on June 23, 1865.

After the war Watie returned to Oklahoma and again took up his successful planting enterprise. In 1866 he served as a delegate for the Southern Cherokee faction during the negotiations that led to the 1866 Cherokee Reconstruction Treaty. After that he retired from public life. Watie died in present-day Delaware County, Oklahoma, on September 9, 1871.

PAUL G. PIERPAOLI JR.

See also

Cherokees; Native Americans and the Civil War; Trail of Tears

References

Cunningham, Frank. *General Stand Watie's Confederate Indians*. Norman: University of Oklahoma Press, 1998.

Franks, Kenny A. *Stand Watie and the Agony of the Cherokee Nation*. Memphis: Memphis State University Press, 1979.

Waunigsootshkau

See Red Bird

Wayne, Anthony
Birth Date: January 1, 1745
Death Date: December 16, 1796

Continental Army officer and commander of the Legion of the United States. Born on January 1, 1745, in Waynesborough, Chester County, Pennsylvania, Anthony Wayne was educated at the Academy in Philadelphia but left school to become a surveyor. He was then a tanner in his father's business.

Elected to the Pennsylvania colonial assembly in 1774, Wayne resigned upon the outbreak of the American Revolutionary War (1775–1783) to raise a regiment of volunteers. Although he had no formal military training, in January 1776 Wayne was commissioned a colonel in the 4th Pennsylvania Regiment. He was wounded in the Battle of Trois Rivières (June 8, 1776), and his action in covering the retreat of U.S. forces from Canada won him promotion to brigadier general in February 1777.

Wayne again distinguished himself in the Battle of Brandywine Creek (September 11, 1777) but was caught by surprise in a British night attack on his camp at Paoli (September 21, 1777). He requested a court-martial, which cleared him of any negligence. He earned praise for his conduct in the Battle of Germantown (October 4, 1777) and performed well in the Battle of Monmouth (June 28, 1778), leading the initial attack and then defending against the British counterattack. He then led a bayonet attack that carried the British position at Stony Point, New York, on July 16, 1779, an action that won him the nickname "Mad Anthony." In January 1781 he ably defused a mutiny of the Pennsylvania line. During the latter stages of the Revolution, Wayne participated in the Yorktown Campaign (May–October 19, 1781) and then campaigned with Major General Nathanael Greene in Georgia until the British evacuated Savannah in July 1782. Wayne was brevetted a major general in September 1783.

After the war Wayne retired to farm in Pennsylvania. He was a member of the Pennsylvania State Assembly in 1785 and was elected to the state convention that ratified the U.S. Constitution. He then relocated to Georgia to manage landholdings that the state had awarded him for his services as Continental Army commander there in 1782. Unsuccessful in securing election to the U.S. Senate from Georgia, he did win election to the U.S. House of Representatives from that state in 1791, but the election was subsequently declared invalid because of voting irregularities.

In April 1792 following two disastrous expeditions against the Native Americans of the Northwest by Brigadier General Josiah Harmar and Northwest Territory governor Arthur St. Clair, President George Washington recalled Wayne as a major general to command the newly authorized 5,000-man Legion of the United States.

Wayne took advantage of extended negotiations with the Native Americans to establish a camp at Legionville in western Pennsylvania and properly train the army. He stressed drill, proper sanitation, field fortifications, and marksmanship. Finally in the summer Wayne led the army, supported by Kentucky militia, west into the

Major General Anthony Wayne, a thorough disciplinarian and meticulous planner, led the Legion of the United States in defeating a Native American force in the Battle of Fallen Timbers on August 20, 1794. Wayne is rightly regarded as the father of the modern U.S. Army. (National Archives)

Ohio Country. In the Battle of Fallen Timbers (August 20, 1794) he defeated Native American forces led by Shawnee chief Blue Jacket. This victory broke the power of the Native Americans in the eastern part of the Old Northwest and did much to restore the prestige of the U.S. Army, which had been so badly tarnished during the earlier Harmar and St. Clair expeditions. As a result Wayne is often called the father of the new U.S. regular army. A year later Wayne concluded the Treaty of Greenville with the Native Americans.

In 1796 Wayne secured the relinquishment to the United States of British forts in the Great Lakes area. While on a military excursion from Fort Detroit to Pennsylvania, Wayne died suddenly at Presque Isle (Erie), Pennsylvania, on December 16, 1796.

PAUL G. PIERPAOLI JR. AND SPENCER C. TUCKER

See also

Blue Jacket; Fallen Timbers, Battle of; Greenville, Treaty of; Harmar, Josiah; Legion of the United States; Little Turtle's War; Old Northwest Territory; St. Clair, Arthur; Washington, George

References

Fox, Joseph L. *Anthony Wayne: Washington's Reliable General.* Chicago: Adams, 1988.

Gaff, Alan D. *Bayonets in the Wilderness: Anthony Wayne's Legion in the Old Northwest.* Norman: University of Oklahoma Press, 2004.

Nelson, Paul David. *Anthony Wayne: Soldier of the Early Republic.* Bloomington: Indiana University Press, 1985.

Wayne's Campaign
Start Date: October 1793
End Date: August 1794

Successful U.S. military campaign occurring from October 1793 to August 1794 in the Ohio Country against Native Americans commanded by Major General Anthony ("Mad Anthony") Wayne. The campaign culminated in the Battle of Fallen Timbers (August 20, 1794), a resounding victory for U.S. forces that essentially ended American Indian resistance in the region.

During the early 1790s, the United States faced open conflict with Native Americans who lived in the Northwest Territory, encompassing the future states of Ohio, Michigan, and Indiana. Many Native Americans in the region resisted the settlement of whites and the selling of large tracts of what they believed to be their ancestral lands. After Brigadier General Josiah Harmar and Major General Arthur St. Clair had been soundly defeated by Native American warriors led by Little Turtle in 1790 and 1791, respectively, President George Washington decided to support another expedition into Ohio, this time led by Wayne.

To provide adequate military resources, Congress expanded U.S. forces and instituted a complete reorganization of the U.S. Army. Known as the Legion of the United States with an authorized strength of 5,000 men, the resulting force was a combined arms organization of infantry, cavalry, and artillery under a single commander. In a training camp near Pittsburgh, Pennsylvania, known as Legionville, Wayne carefully planned the campaign and prepared his army through insistence on rigid discipline and regular organized training.

In October 1793 Wayne led his force on a methodical march through the wilderness along the future Ohio and Indiana border. As the legion advanced, Wayne had the men build forts and blockhouses, among them Fort Greenville, to secure the supply lines back to the Ohio River. When the legion reached the site of St. Clair's defeat (which had occurred on November 4, 1791), Wayne halted his forward movement and established Fort Recovery as a base for beginning the campaign anew in 1794.

In July 1794 the legion was joined by a mounted unit of the Kentucky Militia, which brought the total American force to about 2,700 men. On July 28 Wayne resumed his march north, each night ensuring that his camp was fortified against surprise attack. By August 16 the legion had advanced to the headwaters of the Maumee River. Wayne's troops had burned Native American crops and villages as they marched, trying to force the warriors to make a stand. Finally a Native American force of about 2,200 warriors led by Shawnee chief Blue Jacket sought to ambush the Americans in an area of timber that had been felled by a tornado. Sensing imminent battle, Wayne ordered the construction of Fort Deposit to protect his baggage, causing the warriors to wait several more days in their ambush position. Some grew discouraged and drifted off, while others, who followed a custom of not eating before a battle, became hungry.

On August 20 the warriors fired upon the legion's scouting party and began what became known as the Battle of Fallen Timbers. Wayne deployed the legion into two lines of infantry, ordered them to fire, and then advanced with bayonets. The Native Americans fired once but then fled from the advancing Americans. The mounted militia accelerated the rout, and within an hour the legion had secured a decisive victory. Although the legion lost 26 killed and 87 wounded, the Native Americans suffered about twice as many casualties, including a number of chiefs.

Following the battle, many escaping warriors sought refuge at Fort Miami, an illegal British fort located on U.S. territory, but the British commander refused to shelter them. The defeat at Fallen Timbers and the lack of British support ultimately forced the Native Americans into peace negotiations. On August 3, 1795, the Treaty of Fort Greenville established new frontier boundaries between the United States and the northwestern tribes, who were forced to cede two-thirds of Ohio to the Americans.

Wayne's campaign to Fallen Timbers provided a solid training experience for future national leaders such as William Henry Harrison, who would apply those campaign techniques in later confrontations with the Native Americans. The campaign also did much to restore the prestige of the U.S. Army that had suffered greatly in the previous campaigns of Harmar and St. Clair.

STEVEN J. RAUCH

See also

Fallen Timbers, Battle of; Greenville, Treaty of; Harmar, Josiah; Legion of the United States; St. Clair, Arthur; St. Clair's Campaign; Wayne, Anthony

References

Gaff, Alan D. *Bayonets in the Wilderness: Anthony Wayne's Legion in the Old Northwest.* Norman: University of Oklahoma Press, 2004.

Sword, Wiley. *President Washington's Indian War: The Struggle for the Old Northwest, 1790–1795.* Norman: University of Oklahoma Press, 1985.

Weapons, Edged
See Edged Weapons

Weatherford, William
Birth Date: ca. 1780
Death Date: March 9, 1824

Prominent Creek leader. Born in Creek territory (present-day Alabama) around 1780, William Weatherford (also known as Red Eagle) was the son of Charles Weatherford, a prominent Scottish trader from Georgia, and Sehoy III, a member of the influential Creek Wind Clan. Although only part Creek, Weatherford was raised among the Creeks and rejected white culture and civilization.

By 1812 the Creek Confederation had badly fragmented. Urged by Tecumseh to join a Pan-Indian confederacy to resist American expansion and encouraged by the outbreak of the War of 1812, the Creek faction known as the Red Sticks demanded war against American settlers in Creek territory. Initially counseling neutrality, by the summer of 1813 Weatherford reversed his position and sided with the Red Sticks.

On August 30, 1813, Weatherford and Red Stick leader Peter McQueen led 729 warriors against Fort Mims, roughly 40 miles north of Mobile, Alabama. The fort had become a refuge for white settlers—men, women, and children—attempting to escape the Red Sticks. Although their force successfully captured the fort, neither McQueen nor Weatherford was able to maintain control of their men. The unhappy result was the massacre of 250 to 275 settlers. Upon receiving news of the massacre, Tennessee governor Willie Blount dispatched the state militia under Major General Andrew Jackson to defend white settlers in the area.

Following the Fort Mims Massacre, Jackson and his forces pursued Weatherford and the Red Sticks, striking them at Tallushatchee and Talladega. Finding himself one of the last defenders at the Battle of Econochaca (December 23, 1813), Weatherford managed to escape capture by charging his horse off a 100-foot bluff into the Alabama River below. He was not present for the final defeat of the Red Sticks at the Battle of Horseshoe Bend (March 27, 1814).

With the defeat of the Red Sticks, Weatherford refused to flee south into Spanish Florida. In April 1814 he rode unrecognized into Fort Jackson in Alabama and offered his surrender for the lives of the Creek women and children still hiding in the woods. Impressed by Weatherford's bravery, Jackson spared the Creek leader's life. Weatherford lived out the remainder of his life as a successful planter in Monroe County, Alabama. He died on March 9, 1824, at his Monroe County home.

ROBERT W. MALICK

See also

Creeks; Creek War; Fort Mims, Battle of; Horseshoe Bend, Battle of; Jackson, Andrew; McQueen, Peter; Native Americans and the War of 1812; Red Sticks; Tallushatchee, Battle of

References

Eggleston, George Cary. *Red Eagle and the Wars with the Creek Indians of Alabama.* New York: Dodd, Meade, 1878.

Griffith, Benjamin W. *McIntosh and Weatherford, Creek Indian Leaders.* Tuscaloosa: University of Alabama Press, 1988.

Remini, Robert Vincenti. *Andrew Jackson and His Indian Wars.* New York: Penguin, 2001.

Wells Fargo

Delivery, transportation, and financial services firm that was particularly important in the western United States. Initially begun as a parcel delivery service that spanned the continent, Wells Fargo branched out into subsidiary businesses, including passenger transportation, currency exchange, and mail delivery services. Founded by Henry Wells and William Fargo on March 18, 1852, in New York City as a joint stock association to deliver express services, the company would contribute to communications and transportation on a national scale. In 1850 both men had founded American Express, with which Wells Fargo also shared many board members.

Express companies offered their customers more reliable and secure delivery of packages, which in the era of continued westward expansion and the California Gold Rush was a very profitable business. Fargo was the only founder destined to become president of the company, albeit briefly, and the only one to visit operational offices in the West. Both founders had served as messengers in their previous careers.

Wells Fargo's principal markets were west of the Mississippi River, in particular in the states west of the Rocky Mountains. The company opened its first office on July 13, 1852, in San Francisco, California, with two agents acting on its behalf. Within two years the company had more than 51 offices mostly in California, which accounted for its success. Agents were hired carefully, and they were invariably trusted and active members of their communities. They had the ability to transact the business of the company, including shipping gold, issuing bills of exchange that could be redeemed at other offices, and sending and receiving mail on behalf of patrons, which caused controversy with the U.S. Postal Service. Wells Fargo placed an additional stamp or frank on letters and delivered them at a premium cost. Despite the higher price, however, this was how the vast majority of mail was delivered in California.

Although the blood-red oval-shaped Concord stage coach has come to symbolize the Wells Fargo brand, the company first contracted with the Overland Stage Coach Company, which Wells Fargo later bought and briefly ran between 1865 and 1869. Wells Fargo dominated the stage coach business from 1858 to 1869, transporting passengers, mail, and parcels over a 2,000-mile route with 153 stations between California and Kansas, at which horses would be exchanged or, in the case of home stations, at which meals were served and drivers could rest or change out. Passengers rarely traveled the entire route, which was expensive, dangerous, and uncomfortable. Nevertheless, the stage coach was the most reliable form of transportation to the West until the completion of the transcontinental railroad in 1869, which did more to influence the remaining years of Wells Fargo as an express company than any other event in its history.

With the completion of the transcontinental railroad, passengers, parcels, and mail had a safer and faster means of transportation compared with the stage coach. The railroads would not carry the mail for Wells Fargo, carrying it instead under the Pacific Union Express Company brand and forcing Wells Fargo to reorganize in 1872 and move its headquarters to San Francisco. Lloyd Lewis, who had tried to engage in a joint venture with Wells Fargo during construction of the transcontinental railroad, led the takeover. He ultimately became one of the longest-serving presidents of the firm and oversaw the largest expansion of the number of offices during his 20-year tenure.

Stretched out across the West in largely remote areas, the stage coach stations and the stage coaches themselves were targets of

Wells Fargo & Co.'s Express Office in Virginia City, Nevada, 1866. (Library of Congress)

both white marauders and Indian attacks. Often the remains of victims were not cleared from the trail, and drivers were advised not to tell the tales of previous attacks, particularly if there were women and children traveling in the party. Indian attacks on Wells Fargo stations and offices could occur along the entire route as the lines and demands of the stations encroached on Native American lands, with frequent attacks on stations in Arizona, Colorado, Montana, Utah, and Wyoming occurring during the period of the Indian Wars. In some instances the stations served as forts for both travelers and nearby pioneers, such as at Greely, Colorado, while in other instances the stations were overrun by Native Americans who scalped and killed the station hands and then took the horses and livestock. The attack on Deep Creek Station in western Utah had the distinction of being the first action of the 1863 Goshute War.

After the American Civil War (1861–1865), the U.S. Army afforded some protection to stage coach stations, and peace treaties reopened closed lines and enabled mail traffic to resume. Overland stage coach station managers, like their Wells Fargo city-based agents, took an interest in the plight of the Indians, including supplying local tribes suffering from famine as well as hiring Indians to work the line. Wells Fargo remained an express company until 1913, when it became a traditional bank.

MARCEL A. DEROSIER

See also

Butterfield Overland Mail Route; California Gold Rush; Goshute War; Railroads; Stagecoach

References

Fradkin, Philip L. *Stagecoach: Wells Fargo and the American West.* New York: Simon and Schuster, 2002.

Hungerford, Edward. *Wells Fargo: Advancing the American Frontier.* New York: Random House, 1949.

Wendots

See Wyandots

Werowance

A term describing a male leader or tribal chief (female equivalent, *werowansqua*), as recorded by English observers in the Mid-Atlantic region in the 17th century. The total Native American population of what is present-day Virginia probably comprised some 50,000 people, made up of Algonquian-speaking peoples to the east, Siouan-speaking peoples to the west, and Iroquoian-speaking tribes to the south and southwest. The Virginia Algonquian tribes, which were the first to meet the English in 1607, called eastern Virginia Tsenacomoco, translated by some linguists as "densely populated place."

Some of the Mid-Atlantic Algonquian-speaking tribes, most of which were led by a *werowance* (*weroance*) or *werowansqua*, were organized into paramount chiefdoms in which each tribe paid tribute to a paramount chief in return for military alliance and other support, such as food in lean times, and reciprocal status gifts. The largest of these paramount chiefdoms was governed by the chief known as Powhatan, who held the title of *mamanatowick*, which has been translated as "paramount chief," and who was also a religious leader. Powhatan reportedly inherited 6 tribes from an older relative. By the early 17th century he had increased that number to 30 or more tribes. Powhatan is recognized for his skill as a leader and for his adept interactions with early Jamestown settlers. *Werowances* and *werowansquas* of Powhatan's tributary tribes each led their own chiefdoms. When Powhatan had coerced or persuaded a tribe to become a tributary, he sometimes appointed its *werowance*, replacing leaders who had resisted incorporation.

As described by some English observers, *werowances* had absolute power to reward and punish to the point of life and death. Other observers noted that Algonquian *werowances* often consulted with tribal councils or shamans in decisions. In a culture in which men were judged as hunters and warriors, bravery and skill marked them for positions of authority. Such positions of leadership were a source of pride to Algonquian men and frequently brought additional socioeconomic benefits as well. As these leaders were chosen mostly from certain high-status families, it was not unusual for leaders to be related either to each other or to their paramount chief. In matrilineal Algonquian society, the right to leadership positions passed through the mother's line, not the father's, and *werowansquas* customarily assumed the leadership role when there was no male successor. Powhatan was known to have visited the various territories in his tributary system. Women from these tribes became his temporary wives, and he sometimes appointed his sons by these wives to be the *werowances* of their mother's tribes. Although his primary war chief was his relative Opechancanough, Powhatan also assigned *werowances* to lead specific military actions and rewarded exceptional prowess and deeds of courage.

When the English landed at Jamestown in 1607, the Powhatan paramount chiefdom held a significant presence on the eastern Atlantic seaboard. *Werowances* and their warriors were skilled bow men and hand-to-hand combatants who increased Powhatan's influence by supplying food through hunting and by taking women and children in ritual or reactive military actions. A powerful paramount chief such as Powhatan could quickly organize tribes to repel hostile invaders. Yet the English managed to gain a permanent foothold in Virginia because Powhatan's first response to them was to help them survive in exchange for trade goods and attempt to incorporate them within his own paramount chiefdom.

Europeans attempted their own diplomatic and military means to deal with their indigenous counterparts. Unfamiliar with the Virginia environment, the outnumbered English feared Native American and Spanish threats. Accordingly, Jamestown leader John Smith recorded locations of tribal villages and towns, also estimating warrior numbers in the various tribes. When the Virginia colony began to stabilize after famine and disease, tensions increased between the indigenous peoples and the English. The English agreed in 1614 to settle only in Jamestown, but in a time of peace the colony expanded west into many settlements along the James River.

After Powhatan's death in 1618, tribes led by his successor Opechancanough organized in 1622 and 1644 to punish what was seen as English encroachment onto Indian land. Military defeat and treaties in 1646 and 1677 marked the demise of Native American strength in eastern Virginia. Some tribes endured, however, and currently eight are recognized by the Commonwealth of Virginia. Chiefs and assistant chiefs—the successors to the *werowances*—today continue a tradition of leadership dating back for centuries, although their power is greatly reduced.

Lisa Heuvel and Deanna Beacham

See also

Jamestown; Opechancanough; Powhatan; Powhatan Confederacy; Smith, John

References

Gleach, Frederic W. *Powhatan's World and Colonial Virginia.* Lincoln: University of Nebraska Press, 1997.

Rountree, Helen C. *The Powhatan Indians of Virginia: Their Traditional Culture.* Norman: University of Oklahoma Press, 1989.

Wood, Karenne, ed. *The Virginia Indian Heritage Trail.* 2nd ed. Richmond: Virginia Foundation for the Humanities, 2008.

Wessagusset Raid

Start Date: April 4, 1623
End Date: April 5, 1623

Attack led by the captain general of Plymouth Colony, Myles Standish, against the Native Americans of Massachusetts in the spring of 1623. On February 17, 1621, Standish was appointed the commander of the newly established Plymouth Colony. As such, he had charge of all the colony's military operations.

Direct contact with the natives in the Massachusetts area, especially the Wampanoags, began in March 1621. This was only a few months after the Pilgrims arrived in the New World. At first, relations with the natives were relatively peaceful. However, in 1622 the settlement of Wessagusset (present-day Weymouth, Massachusetts) was founded by a wealthy London merchant, Thomas Weston. Unlike Plymouth, Wessagusset had been established for economic rather than religious reasons. Weston and his settlers constructed a few huts and commenced trade with the Wampanoags. Soon disease, starvation, and other English settlers moving in without permission led to rising tensions with the natives.

After 10 Wessagusset settlers died from starvation or disease, others began stealing from the Native Americans. Led by the Massachusetts tribe, the natives began plotting to exterminate the Wessagusset settlement. Tribal leaders, particularly Wituwaument and Pecksuot, appeared to be threatening not only Wessagusset but also Plymouth. Their plan was to ultimately wipe out the Pilgrims so they would not exact retribution for the killings of those settlers at Wessagusset. At the same time, word of a massacre of Virginia settlers by Native Americans had reached Plymouth. In consequence, the settlers mobilized, and the colony was placed in a high state of readiness.

In the early winter of 1623 Phineas Pratt, the new leader of Wessagusset, heard rumors that the natives were planning to attack both his settlement and Plymouth once the snow melted. Pratt then traveled by foot to Plymouth only to find out that the settlers there had already learned of the planned attack from the Wampanoag sachem (chief) Massasoit. Massasoit, an ally of Plymouth, had been given medical treatment by a Plymouth settler and had informed him of the impending attack. Massasoit urged the English to strike first.

Rather than wait for the natives to carry out their plan, the colony dispatched Standish to deal a preemptive blow. On April 4, 1623, Standish sailed to Wessagusset with 10 men armed with muskets. The next day as Standish and his men met with the native leaders and a large number of warriors inside the stockade, violence erupted. Standish and his men killed 5 natives, among them Wituwaument and Pecksuot. The rest quickly fled. Natives then murdered 3 Wessagusset settlers in retaliation.

The Wessagusset Raid marked the first time that Plymouth Colony used military force to kill natives. The following day, Standish and his crew sailed back to Plymouth. Wituwaument's head was displayed at the fort at Plymouth as a warning against future native plots. Most of the Wessagusset settlers were brought to Plymouth or to fishing stations on the Maine coast. In time, many of them returned to Europe. Standish's effort was not in vain, for the natives' plan to wipe out the colonies in the Massachusetts's territory quickly fell apart.

CHARLES FRANCIS HOWLETT

See also
Massasoit; Standish, Myles; Wampanoags

References
Davis, William T., ed. *Bradford's History of Plymouth Plantation, 1606–1646.* New York: Barnes and Noble, 1952.

Jennings, Francis. *The Invasion of America: Indians, Colonialism, and the Cant of Conquest.* 1976; reprint, Chapel Hill: University of North Carolina Press, 2010.

Moorwood, Helen. "Pilgrim Father Captain Myles Standish of Duxbury, Lancashire." *Lancashire Historical Quarterly* 3 (1999): 47–51, 102–109.

Vaughan, Alden T. *New England Frontier: Puritans and Indians, 1620–1675.* 3rd ed. Norman: University of Oklahoma Press, 1995.

Warner, Russell. *Myles Standish of the Mayflower and His Descendants for Five Generations.* Plymouth, MA: Mayflower Books, 1996.

Western Reserve

Western land claims made principally by the State of Connecticut (sometimes referred to as the Connecticut Western Reserve) in portions of the Old Northwest Territory. As late as the early 1780s, Connecticut claimed lands west of the Pennsylvania border stretching all the way to the Pacific Ocean. Several other states, most notably Virginia, also claimed western lands. In 1786 three years after the American Revolutionary War (1775–1783) had ended and in exchange for the federal government's assumption of their war debts, the states ceded much of this territory to the federal government.

Connecticut was a unique case in that it had engaged in a long-running conflict with settlers in Pennsylvania over which state would control territory in Pennsylvania's Wyoming Valley. Pennsylvanians claimed that the area belonged to them, while Connecticut settlers claimed that the valley should be part of Connecticut. Even after the 1786 cession, however, Connecticut still continued to claim a large area along Lake Erie in what is now northeastern Ohio. The area encompassed about 3 million acres of land.

Settlers were at first slow to move into the region, but in 1796 they began settling the area in greater concentrations. This settlement pattern was aided when the State of Connecticut sold the region in 1796 to eight investors who formed the Connecticut Land Company, which began to subdivide the region and invite settlers to purchase smaller tracts of land for settlement and development. This posed a distinct problem, however, because various Native American tribes also claimed control of the area.

Tensions steadily rose between Native Americans and white settlers but were finally extinguished after the Battle of Fallen Timbers (August 20, 1794) and the resultant Treaty of Greenville (August 1795), which ended Little Turtle's War (1790–1794), also known as the Northwest Indian War. That treaty saw a large confederacy of Native American tribes cede to the federal government millions of acres in the Old Northwest Territory as far west as present-day Chicago. The July 1805 Treaty of Fort Industry elaborated on the earlier treaty, setting the western limits of the United States.

Meanwhile, the Connecticut Land Company, wishing to re-create land-use patterns in Connecticut, divided up most of the Western Reserve into townships, each exactly 25 square miles in area (5 miles on each side). In 1796 Moses Cleaveland, a Connecticut native who had gone to the Western Reserve to survey the area and aid in its settlement, founded what would become the city of Cleveland in northwestern Ohio along the shores of Lake Erie at the mouth of the Cuyahoga River. Cleaveland had encountered initial Native American resistance to his plans, but he engaged them in talks and gave them goods valued at about $1,200. In return he was permitted to lay claim to the area.

During the next several years white settlers slowly made their way into the Western Reserve, which had originally been called New Connecticut. That name gave way to the name "Western Reserve," which is still in use in northeastern Ohio. Case Western Reserve University was so-named because of its location within the original Western Reserve. Numerous towns in northeastern Ohio were soon founded, all of which had a distinctly New England look to them because their founders sought to model them after towns in Connecticut. New England architecture, especially Georgian, Federal, and Greek Revival, typified the area's early buildings.

In 1800 Connecticut finally ceded the remainder of its Western Reserve, which was absorbed into the Northwest Territory. Trumbull County was incorporated later that year. In 1803 the State of Ohio was created out of the easternmost part of the Northwest Territory. The Connecticut claims of the Western Reserve certainly fanned the flames of Native American resentment that led to Little Turtle's War.

PAUL G. PIERPAOLI JR.

See also

Fallen Timbers, Battle of; Greenville, Treaty of; Little Turtle's War; Old Northwest Territory

References

Hatcher, Harlan. *Western Reserve: The Story of New Connecticut in Ohio.* 2nd ed. Kent, OH: Kent State University Press, 1991.

Upton, Harriet Taylor. *History of the Western Reserve.* Chicago: Lewis Publishing, 1910.

Westos

Native American group that migrated from the Great Lakes region into Virginia and then into Carolina and Georgia. The Westos played a key role in the Native American slave trade with the English colonists. Newcomers to the Southeast and armed with guns they acquired in Virginia, the Westos (also known as Eries, Rickahocans, and Chichimecos) terrorized other American Indians in the Southeast with their slave raids during the late 17th century. In the process they changed the sociopolitical landscape of the indigenous peoples of the region.

An Iroquoian-speaking nation originally known as the Eries, the Westo lived around the eastern Great Lakes. Upon losing a war with the Iroquois Confederacy, the Westos were dispersed in 1656. Many Westos fled toward Virginia, with some 600 being captured by the Iroquois before the remaining Westos reached the English colony. In late 1656 those who made it to the Virginia frontier defeated a small number of colonists and their native allies in a battle for control of the native trade in western Virginia.

Known as the Rickahocans to the Virginians, the Westos then formed a trade alliance with Virginia settlers. The Westos provided deerskins and native slaves to Virginians in return for firearms, ammunition, metal knives, hatchets, and other items. By 1659, Westo slave raids brought the Westos into the Southeast, where they attacked those groups that came to be associated with the Creek Confederacy in the 18th century and natives inhabiting the missions of Spanish Florida. The Spanish called these new invaders the Chichimecos.

Thanks to the guns they received from Virginia traders, the Westos held a tactical advantage over other native peoples and, as a result, terrorized the indigenous inhabitants of the South until 1680. Only the mission natives—with the support of Spanish garrisons and guns—were able to defend their territory with any degree of success. The arrival of the Westos in the South led directly to the consolidation of the Tamas from the interior of Georgia with several coastal groups and refugees from the Guale missions to create the people later known to the Spanish and the English as the Yamasees.

In 1670 the English established Charles Town (present-day Charleston, South Carolina) as the first permanent settlement of the Carolina Colony. The Westos soon established a trade alliance with the new colony that allowed them to maintain a monopoly on the Native American slave and deerskin trades by preventing the English from trading directly with other Native Americans.

Despite the fact that the government of South Carolina wanted to maintain the alliance with the Westos, a group of colonists had other ideas. Known as the Goose Creek Men, these individuals armed and encouraged a group of Shawnees known as the Savannahs to attack the Westos. The alliance of the Shawnees and the Goose Creek Men quickly defeated the Westos in the Westo War (1680). Those Westos who remained chose to live among the Cowetas, and their presence among this group of Muskogees assisted the Cowetas in their rise to prominence within the coalescing Creek Confederacy of the late 17th and early 18th centuries.

DIXIE RAY HAGGARD

See also

Captivity of Indians by Europeans; Captivity of Indians by Indians; Creeks; Iroquois; Iroquois Confederacy; Native American Trade; Yamasees

References

Bowne, Eric E. "The Rise and Fall of the Westo Indians: An Evaluation of the Documentary Evidence." *Early Georgia* 28 (2000): 56–78.

Bowne, Eric E. *Southern Frontier, 1670–1732.* Ann Arbor: University of Michigan Press, 1929.

Bowne, Eric E. "Westo and Chisca." *American Anthropologist* 21 (1919): 463–465.

Bowne, Eric E. *The Westo Indians: Slave Traders of the Early Colonial South.* Tuscaloosa: University of Alabama Press, 2005.

Juricek, John T. "The Westo Indians." *Ethnohistory* 11 (1964): 134–173.

Weyapiersenwah

See Blue Jacket

Wheaton, Frank
Birth Date: May 8, 1833
Death Date: June 18, 1903

U.S. Army officer whose long and largely distinguished career included significant service during the American Civil War (1861–1865) and a field command during the ill-fated Modoc War (1872–1873). Born in Providence, Rhode Island, on May 8, 1833, Frank Wheaton attended Brown University but left in 1850 for work on the Mexican-American Border Commission. In 1855 he received a commission as first lieutenant in the new 1st Cavalry Regiment. Over the next five years he saw extensive service against the Cheyennes in Kansas and Nebraska.

On the eve of the Civil War, Wheaton's father-in-law, Adjutant General Samuel Cooper, whose wife was the sister of the powerful Virginia senator James Mason, joined the Confederate service as its ranking officer. Wheaton, now a captain, remained loyal to the Union. On leave from the regular service, he became lieutenant colonel of the 2nd Rhode Island Infantry, which saw heavy fighting in the First Battle of Bull Run (July 21, 1861), losing its colonel. Wheaton thus ascended to command. After an excellent performance during the March–August 1862 Peninsula Campaign, the Seven Days' Battles (June 25–July 1, 1862), and the Battle of Fredericksburg (December 13, 1862), Wheaton assumed command of a brigade in VI Corps, Army of the Potomac, with the rank of brigadier general of volunteers.

After fighting in the April–May 1863 Chancellorsville campaign, Wheaton temporarily commanded a division at the Battle of Gettysburg (July 1–3, 1863). Leading a brigade and occasionally a division, he served throughout the Overland Campaign (May 4–June 12, 1864) and in the defense of Washington. His impressive performance that autumn during Major General Philip Sheridan's Shenandoah Valley Campaign (August 7, 1864–March 2, 1865) won him permanent command of the First Division, VI Corps, which he retained until the end of the war in 1865.

Brevetted through the rank of major general in both the regular and volunteer organizations, Wheaton mustered out of the volunteers in April 1866 and later that year became lieutenant colonel of the 39th Infantry Regiment. As lieutenant colonel of the 21st Infantry, he directed the unsuccessful initial action against

U.S. Army lieutenant colonel Frank Wheaton, who had distinguished himself as a brevet major general in the Civil War, directed the early, unsuccessful army efforts in the Modoc War (1872–1873). (Library of Congress)

Captain Jack's defiant band during the Modoc War (1872–1873), after which efforts to negotiate a settlement resulted in Captain Jack's murder of Brigadier General Edward R. S. Canby during a peace conference in 1873. The following year Wheaton became colonel of the 2nd Infantry Regiment, a position he held for the next 18 years. After serving on Reconstruction duty in Georgia, his regiment was rushed to the Northwest to assist in the Nez Perce War (1877) and in 1878 was engaged again in the same region helping to quell the Bannock-Paiute uprising. After years of relative inactivity, in 1890 Wheaton's regiment was called upon to assist in suppressing the Ghost Dance movement in the Dakota Territory but was not involved in the Wounded Knee tragedy.

Promoted to brigadier general in 1892, Wheaton commanded the Department of Texas for three years. He was promoted to major general prior to his retirement in 1897. Wheaton died in Washington, D.C., on June 18, 1903.

DAVID COFFEY

See also

Bannock War; Canby, Edward Richard Sprigg; Cheyennes; Forsyth, James William; Ghost Dance; Howard, Oliver Otis; Joseph, Chief;

Miles, Nelson Appleton; Modoc War; Nez Perce War; Paiutes, Northern; Wounded Knee, Battle of

References

Chalfant, William Y. *Cheyennes and Horse Soldiers: The 1857 Expedition and the Battle of Solomon's Fork*. Norman: University of Oklahoma Press, 1989.

Coffey, David. *Sheridan's Lieutenants: Phil Sheridan, His Generals, and the Final Year of the Civil War*. Lanham, MD: Rowman and Littlefield, 2005.

Utley, Robert M. *Frontier Regulars: The United States and the American Indian, 1866–1891*. New York: Macmillan, 1973.

Wheeler-Howard Act

See Indian Reorganization Act

White Bird Canyon, Battle of
Event Date: June 17, 1877

Battle fought on June 17, 1877, in the Idaho Territory between the U.S. Army and Nez Perce warriors. White Bird Canyon is situated in present-day central Idaho south of Lewiston and near the Salmon River. The Battle of White Bird Canyon was the first engagement of what came to be known as the Nez Perce War (1877).

The Nez Perce War was caused by white settlers encroaching on lands occupied by the Nez Perces in the rich Wallowa Valley of Oregon. A number of Nez Perces, notably those led by Chief Joseph, had remained in their ancestral lands of the Snake River region of Oregon despite an 1863 treaty that was to remove them to a reservation.

In May 1877 Brigadier General Oliver O. Howard, commander of the Department of the Columbia, having met several times with the Nez Perce leaders, gave Chief Joseph an ultimatum for the Nez Perces to abandon their homes within 30 days or be removed by force. Although Joseph did not recognize the 1863 treaty as binding, he hoped to avoid violence, while other Nez Perces favored armed resistance.

In June 1877, however, any possibility of peaceful resolution was shattered when 3 drunken Nez Perce men from White Bird's band killed 4 white settlers. This action touched off the nearly four-month-long Nez Perce War. When word of what had happened reached Howard at Fort Lapwai, he immediately dispatched Captain David Perry in command of F and H troops (105 men) of the 1st Cavalry Regiment along with 10 Nez Perce scouts to protect settlers in the Salmon River area. They could not prevent the Nez Perces from killing another 15 settlers, however.

Well aware that Howard would be sending soldiers against them, by June 16 the Nez Perces had relocated to the more easily defended canyons of Lahmotta. That night Nez Perce scouts reported soldiers approaching from the north. The Nez Perces then decided to attempt peace negotiations, with the understanding that if these failed they would fight.

On June 17, 1877, an advance party, including 11 Idaho volunteers, approached the Nez Perce camp and encountered 6 warriors under a flag of truce. For some unknown reason, an Idaho volunteer opened fire on the Nez Perce truce party. A full-scale battle then ensued. At the time there were already some 70 Nez Perce warriors in excellent defensive positions. An almost equal number were asleep. When Perry's troops arrived, the army and volunteers numbered some 120 men.

Perry tried to organize a charge, but the Nez Perces proved to be excellent marksmen and attacked the soldiers from both flanks. Perry had difficulty communicating his orders, and a command to consolidate was misinterpreted as an order for a general retreat, which led to near panic and left some soldiers stranded on the battlefield. The U.S. force then began a hasty withdrawal along two routes. The Nez Perces trapped one group. The troops in it ran out of ammunition and were slain. Perry managed to regroup the remaining troops at a nearby ranch and withdraw them under fire to nearby Mount Idaho, where they were reinforced by additional volunteers.

In the Battle of White Bird Canyon, 34 U.S. soldiers died and 2 were wounded; 2 Idaho volunteers were also wounded. The Nez Perces suffered only 3 warriors wounded. The Nez Perces were able to recover a significant number of firearms and some ammunition on the battlefield, which enhanced their military effectiveness. The Battle of White Bird Canyon was a significant victory for the Nez Perces.

ANDREW BYERS AND SPENCER C. TUCKER

See also

Howard, Oliver Otis; Joseph, Chief; Nez Perces; Nez Perce War

References

Lavender, David. *Let Me Be Free: The Nez Perce Tragedy*. New York: HarperCollins, 1992.

Utley, Robert M., and Wilcomb E. Washburn. *Indian Wars*. New York: American Heritage Press, 2002.

Yenne, Bill, *Indian Wars: The Campaign for the American West*. Yardley, PA: Westholme Publishing, 2006.

White Cloud

See Wabokieshiek

Whitestone Hill, Battle of
Event Date: September 3, 1863

Military engagement between U.S. volunteer forces and Sioux Native Americans in southeastern North Dakota. Following Chief Little Crow's Sioux Uprising in Minnesota in 1862, several Santee

Charge by Brigadier General Alfred Sully's cavalry during the Battle of Whitestone Hill in southeastern North Dakota on September 3, 1863, part of the army campaign to punish the Sioux involved in the 1862 Minnesota Sioux Uprising. Illustration from 1863. (Corbis)

Sioux escaped the wrath of Colonel Henry H. Sibley's volunteer command and moved west to link up with the Teton Sioux in Dakota Territory. In 1863 Brigadier General Alfred Sully organized a force of some 1,200 soldiers at Fort Ridgely to join Sibley in what became the 1863–1864 Sioux Campaign.

After almost two weeks of fruitless searching, Sully's column encountered a friendly Native American who told them that the warring band had slipped east of the Missouri River and was traveling along the James River searching for food. Approaching the James River, Sully sent forward a strong reconnaissance force of 300 men from the 6th Iowa Cavalry Regiment in advance of his main body, with orders to find the Sioux camp and report its location. On September 3 Major A. E. House, commander of the reconnaissance effort, discovered a large camp of nearly 500 lodges nestled in ravines near Whitestone Hill in present-day Merricourt, North Dakota.

House immediately dispatched couriers to report the camp to Sully's main column but also decided to move the majority of his command forward in an effort to contain the village and prevent the escape of the Native Americans. Once committed to this course of action, House realized that the Sioux camp held an estimated 1,200 Santee, Yanktonai, Blackfoot, and Hunkpapa warriors. He was thus forced to take a more passive stance until Sully arrived. House left his command in their exposed position and rode to the gathered warriors in an effort to negotiate. The Sioux, thinking that they were threatened by a small command of troops, took their time talking to House, all the while preparing to attack his force.

Just as the Sioux launched their attack, Sully's column struck the assembled warriors from the southeast. The remainder of the 6th Iowa Cavalry broke off from this attack and rode to the defense of House's reconnaissance force. The Sioux meanwhile turned their attention to Sully's larger force. This allowed House to escape, rejoin the rest of the 6th Iowa Cavalry, and then launch a counterattack into the heart of the Sioux camp. Pressed from both sides, the Sioux dissipated their force to meet the threat, and the fighting spread out across the ravine. A charge by the 6th Iowa Cavalry failed to break the Sioux line, and the Sioux in turn failed to flank the soldiers' positions. To add even more confusion, several friendly Native Americans were camped with the Blackfeet and ran to Sully's position for cover. Sully took in 30 men and 90 women and children.

With nightfall the Sioux made good their escape. Sully had sustained 20 dead and 38 wounded. Despite this narrow escape, the Sioux had suffered more than 100 dead, many more wounded, and 156 captured. During the night Sully's soldiers burned some 300 lodges and an estimated 400,000 pounds of buffalo meat.

Patrick R. Jennings

See also
Blackfoot Sioux; Hunkpapa Sioux; Little Crow; Minnesota Sioux Uprising; Nakota Sioux; Sibley, Henry Hastings; Sully, Alfred

References
Clodfelter, Michael. *The Dakota War: The United States Army versus the Sioux, 1862–1865*. Jefferson, NC: McFarland, 1998.

Ferris, Robert, ed. *Soldier and Brave: Historic Places Associated with Indian Affairs and Indian Wars in the Trans-Mississippi West*. Washington, DC: United States Department of the Interior, 1971.

Whitman Massacre
Event Date: November 29, 1847

The murder of Marcus and Narcissa Whitman and 11 other missionaries at Waiilaptu (near Fort Walla Walla in the Oregon Territory) on November 29, 1847. The massacre was perpetrated by members of the Cayuse tribe, with whom the missionaries were working at the time.

The Whitmans had migrated west in 1836 to bring Christianity to Native Americans in the Oregon Territory. The Lewis and Clark expedition of 1804–1806 led to a major movement westward by Americans seeking inexpensive land. In 1831 when representatives of the Nez Perces met with William Clark, head of the Bureau of Indian Affairs for the West, they appeared to be open to receiving missionaries providing information on Christianity. While this was likely not the case, in 1835 the American Board of Commissioners for Foreign Missions, which included several Protestant denominations, sent the Reverend Samuel Parker and Dr. Marcus Whitman by horse to the Oregon Territory to find suitable places to locate missions.

Once in the West, Whitman decided to return home, where on February 18, 1836, he married Narcissa Prentice. Joined by Henry and Eliza Spaulding and William Gray, they set out across the continent in wagons, bound for Oregon. The Spauldings subsequently established a mission near Lapwai, working with the Nez Perces, while the Whitmans set up their mission at Waiilaptu, near Fort Walla Walla, where they worked with the Cayuses.

Over time the mission at Waiilaptu grew in size and achieved some success in teaching the Cayuses new farming techniques. The Cayuses were not interested in Christianity, however. The mission soon became a resting place for travelers on the developing Oregon Trail, and this led to suspicion among the Cayuses that the Americans were really just interested in taking over their

Whitman Mission at Waiilatpu by American painter William Henry Jackson. The mission was on the Oregon Trail near Fort Walla Walla in Washington and was the site of a massacre on November 29, 1847, by the Cayuse tribe whose population had been decimated by a measles epidemic brought to the area by the missionaries. (Hulton Archive/Getty Images)

lands. As the movement of settlers into the area increased, tensions mounted. The missionaries were never fully able to resolve the cultural differences between the settlers and the tribe. At one point the American Board of Commissioners planned to close the mission, believing it to be a failure, but in 1842 Marcus Whitman returned home and convinced the board to keep it open. He then led a wagon train back to Oregon.

In November 1847 a measles epidemic killed as much as half of the Cayuse tribe but affected only a handful of the whites at the mission. This outraged some Cayuses, who blamed Dr. Whitman for the deaths of his patients.

On November 29, 1847, a number of Cayuses, led by Chief Tomahas, killed the Whitmans and 11 others who were staying at the mission. They took an additional 60 people hostage, whom they ransomed a month later.

The Whitman Massacre ended the period of relatively peaceful relations between immigrants and Native Americans in the Pacific Northwest and was followed by a series of Indian wars and uprisings. In 1850 the Cayuses finally surrendered five men, including Chief Tomahas, who were accused of perpetrating the massacre. They were tried, convicted, and executed.

Despite their grisly and untimely deaths, the Whitmans provided a lasting positive legacy as well. Indeed, Narcissa Whitman and Eliza Spaulding are believed to have been the first white women to cross the continent, and their journey demonstrated to potential immigrants that whole families could make the trip.

J. DAVID MARKHAM

See also

Fort Walla Walla; Missionaries; Nez Perces; Oregon Trail

References

Drury, Clifford. *Marcus and Narcissa Whitman and the Opening of Old Oregon.* Eugene, OR: Pacific Northwest National, 1986.

Mowry, William. *Marcus Whitman and the Early Days of Oregon.* Whitefish, MT: Kessinger, 2006.

Sager, Catherine, Elizabeth Sager, and Matilda Sager. *The Whitman Massacre of 1847.* Oakesdale, CA: Ye Galleon, 1997.

Willcox, Orlando Bolivar

Birth Date: April 16, 1823
Death Date: May 10, 1907

U.S. Army officer. Born in Detroit, Michigan, on April 16, 1823, Orlando Bolivar Willcox received education at local schools before entering the U.S. Military Academy at West Point, from which he graduated in July 1847. Commissioned a second lieutenant, he was assigned to the 4th Artillery Regiment. Deployed to Mexico shortly before the Mexican-American War (1846–1848) ended, he arrived too late to see action. In 1850 Willcox, now a first lieutenant, began to combat the monotony of army life by writing novels published under the pen name Major Walter March.

In 1856 and 1857, Willcox pursued Billy Bowlegs's insurgent warriors in the Florida swamps during the Third Seminole War (1855–1858). Willcox resigned his commission in 1857, returned to Detroit, and became a lawyer and a captain in his state's militia.

On the outbreak of the American Civil War (1861–1865), Willcox became colonel of the 1st Michigan Volunteer Infantry Regiment and served in Virginia. For gallantry at the First Battle of Bull Run (July 21, 1861), he received the Medal of Honor (conferred in 1895) and promotion to brigadier general of volunteers. However, he was wounded and captured in the engagement and spent the next 13 months in Confederate prisons before being exchanged. After his release he returned to the Army of the Potomac. He commanded the 1st Division of IX Corps during the Battle of South Mountain (September 14, 1862) and the Battle of Antietam (September 17, 1862). When Major General Ambrose Burnside was chosen to head the Army of the Potomac, Willcox briefly commanded IX Corps. He later commanded in succession the Military District of Central Kentucky, the Military District of Indiana and Michigan, and East Tennessee forces during the Knoxville Campaign. On August 1, 1864, he was brevetted major general of volunteers for conspicuous service during General Ulysses Grant's Overland Campaign. Willcox also won brevets through major general in the regular army.

In 1886 Willcox left volunteer service and reentered the regular army as colonel of the 29th Infantry, later transferring to the 12th Infantry. During the next 12 years he undertook a variety of assignments that included leading occupying forces in Virginia during Reconstruction, becoming superintendent of general recruiting services in New York City, and commanding a regiment in California.

In the spring of 1878 Willcox traveled west to head the Department of Arizona during a period of increased hostilities between the Apaches and white settlers. Willcox's troops responded decisively to Native American attacks, driving bands of hostile warriors out of the territory. After Apache warriors killed several U.S. soldiers at Cibicu Creek in August 1881 and then engaged in raids and ambushes on central Arizona settlers during the spring of 1882, troops in Willcox's department cornered the band, earning an important victory on July 17, 1882, in the Battle of Big Dry Run, the last engagement between army regulars and Apaches on U.S. soil. For these feats the Arizona territorial legislature publicly thanked Willcox for his services, and the town of Willcox, Arizona, was named in his honor. But Willcox drew criticism in the army for his direction of the department and was blamed, perhaps unfairly, for the spike in Apache activity during his tenure. He was replaced in September 1882 by Brigadier General George Crook.

On October 13, 1886, six months before retirement, Willcox was promoted to brigadier general. In 1905 he moved to Coburg, Ontario, Canada. He died there on May 10, 1907.

ANGELA D. TOOLEY AND JIM PIECUCH

See also

Apaches; Apache Wars; Seminole War, Third

References

Herek, Raymond J. *These Men Have Seen Hard Service: The First Michigan Sharpshooters in the Civil War.* Detroit: Wayne State University Press, 1998.

Willcox, Orlando B., and Robert Garth Scott. *Forgotten Valor: The Memoirs, Journals, & Civil War Letters of Orlando B. Willcox.* Kent, OH: Kent State University Press, 1999.

Willem Kieft's War

See Kieft's War

Williams, Roger

Birth Date: December 21, 1603
Death Date: March 15, 1683

English Puritan minister and founder of Rhode Island. Roger Williams was born in London on December 21, 1603, and attended Pembroke College at Cambridge University, graduating in 1627. Ordained to the clergy, shortly thereafter he joined other Puritan dissenters and sailed to the Massachusetts Bay Colony, arriving there in 1631.

During a two-year stay in Plymouth Colony, Williams interacted regularly with the nearby Native Americans. He assiduously studied their language to facilitate mission work among them, and by 1636 he was fully conversant in the Algonquian language. By 1643 Williams had become so well versed in the native culture and language that he published *Key to the Indian Languages,* an indispensable dictionary.

In 1633 Williams accepted a pastorate in Salem (Massachusetts Bay Colony). In October 1635, however, the colony's leadership banished him for claiming, among other things, that the Massachusetts Bay Charter was illegitimate because it ignored the property rights of the natives. By then Williams had already established himself as a champion of sorts of Native American causes.

Williams then fled south from Massachusetts Bay with his followers and established Providence (Rhode Island) in June 1636. He so-named the settlement because he believed that God had cared for him and his supporters after his banishment and had led them to safety.

In Providence, Williams cultivated cordial and strong ties with the Narragansetts, from whom he formally secured land rights to begin building his new settlement. Among other things, Rhode Island's government promoted religious toleration and separated church law from civil law. The Massachusetts Bay authorities soon requested Williams's help, however. By 1636 they feared that the powerful Pequot Nation sought an alliance with the Narragansetts against them.

Williams traveled 30 miles alone by canoe to negotiate with Narragansett sachems Canonicus and Miantonomo. In three days Williams convinced the Narragansetts to abandon their association with the Pequots and instead form an alliance with the English. The Pequots were soon devastated in the Pequot War (1636–1638).

When conflict erupted between the Narragansetts and the Mohegans in the mid-1640s, Williams counseled Massachusetts authorities to remain neutral. His advice was disregarded, but his negotiations did avert war between the Narragansetts and the English. The terms of the agreement, however, punished the Narragansetts rather severely. Again in 1654 Williams tried to prevent the Massachusetts leadership from taking military action against the Niantics and their leader Ninigret for killing other natives on Long Island.

Tensions between the English and the various New England tribes continued to build through the 1670s as the colonists claimed more and more land. At one point in 1671 Williams allowed himself to be taken into the custody of the Wampanoags in order to ensure the safety of their sachem, Metacom (King Philip), during his deliberations with the Plymouth leadership.

By 1675 the English feared a potential Native American alliance led by Metacom. Although the Narragansetts assured Williams that no alliance existed with Metacom, the situation quickly

Roger Williams (1603–1683), the English Puritan minister and founder of Rhode Island, studied Native American culture. Fully conversant in the Algonquian language, he became something of a champion of Native American causes. (Vincent L. Milner, *Religious Denominations of the World,* 1872)

deteriorated. In June 1675 various New England tribes, including the Wampanoags, the Narragansetts, and the Mohegans, united against the colonists in King Philip's War (1675–1676).

Even though Rhode Island officially claimed neutrality in the war, Williams served as one of two captains of the Providence Militia. As a result, his home was burned by natives during an attack. Williams's mediation efforts during King Philip's War proved to be his last major attempt to broker peace between the English and the New England natives. Williams died in Providence on March 15, 1683.

JOSEPH W. WILLIAMS

See also

Algonquins; King Philip's War; Metacom; Miantonomo; Mohegans; Narragansetts; Pequots; Pequot War; Puritans; Sachem; Wampanoags

References

Covey, Cyclone. *The Gentle Radical: Roger Williams.* New York: Macmillan, 1966.

Garrett, John. *Roger Williams: Witness beyond Christendom.* New York: Macmillan, 1970.

Gaustad, Edwin. *Liberty of Conscience: Roger Williams in America.* Grand Rapids, MI: Eerdmans, 1991.

Wilson, Henry

Birth Date: ca. 1794
Death Date: February 21, 1872

U.S. Army officer. Henry Wilson was born in Philadelphia, Pennsylvania, probably in 1794. The precise date of his birth is unknown, as are the circumstances of his youth. In 1813 he secured a commission as an ensign in the U.S. Army during the War of 1812, attaining the rank of second lieutenant before resigning his commission in late 1814. He rejoined the army in 1815 and saw action with Major General Andrew Jackson in the First Seminole War (1817–1818) as well as in the taking of Pensacola in May 1818.

Wilson subsequently married into the prominent Innerarity family of Pensacola, known for its trading with Native Americans. He continued his army career and served in the Second Seminole War (1835–1842) in central Florida and later as commandant of the western district of Florida. He was army agent in Mobile, Alabama, during the Creek removal that occurred roughly from 1834 to 1837. Promoted to major, he was also responsible for the final phases of the move of the Cherokee tribe from western North Carolina and eastern Tennessee to present-day Oklahoma in 1838.

On the outbreak of the Mexican-American War (1846–1848) Wilson, now as lieutenant colonel in the 1st Infantry Regiment, led four companies (known as the First Brigade) to northern Mexico and fought there under Major General Zachary Taylor. Wilson went on to win honors and a brevet promotion to colonel

at the Battle of Monterey (July 7, 1846) and was then transferred to the army of Major General Winfield Scott for the Veracruz Campaign, which began on March 7, 1847, when Scott's forces landed near that port city. Wilson participated in the siege of Veracruz and was appointed military governor of Veracruz on March 28, the day after the city surrendered. He held that post until the end of the war, and his excellent managerial skills helped ensure that the U.S. forces in the Mexican interior would be well supplied, for Veracruz served as the main staging area for Scott's successful Mexico City Campaign.

After the war Wilson served in Texas suppressing Comanche uprisings, earning promotion to colonel of the 7th Infantry in 1851. He also took part in the Utah Expedition of 1857–1858. In 1861 when he resigned his commission due to health reasons, he was the oldest-serving colonel in the U.S. Army. During the American Civil War (1861–1865) he volunteered his services to the Confederate States of America but never received a commission or appointment. Wilson later became a banker in New Orleans and died there on February 21, 1872.

RUSSELL D. JAMES

See also

Cherokees; Comanches; Creeks; Jackson, Andrew; Scott, Winfield; Seminoles; Seminole War, First; Seminole War, Second; Taylor, Zachary; Trail of Tears

References

Johnson, Timothy D. *A Gallant Little Army: The Mexico City Campaign.* Lawrence: University Press of Kansas, 2007.

Semmes, Ralph. *Service Afloat and Vera Cruz Ashore during the Mexican War.* Easton, PA: Easton Area Public Library, 1975.

Utley, Robert M., and Wilcomb E. Washburn. *The American Heritage History of the Indian Wars.* New York: Barnes and Noble, 1991.

Wilson, Jack

See Wovoka

Winnebagos

Native American peoples belonging to the Siouan linguistic and cultural group and linguistically close to the Iowa, Oto, and Missouri peoples. The Winnebagos (Ho-Chunks) are also distantly related to the Dakota Sioux. Unlike many other Siouan peoples, the Winnebagos are culturally affiliated with other Great Lakes nations. The name "Winnebago" likely derives from a Pottawatomi word that loosely translates as "people of the dirty water." The Winnebagos themselves prefer the term "Ho-Chuck," or "Big Fish." The Winnebagos entered written records in 1620 through formerly oral Huron accounts.

The French and their Native American allies claimed that the Winnebagos were extremely warlike and treacherous. The

Winnebago Indians gather around a small table in front of a tipi with a few Euro-Americans, circa 1870. (Library of Congress)

Winnebagos practiced corn-based agriculture in addition to seasonal hunting and gathering. They also subsisted on fish, wild rice, and syrup taken from sugar-maple trees. They engaged in some trade with other Native American tribes and occasionally with Europeans. Because of continual warfare with the Illinois, Ojibwas, and Ottawas as well as possible population expansion, the original Winnebagos split into four groups. They became known as the Iowas, Otos, Missouris, and Winnebagos. By the early 1600s the Winnebagos were firmly established in the Green Bay region (present-day northern Wisconsin).

News of the Winnebagos inhabiting Green Bay in 1620 prompted Samuel de Champlain to send Jean Nicollet to establish a peace in the Green Bay region, yet little is known of the Winnebagos until 1665. By this time they had been reduced to a population of approximately 600 from 25,000. This demographic disaster was the result of warfare with the Fox, Illinois, Ottawa, Ojibwa, and refugee Huron tribes as well as epidemic diseases, most likely spread by Europeans. Around 1665 Nicolas Perrot

concluded a lasting peace with the warring groups in and around the western Great Lakes. After this date the Winnebago population slowly recovered.

As part of the French alliance system, the Winnebagos participated in attacks on the Iroquois, which ultimately led to the Great Peace of 1701. Peace meant that the refugees from the Beaver Wars (1641–1701) living on Winnebago lands were now free to return to their former lands. During the Fox Wars (1712–1737) the Winnebagos were initially neutral (from 1712 to 1716) but then allied with the Foxes from circa 1724 to 1727 and resumed their alliance with the French from 1728 to 1737. The Winnebagos, alongside the Menominees, asked the French to show the Foxes mercy at the end of the war in 1737. During the Ojibwa-Dakota conflict in the 18th century, the Winnebagos remained neutral. This allowed the expansion of villages to the west of Lake Michigan and the pursuit of buffalo on the open prairies.

From 1744 to 1748 and again from 1755 to 1763 during the French and Indian War (1754–1763), the Winnebagos traveled east to aid their French allies. For instance, the Winnebagos participated in the July 13, 1755, defeat of the British expedition against Fort Duquesne led by British major general Edward Braddock and the French campaign in New York. During Pontiac's Rebellion (1763), the Winnebagos sent wampum belts of peace and loyalty to the British. Nevertheless, the Winnebagos exacted revenge on Pontiac's Illinois murderers.

The Winnebagos played a minor role as British allies during the American Revolutionary War (1775–1783), only participating in an ill-fated venture to capture St. Louis. They failed to take part in the western Indian confederacy's battles in the 1790s. Fighting at Prophetstown (Tippecanoe) on November 7, 1811, the Winnebagos experienced heavy losses at American hands. During the War of 1812 the Winnebagos supported Tecumseh and the British. In 1816 the Winnebagos formally made peace with the United States.

During the decades that followed, the Winnebagos signed a number of treaties that resulted in significant land surrenders and the Winnebago War (1827) with the United States, which led to further land loss. A few Winnebagos, including their prophet White Cloud, participated in the Black Hawk War (1832). Despite having captured Black Hawk, the United States forced all the Winnebagos to sign a treaty that would remove the tribe from Wisconsin. Eventually the tribe ended up in Minnesota. Following the 1862 Sioux uprising and despite having played no part in the conflict, the Winnebagos were relocated to South Dakota. From there they migrated to Nebraska, where the United States finally granted them a reservation in 1865.

In 1868 many Winnebagos volunteered as scouts for the U.S. Army against the Dakotas. Other Winnebagos returned to Wisconsin, where they were arrested and returned to Nebraska. By 1875 U.S. authorities gave up trying to fight the Winnebagos and purchased lands for the returnees in Wisconsin, after which the majority of the Nebraska Winnebagos returned to their traditional homeland.

KARL S. HELE

See also

Beaver Wars; Black Hawk War; Braddock, Edward; Braddock's Campaign; Champlain, Samuel de; Dakota Sioux; Fox Wars; French and Indian War; Native Americans and the War of 1812; Ojibwas; Ottawas; Pontiac's Rebellion; Sauks and Foxes; Tecumseh; Tippecanoe, Battle of; Winnebago War; Wyandots

References

Lass, William E. "The Removal from Minnesota of the Sioux and Winnebago Indians." *Minnesota History* 38(8) (1963): 353–364.

Loew, Patty. *Indian Nations of Wisconsin: Histories of Endurance and Renewal.* Madison: Wisconsin Historical Society Press, 2001.

Murphy, Lucy Eldersveld. *A Gathering of Rivers: Indians, Métis, and Mining in the Western Great Lakes, 1737–1832.* Lincoln: University of Nebraska Press, 2000.

Waggoner, Linda M., ed. *"Neither White Men Nor Indians": Affidavits from the Winnebago Mixed Blood Claim Commissions, Prairie du Chien, Wisconsin, 1838–1839.* Roseville, MN: Park General Books, 2002.

Winnebago War
Event Date: Summer 1827

A short conflict between the U.S. Army and local militiamen and members of the Winnebago tribe. The Winnebago War occurred in the summer of 1827. The Winnebago tribe (Ho-chunk-gra, or "People with a Big Voice") resided in the western Great Lakes region (present-day Wisconsin and Illinois). During the 1820s a large number of lead miners began settling on Winnebago lands along the Galena River, located near the present-day Illinois-Wisconsin border. At the time lead prices were steadily rising, and the Winnebagos began digging and selling lead to white traders. Government officials were afraid, however, that the Winnebago practice of selling lead would mean that they would not want to give up their profitable lands in the future. Consequently, officials ordered local Indian agents to prevent the sale of lead by Native Americans.

In March 1826 several members of a white family were attacked and murdered by warriors in their maple sugar camp near Prairie du Chien (in present-day southwestern Wisconsin). Two warriors were arrested and charged with the crime in 1827, and Dakota Sioux militants subsequently spread a false rumor that the captives had been sent to Fort Snelling, Minnesota, for execution. When news reached the Winnebagos in Prairie La Crosse, the tribal council selected Red Bird to uphold the tribe's honor. Based on the frustration and tension caused by widespread white intrusions on Native American land and the prohibition of lead sales, Red Bird believed that other tribes would support them in taking action.

In June 1827 Red Bird, Wekau, and Chickhonsic scalped and murdered a white farmer, Registre Gagnier, and a hired hand, Solomon Lipcap. They also scalped Gagnier's 18-month-old daughter, who miraculously survived. Red Bird returned to his tribe with the scalps, proclaiming that "there are my trophies, now you do the rest." The deed ignited both anxiety and passion among the Winnebagos.

Local settlers and miners in the area feared the Winnebagos and pressured officials to increase the number of garrisons for their protection. Also in June 1827, two Mississippi keelboats stopped in Prairie du Chien at a Winnebago village after making a delivery at Fort Snelling. A number of the boatmen drank rum with the Native Americans and then kidnapped and raped several Native American women. The tribe was enraged by the incident and took revenge on the *General Ashby* and *O. H. Perry* keelboats in the Fever River, which were mistakenly thought to be the same keelboats encountered earlier. In the resultant attack, 4 whites and 12 Winnebagos were killed. This action on June 27, 1827, is considered the only actual engagement of the Winnebago War.

Troops were finally dispatched to deal with the Winnebago militants. The troops included regular forces under Brigadier General Henry Atkinson, volunteers under Illinois governor Ninian Edwards, regulars under Colonel Josiah Snelling from Fort

Snelling, and various miner volunteers. Meanwhile, Governor Lewis Cass of Michigan and U.S. superintendent Thomas McKenney attempted to negotiate with several Wisconsin tribes to isolate the Winnebago rebels. About 125 Menominee, Oneida, and Stockbridge warriors joined the troops. All of these groups converged from different directions to meet the Winnebagos near Portage, Wisconsin.

In an attempt to prevent bloodshed at Butte de Morts, negotiations occurred during the first two weeks of August 1827 between military officials and the Winnebago peace faction led by Four Legs and Nawkaw. Red Bird recognized the military strength arrayed against him coupled with the lack of support received from the other Winnebago bands and decided to surrender to save his people. As a consequence, Red Bird and six warriors involved in the attack on Gagnier's farm and the keelboats were arrested and sent to Fort Crawford at Prairie du Chien, Wisconsin. Red Bird sang his death song while leaving Portage, knowing that he would be executed. However, while waiting for his trial he died of dysentery in January 1828. The others who had been arrested were convicted and sentenced to death but were soon thereafter pardoned.

In August 1829 the Winnebago chiefs were forced to sign their first cession treaty. The Treaty of Prairie du Chien relinquished Winnebago land claims in Illinois and Wisconsin south of the Wisconsin and Fox rivers. A number of Winnebagos were angered by the treaty and continued white settlement. This played a part in the decision by the prophet White Cloud to enter the Black Hawk War in 1832 and in the consequent loss of more land to the government in their defeat.

JUSTIN D. MURPHY AND LORIN M. LOWRIE

See also

Atkinson, Henry; Black Hawk War; Illinois; Red Bird; Winnebagos

References

Nicholas, Roger. *General Henry Atkinson.* Norman: University of Oklahoma Press, 1965.

Wyman, Mark. *The Wisconsin Frontier.* Bloomington: Indiana University Press, 1998.

Winnemucca
Birth Date: ca. 1820
Death Date: October 1882

Influential Northern Paiute leader who worked hard, yet ultimately unsuccessfully, to ensure peaceful relations with nonnatives. The Northern Paiutes traditionally ranged in present-day central and eastern California, western Nevada, and eastern Oregon. Winnemucca was born circa 1820, probably in northwestern Nevada. Prior to assuming responsibility as chief, Winnemucca (also known as Po-i-to or Old Winnemucca) was a medicine man and an antelope charmer.

Historical knowledge of Winnemucca's life begins with his ascent to tribal leadership. When Captain Truckee, Winnemucca's father-in-law, left on an expedition to California, probably accompanying Captain John C. Frémont in the mid-1840s, he appointed Winnemucca the band's leader. Winnemucca's status as chief was recognized internally among the Northern Paiutes, distinguishing him from leaders who were appointed and acknowledged only by nonnatives.

Winnemucca assumed leadership of the Northern Paiutes at a critical moment in Paiute history. Regular contact with whites had begun only a few years earlier, under Truckee's leadership, and changes to everyday life were imminent. Truckee had welcomed whites with open arms because their arrival signaled the fulfillment of a Paiute prophecy. In a dream, however, Winnemucca saw whites bringing bloodshed and destruction among the Northern Paiutes, so he did not celebrate the growing American presence. He sought peaceful relations with whites whenever possible but did not stand idly by to see his people abused.

In 1855 Winnemucca negotiated the Honey Lake Valley agreement with white citizens of Honey Lake, California, to minimize conflict between the communities. According to the agreement, when a member of one party committed a crime against a member of the other, the communities would negotiate and turn over the perpetrator, thereby eliminating the need for continued

Winnemucca ("The Giver") was a noted Paviotso (Paiute) chief in western Nevada who worked diligently and without success to bring about peaceful relations between the Native Americans of the region and whites. (National Archives)

conflict. By 1860 Winnemucca had been accused of not abiding by the terms of his own agreement when he was unhelpful in the investigation of the murder of D. E. Demming, believed to have been committed by Paiutes. But the agreement had collapsed on both sides. Winnemucca would not turn over members of his community each time an American accused a Paiute, and the Honey Lake community was rapidly filling with new citizens who had no regard for the 1855 agreement. At the same time, Winnemucca was outraged by the white exploitation of another agreement in which American cattle herders leased land from Northern Paiutes.

In the spring of 1860 tensions between the Paiutes and Americans grew until they reached a climax in the so-called Pyramid Lake War. Winnemucca participated in the conflict at Pyramid Lake, although by 1862 he was exchanging gifts with Nevada governor James Nye on neutral ground in an effort to maintain peace. In 1865, 30 Paiutes were massacred at Pyramid Lake, including Winnemucca's wives, several daughters, and other family members. Nevertheless, in 1867 Winnemucca sent a letter to the Nevada government at Carson City in hopes of negotiating peace for his people once again.

By this time Winnemucca was widely recognized by the Mormons, other Americans, and some of his own people as the first overall chief of the Northern Paiutes. In 1870 the 5,000 Northern Paiutes still operated in small semiautonomous bands of 50 to 200. Each had its own chief, yet many acknowledged Winnemucca as the overall chief. Notably, Winnemucca never organized all of his subordinate chiefs but was known as the "traveling chief." He negotiated with Indian agents and the military on behalf of his people as they steadily lost land and freedom and became increasingly dependent on government rations for survival.

Following the Bannock War (1878), in the winter of 1879–1880 Winnemucca and his daughter Sarah (who would become famous as an educator and a writer) traveled to Washington, D.C., and met with Secretary of the Interior Carl Schurz and President Rutherford B. Hayes to inform them of the Northern Paiutes' primary concerns: their lack of essential supplies, exploitation by Indian agents, and the government's unfulfilled promises to help them settle in a permanent, peaceful home. Winnemucca continued caring for his people until his death in October 1882 at Coppersmith Station, Utah.

AMY S. FATZINGER

See also
Bannock War; Mormonism; Paiutes, Northern; Winnemucca, Sarah

References
Hopkins, Sarah Winnemucca. *Life among the Piutes: Their Wrongs and Claims.* 1883; reprint, Reno: University of Nevada Press, 1994.

Knack, Martha C., and Omer C. Stewart. *As Long as the River Shall Run: An Ethnohistory of Pyramid Lake Indian Reservation.* Berkeley: University of California Press, 1984.

Winnemucca, Sarah
Birth Date: ca. 1844
Death Date: October 7, 1891

Noted Paiute interpreter, writer, and educator and daughter of Paiute chief Winnemucca. Born in western Nevada probably in 1844, Sarah Winnemucca's birth name was Thocmentony. After learning English and living among whites, she changed her name to Sarah. She is also known as Sarah Winnemucca Hopkins, her married name.

When she was young Winnemucca went to California with her mother and siblings; there she first came in contact with whites. She quickly learned English and for a time attended a Catholic school. Sometime in the 1850s she returned to Nevada and found work as a domestic servant for a prominent white family. In the meantime she began acting as an interpreter between the Paiutes and U.S. military and government officials. Her keen intelligence and fluency in English impressed American officials. During the Snake War (1864–1868) she served as the official interpreter in talks involving U.S.-Paiute relations.

After that conflict Winnemucca continued as an interpreter and a peace diplomat, hoping to bridge the gap between U.S. officials and Native American leaders. She tried unsuccessfully to broker a peace during the 1878 Bannock War. The following year she lectured in San Francisco and was critical of U.S. policies toward Native Americans. In the early 1880s she traveled to Washington, D.C., where she lobbied U.S. officials for the return of Paiute land and the right to self-governance. Although some officials were insulted by Winnemucca's criticism, she had numerous supporters in the U.S. Army, who had not forgotten her efforts to secure peace and her work as an interpreter.

In 1883 and 1884 Winnemucca lectured in numerous eastern cities, speaking about Native American rights. In her travels she met with a number of prominent Americans including Senator Henry Dawes, whose plan to allot land to individual Native Americans came to fruition in the Dawes Severalty Act of 1887. In early 1885 Winnemucca returned to Nevada, where she founded a school for Native American youths. She was perhaps best known for her book *Life among the Piutes: Their Wrongs and Claims,* first published in 1883. She died of tuberculosis on October 7, 1891, in Henry's Lake, Idaho.

PAUL G. PIERPAOLI JR.

See also
Bannock War; Dawes Severalty Act; Paiutes, Northern; Snake War; Winnemucca

References
Hopkins, Sarah Winnemucca. *Life among the Piutes: Their Wrongs and Claims.* 1883; reprint, Reno: University of Nevada Press, 1994.

Knack, Martha C., and Omer C. Stewart. *As Long as the River Shall Run: An Ethnohistory of Pyramid Lake Indian Reservation.* Berkeley: University of California Press, 1984.

Winthrop, John
Birth Date: January 12, 1588
Death Date: March 26, 1649

English Puritan and the first governor of the Massachusetts Bay Colony. John Winthrop was born in Edwardstone, Suffolk, England, on January 12, 1588. He attended Trinity College at Cambridge University but did not receive a degree. For a time he practiced law and oversaw Groton Manor in England. He then decided to leave England on the Puritan expedition to North America. In 1630 he sailed with other Puritans to New England and began serving as the first governor of the Massachusetts Bay Colony that same year.

Conflict soon arose with nearby Native Americans, due in part to Winthrop's assertion that Native American land claims were invalid since they did not improve the land in the English manner. In the mid-1630s tensions heightened with the Pequots in particular. In 1636 the colony's leadership (including Winthrop, now a member of the Standing Council) decided to take action. They sent Captain John Endicott and a force of 90 men to attack those tribes deemed responsible for the killings of several Englishmen. The expedition was also directed to demand retribution from the Pequots, who were seen as complicit in the deaths.

Following Endicott's largely unsuccessful raid, word reached colonial authorities that the Pequots were seeking an alliance with the powerful Narragansetts against the English. Winthrop, who also served as commander of a militia unit, wrote to Roger Williams, the founder of Providence, Rhode Island, and requested his help. Although Winthrop had played a leading role in Williams's recent banishment from the Massachusetts Bay Colony, he recognized the important connections that Williams had forged with the Narragansett sachems. Williams convinced the Narragansetts in October 1636 to abandon their association with the Pequots and instead ally themselves with the English. In the ensuing Pequot War (1636–1638), Winthrop then persuaded Plymouth Colony to join in the effort. The Pequots were badly defeated.

Following the Pequot War, Winthrop worked with other colonial leaders to bring the New England colonies together for mutual defense purposes. By 1643 he was leading a committee that drew up Articles of Confederation among Massachusetts Bay and the colonies of Connecticut, New Haven, and Plymouth. The result was the New England Confederation. In addition to establishing collective defense, the confederation also established a means to settle intercolonial disputes.

Apart from warfare, defense, and civil issues, Winthrop also became involved—perhaps unwisely—in French politics. In 1643 he allowed Charles de Saint Étienne de La Tour to recruit troops in Boston to help him establish his leadership of French Acadia. The Frenchman had been locked in a power struggle with his rival, Charles de Menou d'Aulnay, over control of Acadia. Many colonists condemned Winthrop's association with a Roman Catholic

and questioned the wisdom of participating in a French conflict. Following these events, Winthrop nonetheless continued to play a central role in the politics of the colony until his death on March 26, 1649, in Boston.

JOSEPH W. WILLIAMS

See also
Endicott, John; Endicott Expedition; Narragansetts; Pequots; Pequot War; Puritans; Williams, Roger

References
Bremer, Francis. *John Winthrop: America's Forgotten Founding Father.* New York: Oxford University Press, 2003.

Morgan, Edmund. *The Puritan Dilemma: The Story of John Winthrop.* 2nd ed. New York: Longman, 1999.

Peterson, Harold L. "The Military Equipment of the Plymouth and Bay Colonies." *New England Quarterly* 20 (1947): 197–208.

Winthrop, John (Fitz-John)
Birth Date: March 14, 1637
Death Date: November 27, 1707

English and colonial military officer and governor of Connecticut (1698–1707). John Winthrop, also known as Fitz-John Winthrop, was the grandson of Massachusetts Bay's first governor, John Winthrop. The younger Winthrop was born in Ipswich, Massachusetts, on March 14, 1637, and enrolled at Harvard College but left in 1657 to sail to England and take a commission in the parliamentary forces during the English Civil War (1642–1649). He quickly won promotion from lieutenant to captain, serving in the forces of General George Monck in Scotland and in Monck's march on London in 1660 that led to the restoration of King Charles II to the English throne.

After the Restoration, Winthrop's unit was disbanded, and he returned to Connecticut to take up politics. He soon found himself lured back into martial pursuits, however. Winthrop fought against the Dutch in the Third Anglo-Dutch War (1672–1674) and against Native Americans in King Philip's War (1675–1676). Winthrop also served in Sir Edmund Andros's Governor's Council in the dominion of New England.

In 1690 during King William's War (1689–1697), Winthrop was commissioned a major general and given command of an expedition against Canada. He set out from Hartford, Connecticut, on July 14, 1690, intent on stopping raids by French-supported natives. He also hoped to capture Montreal, but supply problems, poor coordination, and a general lack of support soon caused him to break off the invasion and order a withdrawal. He was briefly arrested and imprisoned for treason because of the failed invasion but was subsequently exonerated by the Connecticut government.

Winthrop became governor of Connecticut in 1698 and was reelected regularly until his death in 1707. During that time he

John (Fitz-John) Winthrop (1637–1707) was a colonial military leader and governor of Connecticut during 1698–1707. (Library of Congress)

struggled to preserve the military autonomy of his province. During Queen Anne's War (1702–1713) he refused to send Connecticut troops outside the colony's boundaries. In fact, in 1704 he even disbanded the provincial militia rather than be pressured into sending Connecticut troops on distant campaigns. Winthrop died in office on November 27, 1707, while in Boston, Massachusetts.

ANDREW C. LANNEN

See also

King Philip's War; King William's War; Queen Anne's War

References

Black, Robert C. *The Younger John Winthrop.* New York: Columbia University Press, 1966.
Dunn, Richard S. *Puritans and Yankees: The Winthrop Dynasty of New England, 1630–1717.* Princeton, NJ: Princeton University Press, 1962.

Wolf Mountains, Battle of
Event Date: January 8, 1877

Military engagement that marked a turning point in the Great Sioux War (1876–1877). The fighting took place about four miles southwest of Birney, Montana, in the Tongue River Valley during a blizzard. U.S. troops led by Colonel Nelson Miles repulsed an attack of some 500 Lakota Sioux and Northern Cheyenne warriors led by Crazy Horse.

The catastrophic defeat of Lieutenant Colonel George A. Custer's 7th Cavalry Regiment in the Battle of the Little Bighorn (June 25–26, 1876) at the hands of the Lakota Sioux and Northern Cheyennes prompted a major retaliation by the United States. Congressional legislation following the debacle authorized a significant increase in the size and scope of U.S. cavalry and infantry forces in an effort to force Native American tribes to cede the Black Hills to the U.S. government and ultimately destroy the tribes' military power.

Colonel Miles was ordered to pursue and force into submission Sitting Bull's warriors, which Miles had achieved by December 1876. However, a number of Cheyennes under Chief Dull Knife, who had been defeated by U.S. troops under Colonel Ranald S. Mackenzie, had managed to move through snow and ice to join with Crazy Horse's warriors camped in the Tongue River Valley. Crazy Horse, recognizing the depleted ranks of Dull Knife's band, decided to negotiate a peace treaty with the army. When a small contingent of U.S. Army Crow scouts killed Crazy Horse's peace delegation, however, the leader became bent on revenge. Crazy Horse then began a series of small raids to draw Miles from his secure position.

On December 29 Miles and a force of some 450 soldiers of the 5th and 22nd Infantry regiments, including Shoshone and Crow scouts, marched out of Cantonment Tongue to the foothills of the Wolf Mountains. Despite blizzards and extremely frigid temperatures, Miles's men camped beside the Tongue River on the southern flank of the Wolf Mountains and established a defensive perimeter on a long ridge. On January 7, 1877, some of Miles's men captured 8 Cheyennes, and Crazy Horse and the remaining Cheyennes at a camp 20 miles distant resolved to rescue them.

On January 8 when daylight broke, Crazy Horse and Two Moons led a combined force of 500 Lakota Sioux and Northern Cheyenne warriors in what they hoped would be a surprise attack against Miles who, however, had anticipated it and had thrown up breastworks. Miles's men repulsed the attack, and when attempts were made to flank the soldiers, reserves quickly thwarted the attempt to overrun the army encampment. The battle ended shortly after Miles ordered an advance and opened artillery fire on the attackers. Captain Edmund Butler of the 5th Infantry Regiment commanded the principal contingent of army troops involved in the battle. With the weather deteriorating, Crazy Horse withdrew.

U.S. casualties in the battle were three dead and eight wounded. Crazy Horse's warriors suffered three dead, including the Cheyenne Big Crow and two Lakotas, and three others wounded, two mortally.

The Battle of Wolf Mountains ended in something of a tactical draw, but it was a strategic victory for the army as a turning point in the Great Sioux War. By early May, Crazy Horse and his followers had surrendered at Camp Robinson and moved to reservations. The battle was the last major conflict of the Great Sioux War, which eventually resulted in the removal of Native American

The Battle of Wolf Mountains on January 8, 1877, between army forces under Colonel Nelson Miles and a confederation of Indians led by Crazy Horse. Sketched by an officer of the expedition, this illustration appeared in *Frank Leslie's Illustrated Newspaper* on May 5, 1877. (Library of Congress)

tribes from the northern Plains and opened the territory to white settlers for farming and ranching.

CHARLES FRANCIS HOWLETT

See also

Black Hills, South Dakota; Cheyennes, Northern; Crazy Horse; Crows; Custer, George Armstrong; Dull Knife; Great Sioux War; Lakota Sioux; Little Bighorn, Battle of the; Miles, Nelson Appleton; Scouts, Native American; Shoshones; Sioux; Sitting Bull

References

Greene, Jerome A. *Yellowstone Command: Colonel Nelson A. Miles and the Great Sioux War, 1876–1877*. Lincoln: University of Nebraska Press, 1991.

Olson, James C. *Red Cloud and the Sioux Problem*. Lincoln: University of Nebraska Press, 1965.

Pearson, Jeffrey V. "Nelson A. Miles, Crazy Horse, and the Battle of Wolf Mountains." *Montana: The Magazine of Western History* 51 (Winter 2001): 53–67.

Rickey, Don, Jr. "The Battle of Wolf Mountains." *Montana: The Magazine of Western History* 13 (Spring 1963): 44–54.

Utley, Robert M. *Frontier Regulars: The United States and the American Indian, 1866–1891*. New York: Macmillan, 1973.

Wooster, Robert. *Nelson A. Miles and the Twilight of the Frontier Army*. Lincoln: University of Nebraska Press, 1993.

Wolf Warrior

See Mortar of the Okchai

Wood, Leonard
Birth Date: October 9, 1860
Death Date: August 7, 1927

Physician, U.S. Army officer, and chief of staff of the U.S. Army. Born in Winchester, New Hampshire, on October 9, 1860, Leonard Wood was forced by financial circumstances to earn a living at a young age. Opting for medicine, he earned a degree from Harvard in 1884. He joined the army as a contract surgeon in 1885 and participated in a protracted pursuit of Chiricahua Apache leader Geronimo through the mountains of southern Arizona and northern Mexico, for which Wood ultimately received the Medal of Honor. Geronimo finally surrendered on September 4, 1886, at Skeleton Canyon, Arizona.

In 1895 Wood was assigned to Washington, D.C., and became friends with President Grover Cleveland. When William McKinley was elected president in 1896, Wood served as personal physician to the president's hypochondriac wife. He also became a close friend of the new assistant secretary of the U.S. Navy, Theodore Roosevelt.

When war between the United States and Spain began in 1898, Wood and Roosevelt received permission from McKinley to recruit their friends into the 1st Volunteer Cavalry Regiment, which was nicknamed the Rough Riders. Wood served as colonel and commander, with Roosevelt as lieutenant colonel and second-in-command.

Wood commanded the Rough Riders in their first skirmish at Las Guásimas after which he was promoted to brigadier general. Wood commanded the 2nd Cavalry Brigade in the Battle of San Juan Hill. Shortly after the Spanish surrendered Santiago de Cuba, Wood was made first military governor of the city and then of the province. He drew upon his medical training to bring disease and starvation under control and proved to be an exceptional, if stern, administrator. His success, coupled with his Washington ties and a talent for political machinations, led to Wood's being named military governor of Cuba in December 1899. In that position he made notable strides in education, public health, and prison reform, and he established a fiscally responsible republican government. Perhaps his most notable accomplishment was his sponsorship of Walter Reed's yellow fever experiments. Immediately after Reed demonstrated the mosquito's role as a carrier of the disease, Wood used his autocratic power to authorize draconian insect-control measures. The campaign transformed Havana from one of the most dangerous cities in the world to one of the healthiest.

Wood had attained the rank of major general in the volunteer army but remained a captain in the medical corps until 1901 when, in a controversial move, Roosevelt, now the president, secured his promotion to brigadier general in the regular army ahead of 509 more senior officers.

Wood turned the government of Cuba over to an elected government in 1902 and was named commander of the Department of Mindanao (Philippines), where he fought to control Islamic insurgents. He was advanced to major general in 1904 and became commander of the Division of the Philippines in 1906. During his tenure in the Philippines, Wood was involved in a number of actions against insurgents in Mindanao, several of which resulted in the deaths of large numbers of civilians.

In 1908 Wood assumed command of the Department of the East, and in 1910 he became chief of staff of the army. In this office, which he held until 1914, he rescued the general staff system from department heads determined to prevent its implementation, introduced techniques of scientific management to the military, and worked to professionalize the officer corps.

From 1914 to 1917 Wood returned to the Department of the East as its commander. Convinced as early as 1910 that the United States would participate in a European war, Wood became a vocal advocate of military preparedness. He advocated universal military training and was a vocal opponent of Woodrow Wilson's neutrality. In 1916 Wood, who repeatedly crossed the traditional line separating military officers from politics, was briefly considered as a Republican candidate for president.

In 1917 when the United States entered World War I (1914–1918), Wilson passed over Wood for command of the American Expeditionary Force in favor of his former subordinate General John J. Pershing. Wood was relegated to training the 89th Division at Camp Funston. When that unit was sent to Europe in May 1918, Wood, at Pershing's specific request, was relieved and reassigned to train the 10th Division.

When Roosevelt died unexpectedly in 1919, Wood became his political heir and narrowly missed receiving the Republican nomination for president in 1920, even though he was still a general officer on active duty. From 1919 until 1921 he commanded the Central Division and then served on a special mission to the Philippines. He retired from active service in late 1921 and then returned to the Philippines, serving as governor-general until 1927. He died in Boston, Massachusetts, on August 7, 1927.

JACK MCCALLUM

See also
Apaches; Geronimo

References
Lane, Jack C. *Armed Progressive: General Leonard Wood.* San Rafael, CA: Presidio, 1978.
McCallum, Jack. *Leonard Wood: Rough Rider, Surgeon, Architect of American Imperialism.* New York: New York University Press, 2006.

Wood Lake, Battle of
Event Date: September 23, 1862

Military engagement between U.S. volunteers and militia and the Santee Sioux led by Chief Little Crow in southwestern Minnesota. Having failed to quell the spreading Minnesota Sioux Uprising and appearing to take too long in his pursuit of the Sioux after the engagement at Birch Coulee, Colonel Henry H. Sibley was pressured into launching a campaign from Fort Ridgely, Minnesota. With a large but mostly untrained force of volunteer infantry, cavalry, and local militia (1,619 men), Sibley departed Fort Ridgely on September 19, 1862.

Once Sibley's command passed the Yellow Medicine Agency, his intentions became clear. Sioux leaders debated whether they should attack, surrender, or flee west to Dakota Territory. Dissension among the Sioux leadership left their leader, Little Crow, with no more than 750 warriors. The remaining Sioux scattered in different directions.

Recognizing that an assault on Sibley's superior force would likely fail, Little Crow decided to set a trap for the advancing column. The idea was simple: the Sioux would allow the advance guard to pass and then fall upon the main body by firing from the tall prairie grass. The Sioux laid their ambush during the night of September 22.

On the morning of September 23 Sibley's soldiers broke camp and prepared to continue their march. Just before the march began, soldiers of Sibley's only veteran regiment, the 3rd Minnesota Infantry, ventured into nearby fields to forage for potatoes and corn. Traveling about half a mile from the main body of troops, the foraging party accidentally triggered Little Crow's ambush, leading to a general engagement. Although the ambush was launched prematurely, Sibley's command had trouble coordinating its response. Confusing bugle calls and conflicting orders caused advance elements of the 3rd Minnesota Infantry to begin withdrawing. At that moment a mounted militia force known as the Renville Rangers rushed forward and stabilized the crumbling line.

This movement by the Renville Rangers gave Sibley sufficient time to organize his effort and push forward while protecting his flanks. The 6th Minnesota Infantry brushed off a Sioux flanking maneuver from one side, while elements of the 7th Minnesota Infantry protected the opposite flank. The majority of Little Crow's ambushing force was posted farther up the road and never entered the fight. Only some 300 warriors fought in the two-hour engagement.

Toward the end of the battle Sibley was able to bring his artillery forward, break the back of Sioux resistance, and end the battle. Little Crow suffered 25 warriors killed and almost twice that number wounded. Among the dead was Chief Mankato, leader of one of the Sioux bands, killed by artillery fire. Sibley lost 7 killed and 34 wounded. Wood Lake was the final battle of the Minnesota Sioux Uprising. The Sioux subsequently disbanded and surrendered, and several hundred were eventually tried, convicted, and sentenced to death. President Abraham Lincoln, after reading trial reports, commuted the death sentences of all but 38, who were hanged at Mankato.

PATRICK R. JENNINGS

See also

Little Crow; Minnesota Sioux Uprising; Sibley, Henry Hastings; Sioux

References

Anderson, Gary Clayton. *Little Crow: Spokesman for the Sioux.* St. Paul: Minnesota Historical Society Press, 1986.

Clodfelter, Michael. *The Dakota War: The United States Army versus the Sioux, 1862–1865.* Jefferson, NC: McFarland, 1998.

Ferris, Robert, ed. *Soldier and Brave: Historic Places Associated with Indian Affairs and Indian Wars in the Trans-Mississippi West.* Washington DC: United States Department of the Interior, 1971.

Wool, John Ellis
Birth Date: February 29, 1784
Death Date: November 10, 1869

U.S. Army general. John Ellis Wool was born at Newburgh, New York, on February 29, 1784. He had little formal education before being apprenticed to an innkeeper and working in a store in Troy,

New York. Wool joined the New York Militia in 1807 and began reading for the law.

In June 1811 Wool secured a militia commission as an ensign. As the nation moved toward war with Britain, in April 1812 Wool helped raise a company of the newly created 13th U.S. Infantry Regiment and secured a commission as its captain. Dispatched that September to the Niagara front with little training, in October Wool's regiment took part in the Battle of Queenston Heights in Upper Canada; the British won the battle. Wool was in the first wave across the Niagara River and was wounded, but he managed to rally his men and capture a British battery before he was evacuated.

On his recovery Wool returned to duty on the Niagara front and was promoted to major and assigned to the new 29th Infantry Regiment in April 1813. He saw action in the Battle of Chateauguay in October 1813, another British victory. He then returned with his regiment to Plattsburg, New York, where in the summer of 1814 with fewer than 300 men he helped retard the advance of the 10,000-man British invasion force from Lower Canada. He then took part in the subsequent Battle of Plattsburg in September. For his role in the battle, Wool was brevetted lieutenant colonel.

Wool remained in the army after the war. In June 1815 he transferred to the 6th Infantry Regiment. He was promoted to

In a military career spanning five decades, Major General John E. Wool distinguished himself in three wars: the War of 1812, the Mexican-American War, and the Civil War. He was involved in numerous conflicts with Native Americans, including the Rogue River War of 1855–1856 in southern Oregon, during which he set himself against genocidal militia tactics. (Library of Congress)

colonel in April 1816 and assumed the post of inspector general of the army. Brevetted brigadier general in 1826, he was ordered to Europe in 1832 to study fortifications. During 1836–1837 he assisted Brigadier General Winfield Scott in the relocation of the Cherokee Nation from the Southeast to Indian Territory (Oklahoma), which resulted in the so-called Trail of Tears. In June 1841 Wool was advanced to permanent brigadier general and took command of the Eastern Department.

In the first six weeks of the Mexican-American War (1846–1848), Wool oversaw the mustering in and training of 10 volunteer regiments (12,000 men) in the Ohio River Valley. The War Department then ordered Wool to San Antonio, Texas, to organize a 3,400-man column for the capture of Chihuahua, Mexico. In December before arriving at his intended destination, Wool received an urgent request from Major General William J. Worth to join him and help meet a threatened attack by 15,000 Mexican troops marching north under General Antonio López de Santa Anna. Wool then led his men to Rancho Agua Nueva south of Saltillo and there joined Major General Zachary Taylor's army. Wool was second-in-command of American forces in the Battle of Buena Vista (February 22–23, 1847) and exercised control over most of the American troop movements. For his role in that battle he received a brevet to major general and a sword from Congress.

From March to November 1847 Wool commanded the Saltillo district. When Taylor left Mexico in November, Wool assumed command of U.S. forces in northern Mexico. Although forced to improvise from lack of instructions, Wool performed effectively, improving security, restoring commerce, opening schools, establishing local Mexican police, and beginning tax collection. He held this command until the end of the war.

Wool commanded in succession the Department of the East (1848–1853), the Division of the Pacific (1854–1857), and then again the Department of the East (1857–1861). He was involved in numerous conflicts with Native Americans, including the Rogue River War (1855–1856) in southern Oregon. In general he deplored the tactics employed by local militias against the Native Americans in the region and wrote numerous editorials denouncing their actions. Some of the militias' actions had bordered on genocide.

Still on duty at the beginning of the American Civil War (1861–1865) at age 77, Wool commanded the Department of Virginia. He managed to keep Union control over Fort Monroe and subsequently directed the Union occupation of Portsmouth and Norfolk, Virginia. That action brought promotion to major general the same month. In June 1862 Wool took command of the Middle Department. The next month he assumed command of VIII Corps, but he returned to administrative duties as commander of the Department of the East in January 1863, in which capacity he helped put down the New York City draft riots in July 1863. He retired from the army in August 1863 at age 79. Wool died in Troy, New York, on November 10, 1869.

SPENCER C. TUCKER

See also
Cherokees; Indian Territory; Rogue River War, Second; Scott, Winfield; Trail of Tears

References
Bauer, K. Jack. *The Mexican War, 1846–1848.* New York: Macmillan, 1974.
Hinton, Harwood P. "The Military Career of John Ellis Wool, 1812–1863." Unpublished doctoral dissertation, University of Wisconsin, 1960.
Lavender, David. *Climax at Buena Vista: The American Campaigns in Northeastern Mexico.* New York: Lippincott, 1966.
Malcomson, Robert. *A Very Brilliant Affair: The Battle of Queenston Heights, 1812.* Toronto: Robin Brass Studio, 2003.

Worth, William Jenkins
Birth Date: March 1, 1794
Death Date: May 7, 1849

U.S. Army general. William Jenkins Worth was born in Hudson, New York, on March 1, 1794. During the War of 1812 he was commissioned a first lieutenant in March 1813. He served as an aide to Brigadier General Winfield Scott, who became both mentor and friend. During the war, Worth distinguished himself in the Battle of Chippewa and in the Battle of Lundy's Lane (where he was seriously wounded) and won brevet promotions to captain and to major.

Worth remained in the army after the war. Beginning in 1820, he served for a year as commandant of cadets at the U.S. Military Academy, West Point. In 1838 he was promoted to colonel and assigned command of the 8th Infantry Regiment. During the Second Seminole War (1835–1842) he distinguished himself under Major General Zachary Taylor.

By 1841 Worth had charge of the U.S. forces in Florida. His strategy of carrying the fight to the Seminoles by the destruction of their crops and dwellings and campaigning in the hot summer months, even at high cost to his own men in sickness, helped bring the war to a victorious conclusion. His accomplishment brought a brevet promotion to brigadier general.

In 1845 Worth was assigned to Taylor's Army of Occupation in southern Texas on the Mexican border. There he became engaged in a feud with Colonel David E. Twiggs over seniority in rank. When President James K. Polk ruled in favor of Twiggs, Worth resigned his commission. Learning of the outbreak of hostilities in 1846, Worth withdrew his resignation.

Rejoining the army on the Rio Grande, Worth commanded a division in Taylor's army and became his second-in-command as a brigadier general. Worth distinguished himself in fighting for the city of Monterrey in September 1846 and was brevetted major general. As the city's military governor, he established order and secured the rights and property of Mexican civilians.

In January 1847 Worth transferred to Major General Winfield Scott's forces preparing for the invasion of Veracruz and the march on Mexico City. On March 9, 1847, Worth led the first division ashore at Collado Beach south of Veracruz. Appointed military governor of the city, Worth instituted the same effective occupation policies as at Monterey.

Worth commanded a division during Scott's march on Mexico City. On August 20, 1847, Worth's division bore most of the fighting at Churubusco and then sustained heavy casualties in the bloodbath of the Battle of Molino del Rey on September 8. Worth's division also played a key role in the final assault on and capture of Mexico City.

A serious falling out with Scott led to Worth's arrest for insubordination, but he was released on orders from President Polk. Restored to command, Worth oversaw the final withdrawal of U.S. troops from Mexico City on June 12, 1848.

Worth then commanded the Department of Texas. He died of cholera in San Antonio, Texas, on May 7, 1849. The city of Fort Worth, Texas, is named for him.

ROBERT W. MALICK AND SPENCER C. TUCKER

See also

Scott, Winfield; Seminoles; Seminole War, Second; Taylor, Zachary

References

Wallace, Edward S. *General William Jenkins Worth: Monterey's Forgotten Hero.* Dallas, TX: Southern Methodist University Press, 1953.

Wheelan, Joseph. *Invading Mexico: America's Continental Dream and the Mexican War, 1846–1848.* New York: Carroll and Graf, 2007.

Wounded Knee, Battle of
Event Date: December 29, 1890

The last major battle between the U.S. Army and Native Americans, fought between the Lakota Sioux and the U.S. 7th Cavalry on December 29, 1890, at Wounded Knee, South Dakota. The Battle of Wounded Knee, also known as the Wounded Knee Massacre, was not premeditated, but it was nonetheless a major military blunder. More than 120 years later, it remains for Native Americans a powerful symbol of their subjugation by whites.

By 1890, most of the western Native American tribes had been relegated to reservations, their lands and culture systematically eliminated. In the early 1870s Wovoka, an influential Northern Paiute medicine man, began preaching a popular peace tenet known as the Ghost Dance that dictated a life of moral behavior combined with traditional Native American customs and above all denounced violence. Many of the beleaguered western tribes embraced this religion. The Sioux, however, distorted this creed into a more militant doctrine against white oppression.

Many of the Lakotas, long fed up with the inept Indian agents of the Pine Ridge Agency, took up the Ghost Dance and moved off their reservations. Military commanders on the northern Plains

Mass burial of Lakota Sioux killed in the Battle of Wounded Knee in South Dakota on December 29, 1890. (Library of Congress)

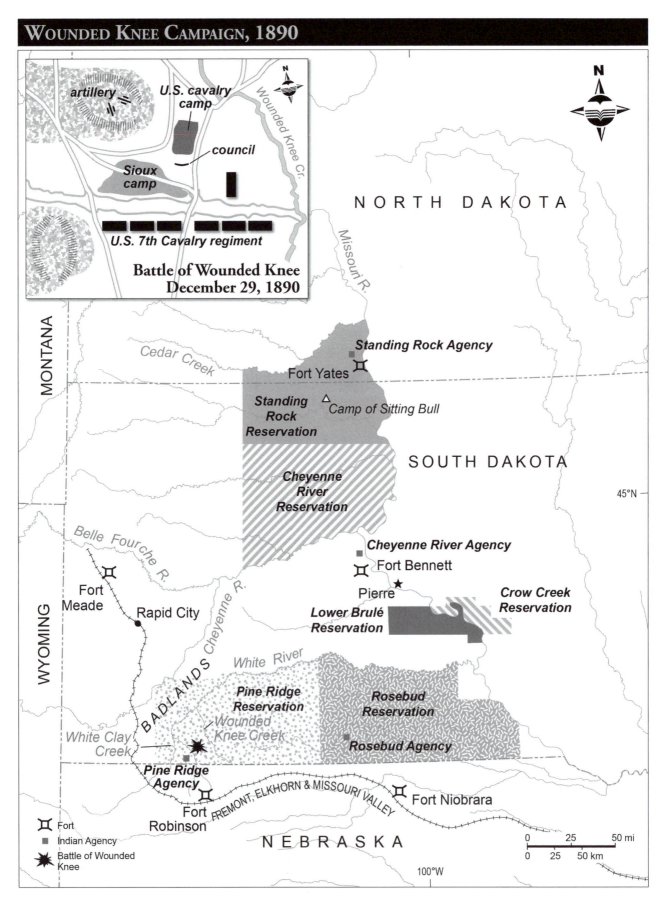

WOUNDED KNEE CAMPAIGN, 1890

artillery

U.S. cavalry camp

council

Sioux camp

U.S. 7th Cavalry regiment

Battle of Wounded Knee December 29, 1890

NORTH DAKOTA

MONTANA

Cedar Creek

Missouri R.

Standing Rock Agency

Fort Yates

Standing Rock Reservation

Camp of Sitting Bull

SOUTH DAKOTA

45°N

Cheyenne River Reservation

Belle Fourche R.

Cheyenne River Agency

Fort Bennett

Fort Meade

WYOMING

Rapid City

Cheyenne R.

Pierre

Lower Brulé Reservation

Crow Creek Reservation

BADLANDS

White River

Pine Ridge Reservation

Wounded Knee Creek

Rosebud Reservation

White Clay Creek

Rosebud Agency

Pine Ridge Agency

Fort Robinson

FREMONT, ELKHORN & MISSOURI VALLEY

Fort Niobrara

Fort

Indian Agency

Battle of Wounded Knee

NEBRASKA

0   25   50 mi

0   25   50 km

100°W

grew apprehensive and worried that other Sioux bands might join the Pine Ridge contingent. Major General Nelson A. Miles, commander of the Division of Missouri, soon ordered the arrest of two prominent Sioux leaders who might bring about this alliance: Sitting Bull and Big Foot. On December 15, 1890, Sitting Bull was killed in a scuffle when police tried to arrest him. The respected Big Foot, whose Miniconjou band resided at the Cheyenne River Agency, agreed to go to Pine Ridge at the invitation of the chiefs there. His mission was to mitigate dissension among the Oglalas and Brulés and not to promote violence. Big Foot and his people managed to evade troops posted to block his path, but they were intercepted at Wounded Knee Creek.

Colonel James W. Forsyth's 7th Cavalry was ordered out to disarm Big Foot's village. Some 500 troops surrounded the encampment on the morning of December 29. The Sioux warriors were lined up and ordered to hand over all weapons. Despite being outnumbered and with four ominous Hotchkiss cannon looming over the encampment, the Native Americans refused to surrender their Winchester repeating rifles. Tension grew as troops began to ransack the lodges and a medicine man known as Yellow Bird began to dance and incite the Sioux to action. A shot went off, and a group of nervous warriors fired into a line of soldiers. The resulting melee exploded into brutal although brief hand-to-hand combat involving clubs, knives, and rifles. Once the fight was over, the four artillery pieces shelled the village. A total of 146 Native Americans lay dead (84 men, 44 women, and 18 children), although some estimates put the number of dead much higher. Big Foot was among the dead. Another 150 Native Americans managed to escape, a number of whom later froze to death. Heaps of bodies were soon covered by fresh snow. Army casualties were 25 killed and 39 wounded.

A related skirmish occurred the following day at Drexel Mission Church, four miles north of Wounded Knee, where a group of Sioux who had escaped the slaughter burned four sheds. They also ambushed a squadron of the 7th Cavalry, killing one trooper and wounding six others. Native casualties are not known. The patrol was rescued by members of the 9th Cavalry Regiment, who had been trailing the Sioux from the White River. This ended the Battle of Wounded Knee.

General Miles, hoping to coerce the Pine Ridge tribes back to their reservations without further violence, surrounded the disgruntled Native Americans at a distance with more than 3,000 soldiers. Miles employed a combination of diplomacy and the threat of force to secure the surrender of the last of the Sioux on January 15, 1891. A grand review was staged on January 21. Hundreds of Sioux looked on as one of the largest parades of soldiers in the West marched past.

Colonel Forsyth, meanwhile, was relieved of command. A court of inquiry concluded that the soldiers did indeed try to avoid killing women and children, but their presence so close to the village made these deaths unavoidable. It was not entirely clear which side fired first. Forsyth was exonerated, but Miles charged him with dereliction of duty. Forsyth was later restored to command.

Prior to the massacre, Forsyth had placed his troops in position to disarm the village; he had not prepared for a confrontation. Although the possibility of combat was remote given the number of soldiers present, Forsyth nevertheless should have been prepared for such a contingency. Furthermore, troops should not have been allowed to mingle so closely with the Native Americans, which Miles had cautioned against.

WILLIAM WHYTE

See also
Big Foot; Cavalry Regiment, 7th U.S.; Forsyth, James William; Ghost Dance; Lakota Sioux; Miles, Nelson Appleton; Pine Ridge Reservation; Sitting Bull; Wovoka

References
Brown, Dee. *Bury My Heart at Wounded Knee.* New York: Holt, Rinehart and Winston, 1970.
Utley, Robert M. *Frontier Regulars: The United States and the American Indian, 1866–1891.* New York: Macmillan, 1973.
Wooster, Robert. *The Military and United States Indian Policy, 1865–1903.* New Haven, CT: Yale University Press, 1988.

Wovoka
Birth Date: ca. 1856
Death Date: September 20, 1932

Native American spiritual leader. A member of the Northern Paiute tribe, Wovoka was born around 1856 in what is now Esmeralda County in western Nevada. When Wovoka was about 14 years old his father died, and Wovoka was raised in the household of David Wilson, a white rancher, where he was exposed to Christian beliefs. Wovoka took the name Jack Wilson and worked for the Wilsons at least until he reached adulthood. At some point he left the Wilson ranch and lived among the Paiutes, perhaps because other Native Americans criticized him for having adopted white ways.

In about 1870 a Northern Paiute prophet named Tavibo began proclaiming that the earth would soon swallow the whites and that dead Native Americans would rise to reclaim their land. Tavibo taught his followers to worship by performing the traditional Paiute Round Dance. He briefly found a following among Native Americans in Nevada, Oregon, and California but was discredited when the events that he had prophesied failed to occur.

Tavibo's teachings evidently influenced Wovoka, and many people later claimed that Tavibo was his father. Other sources indicate that Wovoka's father was probably Numuraivo'o, who was also said to have been a prophet.

On January 1, 1889, Wovoka underwent a profound religious experience. Accounts vary regarding the details of what occurred, but believers agreed that during a total solar eclipse, Wovoka was taken up to heaven. There he spoke with God, who told him to teach the Native Americans to live a moral life, refrain from fighting, work for the whites, and perform the Round Dance as an act

Important Native American Spiritual Leaders

Name	Tribe	Dates
Aripeka	Miccosukee	ca. 1765–1860
Black Elk	Lakota Sioux	1863–1950
Black Hairy Dog	Cheyenne	ca. 1823–ca. 1883
Brave Buffalo	Lakota Sioux	ca. 1840–unknown
Box Elder	Cheyenne	ca. 1795–ca. 1892
Bull Lodge	Gros Ventre	ca. 1802–ca. 1886
Calf Shirt	Blackfoot	ca. 1844–1873
Handsome Lake	Seneca	ca. 1735–1815
Jesse Bushyhead	Cherokee	1804–1844
Kenekuk	Kickapoo	ca. 1790–ca. 1852
Kicking Bear	Lakota Sioux	ca. 1846–1904
Low Horn	Blackfoot	ca. 1822–1899
Molly Ockett	Abenaki	ca. 1744–1816
Nakaidoklini	Apache	ca. 1825–1881
Neolin (Delaware Prophet)	Delaware	ca. 1720–unknown
Passaconaway	Pennacook	ca. 1555–ca. 1665
Piapot	Crow	1816–1902
Popé	Tewa Pueblo	ca. 1620 to 1630–ca. 1690
Porcupine	Cheyenne	ca. 1847–1929
Quanah Parker	Comanche	ca. 1850–1911
Redbird Smith	Cherokee	1850–1918
Short Bull	Lakota Sioux	ca. 1845–1924
Sitting Bull	Arapaho	ca. 1854–1932
Stone Forehead	Cheyenne	ca. 1795–1876
Tenskwatawa	Shawnee	1775–1836
Wabokieshiek	Sauk and Fox	ca. 1794–ca. 1841
White Bird	Nez Perce	ca. 1807–ca. 1882
White Bull	Cheyenne	ca. 1837–1921
Wodziwob	Paiute	ca. 1844–ca. 1918
Wovoka	Paiute	ca. 1856–1932

of worship. Following these commands would lead to the resurrection of dead Native Americans, an end to illness, and the return of wild game.

Wovoka began preaching this message to the Paiutes, reinforcing his prophetic authority with his apparent ability to predict and control the weather. His accurate forecasts of rain during a drought and his alleged power to produce ice in hot weather convinced many Native Americans that his religious authority was legitimate. Wovoka also claimed to be invulnerable to gunpowder and to be able to return to heaven while in a trance. He preached that Jesus was back on earth and would be revealed when the dead arose. Because this resurrection would result from faithful performance of the ritual dances, Wovoka's religious blend of Christianity and Tavibo's teachings was commonly called the Ghost Dance movement.

News of Wovoka's teachings quickly spread eastward to the Native Americans of the Great Plains. Several made the long journey west to hear him preach and returned to share his revelations. The visitors either misunderstood or embellished what they had learned, as they proclaimed that Wovoka was the Native Americans' Messiah: Christ himself returned to earth as a Native American.

The teachings that they related drew as heavily from Tavibo's message as they did from Wovoka. Kicking Bear, a Lakota who in the autumn of 1890 told Sitting Bull of his encounter with Wovoka, asserted that the next spring, Native Americans who performed the Ghost Dance would ascend into the air while new soil appeared and buried the whites. The natural environment would be restored, the buffalo would return, and then the Native Americans would descend again to be united with their risen ancestors. In the meantime, Native Americans who wore Ghost Dance Shirts would be impervious to bullets.

Although Sitting Bull dismissed this version of Wovoka's teachings, large numbers of Native Americans believed it and faithfully performed the ritual dance. Fearing that the movement might spark a new round of warfare with the Native Americans, U.S. government officials decided to suppress the Ghost Dance among the Lakotas. After Sitting Bull was erroneously identified as a leader of the movement, he was arrested, provoking a confrontation that ended in his murder on December 15, 1890. Two weeks later at Wounded Knee, South Dakota, a battle erupted when U.S. troops tried to disarm a Lakota band whose members were adherents of the Ghost Dance movement, resulting in the deaths of more than 150 Native Americans.

Wovoka had never intended for violence to be a consequence of his teaching. In 1891 the Bureau of American Ethnology sent James Mooney to investigate his movement, and Mooney found that Wovoka instructed his followers to pursue peace and good works and to dance every six weeks while awaiting the resurrection. Wovoka's boldest statements were promises to send rain.

By 1892 Wovoka, denounced as a fraud by whites and some disappointed Native Americans, ceased preaching. Although some Native Americans continued to consider him a prophet, he was relegated to selling trinkets to earn a living. Wovoka died on September 20, 1932, near Yerington, Nevada.

JIM PIECUCH

See also
Ghost Dance; Sitting Bull; Wounded Knee, Battle of

References
Brown, Dee. *Bury My Heart at Wounded Knee.* New York: Holt, Rinehart and Winston, 1970.
Hittman, Michael. *Wovoka and the Ghost Dance.* Expanded ed. Edited by Don Lynch. Lincoln: University of Nebraska Press, 1997.

Wright, George
Birth Date: October 21, 1803
Death Date: July 30, 1865

U.S. Army officer. George Wright was born on October 21, 1803, in Norwich, Vermont. He graduated from the U.S. Military Academy, West Point, in 1822 and was assigned to the 3rd U.S. Infantry Regiment. Wright served for a time near the Canadian border and in Florida, where he saw action during the Second Seminole War (1835–1842) during which he was brevetted to major for meritorious service. During the Mexican-American War (1846–1848) he served as a captain in the 8th Infantry Regiment and was brevetted again for his efforts. By 1855 he was colonel of the 9th Infantry Regiment on the West Coast, serving in the Washington Territory.

Beginning in 1857, Wright conducted a campaign against the Spokane tribe in the area of present-day Washington state. He played an important role in the U.S. victory at the September 1, 1858, Battle of Four Lakes (Battle of Spokane Plains), which essentially ended the conflict. In July 1860 he was named commander of the Department of Oregon.

In October 1861 Wright became commander of the Department of the Pacific. He was appointed brigadier general of volunteers on September 28, 1861. Between 1861 and 1863 he supervised construction of a string of coastal forts from Oregon to California. He also stationed troops near the Mexican border to ensure that the French-installed puppet regime of Maximilian I did not aid the Confederacy. Wright negotiated a number of treaties with the region's Native Americans and relocated at least one tribe to a reservation on Santa Catalina Island, off the coast of Los Angeles. He also authorized numerous expeditions including Colonel James H. Carleton's foray into the New Mexico Territory and Arizona, which led to the reestablishment of federal control.

On July 1, 1864, Wright was named to command the Department of California, and in July 1865 he headed the newly created Department of the Columbia, which encompassed Washington, Idaho, and Oregon. He died on July 30, 1865, on his way to his posting when the steamer in which he was a passenger struck a shoal off Crescent City, California, and sank.

PAUL G. PIERPAOLI JR.

See also

Carleton, James Henry; Carleton's Campaign; Four Lakes, Battle of; Spokanes; Yakima-Rogue War

References

Masich, Andrew E. *The Civil War in Arizona: The Story of the California Volunteers, 1861–1865.* Norman: University of Oklahoma Press, 2006.

Warner, Ezra J. *Generals in Blue: Lives of the Union Commanders.* 1964; reprint, Baton Rouge: Louisiana State University Press, 2006.

Wussausmon

See Sassamon, John

Wyandots

Group of Native Americans comprising a broad section of peoples, also known as the Hurons, who lived in the Upper Great lakes region. The name "Wyandotte," or "Wyandot," is derived from the name "Wendat," meaning "islanders" or "People of the Peninsula," the self-designation of the Huron people. The name "Huron" is an archaic French reference to the hair on the head of a wild boar, meaning "boarlike" or "boorish," and referred to the Wyandot's hairstyle; the term is a slur to many Wyandots. The Wyandots are a successor tribe to the Huron Confederacy, which was destroyed in 1650 and consisted of four or five tribes. Contemporary Canadian Huron peoples are known as Hurons-Wendats. Hurons/Wyandots spoke mutually intelligible dialects of a Northern Iroquoian language.

In the 16th century the Hurons lived in the Saint Lawrence River Valley. By 1600 at the latest they inhabited an area known as Huronia, which included land between Georgian Bay (Lake Huron) and Lake Ontario. From a high of between 16,000 and 30,000 people in the early 17th century, the Huron population dropped to about 10,000 people in the mid-17th century and to fewer than 200 people in Canada in the early 19th century.

The tribes of the Huron Confederacy were led by a council formed of chiefs from each tribe. This council had no jurisdiction in purely local matters. The position of chief was inherited matrilineally, but within that context it was subject to merit and a confirmation process. Large villages were governed by clan civil and war chiefs.

There were at least 18 Wyandot villages in the early 17th century. Villages were located on high ground near waterways and woods. The larger ones were often palisaded with up to five rows of sharpened stakes. Public spaces were located between the longhouses. Larger villages had up to 100 longhouses and 2,000 people or more; the average size was perhaps 800 people. Villages were moved every 10 to 20 years after the local soil and firewood were exhausted.

Villages were economically self-sufficient. Women grew corn, beans, squash, and sunflowers. Men may have grown some tobacco. Corn, the staple food, was eaten mainly as a soup with some added foods. Women also gathered blueberries, nuts, and fruits as well as acorns in times of famine. Men hunted deer, bear, numerous other large and small game, and fowl. Women wove mats, baskets, and nets of Indian hemp, reeds, bark, and corn husks. They also made leather bags; these and the baskets were painted or decorated with porcupine quills. Men made wooden items such as utensils, bowls, and shields as well as stone or clay pipes and heavy stone tools such as axes. Some of these items were traded.

Most people traded to acquire goods to give away and thus acquire status. The Hurons were important traders even before the French arrived. They had a monopoly on corn and tobacco, and they also dealt in furs, chert, wampum beads, dried berries, mats, fish, and hemp. Extensive trade routes took the Hurons over much of the eastern Great Lakes and the Saint Lawrence River region and kept their society rich and stable.

The Hurons never achieved the kind of unity of purpose and command essential for defeating or even realistically engaging an enemy as powerful as the Iroquois, their traditional foes. The Hurons probably originated with other Iroquoians in the Mississippi Valley. The Iroquois Wars began in 1641. They were a series of extraordinarily bloody conflicts between members of the

Iroquois Confederation, led by the Mohawks, who sought both to expand their territory and to control the fur trade between the Europeans and native peoples of the western Great Lakes.

The Iroquois were successful in both significantly expanding their territory and destroying several large tribal confederacies that include the Hurons, Eries, and Susquehannocks. The Hurons were driven out of the Saint Lawrence Valley, lands that they may originally have taken by warfare from the Iroquois. Thereafter the Hurons sided with the Algonquins against the Iroquois.

The Hurons had entered the fur trade in the early 17th century, mainly as intermediaries between the French and other tribes. Catholic missionaries soon followed the traders, as did venereal disease and alcohol. Until the late 1640s, the Hurons dominated the French beaver pelt trade. The French, however, were reluctant to sell arms to unconverted Hurons, a policy that was to have disastrous consequences. Severe epidemics in the late 1630s were followed by more Christian conversions and increased factionalism.

The Iroquois, armed with Dutch firearms, launched their final invasion in 1648. These tribes were allied with the Dutch and sought to expand their trapping area and their control over neighboring tribes. Within two years they had destroyed the Hurons. Some Hurons escaped to Lorette, near Quebec City, where they were granted land. They continued to grow crops, hunt, and trap until the end of the 19th century, when craft sales and factory work became the most important economic activities. They also intermarried regularly with the French.

Other Hurons settled among tribes such as the Eries, who were themselves later destroyed by the Iroquois. Many Hurons were adopted by the victorious Iroquois nations. Some escaped to the west, where they joined with the Tionotatis (Petun, or Tobacco, nation), a related tribe. Under continuing pressure from the Iroquois, the Hurons began wandering around the Michilimackinac–Green Bay region, where they hunted and remained active in the fur trade. Although their numbers were small, membership in various alliances allowed them to play an important role in regional affairs.

Jesuits continued to minister to these people, who migrated to Detroit around 1700. They split into pro-British and pro-French groups in the mid-18th century. The latter group became known as the Wyandots and claimed territory north of the Ohio River, where they allowed Shawnee and Delaware (Lenni Lenape) bands to settle. The Wyandots fought the British in Pontiac's Rebellion (1763).

Land cessions to nonnatives began in 1745 and continued into the 19th century. The Wyandots sold their lands on the Canadian side of the Detroit River in 1790 in exchange for reserves, most of which were ceded in the early 19th century; the rest were allotted in severalty later in the century. The Wyandots sided with the British in the American Revolutionary War (1775–1783) and split their allegiance in the War of 1812.

The Wyandots' land claims in Ohio and Michigan were recognized by the United States after the War of 1812, but the tribe ceded most of these by 1819. With the decline of the fur trade, many Wyandots began farming and acculturating to nonnative society.

More land was ceded in 1832, and in 1842 the people had ceded all Ohio and Michigan lands and moved to Indian Territory (Kansas) on land purchased from the Delawares and on individual sections.

An 1855 treaty provided for land allotment (most allotments were soon alienated) and divided the tribe into citizens and noncitizens. Three years later roughly 200 Wyandots settled on the Seneca Reservation. The more traditional (noncitizen) group relocated to the new Indian Territory (Oklahoma) in 1867. The Wyandot Tribe of Oklahoma was created in 1937. It was terminated in the 1950s but was recognized again in 1978. The citizen group remained in Kansas, incorporating as the Wyandot Nation of Kansas in 1959.

BARRY M. PRITZKER

See also

Fur Trade; Iroquois; Iroquois Confederacy; Longhouse; Pontiac's Rebellion; Shawnees

References

Bonvillain, Nancy. *The Huron.* New York: Chelsea House, 1989.
Sioui, Georges E. *Huron Wendat: The Heritage of the Circle.* Lansing: Michigan State University Press, 2000.
Trigger, Bruce G. *The Huron: Farmers of the North.* New York: Holt, Rinehart and Winston, 1969.

Wyoming, Battle of
Event Date: July 3, 1778

Battle fought on July 3, 1778, in northeastern Pennsylvania involving British troops and their Iroquois allies and opposing Patriot forces. The Battle of Wyoming and the resulting massacre were part of the American Revolutionary War (1775–1783). Along the eastern seaboard, the conflict was a war of traditional 18th-century armies employing the principles of European warfare. On the frontier, however, a different war was waged between irregular forces with little concern for established norms of civility or warfare.

The Battle of Wyoming, which unfolded along Pennsylvania's Susquehanna River, was the bloodiest of these frontier engagements, with aftershocks out of proportion to its tactical significance. Major John Butler and his combined force of Loyalist Rangers and Iroquois warriors smashed the American militia that ventured out to meet them on July 3, taking, by Butler's count, some 227 scalps.

The Wyoming Valley comprises a 25-mile stretch of plain along the northern reaches of the Susquehanna River. Prior to the American Revolution, Connecticut's Susquehanna Company had sponsored settlers on the fertile lands based on royal grants that appeared to give the valley to the colony of Connecticut. The terms of William Penn's grant contradicted Connecticut's, however, throwing the area's ownership and administration into dispute. Wyoming's citizens rejected Pennsylvania's claims, and in turn Pennsylvania refused responsibility for providing protection to them. Connecticut could not protect the region because it was too far away. Furthermore, a sizable Loyalist element existed within

Painting of Patriots attacked by Loyalists and Seneca warriors in the Wyoming Valley of Pennsylvania in 1778 during the American Revolutionary War. Patriot propaganda identified this as the Wyoming Massacre. (Christie's Images/Corbis)

the valley's population, and the river offered easy access to the settlements from Iroquois territory.

The Wyoming settlements stood on the frontier at the outbreak of the American Revolution. Settlers had fortified their lands, building a series of forts and blockhouses while organizing the 24th Connecticut Militia to garrison them. The need for such fortifications had become painfully clear by the end of 1777. The Iroquois Confederacy, which American diplomats had diligently worked to keep neutral and the British had courted as potential allies, had split, with the Senecas, Mohawks, and most of the Cayugas supporting the British. Displaced Loyalists from the Mohawk and upper Susquehanna valleys, unified under the command of Major John Butler, provided the operational direction for the combined forces. During the early months of 1778, the combined Loyalist-Iroquois force laid waste to the frontier farming regions of New York and Pennsylvania.

The Wyoming settlement's turn came in late June and early July 1778. Butler's party of 500–600 Iroquois warriors and 100 rangers began moving south from Tioga, a Native American settlement on the Susquehanna near the border with New York. The force

remained undetected until June 30, when it overwhelmed a group of farmers laboring in a cornfield a few miles from Jenkins' Fort. With the help of local Loyalists, Butler proceeded to the vicinity of Wintermoot's Fort and the following day demanded the surrender of its occupants, promising to spare their lives if they capitulated. The local commander agreed to surrender.

On the following morning, Butler secured the surrender of Jenkin's Fort under the same promise. Dispatching his Iroquois and rangers to destroy the farms and fields of the valley, Butler next turned his attention to the main militia garrison of Forty Fort. On the morning of July 3, Butler's messenger arrived with a demand for the fort's capitulation, the surrender of all Continental troops present (there was a company of Continentals there), and the handover of all public stores, especially gunpowder, in exchange for parole and the safety of all civilians.

The combined strength of Continentals and militia in or around Forty Fort amounted to some 375 men. Continental lieutenant colonel Zebulon Butler commanded the American force, with Colonel Nathan Dennison, commander of the 24th Connecticut Militia, as second-in-command. They chose at first to stall, hoping for reinforcements, and then later changed course and ventured forth to do battle.

Zebulon Butler knew little about the strength of his opposition, but he did know from his scouts that they were congregated around Wintermoot's Fort. He moved his soldiers forward to a field north and west of the fort, deploying them in battle line. Many of his soldiers possessed only the most rudimentary training, and their inexperience would tell. Butler advanced, expecting to find his enemy in the woods to his front. John Butler, however, had deployed his men to the front of the advancing Americans and in a swampy thicket along their right flank. Warriors in the swamp, under the command of Sayenqueraghta, the primary Seneca chief, were to hold their fire until the American line had passed and then fall upon its flank and rear.

The plan worked brilliantly. Coming under aimed fire from the front, Zebulon Butler's soldiers responded with volley fire that accomplished little. On order, Sayengueraghta's warriors fell upon the American right flank and crushed it. In the confusion that followed, Zebulon Butler's soldiers fled for their lives, many opting to cross the Susquehanna hoping to find safety on its eastern shore. Few made it to the water before being overtaken, killed, and scalped. Those who tried to surrender met the same fate. Only a handful of soldiers, including Zebulon Butler and Dennison, survived, straggling back to Forty Fort. The fort and its inhabitants capitulated the following day on liberal terms, which included the safety of those who surrendered. John Butler claimed that the attack had resulted in 227 scalps taken, while Dennison tallied the dead at 301.

John Butler's raid into the Wyoming Valley had produced a tactical victory with consequences that reached George Washington's Continental Army. The Susquehanna frontier now disintegrated as inhabitants fled for safety to the lower Susquehanna or eastward toward the Delaware River. Continental Army quartermasters found the procurement of supplies more difficult. Yet the campaign also hurt the British cause. The Battle of Wyoming became known as the Wyoming Massacre in Patriot propaganda and thus increased resentment against the British and their Native American allies. Under pressure from New York governor George Clinton and Pennsylvania governor John Reed, Washington reluctantly dispatched Major General John Sullivan and an army of 4,000 men into the Susquehanna Valley the next summer. When Sullivan's foray was completed, more than 40 Iroquois villages lay in ruins, with croplands decimated. The border war continued until the 1783 peace treaty, but the Iroquois had been dealt a severe blow, although most remained in the fight until the end.

JOSEPH R. FISCHER

See also

Cayugas; Iroquois; Iroquois Confederacy; Mohawks; Native Americans and the American Revolutionary War; Senecas

References

Fischer, Joseph R. *A Well-Executed Failure: The Sullivan Campaign against the Iroquois, July–September 1779.* Columbia: University of South Carolina Press, 1997.

Mann, Barbara Alice. *George Washington's War on Native America, 1779–1782.* Westport, CT: Praeger, 2005.

Williams, Glenn F. *Year of the Hangman: George Washington's Campaign against the Iroquois.* Yardley, PA: Westholme, 2005.

Williamson, James R., and Linda A. Fossler. *Zebulon Butler: Hero of the Revolutionary Frontier.* Westport, CT: Greenwood, 1995.

Y

Yakima-Rogue War

Start Date: 1855
End Date: 1858

The Yakima-Rogue War was one of the largest conflicts fought between whites and Native Americans in the Pacific Northwest. The war, fought from 1855 to 1858, encompassed two conflicts: that with the Yakima (Yakama) tribe, living along the Columbia and Yakima rivers to the lee of the Cascade Mountains in Washington Territory, and that with the Rogue River tribe, ranging farther south in the Oregon Territory.

Although the Yakimas had refused to participate in the Cayuse War (1848), they soon found themselves facing a steady influx of white settlers and prospectors onto their lands. Shortly after Oregon's reorganization into the Oregon and Washington territories in 1853, Isaac Stevens, Washington's first governor, superintendent of Indian affairs, and chief officer of the Northern Pacific Railway Survey, sought land for a proposed railroad route from the Mississippi River to Puget Sound. Along with Joel Palmer, Oregon superintendent of Indian affairs, and James Doty, treaty secretary, Stevens hastily negotiated several treaties at the 1855 Walla Walla Council with the Walla Walla, Cayuse, Umatilla, Nez Perce, and Yakima tribes. The negotiations coerced a total of 14 tribes onto a new Yakima Indian Reservation. In return for the cession of some 10.8 million acres of territory, the government promised a full range of services, generous annuities, and the assurance that removal would occur upon ratification of the treaties in about four years. Although the Yakimas signed the agreement on June 9, 1855, Kamiakin and other leaders refused to accept its terms. Within two weeks of concluding a third treaty, Stevens declared the area east of the Cascades open to settlement. Tensions escalated when settlers and prospectors poured into the region, exacerbated by the discovery of gold along the border of Yakima land and on the recently established reservation itself.

In September 1855, 5 warriors led by Qualchin (son of Kamiakin's uncle Chief Owhi) killed 6 prospectors in retaliation for attacks on the Yakimas. The war began shortly after Andrew Bolon, the Indian agent sent to investigate the incident, was killed by warriors. Several tribes quickly united under Kamiakin, and a force of about 1,500 warriors defeated 102 troops under Major Granville Haller at Toppenish Creek on October 6.

This early success encouraged other tribes to ally with Kamiakin, who became the target of an expedition led by Brigadier General Gabriel Rains. When Kamiakin's force became separated from him at Union Gap, Rains disregarded Kamiakin's request for peace and razed a Catholic mission for supposedly assisting the Native Americans.

The war quickly extended to two fronts when the Rogue River tribe began raiding from the Table Rock Reservation in response to dismal living conditions. On October 8, settler volunteers attacked a Native American camp and killed 23 of its inhabitants. Raids continued until December, when Lieutenant Colonel James Kelly marched 350 settler volunteers through the Walla Walla Valley and eventually discussed peace with Chief Piupiumaksmaks. Rumors of deception resulted in a battle that killed the chief, and reports of his mutilation prompted other tribes to launch attacks throughout the Plateau region.

On February 23, 1856, warriors struck settlements along the lower Rogue River, killing 31 whites and destroying more than 60 homes. Brigadier General John E. Wool of the Pacific Division then sent three columns of troops to the region. During a skirmish at Big Meadows in May, Captain A. J. Smith's column suffered 11 dead and 20 wounded against a large Native American force led by Chief Old John. The Native Americans withdrew when Captain C. C. Augur's relief column arrived. By June, the arrival of more volunteers convinced many Indians to surrender.

On the northern front, the Yakimas attacked a blockhouse in the Cascades, convincing Wool to send Colonel George Wright and members of the 9th U.S. Infantry to occupy the Walla Walla and Yakima valleys. A truce was reached in July following the defeat of the Walla Wallas and Cayuses in Grande Ronde Valley by militia led by Lieutenant Colonel Benjamin Shaw. To strengthen control over the Yakima Valley, Major Robert Garnett supervised construction of Fort Simcoe.

A steady flow of settlers to the area led to renewed hostilities, and in September 1856 Stevens called a second Walla Walla Council, demanding the unconditional surrender of hostile tribes. Most tribes signed the resultant treaty, but Kamiakin, Owhi, and Qualchin fled. Despite efforts by Wool and Wright to restrain encroachment through 1857, trespassing prospectors triggered several Native American attacks, culminating in the renewal of major conflict in 1858. In May 1858 a combined force of more than 1,000 Native Americans defeated 159 troops under Lieutenant Colonel Edward Steptoe at the Battle of Pine Creek. Wright and a force of 570 troops, supported by six howitzers, were now sent to deal with the renewed fighting. Wright inflicted a decisive defeat on the Native Americans near Spokane in the Battle of Four Lakes (September 1, 1858). Howitzers and long-range rifle fire broke a Native American mounted charge, while U.S. dragoons pursued the dispersed warriors. Wright further weakened Indian resistance by killing 800 horses and destroying cattle and food supplies. Kamiakin fled to Montana, while more than a dozen other chiefs were executed or killed trying to escape, including Qualchan and Owhi after they had surrendered. On September 23, Wright imposed a treaty relocating most tribes to a reservation south of present-day Yakima, Washington, thereby restoring peace to the Columbia Plateau.

MICHAEL F. DOVE

See also
Fort Simcoe; Four Lakes, Battle of; Kamiakin; Steptoe, Edward Jenner; Stevens, Isaac Ingalls; Wool, John Ellis; Wright, George

References
Beckham, Stephen Dow, ed. *Oregon Indians: Voices from Two Centuries.* Corvallis: Oregon State University Press, 2006.
Schuster, Helen H. *The Yakimas.* Bloomington: Indiana University Press, 1982.
Stern, Theodore. *Chiefs & Change in the Oregon Country,* Vol. 2. Corvallis: Oregon State University Press, 1996.

Yamasees

Native American group from central Georgia that resettled in large numbers some 100 miles from Charles Town (present-day Charleston, South Carolina). The Yamasees were related to the Hitchitis and the Oconees, two other Muskogean-speaking groups that were part of the Creek Confederacy. At the time of first contact with Europeans, the Yamasees lived on the Oconee River above the fall line in Georgia. The site was along a major east-west trade route.

The Spanish tried to convert the Yamasees to Christianity in 1570 but had little success. However, the Yamasees remained involved in the Spanish trade through the Guale missions on the Georgia coast. They also probably added to their numbers as Guales and Timucuas in the Spanish missions fled northward to escape Spanish rule.

In the early 1660s the slave-raiding Westos arrived in South Carolina and Georgia. Westo raids hit the Yamasees hard. These raids compelled the Yamasees to disperse and resettle in several different areas. Some Yamasees settled among the natives at Spanish missions. Others moved to the lower Chattahoochee River area to live among other groups that spoke various dialects similar to their own.

Although the Yamasees settled among and near the Spanish missions, most did not wish to embrace Christianity. Finally, the Spanish tried to force conversion and participation in their native labor system, known as the *repartimiento* (meaning "to divide" or "to redistribute"). Because of these Spanish demands and the inability of the Spaniards to protect them from French and English pirate raids, many Yamasees moved to the lower Savannah River in the early 1680s. In 1684 the Yamasees established a trade relationship with the English that for a time benefited both parties.

In the years immediately prior to 1715, British colonists began to abuse their Yamasee trading partners. This included fraud, extortion, and physical beatings. The settlers also began to ignore the ceremonial trappings that native people expected to accompany trade. This treatment of the Yamasees, along with Yamasee participation in a growing alliance among the southern tribes dominated by the Creeks, led to the Yamasee War (1715–1717).

In the Yamasee War, almost all of the natives in South Carolina and Georgia took up arms against the Carolina settlers and nearly destroyed the colony. In 1716, however, the colonists managed to defeat the native alliance. Some Yamasees then fled to Florida for protection by the Spanish near St. Augustine. Others sought protection among the Creeks, who were in the process of moving from central Georgia back to the Chattahoochee River. The Hitchitis eventually absorbed most of these Yamasees.

In an attack on the Spanish at St. Augustine in 1727, the British destroyed the Yamasee village located nearby. When the Spanish ceded Florida to the British at the end of the French and Indian War (1754–1763), many of the last of the Spanish Yamasees left with the Spanish for the West Indies. Others remained in Florida and assimilated into the Miccosukee Seminoles during the latter half of the 18th century and the early 19th century. A small number among the Miccosukee Seminoles preserved the Yamasee name until 1812. After that the Yamasees disappeared from the historical record, and it is believed that no descendants remain alive today.

DIXIE RAY HAGGARD

See also

Creeks; Native American Trade; Native American Warfare; Skulking Way of War; Westos; Yamasee War

References

Corkran, David H. *The Creek Frontier, 1540–1783.* Norman: University of Oklahoma Press, 1967.

Hahn, Stephen C. *The Invention of the Creek Nation, 1670–1763.* Lincoln: University of Nebraska Press, 2004.

Oatis, Steven J. *A Colonial Complex: South Carolina's Frontiers in the Era of the Yamasee War, 1680–1730.* Lincoln: University of Nebraska Press, 2004.

Worth, John E. *The Struggle for the Georgia Coast: An Eighteenth Century Retrospective on Guale and Mocama.* Anthropological Papers No. 75. New York: American Museum of Natural History, 1995.

Yamasee War
Start Date: April 15, 1715
End Date: November 1717

A costly frontier conflict that devastated the colony of South Carolina and led to the near extinction of the Yamasee tribe. The Yamasees, a Muskogean-speaking people inhabiting the southern reaches of Georgia at the time the Spanish were occupying nearby Florida, enjoyed cordial relations initially and received Franciscan missionaries until 1680, when the Spanish attempted to deport tribal members to the Caribbean to work as slaves. A war ensued, and the Yamasees migrated northward to the vicinity of St. Helena Island and present-day Hilton Head Island, where the English colony of South Carolina was developing.

Initially the Yamasees and the British were amicably disposed. The Yamasees performed useful services to the British, not the least of which was to act as a buffer between them and the Spanish, residing just to the south. The Yamasees also played a prominent role in the essential deerskin trade and fought on behalf of the English during the Tuscarora War (1711–1713).

Around this time, however, poorly regulated British traders and agents engaged in unscrupulous practices with the Yamasees, including appropriating land without payment, wholesale cheating in trade, and demanding immediate payment for tribal debts estimated at £50,000. When the Yamasees proved unable to comply, the British usually resorted to seizing women and children for the slave market. Such systematic abuse propelled the Yamasees to violence against their antagonists, and they began plotting with neighboring tribes such as the Catawbas, the Apalachees, and the Creeks to initiate military action.

The ensuing Yamasee War began on April 15, 1715 (Good Friday), when native warriors staged carefully orchestrated attacks against British outposts along the South Carolina frontier. Traders and agents were especially targeted for revenge, and upwards of 100 colonials were slaughtered at Pocotaligo. Other war bands struck at the settlement of St. Bartholomew, between the Edisto and Combahee rivers, burning it and scattering the inhabitants. The ensuing crush of white refugees toward Charles Town (present-day Charleston, South Carolina) greatly swelled the population of that region, which gave it the ability to muster sufficient manpower for defense.

Governor Charles Craven proved exceptionally able and energetic in this regard, and in late April he mounted a limited offensive with 240 men. Near Salkehatchie they engaged and defeated 500 warriors. About this same time, a second column under Colonel Alexander Mackay stormed the occupied village of Pocotaligo, dispersing a larger force of Yamasees. In another action fought on July 19, 1715, 120 militiamen under Captain George Chicken pursued a band of warriors into a swamp, surrounded them, and then attacked, killing 40 and freeing several white captives.

Warfare by this time had broken down into large-scale raiding by both sides, with notable actions at New London and Daufuskie Island (adjacent to Hilton Head Island and the Savannah River). The Yamasees and their coalition were unable to withstand the colonial resurgence and began appealing to other tribes for assistance.

Their Creek neighbors agreed to help, providing additional war bands to supplement their original contingent. Thus augmented, the Native Americans were able to resume their destructive raids and in an action near Port Royal on August 1, 1716, killed several defenders. But the South Carolinians, now reinforced by militiamen from North Carolina and Virginia, were able to withstand this new round of native attacks. They soon began to drive the Creeks and the Yamasees back into the nearby swamps of Georgia.

By January 1716 the Creeks felt sufficiently threatened to appeal to their traditional enemy, the Cherokees, who constituted the largest tribe in the Southeast. The Cherokees proved coy initially but, in light of their good relations with the British, announced their decision by slaughtering the Creek emissaries. This combination of colonial militia under Craven's effective leadership, now backed by ample Cherokee manpower, proved too much for the Creeks and the remnants of the Yamasee coalition. Both were soon driven from the colony, the Creeks moving deeper into Georgia and the Yamasees withdrawing completely into Florida, being welcomed by the Spanish as allies. It was not until November 1717 that the Creeks and the British formally concluded a peace treaty. The Yamasees were never a party to this agreement, and from their Florida enclave they launched sporadic raids for more than a decade.

Despite its relatively brief duration, the Yamasee War was one of the most costly conflicts waged by a European colony. South Carolina, with a population of only 5,500 settlers, took proportionately heavier losses than those incurred by New Englanders during King Philip's War (1675–1676). Many frontier communities lay gutted, and the lucrative deerskin trade, heretofore a staple of the local economy, was severely disrupted for many years. And despite Craven's able leadership, the proprietary government's response to the crisis was perceived as sluggish. Thus, in 1719 it was overthrown by the colonists and replaced by royal governance.

The Creeks also drew important lessons from the conflict, realizing that they lacked the power to openly confront both the British and the Cherokees and, moreover, that they could not readily rely on assistance from either France or Spain. The Creeks thereafter embarked on a course of cautious neutrality, partly to offset half a century of enmity toward the Cherokees, which had arisen from this war. But the most negatively impacted were the conflict's instigators, the Yamasees. Driven from their homeland and subject to periodic raids from the new English colony of Georgia, they grew progressively weaker in numbers and were gradually absorbed by their Creek and Seminole neighbors. This once proud and influential tribe had disappeared as an identifiable culture by the end of the 18th century.

JOHN C. FREDRIKSEN

See also

Apalachees; Catawbas; Cherokees; Creeks; Seminoles; Tuscarora War; Yamasees

References

Haan, Richard L. "'The Trade Does Not Flourish as Formerly': The Ecological Origins of the Yamasee War of 1715." *Ethnohistory* 28 (1982): 341–358.

Johnson, David L. "The Yamasee War." Master's thesis, University of South Carolina, 1980.

Oatis, Steven J. *A Colonial Complex: South Carolina's Frontiers in the Era of the Yamasee War, 1680–1730.* Lincoln: University of Nebraska Press, 2004.

Yankton and Yanktonai Sioux

See Nakota Sioux

Yaquis

Native American tribe residing principally in the northwestern Mexican state of Sonora and in southern Arizona (beginning in the late 19th century). In most histories, the December 1890 Wounded Knee Massacre marks the end of the Indian Wars in the continental United States. Yet almost three decades later in the waning years of the decade-long Mexican Revolution, U.S. cavalry engaged in a fierce, if brief, battle with a band of Yaquis in Arizona.

Long before the Spanish conquest of Mexico, the Yaquis had settled the Sonora region of northern Mexico. Although there is evidence of Yaqui contacts with the Toltecs and the Aztecs, the Yaqui lands were located far enough from the centers of those Meso-American empires that their remoteness as well as their

reputation for ferocity spared them from conquest. Indeed, these same variables served the Yaquis well during the first two centuries following the Spanish conquest. In two instances the Yaquis defeated sizable Spanish military expeditions dispatched to subdue them.

Numbering about 30,000 people upon first contact with the Spanish in 1533, the Yaquis counted only about 20,000 people by 1600. By the early 1600s they lived in about 80 rancherias, each having a population of some 250 people. The rancherias were essentially small self-contained villages featuring dome-shaped adobe houses with slightly tapered roofs covered with river cane. After the Jesuits established their missions around 1617, the rancherias were consolidated into eight villages, with 2,000–4,000 people each.

The Yaquis were excellent agriculturalists, raising corn, squash, beans, and amaranth, which grew well in the fertile river valleys. They supplemented this activity with widely available wild foods such as cactus fruit, mesquite beans, succulents, wild grass, and wild game, which included rabbit and deer. They also harvested shellfish and large saltwater fish from the Gulf of California (Sea of Cortez). The Jesuits introduced the Yaquis to peaches, figs, pomegranates, and wheat, which the Yaquis grew with considerable success. By the late 17th century the Yaquis began using plow animals, mainly oxen that had been introduced to them by the Jesuits.

Despite their spirited resistance to Spanish civil authority, the Yaquis welcomed Jesuit missionaries who profoundly transformed Yaqui life in two ways. First, they permitted the Yaquis to blend their traditional religious beliefs and practices with Roman Catholic doctrines and rituals. Thus, while the Yaquis continued to believe that the world consisted of four separate realms—the animal realm, the flower realm, the human realm, and the realm of death—and that the continuation of life depended on maintaining a difficult balance among those realms, Easter became the focal holy day in their spiritual calendar. Second, the Jesuits convinced the Yaquis, who had lived in scattered villages, to concentrate in eight towns, which not only were easier to defend but also gradually became the most important locations in the Yaquis' cultural mythos.

In the middle of the 18th century the Spanish ordered the Jesuits out of the Yaqui territories and eventually subdued the Yaquis. Several subsequent bloody rebellions against Spanish authority occurred. After Mexico became independent of Spain in the 1820s, the Yaquis reasserted their right to autonomy, but the effort led by Juan Banderas ended with his execution in 1833. About a half century later the Yaqui leader Cajeme directed a well-organized and extended rebellion against the Mexican dictator Porfirio Díaz. During this conflict Yaqui towns were ruined, and resistance to the Mexican military was continued for the most part in guerrilla fashion, principally in the Bacatete Mountains. The rebellion finally ended with the defeat of the largest remaining Yaqui force and Cajeme's execution in 1887. Díaz then sought to eliminate the

Yaqui Indians, circa 1910. (Library of Congress)

10,000 Yaquis reside in the United States, 6,000 of whom live in southern Arizona. Approximately 25,000 Yaquis currently reside in Sonora, Mexico.

Martin Kich

See also
Mexico

References
Holden, W. C. *Studies of the Yaqui Indians of Sonora, Mexico.* New York: AMS, 1979.
Moises, Rosalio, Jane Holden Kelley, and William Curry Holden. *The Tall Candle: The Personal Chronicle of Yaqui Indian.* Lincoln: University of Nebraska Press, 1971.
Spicer, Edward H. *The Yaquis: A Cultural History.* Tucson: University of Arizona Press, 1980.

Yavapais

Native American group indigenous to central and western Arizona. The name "Yavapai" is from the Mojave word "Enyaéva Pai," meaning "People of the Sun." The Yavapais are sometimes confused with the Apaches because of their long association and are occasionally (and erroneously) referred to as Mojave Apaches or Yuma Apaches. The Yavapais spoke a dialect (similar to Pai) of Upland Yuman, a Hokan-Siouan language.

Traditionally the Yavapais controlled roughly 10 million acres in present-day west-central Arizona. This transitional area between the Colorado Plateau and the lower deserts provided them with a salubrious mixture of desert, mountain, and plateau plants and animals. Today, Yavapais live on the Fort McDowell, Camp Verde, and Yavapai reservations in Arizona.

The Yavapais were probably descended from the ancient Hakataya peoples. Traditionally they consisted of four major divisions: the Kewevkapayas (southeastern), the Wipukpayas (northeastern), the Tolkepayes (western), and the Yavepes (central). Each was further divided into local bands.

The Yavapais were a nomadic people who followed the ripening of wild foods. The agave plant was a staple; they also harvested wild plants such as cactus fruit, mesquite beans, greens, acorns, piñon nuts, walnuts, seeds, and berries. Women gathered these wild foods. Game included deer, quail, fox, antelope, and rabbit; people also ate lizards, caterpillars, yellow jacket nests, and turkeys. Small amounts of corn, beans, and squash were grown or traded, mostly by the western band.

Contact between the Spanish and the Yavapais first occurred in 1582. After Father Francisco Garces lived with the Yavapais in 1776, this contact became more frequent. Nevertheless, the Yavapais lived traditionally until the 1850s, largely because their country was too rough for the Spaniards, Mexicans, or Anglo-Americans to settle. Some bands, especially the Kewevkapayas, raided with the Apaches. After the Mexican Cession in 1848, more white travelers

threat posed by the Yaquis by forcibly dispersing them as slave labor across the haciendas of southern Mexico.

To escape enslavement, a large number of Yaquis chose to flee north across the U.S.-Mexican border into southern Arizona. There they swelled the small Yaqui communities that had been established over several centuries. These communities were generally located in agricultural areas and near large cities, where Yaquis could find work as laborers.

The decade-long Mexican Revolution began with the overthrow of Díaz in 1911. The Yaquis gradually reconcentrated in their Sonoran homeland, fighting on the side of a succession of leaders who promised to guarantee their autonomy and then defaulted on those promises. When Álvaro Obregón consolidated his power in 1915 and 1916 and decided to distribute some Yaqui territory as land grants to his supporters, the Yaquis resisted and called upon tribal members in Arizona for assistance.

On June 8, 1918, just east of Nogales, Arizona, E Troop of the U.S. 10th Cavalry Regiment intercepted the force of Yaqui volunteers who were on their way to fight against Obregón's forces in Sonora. The Yaquis were turned back because the United States was involved in World War I (1914–1918) and could not afford any further political or military complications with Mexico.

In 1926 the Mexican military launched a yearlong campaign against the Yaquis, blasting the last of the resisters out of the mountains with artillery and bombs dropped from aircraft. For the next half century the Mexican Army maintained forts throughout Yaqui territory to suppress independence efforts. Today almost

View of a Yavapai Native American camp with four women and children cooking outside their wickiups; 1886 photograph by Frank Randall. (National Anthropological Archives, Smithsonian Institution, NAA INV 02048100)

and miners frequented the region, although the Yavapais tried to avoid conflict, owing primarily to their poor weaponry.

Gold was discovered in the Yavapais' region in 1863. Shortly thereafter white settlers arrived, bringing the permanent disruption of Yavapai traditional life. Hungry and under continuous attack, the Yavapais fought back. During 1872–1873, Lieutenant Colonel George Crook's bloody Tonto Basin Campaign against the Tonto Apaches and the Yavapais ended with devastating defeats of the Indians at Skull Cave and Turret Peak. Forced onto the Camp Verde Reservation after disease had killed an additional one-third of their number, the Yavapais and Tonto Apaches dug a five-mile irrigation ditch using discarded army tools and brought in a good harvest. For this they were forcibly relocated in 1875 and settled with the Apaches on the San Carlos Reservation, 180 miles to the east. Within 25 years the Yavapai population fell from 1,500 to 200.

At San Carlos, the Yavapais again tried farming. They also scouted for the U.S. Army against the Chiricahua Apaches and acquired cattle. However, flooding ruined their ditches, miners and ranchers took their land, and they still sought a return to their ancestral home. By 1900, most Yavapai had left San Carlos. Some returned to the Verde Valley, and others returned to Fort McDowell and Fort Whipple.

In 1903 Fort McDowell became a reservation, inhabited mostly by the Kewevkopaya band. The Camp Verde Reservation was established in 1910, with outlying communities such as Middle Verde, Clarkdale, and Rimrock added during the next 60 years. Fort Whipple became a reservation (Yavapai-Prescott) in 1935. The western Yavapais (Tolkepayes) received no reservation and have nearly disappeared.

The Verde River ran through Fort McDowell. The Yavapais tried farming once again, but they were soon involved in a struggle for water rights. Instead of providing funds to improve irrigation and guard against floods, the government wanted to remove the Yavapais to the Salt River Pima Reservation. Largely owing to the efforts of Carlos Montezuma, they were able to remain, but they secured little money or water. During this period, cattle grazing and wage work, both on and off the reservation, became important sources of income. From the 1950s through the 1980s, the Yavapais also fought off construction of a dam (Orme) that would have flooded most of the Fort McDowell Reservation, refusing $33 million in compensation. Finally, in 1990 the Yavapais won the passage of a law granting them sufficient water rights from the Verde River as well as $25 million in compensatory funds.

The Yavapais and Apaches leaving San Carlos settled at Camp Verde around the turn of the century, although Camp Verde is more Apache than Yavapai in character. Unable to make a living on the inadequate reservation lands, most people worked in the nearby copper industry until the 1930s and 1940s.

In 1935 a separate reservation, primarily inhabited by the Yavepe band, was created north of Prescott. Rather than organize under the Indian Reorganization Act, this group maintained the traditional governing structure until 1988. Their land base is surrounded by the city of Prescott.

BARRY M. PRITZKER

See also

Apaches; Crook, George; Indian Reorganization Act; Reservations

References

Braatz, Timothy. *Surviving Conquest: A History of the Yavapai Peoples.* Lincoln: University of Nebraska Press, 2003.

Ruland-Thorne, Kate. *Yavapai: The People of the Red Rocks, the People of the Sun.* Sedona, AZ: Thorne Enterprises, 1993.

Yellowstone Kelly

See Kelly, Luther Sage

Young Joseph

See Joseph, Chief

Yuma War

Start Date: October 1849
End Date: February 1852

Conflict between the U.S. government and Native Americans for control of a strategic crossing over the Colorado River near present-day Yuma, Arizona, fought between October 1849 and February 1852. The significance of the Yuma crossing was recognized early by Spanish missionaries, explorers, and military officers.

Father Francisco Garcés founded Mission San Pedro y San Pablo de Bicuñer in what is today Yuma, Arizona, on January 7, 1781, in hopes of pacifying the local Indians and maintaining control of the crossing over the Colorado River. This endeavor did not last long, however, as warriors from the Yuma (Quechan) tribe attacked the settlement after the Spanish allowed their livestock to trample and eat the Native American crops. In the attack 131 settlers, priests, and soldiers were killed, including Father Garcés and the military commander, Captain Fernando de Rivera y Moncada. Spain and later Mexico made no further effort to control the area.

Control of the Yuma area came under the authority of the United States as a result of the Treaty of Guadalupe Hidalgo, which ended the Mexican-American War (1846–1848). A year later the U.S. government sent a military detail under the command of First Lieutenant Cave J. Couts and Second Lieutenant Amiel W. Whipple into the area to survey the region and also to provide support for the thousands of settlers crossing the country to the goldfields in California. On October 2, 1849, the army established Camp Calhoun on the site of the abandoned Spanish mission. A year later the camp was moved to the banks of the Colorado River, a mile below the mouth of the Gila River, to operate a ferry that served the needs of migrants and the survey team. Established on November 27, 1850, by Captain Samuel P. Heintzelman of the 2nd Infantry, it was renamed Camp Independence.

The Yumas conducted sporadic raids against the earlier encampment beginning in October 1849. However, after the founding of Camp Independence, the number of raids increased, resulting in a bona fide war. The Yumas saw the ferry as a threat to their control over the region and grew increasingly concerned about the number of Americans traveling through their tribal territory. The attacks eventually forced the army to relocate Camp Independence to the original site of Camp Calhoun, which was on a flat mesa. The new camp was completed in March 1851 and named Camp Yuma.

Attacks on the camp and patrols from the camp continued during the spring of 1851. That June the government reduced the camp's garrison in a cost-cutting measure, but a small force remained to protect the people who had settled in the area. By the end of that summer provisions were running low, and the garrison faced possible starvation. That autumn a foraging party was sent to secure provisions, leaving behind a skeleton force of just nine men. The Yumas took advantage of this and laid siege to the camp with hundreds of warriors. The tiny garrison, weakened from the effects of starvation and scurvy, held out for more than a month before deciding to flee after learning that a relief column had been ambushed and turned back. After hiding or burying everything they could not take with them, the men abandoned the fort on December 6, 1851.

Local whites who had settled in the Yuma region also participated in the war. They competed with the Yumas for control of the river ferry. In one incident, a scalp hunter named John Joel Glanton led a group of settlers in an attack on the Yumas then operating the ferry. An unknown number of natives were killed, and the ferry was destroyed. Retribution was swift when a retaliatory attack by the Yumas ended in the deaths of Glanton and many of his followers.

In February 1852 Captain Heintzelman returned to the area with 150 troops and won a decisive battle against the Yumas, repelling 300 warriors and retaking the camp. The army quickly undertook improvements to the camp, which was renamed Fort Yuma. Heintzelman also carried out a successful effort to retake the ferry and to clear the region in a 50-mile radius of any hostile Yumas, pacifying many villages in the process.

Fort Yuma's presence established security in the region and helped to create the Colorado Ferry Company. American success secured the crossing for migrants heading to California and along with the Gadsden Purchase (1853) paved the way for completion of a second transcontinental railroad by the Southern Pacific Railroad Company in 1883.

The Yumas conducted sporadic attacks on white settlers and the garrison at Fort Yuma throughout the 1850s, but the war was essentially over in February 1852. Ironically, the decline in the military strength of the Yumas and their allies, the Mohaves, resulted not from U.S. military actions but instead from a force of Maricopa warriors who killed more than 100 Yumas and Mohaves in 1857 in retaliation for an attack on their settlements.

ROBERT W. DUVALL

See also

California Gold Rush; Mojaves

References

Hart, Herbert M. *Old Forts of the Far West.* Seattle, WA: Superior Publishing, 1965.

Utley, Robert M., and Wilcomb E. Washburn. *Indian Wars.* New York: American Heritage Press, 2002.

Z

Zogbaum, Rufus Fairchild

Birth Date: August 28, 1849
Death Date: October 22, 1925

Leading artist-correspondent of the American West and the Spanish-American War (1898). Rufus Fairchild Zogbaum was born in Charleston, South Carolina, on August 28, 1849. His father, a manufacturer of musical instruments, moved the family to New York City when Zogbaum was a boy. Zogbaum studied at the Art Students' League, an art school established in 1875, in New York City from 1878 to 1879, and from 1880 to 1882 he attended the Académie Julian, an art school established in Paris by Rodolphe Julian in 1868. At the latter school Zogbaum worked under Léon Bonnat, a leading portraitist whose work showed the influence of Diego Velázquez. Zogbaum was heavily influenced by the works of the French military artist Jean Baptiste Edouard Detaille and the French academic painter Alphonse-Marie de Neuville.

In 1884 after returning to the United States, Zogbaum traveled to Montana, where he sketched military life on the frontier. From 1883 to 1899 he contributed seven articles to the popular *Harper's Monthly*. He published his first illustrated article, "War Pictures in Times of Peace," in the August 1883 issue. The 13-page essay about French Army drill tactics was written after the author had spent several months studying the French Army. His second article, "A Home of Tommy Adkins," appeared in the October 1884 issue of *Harper's Monthly*. The 7-page article examined military life in the British Army. His third article, "A Night with the Germans," appeared in June 1885. This 8-page piece profiled life in the German Army. The 6-page article "A Day's Drive

with Montana Cowboys" appeared in the July 1885 issue. "Across Country with a Cavalry Column" was published in September 1885. This 7-page article glorified the U.S. Cavalry. His sixth article, "With the Bluecoats on the Border," was a 12-page piece that appeared in the May 1886 edition of *Harper's Monthly*. Once again covering the U.S. Cavalry, this time Zogbaum examined the interaction of frontier settlers with the U.S. Cavalry. His seventh and final article for *Harper's Monthly*, "Honor to Whom Honor Is Due," appeared in the April 1899 issue. The 7-page article examined U.S. military life, especially in the navy, during the Spanish-American War.

Zogbaum's seven articles in *Harper's Monthly* were illustrated with 24 of his paintings. His painting *Battle of Manila Bay* (1899) vividly depicts Commodore George Dewey directing the battle from his flagship, the cruiser *Olympia*. Zogbaum also published illustrated articles in the *Saturday Evening Post*, *Harper's Weekly*, *Scribner's*, and the *North American Review*. He published two illustrated books, *Horse, Foot and Dragoons: Sketches of Army Life at Home and Abroad* (1888) and *All Hands: Pictures of Life in the United States Navy* (1897).

With the coming of the Spanish-American War, Zogbaum's art depicting scenes of the American West disappeared almost entirely. As with fellow artist Frederic Remington, Zogbaum devoted all of his energies to depicting scenes of American heroism for the duration of the war. Unlike Remington, Zogbaum continued to paint military subjects for the rest of his life. Although Remington is better known, Zogbaum's works predate those of Remington and show greater attention to detail. Zogbaum's paintings, especially his depictions of military scenes done in watercolor and gouache, set the standard for future military artists. His illustrated articles covering the Spanish-American War were especially popular with the American public. After a prolific career, Zogbaum died on October 22, 1925, in New York City.

MICHAEL R. HALL

See also
Remington, Frederic

References

Goldstein, Donald M., Katherine V. Dillon, J. Michael Wenger, and Robert J. Cressman. *Spanish-American War: The Story and Photographs.* Dulles, VA: Potomac Books, 2000.

Zogbaum, Rufus Fairchild. *All Hands: Pictures of Life in the United States Navy.* New York: Harper and Brothers, 1897.

Zogbaum, Rufus Fairchild. *Horse, Foot, and Dragoons: Sketches of Army Life at Home and Abroad.* New York: Harper and Brothers, 1888.

Appendix

Decorations, Medals, and Military Honors

Decorations are symbolic awards conferred by military organizations to recognize gallantry, valor, distinguished service, or meritorious achievement. Medals, which rank below decorations in precedence, recognize service in a war, a campaign, a battle, or periods of long peacetime service. Most modern American decorations and medals consist of a metal badge suspended from a ribbon that has a color scheme unique to that specific award. The badge of the medal generally consists of a round bronze medallion. Decorations generally, but not always, have badges in some shape, with stars and crosses being the most common.

The first permanent American military decorations were introduced only in the mid to late 19th century, at about the same time the Indian Wars were reaching their culmination. Modern military decorations evolved from the system of chivalric and noble orders that existed in Europe for hundreds of years. America, of course, had no tradition of chivalric or noble orders, and for that reason there was widespread resistance to the introduction of permanent military decorations and medals during the American Revolutionary War (1775–1783) period and the early years of the republic. There were, however, other forms of recognition of valorous military conduct and distinguished service, although those honors were almost always restricted to officers. Such distinctions carried no outward badges or devices to be worn on the uniform, but much like modern military decorations, they were entered into an officer's permanent record and became key elements of his professional reputation.

During the American Revolutionary War, the three principal forms of recognition bestowed on military officers by the Continental Congress were, in reverse order of precedence, the Thanks of the Congress, the Congressional Sword, and the Congressional Gold Medal. All three distinctions were expressed through a congressional resolution. The Congressional Sword and the Congressional Gold Medal also included physical tokens of appreciation. But rather than being a military decoration for wear on the uniform, the Congressional Gold Medal was relatively large and was intended for display in a case or on a tabletop. Each individual medal was uniquely designed for the person being honored. The recipient of the first Congressional Gold Medal was General George Washington in March 1776. After the U.S. Constitution was ratified, the U.S. Congress continued all three forms of recognition until just after the American Civil War (1861–1865). The U.S. Congress today continues to confer the Congressional Gold Medal as its highest form of recognition, but the vast majority of those awarded since the start of the 20th century have gone to civilians for nonmilitary achievements. Quite often, the Congressional Gold Medal is confused with or mistakenly equated to the Medal of Honor.

During the American Revolution, three officers received recognition from the Continental Congress for actions against Indians who were allies of the British. Colonel Goose Van Schaick, the commander of the 1st New York Regiment, received the Thanks of the Congress on May 10, 1779, for leading an assault on an Onondaga village. Most of the warriors were away from the village at the time of the attack. Major General John Sullivan received the Thanks of the Congress on October 14, 1779, for leading an expedition against the Six Nations of the Iroquois Confederacy in the Finger Lakes area of New York. Colonel Daniel Broadhead, commander of the Pennsylvania Rifle Regiment, received the Thanks of the Congress on October 27, 1779, for leading an "important expedition against the Mingo and Munsey Indians and that part of the Senecas on the Allegheny River, by which depredations of those savages, assisted by their merciless instigators, subjects of

Great Britain, upon the defenseless inhabitants of the western frontiers, have been restrained and prevented."

Following the adoption of the U.S. Constitution, the U.S. Congress bestowed congressional honors on only two officers for actions against Native Americans, both taking place during the War of 1812. Major General (and future U.S. president) William Henry Harrison received both the Thanks of the Congress and the Congressional Gold Medal for his performance at the Battle of Tippecanoe on November 7, 1811. Colonel Richard M. Johnson, commander of the Kentucky Mounted Militia, received the Congressional Sword for service at the Battle of the Thames in Upper Canada on October 5, 1813, which resulted in the defeat of a combined British and Native American force under the command of Major General Henry Procter and Shawnee chief Tecumseh.

Only the most senior officers received congressional recognition. From the Revolutionary War through the end of the 19th century, the standard method of recognizing officer performance was through the conferral of brevet promotions. Adopted from British practice by the Second Continental Congress in 1775, the brevet promotion was an advancement in rank without an accompanying advancement in pay or assigned position. During the last 100 years of the Indian Wars, brevet promotions were conferred for valor in the presence of the enemy or for distinguished service. Prior to the Civil War, brevet promotions were also conferred upon officers for 10 years of faithful service at the same rank if no regular vacancies were available at the next higher rank. Even though all brevet promotions required confirmation by Congress, the system was prone to overuse and abuse, which ultimately led to its termination at the end of the 19th century.

During the War of 1812, James V. Ball was brevetted to lieutenant colonel for "gallant conduct at the battle with Indians on the Misseneway River, Indiana" on December 18, 1812. Otherwise, brevet promotions for heroic actions during battles against Native Americans were relatively rare until the Second Seminole War (1835–1842). Fifty-five U.S. Army officers received brevet promotions during that conflict, including future U.S. president Zachary Taylor, who was brevetted to brigadier general for distinguished service in the Battle of Kissimmee (Okeechobee) in Florida on December 25, 1837. Taylor also received brevet promotions during the War of 1812 and the Mexican-American War (1846–1848). The only officer brevetted twice for distinguished conduct against the Seminoles was Thomas Childes, who was brevetted to major on August 21, 1836, and to lieutenant colonel on February 1, 1841.

During the Civil War, brevet promotions were awarded indiscriminately and in large numbers. Several scandals arose over brevet promotions awarded to staff officers at the War Department for "faithful and meritorious service" while sitting at their desks. In response, Congress passed an act on March 1, 1869, requiring that all future brevet promotions be awarded only for "distinguished conduct and public service in the presence of the enemy." Only a small handful of brevet promotions were conferred for

actions against Native Americans between the end of the Civil War and the 1869 congressional act, including to Frederick Benteen who was brevetted to colonel for an action at Saline River, Kansas, on August 13, 1868.

The restrictive language of the congressional act effectively put a hold on brevet promotions for the next 25 years. Although officers were nominated for brevet promotions after March 1869 and those nominations were processed and submitted to Congress, the Senate refused to confirm the nominations on the basis that military actions against Native Americans did not qualify under the language of the act that stipulated "in the presence of the enemy." An editorial published in the *New York Times* on January 16, 1888, strongly supported the confirmation of the brevet promotions, noting that "Since for more than 20 years our only wars have been with Indians, it is well that the rising generation of young officers, some of whom were not born when the Civil War ended, should learn that brevet promotion for special valor is not wholly closed against them."

On February 27, 1890, Congress finally passed a law titled "An Act to Authorize the President to Confer Brevet Ranks, &c., for Gallant Services in Indian Wars." Even then, it took more than four years before President Grover Cleveland sent to Congress the consolidated list of the brevet nominations since 1869. The list of 158 officers was submitted on April 20, 1894, but the brevets were confirmed and entered in the officers' records with an effective date of February 27, 1890. Included in that list was Frederick Benteen, who was brevetted to brigadier general for his conduct during the Battle of the Little Bighorn (June 25–26, 1876).

Seven officers received double brevet promotions, including Frank D. Baldwin, brevetted to captain for one action on the Salt Fork of the Red River in Texas on August 30, 1874, and for a second action at McClellan Creek, Texas, on November 8, 1874. Baldwin was also brevetted to major for an action against Sitting Bull's camp on the Red Water River in Montana on December 18, 1876, and for a second action at Wolf Mountain, Montana, on January 8, 1877. Although Baldwin had been nominated for brevet promotion on four separate occasions, the nominations were consolidated into only two promotions by the time they were awarded. Many of the other officers who received a single belated brevet promotion originally had been nominated on two or more separate occasions.

Brevet promotions were far more than merely certificates to hang on the wall, even though Congress on July 15, 1870, passed a law providing that "Hereafter no officer shall be entitled to wear while on duty any uniform other than that of his actual rank, on account of having been brevetted; nor shall he be addressed in orders or official communications by any title other than that of his actual rank." Like other forms of congressional honors, the brevet promotion was recorded in an officer's permanent record and was a mark of honor and high distinction in the small professional military of the 19th century, where most officers knew each other. Although the army and the navy never introduced medals to recognize brevet promotions, the secretary of the navy in 1921 authorized the establishment of the Marine Corps Brevet Medal to recognize marine officers who had received brevet promotions that had been confirmed by the U.S. Senate. Only 23 of the medals were ever awarded, covering the period from the Civil War to the Philippine-American War in the late 1890s and early 1900s. The Marine Corps Brevet Medal ranked in precedence just below the Medal of Honor and above the Navy Cross, although none were conferred for actions during the Indian Wars.

The United States was the first nation to confer military awards on common soldiers. In 1780 the Continental Congress authorized decorations for three New York militiamen to recognize their roles in capturing British intelligence officer Major John Andre, who was Major General Benedict Arnold's contact. The so-called Andre Medals were one-time creations. The first standing American military decoration was the Badge of Military Merit, established by George Washington in 1782. The badge consisted of a purple cloth heart and was awarded only three known times. Sergeant Elijah Churchill of the 2nd Regiment Continental Light Dragoons was the first to receive the badge. After the Revolutionary War, the award fell into disuse until it was reestablished in its modern form in 1932 as the Purple Heart, awarded for wounds (including mortal wounds) received in combat.

The U.S. Army established the Certificate of Merit on March 3, 1847, which was awarded to army privates and noncommissioned officers for acts of heroism, both combat and noncombat. Essentially the enlisted equivalent of the brevet promotion for officers, the Certificate of Merit originally consisted only of a certificate, an entry in the soldier's record, and an extra $2 per month in pay. The award was established during the Mexican-American War, but following that conflict the U.S. Army took the position that it no longer had the authority to confer the award. During the Civil War and the Indian wars immediately following, commanders in the field continued to recommend soldiers for the Certificate of Merit, but the nominations were not acted upon. Following the Battle of the Little Bighorn in 1876, the Certificate of Merit was reinstituted and was awarded through World War I (1914–1918). In 1905 a medal was authorized for all holders of the Certificate of Merit, which became obsolete in 1918. Initially all holders of the Certificate of Merit were authorized to convert their award to the newly established Distinguished Service Medal, the highest decoration for noncombat service. In 1934 an act of Congress authorized the conversion of the Certificate of Merit—including those that previously had been converted to the Distinguished Service Medal—to the more appropriate Distinguished Service Cross, the army's second-highest decoration for combat valor.

Of the 1,206 Certificates of Merit awarded between 1847 and 1918, only 61 were for actions during the Indian Wars. Four soldiers were awarded 2 Certificates of Merit during the Indian Wars, including Sergeant James Bell of the 7th Infantry, who received his first for the engagement on the Bighorn River on July 9, 1876, and his second for an action at Big Hole, Montana, on August 9, 1877.

Twelve African American buffalo soldiers received the Certificate of Merit: 4 from the 9th Cavalry, 2 from the 10th Cavalry, and 6 from the 24th Infantry. Although technically listed as Indian Wars awards, all 8 awarded to the soldiers of the 10th Cavalry and the 24th Infantry were actually for an action fought on May 11, 1889, against robbers who held up an army payroll. The largest number of Certificates of Merit awarded for a single Indian Wars battle was 16 for Milk Creek, Colorado, on September 29, 1879.

America's first permanent military decoration, the Medal of Honor—often erroneously called the Congressional Medal of Honor—was established for the U.S. Navy on December 12, 1861, and for the U.S. Army on July 12, 1862. The highest American military decoration for battlefield heroism, the Medal of Honor today is awarded by the president in the name of Congress to those members of the U.S. armed forces who distinguish themselves by gallantry and intrepidity at the risk of their lives above and beyond the call of duty while engaged in combat against an armed enemy of the United States. Though it was originally authorized only for enlisted men, officers became eligible for the Army Medal of Honor in 1863 and for the Navy Medal of Honor in 1915. The Army and Navy Medals of Honor also differed in that the Army Medal of Honor from the start could be awarded only for acts of combat valor. The Navy Medal of Honor also was awarded for peacetime acts of heroism until 1942.

The first Medals of Honor presented were to the six survivors of the April 1862 Andrews Raid, popularly known as "The Great Locomotive Chase." The first Medal of Honor action occurred in the Arizona Territory during February 13–14, 1861, when U.S. Army assistant surgeon Bernard J. D. Irwin took command of a detachment of troops and led a mission to relieve a force of infantrymen trapped by a band of Chiricahua Apaches under Cochise. For an almost identical action in the summer of 1886, Assistant Surgeon Leonard Wood received the Medal of Honor after taking command of a detachment of infantry during a battle with Apaches under Geronimo. Wood later became the fifth chief of staff of the U.S. Army in April 1910.

A total of 424 Medals of Honor were awarded during the Indian Wars: 46 to officers, 374 to enlisted soldiers, and 4 to civilian scouts. Almost all of the awards were for actions that occurred between March 15, 1865, and December 30, 1891. Four of the Medals of Honor were actually awarded for the May 11, 1889, action against non-Indian outlaws who held up an army payroll wagon. The battle for which the largest number of Medals of Honor was awarded was 25 for the Battle of the Little Bighorn (June 25–26, 1876) followed by 17 for the Battle of Wounded Knee (December 29, 1890). Although most of the citations do not mention the tribe involved in the action, those most identified are the Apaches (38), the Sioux (11), and the Cheyennes (8). The last Indian Wars Medal of Honor was awarded to Private Oscar Burkhard, Hospital Corps, for an action on October 5, 1898, during an uprising of the Chippewas in northern Minnesota. Only 3 Indian Wars Medals of Honor were awarded posthumously:

- Corporal John Given, 6th Cavalry, Wichita River, Texas: July 12, 1870.
- Private George Hooker, 5th Cavalry, Tonto Creek, Arizona: January 22, 1873.
- Private George Smith, 6th Cavalry, Wichita River, Texas: September 12, 1874.

Two soldiers earned the Medal of Honor twice for actions during the Indian Wars. First Sergeant Henry Hogan, 5th Infantry, received his first for a series of actions at Cedar Creek, Montana, between October 1876 and January 8, 1877. His second was awarded for an action at Bear Paw, Montana, on September 30, 1877. Sergeant William Wilson, 4th Cavalry, was awarded his first Medal of Honor for an action at Colorado Valley, Texas, on March 28, 1872, and his second for action at Red River, Texas, on September 29, 1872. Many references identify Patrick Leonard as a double Medal of Honor recipient of the Indian Wars, but they were in fact two different men.

One of the more famous casualties of the Indian Wars, Captain Thomas Custer, who died at the Little Bighorn with his brother Lieutenant Colonel George A. Custer, had earned two Medals of Honor during the Civil War.

Two soldiers received both the Medal of Honor and the Certificate of Merit during the Indian Wars. Sergeant George Jordan, 9th Cavalry, earned the Medal of Honor for action at Fort Tularosa, New Mexico, on May 14, 1880, and the Certificate of Merit for action at Carizo Canyon, New Mexico, on August 12, 1881. Waggoner John Schnitzer, 4th Cavalry, earned the Medal of Honor for action at Horseshoe Canyon, New Mexico, on April 23, 1882, and the Certificate of Merit for action against the Chiricahua Apaches in Sonora, Mexico, on June 8, 1885.

Twenty of the officers who received the belated brevet promotions on February 27, 1890, also earned the Medal of Honor for Indian War actions, and another four had earned the Medal of Honor during the Civil War. Frank D. Baldwin, who retired from the U.S. Army in 1906 as a major general, was a member of both groups. He earned his first Medal of Honor at Peachtree Creek, Georgia, on July 12, 1864, and his second for an action at McClellan Creek, Texas, on November 8, 1874. With two Medals of Honor and two brevet promotions, Baldwin ranks as one of the most highly decorated American soldiers.

The Medals of Honor awarded to the four civilian scouts were revoked in February 1917 after a U.S. Army General Review in 1916 concluded that the original awards had been invalid because civilians were not eligible. The General Review also used the same rationale to revoke the award of Civil War contract acting assistant surgeon Mary E. Walker, the only woman to receive the Medal of Honor. Dr. Walker's Medal of Honor was restored in 1977, and in June 1989 the U.S. Army Board of Correction of Record restored the awards of the four Indian Wars civilian scouts, along with that of a Civil War civilian scout. The Indian Campaign scouts included:

- Amos Chapman, Washita River, Texas: September 12, 1874.
- William F. Cody, Platte River, Nebraska: April 26, 1872.

- William Dixon, Wichita River, Texas: September, 12 1874.
- James B. Doshier, Holliday Creek, Texas: October 5, 1870.

Fifteen Indian scouts earned the Medal of Honor during the Indian Wars. Included in that group were four Black Seminoles, the descendants of escaped slaves from South Carolina and Georgia who settled among the Seminoles in Florida. When the U.S. government moved a large number of the Seminoles to present-day Oklahoma during the 1830s, many Black Seminoles fled to Mexico, fearing that they might be returned to slavery. In 1870 the U.S. Army began recruiting Black Seminoles from Mexico as scouts. Those earning the Medal of Honor were:

- Private Pompey Factor, Pecos River, Texas: April 25, 1875.
- Private Adam Paine, Red River, Texas: September 26–27, 1874.
- Trumpeter Isaac Payne, Pecos River, Texas: April 25, 1875.
- Sergeant John Ward, Pecos River, Texas: April 25, 1875.

The other Indian Scouts who received the Medal of Honor were:

- Sergeant Alchesay, Arizona: Winter 1872–1873.
- Scout Blanquet, Arizona: Winter 1872–1873.
- Scout Chiquito, Arizona: Winter 1872–1873.
- Sergeant Co-Rux-Te-Chod-Ish (Mad Bear), Republican River, Kansas: July 8, 1869.
- Corporal Elsatsoosu, Arizona: Winter 1872–1873.
- Sergeant Jim, Arizona: Winter 1872–1873.
- Scout Kelsay, Arizona: Winter 1872–1873.
- Scout Kosoha, Arizona: Winter 1872–1873.
- Scout Machol, Arizona: Winter 1872–1873.
- Scout Nannasaddie, Arizona: Winter 1872–1873.
- Scout Nantaje, Arizona: Winter 1872–1873.
- Sergeant Rowdy, Arizona: March 7, 1890.

Segregated U.S. Army units with black soldiers and white officers were collectively known as buffalo soldiers and included the 9th and 10th Cavalry and the 24th and 25th Infantry. Eighteen black soldiers and five of their white officers earned the Medal of Honor during the Indian Wars. The Black Seminole Scouts are included in this group, and Factor, Payne, and Ward were actually assigned to the 24th Infantry at the time of the battle for which they received their awards. The two other 24th Infantry Medal of Honor recipients were Sergeant William Brown and Corporal Isaiah Mays, who were both decorated for the May 11, 1889, paymaster robbery rather than for action against Native Americans. The only enlisted soldier from the 10th Cavalry to receive the Medal of Honor was Sergeant William McBryar for an action against the Apaches in Arizona on March 7, 1890. The 9th Cavalry enlisted recipients of the Medal of Honor include:

- Sergeant Thomas Boyne, Mimbres Mountains, New Mexico: May 29, 1879.
- Sergeant John Denny, Las Animas Canyon, New Mexico: September 18, 1879.

- Corporal Clinton Greaves, Florida Mountains, New Mexico: January 24, 1877.
- Sergeant Henry Johnson, Milk River, Colorado: October 2–5, 1879.
- Sergeant George Jordan, Fort Tularosa, New Mexico, and Carrizo Canyon, New Mexico: May 14, 1880, and August 12, 1881, respectively.
- Sergeant Thomas Shaw, Carrizo Canyon, New Mexico: August 12, 1881.
- Sergeant Emanuel Stance, Kickapoo Springs, Texas: May 20, 1870.
- Private Augustus Walley, Cuchillo Negro Mountains, New Mexico: August 16, 1881.
- First Sergeant Moses Williams, Cuchillo Negro Mountains, New Mexico: August 16, 1881.
- Corporal William O. Wilson, Sioux Campaign: 1890.
- Sergeant Brent Woods, New Mexico: August 19, 1881.

Campaign medals are awarded to American military personnel for participation in a war or campaign. Although the first official campaign medals were established in the early years of the 20th century, the membership badges of various veterans' organizations served as unofficial campaign medals and were authorized for wear on U.S. military uniforms through the early 1900s. In the collection of official portraits of the commanding generals and chiefs of staff of the U.S. Army, Major General Henry Dearborn (1812–1815) can be seen wearing the order of the Revolutionary War Society of the Cincinnati. Lieutenant General Samuel B. M Young (1903–1904) and Lieutenant General John C. Bates (1906) are both shown wearing the membership medal of the Civil War Grand Army of the Republic (GAR). The GAR medal looked conspicuously similar to the original design of the Army Medal of Honor, which contributed significantly to the controversy that finally resulted in the establishment of official campaign medals.

President Theodore Roosevelt was the father of the modern American campaign medal. For many years, Congress had steadfastly refused to authorize campaign medals. Roosevelt decided to bypass Congress by declaring that campaign medals were badges, and as commander in chief he had the authority to designate which badges could be worn on military uniforms. In 1905 the secretary of war issued General Order Number 4 establishing a medal for the Certificate of Merit and campaign medals for the Civil War, the Indian Wars, the Spanish-American War, the Philippine-American War, and the China Relief Expedition. Shortly thereafter the army's regulations were changed to stipulate that society medals could not be worn on the uniform if campaign medals were worn.

Introduced in 1907 and awarded retroactively, the Indian Wars Medal was designed by the distinguished American sculptor Francis D. Millet. The chiefs of staff of the U.S. Army who wear the Indian Wars Medal or its ribbon bar in their official portraits include Major General James F. Bell (1906–1910), Major General Leonard Wood (1910–1914), and Major General William W. Wotherspoon (1914). The Indian Wars Medal was authorized for service in 12 distinct campaigns between 1865 and 1891 and also for any other action in which U.S. troops were killed or wounded between 1865 and 1898. The designated campaigns include:

- Southern Oregon, Idaho, northern California, and Nevada: 1865–1875.
- Comanche and allied tribes in Kansas, Colorado, Texas, New Mexico, and Indian Territory (later Oklahoma): 1867–1875.
- Modoc War: 1872–1873.
- Apaches in Arizona: 1873.
- Northern Cheyennes and Sioux: 1876–1877.
- Nez Perce War: 1877.
- Bannock War: 1878.
- Northern Cheyennes: 1878–1879.
- Sheep-Eater, Paiutes, and Bannocks: June and October 1879.
- Utes in Colorado and Utah: September 1879–November 1880.
- Apaches in Arizona and New Mexico: 1885–1886.
- Sioux in South Dakota: November 1890–January 1891.

The only device authorized for the ribbon of the Indian Wars Medal was the Silver Citation Star, a five-pointed star 3-16ths of an inch in diameter. First established in 1918 as a device affixed to the ribbon of the World War I Victory Medal, the Silver Citation Star recognized soldiers who had distinguished themselves in combat as documented in official reports. The Silver Citation Star was an American equivalent to the British Mentioned in Dispatches designation. In 1932 the Silver Citation Star was converted to the Silver Star, America's third-highest decoration for combat valor. Only 11 Silver Citation Stars were awarded retroactively for the Indian Wars Medal: 9 to officers, all second or first lieutenants, and 2 to privates.

DAVID T. ZABECKI

References

Bell, William Gardner. *Commanding Generals and Chiefs of Staff: 1775–1995.* Washington, DC: Center of Military History, 1997.

Decorations, United States Army: 1862–1926. Washington, DC: U.S. Government Printing Office, 1927.

Gleim, Albert F., and Charles P. McDowell. *The Certificate of Merit: United States Army, 1847–1918.* Madison, VA: Foxfall, 2009.

Heitman, Francis B. *Historical Register and Dictionary of the United States Army.* Washington, DC: U.S. Government Printing Office, 1903.

Kerrigan, Evans. *American Medals and Decorations.* London: Apple, 1990.

Lelle, John E. *The Brevet Medal.* Springfield, VA: Quest Publishing, 1988.

Proft, R. J., ed. *Medal of Honor Recipients and Their Official Citations.* Columbia Heights, MN: Highland House II, 1997.

Glossary

---

abatis Defensive obstacle formed of felled trees with sharpened limbs that face the route of enemy advance.

accouterments A soldier's gear except for weapons and clothing.

acculturation The process in which two or more distinct cultures interact and thus yield a blended cultural amalgamation.

adobe An unburned sun-dried brick of clay and straw, often used as a building material.

aide-de-camp The chief military secretary to a superior officer.

assimilation The process whereby individuals or groups of differing ethnic heritage are absorbed into the dominant culture of a society.

ballistics The science of projectiles, divided into interior and exterior ballistics. Its aim is to improve the design of shells/projectiles so that increased accuracy and predictability are the result.

banquette A firing step for infantry at the base of the parapet.

barrage French term for a barrier formed by artillery fire (land) or an antisubmarine net or mine barrier (sea).

bastion A projecting piece of a fortification, often in the form of an irregular pentagon.

battalion Military unit, usually consisting of between 300 and 1,000 individuals and commanded by a commissioned officer, usually a lieutenant colonel.

battery Military unit corresponding to an infantry company and usually composed of about 100 individuals and commanded by a captain.

bayonet A stabbing instrument made of steel and inserted into or around the muzzle of a musket or rifle.

Black Robes French Jesuit missionaries who operated in New France, beginning in 1625.

brigade Military unit usually consisting of between 3,000 and 5,000 individuals and commanded by a commissioned officer, usually a brigadier general (premodern times) or a colonel (modern times).

brigadier general Military rank between colonel and major general, usually denoting the commander of a brigade; often temporary, with the senior colonel of the combined regiments or battalions holding the rank.

buffalo soldiers The term for African Americans soldiers as both cavalry and infantry who served on the western frontier from 1866 to 1917.

canister shot A collection of small shot or other materials, such as nails or shrapnel, enclosed in a wooden or tin cylinder of a size appropriate to fit a cannon's muzzle. Canister shot, also known as case shot, is meant for antipersonnel use at short range.

cannon   A firearm of large enough size that it requires mounting on a carriage. Cannon generally fired solid shot, grapeshot, and canister shot on a flat trajectory.

carriage   The wheeled support vehicle on which an artillery piece is mounted and carried.

case shot   *See* **canister shot**.

cease-fire   A partial or temporary cessation of hostilities. A cease-fire can also involve a general armistice or a total cessation of all hostilities.

colonel   Superior officer of a regiment, ranking above the lieutenant colonel, and who usually has actual command of the regiment. Colonels rank immediately below general officers, specifically brigadiers, and the rank is often honorary and conferred upon princes and distinguished officers.

commissaries   Officials responsible for providing supplies for the military.

commissioned officer   An officer possessing authority over enlisted men and noncommissioned officers whose rank is conferred by a government document (commission).

company   Military unit made up of several platoons and usually commanded by a captain. Several companies make up a battalion.

conquistador   Term used to describe Portuguese and Spanish soldiers, explorers, and adventurers who brought much of the Americas under the control of their two nations from the late 15th century through the 17th century.

corporal   A noncommissioned military officer ranking above a private but below a sergeant.

corps   Military unit, usually consisting of between 30,000 and 50,000 individuals and commanded by a commissioned officer, usually a lieutenant general.

counting coup   The process whereby a Native American warrior won prestige in battle. Any blow struck against the enemy counted as a coup, but it was most prestigious for a warrior to touch an enemy warrior with the hand, bow, or coup stick and then escape unharmed.

coup d'état   A sudden decisive use of force in politics, especially in terms of a violent overthrow of an existing government by a small group often assisted by the military.

court-martial   To subject a military member to a military trial with a court consisting of a board of commissioned officers.

division   Military unit, usually consisting of between 10,000 and 20,000 individuals and commanded by a commissioned officer, usually a major general.

encomienda   An arrangement that involved land allotments—but not grants—as well as a tributary system of labor for Spanish conquistadors.

enfilade   To fire upon the length rather than the face of an enemy position. Enfilading an enemy allows a varying range of fire to find targets while minimizing the amount of fire the enemy can return.

ensign   A commissioned infantry officer of the lowest grade.

envelopment   To pour fire along the enemy's line. A double envelopment is an attack on both flanks of an enemy.

epaulement   A side work to a fortification of fascines, bags of earth, or simply earth heaped up to provide protection from enemy flanking fire.

fascine   A bundle of sticks bound together to fill ditches, strengthen the sides of trenches, and build batteries.

Five Civilized Tribes   Collective name for the Creek, Cherokee, Seminole, Chickasaw, and Choctaw Indian tribes. Whites gave these tribes the name "civilized" because of their greater willingness to accept and adopt Anglo-American customs and practices.

flank   The side of a formation.

forced march   In military usage, a rapid movement of troops over some distance to meet a crisis such as the imperative need to reinforce positions before or during a battle.

glacis   Incline that extends downward from a fort. The glacis protects inner defenses from enemy artillery fire and exposes attacking infantry to artillery and musket fire from the parapet.

grapeshot   Small iron balls bound together with wire or cord, often in a canvas bag or around a wooden spindle, and forming a single charge for a cannon.

grenade   A small bomb or explosive shell detonated by a fuse and thrown by hand.

grenadier
Originally a soldier employed to carry and throw grenades. As grenades declined in use in the early 18th century, the term was retained to denote elite units comprised of the tallest and finest men in a regiment.

guerrilla warfare
A form of irregular warfare that is highly flexible and often decentralized. Nontraditional tactics such as raids and ambushes are employed to compensate for a numerical or technological disadvantage.

gun
Any firearm other than a pistol, but generally the term is applied only to cannon rather than to muskets or rifles.

howitzer
A short artillery piece, usually of light weight, used to fire small bombs or shells. A howitzer was more mobile and had greater range than a mortar but fired smaller projectiles at a lower trajectory. A howitzer differentiated from cannon in that a howitzer had a shorter range and higher trajectory and fired explosive shells.

indirect fire
The process of aiming a large-caliber weapon, usually an artillery piece, by applying a vertical angle of tube elevation for range and a horizontal angle from some fixed reference point for direction.

invest
The action of seizing all of the approaches to a fort or fortress, thus cutting off support.

laager
A defensive formation of wagons or motor vehicles in which the vehicles are formed into a circle or square, with a camp made in the interior of the circle.

land companies
Private investment companies that played a major role in the development of the North American frontier by buying up large tracts of land in America.

lieutenant
Military officer next in rank to captain.

lieutenant colonel
Military officer ranking above a major but below a colonel and having command of a regiment.

loophole
A hole or narrow slit in a wall wider inside than outside through which muskets could be fired.

major
A military officer ranking above a captain but below a lieutenant colonel.

major general
A military officer ranking above a brigadier general but below a lieutenant general. In colonial America, commanders in chief held the rank of major general. Officers appointed to direct campaigns also held this rank, though often temporarily.

Manifest Destiny
A belief held by many Americans that the United States was bound to expand across the North American continent from the Atlantic Ocean to the Pacific Ocean.

mortar
A short artillery piece possessing a large bore and trunnions at the breech and capable of high-trajectory angle of fire. Mortars are used to fire explosive shells or bombs in a high arc.

musket
A muzzle-loading smoothbore long gun that is fired from the shoulder; the standard weapon for an infantryman.

ordnance
Military supplies, particularly weapons and ammunition.

outwork
Fortification built outside the main walls of a fort or fortress.

palisade
Fenced wall of upright and pointed logs fixed into a ground base; also a stockade of sharpened posts for protection.

parapet
A wall of earth or stone used to cover troops from enemy observation or fire. In permanent works, the parapet is placed on top of the rampart as protection from enemy fire.

petroglyph
Engravings made by cutting into the surface of rock using bone, antler, or hard stone chips. Petroglyphs depict spirits, victories, and an association between martial might and supernatural forces.

picket
A small detached body of troops set out in front of a camp or defensive position to warn of an enemy approach.

platoon
Military unit usually consisting of between 30 and 50 individuals and commanded by a commissioned officer, usually a lieutenant.

presidio
Spanish term for a fort or fortified settlement.

private
An ordinary soldier holding no significant rank.

procurement
The act of purchasing. The term "procurement" often refers to the government's purchasing of military equipment or other supplies.

ranging
To move over a region so as to scout or reconnoiter.

regiment
Military unit usually consisting of between 2,000 and 3,000 individuals and commanded by a commissioned officer, usually a colonel.

rifle
An individual firearm designed to be fired from the shoulder and differing from a musket in that the rifle has helical grooves (rifling) in the barrel that is used to impart spin to the projectile. Early rifles were far more accurate than muskets but took much longer to load.

sachem
The term for the leader of certain northeastern Native American groups and associated with one who worked in the best interests of his tribe.

salvo
The simultaneous firing of a number of guns.

scalping
The practice of removing the skin, or scalp, from an enemy's skull with the hair still attached.

scout
A soldier or other person sent out ahead of a main force to gather information about an enemy's position, strength, or movements. In the American Indian Wars, the U.S. Army made frequent use of Native Americans as scouts.

sergeant
A noncommissioned military officer ranking above a corporal.

shot
Cast iron solid shot employed against fortifications and against troops in the open. Shot had the longest range of any artillery projectile.

shrapnel
A hollow thin-walled shell packed with musket balls and fused, timed to explode. Shrapnel is used primarily against enemy troop formations.

spontoon
A short pike or halberd carried by 18th-century infantry officers.

squad
Military unit usually consisting of between 8 and 14 individuals and commanded by a noncommissioned officer.

standing army
A permanent military unit of paid soldiers that exists during both peacetime and times of war.

sutler
Individuals who traveled with troops in the field and sold provisions and other goods to soldiers.

totem
An animal, plant, or other natural object associated with a clan, family, or group of people.

train
General transportation system responsible for supplying necessary equipment and supplies, that is, supporting services for an army (or navy) in the field.

wampum
A Native American form of currency and exchange, also used as a sign of friendship and alliance.

war belt
A form of wampum employed in various diplomatic capacities, primarily among Native Americans of the Northeast and the northern Plains. The colors and designs on the belts transmitted various messages.

war club
A blunt-force weapon employed by Native American warriors for close-in fighting. Usually made of maple or ironwood, the war club possessed a long shaft and a heavy ball end.

wigwam
A type of dwelling often having an arched or conical shape and covered with bark, hides, or mats.

Chronology

January 1493

13   In perhaps the first clash between Europeans and natives in the New World, Christopher Columbus and his ships the *Niña* and *Pinta* are in Samaná Bay in the eastern part of Hispaniola (present-day Dominican Republic) when they encounter a Carib war party. After uneasy negotiations, fighting occurs when more than 50 Caribs attack a Spanish boat party of 7 men. The Spanish weapons intimidate and scatter the Caribs.

April 1513

21   Having discovered Florida on March 27, 1513, Spanish conquistador Juan Ponce de León comes ashore on April 2, 1513, and, despite his efforts to establish friendly contact with the inhabitants, clashes with a party of Ais natives near the mouth of the Saint Lucie River. Two Spaniards are wounded, but a native is taken prisoner to be trained as an interpreter.

May 30, 1539–September 10, 1543

Spanish conquistador Hernando de Soto, newly named Spanish governor of Cuba, lands in Florida with 513 soldiers and 337 horses to begin its conquest. Frequent clashes occur between the Spaniards and natives as de Soto wanders across much of the present-day southeastern United States.

February 1540–October 1542

Spaniard Francisco Vázquez de Coronado leads an expedition north from northern Mexico into New Mexico in an effort to find the legendary Seven Cities of Cibola, reportedly rich in gold and other treasures. Coronado reaches the Zuni village of Hawikuh, supposedly one of the Seven Cities, and captures it on July 7, 1540. Hawikuh and the other supposed Cities of Gold turn out to be simple villages devoid of riches. Coronado presses on nonetheless, passing through present-day New Mexico, Texas, and Oklahoma and even traveling into central Kansas before admitting defeat and returning to Mexico.

January 1599

21–23   Resentful of harsh treatment by the Spanish, the Indians of Acoma Pueblo in New Mexico revolt. Spanish reinforcements scale the mesa and launch a surprise night attack. The following day the Spaniards kill approximately 800 natives.

July 1608

French explorer Samuel de Champlain establishes a trading post at Quebec on the Saint Lawrence River. Allying themselves with the Algonquins, the Hurons, and the Montaignais, the French drive the Iroquois from the Saint Lawrence Valley.

August 9, 1610–April 5, 1614

In the First Anglo-Powhatan War, fighting occurs between the English colonists at Jamestown and Native Americans of the Powhatan Confederacy.

March 1622

22   In widespread coordinated attacks, Native Americans attack the English at Jamestown, Virginia, killing 347

settlers and initiating the Second Anglo-Powhatan War (1622–1632). The colonists retaliate, and in 1623, under promise of peace talks, lure 250 natives to their deaths.

July 1636–September 1638

The Pequot War takes place between the Pequot Native Americans of the lower Connecticut River Valley and the English colonies of Massachusetts Bay and Connecticut. As a result of the fighting, the Pequots are destroyed as an independent people, and most are absorbed by other tribes.

June 1641–1701

The Beaver Wars, also known as the Iroquois Wars and the French and Iroquois Wars, take place. The fighting begins with a skirmish near Trois Rivières in Canada in June 1741. The wars are a series of extraordinarily sanguinary conflicts between the members of the Iroquois Confederacy, who are endeavoring both to expand their territory and control the fur trade with the Europeans, and the native peoples of the western Great Lakes. The conflict pits the nations of the Iroquois Confederacy, led by the Mohawks, against the tribes of the Great Lakes area. The French also take part in the fighting against the Iroquois.

In the early fighting the Iroquois greatly expand their territory, destroying several large tribal confederacies that include the Hurons, Eries, and Susquehannocks. The Iroquois also drive other eastern tribes west of the Mississippi River. A series of setbacks follows, and in 1698 the Iroquois seek peace, increasingly seeing themselves as pawns played by the English against the French. For their part, the French are anxious to have the Iroquois as a barrier between New France and the English colonies to the south. In 1701 in Montreal, Native American chiefs, the English, and the French conclude the Grande Paix (Great Peace), bringing an end to a century of nearly continuous warfare. The Iroquois agree to stop their attacks and to allow remaining refugees from the Great Lakes region to return to their ancestral homes in the east.

1641–1664

Persistent ill will between European settlers in New Netherland and neighboring Algonquian tribes leads to a series of wars: Kieft's War (1639–1645), the Peach War (1655), the First Esopus War (1659–1660), and the Second Esopus War (1663–1664). The outcomes largely favor the Dutch.

April 18, 1644–October 1646

In the Third Anglo-Powhatan War, Opechancanough, chief of the Pamunkeys and leader of the Powhatan

Confederacy, leads an effort to drive out the English colonists in Virginia. The natives kill some 400–500 colonists, but in the reprisal killings that follow the natives again suffer disproportionately and are defeated. Opechancanough is captured in the late summer of 1646 and is brought to Jamestown, where he is murdered by one of his guards. His successor, Necotowance, agrees to a peace treaty in October 1646 in which the Powhatans surrender all their prisoners, firearms, and any runaway servants and agree to cede most of their remaining lands.

June 20, 1675–October 1676

King Philip's War, named for Wampanoag sachem Metacom (known to colonists as King Philip), takes place. Wampanoag warriors attack Swansea in southwestern Plymouth Colony, and conflict quickly spreads. Metacom is killed on August 12, 1676, and many warriors surrender, although the conflict continues for several years in Maine.

1680–1690

Revolt of Pueblo Native Americans against Spanish authorities in New Mexico. The Spanish retake New Mexico in 1690, although not until 1696 do they secure a lasting peace there.

1711–1713

Encroachments by colonists and abuses by colonial traders in North Carolina lead the Tuscaroras to kill some 200 colonists and fight the English-allied Creeks and the Yamasees. The Tuscaroras surrender in March 1713.

1715–1717

The Yamasee Native Americans of South Carolina, angered by settler incursions and abusive English traders, go to war. The Creeks aid the Yamasees, but the South Carolinians are reinforced by North Carolina and Virginia militia and the Cherokees. Peace is concluded between the Creeks and the English in November 1717, but the Yamasees remain at war until 1728.

September 1730

9   The beleaguered Fox tribe, after escaping a monthlong siege of Fox Fort and weeks of near starvation, encounters a combined French and Native American force and loses 200–300 warriors and 300–600 women and children.

May 28, 1754–February 10, 1763

The French and Indian War pits England and France, with their various Native American allies, against each other.

May–November 1763

Pontiac's Rebellion. Ottawa chief Pontiac rouses natives from western New York to the Illinois River and unsuccessfully besieges Fort Detroit, while natives elsewhere capture Fort Sandusky, Fort Miami, and Fort Michilimackinac, capturing a total of eight forts within a two-week span.

August 1763

5–6   Battle of Bushy Run. To relieve Fort Pitt, Colonel Henry Bouquet leads 400 men from Fort Niagara and is set back although not defeated by a large force of Delawares, Wyandots, Mingos, and Shawnees. Bouquet's advance forces the natives to lift the siege of Fort Pitt.

April–October 1774

Lord Dunmore's War. Numbers of frontiersmen attack native settlements in the Ohio River Valley, and when the natives retaliate, Pennsylvanians and Virginians manipulate events as a means of subverting the Proclamation of 1763.

October 1774

10   Battle of Point Pleasant. Chief Cornstalk of the Shawnees leads 1,000 Shawnee, Mingo, Delaware, Wyandot, and Ottawa warriors in an attack against Colonel Andrew Lewis and 1,100 unsuspecting militiamen. Cornstalk fails to defeat the colonists and makes peace on October 19, 1774, surrendering all claims to lands south and east of the Ohio River.

April 19, 1775–September 3, 1783

The American Revolutionary War splits Native Americans' loyalties.

October 1778

6–8   In direct response to Mohawk chief Joseph Brant's raid on German Flats, Lieutenant Colonel William Butler raids and destroys the towns of Unadilla and Uquaga in the Mohawk Valley.

November 1778

11   In response to Butler's destruction of Unadilla, Loyalists and their Iroquois allies massacre 47 people and capture 71 at Cherry Valley, New York.

October 1790

18   Americans under Josiah Harmar come upon 2,500 Indians led by Miami chief Little Turtle in Ohio and are defeated.

November 1791

4   Several factions of different tribes unite under Miami chief Little Turtle, and the new American nation suffers

its greatest defeat against Native Americans in the Battle of the Wabash.

August 1794

20   In retaliation for the defeat at the Wabash, American forces under General Anthony Wayne conquer another tribal coalition under Shawnee chief Blue Jacket, effectively ending Native American resistance in the Old Northwest Territory.

August 1795

3   The Treaty of Greenville, which is essentially negated by settlers, is signed between General Anthony Wayne and several Northwest Indian tribes. The treaty calls for Indians to cede lands in the Ohio River Valley in return for cash payments.

April 30–December 20, 1803

French emperor Napoleon I and Thomas Jefferson conduct the Louisiana Purchase, in which the United States nearly doubles its existing territory for a price of $15 million.

November 1811

7   Indiana governor William Henry Harrison defeats a confederation under Shawnee prophet Tenskwatawa and his absent half brother, Tecumseh, helping to solidify the British–Native American alliance to combat American expansion.

June 1, 1812–February 17, 1815

The War of 1812 between the United States and Great Britain is fought.

1813–1814

The Red Stick War ignites a civil war between different factions of the Creek Nation. The White Sticks favor neutrality, while the Red Sticks want to strike back against the Americans, who they believe are more dangerous than the British.

January 1813

18   After a British victory in the Battle of Frenchtown, between 30 and 60 captives are murdered by drunken Shawnees in what is dubbed the Raisin River Massacre.

July 1813

27   In a surprise attack, Colonel James Caller routs a Red Stick force under Peter McQueen at the Battle of Burnt Corn Creek, marking the beginning of the Creek War between the Red Sticks on one side and the United States

and their White Stick Creek allies in Alabama on the other side.

August 1813

30   A black slave warns the garrison at Fort Mims, Alabama, about approaching hostile Indians, but he is not believed. Some 800–1,000 Red Sticks, led by William Weatherford and Josiah Francis, surprise the garrison and kill hundreds of people there.

October 1813

5   In the Battle of the Thames, the retreating British and Shawnee warriors make a stand against the Americans but are defeated, and Tecumseh is killed.

November 1813

9   In the Battle of Talladega, Americans encircle the Creek Red Sticks, who suffer 299 deaths. Due to lack of supplies, however, the Americans are forced to move north to Fort Schlosser.

December 1813

23   In the Battle of Econochaca, the Americans descend on Creek holy ground, proving false the claims of Creek prophets that it is surrounded by a magic barrier that will strike dead any white who crosses. This battle has a devastating effect on Creek morale.

March 1814

27   Tennessee militia under Major General Andrew Jackson happens upon 1,200 Red Sticks by the Tallapoosa River. In the Battle of Horseshoe Bend, 557 Creeks are killed; another 350 are taken captive.

August 1814

9   Jackson dictates terms to the defeated Creeks, forcing them to cede two-thirds of their lands and shift their villages outside of the settlers' path.

November 20, 1817–October 31, 1818

The First Seminole War is fought. After a number of indecisive battles, Andrew Jackson strikes south with an overwhelming force, eventually seizing a Spanish outpost and hanging two British subjects for allegedly inspiring native uprisings. Jackson's success convinces Spanish officials that Florida is untenable. Spain sells the colony to the United States in 1819.

August 1823

23   In the Arikara War, the Arikaras resist American encroachment up the Missouri River in a pitched battle but are defeated by Colonel Henry Leavenworth at the mouth of the Grand River.

September 1823

Treaty of Moultrie Creek between the U.S. and the Seminoles is signed. The treaty stipulates that in exchange for goods and supplies, the Seminoles will give up claims to land in Florida and move to a reservation in the center of the state.

May 1830

28   The notorious Indian Removal Act is passed at the request of President Andrew Jackson and calls for Indian nations to cede their lands east of the Mississippi River in exchange for lands west of the river in what would be called Indian Territory (present-day Oklahoma).

March 1831

18   In *Cherokee Nation v. Georgia,* William Wirt attempts to defend Cherokee rights before the U.S. Supreme Court.

March 1832

3   In stark contrast to the 1831 *Cherokee Nation v. Georgia,* in *Worcester v. Georgia* the Supreme Court rules that the Cherokee Nation is a distinct community possessing self-government, but Georgia ignores the ruling.

May–July 1832

The Black Hawk War. When Sauk and Fox planters return to Rock Island, Illinois, to sow new crops, panicky American militiamen shoot down one of their men, prompting Sauk chief Black Hawk to authorize cross-border raids; they are defeated at Wisconsin Heights. Black Hawk flees west and is killed in the Battle of Bad Axe.

May 1832

9   The Treaty of Payne's Landing, an agreement between the United States and several Seminole chiefs, is signed and stipulates that the Seminoles are to relocate to the Creek Reservation in Arkansas Territory.

December 28, 1835–August 14, 1842

In the Second Seminole War, the Seminoles ravage farms, settlements, plantations, and army forts. The federal government sends in General Winfield Scott.

March 1836

25   Scott sends three columns into Seminole territory, but they are repeatedly harassed by Seminoles under Osceola, who strike isolated American outposts in the rear.

March 1837

6   After several American victories, three Seminole chiefs request terms. A treaty is signed in which 1,000 Seminoles agree to be transported west of the Mississippi. The plans are publicly criticized, and the Seminoles resume hostilities.

October 1837

27   Seminole war chief Osceola and 94 followers are treacherously seized near Fort Payton, despite having been asked to a parley.

December 1837

25   Colonel Zachary Taylor launches a frontal assault on the Seminoles through a saw grass swamp. His force is riddled with counterfire, and the Seminoles escape.

1838

More than 17,000 Cherokees are rounded up at gunpoint, without provisions or belongings, to be relocated west to Indian Territory (present-day Oklahoma) along the infamous Trail of Tears, a distance of 1,200 miles; 424 Cherokees are officially recorded as having died during the journey, but actual estimates range from 4,000 to 8,000.

1838–1842

The Second Seminole War degenerates into a protracted brush war in which Americans attempt to hunt the Seminoles into extinction and deport hundreds of captives. Disgusted with the war, many U.S. regulars resign from service.

February 1838

7   Major General Thomas Jesup meets with Seminole chief Tuskegee to persuade him to bring his followers to Fort Jupiter on the understanding that they will not have to abandon Florida. When Washington rejects these terms, however, Jesup sends the 2nd U.S. Dragoons to surround and imprison them, thus violating his promise.

1846–1864

Despite a treaty in 1846, 1,000 Navajos attack Fort Defiance. More raids follow, and when an ultimatum fails, Colonel Christopher Houston "Kit" Carson destroys food stores. The Navajos capitulate in January 1864 at Canyon de Chelly, beginning Carson's infamous Long Walk in which 9,022 Navajos are interned at Fort Sumner in New Mexico and thousands more die along the way.

1855–1858

Third Seminole War, the final clash between U.S. troops under Colonel William Harney and the Seminoles under Billy Bowlegs. Bowlegs surrenders on May 7, 1858, and although the hostilities are officially ended, the final remnant of Seminoles never surrenders.

August 17–September 23, 1862

The Dakota Sioux conduct surprise attacks against scores of settlements after not receiving their treaty-guaranteed food. Colonel Henry Sibley quells the uprising and soundly defeats the Sioux at the Battle of Wood Lake. Three hundred three natives are convicted and sentenced to hang, but President Abraham Lincoln commutes all but 39 of the sentences. The Sioux tribes are expelled from Minnesota.

April 1864–October 1867

Cheyenne-Arapaho War. Hoping to acquire statehood, Colorado officials provoke a war and create the 3rd Colorado Cavalry. The war ends with the Medicine Lodge Creek Treaty in 1867, wherein many Cheyennes and Arapahos agree to permanent relocation in Indian Territory.

July 1864

28   In the Battle of Killdeer Mountain (also known as the Battle of Tahkahokuty Mountain), the U.S. 1st Brigade under Brigadier General Alfred Sully scatters a large number of Sioux warriors but is unable to keep them from continuing to raid American settlements.

November 29–December 1, 1864

The Cheyenne-Arapaho War's most notorious event, dubbed the Sand Creek Massacre, occurs. The 3rd Colorado Cavalry under Colonel John Chivington, a Methodist minister, attacks a peaceful Cheyenne camp; 148 Cheyennes die, only 60 of whom are men.

1866–1868

Oglala Sioux chief Red Cloud resists American efforts to build a series of forts along the Bozeman Trail, igniting Red Cloud's War.

December 1866

21   Captain William Fetterman, in an effort to relieve a wood train under attack and ignoring orders, leads his men into a Sioux ambush. All 81 are killed.

August 1867

2   In the Wagon Box Fight, American soldiers under Captain James Powell are able to hold off 1,500 Sioux led by Red Cloud in large part because of the new Springfield Model 1866 Trapdoor .50-caliber breech-loading rifle issued after the Fetterman Massacre.

Mid-August 1868

Cheyenne, Sioux, and Arapaho war bands under Cheyenne chief Roman Nose raid Kansas, killing more than 100 settlers. Major George Forsyth tracks the bands, and Roman Nose is mortally wounded, although the Indians prevail until Forsyth is rescued by the 10th Cavalry Regiment.

November 1868

6   The Fort Laramie Treaty is signed, ending Red Cloud's War. A temporary victory for the Sioux, the treaty closes the Bozeman Trail, and U.S. forts along the trail are evacuated.

27   In the Battle of the Washita, Lieutenant Colonel George Armstrong Custer's 7th Cavalry Regiment attacks Black Kettle's Cheyenne village. Black Kettle is killed, and the village is torched before the Indians regroup.

May 1871

18   While on an inspection tour of Texas, Commanding General William T. Sherman with a small escort passes unmolested before a large Kiowa raiding party that instead strikes a large wagon train just hours later, some eight miles west of Fort Richardson, torturing and killing several teamsters. The experience prompts Sherman to intensify military activity on the southern Plains.

November 27, 1872–June 3, 1873

Clashes between California-Oregon border settlers and the Modocs bring a large regular military response. During a parley, Modoc leader Captain Jack produces a revolver from his jacket and kills Brigadier General Edward Canby, and more skirmishes ensue. The Modocs eventually lose their will to fight. Canby becomes the only general officer to be killed by Indians during the post–Civil War period.

December 1872

Major Joseph Brown runs down and massacres a band of Tonto Apaches at Salt River Ridge. Another victory shortly thereafter secures the surrender of the majority of the remaining Tontos.

May 17, 1873

Colonel Ranald Slidell Mackenzie leads a cavalry column into Mexico on an illegal incursion to curb Kickapoo, Lipan, and Lipan Apache raids. The Indians are completely surprised and are quickly defeated.

June 27, 1874–June 2, 1875

Native Americans of the southern Plains clash with the United States in the Red River War. The U.S. Army

is called to end the uprising, and within five years the southern Plains tribes are pacified.

June 1874

27   Several hundred Comanche and Cheyenne warriors attack a group of 28 buffalo hunters at Adobe Walls in the Texas Panhandle. The hunters, skillfully employing their high-power rifles, hold out while inflicting substantial losses on the attackers.

September 28, 1874

Mackenzie wins a climactic engagement at Palo Duro Canyon against Cheyenne warriors, capturing 1,500 horses and greatly hampering Native American movement.

1876–1877

Discovery of gold in the Black Hills pits Americans against the northern Plains tribes in the Great Sioux War, despite the Fort Laramie Treaty of 1868 that guarantees ownership of the sacred land to Native Americans. The U.S. Army has major successes starting in late 1876.

March 1876

Brigadier General George Crook marches a column out of Fort Fetterman to stop Sioux and Northern Cheyenne raiding parties led by Hunkpapa Sioux chief Sitting Bull. Although the U.S. troops are initially successful, the Indian warriors counterattack and maul the 3rd Cavalry Regiment under Colonel J. J. Reynolds.

June 1876

17   As part of a major three-pronged attack, Crook launches another expeditionary force that collides with 1,000 warriors under Chief Crazy Horse along Rosebud Creek. Crook again withdraws to await reinforcements.

25   In what is known as Custer's Last Stand, Custer inexplicably disobeys orders in an effort to annihilate Sioux leader Sitting Bull's encampment along the Little Bighorn River. After Custer divides his force, his battalion is quickly overwhelmed by warriors under Hunkpapa chief Gall and Oglala Sioux chief Low Dog, and Custer's command is annihilated. The remainder of Custer's regiment under Major Marcus Reno holds out until rescued.

October 1876

Mackenzie's 4th Cavalry Regiment overruns the Northern Cheyenne village of Dull Knife by the Powder River.

June 1877–October 5, 1877

The Nez Perce War is fought between nontreaty Nez Perces under Chief Joseph and the U.S. Army under

Brigadier General Oliver O. Howard and Colonel Nelson Miles, resulting in a running campaign that covers more than 1,600 miles before Joseph surrenders.

August 1877

9–10   Battle of the Big Hole. Nez Perce chief Looking Glass, believing that his band is temporarily safe from attack, insists that they stop to rest, against the judgment of Chief Joseph, and is surprised by a second army column under Colonel John Gibbon. The Nez Perces slip away after 36 hours.

September 1877

About 300 Apaches under Victorio and Loco flee the San Carlos Reservation but surrender at Fort Wingate 11 days later and are taken to the Warm Springs Reservation.

September 30–October 5, 1877

Not far from the salvation of the Canadian border, Nez Perce chief Looking Glass again insists that his band rest, only to be attacked by several companies under Miles. A dispirited Chief Joseph surrenders.

Mid-October 1878

When they learn that they will be repatriated back to the San Carlos Reservation, Victorio and 80 followers flee Warm Springs.

February 1879

Victorio surrenders at Mescalero.

July 1879

Victorio flees to Mexico.

September 1879

Some White River Utes in Colorado ambush a U.S. contingent, killing Major Thomas Thornburgh and several troops before the uprising is put down by Mackenzie.

October 1880

15   Victorio and most of his Apache warriors are killed in a battle with Mexican troops.

April 1882

Apache leaders Geronimo and Juh slip out of the San Carlos Reservation along with several hundred of Loco's Chiricahua followers. Chased by Colonel George Forsyth, they manage to reach Mexico but are ambushed by Mexican troops.

September 1882

Crook resumes command of the Department of Arizona and then crosses the Mexican border to pursue Geronimo.

March 1883

Geronimo's Apaches launch lightning raids throughout northern Mexico, southeastern Arizona, and New Mexico.

May 1883

1   Crook pursues Geronimo into the northern Mexico highlands and along with loyal Apache scouts manages to locate the Apache base camp while the warriors are away raiding. The Apaches surrender, and eventually Crook escorts several hundred back to the San Carlos Reservation.

17   Geronimo again escapes San Carlos along with Chihuahua, Naiché, Nana, and Mangas. Despite the cavalry that Crook had stationed along the Mexican border, Geronimo succeeds in escaping into the Sierra Madres.

January 1886

Captain Emmet Crawford's scouts capture Geronimo's horses and provisions in Mexico, but shortly after opening negotiations with Geronimo, Crawford is killed by Mexican scalp hunters.

March 1886

25   Geronimo agrees to surrender to Crook and serve two years' imprisonment in the East. However, the War Department reneges on this promise and instead ships 77 Chiricahuas to Fort Marion in Florida. Crook resigns, and Geronimo again flees to Mexico. Crook is replaced by Brigadier General Miles.

September 1886

4   Five thousand U.S. regulars and hundreds of Apache scouts hunt Apache leader Geronimo, who finally surrenders to Miles along with 33 followers. Geronimo is dispatched to Fort Pickens in Florida along with the other males, while their families are sent to Fort Marion, also in Florida.

December 1890

29   Battle of Wounded Knee. Near the Pine Ridge Agency, Colonel James Forsyth's 7th Cavalry Regiment intercepts members of Miniconjou Sioux chief Big Foot's band. Fighting breaks out, and U.S. troops kill more than 150 Native Americans, including dozens of women and children. Twenty-five troops die, and 39 others are wounded. The battle brings to a close major warfare between Native Americans and the U.S. Army.

Bibliography

Abel, Annie Heloise. *The American Indian in the Civil War, 1862–1865.* Lincoln: University of Nebraska Press, 1992.

Adams, Alexander B. *Geronimo: A Biography.* New York: Putnam, 1971.

Adams, George Rollie. *General William S. Harney: Prince of Dragoons.* Lincoln: University of Nebraska Press, 2001.

Adorno, Rolena, and Patrick Charles Pautz. *Álvar Núñez de Vaca: His Account, His Life, and the Expedition of Pánfilo de Narváez.* 3 vols. Lincoln: University of Nebraska Press, 1999.

Afton, Jean, David Fritjof Halaas, and Andrew E. Masich. *Cheyenne Dog Soldiers: A Ledgerbook History of Coups and Combat.* Niwot: University Press of Colorado, 1997.

Agnew, Brad. *Fort Gibson: Terminal on the Trail of Tears.* Norman: University of Oklahoma Press, 1980.

Alberts, Don E. *Brandy Station to Manila Bay: A Biography of General Wesley Merritt.* Austin, TX: Presidial, 1981.

Allen, Charles W. *From Fort Laramie to Wounded Knee: In the West That Was.* Edited by Richard E. Jensen. Lincoln: University of Nebraska Press, 1997.

Altshuler, Constance Wynn. *Cavalry Yellow and Infantry Blue: Army Officers in Arizona between 1851 and 1886.* Tucson: Arizona Historical Society, 1991.

Altshuler, Constance Wynn. *Chains of Command: Arizona and the Army, 1856–1875.* Tucson: Arizona Historical Society, 1981.

Ambrose, Stephen E. *Crazy Horse and Custer: The Parallel Lives of Two American Warriors.* New York: Anchor Books, 1996.

Ambrose, Stephen E. *Nothing Like It in the World: The Men Who Built the Transcontinental Railroad, 1863–1869.* New York: Simon and Schuster, 2000.

Ambrose, Stephen E. *Upton and the Army.* Baton Rouge: Louisiana State University Press, 1964.

Anderson, Fred. *Crucible of War: The Seven Years' War and the Fate of the Empire in British North America, 1754–1766.* New York: Vintage Books, 2001.

Anderson, Gary Clayton. *Little Crow: Spokesman for the Sioux.* St. Paul: Minnesota Historical Society Press, 1986.

Anderson, William L., ed. *Cherokee Removal: Before and After.* Athens: University of Georgia Press, 1991.

Anson, Bert. *The Miami Indians.* Norman: University of Oklahoma Press, 1971.

Antal, Sandy. *A Wampum Denied: Procter's War of 1812.* Ottawa: Carleton University Press, 1997.

Appleby, Joyce. *Thomas Jefferson.* New York: Henry Holt and Times Books, 2003.

Aquila, Richard. *The Iroquois Restoration: Iroquois Diplomacy on the Colonial Frontier, 1701–1754.* Detroit: Wayne State University Press, 1983.

Armstrong, David A. *Bullets and Bureaucrats: The Machine Gun and the United States Army, 1861–1916.* Contributions in Military History No. 29. Westport, CT: Greenwood, 1982.

Armstrong, William H. *Warrior in Two Camps: Ely S. Parker, Union General and Seneca Chief.* Syracuse, NY: Syracuse University Press, 1978.

Athearn, Robert G. *Forts of the Upper Missouri.* Englewood Cliffs, NJ: Prentice Hall, 1967.

Atkinson, James R. *Splendid Land, Splendid People: The Chickasaw Indians to Removal.* Tuscaloosa: University of Alabama Press, 2004.

Axelrod, Alan. *Chronicle of the Indian Wars: From Colonial Times to Wounded Knee.* New York: Prentice Hall, 1993.

Axtell, James. *After Columbus: Essays in the Ethnohistory of Colonial North America.* New York: Oxford University Press, 1988.

Axtell, James. *The Invasion Within: The Contest of Cultures in Colonial North America.* New York: Oxford University Press, 1985.

Axtell, James. *Natives and Newcomers: The Cultural Origins of North America.* New York: Oxford University Press, 2001.

Bailey, John W. *Pacifying the Plains: General Alfred Terry and the Decline of the Sioux, 1866–1890.* Westport, CT: Greenwood, 1979.

Bailey, Lynn R. *The Long Walk: A History of the Navajo Wars, 1848–68.* Los Angeles: Westernlore, 1964.

Bailey, Paul D. *Walkara: Hawk of the Mountains.* Los Angeles: Westernlore, 1954.

Baily, M. Thomas. *Reconstruction in Indian Territory: A Story of Avarice, Discrimination, and Opportunism.* Port Washington, NY: Kennikat, 1972.

Bain, David Haward. *Empire Express: Building the First Transcontinental Railroad.* New York: Viking Penguin, 1999.

Baird, W. David. *The Quapaw Indians: A History of the Downstream People.* Norman: University of Oklahoma Press, 1980.

Bakeless, John. *Background to Glory: The Life of George Rogers Clark.* Philadelphia: Lippincott, 1957.

Baker, T. Lindsay, and Billy R. Harrison. *Adobe Walls: The History and Archeology of the 1874 Trading Post.* College Station: Texas A&M University Press, 1986.

Baldwin, Carl R. *Captains of the Wilderness: The American Revolution on the Western Frontier.* Belleville, IL: Tiger Rose, 1986.

Ball, Durwood. *Army Regulars on the Western Frontier, 1848–1861.* Norman: University of Oklahoma Press, 2001.

Ball, Eve. *In the Days of Victorio: Recollections of a Warm Springs Apache.* Tucson: University of Arizona Press, 1970.

Ball, Eve, Nora Henn, and Lynda Sanchez. *Indeh: An Apache Odyssey.* Provo, UT: Brigham Young University Press, 1980.

Ball, Larry D. *The United States Marshals of New Mexico and Arizona Territories, 1846–1912.* Albuquerque: University of New Mexico Press, 1978.

Barbour, Barton H. *Fort Union and the Upper Missouri Fur Trade.* Norman: University of Oklahoma Press, 2001.

Barbour, Hugh, and J. William Frost. *The Quakers.* Westport, CT: Greenwood, 1988.

Barbour, Philip L. *The Three Worlds of Captain John Smith.* Boston: Houghton Mifflin, 1964.

Barbour, Philip L., ed. *The Complete Works of Captain John Smith, 1580–1631.* 3 vols. Chapel Hill: University of North Carolina Press for the Institute of Early American History and Culture, 1986.

Barnard, Sandy. *Custer's First Sergeant, John Ryan.* Terre Haute, IN: AST Press, 1996.

Barnard, Sandy, ed. *Ten Years with Custer: A Seventh Cavalryman's Memoirs.* Terre Haute, IN: AST Press, 2001.

Barnes, Celia. *Native American Power in the United States, 1783–1795.* Teaneck, NJ: Fairleigh Dickinson University Press, 2003.

Barr, Daniel P., ed. *The Boundaries between Us: Natives and Newcomers along the Frontiers of the Old Northwest Territory, 1750–1850.* Kent, OH: Kent State University Press, 2006.

Bartlett, Irving H. *John C. Calhoun: A Biography.* New York: Norton, 1993.

Basso, Keith H., ed. *Western Apache Raiding and Warfare: From the Notes of Grenville Goodwin.* Tucson: University of Arizona Press, 1971.

Bauer, K. Jack. *Zachary Taylor: Soldier, Planter, Statesman of the Old Southwest.* Baton Rouge: Louisiana State University Press, 1985.

Beaver, R. Pierce. *Church, State, and the American Indians.* St. Louis: Concordia Publishing House, 1966.

Beck, Paul N. *The First Sioux War: The Grattan Fight and Blue Water Creek, 1854–1856.* Lanham, MD: University Press of America, 2004.

Belohlavek, John M. *"Let the Eagle Soar!" The Foreign Policy of Andrew Jackson.* Lincoln: University of Nebraska Press, 1986.

Bender, Averam B. *The March of Empire: Frontier Defense in the Southwest, 1848–1860.* Lawrence: University of Kansas Press, 1952.

Bender, Norman J. *New Hope for the Indians: The Grant Peace Policy and the Navajos in the 1870s.* Albuquerque: University of New Mexico Press, 1989.

Bernotas, Bob. *Sitting Bull: Chief of the Sioux.* North American Indians of Achievement. New York: Chelsea House, 1992.

Bernstein, R. B. *Thomas Jefferson.* New York: Oxford University Press, 2003.

Berthrong, Donald. *The Southern Cheyennes.* Norman: University of Oklahoma Press, 1963.

Bieder, Robert E. *Science Encounters the Indians, 1820–1880: The Early Years of American Ethnology.* Norman: University of Oklahoma Press, 1986.

Bilby, Joseph G. *A Revolution in Arms: A History of the First Repeating Rifles.* Yardley, PA: Westholme Publishing, 2006.

Billings, Warren M. *Sir William Berkeley and the Forging of Colonial Virginia.* Baton Rouge: Louisiana State University Press, 2004.

Billington, Monroe Lee. *New Mexico's Buffalo Soldiers, 1866–1900.* Niwot: University Press of Colorado, 1991.

Billington, Ray Allen. *Frederick Jackson Turner: Historian, Scholar, Teacher.* New York: Oxford University Press, 1973.

Bird, Harrison. *War for the West, 1790–1813.* New York: Oxford University Press, 1971.

Black, Jeremy. *Pitt the Elder.* New York: Cambridge University Press, 1992.

Blackhawk, Ned. *Violence over the Land: Indians and Empires in the Early American West.* Cambridge: Harvard University Press, 2006.

Blondheim, Menahem. *News over the Wires: The Telegraph and the Flow of Public Information in America, 1844–1897.* Cambridge: Harvard University Press, 1994.

Bloss, Roy S. *Pony Express: The Great Gamble.* Berkeley, CA: Howell-North, 1959.

Blumer, Thomas J. *Bibliography of the Catawba.* Native American Bibliography Series 10. Metuchen, NJ: Scarecrow, 1987.

Bogue, Allan G. *Frederick Jackson Turner: Strange Roads Going Down.* Norman: University of Oklahoma Press, 1998.

Bold, Christine. *Selling the Wild West: Popular Western Fiction, 1860–1960.* Bloomington: Indiana University Press, 1987.

Bolton, Hebert Eugene. *Coronado: Knight of Pueblos and Plains.* Albuquerque: University of New Mexico Press, 1990.

Bowden, Henry Warner. *American Indians and Christian Missions: Studies in Cultural Conflict.* Chicago History of American Religion. Chicago: University of Chicago Press, 1981.

Braatz, Timothy. *Surviving Conquest: A History of the Yavapai Peoples.* Lincoln: University of Nebraska Press, 2003.

Bradley, James W. *Evolution of the Onondaga Iroquois: Accommodating Change, 1500–1655.* Syracuse, NY: Syracuse University Press, 1987.

Braider, Donald. *Solitary Star: A Biography of Sam Houston.* New York: Putnam, 1974.

Brandão, José António. *Your Fyre Shall Burn No More: Iroquois Policy toward New France and Its Native Allies to 1701.* Lincoln: University of Nebraska Press, 1997.

Brandes, Ray, ed. *Troopers West: Military and Indian Affairs on the American Frontier.* San Diego: Frontier Heritage Press, 1970.

Brasser, Ted J. *Riding on the Frontier's Crest: Mahican Indian Culture and Culture Change.* Ottawa: National Museums of Canada, 1974.

Breitweiser, Mitchell Robert. *American Puritanism and the Defense of Mourning: Religion, Grief, and Ethnology in Mary White Rowlandson's Captivity Narrative.* Madison: University of Wisconsin Press, 1990.

Briceland, Alan Vance. *Westward from Virginia: The Exploration of the Virginia-Carolina Frontier, 1650–1710.* Charlottesville: University Press of Virginia, 1987.

Bridenbaugh, Carl. *Jamestown, 1544–1699.* New York: Oxford University Press, 1980.

Brimlow, George Francis. *The Bannock Indian War of 1878.* Caldwell, ID: Caxton Printers, 1938.

Bross, Kristina. *Dry Bones and Indian Sermons: Praying Indians in Colonial America.* Ithaca, NY: Cornell University Press, 2004.

Brown, D. Alexander. *The Galvanized Yankees.* Urbana: University of Illinois Press, 1963.

Brown, Dee. *Bury My Heart at Wounded Knee.* New York: Holt, Rinehart and Winston, 1970.

Brown, Dee. *Fort Phil Kearny: An American Saga.* New York: Putnam, 1962.

Brown, M. L. *Firearms in Colonial America: The Impact on History and Technology, 1492–1792.* Washington, DC: Smithsonian Institution Press, 1980.

Brown, Mark H. *The Flight of the Nez Perce.* Lincoln: University of Nebraska Press, 1967.

Brown, Roger Hamilton. *The Struggle for the Indian Stream Territory.* Cleveland, OH: Western Reserve University Press, 1955.

Brumwell, Stephen. *White Devil: A True Story of War, Savagery, and Vengeance in Colonial America.* Cambridge, MA: Da Capo, 2005.

Buecker, Thomas R. *Fort Robinson and the American West, 1874–1899.* Lincoln: Nebraska State Historical Society, 1999.

Burke, Charles T. *Puritans at Bay: The War against King Philip and the Squaw Sachems in New England, 1675–1676.* New York: Exposition, 1967.

Butts, Michèle Tucker. *Galvanized Yankees on the Upper Missouri: The Face of Loyalty.* Boulder: University Press of Colorado, 2003.

Calloway, Colin G. *The Abenaki.* New York: Chelsea House, 1989.

Calloway, Colin G. *The American Revolution in Indian Country: Crisis and Diversity in Native American Communities.* Cambridge: Cambridge University Press, 1995.

Calloway, Colin G. *New Worlds for All: Indians, Europeans, and the Remaking of Early America.* Baltimore: Johns Hopkins University Press, 1997.

Calloway, Colin G. *The Western Abenakis of Vermont, 1600–1800: War, Migration, and the Survival of an Indian People.* Norman: University of Oklahoma Press, 1990.

Calloway, Colin G., comp. *North Country Captives: Selected Narratives of Indian Captivity from Vermont and New Hampshire.* Hanover, NH: University Press of New England, 1992.

Calloway, Colin G., ed. *After King Philip's War: Presence and Persistence in Indian New England.* Hanover, NH: University Press of New England, 1997.

Calloway, Colin G., ed. *Dawnland Encounters: Indians and Europeans in Northern New England.* Hanover, NH: University Press of New England, 1991.

Campbell, Randolph B. *Sam Houston and the American Southwest.* Library of American Biography. New York: HarperCollins, 1993.

Canfield, Gae Whitney. *Sarah Winnemucca of the Northern Paiutes.* Norman: University of Oklahoma Press, 1983.

Capps, Benjamin. *The Warren Wagontrain Raid: The First Complete Account of an Historic Indian Attack and Its Aftermath.* Dallas, TX: Southern Methodist University Press, 1989.

Carley, Kenneth. *The Sioux Uprising of 1862.* 2nd ed. St. Paul: Minnesota Historical Society, 1976.

Carlson, Leonard A. *Indians, Bureaucrats and Land: The Dawes Act and the Decline of Indian Farming.* Westport, CT: Greenwood, 1981.

Carlson, Paul H. *The Buffalo Soldier Tragedy of 1877.* College Station: Texas A&M University Press, 2003.

Carlson, Paul H. *"Pecos Bill": A Military Biography of William R. Shafter.* College Station: Texas A&M University Press, 1989.

Carpenter, John A. *Sword and Olive Branch: Oliver Otis Howard.* Pittsburgh: University of Pittsburgh Press, 1964.

Carpenter, John A. *Ulysses S. Grant.* New York: Twayne, 1970.

Carricker, Robert C. *Fort Supply, Indian Territory: Frontier Outpost on the Plains.* Norman: University of Oklahoma Press, 1970.

Carrington, Frances C. *My Army Life: A Soldier's Wife at Fort Phil Kearny With an Account of the Celebration of "Wyoming Opened."* Boulder, CO: Pruett Publishing, 1990.

Carroll, H. Bailey. *The Texas Santa Fe Trail.* Canyon, TX: Panhandle-Plains Historical Society, 1951.

Carroll, John M., ed. *The Black Military Experience in the American West.* New York: Liveright, 1971.

Carroll, John M., ed. *Camp Talk: The Very Private Letters of Frederick W. Benteen of the 7th U.S. Cavalry to His Wife, 1871–1888.* Mattituck, NY: J. M. Carroll, 1983.

Carstens, Kenneth C., and Nancy Son Carstens, eds. *The Life of George Rogers Clark, 1752–1818: Triumphs and Tragedies.* Westport, CT: Praeger, 2004.

Carter, Carroll Joe. *Pike in Colorado.* Fort Collins, CO: Old Army, 1978.

Carter, Harvey Lewis. *The Life and Times of Little Turtle: First Sagamore of the Wabash.* Urbana: University of Illinois Press, 1987.

Carter, R. G. *On the Border with Mackenzie or Winning West Texas from the Comanches.* 1935; reprint, New York: Antiquarian, 1961.

Carter, Samuel, III. *Cherokee Sunset: A Nation Betrayed: A Narrative of Travail and Triumph, Persecution and Exile.* Garden City, NY: Doubleday, 1976.

Castiglia, Christopher. *Bound and Determined: Captivity, Culture-Crossing, and White Womanhood from Mary Rowlandson to Patty Hearst.* Chicago: University of Chicago Press, 1996.

Caughey, John Walton. *McGillivray of the Creeks.* Norman: University of Oklahoma Press, 1938.

Cave, Alfred A. *The Pequot War.* Amherst: University of Massachusetts Press, 1996.

Cayton, Andrew R. L., and Fredrika J. Teute, eds. *Contact Points: American Frontiers from the Mohawk Valley to the Mississippi, 1750–1830.* Chapel Hill: University of North Carolina Press, 1998.

Chalfant, William Y. *Cheyennes at Dark Water Creek: The Last Fight of the Red River War.* Norman: University of Oklahoma Press, 1997.

Chalfant, William Y. *Cheyennes and Horse Soldiers: The 1857 Expedition and the Battle of Solomon's Fork.* Norman: University of Oklahoma Press, 1989.

Champagne, Duane. *Social Order and Political Change: Constitutional Governments among the Cherokee, the Choctaw, the Chickasaw and the Creek.* Stanford, CA: Stanford University Press, 1992.

Chance, Joseph E., ed. *Mexico under Fire: Being the Diary of Samuel Ryan Curtis, 3rd Ohio Volunteer Regiment during the American Military Occupation of Northern Mexico, 1846–1848.* Fort Worth: Texas Christian University Press, 1994.

Church, Benjamin. *Diary of King Philip's War, 1675–76.* Edited by Alan and Mary Simpson. Chester, CT: Pequot, 1975.

Clark, Blue. *Lone Wolf v. Hitchcock: Treaty Rights and Indian Law at the End of the Nineteenth Century.* Lincoln: University of Nebraska Press, 1994.

Clark, Jerry E. *The Shawnee.* Lexington: University Press of Kentucky, 2007.

Clark, Thomas D., and John D. W. Guice. *Frontiers in Conflict: The Old Southwest, 1795–1803.* Albuquerque: University of New Mexico Press, 1989.

Clarke, Dwight L. *Stephen Watts Kearny: Soldier of the West.* Norman: University of Oklahoma Press, 1961.

Clarke, Dwight L. *William Tecumseh Sherman: Gold Rush Banker.* San Francisco: California Historical Society, 1969.

Clarke, Dwight L., ed. *The Original Journals of Henry Smith Turner: With Stephen Watts Kearny to New Mexico and California, 1846–1847.* The American Exploration and Travel Series 51. Norman: University of Oklahoma Press, 1966.

Clayton, Lawrence A., Vernon James Knight Jr., and Edward C. Moore, eds. *The De Soto Chronicles: The Expedition of Hernando de Soto to North America in 1539–1543.* 2 vols. Tuscaloosa: University of Alabama Press, 1993.

Cleaves, Freeman. *Old Tippecanoe: William Henry Harrison and His Time.* New York: Scribner, 1939.

Coel, Margaret. *Chief Left Hand: Southern Arapaho.* Norman: University of Oklahoma Press, 1981.

Coffey, David. *Sheridan's Lieutenants: Phil Sheridan, His Generals, and the Final Year of the Civil War.* Lanham, MD: Rowman and Littlefield, 2005.

Cole, D. C. *The Chiricahua Apache, 1846–1876: From War to Reservation.* Albuquerque: University of New Mexico Press, 1988.

Coleman, William S. E. *Voices of Wounded Knee.* Lincoln: University of Nebraska Press, 2000.

Collins, Charles. *Apache Nightmare: The Battle at Cibecue Creek.* Norman: University of Oklahoma Press, 1999.

Conkling, Roscoe P., and Margaret B. Conkling. *The Butterfield Overland Mail, 1857–1869.* 3 vols. Glendale, CA: Clark, 1947.

Connell, Evan S. *Son of the Morning Star: Custer and the Little Bighorn.* New York: North Point Press, 1984.

Connelly, Donald B. *John M. Schofield and the Politics of Generalship.* Chapel Hill: University of North Carolina Press, 2006.

Cooper, William J., Jr. *Jefferson Davis, American.* New York: Knopf, 2000.

Covington, James W. *The Billy Bowlegs War, 1855–1858: The Final Stand of the Seminoles against the Whites.* Chuluota, FL: Mickler House, 1982.

Covington, James W. *The Seminoles of Florida.* Gainesville: University Press of Florida, 1993.

Coward, John M. *The Newspaper Indian: Native American Identity in the Press, 1820–90.* Urbana: University of Illinois Press, 1999.

Cozzens, Peter. *General John Pope: A Life for the Nation.* Champaign: University of Illinois Press, 2000.

Cozzens, Peter, ed. *Eyewitnesses to the Indian Wars, 1865–1890.* 5 vols. Mechanicsburg, PA: Stackpole, 2001–2006.

Cozzens, Peter, and Robert I. Girardi, eds. *The Military Memoirs of General John Pope.* Chapel Hill: University of North Carolina Press, 1998.

Craig, Reginald S. *The Fighting Parson: The Biography of Colonel John M. Chivington.* Los Angeles: Westernlore, 1959.

Crampton, C. Gregory, ed. *The Mariposa Indian War, 1850–1851: Diaries of Robert Eccleston; The California Gold Rush, Yosemite, and the High Sierra.* Salt Lake City: University of Utah Press, 1957.

Cress, Lawrence Delbert. *Citizens in Arms: The Army and the Militia in American Society to the War of 1812.* Chapel Hill: University of North Carolina Press, 1982.

Cronon, William. *Changes in the Land: Indians, Colonists, and the Ecology of New England.* New York: Hill and Wang, 1983.

Crook, George. *General George Crook: His Autobiography.* Edited by Martin F. Schmidt. Norman: University of Oklahoma Press, 1960.

Crozier, William Armstrong, ed. *Virginia Colonial Militia, 1651–1776.* Baltimore: Southern Book Company, 1954.

Cuneo, John R. *Robert Rogers of the Rangers.* New York: Oxford University Press, 1959.

Cunningham, Frank. *General Stand Watie's Confederate Indians.* Norman: University of Oklahoma Press, 1998.

Cusick, James G. *The Other War of 1812: The Patriot War and the American Invasion of Spanish East Florida.* Gainesville: University Press of Florida, 2003.

Custer, George Armstrong. *My Life on the Plains: Or, Personal Experiences with Indians.* Introduction by Edgar I. Stewart. Norman: University of Oklahoma Press, 1962.

Dacey, Karen H. *In the Shadow of the Great Blue Hill.* Lanham, MD: University Press of America, 1995.

Danziger, Edmund Jefferson, Jr. *Indians and Bureaucrats: Administering the Reservation Policy during the Civil War.* Urbana: University of Illinois Press, 1974.

Dary, David. *The Oregon Trail: An American Saga.* New York: Knopf, 2004.

Davis, William C. *Jefferson Davis: The Man and His Hour.* New York: HarperCollins, 1991.

Dawson, Joseph G., III. *Doniphan's Epic March: The 1st Missouri Volunteers in the Mexican War.* Lawrence: University Press of Kansas, 1999.

De Barthe, Joe. *The Life and Adventures of Frank Grouard.* Norman: University of Oklahoma Press, 1958.

Debo, Angie. *Geronimo: The Man, His Time, His Place.* Norman: University of Oklahoma Press, 1976.

Decker, Peter. *The Utes Must Go: American Expansion and the Removal of a People.* Golden, CO: Fulcrum, 2004.

Delgado, James P. *To California by Sea: A Maritime History of the California Gold Rush.* Columbia: University of South Carolina Press, 1990.

Delo, David Michael. *Peddlers and Post Traders: The Army Sutler on the Frontier.* Salt Lake City: University of Utah Press, 1992.

DeMontravel, Peter R. *A Hero to His Fighting Men: Nelson A. Miles, 1839–1925.* Kent, OH: Kent State University Press, 1998.

Demos, John. *The Unredeemed Captive: A Family Story From Early America.* New York: Knopf, 1994.

Denning, Michael. *Mechanic Accents: Dime Novels and Working Class Culture in America.* London: Verso, 1998.

Dennis, Matthew. *Cultivating a Landscape of Peace: Iroquois-European Encounters in Seventeenth-Century North America.* Ithaca, NY: Cornell University Press, 1993.

Densmore, Christopher. *Red Jacket: Iroquois Diplomat and Orator.* Syracuse, NY: Syracuse University Press, 1999.

Derounian-Stodola, Kathryn Zabelle, and James A. Levernier. *The Indian Captivity Narrative, 1500–1900.* New York: Twayne, 1993.

De Vorsey, Louis, Jr. *The Indian Boundary in the Southern Colonies, 1763–1775.* Chapel Hill: University of North Carolina Press, 1966.

Dickason, Olive Patricia. *The Myth of the Savage and the Beginnings of French Colonialism in the Americas.* Edmonton: University of Alberta Press, 1984.

Dillon, Richard. *Meriwether Lewis: A Biography.* New York: Coward-McCann, 1965.

Dippie, Brian W. *Catlin and His Contemporaries: The Politics of Patronage.* Lincoln: University of Nebraska Press, 1990.

Dippie, Brian W. *Custer's Last Stand: The Anatomy of an American Myth.* Missoula: University of Montana Press, 1976.

Dippie, Brian W., ed. *Charles M. Russell, Word Painter: Letters, 1887–1926.* Fort Worth, TX: Amon Carter Museum, 1993.

Dixon, David. *Hero of Beecher Island: The Life and Military Career of George A. Forsyth.* Lincoln: University of Nebraska Press, 1994.

Dixon, David. *Never Come to Peace Again: Pontiac's Uprising and the Fate of the British Empire in North America.* Norman: University of Oklahoma Press, 2005.

Dobak, William A., and Thomas D. Phillips. *The Black Regulars, 1866–1898.* Norman: University of Oklahoma Press, 2001.

Dobak, William A., and Thomas D. Phillips. *Fort Riley and Its Neighbors: Military Money and Economic Growth, 1853–1895.* Norman: University of Oklahoma Press, 1998.

Doughty, Howard N. *Francis Parkman.* New York: Macmillan, 1962.

Dowd, Gregory Evans. *A Spirited Resistance: The North American Indian Struggle for Unity, 1745–1815.* Baltimore: Johns Hopkins University Press, 1992.

Dowd, Gregory Evans. *War under Heaven: Pontiac, the Indian Nations, and the British Empire.* Baltimore: Johns Hopkins University Press, 2002.

Downey, Fairfax. *Indian-Fighting Army.* New York: Scribner, 1941.

Downey, Fairfax. *Indian Wars of the U.S. Army, 1776–1865.* Garden City, NY: Doubleday, 1963.

Downey, Fairfax, and J. N. Jacobsen. *The Red-Bluecoats: The Indian Scouts.* Fort Collins, CO: Old Army, 1973.

Drake, James D. *King Philip's War: Civil War in New England, 1675–1676.* Amherst: University of Massachusetts Press, 1999.

Drury, Clifford M. *Chief Lawyer of the Nez Perce Indians, 1796–1876.* Glendale, CA: Arthur H. Clark, 1974.

Duncan, David Ewing. *Hernando de Soto: A Savage Quest in the Americas.* Norman: University of Oklahoma Press, 1997.

Dunlay, Thomas W. *Kit Carson and the Indians.* Lincoln: University of Nebraska Press, 2000.

Dunn, Richard S. *Puritans and Yankees: The Winthrop Dynasty of New England, 1630–1717.* Princeton, NJ: Princeton University Press, 1962.

Edmunds, R. David. *American Indian Leaders: Studies in Diversity.* Lincoln: University of Nebraska Press, 1980.

Edmunds, R. David. *The Potawatomis: Keepers of the Fire.* Norman: University of Oklahoma Press, 1978.

Edmunds, R. David. *The Shawnee Prophet.* Lincoln: University of Nebraska Press, 1983.

Edmunds, R. David. *Tecumseh and the Quest for Indian Leadership.* Boston: Little, Brown, 1984.

Edmunds, R. David, and Joseph L. Peyser. *The Fox Wars: The Mesquakie Challenge to New France.* Norman: University of Oklahoma Press, 1993.

Edwards, William B. *The Story of Colt's Revolver: The Biography of Col. Samuel Colt.* Harrisburg, PA: Stackpole, 1957.

Eisenhower, John S. D. *Agent of Destiny: The Life and Times of General Winfield Scott.* New York: Free Press, 1997.

Ellingson, Ter. *The Myth of the Noble Savage.* Berkeley: University of California Press, 2001.

Ellis, Richard N. *General Pope and U.S. Indian Policy.* Albuquerque: University of New Mexico Press, 1970.

Emerson, Everett H. *Captain John Smith.* Twayne United States Authors Series. New York: Twayne, 1971.

Emmitt, Robert. *The Last War Trail: The Utes and the Settlement of Colorado.* Norman: University of Oklahoma Press, 1954.

Endy, Melvin B., Jr. *William Penn and Early Quakerism.* Princeton, NJ: Princeton University Press, 1973.

Ethridge, Robbie. *Creek Country: The Creek Indians and Their World.* Chapel Hill: University of North Carolina Press, 2003.

Faragher, John Mack. *Daniel Boone: The Life and Legend of an American Pioneer.* New York: Holt, 1992.

Faragher, John Mack. *Women and Men on the Overland Trail.* New Haven, CT: Yale University Press, 1979.

Faulk, Odie B. *Destiny Road: The Gila Trail and the Opening of the Southwest.* New York: Oxford University Press, 1973.

Faulk, Odie B. *The Geronimo Campaign.* New York: Oxford University Press, 1969.

Faulk, Odie B. *The U.S. Camel Corps: An Army Experiment.* New York: Oxford University Press, 1976.

Fellman, Michael. *Citizen Sherman: A Life of William Tecumseh Sherman.* New York: Random House, 1995.

Fenton, William N. *The Great Law and the Longhouse: A Political History of the Iroquois Confederacy.* Norman: University of Oklahoma Press, 1998.

Fischer, Joseph R. *A Well-Executed Failure: The Sullivan Campaign against the Iroquois, July–September 1779.* Columbia: University of South Carolina Press, 1997.

Flexner, James Thomas. *George Washington.* 4 vols. New York: Little, Brown, 1965–1972.

Flexner, James Thomas. *Mohawk Baronet: A Biography of Sir William Johnson.* Syracuse, NY: Syracuse University Press, 1989.

Flores, Dan L. *Journal of an Indian Trader: Anthony Glass and the Texas Trading Frontier, 1790–1810.* Southwestern Studies. College Station: Texas A&M University Press, 1985.

Foley, William E. *Wilderness Journey: The Life of William Clark.* Columbia: University of Missouri Press, 2004.

Forbes, Jack D. *Apache, Navaho, and Spaniard.* 2nd ed. Norman: University of Oklahoma Press, 1994.

Fort Phil Kearny/Bozeman Trail Association. *Civilian, Military, and Native American Portraits of Fort Phil Kearny.* Banner, WY: Fort Phil Kearny/Bozeman Trail Association, 1993.

Fougera, Katherine Gibson. *With Custer's Cavalry.* Caldwell, ID: Caxton Printers, 1940.

Fowler, Arlen L. *The Black Infantry in the West, 1869–1891.* Norman: University of Oklahoma Press, 1996.

Fowler, Loretta. *Arapaho Politics, 1851–1978: Symbols in Crises of Authority.* Lincoln: University of Nebraska Press, 1982.

Franklin, Wayne. *The New World of James Fenimore Cooper.* Chicago: University of Chicago Press, 1982.

Franks, Kenny A. *Stand Watie and the Agony of the Cherokee Nation.* Memphis: Memphis State University Press, 1979.

Franz, George W. *Paxton: A Study of Community Structure and Mobility in the Colonial Pennsylvania Backcountry.* Outstanding Studies in Early American History. New York: Garland, 1989.

Frazer, Robert W. *Forts and Supplies: The Role of the Army in the Economy of the Southwest, 1846–1861.* Albuquerque: University of New Mexico Press, 1983.

Frazier, Donald S. *Blood & Treasure: Confederate Empire in the Southwest.* College Station: Texas A&M University Press, 1995.

Freeman, Henry Blanchard. *The Freeman Journal: The Infantry in the Sioux Campaign of 1876.* Edited by George A. Schneider. San Rafael, CA: Presidio, 1977.

Frégault, Guy. *Canada: The War of the Conquest.* Translated by Margaret M. Cameron. London: Oxford University Press, 1969.

Frémont, John C. *The Expeditions of John Charles Frémont.* Edited by Donald Jackson and Mary Lee Spence. 3 vols. Urbana: University of Illinois Press, 1970–1984.

Frey, Rodney. *The World of the Crow Indians: As Driftwood Lodges.* Norman: University of Oklahoma Press, 1987.

Frost, Lawrence A. *The Court Martial of General George Armstrong Custer.* Norman: University of Oklahoma Press, 1968.

Furtwangler, Albert. *Answering Chief Seattle.* Seattle: University of Washington Press, 1997.

Fuson, Robert H. *Juan Ponce de Leon and the Spanish Discovery of Puerto Rico and Florida.* Blacksburg, VA: McDonald and Woodward, 2000.

Gaff, Alan, and Maureen Gaff, eds. *Adventures on the Western Frontier: Major General John Gibbon.* Bloomington: Indiana University Press, 1994.

Gaines, W. Craig. *The Confederate Cherokees: John Drew's Regiment of Mounted Rifles.* Baton Rouge: Louisiana State University Press, 1989.

Galbraith, John S. *The Hudson's Bay Company as an Imperial Factor, 1821–1869.* Berkeley: University of California Press, 1959.

Gallay, Alan. *The Indian Slave Trade: The Rise of the English Empire in the American South, 1670–1717.* New Haven, CT: Yale University Press, 2002.

Galloway, Patricia. *Choctaw Genesis, 1500–1700.* Lincoln: University of Nebraska Press, 1995.

Galloway, Patricia K., ed. *La Salle and His Legacy: Frenchmen and Indians in the Lower Mississippi Valley.* Jackson: University Press of Mississippi, 1982.

Garavaglia, Louis A., and Charles G. Worman. *Firearms of the American West, 1803–1865.* Niwot: University Press of Colorado, 1997.

Garavaglia, Louis A., and Charles G. Worman. *Firearms of the American West, 1866–1894.* Niwot: University Press of Colorado, 1997.

Gibbon, Guy. *The Sioux: The Dakota and Lakota Nations.* Malden, MA: Blackwell, 2003.

Gilbert, Bil. *God Gave Us This Country: Tekamthi and the First American Civil War.* New York: Atheneum, 1989.

Gilman, Rhoda R. *Henry Hastings Sibley: Divided Heart.* St. Paul: Minnesota Historical Society Press, 2004.

Gleach, Frederic W. *Powhatan's World and Colonial Virginia.* Lincoln: University of Nebraska Press, 1997.

Goebel, Dorothy Burne. *William Henry Harrison: A Political Biography.* Indianapolis: Historical Bureau of the Indiana Library and Historical Department, 1926.

Goetzmann, William H. *Army Exploration in the American West, 1803–1863.* New Haven, CT: Yale University Press, 1959.

Goetzmann, William H. *Exploration and Empire: The Explorer and the Scientist in the Winning of the American West.* New York: Knopf, 1966.

Gordon-McCutchan, R. C., ed. *Kit Carson: Indian Fighter or Indian Killer?* Niwot: University Press of Colorado, 1996.

Graham, W. A., comp. *The Custer Myth: A Source Book of Custeriana.* Harrisburg, PA: Stackpole, 1953.

Grant, Ulysses S., III. *Ulysses S. Grant: Warrior and Statesman.* New York: William Morrow, 1969.

Gray, John S. *Centennial Campaign: The Sioux War of 1876.* Norman: Oklahoma University Press, 1988.

Gray, John S. *Custer's Last Campaign: Mitch Boyer and the Little Bighorn Reconstructed.* Lincoln: University of Nebraska Press, 1991.

Graymont, Barbara. *The Iroquois in the American Revolution.* Syracuse, NY: Syracuse University Press, 1972.

Green, Michael D. *The Politics of Indian Removal: Creek Government and Society in Crisis.* Lincoln: University of Nebraska Press, 1982.

Greene, Jerome A. *Morning Star Dawn: The Powder River Expedition and the Northern Cheyennes, 1876.* Norman: University of Oklahoma Press, 2003.

Greene, Jerome A. *Nez Perce Summer, 1877: The U.S. Army and the Nee-Me-Poo Crisis.* Helena: Montana Historical Society Press, 2000.

Greene, Jerome A. *Slim Buttes, 1876: An Episode of the Great Sioux War.* Norman: University of Oklahoma Press, 1982.

Greene, Jerome A. *Washita: The U.S. Army and the Southern Cheyennes, 1867–1869.* Norman: University of Oklahoma Press, 2004.

Greene, Jerome A. *Yellowstone Command: Colonel Nelson A. Miles and the Great Sioux War, 1876–1877.* Lincoln: University of Nebraska Press, 1991.

Greene, Jerome A., ed. *Battles and Skirmishes of the Great Sioux War, 1876–1877: The Military View.* Norman: University of Oklahoma Press, 1993.

Greene, Jerome A., ed. *Lakota and Cheyenne: Indian Views of the Great Sioux War, 1876–1877.* Norman: University of Oklahoma Press, 1994.

Greene, Jerome A., and Douglas G. Scott. *Finding Sand Creek: History, Archeology, and the 1864 Massacre Site.* Norman: University of Oklahoma Press, 2004.

Griffen, William B. *The Apaches at War and Peace: The Janos Presidio, 1750–1858.* Albuquerque: University of New Mexico Press, 1988.

Grossman, James. *James Fenimore Cooper.* American Men of Letters Series. New York: William Sloane Associates, 1949.

Guild, Thelma S., and Harvey L. Carter. *Kit Carson: A Pattern for Heroes.* Lincoln: University of Nebraska Press, 1984.

Gunnerson, Dolores A. *The Jicarilla Apaches: A Study in Survival.* DeKalb: Northern Illinois University Press, 1974.

Gutiérrez, Ramón, and Richard J. Orsi, eds. *Contested Eden: California before the Gold Rush.* Berkeley: University of California Press, 1998.

Haefeli, Evan, and Kevin Sweeney. *Captive Histories: English, French, and Native Narratives of the 1704 Deerfield Raid.* Amherst: University of Massachusetts Press, 2006.

Haefeli, Evan, and Kevin Sweeney. *Captors and Captives: The 1704 French and Indian Raid on Deerfield.* Amherst: University of Massachusetts Press, 2003.

Hafen, LeRoy R., and Ann W. Hafen, eds. *Powder River Campaigns and Sawyers Expedition of 1865: A Documentary Account Comprising Official Reports, Diaries, Contemporary Newspaper Accounts, and Personal Narratives.* The Far West and the Rockies Historical Series, 1820–1875, Vol. 12. Glendale, CA: Arthur H. Clark, 1961.

Hagan, William T. *Quanah Parker, Comanche Chief.* Norman: University of Oklahoma Press, 1993.

Hagan, William T. *United States–Comanche Relations: The Reservation Years.* New Haven, CT: Yale University Press, 1976.

Hahn, Stephen C. *The Invention of the Creek Nation, 1670–1763.* Lincoln: University of Nebraska Press, 2004.

Haille, Edward Wright, ed. *Jamestown Narratives: Eyewitness Accounts of the Virginia Colony; The First Decade, 1604–1617.* Champlain, VA: RoundHouse, 1998.

Haines, Aubrey L. *An Elusive Victory: The Battle of the Big Hole.* West Glacier, MT: Glacier Natural History Association, 1991.

Haley, James L. *The Buffalo War: The History of the Red River Indian Uprising of 1874.* Norman: University of Oklahoma Press, 1985.

Haley, James L. *Sam Houston.* Norman: University of Oklahoma Press, 2002.

Hall, Martin Hardwick. *Sibley's New Mexico Campaign.* Austin: University of Texas Press, 1960.

Hamilton, Allan Lee. *Sentinel of the Southern Plains: Fort Richardson and the Northwest Texas Frontier, 1866–1878.* Fort Worth: Texas Christian University Press, 1988.

Hamilton, Holman. *Zachary Taylor: Soldier of the Republic.* 1941; reprint, Hamden, CT: Archon Books, 1966.

Hamilton, Holman. *Zachary Taylor: Soldier in the White House.* Indianapolis: Bobbs-Merrill, 1951.

Hamilton, Milton W. *Sir William Johnson, Colonial American, 1715–1763.* Port Washington, NY: Kennikat, 1976.

Hammond, George Peter, and Agapito Rey, eds. *Narratives of the Coronado Expedition, 1540–1542.* New York: AMS Press, 1977.

Hampton, Bruce. *Children of Grace: The Nez Perce War of 1877.* New York: Holt, 1994.

Hann, John H. *Apalachee: The Land between the Rivers.* Gainesville: University Press of Florida, 1988.

Hann, John H. *A History of the Timucua Indians and Missions.* Gainesville: University Press of Florida, 1996.

Hann, John H. *Visitations and Revolts in Florida, 1656–1695.* Florida Archaeology, No. 7. Tallahassee: Florida Bureau of Archaeological Research, 1993.

Hann, John H., and Bonnie G. McEwan. *The Apalachee Indians and Mission San Luis.* Gainesville: University Press of Florida, 1998.

Hannon, Leslie F. *Forts of Canada: The Conflicts, Sieges and Battles That Forged a Great Nation.* Toronto: McClelland and Stewart, 1969.

Hanson, James Austin. *Metal Weapons, Tools, and Ornaments of the Teton Dakota Indians.* Lincoln: University of Nebraska Press, 1975.

Harris, Benjamin Butler. *The Gila Trail: The Texas Argonauts and the California Gold Rush.* Edited by Richard H. Dillon. Norman: University of Oklahoma Press, 1960.

Harris, Theodore D., ed. *Black Frontiersman: The Memoirs of Henry O. Flipper, First Black Graduate of West Point.* Fort Worth: Texas Christian University Press, 1997.

Hartley, William, and Ellen Hartley. *Osceola: The Unconquered Indian.* New York: Hawthorne Books, 1973.

Hatch, Thom. *Black Kettle: The Cheyenne Chief Who Sought Peace but Found War.* Hoboken, NJ: Wiley, 2004.

Hatley, Tom. *The Dividing Paths: Cherokees and South Carolinians through the Revolutionary Era.* New York: Oxford University Press, 1995.

Hauptman, Laurence M. *Between Two Fires: American Indians in the Civil War.* New York City: Free Press, 1995.

Hauptman, Laurence M. *The Iroquois in the Civil War: From Battlefield to Reservation.* Syracuse, NY: Syracuse University Press, 1993.

Hauptman, Laurence M. *Tribes and Tribulations: Misconceptions about American Indians and Their Histories.* Albuquerque: University of New Mexico Press, 1995.

Hauptman, Laurence M., and James D. Wherry, eds. *The Pequots in Southern New England: The Rise and Fall of an American Indian Nation.* Norman: University of Oklahoma Press, 1990.

Haviland, William A., and Marjory W. Power. *The Original Vermonters: Native Inhabitants, Past and Present.* Hanover, NH: University Press of New England, 1981.

Haynes, Sam W., and Christopher Morris, eds. *Manifest Destiny and Empire: American Antebellum Expansion.* College Station: Texas A&M University Press, 1997.

Hebard, Grace Raymond, and E. A. Brininstool. *The Bozeman Trail: Historical Accounts of the Blazing of the Overland Routes into the Northwest, and Fights with Red Cloud's Warriors.* Cleveland, OH: Arthur H. Clark, 1922.

Hedren, Paul L. *Fort Laramie in 1876: Chronicle of a Frontier Post at War.* Lincoln: University of Nebraska Press, 1988.

Heidler, David S., and Jeanne T. Heidler. *Old Hickory's War: Andrew Jackson and the Quest for Empire.* Mechanicsburg, PA: Stackpole, 1996.

Heimann, R. K. *Tobacco and Americans.* New York: McGraw-Hill, 1960.

Herr, John K., and Edward S. Wallace. *The Story of the U.S. Cavalry, 1775–1942.* Boston: Little, Brown, 1953.

Herring, Joseph B. *Kenekuk: The Kickapoo Prophet.* Lawrence: University of Kansas Press, 1988.

Heyman, Max L., Jr. *Prudent Soldier: A Biography of Major General E. R. S. Canby.* Glendale, CA: Arthur H. Clark, 1959.

Hickox, Ron G. *U.S. Military Edged Weapons of the Second Seminole War, 1835–1842.* Tampa, FL: Ron G. Hickox, 1984.

Higginbotham, Don. *George Washington and the American Military Tradition.* Athens: University of Georgia Press, 1985.

Hill, Beth, and Ray Hill. *Indian Petroglyphs of the Pacific Northwest.* Seattle: University of Washington Press, 1974.

Hill, Edward E. *The Office of Indian Affairs, 1824–1880: Historical Sketches.* New York: Clearwater, 1974.

Himmel, Kelly F. *The Conquest of the Karankawas and the Tonkawas, 1821–1859.* Elma Dill Russell Spencer Series in the West and Southwest 20. College Station: Texas A&M University Press, 1999.

Hinderaker, Eric. *Elusive Empires: Constructing Colonialism in the Ohio Valley, 1673–1800.* New York: Cambridge University Press, 1997.

Hinderaker, Eric, and Peter C. Mancall. *At the Edge of Empire: The Backcountry in British North America.* Baltimore: Johns Hopkins University Press, 2003.

Hirshon, Stanley P. *Grenville M. Dodge: Soldier, Politician, Railroad Pioneer.* Bloomington: Indiana University Press, 1967.

Hittman, Michael. *Wovoka and the Ghost Dance.* Expanded ed. Edited by Don Lynch. Lincoln: University of Nebraska Press, 1997.

Hoagland, Alison K. *Army Architecture in the West: Forts Laramie, Bridger, and D. A. Russell, 1849–1912.* Norman: University of Oklahoma Press, 2004.

Hoig, Stan. *The Peace Chiefs of the Cheyennes.* Norman: University of Oklahoma Press, 1980.

Hoig, Stan. *Perilous Pursuit: The U.S. Cavalry and the Northern Cheyennes.* Boulder: University Press of Colorado, 2002.

Hoig, Stan. *The Sand Creek Massacre.* Norman: University of Oklahoma Press, 1961.

Hollon, W. Eugene. *The Lost Pathfinder: Zebulon Montgomery Pike.* Norman: University of Oklahoma Press, 1949.

Horsman, Reginald. *Expansion and American Indian Policy, 1783–1812.* East Lansing: Michigan State University Press, 1967.

Horsman, Reginald. *Race and Manifest Destiny: The Origins of American Racial Anglo-Saxonism.* Cambridge: Harvard University Press, 1981.

Hosley, William. *Colt: The Making of an American Legend.* Amherst: University of Massachusetts Press, 1996.

Houze, Herbert G. *Samuel Colt: Arms, Art, and Invention.* Edited by Elizabeth M. Kornhauser. New Haven, CT: Yale University Press, 2006.

Howard, Harold P. *Sacajawea.* Norman: University of Oklahoma Press, 2001.

Howard, James H. *The Canadian Sioux.* Lincoln: University of Nebraska Press, 1984.

Howat, John K. *The Hudson River and Its Painters.* New York: Viking, 1972.

Hoxie, Frederick E., Ronald Hoffman, and Peter J. Albert, eds. *Native Americans and the Early Republic.* Charlottesville: University Press of Virginia, 1999.

Hudson, Charles M. *The Catawba Nation.* Athens: University of Georgia Press, 1970.

Hungerford, Edward. *Wells Fargo: Advancing the American Frontier.* New York: Random House, 1949.

Hunter, William A. *Forts on the Pennsylvania Frontier, 1753–1758.* Harrisburg: Pennsylvania Historical and Museum Commission, 1960.

Hurt, R. Douglas. *The Indian Frontier, 1763–1846.* Albuquerque: University of New Mexico Press, 2002.

Hurtado, Albert L. *Indian Survival on the California Frontier.* New Haven, CT: Yale University Press, 1988.

Hutchins, James S. *Boots and Saddles at the Little Bighorn: Weapons, Dress, Equipment, Horses, and Flags of General Custer's Seventh U.S. Cavalry in 1876.* Fort Collins, CO: Old Army, 1976.

Hutton, Paul Andrew. *Phil Sheridan and His Army.* Lincoln: University of Nebraska Press, 1985.

Hutton, Paul Andrew, ed. *The Custer Reader.* Lincoln: University of Nebraska Press, 1992.

Hutton, Paul Andrew, ed. *Soldiers West: Biographies from the Military Frontier.* Lincoln: University of Nebraska Press, 1987.

Hyde, George E. *Spotted Tail's Folk: A History of the Brulé Sioux.* The Civilization of the American Indian Series 57. Norman: University of Oklahoma Press, 1961.

Innis, Ben. *Bloody Knife: Custer's Favorite Scout.* Bismarck, ND: Smoky Water, 1994.

Innis, Ben. *When Indians Became Cowboys: Native Peoples and Cattle Ranching in the American West.* Norman: University of Oklahoma Press, 1994.

Jackson, Donald. *Custer's Gold: The United States Cavalry Expedition of 1874.* New Haven, CT: Yale University Press, 1966.

Jackson, Donald, ed. *The Journals of Zebulon Montgomery Pike: With Letters and Related Documents.* 2 vols. Norman: University of Oklahoma Press, 1966.

Jackson, Donald, ed. *Ma-ka-tai-me-she-kia-kiak, Black Hawk: An Autobiography.* Urbana: University of Illinois Press, 1955.

Jacobs, Wilbur R. *Dispossessing the American Indian: Indians and Whites on the Colonial Frontier.* New York: Scribner, 1972.

James, Alfred P. *The Ohio Company: Its Inner History.* Pittsburgh, PA: University of Pittsburgh Press, 1959.

James, D. Clayton. *Antebellum Natchez.* Baton Rouge: Louisiana State University Press, 1968.

James, James Alton. *The Life of George Rogers Clark.* Chicago: University of Chicago Press, 1928.

Jamieson, Perry D. *Crossing the Deadly Ground: United States Army Tactics, 1865–1899.* Tuscaloosa: University of Alabama Press, 1994.

Jennings, Francis. *The Ambiguous Iroquois Empire: The Covenant Chain Confederation of Indian Tribes with English Colonies from Its Beginnings to the Lancaster Treaty of 1744.* New York: Norton, 1984.

Jennings, Francis. *Empire of Fortune: Crowns, Colonies, and Tribes in the Seven Years War in America.* New York: Norton, 1988.

Johnson, Dorothy M. *The Bloody Bozeman: The Perilous Trail to Montana's Gold.* New York: McGraw-Hill, 1971.

Johnson, James M. *Militiamen, Rangers, and Redcoats: The Military in Georgia, 1754–1776.* Macon, GA: Mercer University Press, 1995.

Johnson, Patricia Givens. *James Patton and the Appalachian Colonists.* Verona, VA: McClure, 1973.

Johnson, Timothy D. *Winfield Scott: The Quest for Military Glory.* Lawrence: University Press of Kansas, 1998.

Jones, Douglas C. *The Treaty of Medicine Lodge: The Story of the Great Treaty Council as Told by Eyewitnesses.* Norman: University of Oklahoma Press, 1966.

Jones, James Pickett. *"Black Jack": John A. Logan and Southern Illinois in the Civil War.* Tallahassee: Florida State University Press, 1967.

Jones, James Pickett. *John A. Logan: Stalwart Republican from Illinois.* Tallahassee: University Presses of Florida, 1982.

Jones, Landon Y. *William Clark and the Shaping of the West.* New York: Hill and Wang, 2004.

Jordan, David M. *Winfield Scott Hancock: A Soldier's Life.* Bloomington: Indiana University Press, 1988.

Josephy, Alvin M., Jr. *The Civil War in the American West.* New York: Knopf, 1991.

Josephy, Alvin M., Jr. *The Nez Perce Indians and the Opening of the Northwest.* New Haven, CT: Yale University Press, 1965.

Josephy, Alvin M., Jr. *The Patriot Chiefs: A Chronicle of American Indian Resistance.* New York: Penguin, 1989.

Kaplan, Lawrence S. *Thomas Jefferson: Westward the Course of Empire.* Wilmington, DE: Scholarly Resources, 1999.

Karamanski, Theodore J. *Fur Trade and Exploration: The Far Northwest, 1821–1852.* Norman: University of Oklahoma Press, 1983.

Kasson, Joy S. *Buffalo Bill's Wild West: Celebrity, Memory, and Popular History.* New York: Hill and Wang, 2000.

Kastor, Peter J. *The Nation's Crucible: The Louisiana Purchase and the Creation of America.* New Haven, CT: Yale University Press, 2004.

Kavanagh, Thomas W. *Comanche Political History: An Ethnohistorical Perspective, 1706–1875.* Lincoln: University of Nebraska Press, 1996.

Kawashima, Yasuhide. *Igniting King Philip's War: The John Sassamon Murder Trial.* Lawrence: University Press of Kansas, 2001.

Keenan, Jerry. *The Life of Yellowstone Kelly.* Albuquerque: University of New Mexico Press, 2006.

Kehoe, Alice Beck. *The Ghost Dance: Ethnohistory and Revitalization.* New York: Holt, Rinehart and Winston, 1989.

Kelly, Lawrence C. *Navajo Roundup: Selected Correspondence of Kit Carson's Expedition against the Navajo, 1863–1865.* Boulder, CO: Pruett, 1970.

Kelsay, Isabel Thompson. *Joseph Brant, 1743–1807: Man of Two Worlds.* Syracuse, NY: Syracuse University Press, 1984.

Kelsey, Harry E., Jr. *Frontier Capitalist: The Life of John Evans.* Boulder, CO: Pruett, 1969.

Kennedy, J. H. *Jesuit and Savage in New France.* New Haven, CT: Yale University Press, 1950.

Kennedy, Roger G. *Mr. Jefferson's Lost Cause: Land, Farmers, Slavery, and the Louisiana Purchase.* New York: Oxford University Press, 2003.

Kenner, Charles L. *Buffalo Soldiers and Officers of the Ninth Cavalry, 1867–1898: Black and White Together.* Norman: University of Oklahoma Press, 1999.

Kersey, Harry A., Jr. *Pelts, Plumes, and Hides: White Traders among the Seminole Indians, 1870–1930.* Gainesville: University Presses of Florida, 1976.

Kessell, John L. *Kiva, Cross, and Crown: The Pecos Indians and New Mexico, 1540–1840.* Albuquerque: University of New Mexico Press, 1987.

Kessler, Donna J. *The Making of Sacagawea: A Euro-American Legend.* Tuscaloosa: University of Alabama Press, 1996.

Kessler, Henry H., and Eugene Rachlis. *Peter Stuyvesant and His New York: A Biography of a Man and a City.* New York: Random House, 1959.

Kidwell, Clara Sue. *Choctaws and Missionaries in Mississippi, 1818–1918.* Norman: University of Oklahoma Press, 1995.

Kimball, Everett. *The Public Life of Joseph Dudley: A Study of the Colonial Policy of the Stuarts in New England, 1660–1715.* Harvard Historical Studies, Vol. 15. New York: Longmans, Green, 1911.

King, James T. *War Eagle: A Life of General Eugene A. Carr.* Lincoln: University of Nebraska Press, 1963.

Knack, Martha C. *Boundaries Between: The Southern Paiutes, 1775–1995.* Lincoln: University of Nebraska Press, 2001.

Knaut, Andrew L. *The Pueblo Revolt of 1680: Conquest and Resistance in Seventeenth-Century New Mexico.* Norman: University of Oklahoma Press, 1995.

Knetsch, Joe. *Florida's Seminole Wars, 1817–1858.* Charleston, SC: Arcadia Publishing, 2003.

Knight, Oliver. *Following the Indian Wars: The Story of the Newspaper Correspondents among the Indian Campaigners.* Norman: University of Oklahoma Press, 1960.

Knight, Wilfred. *Red Fox: Stand Watie and the Confederate Indian Nations during the Civil War Years in Indian Territory.* Glendale, CA: Arthur H. Clark, 1988.

Kopperman, Paul E. *Braddock at the Monongahela.* Pittsburgh: University of Pittsburgh Press, 1977.

Kraft, Louis. *Gatewood and Geronimo.* Albuquerque: University of New Mexico Press, 2000.

Krech, Shepard, III, ed. *Indians, Animals, and the Fur Trade: A Critique of "Keepers of the Game."* Athens: University of Georgia Press, 1981.

Kroeber, A. L., and C. B. Kroeber. *A Mohave War Reminiscence, 1854–1880.* Berkeley: University of California Press, 1973.

Kroeber, Clifton B., and Bernard L. Fontana. *Massacre on the Gila: An Account of the Last Major Battle between American Indians, with Reflections on the Origins of War.* Tucson, University of Arizona Press, 1986.

Kroeker, Marvin E. *Great Plains Command: William B. Hazen in the Frontier West.* Norman: University of Oklahoma Press, 1976.

Kukla, Jon. *A Wilderness So Immense: The Louisiana Purchase and the Destiny of America.* New York: Knopf, 2003.

Lane, Jack C. *Armed Progressive: General Leonard Wood.* San Rafael, CA: Presidio, 1978.

Langley, Harold D., ed. *To Utah with the Dragoons and Glimpses of Life in Arizona and California, 1858–1859.* Salt Lake City: University of Utah Press, 1974.

Lansing, Ronald B. *Juggernaut: The Whitman Massacre Trial, 1850.* Los Angeles: Ninth Judicial Circuit Historical Society, 1993.

Lapp, Rudolph M. *Blacks in Gold Rush California.* New Haven, CT: Yale University Press, 1977.

Larson, Robert W. *Red Cloud: Warrior-Statesman of the Lakota Sioux.* Norman: University of Oklahoma Press, 1997.

Latorre, Felipe A., and Dolores L. Latorre. *The Mexican Kickapoo Indians.* Austin: University of Texas Press, 1976.

Laumer, Frank. *Dade's Last Command.* Gainesville: University of Florida Press, 1995.

Launius, Roger D. *Alexander William Doniphan: Portrait of a Missouri Moderate.* Columbia: University of Missouri Press, 1997.

Lavender, David. *Bent's Fort.* Garden City, NY: Doubleday, 1954.

Lavender, David. *Let Me Be Free: The Nez Perce Tragedy.* New York: HarperCollins, 1992.

Lavender, David. *Westward Vision: The Story of the Oregon Trail.* New York: McGraw-Hill, 1963.

LaVere, David. *Contrary Neighbors: Southern Plains and Removed Indians in Indian Territory.* Norman: University of Oklahoma Press, 2000.

LaVere, David. *The Texas Indians.* College Station: Texas A&M University Press, 2004.

Lazarus, Edward. *Black Hills/White Justice: The Sioux Nation versus the United States, 1775 to the Present.* New York: HarperCollins, 1991.

Leach, Douglas Edward. *Arms for Empire: A Military History of the British Colonies in North America, 1607–1763.* New York: Macmillan, 1973.

Leach, Douglas Edward. *Flintlock and Tomahawk: New England in King Philip's War.* East Orleans, MA: Parnassus Imprints, 1992.

Leacock, Eleanor B., and Nancy O. Lurie, eds. *North American Indians in Historical Perspective.* New York: Random House, 1970.

Leckie, William H., and Shirley A. Leckie. *The Buffalo Soldiers: A Narrative of the Black Cavalry in the West.* Norman: University of Oklahoma Press, 2003.

Leckie, William H., and Shirley A. Leckie. *Unlikely Warriors: General Benjamin H. Grierson and His Family.* Norman: University of Oklahoma Press, 1984.

Leiker, James N. *Racial Borders: Black Soldiers along the Rio Grande.* College Station: Texas A&M University Press, 2002.

Lekson, Stephen H. *Nana's Raid: Apache Warfare in Southern New Mexico, 1881.* El Paso: Texas Western Press/University of Texas, 1987.

Lemay, J. A. Leo. *The American Dream of Captain John Smith.* Charlottesville: University Press of Virginia, 1991.

Lepore, Jill. *The Name of War: King Philip's War and the Origins of American Identity.* New York: Knopf, 1998.

Levernier, James, and Hennig Cohen, eds. *The Indians and Their Captives.* Westport, CT: Greenwood, 1977.

Lewis, Lloyd. *Captain Sam Grant.* Boston: Little, Brown, 1950.

Lofaro, Michael A. *Daniel Boone: An American Life.* Lexington: University Press of Kentucky, 2003.

Lofaro, Michael A., ed. *Davy Crockett: The Man, the Legend, the Legacy, 1786–1986.* Knoxville: University of Tennessee Press, 1985.

Lofaro, Michael A., and Joe Cummings, eds. *Crockett at Two Hundred: New Perspectives on the Man and the Myth.* Knoxville: University of Tennessee Press, 1989.

Lott, Dale F. *American Bison: A Natural History.* Berkeley: University of California Press, 2002.

Lowe, Percival G. *Five Years a Dragoon ('49 to '54) and Other Adventures of the Great Plains.* Introduction by Don Russell. Norman: University of Oklahoma Press, 1965.

Madsen, Brigham D. *The Bannock of Idaho.* Caldwell, ID: Caxton Printers, 1958.

Madsen, Brigham D. *Glory Hunter: A Biography of Patrick Edward Connor.* Salt Lake City: University of Utah Press, 1990.

Madsen, Brigham D. *The Shoshoni Frontier and the Bear River Massacre.* Salt Lake City: University of Utah Press, 1985.

Mahon, John K. *History of the Militia and the National Guard.* Macmillan Wars of the United States. New York: Macmillan, 1983.

Mahon, John K. *History of the Second Seminole War, 1835–1842.* Rev. ed. Gainesville: University Press of Florida, 1991.

Mails, Thomas E. *Dog Soldiers, Bear Men, and Buffalo Women: A Study of the Societies and Cults of the Plains Indians.* Englewood Cliffs, NJ: Prentice Hall, 1973.

Malone, Patrick M. *The Skulking Way of War: Technology and Tactics among the New England Indians.* Lanham, MD: Madison Books, 2000.

Mancall, Peter C. *Deadly Medicine: Indians and Alcohol in Early America.* Ithaca, NY: Cornell University Press, 1995.

Mancall, Peter C., and James H. Merrell, eds. *American Encounters: Natives and Newcomers from European Contact to Indian Removal, 1500–1850.* New York: Routledge, 2000.

Mandell, Daniel R. *Behind the Frontier: Indians in Eighteenth-Century Eastern Massachusetts.* Lincoln: University of Nebraska Press, 1996.

Mangum, Neil A. *Battle of the Rosebud: Prelude to the Little Big Horn.* El Segundo, CA: Upton, 1987.

Marquis, Thomas B. *Custer, Cavalry, and Crows.* Fort Collins, CO: Old Army, 1975.

Marshall, Joseph M., III. *The Journey of Crazy Horse: A Lakota History.* New York: Viking, 2004.

Marszalek, John F. *Sherman: A Soldier's Passion for Order.* New York: Free Press, 1993.

Martin, Calvin. *Keepers of the Game: Indian-Animal Relationships and the Fur Trade.* Berkeley: University of California Press, 1978.

Martin, Joel W. *Sacred Revolt: The Muskogees' Struggle for a New World.* Boston: Beacon, 1991.

Mathes, Valerie Sherer. *Helen Hunt Jackson and Her Indian Reform Legacy.* Austin: University of Texas Press, 1990.

Mathes, Valerie Sherer, ed. *The Indian Reform Letters of Helen Hunt Jackson, 1879–1885.* Norman: University of Oklahoma Press, 1998.

Mathes, Valerie Sherer, and Richard Lowitt. *The Standing Bear Controversy: Prelude to Indian Reform.* Urbana: University of Illinois Press, 2003.

Mattes, Merrill J. *The Great Platte River Road: The Covered Wagon Mainline via Fort Kearny to Fort Laramie.* Nebraska State Historical Society Publications, Vol. 25. Lincoln: Nebraska State Historical Society, 1969.

Mattes, Merrill J. *Jackson Hole: Crossroads of the Western Fur Trade, 1807–1840.* Jackson, WY: Jackson Hole Museum and Teton County Historical Society, 1994.

May, Robert E. *Manifest Destiny's Underworld: Filibustering in Antebellum America.* Chapel Hill: University of North Carolina Press, 2002.

McCardell, Lee. *Ill-Starred General, Braddock of the Coldstream Guards.* Pittsburgh: University of Pittsburgh Press, 1958.

McConnell, Michael N. *A Country Between: The Upper Ohio and Its Peoples, 1724–1774.* Lincoln: University of Nebraska Press, 1992.

McDermott, John D. *Forlorn Hope: The Battle of White Bird Canyon and the Beginning of the Nez Perce War.* Boise: Idaho State Historical Society, 1978.

McGinnis, Anthony. *Counting Coup and Cutting Horses: Intertribal Warfare on the Northern Plains, 1738–1889.* Evergreen, CO: Cordillera, 1990.

McHugh, Tom. *The Time of the Buffalo.* New York: Knopf, 1972.

McLoughlin, William G. *After the Trail of Tears: The Cherokees' Struggle for Sovereignty, 1839–1880.* Chapel Hill: University of North Carolina Press, 1994.

McLoughlin, William G. *The Cherokee Ghost Dance.* Macon, GA: Mercer University Press, 1984.

McLoughlin, William G. *Cherokees and Missionaries, 1789–1839.* New Haven, CT: Yale University Press, 1984.

McNitt, Frank. *Navajo Wars: Military Campaigns, Slave Raids, and Reprisals.* Albuquerque: University of New Mexico Press, 1990.

McPherson, Robert S. *The Northern Navajo Frontier, 1860–1900: Expansion through Adversity.* Albuquerque: University of New Mexico Press, 1988.

Meadows, William C. *Kiowa, Apache, and Comanche Military Societies: Enduring Veterans, 1800 to the Present.* Austin: University of Texas Press, 1999.

Melvoin, Richard I. *New England Outpost: War and Society in Colonial Deerfield.* New York: Norton, 1989.

Merrell, James H. *The Indians' New World: Catawbas and Their Neighbors from European Contact through the Era of Removal.* Chapel Hill: University of North Carolina Press, 1989.

Merrill, James M. *Spurs to Glory: The Story of the United States Cavalry.* Chicago: Rand McNally, 1966.

Merrill, James M. *William Tecumseh Sherman.* New York: Rand McNally, 1971.

Merritt, Jane T. *At the Crossroads: Indians and Empires on a Mid-Atlantic Frontier, 1700–1763.* Chapel Hill: University of North Carolina Press, 2003.

Merwick, Donna. *The Shame and the Sorrow: Dutch-Amerindian Encounters in New Netherland.* Philadelphia: University of Pennsylvania Press, 2006.

Milanich, Jerald T. *Florida Indians and the Invasion from Europe.* Gainesville: University Press of Florida, 1995.

Milanich, Jerald T., and Charles Hudson. *Hernando de Soto and the Indians of Florida.* Gainesville: University Press of Florida, 1993.

Miller, David Humphreys. *Ghost Dance.* Lincoln: University of Nebraska Press, 1985.

Miller, Joseph, ed. *The Arizona Rangers.* New York: Hastings House, 1972.

Miller, Lee. *Roanoke: Solving the Mystery of the Lost Colony.* New York: Penguin, 2000.

Miller, Mark E. *Hollow Victory: The White River Expedition of 1879 and the Battle of Milk Creek.* Niwot: The University Press of Colorado, 1997.

Miller, Perry. *Roger Williams: His Contribution to the American Tradition.* New York: Bobbs-Merrill, 1953.

Mills, Charles K. *Harvest of Barren Regrets: The Army Career of Frederick William Benteen, 1834–1898.* Glendale, CA: Arthur H. Clark, 1985.

Milner, Clyde A., II. *With Good Intentions: Quaker Work among the Pawnees, Otos, and Omahas in the 1870s.* Lincoln: University of Nebraska Press, 1982.

Minge, Ward Alan. *Acoma: Pueblo in the Sky.* Albuquerque: University of New Mexico Press, 1976.

Mintz, Max M. *Seeds of Empire: The American Revolutionary Conquest of the Iroquois.* New York: New York University Press, 1999.

Moller, George D. *American Military Shoulder Arms.* 2 vols. Niwot: University Press of Colorado, 1993.

Monaghan, Jay. *Custer: The Life of General George Armstrong Custer.* Lincoln: University of Nebraska Press, 1971.

Monnett, John H. *The Battle of Beecher Island and the Indian War of 1867–1869.* Niwot: University Press of Colorado, 1992.

Monnett, John H. *Tell Them We Are Going Home: The Odyssey of the Northern Cheyennes.* Norman: University of Oklahoma Press, 2001.

Moogk, Peter N. *La Nouvelle France: The Making of French Canada—A Cultural History.* East Lansing: Michigan State University Press, 2000.

Moore, Jackson W., Jr. *Bent's Old Fort: An Archaeological Study.* Boulder, CO: Pruett, 1973.

Moore, John H., ed. *The Political Economy of North American Indians.* Norman: University of Oklahoma Press, 1993.

Moore, William Haas. *Chiefs, Agents, and Soldiers: Conflict on the Navajo Frontier, 1868–1882.* Albuquerque: University of New Mexico Press, 1994.

Morgan, Edmund. *The Puritan Dilemma: The Story of John Winthrop.* 2nd ed. New York: Longman, 1999.

Morgan, Edmund S. *Roger Williams: The Church and the State.* New York: Harcourt, Brace, and World, 1967.

Morison, Samuel Eliot. *Samuel De Champlain: Father of New France.* New York: Little, Brown, 1972.

Morris, Roy, Jr. *Sheridan: The Life and Wars of General Phil Sheridan.* New York: Crown, 1992.

Morrison, Kenneth M. *The Embattled Northeast: The Elusive Ideal of Alliance in Abenaki-Euramerican Relations.* Berkeley: University of California Press, 1984.

Moses, Lester G. *Wild West Shows and the Images of American Indians, 1883–1933.* Albuquerque: University of New Mexico Press, 1996.

Moulton, Candy. *Chief Joseph: Guardian of the People.* New York: Tom Doherty, 2005.

Mulford, Ami Frank. *Fighting Indians in the Seventh United States Cavalry: Custer's Favorite Regiment.* Fairfield, WA: Ye Galleon, 1972.

Mulroy, Kevin. *Freedom on the Border: The Seminole Maroons in Florida, the Indian Territory, Coahuila, and Texas.* Lubbock: Texas Tech University Press, 1993.

Murray, Keith A. *The Modocs and Their War.* 1959; reprint, Norman: University of Oklahoma Press, 2001.

Nadeau, Remi. *Fort Laramie and the Sioux Indians.* The American Forts Series. Englewood Cliffs, NJ: Prentice Hall, 1967.

Namias, June. *White Captives: Gender and Ethnicity on the American Frontier.* Chapel Hill: University of North Carolina Press, 1993.

Nash, Gary B. *Red, White and Black: The Peoples of Early North America.* 4th ed. Upper Saddle River, NJ: Prentice Hall, 2000.

Neeley, Bill. *The Last Comanche Chief: The Life and Times of Quanah Parker.* New York: Wiley, 1995.

Nelson, Larry L. *A Man of Distinction among Them: Alexander McKee and British-Indian Affairs along the Ohio Country Frontier, 1754–1799.* Kent, OH: Kent State University Press, 1999.

Nelson, Paul David. *Anthony Wayne: Soldier of the Early Republic.* Bloomington: Indiana University Press, 1985.

Nelson, W. Dale. *Interpreters with Lewis and Clark: The Story of Sacagawea and Toussaint Charbonneau.* Denton: University of North Texas Press, 2003.

Nester, William R. *The Arikara War: The First Plains Indian War, 1823.* Missoula, MT: Mountain Press, 2001.

Nester, William R. *The Great Frontier War: Britain, France, and the Imperial Struggle for North America, 1607–1755.* Westport, CT: Praeger, 2000.

Nester, William R. *"Haughty Conquerers": Amherst and the Great Indian Uprising of 1763.* Westport, CT: Praeger, 2000.

Nichols, David A. *Lincoln and the Indians: Civil War Policy and Politics.* Columbia: University of Missouri Press, 1978.

Nichols, Roger L. *Black Hawk: A Biography.* Wheeling, IL: Harland Davidson, 2000.

Nichols, Roger L. *Black Hawk and the Warrior's Path.* Arlington Heights, IL: Harlan Davidson, 1992.

Nichols, Roger L. *General Henry Atkinson: A Western Military Career.* Norman: University of Oklahoma Press, 1965.

Nichols, Roger L. *Indians in the United States and Canada: A Comparative History.* Lincoln: University of Nebraska Press, 1998.

Nichols, Ronald H. *In Custer's Shadow: Major Marcus Reno.* Norman: University of Oklahoma Press, 2000.

Oberg, Michael Leroy. *Uncas: First of the Mohegans.* Ithaca, NY: Cornell University Press, 2003.

O'Brien, Jean M. *Dispossession by Degrees: Indian Land and Identity in Natick, Massachusetts, 1650–1790.* Cambridge: Cambridge University Press, 1997.

O'Connell, Barry, ed. *On Our Own Ground: The Complete Writings of William Apess, a Pequot.* Amherst: University of Massachusetts Press, 1992.

O'Donnell, Terence. *An Arrow in the Earth: General Joel Palmer and the Indians of Oregon.* Portland: Oregon Historical Society Press, 1991.

Oliphant, John. *Peace and War on the Anglo-Cherokee Frontier 1753–63.* Baton Rouge: Louisiana State University Press, 2001.

Oliva, Leo E. *Soldiers on the Santa Fe Trail.* Norman: University of Oklahoma Press, 1967.

Olmstead, Earl P. *Blackcoats among the Delaware: David Zeisberger on the Ohio Frontier.* Kent, OH: Kent State University Press, 1991.

Olmstead, Earl P. *David Zeisberger: A Life among the Indians.* Kent, OH: Kent State University Press, 1997.

Olson, James C. *Red Cloud and the Sioux Problem.* Lincoln: University of Nebraska Press, 1965.

Osgood, Ernest Staples. *The Field Notes of Captain William Clark, 1803–1805.* New Haven, CT: Yale University Press, 1964.

Ostler, Jeffrey. *The Plains Sioux and U.S. Colonialism from Lewis and Clark to Wounded Knee.* Cambridge: Cambridge University Press, 2004.

Otis, D. S. *The Dawes Act and the Allotment of Indian Lands.* Edited by Francis Paul Prucha. Norman: University of Oklahoma Press, 1973.

Owsley, Frank L., Jr. *Struggle for the Gulf Borderlands. The Creek War and the Battle of New Orleans, 1812–1815.* Gainesville: University Presses of Florida, 1981.

Owsley, Frank Lawrence, Jr., and Gene A. Smith. *Filibusters and Expansionists: Jeffersonian Manifest Destiny, 1800–1821.* Tuscaloosa: University of Alabama Press, 1997.

Palmer, Rosemary Gudmundson. *Children's Voices from the Trail: Narratives of the Platte River Road.* Spokane, WA: Arthur H. Clark, 2002.

Pargellis, Stanley, ed. *Military Affairs in North America, 1748–1765: Selected Documents from the Cumberland Papers in Windsor Castle.* New York: D. Appleton-Century, 1936.

Parker, Arthur Caswell. *Red Jacket: Seneca Chief.* Lincoln: University of Nebraska Press, 1998.

Parker, Watson. *Gold in the Black Hills.* Norman: University of Oklahoma Press, 1966.

Parks, Douglas R. *Traditional Narratives of the Arikara Indians.* 4 vols. Lincoln: University of Nebraska Press, 1991.

Patrick, Rembert Wallace. *Aristocrat in Uniform, General Duncan L. Clinch.* Gainesville: University of Florida Press, 1963.

Paul, R. Eli. *Blue Water Creek and the First Sioux War, 1854–1856.* Norman: University of Oklahoma Press, 2004.

Paul, R. Eli, ed. *Autobiography of Red Cloud: War Leader of the Oglalas.* Helena: Montana Historical Society Press, 1997.

Peare, Catherine Owens. *William Penn: A Biography.* Philadelphia: J. B. Lippincott, 1957.

Peckham, Howard H. *Captured by Indians: True Tales of Pioneer Survivors.* New Brunswick, NJ: Rutgers University Press, 1954.

Peckham, Howard H. *The Colonial Wars, 1689–1762.* Chicago: University of Chicago Press, 1964.

Peckham, Howard H. *Pontiac and the Indian Uprising.* Princeton, NJ: Princeton University Press, 1947.

Peers, Laura. *The Ojibwa of Western Canada, 1780–1870.* St. Paul: Minnesota Historical Society, 1994.

Pencak, William A., and Daniel K. Richter, eds. *Friends and Enemies in Penn's Woods: Indians, Colonists, and the Racial Construction of Pennsylvania.* University Park: Pennsylvania State University Press, 2004.

Perdue, Theda. *The Cherokee.* Indians of North America. New York: Chelsea House, 1989.

Perry, Richard J. *Apache Reservation: Indigenous Peoples and the American State.* Austin: University of Texas Press, 1993.

Peskin, Allan. *Winfield Scott and the Profession of Arms.* Kent, OH: Kent State University Press, 2003.

Peterson, John Alton. *Utah's Black Hawk War.* Salt Lake City: University of Utah Press, 1998.

Peterson, John H., Jr., ed. *A Choctaw Sourcebook.* New York: Garland, 1985.

Peterson, Merrill D., ed. *Thomas Jefferson: A Reference Biography.* New York: Scribner, 1986.

Peterson, Norma Lois. *The Presidencies of William Henry Harrison and John Tyler.* Lawrence: University Press of Kansas, 1989.

Phillips, George Harwood. *Chiefs and Challengers: Indian Resistance and Cooperation in Southern California.* Berkeley: University of California Press, 1975.

Phillips, George Harwood. *Indians and Indian Agents: The Origins of the Reservation System in California, 1849–1852.* Norman: University of Oklahoma Press, 1997.

Phillips, Kate. *Helen Hunt Jackson: A Literary Life.* Berkeley: University of California Press, 2003.

Piecuch, Jim. *Three Peoples, One King: Loyalists, Indians, and Slaves in the Revolutionary South, 1775–1782.* Columbia: University of South Carolina Press, 2008.

Pierce, Michael D. *The Most Promising Young Officer: A Life of Ranald Slidell Mackenzie.* Norman: University of Oklahoma Press, 1993.

Pierce, Richard A. *Russia's Hawaiian Adventure, 1815–1817.* Berkeley: University of California Press, 1965.

Pirtle, Caleb, III, and Michael F. Cusack. *The Lonely Sentinel.* Austin, TX: Eakin, 1985.

Pohanka, Brian C., ed. *Nelson A. Miles: A Documentary Biography of His Military Career, 1861–1903.* Glendale, CA: Arthur H. Clark, 1985.

Poole, D. C. *Among the Sioux of Dakota: Eighteen Months' Experience as an Indian Agent, 1869–1870.* Introduction by R. J. DeMaillie. St. Paul: Minnesota Historical Society Press, 1988.

Potter, Stephen R. *Commoners, Tribute, and Chiefs: The Development of Algonquian Culture in the Potomac Valley.* Charlottesville: University Press of Virginia, 1993.

Powell, Peter John. *People of the Sacred Mountain: A History of the Northern Cheyenne Chiefs and Warrior Societies, 1830–1879, with an Epilogue, 1969–1974.* New York: Harper and Row, 1981.

Price, David A. *Love and Hate in Jamestown: John Smith, Pocahontas, and the Heart of a New Nation.* New York: Knopf, 2003.

Prucha, Francis Paul. *American Indian Policy in the Formative Years: Indian Trade and Intercourse Acts, 1790–1834.* Cambridge: Harvard University Press, 1962.

Prucha, Francis Paul. *American Indian Treaties: The History of a Political Anomaly.* Berkeley: University of California Press, 1994.

Prucha, Francis Paul. *The Great Father: The United States Government and the American Indians.* 2 vols. Lincoln: University of Nebraska Press, 1984.

Prucha, Francis Paul. *The Sword of the Republic: The United States Army on the Frontier, 1783–1846.* New York: Macmillan, 1969.

Puglisi, Michael J. *Puritans Besieged: The Legacies of King Philip's War in the Massachusetts Bay Colony.* Lanham, MD: University Press of America, 1991.

Pulsipher, Jenny Hale. *Subjects unto the Same King: Indians, English, and the Contest for Authority in Colonial New England.* Philadelphia: University of Pennsylvania Press, 2005.

Quinn, David Beers. *Set Fair for Roanoke: Voyages and Colonies, 1584–1606.* Chapel Hill: University of North Carolina Press, 1985.

Rahill, Peter J. *The Catholic Indian Missions and Grant's Peace Policy, 1870–1884.* Washington, DC: Catholic University of America Press, 1953.

Rankin, Charles E., ed. *Legacy: New Perspectives on the Battle of the Little Bighorn.* Helena: Montana Historical Society Press, 1996.

Reddin, Paul. *Wild West Shows.* Urbana: University of Illinois Press, 1999.

Reeves, Carolyn Keller, ed. *The Choctaw before Removal.* Jackson: University Press of Mississippi, 1985.

Remini, Robert Vincenti. *Andrew Jackson and the Course of American Empire, 1767–1821.* New York: Harper and Row, 1977.

Remini, Robert Vincenti. *Andrew Jackson and His Indian Wars.* New York: Penguin, 2001.

Remini, Robert Vincenti. *The Legacy of Andrew Jackson: Essays on Democracy, Indian Removal, and Slavery.* Baton Rouge: Louisiana State University Press, 1988.

Remini, Robert Vincenti. *The Life of Andrew Jackson.* New York: Harper and Row, 1988.

Remini, Robert Vincenti. *The Revolutionary Age of Andrew Jackson.* New York: Harper and Row, 1967.

Rich, Edwin E. *The History of the Hudson's Bay Company, 1670–1870.* London: Hudson's Bay Record Society, 1958.

Richards, Kent D. *Isaac I. Stevens: Young Man in a Hurry.* Provo, UT: Brigham Young University Press, 1979.

Richter, Daniel K. *Facing East from Indian Country: A Native History of Early America.* Cambridge: Harvard University Press, 2001.

Richter, Daniel K. *The Ordeal of the Longhouse: The People of the Iroquois League in the Era of European Colonization.* Chapel Hill: University of North Carolina Press, 1992.

Richter, Daniel K., and James H. Merrell, eds. *Beyond the Covenant Chain: The Iroquois and Their Neighbors in Indian North America, 1600–1800.* Syracuse, NY: Syracuse University Press, 1987.

Rister, Carl Coke. *Fort Griffin on the Texas Frontier.* Norman: University of Oklahoma Press, 1956.

Roberts, David. *Once They Moved Like the Wind: Cochise, Geronimo, and the Apache Wars.* New York: Touchstone, 1993.

Robertson, R. G. *Rotting Face: Smallpox and the American Indian.* Caldwell, ID: Caxton, 2001.

Robinson, Charles M., III. *Bad Hand: A Biography of General Ranald S. Mackenzie.* Austin, TX: State House Press, 1993.

Robinson, Charles M., III. *General Crook and the Western Frontier.* Norman: University of Oklahoma Press, 2001.

Robinson, Charles M., III. *A Good Year to Die: The Story of the Great Sioux War.* New York: Random House, 1995.

Robinson, Charles M., III. *Satanta: The Life and Death of a War Chief.* Austin, TX: State House Press, 1997.

Roehm, Marjorie Catlin, ed. *The Letters of George Catlin and His Family: A Chronicle of the American West.* Berkeley: University of California Press, 1966.

Rogers, J. Daniel. *Objects of Change: The Archaeology and History of Arikara Contact with Europeans.* Washington, DC: Smithsonian Institution Press, 1990.

Rogin, Michael Paul. *Fathers and Children: Andrew Jackson and the Subjugation of the American Indian.* New York: Knopf, 1975.

Rohrbough, Malcolm J. *Days of Gold: The California Gold Rush and the American Nation.* Berkeley: University of California Press, 1997.

Rolle, Andrew. *John Charles Frémont: Character as Destiny.* Norman: University of Oklahoma Press, 1991.

Ronda, James P. *Lewis and Clark among the Indians.* 2nd ed. Lincoln: University of Nebraska Press, 2002.

Ronda, James P., ed. *Thomas Jefferson and the Changing West.* Albuquerque: University of New Mexico Press, 1997.

Rosebush, Waldo E. *Frontier Steel: The Men and Their Weapons.* Appleton, WI: C. C. Nelson, 1958.

Rosenberger, Richard F., and Charles Kaufmann. *The Longrifles of Western Pennsylvania: Allegheny and Westmoreland Counties.* Pittsburgh, PA: University of Pittsburgh Press, 1993.

Rountree, Helen C. *Pocahontas, Powhatan, Opechancanough: Three Indian Lives Changed by Jamestown.* Charlottesville: University of Virginia Press, 2005.

Rountree, Helen C. *The Powhatan Indians of Virginia: Their Traditional Culture.* Norman: University of Oklahoma Press, 1989.

Rountree, Helen C., ed. *Powhatan Foreign Relations, 1500–1722.* Charlottesville: University Press of Virginia, 1993.

Rountree, Helen C., and E. Randolph Turner III. *Before and After Jamestown: Virginia's Powhatans and Their Predecessors.* Gainesville: University Press of Florida, 2002.

Ruby, Robert H. *The Oglala Sioux: Warriors in Transition.* New York: Vantage, 1955.

Rusco, Elmer R. *A Fateful Time: The Background and Legislative History of the Indian Reorganization Act.* Reno: University of Nevada Press, 2000.

Russell, Carl P. *Guns on the Early Frontier: A History of Firearms from Colonial Times through the Years of the Western Fur Trade.* Berkeley and Los Angeles: University of California Press, 1957.

Russell, Don. *The Lives and Legends of Buffalo Bill.* Norman: University of Oklahoma Press, 1960.

Ruth, Kent. *Great Day in the West: Forts, Posts, and Rendezvous beyond the Mississippi.* Norman: University of Oklahoma Press, 1963.

Sajna, Mike. *Crazy Horse: The Life behind the Legend.* New York: Wiley, 2000.

Salisbury, Neal. *Manitou and Providence: Indians, Europeans, and the Making of New England, 1500–1643.* New York: Oxford University Press, 1982.

Samek, Hana. *The Blackfoot Confederacy, 1880–1920: A Comparative Study of Canadian and U.S. Indian Policy.* Albuquerque: University of New Mexico Press, 1987.

Samuels, Peggy, and Harold Samuels. *Frederic Remington: A Biography.* Garden City, NY: Doubleday, 1982.

Sandoz, Mari. *Crazy Horse: The Strange Man of the Oglalas.* 3rd ed. Lincoln: University of Nebraska Press, 2008.

Sarf, Wayne Michael. *The Little Bighorn Campaign, March–September 1876.* Conshohocken, PA: Combined Books, 1993.

Saunt, Claudio. *A New Order of Things: Property, Power, and the Transformation of the Creek Indians, 1733–1816.* New York: Cambridge University Press, 1999.

Scanlan, Peter Lawrence. *Prairie du Chien: French, British, American.* Menasha, WI: George Banta, 1937.

Schaaf, Gregory. *Wampum Belts and Peace Trees: George Morgan, Native Americans, and Revolutionary Diplomacy.* Golden, CO: Fulcrum, 1990.

Schlicke, Carl P. *General George Wright: Guardian of the Pacific Coast.* Norman: University of Oklahoma Press, 1988.

Schmeckebier, Laurence F. *The Office of Indian Affairs: Its History, Activities, and Organization.* Institute for Government Research, Service Monographs of the United States Government, No. 48. Baltimore: Johns Hopkins University Press, 1927.

Schmitt, Martin F., ed. *General George Crook: His Autobiography.* Norman: University of Oklahoma Press, 1986.

Schubert, Frank N. *Black Valor: Buffalo Soldiers and the Medal of Honor, 1870–1898.* Wilmington, DE: Scholarly Resources, 1997.

Schubert, Frank N., ed. *Voices of the Buffalo Soldier: Records, Reports and Recollections of Military Life and Service in the West.* Albuquerque: University of New Mexico Press, 2003.

Schwartz, E. A. The *Rogue River Indian War and Its Aftermath, 1850–1980.* Norman: University of Oklahoma Press, 1997.

Seaver, James E. *A Narrative of the Life of Mrs. Mary Jemison.* Syracuse, NY: Syracuse University Press, 1990.

Seed, Patricia. *American Pentimento: The Invention of Indians and the Pursuit of Riches.* Minneapolis: University of Minnesota Press, 2001.

Shackford, James Atkins. *David Crockett: The Man and the Legend.* Edited by John B. Shackford. Chapel Hill: University of North Carolina Press, 1956.

Shannon, Timothy J. *Indians and Colonists at the Crossroads of Empire: The Albany Congress of 1754.* Ithaca, NY: Cornell University Press, 2000.

Sheehan, Bernard W. *Savagism and Civility: Indians and Englishmen in Colonial Virginia.* Cambridge: Cambridge University Press, 1980.

Sheehan, Bernard W. *Seeds of Extinction: Jeffersonian Philanthropy and the American Indian.* Chapel Hill: University of North Carolina Press, 1973.

Silver, James W. *Edmund Pendleton Gaines: Frontier General.* Baton Rouge: Louisiana State University Press, 1949.

Silver, Peter. *Our Savage Neighbors: How Indian War Transformed Early America.* New York: Norton, 2008.

Silverman, Kenneth. *The Life and Times of Cotton Mather.* New York: Harper and Row, 1984.

Simmons, Marc. *Coronado's Land: Essays on Daily Life in Colonial New Mexico.* Albuquerque: University of New Mexico Press, 1991.

Simmons, Marc. *Massacre on the Lordsburg Road: A Tragedy of the Apache Wars.* College Station: Texas A&M University Press, 1997.

Simmons, Marc, ed. *On the Santa Fe Trail.* Lawrence: University Press of Kansas, 1986.

Simmons, Virginia McConnell. *The Ute Indians of Utah, Colorado, and New Mexico.* Niwot: University Press of Colorado, 2000.

Simmons, William S. *The Narragansett.* New York: Chelsea House, 1989.

Simonelli, Jeanne M. *Crossing between Worlds: The Navajos of Canyon de Chelly.* Santa Fe, NM: School of American Research Press, 1997.

Simpson, Harold B. *Cry Comanche: The 2nd U.S. Cavalry in Texas, 1855–1861.* Hillsboro, TX: Hill Junior College Press, 1979.

Simpson, Howard N. *Invisible Armies: The Impact of Disease on American History.* New York: Bobbs-Merrill, 1980.

Simpson, Leslie Byrd. *The Encomienda in New Spain: Forced Native Labor in the Spanish Colonies, 1492–1550.* Berkeley: University of California Press, 1929.

Skaggs, David Curtis, and Larry L. Nelson, eds. *The Sixty Years' War for the Great Lakes, 1754–1814.* East Lansing: Michigan State University Press, 2001.

Sklenar, Larry. *To Hell with Honor: Custer and the Little Big Horn.* Norman: University of Oklahoma Press, 2000.

Slotkin, Richard, and James K. Folsom. *So Dreadfull a Judgment: Puritan Responses to King Philip's War, 1676–1677.* Middletown, CT: Wesleyan University Press, 1978.

Smith, Bradford. *Captain John Smith: His Life and Legend.* Philadelphia: J. B. Lippincott, 1953.

Smith, David Paul. *Frontier Defense in the Civil War: Texas' Rangers and Rebels.* College Station: Texas A&M University Press, 1992.

Smith, Dwight L., ed. *From Greene Ville to Fallen Timbers: A Journal of the Wayne Campaign, July 28–September 14, 1794.* Indiana Historical Society Publications, Vol. 16, No. 3. Indianapolis: Indiana Historical Society, 1952.

Smith, Elbert B. *The Presidencies of Zachary Taylor and Millard Fillmore.* Lawrence: University Press of Kansas, 1988.

Smith, Jean Edward. *Grant.* New York: Simon and Schuster, 2001.

Smith, Winston O. *The Sharps Rifle: Its History, Development, and Operation.* New York: William Morrow, 1943.

Snow, Dean R., Charles T. Gehring, and William A. Starna, eds. *In Mohawk Country: Early Narratives about a Native People.* The Iroquois and Their Neighbors Series. Edited by Laurence M. Hauptman. Syracuse, NY: Syracuse University Press, 1996.

Sonnichsen, C. L. *The Mescalero Apaches.* Norman: University of Oklahoma Press, 1958.

Sonnichsen, C. L., ed. *Geronimo and the End of the Apache Wars.* Lincoln: University of Nebraska Press, 1990.

Spalding, Phinizy. *Oglethorpe in America.* Chicago: University of Chicago Press, 1977.

Spalding, Phinizy, and Harvey H. Jackson, eds. *Oglethorpe in Perspective: Georgia's Founder after Two Hundred Years.* Tuscaloosa: University of Alabama Press, 1989.

Sprague, Marshall. *Massacre: The Tragedy at White River.* Boston: Little, Brown, 1957.

Stamm, Henry E., IV. *People of the Wind River: The Eastern Shoshones, 1825–1900.* Norman: University of Oklahoma Press, 1999.

Stanley, George F. G. *New France: The Last Phase, 1744–60.* London: Oxford University Press, 1960.

Starita, Joe. *The Dull Knifes of Pine Ridge: A Lakota Odyssey.* Lincoln, NE: Bison Books, 2002.

Starkey, Armstrong. *European and Native American Warfare, 1675–1815.* Norman: University of Oklahoma Press, 1998.

Steele, Ian K. *Betrayals: Fort William Henry & the "Massacre."* Oxford: Oxford University Press, 1990.

Steele, Ian K. *Warpaths: Invasions of North America.* New York: Oxford University Press, 1994.

Steffen, Jerome O. *William Clark: Jeffersonian Man on the Frontier.* Norman: University of Oklahoma Press, 1977.

Steltenkamp, Michael F. *Black Elk: Holy Man of the Oglala.* Norman: University of Oklahoma Press, 1993.

St. Germain, Jill. *Indian Treaty-Making Policy in the United States and Canada, 1867–1877.* Lincoln: University of Nebraska Press, 2001.

Stockel, H. Henrietta. *Survival of the Spirit: Chiricahua Apaches in Captivity.* Reno: University of Nevada Press, 1993.

Stout, Joseph A., Jr. *Apache Lightning: The Last Great Battles of the Ojo Calientes.* New York: Oxford University Press, 1974.

Strong, John A. *The Algonquian Peoples of Long Island from Earliest Times to 1700.* Interlaken, NY: Empire State Books, 1997.

Strong, Pauline Turner. *Captive Selves, Captivating Others: The Politics and Poetics of Colonial American Captivity Narratives.* Boulder, CO: Westview, 1999.

Sugden, John. *Blue Jacket: Warrior of the Shawnees.* Lincoln: University of Nebraska Press, 2000.

Sugden, John. *Tecumseh: A Life.* New York: Holt, 1997.

Sugden, John. *Tecumseh's Last Stand.* Norman: University of Oklahoma Press, 1985.

Sully, Langdon. *No Tears for the General: The Life of Alfred Sully, 1821–1879.* Palo Alto, CA: American West Publishing, 1974.

Sunder, John E. *The Fur Trade on the Upper Missouri, 1840–1865.* Norman: University of Oklahoma Press, 1965.

Svingen, Orlan J. *The Northern Cheyenne Indian Reservation, 1877–1900.* Niwot: University Press of Colorado, 1993.

Swatzler, David. *A Friend among the Senecas: The Quaker Mission to Cornplanter's People.* Mechanicsburg, PA: Stackpole, 2000.

Swauger, James L. *Petroglyphs of Ohio.* Artwork by Carol A. Morrison. Athens: Ohio University Press, 1984.

Sweeney, Edwin R. *Cochise: Chiricahua Apache Chief.* Norman: University of Oklahoma Press, 1991.

Sweeney, Edwin R. *Mangas Coloradas: Chief of the Chiricahua Apaches.* Norman: University of Oklahoma Press, 1998.

Sweet, David G., and Gary B. Nash, eds. *Struggle and Survival in Colonial America.* Berkeley: University of California Press, 1981.

Sword, Wiley. *President Washington's Indian War: The Struggle for the Old Northwest, 1790–1795.* Norman: University of Oklahoma Press, 1985.

Talbert, Charles G. *Benjamin Logan, Kentucky Frontiersman.* Lexington: University of Kentucky Press, 1962.

Tate, Michael L. *The Frontier Army in the Settlement of the West.* Norman: University of Oklahoma Press, 1999.

Taylor, Colin F. *Native American Weapons.* Norman: University of Oklahoma Press, 2001.

Thompson, Gerald. *The Army and the Navajo: The Bosque Redondo Reservation Experiment, 1863–1868.* Tucson: University of Arizona Press, 1976.

Thompson, Jerry. *Henry Hopkins Sibley: Confederate General of the West.* Natchitoches, LA: Northwestern State University Press, 1987.

Thompson, Richard A. *Crossing the Border with the 4th Cavalry: Mackenzie's Raid into Mexico, 1873.* Waco, TX: Texian, 1986.

Thornbrough, Gayle, ed. *Outpost on the Wabash, 1787–1791: Letters of Brigadier General Josiah Harmar and Major John Francis Hamtramck.* Indianapolis: Indiana Historical Society, 1957.

Thrapp, Dan L. *Al Sieber: Chief of Scouts.* Norman: University of Oklahoma Press, 1964.

Thrapp, Dan L. *The Conquest of Apacheria.* Norman: University of Oklahoma Press, 1967.

Thrapp, Dan L. *General Crook and the Sierra Madre Adventure.* Norman: University of Oklahoma Press, 1972.

Thrapp, Dan L. *Victorio and the Mimbres Apaches.* Norman: University of Oklahoma Press, 1974.

Tiller, Veronica E. Velarde. *The Jicarilla Apache Tribe: A History, 1846–1970.* Lincoln: University of Nebraska Press, 1983.

Townsend, Camilla. *Pocahontas and the Powhatan Dilemma.* New York: Hill and Wang, 2004.

Trafzer, Clifford E. *The Kit Carson Campaign: The Last Great Navajo War.* Norman: University of Oklahoma Press, 1990.

Trafzer, Clifford E., and Richard D. Scheuerman. *Renegade Tribe: The Palouse Indians and the Invasion of the Inland Pacific Northwest.* Pullman: Washington State University Press, 1986.

Trask, Kerry A. *Black Hawk: The Battle for the Heart of America.* New York: Holt, 2006.

Trefousse, Hans L. *Carl Schurz: A Biography.* Knoxville: University of Tennessee Press, 1982.

Turner, Frederick Jackson. *The Frontier in American History.* New York: Henry Holt, 1920.

Turner, Frederick Jackson. *The Significance of Sections in American History.* New York: Henry Holt, 1932.

Unrau, William E. *White Man's Wicked Water: The Alcohol Trade and Prohibition in Indian Country, 1802–1892.* Lawrence: University Press of Kansas, 1996.

Upton, L. F. S. *Micmacs and Colonists: Indian-White Relations in the Maritimes, 1713–1867.* Vancouver: University of British Columbia Press, 1979.

Utley, Robert M. *Cavalier in Buckskin: George Armstrong Custer and the Western Military Frontier.* Rev. ed. Norman: University of Oklahoma Press, 2001.

Utley, Robert M. *Frontier Regulars: The United States and the American Indian, 1866–1891.* New York: Macmillan, 1973.

Utley, Robert M. *Frontiersmen in Blue: The United States and the Indian, 1848–1865.* Lincoln: University of Nebraska Press, 1967.

Utley, Robert M. *The Indian Frontier of the American West, 1846–1890.* Albuquerque: University of New Mexico Press, 1984.

Utley, Robert M. *The Lance and the Shield: The Life and Times of Sitting Bull.* New York: Ballantine, 1993.

Utley, Robert M. *The Last Days of the Sioux Nation.* 2nd ed. New Haven, CT: Yale University Press, 2004.

Utley, Robert M., and Wilcomb E. Washburn. *The American Heritage History of the Indian Wars.* New York: Barnes and Noble, 1991.

VanDerBeets, Richard, ed. *Held Captive by Indians: Selected Narratives, 1642–1836.* Knoxville: University of Tennessee Press, 1973.

Vaughan, Alden T. *New England Frontier: Puritans and Indians, 1620–1675.* 3rd ed. Norman: University of Oklahoma Press, 1995.

Vaughan, Alden T. *Puritans among the Indians: Accounts of Captivity and Redemption, 1676–1724.* Cambridge: Harvard University Press, 1981.

Vaughan, Alden T., ed. *New England Encounters: Indians and Euroamericans, ca. 1600–1850: Essays Drawn from the New England Quarterly.* Boston: Northeastern University Press, 1999.

Vaughn, J. W. *Indian Fights: New Facts on Seven Encounters.* Norman: University of Oklahoma Press, 1966.

Vaughn, J. W. *With Crook at the Rosebud.* Harrisburg, PA: Stackpole, 1956.

Vogel, Virgil J. *American Indian Medicine.* Norman: University of Oklahoma Press, 1970.

Volwiler, Albert T. *George Croghan and the Westward Movement, 1741–1782.* 1926; reprint, New York: AMS Press, 1971.

Von Gerstner, Franz Anton Ritter. *Early American Railroads.* Stanford, CA: Stanford University Press, 1997.

Vorpahl, Ben Merchant. *Frederic Remington and the West: With the Eye of the Mind.* Austin: University of Texas Press, 1978.

Wagner, Henry R., ed. *The Discovery of Yucatan by Francisco Hernández de Córdoba: A Translation of the Original Texts with an Introduction and Notes.* Berkeley, CA: Cortés Society, 1942.

Wagoner, Jay J. *Arizona Territory, 1863–1912: A Political History.* Tucson: University of Arizona Press, 1970.

Wainwright, Nicholas B. *George Croghan, Wilderness Diplomat.* Chapel Hill: University of North Carolina Press, 1959.

Wakefield, Sarah F. *Six Weeks in the Sioux Tepees: A Narrative of Indian Captivity.* Edited by June Namias. Norman: University of Oklahoma Press, 1997.

Walden, Howard T., II. *Native Inheritance: The Story of Corn in America.* New York: Harper and Row, 1966.

Wallace, Anthony F. C. *The Death and Rebirth of the Seneca.* New York: Knopf, 1970.

Wallace, Anthony F. C. *Jefferson and the Indians: The Tragic Fate of the First Americans.* Cambridge: Belknap Press of Harvard University Press, 1999.

Wallace, Anthony F. C. *King of the Delawares: Teedyuscung, 1700–1763.* Philadelphia: University of Pennsylvania Press, 1949.

Wallace, Anthony F. C. *The Long, Bitter Trail: Andrew Jackson and the Indians.* New York: Hill and Wang, 1993.

Wallace, Edward S. *General William Jenkins Worth: Monterey's Forgotten Hero.* Dallas, TX: Southern Methodist University Press, 1953.

Wallace, Ernest. *Ranald S. Mackenzie on the Texas Frontier.* College Station: Texas A&M University Press, 1993.

Wallace, Ernest, and E. Adamson Hoebel. *The Comanches: Lords of the South Plains.* 1952; reprint, Norman: University of Oklahoma Press, 1986.

Ward, Harry M. *The United Colonies of New England, 1643–90.* New York: Vantage, 1961.

Ward, Harry M. *Unite or Die: Intercolony Relations, 1690–1763.* Port Washington, NY: Kennikat, 1971.

Ward, Matthew C. *Breaking the Backcountry: The Seven Years' War in Virginia and Pennsylvania, 1754–1765.* Pittsburgh, PA: University of Pittsburgh Press, 2003.

Warde, Mary Jane. *George Washington Grayson and the Creek Nation, 1843–1920.* Norman: University of Oklahoma Press, 1999.

Ware, Eugene F. *The Indian War of 1864.* New York: St. Martin's, 1960.

Washburn, Wilcomb E. *The Assault on Indian Tribalism: The General Allotment Law (Dawes Act) of 1887.* Philadelphia: J. B. Lippincott, 1975.

Washburn, Wilcomb E. *The Governor and the Rebel: A History of Bacon's Rebellion in Virginia.* Chapel Hill: University of North Carolina Press, 1957.

Washburn, Wilcomb E. *The Indian in America.* New York: Harper and Row, 1975.

Webb, Stephen Saunders. *1676: The End of American Independence.* New York: Knopf, 1984.

Weber, David J., ed. *New Spain's Far Northern Frontier: Essays on Spain in the American West, 1540–1821.* Albuquerque: University of New Mexico Press, 1979.

Weddle, Robert S. *The Wreck of the Belle: The Ruin of La Salle.* College Station: Texas A&M University Press, 2001.

Weinstein-Farson, Laurie. *The Wampanoag.* New York: Chelsea House, 1988.

Welch, James, with Paul Stekler. *Killing Custer: The Battle of Little Bighorn and the Fate of the Plains Indians.* New York: Norton, 1994.

Wells, Samuel J., and Roseanna Tubby. *After Removal: The Choctaw in Mississippi.* Jackson: University Press of Mississippi, 1986.

Wert, Jeffrey D. *Custer: The Controversial Life of George Armstrong Custer.* New York: Simon and Schuster, 1996.

Wertenbaker, Thomas Jefferson. *Torchbearer of the Revolution: The Story of Bacon's Rebellion and Its Leader.* Princeton, NJ: Princeton University Press, 1940.

White, Richard. *The Middle Ground: Indians, Empires, and Republics in the Great Lakes Region, 1650–1815.* New York: Cambridge University Press, 1991.

White, Richard. *The Roots of Dependency: Subsistence, Environment, and Social Change among the Choctaws, Pawnees, and Navajos.* Lincoln: University of Nebraska Press, 1983.

Wildes, Harry Emerson. *William Penn.* New York: Macmillan, 1974.

Wilkins, Frederick. *The Legend Begins: The Texas Rangers, 1823–1845.* Austin, TX: State House Press, 1996.

Willert, James. *March of the Columns: A Chronicle of the 1876 Indian War, June 27–September 16.* El Segundo, CA: Upton and Sons, 1994.

Williams, Patrick G., S. Charles Bolton, and Jeannie M. Whayne, eds. *A Whole Country in Commotion: The Louisiana Purchase and the American Southwest.* Fayetteville: University of Arkansas Press, 2005.

Williams, T. Harry. *The History of American Wars from 1745 to 1918.* New York: Knopf, 1981.

Wilson, R. L. *The Colt Heritage: The Official History of Colt Firearms from 1836 to the Present.* New York: Simon and Schuster, 1979.

Wilson, Raymond. *Ohiyesa: Charles Eastman, Santee Sioux.* Champaign: University of Illinois Press, 1983.

Wiltse, Charles M. *John C. Calhoun.* 3 vols. Indianapolis: Bobbs-Merrill, 1944–1951.

Winship, George Parker, ed. *The Journey of Coronado, 1540–1542.* Golden, CO: Fulcrum, 1990.

Winslow, Ola Elizabeth. *Master Roger Williams: A Biography.* New York: Macmillan, 1957.

Wiseman, Frederick Matthew. *The Voice of the Dawn: An Autohistory of the Abenaki Nation.* Hanover, NH: University Press of New England, 2001.

Wishart, David J. *An Unspeakable Sadness: The Dispossession of the Nebraska Indians.* Lincoln: University of Nebraska Press, 1994.

Wood, Peter H., Gregory A. Waselkov, and M. Thomas Hatley, eds. *Powhatan's Mantle: Indians in the Colonial Southeast.* Lincoln: University of Nebraska Press, 1989.

Wood, Raymond, and Thomas D. Thiessen, eds. *Early Fur Trade on the Northern Plains: Canadian Traders among the Mandan and Hidatsa Indians, 1738–1818.* Norman: University of Oklahoma Press, 1985.

Woodworth-Ney, Laura. *Mapping Identity: The Creation of the Coeur d'Alene Indian Reservation, 1805–1902.* Boulder: University Press of Colorado, 2004.

Wooster, Robert. *The Military and United States Indian Policy, 1865–1903.* New Haven, CT: Yale University Press, 1988.

Wooster, Robert. *Nelson A. Miles and the Twilight of the Frontier Army.* Lincoln: University of Nebraska Press, 1993.

Worth, John E. *The Timucuan Chiefdoms of Spanish Florida.* 2 vols. Gainesville: University Press of Florida, 1998.

Wright, J. Leitch, Jr. *Britain and the American Frontier, 1783–1815.* Athens: University of Georgia Press, 1975.

Wright, J. Leitch, Jr. *The Only Land They Knew: The Tragic Story of the American Indians in the Old South.* New York: Free Press, 1981.

Zanjani, Sally. *Sarah Winnemucca.* Lincoln: University of Nebraska Press, 2001.

MATTHEW J. WAYMAN

List of Editors and Contributors

Volume Editor
Dr. Spencer C. Tucker
Senior Fellow
Military History, ABC-CLIO, Inc.

Editors, Documents Volume
James Arnold
Independent Scholar

Roberta Wiener
Virginia Military Institute

Associate Editor
Dr. Paul G. Pierpaoli Jr.
Fellow
Military History, ABC-CLIO, Inc.

Assistant Editors
Dr. David Coffey
Associate Professor and Chair
Department of History and Philosophy
University of Tennessee at Martin

Dr. Jim Piecuch
Associate Professor of History
Department of History
Kennesaw State University

Contributors
Joseph Adamczyk
Independent Scholar

Dr. Stanley J. Adamiak
Department of History and Geography
University of Central Oklahoma

Joseph P. Alessi
Independent Scholar

Charles Allan
East Tennessee State University

Shelley G. Allsop
Independent Scholar

Ralph Martin Baker
Independent Scholar

Richard V. Barbuto
Deputy Director, Department of Military
    History
U.S. Army Command and General Staff
    College

Dr. John H. Barnhill
Independent Scholar

Daniel P. Barr
Department of Social Sciences
Robert Morris University

Dr. Jeffrey D. Bass
Assistant Professor of History
Quinnipiac University

Deanna Beacham
Virginia Indian History Consultant

Michael K. Beauchamp
Visiting Assistant Professor
Texas A&M University

Dr. Randal Beeman
Professor of History
Bakersfield College

Walter F. Bell
Information Services Librarian
Aurora University

Marcia Schmidt Blaine
Plymouth State University

Dr. Thomas John Blumer
U.S. Navy, Retired

Derek N. Boetcher
Independent Scholar

Brigadier General Philip L. Bolté
U.S. Army, Retired

Dr. Stephen A. Bourque
Department of Military History
U.S. Army Command and General Staff
    College

Ron Briley
Assistant Headmaster
Sandia Preparatory School

Robert Greg Brooking
Adjunct Professor
Kennesaw State University

Dr. Stefan M. Brooks
Assistant Professor of Political Science
Lindsey Wilson College

Dr. John Thomas Broom
Associate Program Director and Senior
    Adjunct Professor
Norwich University

William H. Brown
North Carolina Office of Archives and
    History

Dr. Jon L. Brudvig
Professor of History
Dickinson State University

Andrew Byers
Duke University

Dr. Alexander V. Campbell
Independent Scholar

Joshua Adam Camper
Independent Scholar

Dr. Jack J. Cardoso
Professor of History, Emeritus
State University of New York College at
    Buffalo

Roger M. Carpenter
Department of History
University of Louisiana

Dr. James F. Carroll
Associate Professor
Iona College

Dr. Edward J. Cashin (deceased)
Former Director, Center for Georgia History
Augusta State University

Dr. John F. Chappo
Assistant Professor
American Military University

Craig Choisser
Independent Scholar

Dr. Jonathan A. Clapperton
University of Saskatchewan

Richmond L. Clow
University of Montana

Dr. David Coffey
Associate Professor and Chair
Department of History and Philosophy
University of Tennessee at Martin

Chip Colwell-Chanthaphonh
Department of Anthropology
Denver Museum of Nature and Science

David M. Corlett
The College of William and Mary

Dr. Rory T. Cornish
Professor of History
Winthrop University

Jack Covarrubias
Old Dominion University

B. Scott Crawford
Independent Scholar

Lisa L. Crutchfield
Department of History
LaGrange College

Colonel Robert J. Dalessandro
Director, U.S. Army Heritage and Education
    Center

Dr. Mark H. Danley
Catalog Librarian/Assistant Professor
University of Memphis Libraries

Dr. Steven L. Danver
Faculty, Center for Undergraduate Studies
Walden University

Dr. Gregory J. Dehler
Front Range Community College

Jennifer Nez Denetdale
Associate Professor of History
University of New Mexico

Jeffrey W. Dennis
Independent Scholar

Marcel A. Derosier
Independent Scholar

Doug Dodd
Independent Scholar

Michael F. Dove
Department of History
University of Western Ontario
Canada

Dr. Alan C. Downs
Associate Professor
Department of History
Georgia Southern University

Elizabeth Dubrulle
Colonial Society of Massachusetts

Robert W. Duvall
Independent Scholar

Rick Dyson
Information Services Librarian
Missouri Western State University

Alexander Emmerich
Heidelberg Center for American Studies
Universität Heidelberg
Germany

Dean Fafoutis
Department of History
Salisbury University

Amy S. Fatzinger
American Indian Studies
University of Arizona

Stephen D. Feeley
Independent Scholar

Dr. Edward F. Finch
Executive Director
Stephenson Co. Historical Society

Dr. Joseph R. Fischer
Associate Professor of History
U.S. Army Command and General Staff
    College

Billie Ford
Independent Scholar

Andrew K. Frank
Assistant Professor
Department of History
Florida State University

Jason Mann Frawley
Department of History
Texas Christian University

Joseph R. Frechette
University of Maryland

Dr. John C. Fredriksen
Independent Scholar

Dr. Derek W. Frisby
Assistant Professor
Department of History
Middle Tennessee State University

R. J. Gilmore
Independent Scholar

Larry Gragg
Department of History and Political Science
University of Missouri–Rolla

Dr. Pamela Lee Gray
Purdue University

Dr. Charles D. Grear
Assistant Professor of History
Prairie View A&M University

Rick Griset
Historian, 480th Intelligence Wing

Michael P. Gueno
Department of Religion
Florida State University

Dr. Dixie Ray Haggard
Assistant Professor
Department of History
Valdosta State University

Dr. John W. Hall
Ambrose-Hesseltine Assistant Professor of
    U.S. Military History
University of Wisconsin–Madison

Dr. Michael R. Hall
Associate Professor of History
Armstrong Atlantic State University

Frank Harper
Independent Scholar

Dr. Donald E. Heidenreich Jr.
Dean of Institutional Research
Lindenwood University

Karl S. Hele
Department of Anthropology and First
    Nations Studies
University of Western Ontario

Glenn E. Helm
Director, Navy Department Library

Lisa Heuvel
Production Associate, Educational Media
The Colonial Williamsburg Foundation

Dr. Neil Heyman
Department of History
San Diego State University

Adam R. Hodge
Kent State University

Dr. Christopher Howell
Professor of History and Archaeology
Red Rocks College

Dr. Charles Francis Howlett
Associate Professor
Molloy College

Robert H. Jackson
Office of Federal Acknowledgment
Department of the Interior

Russell D. James
Independent Scholar

Dr. Lance Janda
Associate Professor
Department of History and Government
Cameron University

Dr. Patrick R. Jennings
Deputy Director, Center for Oral History
United States Military Academy, West Point

Bruce E. Johansen
Frederick W. Kayser Professor
University of Nebraska at Omaha

Andy Johns
Independent Scholar

Daniel Morley Johnson
Independent Scholar

Kathleen Kane
Associate Professor
Department of English
University of Montana

Dr. Robert B. Kane
Adjunct Professor of History
Troy University

Tom Kanon
Archivist, Tennessee State Library and
    Archives

Jerry Keenan
Independent Scholar

Martin Kich
Professor of English
Wright State University–Lake Campus

Dr. Deborah Kidwell
U.S. Army Command and General Staff
    College

Anna Kiefer
Independent Scholar

Dr. Jeff Kinard
Guilford Technical Community College

Matthew J. Krogman
Independent Scholar

Daniel W. Kuthy
Georgia State University

Janne Lahti
University of Helsinki

Alan K. Lamm
Professor of History
Mount Olive College

Dr. Andrew C. Lannen
Department of History
Stephen F. Austin State University

Dr. Tom Lansford
Dean, Gulf Coast
University of Southern Mississippi

Takaia Larsen
Selkirk College
Canada

Raymond W. Leonard
Assistant Professor of History
University of Central Missouri

Michael Lerma
University of Arizona

Dr. Creston Long
Assistant Professor
Salisbury University

Dr. Brad D. Lookingbill
Department of History
Columbia College of Missouri

Lorin M. Lowrie
Howard Payne University

Jean-François Lozier
University of Toronto

Jeffery P. Lucas
United States Military Academy, West Point

Peter C. Luebke
University of Virginia

Jason Lutz
Kennesaw State University

John R. Maass
Ohio State University

Robert W. Malick
Adjunct Professor of History
Harrisburg Area Community College

Dr. Barbara Alice Mann
Department of English Language and
    Literature
University of Toledo

J. David Markham
President, International Napoleonic Society

Dr. Jerome V. Martin
Command Historian
U.S. Strategic Command

Dorothy A. Mays
Associate Professor
Rollins College

Dr. Terry M. Mays
Associate Professor
Department of Political Science
The Citadel

Dr. Jack McCallum
Adjunct Professor
Department of History and Geography
Texas Christian University

James R. McIntyre
Instructor of History
Moraine Valley Community College

Dr. Andrew Miller
Independent Scholar

Sarah E. Miller
Assistant Professor of History
University of South Carolina–Salkehatchie

Dr. Scott C. Monje
Senior Editor, *Encyclopedia Americana*

Dr. A. Gregory Moore
Department of History
Notre Dame College

Brendan D. Morrissey
Independent Scholar

Matthew S. Muehlbauer
Independent Scholar

Dr. Gene Mueller
Texas A&M University–Texarkana

Dr. Malcolm Muir Jr.
Professor of History
Virginia Military Institute

Dr. B. Keith Murphy
Associate Dean
Fort Valley State University

Dr. Justin D. Murphy
Director, Academy of Freedom;
Brand Professor of History
Department of History, Political Science, and
    Geography
Howard Payne University

Dr. Paul David Nelson
Professor Emeritus of History
Berea College

Dawn Ottevaere Nickeson
Department of History
Michigan State University

Jennifer Bridges Oast
College of William and Mary

Dr. Jaime Ramón Olivares
Professor of American History
Houston Community College–Central

Major Jason N. Palmer
United States Military Academy, West Point

Richard Panchyk
Independent Scholar

Robert Paulett
Independent Scholar

James K. Perrin Jr.
Independent Scholar

Joe Petrulionis
Philosophy and History Instructor
Penn State University–Altoona

Dr. Jim Piecuch
Associate Professor of History
Department of History
Kennesaw State University

M. R. Pierce
Assistant Professor
Department of Military History
U.S. Army Command and General Staff
    College

Dr. Paul G. Pierpaoli Jr.
Fellow
Military History, ABC-CLIO, Inc.

Dr. Raeschelle Potter-Deimel
Independent Scholar

Dr. Steve Potts
Independent Scholar

Barry M. Pritzker
Skidmore College

Dr. Ethan Rafuse
Department of Military History
U.S. Army Command and General Staff
    College

Steven J. Rauch
Command Historian
U.S. Army Signal Center

Lieutenant Colonel Christopher M. Rein
Assistant Professor of History
U.S. Air Force Academy

Dr. Richard Carl Reis
Independent Scholar

Dr. Annette Richardson
University of Alberta

Major Thomas A. Rider II
U.S. Army

Catharine Dann Roeber
Independent Scholar

Charles Rosenberg
Independent Scholar

Anna Rulska
Old Dominion University

Shane A. Runyon
Associate Professor of History
Beacon College

Dr. Patrick R. Ryan
Assistant Professor
Western Connecticut State University

Dr. Richard A. Sauers
Executive Director
Packwood House Museum

Elizabeth D. Schafer
Independent Scholar

Dr. Matt Schumann
Eastern Michigan University

Larry Schweikart
Independent Scholar

Dr. Beccie Seaman
Associate Professor
Elizabeth City State University

Signa Daum Shanks
Independent Scholar

David Sloan
University of Kentucky

Dr. John Howard Smith
Assistant Professor
Texas A&M University–Commerce

Gregory E. Smoak
Assistant Professor
Colorado State University

Dr. Adam Sowards
University of Idaho

Dr. Daniel E. Spector
Historian, U.S. Army Chemical Corps,
    Retired

Dr. Paul J. Springer
Department of Strategy and Leadership
Air Command and Staff College

Dr. Ian Michael Spurgeon
Independent Scholar

Ryan Staude
University at Albany–SUNY

H. Henrietta Stockel
Independent Scholar

Dr. Mary Stockwell
Chair, Department of History
Lourdes College

Theresa L. Storey
Independent Scholar

Cameron B. Strang
University of New Hampshire

Lawrence E. Swesey
Director, American Military Heritage
    Experiences

Mark Thompson
Associate Professor
Department of History
University of North Carolina–Pembroke

Rebecca Tolley-Stokes
Assistant Professor
Media & Communication Studies Program
University of Maryland, Baltimore County

Angela D. Tooley
Independent Scholar

Dr. William Toth
Heidelberg College

Dr. Spencer C. Tucker
Senior Fellow
Military History, ABC-CLIO, Inc.

Dallace W. Unger Jr.
Independent Scholar

José Valente
Independent Scholar

Dr. Mark van de Logt
Research Associate
American Indian Studies Research Institute
Indiana University

Dr. Bruce Vandervort
Virginia Military Institute

Dr. Donald L. Walker Jr.
Professor of History
Arapahoe Community College

Dr. Andrew J. Waskey
Professor of Social Science
Dalton State College

Tim J. Watts
Subject Librarian
Kansas State University

Matthew J. Wayman
Head Librarian, Ciletti Memorial Library
Penn State–Schuylkill

Dr. Seth A. Weitz
Indiana University–Northwest

Major Grant Weller
U.S. Air Force Academy

William Whyte
Adjunct Professor
Northampton Community College

Roberta Wiener
Virginia Military Institute

Dr. Joseph W. Williams
Florida State University

Dr. Bradford A. Wineman
Department of Military History
U.S. Army Command and General Staff
    College

Dr. Anna M. Wittmann
Department of English and Film Studies
University of Alberta

Dr. Brett F. Woods
American Public University System

Dr. Steven E. Woodworth
Professor of History
Department of History
Texas Christian University

Dr. Katja Wuestenbecker
University of Jena
Germany

Dr. David T. Zabecki
Major General
Army of the United States, Retired

Dr. Kyle F. Zelner
Assistant Professor of History
University of Southern Mississippi

Categorical Index

Individuals

American Horse   13
Amherst, Jeffrey   14
Atkinson, Henry   40
Attakullakulla   41
Augur, Christopher Columbus   41
Barboncito   50
Belknap, William Worth   55
Bent, Charles   56
Bent, William   57
Benteen, Frederick William   57
Berkeley, William   58
Bierstadt, Albert   60
Big Foot   61
Billy Bowlegs   63
Black Elk   65
Black Hawk   68
Black Hoof   72
Black Kettle   73
Bloody Knife   78
Blue Jacket   79
Boone, Daniel   82
Bouquet, Henry   84
Boyer, Mitch   86
Bozeman, John   86
Braddock, Edward   88
Brant, Joseph   90
Brims of Coweta   91
Brown, Thomas   94
Buffalo Hump   98
Butler, John   103

Caesar   108
Calhoun, James Silas   109
Calhoun, John Caldwell   110
Cameron, Alexander   115
Canby, Edward Richard Sprigg   117
Canonchet   120
Carleton, James Henry   129
Carr, Eugene Asa   130
Carrington, Henry Beebe   132
Carson, Christopher Houston   132
Catlin, George   135
Chaffee, Adna Romanza, Sr.   149
Champlain, Samuel de   150
Chivington, John   170
Church, Benjamin   175
Clark, George Rogers   176
Clark, William   178
Clinch, Duncan Lamont   182
Cochise   182
Cockacoeske   184
Cody, William Frederick   184
Coffee, John   186
Colorow   187
Colt, Samuel   188
Connor, Patrick Edward   194
Cooke, Philip St. George   198
Cooper, James Fenimore   199
Córdova, Francisco Hernández de   200
Cornplanter   202
Cornstalk   202
Coronado, Francisco Vásquez de   203

Crawford, Emmet   206
Crazy Horse   206
Crockett, David   215
Croghan, George   216
Crook, George   216
Curly   219
Curtis, Samuel Ryan   220
Custer, George Armstrong   221
Custer, Thomas Ward   222
Davis, Jefferson   228
Decanisora   230
Delgadito   233
Dodge, Grenville Mellen   240
Dodge, Henry   241
Dudley, Joseph   245
Dull Knife   246
Duston, Hannah   250
Ecuyer, Simeon   256
Emistisiguo   259
Endicott, John   262
Evans, John   266
Fetterman, William Judd   272
Flacco the Elder   278
Flipper, Henry Ossian   279
Forsyth, George Alexander   280
Forsyth, James William   280
Free, Mickey   308
Frémont, John Charles   309
Gaines, Edmund Pendleton   317
Gall   318
Gatewood, Charles Bare   319

921

Gatling, Richard   320
Geronimo   322
Gibbon, John   327
Girty, Simon   328
Grant, Ulysses Simpson   333
Gregg, John Irvin   349
Grierson, Benjamin Henry   350
Grouard, Frank   351
Gun Merchant of Okchai   352
Haigler   353
Hancock, Winfield Scott   354
Handsome Lake   355
Harmar, Josiah   355
Harney, William Selby   356
Harrison, William Henry   358
Hatch, Edward   360
Hazen, William Babcock   363
Henderson, Archibald   364
Houston, Samuel   370
Howard, Oliver Otis   371
Inkpaduta   391
Jackson, Andrew   397
Jackson, Helen Hunt   398
Jefferson, Thomas   401
Jemison, Mary   402
Jesup, Thomas Sidney   402
Johnson, Sir William   403
Joseph, Chief   405
Kamiakin   407
Kearny, Stephen Watts   408
Kelly, Luther Sage   410
Keokuk   410
Kieft, Willem   412
Kintpuash   423
La Barre, Joseph Antoine Le Fèbvre de   429
Langlade, Charles Michel de   436
La Salle, René-Robert Cavelier, Sieur de   436
Lawton, Henry Ware   437
Lewis, Meriwether   439
Little Crow   447
Little Turtle   448
Little Wolf   451
Logan, Benjamin   4451
Logan, John   452
Lone Wolf   453
Looking Glass   455
Lovewell, John   461
Mackenzie, Ranald Slidell   464
Mangas Coloradas   467
Manuelito   469
Mason, John   472
Massasoit   475

McGillivray, Alexander   476
McQueen, Peter   477
Meeker, Nathan Cook   482
Merritt, Wesley   484
Metacom   486
Miantonomo   491
Miles, Nelson Appleton   494
Mog   510
Moniac, David   516
Mortar of the Okchai   520
Murray, John, Fourth Earl of
    Dunmore   522
Musgrove, Mary   523
Narváez, Pánfilo de   523
Neolin   556
North, Frank Joshua, and Luther Hedden
    North   569
Norton, John   572
Nutimus   573
Oconostota   577
Old Briton   586
Oñate, Juan de   588
Opechancanough   592
Orontony   596
Osceola   597
Otis, Elwell Stephen   598
Ouray   600
Parker, Cynthia Ann   608
Parker, Ely Samuel   609
Parkman, Francis, Jr.   611
Pocahontas   631
Ponce de León, Juan   633
Pontiac   633
Popé   637
Pope, John   638
Powhatan   641
Pushmataha   651
Quanah Parker   654
Red Bird   668
Red Cloud   668
Red Jacket   671
Red Shoe   673
Remington, Frederic   675
Reno, Marcus Albert   676
Reynolds, Charles Alexander   679
Rogers, Robert   684
Roman Nose   687
Rowlandson, Mary White   691
Russell, Charles Marion   692
Sacagawea   697
Samoset   699
Sassacus   705

Sassamon, John   705
Satanta   706
Schofield, John McAllister   710
Schurz, Carl   711
Scott, Winfield   712
Seattle   714
Sequoyah   723
Sheridan, Philip Henry   726
Sherman, William Tecumseh   727
Sibley, Henry Hastings   732
Sieber, Albert   732
Sitting Bull   735
Smith, John   742
Soto, Hernando de   745
Spotted Tail   753
Squanto   755
Standing Bear   758
Standish, Myles   761
St. Clair, Arthur   762
Steptoe, Edward Jenner   764
Stevens, Isaac Ingalls   764
Stuart, John   766
Stuyvesant, Petrus   767
Sully, Alfred   771
Tall Bull   779
Tanaghrisson   780
Taylor, Zachary   782
Tecumseh   783
Teedyuscung   784
Tenskwatawa   786
Terry, Alfred Howe   788
Theyanoguin   791
Tomochichi   798
Turner, Frederick Jackson   804
Uncas   809
Underhill, John   809
Upton, Emory   811
Victorio   815
Wabokieshiek   820
Wamsutta   825
Washakie   829
Washington, George   830
Watie, Stand   834
Wayne, Anthony   835
Weatherford, William   836
Wheaton, Frank   842
Willcox, Orlando Bolivar   846
Williams, Roger   847
Wilson, Henry   848
Winnemucca   851
Winnemucca, Sarah   852
Winthrop, John   853

Winthrop, John (Fitz-John)   853
Wood, Leonard   855
Wool, John Ellis   857
Worth, William Jenkins   858
Wovoka   861
Wright, George   862
Zogbaum, Rufus Fairchild   875

Events

Abenaki Wars   3
Acoma Pueblo, Battle of   4
Adobe Walls, First Battle of   5
Adobe Walls, Second Battle of   6
Albany Conference   9
Albany Congress   10
Aleut Rebellion   11
Anglo-Powhatan War, First   16
Anglo-Powhatan War, Second   17
Anglo-Powhatan War, Third   18
Apache Pass, Battle of   19
Apache Wars   24
Apalachee Revolt   27
Arikara War   35
Ash Hollow, Battle of   39
Augusta, Congress of   42
Bacon's Rebellion   45
Bad Axe, Battle of   47
Bannock War   48
Bascom Affair   51
Bear Paw Mountains, Battle of   51
Bear River, Battle of   52
Beaver Wars   53
Beecher Island, Battle of   54
Big Bend, Battle of   61
Big Hole, Battle of the   62
Birch Coulee, Battle of   64
Birch Creek, Battle of   64
Black Hawk War   69
Black Hills Gold Rush   72
Black Point, Attacks on   74
Bloody Brook Massacre   76
Blue Licks, Kentucky, Action at   80
Braddock's Campaign   89
Brodhead Expedition   92
Brookfield, Siege of   93
Burnt Corn Creek, Battle of   102
Bushy Run, Battle of   102
Cahokia-Fox Raid   109
California Gold Rush   111
Camas Meadows, Battle of   113
Camp Grant Massacre   115
Canby's Campaign   118

Canyon Creek, Battle of   121
Carleton's Campaign   130
Chacato Troubles   149
Cherokees, Campaigns against   155
Cherokee War   156
Cheyenne-Arapaho War   158
Cheyenne Campaign   159
Chickasaw Wars   168
Chillicothe, Ohio, Battles on the Little
    Miami River   169
Choctaw-Chickasaw War   171
Choctaw Civil War   172
Cibecue Creek, Incident at   176
Clark's Garrison, Battle of   179
Clark's Ohio Campaign, First   179
Clark's Ohio Campaign, Second   180
Clearwater River, Battle of   181
Coeur d'Alene War   186
Comanche Campaign   190
Connor's Powder River Expedition   195
Council on the Auglaize   204
Creek-Cherokee Wars   207
Creek-Choctaw Wars   208
Creek War   211
Dade's Massacre   225
Deerfield, Massachusetts, Attack on   230
Devil's Hole Road, Battle of   238
Dover, New Hampshire, Attack on   243
Duck River Massacre   244
Dull Knife Fight   246
Dull Knife Outbreak   247
Dummer's War   248
Dutch-Indian Wars   250
Econochaca, Battle of   256
Emuckfaw Creek, Battle of   260
Endicott Expedition   262
Enitachopco Creek, Battle of   263
Esopus Wars   265
Fallen Timbers, Battle of   269
Falls Fight   271
Falmouth, Battle of   272
Fetterman Massacre   273
Fort Mims, Battle of   289
Four Lakes, Battle of   302
Fox Fort, Siege of   302
Fox Wars   303
French and Indian War   310
Geronimo Campaign   323
Gnadenhutten Massacre   330
Good Friday Massacre   331
Goshute War   332
Grattan Massacre   336

Great Sioux War   344
Great Swamp Fight   346
Hayfield Fight   362
Hillabee Massacre   365
Horseshoe Bend, Battle of   368
Indian Creek Massacre   379
Indian Ring Scandal   384
Johnson's 1780 Campaign   404
Julesburg Raids   406
Kieft's War   413
Killdeer Mountain, Battle of   415
King George's War   416
King Philip's War   418
King William's War   420
Lake Okeechobee, Battle of   429
Lewis and Clark Expedition   440
Little Bighorn, Battle of the   445
Little Turtle's War   449
Lord Dunmore's War   456
Louisiana Purchase   458
Lovewell's Fight   461
Mabila, Battle of   463
Mackenzie's Mexico Raid   465
Marias Massacre   471
Mariposa War   471
Massacre Canyon, Battle of   475
Meeker Massacre   483
Micmac Raids on Nova Scotia   492
Milk Creek, Battle of   499
Minnesota Sioux Uprising   502
Modoc War   507
Mohawk-Mahican War   510
Mojave War   515
Mourning War   521
Muscle Shoals, Grand Council on   523
Mystic Fort Fight   528
Natchez Revolt   535
Natchez War   535
Native Americans and the American
    Revolutionary War   538
Native Americans and the Civil War   542
Native Americans and the War of 1812   544
Navajo Removal   553
Navajo War   555
New Ulm, Battles of   562
Nez Perce War   564
Norridgewock, Battle of   569
Oatman Family Massacre   575
Ogoula Tchetoka, Battle of   580
Ohio Expedition   581
Ojibwa-Dakota Conflict   583
Oriskany, Battle of   594

Palo Duro Canyon, Battle of   604
Paxton Riots   614
Pequot War   618
Petite Guerre, La   620
Pickawillany Massacre   622
Pima Revolts   623
Pine Ridge Campaign   624
Piqua, Battle of   627
Piscataway, Siege of   628
Platte Bridge, Battle of   630
Point Pleasant, Battle of   632
Pontiac's Rebellion   634
Powder River Expedition   641
Pueblo Revolt   647
Queen Anne's War   656
Raisin River Massacre   661
Red Cloud's War   669
Red River War   671
Rogers's Raid on St. Francis   685
Rogue River War, First   686
Rogue River War, Second   686
Rosebud, Battle of the   690
Sand Creek Massacre   701
Seminole War, First   716
Seminole War, Second   717
Seminole War, Third   719
Senecas, French Attack on   722
Sheepeater War   725
Shoshone War   730
Slaughter of the Innocents   737
Slim Buttes, Battle of   739
Snake War   743
Solomon's Fork, Battle of   744
Spirit Lake Massacre   751
Springfield, Massachusetts, Burning
    of   754
Standing Bear v. Crook   759
St. Clair's Campaign   763
Stillman's Run, Battle of   766
Sudbury Fight   769
Sullivan-Clinton Expedition against
    the Iroquois   769
Sully-Sibley Campaigns   772
Summit Springs, Battle of   773
Susquehannock War   775
Swansea, Attack on   777
Tallushatchee, Battle of   779
Taos Revolt   781
Thames, Battle of the   790
Timucuan Revolt   792
Tippecanoe, Battle of   793
Trail of Tears   800

Tres Castillos, Battle of   801
Tuscarora War   806
Uprising of 1747   810
Ute War   813
Wabash, Battle of the   819
Wagon Box Fight   822
Walking Purchase   823
Warren Wagon Train Raid   828
Washita, Battle of the   832
Wayne's Campaign   836
Wessagusset Raid   839
White Bird Canyon, Battle of   843
Whitestone Hill, Battle of   843
Whitman Massacre   845
Winnebago War   850
Wolf Mountains, Battle of   854
Wood Lake, Battle of   856
Wounded Knee, Battle of   859
Wyoming, Battle of   864
Yakima-Rogue War   867
Yamasee War   869
Yuma War   873

American Indian Tribes

Abenakis   1
Algonquins   11
Apaches   20
Apalachees   28
Appomattocks   30
Arapahos   31
Arapahos, Northern   32
Arapahos, Southern   33
Arikaras   34
Athapascans   39
Blackfoot Sioux   67
Brulé Sioux   94
Caddos   107
Catawbas   134
Cayugas   148
Cherokees   153
Cheyennes   160
Cheyennes, Northern   162
Cheyennes, Southern   163
Chickahominys   164
Chickamaugas   165
Chickasaws   166
Choctaws   173
Coeur d'Alenes   185
Comancheros   191
Comanches   192
Creeks   209
Croatans   214

Crows   217
Dakota Sioux   226
Delawares   232
Esopuses   264
Havasupais   361
Hualapais   372
Hunkpapa Sioux   375
Iroquois   391
Karankawas   407
Kickapoos   411
Kiowas   424
Kotsoteka Comanches   425
Kwahadi Comanches   426
Lakota Sioux   430
Lipan Apaches   442
Mahicans   466
Mesquakies   485
Miamis   490
Micmacs   492
Mingos   500
Miniconjou Sioux   500
Modocs   506
Mohawks   511
Mohegans   513
Mojaves   514
Nakoni Comanches   529
Nakota Sioux   530
Nansemonds   531
Narragansetts   532
Natchezes   533
Navajos   554
Nez Perces   563
Nipmucks   567
Nottoways   573
Occaneechees   576
Oglala Sioux   579
Ojibwas   583
Oneidas   590
Onondagas   591
Osages   596
Ottawas   599
Paiutes, Northern   603
Palouses   605
Pamunkeys   605
Pawnees   611
Penateka Comanches   615
Pennacooks   616
Pequots   617
Pottawatomis   639
Pueblos   649
Quapaws   655
Rappahannocks   667

Raritans   667
Red Sticks   674
Sans Arc Sioux   702
Saponis   704
Sauks and Foxes   707
Seminoles   715
Senecas   721
Shawnees   724
Shoshones   729
Sioux   733
Sokokis   744
Spokanes   752
Susquehannocks   774
Tequestas   787
Tunicas   803
Tuscaroras   805
Utes   812
Waccamaws   821
Wampanoags   823
Wappingers   826
Westos   841
Winnebagos   848
Wyandots   863
Yamasees   868
Yaquis   870
Yavapais   871

Groups and Organizations
Arikara Scouts   35
Blackfoot Confederacy   66
Black Robes   74
Buffalo Bill's Wild West Show   97
Buffalo Soldiers   99
Bureau of Indian Affairs   100
Cavalry, Native American   137
Cavalry, U.S. Army   138
Cavalry Regiment, 3rd Colorado   140
Cavalry Regiment, 4th U.S.   141
Cavalry Regiment, 5th U.S.   141
Cavalry Regiment, 6th U.S.   142
Cavalry Regiment, 7th U.S.   144
Cavalry Regiment, 8th U.S.   145
Cavalry Regiment, 9th U.S.   146
Cavalry Regiment, 10th U.S.   147
Conquistadors   196
Digger Indians   238
Dog Soldiers   242
Dragoon Regiments, 1st and 2nd   244
Galvanized Yankees and Rebels   319
Hudson River School   373
Hudson's Bay Company   374
Indian Agents   378

Indians, Confederate   385
Infantry Regiment, 7th U.S.   388
Infantry Regiment, 24th U.S.   389
Infantry Regiment, 25th U.S.   390
Iroquois Confederacy   393
Keepers of the Eastern and Western
    Doors   409
Legion of the United States   438
Militia   497
Missionaries   504
Moravian Church   517
Mounted Riflemen, Regiment of   520
Native Americans   536
New England Confederation   557
Office of Commissioner of Indian
    Affairs   578
Ohio Company of Virginia   580
Pony Express   636
Powhatan Confederacy   642
Praying Towns and Praying Indians   644
Puritans   650
Quakers   653
Scouts, Native American   712
Shawnee Council   724
Texas Rangers   789
War Department, U.S.   827
Wells Fargo   837

Places
Appalachian Mountains   28
Bent's Fort   58
Black Hills, South Dakota   70
Black Swamp   75
Blockhouses   76
Boomtown   81
Boonesborough, Kentucky   83
Bosque Redondo   84
Bozeman Trail   87
Butterfield Overland Mail Route   104
Canada   116
Canyon de Chelly, Arizona   122
Everglades   267
Fort Apache   281
Fort Bascom   283
Fort Laramie   285
Fort Leavenworth   288
Fort Phil Kearny   290
Fort Riley   291
Fort Robinson   292
Forts, Camps, Cantonments, and
    Outposts   293
Fort Sill   295

Fort Simcoe   297
Fort Strother   297
Fort Sumner   299
Fort Walla Walla   300
Fort Washington   301
France   306
Glaize, The   330
Great Britain   337
Great Platte River Road   343
Great Sioux Reservation   344
Great Swamp Fortress   348
Harrodsburg, Kentucky   359
Illinois   377
Indian Territory   386
Jamestown   400
Longhouse   454
Mexico   488
Moravian Indian Missions on the
    Muskingum River   517
New Mexico   558
New Netherland   560
Ojo Caliente Reservation, New Mexico   585
Ojo Oso, New Mexico   586
Old Northwest Territory   587
Old Shawnee Town   588
Oregon Trail   593
Overland Trail   601
Pine Ridge Reservation   626
Prophetstown   646
Reservations   677
Rocky Mountains   682
Russia   692
San Carlos Reservation   699
Santa Fe Trail   703
Spain   746
Staked Plains   757
Standing Rock Reservation   760
Trois-Rivières   802
Western Reserve   840

Ideas and Movements
Cannibalism   119
Captivity of Europeans by Indians   125
Captivity of Indians by Europeans   126
Captivity of Indians by Indians   127
Counting Coup   204
Covenant Chain   205
Encomienda   261
Ghost Dance   325
Grant's Peace Policy   335
Land Rights   434
Manifest Destiny   467

Mormonism   518
Native Americans, Alliances with
    Europeans   537
Nativism, Indian   551
Noble Savage Concept   568
Pan-Indianism   607
Romanticism   688
Scalping   709
Skulking Way of War   736
Slavery among Native Americans   738
Subsistence Agriculture   768
Torture, Ritualized   799

Treaties, Acts, and Other Documents
Amherst's Decree   15
Casco, Treaty of   134
Dawes Severalty Act   229
Dummer's Treaty   248
Dutch-Mohawk Treaty   253
Easton Conference and Treaty   255
Fort Armstrong, Treaty of   282
Fort Harmar, Treaty of   283
Fort Jackson, Treaty of   284
Fort Laramie, Treaty of (1851)   286
Fort Laramie, Treaty of (1868)   287
Fort Stanwix, Treaty of   297
Greenville, Treaty of   348
Hartford, Treaty of   360
Hopewell, Treaty of   366
Indian Removal Act   381
Indian Reorganization Act   383
Iroquois Treaties of 1700 and 1701   394
Logstown, Treaty of   452
Massachusetts Bay–Pequot Treaty   472
Medicine Lodge Treaty   481
Mendota, Treaty of   484
Niagara, Treaty of   566

Northwest Ordinances of 1785 and
    1787   571
Payne's Landing, Treaty of   614
Pettaquamscutt Rock, Treaty of   622
Pine Tree Hill, Treaty of   627
Prairie du Chien, Treaty of   643
Proclamation of 1763   644
Trois-Rivières, Treaty of   803
Virginia-Indian Treaty of 1646   816
Virginia-Indian Treaty of 1677/1680   816

Weapons, Technologies, and Objects
Artillery   36
Barbed Wire   49
Bow and Arrow   85
Canoes   120
Captivity Narratives   123
Carbines   127
Colt Revolver   189
Dime Novels   239
Edged Weapons   257
Gatling Gun   321
Harper's Weekly   357
Indian Presents   380
Lance   432
Muskets   524
Petroglyphs   621
Pistols   629
Railroads   659
Rifles   679
Shield   729
Stagecoach   756
Telegraph   785
Tomahawk   797
Wampum   824
War Belt   826
War Club   827

Other
Agriculture   7
Buffalo   96
Camels   113
Cattle Industry   136
Cherokee Alphabet   151
Corn   200
Corn Liquor   201
Custer's Last Stand in Art   223
Demographics, Historical   234
Film and the American Indian Wars   275
Firearms Trade   277
Fur Trade   312
Great Law of Peace of the Longhouse
    People   343
Horses   366
Land Cessions, Northwest Ordinance   432
Liquor   442
Literature and the American Indian
    Wars   443
Massacre   473
Medicine, Military   478
Medicine, Native American   480
Military Divisions, Departments, and
    Districts   495
Native American Trade   547
Native American Warfare   548
Ranks, U.S. Army   662
Sachem   698
Sagamore   698
Scalp Bounty   708
Smallpox   740
Sutlers   776
Tobacco   797
Werowance   839